German loanwords in English: An historical dictionary is the largest and most up-to-date collection of English words and multiword lexical units borrowed from the German, consisting of over 6,000 items. All major dictionaries in English were surveyed, including the second edition of the *Oxford English Dictionary* and *Webster's Third New International Dictionary* as well as new-words collections, college dictionaries, and specialized dictionaries.

Each dictionary entry gives the first recorded date of the German loan in English, the semantic field, variant forms, etymology, the first recorded date of the German etymon, a definition of the English word, a listing of derivative forms, and often grammatical comment. The sources for each entry are noted along with a notation giving the approximate degree of assimilation in English. All the included terms are separately listed by semantic field and chronologically grouped within fifty-year periods, according to their first recorded occurrence in English.

A substantial part of the book is devoted to nontechnical, discursive essays, which analyze the data and provide considerable information not found in the dictionary entries. The first essay, chiefly by Pfeffer, treats the chronological sequencing of German loans in English, their relationship to historical events and persons, and their semantic fields. The second essay, chiefly by Cannon, deals with the linguistic phenomena, processes, and concepts involved.

GERMAN LOANWORDS IN ENGLISH

GERMAN LOANWORDS IN ENGLISH
AN HISTORICAL DICTIONARY

J. Alan Pfeffer

Stanford University

Garland Cannon

Texas A&M University

CAMBRIDGE
UNIVERSITY PRESS

IN MEMORY OF CURTIS C. D. VAIL (1903–1957)

A true disciple of Gotthold Ephraim Lessing

Published by the Press Syndicate of the University of Cambridge
The Pitt Building, Trumpington Street, Cambridge CB2 1RP
40 West 20th Street, New York, NY, USA
10 Stamford Road, Oakleigh, Melbourne 3166, Australia

Some of the material in this book originally appeared in the German-language study entitled *Deutsches Sprachgut im Wortschatz der Amerikaner und Engländer*, published by Max Niemeyer Verlag in 1987. The publisher and authors gratefully acknowledge permission by Max Niemeyer Verlag to use this material as the basis for a substantial part of this English-language book.

Printed in the United States of America

Library of Congress Cataloging-in-Publication Data
Pfeffer, J. Alan (Jay Alan), 1907–

German loanwords in English : an historical dictionary / J. Alan
Pfeffer and Garland Cannon.

p. cm.

ISBN 0–521–40254–9 (hc)

1. English language – Foreign words and phrases – German –
Dictionaries. 2. German language – Influence on English –
Dictionaries. I. Cannon, Garland Hampton, 1924–. II. Title.
PE1582.G4P49   1994

442'.431'03 – dc20   92-40347
                                                     CIP

A catalog record for this book is available from the British Library.

ISBN 0–521–40254–9 hardback

CONTENTS

ACKNOWLEDGMENTS

For good counsel relating to scope, content, and form of this study, the arrangement of its various parts, and the expert judgments in coordinating the many details the co-authors are greatly indebted to Mr. Sidney I. Landau, editorial director of the North American Branch of Cambridge University Press. For permission to use portions of *Deutsches Sprachgut im Wortschatz der Amerikaner und Engländer* in preparing *German Loanwords in English*, the co-authors are much obliged to Mr. Robert Harsch-Niemeyer, publisher, Max Niemeyer Verlag, Tübingen.

For reading various part of the manuscript the co-authors are most grateful to their colleagues and friends: Virginia Barr (Biology), UCSC (University of California at Santa Cruz); Bruce Bridgeman (Psychology), UCSC; Robert Coats (Mineralogy), of the U.S. Geological Survey and at one time at UC Berkeley; Max Dresden (Mathematics), SUNY (State University of New York) at Stony Brook; Patrick Elvander (Botany), UCSC; Robert Gundry (Theology), Westmont College, Santa Barbara, California; Byron J. Koekkoek (Germanics), SUNY at Buffalo; John Jaros (Physics), Stanford University; Robert I. Pfeffer (Medicine), UC at Irvine. Professors Walther F. W. Lohnes of Stanford University and Professor Harry Steinhauer of the University of California at Santa Barbara, both Germanists and polymaths, read the entire Historical Overview and the Appendix to the Dictionary.

The endless ingathering of details that are a part of the study was made possible by the unstinting help of numerous reference librarians. The co-authors commend highly: Catherine Chambers, UC at Davis; Cheryl Gomez, Fred Yuengling, George Keller, Steven Watkins, and especially Virginia Barr, UC at Santa Cruz. They cite with thanks Garry Decker, Santa Cruz Public Library, and his large staff, including Betty Alice, Benjamin Sawyer, and Merritt Taylor; Heidi Smith and Maxine Zellenbach of the Aptos, CA. Public Library; Bernhard Denham and Henry Lowood, Stanford University; Alan Kaufmann, Oxford University; Dorothy Daetsch, Ithaca College, Ithaca, NY.; Ned Divelbiss, Westmont College, Santa Barbara, CA.

In addition to the help received from those acknowledged in the Introduction, the co-authors were generously assisted in various other ways by Professors George H. Williams and Alan Seabury of Harvard University; Prof. Dr. Günther Drosdowski, editor in chief of the Duden series, Mannheim, Germany; Professor Maria Hornung of the University of Vienna; Professor Willard Daetch of Ithaca College; Professor Gert Sackmeyer of the Bundesgymnasium in Krems, Austria; Dr. Lebrecht Weichsel of the Sächsische Akademie der Wissenschaften zu Leipzig and editor in chief of Poggendorff's biographical dictionary series; Dr. Hans-Joachim

ACKNOWLEDGMENTS

Kann, Studiendirektor, Trier, Germany; Dr. Horst Isak, onetime instructor in German at the University of Pittsburgh, Pa.; and the famed popularizer of English etymology, William Safire.

Lastly and ever, the co-authors owe abiding thanks to their respective spouses whose fate it was to endure and encourage, who alone enabled their husbands to persist in the endless toil demanded by the project, Patricia Cannon and Britt Pfeffer.

PRIMARY SOURCES

GENERAL ENGLISH DICTIONARIES

Algeo, John. *Fifty Years among the New Words: A Dictionary of Neologisms, 1941–1991*. Cambridge: Cambridge University Press, 1991. [Edited from the *American Speech* collections.]

AH. *American Heritage Dictionary of the English Language, The*. Boston: Houghton Mifflin, 1976.

Ayto, John. *The Longman Register of New Words*. Vols. 1–2. Harlow, Essex: Longman, 1989, 1990.

Barnhart, David K. *Barnhart Dictionary Companion Index (1982–85), The*. Cold Spring, NY: Lexik House, 1987.

BDC. *Barnhart Dictionary Companion, The*. 1982– .

B. Barnhart, Robert K., Sol Steinmetz, and Clarence L. Barnhart. *Third Barnhart Dictionary of New English*. New York: H. W. Wilson, 1990. [Includes the first and second Barnhart collections of 1973 and 1980.]

Chambers English Dictionary. 7th ed. Cambridge: Chambers, 1988.

Collins Dictionary of the English Language, The. 2nd ed. Edinburgh: Collins, 1986.

Concise American Heritage Dictionary, The. Rev. ed. Boston: Houghton Mifflin, 1987.

Concise Oxford Dictionary of Current English, The. 8th ed. Oxford: Oxford University Press, 1990.

DA. *Dictionary of Americanisms on Historical Principles*. Ed. Mitford M. Mathews, 2 vols. Chicago: University of Chicago Press, 1951.

DAE. *Dictionary of American English on Historical Principles, A*. Ed. William A. Craigie and James R. Hulbert, 4 vols. Chicago: University of Chicago Press, 1938–44.

DARE. *Dictionary of American Regional English*. Ed. Frederic G. Cassidy and Joan H. Hall. Cambridge, MA: Belknap Press, 1985–   .

Longman Dictionary of the English Language. London: Longman, 1984.

Mort, Simon. *Longman Guardian: Original Selection of New Words*. Harlow, Essex: Longman, 1986.

Oxford English Dictionary, The. 12 vols. London: Oxford University Press, 1884–1928. [Orig. titled *A New English Dictionary on Historical Principles*.]

O. *Oxford English Dictionary, The*. 2nd ed., 20 vols. Oxford: Clarendon Press, 1989. [Incorporates the first ed., the 1933 Supplement, and Burchfield's Supplement.]

0–1933. *Supplement to the Oxford English Dictionary*. London: Oxford University Press, 1933.

0–S. *A Supplement to the Oxford English Dictionary*. Ed. R. W. Burchfield, 4 vols. Oxford: Clarendon Press, 1972–86.

Random House Webster's College Dictionary. New York: Random House, 1991.

R. *Random House Dictionary of the English Language, The*. 2nd ed. New York: Random House, 1987.

12. *12,000 Words*. Springfield, MA: G.&C. Merriam, 1986. [Includes the previous hardcover editions of Merriam's Addenda Sections in W3.]

W2. *Webster's New International Dictionary of the English Language*. 2nd ed. Springfield, MA: G.&C. Merriam, 1934.

WN20. *Webster's New Twentieth Century Dictionary*. 2nd ed. Cleveland: World, 1974.

WNW. *Webster's New World Dictionary of American English*. 3rd college ed. Cleveland: Simon and Schuster, 1988.

W9. *Webster's Ninth New Collegiate Dictionary*. Springfield, MA: G.&C. Merriam, 1983.

Webster's II New Riverside University Dictionary. Boston: Riverside, 1984.

W3. *Webster's Third New International Dictionary of the English Language*. Springfield, MA: G.&C. Merriam, 1961.

OTHER WORKS

Bense, J. F. *A Dictionary of the Low-Dutch Element in the English Vocabulary*. The Hague: Martinus Nijhoff, 1939.

Bentley, Harold W. *Dictionary of Spanish Terms in English*. New York: Columbia University Press, 1932.

Bertoni, Giulio. *L'elemento germanico nella lingua italiana*. Genoa: A. F. Formíggini, 1914.

Brockhaus Enzyklopädie. 20 vols. Wiesbaden: F. A. Brockhaus, 1966–74.

Brown, Charles Barrett. *The Contribution of Greek to English*. Nashville: Vanderbilt University Press, 1942.

The Contribution of Latin to English. Nashville: Vanderbilt University Press, 1946.

Cannon, Garland. *Arabic Loanwords in English*. Wiesbaden: Harrassowitz, 1994.

"Chinese Borrowings in English." *American Speech* 63 (1988): 3–33.

"German Loanwords in English." *American Speech* 65 (1990): 260–5.

Historical Change and English Word-Formation: Recent Vocabulary. Bern: Peter Lang, 1987.

"Japanese Borrowings in English." *American Speech* 56 (1981): 190–206.

"Malay Borrowings in English." *American Speech* 67 (1992): 134–62.

"698 Japanese Loanwords in English." *Verbatim* 9.1 (1982): 9–10.

"Zero Plurals among Japanese Loanwords in English." *American Speech* 59 (1984): 149–58.

Carr, C. T. *The German Influence on the English Vocabulary*. Society for Pure English 41. Oxford: Clarendon Press, 1934.

Chan, Mimi, and Helen Kwok. *A Study of Lexical Borrowing from Chinese into English with Special Reference to Hong Kong*. Hong Kong: University of Hong Kong Centre of Asian Studies. 1985.

Clausing, Stephen. Review of Pfeffer (1987). *Colloquia Germanica* 21 (1988): 376–8.

Deroy, Louis. *L'emprunt linguistique*. Rev. ed. Paris: Les Belles Lettres, 1980.

Duden: Das große Wörterbuch der deutschen Sprache. 6 vols. Mannheim: Bibliographisches Institut, 1977–81.

Fleischer, Michael. *Glossary of Mineralogical Species*. Tucson: Mineralogical Record, 1983.

Grimm, Jakob and Wilhelm. *Deutsches Wörterbuch*. 16 vols. Leipzig: S. Hirzel, 1854–1960.

Haugen, Einar. *The Norwegian Language in America*. 2nd ed. Bloomington: Indiana University Press, 1969.

Höfler, Manfred. *Dictionnaire des anglicisms*. Paris: Librairie Larousse, 1982.

Hope, T. E. *Lexical Borrowing in the Romance Languages*. New York: New York University Press, 1971.

Klappenbach, Ruth, and Wolfgang Steinitz. *Wörterbuch der deutschen Gegenwartssprache*. 6 vols. Berlin: Akademie Verlag, 1978–82.

Kluge, Friedrich. *Etymologisches Wörterbuch der deutschen Sprache*, rev. by Walter Mitzka. Berlin: Walter de Gruyter, 1960; rev. by Elmar Seebold, 1989.

Knowlton, Edgar C. *Words of Chinese, Japanese, and Korean Origin in the Romance Languages*. Stanford, 1959. [Ph.D. dissertation.]

Mackensen, Lutz. *Der tagliche Wortschatz*. Langheim, Württ.: Pfahl-Verlag, 1956.

Mackenzie, Fraser. *Les relations de l'Angleterre et de la France d'après le vocabulaire*. 2 vols. Paris: E. Droz, 1939.

Mencken, H. L. *The American Language* and *Supplement I* and *II*. New York: Alfred A. Knopf, 1936, 1945, 1948.

Meyer, *Meyers Großes Universallexicon*. 15 vols. Mannheim: Bibliographisches Institut, 1981–6.

Mitchell, Richard Scott. *Mineral Names: What Do They Mean?* New York: Van Nostrand Reinhold, 1979.

Paul, Hermann. *Deutsches Wörterbuch*, ed. by Werner Betz, 5 vols. Tübingen: Max Niemeyer, 1966; ed. by Helmut Henne and Georg Objarlei, 1992.

Pfeffer, J. Alan. *Deutsches Sprachgut im Wortschatz der Amerikaner und Engländer*. Tübingen: Max Niemeyer, 1987.

Poggendorff, J. C. *Biographisch-literarisches Handwörterbuch zur Geschichte der exacten Naturwissenschaften*. Leipzig: Barth, 1863– .

Pyles, Thomas, and John Algeo. *The Origins and Development of the English Language*. 3rd ed. New York: Harcourt Brace Jovanovich, 1982.

Rao, G. Subba. *Indian Words in English: A Study in Indo-British Cultural and Linguistic Relations*. Oxford: Clarendon Press, 1954.

Sc. Schönfelder, Karl-Heinz. *Deutsches Lehngut im amerikanischen Englisch*. Halle (Salle): VEB Max Niemeyer, 1957.

Schulz, Hans, and Otto Basler, *Deutsches Fremdwörterbuch*, 6 vols. Berlin: Walter de Gruyter, 1913–42, 1974–83.

Serjeantson, Mary S. *A History of Foreign Words in English*. London: Kegan Paul, 1935.

Skeat, Walter. *An Etymological Dictionary of the English Language*. Oxford: Clarendon Press, 1910.

Sprach-Brockhaus, Der, mit einem Vorwort von F. A. Brockhaus. 7th ed. Wiesbaden: F. A. Brockhaus, 1966.

Steinmetz, Sol. *Yiddish and English: A Century of Yiddish in America*. University: University of Alabama Press, 1986.

Stene, Aasta. *English Loan-words in Modern Norwegian*. London: Philological Society, 1940.

Weinreich, Uriel. *Languages in Contact: Findings and Problems*. New York: Linguistic Circle of New York, 1953.

ABBREVIATIONS USED IN THIS BOOK

DICTIONARIES AND OTHER SOURCES

AH	American Heritage	**O-1**	OED (not in 2nd ed.)
Algeo	Algeo Dictionary	**O-1933**	OED Supplement (1933)
B	Third Barnhart	**O-S**	OED 4-vol. Supplement
BDC	Barnhart Dictionary Companion	**R**	Random House 2nd ed.
DA	Dictionary of Americanisms	**Sc**	Schönfelder
DAE	Dictionary of American English	**12**	12,000 Words
L1	Longman Register 1	**W**	Webster's Third
L2	Longman Register 2	**W2**	Webster's Second
Longman	Longman Dictionary	**W9**	Webster's Ninth New Collegiate
Mort	Longman Guardian	**WNW**	Webster's New World
O	OED	**WN20**	Webster's 20th Century

OTHERS

a.	adjective(s)	**Brit.**	British
abbr.	abbreviation	**c.**	circa
ad.	adaptation	**cap.**	capital(ized)
adj.	adjectival	**Chem.**	Chemistry
Admin.	Administration	**Chin**	Chinese
adv.	adverb	**colloq.**	colloquial
Aeron.	Aeronautics	**comb.**	combining
Agric.	Agriculture	**Crystal.**	Crystallography
AmE	American English	**d.**	died
Anat.	Anatomy	**Dan**	Danish
Anthrop.	Anthropology	**deriv.**	derivative
Ar	Arabic	**dial.**	dialectal
Archit.	Architecture	**dim.**	diminutive
attrib.	attributive	**Du**	Dutch
b.	born	**E**	English
Biochem.	Biochemistry	**Econ.**	Economics
Biol.	Biology	**Ed.**	Education
Bot.	Botany	**erron.**	erroneous

esp.	especially		**NL**	Modern Latin
etc.	et cetera		**nom.**	nominative
fem.	feminine		**Norw**	Norwegian
fig.	figurative		**obs.**	obsolete
Fr	French		**OE**	Old English
freq.	frequentative		**OFr**	Old French
G	German		**OHG**	Old High German
gen.	genitive		**ON**	Old Norse
Geogr.	Geography		**OPol**	Old Polish
Geol.	Geology		**OProv**	Old Provençal
Gk	Greek		**orig.**	originally
Gmc	Germanic		**Ornith.**	Ornithology
Go	Gothic		**ORuss**	Old Russian
Heb	Hebrew		**PaG**	Pennsylvania German
Hung	Hungarian		**Paleon.**	Paleontology
Icel	Icelandic		**part.**	participle
Ichthy.	Ichthyology		**Path.**	Pathology
imper.	imperative		**Per**	Persian
interj.	interjection		**Pg**	Portuguese
irreg.	irregular		**Pharm.**	Pharmacy
ISV	International Scientific Vocabulary		**Philos.**	Philosophy
It	Italian		**Physiol.**	Physiology
L	Latin		**pl.**	plural
LGk	Late Greek		**Pol**	Polish
Ling.	Linguistics		**poss.**	possibly
lit.	literally		**prob.**	probably
Lit.	Literature		**Psych.**	Psychology, Psychiatry
LG	Low German		**Russ**	Russian
LL	Late Latin		**Serb**	Serbian
masc.	masculine		**short.**	shortening, shortened
Math.	Mathematics		**sing.**	singular
Med.	Medicine		**Skt**	Sanskrit
Metall.	Metallurgy		**Sociol.**	Sociology
Meteor.	Meteorology		**Sp**	Spanish
ML	Medieval Latin		**specif.**	specific(ally)
MFr	Middle French		**Sw**	Swedish
MHG	Middle High German		**Tech.**	Technology
Mil.	Military		**Theol.**	Theology
Mineral.	Mineralogy		**transf.**	transferred
MLG	Middle Low German		**transl.**	translation, translated
Mod.	Modern		**ult.**	ultimately
Myth.	Mythology		**usu.**	usually
n.	noun		**v.**	verb
Nat. Sci.	Natural Science		**var.**	variant
NHG	New High German		**Zool.**	Zoology

SEMANTIC FIELD LABELS USED IN THIS BOOK

Admin.	Administration	**Law**		
Aeron.	Aeronautics	**Ling.**	Linguistics	
Agric.	Agriculture	**Lit.**	Literature	
Anat.	Anatomy	**Math.**	Mathematics	
Anthrop.	Anthropology	**Med.**	Medicine	
Apparel		**Metall.**	Metallurgy	
Archaeology		**Meteor.**	Meteorology	
Archit.	Architecture	**Mil.**	Military	
Art		**Mineral.**	Mineralogy	
Astronomy	Astronomy, Astrology	**Mining**		
Beverages		**Music**		
Biochem.	Biochemistry	**Myth.**	Mythology	
Biol.	Biology	**Optics**		
Bot.	Botany	**Ornith.**	Ornithology	
Chem.	Chemistry	**Paleon.**	Paleontology	
Commerce		**Path.**	Pathology	
Crystal.	Crystallography	**Pharm.**	Pharmacology	
Currency		**Philos.**	Philosophy	
Dance		**Physics**		
Ecology		**Physiol.**	Physiology	
Econ.	Economics	**Politics**	Politics	
Ed.	Education	**Pottery**		
Entomology		**Printing**		
Ethnology		**Psych.**	Psychology, Psychiatry	
Food		**Sociol.**	Sociology	
Forestry		**Sports**		
Furniture		**Tech.**	Technology	
Games		**Textiles**		
Geogr.	Geography	**Theater**		
Geol.	Geology	**Theol.**	Theol.	
History		**Trades**		
Ichthy.	Ichthyology	**Transportation**		
Immunology		**Travel**		
Industry		**Zool.**	Zoology	

INTRODUCTION

U NTIL THE PUBLICATION OF PFEFFER'S *Deutsches Sprachgut im Wortschatz der Amerikaner und Engländer* (1987), book-length treatments concerning the impact of
German on the English vocabulary concluded that German was a small and quanti-
tatively minor source. The borrowings were said to be comparatively few, and the majority
of these were characterized as technical items, especially in chemistry and mineralogy, which
the ordinary speaker or reader of English would not encounter.

The great etymologist Walter Skeat had much to do with this still rather prevalent assessment.
He held that the German language was linguistically "the furthest removed from English [by
comparison with major sources like Latin, Greek, French, and Italian], and the one from which
fewest words are directly borrowed, though there is a very popular general notion that the contrary is the case." Although millions of native German speakers settled in America long ago and
have been in constant linguistic intercourse with native English speakers there, Skeat added that
"The number of words in English that are borrowed directly from German is quite insignificant,
and (what is more) they are nearly all of late introduction." He listed only thirty-six items directly borrowed from German (Skeat 1910: xxiii, 764). Mary Serjeantson's *A History of Foreign
Words in English* (1935) proceeded to document seventy-seven items.

C. T. Carr's *The German Influence on the English Vocabulary* (1934) somewhat corrected
Skeat by collecting 820 items that English had taken from German, but he noted that some
were obsolete and that many others were of a scientific nature. Finding only 420 of the 820
in C. T. Onions's *Shorter Oxford Dictionary* (1933), Carr concluded that about half of these
were technical, so that the influence of German on the ordinary English vocabulary was "not
very considerable" and consisted of no more than 200 words (Carr 1934: 88–9).

Also, one of the best current histories, Thomas Pyles and John Algeo's *The Origins and
Development of the English Language* (3rd ed., 1982: 309), continued the belief that "High
German has had comparatively little impact on English," and devoted to German little more
than one page in a twenty-five-page chapter on borrowings into English.

The appearance of Pfeffer's 1987 collection of over 3,000 German borrowings in American
and British English now called for a striking revision of past impressions. Successive book-
length studies of particular language-sources have required historians of the English language
to strengthen and widen their descriptions of the debt to Spanish (Bentley 1932), Dutch (Bense
1939), Greek and Latin (Brown 1942, 1946), Indic and Dravidian languages (Rao 1954),
Cantonese (Chan and Kwok 1985), and Yiddish (Steinmetz 1986), among other major studies
of English borrowings.

Of extensive studies that included mutual borrowings, Frazer Mackenzie's French-English book *Les relations de l'Angleterre et de la France d'après le vocabulaire* (1939) and T. E. Hope's French-Italian analysis *Lexical Borrowing in the Romance Languages* (1971) have suggested useful approaches in the preparation of the present book.

In his *Deutsches Sprachgut* (1987) Pfeffer underlined the fact that the then-impending publication of the fourth (last) volume of Burchfield's *A Supplement to the Oxford English Dictionary* plus his own continuing canvass of more specialized dictionaries in music, philosophy, medicine, and the like would probably disclose new borrowings and necessitate the publication of a supplement to his own book. By 1989 he had collected some 450 additional items. Moreover, new-word dictionaries by the Barnharts, an additional five-year Addenda Section in the reprints of *Webster's Third* (1961), the serial *Barnhart Dictionary Companion* (1982–), and the impending publication of a second edition of the *OED* promised many more.

Cannon was meanwhile pursuing a series of studies of borrowings into English that for the first time was utilizing electronic retrieval of items in the *OED* by means of searches programmed to ferret out entries identified as deriving from certain foreign languages. From this came accounts of English borrowings from Japanese (1981, 1984), Chinese (1988), Malay (1992), and a book-length work on borrowings from Arabic (1994). Cannon's approach held out promise for additional increments to Pfeffer's collection.

Correspondence between Pfeffer and Cannon soon made it clear that a completely new book on German loanwords ought to be the goal and that a collaborative approach would enhance its advent. As a book about English borrowings ought to be easily accessible to students of that language, it was decided that English would be the medium.

As *Webster's Third* does not permit electronic access, it was subjected to an additional conventional search with rewarding results. Victoria Neufeldt generously made electronic searches of the corpus of the 1988 edition of her *Webster's New World Dictionary of American English,* as did Walter C. Daugherty and Lawrence C. Peterson of the Computer Science Department of Texas A&M University for German items in *Webster's Ninth New Collegiate Dictionary* (1983). Both desk dictionaries surprisingly yielded items not identified elsewhere. R. W. Burchfield, who had kept informal lists of certain borrowings as he compiled his huge *Supplement,* obligingly made these available to the co-authors. His succeeding co-editors (Edmund Weiner and John Simpson) and the *New Oxford English Dictionary* department provided other valuable help. Of greatest assistance in collecting additions to the original corpus have been Frank Tompa and the University of Waterloo Centre for the New Oxford Dictionary, whose on-line access to the complete second edition of the *OED* turned up many items that otherwise might never have been found by the co-authors of this collection, particularly since the CD-ROM retrieves items only from the original edition of the *OED*. Further, individual scrutiny of the fine print of the twenty volumes uncovered other unidentified items, as did work on our Historical Overview section. The result was a near-doubling of Pfeffer's original corpus. Indeed, three items were discovered too late for inclusion–*GDR* (Random House) and *S.D.* and *word-hero,* both in the *OED*. And the high frequency of 680 items was demonstrated by their inclusion in the new *Merriam-Webster's Collegiate Dictionary* (10th ed., 1993).

Aside from the expanded coverage and the medium of English, other major changes were agreed upon. The analysis of the materials would take advantage of new sociolinguistic and lexicographic findings, so that scholars in those areas, who may not be particularly interested in English and German per se, might find some data of value. The definitions were systematically revised to reflect recent findings in chemistry, biology, botany, mineralogy, etc; and the co-authors decided to address the common criticism of studies of borrowing in general by positing a degree of naturalization for each of the items included.

At least as important as assembling a complete corpus was the need to make its contents and implications available to a larger readership. For example, in concentrating on the dictionary portion, Pfeffer had limited himself to only ten pages of chronological overview of German borrowings from 1500 to post-1945. Of course, chemists and geologists especially are generally aware of the German contributions to their disciplines. But the co-authors agreed that an extensive chronological overview of each semantic field, represented by the borrowings and highlighted by individual histories, would deepen and broaden their understanding and that of other readers of the richness of the German contributions to these disciplines.[1]

The co-authors also decided that the entries would include etymologies and other data that would shed light on relevant disciplines and the phenomena of borrowing, while still advancing overall knowledge of general and historical linguistics, and that an overview of these aspects would introduce the dictionary. Thus a substantial portion of the book is devoted to an Historical Overview by Semantic Fields that Pfeffer prepared, and a Linguistic Overview that Cannon prepared. The first of these essays treats the chronological sequencing of the German loans in English, their historical relationship to events and persons, and their semantic distribution.

AN HISTORICAL OVERVIEW BY SEMANTIC FIELD

Contrary to previously held views, nine of the 5,380 loanwords in the dictionary proper antedate 1501. The oldest of them to appear in English print is *snorkle*. Its first date of record is 1346, and its origin is to be found in the language of German mysticism. The most recent of the borrowings is *wallpecker*. It was reduced to print in English in 1990; it has its basis in the events accompanying the reunification of Germany in 1989.

Between 1501 and 1750, German loans enriched the English vocabulary at a moderate yet consistent pace. Averaging over one item per year during the two and one-half centuries, they accounted by 1750 for nearly 280 of the borrowings that now make up the store of German loanwords in the British and American lexicon. Some 200 of these early transfers range in somewhat large numbers over ten semantic fields, from theology to currency and some aspects of daily life. The remainder come in ever smaller numbers under the headings of eighteen special areas, extending from chemistry to art.

However, these 280 loans represent but a trickle compared to the near-flood of borrowings from German that was to follow. During the next five decades, from 1751 to 1800, the transfer rate of Germanisms or German loans rose from an average of over one to over two per year. It increased to more than five from 1801 to 1850. And it reached its apex in the following

---

[1]See for example Louis Deroy's monumental *L'imprunt linguistique* (1981) and the best chapters in Fraser Mackenzie's *Les relations de l'Angleterre et de la France d'après le vocabulaire* (1939), Uriel Weinrich's *Languages in Contact* (1953), Einar Haugen's *The Norwegian Language in America* (1969), T. E. Hope's *Lexical Borrowings in the Romance Languages* (1971), and other such studies.

fifty years, with an average of thirty-five attested German loanwords in English per annum. The next five decades, beginning with 1901, witnessed a small decline to about thirty-one each twelve months, despite the upheavals of World War I. World War II drastically reduced the rate of transfer to nearly four a year, barely greater than that which prevailed two hundred years earlier.

Next to mineralogy and chemistry, which account for more than three-tenths of the 5,380 loans, rank in number biology, geology, and botany, which add up to another tenth. In the order of number of loans, biochemistry, philosophy, psychology, zoology, and terms relating to the military make up one-tenth. The borrowings in fifty-eight other semantic areas, from food with 115 loans to trades with five, together represent the other five-tenths.

LINGUISTIC OVERVIEW

A second essay treats the linguistic phenomena, processes, and concepts. The linguistic overview points to the fact that the great bulk of the borrowings having High German etyma moved into English as spontaneous transfers; that few, if any, replaced existing words, instead simply expanding the English lexicon. That overview indicates further that there is little evidence that English borrowed any German sounds or distributions. Short of partial or full translations, there have been small changes in spelling to fit the English graphemic or phonetic pattern. The items that English borrowed are of any form, but principally nouns, adjectives, and verbs in a ratio of 80:8:1. The number of bound forms is statistically small. The transfers include a number of trademarks and eponyms, but there are very few pseudo-Germanisms. Reborrowings are rather uncommon.

PRINCIPLES OF INCLUSION

We use the term *loanword* in a broad sense so as to cover the types of borrowings that German has supplied to English over the centuries. These lexical items, also called *linguistic units,* include items where both the meaning and the form are transferred, as in *Abgesang.* They include few loan blends, where the meaning but only part of the form are transferred, as in *Afrikanerdom,* where *Afrikaner* was borrowed into English but then affixed by the English suffix *-dom* so as to provide a word that Afrikaans never had. We will elaborate on this point shortly. Our loanwords include various types of translations, ranging from partial renditions like *apple strudel* (from *Apfelstrudel*) to full loan-translations like *airship* (from *Luftschiff*). These too will be detailed later. The borrowings also include a small number of semantic loans, that is, senses of German words that were added to existing English forms, such as that of *Kurfürst* to *elector.*

In collecting this corpus of borrowings, and describing and analyzing them, the co-authors have followed the tradition of major studies of borrowings by making several assumptions, which have inevitably affected our results and conclusions.

Most importantly, our corpus, which is presented alphabetically in the dictionary portion, has been collected entirely from English language dictionaries and thus from writing rather than from oral sources or "direct specimens of language," as Clausing (1988) noted in his review of Pfeffer's book. Recorded items are usually dated and can be attested in a variety of printed sources over many years. The co-authors were in no position to attempt to determine how many of the borrowed English written forms still exist in the spoken language and then further to discriminate such forms into the social, regional, and temporal classifications that admittedly could be more revealing and useful in some ways. We agree with Clausing that a dictionary of a language is not language itself. But a dictionary such as the *OED* that presents in its citations words in context can provide many of the insights that oral collections would. Pfeffer was among the first to record German speech on a large scale, distributed over wide areas, and structured sociologically by age, sex, education, and theme; and he is in tune with its implications.[2]

Three other assumptions have been at least as arbitrary. We provide no pronunciation for the entries; we include no item unless it existed in (Early) New High German; and we exclude items that, based on reasonable evidence, were not transferred directly from German into English, but rather by way of an intermediary language.

While the exclusion of phonetic and partly phonetic transcriptions has saved much labor and expense, our chief purpose has been to avoid error, ambiguity, and inevitable incompleteness. Provision of an acceptable bilingual German pronunciation of itself would raise questions. Another argument against the inclusion of pronunciation is that much of our corpus is anglicized or even in the form of partial or full translation, so that we would merely be recording the native English pronunciation, thereby raising the rather irrelevant question of British versus American speech, etc. All of our items, other than those in the Appendix, have been found in British or American dictionaries and are identified by source, so that the reader can go to the given dictionary if interested in a particular pronunciation. Giving pronunciations would clutter the entry with information of doubtful utility: How would a transcription like / *kold kəts* / for *cold cuts* edify a reader?

In excluding an item unless it appears somewhere in Standard High German print, we confront the earlier question of speech versus writing, besides the fact that dictionaries obviously do not include all the written forms of the given language. So we may have excluded some items that should have been included, simply because they were not in the standard German dictionaries consulted. Too, dictionaries often exclude productive or self-defining forms because native speakers know how to construct a near-infinite number of such forms. For example, German adds the suffix *-er* to place-names to form a new noun meaning 'one from X,' as in *Berliner* and *Rhinelander,* which are both in German and English dictionaries and thus appear in our corpus, whereas other German X-er words that English also uses do not appear. Moreover, as English uses the same suffix and process, one might be unable to determine whether a form like *Leipziger* was a German borrowing or had been analogized as an English creation like *New Yorker* (versus *Chicagoan*).

Our arbitrariness does controversially exclude a number of name-based items that might otherwise be accepted into our corpus. English dictionaries include many items consisting of a German personal or proper name + *-(i)an,* as in *Freudian, Kantian,* and *Wagnerian.* We have adopted the practice of most dictionaries by excluding proper names if they are purely

---

[2]See J. Alan Pfeffer and Walter W. Lohnes, *Grunddeutsch: Texte zur gesprochenen deutschen Gegenwartssprache.* 3 vols., Tübingen: Niemeyer, 1984 (*Phonia,* 28, 29, 30). The texts are transcriptions of 400 taped interviews in Germany, Austria, and Switzerland – from Hamburg in the north to Basel in the south, from Arnheim in the west to Cottbus and Vienna in the east.

biographical or geographical rather than characterizing their chief importance, as in *Mindel* (the name of a Bavarian river that empties into the Danube near Gundremingen, Germany, but has also come to mean 'the second stage of European glaciation'), so that *Mindel* is included. We exclude the geographical adjectives that *Webster's Third* idiosyncratically includes as defined by the formula 'of the kind or style prevalent in X' and thus its dozens of geographical adjectives designating German cities and states.

Equally controversial omissions are the many English words built from the names of distinguished Germans, to which has been added a possessive -'s, and/or an English noun that at least partly identifies the Germans' accomplishment. Thus *ohm* 'unit of electrical resistance' utilizes the name of the German physicist Georg Simon Ohm (1787–1854), which Germans also use but evidently borrowed its meaning from English. According to the *OED, ohm* was suggested in 1861 by Sir Charles Bright and Mr. Latimer Clark, and adopted in 1881 at the Congress of Electricians in Paris. Ohm discovered electrical resistance in 1826 and the law derived from that discovery, to which German encyclopedias refer as *Ohm-Gesetz*. They do not mention an etymon for *ohmic resistance*. Where there is direct or circumstantial evidence that the onomastic item was coined first in German, we include it. Nor are *ohmic resistance* and *Ohm's law* in our corpus, though these items directly reflect Ohm's contribution to the world in terms of physics. Without his discovery, the concept, law, and name for these might not have existed for several more decades; and to exclude the words is to exclude German contributions to the world of science but only indirectly to linguistics. *Webster's Third* and the *OED* properly include thousands of such derivative words built from the names of prominent Germans. For the German names that we do include, we have, perhaps redundantly, added a phrase like "from the name of X" to stress the onomastic origin. So when *Bach trumpet* is included, but *Leydig cell* and *Battenberg lace* are not, our arbitrary principle is exemplified.

We did violate the principle a few times in order to show the rich nature of the many items that might otherwise have been included, and to encourage scholars to collect and analyze them in terms of English word-formation. Thus our item *nitwit* comes from Upper German *nit,* which some standard German dictionaries list and thus equate with Standard German *nicht* 'not,' and English *wit* to create a hybrid. This English compound was modeled on old English forms like *half-wit,* so that the German element is pejorated to help create an English term for a person who is implied to be more stupid than a person without any intelligence at all. A more defensible inclusion is our *wisenheimer,* which prefixes English *wise* to German -*enheimer* as analogized on German names like *Guggenheimer* and *Oppenheimer.* A few such pseudo-Germanisms have been created in English, never existed in German to our knowledge, and yet are linguistically as interesting as is *Pappenheimer* to Germans.

Our principle has led us to exclude a number of other items, such as those which German scholars created in another language, particularly in the seventeenth and eighteenth centuries. Writing in Latin, they were given to coining new terms for products and processes that are better analyzed as New Latin. Thus the world, including English speakers, was given the term *laudanum* by Paracelsus (i.e., Theophrastus Bombastus von Hohenheim), and the physics term *inertia* by Johannes Kepler, both in New Latin, as was then the custom. A comparable exclusion is Leibniz's French compound *harmonie préétablie* (German *prästabilierte Harmonie*) that was originally coined in 1696 (see Meyer) and is the centerpiece of his *La Monadologie* (1714). As some German scholars analyze such words as Germanisms, we have included a few like *function* and *safrene* as "cross-references" rather than linguistic contributions to English.

Our principle also excludes what might be termed meaning/culture transfers, or words for which there is no known German etymon reasonably transferrable or anglicizable into English. For example, during World War II there were various synonyms for *V-1* and *V-2,* which are still remembered by Britishers of that time and which appear in standard dictionaries. The above two names clearly came from German, whereas *buzz bomb* describes what many people thought they heard as the missile moved overhead and has no connection with a German etymon. Nor does *doodlebug,* the pejorated synonym for this deadly device, though some Britishers may be more inclined to use one of these two non-German words rather than the actual German borrowings. Nonetheless, we excluded both items from our corpus.

What if an item appears in German and there is a very similar English form possessing an essentially identical sense? Pfeffer's 1987 book rightly followed the principle of excluding possibly acculturated German eponyms in English when they lacked convincing attestation and the necessary chronological verification, a principle that we have continued. We hardly lingered over *spruce beer* before rejecting it, as *Sprossenbier* is a German folk-etymological adaptation of the English term, however long it was known in Danzig and its environs (see Grimm). English did not borrow this German adaptation back, but maintained its original English item.

Such items are often more cultural than lexical in nature and sometimes exist simultaneously, as in Yiddish, especially in the U.S., as documented in Steinmetz (1986). Resisting a reviewer's suggestion to Pfeffer that a word existing in such identical form should be etymologically included at least as a Yiddishism if not as an actual German borrowing, we have maintained Pfeffer's original caution and have silently excluded items like *blintze, chutzpah,* and *gefilte fish* because a similar investigation of Jewish sources showed that Yiddish, rather than German, furnished the etyma for these loanwords into English. If one views Yiddish as the Middle High German variant adopted by Jews who migrated to eastern Europe during the Middle Ages (rather than viewing Yiddish as a separate language), as many Germanists do, then such items may belong alongside other dialectal etyma that have never become Standard High German and thus are outside our corpus anyway. There is an allure in noting that English *gefilte fish* was formed in Yiddish by compounding two German items. The six-volume Duden dictionary of Standard German includes no such compound. And we do note the occasional mistaken analysis in dictionaries of the productive English suffix *-nik* as coming from German, whereas we exclude it because it was derived from Russian or Yiddish. We have recorded a few such items as "cross-references" to this Introduction, as we have excluded them from our corpus. Their small number makes this a marginal matter for us, besides the fact that scholars have fully investigated the subject.

Less controversial is our decision to exclude items not directly transferred from German. To do so would presuppose an entirely different standard of borrowing. Moreover, the German etymon may have undergone phonological, structural, and semantic modification while existing within the intermediary language, which at the extreme could place such distance between the German source and its ultimate English destination that one might question whether the item is German at all. Thus German *Vampir* was transferred into French as *vampire.* French then transferred the etymon into English, and it is properly credited for this loan. Some English dictionaries cite French as the sole source, as though the French etymon was originally of

Romance origin. Actually, the German source goes back to a Slavic source like Serbian *vampir*. The Germans themselves recognize their *Vampir* as a Slavic borrowing.

A complicating reason for this decision is that Germanic accounts for considerable additions to the vocabularies of many European languages, beginning with items contributed to Latin, and later to the diverging Romance languages during the Great Migrations somewhat comparable to the massive infusion of Arabic items into Spanish. Many of the originally Germanic items later passed from Latin or French into English. Sometimes English dictionaries do not cite the ultimate Germanic etyma of such items, either to save space or perhaps because they have not recognized the Germanic source of the given French, Spanish, etc. borrowing into English. This of itself is a disconcerting situation for anyone who is collecting English borrowings that at one time were Germanic, whether or not High German was the direct transmitter. Skeat's Appendixes (1910) list several such examples of English borrowings like *zigzag* via French, *rocket* via Italian, *hetman* via Polish, and *mangle* via Dutch. We exclude such items and will not attempt to defend here a premise that the directly transferring language is the "best" source for the given loanword.

SOURCES OF THE CORPUS

With those purposes, assumptions, and delimitations in mind, we began with Pfeffer's 3,000-word edition, expanding it with electronic retrieval from the second edition of the *OED* and the two desk dictionaries for which such retrieval was possible. Manual checking of the new unabridged *Random House* plus rechecking of *Webster's Third* and *Webster's Second* (*W2*) discovered many additional items, with others coming from the latest editions of six more desk dictionaries. The 1987 index to *The Barnhart Dictionary Companion* furnished convenient access to almost all the German borrowings in that continuing periodical; and manual checking discovered additional, very recent items in John Ayto's 1989 and 1990 volumes of his primarily British *Longman Register of New Words* and Simon Mort's also British *Longman Guardian New Words* (1986). Research for the historical sketch provided most of the rest. Each of these almost 2,400 new items and Pfeffer's original 3,000 was meticulously verified as to its German source, as were the 600 items in the Appendix. Large numbers were quite straightforward because our two major sources (the *OED* and *Webster's Third*) concurred in etymologizing them as coming from German. Even if both sources cited German, we checked the item's etymology, for dictionaries do record mistakes. The *OED* was especially useful, not only for the dates given but also because an entry that is a borrowing sometimes begins with the actual foreign-language passage in which the item is first known to have occurred, or at least with the bibliographical reference that permits one to find that original usage. However, many thousands of items are given no etymology in these two great repositories, posing the overwhelming problem of verifying that each of the unetymologized items was not from German. All that we could do in such cases was to employ a kind of "German sense" in noticing seeming German elements in an item, or to find German contexts in the English citations, whereupon we checked the potential loanword.

Sometimes the evidence was insufficient to document the transfer, whereupon we employed the subjective abbreviation *poss.* 'possibly' or *prob.* 'probably,' as an educated guess is better than nothing, and the alternative was to omit the item. If there was evidence for two or even three sources, we employed a double etymology like "G and Fr" or "Fr or G." When we could date the first known German record, which necessarily must be earlier than the first known English record, we were on firmer ground. But there is no date for the English record of over 700 of our items, so that often even our knowing the first German record was inadequate for deciding a dubious transfer. Still, some chronological information was often available, as when we could roughly date the event or discovery. Also, say, if English word *X* looks and means much like German word *Y*, and if *Y* can be dated as 1900 and *X* first appears in *Webster's Second* (1934), then the earlier *Y* is a possible etymon for the later *X*. But unetymologized German loanwords probably still remain buried in our major sources, with no practical way to find them.

Sometimes the *OED* and *Webster's Third* differ on an etymology, usually involving a German designation by the *OED*, but New Latin by the latter, despite the word's usage in an otherwise all-German passage. An extreme example of the problem of such identification is *Moeritherium*, which is etymologized as New Latin by both the *OED* and *Webster's Third*, but which we included. Fortunately, the *OED*'s bibliographical reference to a German set of *Verhandlungen* caught our eye. We tracked down the actual proceedings and discovered that the word was used by the archaeologist Sir William Andrews, in a German paper published in the German proceedings, though he otherwise wrote only in English. The reader will find dozens of instances where we have given a German source for items that *Webster's Third* etymologizes as New Latin, quietly correcting but always providing enough evidence so that the reader can verify our decision if desired. Sometimes this required us to give the name and dates of the German scholar who coined the term, information that we provided for etymological rather than for informational purposes. Many of our words have fascinating histories pointing back to otherwise unrecorded names of German scholars and others, as can be seen in our Historical Overview.

We might note that our etymologies provide only enough information so that the specialist can construct the details of the total transfer. As our purpose is not to study historical etymology, we usually give the German sources only when they themselves come from non-Germanic languages like Latin and/or Greek (and we transliterate all non-Roman scripts), trusting historical Germanicists to determine such etymologies for themselves. Thus most of our German-derived entries simply cite "G *X*." The ultimately classical ones use a form like "G *P* < MHG *Q* < OHG *R* < ML *S* < Gk *T*" or "G *P* < L *Q* < Gk *R*." A well-known problem is that numbers of German items came from unidentified, probably non-Germanic sources, since the early Germanic peoples ranged throughout central and northern Europe. These sources are often not even identifiable as Indo-European, and we cite "G *X*, of unknown origin" for the few such items, rather than using an etymology like "G *X*" to misleadingly suggest a known Germanic origin. We should further note that additional linguistic and other information is often found in technical handbooks and similar sources, as in mineralogy, where Michael Fleischer's updated *Glossary of Mineral Species* was extremely useful.

FORM OF THE ENTRY

Now we can describe our dictionary entries and the Appendix, with elaboration beyond what has already been said about them. Our entries follow conventional dictionary format and sequence: word, part of speech, first recorded date, semantic area, label, variant forms, etymology and first recorded German date, English definition, productive forms, grammatical remarks, dictionary sources of the word, and degree of assimilation, not all of which appear for every entry. First comes the bold-faced main entry, the first letter of which is capitalized if the item is an active trademark. Next the part of speech is designated in italics. If the item is a noun with the standard -s plural, we simply mark it as *n.*, using traditional abbreviations that are listed in our List of Abbreviations. As the few mass nouns naturally take no plural and usually are so indicated by their definition, we have saved space by marking them, as well as the -s plural types and noun phrases, as being an *n.* Irregular plurals, such as for *achromatic lens* and *albertustaler,* are indicated by ''**-es** *pl.*'' and ''**-ø/-s** *pl.,*'' respectively, the latter meaning that *albertustaler* can take either plural form and that the **-ø** may or may not be the more common plural. As all the verb borrowings are regular, we mark them simply as *v.,* omitting the unnecessary -*ed,* -*ing,* etc. Next comes the parenthesized, earliest known English printed date, usually taken from the second edition of the *OED* as symbolized by *O* at the end of the entry. *Webster's Ninth*'s dates are sometimes earlier than the *OED*'s. Those dates and dates from other non-*OED* sources are symbolized by *W9, DAE,* etc. If only one dictionary source is given at the end of the entry, say *W9,* the *W9* source is not redundantly cited inside the parenthesized date. As few of our borrowings are earlier than 1500, we have made little use of the *Middle English Dictionary,* which otherwise might have supplied some earlier dates than those found even in the second edition of the *OED.*

Next appears the italicized semantic area, such as *Art* or *Ichthy.* (for *Ichthyology*). See our list of Semantic-Field Labels. We have been economical in choosing the designations of the semantic areas, considerably reducing the number used in the *OED* for a vastly larger corpus and employing a four-division semantic taxonomy of sciences, social sciences, arts, and all other areas. Yet some overlapping was unavoidable. For example, *Mining, Geology,* and *Mineralogy* represent significant areas for our corpus, with some items often catalogued in two or even all three of these areas, whereupon we made a single arbitrary choice. The same is true for *Biology, Chemistry,* and *Biochemistry.* Sometimes we needed separate entries for a homonym marked by superscripts, one of which may have, say, a biological meaning and the other biochemical, even though both may have come from the same German etymon. The superscripts make a deliberate distinction to indicate that the same word has been borrowed twice and should be doubly tabulated. By contrast, if a single entry is designated as having both biological and biochemical meanings, the first English meaning was biological (as given first), and from it was developed an English biochemical meaning. Thus the biochemical meaning was not a reborrowing, but was simply a word's gaining a new meaning in the usual way that a vocabulary item expands its senses.

Next may come a label, which we have employed with caution because of the well-known slipperiness of such designations. A word may be slang in one context but entirely nonstigmatized socially in a different context, it may be rare around 1900 but ubiquitous in the 1990s, and it may be marked as British in one dictionary but unmarked in another dictionary of that same decade. The essentially electronic blending of the first edition of the *OED* and its *Supplement* to create the second edition meant that some items labeled as *rare* in the late 1800s retain that label in the second edition but now enjoy rich quotations in the twentieth century. When Burchfield discovered such citations for his *Supplement,* he often included the stipulation that one should disregard the original double tram-lines indicating the foreignness of the given item. Similar care was needed for words in *Webster's Second* that are marked similarly, since decades later, the items might now be entered in standard desk dictionaries and thus are clearly in general English. When such an item appears in *Webster's Third* without a designation of obsolescence, one can normally presume that modern examples were found. We have avoided almost all temporal labels except *obsolete* and *archaic,* using these cautiously. Questions of rarity are partly answered by the degree of naturalization given at the end of each entry, where a *1* or *2* on our scale of 4 indicates that the word is seldom used; thus *rare* would be a subjective and redundant label.

Our two chief social labels are *slang* and *colloq.* (= colloquial), which are used sparingly and are sometimes placed within the definitions in order to apply the label to a particular sense rather than to all senses of the word. Other attitude labels like *derogatory, euphemistic, humorous,* and the like are sparingly attached, as in *dummkopf* (colloq.). While German, like all languages, has obscene or vulgar words, the only such item borrowed from German into English is *dingus* 'penis,' and the originally transferred German meaning of 'someone or something whose name can't be momentarily remembered' was pejorated to the sexual meaning after the item had come into English. Our labeling was chiefly guided by what our dictionary sources have provided, with the reservation that *Webster's Third* labels far fewer words than does the *OED* and that we lacked the massive data needed for us to make original judgments of this sort. (This is admittedly risky. When Cannon was guided by his dictionary source in labeling the items in his 1987 corpus, a Yiddish-speaking reviewer who had access to attitude data rightly criticized the book because several of Barnhart's designations of Yiddish words as slang could be challenged as to whether they were indeed slang.)

Our use of geographical labels reveals a striking but necessary omission. We know that it would have been useful to be able to divide the corpus into items, say, that are purely British, that began as British and then moved by intralanguage transfer into American English or vice versa, or that were borrowed roughly simultaneously by both British and American English. Our two principal regional labels are *Brit.* and *AmE,* again chiefly derived from our dictionary sources and used with caution. For example, if an item does not appear in any American dictionary but appears in the *OED* (and if this entry cites only British usage) and in the equivalent of three British desk dictionaries, none of which marks the item as British, we were hesitant to label it as British and rarely did so. We have also cautiously used an occasional label of *PaG* 'Pennsylvania German,' *Austrian,* etc., in parenthesis, in our German etymologies to indicate that the etymon of the borrowed item was present in that dialect or common in that area as well as in Standard High German. Our fourth kind of label is given to the thirty-six trademarks in our corpus.

Following the label, a dictionary entry may contain one or more bold-faced variants, if so specified in our sources. For example, except for the older German noun borrowings, a German noun etymon begins with a capital, and in the great majority of cases the earliest known English use of the particular noun retains this capitalization. But unless one or more major sources specify the capitalized form as a modern variant, we would have wasted space and misled the reader by listing the capitalized form as a variant. Often what was the standard form in the original *OED* has been changed over time, as witnessed in *Webster's Third* and particularly in the latest desk dictionaries, in which case we sometimes resorted to a double main-entry, separated by a virgule. If recent citations indicate that the earlier form is still viable but evidently not the usual form, we list the earlier form as a variant. In general, we have been conservative in listing variants, as there are sufficient differences between older (and modern) German spelling and American (often vs. British) spelling as to insure goodly numbers of differing forms of many items. We have chosen not to clutter our entries by listing all such variants, even though the *OED* meticulously specified almost all of them on the basis of its comprehensive files, often with a caveat that the particular form was historical, not modern. Our principle has been to list as variants only the forms that are viable today, with enough cross-references to assist the reader to find the main entry for the particular item and later to collect all the variants if such is desired. For items that have had several viable variants over the decades, we have employed the formula "Old var. X" or "Old var. like X" so as to indicate that this item would be a fruitful source for those interested in phonological and graphemic changes.

Next comes the etymology in square brackets, usually beginning "G X" and possibly followed by the German item's etyma. If the English form has undergone comparatively little graphemic change from its German source, beyond the usual dropping of diacritics, or, in the case of a noun, its capitalization, we do not specify "Ad. of G X," reserving this formula for items that have undergone adaptation but not sufficient as to consider the change a translation. Admittedly this distinction may be quite fine, as when we have designated *middlehand* (from *Mittelhand*) and *foreword* (*Vorwort*) as translations, *aegirite* (*Ägirin*) and *automorphic function* (*automorphe Funktion*) as adaptations, and treated *aesthetic* (*ästhetisch*) and *achroite* (*Achroit*) as borrowings without designation. The adaptations are not numerous, though some reflect inconsistencies in the sources. We have called attention to these and also give the present German spelling if it differs from that of the borrowed etymon.

When we specify an item as a translation, there has been major change in the etyma, as in *airship* (*Luftschiff*). The term *partial translation* is employed for items like *brocken specter* (*Brockengespenst*), and *loose translation* for items like *pursuit-flight* (*Reihen*) where all elements of the German etymon have been rendered into English elements that are only roughly comparable semantically. When the etymological evidence is not certain, the qualification *poss.* or *prob.* is used, sometimes with the formula "Prob. orig. formed as G X" for items like *alantolactone* (*Alantolakton*). When the German who created the word or first used it in the particular sense is famous, or the German's identity might shed light on the English definition, we may cite that person's name, as in the formula "Wagner's G X." We cite the earliest date of the given German written word when known, and even the source in which that word occurred if dictionaries disagree about the particular etymology or perhaps provide no etymology at all. Our source for this date is usually the *OED* if the item is recorded there, but it may be any of the other sources listed in our Primary Sources.

To save space, when the spelling of the English form and of the German etymon, irrelevant of any dropped diacritics and capitalization, is identical, we omit the German form. As German spelling underwent some change about the turn of the twentieth century, with c often becoming k or z, ss becoming β, etc., the etymon for affected earlier borrowings includes the formula "(also now G X)" in parenthesis. Calling attention to this change is important because it sheds light on English phonological and graphemic adaptation, which *Webster's Third* unfortunately is none too careful about, so that at times it appears that a mid-nineteenth-century German item (which is spelled in its twentieth-century form) was the etymon. The problem becomes larger when the *OED* gives a different German spelling (perhaps the correct spelling of the day), leaving one to choose between the two forms, barring the possibility that both German spellings were concurrent.

If the German etymon is a shortening, compound, affixation, etc., its word-formation is noted but seldom specified, as in *Ablaut* as coming from *ab* off + *Laut* sound, with no mention of its being compounded from two free forms. We have had difficulty in etymologizing German etyma that utilize combining forms ultimately from Latin or Greek, as the given form might have been the German borrowed element, or else German borrowed the form directly from the classical language so as to create the particular German word (thus suggesting a German paucity of that particular word-formation resource). For example, German *Aerenchym* used an initial *aer-,* which we do not mark as German because the directly preceding etymon was marked as German; this *aer-* was borrowed from Latin *aer-.* Evidence shows that German was already using *aer-* productively by the time it was prefixed to German *-enchym,* and so we indicate this fact in the etymology before citing the original Latin *aer-* from *aero-,* and the original Greek *enchyma.*

Besides the German etymon's structure and etymology, its meaning is also of importance, so as to shed light on any social or other alteration in the meaning transmitted into English. For example, there may be pejoration, as when *Kraut,* shortened from German *Sauerkraut* 'cured cabbage,' borrowed by English, was used to apply disparagingly to a German, especially a soldier. Have there been elevation, generalization, specialization, splitting, or the like? We provide other interesting or important information as to why the particular etyma were used to form the German word. If the etyma are transparent, then there is no reason to explain, say, the forming of *Allomorphit* because the mineral in question seemed strange, as denoted by the prefixing of *allo-.* But the initial positioning of *Allophan* in forming *Allophansäure* is much less transparent and warrants the explanation that the acid was so named because it changes color or appearance.

Following the brackets enclosing the etymology, the English definitions are placed in the order of their earliest known occurrence in English writing. The single English date that is given early in the entry always refers to the first definition in the entry. Lacking the data, we could not provide the dates of the various senses developed from the usually single sense originally borrowed from German, as helpful as such chronology would be in the study of semantic productivity, as in the case of *blitz* and *blitzkrieg.* A necessary delimitation in our definitions was economy. But we have eschewed one-word definitions or other useless senses like ''a mineral,'' inviting the reader to use our one or more symbols at the end of each entry so as to move from our compressed definition to a fuller one if desired. Our debt to the *OED, Webster's Third,* and the unabridged *Random House* dictionaries and others is evident in our definitions, for we began with theirs before refining and checking against more technical sources and then often adding new information. We have made no effort to be comprehensive in noting all the meanings a borrowing may have developed, but have summarized only the most important ones, sometimes excluding obsolete meanings of a semantically productive word. If an item has only one meaning, which is obsolete, that sense is summarized, and the entry is labeled as obsolete, though it may prove later to have been only temporarily in stasis.

Some definitions end with a parenthetical note indicating that the item has different, often earlier senses that came from another language; these are given in the briefest way. The important point is that our German borrowing did not provide those senses, and our definitions must not be thought to be significantly incomplete (as they might be if we did not note the competing senses). If the borrowing is a fairly recent English translation of a German etymon, as *Leader* that was translated from *Führer* into English writing as early as 1934, we anticipate no confusion with already existing senses, and we do not indicate these earlier senses.

The last definition of an entry is sometimes followed by a dash introducing forms developed in English from the borrowed item, listed as run-on forms. The development of such forms is a major index to the state of an item's assimilation. When the suffix unmistakably identifies the part of speech of such a derivative form, we do not provide the part of speech but we use *-ic* marking an adjective or *-ization* marking a noun only when there might be doubt. Nor in most cases do we indicate the process of word-formation involved in the derivation or compounding, etc., a matter that is discussed in our Linguistic Overview. If there is functional shift, as when a noun borrowed from German later gains an adjectival function in English, only the bare data are given, without a specification of functional shift. When there is a list of such run-on items, any functional shift is given first, and succeeding forms are given in the known chronological order of their creation, together with their first known dates when available. When the generated forms are polysyllabic and numerous, we list only their last syllables. We have tried to be comprehensive in listing them; but sometimes a derivative form was developed from an earlier borrowing of a cognate or source word in a different language, as noted in the previous paragraph, and naturally such a form is not included in our run-on list. Our run-on forms are given in boldface. Additional to this possible run-on list may be a grammatical generalization introduced by a heavy dot and ~, where the ~ symbolizes the entry word. The generalization usually notes a symbolization of a chemical element like *In* from *indium*, an abbreviation like *IQ* from *intelligence quotient*, another kind of shortening like *klatsch* from *kaffeeklatsch*, or a translation like *overbelief* from *Aberglaube*. Each of these is given its own cross-reference, as are the variant forms of the entry word. Run-on items are not cross-referenced.

Each entry ends with a symbolized source or sources, as *O, R, W*, plus a numerical degree of naturalization in brackets. As the three major sources of our items are the *OED*, the unabridged *Random House*, and *Webster's Third*, most entries have one, two, or three of these abbreviations – *O, R,* and/or *W* – whether or not each of the sources identifies the given item as a German borrowing. The entry for the given item in any other dictionaries seldom provides additional semantic information and so is not specified for an item appearing in at least one of our major sources. Infrequently an item occurs only in the first edition of the *OED*, the 1933 *Supplement*, or Burchfield's *Supplement*, but not in the second edition of the *OED*, or only in *W2* but not in *Webster's Third*, in which case this omission is noted. Examples are *eis-wool* in the 1933 *Supplement*, but not in *O2*, and *Festspiel* in *W2* but not in *Webster's Third*. If the item is not listed in the expected alphabetical place in the second edition of the *OED*, the particular location is indicated. When the word occurs in none of our three main sources, we symbolize the other sources, usually from *W2*, the *Third Barnhart*, Mort or one of Ayto's two volumes, Merriam-Webster *12,000 Words*, the *Barnhart Dictionary Companion*, or some specified desk dictionary. We feel that the value of such sources to the reader is worth the considerable space required for the symbols needed. Actually, the use of all of the sources can be important, as in determining the spelling of the usual form and in deciding which spellings are modern variants of that form; but an exhaustive symbolizing of the sources would have entailed unacceptable lengthening of entries. The reader who is interested in phonological-graphemic matters should check all the sources, as when an item is recorded as Spelling *A* in nineteenth-century citations in the *OED*, as *B* in *Webster's Third* as of 1961, and as *C* in the 1987 *Random House* and various desk dictionaries. We usually resolved such a situation by choosing *C* as the current form, possibly with *B* sharing the main entry, and often with the *OED*'s *A* still being a viable variant.

DEGREE OF ACCULTURATION

As he had for his Malay corpus (1992), Cannon used a word's appearance in the latest editions of the four American college or desk dictionaries that are constantly updated, and their four British equivalents as one of the criteria in determining the general degree of assimilation of each word in the corpus. "Degree of assimilation" is a valid question that may be raised in connection with any major study of loanwords. A not uncommon reaction to a new study might be: "They found more loans from language X than I thought were in that language, but most of them are big words that I never heard of. So what?" Cannon asked a more precise question about each item: What is its utility? Is it obscure, used only in limited situations by few people to convey a narrow meaning? If so, our book has simply added a lot more words to the known total, while generally verifying Skeat's and Carr's conclusions as to the relative unimportance of German loanwords in the English vocabulary. As the tabulation and discussion of the items in each of the four degrees of assimilation are treated in the Linguistic Overview, the sketch that follows restricts itself to principles and methodology that Cannon used in arriving at this scale.

Granting that an item in certain situations may slide back and forth at least one degree from that assigned to it, and that *utility* may be viewed by some with reason as an unwarranted criterion in the assessment of acculturation, Cannon suggested three "empirical" criteria for ascertaining a general degree of acculturation. First, any study of borrowing must consider productivity. For example, *abraum* was borrowed into English with a single meaning at least by 1753, but has been semantically unproductive because it still has only this single meaning today. By contrast, *allele* was borrowed by 1931 and now has three or four meanings, transferring the original single meaning into analogical senses but not into figurative ones. Our sources record no productive or generative forms of *abraum* like derivatives, compounds, shortenings, functional shifts, etc., whereas they list the derivatives *allelism* and *allelic* (which are also in the desk dictionaries) and the compound *allele frequency*. So *allele* has given rise to suffixations or endings producing a noun and an adjective plus a hybrid compound, and has had more utility than *abraum* has had, data that we have provided in our dictionary entries for the two items.

Second, the English noun *abraum* needed no graphemic anglicization beyond losing the German capital *A*. The English noun *allele* underwent this experience but also gained the usual *-e* for such biological or chemical words, while retaining the uncapitalized German spelling of *allel* as a variant. Though this information is revealing, the occurrence in our three major sources is at least as significant.

So, third, if *abraum* appears only in the *OED* and *Webster's Third*, but *allele* is in these plus the third of our major sources (the unabridged *Random House*), it would seem to have more utility in English writing. We also tabulate appearance in up to eight desk dictionaries.

These are the American *Webster's Ninth New Collegiate Dictionary* (1983), *American Heritage Dictionary* (1985), *Webster's New World Dictionary of American English* (1988), and *Random House Webster's College Dictionary* (1991). The four British equivalents are *Collins Dictionary of the English Language* (1986), *Longman Dictionary of the English Language* (1986), *Chambers English Dictionary* (1988), and *Concise Oxford Dictionary of Current English* (1990). *Abraum* appears in none of these; *allele,* in all nine. All this evidence shows that the latter is far more useful in English than is *abraum* and deserves a higher rank in naturalization and productivity. Comparatively, it merits the highest rank of *4,* with *abraum* having a 3. We reserve the rating of *2* for other items in our dictionary, and perhaps somewhat arbitrarily an implied rating of *1* for those in the Appendix.

The original *OED* editors grappled with the problem of acculturation and included a four-degree scale in their introduction, using the somewhat facetious terms *naturals, denizens, aliens,* and *casuals.* While the *OED* editors deleted all mention of this or any other such scale in their rewritten introduction to the second edition, one should remember that the original editors used this scale in determining the items in their vast corpus that were still sufficiently foreign at that time as to require the double tram-lines with which they tagged such items. The three-degree German scale of *Gastwort, Fremdwort,* and *Lehnwort* continues to be used by some linguists. Finding the German scale more useful than the *OED* one for the 903 items in Cannon's total Malay corpus, Cannon refined both scales into a four-stage measurement. Further details about all three scales can be found in his 1992 Malay article.

Of course, a degree of subjectivity inheres in the assignment of a word to a given stage. Strictly speaking, the scale measures frequency of the word's use and ability to generate new forms. But one should also consider the degree to which loans adapt themselves to their new linguistic environment. *Leitmotiv,* for example, contravenes the concept of productivity; *abgesang,* that of common use. Both words play a significant role in the vocabularies of the semantic areas to which they relate.

THE APPENDIX: SUPPLEMENTARY LOANWORDS

Some of the 621 items listed in the Appendix rather than in the main dictionary section are undoubtedly archaic or rarely used, but many of the rest may be in a state of transition, awaiting inclusion in the principal lexicons that furnished the sources of our dictionary.

About five-sixths of these loanwords were derived from twenty-five specialized English dictionaries; the other sixth was gleaned from the literature on German loanwords in English. A list of Secondary Sources used for the Appendix and a list of Supplementary loanwords arranged by Semantic Fields can be found elsewhere in this volume.

A living language functions like an organism. As it sloughs off archaic parts, it continues to add new ones, by borrowing from other languages and generating new forms of its own. Words that some of us might today regard as esoteric or technical may become common coin tomorrow. This is the rationale for including the unassimilated loanwords of the Appendix, which increases the total loanwords described in this book to 6,001.

PART I
AN HISTORICAL OVERVIEW BY SEMANTIC FIELDS

SEMANTIC FIELD TABLES

As pointed out in our Introduction, eight decades ago the eminent linguist Walter Skeat stated in the preface to the fourth edition of his *Etymological Dictionary of the English Language* (Oxford, 1910, xiii): "Of all the Teutonic languages, German is the one from which fewest words are directly borrowed." In fact, the number of direct loans, he continued, "is quite insignificant, and they are all of late introduction." The tables and the analyses that follow dispel these assumptions.

The English borrowings from German total 5,380 items, and the dates of their transfer extend from about 1340 to 1990. The earliest among them, like *snorkle* (1340) and *ground* (1400), are harvestings of thirteenth-century German mysticism. The most recent of them, such as *Rottweiler politics* (1989) and *wallpecker* (1990), testify to the political conditions in Central Europe of yesteryear.

The distribution of these items spread over 68 semantic fields plus a miscellany is shown in Tables 1 and 2 below. In Table 1 the fields are arranged in the order of the alphabet; and in Table 2, in the order of numerical rank. The total in Tables 1 and 2 is larger than the 5,380 entries in the dictionary, because some of the words in the count pertain to two or more semantic fields. Of the entries, 93 percent are dated. It is on these that the historical analysis by semantic field in the succeeding pages is primarily based. They are subsumed alphabetically under four subject areas: 1. sciences, 2. social sciences, 3. arts and letters, and 4. others, including miscellany.

The borrowings in each field are presented selectively, in part because some of the data are beyond normal reach, "especially those regarding non-academics," as the editor of Poggendorff's renowned multivolume biographical dictionary stated in a recent letter to the authors. Scholars will also observe that instead of being presented as direct outcroppings of historical movements or cultural events, the loanwords are detailed, insofar as it is possible, against the broad spectrum of history and the developments in the arts and sciences, largely because the dates of their origin, where known, and those of their attested acculturation may be close but are more often years, decades, or even a century apart. Thus we find:

Weltinsel (1845) .... *island universe* (1845)
Neuropilem (1890) .... *neuropilema* (1891)
tonofibril (1899) .... *tonofibril* (1901)
Eschatokoll (1854) .... *eschatocoll* (1897)

Table 1

Semantic field		Semantic field		Semantic field	
Administration	12	Ethnology	18	Optics	27
Aeronautics	6	Food	119	Ornithology	18
Agriculture	5	Forestry	6	Paleontology	5
Anatomy	35	Furniture	6	Pathology	52
Anthropology	37	Games	35	Pharmacology	37
Apparel	11	Geography	26	Philosophy	150
Archaeology	9	Geology	318	Physics	118
Architecture	7	History	6	Physiology	46
Art	39	Ichthyology	20	Politics	201
Astronomy	9	Immunology	12	Pottery	12
Beverages	96	Industry	22	Printing	20
Biochemistry	178	Law	7	Psychology	139
Biology	343	Linguistics	101	Sociology	48
Botany	211	Literature	73	Sports	58
Chemistry	687	Mathematics	63	Technology	37
Commerce	7	Medicine	183	Textiles	10
Crystallography	8	Metallurgy	19	Theater	13
Currency	37	Meteorology	24	Theology	70
Dance	12	Military	130	Trades	13
Ecology	29	Mineralogy	857	Transportation	9
Economics	16	Mining	21	Travel	10
Education	34	Music	193	Zoology	122
Entomology	24	Mythology	33	Miscellany	221

Zuwachsbohrer (1818) .... *increment borer* (1889)
Mitteleuropäer (c. 1815) .... *Mittel-European* (1950)

It will also be seen that the scope of the transfer rate of German items into English, as shown in Table 3, is suggestive of the time periods within which they are discussed, i.e., before 1501, 1501–1750, 1751–1950, after 1950.

The review of each semantic field is concluded by a chronological listing of all German loanwords in that field, dated and grouped by fifty-year periods, which is a convenient but arbitrary way to divide their history in English. As many words have the same date of record in English, to save space we have attached the date only to the terminal word in the given sequence. Thus: *X* 1901, *Y, Z* 1902, where the reader assumes that Y is also dated as 1902. Similarly, if there are no words for a given period, as in 1901–50 or Undated, that designation is omitted entirely from the given chronological listing; but it must be emphasized that each listing for the given semantic field includes all dated plus any undated items collected for this book. That principle of economy has dictated other reductions of space in this Historical

Table 2

Semantic field		Semantic field		Semantic field	
Mineralogy	857	Physiology	46	Theater	13
Chemistry	687	Art	39	Trades	13
Biology	343	Anthropology	37	Administration	12
Geology	318	Currency	37	Dance	12
Botany	211	Pharmacology	37	Immunology	12
Politics	201	Technology	37	Pottery	12
Music	193	Games	35	Apparel	11
Medicine	183	Anatomy	35	Travel	10
Biochemistry	178	Education	34	Textiles	10
Philosophy	150	Mythology	33	Archaeology	3
Psychology	139	Ecology	29	Astronomy	9
Military	130	Optics	27	Transportation	9
Zoology	122	Geography	26	Crystallography	8
Food	119	Entomology	24	Architecture	7
Physics	118	Meteorology	24	Commerce	7
Linguistics	101	Industry	22	Law	7
Beverages	96	Mining	21	Aeronautics	6
Literature	73	Ichthyology	20	Forestry	6
Theology	70	Printing	20	Furniture	6
Mathematics	63	Metallurgy	19	History	6
Sports	58	Ethnology	18	Agriculture	5
Pathology	52	Ornithology	18	Paleontology	5
Sociology	48	Economics	16	Miscellany	221

Overview. For example, as almost all the creators of the etyma for our corpus were German and as the context also makes that identity clear anyway, it would have been redundant to speak of, for example, the *German* physician Theodor Fechner.

Alphabetical indexes of semantic fields with subjects (science, social science, arts, and others) in a single amalgamated list follow.

INDEX TO SEMANTIC FIELDS BY SUBJECT

Table 3
(Including Multiple Entries)

Before 1501	12
1501–50	50
1551–1600	65
1601–50	62
1651–1700	64
1701–50	50
1751–1800	137
1801–50	722
1851–1900	1793
1901–50	1629
1951–	203
Undated	696

ALPHABETIC INDEX TO SEMANTIC FIELDS

SCIENCES

Aeronautics

The first of the six German items that have entered English in the field of aeronautics is *airship* (1819). It is a translation of the generic term for dirigible or balloon, *Luftschiff,* coined in 1755, well before the French aeronautical engineer Henry Giffard (1825–82) attempted to fly the first lighter-than-air machine in 1852.

The three loans that followed pertain to dirigibles and airplanes. The German word for *airplane,* be it noted, is *Flugzeug. Zeppelin* was introduced to English in 1900, the year Count Zeppelin built the first rigid dirigible. *Parseval* emerged in English eight years later as a name for the first nonrigid airship, commemorating August von Parseval (1861–1942), who designed the machine in 1906. The borrowing *Messerschmitt* was not popularized in English until 1940. It refers to the German fighter plane, the first model of which (Me 109) was completed in 1934.

The fifth and sixth loans, *hypergol* and *hypergolic,* were formulated in German as *hypergol* and *hypergolisch* to describe the type of fuel Germans began to use during the latter part of World War II as a rocket propellant.

In chronological order, the loanwords in aeronautics are:

1801–50:	airship 1819
1851–1900:	Zeppelin 1900
1901–50:	Parseval 1908, Messerschmitt 1940, hypergol, hypergolic 1947

Agriculture

German contributed only five terms to English in the realm of agriculture, two of which pertain to dairy farming. They are *sennhutt,* from German *Sennhütte* 'Alpine hut,' and *Senn,* unchanged from German *Senn* 'a shepherd in the Alps.' Senn is dated in German as early as 1462 (see Kluge/Mitzka). *Hay-hut,* the third of these borrowings, is the name of a hut that may be seen on any mountainside. The parts of its German etymon, *Heu* 'hay' and *Hütte* 'hut,' have their roots in Germanic times. The fourth term, *crumb structure* 'crumb-like structure (of the soil),' derives from German *Krümmelstruktur* that was first used in *Forschungen der Agrik.-Physik,* 1882, V, 146. The fifth item, *ring rot,* is a translation of *Bakterienringfäule,* describing a bacterial disease of the potato (see Mackensen).

The five words in agriculture are:

1851–1900:	sennhut 1868, Senn 1882
1901–50:	hay-hut 1903, crumb structure 1906, ring rot 1920

Anatomy

Early Greek medicine ranked healing above a knowledge of the human body and its functions. The principles of anatomy were not spelled out in some detail until 1543, when Andreas

Vesalius, Belgian-born physician of German origin, published his *De humani corporis fabrica libri septem,* with anatomic plates by the Dutch painter J. St. van Kalkar. William Harvey's fundamental discovery of the circulation of the blood is dated 1628. Pathological changes began to be investigated in the eighteenth century, and physiology as a special field of study emerged only in the 1800s. The nomenclature of anatomy remained uncodified until 1895.

The earliest of the 35 German items in English anatomy, however, may be among those gleaned from the sources that are without a date. Examples are *ampulla of Vater,* from German *Vatersche Ampulle,* named after Abraham Vater, German anatomist (1684–1751); *column of Türck,* a translation of *Türckische Säule,* from the name of the Austrian physician Ludwig Türck (1810–68); and *corpuscle of Herbst,* a rendition of German *Herbstsches Körperchen,* commemorating the name of the German physician Ernst F. Herbst (1803–92).

In the order of transfer from German to English, the dated borrowings of Latin and/or Greek origin include: *fundiform* (1854), a latinized translation of German *schleuderförmig,* coined in 1841 by Andreas Retzius (1796–1860); *ependyma* (1872), used as *Ependym* by the German physician Rudolf Virchow (1821–1902), the founder of cellular pathology; *delomorphic* (1882), from German *delomorph* (1870), conceived by Alexander Rollett (1834–1903); *chordotonal* (1888), first employed in 1882 in German as *chordotonal* by Veit Graber (1844–92) in a paper published in the *Archiv für mikroskopische Anatomie,* XX, 506; *zoochlorella* and *zooxanthella* (1889), terms created by the German anatomist Karl Andreas Heinrich Brandt (1854–1931); *neuropilema* (1891), formulated in 1890 by Wilhelm His, Swiss anatomist (1831–1904); and *tonofibril* (1901), first used by Martin Heidenhain (1864–1949), German anatomist, in an article that appeared in 1899 in the *Archiv für mikroskopische Anatomie,* LIV, 212.

Examples of more recent neologisms in this field that were transferred into English without significant, if any, change are, briefly, *myoplasm* (1907), formulated by Paul Schiefferdecker (1849–1931) in 1905; *neëncephalon* and *paleëncephalon* (1917), devised in 1908 by the German anatomist Ludwig Edinger (1855–1918); and *nephron* (1932), originated by the German anatomist Hermann Braus (1868–1924) eight years before it surfaced in English.

We offer finally two of numerous additional acculturations in English that came from the pen of less prominent Central European anatomists. They are *spindle* (1894), from German *Spindel* (1863), employed in the anatomic sense by Wilhelm Kühne (1837–1900); and *germ center* (1898), a translation of German *Keimzentrum,* so named in 1884 by Walther Flemming, a German anatomist (1843–1905).

The thirty-five words in anatomy are:

Undated:	ambos, ampulla of Vater, autoscopy, column of Türck, corpuscle of Herbst, corpuscle of Vater, metakinesis[2], neurotrope, pronormoblast, protoblast, rumpf
1851–1900:	fundiform 1854, parametritis 1869, ependyma 1872, clastic 1875, delomorphic 1882, chordotonal 1888, zoochlorella, zooxanthella 1889, neuropilema 1891, spindle 1894, rhomboencephalon 1897, germ center 1898, autoscope 1900
1901–50:	tonofibril 1901, neurotropism 1905, myoplasm, paraganglion 1907, paleostratium 1913, dermatome 1915, neëncephalon, paleëncephalon 1917, Rouget cell 1922, nephron 1932, lipochondrion 1936

Astronomy

The nine German borrowings in astronomy scarcely reflect the contributions made to the field by German astronomers beginning with men such as Georg von Peuerbach (1423–61), who taught astronomy, mathematics, and philosophy in Vienna and not only began the translation of Ptolemy's *Almagest,* but built astronomical instruments, observed the stars, and prepared astronomical tables.

Besides the earliest recorded German loan *trabant* (1617), English lexicons record only the following borrowings between the years 1751 and 1950: *island universe* (1867), a translation of German *Weltinsel,* coined in 1845 by the German natural scientist Alexander von Humboldt (1769–1859); *gegenschein* (1880), attested in German sources since 1854 and denoting a patch of faint, nebulous light that occurs in the elliptic and opposite the sun; *astrophysics* (1890), from German *Astrophysik,* employed in 1854 by the German astronomer Joseph von Fraunhofer (1787–1826); *durchmusterung* (1892), first used by Friedrich Wilhelm August Arglander (1799–1875) in his book *Durchmusterung des nördlichen Himmels,* 1856; *stereocomparator* (1901), introduced as *Stereokomparator* by Max(imilian) Wolf in the *Astronomische Nachrichten* of 1901, 3,749; and *Schmidt telescope* (1939), called in German *Schmidt-Spiegelteleskop* after Bernhard Schmidt (1879–1935), Estonian-born German specialist in optics.

The two German items introduced to English in astronomy after 1950 are *Olbers' paradox* and *Schmidt camera.* The paradox, named after the German astronomer H. Wilhelm Olbers (1758–1840), holds that if enough stars were distributed over an infinite static universe, the sky ought to be as bright at night as it is during the day. The camera that bears the name of the Estonian-born German optician Bernhard Voldemar Schmidt (1879–1935) is a device employing a photographic reflecting telescope.

The nine words relating to astronomy are:

1601–50:	trabant 1617
1851–1900:	island universe 1867, gegenschein 1880, astrophysics 1890, durchmusterung 1892
1901–50:	stereocomparator 1901, Schmidt telescope 1939
1951– :	Olbers' paradox 1952, Schmidt camera 1978

Biochemistry

Because the study of the chemical processes in living things is not very old, it is not surprising to find that all of the dated German biochemical items entered the English lexicon after the year 1800, *Protein* aside,[1] the first dated loans were, in fact, introduced to English from German in the years 1844, 1845, and 1847. These borrowings are, respectively, *humin, biliverdin,* and *crystallin.* A citation in the *OED* associates the Dutch chemist Gerhardus Johannes Mulder (1802–80), sometime professor of chemistry at the University of Utrecht, with *humin,* which appears to have entered English via German. He investigated humus substances and humic acids in 1844 and his work attracted much attention in translation. The Swedish chemist Jöns Jakob Berzelius (1779–1848) is known to have coined *biliverdin* in German in 1840.

[1]*Protein* was apparently also coined in German by the Dutch chemist Johannes Mulder (1802–80) and published in French as *protéine* in the *Bulletin des Sciences Physiques en Néerlande,* III (1838).

And *crystallin,* from German *Kristallin,* a globulin in the crystallin lens of the eye, is connected with German (and possibly Swedish) in *Webster's Third.*

It is well to note here that, in addition to *biliverdin,* Berzelius discovered and named in German *Glycin* in 1848. It passed into English as *glycine* in 1851.

Born about twenty years after Berzelius, the German chemist Justus (von) Liebig formulated in 1853 the term *Kynurensäure.* An English biochemist translated it in 1872 as *kynurenic acid.*

Heinrich Wilhelm Wackenroder (1798–1854), another German biochemist of the time, was the first to isolate *carotene* from carrots (*OED* 1861). He called his 1831 discovery *Carotin.* In 1845 he also discovered the compound *Pentathionsäure* that became English *pentathionic acid.*

The German Nobel laureate in physiology of 1910, Albrecht Ludwig Kossel (1853–1927), who analyzed proteins, protamines, and amino acids, coined a number of terms that found their way into English. They are *Histon* named in 1884 (*histone* 1885), *Histidin, Salmin,* and *Sturin* in 1896 (*histidine, salmine,* and *sturine* 1896), as well as *Proton* in 1898 (*protone* 1898).

Kossel was actually a biochemist, as was his fellow-laureate Heinrich Otto Wieland (1877–1957). Wieland investigated sterols, alcaloids, and pterins. His discoveries include the enzyme *Dehydrase,* named in 1913 in German and registered in English as *dehydrase* in 1914.

The Austro-German chemist Richard Johann Kuhn (1900–67) was awarded the Nobel prize in chemistry for his research in vitamins. He and his associate investigators discovered both *flavin(e)* and *ovoflavin* in 1933. English adopted both terms the same year.

The terms *Chromosom* and *Neuron* were coined by the German biochemist Heinrich Wilhelm Gottfried von Waldeyer-Hartz (1836–1921) in 1888, six years after he had formulated and named *Keratohalin.* Anglicized, these loanwords are *chromosome, neuron,* and *keratohalin(e).* Their dates of first record in English are 1889, 1891, and 1887, respectively.

One of the most prolific stereochemists of the late nineteenth and early twentieth centuries, Hermann Emil Fischer (1852–1919) entered upon his academic career at the University of Munich. He accidentally discovered *Phenylhydrazin* in 1875 (*phenylhydrazine* 1897). In 1891 he added to his string of discoveries the amino acid *Lysin* and the sugar *Ribose.* English transferred them as *lysine* and *ribose* in 1892. In 1903 there followed *Polypeptid* and *Peptid,* which the *OED* records in 1903 and 1906, respectively.

The German biochemist Felix Ehrlich (1877–1942) created *Isoleucin* in 1903. It passed immediately into English as *isoleucine.*

The biochemical term *oligodynamic* (*OED* 1893) was coined in German in 1893 by the Swiss botanist Carl Wilhelm von Nägeli (1817–91). He is known for his micellar theory about the cell structure of plants, a theory long since confirmed.

Another Swiss originator was his fellow countryman Alexander Tschirch (1856–1939). He established the field of pharmacognastics, which he taught at the University of Bern. In 1907 he created *Protopectin.* It has been known in English by that name since 1908.

Adolf Friedrich Johann Butenandt (b. 1903), who shared the 1939 Nobel prize in chemistry with Leopold Ružička, is credited with the discovery of *Pregnandiol* in 1930, *Androsteron* in 1931, and *Progesteron* in 1934 (see Meyer). English dictionaries list *pregnandiol, androsterone,* and *progesterone,* respectively, as of 1930, 1934, and 1935.

Among the dozens of less well-known Germans who contributed loanwords to the expanding English vocabulary in biochemistry between 1751 and 1950, we single out, in conclusion,

Eugen Baumann (1846–89), who is responsible for the neologism *cysteine*. He used it for the first time in German (*Cystein*) in 1882, and its English form followed in 1884. We also note Hans Ernst August Buchner (1850–1902), the discoverer of *alexin* in 1891 (*OED* 1892); Anton Friedrich Robert Behrend (1850–1926), who is credited with creating *uracil* in 1885 (*OED* 1890); Adolf Friedrich Ludwig Strecker (1822–71), who named *choline* in 1862 (*OED* 1869); and Bernhard Christian Friedrich Tollens (1841–1918), who is responsible for finding and coining the name of *polysaccharides* in 1888 (*OED* 1892).

English gained only three German biochemical loanwords after 1950: *macroglobulin, psilocin,* and *siderochrome,* from 1952 to 1961.

The 178 words relating to biochemistry are:

Undated:	chondromucoid, conglutinin, gitoxin, hyalogen
1801–1850:	protein 1838, humin 1844, biliverdin 1845, crystallin 1847
1851–1900:	biochemical, creatinine, glycine 1851, peptone 1860, carotene 1861, picrolichenin 1862, spongin 1868, aleurone, choline, h(a)emoglobin 1869, bilirubin, glutamic acid, proteid, proteide 1871, kynurenic acid 1872, protamine 1874, elastin, urochloralic acid 1875, polyporic acid, zymogen 1877, nuclein 1878, chromophore 1879, biochemistry, enzyme 1881, chromatin 1882, phenylanaline 1883, cysteine 1884, chondroitic acid, histone 1885, hepatin, heteroxanthine, rhodopsin 1886, chemotactic, keratohyalin(e) 1887, rhamnose 1888, chromosome 1889, dispireme, uracil 1890, neuron, sabadine 1891, alexin, lysine, polysaccharide, ribose 1892, oligodynamic 1893, cytosine, glucase, ovomucoid, protochlorophyll, thymine 1894, chondroitin, cytase, nucleon^l 1895, histidine, myogen, salmine, sturine 1896, phenylhydrazine 1897, protone, sitosterol 1898, cephalin, lysin, mucoid 1900
1901–50:	chemosynthesis, isolysin 1901, amboceptor, kinase, nuclease 1902, chemosynthesis, isoleucine, kyrine, oxygenase, polypeptide 1903, guanase, proline 1904, hirudin, pseudo-globulin 1905, peptide, tetrapeptide 1906, nucleoprotein, ph(a)eophytin, phytol, stigmasterol, valine 1907, antigen, coenzyme, haemogregarine, nucleotide, protopectin, volutin 1908, adenosine 1909, carboxylase, cytidine, nucleoside, pheophorbide, polynucleotide, tetrodotoxin, uridine 1911, carotenoid, polyphenol, oxydase, porphyrinogen 1913, dehydrase, mutase, prodigiosin 1914, uroporphyrin 1915, heterophile 1920, ergotamine 1921, elution, ergotaminine 1922, cozymase, sulfatase, uroporphyrinogen 1924, elute, myoglobin, plasmal, plasmalogen 1925, collagenase, dipeptidase 1927, oxyproline, sporonin, wear-and-tear pigment 1928, cathespin, proteinase, zeaxanthin 1929, kallikrein, oligosaccharide, Pasteur reaction, pregnanediol 1930, kynurenine, protoheme, sporopollenin, suprasterol, violaxanthin 1931, lumisterol, phosphomonestrase 1932, flavin(e), grass tetany, lyochrome, ovoflavin, tachysterol 1933, androsterone 1934, heteroauxin, progesterone, riboflavin, testosterone, thiochrome 1935, biotin, pregnenolone 1936, corticosterone, reclamation disease 1937, diaphorase 1938, porphobilin, porphobilinogen, phylloquinone 1939, aldolase, ommatin, ommin 1940, oligopeptide 1941, actin, oligonucleotide 1942, ganglioside 1943, ommochrome, phospholipase 1945, macroglobulinaemia, paraprotein 1949, kallidin 1950
1951– :	macroglobulin 1952, psilocin 1958, siderochrome 1961

Biology

The modern study of the structure, nature, and behavior of living things was given its name *Biologie* in 1802 by Gottlieb Reinhold Treviranus (1776–1837) in his work titled *Biologie oder die Philosophie der lebenden Natur, 1802–22.* (English took note of the term *biology* in 1813.) German, Austrian, and Swiss biologists, anatomists, zoologists, etc., as well as their foreign colleagues writing in German, have since added hundreds of items to the German dictionary of biology, of which 339 have attestedly found their way into English. The following is limited to a sampling of their contributions.

The German biologist Caspar Friedrich Wolff (1733–94), professor at the University of St. Petersburg, for example, developed early the concept *Epigenese* (English *epigenesis,* 1807) to disprove the theory of preformation in favor of the concept of evolution.

In his book, *Das entdeckte Geheimnis der Natur im Bau und der Befruchtung der Blumen,* 1793, Christian Konrad Sprengel (1750–1816) noted the fact that the sexual parts of a single blossom matured at different times and named the phenomenon *Dichogamie,* now English *dichogamy* (1862).

The doctrine that cells are the basic units of structure in plants and mammals was formulated in 1838 by the German botanist Mathias Jacob Schleiden (1804–81) and sustained in 1839 by his friend, the German anatomist and physiologist Theodor Schwann (1810–82). Schwann himself coined the word *metabolisch* in 1839. It entered English in 1845 as *metabolic.* Also, the so-called *Schwann-Zelle* (1839), English *Schwann cell* (1906), bears his name.

Their contemporary, Hugo von Mohl (1805–72) of the University of Tübingen, introduced the notion *Protoplasma* in 1846, which became English *protoplasm* the same year. (The term *Protoplasma* had been used earlier with a different meaning by the Austro-Czech physiologist Johannes Evangelista Purkinje, 1787–1869, in *Übersicht der Arbeiten und Veränderungen der schlesischen Gesellschaft für vaterländische Kultur,* 1839, 2.)

Max Johannes Sigismund Schultze (1825–74), a German anatomist who taught successively at the University of Bonn and of Halle, recognized in 1861 that protoplasm is the physical basis for life. At about the same time, the German biologist Christian Gottfried Ehrenberg (1795–1876) used *Eugenoid* (*eugenoid* 1885) to describe a member of the genus of single-celled aquatic flagellates.

In 1883 August Weismann (1834–1914), professor of biology at the University of Freiburg, published a volume entitled *Keimplasma,* English *germ plasm* (1889). In it he used the term to describe the hereditary portion of the protoplasm and to distinguish it from the remainder of the cell or *Somatoplasma* (English *somatoplasm,* 1889). His synonym for it, *Idioplasma* (1884), passed into English in 1889 as *idioplasm.* Weismann also contributed via German the following words to English biology: *blastogenic* and *somatogenic* (1889), *reduction division* (1891), *determinant* (1893), *id* (1893), *idant* (1893), and *equational division* (1920). In the original German these terms read: *blastogenisch* and *somatogenisch* (1888), *Reduktionstheilung* (1887), *Determinante* (1892), *Id* (1891), *Idant* (1892), and *Aequationstheilung* (1887).

The German zoologist Theodor Boveri (1866–1915), who is viewed as the founder of cytology, is also credited with formulating the term *Centrosom* (1888), now *Zentrosom, Hemikaryon* (1905), and *Oocyt* or *Ovocyt* (1892). They entered English as *centrosome* (1889), *hemikaryon* (1925), and *oocyte* or *ovocyte* (1895).

The botanist who established that the somatic or body cells have a double or *diploid* (1905)

13

number of chromosomes and that the reproductive cells have but a single set or *haploid* (1905) chromosome was Eduard Strasburger (1844–1912) of Jena and Bonn. In addition to *diploid* and *haploid,* which English gained in 1908, he originated the concepts *Chloroplast* (1883), *Anaphase, Metaphase* and *Prophase* (1884), *Kinoplasma* (1892), *Centrosphäre* (1893), *Zygosom* (1904), and *Polyploidie* (1910). English dictionaries now record *chloroplast* (1887), *anaphase* and *metaphase* (1887), *prophase* (1884), *kinoplasm* (1894), *centrosphere* (1896), *zygosome* (1905), and *polyploidy* (1922).

Paralleling Strasburger's contributions to the terminology relating to plants, the German anatomist Walter Flemming (1843–1905) included in his principal work, *Zellsubstanz, Kern und Zelltheilung* (1882): *Cytaster* (now *Zytaster*), *Metakinese, Mitosis* (now *Mitose*), and *Spirem.* In 1887 he added *homöotypisch* and *heterotypisch.* The *OED* records the English forms as follows: *cytaster* (1892), *metakinesis* (1888), *mitosis* (1887), *spireme* (1889), *homeotypic* (1888), and *heterotypic* (1885).

By the 1840s the German physiologist Johannes Peter Müller (1801–58) had conceived the name *Cytoblast* (1840), introduced to English in 1842 as *cytoblast.* In 1858 the German botanist Heinrich Anton De Bary (1831–88) had suggested the term *Mycetozoa* (*OED* 1887) and had expanded on the use of the name for a mutually beneficial association of two types of organisms, *Symbiosis* or *Symbiose.* (A citation in the *OED,* dated 1877, credits a Dr. Brandt, i.e., the German zoologist Johann Friedrich Brandt, 1802–79, with having coined it.) Six years earlier, Maximilan Perty (1804–84) had published his book *Zur Kenntnis kleinster Lebensformen,* 1852, containing the new word *Metabolie* that English has recorded since 1890 as *metaboly.* And the Austrian monk Gregor Mendel (1822–84) had given special meaning to the words *dominierend* and *rezessiv* in 1866, marking the beginning of our precise understanding of genetics. English did not gain these German meanings for the old words *dominant* and *recessive* until 1900.

As numerous as were the contributions to the biological thesaurus by some of the scientists cited above, they were exceeded by those of Ernst Haeckel (1834–1919). This famous German zoologist and philosopher added to the list, among others: *Cytode* (now *Zytode*), *Gonochrist, Gonochorismus* and *Morphon* (1866); *Plankton* (1887); *holoplanktonisch, meritisch, meroplanktonisch,* and *Nekton* (1890); *planktonisch* and *Planktologie* (1891). They were introduced to English beginning in 1873.

Dozens of other biologists, etc. account for the remaining borrowings. Most of them are native to Germany, Austria, and Switzerland. These include Julius Sachs (1832–1897), who coined *Energid* in 1892. It became *energid* in English in 1897. Other such neologisms and their authors are (German) *Euryhalin,* 1871 (English *euryhaline* 1888), by Karl August Möbius (1825–1908); *mixotroph,* 1897 (*mixotrophic* 1900) by Wilhelm Pfeffer (1845–1920); *Enchylema,* 1880 (*enchylema* 1886) by Johann Ludwig von Hanstein (1822–81); *Spongioplasma,* 1885 (*spongioplasm* 1886) by Franz von Leydig (1821–1908); *holopneustisch,* 1877 (*holopneustic* 1892) by Johann Axel Palméns; *Idioblast,* 1893 (*idioblast* 1893) by Oscar Hertwig (1849–1922); *epitok,* 1868 (*epitocous* 1896) by Ernst Ehlers (1857–1927); and *Chromosom,* 1888 (*chromosome,* 1889), *Neuron,* 1891 (*neuron* 1891), and *Organisator,* 1921 (*organizator* 1924) by Heinrich Wilhelm Gottfried Waldeyer-Hartz (1836–1921). There are also *Myoplasma,* 1905 (*myoplasm* 1907), by Paul Schiefferdecker (1841–1931); *Treponema,* 1905 (*treponema* 1908) by Fritz Richard Schaudinn (1871–1906); *Rezeptor,* 1900 (*receptor* 1900) and *neutral,* 1880 (*neutral* 1893) by Paul Ehrlich (1854–1915); *Plasmotomie,* 1898 (*plasmo-*

tomy 1902) by Franz Doflein (1873–1924); and *Auslöser,* 1935 (*releaser* 1937) by Konrad Lorenz (1903–79).

Finally, some of the non-German biologists, etc., who created and published their neologisms in German are the Polish-American biochemist of German origin Casimir Funk (1884–1967), who is responsible for the term *Vitamin* in 1912 (English *vitamin* 1912); the Dutch botanist and geneticist Hugo De Vries (1845–1915), who included *Mutante* and *Mutation* (English *mutant* and *mutation* 1901) in his work *Die Mutationstheorie* (1901–3); the German-Dutch zoologist Ehrich Wasmann (1859–1937), whose basic work on the communal life of insects, *Instinkt und Intelligenz im Tierreich* (1897), yielded the term *Syntrophie* (English *syntrophy* 1897); and the American zoologist of German origin Richard Goldschmidt (1878–1958), who developed the theory of sex determination and named *Dominogen,* 1935 (*dominogene* 1938) and *Phänokopie,* 1935 (*phenocopy* 1937).

The 343 words in biology are:

Undated: alloplasm, amphicaryon, Artenkreis, aula², -biont, chiasto, chondri(o)-, chondriome, chondriomere, chondriomite, chondriosphere, cytolymph, cytomere, cytomicrosome, cytosome, diplokaryon, double assurance, epichordal, eutely, flimmer, formenkreis, idiobiology, mastocyte, mesectoderm, mesendoderm, morpho-, neustic, -plasm, plastein, quellung

1501–50:   spin 1525

1601–50:   trabant 1617

1801–50:   epigenesis 1807, biology 1813, heteronomous 1824, morphology¹ 1830, albinism 1836, chondrin 1838, cytoblast 1842, metabolic 1845, protoplasm 1846

1851–1900:   organoid 1857, blastoderm, cyto- 1859, dichogamy 1862, myelin¹ 1867, trivalent 1868, protagon 1869, heteronomous 1870, fibrinogen, osteoclast 1872, morphon 1873, cytoplasm 1874, autogeny, osteoblast, phenological, phylogenesis, polyphyletic 1875, blast(o)-, gonochorism, outwandered, plasmogony, plastid 1876, plastidule, symbiosis 1877, promorphology, retinula 1878, bacillus, cytode, palingenesis, physiogeny, plasson 1879, phyletic 1881, cytostome, ektogenous, tectology 1883, eutrophic, poikilothermic, prophase 1884, euglenoid, lithistid (n.), microsome 1885, arginine, enchylema, eosinophil(e), hyaloplasm, leucoplast, spongioplasm, systrophe 1886, anaphase, chloroplast, linin, lipochrome, metaphase, mitosis, mycetozoa, ovogenesis, somatoplasm, symbiont 1887, amitotic, cytopyge, euryhaline, eurytherm, homeotypic, mensenchyme, metakinesis, mitome, paramitome, plasma cell, trivalence 1888, blastogenic, centrosome, chromomere, chromosome, germ plasm, gnathostome, hyalosome, idioplasm, nucleoplasm, plastin, somatogenic, heterotypic, spireme 1889, mast cell, metaboly, microphage, ovoplasm, tryptophan, vagile 1890, holoparasite, mitosome, neritic, plankton, reduction division 1891, anlage, cytaster, holopneustic, lithistid (a.) 1892, biophore, determinant, holoplanktonic, id¹, idant, idioblast¹, idiosome, meroplanktonic, milk line, nekton, neutral, planktology, planktonic, thrombocyte 1893, kinoplasm 1894, autobasidiomycete, oocyte, oogonium, orthogenesis, oxychromatin, plasome, platelet, pyronin(e), telophase 1895, astrosphere, centriole, centrosphere, epitokous, ergastic, heterotrophy² 1896, energid, genotype, parasymbiosis, syntrophy 1897, hyperchromatosis, nebenkern, univalent 1898, hyalosome, idiozome, pangen, phototropism, pycnomorphous, sarcosome, symphily, taxis 1899, autotrophic, dominant, ectogenic, gonotome, metatrophic, mixotrophic, nucleocentrosome, paratrophic, receptor, recessive 1900

1901–50: chromatoid, lampbrush, mutant, mutation 1901, autolysis, basichromatin, chromatoplasm, diakinesis, hookworm, melanoblast, plasmotomy, potamoplankton, regulation, X-chromosome 1902, gonomere, melanophore, pseudomonas 1903, arginase, diptoicin, gonochorist, myeloblast, polyblast 1904, gonotokont, kinesis, ovocyte, Phytin, postreduction, prereduction, zygosome 1905, biotype, chromidium, prochromosome, pure line, Schwann cell 1906, myoplasm 1907, diploid, haploid, phytase, treponema 1908, adenosine, cryptomere, cytophilic, cytotropism, milk ridge, mycobacterium, organelle, placode, syndesis, trophochromatin 1909, autoagglutination, chondriosome, liposome, paedogamy 1910, chimera, chondricont, gene, lampbrush chromosome, neuron, phenolase, phenotypical, phenotype 1911, agamont, chromidiogamy, chromidiosome, gamont, nannoplankton, parabasal, peridinian, plasmogamy, vitamin 1912, interphase, monocyte, phenol oxydase 1913, polymery 1914, intersexuality, periclinal, chim(a)era, seston, Z line 1916, intersex 1917, equational division 1920, haplont, polyenergid, polyploid 1920, Urschleim 1921, polyploidy 1922, biological value, organizator 1924, centromere, chromonema, diplont, diplophase, hemikaryon, heteropycnosis, monoblast, pericyte 1925, cyclomorphosis, euploid 1926, organization center, pluripotency, polygenic, provitamin, restitution nucleus 1927, allopolyploidy, monoploid, neuston, osteon 1928, mesophase 1929, fetalization, genom(e) 1930, allele, aneuploid, mixoploid, tripton 1931, euchromatin, heterochromatin, plasmon, saprobe 1932, isogenic 1933, aneuploidy, penetrance, tropotaxis 1934, holomictic, meromictic, monolimnion, phenocopy, polysomatic[2], polysomaty, releaser 1937, autotroph, dauermodification, dominogene, nucleoid, phenogenetics, spinnbarkeit, X organ 1938, pinosylvin(e), pleiotropy 1939, monoxenous 1940, endomitosis, plasmoblast 1942, spinnbar 1944, eurytopic 1945, somatogamy 1949

1951– : thiobacillus 1951, scotophil 1952, cladogenesis 1953, plastome 1954, Z disc 1972, psychrotolerance 1977

Botany

The earliest of the 211 German botanical items borrowed into English is *raff*, from *Reff*, originally meaning 'timber' in OHG. It appears to have come into the English language around 1440, possibly in connection with mining operations in which Germans are known to have been engaged as early as the thirteenth century in Cornwall.

Between 1501 and 1750, the presence in English of a comparatively large number of botanical names derived from German is not surprising. Three of the five best herbalists in the early sixteenth century were German: Otto Brunfels (c. 1488–1534), Hieronymus Bock (1498–1534), and Leonhart Fuchs (1501–66), now often called ''the father of botany.'' The other two were English: John Gerard (1548–1612) and William Turner (d. 1568). Of the two, Turner traveled widely and repeatedly in Germany and collected plants in many parts of the German Rhineland, as well as in Holland. He had access to Fuchs's *New Kreuterbuch* (1543) and introduced many botanical names from German in his *Names of Herbs* (1548) and a *New Herbal* (1551, 1568). Exemplifying the thirty-five borrowed botanical names, better called *herbals,* are *sneeze-wort* and *swallowwort, sorb apple* and *thoroughwax, devil's milk* and *devil's dung.*

Three hundred years after Turner's death the store of English botanical terms once more began to be augmented by a considerable number of German terms. However, very few among them like *springwort* (1889), *plank buttress* (1903), and *prop root* (1905) retained the ring of the vernacular tradition of the 1600s. Also, most of the German botanical terms introduced to English between 1501 and 1750 were names of herbals. Moreover, the vast majority of those that now followed reflected the advances in the study of plant morphology, anatomy, physiology, and, above all, in classification.

Although the first known attempt at describing and classifying plants was that of the Greek philosopher Theophrastus (c. 372–287 B.C.), who succeeded Aristotle as the leader of the peripatetic school he founded, Theophrastus's work was still one of the three standard botanical sources when Bock, Brunfels, and Fuchs published their descriptions of plants in the sixteenth century.

First to demonstrate that pollen is necessary for fertilization and seed formation was Rudolf Jakob Camerarius (1665–1721), appointed in 1688 professor of medicine and director of the Botanic Gardens of the University of Tübingen. His discoveries, published in Latin, were popularized in M. Mobius's translation, *Über das Geschlecht der Pflanzen* (1694).

Almost two hundred years later there began to appear Adolf Engler's *Die natürlichen Pflanzenfamilien,* now in thirty-two volumes, published by Engelmann, Leipzig, 1891–1911. His *Syllabus der Pflanzenfamilien,* in its thirteenth edition, was published by the Gebrüder Bernschläger in 1983 in Berlin. In its fifth edition, edited by O. Mügger, 1924–7, is Harry Rosenbusch's *Mikroskopische Physiographie* (2 vols. Stuttgart, Schweizerbärtscher Verlag, 1873).

Of the 156 dated English botanical terms for which English is indebted to German scholarship after 1750, 144 have first dates of attestation extending from 1851 to 1950. Examples are below under the headings of taxonomy, morphology, physiology, anatomy, and ecology.

An illustrative English borrowing from German relating to plant taxonomy, or classification, is, first, *pteridophyte* (1880), from German *Pterydophyt,* coined by Ernst Haeckel (1834–1919) in his *Generelle Morphologie der Organismen* (1866). It refers to a plant such as a fern or fern ally. Another such term is *taxon* (1929), from German *Taxon,* which the German botanist Adolf Meyer-Abich (1893–1971) first used as a name for a taxonomic group such as a genus or species, in his *Logik der Morphologie* (1926). A third example is *phycomycete* (1887), from German *Phycomycet,* a neologism that the German botanist Anton de Bary (1831–88) drew upon for the first time in his *Morphologie und Physiologie der Pilze* (1866) to label a fungus belonging to the class of Phycomycetes.

Among loanwords in English that are descriptive of plant morphology, one might list *oocyst* (1875), derived from De Bary's *Oocyst,* formulated in his above-cited volume in 1866 as a name for "a chamber for the ova of some Polyzoa." One could add *xylem* (1873), from German *Xylem,* as formed by the Swiss botanist Carl Wilhem Nägeli (1817–91) to describe the wood portion of a vascular bundle in his *Beiträge zur wissenschaftlichen Botanik* (1858). And one might conclude with *speltoid* (1920), from German *Speltoid,* as used in a German context in 1917 by the Swedish botanist of German origin Herman Nilsson-Ehle (b. 1873) for a type of wheat having some of the characteristics of spelt.

A similar sampling of lexical transfers in plant physiology could include *phycobilin* (1945), from German *Phycobilin* (1929); *guttation* (1889), from *Guttation* (1887); and *geotropism* (1875), from *Geotropismus* (1868). These terms emanate from studies by Rudolf Lemberg (b. 1892), Alfred Burgerstein (b. 1892), and Albert Bernard Frank (1839–1900) in *Naturwissenschaften* (XVII, 541/2), *Verhandlungen der zoologisch-botanischen Gesellschaft in Wien* (XXXVII, 692), and *Beiträge zur Pflanzenphysiologie* (1868).

Of terms relating to plant anatomy, three readily present themselves. They are *stomium* (1905), *proembryo* (1849), and *phloem* (1875). The German botanist Karl Goebel (1855–1932) used *Stomium* in his *Organographie der Pflanzen* (1901) to denote the thin-walled cells of a fern annulus. *Proembryo* is found for the first time in Mathias Jacob Schleiden's *Grundzüge der wissenschaftlichen Botanik* (1843) as a name for the group of cells in plants developed before the formation of a true embryo. *Phloem,* the name for a vascular bundle in higher plants, is traceable to Nägeli's above-mentioned book of 1858.

As examples of words relating to plant ecology, one could list four examples coined, respectively, by Andreas Franz Wilhelm Schimper (1856–1901), Ernst Georg Pringsheim (b. 1881) and Lorenz Hiltner (b. 1923). Their names and sources, in that order, are *monsoon forest* (1903), from German *Monsunwald* meaning an open forest found in tropical areas with seasonal heavy rainfall or prolonged drought, in *Pflanzengeographie,* 1898; *photoautotrophic* and *photoheterotrophic* (1945), from *photoautotrophisch* and *photoheterotrophisch,* referring to the autotrophic and heterotrophic ability of plants to obtain energy from light, in *Naturwissenschaften,* 1932, XX, 475; and *rhizosphere* (1929), from *Rhizosphäre,* formulated as a name for the sphere of chemical and bacterial influence of the roots on a plant, in *Arbeiten der Landwirtschaftsgesellschaft,* 1904, XCVIII, 69.

After 1950, the English botanical vocabulary gained only three terms from German: *reserpine* (1952), *thylacoid* (1962), and *isochar* (1963). Their German etyma are *Reserpin, Thylakoid,* and *Isochar* and are documented in the *OED,* respectively, as of 1952, 1961, and 1938.

The 211 words pertaining to botany are:

Undated:	alant, alraun, altha(e)in, amarelle, cataphyll, chlorophyllase, chlorophyllide, cleisto-, clinostat, hypsophil, -nastie, physode, polster, steckling, ventral canal cell, waldmeister
Before 1501:	raff (a.) 1440
1501–50:	larch, masterwort, neeze-wort, pestilence-wort, shabub, sindaw, sorb apple, spindle tree, swallowwort, thoroughwax 1548
1551–1600:	cornel tree, hazelwort 1551, hirse, speltz 1562, swordling 1562, digitalis 1568, linden 1577, aconite, amelcorn, bertram, butterflower, cornel berry, devil's dung, devil's milk, Good King Henry, ground-hele, haskwort, holewort, hollow root, jacobaea, knawel, rosewort, trollflower 1578, crowberry, water violet 1597
1601–50:	cranberry 1647
1651–1700:	raff (n.) 1667
1701–50:	maw (seed) 1730
1751–1800:	mangel-wurzel 1767, cembra(n) pine 1785
1801–50:	inulin 1813, Gravenstein 1821, cyclosis, intine 1835, funkia, periderm 1839, proembryo 1849

1851–1900:   cystolith 1857, dasylirion 1858, dichogamy, edelweiss 1862, sinker 1863, chromato-phore, zygospore 1864, dinkel 1866, coniferin 1867, contabescent 1868, phylogeny, protandrous, protogynous, wineberg 1870, periblem, xylem 1873, homogamy, zygo-mycetes 1874, colleter, eucyclic, geotropism, hyponasty, oocyst, paratonic, phloem, plerome, root pressure, tracheid, trichome 1875, plasmogony 1876, autogamy 1877, high forest, knopper 1879, klinostat, pteridophyte 1880, cleistogamy 1881, heteroecious, plagiotropic, trichoblast, phototactic 1882, Chlamydomonas, einkorn, exine, proto-phloem 1884, chromoplast, mestome, stereome, trophoplast 1885, ph(a)eoplast, plagi-otropism, rhodoplast 1886, homostyly, hydroid, neck canal cell, phellem, phycomycete, protoxylem 1887, tonoplast 1888, aerotropism, guttation, springwort 1889, heterotro-phy[1], holosaprophyte 1890, hemiparasite, mesarch[1] 1891, aerenchyma, limnoplankton, metaphyte, phototaxis 1893, granum, symplast[1] 1894, hemisaprophyte, hydathode, my-corrhiza, ombrophilous, ombrophobous, perine 1895, sclereid 1896, individualism, par-asymbiosis, ectotrophic 1897, hadrome, leptome, photosynthesis 1898, endotrophic, polytropic[2] 1899, emmer, geophyte, haptotropism, heterotrophy[3], hexenbesen, hy-drom(e), prototrophic, pseudogamy, purple bacterium, stemform 1900

1901–50:   gas vacuole, porogamy 1902, monsoon forest, rain forest, plank buttress 1903, plas-modesma, prop root, stomium 1905, nyctinastic 1906, nastic 1908, chomophyte 1909, parthenocarpy, prototrophic, sclerophyll 1911, phragmoplast 1912, alpenrose 1914, cryptobiotic, heterokaryotic, homokaryotic 1916, afrormosia, orthoploid, rhynchospor-ium, speltoid 1920, rhizobium, wound hormone 1921, suction pressure 1922, mesosa-probic, solarization 1925, heteroploid 1926, mesosaprobe, mycotrophy, sectorial (chimaera) 1927, plastochron, rhizosphere, taxon 1929, phytohormone 1933, auxin 1934, telome 1935, nasty, nyctinasty 1936, symplast[2] 1938, pinosylvin(e) 1939, pho-toautotrophic 1943, isoflor 1944, photoheterotrophic, photophilic, phycobilin, syncy-anosis 1945, zebrina 1946, allelopathy 1948, photophilic, phytoalexin 1949

1951– :   reserpine 1952, thylakoid 1962, isochar 1963

Chemistry

The 687 English borrowings from German in the field of chemistry rank in number imme-diately below those in mineralogy, which leads all other semantic areas with its 857 items.

Together these transfers reflect the paramount role that German chemists played in the development of the field. The earliest examples among them are *wismuth* (1587), *zinc* (1641), *Cologne brown* (1658), and *cobalt* (1683).

The metal *wismuth* or *bismuth* was known in the Middle Ages. In Late MHG it was called *wismāt*. Agricola described the methods of mining the metal in 1555. The metal *zinc*, from German *Zink*, possibly from German *Zinke* 'tine, spike,' probably derives its name from the form or manner in which the metal distillate forms on the walls of the melting oven. In OHG times it was called *zinko*. *Cologne brown* (or *earth*) is a translation of German *Kölner Braun*. It is the name of a pigment obtained from lignite, originally from a bed near the city of Cologne. Of more mysterious origin is the name of the metal *cobalt*, from *Kobalt*, which folk etymology associated early with *Kobolt* 'sprite,' because miners originally considered the mineral to be worthless and capriciously scattered among precious metals by mountain spirits and because it had a mysterious effect on miners' health due to the arsenic and sulfur with which it was combined.

Among the earliest examples of seventeenth-century loanwords in chemistry are *zirconium, uranium, titanium,* and *tellurium.* All four were discovered by a leading scientist of the time, Martin Heinrich Klaproth (1742–1817), professor of chemistry at the University of Berlin. Their dates of identification and of emergence in the English lexicon are but few years apart, i.e., 1789/1808, c. 1790/1797, 1795/1796, and 1798/1800.

One of the next loans in chemistry to be introduced to English, *Scheele's green* (1819), from German *Scheeles Grün* (1778), commemorates the name of the founder of organic chemistry, the German-born Swedish chemist Carl Wilhelm Scheele (1742–86).

The equally noted Swedish chemist Jöns Jakob Berzelius (1779–1848) announced in 1818 in a German journal (in German) his discovery of *selenium.* It was noted in English that same year, a few months after its name was published. In 1830 and 1833 Berzelius also coined in German the terms *Polymer* and *polymerisch* that became English *polymer* (1866) and *polymeric* (1833). In 1830, too, his Austrian contemporary Franz Josef Müller (1740–1825) discovered and named *Paraffin.* English adopted the name unchanged in 1838. Soon thereafter Müller added *Creosot* (1832) and *Pittical* (1835) to his list of discoveries. English recorded both *creosote* and *pittical* in 1835.

In 1819 Eilhard Mitscherlich (1794–1863), the German chemist who was the first to see the similarity between crystals of arsenates and phosphates, reported the law of *Isomorphismus.* The earliest date for *isomorphism* in English is 1828. In 1833 he discovered a compound that he named *Benzin,* which English rendered into *benzene* in 1835. (It is not to be confused with the light petroleum distillate that now means gasoline or petrol in some parts of Europe.) In 1834 Justus von Liebig substituted for it the term *Benzol.* The *OED* dates *benzol* as 1838.

Liebig (1803–73), who taught at the University of Giessen and of Munich, was one of the giants in chemistry. Not only did he develop a successful method of measuring amounts of carbon and hydrogen in compounds in 1830, but his name is associated with the discovery of many new chemical substances or groups like *chloral* (1831), *ethyl* (1838), *aldehyde* (1846), *mellon* (1835), and *sarcosine* (1848), in the order of their coinage in German as *Chloral* (1831), *Ethyl* (1834), *Aldehyd* (c. 1834), *Mellon* (1834), and *Sarkosin* (1847).

In 1805 the German pharmacist Friedrich Wilhelm Sertürner (1783–1841) isolated a crystalline substance from opium, which he described in detail in 1816. He called the substance *Morphin,* now known in English (1828) as *morphine.*

Friedrich Ferdinand Runge (1795–1867) was a professor of chemistry at the University of Breslau before he entered industry and became a pioneer in the chemistry of dyes. He isolated *Koffein* from the coffee bean around 1828. It entered English in 1830 as *caffeine.*

One of the co-founders of physiological chemistry, Leopold Gmelin (1788–1853) is remembered particularly as the discoverer of esters in 1848, cited in English as esters beginning with 1852. His three-volume *Handbuch der theoretischen Chemie* (1817–19), now called *Handbuch der organischen Chemie,* is still in print.

The fame of Friedrich Wöhler (1800–82), a student of Gmelin's, rests not only on the fact that he isolated the elements aluminum, beryllium, silicon, and boron, respectively, in 1827, 1828, 1855, and 1856, but also on his having obtained in 1828 *urea* from the inorganic compound ammonium cyanate. He also discovered *cyanuric acid* (1838) (German *Zyanursäure,* 1822) and *silicon(e)* (1863) (*Silicon,* now *Silikon,* 1863).

The term *primary* (1864), from German *primär* (1864), as applied to alcohols, is the creation of Adolf Wilhelm Hermann Kolbe (1818–84), successively professor of chemistry at the University of Marburg and of Leipzig. In 1864 he also discovered what he called *Isobuttersäure* (English *isobutyric acid,* 1871). Twenty years later he added to his list of discoveries *Isatosäure,* which was transferred to English as *isatoic acid* (1885).

While still one of Justus von Liebig's assistants, August Wilhelm von Hofmann (1818–92), who later became professor of chemistry at the University of Berlin, conducted extensive work on coal tar. He is now viewed as the founder of the chemistry of dyes. In 1843 he proved that the amine named *aniline* (*OED* 1850), German *Anilin,* derived variously, as by the German chemist Otto Unverdorben (1806–73) from indigo in 1826, by Friedrich Ferdinand Runge (1795–1867) from coal tar in 1834, by Karl Julius Fritsche (1808–71) from anthranilic acid in 1841, and the same year by Nikolai Zinin (1812–80) by reduction from nitrobenzene, were one and the same. Besides adding other terms, Hofmann added *psilocybin* to the German and English chemical vocabularies in 1858.

The German chemist Albert Ladenburg (1842–1911) was the first to suggest a prism structure for the cyclic compound benzene, which had been discovered by Faraday. In 1881 he discovered and named *Alkyn,* which made its way into English as *alkyne* in the following year.

Emil Fischer (1852–1919), one of Germany's most prolific stereochemists, worked out the structure of glucose and related sugars toward the end of the nineteenth century. He is credited specifically with a wide range of discoveries. They include *Phenylhydrazin* (1875), *Osazon* (1884), *Hydrazon* (1888), *Glucoson* (1889), *Nonose* (1890), and *Octose* (1890). These passed into English as *phenylhydrazine* (1897), *osazone* (1888), *hydrazone* (1888), *glucosone* (1889), *nonose* (1890), and *octose* (1890).

In 1887 Theodor Curtius (1857–1928) termed his newly found compound *Hydrazin* (English *hydrazine,* 1887), and one year later Otto Rudolph called his finding *Phenylhydrazon* in his 1888 inaugural dissertation at the University of Würzburg (English *phenylhydrazone,* 1889).

At about the same time Peter Conrad Laar (1853–1929) introduced the concept *Tautomerismus* (1885) that English adopted as *tautomerism* in 1886.

The German chemist and professor at the University of Jena, Ludwig Knorr (1859–1921), worked on acetoacetic esters. Among the names of cyclic compounds associated with him that found their way into English are *pyrazole* (1887), *pyrazoline* (1887), and *pyrazolone* (1887).

Many other German chemists created and named chemical substances and coined technical terms in the late nineteenth and early twentieth centuries. Mention of four of them will illustrate their reach.

Walther Nernst (1864–1941), who taught at the University of Göttingen, proposed the third law of thermodynamics, which was first described in German as *das Nernstsche Wärmetheorem* in 1906. It is now called the *Nernst-Wärmetheorem.* English reduced the latter to *Nernst's (heat) theorem* in 1913. Friedrich Kohlrausch (1840–1910) showed in 1874 that every ion has a characteristic mobility. He referred to it as *Mobilität.* Its earliest date in the *OED* is 1895. Walter Kossel (1888–1956) recognized the heteropolar nature of chemical compounds, and ten years later Richard Abegg (1869–1910) conceived the terms *heteropolar* and *homopolar* (1906). Their earliest date in English is 1922. Besides coining other terms, Kossel added *Hexon(base)* in 1898. It was immediately introduced into English as *hexone.*

Lastly, in the early twentieth century, Hans Fischer (1881–1945) established the structure of chlorophyll, worked on the analysis and synthesis of porphyrins, and succeeded in synthesizing *Hämin* in 1929 (English *hemin,* 1955), the year in which he also coined *Dithizon* (English *dithizone, 1929).* He received the Nobel prize in chemistry in 1930, the tenth German or Austrian chemist to be so singled out. The latest to be so honored before 1951, the period here under review, was Adolf Windaus (1876–1859), who deduced the structure of the *vitamins* D_2 and D_3 and that of their provitamins in 1928. *Vitamin* D_2 is cited in the *OED* beginning with 1932; *vitamin* D_3, as of 1936.

From 1850 to 1900 an average of nearly seven chemistry items a year found their way into English. That number decreased to less than four by 1950. Since then, English has acquired only ten such additions, at a rate of borrowing approximating one in five years. The terms *sarin* (1951) and *ylid(e)* (1951) may well represent the ten. *Sarin,* a trade name for a nerve gas, was developed in Germany during World War II and was well known abroad by the end of that conflict. *Ylid* is the name the German chemist Georg Wittig (b. 1897) gave to his discovery in 1944 that there are neutral compounds containing negatively charged carbon atoms directly bonded to positively charged atoms in another compound. In 1979 he and the American chemist Herbert Charles Brown (b. 1912) were jointly awarded the Nobel prize in chemistry.

The 687 words relating to chemistry are:

Undated:	Abderhalden reaction, acoine, alantic acid, alantolactone, aldehydine, alkamine, allose, ammino-, bathochrome, bebeerine, benzamide, Biebrich scarlet, Bohemian earth, Bremen blue, Bremen green, Brunswick black, Brunswick blue, Brunswick green, caffeol, canadol, carmoisin, carnosine, Caro's acid, Casselmann's green, cedriret, chalcone, chloralide, chrysogen, civetone, coniceine, coumaran, cuminoin, curine, cuscohygrine, cusconine, cyan(o)methemoglobin, cyanuramide, cyaphenine, cytoglobin, delatynite, elemicin, ergocristine, estragole, fillmass, fulgide, fulvene, hydatomorphic, hydrocotarnine, -il, Karlsbad salt, lupeol, melis, Neuwider green, Neuwied blue, nitrolamine, nitrosate, nitrosite, nutch filter, oenin, oligopyrene, osamine, persis, phenanthridine, phenmiazine, phylloporphyrin, pseudonitrole, ribonic acid, sterone, stupp, tourill, urazine, urazole, xerogel
1551–1600:	wismuth 1587
1601–50:	zinc 1641
1651–1700:	Cologne brown 1658, bismuth 1668, cobalt 1683
1751–1800:	wolfram 1757, titanium 1796, uranium, zirconium 1797, salmiac 1799, tellurium 1800
1801–50:	polychrome 1801, chloride 1812, selenium 1818, Scheele's green 1819, strass 1820, cadmium 1822, xanthogen 1823, iridosmine 1827, caffeine, isomorphism, morphine 1828, senegin 1830, alkaloid, chloral, coniine 1831, polymeric 1833, mercaptan 1834, benzine, creosote, melam, melamine, mellon, pittacal, pyrrole, rosolic acid, vanadite 1835, atropine, bromate, picamar 1836, dyestuff 1837, benzol, corydaline, croconic acid, cyanic acid, cyano-, cyanuric acid, emulsin, ethyl, fagine, menthene, murexide, paraffin, petrolene, sinapine, xanthine 1838, acetone 1839, Mitis green, rhodizonic acid 1839, ozone 1840, anemonin, natrium 1842, xylite 1843, carbyl sulfate, mandelic acid 1844, allantoin, cyanate, idryl, niobium, rhodeoretin 1845, aldehyde, uroglaucin(e),

urostealith, uroxanthine, urrhodin(e) 1846, aconitine, alantin, amanitine, amide, colchicine 1847, card(ol), rubiacin, sarcosine 1848, neroli oil, pentathionic acid 1849, aniline, cumidine, curcumin, fusel oil, styphnic acid 1850

1851–1900   ketone, pyromellic acid, stannite 1851, amorphism, ester, euxanthic (acid), euxanthone, xyloretin 1852, acetal, alloxan, alloxantin, catechin, quinone 1853, carvacrol, Krems white 1854, benzoyl, inosinic acid, jalapinolic acid 1855, amyloid, cotarnine, rutin 1857, hyoscyamine, sarcine 1858, berberine[2], cesium, rubidium 1861, sapogenin 1862, alanine, allophanic acid, alloxanic acid, anilide, cresotinic acid, crocin, silicone 1863, chrysaniline, ecgonine, frangulin, fraxin, fustin, globularin, indium, physostigmine, primary, secondary 1864, filicic acid, fisetin, hydroquinone 1865, barbituric acid, benzaldehyde, eosin(e), guaiaretic acid, isomer, pinacoline, pinacone, polymer, thionyl 1866, butyne, ozonide 1867, stictic acid, trivalent, umbelliferone, xyloretinite 1868, aurin, biuret, cresol, indole, isocitric acid, piperonal, valence 1869, meth(a)emoglobin 1870, codamine, geraniol, isobutyric acid, lactonic (acid), laudanine, laudanosine 1871, dehydracetic acid, formaldehyde, hydantoin, itatartaric acid, muscarine, sulfone 1872, acetamide, cerulignone, cinnamene, Fehling's solution, nicotinic acid, perchloroethylene 1873, cocaine, Cremnitz white 1874, bromal, hydroxamic acid, thermolysis 1875, anorganology, berberine[1], menthol, septicine, wine yellow 1876, furfuran, glycosamine, hydrobenzoin, neptunium, quinquevalent, sylvestrene, synantherin, thioglycol(l)ic acid 1877, benzidene, fluoranthene, juglone, nitrosamine, vaporimeter 1878, alkyl, cinchoninic acid, conglutin, cotoin, dextran, echitamine, flavopurpurin, mercapturic acid, naringin, pararosaniline 1879, diosphenol, lactone, saccharine, serine 1880, cobaltammine, gallacetophenone, ligroin, oxonic acid 1881, alkyne, galangin, glucuronic acid, phenanthrene, phenanthroline 1882, celloidin, cerulignol, cinnoline, coumarone, imine, isoeugenol, isonicotinic acid, kairoline, lactam, lactim, phenosafranine, semipermeable 1883, antipyrine, auramine, gallisin, glucovanillin, indazole, pyrroline, quinoxaline 1884, adenine, Bismarck brown, condurangin, Congo red, galactonic acid, haematoporphyrin, iodine number, isatoic acid, Kolbe reaction, lanolin, neodymium, pinene, polyterpene, praseodymium, pyrimidine, pyrrolidine, scopoleine, vesuvin 1885, chondrosine, dicoumarin, formose, galactan, germanium, tautomerism 1886, blood meal, hydrastinine, hydrazine, irisin, isohydric, linolenic acid, pyrazine, pyrazole, pyrazoline, pyrazolone, quinazoline, saprine 1887, lacmoid pre–1888, galli(si)ze, gentianose, glycerose, hydrazone, indamine, keto-, Kohlrausch's law, lanthopine, mannose, osazone, oxazole, piperazine, rhodamine, trivalence 1888, chloralamide, chloropicrin,-eka-, glucosone, icosa-, lactobionic acid, morpholine, osone, pyrrolidone, sulfonal 1889, carbinol, derrid(e), glucoheptose, haematogen, multirotation, nonose, octose, pentose, stachyose, stereochemical, stereochemistry, turanose 1890, alicyclic, azoimide, coriandrol, dipeptide, fenchene, fenchone, gulose, guvacine, hemicellulose, homogentisic (acid), isomaltose, isoxazole, linalool, liquid crystal, oxime, pyrone, rubeanic acid, sabadine, sapotoxin, xylitol 1891, Amidol, araban, filicin, hypsochromic, imidazole, linamarin, nucleic acid, organosol, pentaërythritol, pentosan, rhodinol, scopolamine 1892, adonitol, auxochrome, chromotrope, corycavine, Metol, phthalazine, semidine 1893, butanol, corybulbine, ionene, ionone, irene, iretol, iridin[1], irigenin, irone, isoborneol, ketazine, maltol, syn-, thymine 1894, diazonium, heat tonality, mobility, pellotine, pyronin(e), zinnober 1895, Chinosol, factice, lyxose, mescaline, polymolecular, triacid (solution) 1896, ammine, Brix, flavone, metastable[1], new blue, phallin, phenylhydrazine, phenylhydrazone 1897, flavonol, fluorophor(e), hexone, isolichenin, purine 1898, acyl, Adurol, chromotropic acid, geranial, gossypol, guanylic acid, hadromal, hexite, isatoic anhydrite, knall-gas, melibiase, melibiose, partial valency, pseudoacid, pseudo base 1899, acetoacetic acid, aluminothermy, collargol, enantiotropy, galactosamine, hedonal, peracid, phototropy, rhodinal, sabinene, Thermit, Thiazine 1900

1901–50: glycyl, liquidus, osmophilic, osmophoric, sapropelic, solidus, threose 1901, cytotoxin, flavanthrone, halochromism, mole, monotropy, saponarin, terpane 1902, chromaffin, geochemistry, isoleucine, nerol, tripeptide, Veronal 1903, farnesol 1904, chemiluminescence, ketene 1905, aminophenol, aryl, atoxyl, nitron, zwitterion 1906, arsanilic acid, mesothorium, ol, -ol, overvoltage, permutite, phytane 1907, coordination number, hydronium (ion), indigoid, ketoketen(e), mononucleotide, platinum blue, spir(o)-, stand oil 1908, Bakelite, guanosine, pH, protopetroleum, suspensoid, tetryl 1909, Bayer process, cupferron, depside, methyl red, perylene, porphyrin, Salvarsan 1910, Adalin, epi, epimer, epimerism, lyophobic, rotameter, spiran(e), thermochromism, Walden inversion 1911, ionogenic 1912, norleucine, photocatalytic, resite, resitol, resol(e) 1913, anthocyanidin, cyanidin, delphinidin, pelargonidin, pelargonin 1914, isocolloid, lyophile, peonidin, peonin, polydisperse 1915, borane, misch metal, silane, solvolysis 1916, dopa, galacturonic acid, propylene imine, siloxane 1917, chrysanthemin, protactinium, radon, thoron 1918, isostere[2], lupulon(e), tropane 1919, phosphazene, topochemical 1920, norvaline 1921, batyl alcohol, Bayer 205, chromatogram, heteropolar, homopolar, selachyl alcohol 1922, hexogen, icosenic acid, pristane, scopine 1923, chimyl alcohol, coproporphyrin, pyrethrin, synthol 1924, aglycon, Coramine, hydroxonium (ion), isobestic, lactol, masurium, pseudohalogen, rhenium 1925, apozymase, lanthanide contraction, porphin, tall oil, xanthopterin 1926, choleretic, hydroborane, oxine, thixotropy 1927, hydrotropy, raffinate, reineckate 1928, dithizone, hemin, macromolecule, orthohydrogen, parahydrogen, tactoid, tactosol 1929, aprotic, heteropolymerization, homopolymerization, xanthophyll 1931, cocarboxylase, pregnane, vitamin D_2 1932, Fischer-Tropsch process, holocellulose, lactoflavin, septanose, terpenoid 1933, androsterone, cryptoxanthin, pterin 1934, dehydrocholesterol, depsidone, electroviscous, lumichrome, manool, phorbol 1935, antiferromagnetic, Buna, polycondensation, vitamin D_3 1936, chromatography, diosgenin 1937, adermine, cyan(o)-, Perbunan, phalloidin(e), tosyl 1938, pyrrolizidine 1939, helvetium 1940, adduct, invert soap, Perlon 1941, neuraminic acid 1942, pteridine 1943, ergocornine 1944, lycomarasmin 1945, amidone 1946, heteropolymer, polyaddition 1948, aldrin, ionotropy 1949

1951– : oligohaline, sarin, ylid(e) 1951, iridin[2] 1953, sulphane 1955, psilocybin 1958, phalloin 1959, endosulvan, free 1965, resinophore (group) 1972

Crystallography

See *Geology*.

Ecology

The branch of biology concerned with the interrelationships of organisms and their environment was named *Ökologie* in 1866 by the German zoologist and philosopher Ernst Haeckel

(1834–1919). The first use of it in English in this broad sense is dated 1873, following Thoreau's use of *ecology* in a more restricted sense in 1858.

Concern about the environment, i.e., the *world about us,* had induced the Danish traveler, poet, and philosopher Jens Immanuel Baggesen (1764–1826) even earlier to coin in 1800 in German the term *Umwelt.* Carlyle translated it in 1827 as *environment.*

Toward the end of the nineteenth century, in 1898, Carl Schröter (1855–1939) and Oskar von Kirchner (1850–1925) in Germany supplied a name for the division of ecology that studies the interrelationships between individual organisms and their environment. That name was *Autoökologie.* English adopted it in 1910 as *aut(o)ecology.* In 1902 these same scholars turned their attention to the branch of ecology that concerns the interaction between plants and animals. In their book *Die Vegetation des Bodensees* they named that interrelationship *Synökologie.* In consequence English has been calling it *synecology* since 1910.

Before Schröter and Kirchner, the Austrian ecologist August von Jilek (1818–98) had delineated in his text, *Lehrbuch der Oceanographie* (1859), another area of interest to modern ecologists. *Oceanography,* as it has been called in English since then, is the branch of physical geography that deals with the oceans and the phenomena relating to them.

Specific German items relating to the environment begin to turn up in English in 1840 and 1864, respectively.

In 1830 the German chemist Christian Friedrich Schönbein (Schonbein) (1799–1868) discovered the allotropic triatomic form of oxygen that shields humans from excessive ultraviolet radiation of the sun. He spoke of it as *Ozon.* Soon thereafter he invented the device that he called *Ozonometer.* The *OED* records the terms as *ozone* and *ozonemeter,* respectively.

In 1838 the German botanist August Grisebach (1814–79) adopted in *Linnaea,* XII, 160 the word *Formation,* still in use today, to refer to a community of species, such as a group of plants that have adapted themselves to similar climatic conditions. The earliest reference to *formation* in this sense in the *OED* is dated 1898. Sixty years later, the German botanist and philosopher Andreas Franz Wilhelm Schimper (1856–1901) provided the term *edaphisch* (*edaphic* 1900) in his *Pflanzengeographie* (1898) to name the change produced in ecological formations that are influenced by the soil.

Illustrating later additions of German items to the store of English ecological terms is, first, *biochore* (*OED* 1913). It was formulated in 1900 as *Biochore* by Wladimir Köppen (1846–1940) to define the climate boundary of an area. Next are the neologisms *saprobic* (1913, from German *saprobisch*), *oligoprobic* (1925, from *oligoprobisch*), and *polysaprobic* (1925, from *polysaprobisch*) all three created in 1902 by the German ecologists Richard Kolkwitz (b. 1873) and Theodor Friedrich Marsson (1816–92) to denote an aquatic environment containing organic matter, or one deficient in plant nutrients yet containing abundant oxygen, or one rich in decaying organic matter and having little or no oxygen. A later example is the term *edaphon* (1927), borrowed from the title of the book *Das Edaphon* (1913), by Raol Heinrich Francé (1870–1943), and used as a name for a community of plant and animal life in the soil.

Post-1950 examples are *vicariant* (1952), *thanatocoenosis* (1953), and *trophogenic* (1957). *Vicariant* is an adaptation of German *vikarirende Spezies* (now, more likely, *vikariierende Pflanzen*) that was first used by the German botanist Franz Joseph Andreas Nikolas Unger (1800–70) in his book *Ueber den Einfluss des Bodens auf die Vertheilung der Gewächse*

(1836) as a name for one group of plants or animals that have evolved from an ancestral stock out of effective contact with another. *Thanatocoenosis* (now *Thanatozönose*) was formed in 1926 by the German biologist Ehrich Wasmund (b. 1902) in a paper published in the *Archiv für Hydrobiologie, XVII, 6.* Finally, *trophogen,* the German source for *trophogenic,* is to be found in the thesaurus *Limnologische Terminologie* published by the Swedish biologist of German origin Einar Christian Leonard Naumann (1891–1934).

The twenty-nine words relating to ecology are:

Undated:	zonolimnetic
1801–50:	environment 1827, ozone 1840
1851–1900:	oceanography 1859, ozonometer 1864, ecology 1873, zoochlorella, zooxanthella 1889, formation 1898, edaphic 1900
1901–50:	autoecology, synecology 1910, biochore, saprobic 1913, mesarch[2] 1923, synusia 1924, oligosaprobic, polysaprobic 1925, biotope, edaphon 1927, mull, oligotrophic, profundal 1928, dystrophic 1931, vicari(i)sm 1939
1951– :	vicariant (n.), vicariant (a.) 1952, thanatocoenosis 1953, trophogenic 1957

Entomology

English borrowed twenty-four German items in entomology, the branch of biology concerned with the physiology, morphology, and classification of insects as well as their impact on the ecology and on humans.

The first item is *Maychafer* (1827), which is a translation of *Maikäfer.* Kluge/Mitzka traces it to Early NHG *Megenkefer* that was recorded in 1517.

The most recent of these words, *Varroa,* was introduced into English in 1974. It is the name the Dutch entomologist Anthonie Cornelis Oudemans (1858–1943) gave in 1904 to a small mite that is a fatal parasite of the honeybee in East Asia.

The German items that entered the English lexicon between 1827 and 1974 include terms coined by German and non-German entomologists writing in German.

Ehrich Wasmann (1859–1937) represents the latter. This Dutch scholar of German origin formed *Physogastrie* to describe in brief a mutually helpful symbiosis between ants and termites. See his *Kritisches Verzeichnis der myrmekophilen und termitophilen Anthropoden* (1894). English adopted the term in 1903 as *physogastry* and *physogastrism.* Two years earlier English had incorporated *macroergate,* which Wasmann had used for the first time in 1895/6 as a name for a large worker ant. English had already gained in 1899 *synechthry* from Wasmann's 1896 German term *Synechthrie.* His principal work was *Instinkte und Intelligenz im Tierreich* (1897).

Among German scholars who enriched the vocabulary of English entomologists, there are Veit Graber (1844–92), Martin Heidenhain (1864–1949), Odo M. Reuter (1850–1913), and Hermann Julius Kolbe (b. 1855).

Graber's coinages are *Scolopophor* (1881, English *scolopophore* 1888) for an insect's integumentary sense-organ, *Scolopale* (1882) (*OED scolopale* 1912) for the rod-like structure inside the sheath of a scolopodium, and *scolopophor* (1881) (*scolopophorous* 1935) for an insect that has an elongated sensory end-organ.

Heidenhain contributed *Tonofibrille* in 1899 (*tonofibril* 1901). Reuter added *Parasitoide* (1913, *parasitoid* 1922). And Kolbe introduced *Prothetelie* (1903, *prothetely* 1934). The meanings assigned to these three terms are an insect having a greatly distended abdomen due to the growth of ovaries, etc.; an insect whose larva lives as an internal parasite which eventually kills its host; and the development in certain insects of one part of the body at a faster rate than that of the others.

The twenty-four words in entomology are:

1801–50:	Maychafer 1827, polytropic[1] 1838
1851–1900:	morpho 1853, frass 1854, trichome 1875, acrostichal 1884, oenocyte 1886, scolopophore 1888, holopneustic 1892, trichogen 1898, ologotropic, synechthry 1899
1901–50:	macroërgate, tonofibril 1901, physogastry, symphilism 1903, scolopale 1912, parasitoid 1922, mycetocyte 1924, prothetely 1934, scolopophorous, scolops 1935, scolopodium 1939
1951– :	Varroa 1974

Forestry

The earliest of the six German items in English relating to forestry, and in a remote sense to botany, is *raff,* from OHG *Reff* 'timber.' It appears to have come into the English language in its adjectival form around 1440 and as a noun in 1667, possibly in connection with mining operations by Germans known to have been working in Cornwall as early as the thirteenth century.

Only four of the thousands of German loanwords that have become a part of the English vocabulary since then can in any sense be said to relate to forestry. Three of these were added before 1950. They are *increment borer* (1889), a translation of German *Zuwachsbohrer* that was coined by Maximilian Robert Pressler and included in his volume *Zur Forstzuwachskunde,* 1868; *krummholz* (1903), adopted by August Heinrich Rudolph Grisebach as the name for stunted forest or elfin wood in his book *Vegetation der Erde* (1872); and *rain forest* (1903), a rendering of *Regenwald,* as used by Andreas Hans Wilhelm Schimper in his *Pflanzengeographie* (1898). The fourth, *widow-maker* (1975), is a translation of the vernacular German *Witwe(n)macher* (see *OED*).

The six words relating to forestry are:

Before 1501:	raff (a.) 1440
1650–1700:	raff (n.) 1667
1851–1900:	increment borer 1889
1901–50:	krummholz, rain forest 1903
1951– :	widow-maker 1975

Geology, Mineralogy, Crystallography

German has contributed large numbers of mineralogical terms to English. In number of transfers, mineralogy, indeed, ranks first among the 69 semantic areas that we have tabulated. Geology (including petrology and petrography) ranks fourth, and crystallography stands in 59th place.

The earliest and latest dated German loanwords in mineralogy are *glance* (1457) and *imhofite* (1965); those in geology are *toadstone*[1] (1558) and *Q scale* (1970); and those in crystallography, *cuproid* (1864) and *layer lattice* (1929). Of the three groups, the very first attested transfer in English, and the only one prior to 1501, is *glance*. The name of the "mineral with a metallic luster" or the "ore with a gleam" is recorded in English along with a variant, *glanz*. *Glanz,* German 'gleam,' suggests that *glance* is an obvious borrowing from German rather than from Dutch *glans,* as Carr assumes (p. 39).

From 1501 to 1750 at least 23 German terms in geology and mineralogy were added to the English scientific vocabulary. (There were none in crystallography.) As do those in mining and metallurgy of this period, they initially reflect an oral tradition. Thus we find *shruf(fe)* (1541–2) and *spaad* (1594), *glimmer* (1683) and *blende* (1683), *mispickel* (1683) and *spalt* (1733), *shiffer* (1683) and *schlich* (1677), all of them with their roots in MHG and/or OHG. They scarcely presage the large store of German technical terms one has come to associate with these semantic areas after 1750. The term *fluor* (1661) is the latinized form that Georgius Agricola (1494–1555) gave to the German miners' word for *flusse* in his *De re metallica* (published posthumously in 1556, nearly a hundred years earlier than the appearance of the term in English).

Between 1751 and 1950 English absorbed an additional 951 loanwords in these fields, six of them in crystallography. To better grasp the reason for that surge, one must briefly consider the evolution of these fields.

The acknowledged founder of modern or scientific geology is the Catholic ecclesiastic Nicholas Steno (Stensen) (1638–86), at one time bishop of Hamburg, Germany. But the first practical ideas concerning the evolution of the earth are those of René Descartes (1591–1650), which were enlarged and organized by the German philosopher and polymath, Wilhelm Gottlieb Leibni(t)z (1646–1716). The most famous geologist of the eighteenth century was Abraham Gottlob Werner (1749–1817), docent at the School of Mines in Freiberg, Saxony. He defined the boundaries between petrology and geology. Many of the most widely used books in geology and petrology of the late nineteenth and early twentieth century are German, such as Karl Alfred von Zittel's *Geschichte der Geologie und Paläontologie* (R. Oldenburg, Munich, 1899); Friedrich Rinne's *Gesteinskunde* (Leipzig, Hannover, M. Janicke, 1901, 1937); Harry Rosenbusch's *Mikroskopische Physiographie* (Stuttgart, Schweizerbärtsche Verlag, 1879, 1928).

The advent of mineralogy as the science specifically dedicated to the study of the constituent elements of the earth's crust was signaled by the publication of Agricola's *De re metallica* in 1556. (The oldest existing treatise on the subject, Theophrastus' *perí tõn líthon (On Stones)* dates back to 315 B.C. It was followed by Pliny's *Historia Naturalis,* written about A.D. 77, and, much later, by Albertus Magnus's *De Mineralibus* around 1262.)

A decade after Agricola's death there appeared, in 1565, the first systematic treatise on minerals authored by the Swiss German polymath Conrad Ges(s)ner (1516–65). It heralded the role that German mineralogy was to play and hence the imprint it was to make on the English lexicon in future centuries. Martin Heinrich Klaproth (1741–1817), who became professor of chemistry at the University of Berlin in 1792, is now ranked as the leading mineralogical analyst of his time. No less significant were the discoveries in crystallography made a few years later by Christian Wilhelm Weiss (1780–1856).

Based on his innovative concept of axial symmetry, Johann Christian Hessel (1796–1872) established in 1830 the classification of crystals, as we now know it, and Gustav Rose (1798–1873) completed his classification of minerals twenty-two years later. Toward the end of the nineteenth century Paul Ritter von Groth (1843–1927), who first taught at the University of Strassburg and then at the University of Munich, consolidated the knowledge of his predecessors in the field. His books are valued as reference tools to this day.

Klaproth and Werner discovered and named many minerals, as did numerous other German mineralogists. The names of these minerals introduced into English in the years from 1751 to 1950 in such large numbers range from *acmite* (1837), *bieberite* (1854), and *chlorite* (1794) to *vogesite* (1891), *wüstite* (1928), and *zeunerite* (1873). The names that German geologists created extend from the scientific designations *anamesite* (1876), *aplite* (1879), *dacite* (1878), and *ijolite* (1897) to *tectonite* (1933), *tillite* (1907), *rhythmite* (1946), and *suevite* (1938) in geology. Those that they coined in petrography and petrology, conveniently also catalogued under geography, range respectively from *adamellite* (1896) to *grorudite* (1896), and from *hedrumite* (1896) to *kinzigite* (1878). The loans of their creations in crystallography include *cuprid* (1864), *enantiomorph* (1885), and *layer lattice* (1929). The overall prolific mineralogical output is exemplified by the fact that there were 67 such borrowings in 1868 alone.

Meanwhile, such scientific designations continued to be paralleled during the years from 1751 to 1950 by relatively large numbers of loans of folk origin, a trend noted in the overview of the periods preceding 1751. Some of these are *hornstone* (1728), *horn silver* (1770), *fahlerz* (1796), *grunstein* (1796), *silver glance* (1805), *salamstone* (1816), *needle stone* (1820), *felstone* (1858), *nickel iron* (1875), and *zinc bloom* (1942).

The gradually diminishing nineteenth-century flood of terms in geology and mineralogy continued only as a trickle after 1950, with nine loanwords documented in the former and twelve recorded for the latter.

One example in geology is *pseudogley* (1953) 'a gley produced by water logging rather than by a higher water table.' It was introduced in 1953 by the Austrian geologist Walter Kubiëna (b. 1897) in his *Bestimmungsbuch und Systematik der Böden Europas*. Another such loan is *tower karst* (1954), a partial translation of *Turmkarst*, which the noted German geologist Hermann von Wissmann (b. 1895) used in 1954 in *Erdkunde*, VIII, 121, 1 to describe a type of karst characterized by isolated steep hills. A third is *lebensspur*, adopted in the *OED* in 1960 in the original German. It was coined in 1912 by the Austrian paleontologist Othenio Abel (1875–1946) and included in his *Grundzüge der Paläographie der Wirbeltiere*.

Exemplifying mineralogical loanwords during the second half of the twentieth century are *tertschite* (1953), *stranskiite* (1960), and *imhofite* (1965). With some associates, the mineralogist Conrad Burri (b. 1900) named *Imhofit* 'a sulfide of thallium and arsenic' in 1965 after the twentieth-century Swiss collector of minerals Josef Imhof. The Austrian mineralogist Hermann Strunz (b. 1910) honored the Bulgarian-born German chemist Iwan N. Stranski (1897–1979) in 1960 by naming an arsenate of zinc and copper as *Stranskiit*. And in 1953 the

Austrian mineralogist Heinz Meixner chose the name of his countryman Hermann Tertsch (1880–1962) for a hydrated, fine-fibered calcium borate that he discovered.

The scanty flow of transfers in crystallography dried up entirely after 1929.

The 318 words in geology are:

Undated: akerite, alboranite, allochetite, allothimorph, alnoite, alsbachite, anchiëutectic, apachite, arsoite, aschaffite, atlantite, augitite, berg crystal, bergmehl, chassignite, damkjernite, decke, decken structure, diogenite, einkanter, endrumpf, felsophyre, gang, grano-, granoblastic, gruss, hairstone, hysterocrystalline, lepidoblastic, leucitite, liparite[2], lujau(v)rite, plutonite, polygene, protoclastic, quader, Rot(h)liegende, sideromelane, slickens[1], taxite, wiesenboden

1551–1600: toadstone[1] 1558

1601–50: matted 1648

1651–1700: spalt (n.) 1668, schlich 1677, shiffer 1683

1701–50: shiver (v.) 1728, shiver (n.) 1729, spal (v.) 1733, shale 1747

1751–1800: druse 1753, riffle (v.) 1754, gneiss 1757, gletscher 1762, sinter 1780, pitchstone, toadstone[2] 1784, graywacke, speckstone 1794, trass 1796, mandelstein 1799, pearlstone 1800

1801–50: wacke 1803, schalstein, sparglestone, stinkstone 1804, greenstone, iron glance 1805, nagelfluh 1808, salband 1811, lydite 1816, lauwine 1818, spherulite, Zechstein 1823, flysch 1827, geest, phonolite 1828, Jura 1829, Bunter, Kupferschiefer 1830, bucholzite, thalweg 1831, lehm, loess, Muschelkalk, perlite 1833, hypersthenite, mimophyre, Triassic (n.), Triassic (a.) 1841, bergschrund, Keuper 1844, stoss 1848, hydrothermal 1849, andesite 1850

1851–1900: Eifelian 1853, hornfels, miascite, sepiolite, sinter coal 1854, bergfall 1856, Oligocene, psarolite 1859, epidosite, nephelinite, palagonite 1863, liparite[1] 1865, chondritic, tholeiite 1866, interglacial, predazzite 1867, limnite, mesosiderite, pallasite, picrite[2], rhyolite, trichite 1868, schrund 1870, Tithonian 1871, kieselguhr, riffle (n.) 1875, anamesite, corsite, rille 1876, clastic, Paleocene 1877, dacite, greisen, kinzigite, microlite, minette, peridotite 1878, aplite, leucitophyre, tonalite 1879, fahlband 1880, cryptoclastic, granophyre, Paleogene, sparagmite, spilosite, vitrophyre 1882, chondrite, fastland, overfold, troctolite 1883, augengneiss, karrenfeld, microperthite, schlieren, stratovolcano, Tortonian 1885, petrographic province 1886, allothogenic, authigenic, effusive, flaser, homeocrystalline, hyalopilitic, polysomatic[1], trachybasalt 1888, intratelluric, keratophyre 1889, chloritization, dahllite, harzburgite, lamprophyre 1890, monchiquite, vogesite 1891, nepheline-syenite 1892, deflation, horst, intersertal, tinguaite 1893, karren, karst 1894, camptonite, hypabyssal, miarolitic, nordmarkite, orthophyric 1895, adamellite, centrosphere, Gondwanaland, graben, grorudite, hedrumite, moldavite, pneumatolysis, pneumatolytic 1896, ijolite 1897, theralite 1898, biosphere, eucrite 1899, autochthonous, overdeepened 1900

1901–50: heumite, petrogenesis 1901, klippe,[1] orthogneiss, paragneiss 1902, batholith, dreikanter, lateritization, laterization, piezocrystallization, Pliensbachian, polygenetic, epigenetic, felsenmeer 1905, biolith, eustatic, ortstein, Variscan 1906, Fennoscandian, inselberg, juvenile, sapropel, tillite 1907, stratosphere 1908, australite, billitonite, leucocratic, melanocratic, sima, syntaxis, tektite 1909, augen, Günz, Günz-Mindel, Mindel, riegel, Riss, Riss-Würm, Würm 1910, allochthonous, limnic, paralic, shield volcano, shotter 1911, pedology 1912, crystalloblastic 1913, concordant, interstadial 1914, myrmekite, stromatolith, symplectic 1916, leptomology, ring fracture 1919, homeoblastic, hyaloophitic, idioblast[2], laterize, poikiloblastic, porphyroblastic 1920, cryptovolcanic 1921, sial, trondhjemite 1922, kratogen, lithophile, orogen, siderophile, taphrogenesis 1923, knickpoint, Pangaea, polygonboden 1924, fenster, piercement 1925, heteroaxial 1926, Laufen, parautochthonous 1927, ooid, periglacial, solum 1928, Wildflysch 1929, orterde, stromatolite 1930, Pfalzan, polymict, Saalian 1931, ignimbrite, (k)nick, poikiloblastic 1932, petrotectonics, pluton, siallite, tectonite 1933, randkluft, Weichsel 1934, orthogeosyncline, parageosyncline, synorogenic 1936, Saale, rheomorphism, tectogene, tectogenesis 1937, suevite 1938, geoscience, miogeosynclinal, tafoni 1942, craton, polytypism, superstructure 1944, cryoturbation, rhythmite 1946, phyllosilicate 1947, transfluence 1949

1951– :   pseudogley 1953, tower karst 1954, orthotectonic, paratectonic 1956, lebensspur, vergence 1960, tonstein 1961, pseudotillite 1963, Q scale 1970

The 857 words in mineralogy are:

Undated: achroite, ader wax, agricolite, akermanite, alabandite, alluaudite, altaite, anapaite, andorite, anomite, anorthoclase, aphrosiderite, arcanite, ardealite, ardennite, arnimite, arzrunite, astrakhanite, atelestite, atlasite, baikerinite, baikerite, barthite, beraunite, beringite, berzeliite, bildstein, bindheimite, bischofite, bismuthite, bismutite, bismut(o)-, bloedite, boronatrochalcite, brackebuschite, breithauptite, brownmillerite, buchite, buetschliite, cacoxenite, chalmersite, chevkinite, -clasite, -clastic, clinozoisite, cohenite, cryolithionite, cumengite, darapskite, dehrnite, dietzeite, douglasite, dravite, duftite, earth pitch, egeran, enigmatite, epididymite, epigenite, erikite, eschynite, ettringite, eusynchite, germanite, geocerite, glaucocerinite, glessite, gorceixite, hyalobasalt, jaulingite, kalkowskite, kotoite, kraurite, leptochlorite, leucitite, leucosphenite, leucoxene, lime uranite, longulite, loranskite, magnochromite, magnoferrite, manganosiderite, manganotantalite, manganpectolite, melanostibian, melanterite, mercallite, milarite, mizzonite, molybdite, monomict, muckite, muthmannite, navite, neftgil, oligonite, onegite, phoenicite, piotine, plumboniobite, podolite, pyrodmalite, pyrophanite, rosickyite, salite, schapbachite, scholzite, schönfelsite, seligmannite, stylotypite, swedenborgite, szomolnokite, triachalcite, trigonite, vashegyite, voglite, walpurgite, waltherite, wattvilleite, weinschenckite, weisbachite, woehlerite, wolfachite, yttrofluorite, zeophyllite, zirklerite

Before 1551:   glance 1457

1501–50:   schruff 1541

1551–1600:   spaad 1594

1601–50:   quartz 1631

1651–1700:   fluor 1661, spady, blende, glimmer, mispickel 1683

1701–50:   mountain green 1727, copper nickel, hornstone, shiver (v.) 1728, shiver (n.) 1729

1751–1800:   druse 1753, nickel 1755, feldspar 1757, iolite 1758, surturbrand 1760, schorl 1761, marienglas(s) 1762, spath 1763, hornblende, horn silver, pitchblende 1770, plasma 1772, cobalt bloom 1776, meerschaum 1784, wood tin 1787, heavy spar, loch 1789, hornslate 1791, baikalite, chlorite, cyanite, hyalite, nephrite, semiopal, schorlite, swine-stone, uranite, witherite, zircon 1794, hair salt, prehnite 1795, fahlerz, graphite, grunstein, lepidolite, porcellanite, schiller spar, thumerstone, vesuvian 1796, leucite, muriacite 1799

1801–50:   chalcolite, cimolite, cryolite, mellite 1801, gadolinite, hepatite, scapolite 1802, apatite, aragonite, menacane, rutile 1803, celestine, celestite, chiastolite, schiller, schiller stone, shiver spar 1804, crystallite, iserine, laumontite, natrolite, nigrine, pharmacolite, pinite, silver glance, zoisite 1805, cobalt glance 1806, lazulite, melanite, sahlite, sassolin(e), schieferspar 1807, collophonite, datolite, gahnite, petalite, pyrodmalite, zirconium 1808, boracite, lead glance 1810, clinkstone, gangart 1811, fassaite, lievrite, moroxite, paulite, picrite[1], pyromorphite 1814, sanidine 1815, bronzite, el(a)eolite, ilvaite, picrolite, pyrosmalite, rhaetizite, salamstone, wood opal 1816, gehlenite, orthite 1817, helvite, knebelite, pargasite, polyhalite 1818, lucullite, physalite 1819, needlestone, olivenite 1820, calcspar, calc-tufa, mesolite, pyrallolite 1822, calc-sinter, cronstedtite, cyprine, gismondite, goethite, humboldtite, lepidocrite, limonite, picropharmacolite, rhodonite, sapphirine, scolecite, scorodite, stilpnosiderite, strahlite, vivianite 1823, hyalosiderite 1824, breunnerite, euchroite, picrosmine, wagnerite 1825, chloropal, dialogite, elaterite, epistilbite, humboldtilite, pitticite 1826, cotunnite, ilmenite, iridosmine 1827, amblygonite, caffeine, herderite, mesitine, omphacite, pectolite, pistacite, pyrolusite 1828, polybasite, pyrochlore, pyrophyllite, rhyocolite 1830, anhydrite 1831, chalcotrichite, hedyphane, libethenite, oligoclase 1832, actinolite 1833, phenacite 1834, crocidolite, hydroboracite, johannite, melanochroite, pharmacosiderite, plagionite, pseudomalachite, stromeyerite, uralite, voltzite, zinkenite 1835, glauconite, metaxite, monazite, myrargyrite, nickel glance, nosean, rhodizite, rhodochrosite, rubinglimmer, triphylite, weissite 1836, acmite, aegirine, aegirite, alexandrite, allomorphite, annabergite, argentite, bastite, eudialyte, gallizinite, hydromagnesite, ozokerite, sea-foam, scheelite, uvarovite 1837, braunite 1839, chromite, perovskite 1840, edenite, zinc blende, zinc bloom 1842, ankerite, marmatite, spadaite, xylite 1843, aurichalcite, cancrinite, carpholite, chloritoid, coquimbite, crocoite, euxenite, fayalite, fibroferrite, fuchsite, heteroclin(e), lepidomelane, leuchtenbergite, linarite, periclase, pyrrhite, schrötterite, symplesite, thrombolite, thuringite, volkonskoite, xanthophyllite 1844, polycrase, susannite 1845, fischerite, loxoclase, monradite, mosandrite, parisite 1846, apjohnite, bornite, eucolite, grossularite, hauerite, pollux 1847, leonhardite 1848, calcite, gersdorffite, glaucophane, goslarite, hercynite, hessite, lanthanite, linn(a)eite, löllingite, malthacite, margarodite, microcline, nagjagite, naumannite, orthoclase, paragonite, petzite, phoenicochroite, phosgenite, platternite, polianite, pyrrhotine, pyrargyrite, samarskite, saponite, schreibersite, stephanite, wulfenite 1849, anauxite, carphosiderite, cerussite, chalcophyllite, chrysotile, clinoclase, coccinite, conichalcite, copiapite, cornwallite, crednerite, cuprite, diadochite, digenite, domeykite, embolite, fireblende, freieslebenite, glaucodot, kreittonite, phlogopite, ripidolite, siderite, siserskite, skutterudite, stilpnomelane, struvite, tetradymite, tharandite, triplite, uranocircite, variscite, violan(e), willemite 1850

1851–1900:   branchite, dechenite, magnetite, martite, mendipite, zeilanite 1851, eliasite, enargite, manganocalcite, mimetite, safflorite, torbernite 1852, bieberite, catapleite, cyanotrichite, delanovite, delvauxite, embrithite, fluocerite, hydrozincite, jarosite, kämmererite, kremersite, malacon, marialite, millerite, mirabilite, muromontite, myelin[2], neotocite, nevjanskite, niobite, oncosine, partschinite, piedmontite, prosopite, rammelsbergite, sericite, tyrolite, zincite, zippeite 1854, hyalophane, radiolite, vanadinite 1855, felsobanyite, freibergite, placodine, tritomite 1856, chalcanthite, emplectite, enstatite, lindackerite, svanbergite 1857, chalybite, felstone, gramenite, saynite, titanite 1858, saccharite, thermonatrite 1859, valentine 1860, dianite, grünerite, hydrohalite, ilmenorutile, nickel bloom, pisanite, wehrlite, zinnwaldite, zwieselite, zyagdite 1861, andesine, antigorite, biotite, kieserite, loeweite, xylochlore, pyrosclerite, wehrlite 1862, dopplerite, hartite, kischtimite 1863, plumosite, tachylite, wolframite, xylotil(e) 1864, botryogen, liparite[1], lonchidite 1865, laurite, pachnolite, pyromeline, pyropissite, szaibelyite, tarnowitzite 1866, huebnerite 1867, aluminite, aphrite, arendalite, augelite, boulangerite, brandisite, castorite, chalcostibite, chiviatite, cubanite, diaphorite, dihydrite, eulytite, ferberite, forbesite, galenite, globosite, gummite, hemimorphite, hisingerite, hoernesite, jalpaite, jordanite, joseite, kainite, klipsteinite, kochubeite, krantzite, mesitite, oosite, palygorskite, penninite, phengite, picrite[2], pilsenite, plagioclase, pyrochroite, pyroretin, pyrrholite, rébányite, richterite, roesslerite, sinopite, sphalerite, staffelite, stolzite, studerite, taenite, tagilite, tauriscite, tephroite, teratolite, tetrahedrite, tiemannite, tridymite, troilite, tschermigite, ullmannite, uranophane, uranopilite, uranosphaerite, uranotantalite, uranothallite, uranothorite, uranotil, wittichenite, wittingite, xanthoconite, xanthosiderite, xonolite 1868, gümbelite, ilsemannite, lithiophorite 1871, heterogenite, isoclasite, klaprotholite, luenebergite, polyargyrite, pucherite, speiskobalt, trögerite, walpurgite 1872, zeunerite 1873, rhagite 1874, alloclase, calc-, copper-slate, diabantitie, famatinite, foresite, grochauite, guadalcazarite, hydrophilite, kaluszite, ludwigite, maskelynite, nickel iron, osteolite, schröckingerite, strigovite, syngenite, vesszelyite 1875, carnallite, ihleite 1876, clastic, heubachite, manganophyllite, roemerite, sarcopside, sphaerocobaltite 1877, foyaite, krennerite, orthoclastic, polydymite, pseudobrookite, rhabdophane 1878, belonite, hannayite, hydrotalcite, melanophlogite, Mohs scale, newberyite, uraninite 1879, koppite, osmiridium 1880, eleonorite, herrengrundite, homilite, strengite, trippkeite 1881, cossyrite, dietrichite, fluorapatite, granophyre, leopoldite, limbachite, mixite, sarawackite 1882, lautite, leucochalcite, szaboite 1883, chalcosiderite, karstenite, maranite, rezbanyite 1884, endlichite, microclase, pinnoite, schuchardtite, uranospinite 1885, argyrodite, polylithionite, rinkite, sphaerite 1886, allotriomorphic, epidiorite, gedanite, kaliophilite, långbanite, laurionite, manganosite 1887, cristobalite, hohmannite, lansfordite, laubanite, quenstedtite 1888, avalite, inesite, pseudocotunnite, riebeckite 1889, amaranite, hambergite, heliophyllite, iodobromite, johnstrupite, kamacite, pinakiolite, tamarugite 1890, flinkite, heintzite, hintzeite, umangite 1891, castanite, collophane, demantoid, fiedlerite, ganophyllite, hiortdahlite, kaliborite, kallilite, klementite, lautarite, lazurite, lillianite, noselite, piemontite, protolithionite, rhabdophanite, rumänite, schungite, synadelphite, szmikite 1892, brazilite, cylindrite, franckeite, hauchecornite 1893, rhodusite 1894, kamarezite, larvikite, miarolitic 1895, brandtite, knopite, kyrosite, melanocerite, schraufite, stannite, strüverite, sylvinite, trimerite 1896, leonite, rathite, siderotil 1897, grunlingite, langbeinite, mossite, raspite 1898, lamprophyllite 1899, conchite, morphotropy, picroilmenite, titanmagnetite 1900

1901–50:   molybdophyllite, synchisite 1901, brunsvigite, koenenite, natro-, vanthoffite 1902, hellandite, orthopyroxene, pycnochlorite 1903, otavite 1906, hibschite, kleinite, kutnahorite, priorite, rutherfordine 1907, natrochalcite 1908, melanocratic, rinneite, stellerite 1909, chromitite, jordisite, samsonite 1910, hydroxylapatite, thortveitite 1912, heliodor, maucherite, mineraloid, tsumebite, vaterite, vrbaite 1913, holmquisite, hügelite 1914, roscherite 1916, katoptrite, monomineral(ic) 1917, pyrobelonite, xanthoxenite, xenoblast 1920, phosphoferrite, phosphophyllite 1921, kalcinite, schafarzikite 1922, parsettensite, tinzenite 1924, pseudowavellite 1925, bromellite, magnetoplumbite, quensilite 1926, ianthinite 1927, gudmundite, kolbeckite, sursassite, wüstite 1928, isotypic 1929, ramdohrite 1931, letovicite 1932, titanaugite 1933, heteroauxin 1935, iron monticellite 1937, isotypy 1938, boehmite, klockmannite, phosphorroesslerite, protoenstatite 1939, zinc bloom 1942, tectosilicate 1947, hühnerkobelite, shandite 1950

1951– :   tertschite 1953, värynenite 1954, stilleite 1957, strunzite 1958, novákite 1959, oregonite, stranskiite 1960, nickel antigonite, nickel chlorite, nickel spinel 1961, sudoite 1963, imhofite 1965

The eight words relating to crystallography are:

Undated: birne, Bohemian ruby

1851–1900:   cuproid 1864, enantiomorph 1885, automorphic 1888, point group 1895

1901–50:   space group 1901, layer lattice 1929

Ichthyology

See *Zoology*.

Immunology

The English vocabulary in immunology as yet includes only twelve German items.

The first serious experiments in immunology were not performed until the end of the eighteenth century. It was not until 1890 that a German physiologist, Emil Adolf von Behring (1854–1917), discovered the principle of immunity. He found that immunity to infectious diseases depends on the presence of certain molecules circulating in the bloodstream. He called these molecules *Antikörper* or *antibodies,* as they have been known in English translation since 1901. In that same year the Austrian immunologist Karl Landsteiner (1868–1943) discovered the human blood types, for which he was awarded the Nobel prize in physiology in 1930. In 1902, he created the compound that is sometimes used as a synthetic antigen. He termed it *Azoprotein.* English added it in 1918. Soon thereafter, in 1921, English added another of Landsteiner's coinages, *hapten,* to identify a nonantigenic substance that can become an antigen when conjugated to a carrier protein.

Three concepts in the theory of immunology, originated by the German physiologist Paul Ehrlich (1854–1915), had previously found acceptance as well. They are *passiv* (1892), the state caused by the introduction into the body of external antibodies (English *passive* 1895);

34

Haptophor (1898), denoting the ability to enter into combination, as atoms in a toxin's molecule that can combine with the corresponding receptors of a cell (*haptophore* 1899); and *Haptin* (1900), referring to a type of free receptor (*haptine* 1900). For his work, Ehrlich was awarded the Nobel prize in physiology and medicine in 1908.

To those items in immunology we can add other examples. *Isoagglutination* is a name for the agglutination of one individual's cells by the serum of another individual of the same species. It was first used in 1902 by the German immunologist A. Klein in the *Wiener klinische Wochenschrift,* XV, 415, 1 (English *isoagglutination* 1907); *Reagin* (1911), or *Wassermann antibody,* discovered c. 1910 by the German immunologist Alfred Wolff-Eisner (b. 1877). *Paraprotein* is a protein found in the blood of patients suffering from myelomatosis. It was named in 1940 by the German immunologist Karl Apitz in *Virchows Archiv,* CCCVI, 685 and introduced to English in 1949 as *paraprotein.* Apitz's *Paraproteinämie* (1958) is the most recent term to be added to English. The *OED* cites *paraproteinemia* beginning with 1958.

The twelve words relating to immunology are:

Undated: H antigen, O antigen

1851–1900:   passive 1895, haptophore 1899, haptine 1900

1901–50:   antibody 1901, isoagglutination 1907, reagin 1911, azoprotein 1918, hapten 1921, paraprotein 1949

1951– :   paraproteinemia 1958

Mathematics

One of the oldest sciences, originally concerned with counting, calculating, and measuring, mathematics became by David Hilbert's time, around the turn of the nineteenth century, the science of formal systems. Prior to Hilbert, perhaps the most prolific author in mathematics of all time, the Swiss mathematician Leonhard Euler (1707–83) wrote some 900 papers, principally in Latin, among them the foremost textbook, *Introductio in analysin informatiorum,* 1748. His name survives in scores of mathematical concepts like *Euler's formula, Euler's solution, Euler's conclusion,* and *Euler's numbers,* but none as borrowings from German (see *OED*).

Some of the earliest of the sixty English adaptations of German mathematical terms in the years from 1751 to 1950 – there were none before 1751 – like *ideal* (1898) and *ideal number* (1860), *velocity potential* (1867) and *precision* (1885) are associated, respectively, with the names of Ernst Eduard Kummer, Richard Dedekind, Hermann von Helmholtz, and Wilhelm Lexis.

Kummer (1810–93), who taught at the University of Breslau and of Berlin and worked especially on the theory of functions, originated in 1846 the use of *ideal* in its mathematical sense. Dedekind (1831–1916), who succeeded Carl Friedrich Gauss at the University of Göttingen, and who was one of the independent discoverers of non-Euclidian geometry, combined *ideal* with *Zahl* to form *ideale Zahl* in 1846 (*OED ideal number* 1860). He is also the author of the term *Modul* (1871), which the *OED* lists as *module* (1927). Helmholtz (1821–94) was one of the great natural scientists of the nineteenth century. His work ranged from mathematics and physics to music and philosophy. He coined the word *Geschwindigkeitspotential* in 1858

OED (*velocity potential* 1867). Lexis (1837–1914), founder of the first department of insurance at a German university and author of *Zur Theorie der Massenerscheinungen in der menschlichen Gesellschaft* (1877), was the first to use *Präzision* (*OED precision* 1885) to mean degree of agreement of repeated measurements.

In 1888 English recorded for the first time the borrowed special sense of *primitive* (German *primitiv*) from Sophus Lie's book *Theorie der Informationsgruppen* (1888); Lie; 1842–99,) was a Norwegian mathematician who also wrote in German.) *Ludolph's number* entered English in 1886. The Britannica of 1952 cites it along with its German form, *Ludolphsche Zahl*, which is named after Ludolph van Ceulen (1540–1610), a German mathematician who calculated the number π to 35 decimal places. (The Chudovsky brothers carried it to 480 million digits in 1989. See *The New Yorker,* March 2, 1992, 36 ff.)

To Felix Klein (1849–1925), who became famous in 1872 for his *Erlangen Programm* in which he pointed out the unifying role of the group concept in geometry, the English lexicon is indebted for the term *automorphic function* in 1892 (German *automorphe Funktion* 1890).

In his book *Die lineale Ausdehnungslehre,* 1844, Hermann Günther Grassmann (1809–77) was the first to use the concept *inneres* and *äusseres Produkt,* now *inner* (1909) and *outer product* (1929) in English.

One of the German mathematicians to offer definitions of irrational numbers, along with Dedekind, was Georg Cantor (1845–1918), a German mathematician of Danish descent and the author of *Beiträge zur Begründung der transfiniten Mengenlehre* (1895–7). In it he developed the concepts of *transfinit* (English *transfinite* 1903) and *wohlgeordnet* (*well-ordered* 1902).

Adopted in English the same year as Cantor's *transfinite* were two other neologisms, *null plane* and *null point* (German *Nullebene* and *Nullpunkt*) from the *Lehrbuch der Statistik* (1837), by August Ferdinand Möbius (1790–1868).

The first of the coinages of David Hilbert (1862–1943), *Kern* in the mathematical sense (1904), was added to English as *kernel* in 1909. In 1924 there followed in English his *metamathematics,* from German *Metamathematik,* 1923; *recursive* in 1934, from *rekurrent,* 1904; and (*primitive*) *recursion* (1934), from *primitive Rekursion,* 1934. The borrowing *decision problem* (1939), from *Entscheidungsproblem* (1922), also originated with him. In 1928 Hilbert and Friedrich Wilhelm Ackermann (1896–1962) introduced the term *Prädikatenkalkül* in their *Grundzüge der theoretischen Logik* (1928). English added it as *predicate calculus* in 1950.

The term *Vierervektor* (1910), formulated by the German physicist (and sometime mathematician) Arnold (or Alfred) Sommerfeld (1868–1951), was translated into English as *four-vector* in 1914.

Felix Hausdorff (1868–1942) – German mathematician and novelist, who taught at the University of Leipzig, of Greifswald, and of Bonn – included in his *Grundzüge der Mengenlehre* (1914) the terms *topologischer Raum* and *metrischer Raum.* The former became *topological space* in English in 1926; the latter, *metrical space* in 1927.

Also in 1927, *metrizable* and *metrization,* from German *metrisierbar* and *Metrisation* (1924), formed by the Russian mathematician Pawel Urysson (1898–1924), entered English. One year prior to that it was *ergodic,* from German *ergoden* (1887), conceived by the Austrian physicist Ludwig Boltzmann (1844–1906).

Here are more modern loanwords: *factor group,* 1897, from German *Factorgruppe,* 1889, by Otto Hölder (1859–1937); *monotone,* 1905, from *monoton,* 1881, by Carl Gottfried Neumann (1832–1925); *extremal,* 1901, from *Extremale,* 1900, by Adolf Kneser (1862–1930); *holonomic,* 1899, from *holonom,* 1894, by Heinrich Hertz (1857–1894); *polytope,* 1908, from *Polytop,* 1882, by Reinhold Hoppe (1816–1900); and *isopleth,* 1909, from *Isoplethe,* 1877, by Christian August Vogler (b. 1841).

Three terms in mathematics were added to English after 1951. They are *finitary, ordination,* and *square-free.* Of these, two can be readily traced. *Ordination* is an unusual borrowing. It is a translation of German *Ordnung* 'arrangement,' which David W. Goodall (b. 1914) introduced in 1954 "because there appears to be no other word in English which one can use . . . (in) factor analysis as an antonym to 'classification.' " *Ordnung* has been in use in German for some time in mathematics and statistics for 'structure of an ordered group.'

Finitary (1952) is an English rendering of Hilbert's *finit.* See his *Grundlagen der Mathematik* (1934), written with the Swiss mathematician Paul Bernays (1888–1977).

The sixty-three words in mathematics are:

1751–1800:   statistics 1787, statistic 1789

1801–50:   statist*[l]* 1802

1851–1900:   ideal number 1860, velocity potential 1867, entropy 1868, cyclotomy 1879, precision 1885, Ludolph's number 1886, primitive 1888, automorphic function 1892, conformal, Riemann surface 1893, point group 1895, factor group 1897, augend, ideal 1898, holonomic 1899

1901–50:   element, extremal, monotonic 1901, well-ordered 1902, transfinite, null plane, null point 1903, extremum 1904, monotone 1905, polytope 1908, inner product, isopleth, kernel 1909, four-vector 1914, homotopic, homotopy 1918, Goldbach's conjecture 1919, entscheidungsproblem 1922, autological, eigenfunction, ergodic, metamathematics, topological space 1926, metric space, metrizable, metrization, module 1927, outer product 1929, eigen-, recursion formula, u^{l} (= ungerade) 1930, Gödel's theorem 1933, formalism, recursion, recursive 1934, orientable, ring 1935, decision problem, Hilbert space 1939, Leibniz's law 1941, schlicht 1944, predicate calculus 1950

1951– :   finitary 1952, ordination 1954, square-free 1960

Medicine

The borrowings in the field of medicine prior to 1751 were from the German vernacular. *Mase* (1527) 'spot, freckle' derives from OHG *maser* 'gnarl.' Obsolete *masers* (1527) 'measles' from German *Masern,* has its origin in OHG *masala,* which Paul/Betz traces to LG. Kluge/ Mitzka's earliest source for *Masern* is dated 1579. *Joint water* (1599) 'synovia' is a translation of German *Gelenkwasser* 'lubricating fluid in joints.' According to Paul/Betz, Early NHG *gelenk(e)* already referred to all joints, and OHG *wazzer* is documented in blendings related to medicine of that period.

About fifteen percent of the German items in medicine introduced to English during the years that followed and well into the nineteenth century continued to have their base in popular speech. The English-speaking travelers who took the waters on the Continent began to bring back with them from the world-renowned spas in Germany and German-speaking Bohemia such additions to their vocabulary as *Kur* (*OED* 1885), a term familiar to Germans at least since 1526. Or they might recount tales about their *water cure* (1842) (from German *Wasserkur*), or *air-cure* (1876) (from *Luftkur*), or indeed *Kneipp cure* (1890), the name given to a treatment of disease by hydrotherapic means. They took these cures at a *kurort* 'spa' (1849), in a *Kurhaus* 'main building (in a watering spa)' (1855), or in the case of waters, in a *Trinkhalle* 'casino' (1873). Some subjected themselves to a *hacking* (1890), from German *Hackung*, a massage with the edge of the hand, before they gathered in a *kursaal* (*OED* 1849).

Those who did not travel abroad, as might those who did, may have heard their physician use such a mundane term as *rötheln* (1873), German for 'measles.' They might also have heard him use the common German word for the pain between menstrual periods, *Mittelschmerz* 'midpain or intermenstrual pain' (*OED* 1895) and a reference to the nematode worm, *hookworm* (1902), from German *Hakenwurm* (1789). The doctor might even have told patients that he wished to *prove* (1833), i.e., *prüfen* 'to test' a medication, and that he wanted to examine for *occult bleeding* (1901), or *innere Blutung*, as Germans refer to it in their daily speech.

As the art of healing increasingly traveled the ways of science beginning with the early 1800s, its vocabulary acquired the aspect of learning that marks the language of science in general. By 1825 the English travelers to Gräfenberg, Germany, seeking a water cure, would receive a kind of medical treatment, which its originator, Vincenz Preissnitz, called *Hydropathie* 'water cure.' At home they would then speak of it as *hydropathy* (*OED* 1843). In the years from 1825 to 1950 their doctors would diagnose, for example, as the occasion might warrant, *angioneurosis* (1887), *dyslexia* (1888), *chorioepithelioma* (1901), or *nephrosis* (1916). These terms originated, in that order, with H. I. Quincke in 1882, R. Berlin in 1883, F. Marchand in 1898, and F. v. Müller in 1905. (Quincke was at one time professor of medicine at the University of Bern, of Kiel, and of Frankfurt, and Müller was professor of medicine at the University of Bonn, of Basel, and of München.) Berlin and Marchand published, respectively, in the *Medicinisches Correspondenz Blatt des Württembergischen ärztlichen Landesvereins,* vol. 53 (1883), 209, and the *Zeitschrift für Geburtshilfe und Gynekologie,* vol. 39 (1896), 255.

The doctor might then proceed to use the appropriate mode of treatment, including some that Germans had developed like *diathermy* (1909), from German *Diathermie* (1909); *chemotherapy* (1907), developed by Paul Ehrlich in 1907 as *Chemotherapie;* or *cyclodialysis* (1908), from *Cyclodialyse* (1905).

In all, German medicine enlarged English medical terminology with some 60 names for diseases or conditions of malfunction, including *Alzheimer's disease* (1912), named after Alois Alzheimer, the German neurologist who identified it; *Fröhlich's syndrome* (1912) (German *Fröhlich Krankheit*), adiposogenital distrophy, which bears the name of its discoverer, the Austrian neurologist Alfred Fröhlich; *Pick's disease* (1931), a slowly progressive dementia, most often beginning in middle age, named for the Austrian psychiatrist and neurologist Arnold Pick; and *Perthes disease* (1915), a children's disease leading to the deformity of the femur, bearing the name of the German surgeon Georg Clemens Perthes (1869–1927), who was the first to describe it.

Among medically related substances an English doctor might mention are *alkapton* (1888), a reducing substance found in urine; *Avertin* (1927), the anesthetic tribromethanol; and *lepromin* (1932), an extract from leprous tissue used in skin tests for leprosy. They, too, are of German provenance.

After 1950 the physician's vocabulary might include some of the five loanwords that German continued to contribute to English. One of these is Hans Eppinger's (1876–1933) 1920 neologism *Thrombocytopenie* 'persistently restricted number of blood platelets' (*thrombocytopenia* 1923), published in Leo Langstein's *Enzyklopädie der klinischen Medizin* (1920). The 183 words related to medicine are:

Undated:	allotriophagy, Altmann's granules, Auerbach's plexus, bioblast, Borna disease, -caine, carcinolytic, cartilage of Wrisberg, Credé's method, dauerschlaf, diener, geomedicine, grenz ray, hyperergy, leuma, milzbrand, -path, sensibilism, stromuhr, treppe
1501–50:	mase, masers 1527
1551–1600:	joint water 1599
1601–50:	weapon salve 1631
1701–50:	Glauber's salt 1736
1751–1800:	animal magnetism 1784
1801–50:	sweeny 1813, potentiate 1817, homeopathy 1826, policlinic 1827, allopath, allopathic, homeopath, homeopathic 1830, prove 1833, cruorin 1840, allopathy, enanthem, hydropath, stearrhoea, water cure 1842, hydropathy 1843, Lieberkühn's gland, pepsin 1844, psychiatry 1846, bacterium, pseudoplasm, osteoid 1847, dacryoadenalgia 1848, kursaal 1849
1851–1900:	Kurhaus 1855, keratoplasty, polycyth(a)emia, potentize 1857, physiatrics 1858, rinderpest 1865, defervescence 1866, kymograph, ochronosis 1867, Kurort 1868, fibrinogen 1872, rötheln, Trinkhalle 1873, pernicious anemia 1874, air-cure, periarteritis (nodosa) 1876, visual purple 1877, botulism, odontoblast, polymastia, psychophysics 1878, crematorium, endothelioma 1880, anarthria, pneumoconiosis 1881, rhinophyma 1882, cataplexy, pseudomucin, urning 1883, Kur, polioencephalitis 1885, myotonia congenita 1886, angioneurosis 1887, alkapton, dyslexia 1888, ephedrin 1889, hacking, Kneipp cure, siderosis[1] 1890, neuron 1891, petri dish 1892, neutrophil 1893, mosaic disease, toxoid 1894, Mittelschmerz, uranism, urotropin 1895, pseudotuberculosis 1896, multiple myeloma 1897, Protargol 1898, aspirin, reticulin, Rinne's test, toxophore 1899, extrasystole, menarche, pyocyanase 1900
1901–50:	choriocarcinoma, chorioepithelioma, heterolysin, punctograph 1901, erespin, hookworm, pentosuria, toxophorous 1902, electrocardiogram, occult bleeding, orthodiagraphy, plomb 1904, Alypin, trypan red 1905, aggressin, lipoid 1906, chemotherapy 1907, cyclodialysis, serum sickness, symplasma, treponema 1908, diathermy, Giesma stain, photodynamic, trypan blue, Wassermann reaction 1909, transvestite 1910, Alzheimer's disease, Fröhlich syndrome, reticulum cell, twilight sleep 1912, roentgenkymogram, roentgenkymography, transvestism 1913, Perthes disease, laparoscopy, nephrosis, past pointing 1916, transvestitism 1919, leucosis, pyknolepsy 1922, thrombocytopenia 1923, reticuloendothelial 1924, karyotin 1925, reticuloendothelios 1926, Avertin, myxomatosis 1927, pheochromocyte, pheochromocytoma, stab (n.), stab (a.) 1929, osteodystrophia fibrosa, osteodystrophy 1930, leptosome (a.), leptosome (n.), Pick's disease, struma 1931, electron microscope, lepromin, reticulosis, Thorotrast 1932, electroencephalogram, sympathogonia 1934, salpingography, thrombastenia, to-

mography 1935, citrin, tomogram 1936, dextran 1946, Marek's disease 1947, prosopagnosia 1950

1951– : lignocaine 1954, pharmacogenetics 1960, Creutzfeld-Jakob disease, thrombocyth(a)emia 1966, stab cell 1972

Metallurgy

See *Mining*.

Meteorology

Prior to the seventeenth and eighteenth centuries, Aristotle's *Meteorologia* was the only serious attempt to explain the behavior of the atmosphere. The application of scientific principles to the phenomena of the upper reaches of the air was first made possible by the development of the thermometer and the hygrometer, beginning with Galileo (1564–1642) and Sir John Leslie (1766–1832).

A certain Wilhelm Köpper, cited in the *OED*, attests the use of *Aerologie* in German in 1906. English sources cite *aerology* as early as 1736, but they do not refer to it as a branch of meteorology concerned with the phenomena of the upper air until 1912.

The invention of the telegraph in the nineteenth century made it possible to gather and transmit observations regarding atmospheric conditions from afar and hence to compile daily weather maps. But the German items that entered English in the first half of the nineteenth century derive, without exception, from observations of the folk. Among them one might note *brocken specter* (1801), from *Brockengespenst,* and *cloudburst* (1817), from *Wolkenbruch,* both attested in Grimm, as well as *wind rose* (1846) 'a diagram indicating the strength, direction, and frequency of winds,' documented in German since 1794 (see Kluge/Mitzka).

The same holds true for the meteorological terms that enriched the English vocabulary from 1850 to 1900. They include *firn (snow)* (1853), from German *Firn,* used in the Swiss Alps since the sixteenth century (see Kluge/Mitzka); *ball lightning* (1857), a translation of *Kugelblitz,* found in Grimm and denoting a very rare type of lightning that appears in the form of blazing spheres; *foehn* (1861), so named in German since the fourteenth century, after Latin *flavonius,* a gentle west wind blowing through the Alps; and *alpenglow* (1871), a rendering of *Alpenglühen,* defined in Grimm as a phenomenon seen near sunset or sunrise on an Alpine summit.

Here are some other loanwords of this period: *graupel* (1889), the verb form of which (*graupeln*) Kluge/Mitzka dates as early as 1691 in German; and *snow eater* (1886), a literal translation of the homespun name for a type of chinook wind, *Schneefresser* (see Grimm). A later addition to this group is *storm collar* (1908), from *Sturmkragen,* commonly referring to a long, low roll of cloud that accompanies a squall or thunderstorm (see Grimm).

Thanks to the development of kites, balloons, and aircraft, meteorology made immense progress after 1900 in observing and obtaining data regarding the atmosphere, as the loanwords of these years attest. Albert Ritter von Miller-Hauenfels's term *Isoster,* used initially in his book *Theoretische Meteorologie* (1883), made its entry into English in 1900. (Miller-Hauenfels's dates are 1818–97.) Wilhelm Zenker's coining *Ozeanität,* used in his volume *Der thermische Aufbau der Klimate* (1895), passed into English as *oceanity* in 1922. (Zenker lived from 1829 to 1899.) Tor Bergeron's name for the formation of a weather front, *Frontogenese,* in his book *Über die dreidimensional verknüpfende Wetteranalyse* (1928), passed into English as *frontogenesis* in 1931. (Bergeron was born in 1891 and died in 1977.)

Besides those loanwords, we find in English during the first half of the twentieth century meteorological transfers from G *Kernzähler* (1913), like *kern counter* (1941), 'a device that counts dust and other nuclei particles,' originated by Albert Wigand, German meteorologist (1878–1944), and *langley* (1947), for a unit of solar energy per unit of area, first used in 1942 by Karl Wilhelm Franz Linke, German meteorologist (1878–1944).

The newest word is *rotor* (*OED* 1949), which the German-American meteorologist Joachim Küttner (Kuettner) (b. 1909 in Breslau, emigrated to the U.S. in the 1930s) used in 1938 to describe 'a large eddy where the air circulates around a horizontal axis' (see *Beiträge zur Physik der freien Atmosphäre,* XXV, 108).

The twenty-four words relating to meteorology are:

Undated:	austausch, hypsoisotherm
1801–50:	brocken specter 1801, cloudburst 1817, wonder-sight 1845, wind rose 1846
1851–1900:	firn (snow) 1853, ball lightning 1857, foehn 1861, alpenglow 1871, snow eater 1886, graupel 1889, isostere¹ 1900
1901–50:	bar 1903, storm collar 1908, aerology 1912, oceanity 1922, frontogenesis 1931, radiosonde 1937, kern, kern counter 1941, langley 1947, rocketsonde, rotor 1949

Mineralogy

See *Geology.*

Mining, Metallurgy

Evidence of a German presence in fifteenth-century British metalliferous mining in the years preceding 1501 is provided by the metallurgical English terms *glance-ore* (1457) and *work-lead* (1471). The "ore with a gleam," *glance* (see Mineralogy) is recorded along with a variant, *glanz,* an obvious loan of G *Glanz* rather than Du *glans,* as Carr states (p. 39). Given the derivation of English *glance,* the term *glance-ore,* recorded in the same year, can easily be seen as an English adaptation of *Glanzerz.* The basis for etymologizing *work-lead* (1471–2) as a translation of German *Werkblei* is a notation in the *Extracts from the Account Rolls of the Abbey at Durham,* 1278–1580. Moreover, Carr (p. 44) reminds us that as early as the thirteenth century Richard of Cornwall brought German miners to work in the mines of Cornwall.

A string of mining terms – also springing from the German vernacular and including *stempel, bosh, stulm, kibble* and *guhr,* as well as *bargh, berman, barmaster,* and *barmote* – attest to the growing significance of that presence in the seventeenth and early eighteenth centuries.

A favorite theme among students of mining is that the British were obligated to foreigners, and to the Germans in particular, for introducing gunpowder to blast rocks in sinking shafts and for importing improved draining machinery that permitted fuller exploitation at greater depths. (See John Ulric Neff, *The Rise of the British Coal Industry,* 2 vols., London, 1966, I, 241.) Basing his findings on William Cunningham's *Alien Immigrants in England* (London, 1897), Carr (p. 45) points out that Henry VIII himself called on German know-how to develop the mineral resources of England. In 1528 Joachim von Hoechstetter, a member of Germany's third-largest trading company at that time, was appointed principal surveyor and master of all the mines in England and Ireland. His son Daniel followed him in that office in the second half of the century.[2] In 1563 a German mining company at Keswick brought over 300 to 400 German workmen. Two years later German investors obtained mining rights in the Forest of Dean. And in the seventeenth century, James I authorized James Malynes to bring over German miners to work in the Yorkshire lead mines and the silver mines in Durham.

There are ten transfers from German to English in mining during the two centuries from 1751 to 1900. As in the previous centuries, they continue to have their roots in the German vernacular, as, for example, *abraum* (1753), *stull* (1778), *loch* (1789), and *trommel* (1877). At least one of these, *stockwork* (1808), indirectly confirms the fact, referred to above, that German mining methods introduced in the sixteenth century made possible a fuller exploitation of English mines at greater depths.

The borrowings in metallurgy, somewhat newer but fewer than those in mining, point linguistically backward and forward. Loanwords such as *speiss* (1796), *flitter* (1800), *kish* or *keesh* (1812), *floss* (1839), *spiegeleisen* (1868), and *pilger* (1902) are among those that transmit the simple language of the folk in the mines. But newer ones like *ledeburite* (1912), *silumin* (1922), and *peritectic* (1924) indicate that a terminology coined by scientists is in the ascendance.

The twenty-one words in mining are:

Undated:	zimentwater
Before 1501:	glance-ore 1457
1651–1700:	stempel 1653, barmaster, barmote 1662, kibble 1671, berman 1677, slick 1683, stulm 1684, guhr 1686, bargh 1693
1751–1800:	abraum 1753, stull 1778, loch 1789
1801–50:	glance coal 1805, stockwork 1808, shicer 1846
1851–1900:	slum 1874, Abraum salts 1875, trommel 1877, stock*[1]* 1882

In metallurgy the nineteen borrowings from German are:

Undated:	Augustin process, brown iron ore, mirror iron
Before 1501:	work lead 1471
1651–1700:	slacken 1670, bosh 1679, slackstone 1683
1751–1800:	speiss 1796, flitter c.1800

[2] "By the advice of her Council, Queen Elizabeth I sent over for some Germans experienced in mines, and being supplied, she, on the tenth of October 1561 . . . granted mining rights . . . in eight counties to (Daniel) Houghsetter (or Haughstetter), a German, . . . he having skill and knowledge of and in all manner of mines, of metals, and of minerals." See Georgius Agricola, *De re metallica,* translated from the first Latin edition of 1556, by Herbert Clark Hoover and Lou Henry Hoover, *Mining Magazine* (1912), p. 283.

1801–50:   kish 1812, floss 1839

1851–1900:   spiegeleisen, talmi gold 1868

1901–50:   pilger 1902, ledeburite 1912, silumin 1922, peritectic 1924, Laves phase 1940, pole figure 1943

Optics

The earliest German contribution to the English vocabulary in optics was perhaps that of a certain "Dr. Schmidt of Vienna." According to an entry in the *OED,* dated 1818, Schmidt coined the term *iritis* in 1801 to name an inflammation of the iris of the eye. Other such coinages began to follow in the second half of the nineteenth century.

The German ophthalmologist Gustav von Runge (1844–1920) used the term *Siderosis* or *Siderose* in 1891 to name a condition in which the lens of the eye is stained by rust from an embedded iron particle. *OED* sources begin to record *siderosis* in 1895. In 1897 the German physiologist Johannes von Kries (1853–1928) created *Deuteranope* (English *deuteranope* 1902) as a name for a person who is red-green color-blind due to a deficit in the optic nerve, and *Protanop(e)* (English *protanope* 1908) to classify a person who is red-green color-blind due to a defect in the receptive mechanism in the retina. In 1911 von Kries added *Tritanopie* to his list of neologisms. English adopted it in 1915 as *tritanopia.*

To identify a person with a form of anomalous trichromatism, the German physiologist and optical engineer Willibald Nagel (1870–1911) created in 1907 the name *Protanomale,* which English sources have been using since 1915 as *protanomal.*

Among the loanwords for viewing devices invented by Germans, two stand out. One is the *ophthalmoscope.* Its creator was the German physicist and physiologist Hermann von Helmholtz (1821–94), who called it *Ophthalmoskop.* He completed the instrument in 1850–1, but English scientists did not use its name in print until 1857. They were even less alert in acknowledging the advent of the second viewing device, the *anomaloscope.* It was invented in 1898 by Willibald Nagel. The first known reference in English to this new instrument for testing color vision, called *Anomaloskop* in German, is dated 1923.

Antedating this was an apparatus devised in 1862 by the German physicist August Toepler (Töpler) (1836–1912) to observe and record the presence of schlieren, or streaks, in transparent media. He called it *Schlierenapparat,* which English borrowed as *schlieren apparatus* in 1895.

Examples of names for lenses originated by German scientists are *anastigmat* and *aplanat,* both cited in the *OED* as of 1890. *Anastigmat* is the name for a lens free of astigmatism that was developed in 1889 by the physicist Paul Rudolph (1858–1935). The optical firm Carl Zeiss of Jena, Germany, patented it in 1890. *Aplanat* designates a lens corrected for spherical aberrations. The optician who built and named it in 1866 was Hugo Adolph Steinheil (1832–93).

To illustrate additional earlier optical items, one could single out *neuroepithelium* (1885) and *eucone* (1885). The German physiologist Gustav Schwalbe (1844–1916) created the former in 1874 to identify in brief a modified epithelium in organs of special sense, as the nose or the eye. *Eucone* was first employed in 1877 by the German entomologist Hermann Grenacher (1843–1925) to describe eyes of certain insects and crustaceans that have a fully developed cone in the ommatide.

Only two German items found their way into English in optics or ophthalmology after 1950. One of these, *pleoptics* (1955), was formed in 1953 as *Pleoptik* by the Swiss ophthalmologist Alfred Bangerter (b. 1909).

The twenty-seven words pertaining to optics and/or ophthalmology are:

Undated:	meter angle, Schlemm's canal
1801–50:	iritis 1818
1851–1900:	ophthalmoscope 1857, Lieberkühn 1867, gitter 1876, optogram 1878, eucone, neuro-epithelium 1885, anastigmat, anastigmatic, aplanat 1890, schlieren apparatus, siderosis[2] 1895, Hefner candle, Schröder stairs 1898, schlieren method 1899, achromat 1900
1901–50:	deuteranope 1902, papill(o)edima, protanope 1908, protanomal, tritanopia 1915, anomaloscope 1923, protanomaly 1938
1951– :	pleoptics 1955, achromatic lens 1982

Ornithology

See *Zoology.*

Paleontology

Fossilized remains of animals and the like surely attracted humans' attention long before the publication in 1558 of Agricola's *De natura fossilium.* But it was perhaps Karl Alfred von Zittel, a German geologist and paleontologist (1834–1904), who established the study of fossils as a distinct science. Fittingly, the first of the dated German items in the English vocabulary of paleontology, *pseudosuchian,* from German *Pseudosuchier,* is to be found in his *Handbuch der Paläontologie* of 1890. The earliest citation in the *OED* that refers to *pseudosuchian* is dated 1913. The second such item, *Leptonologie* (1916), appears in Friedrich Rinne's *Gesteinskunde,* originally published in 1901 and now in its twelfth edition (1937). English added *leptonology* a year after its coining in 1917.

The remaining two dated loanwords concerning fossils are *prosauropod* (1951) (from German *Prosauropode* 1920) and *trace fossil* (1956), a translation of *Spurenfossil.* Friedrich Ritter von Huene (b. 1875) included the former in his paper in the *Zeitschrift für induktive Abstammungs- und Vererbungslehre,* 1920, XXII, 211. Karl Krejci-Graf (b. 1898) employed the latter in his study published in 1932 in *Senckenbergiana,* XIV, 21.

The undated borrowing, *steinkern,* Grimm tells us, was already present in German in 1778.

The five words in paleontology are:

Undated:	steinkern
1901–50:	pseudosuchian 1913, leptonology 1917
1951– :	prosauropod 1951, trace fossil 1956

Pathology

Pathologia, the name for the branch of medical science that deals with the causes and nature of disease and the way the body combats them, may already be found in the writings of the Roman physician of Greek origin, Claudius Galen (?129–?199). But it was not until 1761 that the Italian anatomist Giovanni Battista Morgagni (1682–1771) delineated the parameters of pathology in terms of situs and cause in the organs, the French physician François Xavier Bichat (1771–1802) sought them in the tissue, and the German physician Rudolph Virchow (1821–1902) traced them to the cells.

The year of Virchow's establishment of his Institute of Pathology at the University of Berlin (1856) roughly coincides with the date (1855) when one of the first German pathological items was added to English. *Leuk(a)emia,* which he coined in 1848 as *Leukämie,* describes the disorder characterized by an excessive production of white corpuscles in the blood.

In 1855 the German pathologist Friedrich Theodor von Frerichs (1819–85) coined *Melanämie,* English *melan(a)emia* (1860), to label an abnormal condition in which the blood contains melanin resulting in malaria.

During the remainder of the century English gained a number of such German loanwords. In 1882 the Viennese pathologist Friedrich Schultze (1848–1934) saw the need for *Gliose* (English *gliosis* 1890) and *Gliomatose* (*gliomatosis* 1886) to denote 'a proliferation of the glia' and 'a diffuse overgrowth of the glia cells.' The German pathologist Julius F. Cohnheim (1839–84) introduced in his *Untersuchungen über die embolischen Processe* (1872) the neologism *Endarterie,* and in his *Vorlesungen über allgemeine Pathologie* (1877) he added *Koagulationsnekrose.* English added *endartery* in 1880 and *coagulation necrosis* in 1883.

Further transfers in the late nineteenth century included *Erysipelas,* first used in 1887 by the German microbiologist Anton Johann Friedrich Rosenbach (1842–1923) for a type of dermatitis of the hands; and *Weilskrankheit,* named in 1886 for the German physician Adolf Weil (1848–1916), who described the illness. These words became English *erysipeloid* (1888) and *Weil's disease* (1889). Others were *chondriodystrophy* (1893), from German *Chondrio-dystrophie* as formed in 1892 by the German pathologist Eduard Kaufmann (1860–1931) as a name for a cartilage condition that results in dwarfism; *muscle spindle* (1894), a translation of *Muskelspindel* (1863), which the pathologist Friedrich Wilhelm Kühne (1837–1900) coined to describe any of numerous sensory end organs within a muscle that respond to muscle stretching and contraction; and *hypotrichosis* (1896), from *Hypotrichose,* employed in 1892 by the German embryologist Robert Bonnet (1851–1921) to refer to a congenital deficiency of hair.

The number of German items introduced into English during the first half of the twentieth century is even more appreciable. We counted eight in the first decade, eleven in the second, five in the 1920s, and three between 1937 and 1950. Representative of the seven are *Oto-sclerose* (English *otosclerosis* 1901), which appeared initially in Adam Politzer's *Lehrbuch der Ohrenheilkunde* (4th ed., 1901) to name an ear disease gradually leading to deafness; *Koilonychia* (*koilonychia* 1902), which originated in 1897 with the German physician Julius Heller (1864–1931) to name an abnormal condition of the fingernails; and *Fibrinoid* (*fibrinoid* 1910), which the anatomist Ernst Neumann (1834–1918) employed in 1880 for a substance that stains fibrin.

Here are samples of the items that entered English between 1911 and 1919: *Allergie,* which the Viennese pediatrician Clemens Pirquet (1874–1929) identified and named in 1906, and which was incorporated in English in 1911 as *allergy; Diaschisis* (1915), used in 1906 by the Swiss neurologist Konstantin von Monakow (1853–1930) as the technical term for the loss of a pattern of brain activity caused by a localized injury; and *Thynome* (*OED thynoma* 1919), coined by the French pathologist Albert Grandhomme (b. 1859) in his Heidelberg dissertation *Über Tumoren des vorderen Mediastinums* (1910) for a potential tumor in the thymus gland.

The 1920s witnessed, among others, the addition to English of *erythroblastosis* (1923), *Reiter's disease* (1923), and *dysplastic* (1925). They derive, respectively, from *Erythroblastose,* coined in 1912 by the German pathologist Hermann Rautmann (1885–1956); *Reiter Krankheit,* commemorating since 1916 the name of the bacteriologist Hans Reiter (1881–1969), who first described the disease; and from *dysplastisch,* which the psychiatrist Ernst Kretschmer (1888–1964) used in his treatise *Körperbau und Charakter* (1921) to mean 'abnormal growth.'

An example of the German items introduced to English in more recent years is *proteinosis* (1937) (German *Proteinose*), which Erich Urbach (b. 1893) introduced in the *Handbuch der Haut- und Geschlechtskrankheiten* (1932) by Josef Jadassohn (1863–1936). One of the newest pathological terms from German is *sideroachrestic* (1961). It was used in 1957 by the German internist Ludwig Heilmeyer (1899–1969) and his assistants as *sideroachrestisch* in an article in the *Schweizer medizinische Wochenschrift,* LXXXVII, 1237/2 in relation to hypochromic anemia.

The fifty-two words in pathology are:

Undated:	Cohnheim's area
1801–50:	iodism 1832, cystolith 1846
1851–1900:	leukemia 1855, melanaemia 1860, asymbolia, morbility 1876, saltatoric 1877, endartery 1880, coagulation necrosis 1883, gliomatosis 1886, erysipeloid 1888, Weil's disease 1889, erythroblast, gliosis 1890, chondrodystrophy 1893, epidermolysis, muscle spindle 1894, hypotrichosis 1896, polychromatophil(e) 1897, dermatomyositis 1899, algolagnia, pseudocirrhosis, pseudoxanthoma (elasticum) 1900
1901–50:	otosclerosis 1901, koilonychia 1902, hamartoma 1904, plasmacytoma 1907, erythremia 1908, allergen, atherosclerosis, fibrinoid 1910, allergy 1911, furunculosis, kernicterus 1912, neurinoma 1913, diaschisis 1915, diverticulosis, poikiloderma 1917, heterogenetic, spongioblastoma 1918, thynoma 1919, marble bone (disease) 1922, erythroblastosis, porphyrism, Reiter's disease 1923, dysplastic 1925, proteinosis 1937, Sjögren's (syndrome) 1938, panencephalitis 1950
1951– :	sideroachrestic 1961, scleromyxoedema 1964

Pharmacology

Although the science that concerns itself with pharmaceuticals has its roots in the distant past, the preparation of medications on a scientific basis did not begin until around 1900.

The oldest German pharmacological item to be introduced into English is *digitalis*. It is a latinization of German *Fingerhut* in 1542 by the German botanist Leonhard Fuchs (1501–66), the year in which the first pharmacopia was published in Nürnberg. English sources begin to refer to *digitalis* in 1568. But the ameliorating effect of the drug on heart disease was not discovered until the twentieth century.

Thirty-five German names of pharmaceuticals have been added to the English pharmacopia since *digitalis*. *Phlorizin* (*OED* 1835), from German *Phloridzin* (1835), was the earliest drug used in diabetic experiments. It was discovered and named in German by the Belgian physician and philosopher Laurent Guillaume de Koninck (1809–87).

Forty-five years later, in 1880, the German chemist Albert Ladenburg (1842–1911) developed *Homatropin* (*homatropine,* 1880), a medication that is used to dilate the pupil of the eye. Soon thereafter, in 1882, the Dutch chemist Pieter Cornelis Plugge (1847–97) found the poisonous crystalline amaroid that he named in German *Andromedotoxin*. English began to use this word in 1883.

The preparation in 1896 by Heinrich Dreser (1860–1924) of *Heroin,* a crystal derivative of morphine, caught the world's immediate attention (*heroin,* 1898). In 1898 references in the *OED* began to cite another new drug, the antipyrine *Pyramidon,* which the German pharmacologist Wilhelm Filehne (1844–1927) had described in 1896 in the *Berliner klinische Wochenschrift,* XXXIII, 1,061. Also significant was the discovery of *Helmitol* in 1902 by the chemist Arthur Eichengrün (1867–1949). It is a preparation of formamol that is used in the treatment of rheumatism. The earliest reference to it in the *OED* is dated 1903.

Paul Ehrlich's (1854–1915) discovery of *Salvarsan* in 1907 was not introduced until 1909 in the treatment of syphilis and marked another milestone in the advance of pharmacology. English began to use the word in 1910. Conditions brought about by World War I enabled a Dr. M(orris?) Goldschmidt in 1913 to put to successful use *Optochin,* a quinine derivative that he had prepared a few months earlier for the treatment of the eye. The *OED* attests *optochin* in 1914.

The Polish-American biochemist of German origin Casimir Funk (1884–1967) found a certain substance to be essential to normal development and health and in 1912 named it *vitamin* (English, 1912), from Latin *vita* 'life.' Subsequently, Adolf Otto Reinhold Windaus (1876–1959) independently and later with associates synthesized and named *vitamin D_2* in 1931 (*OED* 1932). In 1936 Windaus added *vitamin D_3* (*OED* 1936) to the growing list of these nutritional additives. The Austro-Hungarian physiologist Paul György (b. 1893) meanwhile produced *vitamin H* (*OED* 1937).

The most recent contribution to pharmacology was the development in 1957 by the German pharmacologist Eugen Stahl (b. 1890) of the process that he called *Dünnschicht-Chromatographie,* which English borrowed as *thin-layer chromatography.* By means of it, compounds are separated on a thin layer of absorbent material like silica gel for a variety of analytic procedures.

The thirty-seven words in pharmacology are:

Undated:	acetopyrine, eurobin, Mohr balance
1551–1600:	digitalis 1568
1801–50:	phlorizin 1835, phenetole 1850
1851–1900:	vaseline 1874, homatropine 1880, andromedotoxin 1883, Holocaine 1897, heroin, Pyramidon, tubocurarine 1898, dionin(e), iodipin 1899
1901–50:	Helmitol 1903, helvellic acid 1906, Salvarsan 1910, Neosalvarsan, vitamin S-66 1912,

optochin 1914, Plasmochin 1926, synthalin 1927, pantocain 1931, vitamin D_2 1932, testosterone 1935, neohesperidin, prontosil, prostaglandin, vitamin D_3 1936, mimosine, vitamin H 1937, Resochin 1946, LSD (25) 1947

1951– :   pyridostigmine 1953, valinomycin 1955, thin-layer chromatography 1957

Physics

Greek and Roman philosophers reflected on matter and energy and on their interaction. But Galileo was the first to arrive experimentally at the law of free fall, in 1609, marking the emergence of classical physics concerned with all the observable phenomena in nature. Modern physics, as represented by Planck, Einstein, and Heisenberg, can be said to have begun at the turn of the nineteenth century.

The first German item of record to be introduced into English physics antedates 1800. *Fahrenheit,* the name of the thermometer scale still in use in the United States and Great Britain, was added in 1753. It is named after the German physicist Daniel Gabriel Fahrenheit (1686–1736), who invented the scale in 1714. The expression *Chladni figures* may also have entered English in the eighteenth century as a translation of *Chladni-Figuren,* named after the founder of experimental acoustics, the German physicist Ernst Florens Chladni (1756–1827) and for the figures that are formed by vibrations in a powder or the like with which an agitated metal disk may be covered.

The first documented German loanword in English in the nineteenth century is *tellurism.* It was proposed by the German physicist Dietrich Georg Kieser (1779–1862) in 1822 to describe a magnetic force or principle then supposed to pervade all nature and all organisms therein. Its earliest presence in English is dated 1843.

Between 1851 and 1900 twenty-eight terms were added to the English vocabulary in physics. These divide into two groups. One is made up of new concepts coined by Clausius, Listing, Nägeli, Wiedemann, and Betzold. For example, the German mathematical physicist Rudolf Julius Emanuel Clausius (1822–88), who introduced statistical methods in kinetic theory, coined *Entropie* in 1865 (English *entropy,* 1868) to name the measure of the amount of disorder in any physical system and the limitations it imposes on extracting energy from that system. Next, Johann Benedikt Listing (1808–82), a German mathematician and physicist of Czech origin, employed the term *Geoid* for the first time in his book *Über unsere jetzige Kenntnis der Gestalt und Grösze der Erde* (1872). *Geoid* (*OED* 1881) denotes the true contour of the earth's surface.

The Swiss botanist Carl Wilhelm (von) Nägeli (1817–91) used within his theory, formulated in 1877, the concept of *Micell,* to name a unit of structure comprising polymeric molecules or ions (*micelle,* 1881). Eilhard Ernst Wiedemann (1852–1928) discovered and named *Luminescenz* and *Photoluminescenz* in 1888. Entries in the *OED* date *luminescence* and *photoluminescence* one year later.

The first professor of meteorology at a German university (the University of Berlin), Wilhelm von Bezold (1837–1907), created in 1888 the term *potentielle* (now more commonly *potentiale*) *Temperatur* for the temperature that a body of gas or liquid attains if brought adiabatically to a pressure of 1,000 millibars. The *OED* cites the expression as *potential temperature* (1891).

The second group of the 1851 to 1900 words includes neologisms named after Lenz, Gauss, Hefner, Röntgen, and Boltzmann. Thus *Lenz's law* (1866), from German *Lenz-Gesetz* or *Lenz-Regel* was first used in 1834. It honors the Russian physicist of German origin, Heinrich Friedrich Ernst Lenz (1804–65), who not only formulated this law but also discovered that electrical resistance varies with temperature.

One of the most eminent polymaths of the early 1800s, Karl Friedrich Gauss (1777–1855) is remembered especially for the cgs unit of electromagnetic induction on magnetic fields, the *Gauss,* named after him in Germany and eventually introduced in print in English in 1882.

Friedrich Hefner von Alteneck, an electrical engineer (1845–1904), designed the lamp that was named after him in 1872–3. English physicists translated *Hefnerlampe* into *Hefner lamp* in 1891.

Wilhelm Conrad Röntgen (1845–1923), who was honored with the first Nobel prize in physics in 1901, discovered in 1895 the rays that he called *X-Strahlen*. English has been referring to these as *X rays* since 1896.

The Austrian theoretical physicist Ludwig Eduard Boltzmann (1844–1906), who expanded the meaning of the term *entropy* to include 'a measure of randomness or disorder in a system,' also related the kinetic energy of molecules to their temperature with a constant, spoken of thereafter in German as the *Boltzmann-Konstante* and in English since 1910 as *Boltzmann's constant*. In 1884, moreover, Boltzmann formulated the law that relates the radiation of black bodies to their temperatures. His teacher at the University of Vienna, Josef Stefan (1835–93), had already arrived at the law empirically in 1879. English dictionaries and German sources have been referring to this law since 1898, respectively, as the *Stefan-Boltzmann law* and the *Stefan-Boltzmann-Gesetz*.

Between 1901 and 1950 the English vocabulary of physics gained an additional seventy-five borrowings from German. Some examples are *Piezomagnetismus* and *Pyromagnetismus,* coined by Woldemar Voigt (1850–1919) in 1901, and *Tensor,* which he included in his book *Die fundamentalen physikalischen Eigenschaften der Kristalle,* published in 1898 (English *piezomagnetism* and *pyromagnetism,* 1901 and *tensor,* 1916). Other examples are *Paschen-Gesetz,* established in 1889 and named for the physicist Louis Carl Heinrich Friedrich Paschen (1865–1947) (*Paschen's law,* 1903); *Kanalstrahlen,* discovered in 1886 by the German physicist Eugen Goldstein (1850–1930) (*canal rays,* 1904); and *Doppler-Effekt,* first observed by the Austrian physicist Christian Doppler (1803–53) in 1842 and described in a paper in 1843 (*Doppler effect,* 1905).

Other English borrowings during the first decade of the twentieth century are *Planck's radiation law* in 1905, from *Planck-Strahlungsgesetz,* so named in 1900 after its discoverer Max Karl Ernst Ludwig Planck, German physicist (1858–1947); *quantum theory,* initially *quanta theory* (1911), from *Quantentheorie,* known among physicists the world over to have been developed from Planck's concept of radiant energy in his paper of 1900, extended by Einstein in 1905, and Niels Bohr in 1913 in relation to atomic structure; and *polytropic* in 1907, from German *polytropisch,* named by Gustav Anton Zeuner (1828–1907) in his *Technische Thermodynamik,* 1887.

Among the loanwords in the 1910s attributable to German physicists, two originated with

Arnold (Alfred) Sommerfeld (1868–1951) and two with Claus Hugo Hermann Weyl (1885–1955). Sommerfeld's concepts, *Raumwelle* (1911) and *innere Quantenzahl* (1920), passed into English in 1913 and 1923, respectively, as *space wave* and *inner quantum number*. Sommerfeld added *Feinstruktur* to his list of coinages in 1916. Its translation, *fine structure,* turned up in English in 1918.

Weyl's 1918 book, *Raum, Zeit, Materie,* included the phrase *Raum-Zeit(-Welt)* to explain in full his earlier notion of a unified world theory. (An article in *Nature* of March 10, 1956, 458/1, reminds us that Weyl discovered the first "unified field theory.") In 1918 Weyl also added *Maßstab* to the physics vocabulary in the sense of *gauge* (1920).

The items *worldline* (1916) and *world point* (1923) derive from German *Weltlinie* and *Weltpunkt,* which relate to the geometry of numbers as used by the German mathematician Hermann Minkowski (1864–1909) in his essay published in *Das Relativitätsprinzip* in 1913. *Photophorese* (English *photophorisis* 1919) was coined by the Austrian physicist Felix Ehrenhaft (1879–1952), who identified the phenomenon; and *metastabil* (*metastabile* 1922) was used first in 1919 by the German-American physicist James Franck (1882–1964) together with the German physician Hugo Wilhelm Knipping (b. 1895).

Representative of the loanwords of the 1920s are *Wien bridge, Geiger counter,* and *polytrope. Wien bridge* (1922), from German *Wien Brücke,* commemorates the German physicist Max Carl Werner Wien (1866–1938), who is noted for his trenchant contributions to our understanding of the electrical conductivity of electrolytes and the development of high-frequency technology. *Geiger counter* is a 1924 translation of *Geigerzähler.* The counter is named after the physicist Hans Geiger (1882–1945), who helped develop it in 1913. The term *polytrope,* in the *OED* since 1926, has its origin in the German *Polytrop,* created by the Swiss physicist Robert Emden (1862–1940) in his principal work, *Gaskugeln,* 1907.

At least six English borrowings merit citing to illustrate the twenty-two transfers in the 1930s and 1940s. The term *damping capacity* surfaced in 1931 as a translation of German *Dämpfungsfähigkeit* that was originated in 1923 by August Föppel (Foeppel) (1854–1924), for many years professor of physics at the Technical University of Munich. The founder of the first department of low energy studies (at the Institute of Technology in Dresden), Heinrich Barkhausen (1881–1956), is responsible for the coinage *Phon* in 1926, which English has been using as *phon* since 1932. The principal developer of the *electron microscope* (1932) was the German physicist Ernst Brüche (b. 1900), who described and named it *Elektronenmikroskop* in 1932.

The term *Umklapprozess* did not enter English as *Umklapp process* until 1937, although it was abroad among German physicists since 1919, the year it was coined in German by the British physicist of German origin Rudolf Peierls (b. 1907), who is known for his original work on the structure of matter. The Swiss physicist Walter Heinrich Heitler (1904–81) used *Bremsstrahlung,* beginning in 1936, to explain the electromagnetic radiation produced by the abrupt retardation of a moving charged particle. English-speaking physicists have been using the term since 1939. Our sixth example is *Matrix-S,* which Werner Karl Heisenberg (1901–76), the German Nobel laureate in physics in 1932, used in 1943 to define a matrix of probability amplitudes describing the scattering of an initial state into all possible final states. Its first citation in the *OED* as *S-matrix* is dated 1945.

An example of the eight English borrowings after 1954 is *Hz* (1958). It has been the international symbol for a unit frequency equal to one cycle per second since 1934. In use in English also as *Hertz* since 1928, and almost universally in German technical literature for nearly half a century, both *Hz* and *Hertz* derive from the name of the physicist Heinrich Rudolf Hertz (1857–94), who discovered radio waves in 1886–8 and the photoeffect in 1887.

The 118 words pertaining to physics are:

Undated:	barycenter, bremsung, Chladni figures, gegenion, ka (= Kathode)
1751–1800:	Fahrenheit 1753
1801–50:	tellurism 1843
1851–1900:	ohm 1851, spectroscope 1861, telestereoscope 1864, Lenz's law 1866, clang, clangful, overtone 1867, entropy 1868, Kirchhoff's law 1869, virial 1870, spectrometer 1874, weber 1876, etch(ing) figure 1879, cathode ray 1880, geoid, micelle 1881, gauss 1882, piezoelectricity 1883, luminescence, photoluminescence 1889, Hefner lamp, potential temperature 1891, mobility 1895, X ray 1896, thermoluminescence 1897, Stefan-Boltzmann law, Poggendorff illusion 1898, Nernst lamp 1899
1901–50:	h (= Planck's constant), k (= konstant), piezomagnetism, pyromagnetism 1901, quantum, virial coefficient 1902, activate, Paschen's law, Seebeck effect 1903, canal rays 1904, Doppler effect, Planck's radiation law 1905, free 1906, polytropic[3] 1907, valence electron 1908, Boltzmann('s) constant, Planck's constant, phosphor, Reststrahl 1910, quantum theory 1911, elastic (collision) (a.), Nernst's theorem, optophone, space wave 1913, Lauegram, space-time 1915, Hittorf dark space, proper, proper time, tensor, worldline 1916, fine structure 1918, photophoresis 1919, gauge 1920, Magnus effect 1921, metastable[2], Wien bridge 1922, elastic (collision) (n.), inner quantum number, nucleon[2], world point 1923, Barkhausen effect, Geiger counter, Wiedemann-Franz law 1924, Schottky-effect 1925, eigenfunction, s (= spin), polytrope 1926, eigenvalue, hyperfine structure, street 1927, Hertz 1928, eigen-, g (= gerade), Helmholz resonator, photocathode, Ramsauer-Townsend effect, u (= ungerade) 1930, damping capacity, spinor 1931, electron microscope, electron optics, phon 1932, order, Prandtl number 1933, raster 1934, ferrometer, spark counter 1935, posit(r)on, Umklapp (process), Weber number 1937, bremsstrahlung 1939, eigentone 1940, S-matrix 1945, Schottky-barrier 1949
1951– :	eigenfrequency, eigenstate, eigen vector 1955, Pockels effect 1957, Hz 1958, Leidenfrost phenomenon 1967, Q scale 1970, thermal bremsstrahlung 1972

Physiology

The eminent Swiss poet, anatomist, physiologist, and botanist Albrecht von Haller (1708–77) published in 1747 the first manual on physiology or the study of the normal functions of the body. The development of physiology as a distinct discipline utilizing chemical, physical, and anatomical methods of analysis, however, had to await the coming of the nineteenth century.

The first of the forty-three dated German borrowings in physiology was introduced into English in 1872. At least twelve more items were borrowed by 1899, with another twenty-seven between 1901 and 1944, and three in the 1960s and 1970s.

In the 1870s and 1880s English gained, among other borrowings, *fibrinferment* (1876), from German *Fibrinferment,* which the German physiologist Alexander Schmidt (1831–94) first used in 1872 as a name for the proteolytic enzyme thrombin; and *metaphasis* (1888), from *Metaphase,* which was Eduard Strasburger's term for the stage in nuclear division that follows prephase and precedes anaphase. It was introduced in his paper "Generelle Morphologie der Organismen" (1884), in the *Archiv für mikroskopische Anatomie,* XXIII, 260.

Examples of five loanwords in the 1890s are *heteromorphosis* (1891), from *Hetromorphose,* which designates an organism's regenerative development of an abnormal or misplaced part, as used in the *Untersuchungen zur physiologischen Morphologie der Thiere* (1891) by the physiologist Jacques Loeb (1859–1924); and *isotonic²* (1891), not to be confused with *isotonic,¹* which was used by the physiologist Adolf Fick (1829–1901) as *isotonisch* in his book *Mechanische Arbeit und Wärmeentwicklung bei der Muskelthätigkeit* (1882) to explain the characteristic of exhibiting equal tension; *fusion* (1882), a translation of *Verschmelzung,* which was introduced by the philosopher and physiologist Johannes Friedrich Herbart (1776–1841) in his *Psychologie als Wissenschaft* (1825) for a blend of separate, simultaneous sensations or ideas; and *barotaxis* 'a taxis where pressure is the orienting mechanism' and *biogen* 'a hypothetical protoplasmic unit,' both borrowed in 1899 from German *Barotaxis* and *Biogen* as formed by the physiologist Max Verworn (1863–1921) in his *Allgemeine Physiologie* (1894/5).

Beginning with the 1900s, new names of German and non-German physiologists writing in German come to the fore, some belatedly. A number of their coinages have found a permanent place in English. Representative of the German group are Höber, Ranke, and Aschoff.

In his *Physiologische Chemie der Zelle und der Gewebe* (1902), Rudolf Höber (1857–1930) speaks of an animal whose body fluids vary osmotically with the fluctuations in the surrounding medium as being *pökilo-* or *poikilosmatisch* (English *poikilosmatic* 1905). In a 1906 edition he refers to 'the process of maintaining a somewhat constant osmotic pressure in an organism's body fluid' as *Osmoregulation* (*OED* 1927). Johannes Ranke (1836–1916) used the phrase *ermüdender Stoff* or *ermüdende Substanz* in *Tetanus,* XIV, 329, as early as 1865 to denote an accumulation of toxic material in muscles, once thought to cause fatigue due to overexertion. English physiologists translated the concept as *fatigue products,* but evidently not until 1909. In a paper in *Folia Haematologica,* XV, 386, co-authored with one of his students, Ludwig Aschoff (1866–1942), who was one of the founders of anatomical study based on morphological findings, coined the term *Histiozyt* in 1913 to mean a large phagocyte cell. English sources first record *histiocyte* in 1924.

Among significant non-German contributors of German physiological transfers, one may list Bernhard Zonde, Leopold Ružička, and Hendrik Zwaardemaker. The onetime professor of medicine at the University of Berlin and later an Israeli physiologist, Zondex (1891–1966) is credited with *Prolan,* which he coined in 1929 (English *prolan,* 1931), and *Intermedin (intermedin,* 1932), cooperatively created with a student in 1932. Prolan is a female sex hormone, now understood to consist of prolan A and prolan B. Intermedin is a melanocyte-stimulating hormone.

The Swiss chemist of Croatian origin Ružička (1887–1976) created the word *Osmorezeptor* in 1920 as a label for a receptor sensing smell. It did not appear in English as *osmoceptor* until 1944. Hendrik Zwaardemaker (1857–1930), a Dutch otolaryngologist, is cited in English sources in 1919 as the originator of the term *odoriphor.* He had used *Odoriphor* 'a chemical carrier in molecules that causes a compound to have an odor' in 1895 in his study on odors, *Die Physiologie des Geruchs.*

Of the three post-1950 transfers, *Pseudopupille* is quite interesting. English appears not to have discovered the term until 1971 (English *pseudopupil*), although Franz Serafin Exner (1849–1926), the Austrian physiologist and professor at the University of Vienna and the brother of Sigmund Ritter von Erwarten (1846–1926), had used it as early as 1891 in *Physiologie der facettirten Augen von Krebsen und Insekten* for 'a black spot in the center of an insect's eye that always points in the direction of the observer.'

The forty-six words relating to physiology are:

Undated:	euryene, mesene, mesocranial
1851–1900:	Reissner's membrane 1872, fibrinferment 1876, h(a)emosiderin 1885, metaphasis 1888, karyosome 1889, isometric, heteromorphosis, isotonic^2 1891, fusion 1892, isotonic^1 1895, prothrombin 1898, barotaxis, biogen 1899
1901–50:	antibody 1901, secretin 1902, inotropic 1903, rhinion 1904, microrespirometer, photokinesis, poikilosmotic 1905, chemoreceptor, renin 1906, critical fusion frequency 1907, fatigue products 1909, osmoregulatory 1911, odoriphore 1919, poikilotherm 1920, histiocyte, leucophore 1924, pneumotachogram, pneumotachograph 1926, osmoregulation, phonolyte 1927, prolan 1931, intermedin 1932, brei, progesterone 1935, secretor 1941, plasmolyticum 1943, osmoceptor 1944
1951– :	zeitgeber 1964, pseudopupil 1971, paracrine 1972

Zoology, Ornithology, Ichthyology

The *OED* cites only one German item in zoology (*hummel*) that entered English by 1500. German *Hummel* has its origin in OHG *humbal*, which is assumed to be of echoic provenience.

Among the names of animals that English borrowed between 1501 and 1750 are *flittermouse* (1547), *ermeline* (1555), *hazelhen* (1661), and *steinbock* (1683). All of their German etyma (*Fledermaus, Hermelin, Haselhenne,* and *Steinbock*) are rooted in MHG and/or OHG times. The German names of birds added in the two hundred years after 1500 are somewhat less numerous. Examples are *siskin* (1562), *smiring* (1655), *roller* (1663), *silktail* (1685), and *woodchat* (1705). Their etyma (*Zeischen, Schmiering, Roller, Seidenschwanz,* and *Waldkatze/ Waldkater*) invariably derive from MHG and/or OHG, rather than themselves coming from Latin or Greek.

The English acquisitions of fish names during this period are even fewer than those of birds, but are appreciable in number. They include *sheathfish* (1589), *dorse* (1610), *smerlin* (1627), *streamling* (1694), *orfe* (1706) and *hausen* (1745). These are translations and/or adaptations of German *Schaid(e), Dorsch, Schmerling, Strömling, Orf(e),* and *Hausen* and are similarly sprung from etyma of the distant German past.

These names of animals, birds, and fish total twenty-nine, and all have sprung from the folk. In the centuries that followed, English gained an additional ninety-three zoological items, again with the names of animals and such items (eighty-four) in the dominance; these loans begin to reflect the impact of scientific discoveries, especially in zoology.

Three of the sixteen transfers between 1751 and 1850 are now of a scientific nature. They are *protozoa* (1834), coined in 1818 by the German zoologist August Goldfuss; *tellurism* (1843), discovered by the chemist Heinrich Klaproth in 1798; and *dasypeltis* (1849), described by the zoologist J. G. Wagler in 1830. The remaining items, variously adapted, continue to be in the language of the folk. Examples are *rell-mouse* (1752), *nutcracker* (1758), *aurochs* (1766), *eiderdown* (1774), *balm cricket* (1783), *wolfhound* (1786), *dachshund* (1840), and *spitz* (1842).

In the period 1850–1950, the ratio between vernacular and scientific transfers increased to 1:3. Representative of items springing from the folk are *powder-down* (1861), *brant-fox* (1864), *baum martin* (1879), *krieker* (1890), and *affenpinscher* (1903). Examples of a scientific nature include *theca* (1857), so named in German by G. E. von Baer in 1837; *Ondatra* (1867), adopted by H. F. Link in his *Beyträge zur Naturgeschichte* (1795); *perihaemal* (1881), from H. Ludwig's paper in *Zeitschrift für wissenschaftliche Zoologie, 30* (1877), 123; and *chlora-gogen* (1894), coined by W. Kükenthal (see *Jenaer Zeitschrift für Naturwissenschaften,* 1885, XVIII, 332). Our dictionary entries and the *OED* provide data for the other items. Yet these do not adequately show that, among German zoologists before and after Darwin, the names of J. F. Meckel (1781–1833), Karl Enst Ritter von Baer (1792–1876), Fritz Müller (1821–97), and Ernst Haeckel (1834–1919) rank high among those who contributed greatly, directly or indirectly, to the development of zoology as a science.

The number of transfers in ornithology in the years from 1751 to 1950 is small and almost evenly divided between popular names of birds and terms that science then began to supply. Compare, for instance, the vernacular terms *zizel* (1785), *snow-hammer* (1802), and *sprosser* (1871) with the scientific names *pteryla* and *pterylography* (1867), both coined by the German ornithologist Christian Ludwig Nitsch in 1840, as well as *isepiptesis* (1875), the brainchild of A. T. von Middendorff in 1855, who described the Russian flora and fauna in his *Reise in den äußersten Norden und Osten Sibiriens während der Jahre 1843–1844* (4 vols., 1848–75).

The names of fish that English borrowed between 1751 and 1950 derive solely from the tradition of the folk. Among them, familiar to some fishermen, are *huchen* (1829), *zander* (1854), *bitterling* (1880), *wels* (1880), *zope* (1880), *kilch* (1881), and *grindle* (1884).

Except for the loss of capitalization and *Gründel,* all these folk items were borrowed without change.

English borrowing of German items in zoology did not cease in 1950, unlike those in ichthyology and ornithology. Representative of the five zoological items added since then are *waggle dance* (1952) and *rhynchokinesis* (1963). The former is a translation of *Schwänzeltanz,* which denotes the movement performed by honeybees at their hive, believed to signal to other bees the direction of the location of food. It was formed in 1923 by the German and Austrian zoologist Karl Ritter von Frisch (b. 1886). Frisch shared the Nobel prize in medicine in 1973 with the Austrian zoologist Konrad Lorenz (b. 1903) and the Dutch zoologist Niklaus Tinbergen (b. 1907). The German zoologist Helmut Hofer (b. 1912?) coined *Rhynchokinetik* in 1949 to express the capacity of some birds and lizards to raise their upper bill relative to the cranium by extensively bending nasal and premaxillary bones.

The 122 items in zoology are:

Undated:	allopelagic, distelfink, drahthaar, gems(e), Lakenvelder, Pinzgau, ringelnatter, sandnatter, Schwyz, sarmatier
Before 1501:	hummel 1500
1501–50:	lucern 1532, flittermouse 1547

1551–1600:	ermeline 1555, kafer 1599
1601–50:	hamster 1607, water weasel 1611, blaze 1639
1651–1700:	wolf dog 1652, hazelhen 1661, glutton 1674, steinbock 1683
1701–50:	amsel 1705, rainworm 1731, eider 1743
1751–1800:	rell-mouse 1752, nutcracker 1758, aurochs 1766, eiderdown 1774, gemsbock 1777, balm cricket 1783, sisel 1785, wolfhound 1786
1801–50:	angora 1819, poodle, poodle dog 1820, protozoa 1834, dachshund 1840, spitz 1842, tellurism 1843, dasypeltis 1849
1851–1900:	theca (folliculi) 1857, bilharzia 1859, powder-down 1861, badger dog, brant-fox 1864, Holstein 1865, wisent 1866, Ondatra 1867, Monera 1869, homoiothermic 1870, meta-zoa 1874, infusoriform 1877, coelom 1878, baum marten 1879, perihaemal, stenother-mal 1881, biogenetic law, oocyst 1882, coenoblast 1883, taster 1884, stereome 1885, dachs 1886, rheotropism, scapulet(te) 1887, polyclad 1888, protist 1889, krieker, mops 1890, breitschwanz, broadtail 1892, pole cell 1893, chloragogen, rhynchodaeum, rhynchstome 1894, hypertely, nephrotome, protonephridium 1895, nephrocyte, atoke, dissogeny 1896, protandrous, trichoplax 1897, acrosome 1899, rheotaxis, schizont 1900
1901–50:	neoteny, spasmoneme, streptostylic 1901, Moeritherium 1902, affenpinscher, Em(b)den, xanthophore 1903, olm 1905, Rottweiler 1907, turbary pig, turbary sheep 1908, buck-ling 1909, Lippizaner, parasyndesis 1911, Doberman pinscher 1917, schnauzer 1923, guanophore, mycetome, troglobiont, troglophil(e) 1924, sensillum 1925, metanephri-dium, paratomy, pursuit-flight 1930, protrichocyst 1933, boxer, telotaxis 1934, sinus gland 1938, Weimaraner 1934, stenotopic 1949, round dance, waggle dance 1950
1951– :	somatocoel 1955, ecdyson(e) 1956, prokinesis 1962, rhynchokinesis 1963

The twenty words in ichthyology are:

1551–1600:	sheatfish 1589
1601–50:	dorse 1610, smerlin 1627
1651–1700:	setzling 1688, streamling 1694
1701–50:	orfe 1706, hausen 1745
1751–1800:	crucian carp 1763
1801–50:	zingel 1803, schnapper 1827, huchen 1829, gibel 1841
1851–1900:	zander 1854, bitterling, wels, zope 1880, kilch 1881, grindle, saibling 1884, schill 1885

The eighteen words in ornithology are:

Undated:	pirol
1500–50:	witwall 1544
1551–1600:	siskin 1562
1651–1700:	smiring 1655, roller 1663, silktail 1685, sugarbird 1688

1701–50:   woodchat 1705

1751–1800:   zizel 1785

1801–50:   snow-hammer 1802, lammergeier 1817

1851–1900:   pteryla, pterylography 1867, sprosser 1871, isepiptesis 1875

1901–50:   waldrapp 1924, anting 1936, Zugunruhe 1950

SOCIAL SCIENCES

Anthropology

The development of biological studies during the nineteenth century also led to the emergence of anthropology in its modern form. All of the twenty dated German loanwords that entered English by 1950 were, in fact, acquired after 1800.

Two of these were transferred between 1806 and 1832. They are *craniology* (1806) and *animism* (1832). The former derives from German *Kraniologie*, as coined by the physician Franz Joseph Gall (1758–1828), founder of the study of the subject, which was proscribed in Germany in 1802. The term *Animismus* was conceived as long ago as 1720 by the German philosopher Georg Ernst Stahl (1660–1734) as a name for the doctrine that views the immaterial soul as the vital principle underlying all organic development.

Ten of the dated loans were added to English between 1851 and 1900. Exemplifying them are *Book of the Dead* (1853), coined in German as *Totenbuch* by Carl Richard Lepsius (1810–84), professor of Egyptology at the University of Berlin, to describe a collection of ancient Egyptian papyrus books containing magical formulae; *Neanderthal* (1861), the name of the valley of the river Düsel between the cities of Wuppertal and Düsseldorf, where, in 1856, the first or oldest human remains were discovered in the Feldhofer Grotte, one of the caves lining the shores of the Düsel; *pithecanthropus* (1876), a term coined in 1868 by the German zoologist and philosopher Ernst Haeckel (1834–1919) to denote what he conjectured to be the link between man and ape; *stem father* (1879), from *Stammvater* 'tribal ancestor,' the 1741 use of which is documented in Paul/Betz; *Armenoid* (1899), which the Austrian anthropologist Felix von Luschan (1854–1924) used in 1892 to refer to the eastern branch of Alpine people of ancient West Asia; and *endocannibalism* (1900), from *Endokannibalismus* (1896), a word created in German by the Dutch ethnologist and sociologist Sebald Rudolph Steinmetz (1862–1940) to describe the practice of eating members of one's own family or tribe.

Representative of the eight loanwords between 1901 and 1950 are *Austronesian* (1903), from *austronesisch,* coined by Wilhelm Schmidt (1868–1954), founder of the Vienna School of Ethnology, to refer to the Malayo-Polynesian language family; Friedrich Nietzsche's *blond beast* (1907), conjured up in German as *blonde Bestie* in 1887 in his book *Zur Genealogie der Moral,* partly to delineate a type of primitive, predatory inhabitant of northern Europe; and *pyknic* (1925), originally *pyknisch,* which the physiologist Ernst Kretschmer (1888–1964) used to describe a 'stocky physique' in his study on *Körperbau und Charakter* in 1921.

One of the most recent items is *hominine* (1961). It was coined in 1949 by the eminent German anthropologist Gerhard Heberer (1901–73) as a name for a large-brained hominoid. His principal, three-volume work, *Die Evolution der Organismen* (1943), is in its third edition.

The thirty-seven words in anthropology are:

Undated:	chamaerrhine, culture-historical, homophyletic, hyperchamaerrhine, hypereuryprosopic, hypereuryprosopy, hyperleptoprosopic, hyperleptoprosopy, hypsicranial, leptene, mesocranial, orthocranic, Rassenkreis, tapeinocranic
1801–50:	craniology 1806, animism 1832
1851–1900:	Book of the Dead 1853, Neanderthal 1861, pithecanthropus 1876, stem father 1879, homophyly 1883, chamaeprosopic 1886, leptoprosopic 1889, oxycephaly 1895, Armenoid 1899, endocannibalism 1900
1901–50:	chamaecranial 1902, Austronesian 1903, blond beast 1907, Neanderthaler 1913, pyknic 1925, culturology 1939, sibling species 1940, Kulturkreis 1948
1951– :	hominine (n., a.), Kulturbild 1961

Archaeology

Organized study of the material remains of the past may be said to have begun with the rise of humanism in the late fifteenth and early sixteenth centuries. And, although serious efforts to collect antiquities were accelerated by the excavations of Herculaneum and Pompey beginning in 1709, some view the publication of the *Geschichte der Kunst des Altertums* by Johann Joachim Winckelmann (1717–68) in 1764 as the start of modern archaeology. There are only nine archaeological German items in English, of which two are undated.

The undated loans are *Reihengräber,* adjective and noun, '(of) long barrows of prehistoric graves' known to have been in use in the Neolithic Age (see Meyer).

Of the dated loans, two surfaced in English prior to 1901; *conodont* and *isochronous.* Christian Heinrich Pander (1794–1865) coined the former in his *Monographie der fossilien Fische des silurischen Systems des Russisch-Baltischen Gouvernments* (1856) to name a very toothlike fossil found in large numbers in marine sediments. English gained it in 1859. *Isochronous* 'originally found in the same period' was introduced into English in 1895. Its source is *Die Cophalopoden der Hallstätter Kalke* (1893) by the Austrian paleontologist Edmund Mojsisovics (1839–1907).

After 1900, names for three types of pottery were added to English phonetically between 1902 and 1929: *schnurkeramik* (and in translation as corded ware), *Bandkeramik,* and *Buckelkeramik.* Originally formulated to describe three different cultures of the Neolithic Age in terms of the ornamentation of the pottery produced during these periods, at least one appears to have originated with Adolf Kopfleisch in his *Vorgeschichtliche Alterthümer der Provinz Sachsen* (1883), and one with Wilhelm Dörpfeld in his book *Troja und Ilion* (1902).

The last of the dated borrowings in archaeology is *Urheimat* 'original home,' which the *OED* documents beginning with 1934. Note that some German compounds with *ur-,* meaning 'archetypal, original,' date back to the seventeenth century. *Urheimat* was very likely formed somewhat later, as is suggested by Johannes Schmidt's use of it in the title of his 1890 book, *Die Urheimat der Indogermanen.*

The nine loanwords in archaeology are:

Undated:	Reihengräber*1*, Reihengräber*2*
1851–1900:	conodont 1859, isochronous 1895

1901–50:   schnurkeramik 1902, Bandkeramik 1921, corded ware 1928, Buckelkeramik 1929, Ur-heimat 1934

Economics

Only sixteen German terms bearing on economics found their way into English dictionaries prior to the publication of the present study. Three of them are undated.

The oldest of the dated transfers is *autarky* (1617), from German *Autarkie,* denoting 'a self-sufficient national or regional economy' and/or 'a self-sufficiency in the realm of ethics or theology.' The citations in the *OED* refer to it as also meaning 'a self-sufficiency that dwells in the divine.'

After 1617 and before 1901 English adopted in its original German form, among other items, the term *Zollverein* (1843), an abbreviation of the name for the German customs union, *Deutscher Zollverein,* initiated in Prussia in 1818, and which the state of Hannover was last to join in 1854. In 1850 the English lexicon added, unchanged, *Wirtschaft* for 'domestic economy (of a state),' the sense of which prior to the eighteenth century had been restricted to 'domestic economy' in German. See Paul/Betz. The adjective *sparsam* 'economical, thrifty,' which the German poet Johann Fischart (1546–c.1590) used as early as 1578 (see Paul/Betz), emerged as English *sparesome* in its first citation in the *OED* of 1864. Before the end of the century, German transmitted to English unaltered two terms borrowed from Italian in the seventeenth century: *valuta* 'foreign exchange' (1893) and *giro* 'a system of transferring credits between banks' (1896). English assimilated the term *iron law of wages* (1896), a translation of German *ehernes Lohngesetz,* a concept that was coined in 1863 by Ferdinand Lassalle (1825–64), German labor leader.

Between 1901 and 1950 German enriched the English vocabulary in economics with *cameralist* and *cameralism* (1909), denoting, respectively, a person and the field concerned with seventeenth- and eighteenth- century policies designed to strengthen the economic position of a Central European ruler. German also supplied English with the name for a *value-added tax* (1935), from German *Mehrwertsteuer,* based on the expression *Mehrwert* 'value added,' which Karl Marx employed in the later part of the nineteenth century. The notion of *roof organization* (1948) represents German *Dachorganisation* and its more recent equivalents or near synonyms *Spitzenorganisation, Spitzengesellschaft,* and *Rahmengesellschaft* (see Mackensen, Sprach-Brockhaus, and Klappenbach/Steinitz).

German contributed two concepts to the English roster of expressions in economics after 1950. One of these is *Wirtschaftswunder,* of which *OED* sources took note in 1959, and which has since become a commonplace in the English-speaking world. It is associated with the economic miracle or lasting recovery in the economic state and standard of living in Germany, especially in the German Federal Republic, following World War II. The recovery was sparked by the monetary conversion of the Reichsmark to the Deutsche Mark or D-Mark on June 21, 1948. The term describing the economic miracle had its origin in German in the mid-fifties.

The second of the post-1950 additions is *Mitbestimmung.* The word for the legal right of German labor representatives to sit on management boards and help make decisions is found in a draft for the regulation of trade prepared for the Assembly that met in Frankfurt in 1848. *Mitbestimmung* entered English in 1970, twenty-one years after *codetermination,* its English rendition, had gained a foothold across the Channel and in the United States, thus providing an interesting linguistic competition between the two forms.

The sixteen words in economics are:

Undated:	cameralistic, cameralistics
1601–50:	autarky 1617
1801–50:	Zollverein 1843, Wirtschaft 1850
1851–1900:	sparesome 1864, valuta 1893, giro, iron law of wages 1896
1901–50:	cameralism, cameralist 1909, value added tax 1935, roof organization 1948
1951– :	Wirtschaftswunder 1959, Mitbestimmung 1970, ergonomy 1987

Ethnology

The science that deals with the division of humans into racial groups and investigates their characteristics, customs, and institutions initially followed a historical-philological bent, as reflected in the publications of the Brothers Grimm. Accordingly, nearly all of the eighteen ethnological loanwords from German are names of tribes, members of tribes, or of languages or speakers thereof. These include *Lett* (1589), *Swab* (1663), Wend (1786), *Sorb* (1843), *Yugoslav* (1853), and *Lech* (1893). Among borrowed adjectives that pertain to such languages are *Semitic* (1813) and *Gutnish* (1927).

The concepts *Mitteleuropean* (1937, 1950), taken nominally and adjectivally from German *Mitteleuropäer* and *mitteleuropäisch,* are coinages that had their origin in the days of Metternich.

Untermensch (1964), the most recent item to be transferred with particular reference to the Nazi regime, was actually coined at the beginning of the eighteenth century as an appositive to *Hochmensch* that somehow seems to echo in *Übermensch* or superman (see Paul/Betz).

The eighteen words in ethnology are:

1551–1600:	Lett 1589
1601–50:	Wendish (a.), Wendish (n.) 1617
1651–1700:	Swab 1663
1751–1800:	Wend 1786
1801–50:	Semitic 1813, Lettish 1831, Sorb, Szekler 1843
1851–1900:	Yugoslav 1853, Tungan 1875, Lech 1893
1901–50:	Luwian (a.) 1923, Gutnish 1927, Mitteleuropean (n.) 1937, (a.) 1950
1951– :	Luwian (n.) 1952, Untermensch 1964

Geography

Despite the role that German geographers like Phillip Clüver (1580–1622), Bartholomäus Keckermann (1571–1610), Alexander von Humboldt (1769–1859), and Carl Ritter (1779–

1859) played in formulating and establishing modern geography, German has supplied only twenty-six geographical loanwords to English.

The earliest dated item was *Hamburger* 'resident of that German city' (1616). An important term was *watershed* (1803). Its etymon, *Wasserscheide,* was already in common use in German as a scientific term by 1800. Compounds with *Scheide* were also present in OHG (Kluge/Mitzka). The name for a volcanic crater (lake), *maar,* was added to English in 1826. German *Maar* itself probably derives from ML *mara* 'standing body of water,' which is ultimately from L *mare* 'ocean.'

Morning-land, which passed into English in 1842, is a translation of *Morgenland,* Luther's rendition of Greek *anatolē* 'sunrise.' In Switzerland *Morgenland* has been in use as a name for the Orient since 1558 (Kluge/Mitzka). In 1859 came *haff* 'a shallow freshwater lagoon,' which German etymological dictionaries trace back to Middle Low German.

To specify 'on the Austrian side of the river Leitha,' in the text of the 1867 treaty between Austria and Hungary, its authors coined *zisleithanisch,* the etymon for English *cisleithan* (1870). The term *photogrammetry* (1875) is an adaptation of *Photogrammetrie,* which the German architect Albrecht Meydenbauer (1834–1921) first employed in 1858 to describe his technique for measuring buildings.

German *Hinterland* was used as early as 1877 to refer to the surrounding countryside of a capital. English geographers employed it by 1890 with an ever-expanding range of senses, and five years later they took *anthropogeography* from the two-volume study by Friedrich Ratzel (1844–1904), *Anthropogeographie* (1882–91).

Ferdinand von Richthofen's (1833–1905) adoption in 1886 of *Ria* as a technical term for a long, narrow inlet of the sea, gained acceptance among English geographers as *ria* in 1899. In 1888 the German geographer Eduard Suess (1831–1914) introduced in his book *Das Antlitz der Erde,* II, iii, ii, 42, the term *Schild* in the sense of a seismically stable mass of chiefly Precumbrian rock. That sense was added to English *shield* in 1906.

The most recent transfers are *shelf ice* (1910) and *Mitteleuropa* (1918, 1931). Otto Nordenskjöld used the German etymon *Schelfeis* in a paper published in the *Zeitschrift der Gesellschaft für Erdkunde zu Berlin,* XLIII, 618, to describe an extensive ice sheet that extends into the water. *Eis* can be found in OHG, and *Schelf* appears to derive from MLG *Mitteleuropa* as a concept for Central Europe already current in the days of Metternich.

The twenty-six words in geography are:

Undated:	Bottrop, Danziger, hochmoor, hylean, joch, umland
1601–50:	Hamburger 1616
1651–1700:	Carpathian 1673
1801–50:	watershed 1803, maar 1826, sastruga 1840, morning-land 1842
1851–1900:	haff 1859, cisleithan 1870, photogrammetry 1875, Carlsbad 1885, hinterland 1890, polje 1894, anthropogeography 1895, ria 1899
1901–50:	ria coast 1902, shield 1906, Sudetic 1907, shelf ice 1910, Mitteleuropa (n.) 1918, Mitteleuropa (a.) 1931

History

As a record of humans as a whole, history is said to have its beginnings in the Renaissance. Its emergence as a more objective discipline is associated with the Enlightenment. Modern history is assumed to be indebted in good measure to such nineteenth century German historians as Leopold von Ranke (1795–1886) and Barthold Niebuhr (1776–1831), who are known for their critical use of sources.

The oldest of the six historical lexemes that entered English from German, *Vorwelt,* is in fact attributed ultimately to the German poet Martin Opitz (1597–1639). But its translated use in English as *foreworld* in 1796 is associated with Friedrich Gottlieb Klopstock's (1724–1803) popularization of the term in his late eighteenth-century poetical works.

Weltgeschichte is known to have been used in 1691 by the poet and lexicographer Caspar (Kaspar) von Stieler (1632–1707). It was given wider circulation in German at the end of the eighteenth century by the poet and theologian Johann Gottfried von Herder (1744–1803), before its translation as *world history* (1837). The German concept *Kulturgeschichte* or *history of civilization* gained acceptance in English in 1876, sixteen years after it had won German currency in 1860 following its appearance in Jacob Burckhardt's *Die Cultur der Renaissance in Italien.*

Adopted phonetically in English in 1879, the word *Kulturkampf* was the name given to the political war that Bismarck waged against the Catholic Church between 1872 and 1887 to gain control of education and church appointments in Prussia, hitherto exercised by the Vatican. The term is attested in German as early as 1840. It was used by Rudolf Virchow (1821–1902), renowned pathologist and then a member of the Prussian Parliament, in his opposition to Bismarck's actions.

The view or theory that all social and cultural phenomena are historically interrelated gained ascendance in Germany in the second half of the nineteenth century. It was given the name *Historizismus,* which was shortened to *Historismus.* It gained acceptance around the time of the founding of the German Reich in 1871. The *OED* records both forms, *historism* without date and *historicism* as of 1895, as the last of the German historical loans.

The six borrowings in history are:

Undated:	historism
1751–1800:	foreworld 1796
1801–50:	world history 1837
1851–1900:	Kulturgeschichte 1876, Kulturkampf 1879, historicism 1895

Law

In view of the differing types of law, i.e., Roman law versus common (English) law, that obtain in the German- and English-speaking worlds, respectively, the number of German legal concepts that were transferred to English is understandably small. The oldest was *cameral* (1762). The next oldest was *raven-stone* (1817), from German *Rabenstein,* the stone or place of execution where ravens gather, a designation made popular in medieval German literature. *Fist-law* (1831), from *Faustrecht*, was perhaps fist used by Luther.

More recent borrowings are *eschatocol* (1897), *father-right* (1899), and *exlex* (1909). *Eschatocol*, from German *Eschatocoll* 'the concluding part of a protocol or document containing attestation, date, etc.,' is a coinage that gained special attention with the establishment in Vienna in 1854 of the first institute dedicated specifically to the study and evaluation of historical documents. *Father right* is a translation of *Vaterrecht*, which Grimm derives from MHG *vater recht*. *Exlex* is transferred from German (ultimately Latin) *ex lex*, meaning beyond the pale of the law. In English it has come to mean 'without legal authority.'

The most recent loanword is *criminalistics* (1943), from *Kriminalistik*, now labeled 'antiquated' in German. It was coined by the Austrian criminologist Hans Gross (1847–1915) in 1897 to describe the branch of criminology dedicated to the prevention and solution of crime.

The seven words relating to law are:

1751–1800:	cameral 1762
1801–50:	raven-stone 1817, fist-law 1831
1851–1900:	eschatocol 1897, father right 1899
1901–50:	exlex 1909, criminalistics 1943

Linguistics, Language

Lett (1589) is the earliest of the 101 German loanwords in English related to linguistics, chiefly denoting a language and/or its speakers. In OHG *letto* means 'clay,' *Lettland* being the country with clay-like soil. The second is *Wendish* (1617) (German *Wendisch*). It is cited in the *OED* as "the language of the Saxons," but is actually the language of a Slavic tribe that lived in what is now Saxony before the beginning of the sixteenth century. The only other loan that English dictionaries record prior to 1813 is *High German* (1706), a translation of *hochdeutsch*. Kluge/Mitzka traces it to the second half of the fifteenth century, when it referred to the language spoken in the highlands of the South, and as an appositive to *niederdeutsch*, the German tongue spoken in the lowlands of the North. (English gained the term *niederdeutsch* in translation in 1838 as *Low German*.)

In the years from 1813 to 1950 English borrowed at least eighty-four terms pertaining to linguistics or, as in German, *Linguistik*.[3] An appreciable number of these denote languages or dialects, as *Lettish* (1831, from *Lettisch*), the language of the Letts, who still live in Latvia; *Semitic* (1813), from *Semitisch*, a term coined in 1781 by August Ludwig Schlözer (1735–1809), one of the most prominent German historians of the Enlightenment, for a group of languages ranging from Babylonian and Assyrian to Hebrew and Aramaic; *Rotwelsch* (1841), a form of cant, documented in German since 1250 as the language of "foreign vagrants"; *Sorb* (1843, from *Sorbisch*), the language of a West Slavic tribe that settled between the Saale

[3]*Webster's Third* defines *linguistics* as "the study of human speech." *Philology* is explained first as "historical and comparative linguistics," and secondly as "the study of human speech." Meyer is more direct than Duden. He explains the meaning of *Linguistik*, as Webster describes *philology*, namely as "philology" (or diachronic and comparative linguistics) in the first instance, and as (synchronic, or structural, or glossomatic) "linguistics" including generative grammar in the second.

and the Neisse rivers in the Middle Ages. There are also *Rhaeto-romanic* (1867), from *rätisch-romanisch*, spoken in the Swiss canton of Graubünden before the nineteenth century and still the fourth official language of Switzerland; *Polabish* (1877, from *Polabisch*), the language of an extinct West Slavic tribe that lived along the Elbe river and the Baltic Sea, still spoken in the eighteenth century but now extinct; *Lechish* (1888, from *Lechisch*), the language of another northern group of West Slavs, now also extinct; *Luwian* (1923, from *Luwisch*), one of the Luwian group of Indo-European languages, spoken by a people that moved into Asia Minor at the beginning of the second century B.C.; *Tocharic* (1910, from *Tocharisch*), the language of the inhabitants of Turkestan that became extinct after the eighth century; *Austric* (1927, from *Austrisch*), a member of the Austro-Asiatic and Austronesian family of languages, described in 1906 by Wilhelm Schmidt, German ethnologist (1868–1954), in his book *Die Mon-Khmer-Völker;* and *Nostratic* (1931, from *nostratisch*), a hypothesized parent language of the Indo-European, Hamito-Semitic, etc. group cited in Holger Pedersen's *Vergleichende Grammatik der keltischen Sprachen,* 2 vols., 1909–13.

The term *High German* was introduced to English in 1706, but *Low German* and *Middle English* did not follow until 1838 and 1836. *High German* and *Low German* are translations of *Hochdeutsch* and *Niederdeutsch,*[4] both of which had been in use in German as early as 1457 (see Kluge/Mitzka). *Mittelenglisch,* the source for *Middle English,* was coined in 1802 by the brilliant phonetician Jakob Grimm, whose name was used in *Grimm's law,* the fundamental explanation of Germanic consonantal shifts.

The names for the fields of study and those engaged therein, *Germanist* (1831) and *Anglist* (1888), as well as *Germanistics* (1881) and *Anglistics* (1930), have a more recent history. Although *Germanist* dates back to about 1800, Grimm still used it in 1839 in the sense of 'an expert in Germanic law.' On the other hand, Carlyle's use of it in 1831 as 'a person versed in German language and philology' indicates that the linguistic meaning was already known in English, well before the first *Germanistenversammlung* (Meeting of Germanists) in Frankfurt am Main in 1846 (see Kluge/Mitzka). The German name for their field of study, *Germanistik,* was well-established by the middle of the nineteenth century; but that for *Anglistik* did not come into full use until the latter part of that century, when the study of English language and literature reached its first height in Germany under the guidance of Eduard Sievers.

Klaproth originated the term *indogermanisch* in 1823. The *OED* cites *Indo-Germanic* as of 1823. The division of Indo-Germanic or Indo-European into *centum* and *satem* languages – from German *Kentum-* and *Satemsprachen* – was formulated by Peter von Bradke in his volume *Über Methode und Ergebnisse der arischen Alterthumswissenschaft* (1890). English borrowed the shortened form of the two adjectives in 1901.

The number of Jakob Grimm's terms that found their way into English beginning with 1819 include *anlaut* (1881), *auslaut* (1881), *inlaut* (1892), *breaking* (from *Brechung*) (1883), *sound law* (a translation of *Lautgesetz* in 1874), and *sound shifting* (a rendering of *Lautwandel* or *Lautverschiebung* in 1886). *Strong* (1841) and *weak* (1833), as equivalents for Grimm's connotative use of *stark* and *schwach,* and *Umlaut* (1844), although already present in Justus Georg Schottel's dictionary (1641) and in Joachim Heinrich Campe's dictionary (1807–11),

---

[4]The synonym for *Niederdeutsch, Plattdeutsch* entered English in 1814. Kluge's earliest date for it in German is 1524.

were popularized by Grimm in 1819. *Grade* (1872), from *Stufe* as in *Hochstufe* and *Schwund-stufe,* has its source in Luther's Bible translation.

Examples of later German constitutive concepts that entered English linguistic terminology are August Schleicher's *Stammbaumtheorie* of 1863, which was translated as *family-tree theory* (1933); Johann Schmidt's *Wellentheorie,* enunciated in 1872 and translated in 1933 as *wave theory;* Eduard Sievers's *Schallanalyse,* described in his *Ziele und Wege der Schallanalyse,* 1924, that was phonetically transferred in 1930; and Eberhard Zwirner's *Phonometrie* (1927), elucidated in his and Kurt Zwirner's *Grundfragen der Phonometrie* (1936) as a statistical analysis of instrumentally measured speech sounds. The *OED*'s account of *phonometry* is dated 1936.

A major late nineteenth-century German linguistic influence was that of the *Junggrammatiker,* a group of linguists formed around 1880. They admitted to no exceptions in sound laws. English adopted their name in 1885 as *neo-grammarians* and again in 1922 in the original German.

To conclude this selective overview of the transfers prior to 1950, we will list a few other important items: *Ursprache* (English, 1908) and *Urheimat* (*OED* 1934) (see Eduard Hermann (1869–1950) and Matthias, *Archiv für die gesamte Physiologie,* 1908); *Mischsprache* (*OED* 1930) (see "Mischsprachen und Sprachmischungen," in *Sammlung gemeinschaftlicher wissenschaftlicher Vorträge,* XX, 613 (1930) by Max Grünbaum, as cited in the *OED*): *Umgangssprache* (*OED* 1934), coined by the Leipzig School of Linguists in 1885 (see Paul/Betz); and *Schriftsprache* (*OED* 1931), used in *Der Teutsche Merkur* in 1782.

After 1950 only three loanwords found their way into English. The first is *Stammbaumtheorie* (1954). The last is *text linguistics* (1973), from German *Textlinguistik.* The concept *Stammbaumtheorie* can actually be found in American textbooks on German linguistics published in the 1930s. The term itself was first used in 1863 by the linguist August Schleicher (1821–68), whose *Compendium der vergleichenden Grammatik der indogermanischen Sprachen* in two parts (1861–2) was reprinted in 1982. Overall, in American and, generally, in English-speaking linguistics, there are perhaps as many German loanwords as there are native creations.

The 101 words relative to linguistics are:

Undated:	ach-laut, augenphilologie, Benrath line, dehnstufe, Germanistics, ground form, ich-laut, lautverschiebung, New English, rückumlaut, stosston
1551–1600:	Lett 1589
1601–50:	Wendish 1617
1701–50:	High German 1706
1801–50:	Semitic 1813, Plattdeutsch 1814, Indo-Germanic 1823, Germanist, Lettish 1831, weak 1833, Middle English 1836, Low German 1838, Rotwelsch, strong 1841, idioticon 1842, Sorb 1843, umlaut 1844, ablaut 1849
1851–1900:	anomalist 1860, word-lore 1861, Rhaeto-Romanic 1867, morphology[2] 1869, i-umlaut, stem building 1870, grade 1872, loanword, sound law 1874, Tungan 1875, Polabish 1877, affricate, sound shifting 1880, anlaut, auslaut, folk etymology 1882, breaking,

Slovene 1883, anlauting 1884, neogrammarian 1885, Anglist, combinative, Lechish, speech island 1888, back-formation 1889, Gutnish (n.), inlaut 1892, haptics, schwa 1895

1901–50:   centum, constative, East Germanic, formant, satem 1901, Sprachgefühl 1902, Ursprache 1908, Tocharish 1910, -ismus, lenition 1912, word class 1914, Junggrammatiker, young grammarian 1922, Luwian 1923, isogloss 1925, grammatical change 1926, Austric 1927, autosemantic, synsemantic 1929, Anglistics, Mischsprache, Schallanalyse 1930, Nostratic, Schriftsprache 1931, Urtext 1932, family tree, family-tree theory, loan translation, sound-history, wave theory 1933, Lechitic, Schwyzertütsch, Umgangssprache, Urheimat 1934, Lechitic (a.) 1935, phonometry 1936, Wörter und Sachen 1937, sema 1938, second fronting, Stammbaum 1939, coarticulation 1942

1951– :   Stammbaumtheorie 1954, junggrammatisch 1958, text linguistics 1973

Philosophy

The 150 philosophical borrowings from German place that discipline eleventh among the sixty-nine semantic fields tabulated. The dated items include 3 before 1787, 137 between 1787 and 1947, and 6 after 1954.

The oldest terms with dates are *ownhood* and *selfhood* (1649), and *teleology* (1740). *Ownhood* is a translation of Jakob Böhme's *Eigenheit.* Contemporary English philosophers sometimes referred to this German mystic, philosopher, and theosopher (1575–1624) as *Behmen.* His influence began to make itself felt with the publication in 1619 of his *Beschreibung der drei Principien göttlichen Wesens. Selfhood,* an early rendering of his term *Selbheit,* is now seen as the equivalent of the concepts *Ichheit, Meinheit,* and *Eigenheit. Teleology* may go back, directly or indirectly, to Christian Wolff's *Teleologie* (1728) (see *OED*), since he published in both German and Latin,[5] unlike Böhme, who was the first to publish in his field solely in German.

Baruch Spinoza (1632–77) published his principal work on pantheism in Latin, and the monadology of Gottfried Wilhelm Leibni(t)z (1646–1716) appeared in French. Hence they impacted the English philosophical vocabulary only indirectly. Among the exceptions may be Spinoza's *voluntarianism* (1896), which was given vogue in the works of Ferdinand Tönnies (1855–1936). Also, *monadological* (1895) was taken over and transmitted from German to English either by Christian Wolff or his most prominent pupil, Alexander Gottlieb Baumgarten (1714–62), at one time professor of philosophy at Halle-Saale and Frankfurt. Baumgarten coined the terms *Ästhetik* and *ästhetisch,* which English later adapted as *aesthetics* (1803) and *aesthetic* (1798).

The largest number of philosophical transfers, including lexemes and senses, that flowed from the pen of one philosopher came from Immanuel Kant (1724–1804). Some of his coinages speak to us directly from the titles of his key works, such as the undated *Vernunft* and its translation *reason* (1809), as well as the undated translation of *Urteilskraft* as *determinative*

---

[5]See Wolff's *Vernünfftige Gedanken von den Kräften des menschlichen Verstandes* . . . (1713, 1754, 14th ed.); *Vernünfftige Gedanken von Gott, der Welt und der Seele des Menschen* . . . (1720, 1752, 10th ed.); and *Philosophia rationalis sive logica* (1828, 1736, 2nd ed.).

judgment.[6] Others are *Grenzbegriff* 'limiting sense or concept of experience' (1781, see *noumenon*), *idealism* (1796), *noumenon* (1796) and its translation *idea* (1801), *schema* (1796), *thing-in-itself* (1798) and also the original German *an sich* and *ding an sich* (both in 1846), *transcendental* (1798), the special sense of *form* (1803), *transcendent* (1810), *transcendentalism* (1803), *Vorstellung* 'mental image' (1807), *(the) conditioned* (1829), *categorical imperative* (1827), and *Anschauung* 'perception' (1856).

Philosophy associates with Kant some terms that originated with colleagues who came before him or who treated the specific topic more comprehensively afterward. Notable examples are *phenomenology* (1875), which derives from its chief exponent Johann Heinrich Lambert (1728–77); *eudaemonism* (1827) 'the doctrine of happiness' that Thomas De Quincey found in Kant's works, but which has a long philosophical history; and *as if* (1892), used equally frequently in English and in the original German *als ob* (undated), which was treated systematically by Hans Vaihinger (1852–1933), author of *Die Philosophie des Als ob* in 1911.

In 1776 Adam Weishaupt (1748–1830), professor of philosophy at Ingolstadt, founded a deistic group named *Die Illuminaten*. English lists *Illuminati* since 1797. His notion of *illumination*, the form in which the *OED* records it as of 1798, became one of the guiding principles of the Aufklärung that Kant also shared.

Another of Kant's contemporaries, Friedrich Wilhelm Joseph von Schelling (1775–1854), sought to reestablish harmony between humans and nature.[7] Examples of his contributions are *Naturphilosophie* (*OED* 1817), also conveyed into English as *physiophilosophy* (1847) and later translated as *philosophy of nature; Identitätsphilosophie* (*OED* 1866), now also known as *philosophy of identity*; and *intellectualism* (1829). Among items contributed by some of his other contemporaries we find Johann Gottlieb Fichte's *Wissenschaftslehre* (*OED* 1846), coined in 1794; Johann Georg Jacobi's *nihilism* (1817), from his *Nihilismus* in 1799; and Karl Christian Friedrich Krause's *panentheism* (1874), from his *Panentheismus* in 1828 to describe the view that all reality is part of the being of God.

The vision central to the *Geschichtsphilosophie* of Georg Wilhelm Friedrich Hegel (1770–1831) left its mark in 1846, when the notion of *Weltgeist* appeared in English print as *world spirit* together with *Dasein,* to which he had attached the special meaning of 'determinant being' as early as 1807.

Although English *existentialism* (1919) was adapted from German *Existenzialismus* or *Existentialismus* (1902), both words build on Sören Kierkegaard's original philosophical reflections revolving around "Existents" as early as 1846.

A major modern philosopher was Friedrich Nietzsche, who viewed the approaching twentieth century as an age of *Immoralismus* and *Sklavenmoral* that could be overcome only by an *Übermensch,* a man driven by a *Willen zur Macht* 'a will to power.' English added the first two terms of this quartet in 1907 as *immoralism* and *slave morality*. Nietzsche's designation *Übermensch* was translated as *overman* (1895), *beyondman* (1896), and in 1903 as *superman* by George Bernard Shaw in his play *Man and Superman. Superman* is probably the most famous philosophical transfer into English. Of the six items that English gained after 1954, *critical theory* (1968) and *situation ethics* (1955) are notable. The originator of the

---

[6]See Kant, *Kritik der reinen Vernunft* (1781); *Kritik der praktischen Vernunft* (1788); and *Kritik der Urteilskraft* (1780).

[7]See his *Ideen zu einer Philosophie der Natur,* 1797; En-

twurf eines Systems der Naturphilosophie (1798–9); and Über das Wesen der menschlichen Freiheit (1809).

German etymon *Kritische Theorie,* in the early 1930s, was Max Horkheimer (1895–1973), social philosopher and founder of the Institute for Social Research at the University of Frankfurt. After the demise of the Nazi regime, he and Theodor Adorno (1903–69) returned to Frankfurt in 1949 or 1950 and founded the so-called Frankfurt School, which insisted that critical theories must be gauged by the degree to which they pass the test of practical reason. Horkheimer's definitive, two-volume work on the subject was *Kritische Theorie,* published in 1967.

The German Jesuit Karl Rahner (1904–84) published an essay in 1950 in the Catholic periodical *Stimmen der Zeit,* CXLV, 330, with the heading "Situationsethik und Sündenmystik," which gained instant, widespread attention. It expressed the belief that individual circumstances or particular situations may require flexibility in the application of moral laws. The Vatican took note of it and invited him to assist with the planning of the Second Vatican Council held in 1962–5. The English translation *situation ethics* meanwhile appeared in 1955.

The 150 words relating to philosophy are:

Undated:	als ob, anstoss, determinative judgment, hypothetical imperative, ideal realism, noematic, notion, prestabilism, somewhat, urgrund, Vernunft, Verstand, Verstehen
1601–1650:	ownhood, selfhood 1649
1701–50:	teleology 1740
1751–1800:	Grenzbegriff 1787, idealism, noumenon, schema 1796, Illuminati 1797, aesthetic, heteronomy, illumination, thing-in-itself, transcendental 1798
1801–50:	element, terminology 1801, aesthetics, form, transcendentalism, transcendent (a.) 1803, Vorstellung 1807, reason, understanding 1809, transcendent 1810, foundations, Naturphilosophie, nihilism, realism 1817, eudaemonist 1818, categorical imperative, eudaemonism 1827, (the) conditioned, intellectualism, nonego 1829, Naturphilosoph 1834, monist 1836, occasionalism 1842, an sich, Dasein, ding an sich, Hegelianism, transcendentality, Wissenschaftslehre, world spirit 1846, physiophilosophy, worldall 1847, cosmos, heuristic (a.), world soul 1848, od 1850
1851–1900:	Anschauung 1856, world view 1858, chain argument, henotheism, heuristic (n.) 1860, monism 1862, enlightenment, Schellingism 1865, Identitätsphilosophie, noematic 1866, criticism 1867, Weltanschauung 1868, panlogism 1871, Aberglaube 1873, dysteleology, panentheism 1874, phenomenology, Weltschmerz 1875, (the) determinable 1878, henism, illumination, Neo-Kantian 1881, heterogony of ends, physiophilosoph(er) 1887, Neo-Kantianism 1888, as if, value judgment, Weltansicht 1892, Pan-Satanism 1894, empirio-, energism, monadological, overman 1895, beyondman, psittacism, superhuman, voluntarianism 1896, empiriocriticism 1897, introjection*[1]* 1899
1901–50:	element, form quality, immanence philosophy 1901, Übermensch 1902, humanism, superman, truth value 1903, henid 1906, immoralism, slave morality 1907, contentual, Geisteswissenschaft, truth-function, wertfrei 1909, perspectivism 1910, categorial 1912, anthroposophy 1916, existentialism 1919, übermenschlich 1920, Spielraum, truth table 1921, formal concept, Sachverhalt 1922, heterological 1926, physicalism, protension, übermenschlichkeit 1931, three-valued, Wiener Kreis 1932, mathematicism 1933, many-valued, Vienna circle 1934, protocol statement 1935, universal quantifier 1936,

sentential calculus 1937, geisteswissenschaftler 1938, decision problem 1939, life-world, protothetic 1940, positive logic 1943, facticity, thought experiment 1945, thought-world 1947

1951– : Mitsein, situation ethics 1955, Gedankenexperiment 1958, Lebenswelt 1962, Umwelt 1964, critical theory 1968

Politics

As the Age of Discovery further changed England from a land at the edge of the known world to a hub of maritime routes, German concepts like *landgrave* (1516) and *Junker* (1554), *burgher* (1568) and *Landtag* (1591), and *Rathaus* (1611) and *burghermaster* (1676), as well as *mark* (1726) began to enter the English language, political consciousness, and literature. The motto of every successive Prince of Wales, *ich dien,* turned up in English print for the first time in 1529. An older and now the standard German form, *ich diene,* was engraved on the tomb of the Black Prince, Edward Prince of Wales, at Canterbury in 1376.

The time frame within which these concepts and words found a place in the English lexicon extends from Early New High German times to about 1750. Kluge/Mitzka, Paul/Betz, and other pertinent sources cited in our Primary Sources give the High German etyma for these borrowings. *Landgraf,* from MHG *lant grāve,* an equivalent of Latin *comes provinciae,* since the thirteenth century generally has been the title for a ruler of a German county. *Junker,* from OHG *junchhērro,* originally the son of a member of the landed gentry prior to being knighted, came to mean the son of a 'duke' or 'count' in the Middle Ages. *Bürger,* from OHG *burgāri,* came to mean quite early an inhabitant of a Burg. *Landtag,* from MHG *lant tac* 'provincial diet,' continued to serve into the sixteenth century as an equivalent of today's *Gerichtsversammlung* or 'sitting court' as well (see Paul/Betz). *Rathaus,* the meeting place of the *beratende Versammlung* 'assembled council' since the fourteenth century, is a building such as that in Münster or Cologne, patterned after the city halls built in Italy since the twelfth century. *Bürgermeister* is from Middle High German as a rendering of Latin *magister civium. Mark,* from OHG *mar(h)a,* initially meant 'border,' then 'security zone,' and eventually 'borderland.' It also survives in the name *Mark Brandenburg* 'Marches of Brandenburg.'

The political loanwords added to English between 1751 and 1950 number 131. Of that total, 5 entered English during the first fifty years, 15 during the next half century, 28 in the period 1851–1900, and 83 in the years from 1901 to 1950, reflecting the sharply rising trend of transfers in politics until roughly the 1950s.

Viewed against the historical background, these words portray the increasingly important role that Central Europe played in the political life of the English-speaking world. To some extent they also reveal the causes or forces that moved Prussia, then Germany, closer to center stage of world politics. *Fürstenbund* (n.d.) and *co-state* (1795), for instance, tell of Prussia's place to come in the years ahead. *Fürstenbund* is the name given to a pact between Prussia and its neighboring princess, concluded on July 23, 1785, at the urging of Frederick the Great to counter Austria's effort at isolating his country. *Co-state* is a translation of German *Mitstaat,* which calls to mind the fact that Friedrich Wilhelm II so addressed the members of the Germanic League in one of his declarations. The *Annual Register* of 1795 (p. 227) quotes him, in translation, as having named the members "Most High Colleagues, Co-states of the German Empire."

The loanwords *Bund* (1850), *mediatize* (1830), and *states-system* (1834) and, concommitantly, *Pan-Slavism* (1846), *particularism* (1853), and *Reichsrath* (1858) speak to further developments that lay ahead. Nineteenth-century European history informs us that *Der Deutsche Bund,* shortened to *Bund,* was a confederation, originally of thirty-eight states, formed at the Congress of Vienna in 1815, in the wake of the Napoleonic wars. As a result of this Congress, a number of German princes or states were *mediatized,* that is, deprived of the sovereignty they had held as vassals of the Holy Roman Empire of the German nation and were placed under the rule of another sovereign. Thereupon contiguous states, drawn together by a reciprocity of interests, now entertained the notion of a *Staatensystem,* eventually translated into English *states-system.*

By the 1830s, a movement stressing the cultural ties of various Slavic peoples was under way. That movement gradually turned political. Its German name, *Panslavismus,* became English *Pan-Slavism* in 1846. Around 1850 a new catchword surfaced in German politics, *Partikularismus,* adapted into English in 1853 in *Tait's Magazine* (XX, 387) as *particularism.* It decried the efforts to create such socioeconomic or geopolitical entities. By 1851, the first consultative assembly was convened in Austria as a *Reichsrath* (English 1858).

Soon English gained unpleasant political items like *blood and iron* (1869), *mailed fist* (1897), *lebensraum* (1905), and *Drang (nach Osten)* (1906). A review of the origin of these items reveals further bits of history. On Sept. 2, 1862, for example, Bismarck told the budget committee of the Prussian parliament: "Nicht durch Reden und Majoritätsbeschlüsse werden die großen Fragen der Zeit entschieden ... sondern durch Eisen und Blut." (The important decisions of our time are not arrived at by talk and majority vote ... but by iron and blood.) Euphony changed *Eisen und Blut* to *Blut und Eisen.* When Wilhelm I ascended the throne in 1871, the concept of *Lebensraum* had already taken hold as an extension of social Darwinism to justify the drive for territorial expansion, and twenty-five years later English gained that term. By then, Wilhelm II, who became kaiser in 1888, had recommended a *gepanzerte Faust* as one means of achieving *lebensraum.* That concept was translated into English as *mailed fist* in 1897. A similar product of the 1860s and 1870s is the phrase *Drang (nach Osten),* the name for the imperialistic foreign policy of Germany to expand into eastern and southeastern Europe. The *OED* records that phrase in English beginning with 1906.

Wilhelmstrasse, kaiserdom, and *Dreibund* were all added to English in 1914 and recall the era of World War I. The Berlin street connecting Unter den Linden and Stresemannstrasse was given the name *Wilhelmstrasse* in Wilhelmine days. Because Germany's foreign office was located on it until 1945, this street name came to be used in English as a synonym for the foreign office. Another linguistic bequest of the Wilhelmine empire or of Austria is *kaiserdom* or its more popular equivalent, *Kaiserreich.* Somewhat older in origin is *Dreibund,* the name for the Triple Alliance formed between Germany, Austria, and Italy as a secret defense pact on May 20, 1882.

Traces of the period between 1918 and 1933 survive in English loanwords like *spartacist* (1919), *putsch* (1920), and *Schutzbund* (1927). A spartacist was a member of an Austrian movement organized on November 11, 1918, the *Spartakusbund,* dedicated to the establishment of a socialist government. *Putsch,* probably first used in the modern sense in Switzerland in 1839, was very much in the air in Austria at the time of the demise of the Austro-Hungarian empire. *Schutzbund,* an offshoot of the Austrian Social Democratic Party founded in 1888–9, was organized in 1923, initially to counteract the inroads of Austrian communism, later of clericalism and conservatism.

During the 1930s and 1940s, by far the greatest number of political etyma was generated by National Socialism. Among the earliest to be added to many of the world's languages in phonetic form or in translation was the concept of English *Third Reich.* It was translated within months from the title of Arthur Moeller van den Bruck's book *Das Dritte Reich* (1923). Soon came *Nazi* (1930) and *Nazism* (1934), the latter from *Nazismus,* reportedly formulated by Hitler himself, *Reichstag fire* (1933), *gleichschaltung* (1933), and *rassenschander* (1937). The next decade gave English *blood and soil* (1940), *New Order* (1940), and *Sieg Heil* (1940). The final years of Hitler's rule account for English items like *Thousand-Year Reich* (1946), *Judenrat* (1950), and *Mussulman* (1950).

German had transmitted to English in 1935 the word *Rechtsstaat,* the name for a country where the rule of law prevails. Though that concept could describe the government of West Germany following the German defeat in 1945, it could hardly fit Soviet-dominated East Europe prior to 1990.

The incisive role that politics continues to play in modern times is reflected in the type of German items and in their large number, i.e., twenty-six, more than in any other semantic field, that have become a part of English since 1950. Thus politics is the most dominant influence on Present-Day English. Three examples will suggest their sense and range: *Sonderkommando* (1951), *Überfremdung* (1965), and *filzokratie* (1981). *Sonderkommando* is a term that emerged in the late 1930s to denote a group of prisoners in Nazi concentration camps, who were assigned the task of disposing of their dead fellow inmates. Nearly two decades elapsed before the bibliographers of the *OED* found references to it in English print. German dictionaries of the 1980s have extended its meaning to 'special service corps,' an ameliorated sense that English has not yet borrowed.

Überfremdung 'the inundation of a Central European country by foreigners, especially foreign laborers,' is a back-formation of the verb *überfremden* that had its origin around the beginning of the twentieth century (see Paul/Betz). Finally, English and German dictionaries were prompt in including the neologism *filzokratie,* blended on the analogy of *Demokratie* 'democracy' in compound with German *Filz* 'slovenliness.' This blend conveys the public's disgust with the shoddy systems of government today. The *Barnhart Dictionary Companion* dates it as 1981. Duden's *Deutsches Universalwörterbuch* of 1983 is apparently the first German dictionary to record it.

The 201 loanwords in politics are:

Undated:	Abgeordnetenhaus, amman, Ausgleich, Bundesstaat, crownland, Deutsches Reich, Erzherzog, erzherzogin, Festung Europa, folk state, Forty-eighter, Free Democrat, Fürst, Fürstenbund, gemeinde, gräfin, Hakenkreuzler, herzog, kreis, landvogt, reichsstadt, Staatenbund, Weltpolitik
1501–50:	landgrave 1516, elector, ich dien 1529, Pole 1533, Protestant 1539, fussefall 1547, burgrave 1550
1551–1600:	markgraf 1551, Junker 1554, burgher 1568, Landtag 1591

1601–50:	Rat(h)haus 1611, Graf 1630, stadthouse 1646
1651–1700:	burghermaster 1676, landgravine 1682
1701–50:	starosty 1710, czarin 1716, czarina 1717, mark^2 1726
1751–1800:	vogt 1762, Alemannic (a.) 1776, crown prince 1791, co-state 1795, landamman(n) 1796
1801–50:	kaiser^1 1807, Alemannic (n.) 1814, ritter 1824, Fehme, Vehmgericht 1829, mediatize 1830, states-system 1834, Englander 1836, Geheimrat 1837, Stadthaus 1839, Residenz 1840, gau 1845, Pan-Slavism, snollygoster 1846, Sonderbund 1847, bund 1850
1851–1900:	Vaterland 1852, particularism 1853, Völkerwanderung 1855, Reichsrat(h), Rhinelander^1 1858, (the) fatherland 1864, world power 1866, Reichstag 1867, blood and iron 1869, social democratic 1870, Bundesrat 1872, Social Democrat 1877, honest broker 1878, Bundestag, state socialism, state socialist 1879, Judenhetze 1882, Slovene 1883, kaiser^2, kaiserin, social democracy 1888, Pan-German 1892, will to power, world politics 1896, mailed fist 1897, fatherlandless 1898, los von Rom 1899
1901–50:	geopolitical 1902, Weltpolitik 1903, geopolitics, palace revolution 1904, lebensraum 1905, Drang (nach Osten) 1906, activism, activist, trialism 1908, (The) Day, Dreibund, hymn of hate, kaiserdom, optant, real politik, Wilhelmstrasse 1914, strafe 1915, Klein-deutsche(r), machtpolitik 1916, Hakenkreuz (n.), Spartacus group 1918, spartacist 1919, land, putsch 1920, Reich, S.P.D. 1921, National Socialist, Schupo, Sturmabteilung, Third Reich, Anschluss, lumpenproletariat 1924, Kulturstaat 1925, Schutzbund 1927, illustriousness, power politics 1929, Hitler (a.), Nazi (n.), Nazi (a.), realpolitiker 1930, Hakenkreuz (a.), National Socialism, SA 1931, S.S. 1932 (see Schutzstaffel), diktat, Gleichschaltung, praxis, Reichsführer, Reichstag fire, (Das) Volk 1933, Führer, Gestapo, Leader, Nazism 1934, Recht(s)staat 1935, Ausländer, Gauleiter 1936, Führer principle, Horst Wessel (lied), Mittel-European (a.), rassenschander, volksdeutsch 1937, völkisch 1939, blood and soil, New Order, Reichsmarschall, Sieg Heil 1940, geopolitician 1941, judenrein 1942, Totenkopf (a.) 1943, Festung Europa, Volkssturm 1944, Iron Curtain, kleindeutsch, werewolf 1945, big lie, grossdeutsch, Thousand-YearReich 1946, Sich-erheitsdienst 1947, Volkskammer 1949, Judenrat, Mittel-European (n.), Mussulman, reprivatize 1950
1951– :	Sonderkommando 1951, Saarlander 1955, Bundist 1956, provisorium 1957, Ostpolitik, residence city, Residenzstadt, Volksdeutscher 1961, Grepo, Volkspolizei, Überfremdung 1965, N.P.D. 1966, über alles 1967, S.D.S. 1968, Amerika 1969, Westpolitik 1970, Juso 1971, Abgrenzung 1972, Schutzbündler 1974, Volkspolizist, Berufsverbot 1976, Filz, filzokratie, Totenkopf (n.) 1981, gorbasm 1989, Rottweiler politics 1989

Psychology, Psychiatry

Prior to the nineteenth century, psychology or "the study of the soul" was a branch of philosophy that had its origin in antiquity. The Greeks had no word for it. Its designation as *psychology* derives from Latin *psychologia*, which Philipp Melanchthon is reported to have used (in Latin) in the first half of the sixteenth century. The use of Latin *psychologia* is also attested in Germany in 1575, 1590–7, and later in Christian von Wolff's *Psychologia Empirica* (1732). The German form, *Psychologie*, did not surface before 1745, more than fifty years after English added the term *psychology* (1693). *Psychiatrie,* on the other hand, did originate in German with Johann Christian Reil in 1808. Its transfer as English *psychiatry* is dated 1846.

The earliest among the 129 dated items in English actually relating to psychology or psychiatry prior to 1951 are *genial* (1825), *psychiatric* (1847), *psychopathy* (1847), *psychopathic* (1847), *psychopathology* (1847), and *angst* (1849).[8] *Genial* derives from German *genialisch,* as used in 1777 by the Swiss German poet, philosopher, and cleric Johann Caspar Lavater (see Paul/Betz). According to the *OED, Psychopathie, psychopathisch,* and *Psychopathologie,* three of the etyma for this early group, appear in the address of 1844 to the psychopathic physicians of Germany by Ernst Freiherr von Feuchtersleben, who was then a member of the medical faculty of the University of Vienna. English *Angst* evidently first appears in George Eliot's letter of August 5, 1849, in which she anticipated Freud. "Die Angst," she says, "often brings on a pain at her heart." As 'pain,' physical and perhaps spiritual or mental, *Angst* has a long tradition in German (see Kluge/Mitzka).

Modern psychology is said to have its beginnings in the investigations of three experimentalists: Weber, Fechner, and Müller. Ernst Heinrich Weber (1795–1878) was among the first to examine the range of physical stimuli and responses with a view to establishing norms or thresholds. Fechner called these norms the *Weber-Gesetz,* which was translated as *Weber's law* (1890). The German term for *threshold* is *Schwelle.* Johann Friedrich Herbart (1776–1841) used it in 1824, and English rendered it in its Latin equivalent *limen* (1895). Continuing Weber's work, Gustav Theodor Fechner (1801–87) arrived at additional norms that came to bear the name *Fechner-Gesetz.* Among English psychologists it has been referred to since 1874 as *Fechner's law.* Fechner's coinage of *Psychophysik* in 1859 or 1860 became *psychophysics* in English in 1878.

Among other German psychologists preceding the more prominent Wundt, Ehrenfels, Freud, Jung, and Adler were Rudolf Hermann Lotze, who created the concept *Lokalzeichen* (1841), translated as *local sign* (1874); Emanuel Mendel, the author of the study *Manie* (1881), which contains the word *Hypomanie,* in English writing as *hypomania* since 1882; and Moritz Lazarus (1824–1903) and Hajim Steinthal (1823–99), who established a new discipline titled *Völkerpsychologie* in 1860. English transferred this as *ethnopsychology* (1886) or, more commonly, as *folk psychology* (1889).

To Wilhelm Wundt, who founded the first experimental psychology laboratory and taught at the University of Heidelberg, of Zurich, and of Leipzig, psychology is indebted for *Lustprinzip* (1894) and *Affekt* (attested in Kluge/Mitzka since 1526). English transferred the pair as *pleasure principle* (1912) and *affect* (1891), respectively.

From Christian Freiherr von Ehrenfels's treatise *Über Gestaltqualitäten* (1890), and, more immediately, from the so-called Berlin School under the leadership of Wolfgang Köhler, derive *gestalt* (1890) and its English translation, *configuration* (1925). There followed *Gestaltqualität* (1909) and, partially translated or adapted, *gestalt psychologist* (1922), *Gestalt psychology*

---

[8]The terms *Vorstellung* (1807) and *narcissism* (1820) appear to antedate *genial* (1825). But the ninth edition of Paul's *Deutsches Wörterbuch* and early citations in the *OED* indicate that Coleridge, for example, still used *Vorstellung* in 1820 in the sense of 'idea, mental picture,' a meaning it had acquired in German in the seventeenth century. The more specifically psychological sense of 'a permanently existing idea' emerged in German at the beginning of the eighteenth century and in English in 1890, perhaps with William James. Coleridge's reference to *narcissism* in 1822 in the narrower sense of 'self-admiration' similarly does not yet anticipate Paul Adolf Näcke's (1851–1913) *Die sexuellen Perversitäten* (1899), in which he employs the term in the sense consonant with Freud's use of it.

(1924), *gestalt theory* (1925), *gestaltist* (1931), and *gestaltism* (1938), with dates of origin in German between 1890 and 1912. This concept has had large intellectual, worldwide impact.

Most numerous among these loanwords, especially in the early decades of the twentieth century, are those attributable to Sigmund Freud (1856–1939). They include *psychoanalysis* (1898), *psychoanalytic* (1906), *libido* (1909), *forepleasure* (1910), *censor* (1912), *dreamwork* (1913), *sublimation* (1916), *transference* (1916), *alloerotic* (1921), *death instinct* (1922), *fusion* and *defusion* (1927), and *alloeroticism* (1934). Their etyma are *Psychoanalyse* and *psychoanalytisch* (1896), *Libido* (1909), *Vorlust* (1905), *Zensur* (1912), *Traumarbeit* (1900), *Sublimierung* (1916), *Übertragung* (1895), *alloerotisch* (1921), *Todestrieb* (1923), *Mischung* and *Entmischung* (1923), and *Alloerotizismus* (1899). Freud's genius shows in these rich, worldwide loans.

Carl Gustav Jung's bequests to the English vocabulary include *extraversion* (1915), *extroverted* (1918), and *depth psychology* (1927), formed in German as *Extroversion, extrovertiert,* and *Tiefenpsychologie* between 1915 and 1923.

English students of psychology are indebted to Alfred Adler (1870–1937), the Austrian founder of individual psychology, for the compound *overcompensation* (1917), which he coined in 1907 in German as *Überkompensation* or *übersteigerte Kompensation.*

English psychological borrowings did not end with the contributions of modern titans like Freud, Jung, and Adler. Their contemporary or near-contemporary colleagues added more. Julius Friedrich Bahnsen, for example, crystallized the study of character development, which he called *Charakterologie* (1867) (see his *Beiträge zur Charakterologie,* 1867), and which English took over as *characterology* (1903). Theodor Lipps gave special meaning to the notion *Einfühlung* (1903). English psychologists have been using it since 1904 in phonetic form or in translation as *empathy.* The German psychiatrist Richard von Krafft-Ebing (1840–1902) originated the term *Masochismus* in 1886 (English *masochism,* 1893) to describe a form of sexual perversion. In 1904 Richard Semon established the concept of neural imprints, which he called *Engramme* (singular: *Engram*). By 1908 *engram* was a part of the English vocabulary. Psychologists everywhere now also speak of *engrams* as *neurograms.*

A later, important coinage was by Victor Emil Frankl (b. 1905), who, in his search for methods of diagnosing and treating disfunctions of humankind's sentiments and mind, founded the school of existential analysis. That coinage, which also succinctly describes his method, is *Logotherapie* (1947). It became English *logotherapy* (1948).

Since 1955 English has added three more psychological loanwords: *aktograph* (1956), *reafference* (1965), and *Ganzfeld* (1973). *Reafference* is a telling example. Coined in 1950 by the German psychologist Erich von Holst (1908–62) and his assistant Horst Mittelstaed as *Reafferenz* to describe in sum the sensory stimulation changes that result when an object moves in response to a stimulus, the term has gained wide acceptance among psychologists worldwide.

Overall, though the borrowings in psychology are only in twelfth place among the semantic areas in which German has contributed to English, the importance of numbers of these items is such as almost to transcend, for example, the much more numerous loanwords in mineralogy and chemistry. This fact underlines the danger of one's concluding that German was somehow greatly more useful to English in terms of mineralogy and chemistry because those areas gave many more words than psychology gave to English. Items like *extroverted, psychoanalysis,* and *schizophrenia* are as vital to English in their own way as are items like *blende, quartz, uranium,* and *zinc.* Words are simply not equal in terms of their usage, whether scholarly or general.

The 139 words pertaining to psychology and psychiatry are:

Undated: appersonation, aussage test, Bewusstseinslage, existenz, Gegenstandstheorie, mnestic, mycotic

1801–50:   Vorstellung 1807, narcissism 1820, genial 1825, psychiatry 1846, psychiatric, psycho-pathic, psychopathology, psychopathy, 1847, angst 1849

1851–1900:   schadenfreude 1852, Fechner's law, local sign 1874, Grübelsucht 1876, symbiosis 1877, psychophysics, self-estrangement 1878, color hearing, hypomania 1882, ethnopsychol-ogy 1886, catatonia 1888, folk psychology 1889, gestalt, Weber's law 1890, affect 1891, feeling tone, fusion^1 1892, masochism 1893, pleasure-pain, suppression 1894, clang, clang unity, haptics, limen 1895, death wish 1896, autoeroti(ci)sm, hypnoid(al), Poggendorff illusion, psychoanalysis 1898, epiphenomenon 1899

1901–50:   wish-fulfillment 1901, Aufgabe, somatopsychic 1902, characterology 1903, einfühlung, empathy 1904, phoneme 1905, psychoanalytic 1906, complex, critical flicker/fusion frequency, psychogalvanic (reflex) 1907, engram, neurokyme 1908, autopsychic, Ges-taltqualität, libido, repress 1909, forepleasure, sublimation 1910, psychoanalyst, schmerz 1911, abreact, abreaction, ambivalence, censor, introversion, overcompensa-tion, pleasure principle, schizophrenia 1912, condensation, dreamwork, elastic (colli-sion), mneme 1913, extraversion, foreconscious, horme 1915, ambivalent, imago, introjection^2, narcissistic, tendency wit, transference 1916, ecphore, ecphoria, pansex-ualism 1917, extroverted, psychogram 1918, unpleasure 1919, alloerotic, cyclothymia, psychography 1921, cathexis, death instinct, gestalt psychologist, reflexology 1922, depth psychology, eidetic, Gestalt psychology, id^2 1924, configuration, gestalt theory, Prägnanz, schizoid, schizophrene, syntony 1925, hormic, psychotechnics 1926, defu-sion, depth psychology, fusion^2, psychotechnical 1927, pecking order 1928, narcissist 1930, gestaltist 1931, psychodiagnostics, Unding 1932, object libido 1933, alloeroti-cism, catathymia 1934, simultanagnosia 1936, releaser 1937, gestaltism, numinous 1938, mixoscopia 1939, schizoidia 1940, ressentiment 1941, logotherapy 1948, inten-tion movement, metacontrast 1950

1951– :   aktograph 1956, reafference 1965, Ganzfeld 1973

Sociology

In its broadest sense, sociology may be said to concern itself with all the structural as well as functional aspects of society. Yet of all the thousands of German items added to English over the years, only forty-eight bear directly or indirectly on sociology.

Quite early to find its way into English was *weakling* (1526), Tyndale's translation of Luther's *Weichling* for the unmanly person. There followed: *schloss* (1617) and *stem-house* (1762). In OHG and Early MHG, *sloz* meant 'house' in an extended sense. It did not come to denote 'residence of a person of distinction' until the end of the thirteenth century. In the sense of 'generation' (German *Geschlecht*), *Stamm* was already in wide use in the sixteenth century; and *Stammhaus,* the etymon for *stem-house* (1762) 'ancestral home' may be almost as old (Paul/Betz).

Among the transfers connoting some form of social structure, four are quite interesting: *Verein* (1853), *matriarchate* (1885), *gemeinschaft* (*OED* 1887), and *Gesellschaft* (1887). Paul/ Betz authenticates *Verein,* the German name for a social or political organization, as of the eighteenth century. The *OED* gives 1853 as a date for its first English use. The Swiss legal historian and anthropologist Johann Jakob Bachofen (1815–87) provided the modern name for a matriarchal community. He called it *Matriarchat* in his 1861 volume *Das Mutterrecht. Matriarchate* found its way into English in 1885.

The borrowings *Gemeinschaft* and *Gesellschaft* were accorded more immediate acceptance in English. Both were popularized in 1887 in German by the German sociologist and philosopher Ferdinand Tönnies (1855–1936) and introduced abroad in the same year, the one as a name for 'an instinctive community,' the other with the acquired sense of 'structured association.' The original, basic OHG meaning of *giselschaft* was 'company.'

Indicative of the principles stirring these social structures are *time spirit* (1831) and its untranslated etymon *Zeitgeist* (*OED* 1848) 'spirit of the age'; *Volksgeist* (*OED* 1936), best rendered as 'genius of a people,' in use in German since 1794 as a substitute for *Nationalgeist* 'national spirit' (Kluge/Mitzka); and *Wertfreiheit* (*OED* 1944), which the German sociologist Max Weber (1864–1920) proposed in 1904 as a judgmentally unencumbered basis for examining economic and social phenomena.

Some modern loanwords relating to social stratification are the unaltered *hochgeboren* (1905), *salonfähig* (1905), *Herrenvolk* (1940), and *Untermensch* (1964). Kluge/Mitzka traces *hochgeboren* 'of high station' to MHG *hôchgeborn.* More colorful are the etymologies of the other three examples. *Salonfähig* is a blending of German *fähig* 'able, capable of' and *Salon,* which is an eighteenth-century importation from France. Salons had become the vogue in seventeenth-century France as meeting places for groups such as *Les Précieuses* and *Les Femmes Savantes,* in contrast with Nietzsche's *Herrenvolk* in his famous *Also sprach Zarathustra* (1883–5). As a fundamental tenet in Nazi ideology, it and its loose rendering *master race* were added to English in 1940. *Untermensch,* the most recent English gleaning from the Nazi lexicon, is structurally related to the *untermenschlich* that was used in 1775 by the Swiss theologian and poet Johann Kaspar Lavater (1741–1801). By the end of the eighteenth century the notion of *Untermensch* well nigh invited Nietzsche's coinage of the philosophical item *Übermensch,* which has achieved worldwide usage as *superman* both as the comic-strip character and as someone with great powers.

Borrowings from German that are descriptive of social ills, such as *Blue Monday* (1801), *English sickness* (1963), *Torschlusspanik* (1963), and *Mauerkrankheit* (1981) also offer interesting histories. Paul/Betz, for instance, conjectures that *Blue Monday,* from German *Blauer Montag,* may have its origin in the "Monday before fasting," the day on which the prescribed liturgical color was blue. Kluge/Mitzka offers other explanations. To be tinted blue, in the olden days wool had to be submerged in the dye for twelve hours and then allowed to oxidize in the open air for additional hours. Because no wool was removed from the dye on Sunday, it was left to dry on Monday, leaving the idled dyers to their own devices. Both sources add that *blau* in the sense of 'drunk' may derive from the color associated with the nose tips of habitual imbibers.

The term *English disease* was initially the German colloquial name for *rachitis,* the disease that was first identified and fully described in the 1770s in Great Britain. In the late 1950s and early 1960s, it came to be widely used in Europe to describe the economic inefficiency, excessive absenteeism, and other disruptive labor practices that came to full flower in the early 1970s.

The German name for 'the fear that life's opportunities have passed one by,' *Torschluß-panik,* is a 1950s compounding of *Panik* 'panic,' borrowed from English in 1840, with *Torschluß,* which was already in use in German around 1750 to refer to the closing of the city gates at sunset. The word becomes fully clear in light of the phrase *kurz vor Torschluß* 'at the last moment' that Goethe used in his letter of February 13, 1818.

One of our newest loans, *Mauerkrankheit* (1981), testifies to the ills generated by the Berlin Wall, from German *Berliner Mauer* (1961). The Wall and some of its effects are now past history. But the etyma of *Mauer* (from Latin *murus* 'stone wall') and *Krankheit* (from MHG *krancheit* 'weakness') continue to be of interest.

The forty-eight words relating to sociology are:

Undated:	cultural sociology, mite, Zips
1501-50:	weakling 1526
1601–50:	schloss 1617
1751–1800:	stem-house 1762
1801–50:	Blue Monday 1801, cram 1810, time spirit 1831, Zigeuner 1841, Zigeunerin 1845, folklore 1846
1851–1900:	Verein 1853, Wesen 1854, Frauendienst 1879, matriarchate 1885, gemeinschaft, Gesellschaft 1887
1901–50:	class-consciousness 1903, hochgeboren, salonfähig 1905, underman 1910, Kultur, plunderbund 1914, cultish 1926, ideal type 1928, belongingness 1931, verstehende 1933, Verstehen*,* Weltbild 1934, Volksgeist 1936, Lebensform, master race 1937, untergang 1938, Herrenvolk 1940, immiseration 1942, Wertfreiheit 1944, Verfremdung 1945
1951– :	species being 1959, Tobias night 1960, English disease, Torschlusspanik, Zigeunerbaron 1963, gemeinschaft-like, Gesellschaft-like, Untermensch 1964, Mauerkrankheit, Wohnbereich 1981

ARTS AND LETTERS

Architecture, Art, Pottery

A review of the seven pertinent words that English borrowed from German between 1340 and 1990 suggests that in the history of architecture of these times, Central European originality asserted itself only twice. Its first manifestation was in the so-called *Hallenkirche,* which English dictionaries record in translated form as *hall church,* without date. The term *Jugendstil* (*OED* 1928) is covered below under *Art.* In 1919 the *Bauhaus* was established in Weimar. The style of architecture that it promoted was soon known in English as the *Bauhaus* (*OED* 1923) or 'international style.'

Perhaps relating to structures connected with mining, in which Germans played a significant role in sixteenth-century England, are the borrowings *slight* (1640) and *postament* (1738). The latter is suggestive of classical architecture, as is the loanword *knosp* (1808), from German *Knospe*, the decorative element 'bud.' Kluge/Mitzka traces *schlicht*, the etymon of *slight*, back to the early seventeenth century as a back-formation of the verb *schlichten* 'to smooth.' The Paul/Betz etymon for *Knospe* is found in late MHG mysticism.

In representative art, the linguistic traces of English-German interaction begin a century later and outnumber those in architecture by six to one. These thirty-nine borrowings denote trends or styles in art, providing names for methods of reproducing that art and including terms in art criticism.

Representative of the trends or artistic styles are *Secession* (1890), *Biedermeier* (1903), *expressionism* (1925), *Jugendstil* (1928), and *Neue Sachlichkeit* (1929). Historically, *Sezession*, a radical movement in German art, began in Vienna in 1881. Its influences moved into Munich in 1892 and then took hold in Berlin in 1898. These movements were approximately contemporaneous with French *art nouveau*. *Biedermeier* refers to 'a humdrum style that is intellectually and stylistically lacking,' as coined from the name of the imaginary author Gottlieb Biedermeier, in pejoration of a Swabian rhymester of hackneyed verses, S. F. Sauer. *Expressionismus*, the etymon for English *expressionism* (1925), was coined in 1911 by the German author and art critic Herwarth Walden (1878–1914) as a name for the style that depicts the artist's inner, subjective emotions. The term *Jugendstil*, for *art nouveau*, owes its origin to the founding in 1896 of the cultural periodical *Jugend* 'Youth.' *Neue Sachlichkeit*, a new realism, evolved in the German-speaking countries in the 1920s as a reaction against impressionism.

Examples of the names for methods of reproduction are *hausmalerei* (1935), *nature printing* (1855), *lithography* (1813), and *stereochromy* (1945). The handpainted decoration of porcelain, referred to in English also as *Hausmalerei*, was at its height in the seventeenth and eighteenth centuries in Nuremberg, where Johann Schaper was its leading representative. The shortened translation *nature printing*, from *Naturselbstdruck*, was inspired by Peter Kyhl of Copenhagen and realized by Aloys von Auer in 1852 in Vienna. *Lithographie*, a method of reproducing art on zinc or aluminum plates, was developed by the Austrian Aloys Senefelder (1771–1834) in 1796–7. *Stereochromie* was coined and used in the title of an 1804 book by the distinguished Munich chemist Johann Nepomuk von Fuchs (1774–1856).

Belonging to the vocabulary of art criticism are *kitsch* (1926) and *stylize* (1898). According to Kluge/Mitzka, *kitsch* came into vogue in Munich art circles around 1870 to describe a tasteless work of art. According to Paul/Betz, the term made its first impact on the Berlin art world in 1881. *Stilisieren* antedates its English form, *stylize*, by about 250 years. Paul/Betz dates this verb around 1650.

Among the German names relating to china and pottery that English gained between 1735 and 1950 are *Dresden* (1735), *Böttger ware* (1850), *Meissen* (1863), and *Ludwigsburg* (1863). The German maker of porcelain Johann F. Böttger of Dresden (1682–1719) is viewed as the father of the industry that began to produce a type of fine red stoneware in 1707, called *Böttger Steinzeug*. By 1710 *Meissen* began to make the famous 'China ware' of hard-paste porcelain. A variety of this has gone by the name of *Dresden* since 1735. Another was manufactured in *Ludwigsburg* from 1758 to 1824. Meissen is still one of the great china-producing cities of the world.

After 1965, English added five loanwords relating to pictorial art, whereas there have been no additions in architecture since 1928 and none in pottery since 1925. Several of these art terms hark back to the past. Thus *kitchy* (1967), from German *kitschig,* points to *Kitsch,* coined nearly two hundred years earlier. *Secessionist* (1972) and *secession style* (1973) are offshoots of *Sezession,* the breakaway movement in art at the end of the nineteenth century. Seemingly recent is *Kunstforschung* (1966). However, it too has its roots in the nineteenth century, in the string of synonyms like *Kunstgeschichte, Kunstgeschichtler,* and *Kunstforscher. Kunstgeschichte* 'art history' was established as an academic discipline in Germany at the end of the 1800s.

Interesting, too, is *Bürolandschaft* (1968). This German name for the style of office decoration that uses screens or plants as dividers has not yet made its way into Duden's latest *Universalwörterbuch* (1989). Its editor-in-chief, Professor Günther Drosdowski, was kind enough to send us in 1991 copies of the three citations that Duden had collected of *Bürolandschaft* as of that time, so that this word is quite new but has already made its way into English-speaking art circles.

The seven loans in architecture are:

Undated:	aula, hall church
1601–50:	slight 1640
1701–50:	postament 1738
1801–50:	knosp 1808
1901–50:	Bauhaus 1923, Jugendstil 1928

The thirty-nine words in art are:

Undated:	Blaue Reiter, Deutsche Blumen, Dortmund
1701–50:	Dresden 1735
1801–50:	lithography 1813, autoportrait(ure) 1828, self-portrait 1831
1851–1900:	stereochrome 1854, nature printing 1855, epigone 1865, staffage 1872, docent 1880, Secession 1890, Kunstgeschichte 1892, passglas 1897, stylize 1898, Kunstforscher 1899
1901–50:	(Die) Brücke 1903, Biedermeier 1905, folk art 1921, expressionism 1925, kitsch 1926, Jugendstil 1928, will to art, Neue Sachlichkeit 1929, Sachlichkeit 1930, scissor cut 1931, malerisch 1933, hausmaler, hausmalerei 1935, Modernismus 1934, Kunsthistoriker 1937, Gesamtkunstwerk 1939, stereochromy 1945
1951– :	Kunstforschung 1966, kitchy 1967, Bürolandschaft 1968, Secessionist 1972, secession style 1973

The twelve words in pottery are:

Undated:	Hafner ware, Höchst, protoporcelain
1701–50:	Dresden 1735
1801–50:	Böttger ware 1850

1851–1900:	massa bowl 1858, Frankenthal, Ludwigsburg, Meissen 1863, lithophane 1890
1901–50:	Urfirnis 1912, schwarzlot 1925

Art

See *Architecture*.

Dance

If music is a universal language, then dance ought not to lag far behind. Yet the twelve German loans in English that pertain to dance are greatly outnumbered by the 193 items relating to music.

The earliest dance item is the common *waltz* (1712). A Bavarian ordinance of 1760 proscribed waltzing, i.e., the turning of feet while dancing as opposed to hopping (see Kluge/Mitzka). There was presumably no communal objection to *redowa*, a Bohemian dance resembling a waltz, let alone a polka, that found its way into English in 1845. Again the intermediaries in 1849, German dancers popularized – for English – the *schottische,* a Scottish round dance. An indigenous Central European dance, the *ländler* or Austrian couple dance, followed in 1876. It was joined by the *Rheinländler* (*OED* 1887), a German form of polka, as well as by the *schuhplattler* (*OED* 1905), a Bavarian and Austrian courtship dance.

Three more recent German dance terms added to English include the generic concept *folk dance* in 1909, from German *Volkstanz* (Grimm, 1798); the expression *jump turn* (1924), from German *Umsprung;* and *eurythmy* in 1949, as conceived and spelled by the Austrian anthroposophist Rudolf Steiner (1861–1925).

The twelve words in dance are:

1701–50:	waltz (v.) 1712
1801–50:	redowa 1845
1851–1900:	schottische 1849, Schuhplattltanz 1874, ländler 1876, furiant 1881, Rhinelander[2] 1887, schuhplatteln 1895
1901–50:	schuhplattler 1905, folk dance 1909, jump turn 1924, eurythmy 1949

Literature

German loans in English total seventy-one items in literature, making it second only to music as a major lexical contributor in the arts. Prior to 1799, English borrowed only *tabulatur* (1574), the name for the system of rules for musical and poetical compositions established by the Meistersinger, of which mention is made in German sources since 1511, and *ship of fools* (1509), the name of a mythical ship whose passengers symbolize various types of folly or vice, in an allusion to the *Narrenschiff* by Sebastian Brant, 1494.

The greater portion of the loans relating to literature that entered English between 1799 and 1950 describe genre. The balance falls within the province of the literary historian, the student of poetry in particular, and those interested in literature in general. Connoting genre in the collective sense of *minnelied* (1876) are the English renditions of *Minnesang: minnesong*

(1845), *Minnepoesy* (1845), and *Minnepoetry* (1887). Although the largely aristocratic German lyric poetry of minnesong flourished in the twelfth to fourteenth centuries, full English attention was first turned to it in Edgar Taylor's *Lays of the Minnesingers, or German Troubadours* (1825), Sir Walter Scott's *Anne of Geierstein* (1829), and Henry Wadsworth Longfellow's *Poets and Poetry of Europe* (1845).

In German literature, the concept of *Tendenz* or purpose that influences the content and structure of a literary work dates back to 1791. The genre "engaged literature," reflected in the terms *Tendenzdrama* and *Tendenzroman,* also gained ground in Germany at the end of the eighteenth century, but it did not surface in English until the middle of the nineteenth century in the terms *tendency drama* (1838), *tendenzroman* (1855), and *tendency writing* (1875).

The notions of *Bildungsroman* and *Künstlerroman,* documented in English as of 1910 and 1941, crystallized in the Sturm und Drang period and in the age of German classicism, at the end of the eighteenth and the beginning of the nineteenth centuries, respectively, with J. J. W. Heinse's *Ardinghello und die glückseligen Inseln* (1787) and Goethe's *Wilhelm Meister* (1795–6) as the model. Johann Gottfried Herder's coinage of *Volkslied* in 1771 (in print since 1773) is encountered seven decades later in English as *folk song* (1847), as well as in its original German form in 1858.

The Brothers Grimm established *Märchen* in the sense of 'fairy tale' in 1812, but English did not gain that word until 1871. The term *Rahmenerzählung* for a story told within a story appears to have its origin in German (see Grimm). It was transferred to English as *frame story* in 1924. (The name of the astute queen of the archetypal frame story, *Scheherazade* of *A Thousand and One Nights,* reportedly was introduced to English via the same route in 1851 – see Meyer.) Germans were enormously interested in exotic literature such as from Arabic and Sanskrit. Germanic literary myths are reflected in loans like *Lohengrin, Parsifal, Siegfried, Nibelungenlied,* and *Rumpelstiltskin.*

Of four dated borrowings in the 1751–1950 group of loans, two entered English both in the original form and in translation, and two in the original German only. The former two were *Auflklärung* (1801) and *Sturm und Drang* (1844). Although it had been in use in German as early as 1691, *Aufklärung* was not fully established as a literary term until 1791 (see Kluge/ Mitzka and Paul/Betz). It describes the Age of Reason and the Enlightenment in German literature that reached its apex in Gotthold Ephraim Lessing's drama *Nathan der Weise* (1779). Its English translation, *enlightenment,* documented in the *OED* since 1865, still has its focus in philosophy. *Sturm und Drang* was the title of a play by Friedrich Maximilian Klinger, originally titled *Wirrwarr* 'Confusion' but renamed by Christian Kaufmann in 1776. It mirrors the mood of passion or emotion in German literature from the mid-1760s to the end of the 1780s and was translated as *Storm and Stress* (1838).

The first definitive use of *Expressionismus* to describe the practice in art, music, and literature of depicting subjective emotions rather than objective reality was by the German art and literary critic Herwarth Walden in 1911. Its first citation in the *OED* is dated 1925, as the earlier dates for this word, beginning with 1908, have a somewhat different meaning. The last of this quartet of loanwords referring to a literary and artistic period is *(Die) Neue Sachlichkeit* (1929), coined by Gustav Friedrich Hartlaub in 1925 to describe the neorealism developing in Germany in the 1920s as a reaction against impressionism.

Some other borrowings of interest to the student of poetry during the two-hundred-year period after 1751 are *stave rime* (i.e., alliteration) (1888), from German *Stabreim* ("kaum vor 1838," states Kluge); *dip* (1894), a translation of *Senkung* that most likely goes back to the metric reforms instituted by Martin Opitz in his *Buch von der deutschen Poeterey* in 1624 (see Grimm); and *on-verse* and *off-verse*, 1935 English translations of *Anvers* and *Abvers* that appear to have surfaced among German Anglicists at the beginning of the twentieth century and refer, respectively, to the first and second half-line of a line of Old English poetry. *Priamel* (1950) is a kind of epigrammatic verse that Hans Rosenplüt popularized in the second half of the fifteenth century. A person versed in such aspects of poesy is, according to Sir Walter Scott, a *reim-kennar* (1821), from *Reimkenner,* someone who knows or is knowledgeable about rhymes.

Some loans during the 1751–1950 period generally bear on the creation, transmission, or purpose of literature. Thus we find *nachlass* 'posthumous works' (1842), in use in German since the beginning of the eighteenth century; *fragmentist* (1874), the author who leaves only fragments of work done, as Grimm put it; *epigone* (1865) 'follower and inferior imitator,' coined by Karl Immermann in 1830; and *Verfremdung* 'alienation' (1945), originated by Bertold Brecht in his theory of the epic or "dialectic" theater, developed fully in his *Der Messingkauf,* completed in 1939–40.

Four literary items were borrowed after 1950. The first was *Verfremdungseffekt* (*OED* 1951), as Brecht termed the effect intended to break a theatrical illusion that can mesmerize the audience into witless passivity. Seven years later came *Quellenforschung,* the name given to the principal tool of nineteenth-century German positivists like the literary historian Wilhelm Scherer (1841–86), who sought to discover the effect that one's sources had on one's literary work. By 1958 English became aware of the term *stemmatic,* which the German classical philologist Paul Mass (1880–1964) had coined in 1949 as *stemmatisch* to label the process of reconstructing the interrelationship between the readings of varying manuscripts of a text. The newest loan is *Totentanz* (*OED* 1964). The *danse macabre* originated in France around 1400 and was widespread in Central Europe in the fifteenth and sixteenth centuries in ritual or miracle play form when Hans Holbein, Jr., recorded it in a series of woodcuts titled *Totentanz* in 1522–6. This less-frequent synonym of the old French borrowing invokes Holbein's figures.

The seventy-one borrowings in literature are:

Undated:	Abgesang, Blue Flower, Brunhild, entwicklungsroman, Germanistics, Lohengrin, meistergesang, meisterlied, Nibelungenlied, Parsifal, Siegfried, stollen
1501–50:	ship of fools 1509
1551–1600:	tabulatur 1574
1751–1800:	obscurant 1799
1801–50:	Aufklärer, Aufklärung 1801, Meistersinger 1810, reim-kennar 1821, minnesinger 1825, Weltliteratur 1827, aesthetic tea, Germanist, world literature 1831, (das) Ewigweiblich 1832, tendency drama 1838, nachlass 1842, Sturm und Drang 1844, Minnepoesy, minnesong 1845, folklore 1846, Robinsonade 1847
1851–1900:	Scheherezade 1851, Storm and Stress, tendenzroman 1855, Volkslied 1858, epigon(e) 1865, märchen 1871, fragmentist 1874, tendency-writing 1875, minnelied 1876, Min-

nepoetry 1887, Anglist, stave rime 1888, (the) eternal feminine, value judgment 1892, dip 1894, tendenz 1896, tendentious 1900

1901–50:   Bildungsroman 1910, hymn of hate 1914, form criticism, Formgeschichte 1923, frame story 1924, expressionism 1925, kitsch 1926, magic realism 1927, Neue Sachlichkeit 1929, Anglistics 1930, off-verse, on-verse 1935, Kunstprosa 1936, Künstlerroman 1941, Verfremdung 1945, Rumpelstiltskin, stemmatics 1949, priamel 1950

1951– :   Verfremdungseffekt 1951, Quellenforschung, stemmatic 1958, Totentanz 1964

Music

The first organ to reach Europe was a gift to Pippin III from Emperor Constantin V. Kopron-ymos in 757. Following Charlemagne's receipt of a similar gift from Byzantium in 811, the organ assumed a significant place in the religious services of the Church. By 950 an impressive organ is reported to have been installed in Winchester (see Meyer). In an 1852 translation of Johann Julius Seidel's *Die Orgel und ihr Bau* (1843), we read (on p. 52) that ''in 1515 . . . an organ in St. Mary's, at Danzic . . . contained . . . hohlflute, gemshorn, etc. (stops).'' Begin-ning with 1555 English contained German names for organ stops like *fife, hohlflute,* and *posaune.* Other musical loans followed, totaling 193.

By 1750 at least seven musical terms had been transferred, with another four coming into English within the next quarter of a century: two names of instruments (*pantaleon* 1757 and *zinke* 1776); the name of a song memorializing or performed at approaching death, *death song* (1778), from *Todesgesang;* and the name of a dance, *waltz* (1781). The period from 1806 to 1940 witnessed a surge in transfers. As if foreshadowed by the earliest loans in music, the new items pertained to a considerable extent to the organ, as in *gemshorn* (1825), *glockenspiel* (1825), *portunal* (1852), *waldflute* (1852), *waldhorn* (1852), *krummhorn* (1864), *rauschpfeife* (1876), and *gedackt work* (1904). The many items naming musical instruments included *sal-icional* (1843), *clavier* (1845), *doodlesack* (1847), *melodion* (1847), *panharmonicon* (1848), *zither* (1850), *waldhorn* (1852), *flugelhorn* (1854), *althorn* (1859), *alpenhorn* (1864), *querflöte* (1876), *heckelphone* (1905), *zimbalon* (1910), *Schreierpfeife* (1939), and *wind cap* (1940). Other items memorialized the names or works of composers like Johann Sebastian Bach, Richard Wagner, Johann Strauss, and Arnold Schönberg: *Bach trumpet* (1898), *leitmotiv* (1876), *waltz king* (1908), and *Sprechstimme* (1925).

Borrowings related to voice, such as *Sprechstimme,* extended to *yodel* (1838), *chorale* (1841), *lied* (1852), *Saengerbund* (n.d.), and *heldentenor* (1926). Other items reflected types of music: *kunstlied* (1880), *symphonic poem* (1864), *Romanze* (1883), *Tafelmusik* (1876), and *Gebrauchsmusik* (1930). Still others reflected theory: *clang tint* (1867), *overtone* (1867), *up-beat* (1869), and *nachschlag* (1879). Tempo was reflected in *mässig* (1849) (and *fröhlich, lebhaft,* and *lieblich* that are undated). There were even words for the leader and subleader of the band or orchestra, the *Kapellmaster* (1838) and *concertmaster* (1876), from German *Ka-pellmeister* and *Concertmeister* (now *Konzertmeister*).

Clearly, German musical loanwords denoting the voices of the organ have a venerable history. The origins of some of the other musical terms are just as interesting. For instance, the noun *waltz* is attested in English beginning with the year 1781, the same date of its first record in German, according to Paul/Betz. One reason for its instant transfer may be provided by the Bavarian edict of 1760 that forbade *walzende Tänze* 'revolving dances.'

The earliest English source to quote *leitmotiv* is dated 1876. Like *waltz*, this term achieved immediate attention abroad. We learn from Kluge/Mitzka that the word denoting 'a recurring melodic phrase,' in which Wagner's operas are replete, originated not with Wagner but with one of his younger friends. Wagner did use it and he speaks of it in his *Mein Leben* (1865–80). Its instant fame, initially inverse, was due to the ridicule it received in 1877 from the German author and onetime dramaturg Karl Gutzkow (1811–78), and later from other prominent German critics.

Associated with the name of the Austrian composer Franz Schubert (1797–1828) is the loan *durchkomponiert* 'through-composed' (1897). It describes a libretto set to music without narrative passages or regard to its strophic form. A well-known example is Goethe's *Erlkönig* 'Erlking' (1815).

In 1922 English-speaking musicologists began to use the term *Sprechstimme*, literally, 'speaking voice' in German. In 1925 they added *Sprechgesang* for "a dramatic voice style intermediate between speaking and singing." Originator of both terms was the Austrian composer Arnold Schönberg (1874–1951), who called for both in the introduction to his musical composition *Pierrot Lunaire für Sprechstimme und fünf Instrumentalisten* (1911).

At least five musical loanwords have been added since 1952. Thus we find *Scheitholt (Scheitholz)*, an early stringed instrument, a precursor of the zither. Its use in German extends from the Middle Ages to the end of the nineteenth century. *Innigkeit* (1964) expresses 'deepfelt sincerity.' Paul/Betz cites its general etymon as Middle High German *innecheit*. *Schrammelmusik* (1967) describes music that was initially arranged for and played by the Schrammel Quartet, which included the brothers Johann (1850–93) and Josef (1852–95) Schrammel.

The 193 words in music are:

Undated:	abendmusik, aerophor, Albumblatt, auftakt, auftaktigkeit, bebization, becken, Beckmesser, birn, blockflöte, bobization, character piece, clarina, clavieristic, concertstück, Doppleflöte, dur, erzähler, fackeltanz, fagott, fantasie, fantasiestück, fernflöte, flugel, fröhlich, gedeckt pommer, geige, geigen principal, geistlich, grossflöte, kapelle, kapellmeister music, klangfarbe, klavierstück, koppelflöte, lautenclavicymbal, lebhaft, lieblich, Männerchor, nachthorn, nachtmusik, nasat, Parzifal, quintaton, rauschquinte, rohr bordun, rohr nasat, rohr quinte, saengerbund, schalmei, scharf, schnell, schwegel, Siegfried, sifflöt, sinfonie, spillflöte, stark, stollen, takt, trinklied, tusch, zauberflöte, zwischenspiel
1551–1600:	fife 1555, tabulatur 1574, moll 1597
1651–1700:	hohlflöte 1660, krummhorn 1694
1701–50:	waltz (v.) 1712, posaune 1724
1751–1800:	pantaleon 1757, zinke 1776, death song 1778, waltz (n.) 1781
1801–50:	mordent 1806, mastersinger 1810, doodle 1816, gemshorn, glockenspiel 1825, colo; ture, septet(te) 1828, accordion 1831, basset horn 1835, Kapellmaster, physharmonica, yodel 1838, melodeon 1840, chorale, pralltriller, sextet 1841, salicional 1843, Boehm, clavier 1845, doodlesack, folk song, panharmonicon 1848, zither 1850
1851–1900:	lied, portunal, salicet, Waldflute, waldhorn 1852, flugelhorn, sextole 1854, gedackt, rohrflöte, spitzflöte 1855, Liederkranz[1] 1858, althorn, spiel[2] 1859, tremulant 1862, al-

penhorn, clarinet(t)ist, krummhorn, symphonic poem 1864, saengerfest 1865, clang tint, klang, stroh, overtone 1867, Schubertiad, upbeat 1869, song without words 1871, tone poet 1874, concertmaster, leitmotiv, querflöte, racket(t), ranket, rauschpfeife, Singspiel, Tafelmusik, ventil, Vorspiel 1876, pommer 1878, arpeggione, bebung, cassation, nachschlag 1879, clavicylinder, humoresque, kunstlied, yodeler 1880, furiant, tone color 1881, claviature, Romanze 1883, mässig, song form 1884, fagottist 1886, janizary music 1888, Liebestod, tone poem 1889, Wunderkind 1891, agogic, agogics 1893, durchkomponiert, Rhine daughter, tone painting 1897, Bach trumpet 1898, song cycle 1899

1901–50: stroh fiddle 1902, through-composed 1903, gedacktwork 1904, heckelphone 1905, waltz king 1908, zimbalon, zimbel 1910, galanterie 1911, songfest 1912, sprechstimme 1922, Schrammelquartet 1924, bandonion, expressionism, Sprechgesang 1925, heldentenor 1926, Volksoper 1928, Gebrauchsmusik 1930, trautonium 1931, Lieder singer, tone-row 1936, zugtrompete 1938, Gesamtkunstwerk, Schreierpfeife 1939, idiophone, wind cap 1940, galant (n.) 1949

1951– : galant (a.) 1953, klangfarbenmelodie 1959, Scheitholt 1961, Innigkeit 1964, Schrammelmusik 1967

Pottery

See *Architecture, Art, Pottery.*

Theater

The German loans relating to the theater total only thirteen, of which nine are dated. The oldest of these is *dramaturgy* (1801), from *Dramaturgie*. Originator of the term was the critic and dramatist Gotthold Ephraim Lessing (1729–81), who included it in the title of his book on the theory of the theater, *Die Hamburgische Dramaturgie* (1767–9). The etymon for Lessing's coinage may have been the term *Dramaturg* suggested by the German dramatist Johann Elias Schlegel (1719–49) in 1747. Not until 1859 did English borrow *dramaturge* as the designation for someone skilled in writing and revising plays, as well as in selecting and arranging a repertoire. English reborrowed the title in 1988 in the form of *dramaturg*. To differentiate between the *Dramaturg* and the administrator of the theater or opera, German introduced before 1775 the title *Intendant* (see Schulz/Basler). In the France of Richelieu, whence German took the word, an intendant was a governor of a province. English borrowed the German meaning in 1903.

Inscenation appears to have followed a similar course. The phrase *mise en scène,* in use in the French theater around the beginning of the nineteenth century, likely yielded the German form *Inszenierung*. George Bernard Shaw is then assumed to have rendered the German into English *inscenation* in 1897.

Supernumeraries or 'walk-ons' appear on many stages. Germans were calling them *Statisten* as early as the seventeenth century. Lessing refers to them, and the *OED* dates *statist* beginning with 1807.

Four loans refer to types of plays: *Festspiel* and *Kammerspiel* (undated), *passion play* (1870), and *kinderspiel* (1902). *Passion play* derives from *Passionsspiel,* which was in use in

German when the town of Oberammergau performed the play of the Passion of Christ for the first time in 1634 to give thanks for having escaped the plague. Its name and fame have continued to spread, since the play continues to be performed every ten years. Far less well known is the *Kinderspiel,* a name probably coined in the nineteenth century (see Grimm) on the analogy with *Lustspiel* 'comedy' and *Trauerspiel* 'tragedy' to describe a dramatic presentation performed by the *Kinder* 'children.'

A bit remote from the theater is *tingle-tangle,* which entered English print in 1911. Its German etymon, the echoic *Tingeltangel,* describes a type of cabaret or nightclub that emerged in Berlin after 1870.

The thirteen words in theater are:

Undated:	Festspiel, Hanswurst, Kammerspiel, kino
1801–50:	dramaturgy 1801, statist[2] 1807
1851–1900:	dramaturge 1859, passion play 1870, inscenation 1897
1901–50:	kinderspiel 1902, intendant 1903, tingle-tangle 1911
1951– :	dramaturg 1988

OTHER SEMANTIC FIELDS

Administration

The first of the twelve German terms in administration to be introduced into English was *court-marshal* (1692), from *Hofmarschall* 'administrator of a prince's household.' That loanword is now obsolete and is not to be confused with the modern English military homonym, *court-martial.* Other now-antiquated transfers took place between 1762 and 1909: *cameral* (1762), *cameralism* and *cameralist* (1909), *Wildgrave* and *Wildgravess* (1762), and *Geheimrat* (1837). These tell of bygone Central European institutions and personages. Thus we find the *cameralist,* whose pursuits were *cameral* and who advocated *cameralism,* that is, policies in seventeenth- and eighteenth-century Central Europe designed to strengthen the ruler's economic position. In recent times, *cameralist* has come to apply to an economist whose policies are strongly guided by political factors.

Equally anachronistic are the names for those who formerly ruled and/or administered a given forest region in Germany. *Wildgrave* and *Wildgravess,* from *Wildgraf* and *Wildgräfin,* are derived from German *Wild* 'game of the forest' and *Graf* or *Gräfin,* meaning 'count' or 'countess.' The outmoded, euphemistic title *Geheimrat* was actually a popular contraction of *Geheimer Rat* 'privy councillor,' who, in the sixteenth and seventeenth centuries, was a member of a council that advised an absolute ruler of a German realm.

Overall, Administration is one of several fields included in this fourth division of the Semantic Overview that exhibit few words and usually nonmodern and often uncommon ones. Thus our latest administrative item is dated 1909.

The twelve words in administration are:

Undated:	cameralistic, cameralistics, waldgrave, waldgravine
1651–1700:	court-marshal 1692

1751–1800:   cameral, Wildgrave, Wilgravess 1762

1801–50:   Geheimrat, personnel 1837

1901–50:   cameralism 1909, cameralist 1909

Apparel

Five of the eleven apparel loanwords denote characteristically German attire: two items of clothing in general, two furs or pelts, and a common handkerchief. These are *blucher* (1831), *Homburg (hat)* (1894), *lodenmantle* (1914), *lederhosen* (1936), and *dirndl* (1937). *Bluchers* are the sturdy half-boots or high shoes named for the Prussian field marshal Gebhart L. von Blücher (1742–1819). The *Homburg hat* gets its name from the town of Homburg, near Frankfurt. Meyer tells us that this soft felt hat with curled brim and creased high crown was fashioned in Homburg at the behest of the Prince of Wales, who was to become Edward VII of Great Britain, on the occasion of his visits to the spa. The name of the cloak or coat *lodenmantle* (German *Lodenmantel*), made of thick, originally Tyrolean woolen water-resistant Loden cloth, reaches back to Old High German times, as does *Lederhosen,* the knee-length leather trousers worn in Bavaria and other Alpine regions. According to Paul/Betz, that is not true of *dirndl,* shortened from *Dirndlkleid,* literally 'girl's dress.' This dress with a close-fitting bodice, short sleeves, low neck, and skirt was not copied from the attire worn by Alpine peasants until around 1930.

Two names of articles are not solely a part of a German's wardrobe, *schlafrock* (1836) and *sontag* (1862). *Schlafrock* 'dressing gown' has its antecedent in the fourteenth century (Paul/Betz). Not popularized until the first half of the nineteenth century, *Sontag* was named after the German vocalist Henriette Sontag (1806–54), who brought the cape into vogue. Two items relate only peripherally to garments: *grotzen* (undated) and *krimmer* (1834). The former refers to 'the darker center of a fur pelt'; *krimmer,* to 'a gray fur resembling astrakhan,' originally from a breed of karakul sheep raised in the Crimea (German *Krim*). Another item is *stook* (1859), probably from *Stück* 'piece,' i.e., piece of cloth, linen, etc., meaning 'handkerchief.' Synonyms for everyman's pocket accessory of this kind recorded in Paul/Betz and Kluge/Mitzka are *Taschentuch, Sacktuch, Schnupftuch* and, the oldest among them dating back to the fifteenth century, *Fazzilet* and *Fazzenetlin.* However, they do not include *Stück.*

The most recent loan is *dirndl skirt* (1957), a partial translation of *Dirndlrock.* Duden lists *Dirndlrock* along with *Dirndl, Dirndlkleid, Dirndlbluse,* and *Dirndlschürze,* i.e., the ensemble, as well as its parts. Paul/Betz notes that their popularity is only recent: ''*Dirndlkleid,* seit 1930.''

The eleven borrowings in apparel are:

Undated: grotzen

1801–50:   blucher$^/$ 1831, krimmer 1834, schlafrock 1836

1851–1900:   stook 1859, sontag 1862, Homburg (hat) 1894

1901–50:   lodenmantle 1914, lederhosen 1936, dirndl 1937

1951– :   dirndl skirt 1957

Beverages

See *Food, Beverages.*

Commerce

English sources record only seven German loans that relate to commerce. Surprisingly however, together with *raff* and *Minster* (noted under Botany and Textiles, respectively), these few words document an east-west trade as well as one that extended from south to north. *Raff* originally meant 'timber,' then 'pole' or 'slat.' It was imported to the British Isles from northern Germany in the fifteenth century. *Minster,* a kind of linen cloth made in Münster, Germany, is reported to have been exported to England in the sixteenth century.

The *OED* defines the noun *brack* (1734) as 'a method of selling or sorting goods at Baltic ports in the eighteenth century.' The verb *brack* (1858) correspondingly means 'to select or sell goods or produce at Baltic ports.' Kluge/Mitzka identifies their German etyma, *Brack* and *bracken,* as commercial expressions in use in North German trade since the fourteenth century, the noun originally meaning 'ware' and eventually 'seconds' or 'rejects,' and the verb 'to trade these wares.'

Crame ware (1667), from German *Kramwaare,* went with the German traders to the north and into Slavonic and Lithuanian territories. In OHG, *Kram* originally meant 'tent,' then 'stall,' and ultimately 'wares sold in either.' Hailing from farther south is *firm* (1744). German had borrowed *Firma* – 'the title of a firm or business' – from Italian in 1733, just as in the seventeenth century it had borrowed from French the term *Kartell* 'an international combination of business houses that agree to limit competition among its members.' English did not transfer this German item as *cartel* until 1902, but it now has enormous utility in the language. A less useful loan was *Reichsbank* (1879), Germany's state bank, established in 1876.

The newest is in reality not a loan. English, having acquired from German in 1940 the word *blitz* and its complete etymon *Blitzkrieg,* both descriptive of the lightning warfare unleashed on Poland in 1939, extended the semantic range of *blitz* to a football play and a lightning sales campaign.

The seven borrowings in commerce are:

1651–1700:	crame ware 1667
1701–50:	brack (n.) 1734, firm 1744
1851–1900:	brack (v.) 1858, Reichsbank 1879
1901–50:	cartel 1902, blitz 1940

Currency

Although the German loanwords relating to currency total only thirty-seven, the circulation in English as early as the 1600s and early 1700s of the names of coins like *silverling* (1526), *kreutzer* (1547), *heller* (1575), *groschen* (1617), *batz* (1625), and *friedrichsdor* (1741) evinces the growing trade and other interchanges between the peoples of the British Isles and the heart of Europe. *Heller,* for example, at first a bronze and later a copper penny, was originally minted in Schwäbisch Hall in the thirteenth century, hence its initial name *Haller,* i.e., from Hall. That name was eventually changed to *Heller.* It was a popular coin, widely used in commerce. The appearance of *friedrichsdor* in English in 1741, the same year it was minted by Frederick the Great, indicates the immediacy of monetary exchanges during that period.

Some of the thirteen words that denote various denominations of Swiss, Austrian, and German currency, which entered English during the years from 1751 to 1950, are equally of interest. The Swiss penny, called *batz* or *bätz,* was so named because of its hefty, lumpy appearance. Similarly jocular is the sobriquet for another Swiss coin, *rappen* 'raven.' Minted since the fourteenth century, its embossing is actually that of an eagle. It was not introduced into English until 1838. Two coins that were at one time or still are basic monetary units in Austria, the *schilling* and the *krone,* have been known to the English-speaking world since 1753 and 1895, respectively. Minted since Carolingian days, the *Schilling* was at times used as a subsidiary monetary unit in some parts of Germany, as late as 1855 in Hamburg. *Krone* continued as legal tender in Austria from 1892 until 1924.

The *taler* or *thaler* was one of many large silver coins issued by some German states from the fifteenth to the nineteenth centuries. The first record of it in the *OED* is dated 1787. (For *Joachimsthaler,* see *taler* in our dictionary.)

Mark, at first the name for a weight, has been in use in Scandinavia since the ninth century, and since the eleventh century in northern Germany. It has been the name of a coin there since the sixteenth century. The *Mark* became the legal tender of the German Reich in 1871. It was then also known as the *Reichsmark.* In 1923, following the collapse of the Reich after World War I, its name was changed to *Rentenmark,* and then was altered officially to *Reichsmark* in 1934. After World War II it was first referred to as *Deutsche Mark.* Upon the division of Germany into eastern and western parts in 1948, it accordingly became the *Ostmark* and the *Westmark.* And the legal tender of the reunited parts is *Deutsche Mark* or *Deutschmark.* The mutations of the *mark* are recorded in the *OED: mark* (1839), *reichsmark* (1874), *Rentenmark* (1923), *Deutsche Mark* (1948), and *Westmark* and *Ostmark* (1948). The latter items are the newest currency loans from German, a fact that historians might view as being indicative of economic strength and political calm, especially since the Deutsche mark is quoted daily on worldwide currency markets. We lastly cite *notgeld.* It did not surface in English until 1970, but the German term for 'supplementary currency or scrip' actually harks back to World War I.

The thirty-seven words relating to currency are:

Undated:	albertustaler, albus, angster, blaffert, frank*¹*, guldengroschen, guldentaler, klippe², neugroschen, reichspfennig, reichst(h)aler, speciestaler, zehner
1501–50:	silverling 1526, gelt 1529, dollar 1543, kreu(t)zer, pfennig 1547
1551–1600:	heller 1575
1601–50:	groschen, mariengroschen 1617, batz 1625
1701–50:	friedrichsdor 1741
1751–1800:	schilling 1753, taler 1787

1801–50:   zwanziger 1828, rappen 1838, mark¹ 1839

1851–1900:   shice (n.) 1859, reichsmark 1874, krone 1895

1901–50:   Rentenmark 1923, deutsche mark, D-mark, Westmark, Ostmark 1948, notgeld 1970

Education

The dated German borrowings that enriched the English vocabulary in education total thirty. Two of these touch on preschooling. None relates to elementary education, and a few pertain to secondary training. Most of the rest concern teaching and learning at higher levels.

The term *kindergarten,* which English borrowed phonetically in 1852, was coined by the Swiss educator Friedrich Fröbel (1782–1852) or Froebel, when he established in 1840 a school for the training of children of preschool age. Those who attend that school are now called *kindergarteners* (1881) in English, a name that is not to be confused with German *Kindergärtner* 'a teacher who teaches kindergarten.' Examples of loans descriptive of secondary schools are *gymnasium* (1691), *gymnasiast* (1828), *Abiturient* (1863), and *repetitor* (1770). German academic secondary schools, called *Gymnasien* (sing. *Gymnasium*), have been in existence since the sixteenth century. Their students still go by the name of *Gymnasiasten.* Those who pass the leaving examination, the *Abitur,* are referred to as *Abiturienten,* a German word used as early as 1652. Those who do not pass often engage a tutor, whom they call *Repetitor.*

Some vital borrowings relating to higher education are *semester, seminar, handbook, source book, famulus, doctorand, habilitate, docent, privatdocent, academic freedom,* and *Festschrift.* In use since the fifteenth century to designate a half year of study in a German gymnasium, *semester* was formally introduced into the German academic calendar as early as 1773. English sources first used it in 1827. *Seminar* was already in use in German in 1524. English began to utilize it in 1889 for a course in which a professor guides students' efforts at research. Professors wrote (and still write) and students used (and still use) *Handbücher. Handbuch* 'a survey of a specific field of study' has been known as English *handbook* since 1814. Nuremberg sources mention *Handbuch* in 1482 as the German equivalent for the Latin *manuale,* of which every student in theology was required to have a copy. The student who assisted and still assists the professor is called a *Famulus,* a word cited in German sources in 1558 and first used in English print in 1832.

The student who reaches the stage of writing a dissertation is still called *Doktorand* (in German since 1644), a word that did not appear in English until 1912. After completing the requisite studies, the *doctor,* or *Doktor* as the word is now spelled in German, must *habilitate* himself or herself. This verb was added to English in 1881. In a German university, *sich habilitieren* (1684) is to qualify for a *venia legendi,* an invitation or certification to teach there. The person so qualified is a *Dozent,* a term in use by 1755. It turns up in English 125 years later as *docent* (1880). A *privatdocent* (1881, from German *Privatdozent,* 1697) is an unsalaried docent who depends only to a small extent on students' tuition fees.

In teaching and research a German professor has had *akademische Freiheit* since 1737, when the University of Göttingen, at its founding, resolved to separate Church and Gown. The concept of *academic freedom* (1901) is equally fundamental in English. A professor who retires with distinction is honored by colleagues and students with a collection of essays called a *Festschrift,* a term used in an anniversary volume of 1883, "dem Andenken Albrecht von Haller dargebracht von den Ärzten der Schweiz am 12. Dezember 1877."[9] English added this term in 1898.

A few loans do not directly relate to education or pedagogy, such as *Wissenschaft,* naming '(a field of) learning, knowledge, science' since the seventeenth century in German and introduced into English in 1834. In 1836 followed *Gelehrte(r),* already used around 830 in *Tatian* as a translation for 'scribe.' The first English citation in the *OED* likens *Gelehrter* to 'savant.' The next borrowing was *intelligence quotient* (1916), from the *Intelligenzquotient* coined in 1912 by Louis Wilhelm Stern, German psychologist and philosopher (1871–1938). The series of tests on which the term is based was, in fact, developed by the French psychologist Alfred Binet (1857–1911). The most recent term, *technicum* (1932), was borrowed both from Russian and German. We might note that one undated term, *K* from the German abbreviation for *Kindergarten,* enjoys high English frequency in educational-level designations like *K-12.*

The thirty-four words pertaining to education are:

Undated: Grundriss, K (= Kindergarten), oberrealschule, Paideia

1651–1700:   gymnasium 1691

1751–1800:   registrature 1762, repetitor 1770, proseminary 1774

1801–50:   handbook 1814, clerisy 1818, programma 1820, semester 1827, gymnasiast 1828, famulus 1831, humanism 1832, Wissenschaft 1834, Gelehrte(r) 1836

1851–1900:   kindergarten 1852, realschule 1853, Abiturient 1863, docent 1880, habilitate (oneself), kindergartener, privatdocent 1881, seminar 1889, Festschrift 1898, predicate, sourcebook 1899

1901–50:   academic freedom 1901, practicum 1904, holiday course 1906, doctorand 1912, intelligence quotient 1916, technicum 1932

Food, Beverages

The total 215 German loanwords for food and drink can best be seen from two perspectives–topical and historical. A preference for certain types of edibles and beverages is part of a people's heritage that may not be readily transferred. But by the middle of the seventeenth century German loans such as *sauerkraut* and *speck* were well established in English, along with *marzipan, hock,* and *mum.* After 1750, British and American dictionaries began to record in ever larger numbers various names for German foods and beverages that found their way abroad. Leading the foods are sausages like *leberwurst* or *liverwurst* (1855), *frankfurter* (1877), *wienerwurst* (1889), *mettwurst* (1895), *bratwurst* (1888), *Thuringer* (1923), and *knackwurst* (1929). Following closely, besides *delicatessen* (1877), are such meat dishes as *schinken*

---

[9]Albrecht von Haller (1708–77), poet and distinguished physician, was the first professor of medicine at the University of Göttingen founded in 1737. Even earlier than Haller's memorial was the *Festschrift zum hundertjährigen Jubiläum der königl. sächs. Bergakademie zu Freiberg am 30. Juli 1866,* published in several parts in 1866–7 by C. C. Meinhold and Söhne in Dresden.

(1848), *Wiener schnitzel* (1862), *hamburger steak* (1889), *sauerbraten* (1889), *hasenpfeffer* (1892), and *klops* (1936).

British and American tastes for German baked goods appear to outweigh those for cheeses, as evinced by the number of loans like *kuchen* (1854), *pfefferkuchen* (1877), *Linzer torte* (1906), *Sacher torte* (1906), *streusel kuchen* (1910), *krapfen* (1845), *ponhas* (1869), *strudel* (1893), and *pfeffernuss* (1934). These contrast with *smearcase* (1829), *Schabziger* (1837) as later reduced to *sapsago* (1846), *Emmenthaler* (1902), *Liptauer* (1902), and *Tilsit* (1932). Other edibles, made at least partly with flour, are *pretzel* (1824), *zwieback* (1894), *nockerl* (1855), *knödel* (1827), and *spaetzli* (1933). The names of fruits include only *Gravenstein* apples (1821) and *snow pears (Schneebirnen)* (1860); of vegetables, only *kohlrabi* (1845) and *kraut* (1845).

Among the names of wines transferred into English between 1797 and 1950 are *Rudes-heimer* (1797), *Marcobrunner* (1825), *Niersteiner* (1825), *Liebfraumilch* (1833), *Steinberger* (1833), *Riesling* (1833), *Auslese* (1851), *Traminer* (1851), *Carlowitz* (1858), *Bernkasteler* (1875), *Vöslauer* (1920), *Sylvaner* (1928), and *tafelwein* (1972). The loans naming German liqueurs and beers during this period are fewer. We find nonbeers like *schnapps* (1818), *kirschwasser* (1869), *(Danziger) goldwasser* (1848), and *kümmel* (1864), as well as *schenk beer* (1850), *lager beer* (1855), *bock beer* (1856), and *Pilsner* (1877). The words for containers in which these drinks are served range from *krug* (1866) and *pokal* (1868) to *stein* (1885) and *seidel* (1908). One drinks these beverages in a *beer garden* (1863), *beer hall* (1882) and *bierstube* (1909), *Weinstube* (1899), *wine hall* (1906), *rathskeller* (1900), or *Stube* (1946). At such establishments one may use or hear terms like *prosit* (1846), *cookbook* (1809), *wine card* (1851), *Mittagessen* (1880), and *konditorei* (1935).

Historically, the first of the borrowed names for sausages, *Leberwurst*, goes back to Old High German *leparawurst* (Paul/Betz). The German satirist Johann Fischart (1546–c. 1590) employed the noun *Mettwurst* in 1575. Despite the meaning inherent in the MHG root *brät* 'to roast, broil,' as Paul/Betz points out, *Bratwurst* is a sausage that can be stored. It is not intended to be broiled or roasted. *Knackwurst*, giving off a cracking sound when bitten into, was already a favorite in the sixteenth century. There are reportedly some 3,000 types of sausages made in Germany and Austria, of which about 300 bear regional labels (see Meyer) such as *Frankfurter (Würstchen)*, *Wiener Würstchen*, or *Thüringer (Wurst)*, named after the locale in which they are or were originally made.

German sources provide a date for only one of the two legume loanwords: *kohlrabi*, 1691. The other, *Kraut*, derives from OHG *krūt*. Paul/Betz dates *sawer craut* (1400), but offers no year for *Sauerbraten*. *Wiener Schnitzel*, we are informed, was already being served in Vienna around 1850, and *Schinken* could be found on German tables as early as the eleventh century. *Klöpse* were a staple food in 1759 in East Prussia. And *Delicatesse*, the word for a culinary delicacy, was not transmitted to English until 1877, over one hundred years after German had taken the word from French around 1750–60. This raises an interesting question: Why did not French give it to English?

The oldest of the names of German and Austrian wines that crowd English wine lists is *Traminer*, which has been grown in the Southern Tirol for 1,500 years. The beginnings of the wine industry that produced the *Vöslauer* in the Austrian town of Bad Vöslau are traced to the twelfth century, as are those of the *Rüdesheimer* along the Rhine and the *Sylvaner* in Transylvania. The *Bernkasteler* grape, Meyer indicates, has been grown in the Palatinate since the fifteenth century, that of the *Riesling* along the Rhine since the sixteenth. The grape used to produce the *Auslese* is mentioned in the 1800s (see also Paul/Betz). *Tafelwein* was a widely used concept before 1972 (see Richard Perkun, *Das deutsche Wort,* Heidelberg, 1933, 3rd ed., 1953). The newest wine loanword is *ice wine* (1982).

Oldest among the *Danziger Goldwasser* liqueurs is the Danziger Lachs of 1598. The word *Schnapps* is dated 1780 in Adelung, and Paul/Betz attests *kümmel* as about 1800. The term *beer,* German *Bier* is from MHG *bier,* maybe an acculturation of Latin *bibere* 'to drink.' There is mention of *Ausschank* (see *schenk-beer*) in the fifteenth century. Famous for their brews are Bavaria and Bohemia, the latter for *Pilsner,* brewed perhaps as early as the eleventh century. *Bock beer* obtained its name around 1800 from the town of Einbeck (Bavarian *Aim-bock* or *Oambock*).

Tacitus and Caesar mention cheeses made by the Germani. By the Middle Ages the inhabitants of Central Europe had learned to produce hard, less perishable cheeses such as that eventually made in the *Emmenthal.* German *Schabziger* derives from MHG *schaben* 'to scrape, grate' and MHG *ziger* 'a type of whey cheese.'

Gravenstein, the name for the apple borrowed from the German, comes from a village in Denmark that was formerly Schleswig-Holstein, Germany. Trees bearing this apple, considered to be the best-flavored apple in North Germany and Denmark, were brought early to England and the United States. The *Pyrus nivalis* or *snow pear,* from German *Schneebirne,* comes into season after snow has fallen and has been cultivated for centuries in South Austria.

We conclude with three items not directly concerned with eating and drinking: *Pokal* from the sixteenth century; *Konditor* (1646), the etymon for *konditorei;* and *ratskeller,* the inevitable part of a *Rathaus* (as illustrated in the *Sprach-Brockhaus*), which German towns have constructed since the fourteenth century.

Overall, numbers of these food and beverage items have long been household words in English. English speakers worldwide enjoy sauerkraut, punpernickel, wieners, hamburger (steak), (apple) strudel, and cold cuts, as well as beer, seltzer, lager, and cold duck. This is a major German culinary contribution to English-speaking culture, but far outnumbered by French loanwords in this semantic area. Can this quantitative fact, plus the much-earlier infusion of French food-and-drink items into English, cast light on why French restaurants considerably outnumber German ones in America?

The 119 words relating to food are:

Undated:	aleuronat, Backstein, bierkäse, brötchen, butterbread, grieben, king's paprika, kipfel, klösse, lebkuchen, Liederkranz², mett sausage, napfkuchen, noodle (v.), Romadur, schnecken, schnitz, schwarzbrot, schweizerkäse, semmel, springerle, sulze, stippen, zieger
Before 1501:	marzipan 1494
1501–50:	boor's mustard 1548
1551–1600:	torte 1555, Welsh bean 1585
1601–50:	sauerkraut 1617, speck 1633
1651–1700:	pumpernickel 1663
1751–1800:	smouse 1775, noodle (n.) 1779, runcle 1784, sots 1799

1801–50:   kohlrabi 1807, cookbook 1809, Gravenstein 1821, pretzel 1824, knödel 1827, smearcase 1829, Schabziger 1837, quetsch[2] 1839, krapfen, kraut 1845, sapsago 1846, schinken 1848

1851–1900:   kuchen, schnitzel 1854, leberwurst, liver sausage, liverwurst, nockerl, wurst 1855, blood sausage, blutwurst 1856, snow pear 1860, Wiener schnitzel 1862, black bread 1863, wiener 1867, ponhaus, schnitz and knepp 1869, pfefferkuchen 1870, Speisesaal 1871, delicatessen[2], frankfurter 1877, Mittagessen 1880, hamburger 1884, erbswurst 1885, gugelhupf, kugelhop(f) 1886, bratwurst 1888, hamburger steak, sauerbraten, wiener-wurst 1889, hasenpfeffer, Lucullic, sand cake 1892, delicatessen[1], strudel 1893, zwieback 1894, mettwurst 1895

1901–50:   Emment(h)aler, Liptauer 1902, frank[2] 1904, paprikahuhn, schmierkase 1905, Linzer torte, Pfannekuchen, Sacher torte, stollen 1906, schlagsahne 1907, bückling, streusel 1909, streuselkuchen 1910, rollmops 1912, Dobos torte 1915, apple strudel, lachsschinken, Thuringer 1923, knackwurst, palatschinken 1929, Bismarck herring 1931, Tilsit (cheese) 1932, spaetzli 1933, Braunschweiger, pfeffernuss 1934, konditorei 1935, klops 1936, schlagobers, Stammtisch 1938, burger, -burger 1939, schalet(e) 1943, cold cuts 1945

1951– :   roesti 1952, Weisswurst 1963, Schinkenwurst 1967, schlag 1969

The ninety-six borrowings relating to beverages are:

Undated: Allasch, bocksbeutel, Danziger goldwasser, krausen (n.), krausen (v.), lauter, lauter tub, Oktoberfest, Oppenheimer, trub, weiss beer, zwetschenwasser

1501–50:   wine stone 1526, wine-bibber, winegarden, wine gardener, wine harvest, wine kernel, wine stock 1535

1551–1600:   carouse 1567

1601–50:   mosse, steifkin, wine vinegar 1617, hock 1625, mum 1640

1651–1700:   rummer 1654, hockamore 1673, Moselle 1687

1701–50:   corn brandy 1704, beer cellar 1732, seltzer (water) 1741

1751–1800:   Rudesheimer 1797

1801–50:   schnapps 1818, Johannisberger 1822, Marcobrunner, Niersteiner 1825, Liebfraumilch, Riesling, Steinberger, steinwein 1833, beer stube 1840, Rhine wine 1843, prosit 1846, goldwasser 1848, May-drink, schenk beer 1850

1851–1900:   Auslese, ohm, Traminer, wine card 1851, lager (n.), lager beer 1853, bock (beer) 1856, Carlowitz, Maitrank 1858, beer garden 1863, kümmel 1864, krug 1866, pokal 1868, kirsch(wasser) 1869, wineberg 1870, shenk-beer 1872, Bernkasteler 1875, Pilsner 1877, minne drinking 1880, beer hall 1882, stein 1885, glühwein, Weinstube 1899, rathskeller 1900

1901–50:   Saar 1905, wine hill 1906, seidel 1908, bierstube 1909, Sekt, Vöslauer 1920, Spätlese 1926, keller 1927, Sylvaner 1928, bierhaus 1930, heurige 1934, spritz 1935, quetsch(e) 1936, klatsch 1941, lager (v.), Stube 1946, spritzig 1949

1951– : Steinhäger 1959, spritzer 1961, Trockenbeerenauslese 1963, cold duck 1969, bierkeller, gewürztraminer 1970, Qualitätswein, tafelwein 1972, ice wine 1982

Furniture

In addition to the highly useful noun (1702) and verb *veneer* (1728), and the participial noun *veneering* (1706), which German took from French *fournir,* only three other German items relating to furniture have found their way into English.

Schrank (undated) 'wardrobe' has been used in Middle German and Upper German since the fifteenth century (Kluge/Mitzka). *Biedermeier* (1905), coined in 1853 to apply to uninspired poetry, came to mean simple, practical furniture around 1900 (see Paul/Betz). *Bürolandschaft* (1968) is a neologism used for a style of office equipment, where functional dividers like screens or plants replace walls.

The six loans relating to furniture are:

Undated:	schrank
1701–50:	veneer (n.) 1702, veneering 1706, veneer (v.) 1728
1901–50:	Biedermeier 1905, Bürolandschaft 1968

Games

Between 1830 and 1950 nineteen dated terms denoting or relating to various forms of games were introduced to English from German. Fourteen of these pertain to cards, three to chess, and two to other games.

Card-game terms are *pinochle* (1864) and the verb and noun *meld* (1897), employed in playing it; *poker* (1836); *rounce* (1855); *sheepshead* (1886), with *schwarz* (1880) and *schneider* (1886) as the names of activities within the game; *skat* (1864), together with *grand* (1893) and *schneider* (1886) that make up a part of the terminology of that game; and *slobberhannes* (1877), a version of the game of hearts.

In the vocabulary of most chess players are the three borrowings *zugzwang* (1904), *zwischenzug* (1941), and *patzer* (1948). The other two dated loans are *Ouija* (1891) and *salta* (1901).

The thirty-five words relating to games are:

Undated:	blucher[2], endhand, forehand, frage, hinterhand, jass, middlehand, mittelhand, passt-mir-nicht, rams, roodle, schafskopf, schmeiss, stich, tournee, wenzel
1501–50:	landsknecht 1530
1801–50:	bower 1830, poker 1836
1851–1900:	rounce 1855, pinochle, skat 1864, slobberhannes 1877, schwar(t)z 1880, schneider, sheepshead 1886, Ouija 1891, klaberjass 1892, grand 1893, meld (n.), meld (v.) 1897
1901–50:	salta 1901, zugzwang 1904, zwischenzug 1941, patzer 1948

Industry

Latin *industria* is defined as 'diligence, application.' Today we also mean by *industry* the procurement and manufacture of raw materials into products, tools, machines and apparatuses, and all such activity. Yet German has transferred only twenty-two items in industry. These include labor, as reflected in the loans *Gastarbeiter* (1970), in the original German, and by *guest worker* (1970), its translation. This is the name for a foreign worker employed in a Central European country beginning with the early 1960s. In the late 1960s a worker's ability to arrange to work any hours between 7:00 a.m. and 7:00 p.m., provided he or she is on the job from 10:00 a.m. to 3:00 p.m., came to be called *gleitende Arbeitszeit*. Shortened to *Gleitzeit*, it entered English in 1971. *Flextime*, its translation, has been in English since 1972. *Mitbestimmung*, the term for the legal right of German labor representatives to sit on management boards and help make decisions, is found in a draft for the regulation of trade prepared for the Assembly that met in Frankfurt in 1848. Its English rendition, *codetermination*, did not gain a foothold in England and the United States until 1949. In 1905 the German social economist Max Weber (1864–1919) used the word *Rationalisierung* as the name for the organization of industry along scientific lines. English adapted this term as *rationalization* in 1927.

Names of products include *schmelz* in English as of 1854. Paul/Betz traces the shortened form of German *Schmelzglas* 'a type of decorative glass' back to OHG *smelzi*. English has been using *litzendraht* since 1921 and its partial translation *litz wire* (1927) as a name for a copper wire made from individually enameled strands braided together. Paul/Betz traces German *Litze* to Latin *licium* 'rope.' The meaning 'braided twine or rope' was added in time. *Draht* derives from OHG *drāt* that originally meant 'twisted thread of flax or wool yarn.' It did not come to mean 'wire' until much later.

Over the years, English also borrowed the names for several apparatuses such as *deckle* (1810), short for *deckle edge* or *strap*. Paul/Betz attests *Deckel* in Late New High German. Grimm speaks of it as a rectangular frame fastened by two straps to the press, long in use among printers. Two others are *dynamo (electric machine)* (1875), from German *Dynamo(elektrische) Maschine*, so named by its designer Werner von Siemens (1816–92); and *diesel* (1894), a shortening of *Dieselmotor*, which bears the name of the German engineer Rudolf Diesel (1858–1913), who developed it in 1893 and perfected it in 1897.

The twenty-two words relating to industry are:

Undated:	DIN system, dynamoelectric, waldglas
1551–1600:	salt works 1565
1801–50:	deckle 1810, ricker 1820
1851–1900:	schmelz 1854, dynamo (electric machine) 1875, Welsbach 1887, kollergang 1890, staff^2 1892, diesel 1894
1901–50:	kraft (paper) 1907, litzendraht 1921, litz wire, rationalization 1927, Schmelzglas 1935, codetermination 1949
1951– :	Gastarbeiter, guest worker 1970, Gleitzeit 1971, flextime 1972

Military

The continuing upheavals on the Continent in the 1500s, 1600s, and beyond, culminating in the Peasants' War of 1524–5 and later in the Thirty Years War (1618–48), left a legacy of German items, which English borrowed as *landsknecht, reiter, dragooner,* and *sharpshot,* as well as *rittmaster* and *field marshal.* The upheavals also provided *swine's feather, howitz,* and *plunder,* the unsavory companion-word to *war.* Because politics and military affairs are often intimately related if not sometimes overlapping, it is surprising that the 159 political loans taken into English between 1751 and 1950 are about a third more numerous than the 98 military loans from German during that period. Among the earliest of these were *hunter* (1753) and *uhlan* (1753). Both came via Prussia. Jonas Hanway mentions *hunter* in his *Historical Account of the British Trade over the Caspian Sea, with a Journal of Travels from London into Persia and Back,* I, vii, xciii, 428, 1753 (1762): "Beside the hussars, the king – Frederick II – has a small body of men whom they call hunters." Toward the end of the eighteenth century Frederick II formed the first standing company of such hunters, called *Jäger* in German (see Meyer). The original German form turns up in the *OED* in 1776 as *jaeger* and in 1804 as *yager.* Though Saxony introduced *uhlans* (now spelled *Ulanen* in German) in the 1730s, it was Frederick II who described the lancers in 1742 as *hulahnen* (see Kluge/Mitzka).

Also traceable to Prussia and Frederick II is English *f(l)ugelman* (1804), from German *Flügelmann* (see Thomas Carlyle's *History of Frederick II of Prussia, called the Great,* 1858–65). Moreover, Prussia is the source for English *landsturm* (1814) and *landwehr* (1815). In 1813–14 its *Landwehr* consisted of reservists between the ages of twenty and thirty-two or thirty-nine, and its *Landsturm* was made up of all men between seventeen and fifty who were neither in the Prussian army nor in its reserves (see Meyer).

At the beginning of the nineteenth century Prussia popularized the concept of *war game* (*OED* 1828), first transmitted to English in the original German *kriegsspiel* (1811), although the *Quarterly Review* of May 1811 (p. 403) notes that "In Switzerland a game has lately been made of war (*Das Kriegsspiel*)." Furthermore, while A. B. Granville mentions in his *St. Petersburgh,* 1828, II, 75, a "war-game table, on which the present Emperor [i.e., Nicholas I], when Grand-duke, used to play," it is Friedrich Schiller who, in his trilogy *Wallenstein,* has Ferdinand II's famous general Wallenstein use the term as early as 1800.

Also somewhat misleading are the dates of first use in English as cited in the *OED* for *footfolk* (1859), *war-lord* (1856), *Iron Cross* (1871), and *pickelhaube* (1875). *Footfolk* (German *Fußvolk* 'foot soldiers,' as opposed to *Rittertum* in the more modern sense of 'mounted men') and *warlord* (German *Kriegsherr* 'commander-in-chief,' especially in the nineteenth century) likely owe their wider use in the 1800s and transfer to English to Karl von Clausewitz's *Vom Kriege,* 1832–4. Grimm cites two sources for *Kriegsherr.* One usage, dating back to 1479, means 'warlord.' The second, going back to 1846, signifies 'commander-in-chief.' Meanwhile, Frederick Wilhelm III of Prussia established the decoration *Iron Cross* (German *Eisernes Kreuz*) in 1813. It was the Prussian army that adopted the use of the *Pickelhaube* in 1842.

A loan more nearly synchronous in origin and transfer in the years that followed is *Mauser.* The Waffenfabrik Gebrüder Mauser began to manufacture this handgun in 1872 in Oberndorf am Neckar. The *OED*'s first English reference to it is 1880. Other military loans near the end of the nineteenth and the beginning of the twentieth century are *Fritz* and *Heinie.* Two years into World War I, the British began to call their German enemy *Fritz*. The *Daily Chronicle* pointed out on August 25, 1917, ''Canadians call(ed) their enemy *Heinie* not *Fritz*.'' Actually, the British had used *Fritz* deprecatingly as early as Feb. 1, 1883 (see George Meredith's *Letters,* 3 vols., edited by C. L. Cline, 1970). *Heinie* is attested as of 1904. According to Meyer, the name *Fritz* came to mean 'German soldier' in England and France at the beginning of the twentieth century and is still used pejoratively by Russians for all Germans.

Several items are of distinctly World War I origin, such as *Big Bertha* (1914) and *kamerad* (1914). The German gun with a 42 cm bore was employed for the first time on March 23, 1918, to bombard Paris. German soldiers used *kamerad* as early as 1914 as a cry of surrender. *Field gray* (1915), a translation of *feldgrau,* was the color of the uniforms these German soldiers wore during this war and in World War II. In both wars the soldiers themselves came to be known in German as *die Feldgrauen* and in English as *the field gray/grey*. In World War I they used *flame throwers* (1915), christened *Flammenwerfer* in German; monoplanes called *Tauben* (1913), ironically meaning 'doves'; and *U-boats* (1916), that is, *U-Boote* or *Unterseeboote* 'submarines.'

Additional military terms were transferred during the years between the two world wars: *Siegfried line* (1918), *Reichsbanner (Schwarz-Rot-Gold)* (1924), *Stahlhelm* (1927), and *Schutzstaffel* (1930). The *Siegfried Line,* a series of German fortifications facing the French, was completed in 1917. English first used the item in print in 1918. *Reichsbanner,* a powerful paramilitary group of left-wingers flying the imperial banner, was borrowed by English writers almost immediately after the group was founded in reaction to their opponents' organization, the *Stahlhelm,* a veterans' association founded on Dec. 25, 1918 (see Meyer). The *Schutzstaffel,* created in 1930 as a bodyguard for Hitler and other Nazi functionaries, eventually incorporated a large number of the members of the Stahlhelm into its own ranks.

World War II furnished its own group of loans like *blitzkrieg* (1939), *coventrate* (1941), *panzer* (1940), and *stuka* (1940). Germans named the sudden massive aerial and ground attack on Poland on Aug. 23, 1939 *Blitzkrieg*. Its first citation in the *OED* is dated Oct. 7, 1939. The aerial devastation of Coventry began on Oct. 2 and continued to Nov. 26, 1940, by which time the German verb *coventrieren* was born and soon tranferred to English. When Germans began to equip treaded motorized vehicles with armor, they called them *Panzerwagen, Kampfpanzer,* or *Panzer* 'armor' for short. They began to send panzers into battle in large numbers in 1940, the year the term passed into English. Similarly, Germans called their divebombers *Stuka,* which is a contraction of *Sturzkampfflugzeug* (see our dictionary entry). It was code-named *Ju87* and first produced in 1936 by the Junker Flugzeug- und Motorenwerke, located in Dessau. Its name was introduced to English in 1940. Then there were the terrifying *V-one* and *V-two* noted in 1944.

The nazified rank of major echoes in the loanwords *SS* (or perhaps more accurately *SA*) and *Sturmbannführer* (1955). *Walther* (1968), a shortening of *Walther Selbstladepistole,* is reminiscent of early post-World War I days.

The 130 words pertaining to military matters are:

Undated:	Abwehr, Bundeswehr, dusack, free corps, Klappvisier, Krieg, spitzer, wolf-pack tactics, zischägge, zwinger
1501–50:	lance-knight, landsknecht 1530

1551–1600:   reiter 1584, halt (n.) 1591

1601–50:   field marshal 1614, haiduck 1615, shield knave 1627, plunder 1632, swine's feather 1635, morgenstern, proviant, still-stand 1637, dragooner, spanner 1639, rit(t)master 1648

1651–1700:   halt (v.) 1656, morning star 1684, howitz 1687, staff' 1700

1701–50:   velt-marshal 1709, sharpshot 1725

1751–1800:   hunter, uhlan 1753, jaeger 1776

1801–50:   sharpshooter, Warasdin 1802, fugelman, yager 1804, goose-step 1806, shabrack 1808, kriegsspiel 1811, landsturm 1814, landwehr 1815, war game 1828, crown-eater 1845, carthoun 1849

1851–1900:   war-lord 1856, footfolk 1859, drillmaster 1869, Iron Cross 1871, ersatz reserve, pickelhaube 1875, Mauser (rifle) 1880, dolman, Fritz 1883, westfalite 1896

1901–50:   Heinie 1904, High Sea Fleet 1907, Taube, U-boat 1913, Big Bertha, frightfulness, kamerad 1914, devil dog, field gray, flame thrower, minenwerfer, mine thrower, Schrecklichkeit, strafe, strongpoint 1915, drumfire 1916, minnie, shock troops, storm troops, unteroffizier 1917, Kraut, Siegfried Line, Spandau, spurlos versenkt 1918, Schlieffen (plan) 1919, reichswehr, Walther (a.) 1920, Reichsbanner 1924, Steel Helmet 1925, Stahlhelm 1927, feldgrau (a.) 1929, Schutzstaffel 1930, Heimwehr 1931, Brownshirt 1932, feldgrau (n.) 1934, Luftwaffe, Wehrmacht 1935, Kommandatura 1937, flak 1938, bunker, blitzkrieg 1939, blitz, coventrate, panzer, panzer division, Sea Lion (= Operation Sea-lion), sitzkrieg, stuka 1940, ilag, moaning minnie, Oflag, stalag, wolf pack 1941, R-boat 1942, nebelwerfer, Standartenführer, Teller mine, Totenkopf, Totenkopf division, Totenkopfverband, Waffen SS 1943, kriegie, schnorkel, Schu mine, S-mine, volkssturm, V-bomb, V-one, V-two 1944, Stalag Luft 1947, Schmeisser 1950

1951–   :   Sturmbannführer 1955, Walther (n.) 1968, widow-maker 1975

Mythology

The earliest samplings of German mythology to seize the imagination of English speakers tell of spirits or monsters rather than of heroes or gods. They speak darkly of the *wassermann* (1590), the sea monster partly in the form of a man, that destroys ships. Could the sailors of the Hanseatic League have carried word of his deeds to England? The early loans include *Mephistopheles* (1590), the beguiler of humans, who describes himself in Goethe's *Faust* as ''der Geist, der stets verneint'' – the spirit who always denies. Other scary myths, no doubt from the store of the German miners' myths about the English mines in the sixteenth century (see *Mining*), speak of the *kobold* (1635), the mischievous gnome that is said to dwell in caves, and tell of the *barghest* (1732), the portentous goblin that roams the miners' realm.

After 1767 the loans in German myth begin to include elements of German or Germanic legend like *Valhalla* (1768), *Valkyrie* (1768), and *Twilight of the Gods* (1768), from German *Götterdämmerung*, which English also borrowed phonetically in 1909. Now the myths take on vast, cataclysmic overtones. Beginning with the mid-nineteenth century, Richard Wagner's musical works provide the etyma for English *tarn cap* (1856), *tarnhelm* (1877), *Venusberg* (1885), and *Swan Knight* (1911). Other items come from the spreading fame of the poets

Goethe and Heine and the novelist La Motte-Fouqué: *erlking* (1797), *Walpurgis Night* (1822), *Lorelei* (1878), and *undine* (1821).

Other mythological concepts abroad in Central Europe prior to 1941 – none has appeared in English since then – that gained a hold across the Channel and the Atlantic extend from *overbelief* (1897, from archaic German *Aberglaube,* i.e., 'superstition') to *spook* (1801) and *nixie* (1816), as well as *poltergeist* (1848) and *snallygaster* (1940), presumably an adaptation of German *schnelle Geister,* perhaps best rendered as 'fleeting spirits.'

The thirty-three words bearing on mythology are:

Undated:	Gunther, Knecht Ruprecht, Isolde, swan shift
1551–1600:	Mephistopheles, wassermann 1590
1601–50:	kobold 1635
1651–1700:	killcrop 1652
1701–50:	barghest 1732
1751–1800:	Twilight of the Gods, Valhalla, Valkyrie 1768, erlking 1797
1801–50:	spook 1801, nixie 1816, undine 1821, Walpurgis Night 1822, Kriss Kringle 1830, swan song 1831, nix*¹* 1833, poltergeist 1848
1851–1900:	tarn cap 1856, Nibelung 1861, thumbling 1867, swan maiden 1868, tarnhelm 1877, Lorelei 1878, Venusberg 1885, overbelief 1897
1901–50:	earth mother 1902, Götterdämmerung 1909, Swan Knight 1911, snallygaster 1940

Printing

Twenty German loans relate to printing. Three designate typefaces or fonts, nine describe books or parts thereof, five pertain to apparatuses for or processes of reduplication, one identifies an ink used in printing, and one names a part of a hand printing press.

The oldest among the typefaces is the *textura,* for which the earliest date given in the *OED* is 1922. The etymon *textur(a)* is the name of the script used in Gutenberg's bible printed in 1456. One fifteenth-century black-letter typeface is named *Schwabacher,* after the central Bavarian town *Schwabach,* where it was first used. English literature on printing does not use it until 1910. *Fraktur* (1886), a shortening of German *Frakturbuchstabe,* dates back to 1571 (see Kluge/Mitzka). Today it is a synonym for Gothic script.

As for books, we now refer to those printed before 1500 as *incunabula* (*OED* 1861), because printing was then in its infancy, and the Latin word for *crib* is *incunabulum.* A bookdealer from Emmerich, Westphalia, a town near the Dutch border, popularized the word in 1677 with his book *Incunabula typographica* in Germany, where it was eventually clipped to *Inkunabel.* The name for a journal or memorandum book in the sixteenth century was *Stammbuch* (see Paul/Betz), which English borrowed as *stambook* in 1662. In Modern German, *Stammbuch* is a 'family register.'

Format has been used in German since 1634 to denote shape and size of a publication (Kluge/Mitzka). The earliest use of it in English was 1840. Since 1842, the prefatory matter of a book has been called a *foreword,* as translated from *Vorwort,* from OHG *furiuurti* (Paul/

Betz). Its German use in the sense of Latin *proverbium* 'preface' originated in the sixteenth century.

The borrowings *heft, offprint,* and *separate,* denoting parts of a book, were introduced to English in 1885–6. *Heft* was a German back-formation of the sixteenth-century verb *heften* 'to fasten.' Meaning 'fascicle,' it has been a part of the German bookbinder's vocabulary since the eighteenth century (Paul/Betz). *Offprint,* a translation of *Abdruck* 'reprint,' has a more august history. This back-formation of *abdrucken* was used in 1356 to mean 'reproducing' the Golden Bull issued by Charles IV to regulate the election and coronation of an emperor of the Holy Roman Empire of the German Nation, but was restricted to printing after the advent of Gutenberg. *Separate* (1886) corresponds to Latin *separatum,* which German has used as a learned synonym for *Sonder(ab)druck.*

Christian Bernhard, Baron von Tauchnitz (1816–95), in 1841 published a collection of volumes on British and American authors for sale on the Continent. By 1856 the name *Tauchnitz* was an eponym for these books in England. Also well established was *kettle stitch* (1818), from *Kettelstich* or *Kettenstich,* used in early bookbinding to describe a knot formed in the sewing thread at the end of a book section to fasten it to the next section.

Till (1611), the name for a part of an early handpress, is from German *Tülle* 'socket,' from MHG *tülle* and OHG *tulli.* A later addition is *tusche* (1885), the name for a type of India ink used in printing. Its German etymon is an early eighteenth-century back-formation of the verb *tuschen* 'to touch up,' which was developed from *touchieren,* from French *toucher* having the same sense.

Names of apparatuses or processes include *chromatotypography* (1851), a likely adaptation of German *Chromatotypographie* 'the method of printing in chromatic colors.' *Hectograph* (1880), now German *Hektograph,* names a device for making copies by transferring a manuscript or drawing to a gelatin slab treated with glycerin and then taking impressions from the gelatin. *Algraphy* (1897), a shortening of German *Aluminographie* 'the art of printing from aluminum plates,' was invented by Johann Scholz (b. 1833). *Albertype* (1875) is a photochemical process on the lithographic principle, devised by and named in German *Alberotypie* for Joseph Albert, a German photographer (1825–86). And *Klischograph* is a modern machine for making printers' blocks, produced since 1955 by the firm of Rudolf Heil in Kiel-Dietrichsdorf.

The twenty words relating to printing are:

1601–50:	till 1611
1651–1700:	stambook 1662
1801–50:	kettle stitch 1818, format 1840, foreword 1842
1851–1900:	chromotypography 1851, Tauchnitz 1856, incunabula 1861, albertype 1875, hectograph 1880, offprint, tusche 1885, Fraktur, heft, separate 1886, algraphy 1897
1901–50:	Schwabacher 1910, textura 1922
1951– :	Klischograph 1955, vorlage 1965

Sports

"Apart from card games this [*langlauf*] is the only sporting term borrowed from German into English," stated Carr (p. 87) in 1934. In reality, even the number of dated German sports loans total twenty-five by 1933, with a total of thirty-nine dated items by 1949, and only ten items that precede 1889. Together they represent ten different sports, with bowling, diving, dressage, and swimming having only one term each: *kegler* (1932), *snorkel* (1947), *levade* (1944), and *Strandbad* (1939).

Skiing has provided the largest number of sports loans, as in *stem* (1904), *outrun* (1913), *jump turn* (1924), *langlauf* (1927), *langläufer* (1929), *geländeläufer* (1933), *Vorlage* (1936), *schuss* (a. and v., 1937), and *forerunner* (1949). Mountain climbing ranks second, with gymnastics in third place. Examples are *alpenstock* (1829), *alpenstocker* (1864), *kletterschuh* (1920), *carabiner* (1920), *abseil* (1933), and *turnverein* (1852), *turner* (1853), *turnfest* (1856), and *kip* (1909). Hunting or marksmanship and boating or Zyachting follow next, as in *sonder* (1909) or *sonderclass* (1913), *faltboat* (1926) or *foldboat* (1938), and *schuetzenfest* (1870).

British and American sportspeople climbing the Alps and the Dolomites returned with the cited terms in mountain climbing. British and American skiers abroad and later their imported instructors account for an appreciable number of the loans in skiing. By contrast, borrowings in gymnastics and marksmanship largely owe their presence in the English vocabulary to German immigrants to the United States. Early references to yachting as a sport founded by Friedrich Ludwig Jahn (1778–1852), with E. W. B. Eiselen (author of *Deutsche Turnkunst*, 1816), go back to 1856 in the United States, and to 1860 in Britain. The first English loans in yachting point to the United States as the original recipient, whereas those pertaining to boating identify England as the recipient.

All but one of the post-1950 sports loans pertain to skiing. They range from *giant slalom*, adapted in 1952, to *K-point*, which entered English in 1982. They include *fall line, mogul, vorlaufer, wedeln* (v.), and *seilbahn*. The exception among the recent acquisitions is *schooner-sail* (1952). German adapted English *schooner* as *Schoner* in the eighteenth century and then developed a hybrid compound, which was no doubt translated because of the recent increase in competitive sailing. Clearly, German sports are continuing to influence the English language.

The fifty-eight words relating to sports are:

Undated:	bergstock, dauerlauf, forward lean, kanone, passgang, quersprung, shortswing, skimaster, stock^2, turnhalle
1651–1700:	huntmaster 1691
1801–50:	alpenstock 1829, querl 1830
1851–1900:	turnverein 1852, turner 1853, turnfest 1856, alpenstocker 1864, schuetzenfest 1870, turn 1888
1901–50:	stem (n.) 1904, kip, sonder 1909, outrun, sonderclass 1913, carabiner, kletterschuh 1920, jump turn 1924, faltboat 1926, heil, langlauf 1927, langläufer 1929, geländesprung 1931, kegler 1932, abseil (n.), geländeläufer 1933, sitzmark, strength through joy 1935, Vorlage 1936, schuss (a.), schuss (v.) 1937, foldboat, kegling 1938, Strandbad 1939, blitz 1940, abseil (v.) 1941, levade 1944, schuss (n.), snorkel 1947, forerunner 1949
1951– :	giant slalom, schooner-sail 1952, wedeln (n.) 1957, fall line, mogul, vorlaufer, wedeln (v.) 1961, seilbahn 1963, K-point 1982

Technology

The semantic area subsumed under technology embraces a variety of practical activities that provide goods and services for human welfare. They furnish transportation, communication, etc., which the industrial revolution enhanced, and which recent technological advances continue to improve. Yet the English technological loans from German include only five rather obscure undated loans and thirty-two dated ones, mainly referring to devices and products.

The earliest item to denote a device is *lehr* (1598), a shortening of German *Lehrofen*. Histories of glassmaking tell us that the Romans had built early glass manufactories along the Rhine, that these spread eastward and later westward, and that they included long ovens in which glassware was annealed on a continuous belt, i.e., *Lehröfen*. A 1662 citation in the *OED* informs us that Agricola, who died in 1555, referred to such a *leer*.

In 1721 English acquired the word *ratsch* as a name for a rachet or ratchet wheel. Kluge/Mitzka derives the term ultimately from MGH *ratzen* 'to rattle.' Then in the nineteenth century other names of devices were transferred, such as the *melanoscope* (1876) devised in 1871 by Eugen Cornelius Joseph von Lommel (1837–99), a professor of chemistry at the University of Erlangen, as a means of exhibiting certain optical properties of chlorophyll. The *tachyscope* (1889), from German *Tachyskop,* was an early animated picture machine invented in 1885 by Ottomar Anschütz (Anschuetz) (1846–1907), German photographer and pioneer in cinematography. The *phase meter* (1898), coined as *Phasenmeter,* was invented by the Russian-born German engineer Michail Dolivo-Dobrowelsky (1862–1919). He created the instrument in 1894 to measure the phase difference between two oscillations having the same frequency.

The twentieth century witnessed the adding of three more names of German devices. In 1901 the physicist Ernst Walter Ruhmer (1878–?) built a scientific marvel for the day, a *Photographophon,* to record and produce a series of sounds of the human voice. His word was transferred into English as *photographophone* that same year. Though *stereoplanigraph* was not borrowed until 1906, this device to plot topographic maps was built by the inventor Carl Pulfrich (1858–1927) and was already being manufactured by the Carl Zeiss firm in 1896. Associated with the name of the mechanical engineer Felix Wankel (1902–88) is the loanword *Wankel engine,* used in English since 1961 but invented in 1953.

The names of products or materials that were borrowed include *Zyklon* (1926), a hydrogen cyanide used as a fungicide and as a poison gas in World War II for mass extermination. It was patented in 1926, in Germany and abroad, by the Deutsche Gesellschaft für Schädlingsbekämpfung. A better-known example is *Plexiglas* (1935), a substance used as a plastic that was patented by the firm of Röhm and Haas of Darmstadt in 1935. Its name and use became known immediately all over the world, competing favorably in usage with other English technological household words like *automat* and the *glitch* that has swept the computer and space worlds.

The thirty-seven words associated with technology are:

Undated:	four-hundred-day clock, kominuter, quetsch*, schrother, shrend
1551–1600:	lehr 1598
1651–1700:	way wiser 1651
1701–50:	ratsch 1721, post 1727

1801–50:	aspirator 1804
1851–1900:	waterdust 1873, melanoscope 1876, slickens[2] 1882, afterburning 1887, tachyscope 1889, diesel (n.), Seger cone 1894, Brix scale 1897, phase meter 1898
1901–50:	photographophone 1901, automat 1903, presspahn 1904, stereoplanigraph 1906, litz-endraht, shot effect 1921, Zyklon, Schering bridge 1926, litz wire 1927, Spackle 1928, Plexiglas 1935, Magnetophone 1946, afterburner 1947
1951– :	Schmidt number 1955, reprography 1956, Wankel engine 1961, glitch 1962, user-friendly 1977

Textiles

Though Italy was the principal center of the textile industry in Europe as early as the twelfth and thirteenth centuries, in the Tyrol a thick, coarse, woolen cloth was already being made in Old High German times. It was called *lodo,* the current German name for which is *Loden.* However, English records do not allude to *loden* until 1911 (see Kluge/Mitzka).

The name of a strong, durable, triple cotton weave, called *drilling,* surfaced in English by 1640. Its origin, too, can be traced to the Old High German period. Kluge/Mitzka derives its German etymon *Drillich* from OHG *drilich* and ultimately from Latin *trilix* 'triple weave.' Reported to have been exported to England as early as the sixteenth century is a kind of linen cloth that English writers began to refer to in 1612. Its name is *Minster,* taken from *Münster,* a town in the Upper Alsace that was granted imperial status under Frederick II in 1354.

Rhine, a shortening of German *Rheinhanf* (from *Reinhanf* 'pure hemp'), was the best hemp brought to England from Prussia and Riga in the sixteenth and seventeenth centuries. Citations in the *OED* use *rhine* beginning with 1641. From Bohemia, then under the rule of the house of Hapsburg, Great Britain also imported in the seventeenth century a particular quality of woolen material. English writers converted this *Kronrasch* to *crown-rash* beginning in 1710.

English next added *ravenduck* (1753) to its linguistic imports. The German history of this canvas called *Rabentuch* eludes us and the editorial staff of the *Duden,* as does that of *Eiswolle,* a fine glossy wool yarn that lends itself especially to making shawls. English writers began to use *eis wool* in 1852. By 1885 they added the loan *schappe,* a fabric or yarn originally made of spun silk and now also of a type of rayon. *Schappe* is a dialectal Swiss clipping of German *Schappeseide.*

The most recent German textile loan is *raschel* (1940), a clipping of German *Raschelmaschine* as named in the nineteenth century after the French actress Elisa Rachel Félix (1821–58). She popularized the tricot spun on such a machine by wearing dresses made of it. Actually, *raschel* is a phonetic rendition of the French pronunciation of German *Rachel.*

The ten words relating to textiles are:

Undated:	Bielefeld
1601–50:	Minster 1612, drilling 1640, rhine 1641
1701–50:	crown-rash 1710
1751–1800:	ravenduck 1753

1851–1900:   eis wool 1882, schappe 1885

1901–50:   loden 1911, raschel 1940

Theology

A close reading of the quotations in the *OED* that document the now-obsolete entries *snorkle* and *greathede* (both 1340), as well as *ground* (1400), suggests that the concepts of all three originated in German mysticism and are among the earliest of all German borrowings in English. Such terminology appeared in Mechtild von Magdeburg's *Das fliessende Licht der Gottheit,* as written down by the Dominican monk Heinrich von Halle around 1290. It was particularly augmented in the works and sermons of Meister Johannes Eckhart (c.1260–1327), the famous Dominican theologian and exponent of German mysticism.

With reference to Christ's kirtle, the *OED* derives English *snorkle* '? a wrinkle, crease' from *Schnörkel* 'flourish.'[10] In Henry Bradley's edition of Franz Heinrich Stratmann's *Middle-English Dictionary* (Oxford, 1971), it is defined as 'pleat,' but is perhaps best rendered as 'curlique.' Paul/Betz identifies it as an heraldic term meaning 'geschmacklose Verzierung' or 'tasteless adornment.' Kluge/Mitzka's deriving Danish *snørkl* from German *Schnörkel* further suggests this German item to be the source of English *snorkle.*

In the *OED,* English *greathede* is given as a cognate of Dutch *grootheid* and German *Groszheit.* Grimm's dictionary notes that *Groszheit* 'greatness, magnitude, magnificence' appears to be essentially from Low German *groetheit* but that it is frequently found in late MHG and early New High German glosses as a term of 'die oberdeutsche Mystik.'

The borrowing *ground* 'Godhead, divine essence' derives from German *Grund,* as used by the fourteenth-century mystics Johannes Eckhart and John Tauler in that great century of European mysticism.

The doctrinal changes occasioned during the sixteenth and seventeenth centuries by the Reformation left more lexical traces of German in English than did the rise and waning of mysticism. By 1521 English traveling scholars and merchants had already brought back from the Continent the doctrines of the Reformation to the University of Cambridge. Soon thereafter orders were issued by the ensconced English clergy for the discovery of their heretical books. Still, terms like *mercy seat, shewbread* or *showbread,* and *weakling* have come down to us in William Tyndale's rendition of the New Testament in 1525, closely patterned after Luther's German translations *Gnadenstuhl, Schaubrot,* and *Weichling.* Miles Coverdale (1488–1568), continuator of Tyndale, added *firstling* and *sinflood* (recorded in the *OED* under *flood*). Luther spoke of them as *Erstling* and *Sintflut* (altered by folk etymology to *Sündflut*). Other coinages or uses associated with Luther or his adherents and successors that entered English between 1523 and 1698 are *Romanist, God's acre, theologaster, stift,* and *shaman* (ordered chronologically). They derive from German *Romanist, Gottesacker, Theologaster, Stift,* and *Schamane.*

Theology does not loom large in the scheme of loans from 1751 to 1950. It accounts for only thirty-six dated loans out of over 4,000 German total items transferred during these years.

---

[10]Drawing on the analogy in verse 16 of Psalm 147 of David, ''[God,] qui dat nivem sicut lanam,'' the English hermit Richard Rolle of Hampole envisions Christ's kirtle made of divine wool, without ''spot and snorkil,'' i.e., blemish and disfigurement, so that He can, as snow yields (divine) wool, turn humans from sin to love. Rolle was well acquainted with the religious treatises of his time.

Although two hark back to the early days of the Reformation, they were not attested in English until 1845. Both *Stolgebühr(en)* (English *stole fee*) and *Sakramenter* (*sacramentarian*) relate to the sacraments. Luther had inveighed against both concepts in his polemical writings of the 1520s. In addition, the name for the institution that Luther spurned, *Kloster,* itself a derivative from sixth-century Latin, is attested in English in 1844. The name of the legal representative of the kloster, then called *Vogt* in German (from Latin *advocatus* 'advocate'), was recorded in English as *vogt* by 1762.[11]

Two theological isms transmitted to English in the two centuries after 1750 are of interest: *terminism* (1860) and *monergism* (1893). The first, envisioning a time limit during which an individual has the opportunity to seek a return to divine grace, was conceived by the Leipzig theologian Adam Rechenberg (1642–1721). The second, concerning regeneration solely through the Holy Spirit, is a Lutheran doctrine.

The application of modern historical and literary criticism to the Bible as, for example, at the University of Tübingen School of Theology, accounts for borrowings like *Q* (1901), *form criticism* (1923), *Interimsethik* (1910), interim ethics (1947), *subsidiaritity* (1936), *scandal of particularity* (1930), and *Sitz im Leben* (1934).[12] Martin Buber's *I-thou* (1937) reflects the twentieth-century human search after a personalized relationship to a guiding or divine principle, motivated by an overriding dedication to love.

We also find names like *Amish* (a., 1844) and *Schwenkfelder* (1882), which bear witness to a splintering of the faithful in the wake of the Reformation. Others, like *theonomy* (1890) and *heortology* (1900), connote a proposed subordination of the state to divine rule, as well as the study of the origins and development of religious feasts. Such feasts are memorialized in items like *Christmas tree* (1789), *blue Monday* (1801), and *Fasching* (1911). Our two 1950s loans are the adjective *heilsgeschichtlich* and *religionless Christianity*.[13]

The seventy loans in theology are:

Undated:	Amanist, Augsburg, fastnacht, Gott mit uns, heiligenschein, inner mission, Ronsdorfer, Taufer, Zwickau prophet
Before 1501:	greathede, snorkle 1340, ground 1400
1501–50:	Romanist 1523, weakling 1526, mercy seat, shewbread 1530, field devil, firstling 1535, Care Sunday 1536, sinflood 1550
1551–1600:	Mennonite 1565, Swermer 1585
1601–50:	God's acre 1617, theologaster 1621, Rosicrucian 1624, stift 1637, Taborite 1646
1651–1700:	substantialist 1657, Pietism, Pietist 1697, shaman 1698
1701–50:	Herrnhuter 1748
1751–1800:	vogt 1762, Christmas tree 1789, Illuminati 1797
1801–50:	blue Monday 1801, patristic 1828, Christ Child 1842, Amish (a.), kloster 1844, sacramentarian, stole fee 1845, catechetics 1849

[11]*Vogt* has a wide semantic range in German. Thus Friedrich Schiller's *vogt,* in the drama *William Tell,* signifies 'governor.'

[12]The Tübingen School of Theology rose to eminence in the late eighteenth century. It retains that prominence today in both its Evangelical and Catholic branches of study.

[13]Religious modification in accordance with modern research brings to mind Cicero's definition of *religio* as a derivative of *religere,* meaning to observe or examine carefully.

1851–1900:	terminism 1860, soteriology 1864, world power 1866, passion play 1870, soteriological 1879, Schwenkfelder, soterology 1882, Amish (n.) 1884, theonomy 1890, monergism 1893, cultic 1898, heortology 1900
1901–50:	Q (= Quelle) 1901, putz 1902, binitarian (n.) 1908, Interimsethik 1910, Fasching 1911, form criticism, Formgeschichte 1923, scandal of particularity 1930, Modernismus, Sitz im Leben 1934, subsidiarity 1936, I-thou 1937, Heilsgeschichte 1938
1951– :	heilsgeschichtlich 1952, religionless Christianity 1953

Trades (Callings)

Except for loanwords like *barmaster* (1662) 'a local judge among English miners' and possibly *goosegirl* (1828), a translation of *Gänsemädchen* 'a girl gooseherd,' German has given English few items that relate to vocation, calling, or trade. Among these are the generic term *Fach* (1842), denoting field or type of work, and *professionist* 'specialist' (1804), now signifying a qualified mechanic or tradesman. The Briticism *bushel(l)er* (1847), a tailor who mends clothes and does alterations, appears to derive from German *Bossler* or *bosseln* 'to repair or alter.' Since 1927 some English speakers have come to know *Putzfrau* 'char or cleaning lady.'

Lehrjahre (1865) 'years of apprenticeship' and the partly travel term *wanderyear* (1880) 'a journeyman's requisite stint of broadening travel' are most likely English popularizations from the titles of Goethe's developmental novels *Wilhelm Meisters Lehrjahre* (1795–6) and *Wilhelm Meisters Wanderjahre* (1821–9).

English adaptations of the names of three tools or devices suggest fields or trades in which German workers no doubt excelled at the time. These are *spanner* (1639), a device for spanning the spring in a wheel-lock firearm; *riffler* (1797), a tool to carve grooves into an object, used by sculptors and woodcarvers; and *bott-hammer* (1858) or *bushhammer* (1885), a mason's hammer with serrated face for dressing concrete or stone.

The thirteen words pertaining to trades are:

1601–50:	spanner 1639
1651–1700:	barmaster 1662
1751–1800:	riffler 1797
1801–50:	professionist 1804, goosegirl 1828, Fach 1842, bushel(l)er 1847
1851–1900:	bott-hammer 1858, Lehrjahre 1865, bushel 1877, wanderyear 1880, bushhammer 1885
1901–50:	Putzfrau 1927

Transportation

The early means of transportation in Europe were beasts of burden, two-wheeled barrows, and boats. Later, four-wheeled wagons, coaches, chaises, and ships were added. The coming of the industrial age witnessed the introduction of trains and automobiles and roadways to carry them.

The two earliest vehicular loans in English were *landau* (1743) and *barouche* (1801). Paul/

Betz tells us that Joseph I of Austria, who became emperor in 1705, rode in a *Landauer* in 1702. The four-wheeled carriage with a folding top was first made in Landau, Bavaria, hence its German name. Reports of a *barouche,* from German *Barutsche,* reached England in 1801. By then it had become a shallow, four-wheeled carriage, although its etymon, ultimately derived from Latin, designated a two-wheeled vehicle. Its vogue in Germany may date as early as 1721.

In 1817 Baron Karl von Drais invented a cumbersome, two-wheeled velocipede that was named for him, *Draisine.* Its popularity, though temporary, carried its name across the Channel as *draisine* by 1818. Another Central European inventor, Siegfried Marcus, is said to have built, in 1875, the first gasoline-driven motorcar in Vienna, purportedly also equipped with a *Taxonometer* to record the distance the car traversed. Shortened to *taxameter,* this name surfaced in England in 1890 (see Meyer and the 1890 German Patent Specifications 56310 of the Taxameter-Fabrik Westendorp & Pieper of Hamburg, Germany).

By the twentieth century, freeways or turnpikes began to be built throughout Europe. The first section of the Reichs*autobahn,* Bonn–Cologne, was opened to traffic in 1932. Frankfurt–Darmstadt followed in 1935. English adopted the name *autobahn* in 1937. That year marked the founding of a plant for the manufacture of small cars intended for popular use, the Volkswagenwerk in Wolfsburg. The abbreviation of the name *Volkswagen* to *VW* became a household word in Europe and abroad by mid-twentieth century. In English (1958), *VW* also soon superseded its full form.

The first German subway, named *Untergrundbahn,* was built in Berlin in 1902 and quickly rechristened *U-Bahn.* Thirty-six years passed before anyone recorded that shortening in English (*OED U-bahn* 1938). Another quarter of a century passed before English gained *S-bahn* in 1962. It is a shortening of *Stadtschnellbahn,* the German name for a high-speed railway or train line initiated in Berlin in 1871. The loans relating to air transportation, *Zeppelin* (*OED* 1900) and *Parsefal* (*OED* 1908), are discussed under *Aeronautics.*

The nine words in transportation are:

1701–50:	landau 1743
1751–1800:	barouche 1801, draisine 1818
1851–1900:	taxameter 1890
1901–50:	Rheingold 1935, autobahn 1937, U-bahn 1938
1951– :	VW 1958, S-bahn 1962

Travel

The coming of the industrial age in the eighteenth and nineteenth centuries enlarged the means and opportunities for travel. English men and women and, later, Americans journeying abroad, perhaps at first to take the waters and later to study at German universities, began to bring back the words for inns in which they stayed. These included *Wirtshaus* in 1829, *gasthof* in 1832, *gasthaus* in 1834, and eventually *Wirtschaft* as a shortening for *Gastwirtschaft* (1903). In 1929 the younger traveler came to know of German *youth hostels.* The loan *wanderlust* (*OED* 1902) attests to an urge to travel.

Of these accommodations, *Gasthaus* was known as *gasthus* in OHG times. The earliest date given for the use of *Gasthof* is 1420 (see Paul/Betz). *Wirtshaus,* in the sense of a *Gasthaus auf dem Lande,* i.e., a country inn, very likely is a sixteenth-century coinage (see *Wirth* below). *Wirtschaft,* a shortening of *Gastwirtschaft,* definitely has its semantic base in the sixteenth century (see Paul/Betz). The first German *youth hostel,* from the name *Jugendherberge* given by its founder, was built in 1909 (see Meyer).

Kluge/Mitzka informs us that *Wirt* or *Wirth,* originally meaning 'host,' came to denote 'owner of a *Wirtshaus*' as well. English added *wirt(h)* in 1858. To find their way to the accommodations ranging from *gasthaus* to *youth hostel,* English-speaking travelers could in time rely on the help of a *Baedeker* (1863), a travel guide named for Karl Baedeker (1801–59), who published the first such guide in 1827.

Our remaining two borrowings, *wander-book* (1844) and *wanderyear* (1880), bring to mind the age of the guilds. Upon completing their training, journeymen would, *Wanderbuch* in hand, enter upon a *Wanderjahr* to broaden their knowledge and outlook on the world. Goethe poetically popularized that prospect, although with some degree of renunciation, in his *Wilhelm Meisters Wanderjahre* (1821–9).

The ten words relating to travel are:

1801–50:   Wirtshaus 1829, gasthof 1832, gasthaus 1834, wander-book 1844

1851–1900:   Wirt(h) 1858, Baedeker 1863, wanderyear 1880

1901–50:   wanderlust 1902, Wirtschaft 1903, youth hostel 1929

Miscellany

We must also take account of 221 dated or undated German loans appearing in English between 1340 and 1990, the chronological limits of this book. Some of these items are too general or otherwise difficult to classify, while others apply to multiple aspects of daily life. Even when semantic classification is possible, the items are fewer than the arbitrary number of five that we have used to justify a separate semantic classification for items in the dictionary section. Yet numerous items that are placed in this ''Miscellany'' section are sufficiently interesting to warrant this final sketch.

Examples of the first group of these are *one-sided* (1813), *epoch-making* (1863), and *chain-smoker* (1890), as translated from *einseitig, epochemachend,* and *Kettenraucher.* Other loans, adopted phonetically, include *ersatz* (1875), *halt* (1796), and *Verstandsmensch* (1879).

The second largest group mirroring everyday activities includes pejoratives, denigrations, oaths and interjections, salutations, terms of endearment, and other appellations. For lack of a better repository, it also encompasses samples of student speech. Some common German pejorations transmitted to English are *swindler* (1775), *dummkopf* (1809), *bum* (1864), *hoodlum* (1871), *mucker* (1891), and *wisenheimer* (1904). More sophisticated is the label *Philister* or *Philistine* (1802), which Goethe is reported to have attached to the unenlightened and uncultured masses.

The denigrations *schelm* (1584), *shark* (1599), *shirk* (1639) or *trull* (1519), *trollop* (1615), and *slattern* (1639) as well as *bantling* (1593) and *killcrop* (1652) might be explained by the presence of large numbers of German miners in the British Isles in the 1500s and 1600s.

The introduction of *Heimweh* into English in 1721, followed by its translation *homesickness* in 1756, should probably be attributed to Matthew Prior, who used it in his *Essay upon Dialogue* (1721).

Characteristic of the oaths, including the generic term *Schimpfwort* (1949), are *sapperment* (1815), *phooey* (1866), *Schweinerei* (1906), and *pfuiteufel* (1922), as well as *mein Gott* (1838) and *lieber Gott* (1898).

Sample interjections are *ouch* (1837), *hoch* (1867), and *gesundheit* (1914).

Sample salutations include *guten Morgen, guten Tag, guten Abend, gute Nacht* (undated), and *auf Wiedersehen* (1885). In addition to the forms of address *Herr* and *fraülein,* which English acquired in 1653 and 1689, respectively, it added *frau* in 1813 and *mein Herr* in 1922. (Note the use of the lower case in the English spelling of *fraülein* and *frau.*)

Centuries after English borrowed the endearing *kinchin Kindchen* '(dear) child' in 1561, it began to use the pet names *Liebling* 'darling' in 1868, *Liebchen* 'sweetheart' in 1876, *mutti* 'mom' in 1906, and *Schatz* 'treasure' in 1907. English *hausfrau* 'lady of the house' or 'house-keeper' surfaced in 1798 and *housemother* (from *Hausmutter*) in 1834.

Primarily associated with German students' informal speech are *fidibus* (1829), *bursch* (1830), *Stammtisch* (1938), *Kneipe* (1854), *commers* (1855), *corpsbruder* (1904), and *mensur* (1911), which English-speaking students will eschew for their own English equivalents of *paper spill, frosh, regular table, tavern, beer party, fraternity brother,* and *duel.*

Illustrative of the variety of other adaptations included in this sketch are *meiler* (1893) 'a charcoal kiln,' *dingus* (1876) 'thingamabob, a contraption or thing whose name momentarily escapes one's memory,' and *denkmal* (1877) 'a memorial or monument.' There are also some very recent loans: *kletten prinzip, rollade,* and *wallpecker* (1988–90).

The 221 words grouped under Miscellany are:

Undated:	Achtung, aphro-, bitte, bringsel, burschenschaft, danke, danke schön, desemer, diatoric, folk, futurological, geoscience, glucke, guten Abend, gute Nacht, guten Morgen, guten Tag, -il, mauger, rutsch, schläger, sorge, strubbly, stummel, u^2, usw, von, weissnichtwo, Wie geht's, wunderbar, zum Beispiel
Before 1501:	snorkle 1340
1501–50:	trull 1519, splitter (n.) 1546, verst 1555
1551–1600:	kinchin 1561, buss 1570, masterpiece 1579, schelm 1584, fantast 1588, crants, stembook 1592, bantling 1593, halper 1596, shark 1599
1601–50:	stroll 1603, statelich 1610, trollop 1615, grobian 1621, schelmisch 1634, shirk, slattern 1639
1651–1700:	fob, Herr 1653, slenker, 1658, centner 1683, fräulein 1689
1701–50:	houndsfoot 1710, hurrah 1716, coal blower, Heimweh 1721
1751–1800:	homesickness 1756, swarmer 1765, swindler 1774, nix (adv.) 1776, swindle (v.) 1782, nix^2 (n.) 1789, halt 1796, hausfrau 1798, hell (v.) 1799
1801–50:	Philister 1802, Prater 1803, dummkopf 1809, motiviert 1812, frau, one-sided 1813, sapperment 1815, storm-clock 1819, berg, dumb 1823, goosegirl 1826, alp^1, markworthy 1827, fidibus, standpoint 1829, bursch, Doppelgänger, loafer 1830, swindle (n.) 1833, housemother 1834, alp^2 1836, brool, ouch, storm-bell, world-famous 1837, mein

Gott 1838, meiler 1839, world-old 1840, schwärmerei 1845, Sehnsucht 1847, fresh, grauly, wirble (n.,v.), katzenjammer, sitz bath 1849

1851–1900: wonderworld 1851, gemütlich 1852, Kneipe, swatchel 1854, bummer[1], commers, saal 1855, Ewigkeit, foozle 1857, unberufen 1858, Berliner 1859, interimistic, spieler 1859, splitter (v.) 1860, bum (v.), epoch-making 1863, bum (n.), ur- 1864, fest, wirwarr 1865, Motivierung, phooey, rucksack 1866, hoch, Versöhnung 1867, Liebling 1868, spiel[1] (v.) 1870, Geist, hoodlum 1871, guest-friend 1873, ersatz (a.), überhaupt 1875, dingus, Liebchen 1876, denkmal, unheimlich 1877, Verstandsmensch 1879, flimmer (v.), schwärmer 1884, auf Wiedersehen, mit, und so weiter, Wein Weib und Gesang 1885, backfisch, kaffeeklatsch 1888, chain smoker, lebenslust, toot 1890, bummel (v.), mucker, overnight, ersatz (n.), Gemütlichkeit 1892, servus 1893, schärmerisch 1894, kaput 1895, spiel (n.) 1896, hexerei, lieber Gott 1898, bummel (n.), kinder, kirche, küche 1899

1901–50: gallows humo(u)r 1901, wanderlust 1902, Lokal 1903, wisenheimer, corpsbruder 1904, pathbreaker 1905, mutti, Schweinerei 1906, quatsch, Schatz, Wehmut 1907, Stimmung 1909, Auguste 1910, mensur, sympathisch 1911, galgenhumor, verboten 1912, schwärm (v.) 1913, pathbreaking, gesundheit 1914, echt 1916, breakthrough 1918, Kulturträger 1920, mein Herr, nitwit, pfuiteufel 1922, nicht wahr, wander-bird 1924, schwärm (n.) 1926, Putzfrau, schwärmerin 1927, Wandervogel 1928, Sitzfleisch 1930, Stammtisch, nachtlokal 1939, schwein(e)hund 1941, Kulturhound, futurology 1946, nacht und nebel 1947, Schimpfwort 1949

1951– : Kulturgut 1952, Methodenstreit 1958, schlamperei 1961, meister 1965, bummer[2] 1967, sandburg 1970, popo 1972, welcome money 1977, kletten prinzip 1988, rollade, Rottweiler (a.) 1989, wallpecker 1990

PART II
LINGUISTIC OVERVIEW

LINGUISTIC OVERVIEW

THE SIZE OF OUR LEXICAL CORPUS MAKES IT QUITE DAUNTING TO COMPOSE AN OVER-view of the linguistic ramifications beyond what is treated in the Introduction and An Historical Overview by Semantic Fields. Collectively, the 5,380 items in our Dictionary proper illustrate the phonological (chiefly graphemic), morphological, syntactic, and semantic ways by which a major modern language – in this case German – enriches and expands the vocabulary of another major modern language, one which probably enjoys a greater worldwide distribution and use than any previous language has had.

The great bulk of High German etyma evidently moved into English as spontaneous trans-fers, rather than as deliberate insertions, like the inkhorn terms borrowed into English from the classical languages, especially during the Renaissance. Few if any of our German items replaced existing English words; instead, they simply expanded the English lexicon. Nor did they come in during a military or political conquest, as when a conquering people overrun an area whose population speaks a language different from that of the conquerors. Thus, during the medieval period, the Great Migrations introduced large numbers of Germanic words into the widespread areas of the Roman Empire. This was particularly true for transfers into the French areas, even giving the Frankish word *France;* and the ensuing Norman conquest of England brought huge numbers of Norman-French words into the English lexicon, ultimately at the expense of the majority of the directly descended West Germanic items in English. As our corpus by definition excludes Old High German and Middle High German items, though many of our German direct transfers into English did derive from Middle High German, it is only of historical interest to illustrate with examples like the addition of Norman-French *baron.* The dimensions and effects of such partly coercive transfers can be seen in Bertoni's study (1914) of 1,187 Germanic borrowings into Italian following the "invasioni teutoniche nei paesi latini." Comparably, more than 300 more modern German items moved into standard Hungarian usage, not to mention thousands of dialectal, more peripheral parts of the Hungarian vocabulary. German has had similar lexical influence on other, principally European vocab-ularies.

An immediate question for our corpus concerns the form in which a borrowing is trans-mitted. Generally, one expects that two languages in contact may transfer items in roughly their phonetic form (rather than in translation or its equivalent) when they have descended from the same parent, and our statistics demonstrate this hypothesis. Thus when exposed to Language B, speakers of A will take some foreign features of B into their vocabulary, naturally encountering less difficulty in borrowing these features when a language group in common

(West Germanic) was the parent of both A and B, as is true for English and German. When there is long, intimate contact through millions of bilingual speakers as in the American Midwest and Pennsylvania, one might further expect intensified cultural pressures. A general example is English *press conference,* French *conférence de presse,* and German *Pressekonferenz* (as opposed to *Gipfelkonferenz*), all of which come from the original Latin etyma.

The greater the typological differences between two languages, when the forms and patterns of one language do not appear in the other, the greater the interference in the linguistic transferring. This does not mean that two greatly differing languages – like Japanese and English, or Cantonese and Portuguese – cannot mutually transfer many lexical items; for history has shown that large numbers of items were borrowed within these two pairs. A language borrows what it needs, regardless of typological differences, but borrows more easily when there is less interference, which often means that it ultimately gains the best form out of all the possible transfers that might have been made. In the transfer of forms from German into English, there is comparatively little interference.

Let us now consider the phonological, grammatical, and semantic aspects of our High German loanwords, concluding with generalizations as to overall utility and with sample lists of two kinds of German items that we have arbitrarily excluded from our corpus – intermediately transferred items and dialectal ones.

PHONOLOGY AND GRAPHEMICS

Because we have not analyzed (or represented in the Dictionary section of this book) the pronunciation of our items, our data relate more to graphemics than to speech. Even so, there is little evidence that English has borrowed German sounds or distributions. Of course bilingual speakers are likely to use their German glottal stop and /x/ in English, regardless of the anglicization and length of time that the given borrowing has experienced in English. Apparently the German sounds and distributions are at least partly converted to English equivalents at once by the monolinguals who begin to use the German loanword, so that *Achtung* immediately gains the /-k-/ replacement for the German /-x-/, and *Tsarina* is spelled and pronounced in the English pattern of *czarina* as /z-/. Except for bilinguals and music appreciators, English pronunciation of the name of the famous German composer *Bach* is likely to be with /-k/. However, a language seldom borrows a new phoneme. English, for example, even after centuries still has not phonemically accepted the French /ž-/ initially, despite the many words in which English speakers now use /ž/ medially and terminally, both in naturalized French loanwords and in native English items. Even so, many speakers use /-ǰ/ rather than /-ž/ in words like *garage.* Even when the German sound is an existing variant of an English sound, anglicization may occur. Thus there has often been voicing as an English /z/ of the terminal German *-s* (pronounced as /-s/), and Americans have routinely converted the trilled and the uvular German /r/ to their flapped variety. The German *th* (not a fricative) is pronounced as the German /t/. As German vowels and diphthongs are not nearly so unphonetically spelled as are the English ones, these are often respelled, especially the diphthongs and umlauted vowels. Though the German *j* is not respelled, sometimes it is pronounced as the German and English /y/ as in *jass,* but sometimes is erroneously changed to spelling pronunciation (*jarosite*). Our Introduction has treated the problem of English pronunciation of German *v* and *w.*

As for graphemics, we will repeat what was said in the Introduction. That is, *z* has usually become *c,* as in respelling *Zedriret* to *cedriret* and retaining this fricative as /s/, and similarly in changing *Chemorezeptor* to *chemoreceptor.* German *k* has often become *c,* as in changing *Klang* to *clang.* This alteration has sometimes been unnecessary since about 1900, when the German *c* often became *k,* so that German *Keten* was easily retained as English *ketene.* This example illustrates another small change to fit the English pattern, when the common German noun ending of *-ie* becomes *-y.* We will delay describing the other spelling changes until we discuss adaptation.

For those who are statistically interested in the initial letters of our 5,380 main-entry loanwords, which are naturally spelled in their English form, we present the following tabulation:

A	332	G	230	L	221	Q	23	V	96
B	245	H	292	M	313	R	218	W	170
C	387	I	144	N	145	S	682	X	22
D	158	J	29	O	136	T	245	Y	8
E	177	K	186	P	600	U	70	Z	63
F	188								

We will not tabulate the initial semivowels and vowels as compared with the initial consonants, or compare the number of initial stops vs. fricatives, etc.; but it may be of interest to note that 858 items (16%) are spelled with one of the five traditional vowels initially.

In view of the spelling differences just noted, including some inconsistencies caused by the many changes in German spelling at the beginning of the twentieth century, the number of English variants seems relatively small. There are few problems of transliteration, as in the case of Japanese or Arabic, where, predictably, the non-Roman orthography has led to a large percentage of English variant main-forms and particularly of secondary variants. Let us first consider the 305 main entries (5.6%) that have two spellings. One trivial difference is punctuation. German nouns and words used as nouns are capitalized, and most of these capitals have been converted to lower case in English. In less-anglicized items the capital is retained as the single main entry *(Aberglaube),* and some entries have a capitalized second form *(ach-laut/Ach-laut).* The umlaut is occasionally retained in variant main entries *(gluhwein/glüh-wein),* sometimes resulting in a variant vowel spelling because of conscious translation *(hohlflöte/hohlflute).* As English-language publishers commonly avoid diacritics, this general omission of German diacritics is more a reflection of publishers' practice rather than of historical graphemic alteration. The British hyphenation may also produce a second version *(Good(-)King(-)Henry),* as does British spelling like *bushel(l)er, Pang(a)ea, papill(o)edema,* and *gallows humo(u)r.* The German spelling may cause a variation, as in *eosin(e), extrovert(ed)/extravert(ed), Führer prinzip/principle,* and the already mentioned *c/k (ecphore/ek-phore).* The largest number of main-entry variants occurs in the entries *Lip(p)i(z)zaner Emment(h)al(er)/emment(h)al(er).*

Overall, there are few significant differences between the two spellings of a main entry. Infrequently the article is retained, as translated in *(the) Day* or preserved in *(Die) Brücke.* A German item may be shortened, as in *Drang (nach Osten),* or only partially translated, as in *grass tetany/staggers* and *Horst Wessel (lied/song).* When the German etyma themselves present a variant, this choice may be retained in English, as in *Liptauer (cheese).* The anglicized

German possessive form is infrequently retained, as in *Planck('s) radiation law*. Addition of an English suffix may provide two forms, as when the German adjective *delomorph* becomes *delomorphous/delomorphic*.

Some main entries with at least two spellings also have secondary variants. Overall, 1,015 main entries (18.9%) have at least one secondary variant. As previously stated, we have not cluttered our entries by including superseded variants except in special cases to indicate that there was a considerable number in the given item's history in English, and for such cases the reader can turn to the *OED*'s comprehensive recording. Our most unstandardized main entry is *ponhaus/ponhaws/ponhoss*, for which we have listed seven viable secondary variants – *pawnhaus, panhas, pannhaas, pan(n)haus, ponhass,* and *ponhos*. Though these ten forms constitute an exceptional number for a rather old, comparatively well-known synonym for *scrapple*, they pale beside the multiple forms for Arabic etyma such as the twenty-eight for *mosque*. The patterns in the secondary variants are like those described for the main entries, as in the four versions of *commers (commerz, commerce, kommerz, kommers)*. When there are multiple secondary variants, these are usually sufficiently similar to the main entry that one would have little difficulty in locating the main entry in a dictionary, as in the variants *accordeon* and *accordian* for *accordion*. But there are a few exceptions, like two for *aurochs (aurox, urochs)*. Seldom are there short forms, as in the *D-mark* and *DM* for *Deutsche mark*. Perhaps predictably, when we have recorded at least one secondary variant and when the German form is preserved among the total variants, the German form is likely to be the secondary variant, as in the two secondary forms for *intersexuality (intersexualism, Intersexualität)*.

GRAMMAR

In shifting our attention to grammar, we raise the important question of the kinds of items that are transferred into a borrowing language. Has English, for example, taken proportionately more compounds from German than it has from another Indo-European language like French? Has it taken more derivative forms from Spanish? In borrowing from an exotic language like Mandarin Chinese, has English usually added an English suffix so as sufficiently to anglicize the form from the outset, by comparison with transfers from German? Is English today taking many back-formations or shortened forms like abbreviations and acronyms, as in the case of some recent German transfers? Our scope permits us to generalize only that English has successfully borrowed German items of any form and is continuing to do so. The great majority of these loanwords come from compounds or derivatives. Few blends have been transferred, as in the recent *gorbasm (Gorbachev + Orgasm)*. Likewise, few items have originally come from English, as in *shelf ice* (where German *Schelf* is from English *shelf* as compounded with *Eis*) and *boxer* 'dog' (which came from English and then was borrowed back into English). There are few echoic sources *(quatsch)*.

Despite the rapidly increasing frequency of English abbreviations and acronyms, our dictionary evidence seldom justifies giving a main entry to the shortened form, even when we know that the short form has widespread usage that may even supersede that of the full form. Thus our entry is *intelligence quotient*, for *IQ* is not an *English* shortening of the same German etyma that gave the full form to English. Rather, *IQ* is an *English* abbreviation of the English *intelligence quotient* and so becomes a secondary, productive item rather than an actual borrowing. In this sense, the full form might mislead one in terms of usage, though we have included *IQ* as a cross-reference. The later abbreviating or symbolizing of full forms is particularly true for numerous borrowings in physics and chemistry. In a few cases English does abbreviate or symbolize the German full form at roughly the same time that it is borrowing the full form, so that both forms come competitively into English as borrowings. As the two linguistic processes are different, each form requires its own main entry, with a cross-reference included in one entry, as in *h* and *Planck's constant, Hz* and *Hertz*, and *SA* and *Sturmabteilung*. Sometimes English borrows only the German abbreviation, as when *N.P.D.* was transferred but not the original *Nationaldemokratische Partei*. Other examples are *Q, s, S.D.S., S.P.D.,* and even *VW*, where our dictionary sources do not include the full name of this famous car and thus compel us to cite the full name only as a cross-reference to *VW*.

In turning to parts of speech, we begin with the fact that English seldom shifts the part of speech when borrowing the German etymon. Thus a noun is transferred as a noun, an adjective as an adjective, etc. This is hardly surprising, as there would be considerable syntactic wrenching for a German noun to be pressed into service initially as an English verb; if other parts of speech are needed later for the particular phonemic sequence, then functional shift normally effects this vocabulary addition. Two notable exceptions are the transferring of the verbs *sensibilieren* and *staffieren* as the English nouns *sensibilisin* and *staff*. Let us now tabulate the parts of speech of our 5,452 entries (note that these outnumber the main entries, as some main entries serve for two forms like a noun and an adjective):

noun	4,797	(88.0%)	bound forms	39	(0.7%)
adjective	503	(9.2%)	preposition	2	
verb	60	(1.1%)	conjunction	1	
interjection	21	(0.4%)	unmarked*	20	(0.4%)
adverb	9	(0.2%)			

*phrases, sentences, etc.

The usual projection for German and French proportions is four nouns to two verbs and one adjective, but few relatively comprehensive statistics are available for comparison. Haugen's statistics for American Norwegian (1969: 406–7) mainly differ from ours in verb and adjective proportions, with 75.5% nouns, 18.4% verbs, and 3.4% adjectives. Rao's statistics for English borrowings chiefly from Hindi and Urdu (1954: 51–4) are extremely close to ours: Cannon's 1987 statistics for 1,029 recent borrowings are of interest here: 89% nouns, 8% adjectives, 1.2% verbs, 0.3% interjections, and others. His yet-unpublished findings for recent Spanish loanwords in English reveal 86.6% nouns, 12.7% adjectives, and 0.7% verbs. The most applicable may be his percentages for Chinese, Japanese, and Malay loanwords unrestricted by time (1988, 1981, 1992):

	Noun	*Adj.*	*Verb*	*Adv.*	*Others*
German	88%	9.2%	1.1%	0.2%	1.5%
Chinese	83	14.5	1.9	0.1	0.5
Japanese	89.5	10			0.5
Malay	95.4	4.4		0.2	

Thus, some languages mainly transfer nouns, which presumably offer the least resistance and the greatest utility. Our German nouns include only 29 that are transferred in plural form (.6%), a not unsurprising finding in view of the modern trend for English nouns to be made into count nouns at will, as in *two milks/popcorns*. Even when an item is a uniquely mass noun, as for *Führer* to mean the Nazi leader, it can be made into a common noun and pluralized if need be. (We have not tabulated the number of German mass nouns transferred as count nouns or at least made so during their naturalization, or the German count nouns – probably few if any – transferred as mass nouns.) Almost all the nouns take the English analogical plural *-(e)s* (or *-ies* when the base form has *-y*). Of the 29 transferred plurals, 15 are translations and thus contain usual plurals like *-s (foundations)*, *-i (Illuminati*, where the German *-en* becomes the Latin *-i* plural), and *-ø (footfolk)*. Except for *schnitz and knepp,* the other plurals retain their German form (*Aufklärer, augen, klösse*). Structurally, our nouns exemplify every kind of formation, but come mainly from German compounds and suffixations and/or prefixations, with numbers of items formed from two or even three bound forms (*metaphase*, which illustrates a major new kind of modern word-formation, especially for technical words, that Modern German, English, and other Western languages utilize).

Our 503 adjectives provide few surprises derivationally, as 344 contain a common English adjectival suffix, and few others are structurally unusual for English. Cannon's 1987 statistics for new items (including borrowings, but mainly nonborrowings) may be of interest here, as they tabulate the suffixes found in recent English adjectives. There follow the statistics for our German adjectival borrowings, with the 1987 number for the same suffix given in parenthesis: 180 *-ic* (43), 33 *-(i/y)al* (19), 21 *-(i)ous* (13), 19 *-oid* (6), 11 *-ical* (11), 10 *-(i/e)an* (56), 9 *-ed* (20), 7 *-y* (33), and 6 each of *-ish* (3), *-ive* (7), and *-lich.* So our adjectives borrowed from German broadly exemplify these patterns, with *-(i/e)an* and *-y* being the most different proportionately. The suffix *-able* has only 5 occurrences (vs. 21), with only one each of the native English suffixes *-ful, -less* (12), *-ly* (3) and *-some.* Thus our corpus also exemplifies the further nonuse of these once high-frequency Germanic suffixes, which were generally replaced in English by classical ones. The 6 *-lich* words and 5 items with *-isch* are our only adjectives to retain their German suffix. Unlike the noun borrowings, which are roughly balanced as between compounds and derivatives, there are somewhat more derivatives among our adjectives, so that the adjectives are generally a bit shorter than the nouns.

Our 60 verbs are among the shortest of the borrowings, with 23 items of one syllable (38.3%, as in *blitz*), 24 of two syllables (40%, *plunder*), 9 of three *(bushhammer)*, and 4 of four syllables *(mediatize).* As compared with the 1987 corpus (where 49 of the 52 new verbs containing suffixes have *-ize*), only 6 of our verbs (10%) have *-ize (laterize)*, and 4 have *-ate (activate).* The 1987 corpus has only 2 verbs with *-ate*, as well as *limpen*, which is ultimately related to the Middle High German verb *limpfen*, extinct in Modern German. Thus our German transferred verbs are rather different derivationally from new English verbs, as well as being among the most structurally different from other parts of speech in our corpus, particularly because many are formed by the clipping of their German suffix. Only 3 items (5%) preserve this suffix (*krausen, schuhplatteln*, and *wedeln*, which has the clipped variant of *wedel*).

Perhaps predictably, the 21 interjections are among the least graphemically altered of items in our corpus. Five are compounds (*auf Wiedersehen, guten Tag, Sieg Heil, mein/lieber Gott*), 4 are monosyllabic (*halt, heil, hoch, ouch*), and there are some derivatives (*gesundheit*). Five of our 9 adverbs *(carouse, geistlich, mässig, nix, schnell, stark, statelich, überhaupt, übermenschlich)* retain their German affixes. None has *-ly*, which characterizes one-seventh of the new adverbs in the 1987 corpus. There are 2 prepositions *(mit, von)* and a conjunction *(u,* which is the abbreviation of *und* 'and').

Though our bound forms are statistically small, many of these 34 combining forms and 5 affixes have been and are continuing to be quite productive in English. Here our desk-dictionary criterion can be occasionally misleading, as only 15 of the bound forms appear in enough desk dictionaries (along with other criteria that will be discussed later) to justify their being given the highest degree of naturalization. When we consider the many common words in English that contain *amino-, -burger, cyan(o)-, -cyto, keto-, morph(o)-, -ol, -path,* and *–plasm* (much less the more technical items), we begin to comprehend their real utility in English.

Twenty of our items are grammatically unlabeled, though a few might be considered conjunctive nouns, as in *Wein, Weib, und Gesang* and *nacht und nebel.* There are phrases like *mein Herr, über alles,* and *zum Beispiel,* formulas like *danke (schön)* and *und so weiter* (its German abbreviation *usw* is also borrowed), and telescoped sentences like *ich dien, los von Rom,* and *Gott mit uns.* The only translations are *as if, will to art,* and *will to power.* These 20 items are among the most grammatically interesting in our corpus, as they must be plugged into precise slots in English structures, paralleling the way that a bilingual casually interpolates German items when speaking English to another bilingual.

WORD-FORMATION PROCESSES

What happened to these 5,452 grammatical items during their transfer? In what proportions are the German forms adapted or translated, and what word-formation processes are involved? Most of the noun adaptation, when it occurs at all, is straightforward. When we were able to see the English passage in which the given noun is first known to have appeared, the noun virtually never has case and gender designations. Because of the generally uninflected English pattern, the German article is almost always replaced by the appropriate English one, the noun is almost always capitalized, and any umlaut or other diacritic is preserved. This punctuation is usually eventually lost, the maximum preservation being the retaining of the capitalization in a variant (non-main entry) form. Four common German noun patterns are usually eventually anglicized, as in these examples: *Aktivismus* to *activism, Laparoskopie* to *laparoscopy, Orthogeosynklinale* to *orthogeosyncline,* and *Chondriomer* to *chondriomere* (the latter particularly for chemical names). In one instance an *-ismus* form is anglicized (*botulism*), but then a later compound arises as *botulismus toxin.* Note also *expressionismus* preserved as a variant of *expressionism.* Possessives are almost always anglicized *(Olbers-Paradoxen* to *Olbers' paradox).* Sometimes there is shortening to fit an existing English pattern, as when English *uroporphyrin* entails a clipping of the initial German *Urin* plus the adding of a linking *-o-* vowel. Such loss is not uncommon, as when *Urorhodin* provides English *urrhodin.*

Anglicization of verbs is sometimes less straightforward, often utilizing sufficient graphemic and phonemic change as to lead one to characterize the transfer as translation rather than as adaptation. In theory, all that has to be done is to drop the German *-(e)n* infinitive suffix, so as to transfer *meld, plunder,* and *turn,* for example. But the goodly number of examples like the changing of *reprivatisieren* to *reprivatize* would complicate the devising of word-formation rules so as automatically to adapt the verb to an English form.

Adaptation of some adjectives poses considerable difficulty for English, with all case and gender inflections immediately dropped. When the adjective contains a suffix, the process is usually rather regular, as when *wendisch* becomes *Wendish,* and *triassisch* is altered to fit the *-ic* pattern in *Triassic* and is capitalized because it is a name. Such changes are so slight and even automatic that we do not designate them as adaptation. However, as *-isch* is also the equivalent of English *-ical,* sometimes either this German suffix is replaced sequentially by both morphemes in a single operation, or else it first becomes the *-ic* form and later gains the *-al* suffix. In the case of *topochemisch,* the lack of a **chemic* form has motivated the single-step change to *topochemical.* Thus, though the adjectival *-isch* is usually replaced by *-ic,* it infrequently becomes *-ical (phenological), -ous (protandrous),* or *-ory (osmoregulatory).* On the rare occasions when *-isch* is replaced by a quite different suffix like *-in (trophochromatisch* to *trophochromatin),* the addition of the noun suffix *-in* is part of the grammatical change of the erstwhile adjective to an English noun, in a phenomenon resembling back-formation. There are also a few low-frequency forms, as in the change of the adjective *secundär* to *secondary.*

As many German adjectives contain no suffix, such forms usually gain an English adjectival suffix like *-ic* (as added to *allothigen*) or *-ous* (to *allochthon*). The addition must be phonologically compatible, but is often not so mechanical as to be rule-governed, inasmuch as *allothigenous* (which is now a variant) would seem to be as compatible as the main-entry form *allothogenic.* Overall, the anglicization or adaptation of any part of speech eventuates in an English spelling-pattern, as in changing the interjections *autsch* to *ouch,* or even *pfui* (which remains a variant) to *phooey.* Such changes shed light on phonotactics in both languages, as well as on English word-formation.

Thus we have seen three general alterations of the German etyma: (1) no change or such slight change of the graphemic form that there is anglicization rather than adaptation (*echt* unchanged, and *Barkhausen-Effekt* to *Barkhausen effect*); (2) adaptation, in which the graphemic form is not substantively altered *(Muskelspindel* to *muscle spindle);* and (3) translation, which we can categorize into five types. Unfortunately, we could discover no guiding principle for a substantive matter: Why is one German word adapted, whereas another is translated? Obviously, a rather close graphemic (and even phonemic) similarity to an English form usually dictates adaptation. Beyond that, it is difficult to generalize. There is no discernible reason for translating a German etymon when it already generally fits an English pattern (and yet this source is translated rather than adapted), or for adapting a German source for which there is no English analogue (and yet *nachschlag* is not immediately translated into something like *afterbeat,* which would fit the common English pattern of *after* + Noun). Our corpus contains few old instances where a German source that might lend itself as easily to adaptation as to translation has come into English in both forms, with usage eventually determining the dominant form. Rather, an item comes into English essentially as a phonemic or a translated form and is never replaced by its putative competitor once the original, perhaps arbitrary choice is made. There have been double forms in recent years, where both the phonetic form *(Gastarbeiter)* and a translation presumably primarily for nonbilinguals *(guest worker)* enter into English at about the same time, in a situation prompting us to tabulate two items for our corpus, even though they are synonyms. An extreme case is *Übermensch, beyond-man, overman,* and *superman.* We will analyze this phenomenon shortly.

The term *loanblend* has been suggested for items like our *brant-fox,* where the initial *Brand* morpheme in the German compound has been altered graphemically, but *Fuchs* has been translated. As we use the term *blend* in a technical sense in this book, we prefer to analyze items like *brant-fox* as a partial translation, the first of our translation types. A reverse example is *liverwurst,* where initial German *Leber* is translated, but *wurst* is unchanged. All the 57 partial translations in our corpus (1%) exemplify this half-and-half transfer, except for the medial translation of the colloquial German *un* in *schnitz and knepp.* No pattern appears in these, beyond the fact that 44 have a terminal (i.e., headword) translation, as in *stambook,* and only 12 have an initial one *(apple strudel). Isochar* might be posed as a 58th example, as German *Isopsepher* undergoes a translation of terminal *Psepher* to *character,* which is then clipped.

The second type contains 737 (13.7%) full translations, which are often called *loan translations.* The only frequent terminal element is *acid,* of which there are 54 occurrences *(allophanic acid).* Otherwise, there is a wide variety of English elements, usually nouns rather than particles (as in *breakthrough*) or suffixes *(breaking, combinative).* The initial elements are even more varied, the most frequent being the 11 items with each of *wine* or *world (winegarden, world history)* and the 8 with *folk (folk song).* Only 113 items are derivative forms, but we might note that dozens of the items which we have classified as compounds contain an affix that makes them partly derivative *(double assurance).* A few full translations also involve a shortening or abbreviation, as when *K-point* is transferred from *kritischer Punkt.* Others are *mercapturic acid (< Bromphenyl-mercaptursäure)* and *suppression (< Verdrängung* + a long phrase).

Moaning minnie (< Minenwerfer) has lost the *werfer* but gained the *moaning* to suggest the sound of the shell. This seeming expansion does not particularly violate our exclusionary criterion and does offer a sample of the many items that might have been added to our corpus, particularly if we permitted English composites constructed from German proper nouns as expanded by English nouns and/or suffixes. We have added only a few such items as a tiny third type of translation, which express the German semantic implication that is not specifically expressed in the German etymon. For example, our *Rudel* means 'pack, as of wolves,' and the English translation becomes *wolf pack* to designate such attackers of Allied convoys during World War II. Other examples of such limited, permitted expansion are *massa bowl, plunderbund, Q scale,* and *rocketsonde (< Sonde,* as patterned on German *Radiosonde).*

To these types we can add a handful of translations into fairly technical, naturalized elements from Latin and/or Greek. Dictionaries sometimes obscure this process by omitting the etymology of such items. Two examples are *protozoa* (where the *ur-* of German *Urthiere* is translated into *proto-,* and the *Thiere* into *zoa*) and *psarolite (< Starstein).*

The fifth, final type includes about a dozen items where all elements undergo a translation that is not quite literal or is even erroneous. Thus the *Big* in *Big Bertha* does not convey the original German meaning of *dick* 'thick, clumsy,' as compounded with *Bertha,* the name of the wife of the onetime owner of the Krupp Works. One can check our Dictionary section for these seven loose translations – *glutton, lampbrush, master race, pursuit-flight, schenk beer, V-bomb,* and *waterdust.* The mistranslations, which we specify as such, include *censor* (vs. *repression), goose-step, storm-clock,* and *woodchat.* As only about 815 (15%) of our main entries contain at least some translation, we have answered an earlier question: Our corpus chiefly consists of phonetic borrowings rather than translations.

Before turning to some aspects of semantics that we have not previously discussed, we might look for a moment at shortenings in general, since this process is often important in word formation. There are only 56 examples (1%) of significant shortening, and many of these can be explained as clippings of the sort that characterizes many English items. Most are back-clippings, as in *blitz* (which lost *krieg*), *hamburger (steak)*, and *Backstein (Käse)*. A rare back-formed borrowing developed when the adjective *plutonisch* was clipped to form the noun *pluton*. There are a few abbreviations of German full forms (*K < Kindergarten*) and the acronym *LSD* from its long German full form. A common kind of modern shortening is illustrated by English *Chicom* (< *Chinese Communist*); and in our corpus only *Oflag* (< *Offizierslager*) follows this pattern, which exhibits an interesting process in borrowing inasmuch as *Offizierslager* was apparently never in English, thereby hopelessly obscuring the kind of otherwise fairly transparent source and meaning. Some examples of the few front-clippings are *(ham)burger* and *(ice)berg*. Perhaps the most complicated shortening reduces the sentence *Gott strafe England* to a medial transfer of only the verb *strafe*. Overall, though some of these insights into word formation are interesting, shortening is of comparatively little importance in our corpus.

SEMANTICS

Now let us consider the semantic matters of names, trademarks, and labels. We have said that our corpus is rich in names, perhaps predictably so because the German contribution to English-speaking culture was chiefly made by specific people in specific places that often gave their names to the particular discovery or thing. These onomastic creations did not come about because of the given scientist's egotism or often not because of someone's geographical pride, as the name for the given mineral, say, may not have been coined until after its discoverer was dead. At least 473 items contain the names of real or imaginary beings, another 337 of places, and 19 more of peoples or ethnic groups, as well as 36 trademarks. These total 15.1% of our corpus. Most of the beings named refer to real persons; and specialists in the given field will recognize the Vater named in *ampulla of Vater*, the Trautwein named in *trautonium*, and the Bilharz named in *bilharzia*. Though most of these persons are German, numerous items memorialize other ethnic backgrounds, as in *Pasteur reaction* and Galvani in *psycho-galvanic*. Sometimes the German name contains no suffix or other element, providing English with numbers of eponyms like *Baedeker, Fahrenheit, gauss, Hertz, Mauser*, and *Messer-schmitt*. Eponyms of imaginary beings are similarly transferred, as in the German mythological *Brunhild, Gunther, Lorelei, Parsifal, Siegfried, Swan Knight, Valkyrie*, and *Rumpelstiltskin*. German provides the Persian name of *Scheherazade* to English. Classical names are embedded in items like *narcissism* and *titanaugite;* religious names, in *Pan-Satanism, Semitic*, etc. There are two onomastic interjections–*lieber/mein Gott*.

As can be observed in these items, the originating name is usually transparent. Exceptions arise when the name is buried medially (*Nicot* in *isonicotinic acid*, and *Brooke* in *pseudo-brookite*), when it is shortened (*Adonis* in *adonitol*), and when it was considerably altered when borrowed by German (Latin *Caesar* as adapted to *Kaiser*). This situation also obtains for the items utilizing place-names, as illustrated in the Danube tributary *Leitha* in *cisleithan* and in the Austrian *Pinzgau* in *affenpinscher* and *pinscher*. In general, the adjectives and nouns built from place-names are as straightforward as are the person-based ones, usually being derivatives (*andesine*) or compounds (*Congo red*). In this group we find a few *-er* forms like *Berliner* and *wiener* (< *Wien* 'Vienna'). There are about a dozen eponyms like *landau, Meissen, Neanderthal, seltzer, Spandau,* and *Valhalla.* The only onomastic verb, *coventrate,* gains its unpleasant meaning of 'pulverize' from the name of the much-bombed city of Coventry.

Several of the ethnic or religious names are well known *(Pole, Protestant, Slovene, Yugoslav)* and have been borrowed into many of the world's languages. Some designate linguistically important peoples such as the *Sorb, Tocharish* 'Tocharian,' and *Wend.* There are a dozen or so miscellaneous names of associations, genera, and the like *(burschenschaft, Sonderbund).*

Trademarks or proprietary names constitute somewhat more of our corpus (0.7%) than they do of Cannon's 1987 corpus of borrowings (0.4%), but still are a tiny percentage. (It might be noted that dictionaries eschew trademarks unless these names have moved beyond the technical and legal literature into other areas of usage, so that the seeming paucity of German trademarks does not mean that Germans are not as busily creating new products and methods as other advanced peoples are.) Because products are carefully named so as to attract purchasers (see Cannon 1987: 248–9), the structure of trademark names is of little linguistic interest. *Heroin* and *Ouija* have probably suffered the greatest pejoration among our trademarks (few items in our corpus have undergone pejoration or amelioration). Several others are also internationally known, as in *automat, Bakelite, Buna, Plexiglas, snorkel,* and *Vaseline.*

Labels are important in any corpus, as they indicate a limitation on the given item. Ninety-four of our items (1.8%) merit at least one label; and at this point we should reiterate that we did not have the resources and scope to check each of our items or even systematically to verify all labels on relevant items in the various dictionaries, and have had to rely on the judgments of the experienced lexicographers who composed those dictionaries. Sometimes this judgment varies from dictionary to dictionary. The 60 temporal labels (40 archaic and 20 obsolete) constitute 1.1% of our corpus. Most of these items were designated in the original edition of the *OED* as being used only historically as of that date, and that judgment has often been verified by our affixing an archaic or even obsolete label on the basis of modern dictionaries' labels. But other such temporal or usage designations were passed on into the second edition of the *OED* by repeating the double tram-lines or the qualifying word *rare,* which we have quietly corrected on the basis of adequate modern evidence for the given item.

The 24 social labels (0.4%, as compared with the exactly equal 0.4% of Cannon's 1987 corpus of recent borrowings) consist of 12 items marked as colloquial *(bummer, dumb),* 11 as slang *(glitch, kaput),* and the interjection *phooey* as informal. We might note that the 1987 corpus was collected from some of the sources that produced our German corpus (the slang *patzer* is in both corpora), and all of Cannon's socially marked borrowings except the Yiddish translation *instance* are labeled as slang. Four of our slang items also have a geographical label – 3 as U.S. *(mucker, popo, schnitz and knepp)* and the British *kinchin.* As for the 16 geographical labels, 7 of the 12 British items are so marked because of spelling, with 5 *sulphur* items *(sulphane), stylise,* and *value judgement.* The others are *cookery book* (vs. U.S. *cook book), doodle, kibble, kinchin,* and *note row.* The U.S. items are the 3 previously mentioned ones and *sonder.*

Before we leave semantics, including semantic transfers like *weak* and *strong* from Grimm's special senses of *schwach* and *stark,* and turn directly to the overall utility of our items, we might consider their international quality. Are they essentially unique transfers into English, or do they represent common activities or things that are potentially worldwide and so may be international words appearing in many languages? If the latter is true, then one will have little worry about contextual misunderstanding of the given item, as there is a kind of basic international meaning that varies little from language to language. Of course many of our items demonstrate that a borrowing often develops additional meanings from the originally transferred sense, resulting from semantic change during its sometimes long process of naturalization. But a German can still fairly confidently move from the German *Aprikose* to the Czech *aprikoze* or English *apricot* without particular worry about the basic meaning (see Deroy 1980: 335, 143–4). Although this fruit originated in China, Arabic gave *al-barqūq* to the world. The Romance languages kept the Arabic article, resulting in Portuguese *albricoque,* Spanish *albaricoque,* French *abricot,* etc. There are Dutch *abrikoos,* Russian *apricos,* etc. Our German corpus contains only a few dozen truly international words like *apricot,* as in chemical terms like *cobalt* and *nickel,* minerals like *blende,* psychological terms like *psychoanalysis,* and biological ones like *protozoa.* Yet despite this seeming semantic limitation, the bulk of our corpus have long since lost their German context, which is a necessary condition if a loanword is to become really productive in another language. Thus internationally transferred words like Malay *orangutan,* Arabic *imam,* Japanese *karate,* and Chinese *chow mein* have retained their Asian context and are relatively unproductive in providing compounds and derivatives, despite their long high frequency in many languages. As we turn now to the degree of naturalization of our German items, we will discover that their general loss of native context promises a higher productivity in English than if they had been international words bound to a German environment, even though the majority have not yet reached the maximum degree of our Stage 4.

DEGREE OF NATURALIZATION

Obviously a word is likely to be of greater overall utility in a language if it has been accepted into general writing and speech and is used without restriction temporally, socially, and geographically. Let us begin with a word that is in Stage 1, which one might expect to move to higher stages over the years or else never be adopted by many speakers and thus die, being useful only in historical contexts. A word could hardly be permanently in Stage 1, a condition that the technical and some other limited words in our Appendix seem to contradict. We reserve Stage 1 for an unadapted item that is often newly adopted and almost always requires glossing and punctuation either in quotation marks or italics. It may be noticeably foreign-looking, is used by restricted groups of people, and may be transitory, conditions that some of the words in the Appendix fulfill. But as others do not even merit a *1,* in contrast to a few colloquial oral items that merit a *4,* we will not rank these restricted words composing the Appendix.

By contrast, all the items in the corpus recorded in our Dictionary, which were collected from general dictionaries, merit at least a *2.* Of course, lexicographers do make mistakes, sometimes admitting a word to their collections on rather inadequate evidence of usage but then finding that people unaccountably do not continue to use the item. Or there might be adequate contemporary evidence for including the item in their dictionary, and the word is never accepted later by English speakers and writers. Thus *Webster's Second* was the only one of our sources to admit *Erzherzog* and *Erzherzogin* 'Archduke' and 'Archduchess,' respectively. The two entries provide no citations; but the words preserved the German *-e* and *-nen* plural inflections, and no other dictionaries recorded them, not even *Webster's Third*. Nor do the entries include any evidence of productivity. We were confident that no modern desk dictionary would include them either, a conclusion that we verified. As *Webster's Second* was a major lexicographic accomplishment, we included the words in our dictionary and gave them a *2,* anticipating that the usages found by those editors are still available and being read today, if only in an historical sense. Had our scale been applied in 1934, a *2* might still have been given, and we feel that these words still merit a *2* today. Comparably, a Stage 2 item might appear only in the 1933 *Supplement* of the *OED,* omitted both from Burchfield's volumes and the second edition of the *OED.*

Stage 2 designates partial adaptation of items enjoying a fairly wide range of usage, in contrast to the unadapted or unspecified condition represented by Stage 1. Other Stage 2 items in our corpus, for which there is citational evidence, usually require no glossing or special punctuation, but yet have enjoyed little or no usage (general or restricted) in modern decades. They have evidently advanced from Stage 1 on the way toward potential acceptance in general English, though they may well be frozen at that stage for many years or even become static and eventually archaic, being chiefly useful in an historical sense. Few items in our corpus seem to have avoided this otherwise necessary sequence and to have burst abruptly into English and other languages in Stage 4 or at least in Stage 3, as did Arabic *intifada* and Russian *perestroika,* the latter primarily first from the title of Gorbachev's 1987 book. When Europeans experienced blitzkriegs in 1939, that German word went immediately into English and other languages as probably Stage 4.

An item in Stage 3, by contrast with Stage 2 items, has generally finished adaptation, whether or not it has adapted the English forms of inflection and the like (one thinks of centuries-old Latin borrowings like *radius* that are only now gaining the analogical variant plural, *radiuses*). It usually fits English morphological and phonological patterns (if it is not a highly useful word like *radius*), and it occurs without glossing or special punctuation. It appears in enough desk dictionaries as to suggest that it is almost or partly a part of general English. Yet it is still not fully configured with English, which is the characteristic of Stage 4 words, all of which are in general international English, as is illustrated by *allele*.

As an example of a Stage 3 item, let us begin with *Abderhalden reaction,* which required little change from the original German. *Reaktion* is obviously a cognate of English *reaction,* and it is easy for one to learn the relevant details of the achievement of the Swiss chemist Emil Abderhalden. Although the item occurs only in *Webster's Third* (evidently being too recent to have been in *Webster's Second*), and there are no citations, no gloss or special punctuation is needed. Yet we know of no productive forms, and all eight desk dictionaries eschew the item. The wider, more general scope of the fairly contemporary *Webster's Third* places the item somewhat above Stage 2, though certainly at the lower level of Stage 3. The fact that the more recent *OED Supplement* and unabridged *Random House* do not record the item suggests that it is not a part of general English and may never be. Indeed, if the reaction in question were later proved to be false or otherwise dubious, the item might become an historical relic.

By contrast, the mineral *aegirite* possesses all the above qualities, while also appearing in the *OED* as cited at least by 1837, in *Webster's Second,* and also in the recent unabridged *Random House.* Though lacking productive forms and appearance in any desk dictionary, *aegirite* merits a higher place in Stage 3 than does *Abderhalden reaction.* It too may not yet be in general English, for it is chiefly a less-used synonym for *acmite.* In short, Stage 3 items occur in few or even possibly in no desk dictionaries, have few or even no productive forms, and lack those final qualities that make them an undeniable part of general English; but they are ready for that status.

Stage 4 items, which are fully configured with English, also have internal levels. The mineral *alexandrite* is recorded in all three of our main sources and in all four British and four American desk dictionaries, but is evidently without productive forms. Except that it is a variety of *chrysoberyl* (a word that is more likely to be used than our German borrowing unless one wishes to specify only this mineral variety), it might enjoy a higher level in Stage 4. We have seen *allele,* which sits at the middle or a slightly higher level because it is in all eight desk dictionaries (named in our Introduction) and has two productive forms that also have high frequency. *Allergen* at least equals *allele,* because it appears in seven instead of eight desk dictionaries and has at least equivalent high-frequency productive forms, but also enjoys such wide, nontechnical usage that it approaches the status of a household word. One of the maximum examples of such a household word in Stage 4 is *angora,* which we have had to qualify as *probably* coming from German (the lesser possibility being that it was transferred from French). By at least 1833 we find *angora* in English to mean a kind of goat, and soon with transferred senses to a cat or a rabbit, to yarn from this hair, and to the wool itself. Besides this semantic productivity, there has been high linguistic productivity in compounds like *Angora cat/goat/rabbit/wool,* besides flourishing adjectival use as in *angora sweater* and of course occurrence in all desk dictionaries.

Now let us consider any differences in degree of naturalization according to part of speech. That is, are there proportionately more nouns in our German corpus, say, in Stage 4 than there are adjectives or verbs? The rounded-off percentage of the particular stage is given in the following list:

	Stage 2	*Stage 3*	*Stage 4*
4,795 nouns	4.0%	65.6%	30.3%
503 adjectives	3.0	59.2	37.8
60 verbs	1.7	53.3	45.0
21 interjections	23.8	33.3	43.0
9 adverbs	33.3	44.4	22.2
2 prepositions	50.0	50.0	
1 conjunction		100.0	
39 bound forms		62.0	38.0
20 unmarked	30.0	60.0	10.0

These statistics speak for themselves and pose few surprises. As verbs are the central part of a sentence, one might expect verbs to have the highest percentage of items in Stage 4. The rather unique syntactic freedom of interjections may suggest their also high percentage. There is little difference between nouns and adjectives in this regard, and adverbs are among the least naturalized. As function words are seldom borrowed, it is not surprising that the single conjunction and two prepositions are even less naturalized than the adverbs are. The utility of bound forms for creating new items may explain why they have a higher number of post-2 stages (none is in Stage 2). When we total these figures, 55.7% of our corpus are in Stage 3, 23.7% are in Stage 4, and 20.6% are in Stage 2, percentages that can be compared with those for the individual parts of speech given in the table above. Cannon's statistics for his Malay corpus (1992) are a bit inapplicable, as he includes 40 Malay items that are in Stage 1 and thus would have been excluded from our German corpus and would have appeared in our Appendix. If we disregard those, then the Malay statistics would be 67.1% in Stage 2, 23.4% in Stage 3, and only 9.4% in Stage 4. So our German corpus greatly surpasses the much-smaller Malay one in utility based on this naturalization criterion, as might be expected from a corpus of items heavily tied to their Asian context. Almost a quarter of our German items are in general international English.

As we did not have the scope to construct a reverse dictionary of our corpus, we have not considered utility in terms of high-frequency terminal elements, but can provide statistics for the initial elements. The most frequent are combining forms borrowed from Latin or Greek, usually ultimately going back to a Greek etymon and always being a homonym for a long-naturalized English form (thus making it easier for a German word to move into English). In descending order, the most frequent are 44 items with *poly- (polytropic)*, 30 *iso- (isotonic)*, 25 *hetero- (heterotypic)*, 22 *hydro- (hydroid)*, and 20 each with *chromo- (chromoplast)* and *pseudo- (pseudomonas)*. All of these are also of high frequency in Cannon's 1987 total corpus for English neologisms; but our German corpus lacks items with his high-frequency *immuno-* and *mini-*, and has a generally lower occurrence of other initial bound-forms that are quite productive in English today *(micro-, multi-, neo-, neuro-)*. Our German corpus also contains 15–19 items each with *allo-, auto-, bio-* (versus 57), *chondr-, cyto-, mon(o)-, para-, phen (a/o)-, photo-, plasm(a/o)-, proto-,* and *pyro-*.

There are few free forms among our initial higher-frequency elements. The only purely German ones are *Volk* and *Kultur*, and they seem to offer no particular productivity for future English items as opposed to the demonstrated productivity of the German combining-forms seen in our corpus. German has made enormous use of classical combining-forms in its own lexicon, and these massively appear in our corpus. When we consider the equally enormous English productivity of combining forms and affixes borrowed from the classical languages and Middle French during the Middle Ages and the Renaissance (often with a consequent loss of Germanic-descended affixes), no German element can compare with any of these. Indeed, German has added only five affixes to English. For example, there are few items with the suffixes *-isch, -ismus, -ung,* etc., and no evidence that the words containing them are likely to become sufficiently productive as to be clipped to furnish new bound-forms for English. But German has transferred two international combining-forms to English and other languages. In the 1930s H. L. Mencken collected 30 composites utilizing *-burger*, and now there are numerous others. All are a kind of food (even to *dogburger*), and international fast-food chains have brought the now-English *-burger* into many languages to serve this semantic function. Interestingly, it was a kind of folk etymology that erroneously front-clipped the German *Hamburger* 'resident of Hamburg' to produce this high-frequency combining-form. The second international combining-form given by German is *-fest*, for which Mencken and Schönfelder independently collected more than 80 composites (even to *nudefest*). Of course frequency statistics can be misleading. In one sense the presence of 44 items with *poly-* among our transfers indicates much greater potential utility than do the 5 items with *schiz-*. Yet English already had the combining form *poly-*; and when we consider the wide usage of *schizophrenia*, another international word, we realize the utility in English of just this one word. And we must underline the great utility of *-burger* and *-fest*.

It is well known that English contains numbers of pseudo-loanwords, ranging from the pidgin *chop-chop* (from Chinese) to the back-formed *Chinee* and *Japanee*. Some recently formed pseudo-Spanishisms are *el cheapo* and *Tio Taco,* paralleled in our German corpus by the hybrid *nitwit* and the pseudo-Germanism *wisenheimer*. Yiddish contains many hybrid compounds built from German etyma, as in the *schlockmeister* that was recently borrowed into English from Yiddish and so is excluded from our corpus. But when we consider the utility of our corpus in terms of constructing pseudo-Germanisms, their small number means that German has had virtually no influence on English in this sense.

Three other measures of utility are double entries, reborrowing, and productive forms. An infrequent phenomenon in recent English is simultaneous borrowing of a meaning in two forms, as in the French transfer of *black comedy* and *comédie noire,* and the Spanish *refried beans* and *frijoles refritos,* where neither the phonetic transfer nor the loan translation is dominant. Our German corpus contains 58 double entries, some of which have been in English for many decades and show no evidence that one or the other form may become dominant and eventually squeeze out its presently competing form. The degree of naturalization sheds no particular light on future longevity, as sometimes the phonetic form is in Stage 4 (*dachshund,* with the translation *badger dog* in Stage 3), or vice versa (*blood sausage* in Stage 4 and *blutwurst* in 3), or both forms in the same stage (*minnelied* and *minnesong* in 3). Sometimes the evidence places both forms in Stage 4, though we may intuitively feel that Form A is dominant over B, as, for example, *gestalt* is more common than *configuration*. (The derivatives *configurationism* and *configurationist* and other evidence require that *configuration* be given its own entry.) As *Junggrammatiker* has produced three forms – *Junggrammatiker, neogrammarian,* and *young grammarian* – 58 German etyma have given English a total of 117 main entries (2.16%). Though there are no statistics on double entries borrowed from other languages into English (or perhaps in any language), Cannon's work with borrowings from five exotic languages into English suggests that German is rich by comparison. Why this is so is unclear, as, though the majority are compounds (*meerschaum* and *sea-foam),* there are also prefixations and suffixations (*vorlaufer* and *forerunner, jaeger* and *hunter),* phrases (*ding an sich* and *thing-in-itself),* and conjunctive phrases (*Sturm und Drang* and *Storm and Stress).* There are no monosyllabic examples, which would likely be transferred in phonetic form anyway. Thus the form of the German source sheds no light on the kind of structure that might come into English in two or even three forms.

Reborrowing is another phenomenon that is occurring in English today, and German seems to be rich in this kind of utility too. Thirty-five etyma have been borrowed at least twice, with three sources borrowed three times. *Heterotrophy* gave two separate meanings in botany and one in biology. Two other etyma were reborrowed in derivative forms: *polygene, polygenetic,* and *polygenic* to give two meanings in geology and one in botany, respectively; and *statist, statistic,* and *statistics* to give three meanings in mathematics. Only for *brack* (noun and verb) are different parts of speech involved, and *Iron Curtain* is the only loan translation (giving meanings in theater and politics). Usually the semantic areas are related, as in the *metakinesis* that gave meanings in both biology and anatomy. It should be stressed that reborrowing differs from the usual semantic shifting of a loanword in a lexicon, where extended, transferred, and other senses are added over the years to an original core of meaning. In reborrowing, there is a return to the original etymon to procure another sense, usually in a different semantic area.

A last, much more important measure of a loanword's utility in a language is its productivity after it has been at least partly naturalized. This action may require decades, as seen in the noun *breakthrough* (1918), which gained an adjectival use in 1944, and a verb use in 1968. We consider such functional shift also to be an expansion of vocabulary, as when German *Durchbruch* thereby ultimately gave English three items (note that this is not a reborrowing). Functional shift, as indicated by certain run-on forms in 338 of our main entries (6.3%), has occurred for 284 nouns, 41 adjectives, 9 verbs, and 4 interjections. The nouns have produced 231 adjectives *(mountain green)*, 50 verbs *(offprint)*, and 3 combining forms *(Lett-)*. The adjectives have produced 38 nouns *(effusive)*, 2 verbs *(lauter, pilger)*, and the adverb *echt*. The verbs have produced 9 nouns *(yodel);* the interjections, 3 verbs *(heil, hurrah, kamerad)* and the adjective *hurrah*. Perhaps predictably, the shorter, noncompound forms provide most of the shifts, including numbers of monosyllabic or disyllabic items like the other 8 shifts of a verb to a noun *(foozle, mite, plunder, querl, spritz, strafe, stroll,* and *swindle)*. Cannon's 1985 study of the 567 functional shifts in recent English items that were usually not loanwords (4.1% of the total items in his 1987 corpus) is not quite comparable, but his findings are useful for measuring our German transfers over the years. His largest shifts, in descending order, are as follows, with the German totals in parenthesis:

189 nouns	to verbs	(50)
121 adjectives	to nouns	(38)
114 verbs	to nouns	(9)
77 nouns	to adjectives	(231)
19 verbs	to adjectives	(0)
11 adjectives	to verbs	(2)

As all of the kinds of our German shifts appear in his 1985 corpus, none of ours is unusual; but ours evince a striking noun-to-adjective dominance, which may be partly explained by the fact that nouns constitute about 88% of our corpus.

Actually, our functional shifts are a minority of the kinds of one or more items listed in the 1,291 main entries (24%) that have run-on forms. Despite the lack of such statistics from other sets of borrowings, the fact that almost a fourth of our corpus have contributed at least one other item demonstrates that German has been quite useful to English vocabulary in this sense. These contributions span the structural gamut, producing shortenings like abbreviations, acronyms, various kinds of clippings, and symbols. Numerous derivatives and compounds have been produced by borrowings like *creosote, ethyl, folk, paraffin,* and *peptide*. Numerous derivatives have been provided by *cartel, cobalt, Hitler, isomer, spook, sulfone,* etc. A good example of productivity is the noun *burgher*, which gives a combining form and derivatives with suffixes like *-age, -dom, -ess, -hood, -ly,* and *-ship*. We have mentioned the high productivity of *-burger* and *-fest*.

NONDIRECT LOANWORDS

Finally, we can turn to samples of two kinds of items arbitrarily excluded from our corpus, which are nonetheless of considerable linguistic interest. Since the statistical conclusions presented in the Linguistic Overview are based solely on a corpus of direct loans, as that derived from our primary sources, it may be argued that German items transmitted to English by another, intermediate language present a very different aspect of the borrowing process that ought not to be neglected.

Items with particular use presumably go directly and quickly into the given language, without having to wait years or even decades in undergoing indirect transmission. But however slow and even multiple-sourced the ultimate transferral may be, some of the original semantic and phonological influence is likely to remain in the etymon ultimately transferred, unless the item is translated. Study of such items can throw light on questions like survivability and interference versus ease of transmission. For example, why does one item go directly from Language A into B and soon become a permanent part of the vocabulary of B, whereas another item undergoes a transitory but unsuccessful transfer to B and only later actually moves into B by transferral from C? The latter situation raises detailed questions like the phonological and other conditions that must be present before there can be direct transfer, not to mention that the proportion of direct to indirect transfer is itself of interest. If the indirect items had been included in our corpus, they would have had to be tagged to indicate that they presumably possess additional or special qualities that militated against their being lumped indivisibly with the direct borrowings. Also, if German gives an item to English (and is thus in our corpus), what if German itself is only an intermediary in transferring a Latin or Greek etymon that has been changed little by its stay in German? An example is our *dolman,* which we have etymologized as coming from French and/or German into English. But the real semantic and phonetic transfer is from the original Turkish *dolama,* not to mention that the item may have had a residence in Hungarian before Hungarian passed it on to German. We have mentioned the excluded *vampire,* and a similar example is the *guerrilla* given to English by Spanish. In its modern form the ultimate descent of *guerrilla* from a Germanic stem is no longer perceptible to modern speakers of Romance and Germanic languages, a fact that German linguists recognize by considering the item as a Spanish loan. Perhaps *guerrilla* is related or even descended from High German *Wirren* 'disturbances, confusions' (as in the idiom *die Wirren des Krieges*) and also to the noun *Wehr* 'defense, resistance, as opposed to *Krieg*.' Inclusion of *guerrilla* in a dictionary of Germanic transfers into English would raise many such problems that considerably motivated our excluding such items.

Here are samples of German transfers into English by way of five other languages:

Dutch: etch, mangle, schelm

French (Skeat 1910: 764 lists 55 of these, with many errors):
    calash, haversack, Papiste, psychological moment, reister, sabretasche,
    vampire, vermouth, widerkom, zigzag

Italian: brindisi, suabe (flute)

Polish: hetman

Russian: feldscher, residént

DIALECTAL ITEMS

Our other kind of exclusion is dialectal items that are not found in Standard High German sources, even though they appear in dictionaries of the English language, especially American ones. These come primarily from Pennsylvania German, a viable if seriously endangered regional variety of German still spoken in parts of the United States. Admittedly, the tagging of an item as dialectal is tricky, as it might be dialectal in one context but not socially or otherwise conspicuous in another context. Thus a standard German etymon may be transferred into an English form, as was our included *hexerei,* while part of that same etymon, the excluded *hex,* came into English via Pennsylvania German. A few such, chiefly Pennsylvania German dialectal items that appear in standard American and/or English dictionaries, but are not in our corpus are: *clapholt, dunker, grex,* the verb and noun *hex, hexafoos, overden, schiffli,* and *schnitz un knepp* (vs. our included *schnitz and knepp*).

Similarly, although German linguists now generally consider Jüdisch-Deutsch archaic for Old or Middle or West Yiddish, with Yiddish as the language of the unassimilated Ashkenazi Jews, some scholars still view it as a German dialect. Whether dialect or language, we exclude such well-known Yiddish loanwords in English as *gefilte fish, heinisch, klutz, kugel, kvetch, landsman, macher, mensch,* and *narrischkeit,* regardless of their etymology. *Nebbish* also comes into English from Yiddish, which borrowed the item from a Slavic source without any connection to German and thus provides an excellent example to justify our excluding such items from our German-derived corpus.

CONCLUSION

The present study is in good part an evolution of Pfeffer's *Deutsches Sprachgut im Wortschatz der Amerikaner und Engländer,* which, on publication, was viewed as being "by far the best and most comprehensive collection of German lexical transfers into English"—see *American Speech,* 65.3 (1990): 260–6. Prefaced by two overviews, one historical and one linguistic, the Dictionary portion of the new study details 5,380 English borrowings from German, and its Appendix catalogs an additional 621 items, thereby totaling 6,001 items.

A last comment concerns the extent of the German linguistic contribution to English. Although the large size of our corpus considerably elevates German as a direct transmitter over the centuries, in the hierarchy of languages that have directly transmitted quantities of loanwords, the lack of comparable, comprehensive studies makes it impossible for us to conclude, for example, that German may now be the third or the sixth largest contributor. The huge quantities of attested items from Latin and French would seem to leave them unchallenged as the leading suppliers. Except that so many of the ultimately Greek etyma were conveyed by those two and other languages including German as intermediate suppliers, Greek would likely be at least third. The huge number of direct German loanwords may now be challenging

Italian if not Spanish. If one separates the directly transmitted Old Norse etyma from the Old Icelandic ones etc. (when this can be done), Serjeantson's conclusion that ''Scandinavian'' is in third place (1935: vii, 183) would be challenged. Thus, for lack of quantitative evidence, we leave Latin and French, probably in that order, in first and second places. We project German, Greek, Italian, and Spanish (in an order yet to be determined), in third through sixth places, with Old Norse perhaps trailing fairly closely in seventh place.

As our study documents the impossibility of making a qualitative judgment alongside this subjective quantitative one, we can only repeat that German loanwords have been and continue to be extremely useful in English, by comparison with items from other languages. However, Cannon's continuing studies on current loanwords show that Spanish (and Japanese, which starts from a far-smaller word-base in English) are rapidly elevating their quantitative status in English, so that, if German, say, presently surpasses Spanish in total quantity, the current rate of Spanish inflow will probably exceed within a few decades the German totals (and the Spanish total may already be higher). As German is in seventh place in current inflow, as compared with Arabic's eleventh place (Cannon 1987: 89), the smaller word-base of Arabic means that Arabic is at best in tenth place, probably trailing Hebrew, Old Norse, and Portuguese, if not Sanskrit.

PART III
DICTIONARY OF GERMAN LOANWORDS
IN ENGLISH

A

A, *see* alanine

Abderhalden reaction, *n. Chem.* [G *Abderhalden-Reaktion* < the name of Emil *Abderhalden,* Swiss chemist and physiologist (1877–1950) + G *Reaktion* reaction] The reaction occurring in body fluids of certain proteolytic enzymes. W [3]

abendmusik, -en *pl. Music* [G < *Abend* evening + *Musik* music < L *mūsica* < Gk *mousikē*] Usu. an evening performance of religious or sacred music; this music. W [3]

Aberglaube, *n.* (1873) *Philos.* [G < (the archaic meaning of) *aber* false or alternate + *Glaube* belief] An antiquated or superseding belief additional to what is certain and verifiable; superstition. • ~ is transl. as **overbelief** (1897, q.v.). 0–1933 [2]

Abgeordnetenhaus, *n. Politics* [G < *Abgeordneten* (*pl.*) deputies, representatives + *Haus* house] Formerly in Prussia and Austria, the lower house of the legislature; in 1950–90 the parliament of West Berlin. W2 [2]

Abgesang, *n. Lit.* [G < *ab* down + *Gesang* singing, song] Epistrophe, esp. the concluding section of a medieval stanza or bar. W [3]

Abgrenzung, *n.* (1972) *Politics* Var. **abgrenzung** (1973) [G delimitation] Preceding reunification, the policy of total separation of East Germany from West Germany. B [2]

Abiturient, -en *pl.* (1863) *Ed.* Var. **abiturient** (1863) [G (1652) < ML *abiturire* to want to leave < L *abīre* to leave, graduate] In Germany, a pupil who is graduating from a gymnasium or high school to enter a university.— **abiturient,** *a.* (1917). O [3]

ablaut, *n.* (1849) *Ling.* [G < *ab* off + *Laut* sound, i.e., vowel gradation, change in vowel] Gradation: systematic variation of the vowels in the same or related roots or affixes in Indo-European languages. O, R, W [4]

abraum, *n.* (1753) *Mining* [G top layer of soil, etc. over mineral veins < *abräumen* to remove] A red ocher used for darkening mahogany. O, W [3]

Abraum salts, *pl.* (1875) *Mining* [Partial transl. of G *Abraumsalze* (1753) < *Abraum* abraum (q.v.) + *Salz* salt] Mixed salts lying above the pure rock-salt, used for producing potassium chloride. O [3]

abreact, *v.* (1912) *Psych.* [Transl. of G *abreagieren* < *ab* off, away from, down + *reagieren* to react < NL *reagere*] To release emotional energy previously forgotten or repressed. O, R, W [4]

abreaction, *n.* (1912) *Psych.* [Transl. of G *Abreagierung* < *abreagieren* to abreact (q.v.)] The release of emotional energy supposedly attached to a repressed idea. —**abreactive** (1944). O, R, W [4]

abseil, *n.* (1933) *Sports* Var. **abseiling** (1941) [G *abseilen* < *ab* down + *seilen* to lower by rope] The technique of descending a steep face by means of a rope looped over a projection above the climber. O, R, W [4]

abseil, *v.* (1941) *Sports* [G (*sich*) *abseilen* to lower oneself or someone down a cliff with the aid of a rope] To abseil

(q.v.) or rappel. —**abseiling,** *verbal n.* (1941); **abseiler.** O, R [3]

Abwehr, *n. Mil.* [G defense, resistance < *abwehren* to ward off] The German office for espionage, counterintelligence, and sabotage in World War Two. R [3]

academic freedom, *n.* (1901) *Ed.* [Transl. of G *akademische Freiheit* < *akademisch* academic (< NL *academia*) + *Freiheit* freedom] Freedom to teach or learn according to personal convictions, without fear of reprisals. O, R, W [4]

accordion, *n.* (1831) *Music* Var. **accordeon, accordian** [G (now *Akkordeon*) (1829) < *Akkord* + *-ion* -ion < Fr *accord* < *accorder* to tune instruments] A portable keyboard instrument in which a hand-operated bellows forces the wind past free metallic reeds. —**accordion,** *a.* (1885); **piano accordion** (1860); **accordionist.** O, R, W [4]

acetal, *n.* (1853) *Chem.* [G (now also *Azetal*) < *Acet-* (< a short. of L *acētum* vinegar) + G *Alkohol* (ult. < Ar) alcohol] A colorless liquid or any of a class of organic compounds usu. obtained from aldehydes or ketones, used in medicines, cosmetics, etc. • ~ appears in numerous composites like **acetaldol, acetalize, acetaldehydase, acetaldehyde.** O, R, W [4]

acetamide, *n.* (1873) *Chem.* Var. **acetamid** [G *Azetamid* < *Azet-* + *Amid* amide < L *acet-* < *acētum* vinegar] A white, water-soluble, crystalline amide of acetic acid, used as a solvent; a series of analogous compounds. —**acetamido-.** O, R, W [4]

acetoacetic acid, *n.* (c.1900 *W9*) *Chem.* Var. **acetacetic acid** [Transl. of G *Azetessigsäure* < *Azet-* (< L *acet-*) acet- + G *Essigsäure* acetic acid] An unstable acid sometimes found in the urine of diabetics and some other patients; also called *diacetic acid.* O, R, W [4]

acetone, *n.* (1839) *Chem.* [G *Aceton* (now also *Azeton*) < *Acet-* + *-on* -one < L *acētum* vinegar < Gk *-onē* fem. patronymic suffix] A volatile, fragrant, liquid ketone used as a solvent and in organic synthesis. —**acetone,** *a.* (1928); **acetonic** (1873); and many other composites like **acetone body** (1928). O, R, W [4]

acetopyrine, *n. Pharm.* [G *Acetopyrin* (now also *Azetopyrin*) < *aceto-* + *Antipyrin* < L *acētum* vinegar + *anti-* against + Gk *pyretós* fever + G *-in* -in(e)] A white compound of aspirin and antipyrin. W [3]

ach-laut/Ach-laut, *n. Ling.* [G the fricative /x/ as it is pronounced in German after *a, o, u* < *ach* ah, alas + *Laut* sound] The voiceless velar fricative as represented by the *ch* of German *ach.* W [3]

achroite, *n. Mineral.* [G *Achroit* < *achro-* + *-it* -ite < Gk *áchrous* colorless] A colorless variety of tourmaline; a gem cut from this. O, R, W [3]

achromat, *n.* (1900) *Optics* [G (1897), a short. of *achromatische Linse* < *achromatisch* achromatic + *Linse* < NL < Gk *achrōmatos* colorless] Achromatic lens. O, R, W [4]

achromatic lens, -es *pl.* (1982) *Optics* Var. **achromat lens** (1982) [Transl. of G *achromatische Linse* acromat(ic) (q.v.) lens] A compound lens with differing focal powers. O, R, W [4]

Achtung, *interj.* [G attention, caution] Attention, caution. R [2]

acmite, *n.* (1837) *Mineral.* [G *Akmit* (1821) < Gk *akmḗ* point, top, summit + G *-it* -ite, discovered by Friedrich Stromeyer, German chemist (1776–1835)] A brittle mineral of the pyroxene group of silicate of sodium and iron; also called *aegirite.* O, R, W [3]

acoine, *n. Chem.* Var. **acoin** [Prob. < G *Akoin,* prob. an anagram of *Kokain* cocaine (q.v.)] A crystalline derivative of guanidine used as an antiseptic and local anesthetic. W [3]

aconite, *n.* (1578) *Bot.* Var. **aconitum** (1597) [Poss. < G *Akonit,* but more prob. < Fr *aconit* < L *aconītum* without dust] A genus or plant of *Aconitum* with a poisonous root; an extract or preparation of this plant, used in dentistry and formerly as a sedative. —**aconite,** *a.* (1741); **winter aconite** (1794); **aconitic** (1873); **aconite violet**; and numerous other composites. O, R, W [4]

aconitine, *n.* (1847) *Chem.* [G < *Akonit* aconite (q.v.) + *-in* -ine] An extremely poisonous alkaloid obtained from aconite (q.v.). O, W [3]

acrosome, *n.* (1899) *Zool.* [G *Akrosoma* (1898) < *akro-* + *-soma* < Gk *ákros* the highest, outermost + *sṓma* body] An anterior cap or hooklike prolonging of a spermatozoon. —**acrosomal** (1940), **acrosomic** (1952). O, R, W [4]

acrostichal, *a.* (1884) *Entomology* [G (now *akrostichal*) (1878) < *acro-* + *-stichal* < Gk *ákros* the highest, outermost + *stíchos* row, rank] Situated in the highest row or rank, as in certain bristles on muscoid flies' mesonotum. —**acrostichal,** *n.* (1961). O, W [3]

actin, *n.* (1942) *Biochem.* [G *Aktin* < *akt-* + *-in* -in < L *āctus* act, motion] A protein in muscle that, with myosin, is active in muscular contraction and relaxation. O, R, W [4]

actinolite, *n.* (1833) *Mineral.* [G *Actinolith* (now *Aktinolith*) < *actino-* + *-lith,* and also an E transl. of *Strahlstein* (< *Strahl* + *Stein*) < Gk *actís* (gen. *actînos*) ray + *líthos* stone] A green variety of amphibole. —**actinolitic** (1878). O, R, W [4]

activate, *v.* (1903) *Physics* [Transl. of G *aktivieren* to activate < Fr *activer* to set in motion < L *āgere*] To make radioactive (this is different from the old meaning of "to make active"). —**activated,** *a.* (1903); **activating,** *a.* (1938). O, R, W [4]

activism, *n.* (1907) *Politics* [G *Aktivismus* < *aktiv* + *-ismus* < L *āctīvus* active, energetic + *-ismus*] A philosophical theory about the activity of the mind; a doctrine or practice that stresses energetic action, as in using force for political means. O, R, W [4]

activist, *n.* (1907) *Politics* [G *Aktivist* < *aktiv* + *-ist* -ist] One who advocates or practices activism (q.v.). —**activistic** (1907). O, R, W [4]

actograph, *see* aktograph

acyl, *n.* (1899) *Chem.* [G (now also *Azyl*) (1888) < *ac-* + *-yl* < L *acidus* sour, sharp] An organic radical derived from a carboxylic acid. —**acyl,** *a.* (1901); **acylate,** *v.*

(1907); **acylation** (1910); **acylal; acylamino; acylase; acyl,** *n.;* **acyloin; acyloxy.** O, R, W [4]

Adalin, *n.* (1911) *Chem.* Var. **Adaline** (1911) [G *Adalin* (1910), a proprietary name] A sedative for sleeping. O [3]

adamellite, *n.* (1896) *Geol.* [G *Adamellit* (1890) < *Adamello,* the name of a mountain in northern Italy + G *-it* -ite] Any of several kinds of quartz, as from Adamello. O, W [3]

added-value tax, *see* value-added tax

adduct, *n.* (1941 W9) *Chem.* [G *Addukt* (1931), coined by the German chemists Otto Siels (1876–1954) and Kurt Alder (1902–58) (see *Annalen der Chemie,* 1931, p. 191) as a blend < *Addition* addition + *Produkt* product, seemingly < L *adductus,* past part. of L *addūcere,* lit., to lead to] A chemical addition product. O, W [3]

adenine, *n.* (1885) *Chem.* [G *Adenin* (1885) < *Aden* + *-in* -ine < Gk *adḗn* gland] A purine base extracted from certain glands and animal and vegetable tissue. O, R, W [4]

adenosine, *n.* (1909) *Biochem.* [G *Adenosin* (1909), a short. of *Adenin* adenine (q.v.) + *Ribose,* a short. and metathesis of *Arabinose* + *-in* -ine] A crystalline nucleoside occurring mainly in muscle tissue and obtainable from ribonucleic acid. —**adenosine diphosphate** (1938)/**triphosphate** (1939)/**monophosphate** (1950)/**arabinoside/cyclic monophosphate/deaminase (deficiency)/triphosphatase.** O, R, W [4]

adermine, *n.* (1938) *Chem.* [G *Adermin* (1938) < *a-* + *derm-* + *-in* -ine < Gk *a-* not + *dérma* skin] Vitamin B_6, pyridoxin. O, W [3]

ader wax, *n. Mineral.* [Prob. ad. of G *Aderwachs,* a popular name for *Ozokerit* < *Ader* vein + *Wachs* wax] Ozokerite (q.v.). W [3]

adonitol, *n.* (1893) *Chem.* [G *Adonit* (1893) < *adon-* + *-itol* < NL (< Gk) *Adonis* Adonis + G *-t-* + E *-ol*] A crystalline pentahydroxyl alcohol found in *Adonis vernalis;* also called *ribitol.* O, W [3]

Adurol, *n.* (1899) *Chem.* [G a trademark] Either of two crystalline agents used in photographic developing. O, W [3]

aegirine, *n.* (1837) *Mineral.* Var. **aegerite** (q.v.) [G *Ägirin* < *Aegir,* the name of an ancient Scandinavian sea god + *-in* -ine] Acmite (q.v.). O, R, W [4]

aegirite, *n.* (1837) *Mineral.* [Ad. of G *Ägirin* < *Aegir,* the name of an ancient Scandinavian sea god, by adding the conventional E mineral suffix *-ite*] Acmite (q.v.). O, R, W [3]

aenigmatite, *see* enigmatite

aerenchyma, *n.* (1893) *Bot.* Old var. **aerenchym(e)** (1911, 1908) [G *Aerenchym* (1889) < *aer-* + *-enchym* < the comb. form of L *āēr* aero- air + Gk *énchyma* infusion] One of various tissues with large intercellular spaces, as found in many aquatic plants. O, R, W [4]

aerology, *n.* (1912) *Meteor.* [G *Aerologie* (1906) < *aero-* + *-logie* < L *āēr* air + Gk *lógos* word, study] Meteorology, esp. that branch concerned with the phenomena of the upper air. —**aerologist** (1847), **aerological** (1932), **aerologically.** O, R, W [4]

aerophor, *n. Music* Var. **aerophore** [G < *aero-* + *-phor* < L *āēr* air + Gk *phóros* bearing, carrying] An instrument using a foot bellows to sustain a tone on a wind instrument (not to be confused with the word that gave the meaning of "a respirator used in mines"). W [3]

aerotropism, *n.* (1889) *Bot.* [G *Aerotropismus* (1885) < *Aerotrop* + *-ismus* < L *āēr* air + Gk *tropé* turning < *tréptein* to turn + L *-ismus*] The direction-changing property exhibited esp. by plants' growing roots. —**aerotropic** (1898). O, W [3]

aeschynite, *see* eschynite

aesthetic, *a.* (1798) *Philos.* Var. **esthetic** [G *ästhetisch* < NL *aestheticus* < Gk *aisthētikós* of sense perception] Relating to aesthetics or the aesthetic; concerning the beautiful as distinguished from the pleasing, moral, or practical. O, R, W [4]

aesthetics, *n.* (1803) *Philos.* Var. **esthetics** [G *Aesthetik* (1750) (now *Ästhetik*) < NL *aesthetica* < Gk *aisthētikós* of sense perception] A branch of philosophy concerned with beauty and the beautiful; the science or philosophy of art. O, R, W [4]

aesthetic tea, *n.* (1831) *Lit.* [In Carlyle's *Sartor Resartus* (1858), poss. a transl. of G *ästhetischer Thee* < *ästhetisch* aesthetic (q.v.) + *Thee* (now *Tee*), ult. < Chin *t'e* tea, orig. a euphemism for a gathering at a salon of Romanticists, as of the notorious *Dresdener Dichter,* the Dresden Circle of Poets] Such a gathering; a more general appreciation or criticism of the beautiful. O [3]

affect, *n.* (1891) *Psych.* [G *Affekt* < L *affectus* < *afficere* to place in a mood] The conscious, subjective part of an emotion, as distinct from bodily changes. O, W [4]

affenpinscher, *n.* (1903) *Zool.* [G < *Affen,* pl. of *Affe* monkey + *Pinscher* a breed of monkey-faced dogs named for *Pinzgau,* Austria, where they are bred] A small breed of dog, related to the Brussels griffon. O, R, W [4]

affricate, *n.* (1880) *Ling.* Var. **affricative** (1880) [Prob. < G *Affrikata* < L *affricāta* + *affricāre* to rub against] An alveopalatal consonant that begins as a stop and ends as a fricative, often described as an affricated stop. —**affricate,** *v.* (1891); **affricated,** *a.* (1891), **affrication** (1934); **affricative,** *a.* O, R, W [4]

afrormosia, *n.* (1920) *Bot.* [G (1906), a combining of *Afr-* < *Afrikaner* African < L *Africanus* + G *Ormosia* a genus of shrubs and trees] A genus of tropical African trees and shrubs of the legume family; a tree of this genus. O, R [4]

afterburner, *n.* (1947) *Tech.* [Transl. of G *Nachbrenner* < *nach* after + *Brenner* burner < *brennen* to burn] An auxiliary burner attached to the exhaust pipe of a turbojet engine to give it more power. O, R, W [4]

afterburning, *n.* (1887) *Tech.* [Prob. trans. of G *Nachbrennen* < *nachbrennen* to burn additionally] In internal combustion or jet engines, the diminishing combustion that follows the full force of the explosion; the use of an afterburner. O, R, W [4]

agamont, *n.* (1912) *Biol.* [G (1904) < *a-* + *Gamont* < Gk *a-* not + *gameté* spouse + *ón* (gen. *óntos*) being] A schizont, a protozoan's cell that does not produce gametes. O, W [3]

aggressin, *n.* (1906) *Med.* Var. **aggressine** (1906) [G < L *aggressio* attack + *-in* -in] A hypothetical substance that increases the toxic effect of bacteria in the host's body. O, W [3]

aglycon(e), *n.* (1925) *Chem.* Var. **aglucone** (1925) [G *Aglykon* (1925) < *a-* + *glyk-* (< Gk *a-* not + *glykýs* sweet) + G *-on* (< Gk *-ōnē* fem. patronymic suffix) -one] An organic compound combined with the sugar portion of a glycoside, obtained by hydrolysis. O, W [3]

agogic, *a.* (1893) *Music* Var. **agogical** (1922) [G *agogisch* (1884) < *agog-* + *-isch* -ic < Gk *agōgós* directing, guiding] Pertaining to variations in tempo within a musical piece or movement. —**agogic accent** (1883). O, R, W [3]

agogics, *n.* (1893) *Music* [G *Agogik* (1884) < *agog-* + *-ik* -ics < Gk *agōgós* directing, guiding] The musical theory that rhetorical emphasis includes dynamic stress as well as emphasis in the greater relative length of the tones being emphasized. O, R, W [3]

agricolite, *n. Mineral.* [G *Agricolit,* named after Georgius *Agricola,* the latinized form of Georg Bauer (1494–1555), German mineralogical pioneer] Eulytite, a monoclinic bismuth silicate. W [3]

air-cure, *n.* (1876) *Med.* [Transl. of G *Luftkur* < *Luft* air + *Kur* cure] A cure by the use of air. 0 [3]

airship, *n.* (1819) *Aeron.* [Transl. of G *Luftschiff* < *Luft* air + *Schiff* ship] A motor-driven dirigible, lighter than air, usu. cigar-shaped and elongated; applied in the U.S. generally to other types of aircraft. —**airshipman** (1904). O, R, W [4]

akerite, *n. Geol.* [G *Åkerit,* named after *Åker,* a district near Oslo, Norway + G *-it* -ite] A variety of quartz-syenite rock. W [3]

akermanite, *n. Mineral.* [G *Åkermanit,* named after Anders Richard *Åkerman* (1837–1922), Swedish metallurgist + G *-it* -ite] Calcium magnesium silicate. W [3]

aktograph/actograph, *n.* (1956) *Psych.* [G *Aktograph* < *akto-* + *-graph* < L *āctus,* past part. of *ágere* to do, drive + Gk *gráphein* to write, record] A device that records the movements of caged experimental animals. O, W [3]

Ala, *see* alanine.

alabandite, *n. Mineral.* [G *Alabandit,* named after *Alabanda,* an ancient city in what is now Turkey + G *-it* -ite] A native manganese sulfide, also called *manganblende.* O, R, W [3]

Alamannic, *see* Alemannic

alanine, *n.* (1863) *Chem.* Var. **alanin** [G *Alanin* (1849), a combining of *Aldehyd* aldehyde (q.v.) + *-in* -ine with the infixing of *-an-*] A white crystalline amino acid formed by hydrolyzing proteins; an amino acid found in muscle and made synthetically. • ~ is short. to **Ala** and symbolized as **A.** O, R, W [4]

alant, *n. Bot.* [G < MHG < OHG *alant* sneezeweed] Sneezeweed, a North American herb that may cause sneezing. W [3]

alantic acid, *n. Chem.* [Partial transl. of G *Alantsäure* < *Alant* alant (q.v.) + *Säure* acid + E *-ic*] A crystalline acid derived from alantolactone (q.v.). W [3]

alantin, *n.* (1847) *Chem.* [G < *Alant* the Elecampane, a plant in the Compositae family that causes sneezing + *-in* -in] Inulin (q.v.). O, W [3]

alantolactone, *n. Chem.* [Prob. orig. formed as G *Alantolakton* < *Alant* alant (q.v.) + *-o-* + *Lakton* lactone (< L *lāc,* gen. *lactis* milk)] A crystalline lactone obtained from elecampane root. W [3]

albertustaler, -ø/-s *pl. Currency* [G (1612) < Du *alber-tusdaalder* < the name of *Albert* VII (1559–1621), archduke of Austria and regent of the Netherlands + Du *daalder* < G *Taler* (see *dollar*)] A silver coin worth three gulden. W [2]

albertype, n. (1875) *Printing* Old var. **Albert-type** (1875) [G *Albert(t)ypie* < the name of Joseph *Albert* (1825–86), German photographer + *-typie* -type] Collotype, a photomechanical process on the lithographic principle; a print made from this. O, W [3]

albinism, n. (1836) *Biol.* Var. **albinoism** (1868) [Fr *albinisme* (< G *Albinismus* < *Albino* + *-ismus* -ism) or directly < G, ult. < L *albus* white] The quality or condition of being an albino; mammals' and others' incapacity to produce pigment. —**albinistic** (1880). O, R, W [4]

alboranite, n. *Geol.* [G *Alboranit* < the name of the Spanish island *Alborán* + G *-it* -ite] A hypersthene-basalt of porphyritic texture. W [3]

Albumblatt, -blätter/-blatts *pl. Music* [G < *Album* (< L) album + *Blatt* leaf < OHG *blat*] A short instrumental work, usu. for piano. W [2]

albus, -es *pl. Currency* [G < ML < L *albus* white] A minor bullion coin in Germany and the Low Countries in the 13th and 14th centuries. W [3]

alcamine, *see* alkamine

alcapton, *see* alkapton

aldehyde, n. (c.1846 *W*9) *Chem.* [G *Aldehyd* < NL *al dehyd,* a short. of L *alcoholus dehydrogenātus* dehydrogenated alcohol] Acetaldehyde; one of a large class of highly reactive organic compounds. —**aldehydic** (1882), **aldehydo, aldehydo-,** and in compounds like **aldehyde ammonia** (1863)/**green/resin.** O, R, W [4]

aldehydine, n. *Chem.* [G *Aldehydin* < *Aldehyd* aldehyde (q.v.) + *-in* -ine] Methylethylpyridine; one of a class of solid bases containing an imidazole ring. W [3]

aldolase, n. (1940) *Biochem.* [G (1936), a combining of *Aldehyd* aldehyde (q.v.) + *Alkohol* alcohol (ult. < Ar) + *Diastase* < Gk *diástasis* separation] A crystalline enzyme widely present in animal muscle and plant cells; also called *zymohexase.* O, R, W [3]

aldrin, n. (1949) *Chem.* [G < the name of Kurt *Alder* (1902–58), German chemist + *-in* -in] A crystalline insecticide consisting of a chlorinated tetracyclic derivative of naphthalene. O, R, W [4]

Alemannic, a. (1776) and n. (1814) *Politics, Ling.* Var. **Alemannian** (n. 1879, a. 1951), **Alemanic, Alamannic** [G *alemannisch* and *Alemanne* < LL *Alemannicus* < *Alemanni* (pl.), ad. Gmc **Alamanniz,* prob. *all* + *man,* denoting a wide alliance of peoples] (Of or relating to) a federation of Germanic tribes living in the territory between the Main and the Danube rivers; (of) the dialects of Old High German spoken by them or their modern descendants in Alsace, Switzerland, and southwestern Germany. —**Alemannish,** n. (1813) and a. O, R, W [4]

aleuronat, n. *Food* [G < *Aleuron* (< Gk wheat flour) + G *-at* -at] A flour made of aleurone (q.v.), used for bread for diabetics. W [3]

aleurone, n. (1869) *Biochem.* Var. **aleuron** (1879) [G *Aleuron* (< Gk wheat flour) or directly < Gk] Ergastic protein matter occurring as amorphous granules in endosperm and some plant seeds. —**aleuronic** (1879). O, R, W [4]

alexandrite, n. (1837) *Mineral.* [G *Alexandrit* < the name of *Alexander I* (1777–1825), Russian czar and emperor + G *-it* -ite] A grass-green variety of chrysoberyl (q.v.). O, R, W [4]

alexin, n. (1892) *Biochem.* Var. **alexine** (1949) [G (1891) < Gk *aléxein* to ward off, defend + G *-in* -in] A class of thermolabile substances occurring in blood serum and having the capacity to help destroy bacteria, etc. —**alexinic.** O, R, W [3]

algolagnia, n. (1900) *Path.* [G *Algolagnie* (1892) < NL *algolagnia* < Gk *álgos* pain + *lagneía* pleasure] Sexual gratification derived from inflicting or enduring bodily pain. —**algolagnistic** (1908), **algolagnic, algolagnist.** O, R, W [4]

algraphy, n. (1897) *Printing* [G *Alagraphie* (1896), a short. of *Aluminium* aluminum + *-graphie* (< Gk *graphía* writing < *gráphein* to write)] The process or art of printing from aluminum plates; also called *aluminography.* —**algraphic** (1898). O, R, W [3]

alicyclic, a. (1891) *Chem.* [G *alicyclisch* (now *alizyklisch*) (1889), a short. of *aliphatisch* (< Gk *aleiphat-, áleiphar* unguent, fat) + G *cyclisch* < Gk *kyklikós* cyclic] Of organic compounds having the properties of both aliphatic and cyclic substances. O, R, W [4]

alkaloid, n. (1831) *Chem.* [G < *Alkali* + *-oid* -oid < Sp *álcali* potash (ult. < Ar *al-qili*) + Gk *-oeidēs* similar] Any of a numerous group of organic bases containing nitrogen, usu. in seed plants. —**alkaloid(al),** a. (1859, 1879). O, R, W [4]

alkamine/alcamine, n. *Chem.* [G *Alkamin,* a blend of *Alkohol* alcohol (< Sp *alcohol* < Ar *al-kuhul* lead glance, used for coloring eyebrows) + G *Amin* amine] Amino alcohol, which combines the properties of an alcohol and an amine. W [3]

alkapton, n. (1888) *Med.* Var. **alcapton** (1888), **alcaptone** [G *Alcapton* (now *Alkapton*) (1861) < Sp *álcali* potash (ult. < Ar) + Gk *kápton* < *káptein* to swallow greedily] Homogentisic acid, a reducing substance found in urine in persons having alkaptonuria. —**alkaptonuria** (1888); **alcapton,** a. (1899); **alkaptonuric,** a. and n. (1899, 1905). O, R, W [3]

alkyl, n. (1879) *Chem.* [G < *Alkohol* alcohol (ult. < Ar) + *-yl* -yl] A noncyclic saturated hydrocarbon radical; a compound with one or more alkyl radicals with a metal. —**alkyl,** a. (1882). • ~ appears in many derivatives like **alkylated** (1889); **alkylating** (1900); **alkylation** (1900); **alkylate,** v. and n. (1903, 1904); **alkylene; alkylic;** and in some compounds like **alkyl group/halide.** O, R, W [4]

alkyne, n. (1882) *Chem.* Var. **alkine** (1882) [G *Alkin* (now *Alkyne*) (1881) < *Alkohol* alcohol (ult. < Ar) + *-in* -ine] Any of a series of aliphatic hydrocarbons having a triple bond. —**alkyne series** (1844), **alkynl.** O, R, W [4]

allantoin, n. (1845) *Chem.* [Prob. < G < *Allantois* < NL < Gk *allântos* sausage (i.e., vascular fetal membrane) + G *-in* -in, so named because it was found in the allantoinic liquid of cows, G *Allantoiswasser*] A crystalline oxidation found in most mammals' urine and in many plants, used as an antiseptic. —**allantoinase.** O, R, W [3]

Allasch, -es *pl. Beverages* [G < *Allasch,* the name of a town near Riga, Latvia] A sweet kümmel, a kümmel liqueur. W [3]

allele, *n.* (1931) *Biol.* Var. **allel** (1953) [G *Allel,* a short. of *Allelomorph* < *allelo-* + *-morph* < Gk *allélōn* mutual, one another + *morphé* form, shape] Either of a pair of alternative Mendelian qualities; allelomorph; a gene as the vehicle of an allele. **—allelism** (1935), **allelic** (1940), **allele frequency.** O, R, W [4]

allelopathy, *n.* (1948 *W9*) *Bot.* [G *Allelopathie* < *allelo- .* + *-pathie* (or < Fr *allélopathie*) < Gk *allélōn* mutually, one another + *pátheia* suffering] The supposed noxious influence of a living plant upon some other due to toxic substances secreted. **—allelopathic.** R, W [4]

allergen, *n.* (1910 *W9*) *Path.* [G < *all-* + *-ergen* < Gk *állos* other + *érgon* work, effect + *génos* type] An alergy-inducing substance. **—allergenic** (1913), **allergenicity.** O, R, W [4]

allergy, *n.* (1911) *Path.* [G *Allergie* (1906) < *all-* + *-ergie* < Gk *állos* other + *érgon* work, effect] An altered bodily reactivity following a first exposure; a reaction like sneezing, rashes, etc. to situations or foreign material such as particular foods, pollens, or medication; medical practice concerned with allergy; a feeling of antipathy to some person or thing. **—allergic** (1911), **allergist** (1945), **allergology, allergic rhinitis.** O, R, W [4]

allochetite, *n. Geol.* [G *Allochetit,* named after *Allochet,* a valley in the Austrian Tirol + *-it* -ite] A porphyritic dike rock containing phenocrysts in a dense groundmass. W [3]

allochtonous, *a.* (1911) *Geol.* [G *allochthon* (1888) < *allo-* + *-chthon* < Gk *állos* other + *chthṓn* earth, land + E *-ous*] Of a transported substance like coal or limestone that was formed elsewhere than where found. **—allochthon,** *n.* (1942). O, R, W [4]

alloclase, *n.* (1875) *Mineral.* [G *Alloklas* (1866) < *allo-* + *-klas* < Gk *állos* other + *klásis* fracture, so named because it has a different cleavage from that of minerals with which it has been confused] Alloclasite, a mineral in the pyrite group. O [3]

alloerotic, *a.* (1921) *Psych.* [G *alloerotisch* (1899) < *allo-* + *erotisch* < Gk *állos* other + *erōtikós* concerning love] Relating to Freud's concept of eroticism aroused by another person. O, W [3]

alloerotism, *n.* (1934) *Psych.* Var. **alloeroticism** [G *Alloerotizismus* (1899) < *allo-* + *Erotizismus* < Gk *állos* + *eros* love, *erōtikós* concerning love + L *-ismus* -ism] Sexual feeling or activity directed toward someone else, in contrast with autoerotism. O, W [3]

allomorphite, *n.* (1837–80) *Mineral.* [G *Allomorphit* (1838) < *allo-* + *-morphit* < Gk *allómorphos* strange in form, shape] Barite, a mineral resembling anhydrite. O, W [3]

allopath, *n.* (1830) *Med.* [G < *allo-* + *-path* < Gk *állos* other + *-patheia* suffering, illness] One who practices or believes in allopathy (q.v.). O, R, W [4]

allopathic, *a.* (1830) *Med.* Var. **allopathical** [G *allopathisch* < *allo-* + *-pathisch* < Gk *állos* other + *-patheia* enduring illness] Of or pertaining to allopathy (q.v.). **—allopathically** (1842). O, R, W [4]

allopathy, *n.* (1842) *Med.* [G *Allopathie* < *allo-* + *-pathie* < Gk *állos* other + *-patheia* enduring illness] Treating a disease by using remedies that produce a condition different from the condition being treated; the most common

system of medical practice. **—allopathist** (1844). O, R, W [4]

allopelagic, *a. Zool.* [G *allopelagisch* < *allo-* + *pelagisch* < Gk *állos* other + L *pelagicus* < Gk *pélagos* the sea] Of or pertaining to marine organisms living or growing in the surface or at varying depths. R, W [3]

allophanic acid, *n.* (1863) *Chem.* [Transl. of G *Allophansäure* < *Allophan* + *Säure* acid < Gk *allophanés* appearing otherwise, so named because the acid changes color or appearance] An acid like an ester that is found only as a derivative. O, W [3]

alloplasm, *n. Biol.* [Short. of G *alloplasmatisch* < *allo-* + *plasmatisch* < Gk *állos* other + *plasmatikós* imitative] Differentiated active protoplasm or certain protoplasmic derivatives. **—alloplasm(at)ic.** W [3]

allopolyploidy, *n.* (1928) *Biol.* [G *Allopolyploidie* (1927) < *allo-* + *Polyploidie* < Gk *állos* other, different + *polýs* much + *-ploos* -fold (as in *manyfold*)] The situation where a polyploid's sets of chromosomes have been derived from at least two different ancestral species. **—allopolyploid,** *n.* (1928) and *a.* (1953). O, R, W [4]

allose, *n. Chem.* [G < *allo-* + *-ose* (a short. of *Glucose*) < Gk *állos* other + *glykýs* sweet + *-ose* denoting a carbohydrate] A sugar that is obtained as a syrup synthetically. W [3]

allothimorph, *n. Geol.* [Orig. formed as G < *allothi-* (< Gk) elsewhere + G *-morph* < Gk *morphé* form] A constituent, as in a metamorphic rock, that preserves its original crystal boundaries. **—allothimorphic.** W [3]

allothogenic, *a.* (1888) *Geol.* Var. **allothigenic, allothigenous, allothogenous** [G *allothigen* (1880) < *allo-* + *-thigen* < Gk *állothi* elsewhere + *génein* to generate + E *-ic*] Formed in a place different from where found, as in clastic rocks: allogenic. O, W [3]

allotriomorphic, *a.* (1887) *Mineral.* [G *allotriomorph* (1886) < *allotrio-* + *-morph* < Gk *allotriós* belonging to another + *morphé* form + E *-ic*] Not possessing a characteristic form because of special circumstances. **—allotriomorphically** (1888). O, R, W [3]

allotriophagy, -ies *pl. Med.* Var. **allotriophagia** [G *Allotriophagie* < *allotrio-* + *-phagie* < Gk *allotriós* strange, foreign + *phageîn* to eat] Pica, a desire for and eating of unnatural substances. O, W [3]

alloxan, *n.* (1853) *Chem.* [G (1838) < a short. and combining of *Allantoin* allantoin (q.v.) + *Oxalsäure* oxalic acid (so named because these are its constituents) + *-an* -an] A crystalline compound, formed by oxidizing uric acid, that causes diabetes mellitus. **—alloxanate,** *n.* (1863); **alloxanic,** *a.* (1863); **allox-.** O, R, W [4]

alloxanic acid, *n.* (1863) *Chem.* [Transl. of G *Alloxansäure* (1838) < *Alloxan* alloxan (q.v.) + *Säure* acid] A crystalline acid obtained by hydrolyzing alloxan. O, W [3]

alloxantin, *n.* (1853) *Chem.* [G < *Alloxan* alloxan (q.v.) + connective *-t-* + *-in* -in] A crystalline compound obtained by oxidizing uric acid or from the reaction of alloxan and dialuric acid. O, W [3]

alluaudite, *n. Mineral.* [G *Alluaudit,* named after François *Alluaud* (1815–65), French mineralogist + G *-it* -ite] A rare phosphate of sodium, iron, and manganese. W [3]

alnoite, *n. Geol.* [G *Alnoit,* named after the Swedish island

Alnö + G -*it* -ite] A rare basaltic rock of the composition of a melilite-basalt. W [3]

alp¹, *n.* (1827) [G *Alp(e)* mountain pasture < MHG *albe* < OHG *albun, alpun* < L *Alpes*] A mountain pasture (this is different from the old meaning of "high mountain"). O, W [4]

alp², *n.* (1836) [G < OHG *alp, alb* mysterious being, demon] Nightmare. O [3]

alpenglow, *n.* (1871) *Meteor.* [Prob. < partial transl. of G *Alpenglühen* < *Alpen* (ult. < L) Alps + *Glühen* glow] A reddish glow or entire light phenomenon observable near sunset or sunrise on an Alpine summit or on any other mountain. O, R, W [4]

alpenhorn, *n.* (1864) *Music* Var. **alphorn, alpine horn** [G < the comb. form of *Alp* (ult. < L) Alp + *Horn* horn, ult. < Gk *kéras*] A straight horn with a cupped mouthpiece used by Swiss herdsmen. —**alp(en)horn,** *a.* (1895). O, R, W [4]

alpenrose, *n.* (1914) *Bot.* [G < the comb. form of *Alp* (ult. < L) Alp + *Rose* rose < L *rosa*] Rose of the Alps, the common name for at least two species of Alps rhododendron. O [3]

alpenstock, *n.* (1829) *Sports* [G < the comb. form of *Alp* (ult. < L) Alp + *Stock* staff, stick] A long, metal-pointed staff orig. used in the Alps and now in mountain climbing anywhere. O, R, W [4]

alpenstocker, *n.* (1864) *Sports* [G < the comb. form of *Alp* (ult. < L) Alp + *Stock* staff, stick + *-er* -er] One who uses an alpenstock (q.v.): a mountain climber. O [3]

alphorn and **alpine horn,** *see* alpenhorn

alraun, *n. Bot.* [G *Alraun(wurzel)* < *Alb, Alp* mysterious being + *raunen* to speak mysteriously (in whispers) (+ *Wurzel* root)] The mandrake root, formerly used in magic or as an aphrodisiac. W [3]

alsbachite, *n. Geol.* [G *Alsbachit,* named after *Alsbach,* a village in Germany + *-it* -ite] A porphyritic aplite often containing garnets. W [3]

als ob, -ø *pl. Philos.* [G < *als* as + *ob* if, as frequently used by Kant] An assumption, esp. one made to permit thought, action, or further assumption. • ~ is transl. as **as if** (1892). W [3]

altaite, *n. Mineral.* [G *Altait,* named after *Altai,* an Asian mountain range + G -*it* -ite] Lead telluride. O, W [3]

althaein/althein, *n. Bot.* [Orig. formed as G *Althein* < NL *Althaea* a genus name of *Althaea rosea* + G -*in* -in] A crystalline pigment derived from the hollyhock. W [3]

althorn, *n.* (1859) *Music* Var. **alto horn** [G < *alt* alto (< It *alto*) + *Horn* horn, ult. < Gk *kéras*] An instrument of the saxhorn family; an alto or tenor saxhorn. O, R, W [4]

Altmann's granules, *pl. Med.* [Transl. of G *Altmannsche granula* < the name of Richard *Altmann* (1852–1901), German histologist + G *Granula* (< L) granules] Minute granules in protoplasm, equated with mitochondria. W [3]

aluminite, *n.* (1868) *Mineral.* [G *Aluminit* (1807) < *Aluminium* aluminum < L *alūmen* (gen. *alūminis*) alum + G -*it* -it, so named because of its natural occurrence in alum earth] An opaque, hydrous aluminum sulfate; also called *websterite.* O, R, W [3]

aluminothermy, *n.* (1900) *Chem.* [G *Aluminothermie* (1900) < *alumino-* + -*thermie* < the comb. form of L *alūmen* (see *alūminite*) + Gk *thérmē* warmth, heat] A

process that produces high temperatures by combining aluminum and oxygen. —**aluminothermic(s)** (1904, 1904), **aluminothermic process** (1916). O, R, W [3]

Alypin, *n.* (1905) *Med.* Var. **alypine** (1908) [G (1905) < *alyp-* + -*in* -in < Gk *álypos* painless] A trademark for a glycerin derivative used as a local anesthetic. O [3]

Alzheimer's disease, *n.* (1912) *Med.* [Transl. of G *Alzheimersche Krankheit* < the name of Alois *Alzheimer* (1864–1915), German neurologist + *Krankheit* disease] Presenile dementia. O, R, W [4]

Amanist, *n. Theol.* Var. **Amanite** [Short. of G *Amana-Gesellschaft* Amana Society < the biblical name *Amana* for a range of the Lebanon mountains (see *Songs of Solomon,* 4:8) + E -*ist*] A member of the communal Amana Church Society developed in Germany in 1714, and finally located at Amana, Iowa, in 1855. • *DA* cites **Amana Society** (1885) and **Amanite** (pre-1901). R, W [3]

amanitin(e), *n.* (1847) *Chem.* [G *Amanitin,* named after *Amanita* (prob. < Gk *amanîtai*) the genus of death angel + G -*in* -ine] A poisonous cyclic peptide produced by the death cup that selectively inhibits RNA polymerase in mammalian cells. O [3]

amarantite, *n.* (1890) *Mineral.* [G *Amarantit* (1888) < *Amarant,* the name of a plant of the genus of foxtail plants (< Gk *amárantos* immortal) + G -*it* -ite] A brownish-red, hydrous ferric sulfate. O [3]

amarelle, *n. Bot.* [G < ML *amarellum* < L *amārus* bitter, sour] Any of various cultivated cherries derived from the sour cherry, as distinguished from the morellos. R, W [3]

ambivalence, *n.* (1912) *Psych.* Var. **ambivalency** (1912) [G *Ambivalenz* (1910–11) < *ambi-* + *Valenz* < L *ambi-* from both sides + *valēns* (gen. *valēntis*) strong, powerful] A person's having coexisting, contradictory feelings or attitudes, such as love and hatred, toward someone or something; continual oscillation, as between two opposite things; uncertainty as to which attitude, method, or treatment to follow. O, R, W [4]

ambivalent, *a.* (1916) *Psych.* [G < *ambi-* + -*valent*—see *ambivalence*] Distinguished or motivated by, or showing or suggesting ambivalence; extended to literary and general use. —**ambivalently.** O, R, W [4]

amblygonite, *n.* (c.1828 *W9*) *Mineral.* [G *Amblygonit* (1817) < *Amblygon* (< Gk *amblygónios* obtuse-angled) + G -*it* -ite] A basic lithium aluminum phosphate; also called *hebronite.* O, R, W [4]

amboceptor, *n.* (1902) *Biochem.* [G < *ambo-* + -*ceptor* < L *ambo-* both + *receptor* receiver] (From Paul Ehrlich's immunization theory) an intermediary body or antibody that acts as a detached receptor; a lytic antibody used for complement-fixation testing. O, R, W [4]

ambos, -es *pl. Anat.* [G *Amboß* anvil < OHG *anaboz*] An incus, the middle bone of the chain of three small bones in mammals' ears. W [3]

amelcorn, -ø *pl.* (1578) *Bot.* [G *Amelkorn* < L *amylum* starch + G *Korn* grain < MHG, OHG *korn*] Emmer, a poor type of wheat cultivated in Europe for starch. O, W [3]

Amerika, *n.* (1969) *Politics* Var. **Amerikkka** (1970) [G *Amerika*] The racist or fascist aspect of American society. —**Amerik(kk)an,** *a.* (1969) < the distorted use of the German spelling of *America,* by likening the U.S. to Nazi (q.v.) Germany or by spelling the word by including the initial letters of *Ku Klux Klan.* O [3]

amide, *n.* (c.1847 *W9*) *Chem.* [G *Amid* < *Am-* (< *Ammoniak* ammonia) + *-id* (< Fr or L *-id*) *-ide*] Any of a class of crystalline compounds obtained from ammonia; the generic name of various compound ammonias or amines. — **amidic** (1877). O, R, W [4]

Amidol, *n.* (1892 *W9*) *Chem.* [G a trademark, an anagram of *Diaminophenol*] A colorless crystalline salt used in photographic developing. O, R, W [4]

amidone, *n.* (1946) *Chem.* [Prob. < G *Amidon,* a short. of Dimethyl*amino-d*iphenyl-heptan*on*] Methadone, a narcotic. O, W [3]

aminophenol, *n.* (1906) *Chem.* Var. **amino phenol** [G < *amino-,* the comb. form of *Amin* + *Phenol*] One of three crystalline compounds obtained from phenol, used in dyes and photographic developing; any amino derivative of a phenol. O, R, W [4]

Amish, *a.* (1844) *Theol.* [G *amisch* < the name of Jacob *Amman* or *Amen* (fl. 1693), a Swiss Mennonite bishop + G *adj. suffix -isch -ish*] Concerning or belonging to a sect of Mennonite followers of Amman that moved to America. O, R, W [4]

Amish, *n.* (1884) *Theol.* [G *Amische(r)* Amish] The Amish (q.v.) people. —**Amishman.** O, R, W [4]

amitotic, *a.* (1888) *Biol.* [G *amitotisch* (1882) < *a-* + *mitot-* + *-isch -ic* < NL *amitosis* < Gk *a-* not + *mítos* thread, filament] Of or relating to a division of a nucleus and thus of a cell without mitosis. —**amitotically** (1894), **amitosis** (1894). O, W [3]

amman, *n.* *Politics* [(Swiss) G *Ammann* < a blend of G *Amt* office + *Mann* man] A district officer in certain Swiss cantons. WN20 [2]

ammine, *n.* (1897) *Chem.* [G *Ammin* (1897) < *Ammoniak* ammonia + *-in -ine*] A compound with ammonia or possibly an amine considered as a coordination complex; an ammonia molecule existing in a coordination complex. O, R, W [4]

ammino-, *comb. form Chem.* [Prob. < G < *Ammin* ammine (q.v.)] Ammine, as in *amminochloride.* W [3]

amorphism, *n.* (1852) *Chem.* [G *Amorphismus* < *amorph* + *-ismus* (< L) *-ism* < Gk *ámorphos* want of a regular form] Lacking a crystalline or regular form, as in amorphous minerals. O, R, W [4]

amphikaryon, *n.* *Biol.* [G < *amphi-* + *Karyon* < Gk *amphi-* both-sided, roundabout + *káryon* nut kernel] A cell nucleus with two haploid groups of chromosomes. —**amphikaryotic** (1909). R, W [3]

ampulla of Vater, *n.* *Anat.* [Transl. of G *Vatersche Ampulle,* named after Abraham *Vater* (1684–1751), German anatomist + *Ampulla* a globular vessel < L *ampulla,* the dim. of *amphora,* an ancient oval-bodied vessel] A trumpet-mouthed dilatation of the duodenal wall. W [3]

amsel/amzel, *n.* (1705) *Zool.* (archaic) [G < MHG *amsel,* OHG *ams(a)la* < unknown origin] A blackbird or ring ouzel, i.e., a thrush. O [3]

amyloid, *a.* (1857) *Chem.,* (1859) *Path.* [G (1839) < *amyl-* + *-oid* < L *amylum* starch + Gk *-oeidēs* similar] *Chem.*: having the form or nature of starch or gelatinous hydrated cellulose; *Path.*: applied to a form of degeneration of various organs. —**amyloid,** *n.* (1872); **amyloid degeneration**

(1859); **amyloidal,** *a.* (1872); **amyloidosis** (1900). O, R, W [4]

amzel, *see* amsel

anamesite, *n.* (1876) *Geol.* [G *Anamesit* (1832) < *anames-* + *-it -it* < Gk *anámesos* of medium size] A fine-grained type of basalt. O [3]

anapaite, *n. Mineral.* [G *Anapait,* named after *Anapa,* seaport on the Black Sea + G *-it -ite*] A calcium ferrous iron hydrous phosphate. W [3]

anaphase, *n.* (1887) *Biol.* [G (1884) < *ana-* + *Phase* < Gk *aná* back, again + *phásis* phenomenon] A late stage in mitosis, when the chromosome halves move apart toward the opposite poles. —**anaphasic.** O, R, W [3]

anarthria, *n.* (1881) *Med.* [G *Anarthrie* (1867) < NL *anarthria* < Gk *anarthrós* lacking in strength] A person's severely defective articulation eventuating in speechlessness. —**anarthric,** *a.* (1889). O, R, W [3]

anastigmat, *n.* (1890) *Optics* [G back-formation < *anastigmatisch* anastigmatic (q.v.)] An anastigmatic lens or lens system. O, R, W [4]

anastigmatic, *a.* (1890) *Optics* Var. **anastigmat** (1902) [G *anastigmatisch* < *ana-* + *-stigmat* + *-isch -ic* < Gk *an-* not + *a-* not + *stígma* (gen. *stígmatos*) dot] Free of astigmatism, as in lens that corrects the aberration. O, R, W [4]

anauxite, *n.* (1850) *Mineral.* [G *Anauxit* (1838) < *an-* + *-auxit* < Gk *anauxés* not increasing + G *-it -ite*] A hydrous aluminum silicate found in certain clays. O, W [3]

anchieuctetic, *a. Geol.* [G *anchi-eutektisch* < *anchi-* + *eutektisch* < Gk *ánchi* almost + *eútēktos* easily melted + G *-isch -ic*] Containing minerals in essentially eutectic proportions. W [3]

andesine, *n.* (1862) *Mineral.* [G *Andesin,* named after the *Andes,* a mountain range in South America + G *-in -ine*] A triclinic feldspar. —**andesinic, andesinite.** O, R, W [3]

andesite, *n.* (1850) *Geol.* [G *Andesit,* named after the *Andes,* a mountain range in South America + G *-it -ite*] An extrusive rock consisting principally of oligoclase or andesine feldspar with one or more mafic minerals. —**andesitic** (1876). O, R, W [4]

andorite, *n. Mineral.* [G *Andorit,* named after *Andor* von Semsey (1833–1923), Hungarian nobleman + G *-it -ite*] A prismatic compound of silver, antimony, lead, and sulfur. W [3]

androgenesis, *n.* (c.1900 *W9*) *Biol.* [G *Androgenese* (1891) < *andro-* + *-genese* < Gk *anér* (gen. *andrós*) man + *génesis* origin, generation] Male parthenogenesis, the development of an individual from a male cell. —**androgenetic** (1918), **-genetically, -genous.** O, W [3]

andromedotoxin, *n.* (1883) *Pharm.* [G (1882), a compound < *Andromeda* (< NL), the name of a mythological Ethiopian princess who was fastened to a rock for a sea monster to devour but was rescued by Perseus + G *Toxin* an organic poison < Gk *tóxon* arrow] A poisonous crystalline amaroid found in some ericaceous plants, esp. of the genus *Andromeda.* O, W [3]

androsterone, *n.* (1934) *Chem.* [G *Androsteron* (1931) < *andro-* + *Steron* < Gk *anér* (gen. *andrós*) man, human being + *stéreos* firm, limited] An androgenic hormone, found esp. in male humans' urine. —**androstane.** O, R, W [4]

anemonin, *n.* (1842) *Chem.* [G < *anemon-* + *-in* -in < NL *anemone* (< Gk) anemone] An acrid, toxic, crystallizable dilactone obtained from plants of the genera Anemone and Ranunculus. O, W [3]

aneuploid, *a.* (1931) *Biol.* [G (1922) < *an-* + *-euploid* < Gk *an-* not + *eú* < *eús* good + *diplóos* double, twofold] The chromosomic state of not being euploid. —**aneuploid**, *n.* (1939). O, W [4]

aneuploidy, *n.* (1934) *Biol.* [G *Aneuploidie* < *an-* + *-euploid* + *-ie* -y —see *aneuploid*] An aneuploid condition. O, W [4]

angioneurosis, -oses *pl.* (1887) *Med.* [G *Angioneurose* (1882) < *angio-* + *Neurose* < Gk *angeîon* vessel + *neûron* nerve] An intermittent, severe edematous condition due to unstable vasomotor reactions. —**angioneurotic** (1887). O [3]

Anglist, *n.* (1888) *Ling., Lit.* [G inhabitant of *Anglia* < ML *angli* < L *Anglii* Angles, inhabitants of Anglia + G *-ist* -ist] Anglicist, a student of or an expert in English language and literature. O, R, W [4]

Anglistics, *n.* (1930) *Ling., Lit.* [G *Anglistik* English language and literature (see *Anglist*)] The study of the English language and/or literature, O, R, W [3]

angora, *n.* (1819) *Zool.* Var. **Angora** [Prob. < G, named after a town in Asia Minor (now *Ankara*, capital of Turkey), as in *Angorakatze* Angora cat, *Angorakaninchen* Angora rabbit, *Angorawolle* Angora wool] A species of goat or its silklike wool, a long-haired type of rabbit or its fine white fur, or a fabric made from this fur, all named for the town *Angora*. —**Angora**, *a.;* **Angora cat** (1819)/**goat** (1833)/**rabbit** (1849)/**wool** (1875); **angola** (1867). O, R, W [4]

angst, ängste *pl.* (1849) *Psych.* [G fear, concern, sense of danger] Anxiety, anguish, neurotic fear. • ~ appears in adj. compounds like **angst-forming** (1944)/**-ridden** (1958)/**-wrought** (1958). O, R, W [4]

angster, *n.* *Currency* [G < a folk-etymological short. of G *Angesichter*, pl. of *Angesicht* face, countenance < MHG *angster* < ML *angustus* thin] An old Swiss copper coin. W [3]

anhydrite, *n.* (1831) *Mineral.* [G *Anhydrit*, named by Abraham B. Werner (1749–1817), German mineralogist < *anhydr-* + *-it* -ite < an ad. of Gk *ánhydros* waterless] An anhydrous calcium sulfate. O, R, W [3]

anilide, *n.* (1863) *Chem.* [G *Anilid*, a blend of *Anilin* analine (< Ar *anil* dark blue) + G *Amid* amide (q.v.)] A type of amide; an N-acyl derivative of aniline; arylide. —**anilidic**. O, R, W [3]

aniline, *n.* (1850) *Chem.* Var. **anilin** [G *Anilin* (1826) < *anil-* + *-in* -ine < Ar *anil* dark blue < Skt *nīlī* indigo] An oily toxic amine important in industry and the arts as the source of pharmaceuticals, resins, and numerous beautiful dyes. • ~ appears in initial or terminal position in many compounds like **aniline dye** (1864)/**black/series** and **rosaniline** (1872), and **chrysaniline** (1875). O, R, W [4]

animal magnetism, *n.* (1784) *Med.* [Transl. of G *animalischer Magnetismus* (1775), coined by Friedrich Anton Mesmer (1734–1815), German physician < *animalisch* animalistic + *Magnetismus* (< NL) magnetism] Mesmerism, a spiritlike force; in Christian science, error or mortal mind. —**animal magnetist** (1792). O, R, W [4]

animism, *n.* (1832) *Anthrop.* [G *Animismus* (1720) < *anim(i)-* + *-ismus* -ism < L *anima* soul + *-ismus*] The doctrine advanced by the German philosopher Georg Ernest Stahl (1660–1734) asserting that the immaterial soul is the vital principle underlying all organic development; attribution of a living soul to every concrete form of reality (stones, plants); belief in a spiritual world or spiritualism. O, R, W [4]

ankerite, *n.* (1843) *Mineral.* [G *Ankerit*, named after Mathias Joseph *Anker* (1771–1843), Austrian mineralogist + G *-it* -ite] A variety of dolomite, in which the magnesium is mainly replaced by iron. O, R, W [3]

anlage, -n/-s *pl.* (1892) *Biol.* [G hereditary factor, (pre)disposition < *anlegen* to establish] The initial development of cells in an embryo. O, R, W [4]

anlaut, -e/-s *pl.* (1881) *Ling.* [G initial sound] The initial sound or position of a word or syllable. O, R, W [3]

anlauting, *a.* (1884) *Ling.* [Ad. of G *Anlauten* < *anlauten* to serve as the initial sound] Functioning as the initial sound of a word or syllable. O [3]

annabergite, *n.* (1837) *Mineral.* [G *Annabergit*, named after *Annaberg*, a town and mountain in Saxony, Germany + *-it* -ite] A hydrous nickel cobalt arsenate. O, R, W [4]

anomalist, *n.* (1860) *Ling.* [Poss. < G < *anomal-* + *-ist* -ist < Gk *anómalos* irregular] An advocate of certain early Greek grammarians' view that in language the connection between the word and the idea is arbitrary. —**anomalistic** (1882). O, W [3]

anomaloscope, *n.* (1923) *Optics* [G *Anomaloskop* (1898) < *anomalo-* + *-skop* < L *anōmalus* (< Gk) irregular + Gk *skōpé* viewer] An instrument invented by the German optical scholar Wilibald Nagel (1870–1911) that tests color vision. O, W [3]

anomite, *n.* *Mineral.* [G *Anomit* < *anom-* + *-it* -ite < L *anōmalus* (< Gk) irregular] A variety of mica that differs optically from ordinary biotite. R, W [3]

anorganology, *n.* (1876) *Chem.* [G *Anorganologie* < *anorgano-* + *-logie* < Gk *anórganos* without organs + *lógos* word, study] That part of natural science concerned with inorganic objects and phenomena explicable by chemical and mechanical principles. O [3]

anorthoclase, *n.* *Mineral.* [G *Anorthoklas* < *anortho-* + *-klas* < Gk *an-* not + *orthós* straight + *klásis* break] A feldspar, mainly of sodium potassium aluminum silicate, which is triclinic rather than the monoclinic found in orthoclase. R, W [3]

Anschauung, -en *pl.* (1856) *Philos.* [G point of view, perception < *anschauen* to look at + *-ung* -ing] Sensory intuition; in Kantian philosophy, the part of knowledge that is derived directly from sense awareness; an attitude or point of view. • ~ is loosely transl. as **intuition**. O, R, W [3]

Anschluss, -es *pl.* (1924) *Politics* [G *Anschluß* joining, connection, annexation] Annexation or union, as of Austria to Germany in 1938 or of Tibet to China; (extended to) economic union. —**anschluss**, *v.* (1945). O, R, W [4]

an sich (1846) *Philos.* [G in itself, as such < *Ding an sich* the thing in itself] In itself; abstractly, without reference to anything else. O [3]

anstoss, -stösse *pl.* *Philos.* [G *Anstoß* resistance, objection] In the philosophy of Johann Gottlieb Fichte (1762–1814),

German philosopher, any of up to six successive steps whereby the absolute ego is limited or checked and thus gains self-knowledge. R [3]

anthocyanidin, *n.* (1914) *Chem.* [G (now *Anthozyanidin*) (1913) < *antho-* + *Zyanidin* < Gk *ánthos* flower + L *cyanus*, Gk *kýaneos* dark blue + G *-in* -in with an infixed *-d-*] A sugar-free plant pigment formed by hydrolyzing an anthocyanin. O, W [4]

anthropogeography, *n.* (1895) *Geogr.* [G *Anthropogeographie* (1882) < *anthropo-* + *Geographie* < Gk *ánthrōpos* man + *gê* earth + *gráphein* to write, describe] The branch of geography that deals with the relations of the earth to humans and its other inhabitants. —**anthropogeographer** (1899), **-geographic(al)** (1940, 1939). O, R, W [3]

anthroposophy, *n.* (1916 W9) *Philos.* [G Anthroposophie (1913) < *anthropo-* + *-sophie* < Gk *ánthrōpos* man + *sophía* wisdom] A spiritual, mystical doctrine developed from the teachings of Rudolf Steiner (1861–1925), Austrian social philosopher (this is different from the meaning of "knowledge of human nature and wisdom"). —**anthroposophical** (1914), **-sophist** (1916), **-sophic.** O, R, W [4]

antibody, -ies *pl.* (1901) *Physiol.* [Transl. of G *Antikörper* < *anti-* (< Gk) against + G *Körper* body < L *corpus*] Any globulin, either naturally present in the body or produced by infection or administered antigens, which reacts with antigens; extended to human life in general; also called *immunoglobulin.* O, R, W [4]

antiferromagnetic, *a.* (1936) *Chem.* [G *antiferromagnetisch* (1936) < *anti-* + *ferromagnetisch* < Gk *antí* against + L *ferrum* iron + *māgnēs* (gen. *māgnētis*) < Gk *líthos magnétēs* magnet stone, actually stone from *Magnesia,* a region in ancient Greece] Magnetic behavior where there is thought to be oppositely directed alignment of electron spin. —**antiferromagnetism** (1938). O, R, W [4]

antigen, *n.* (1908) *Biochem.* [G (1905) < *anti-* + *-gen* < Fr *antigène* < Gk *antí* against + *génos* type] A protein or carbohydrate substance that, upon being introduced into the body, helps produce an antibody; a substance that reacts with an antibody to form a complement. —**antigenic(ally)** (1913, 1946), **antigenicity** (1946). O, R, W [4]

antigorite, *n.* (1862) *Mineral.* [G *Antigorit,* named after *Antigorio,* a valley in the Italian Piedmont + G *-it* -ite] A lamellar variety of serpentine. —**antigoritic.** O, R, W [3]

anting, *n.* (1936) *Ornith.* [Transl. of G *Einemsen* (1935) < *ein* in + *Ameisen* ants, i.e., the act of rubbing in insects] The action of birds in rubbing live ants or other insects onto their plumage. —**ant,** back-formed as *v.* (1944). O, W [4]

antipyrine, *n.* (1884) *Chem.* Var. **antipyrin** (1884) [G *Antipyrin* (1884) < the G trademark < *anti-* + *-pyrin* < Gk *antí* against + *pyretós* fever] The commercial name of an antipyretic, analgesic derivative of pyrazolone. O, W [4]

apachite, *n.* *Geol.* [G *Apachit,* named after the *Apache* Mountains, Texas, U.S.A. + G *-it* -ite] A phonolithic rock containing much amphibole and enigmatite. W [3]

apatite, *n.* (1803) *Mineral.* [G *Apatit* (1786) < *apat-* + *-it* -ite < Gk *apátē* deceit] One of a group of calcium phosphates containing other elements or radicals, used as a fertilizer. —**carbonate/chlora-/hydroxyl apatite.** O, R, W [4]

aphrite, *n.* (1868) *Mineral.* [G *Aphrit* < *aphr-* + *-it* -ite

< Gk *aphrós* foam] A pearly type of carbonate of calcite. O, W [3]

aphr(o)-, *comb. form* [G *aphr-* < Gk *aphrós*] Foam, as in *aphrite, aphrometer.* W [3]

aphrosiderite, *n.* *Mineral.* [G *Aphrosiderit* (1847) < *aphro-* + *Siderit* < Gk *aphrós* foam + *sídēros* iron + G *-it* -ite] A hydrous silicate of the chlorite group. O, W [3]

apjohnite, *n.* (1847) *Mineral.* [G *Apjohnit,* named after James *Apjohn* (1796–1886), Irish chemist + G *-it* -ite] A manganese aluminum sulfate. O, W [3]

aplanat, *n.* (1890) *Optics* [G (1866), back-formed from *aplanatisch* aplanatic (q.v.)] A lens corrected for spherical aberration. —**aplanat,** *a.* (1951). O, W [4]

aplanatic, *a.* (1794) *Optics* [G *aplanatisch* < *aplanat-* + *-isch* -ic < Gk *aplánētos* free of blemish] Concerning a lens that has no spherical aberration. —**aplanatism** (1869), **aplanatically.** O, R, W [4]

aplite, *n.* (1879) *Geol.* Var. **aplit** (1879), **haplite** [Prob. < G *Aplit,* a variant of *Haplit* < *hapl-* + *-it* -ite < Gk *haploós* simple, single] A fine-grained differentiation rock used in making glass, enamel, etc. —**aplitic.** O, R, W [4]

apozymase, *n.* (1926) *Chem.* [G (1925) < *apo-* + *Zymase* < Gk *apó* down, away + *zýmē* yeast + *-ase* denoting a destroying substance] The protein part of a zymase. O, W [3]

appersonation, *n.* *Psych.* Var. **appersonification** [Transl. of G *Appersonierung* < *ap-* + *Person* + *-ierung* -tion < L *ad* up to, to(ward) + *persōna* mask, *persōnātus* person represented by the mask] The incorporating of characteristics of persons or external objects by means of ego extension. —**appersonate,** *v.* R, W [3]

apple strudel, *n.* (1923) *Food* Var. **apfelstrudel** (1936) [Partial transl. of G *Apfelstrudel* < *Apfel* apple + *Strudel* strudel (q.v.)] A baked spicy mixture of apples wrapped in flaky pastry; strudel. O [3]

aprotic, *a.* (1931) *Chem.* [G *aprotisch* (1930) < *a-* + *prot-* + *-isch* -ic < Gk *a-* not + *prōton,* neuter of *prōtos* first] A liquid incapable of acting as a proton donor or acceptor or as an acid or a base. —**aprotic solvent** (1965). O, R, W [3]

araban, *n.* (1892) *Chem.* [Ad. of G *arabisch* Arabic (ult. < Ar) + E *-an*] A pentosan that yields arabinose upon hydrolysis. O, R, W [3]

aragonite, *n.* (1803) *Mineral.* [G *Aragonit* (1800), named after *Aragon,* a province in Spain + G *-it* -ite] A lime carbonate, crystallizing in orthorhombic prisms. —**aragonitic.** O, R, W [4]

arcanite, *n.* *Mineral.* [G *Arcanit* (now *Arkanit*) < NL *arcanum* < L *arcānus* mysterious, hidden + G *-it* -ite] Potassium sulfate, also called *aphthitalite.* O, W [3]

ardealite, *n.* *Mineral.* [G *Ardealit,* named after *Ardeal,* a region in Transylvania, Rumania + G *-it* -ite] A hydrous acid calcium phosphate-sulfate. W [3]

ardennite, *n.* *Mineral.* [G *Ardennit,* named after the *Ardennes,* a mountain range in Belgium + G *-it* -ite] A crystalline vanadosilicate of aluminum and manganese. W [3]

arendalite, *n.* (1868) *Mineral.* [G *Arendalit* (1800), named after *Arendal,* a town in Norway + G *-it* -ite] A variety of epidote. O, W [3]

Arg, *see* arginine

argentite, *n.* (1837) *Mineral.* [G *Argentit* < L *argentum* silver + G -*it* -ite] A native silver sulfide occurring in veins in granite, etc.; also called *silver glance*. O, R, W [4]

arginase, *n*. (1904) *Biol.* [G (1904) < a combining of *Arginin* arginine (q.v.) (< L *argentum* silver) + G -*ase*, denoting a destroying substance] A crystalline enzyme capable of hydrolyzing arginine into urea and ornithine. O, R, W [4]

arginine, *n*. (1886) *Biol.* Var. **arginin** (1919) [G *Arginin* (1886) < *argin*- (< Gk *arginóeis* bright, white) + G -*in* -ine] A basic amino acid occurring in many animal proteins (as in rats) and some vegetable tissues. • ~ is short. to **Arg.** O, R, W [4]

argyrodite, *n*. (1886) *Mineral.* [G *Argyrodit* (1886) < Gk *argyrodés* rich in silver + G -*it* -ite] A mineral containing silver, germanium, and sulfur. O, W [3]

Armenoid, *a*. (1899) *Anthrop.* [G (1892) < a blend of *Armenier* Armenian (< L *Armenia*) + -*oid* < Gk -*oeidēs* similar] Of or relating to the eastern branch of Alpine people of ancient west Asia. —**Armenoid,** *n*. (1911). O [3]

arnimite, *n*. *Mineral.* [G *Arnimit,* named after the von *Arnim* family, owners of a mine near Planitz, Germany + -*it* -ite] A basic copper carbonate. W [3]

arpeggione, *n*. (1879) *Music* [G < It *arpeggio* production of the tones of a chord in succession < *arpeggiare* to play the harp < *arpa* harp < LL *harpa* < Gmc **harpa* harp (Mod G *Harfe*)] A bowed instrument of the early 19th century, the size of a cello but with six strings. O, W [3]

arsanilic acid, *n*. (1907) *Chem.* [Transl. of G *Arsanilsäure* (1907), a combining of the clipping *Arsan* (< Gk *arsenikón* arsenic) + G *Anilin* (< Fr *anil* indigo plant) + G *Säure* acid] A para isomer used in preparing organic arsenical medicines. O, W [3]

arsoite, *n*. *Geol.* [G *Arsoit,* named after *Arso,* a mountain on the Italian island of Ischia + G -*it* -ite] A dark-gray, porous trachyandesite. W [3]

Artenkreis, -e/-es *pl. Biol.* [G < *Arten,* pl. of *Art* type, species + *Kreis* circle, group] A group of species that replace one another in geographic succession and presumably ult. stem from a common ancestral form. W [3]

aryl, *n*. (1906) *Chem.* [Prob. < G *Arryl* (now *Aryl*) (1899), a blend of *aromatisch* aromatic (< L *aromat*- < Gk) + -*yl* -yl] A monovalent, aromatic hydrocarbon radical like phenyl, obtained from an arene; a compound formed from one or more aryl radicals and a metal. —**arylation** (1918), **arylate, arylene, arylide, aryloxy, arylamine.** O, R, W [4]

arzrunite, *n*. *Mineral.* [G *Arzrunit,* named after Andreas *Arzruni* (1847–98), German mineralogist + -*it* -ite] A basic copper sulfate with incrusted copper chloride. W [3]

aschaffite, *n*. *Geol.* [G *Aschaffit,* named after *Aschaffen-* burg, a city in Bavaria, Germany + -*it* -ite] A lamprophyric dike rock with phenocrysts, related to quartz diorites. W [3]

as if (1892) *Philos.* [Transl. of G *als ob* (q.v.)] A rhetorical supposition or assumption, made to permit thought, action, or further assumption. —**as-ifness** (1940). O, W [4]

aspirator, *n*. (1804 *W9*) *Tech.* [G < L *aspīrātus* < *aspīrāre* to inhale, suck + G -*or* -or] A suction device for moving liquids, gases, and some substances through a tube; a suction device to collect material; respirator. O, R, W [4]

aspirin, *n*. (1899) *Med.* [G (1899), coined from *Acetyl* (now *Azetyl*) the radical of CH₃CO- of acetic acid + *Spirsäure* spiraeic acid + -*in* -in] A white crystalline compound, also called *acetylsalicylic acid;* a tablet or dose of this, used worldwide as an antipyretic and analgesic. —**aspirin,** *a*. (1924). O, R, W [4]

astrakhanite, *n*. *Mineral.* Var. **astrakanite** [G *Astrakanit,* named after *Astrakhan,* a city in Russia famed for its wool and cloth + G -*it* -ite] A variety of bloedite (q.v.). W [3]

astrophysics, *n*. (1890) *Astronomy* [G *Astrophysik* < *astro*- + *Physik* (< Gk *ástron* star(s), constellation + L *physica* natural science) + E -*s*] A division of astronomy concerned mainly with the physical, chemical, and evolutionary natures of heavenly bodies. —**astrophysical** (1956), **astrophysicist.** O, R, W [4]

astrosphere, *n*. (1896) *Biol.* [G *Astrosphäre* (1891) < *astro*- + *Sphäre* < Gk *ástron* stars, constellation + *sphaîra* realm] The centrosphere, the central part of the aster, excluding the astral rays; the entire aster, excluding the centrosome. O, R, W [3]

asymbolia, *n*. (1876) *Path.* [G *Asymbolie* (1870) < NL *asymbolia* < L *a*- not + *symbolus* < Gk *symbolía* application, use of symbols] A form of aphasia or one's inability to understand or use previously familiar words or signs, usu. because of brain lesion. O, W [3]

atelestite, *n*. *Mineral.* [G *Atelestit* < Gk *atélestos* incomplete + G -*it* -ite] A basic bismuth arsenite, found in tiny yellow crystals. W [3]

atherosclerosis, -oses *pl*. (1910) *Path.* [G *Atherosklerose* (1904) < *ather(o)*- + *Sklerose* < Gk *athér(e)* groats, porridge + *sklērós* hard, brittle] A stage of arteriosclerosis where there is artheromatous degeneration of blood-vessel walls. —**atherosclerotic,** *a*. and *n*. (1914, 1958); **atherosclerotically.** O, R, W [4]

atlantite, *n*. *Geol.* [G *Atlantit* < *Atlantik* Atlantic + -*it* -ite] A rock of melanocratic nephelite-basalt. W [3]

atlasite, *n*. *Mineral.* [G *Atlasit* (1865) < *Atlas* (< Ar *atlas* smooth, bare) + G -*it* -ite] A copper carbonate containing some chloride, of silky or vitreous luster. O [3]

atoke, *n*. (1896) *Zool.* [Poss. < G (1868) (< Gk *átokos* without offspring) or directly < Gk] The sexless part of certain polychaetous worms. —**atokous** (1896), **atokal** (1904), **atocous.** O, W [3]

atoxyl, *n*. (1906) *Chem.* [G (1902) a trade name derived from the poison in which arrows were dipped < *a*- + *toxyl* < Gk *a*- not + *tóxon* arrow + *hýlē* wood, substance] An organic arsenic compound, formerly used to treat syphilis and sleeping sickness but frequently causing blindness. O, W [3]

atropine, *n*. (1836) *Chem.* [G *Atropin* < NL *Atropa (belladonna)* Belladonna + G -*in* -ine] A poisonous alkaloid occurring in belladonna and in the seeds of the thorn apple, often used in sulfate form as a medication; racemic hyoscyamine. —**atropine,** *a*. (1879); **atropic** (1863); **atropinized** (1875); **atropinism** (1876); **atropinization** (1880); **atropism; atropinize.** O, R, W [4]

Auerbach's plexus, *n*. *Med.* [G *Auerbachscher plexus,* named after Leopold *Auerbach* (1828–97), German anatomist + *Plexus* (< L) web] A network of ganglia and nerve fibers between the circular and longitudinal muscle layers of the intestine. W [3]

Aufgabe, -n *pl*. (1902) *Psych.* [G task, problem < *aufgeben* to assign] In psychology, an experimental task or test; an exercise. O, W [3]

Aufklärer, *pl.* (1801) *Lit.* [G < *aufklären* to enlighten] The members of the Aufklärung (q.v.). O [2]

Aufklärung, *n.* (1801) *Lit.* [G enlightenment < *aufklären* + nom. suffix *-ung* -ment] The 18th-century (German) Age of Reason or Enlightenment. • ~ is trans. as **Enlightenment** (1865). O, R, W [3]

auftakt, *n. Music* [G upbeat < *auf* up + *Takt* beat, measure] Upbeat; anacrusis. • ~ is transl. as **upbeat** (q.v.). W [3]

auftaktigkeit, *n. Music* [G < *Auftakt* auftakt (q.v.) + adj. suffix *-ig* + nom. suffix *-keit,* together, forming an abstract noun] The principle that all musical phrases begin on an upbeat. W [3]

auf Wiedersehen, *interj.* (1885 *W9*) [G transl. of Fr *au revoir* until we see each other again] Au revoir, good-bye. R, W [4]

augelite, *n.* (1868) *Mineral.* [Prob. < G *Augelith* < Gk *augé* brightness, luster + *líthos* stone] A basic aluminum phosphate. O, W [3]

augen, *pl.* (1910) *Geol.* [G eye-shaped masses of quartz or feldspar < the *pl.* of *Auge* eye] A variety of gneissic rock; augengneiss (q.v.). • ~ is transl. as **eye** (1906). O [3]

augend, *n.* (1898) *Math.* [Poss. < G (1898) < L *augendum, augendus* increase] The quantity to which an addend is added. O, R, W [4]

augengneiss, *n.* (1885) *Geol.* [G *Augengneis* < *Augen* eyes + *Gneis* gneiss (q.v.). Porphyritic gneiss. O [3]

augenphilologie, *n. Ling.* [G < *Augen,* pl. of *Auge* eye + *Philologie* philology] Linguistics that misrepresents the phonological facts because of an overemphasis on spelling. W [3]

augitite, *n. Geol.* [Prob. orig. formed as G *Augitit* < *Augit* < Gk *augé* shine, glimmer + G *-it* -ite] An extrusive porphyritic rock essentially composed of augite. W [3]

Augsburg, *a. Theol.* [G *Augsburger,* the attrib. form of *Augsburg,* a city in Bavaria, Germany, famous for the Augsburg Confession (*Augsburger Bekenntnisse,* 1530) and the (Religious) Peace of Augsburg (*Augsburger Religionsfriede,* 1555)] Of or pertaining to the city of Augsburg or the style there. R, W [3]

August(e), *n.* (1910) [Fr (<G) or G *August* < (*der dumme*) *August* addlepate] A type of circus clown with a mainly slapstick routine. O, W [4]

Augustin process, *n. Metall.* [Transl. of G *Augustinverfahren* < the name of *Augustin* Augustin + G *Verfahren* process] A method of extracting silver by converting it into chloride. W [3]

aula¹, -s/-e *pl. Archit.* [G (1617) < L *aula* court, large hall < Gk *aulê*] Assembly hall, as in a German school or university. W [3]

aula², *n. Biol.* [G < NL < L *aula* entrance way < Gk *aulê*] The anterior part of the brain's third ventricle leading to the lateral ventricles. W [3]

auramine, *n.* (1884) *Chem.* Var. **auramin** [G *Auramin* (1884) a proprietary term < *aur-* (< L *aurum* gold) + G *Amin* ammine] A synthetic yellow ketonimine dyestuff, used in coloring paper, biological stains, etc. O, R, W [3]

aurichalcite, *n.* (1844) *Mineral.* [G *Aurichalcit* (now *Au-*

richalzit) (1839) < L *aurichalcum* < Gk *ereíchalcon* golden copper + G *-it* -ite] A pale green or blue basic carbonate of copper and zinc. O, W [3]

aurin, *n.* (1869) *Chem.* Var. **aurine** (1883) [Prob. < G (1861) < *auri-* (< L *aurum* gold) + G *-in* -in(e)] A toxic red dye obtained from triphenylmethane and used as a dye intermediate. O, W [3]

aurochs, -ø/-es *pl.* (1766) *Zool.* Var. **auroch, aurox, urochs** [G (now *Auerochse*) < MHG *ūrochse* ancient ox] European bison: wisent (q.v.); extinct European wild ox: urus (q.v.). O, R, W [4]

aurox, *see* aurochs

Ausgleich, *n. Politics* [G settlement, agreement < *ausgleichen,* lit., to even out, fig., to settle a dispute] The 1867 agreement between Austria and Hungary. R [3]

Ausländer, *n.* (1936 *W9*) *Politics* Var. **auslander, auslander** [G foreigner < *Ausland* foreign country + *-er* -er] Foreigner, stranger. R, W [3]

auslaut, -e/-s *pl.* (1881) *Ling.* [G sound at the end of a word or syllable < *aus* out + *Laut* sound] The final sound or position in a word or syllable. O, R, W [3]

Auslese, -s/-n *pl.* (1851) *Beverages* Var. **auslese** [G selection < *aus* out, from + *Lese* gleaning, vintage] A wine made in Germany from carefully selected ripe grapes; a wine of this official category of German wine. O, R [3]

aussage test, *n. Psych.* [G < *Aussage* deposition, statement < *aussagen* to testify, declare + *Test* test] A test of a subject's reliability of testimony in describing a given event. W [3]

austausch, -e *pl. Meteor.* [G interchange, exchange < *austauschen* to exchange] An atmospheric effect of turbulent motion; the effect of this on the viscosity coefficient for horizontal flow. W [2]

australite, *n.* (1909) *Geol.* [G *Australit* (1901), named after *Australien,* the G variant for *Australia* + *-it* -ite] A form of meteoric glass found in Australia and neighboring areas. O, W [3]

Austric, *a.* (1927) *Ling.* [G *austrisch* (1906) < *austr-* (< L *auster* south) + G *-isch* -ic] Belonging to or concerning a vast language family within which the related Austroasiatic and Austronesian families are considered as subfamilies. O, W [3]

Austronesian, *a.* (1903) *Anthrop.* [G *austronesisch* (1899), a blend of *austro-* (< L *austro-* < *auster* south) + G *polynesisch* relating to Polynesia, ult. < Gk *polýs* many + *nêsos* island] A modern name for the Malayo-Polynesian language family. —**Austronesian,** *n.* O, R, W [4]

autarky, -es *pl.* (1617) *Econ.* [G *Autarkie* < Gk *autárkeia* personal self-sufficiency] Self-sufficiency, independence; a completely self-sufficient national or regional economy. —**autarkic** (1883); **autarkist,** *a.* and *n.* (1938, 1939); **autarkical(ly).** O, R, W [4]

autecology, *n.* (1910) *Ecology* Var. **autoecology** [Ad. of G *Autoökologie* (1898) < *auto-* + *Ökologie* < Gk *autós* self + *oîkos* habitation + *lógos* word, study] The ecological branch that studies the interrelationships between individual organisms or species and their environment. —**autecological** (1926), **autecologic(ally).** O, R, W [4]

authigenic, *a.* (1888) *Geol.* Var. **authigenous** [G *authigen* (1880) < Gk *authigenês* native-born + E *-ic*] Concerning particles in rocks formed by crystallization in the place where the rocks naturally occur. O, R, W [3]

autoagglutination, *n.* (1910) *Biol.* Var. **auto-agglutination** (1910) [G < *auto-* + *Agglutination* < Gk *autós* self + L *agglūtinātio*] Spontaneous agglutination of an individual's red blood cells, esp. that produced by autoantibodies. O, W [3]

autobahn, -s/-en *pl.* (1937) *Transportation* [G < *Auto* automobile + *Bahn* roadway (cf It *autostrada*, which was in E by 1927)] In Germany a fast motorway or turnpike. O, R, W [4]

autobasidiomycete, *n.* (1895) *Biol.* [G *Autobasidiomyzet* (1889) < NL *Autobasidiomycetes* < Gk *autós* self + NL *basidium* basis + Gk *mýkēs* mushroom] A fungus belonging to a subclass of Basidiomycetes, including mushrooms, toadstools, etc. O [3]

autochthonous, *a.* (1900) *Geol.* [G (< Gk) *autóchthōn* (1888) indigenous + E *-ous*] Made of or formed from indigenous material; formed where the rock is found; not displaced by overthrusting (this is different from the old meaning of "native or aboriginal"). —**autochthon,** *n.* (1942). O, R, W [4]

autoecology, *see* autecology

autoeroti(ci)sm, *n.* (1898) *Psych.* Var. **auto-erotism** (1898) [G *Autoërotismus* (1899) < *auto-* + *Erotismus, Erotizismus* (< L *auto* self + Gk *erotikós* concerning love + L *-ismus* -ism)] Sexual gratification aroused or obtained by oneself, as in masturbation; sexual desire without a known external stimulation. —**autoerotic.** O, R, W [4]

autogamy, *n.* (1877) *Bot.* [G *Autogamie* (1876) < *auto-* + *-gamie* < Gk *autós* self + *gameîn* to wed] Self-fertilization, the fecundation of a flower by its own pollen. —**autogamic** (1881). O, R, W [4]

autogeny, -ies *pl.* (1875) *Biol.* Old var. **autogony** (1875) [G *Autogonie* < Gk *autogenés, -gónos* self-produced] A mode of spontaneous generation; self-generation. O, W [4]

autological, *a.* (1926) *Math.* [G *autologisch* (1907) < *auto-* + *-logisch* < Gk *autós* self + *lógos* word] Concerning something's quality or property that is easily discerned from its name. O [3]

autolysis, *n.* (1902) *Biol.* [G *Autolyse* (1900) < *auto-* + *-lysis* < Gk *autós* self + *lýsis* dissolution] The action of self-digestion or disintegration by plant and animal tissues. —**autolytic** (1902); **-lyze,** *v.* (1903); **-lysate,** *n.* (1927); **-lysing** and **-lysed,** *a.* (1932, 1933); **-lysin** (1964). O, R, W [4]

automat, *n.* (1903) *Tech.* Var. **Automat** [G (1520), poss. < Fr *automate*, ult. < Gk *autómatos* self-propelling] Orig. a trademark for a cafeteria where food can be obtained from viewable compartments by inserting a coin or token; automaton, as in a vending machine, receiving receptacle, or a robot. O, R, W [4]

automorphic, *a.* (1888) *Crystal.* [G *automorph* (1885) < *auto-* + *-morph* < Gk *autós* self + *morphē* form, shape + E *-ic*] Idiomorphic, said of a rock whose crystals have the proper form or shape (this is different from the old meaning of "patterned after self"). —**automorphicgranular,** *a.* O, R, W [3]

automorphic function, *n.* (1892) *Math.* [Ad. of G *automorphe Funktion* (1890) < *automorph* (see *automorphic*) + *Funktion* function < L *fūnctio* performance] A function that is unchanged by the substitution of a discontinuous group, regardless of the nature of the group. O [3]

autoportrait(ure), *n.* (1828) *Art* Var. **auto-portrait** (1828) [Transl. of G *Selbstportrait* < G *selbst* self + *Portrait* portrait (< MF, past part. of *portraire*] A self-portrait. O [3]

autopsychic, *a.* (1909) *Psych.* [G *autopsychisch* (1892) < *auto-* + *psychisch* < Gk *autós* self + *psychikós* of the soul] Of or relating to self-consciousness or one's own mind. O, W [3]

autoscope, *n.* (1900) *Anat.* [Prob. < G *Autoskop* < *auto-* + *-skop* < Gk *autós* self + *skopós* viewer] An instrument to record or magnify a body's small, involuntary movements. —**autoscopic.** O, W [4]

autoscopy, *n.* *Anat.* [Prob. < G *Autoskopie* < *auto-* + *-skopie* (see *autoscope*)] Visual hallucination of one's own body image; the use of an autoscope. O, W [3]

autosemantic, *a.* (1929) *Ling.* [G *autosemantisch* (1908) < *auto-* + *semantisch* < Gk *autós* self + *semantikós* significant + G *-isch* -ic] Concerning a word or phrase with a meaning outside a context; meaningful in isolation. O [3]

autotroph, *n.* (1938) *Biol.* Var. **autotrophe** (1938) [G < *auto-* + *-troph* < Gk *autós* self + *trophé* nutrition] An organism capable of self-nourishment: autophyte. —**autotrophy,** *n.*; **autotroph hypothesis.** O, R, W [4]

autotrophic, *a.* (c.1900 W9) *Biol.* [Prob. < G *autotroph* autotroph (q.v.) + E *-ic*] Capable of self-nourishment. —**autotrophically.** O, R, W [4]

auxin, *n.* (1934) *Bot.* [G (1931) < *aux-* + *-in* -in < Gk *aúxein* to increase] Any organic substance that promotes and directs plants' growth; a growth hormone. —**auxinic(al), auxinically.** O, R, W [4]

auxochrome, n. (1893) *Chem.* [G *Auxochrom* (1888) < *auxo-* + *-chrom* < Gk *aúxein* to grow + *chrōma* color] A salt-forming group that, when combined with a chromogen, provides a dye. —**auxochromic** (1892), **auxochromous** (1902). O, R, W [4]

avalite, *n.* (1889) *Mineral.* [G *Avalit* (1884), named after *Avala*, a mountain near Belgrade, Serbia + G *-it* -ite] An earthy green mineral containing chromium oxide. O [3]

Avertin, *n.* (1927) *Med.* [G (1927) a trade name < *avertieren* to avert or ward off] A trademark for the anesthetic tribromoethanol (this is different from the old Fr borrowing that means "a sheep disease or mental disease"). O, R, W [3]

azoimide, *n.* (1891) *Chem.* Var. **azoimid** [G *Azoimid* < *azo-* (< Fr *azote* nitrogen) + G *Imid*, altered from *Amid* amide] Hydrazoic acid, a volatile, explosive liquid. O, R, W [3]

azoprotein, *n.* (1918) *Immunology* [G (1917) < *azo-* + *Protein* < Gk *a-* not + *zōé* life + *prōtos* first] A compound produced by coupling a protein with a diazotized amine, which is sometimes used as a synthetic antigen. O, W [3]

B

bachfisch, *see* backfisch

Bach trumpet, *n.* (1898) *Music* [Ad. of G *Bachtrompete* < the name of Johann Sebastian *Bach* (1685–1750), German composer + *Trompete* trumpet] A three-valved trumpet designed orig. for performing the high trumpet parts of Bach's works and now also for other compositions with high pitch: the clarion trumpet. O, R, W [4]

bacillus, *pl.* **bacilli** (c.1879 W9) *Biol.* [G *Bazillus* (1872) < NL *bacillus* little rod < L *baculus,* a var. of *baculum* rod, stick, coined in this sense, according to *Duden,* by Ferdinand Cohn (1828–98), German bacteriologist] A genus of rod-shaped bacteria producing endospores; (when not cap.) a member of this genus or a disease-producing bacterium. —**bacillicide** (1885), **bacillicidal** (1894), **bacillus Calmette-Guerin, Bacillus thuringiensis.** O, R, W [4]

backfisch, -e *pl.* (1888) Old erron. var. **bachfisch** (1888) [G actually, a fish too small to be boiled but large enough to be baked; fig., a girl between 14 and 17 < *backen* to bake + *Fisch* fish] A bobby-soxer, teen-age girl. O, W [3]

back-formation, *n.* (1889) *Ling.* [Transl. of G *Rückbildung* < *rück-* (comb. form of *zurück* back, again) + *Bildung* formation] The formation of a new word by subtracting a supposed affix from an already existing word, usu. resulting in a change of word class; such a word formed by this analogical process. O, R, W [4]

Backstein, *n.* *Food* Var. **backsteiner** [Short. of G *Backstein-käse* < *Backstein* brick + *Käse* cheese, i.e., Limburger cheese in the form of bricks] A German cheese resembling Limburger brick cheese. W [3]

bacterium, -ria *pl.* (1847) *Med.* [Poss. < G *Bakterium* (1838) (now *Bakterie*) < NL *bacterium* < Gk *baktḗrion,* the dim. of *báktron* stick, staff, prob. first coined in this sense in *Infusoria* (1838) by Christian Gottfried Ehrenberg (1795–1876), German bacteriologist] Any of various unicellular, rod-shaped bacteria without flagella or spores. O, R, W [4]

badger dog, *n.* (1864) *Zool.* [Transl. of G *Dachshund* dachshund (q.v.)] Dachshund: a long-bodied, short-legged dog of an orig. German breed, useful in hunting badgers etc. O, W [3]

Baedeker, *n.* (1863) *Travel* [G (1827) < the name of Karl *Baedeker* (1801–59), German author of European guidebooks] Any of a series of guidebooks published by Baedeker or his successors; any guidebook or handbook. — **Baedeker raid** (1942). O, R, W [4]

baikalite, *n.* (1794) *Mineral.* [G *Baikalit,* named after Lake *Baikal* in southern Siberia + G *-it* -ite] A dark-green variety of hedenbergite. O, W [3]

baikerinite, *n.* *Mineral.* [G *Baikerinit,* a blend of G *Baikerit* (< irreg. form of Lake *Baikal* in southern Siberia) + G *-it* -ite with the insertion of *-in*] A tarry hydrocarbon of which about one-third is baikerite (q.v.). O, W [3]

baikerite, *n.* *Mineral.* [G *Baikerit,* irreg. form of Lake *Bai-* *kal* in southern Siberia + G *-it* -ite] A mineral wax containing ozokerite and other hydrocarbons. O, W [3]

Bakelite, *n.* (1909) *Chem.* [G trademark *Bakelit* (1909) < the name of L H. *Backland* (1863–1944), its Belgian inventor + G *-it* -ite] A trademark for a condensation plastic obtained from phenol or cresol, used for kitchenware, electric insulators, etc. O, R, W [4]

ball lightning, *n.* (1857) *Meteor.* Var. **kugelblitz** (1968) [Transl. of G *Kugelblitz* < *Kugel* ball, sphere + *Blitz* lightning] A very rare type of lightning that appears in the form of blazing spheres that move slowly and disappear without an accompanying sound. O, R, W [4]

balm cricket, *n.* (1783) *Zool.* Var. **balm-cricket** (1783) [By folk etymology and partial transl. of G *Baumgrille* < *Baum* tree + *Grille* cricket] The cicada. O, W [3]

Bandkeramik, *n.* (1921) *Archaeology* [G (1883) < *Band* band + *Keramik* pottery < Gk *keramikē* (*téchnē*)] A European Neolithic pottery with banded decorations. —**band-keramik,** *a.* (1940). • ~ is transl. as **band ceramic** (1936). O, R, W [3]

bandonion/bandoneon, *n.* (1925) *Music* [G *Bandonion* (c. 1845) (now also *Bandoneon*) < the name of its inventor, Heinrich *Band* (1821–60), German musician + *-on* (as in *Harmonika* harmonica + *-ion*/*-eon* to form *Akkordeon*] A square-built button accordion popular in South America. O, W [3]

bantling, *n.* (1593) [Prob. ad. < G *Bänkling* bastard < *Bank* bench + *-ling* -ling, denoting one of a kind or condition, or of youth or smallness, as in the sense of a child begotten on a bench rather than in the marriage bed] Formerly, a bastard; now usu. disparaging for an infant or small child; a brat; fig. in the sense of vices, poor poetry, etc. O, R, W [4]

bar, *n.* (1903) *Meteor.* [G < Gk *báros* weight] A unit of pressure equaling one million dynes per square centimeter; the absolute cgs unit of pressure. O, R, W [4]

barbituric acid, *n.* (1866) *Chem.* [Transl. of G *Barbitur-säure* (1863) < *Barbitur,* irreg. < the name of *Barbara* + *-ur* < L *ūrīna,* Gk *oûron* urine + G *Säure* acid] Malonylurea, a crystalline acid derived from pyrimidine, used as a hypnotic. O, R, W [4]

bargh, *n.* (1693) *Mining* (archaic) [By folk etymology < G *Berg* mountain] A mine. O [3]

barghest, *n.* (1732) *Myth.* Var. **barguest** (1732) [Poss. < G *Berg* mountain + *Geist* demon] A goblin portending misfortune and fabled to appear often as a large, horrible dog. O, R, W [3]

barghmaster, *see* barmaster

barguest, *see* barghest

Barkhausen effect, *n.* (1924) *Physics* Var. **Barkhausen oscillation** (1925) [G *Barkhausen-Effekt* (1919) < the name of the German scientist Heinrich *Barkhausen* (1881–1956) + *Effekt*] The series of short, sudden changes in the magnetization of a substance when the magnetizing force is gradually altered. —**Barkhausen oscillator** (1940). O, R, W [3]

barmaster, *n.* (1662) *Mining* Var. **barghmaster** (1721) [By folk etymology and partial transl. of G *Bergmeister* < *Berg* mountain + *Meister* master] A local judge among English miners; an officer of the barmote (q.v.). O, W [3]

barmote, *n.* (1662) *Mining* [Ad. of *barghmoot*, which was prob. an ad. and compounding of G *Berg* mountain + E *moot* assembly, court] A Derbyshire court for deciding controversies among miners. O, W [3]

barotaxis, -taxes *pl.* (1899) *Physiol.* [G (1894) < *baro-* + *-taxis* (< NL) < Gk *báros* weight + *táxis* arrangement, grouping] A taxis where pressure is the orienting mechanism. —**barotaxy**, *n.* (1906). O, W [3]

barouche, *n.* (1801) *Transportation* [Ad. of G *Barutsche* < It *baroccio* < LL *birotus* two-wheeled] A four-wheeled shallow carriage. —**barouche**, *a.* (1805); **barouchet(te)** (1807, 1816). O, R, W [4]

barthite, *n.* *Mineral.* [G *Barthit* < the name of W. *Barth*, a German mining engineer at the Otavi mine, South-West Africa (now Namibia), where it was found + G *-it* -ite] Conichalcite (q.v.). W [3]

bartram, *see* bertram

barycenter, *n.* *Physics* [Ad. of G *Baryzentrum* < *bary-* + *-zentrum* < Gk *barýs* + *kéntron* center] Center of mass. —**barycentric (coordinate) system.** W [3]

basichromatin, *n.* (1902) *Biol.* [G (1894) < *basi-* + *-chromatin* < L *basis*, Gk *básis* basis + *chrôma* color] Chromatin that can be readily stained with a basic dye; basophilic chromatin. —**basichromatinic.** O, W [3]

basset horn, *n.* (1835) *Music* [Prob. < G *Bassetthorn* (c. 1770) < It *bassetto* small double-bass + G *Horn* horn, ult. < Gk *kéras*] A tenor clarinet. O, R, W [4]

bastite, *n.* (1837) *Mineral.* [G *Bastit* < *Baste*, the name of a town near Harzburg, Germany + *-it* -ite] Schiller spar (q.v.). O, W [3]

bathochrome, *n.* *Chem.* Var. **bathychrome** [G *Bathychrom* < *batho-* + *-chrom* < Gk *báthos* depth, *batýs* deep + *chrôma* color] An atom or a group introduced into a compound like a dye to cause a visible deepening of color. —**bathochromic.** W [3]

batholith, *n.* (1903) *Geol.* Var. **batholite** (1904), **bathylith** (1905), **batholyth, bathylite** [G *Batholith* (1892) < *batho-* + *-lith* < Gk *báthos* depth + *líthos* stone] A great, dome-shaped mass of intruded igneous rock without a known depth. —**batholithic** (1912), **batholitic, bathylit(h)ic.** O, R, W [4]

bathychrome, *see* bathochrome

batyl alcohol, *n.* (1922) *Chem.* [G *Batylalkohol* (1922) (< NL) < L *Batis* genus of fishes < Gk *batís* flatfish + G *Alkohol* (ult. < Ar *al-kuhul* alcohol] A colorless crystalline alcohol. O, W [3]

batz, -en/-es *pl.* (1625) *Currency* [G *Batzen* (1495) clump, lump (also called *betz* in Bern); a thick penny, so called because of its appearance, originally minted in Bern and Salzburg] A small, obs. copper coin with a mixture of silver, worth four kreuzers in South Germany; now a Swiss unit of value. O, W [3]

Bauhaus, *a.* (c.1923 *W9*) *Archit.* [G < *Bau* structure, building + *Haus* house, i.e., an art academy located in Weimar from 1919 to 1933, and later in Dessau, Germany, which sought to blend into a Gesamtkunstwerk (q.v.) the various arts in the style of early 20th-century ''Sachlichkeit''] Relating to or characteristic of the art principles of the Bauhaus. O, R, W [4]

baum marten, *n.* (1879) *Zool.* [Partial transl. of G *Baummarder* < *Baum* tree + *Marder* marten] The European pine marten or its fur. O, R, W [3]

Bayer process, *n.* (1910) *Chem.* [Prob. transl. of G *Bayer-Verfahren* < the name of Karl J. *Bayer* (1847–1904), Austrian chemist + G *Verfahren* process] A process for producing alumina from bauxite. O, W [3]

Bayer 205, *n.* (1922) *Chem.* [G (1920) < the name of Friedrich *Bayer* & Co., a German chemical firm] Suramin, a synthetic trypanocidal drug. O, W [3]

bebeerine, *n.* *Chem.* [G *Bebeerin* < *Bebeerubaum* bebeeru tree < Sp and Pg *bibirú* + G *-in* -ine] A crystalline alkaloid, esp. that obtained from the bebeeru tree and used in medicines. R, W [4]

bebization, *n.* *Music* [G *Bebisation* < *be* a note of this scale + *-isation* -ization] An obsolete musical solmization proposed by Daniel Hitzler in 1628 that uses the syllables *la, be, ce, de, me, fe, ge.* W [3]

bebung, -en *pl.* (1879) *Music* [G tremor, trill < *beben* to tremble] A tremolo effect similar in sound to a violin vibrato, peculiar to the clavichord. O, W [3]

becken, *pl.* *Music* [G, lit., basin < OHG *beckin* < LL *bacchinon*] Cymbals. W [3]

Beckmesser, *n.* *Music* [G < the name of Sixtus *Beckmesser*, German pedantic musical philistine in Richard Wagner's opera *Die Meistersinger von Nürnberg* (1867)— Beckmesser (or Peckmesser or Beckmeserer) was actually a meistersinger who lived in Nürnberg around 1500 and died before 1539. One of the texts to his songs survives, and his tunes were still popular in the 17th century] A pedant, usu. a music critic or teacher. W [3]

beer cellar, *n.* (1732) *Beverages* Var. **beer-cellar** (1817) [Transl. of G *Bierkeller* < *Bier* beer + *Keller* basement, cellar] A cellar for storing beer; a rathskeller (q.v.) or bierkeller (q.v.). O, W [3]

beer garden, *n.* (1863) *Beverages* [Transl. of G *Biergarten* < *Bier* beer + *Garten* garden] A garden (restaurant) where beer and other liquors are served at outdoor tables. O, R, W [4]

beer hall, *n.* (1882) *Beverages* [Transl. of G *Bierhalle* < *Bier* beer + *Halle* hall] Earlier, a public hall in South Africa where nonwhites could purchase Kaffir beer; a spacious establishment in which beer is served and usu. offering dancing, music, etc. (see *DA*). O, R, W [4]

beer stube, *n.* (1840 *DA*) *Beverages* Var. **bierstube** (1909, q.v.), **Beer-Stube** (1944), **beer-stube** (1950), **Beerstube** (1952) [G < *Bier* beer + *Stube* parlor, room] Beer parlor. O [3]

belongingness, -es *pl.* (1931) *Sociol.* [Transl. of G *Zugehörigkeit* < *zugehören* to belong to, be a part of] The state or condition of belonging, of being an essential or integral part. O, R, W [3]

belonite, *n.* (1879) *Mineral.* [G *Belonit* < Gk *bélonē* needle, arrow tip + G *-it* -ite] An elongated crystallite with pointed or rounded ends. O, W [3]

Benrath line, *n.* *Ling.* [Transl. of G *Benrather Linie* < the name of *Benrath,* a town now a part of Düsseldorf, a line that derives its name from Benrath, near which the isogloss for HG *machen* to make, corresponding to LG *maken,* crosses the Rhine + *Linie* line] A line of bundles of isoglosses that divide southern High German from the rest of the speech developed from West Germanic. W [3]

benzaldehyde, *n.* (1866) *Chem.* [G *Benzaldehyd,* a blend of *Benzoesäure* benzoic acid + *Aldehyd* aldehyde] A colorless liquid aldehyde with the odor of bitter almonds, which is used in perfumery, flavoring, and pharmaceuticals. —**benzaldoxime.** O, R, W [4]

benzamide, *n. Chem.* [G *Benzamid,* a blend of *Benzoe* benzoic (< ML *benzol,* It *bengiui* < Ar *luban jáwi* frankincense of Java) + G *Amid* amide < *Ammoniak* ammonia + Fr or L *-id* -ide] A colorless crystalline compound obtained usu. from benzoyl chloride; benzoic amide. —**benzamido-.** W [3]

benzidine, *n.* (1878) *Chem.* [Prob. < G *Benzidin* < *Benzin* with the insertion of *-di-* (see *benzine*)] A crystalline base prepared by a series of reactions from nitrobenzine, used esp. in synthesizing certain azo dyes. —**benzidine yellow** (1967). O, R, W [4]

benzine, *n.* (1835) *Chem.* Var. **benzin** (1853) [G *Benzin* (1833) (now *Benzol*) < ML *benzoe* Javanese incense (G *Benzin* now corresponds to the American *gasoline* and British *petrol*) + G *-in* -ine] Benzene: a volatile, flammable, petroleum distillate that is used esp. as a motor fuel or solvent. —**benzine-collas** (1864), **benzine cup, benziner.** O, R, W [4]

benzol, *n.* (1838) *Chem.* Var. **benzole** (1838) [G (1834) < *benz-* (< ML *benzoe* Javanese incense) + G *-ol* (< G *Alkohol* alcohol, ult. < Ar) -ol] Benzene or an impure form of benzene, used as a solvent or cleaning agent. —**amido-benzol** (1869), **benzoline** (1874), **nitro-benzol** (1875), **benzolize.** O, R, W [4]

benzoyl, *n.* (1855 W9) *Chem.* [G < *benzo-,* the comb. form of *Benzoin* benzoin + *-yl* (first used in G *Benzoyl*—see *benzine*) < Gk *hýlē* wood, matter] The radical of benzoic acid. —**benzoyl,** *a.;* **benzoylate,** *v.;* **benzoylic.** • ~ appears in many compounds like **benzoyl chloride/peroxide.** O, W [4]

beraunite, *n. Mineral.* [G *Beraunit* < *Beraun* Beroun, the name of a town in Czechoslovakia + G *-it* -ite] A hydrous basic iron phosphate. W [3]

berberine[1], *n.* (1876) *Chem.* [G *Berberin* < NL *Berberis* the name of the genus, barberry (< Ar *barbáris*) + G *-in* -ine] Bitter crystalline yellow alkaloid obtained from barberry roots and other plants and used in medicines. • ~ appears in numerous technical compounds. O (not in 2nd ed.), R, W [4]

berberine[2], *n.* (1861) *Chem.* Var. **berberine tree** [G *Berberin*—see *berberine[1]*] An African tree from which a yellow dye containing berberine is obtained. O, W [3]

berg, *n.* (1823) [Short. of E *iceberg* (q.v.) < G *Eisberg* < *Eis* ice + *Berg* mountain] Iceberg. O, R, W [4]

berg crystal, *n. Geol.* [Partial transl. of G *Bergkristall* < *Berg* mountain + *Kristall* crystal] Rock crystal; transparent quartz. W [3]

bergfall, *n.* (1856) *Geol.* [G < *Berg* mountain + *Fall* fall] An avalanche of stone down a mountain. O [3]

bergmehl, *n. Geol.* [G < *Berg* mountain + *Mehl* meal, flour] An earthy material of the fineness of flour or meal, consisting of the shells of diatoma. WN20 [3]

bergschrund, *n.* (1843) *Geol.* [G < *Berg* mountain + *Schrund* crevasse] A deep, often broad crevasse formed at the head of a glacier. O, R, W [3]

bergstock, *n. Sports* [G < *Berg* mountain + *Stock* staff, stick] Alpenstock (q.v.). W [3]

beringite, *n. Mineral.* [G *Beringit* < the name of *Bering* island, Kamchatka, Siberia + G *-it* -ite] A dark-colored barkevikite andesite. W [3]

Berliner, *n.* (1859) [G < the name of the city of *Berlin,* capital of Germany + the nom. suffix *-er* -er] A native or inhabitant of this city. O, R, W [4]

berman, *n.* (1677) *Mining* (archaic) [G *Berghman* (now *Bergman*) miner] A miner. O [3]

Bernkasteler, *n.* (1875) *Beverages* Var. **Bernkasteler Doctor** (1875) [G < *Bernkasteler* (*Wein/Doktor*) < the name of *Bernkastel,* a village on the Moselle river, near Trier (+ *Wein* wine or *Doktor* doctor) + *-er* -er] One of various Moselle wines produced in Bernkastel and Cues. O [3]

bertram, *n.* (1578) *Bot.* Var. **bartram** (1578) [G *Bertram/ Berchtram* < a folk etymological var. of L *pyrethrum,* Gk *pýrethron* pellitory-of-Spain] An old name for the *Anacyclus pyrethrum,* a plant of which parts were chewed to relieve a toothache. O [3]

Berufsverbot, -e *pl.* (1976) *Politics* [G < *Berufs* (the gen. of *Beruf* vocation, job, employment) + *Verbot* prohibition] The West German policy of prohibiting civil-service employment to persons suspected of radical political tendencies. B [3]

berzeliite, *n. Mineral.* Var. **berzelite** [G *Berzeliit* < the name of Jons Jacob von *Berzelius* (1779–1848), Swedish chemist + G *-it* -ite] A yellow arsenate of magnesium, calcium, and manganese. O, W [3]

Bewusstseinslage, -n *pl. Psych.* [G *Bewußtseinslage* < the gen. of *Bewußtsein* consciousness + *Lage* state] A state of consciousness or a feeling without sensory qualities. W [2]

beyondman, *n.* (1896) *Philos.* Var. **beyond-man** (1896) [Transl. of Nietzsche's G *Übermensch* superman (q.v.)] An early synonym for *superman* or *overman.* O [3]

Bi, *see* bismuth

bieberite, *n.* (1854) *Mineral.* [G *Bieberit* (1845) < *Bieber,* the name of a town near Hanau, Germany + *-it* -ite] Hydrous cobalt sulfate, found in red crusts and stalactites. O, W [3]

Biebrich scarlet, *n. Chem.* [Transl. of G *Biebricher Scharlach* (1879) (now also *Altscharlach*) < the name of the town of *Biebrich* (now a part of Wiesbaden) in Germany + *Scharlach* scarlet] An acid diazo dye used in wood dyeing and biological staining. W [3]

Biedermeier, *a.* (1905) *Art, Furniture* Var. **Biedermeyer** (1914) [G (1854), named after Gottlieb *Biedermeier,* satirizing a fussy, uninspired German bourgeois, imaginary author of the "Gedichte des schwäb. Schullehrers Gottlieb Biedermeier" (in reality the hackneyed verses of the Swabian rhymster S. F. Sauer), which Ludwig Eichrodt and Adolf Kußmaul published together with their own parodies in the "Fliegende Blätter" in 1855–57] Simple, humdrum; pertaining to simple, practical furniture; relating to the artistic, literary, philosophical, and political movements of the time marked by "Weltschmerz" and "Tränenseligkeit"; derogatory as intellectually and artistically lacking. —**Biedermeier**, *n*. O, R, W [4]

Bielefeld, *a. Textiles* [G < the name of *Bielefeld*, a German city in Nordrhein Westphalia, famous for its linens since the 16th cent.] Of the kind or style (as in linens) prevalent in Bielefeld. W [3]

bierhaus, -es *pl.* (1930) *Beverages* [G < *Bier* beer + *Haus* house] A German-style tavern used primarily for the serving of beer. O [3]

bierkase, *n. Food* [G < *Bier* beer + *Käse* cheese] Originating in Germany, a strong white cow's milk cheese that is often eaten with beer. R [3]

bierkeller, *n*. (1970) *Beverages* [G < *Bier* beer + *Keller* cellar, basement] Beer cellar (q.v.). • ~ is a recent reborrowing, this time in its phonetic form rather than as a transl. B [3]

bierstube, -s/-n *pl.* (1909) *Beverages* Var. **Bierstube** (1952) [G < *Bier* beer + *Stube* room] A room or other place, as in a German-style café or tavern, used primarily for the serving of beer, food, etc. O, R, W [3]

Big Bertha, *n*. (1914) *Mil.* Var. **Bertha** (1914) [Loose transl. of G *dicke Bertha* < *dick* thick, clumsy, unwieldy + the first name of Frau *Bertha* Krupp von Bohlen und Halbach, the wife of the onetime owner of the Krupp Works in Essen, Germany] A German gun of large bore used in World War One; a tool or machine that is large and cumbersome; a long-range camera or photographic lens. O, R, W [4]

big lie, *n*. (1946) *Politics* [Transl. of G *große Lüge* < *groß* big + *Lüge* lie] Falsehood on a large scale used as a propaganda technique, as the Nazis did, on the assumption that a big lie was more likely to persuade than would a small one. O, W [4]

bildstein, *n. Mineral.* [G < *bilden* to form, shape + *Stein* stone] Agalmatolite, figure stone, or pagodite (used esp. in China as a kind of modeling clay). WN20 [3]

bildungsroman, -e/-s *pl.* (1910) *Lit.* Var. **Bildungsroman** [G < the gen. of *Bildung* development, education + *Roman* novel, ult. < L *Rōmānicus*] A developmental novel, one concerned with a character's early development or spiritual or intellectual education. —**Bildungs(roman) hero** (1962, 1962). O, R, W [3]

bilharzia, *n*. (1859) *Zool.* [G < NL *Bilharzia* < the name of Theodor *Bilharz* (1825–62), a German physician who discovered the parasite in 1852] Schistosoma or schistosome, a genus of parasitic trematode worms or a worm of this genus; schistosomiasis. —**bilharzial** (1893), **bilharziasis** (1900), **bilharzic** (1903), **bilharzially**. O, R, W [4]

bilirubin, *n*. (1871) *Biochem.* [G (1864) < *bili-* + *rubin* < L *bīlis* bile + *ruber* red + G *-in* -in] A crystalline pigment occurring in bile, etc. —**bilirubin**, *a*. (1961); **bilirubin(a)emia**; **bilirubinuria**. O, R, W [4]

biliverdin, *n*. (1845) *Biochem.* [Sw or G (1840) < *bili-* + *verdin* < L *bilis* bile + Fr *vert*, L *viridis* green + Sw or G *-in* -in] A green crystalline pigment occurring in amphibians' and birds' bile. O, R, W [4]

billitonite, *n*. (1909) *Geol.* [G *Billitonit* (1901), named after *Billiton* Belitung, an Indonesian island + G *-it* -ite] A kind of tektite found in the East Indies. O [3]

bindheimite, *n. Mineral.* [G *Bindheimit* < the name of

Johann Jacob *Bindheim* (1750–1825), German chemist + *-it* -ite] An amorphous, hydrous lead antimonate. R, W [3]

binitarian, *n*. (1908) and *a*. (1910) *Theol.* [G *binitarisch* (1898) < L *bīnī* twofold, double, after G *trinitarisch, Trinitarier* (ad. L *trīnitās*) trinitarian (of) one who subscribes to the doctrine of the Trinity] *a.*: of or adhering to the belief in a Godhood of two persons only; *n.*: a follower of this doctrine. —**binitarianism** (1928). O [3]

bioblast, *n. Med.* [G < *bio-* + *-blast* < Gk *bíos* life + *blastós* germ, sprout] Altmann's granules (q.v.). —**bioblastic**. O, W [3]

biochemical, *a*. (1851) *Biochem.* Var. **biochemic** (1881) [G *biochemisch* < *bio-* + *chemisch* chemical < Gk *bíos* life + ult. Ar *al-kimiyā*] Of or relating to biochemistry. —**biochemically** (1887), **biochemical oxygen demand**. O, R, W [4]

biochemistry, *n*. (1881) *Biochem.* [G *Biochemie* < *biochemisch* < Gk *bíos* life + G *Chemie*, prob. < *Alchemie*, ult. < Ar *al-kimiyā*] The chemistry of animal and plant life; chemistry concerned with life processes. —**biochemist** (1897). O, R, W [4]

biochore, *n*. (1913) *Ecology* [G *Biochore* (1900) (also *Biochorion*) < *bio-* + *-chore* < Gk *bíos* life + *chóra* place, space] The climate boundary of an area; a group of similar biotopes such as a temperate forest; the largest area or division of plant and animal environment. O, W [3]

biogen, *n*. (1899) *Physiol.* Var. **biogene** (1909) [G (1895) < *bio-* + *-gen* < Gk *bíos* life + *génesis* generation, origin] A hypothetical protoplasmic unit; a biophore. O, R, W [4]

biogenetic law, *n*. (1882) *Zool.* [Transl. of G *biogenetisches Grundgesetz* < *biogenetisches* biogenetic + *Grundgesetz* < *Grund* basis + *Gesetz* law] Recapitulation theory, the theory of the German biologist Ernst Heinrich Haeckel (1834–1919) that a developing organism successively recapitulates approximately the series of ancestral types out of which it evolved. O, W [4]

biolith, *n*. (1906) *Geol.* Var. **biolite** [G (1854) < *bio-* + *-lith* < Gk *bíos* life + *líthos* rock] A rock of organic origin. O, W [3]

biological value, *n*. (1924) *Biol.* [Transl. of G *biologische Wertigkeit* (1909) < *biologische* biological + *Wertigkeit* value] A measure of a protein's digestive efficiency in a foodstuff. O, W [3]

biology, *n*. (1813 *W9*) *Biol.* [G *Biologie* (1802) < *bio-* + *-logie* < Gk *bíos* life + *lógos* word, account] The science of life; ecology; the plant and animal life of a given region or environment viewed as a unit; the conditions and laws relating to an organism or group of organisms; a biological treatise; animal magnetism. —**biologism** (1852), **-gize** (1862), **-gic(al)** (1864, 1859), **-gically** (1875), **-gistic** (1948). • *biological* appears in many compounds, as in **biological species** (1902)/**control** (1923)/**clock** (1955)/**warfare** (1946). O, R, W [4]

-biont, *comb. form Biol.* [G, poss. < Gk *bíon tiná* to have (an) existence, (a) life] One having a specified mode of living, as in *aerobiont*. W [3]

biophore, *n*. (1893) *Biol.* Var. **biophor** (1893) [G *Biophor* < *bio-* + *-phor* < Gk *bíos* life + *phorós* bearing, bringing] The ultimate supramolecular vital unit underpinning the theory of the German biologist August Weismann (1834–1914), a unit which is now disproved. O, W [3]

biosphere, *n.* (1899) *Geol.* [G *Biosphäre* (1875) < *bio-* + *Sphäre* < Gk *bíos* life + *sphaîra* realm] That part of the world and atmosphere occupiable by living organisms; those beings plus their environment, including on other worlds or on artifically created ones. —**biospheric.** O, R, W [4]

biotin, *n.* (1936) *Biochem.* [G (1936) < Gk *biōtikós* pertaining to life + G *-in* -in] A crystalline growth vitamin of the vitamin B complex. O, R, W [4]

biotite, *n.* (1862) *Mineral.* [G *Biotit,* named after Jean B. Biot (1774–1862), French physicist + G *-it* -ite] Black or magnesia mica. —**biotitic, biotitize.** O, R, W [4]

biotope, *n.* (1927) *Ecology* Var. **biotop** (1927) [Prob. < G *Biotop* < *bio-* + *-top* < Gk *bíos* life + *tópos* space, place] An area characterized by high uniformity in its environmental conditions and in its animal and plant life. O, R, W [4]

biotype, *n.* (1906) *Biol.* [G *Biotypus* < *bio-* + *Typus* < Gk *bíos* life + L *typus* type] All the organisms having the same genotype; such a shared genotype; in a transf. sense to individuals sharing many psychological traits. —**biotypology** (1937), **biotypic, biotypogram.** O, R, W [4]

birn, *n. Music* [G (now usu. *Birne*) pear < MHG *bir* < OHG *bira* < ML *pira*] An instrument of the clarinet class into which a mouthpiece is inserted. O, W [3]

birne, *n. Crystal.* [G — see *birn*] A boule, or pear-shaped artificial ruby, sapphire, etc. used for watch or instrument bearings. W [3]

bischofite, *n. Mineral.* [G *Bischofit* < the name of Gustav Bischof (1792–1870), German geologist + *-it* -ite] A hydrous magnesium chloride. W [3]

Bismarck brown, *n.* (1885) *Chem.* [Transl. of G *Bismarck-braun* < the name of Prince Otto von *Bismarck*-Schönhausen (1815–98) + *braun* brown] One of various brown colors; a basic diazo dye or various other dyes. O, W [3]

Bismarck herring, *n.* (1931) *Food* [G *Bismarckhering,* named after Prince Otto von *Bismarck*-Schönhausen (1815–98) + *Hering* herring] A marinated, filleted salt herring that is served as a cold hors d'oeuvre. —**bismarcked** (1945). O, R, W [4]

bismuth, *n.* (1668) *Chem.* Old var. like **bismute** (1668) [G (1629) < L *bismutum,* latinization of G *Wismuth* (now *Wismut*)] A heavy, brittle, metallic element. • ~ is symbolized as **Bi** and appears in numerous derivatives like **-thic** (1799), **-thane** (1812), **-thous** (1881), **-thine, -thinite, -thyl,** and in many compounds like **bismuth ocher** (1796)/**glance** (1839)/**blende/oxide.** O, R, W [4]

bismuthite, *n. Mineral.* [G *Bismutit* < *Bismut* bismuth (q.v.) + *-it* -ite] A bismuth nitrate. O, W [3]

bismutite, *n. Mineral.* [G *Bismutit* < *Bismut* bismuth (q.v.) + *-it* -ite] An amorphous bismuth carbonate. O, R, W [4]

bismut(o)-, *comb. form Mineral.* [G *Bismuth* (1629) bismuth (q.v.)] Pertaining to bismuth, as in *bismutotantalite.* W [3]

bitte, *interj.* [G imper. or first person sing. of *bitten* to beg, ask] Please; beg your pardon; you're welcome. AH, WN20 [3]

bitterling, *n.* (1880) *Ichthy.* [G < *bitter* (< OHG *bittar* <

a transl. of L *amārus*) bitter + G *-ling* -ling] A small cyprinid fish used in the bioassay of mammalian hormones. —**bitterling test, Japanese bitterling.** O, R, W [4]

biuret, *n.* (1869) *Chem.* [G (1847) < L *bi-* two + *ūrīna* urine + G *-et* -et] A crystalline compound obtained by heating urea; also called *allophanamide.* —**biuret reaction** (1883). O, R, W [4]

black bread, *n.* (1863) *Food* [Transl. of G *Schwarzbrot* (q.v.)] A dark bread, esp. the sour, whole-grain rye bread eaten in north and central Europe. O, R, W [4]

blaffert, *n. Currency* Var. **plappert** [G < MHG *blaffert* pale, because of its color] A 15th-century silver coin used in Switzerland and Germany. W [3]

blast(o)-, *comb. form* (1876) *Biol.* [G *blasto-* < Gk *blastós* shoot, germ, sprout] Embryo in its early stages, used in many biological terms like *blastoderm* (q.v.). O, R, W [4]

blastoderm, *n.* (1859) *Biol.* [G < *blasto-* + *-derm* < Gk *blastós* bud + *dérma* skin] A completed blastodisc; the part of certain invertebrate embryos corresponding to the vertebrate blastoderm. O, R, W [4]

blastogenic, *a.* (1889) *Biol.* [G *blastogenisch* (1888) < *blasto-* + *-genisch* < Gk *blastós* bud + *génesis* origin, generation] Of or originating in the germ plasm; of the genetic determination of insects' social castes; initiating or promoting tissue proliferation. O, W [3]

Blaue Reiter, *n. and a. Art* [G *Der blaue Reiter* (1911) < *der* the + *blau* blue + *Reiter* rider] (Of) a short-lived group of German artists founded by Kandinsky in 1911 and characterized by their use of Fauve color. • ~ is transl. as **Blue Rider (School).** R, W [3]

blaze, *n.* (1639) *Zool.* [G *Blas* (now *Blesse*) < MHG *blasse,* OHG *blassa* paleness, i.e., a white mark or stripe on the forehead or bridge of certain domestic animals, including horses, cows, etc.] Such a white mark on the face of a horse, ox, etc.; a facial pattern in certain cats; a mark made on a tree to indicate a trail or road; such a route marked out by blazes; something serving as a means of identifying a course or way to be followed. —**blazed** (1685), **blaze the/a way** (1750). O, R, W [4]

blende, *n.* (1683) *Mineral.* [G, orig., a deceptively gleaming mineral < *blenden* to deceive] Sphalerite; a metallic sulfide or worthless ore. O, R, W [4]

blitz, -es *pl. a.* (1940), and *v.* (1939) *Mil., Sports, Commerce* [Short. of G *Blitzkrieg* (q.v.)] *n.* and *a.*: (of) an all-out, intensive aerial campaign or attack; a transf. sense, as in a defense rush on a passer in football, in a quick and intensive political campaign, or in the offer of unusual discounts in advertising a product; *v.*: to make a military, political, or other blitz. —**blitzing,** *verbal n.* (1940); **blitzed,** *a.* (1941); **blitzer** (football, 1963); **blitz buggy** (*Algeo* 1942)/**can; blitzweed.** O, R, W [4]

blitzkrieg, *n.* (1939) Var. **Blitzkrieg** (1939) *Mil.* [G < *Blitz* lightning + *Krieg* war(fare)] A war conducted with great force and speed; any sudden overpowering bombardment, as in propaganda, advertising, etc. —**blitzkrieg,** *v.* O, R, W [4]

blockflöte, -s/-en *pl. Music* Var. **blockflote** [G < *Block* block of wood (used to block the mouthpiece) + *Flöte* flute] A recorder; a flute organ stop. R, W [3]

blödite, *see* bloedite

bloedite, *n. Mineral.* Var. **blödite, blodite** [G *Blödit* < the name of Carl August von *Bloede* (1773–1820), German chemist and mineralogist + *-it* -ite] A hydrous sodium magnesium sulfate. W [3]

blond beast, *n.* (1907) *Anthrop.* [Transl. of G *blonde Bestie* (1887) < *blond* blond + *Bestie* beast < Fr *blond* + L *bēstia*] A blond type of primitive person of northern Europe, often regarded, as by Nietzsche in his *Zur Genealogie der Moral,* as a superior, ideal physical specimen; any predatory being. O, W [3]

blood and iron, *n.* (1869) *Politics* [Transl. of G *Blut und Eisen* < *Blut* blood + *und* and + *Eisen* iron] (A phrase coined by Bismarck which extols) the use of military force rather than normal diplomatic means. O, W [3]

blood and soil, *a.* (1940) *Politics* [Transl. of G *Blut und Boden* < *Blut* blood + *und* and + *Boden* soil] A catch-phrase denoting a literary movement espousing Nazi ideology. O [3]

blood meal, *n.* (1887) *Chem.* [Transl. of G *Blutmehl* < *Blut* blood + *Mehl* meal] Dried animals' blood used for feeding animals and as a nitrogenous fertilizer. O, R, W [3]

blood sausage. *n.* (1856) *Food* Var. **blutwurst** (1856), **black pudding** (1873), **blood pudding** [Transl. of G *Blutwurst* < *Blut* blood + *Wurst* sausage] A dark sausage with a high content of blood. O, R, W [4]

blucher[1], *n.* (1831) *Apparel* (1864) *Transportation* [G < the name of the Prussian field marshal Gebhard L. von *Blücher* (1742–1819)] A sturdy leather half-boot or high shoe; an unlicensed cab. O, R, W [4]

blucher[2], *n.* *Games* [G *blüchern* < the name of the Prussian field marshal Gebhard L. von *Blücher* (1742–1819) + G verbal ending *-n*] The highest bid in the game of napoleon. —**blucher,** *v.* W [3]

Blue Flower, *n.* *Lit.* [Transl. of G *Blaue Blume* < *blau* blue + *Blume* flower, i.e., the symbol of poetry in Novalis' *Heinrich von Ofterdingen* (1802)] The mystic object of romantic longing. W [3]

blue Monday, *n.* (1801) *Theol., Sociol.* [Transl. of G *der blaue Montag,* lit., the blue Monday, orig. the Monday before Ash Wednesday, named after the traditional blue coverlet on the altar that day; later, a wasted day on which workmen are idle, because of the carousing on the preceding day] The day before Lent; transf. sense for a trying, depressing Monday workday, following a relaxing weekend. O, R, W [4]

Blue Rider, *see* Blaue Reiter

blutwurst, *n.* (1856) *Food* Var. **plutworst** [G < *Blut* blood + *Wurst* sausage] Blood sausage (q.v.). O, W [3]

bobization, *n.* *Music* [G *Bobisation* (1628) < the obsolete musical solmization proposed by Daniel Hitzler in 1628] Hitzler's obsolete solmization. • ~ has the same meaning as **bebisation** (q.v.), but merits its own entry because it comes from a different etymon. W [3]

bock (beer), *n.* (1856) *Beverages* Var. **buck beer** (1869 *Ks*) [G *Bock(bier)* < the name of the town of Einbeck, Niedersachsen, Germany, called *Aimbok* or *Oambock* in the older Bavarian dialect, and famous for its beer made of hops] A strong dark beer usu. sold in early spring; a glass of this or another beer. O, R, W [4]

bocksbeutel, *n.* *Beverages* [G < the gen. of *Bock* he-goat + *Beutel* bag, purse, scrotum (because of the similarity of its shape to a goat's testes) A bulbous, short-necked bottle

for white wine produced along the Main river in Germany or for similar wine. W [3]

Boehm, *a.* (1845) *Music* [G (1832) < the name of Theobald *Böhm* (1794–1881), German musician] Of the system of keys and fingering and also the flute that he designed. —**Boehm system/clarinet** (1905, 1954). O [3]

boehmite, *n.* (1939 *W9*) *Mineral.* Var. **bohmite, Boehmite** [G *Böhmit,* named after Johannes *Böhm* (1857–1938), German mineralogist + *-it* -ite] Hydrous aluminum oxide, found in bauxite. R, W [4]

Bohemian earth, *n.* *Chem.* [Prob. transl. of G *Böhmische Erde* < *böhmisch* Bohemian + *Erde* earth] Terre verte, a variable pigment-color. W [3]

Bohemian ruby, *n.* *Crystal.* [Prob. transl. of G *Böhmischer Rubin* < *böhmisch* Bohemian + *Rubin* ruby] A red variety of rock crystal. W [3]

bohmite, *see* boehmite

Boltzmann('s) constant, *n.* (1910) *Physics* [Transl. of G *Boltzmann-Konstante* < the name of Ludwig *Boltzmann* (1844–1906), Austrian physicist + G *Konstante* constant < L *cōnstāns* (gen. *cōnstāntis*), present part. of *cōnstāre* to be certain, fixed] A formula in physics and chemistry symbolized as k (q.v.). O, R, W [3]

Book of the Dead, *n.* (1853) *Anthrop.* [Transl. of G *Totenbuch* < the gen. of *Toten* (pl.) (of the) dead + *Buch* book] A collection of ancient Egyptian papyrus books containing magical formulas etc. for the behavior of the souls of the dead in the hereafter. O, R [4]

boor's mustard, *n.* (1548) *Food* [Partial ad. and transl. of G *Bauernsenfe* < *Bauer* peasant + *Senf* mustard] A British wild plant: *Thlaspi arvense,* so named by herbalists since Turner; or *Lepidium ruderale,* as named by Gerard. O [3]

boracite, *n.* (1810) *Mineral.* [G *Boracit* (now also *Borazit*) < ML *boracum, borax* < Ar *bawraq* < Per *búrah* + G *-it* -ite] A borate and chloride of magnesium that is highly pyroelectric. O, R, W [4]

borane, *n.* (1916) *Chem.* [G *Boran* (1916) < ML *borax* (see *boracite*) sodium borate + G *-an* -ane] Boron hydride; a borane derivative. O, R, W [4]

Borna disease, *n.* *Med.* Var. **borna disease** [Transl. of G *bornasche Krankheit (der Pferde)* < the name of the city of *Borna,* Saxony, Germany, where the disease was esp. prevalent in the 1890s + *Krankheit* disease (+ the gen. pl. of *das* of + *Pferde* horses)] A virus disease of equines. W [3]

bornite, *n.* (c.1847 *W9*) *Mineral.* [G *Bornit,* named after Ignatius von *Born* (1742–90), Austrian mineralogist + G *-it* -ite] A valuable, brittle sulfide of copper and iron; also called, among other names, *purple copper ore* and *erubescite.* —**bornitic.** O, R, W [4]

boronatrocalcite, *n.* *Mineral.* [G *Boronatrokalzit* < ML *borax* (see *boracite*) + Sp *natrón* (< Ar *natrún* < Gk *nítron*) bicarbonate of sodium + L *calx* (gen. *calcis*) lime + G *-it* -ite] Ulexite, a hydrous sodium calcium borate. W [3]

bosh, *n.* (1679) *Metall.* [Prob. < G *Böschung* slope < *Bosch(en)* shrub < MHG *bosch* bush, (actually) a slope retained by shrubs] The lower sloping part of a blast furnace; a trough where ingots and tools are cooled; a tank used for washing metal parts. O, R, W [3]

botriogen, *see* botryogen

botryogen, *n.* (1865) *Mineral.* Old var. botriogen (1865) [G (1828) < Gk *botrýs* bunch of grapes + *genés* producing, generated] A hydrous sulfate of magnesium and iron. O-1933, W [3]

Böttger ware, *n.* (1850) *Pottery* [G (1707) < a short. and partial transl. of *Böttger Steinzeug* Bottger stoneware, after Johann F. *Böttger* (1682–1719), a German maker of porcelain] A type of fine red stoneware. O, W [3]

bott-hammer, *n.* (1858) *Trades* [G < *botten* to break flax + *Hammer* hammer] A wooden hammer having flutings or channels under its face to break the stalks of flax. O [3]

Bottrop, *a. Geogr.* [G < the name of *Bottrop*, a city in the Ruhr region, Germany] Of or from Bottrop; of the kind or style prevalent there. W [3]

botulism, *n.* (1878) *Med.* [G *Botulismus* < *botul-* + *-ismus* (< L) *-ism* + L *botulus* sausage] An often fatal poisoning caused by eating food, usu. poorly preserved, that contains botulin. —botulismus toxin. O, R, W [4]

boulangerite, *n.* (1868) *Mineral.* [G *Boulangerit* < the name of Charles Louis *Boulanger* (1810–49), French mining engineer + G *-it* -ite] A native sulfide of antimony and lead. O, R, W [3]

bower, *n.* (1830 *DA*) *Games* [Folk etymology of G *Bauer* jack (in cards), peasant] In the games of euchre and five hundred, the jack of trumps and the jack of the same color, called *right* and *left bower*, respectively. O, R, W [4]

boxer, *n.* (1934) *Zool.* [G (< E *boxer*) a bulldog type of hound] A short-haired, square-built breed of dog of the bulldog type, originating in Germany. O, R, W [4]

brack, *n.* (1734) *Commerce* (archaic) [Back-formation < G *bracken* to sort or inspect goods] The official method of sorting goods or produce in use in the principal Baltic ports as of the 18th century. O [3]

brack, *v.* (1858) *Commerce* [G *bracken* to select or sort goods] To select or sort goods or produce (as at Baltic ports). —bracked (1883). O [3]

brackebuschite, *n. Mineral.* [G *Brackebuschit*, named after Ludwig *Brackebusch* (1849–1906), German mineralogist in Argentina + G *-it* -ite] A basic vanadate of lead, manganese, and iron. W [3]

branchite, *n.* (1851) *Mineral.* [G *Branchit* (1842), named after the mineralogist J. *Branchi* from Pisa, Italy + G *-it* -ite] A mineral resin found in fossil pinewood. O [3]

brandisite, *n.* (1868) *Mineral.* [G *Brandisit* (1846) < the name of Clemens, Count von *Brandis*, governor of the Tirol + G *-it* -ite] Clintonite, a mica. O [3]

brandtite, *n.* (1896) *Mineral.* [Sw or G *Brandtit* < the name of Georg Brandt (1694–1768), Swedish chemist + Sw or G *-it* -ite] A hydrous arsenate of calcium and manganese. O, W [3]

brant-fox, *n.* (1864) *Zool.* [Partial transl. of G *Brandfuchs* < *Brand* burn, i.e., dark red + *Fuchs* fox] A variety of fox, chiefly characterized by its greater admixture of black in its fur. O [3]

bratwurst, -s/-e *pl.* (c. 1888 *W9*) *Food* [G fried sausage < *braten* to fry + *Wurst* sausage] A highly seasoned, fresh sausage of veal or pork. O, R, W [4]

braunite, *n.* (1839) *Mineral.* [G *Braunit*, named after W. *Braun* (1790–1872), German Councilor + *-it* -ite] A brittle manganese silicate. O, R, W [4]

Braunschweiger, *n.* (c.1934 *W9*) *Food* Var. brownswager [G *Braunschweiger* (*Wurst*) < the name of *Braunschweig* Brunswick, German region and city (+ *Wurst* sausage)] A spiced, usu. smoked liver sausage. R, W [4]

brazen law of wages, *see* iron law of wages

brazilite, *n.* (1893) *Mineral.* [G *Brazilit* (1892) < *Brazil*, the name of the country where the mineral was discovered + G *-it* -ite] Baddeleyite, a zirconium oxide used as a chief source of zircon. O [3]

breaking, *n.* (1883) *Ling.* Var. fracture (1891) [Transl. of G *Brechung* brake, fracture] The development of a diphthong from a single vowel, usu. due to the influence of certain consonants that follow. O, R, W [4]

breakthrough, *n.* (1918) Var. break-through (1918) [Poss. a transl. of G *Durchbruch* < *durch* through + *Bruch* break] An act of breaking through some kind of barrier or, fig., as through an existing price-level or state of knowledge; a successful military thrust; the place where a breakthrough occurs. —breakthrough, *a.* (1944) and *v.* (1968). O, R, W [4]

brei, *n.* (1935) *Physiol.* [G pulp, mash < OHG *brīo*] A uniformly, finely divided tissue suspension used in metabolic experiments. O, R, W [3]

breithauptite, *n. Mineral.* [G *Breithauptit* < the name of J. F. *Breithaupt* (1791–1873), German mineralogist + *-it* -ite] Nickel antimonide. O, W [3]

breitschwanz, -es *pl.* (1892) *Zool.* Var. breitswanz (1927), breitschwantz (1928) [G < *breit* broad + *Schwanz* tail] Broadtail (q.v.). • ~ is a simultaneous borrowing in its phonetic form alongside its translation. O, W [3]

Bremen blue, *n. Chem.* [Prob. transl. of G *Bremerblau* < the name of *Bremen*, city, state, and North Sea port in Germany + *blau* blue] A moderate bluish green; any of various bluish green or greenish blue pigments, mainly consisting of copper hydroxide. W [3]

Bremen green, *n. Chem.* [Prob. transl. of G *Bremergrün* < *Bremen* (see *Bremen blue*) + *grün* green] Malachite green; a green pigment similar in composition to Bremen blue. W [3]

bremsstrahlung, *n.* (1939 *W9*) *Physics* [G braking radiation < *bremsen* to retard, brake + *Strahlung* radiation] The electromagnetic radiation produced by the abrupt retardation of a moving charged particle. O, R, W [4]

bremsung, *n. Physics* [G retardation < *bremsen* to brake, retard + *-ung* -ing] The sudden retardation of a moving charged particle upon entering an opposing electric field. W [3]

breunnerite, *n.* (1825) *Mineral.* [G *Breunnerit* (1825) < the name of Count *Breu(n)ner*, a 19th-century Austrian nobleman + G *-it* -ite] Impure magnesite containing up to 30% iron carbonate. O, W [3]

Bridge, *see* Brücke

bringsel/brinsell, *n.* Var. bringsal [G *Bringsel* < *bringen* to bring + nom. suffix *-sel* -sel] A device suspended from the collar of a trained dog, which it takes into its mouth to signal the handler that it has located the objective such as a wounded man. W [3]

Brix, *n.* and *a.* (1897, 1897) *Chem.* [G < a short. of *Brix-*

Skala Brix scale (q.v.)] (Of) Brix's calibrated hydrometer. O, W [3]

Brix Scale, *n.* (1897) *Tech.* [Transl. of G *Brix-Skala* < the name of Adolf W. *Brix* (1798–1890), German scientist + *Skala* scale] A scale for measuring the percentages by weight of sugar in a solution. O, R, W [4]

broadtail, *n.* (1892) *Zool.* Var. **breitschwanz** (q.v., 1892) [Transl. of G *Breitschwanz* < *breit* broad + *Schwanz* tail] The wavy, moirelike pelt or fur of a very young or stillborn karakul lamb. O, R, W [4]

brocken specter/bow (as in rain*bow*), *n.* (1801) *Meteor.* [Partial transl. of G *Brockengespenst* < the name of *Brocken*, the highest of the Harz Mountains in Saxony, Germany + *Gespenst* specter, ghost] An optical phenomenon sometimes seen from mountain summits (as on the Brocken) or from an airplane, when the viewer is between the sun and a cloud mass; a dramatic representation of revels on Walpurgis night. O, R, W [4]

bromal, *n.* (1875) *Chem.* [G < a blend of *Brom* bromine (< Gk *brõmos* foul smell) + G *-al* < G *Alkohol* (< Sp *alcohol* < Ar *al-kuḥul* alcohol)] An oily, colorless liquid produced by the action of bromine on ethyl alcohol and used as an anodyne and hypnotic. O, R [3]

bromate, *n.* (1836) *Chem.* [Prob. < G *Bromat* < Gk *brõmos* foul smell + G nom. suffix *-at* (< L past part. suffix *-atus*) *-ate*] A salt of bromic acid. —**bromate,** *v.* O, R, W [4]

bromellite, *n.* (1926) *Mineral.* [G *Bromellit* (1925) < the name of Magnus von *Brommel* (1679–1731), Swedish mineralogist + G *-it* *-ite*] Beryllium oxide, occurring in white hexagonal crystals. O, W [3]

bronzite, *n.* (1816) *Mineral.* [G *Bronzit* < *Bronze* (< Fr) alloy of copper and tin + G *-it* *-ite*] Ferroan enstatite, a natural silicate of iron and magnesium that often has a bronzelike luster. O, R, W [3]

brool, *n.* (1837) [Prob. ad. of G *brüllen* to roar, *(Ge)brüll* roar, ult. of an imitative origin] A low roar or deep humming sound. —**brooling,** *verbal n.* (1837). O, W [3]

brötchen, *-s/-ø pl. Food* [G a (baked) roll < *Brot* bread + *-chen,* dim. suffix] (Baked) roll. W [3]

brown iron ore, *n. Metall.* [Transl. of G *Brauneisenstein* < *braun* brown + *Eisen* iron + *Stein* stone, ore] Limonite, a native hydrous ferric oxide. W [3]

brownmillerite, *n. Mineral.* [G *Brownmillerit,* named after Lorrin Thomas *Brownmiller* (1902–), American chemist + G *-it* *-ite*] Celite, a mineral found in portland cement that is an oxide of calcium, iron, and aluminum. W [3]

Brownshirt, *n.* (1932) *Mil.* Var. **brown shirt** (1932), **Brown-shirt** (1939), **Brown Shirt** [Transl. of G *Braunhemd* < *braun* brown + *Hemd* shirt] A member of the Nazi Sturmabteilung, or storm troopers (wearing a brown shirt as part of his uniform); any fascist. —**brown-shirted** (1934). O, R, W [4]

brownswager, *see* Braunschweiger

(Die) Brücke, *n. Art* [G (1903) (the) bridge] The name of a group of early 20th-century German painters who experimented with distorted forms and Fauve color. • ~ is transl. as **Bridge.** R [3]

Brunhild, *n. Lit.* Var. **Brunhilde, Brünnhilde** [G < the name of the queen *Brunhild,* in Germanic legend won by the epic hero Siegfried (q.v.) for Gunther] The queen in this legend. R [4]

Brunsvigite, *n.* (1902) *Mineral.* [G *Brunsvigit* (1902) < Dan *Brunsvig* Brunswick + G *-it* *-ite*] An oxidized chlorite occurring in gabbro in the Radautal, Germany. O [3]

Brunswick black, *n. Chem.* [Transl. of G *Braunschweiger Schwarz* < the name of *Braunschweig* Brunswick, region and city in Germany + *schwarz* black] A black varnish. O, W [3]

Brunswick blue, *n. Chem.* [Transl. of G *Braunschweiger Blau* < the name of *Braunschweig,* Germany + *blau* blue] A pigment containing a mixture of an iron blue with much barium sulfate; Prussian blue. W [3]

Brunswick green, *n. Chem.* [Transl. of G *Braunschweiger Grün* < the name of *Braunschweig* Brunswick, Germany + *grün* green] A green pigment formerly consisting of an oxychloride of copper; chrome green; deep/light/middle Brunswick green. O, W [3]

buchite, *n. Mineral.* [G *Buchit* < the name of Baron Christian Leopold von *Buch* (1774–1853), German mineralogist + *-it* *-ite*] A vitreous metamorphic rock. W [3]

bucholzite, *n.* (1831) *Geol.* [G *Bucholzit* (1819) < the name of Christian Friedrich *Bucholz* (1770–1818), German chemist + *-it* *-ite*] A variety of sillimanite, an aluminum silicate. O [3]

Buckelkeramik, *n.* (1929) *Archaeology* [G (1902) < *Buckel* hump + *Keramik* ceramics < Gk *keramikē* (*téchnē*)] A variety of late Bronze Age pottery with protruded decorative knobs. O [3]

buckling/bückling, **-e** *pl.* (1909) *Zool.* [G bloater] A smoked herring or bloater. O [3]

buetschliite, *n. Mineral.* Var. **butschliite** [G *Buetschliit* < the name of Otto von *Bütschli* (1848–1920), German zoologist + *-it* *-ite*] A hydrous carbonate of potassium and calcium. W [3]

bum, *n.* (1864) (colloq.) [Poss. < G *Bummler* loafer, tramp] A loafer or tramp; a lazy, dissolute person. O, R, W [4]

bum, *v.* (1863) (colloq.) [Poss. < G *Bummler* loafer, tramp or < *bummeln* to loaf] To idle about; to wander and act like a tramp. O, R, W [4]

bummel, *n.* (1900) [G a leisurely walk] A leisurely stroll. O [3]

bummel, *v.* (1891) [G *bummeln* to take a leisurely walk, to loaf] To take a leisurely stroll. —**bummeling,** *verbal. n.* (1900). O, W [3]

bummer[1], *n.* (1855) (colloq.) [Prob. < G *Bummler* loller, loafer] Loafer or tramp; marauder or plunderer. —**bummerish** (1872). O, W [4]

bummer[2], *n.* (1967 *W9*) (colloq.) [Prob. extension by folk etymology of G *bummer*[1] (q.v.), presumably < G *Bummler* idler, tramp] A bad experience; something that is of low quality or disappointing. R [4]

Buna, *n.* (1936) *Chem.* Var. **buna** [G < a short. of *Butadien* butadiene + *Natrium* (< Ar *natrūn* < Gk *nítron*) sodium] A trademark for synthetic rubber and rubbery materials, first developed in Germany. O, R, W [4]

bund, **-s/-e** *pl.* (1850) *Politics* Var. **Bund** (1851) [G league, association, confederation < MHG *bunt*] A confederation of German states (formed in 1815) or another federation or association, esp. a politically oriented one as in the

American pro-Nazi organization founded in 1936. • ~ appears terminally in **saengerbund** (q.v.) and **turnerbund** (1880 *DA*). O, R, W [4]

Bundesrat, *n.* (1872) *Politics* Var. **Bundesrath** (1872) [G *Bundesrath* (now *Bundesrat*) < *Bund* (gen. *Bundes*) confederation + *Rath* (now *Rat*) council] A federal council, as in the upper house of the German and Austrian parliaments, or the federal council of Switzerland. O, R, W [4]

Bundesstaat, *n.* *Politics* Var. **bundesstaat** [G < *Bund* (gen. *Bundes*) confederation + *Staat* state] A federated state or federation (cf. *Staatenbund*). W [3]

Bundestag, *n.* (1879) *Politics* Var. **bundestag** (1879) [G < *Bund* (gen. *Bundes*) confederation + *-tag* < *tagen* to meet, be in session] An assembly of representatives of a bund or confederacy, esp. since 1949 the German lower house of parliament. O, R, W [4]

Bundeswehr, *n.* *Mil.* [G < *Bund* (gen. *Bundes*) confederation + *Wehr* defense] The German armed forces. R [3]

Bundist, *n.* (1956) *Politics* [G *Bund* (q.v.) + E *-ist*] A member of a pro-Nazi bund, founded in 1936. O, R, W [3]

bunker, *n.* (1939) *Mil.* [G (underground) concrete shelter, borrowed during World War One < E *bunker* storage bin, shelter, and then borrowed back into E with the G meaning] A reinforced concrete shelter used in military defence. O, R, W [4]

Bunter, *n.* (1830) *Geol.* Var. **Bunter Sandstein** (1830) [Short. of G *bunter Sandstein* mottled sandstone < *bunt* variegated + *Sandstein* sandstone] The lowest division of the European Triassic. —**Bunter,** *a.* O [3]

burger, *n.* (1939) *Food* [Short. of G *Hamburg(er) (Steak)* < the name of the city of *Hamburg,* Germany] A usu. fried patty of ground or chopped meat or meat substitute; a sandwich made of such a patty in a split bun. O, R, W [4]

-burger, *comb. form* (1939) *Food* [A false etymological short. of G *Hamburger*—see *burger*] The productive source of items like fishburger and clamburger (Mencken lists 30 such derivatives). O, R, W [4]

burgher, *n.* (1568) *Politics* [G and D *Burger,* Mod G *Bürger,* in the 16th century, an inhabitant of a *Burg* or fortified town, afterward altered to E *burgh* borough] An inhabitant of a burgh or town; a prosperous citizen or member of the middle class; a Sri Lankan of mixed blood, esp. of Dutch descent; a Scottish Antiburgher. • ~ appears in derivatives like **-ship** (1725), **-ly** (1762), **-age** (1858), **-dom** (1884), **-hood** (1885), **-ess** (1901). O, R, W [4]

burghermaster, *n.* (1676) *Politics* [Ad. of G *Bürgermeister* burgomaster, mayor, to become a var. of *burgomaster* as used in English] Burgomaster, mayor. O [3]

burgrave, *n.* (1550) *Politics* [Ad. of G *Burggraf* (< MHG *burcgrāve*) < *Burg* castle + *Graf* count] Orig., the mili-

tary governor of a German town or castle in the Middle Ages; later, a noble who hereditarily rules such a domain. —**burgraviate** (1762). O, R, W [4]

Bürolandschaft, *n.* (1968) *Furniture, Art* Var. **burolandschaft** (c. 1973) [G < *Büro* office + *Landschaft* landscape] A style of office decoration, where functional dividers like screens or plants replace walls so as to permit changes in the area for work units. B [3]

bur principle, *see* kletten principle/princzip

bursch, **-en** *pl.* (1830) [G (now also *Bursche*) fellow (student) < MHG *burse* < ML *bursa* bag, purse] A (full) member of a burschenschaft, a university students' association; a student in a German university. —**burschenism** (1830). O [2]

burschenschaft, **-en** *pl.* [G < *Burschen,* pl. of *Bursch* bursch (q.v.) + nom. suffix *-schaft* -ship] A German students' association, orig. to promote Christian conduct, patriotism, etc., but now mainly as social fraternities. R [3]

busaun, *see* posaune

bushel, *v.* (1877) *Trades* [Prob. ad. of G *bosseln* to labor at, patch < MHG *bozeln*] To repair or alter, as men's garments; to do odd jobs. —**bushelwoman** (1889), **bushelman.** O, R, W [4]

bushel(l)er, *n.* (1847) *Trades* [Prob. ad. of G *Bossler* < *bosseln* (see *bushel*) + *-er* -er] One who bushels or repairs garments for tailors. O, W [4]

bushhammer, *n.* (1885) and *v.* (1884) *Trades* Var. **bush hammer** [Folk etymological ad. of G *Bosshammer* a hammer for dressing stone < obs. G *bossen* to beat + *Hammer* hammer] *n.*: in the U.S., a mason's hammer with serrated face for dressing concrete and stone; *v.*: to use a bushhammer. O, R, W [4]

buss, **-es** *pl.* (1570) [Prob. a short. of Upper G < G *Busserl* kiss] A kiss; kissing. —**buss,** *v.* (1571). O, R, W [4]

butanol, *n.* (1894) *Chem.* [G < *Butan* saturated gaseous hydrocarbon < L *būtryum* butter + G *-ol* (< G *Alkohol* alcohol, ult. < Ar < Gk) -ol] Either of two butyl alcohols. —**butanolide.** O, R, W [4]

butschliite, *see* buetschliite

butterbread, *n.* *Food* [Transl. of PaG *Budderbrot* and G *Butterbrot* < *Butter* butter + *Brot* bread] In parts of Pennsylvania, U.S.A., a piece of bread and butter. R, W [3]

butterflower, *n.* (1578) *Bot.* Var. **butter-flower** (1607) [Transl. of G *Butterblume* a common collective name for the dandelion, buttercup, etc. < *Butter* butter + *Blume* flower] Buttercup, a plant of the genus *Ranunculus.* O, W [3]

butyne, *n.* (1867) *Chem.* Old var. **butine** (1867) [G *Butin* (1853) < the name given to a substance found in butter < L *būtryum* butter + G *-in* -ine] Orig., this substance as found in butter; either of two isomeric hydrocarbons. O, W [3]

C

cacoxenite, *n. Mineral.* Var. **cacoxene** [G *Kakoxen* cacoxenite < Gk *kakós* bad + *xénos* guest + E *-ite,* so named because its presence in iron ore is injurious] A hydrous iron phosphate. O, W [3]

cadmium, *n.* (1822) *Chem.* [G (1817) (now also *Kadmium*) < NL *cadmium,* discovered by Friedrich Stromeyer (1776–1835), German chemist < L *cadmia* < Gk *kadmía* zinc ore] A tin-white malleable ductile metallic element, used in electroplating etc. • ~ appears in many compounds, esp. with names of colors, such as **cadmium red** (1886)/**yellow** (1895)/**orange** (1895)/**cell** (1908)/**green** (1934). O, R, W [4]

caffeine, *n.* (1828 *W9*) *Mineral.* Var. **caffein** (1830), **caffeina** [G *Kaffein* (now also *Koffein*) < *Kaffee* coffee < Turk *kahve* < Ar *gahwah* coffee + G *-in* -ine] A bitter crystalline compound found in coffee and tea, used as a nerve stimulant and diuretic. —**caffeism** (1886), **caffeinism** (1889), **caffeinic, caffeine citrate.** O, R, W [4]

caffeol, *n. Chem.* Var. **caffeone** [G *Kaffeol* < G *Kaffee* coffee (see *caffeine*) + *-ol* (< L *oleum* oil) -ol] A fragrant oil obtained by roasting coffee. W [3]

-caine, *comb. form Med.* [G *-kain* < *Kokain* cocaine (q.v.)] (Denoting a) synthetic alkaloid anesthetic. W [3]

calc-, *comb. form* (1875) *Mineral.* [G (now *Kalk*) lime < L *calx* (dat. *calcem*) lime] Calcium. O, R, W [4]

calcite, *n.* (1849) *Mineral.* [G *Calcit* (1845) (now also *Kalzit*) < L *calx* (gen. *calcis*) lime + G *-it* -ite] Native crystalline rhombohedral anhydrous carbonate of lime, such as calcareous spar. —**calcitic.** O, W [4]

calc-sinter, *n.* (1823) *Mineral.* [G *Kalksinter* < *Kalk* lime + *Sinter* slag] Travertine, a calcareous sinter. O, R, W [3]

calcspar, *n.* (1822) *Mineral.* Var. **calc-spar** (1822) [Partial transl. of Sw or G *Kalkspat,* ult. < L *calx* (gen. *calcis*) lime + Sw or G *Spat,* akin to OHG *sparro* a mineral (English, Danish, and Swedish *spat* derive from HG *Spat*—see *Kluge*)] Calcite (q.v.). O, R, W [3]

calc-tufa/calf-tuff, *n.* (1822) *Mineral.* [G < *Kalktuff* < *Kalk* lime + *Tuff* tufa] Calcareous tufa. O, R, W [4]

cameral, *a.* (1762) *Admin., Law* [G (now *kameral*) < ML *cameralis* < L *camera* treasury, chamber] Of or pertaining to the management of ducal property in 17th- and 18th-century Germany, or to a judicial or legislative chamber; cameralistic (q.v.). O, W [3]

cameralism, *n.* (1909) *Admin., Econ.* [G *Cameralismus* (now *Kameralismus*) < ML *cameralis* < L *camera* treasury, chamber] The theories and practices of a cameralist (q.v.). O, R, W [3]

cameralist, *n.* (1909) *Admin., Econ.* [G (now *Kameralist*) < NL *cameralista* < ML *cameralis* < L *camera* treasure, chamber + G *-ist* (< L *-ista*) -ist, i.e., one who administered ducal property in the 17th and 18th centuries in Germany] A mercantilist who advocated economic policies in 17th- and 18th-century Europe to strengthen the position of the country's ruler; an economist whose policies strongly emphasize political factors. O, R, W [3]

cameralistic, *a. Admin., Econ.* [G *cameralistisch* (now *kameralistisch*) < *Kameralist* cameralist (q.v.) + *-isch* -ic] Of or concerning public finance or cameralism. O, R, W [3]

cameralistics, *n. Admin., Econ.* [G *Cameralistik* (now *Kameralistik*) < *Kameralist* cameralist (q.v.) + *-ik* -ics] The science of public finance. O, R, W [3]

camptonite, *n.* (1895) *Geol.* [G *Camptonit* (1887) (now also *Kamptonit*) < the name of *Campton* Falls, New Hampshire + G *-it* -ite] A dark, lamprophyric, porphyritic rock found in dikes. O, R, W [3]

canadol, *n. Chem.* [G *Kanadol* < *Kanada* Canada + *-ol* -ol < L *oleum* oil] A light green ligroin. W [3]

canal of Schlemm, *see* Schlemm's canal

canal rays, *pl.* (1904) *Physics* [Transl. of G *Kanalstrahlen* (1886) < *Kanal* channel + the plural form of *Strahl* ray] Positive rays, named from the openings in the cathode through which ions pass. O, W [4]

cancrinite, *n.* (1844) *Mineral.* [G *Cancrinit* (now also *Kankrinit*) < the name of Count Georg *Cancrin* (1774–1845), Russian statesman of German descent + G *-it* -ite] An aluminosilicate and carbonate of calcium and sodium. O, W [3]

capelle, *see* kapelle

carabiner/karabiner, *n.* (1920 *W9*) *Sports* Var. **karibiner** (1933) [G, a short. of *Karabinerhaken* spring hook < *Karabiner* (< Fr *carabine* rifle) + G *Haken* hook (used to fasten a carbine to a bandoleer)] A metal ring with a spring clip used in mountain climbing to attach a climber to a rope. O, R, W [4]

carbinol, *n.* (c.1890) *Chem.* [G (c.1868) (now also *Karbinol*) < L *carbō* (gen. *carbōnis*) coal + G *-ol* (< *Alkohol,* ult. < Ar alcohol) -ol] Methanol or an alcohol derived from it. O, R, W [4]

carboxylase, *n.* (1911) *Biochem.* [G *Karboxylase* (1911) < L *carbō* (gen. *carbōnis*) coal + Gk *xýlon* wood + G *-ase* (denoting a destroying substance) -ase] One of two kinds of enzymes that catalyze carboxylation or decarboxylation. O, R, W [4]

carbyl sulfate/sulphate, *n.* (1844) *Chem.* Var. **sulphate/sulfate of carbyle** (1844) [G *Carbylsulphat* (1839) < *Carbyl* < L *carbō* (dat. *carbōnem*) coal + G *-yl* (< Gk *hýlē* matter, substance) -yl + G *sulphat* sulfate < L *sulfur* + G *-at* -ate] Ethionic anhydride. O, W [3]

carcinolytic, *a. Med.* [Prob. orig. formed as G *carcinolytisch* (now also *karzinolytisch*) < Gk *karkínos* cancer + *lytikós* able to loose] Destructive of cancer cells. W [3]

cardol, *n.* (1848) *Chem.* [G (1847) < NL *(ana)card(ium)* generic name of the cashew tree + G *-ol* (< *Alkohol,* ult. < Ar alcohol) -ol] A vesicatory oil obtained from cashew nuts. O [3]

Care Sunday, *n.* (1536) *Theol.* Old var. **Cair Sunday** (1538)

[Prob. transl. of unrecorded G *Karsonntag* Care Sunday, patterned after *Karfreitag* Good Friday < OHG *chara*, OE *caru* care, in its earlier sense of "sorrow, trouble, grief"] Earlier, the Sunday immediately preceding Good Friday, but later the fifth Sunday during Lent. O [3]

Carlowitz, -es *pl.* (1858) *Beverages* Var. **Karlowitz(er)** (1858) [G *Carlowitzer* (now *Karlowitzer*) < the name of *Karlovci* Sremski, a town in Croatia < *Karlowitzer Ausbruch* a Karlowitz wine made from select grapes] A sweet, strong red wine. O, W [3]

Carlsbad, *a. Geogr.* (1885) [G < the name of *Karlovy Vary*, a town in Czechoslovakia] Used attributively in *Carlsbad plum*, a dark dessert plum. O [3]

carmoisin, *n. Chem.* [Prob. < G *Karmoisin* carmine, not < *karmo(i)sieren* to surround a large precious stone with a setting of smaller precious stones, both of which are < It *carmesino* < Ar *quirmizi* kermes-colored] Azo rubine, a mordant acid azo dye used for dyeing wool. W [3]

carnallite, *n.* (1876) *Mineral.* [G *Carnallit* (1856) (now also *Karnallit*) < the name of Rudolf von *Carnall* (1804–74), German geologist + *-it* -ite] A hydrous chloride of potassium and magnesium used chiefly as a source of potassium. O, R, W [4]

carnosine, *n. Chem.* [G *Carnosin* (now also *Karnosin*) < L *carnosus* fleshy + G *-in* -ine] A crystalline dipeptide occurring in most mammals' muscles; B-alanyl histidine. W [3]

Caro's acid, *n. Chem.* [Transl. of G *Caro'sche Säure* < the name of Heinrich *Caro* (1834–1910), German chemist + *Säure* acid] Permonosulfuric acid. W [3]

carotene, *n.* (1861) *Biochem.* Var. **carotin** (1861), **carrotene**, **carrotin** [G *Carotin* (1831) (now also *Karotin*) < L *caröta* carrot + G *-in* -in] An orange or red carotenoid hydrocarbon found in plants and plant-eating animals, used in food coloring and as a source of vitamin A. —**carotin(a)emia** (1919), **caroten(a)emia**, **carotenol**. O, R, W [4]

carotenoid, *n.* (1913) *Biochem.* Var. **carotinoid** (1913) [G *Carotinoïd* (1911) (now also *Karotenoïd*) < G *Carotin* carotene (q.v.) + *-oid* (< the Greek suffix meaning 'similar') -oid] A highly unsaturated pigment like carotene or xanthophyll found in many plants and animals. —**carotenoid,** *a.* (1930). O, R, W [4]

carouse, *adv.* (1567) *Beverages* (obs.) Var. **garaus** (1609), **carous** [Ad. of G *gar aus* completely over, entirely at an end (as used in the earliest recorded instance in Regensburg, Germany, in 1498 to announce *the end of the day* at the tolling of the bell—see Kluge/Mitzka and Paul/Betz); the semantically linked or bonded verbal object *gar aus* or *garaus* entirety or end, turns up in Rabelais in the 16th century as *boire carrous,* rendering *gar aus* and *gar-aus trinken* (see Grimm) in the sense of drink to the bottom, with MFr *carousse* then giving the Mod E *v.* and *n. carouse*] Drinking completely, entirely, in the phrase "to drink/quaff/pledge carouse." • ~ as *n.* (1559) and *v.* (1567) preserve this old meaning, which is different from the Middle French-derived one. O, R, W [4]

Carpathian, *a.* (1673) *Geogr.* [Prob. < G *Karpathen* (now *Karpaten*) Carpathian Mountains < L *Carpatus* < Gk *Kárpatos* + E *-ian*] Of or situated in the Carpathian Mountains. —**Carpathian,** *n.* (1694). O, W [4]

carpholite, *n.* (1844) *Mineral.* [G *Karpholith* (1819) < Gk

kárphos straw + G *-lith* (< Gk *líthos* stone) -lite] A straw-yellow hydrous silicate of aluminum and manganese. O, W [3]

carphosiderite, *n.* (1850) *Mineral.* [G *Karphosiderit* < Gk *kárphos* straw + *sídēros* iron + G *-it* -ite] Hydronium jarosite, a straw-colored iron sulfate. O, W [3]

carrotene, *see* carotene

cartel, *n.* (1902) *Commerce* [G *Kartell* < Fr *cartel* contract, alliance < OIt *cartello*] A frequently international combination of business houses or nations that agrees to limit its members' competitive activities, as in the production of oil by OPEC (this is a different meaning from the MFr borrowing *cartel* meaning "written challenge, letter of defiance, etc." —**cartelization** (1923); **cartelist** (1925); **cartelism** (1926); **cartel(l)ized** (1927); **cartelizing,** *a.* (1935); **cartelistic; cartelize.** O, R, W [4]

carthoun, *n.* (1849) *Mil.* [Ad. of G *Karta(u)ne* < It and ML *quartana,* which was transl. into G *Viertelsbüchse* quarter gun] A 25-pounder cannon, as compared with the 100-pounder siege cannons of the day (see *Kluge*). O [3]

cartilage of Wrisberg, *n. Med.* [Transl. of G *Wrisberger Knorpel* < the name of Heinrich August *Wrisberg* (1739–1808), German anatomist + *Knorpel* cartilage] A cuneiform cartilage. W [3]

carvacrol, *n.* (1854) *Chem.* Old var. **carvacrole** (1854) [G (1841) < NL *carvi* in *Carum carvi* the botanical name of the caraway + L *acris* bitter + G *-ol* (< *Alkohol,* ult. < Ar) -ol] A liquid phenol obtained from various plants of the mint family and used as a disinfectant and fungicide. O, R, W [4]

cassation, *n.* (1879) *Music* [G (now also *Kassation*) < It *cassazione* leave taking; hence G *Kassation gehen* to roam the streets at night serenading or romancing the ladies] An 18th-century instrumental composition, often performed outdoors, that is similar to the divertimento and the serenade (this is a different word from the MFr legal borrowing *cassation*). O, R, W [4]

Casselmann's green, *n. Chem.* [Prob. transl. of G *Casselmanns Grün* < the name of Arthur *Casselmann,* a German chemist who was active around 1890 + *grün* green] A copper sulfate used as a pigment. W [3]

cassium, *see* cesium

castanite, *n.* (1892) *Mineral.* [G *Kastanit* (1890) < Gk *kástana* chestnut (from its color) + G *-it* -ite] Hohmannite (q.v.). O [3]

castorite, *n.* (1868) *Mineral.* Var. **castor** [G *Castor* (now also *Kastor*) < L *Castor,* the name of a personage in Greek mythology + E *-ite,* so named because of its occurrence with pollucite (orig. named *Pollūx,* the name of Castor's twin brother] A colorless variety of petalite. O, W [3]

cataphyll, *n. Bot.* [G < *cata-* + *-phyll,* intended as a transl. of *Niederblatt* < *nieder* lower + *Blatt* leaf] A rudimentary scalelike leaf preceding a plant's foliage leaves. —**cataphyllary,** *a.* (1875). R, W [3]

catapleiite, *n.* (1854) *Mineral.* [G *Catapleiït* (1850) (now *Katapleiït*) < Gk *katá* together with + *pleíōn* more + G *-it* -ite, so named because of its occurrence with several other rare minerals] A hydrous silicate of zirconium, sodium, and calcium. O, W [3]

cataplexy, *n.* (1883) *Med.* [G *Kataplexie* < Gk *katáplēxis* stupefaction] A sudden loss of muscle power in animals and humans following a strong emotional experience, as in near-death. —**cataplectic**. O, R, W [4]

catathymia, *n.* (1934) *Psych.* [G *Katathymie* (1912) < NL *catathymia* < Gk *katá* according, together with + *thymós* spirit] A condition in which the mind is controlled by the emotions. —**catathymic(ally)** (1934, 1934). O [3]

catatonia, *n.* (1888) *Psych.* Var. **katatonia** (1888), **catatony** [G *Katatonia* (1863) (now *Katatonie*), coined by Karl Ludwig Kahlbaum (1828–99), German psychiatrist < *kata-* + *-tonia* < Gk *katá* down + *-tonia* < *tónos* tone] Catalepsy; catatonic schizophrenia. —**catatonic**, *a.* (1908) and *n.* (1917). O, R, W [4]

catechetics, *n.* (1849) *Theol.* [G *Katechetik* < NL *catechetica* < Gk *katéchēsis* oral instruction] Practical Christian theology dealing with oral instruction in religious teachings. O, W [3]

catechin, *n.* (1853) *Chem.* [G *Cathechin* (now also *Kathechin*) < NL *catechu* catechu (< Malay, ult. of Dravidian origin) + G *-in* -in] An amorphous yellow compound obtained from catechu and used in tanning and dyeing. O, R, W [4]

categorial, *a.* (1912) *Philos.* [G *kategorial* (1880) < L *catēgoria*, Gk *katēgoría* basic fact] Concerning or involving categories, esp. in logic and linguistics. —**categorially** (1959). O, R, W [4]

categorical imperative, *n.* (1827) *Philos.* [Transl. of G *kategorischer Imperativ* < LL *catēgoricus* pertaining to basic fact + (*modus*) *imperātīvus* imperative (form)] Orig. from Kantian ethics, a moral obligation to act in consonance with universal ethical law. O, R, W [4]

cathepsin, *n.* (1929) *Biochem.* [G *Kathepsin* (1929) < Gk *kathépsein* to boil down] Any of various proteases present in most animal tissues, which help autolyze dead or diseased cells. —**catheptic**. O, R, W [4]

cathexis, -exes *pl.* (1922) *Psych.* [G (< NL) < Gk *káthexis* holding, retention, intended as a rendering of G (*Libido*)*besetzung* (Freud)] The investing of libidinal energy in an activity, idea, person, etc.; the energy so invested. —**cathectic**. O, R, W [4]

cathode ray, *n.* (1880) *Physics* [Transl. of G *Kathodenstrahl* < *Kathode* cathode < Gk *káthodos* (the) way down, descent + G *Strahl* ray] One of the high-speed electrons projected in a stream from the cathode of a vacuum tube under the action of a strong electric field; a stream of such electrons. —**cathode-ray tube** (1934)/**oscillograph** (1922)/**oscilloscope** (1951). O, R, W [4]

catoptrite, *see* katoptrite

cattle plague, *see* rinderpest

cedriret, *n. Chem.* [G *Zedriret* < L *cedrium* cedar oil + *rēte* net] Cerulignone (q.v.). W [3]

celestine/coelestine, *n.* (1804) *Mineral.* [G *Zölestin* celestite] Celestite (q.v.). O, W [3]

celestite, *n.* (1804) *Mineral.* Var. **celestine** (1804) [Ad. of G *Zölestin* < L *caelestis* celestial + G *-in* -ine, so named for its occasional sky-blue color] A native strontium sulfate. O, R, W [4]

celloidin, *n.* (1883) *Chem.* [Prob. < G *Zelloidin* < L *cellula* small cell + *-oid-* (derived from the Greek denoting) similar + G *-in* -in] A pure form of pyroxylin used in microscopy and photography. O, R, W [4]

celom, *see* coelom

cembra/cembran pine, *n.* (1785) *Bot.* [Partial latinization and/or transl. of G *Zimmer*, dial. *zember* < MHG *zimber*] Swiss stone pine, *Pinus cembra.* O, W [3]

censor, *n.* (1912) *Psych.* [Mistransl. of G *Zensur* (1899) censorship (as introduced into psychology in A. A. Brill's transl. of Freud's *Die Traumdeutung* titled *The Interpretation of Dreams*) < L *cēnsūra*] The mental agency or capacity that represses unconscious, unacceptable notions before they become conscious (this is different from the old Latin borrowing meaning "an ancient Roman magistrate"). O, R, W [4]

centner, *n.* (1683) [G (now *Zentner*) < ML *centenarius* hundred < L *centum* hundred] A German hundredweight. O, R, W [4]

centriole, *n.* (1896) *Biol.* [G *Centriol* (now also *Zentriol*) < NL *centriolum*, dim. of *centrum* center, dot] A minute body composing the center of a centrosome; the centrosome itself; central apparatus. O, R, W [4]

centromere, *n.* (1925) *Biol.* [G *Zentromer* (1903) < Gk *kéntron* center + *méros* part] That part of a chromosome to which a spindle fiber evidently attaches in mitosis. —**centromeric** (1960). O, R, W [4]

centrosome, *n.* (1889) *Biol.* Old var. **centrosoma** (1889) [G *Centrosoma* (1888) (now *Zentrosom*) < transl. of Fr *corpuscle central* < L *centrum* + Gk *sōma* body] A minute protoplasmic body in the cytoplasm of many animal and some plant cells; centriole (q.v.); centrosphere (q.v.). —**centrosomic** (1912). O, R, W [4]

centrosphere, *n.* (1896) *Biol., Geol.* [G *Centrosphäre* (1893) (now *Zentrosphäre*) < *centro-* + *Sphäre* < Gk *kéntron* center + *sphaîra* ball, sphere] The cytoplasmic layer surrounding the centriole within the centrosome; the dense, central part of the earth; centrosome (q.v.). O, R, W [4]

centum, *a.* (1901) *Ling.* [Transl. of G *Kentum(sprachen)* (1890) < L *centum* hundred + G *Sprachen* languages, so named because the initial sound of L *centum* is a velar stop rather than a sibilant] Of the western group of Indo-European languages, in which the palatals did not become sibilants, as happened in the eastern group, or satem (q.v.). O, R, W [4]

cephalin, *n.* (1900) *Biochem.* Var. **kephalin** [G (now *Kephalin*) < Gk *kephalē* head, *képhalos* brain + G *-in* -in] An acidic phosphatide similar to a lecithin but without choline, occurring esp. in the brain's nervous tissue (this is a different word from the Fr zoological borrowing *cephalin*). O, R, W [4]

cerulignol, *n.* (1883) *Chem.* Var. **coerulignol** (1883) [G *Cärulignol* (1882) (now also *Zärulignol*) < L *caeruleus* dark blue + *līgnum* wood + G *-ol* (< *Alkohol* alcohol, ult. < Ar) -ol)] A colorless oily phenol with astringent properties and a burning taste, obtained from wood-tar oils. O, W [3]

cerulignone, *n.* (1873) *Chem.* Var. **coerulignone** (1874) [G *Cörulignon* (1872) (now also *Zörulignon*) < L *caeruleus* dark blue + *līgnum* wood + G *Quinon/Chinon* quinone] A dark blue quinone obtained from beechwood tar. O, W [3]

cerussite, *n.* (1850) *Mineral.* Var. **cerusite** [G *Cerussit*

(1845) (now also *Zerussit*) < L *cerussa* waxy + G -*it* -ite] White lead ore. O, R, W [4]

cesium, *n.* (1861) *Chem.* Var. **cassium** (1861) [G *Caesium, Cäsium* (1860) (now also *Zäsium*) < L *caesius* blue-gray, first discovered as two spectral lines by Robert Wilhelm Bunsen and Gustav Robert Kirchhoff, and produced in a pure state by Carl Setterberg in 1882] A rare metallic element used esp. in electron tubes and photoelectric cells. • ~ is symbolized as **Cs.** —**cesium,** *a.* (1873). O, R, W [4]

chain-argument, *n.* (1860) *Philos.* [Transl. of G *Kettenschluss* < the comb. form of *Kette* chain + *Schluss* conclusion, inference] A sorites, or propositional argument. O [3]

chain smoker, *n.* (1890) [Transl. of G *Kettenraucher* < the comb. form of *Kette* chain + *Raucher* smoker] One who smokes continuously, lighting each cigarette or cigar from the previous one. —**chain-smoking,** *verbal n.* (1930); **chain-smoke** (1934). O, R, W [4]

chalcanthite, *n.* (1857) *Mineral.* [G *Chalkantit* (1853) < L *chalcanthum* < Gk *chalkós* metal ore, copper + *ánthos* flower + G -*it* -ite] A native blue vitriol or bluestone. O, R, W [3]

chalcolite, *n.* (1801) *Mineral.* [G *Chalkolith* < Gk *chalkós* copper, metal ore + *líthos* stone + G -*it* -ite, so named because it was first thought to be copper ore] Torbernite (q.v.). O, R, W [3]

chalcone, *n. Chem.* Var. **chalkone** [G *Chalkon* < Gk *chalkós* copper + G -*on* -one] A yellow crystalline ketone or a derivative of this compound. W [3]

chalcophyllite, *n.* (1850) *Mineral.* [G *Chalkophyllit* < Gk *chalkós* copper, metal ore + *phýllon* leaf] A green arsenate and sulfate of copper and aluminum. O, W [3]

chalcosiderite, *n.* (1884) *Mineral.* [G *Chalkosiderit* < Gk *chalkós* metal ore, copper + *síderos* iron + G -*it* -ite] A hydrous, green phosphate of iron, copper, and aluminum. O, W [3]

chalcostibite, *n.* (1868) *Mineral.* [G *Chalkostibit* (1847) < Gk *chalkós* metal ore, copper + *stibi* < L *stibium* antimony + G -*it* -ite] A lead-gray antimony copper sulfide. O, R, W [3]

chalcotrichite, *n.* (1832) *Mineral.* [G *Chalkotrichit* < Gk *chalkós* metal ore, copper + *trich-* < *tríx* hair + G -*it* -ite] A capillary variety of cuprite (q.v.). O, R, W [3]

chalmersite, *n. Mineral.* [G *Chalmersit* < the name of G. *Chalmero,* Brazilian director of mines around 1902 + G -*it* -ite] Cubanite (q.v.). W [3]

chalybite, *n.* (1858) *Mineral.* [G *Chalybit* (1847) < L *chalyb-* steel + G -*it* -ite] Siderite (q.v.). O, R, W [3]

chamaecranial, *a.* (1902) *Anthrop.* Var. **chamaecranic** [G *chamäkran* < *chamä-* < Gk *chamaí* low + *kraníon* skull + E -*ial*] Having a low flat skull. —**chamaecrany,** *n.* O, W [3]

chamaeprosopic, *a.* (1886) *Anthrop.* [G *chamäprosop* < *chamä-* < Gk *chamaí* low + *prósōpon* face + E -*ic*] Having a low broad face. —**chamaeprosope** (1900), **chamaeprosopy** (1902). O, W [3]

chamaerrhine, *a. Anthrop.* [G *chamärrhin* < *chamä-* < Gk *chamaí* low + -*rrhin-, rhís* nose + G -*in* -ine] Having a short broad nose. W [3]

chappe, *see* schappe

Chapsager, *see* Schabzieger

characteristic vector, *see* eigenvector

characterology, *n.* (1903) *Psych.* [G *Charakterologie* (1867) < *Charakter* (< L *charactēr* < Gk *charaktḗr*) + -*o-* + Gk *lógos* word, study + G -*ie* (< Gk -*ia*) -y] The study of character development and individuals' differentiation. —**characterological(ly)** (1916, 1963), **characterologist** (1958). O, W [3]

character piece, *n. Music* [Transl. of G *Charakterstück* < *Charakter* character (< L *charactēr* < Gk *charaktḗr*) + G *Stück* piece] A short musical piece, esp. for piano, conveying a single mood or programmatic idea. R, W [3]

chassignite, *n. Geol.* [G *Chassignit* < *Chassigny,* the name of a region in eastern France + G -*it* -ite] An achondritic meteorite of chromite and olivine. W [3]

chemiluminescence, *n.* (1905) *Chem.* [G *Chemilumineszenz* (1905) < *Chemie* chemistry, a short. of *Alchemie* (ult. < Ar *al-kimiyā'*) alchemy + G *Lumineszenz* luminescence] Emission of light due to chemical reaction. —**chemiluminescent** (1913). O, R, W [4]

chemoreceptor, *n.* (1906) *Physiol.* [G *Chemorezeptor* < the comb. form of *Chemie* chemistry, a back-formation from *Alchemie* alchemy (ult. < Ar) + G *Rezeptor* < L *receptor* receiver] One of the side chains or receptors in a living cell sensitive to chemical stimuli that result in a specific response by the cell. —**chemoreception** (1919), -**receptive,** -**receptivity.** O, R, W [4]

chemosynthesis, -theses *pl.* (1901 W9) *Biochem.* [G *Chemosynthese* < *chemo-* (< *Chemie,* ult. < Ar) + G *Synthese* < L (< Gk) *sýnthesis* synthesis] Synthesis of organic compounds with energy derived by chemical reactions. —**chemosynthetic** (1959), -**synthetically,** -**synthetic bacteria.** O, R, W [4]

chemotactic, *a.* (1887 W9) *Biochem.* Var. **chemotactical** (1908) [G *chemotaktisch* (< NL *chemotaxis*) < the comb. form of G *Chemie* chemistry, ult. < Ar + Gk *taktikós* of order + G -*isch* -ic] Involving or exhibiting chemotaxis or cell activity in relation to chemical agents. —**chemotactically.** O, R, W [4]

chemotherapy, *n.* (1907) *Med.* [G *Chemotherapie* (1907) < the comb. form of *Chemie* chemistry, a short. of *Alchemie* (ult. < Ar) alchemy + G *Therapie* < Gk *therapeía* healing] The use of chemical agents to treat or prevent cancer or esp. infectious disease in people, animals, or plants. —**chemotherapeutic(al)** (1907, 1911), -**therapeutics** (1913), -**therapist, chemo** O, R, W [4]

chevkinite, *n. Mineral.* [G *Tschewkinit* < the name of General Konstantin V. *Chevkin* (G *Tschewkin*) (1802–75), Chief of the Department of Mines of Russia + G -*it* -ite] A silicotitanate of the cerium metals with iron and calcium. W [3]

chiasto-, *comb. form Biol.* [G < Gk *chiastós* crosswise] Characterized by or marked with a cross; crossed at right angles. W [3]

chiastolite, *n.* (*1804*) *Mineral.* Old var. **chiastolith** (1804) [G *Chiastolith* (1800) < Gk *chiastós* crosswise + *líthos* stone + G -*it* -ite] A variety of andalusite, a cross section of which often exhibits the figure of a cross. —**chiastolite slate** (1849). O, R, W [3]

chimera, *n.* (1911) *Biol.* Var. **chimaera** (1911) [G *Chimäre* (1907) (now also *Schimäre*) (< L *chimaera*) illusion, named for the monster of Greek mythology, ult. < Gk *chímaira* she-goat] An organism containing two or more genetically different tissues (this is a different meaning from the old Latin mythological sense of *chimaera*). O, R, W [4]

chimyl alcohol, *n.* (1924) *Chem.* [G *Chimylalkohol* (1924) < *Chimäre* phantasmagoria, named for the monster in Greek mythology, ult. < Gk *chímaira* she-goat + G *-yl* -yl + *Alkohol* (ult. < Ar) alcohol] Cetyl-a-glyceryl ether, obtained from the liver oils of fishes and from cows' bone marrow. O, W [3]

chinone, *see* quinone

Chinosol, n. (1896) *Chem.* Var. **chinosol** (1896) [G < the comb. form of *china* < Peruvian Sp *quina* china bark, a short. of *quinaquina* bark of barks, i.e., the best of barks < Quechua + G *-sol* -sol] The proprietary name of 8-hydroxy quinoline sulfate, a crystalline substance used for its antiseptic and deodorant properties. O [3]

chiviatite, *n.* (1868) *Mineral.* [G *Chiviatit* (1853) < *Chiviato,* the name of a town in Peru + G *-it* -ite] A lead bismuth sulfide. O, W [3]

Chladni figures, *pl. Physics* [Transl. of G *Chladnische (Klang)figuren* (1802), named after Ernst F. *Chladni* (1756–1827), German physicist + (*Klang* sound) + *Figuren* figures] Sonorous figures: figures formed by vibrations when a substance is emitting a musical tone. W [3]

Chlamydomonas, *n.* (1884) *Bot.* [G (1883) < NL < Gk *chlamýs* (gen. *chlamýdos*) cloak + *monás* (gen. *monádos*) one, single] A genus of biflagellated plantlike flagellates or green algae that multiply so fast as to be a nuisance to filtration plants; (when in lower case) the individual form of this. O, W [3]

chloragogen, *a.* (1894) *Zool.* Var. **chloragogenous** (1894), **chloragogue** [G (1885) < NL *chloragogena* < G *Chlor* < Gk *chlōrós* yellow green + *agogós* carrying away, leading] Of, concerning, or being certain cells lining the surface of the alimentary canal in annelids like earthworms. O, W [3]

chloral, *n.* (1831) *Chem.* [G, coined by the German chemist Justus von Liebig (1803–73) < *Chlor(in)* < Gk *chlōrós* yellow green + *Al(kohol)* < Ar *al-kuhul* alcohol] A colorless, oily liquid with a pungent odor; chloral hydrate. O, R, W [4]

chloralamide, *n.* (1889) *Chem.* [G *Chloralamid,* a short. of *Chloralformamid* < Gk *chlōrós* yellow green, yellow + G *-al* (< *Alkohol* alcohol, ult. < Ar) -al + G *Amid* amide (q.v) + *-id* -ide] Chloral formamide, used as a sedative and a hypnotic. O [3]

chloralide, *n. Chem.* [G *Chloralid* < Gk *chlōrós* yellow green, yellow + G *-al* (< *Alkohol,* ult. < Ar) -al + *-id* -ide] A white crystalline cyclic compound; a compound obtained by condensing chloral with an alpha-hydroxy acid. W [3]

chloride, *n.* (1812) *Chem.* [G *Chlorid* < Gk *chlōrós* yellow green + G *-id* -ide] A simple compound of chlorine with metal or an organic radical. —**chloridize** and **chlorodize,** *v.* (1870, 1884); **chlorider** (1874); **chloridization** (1877); **chloridizing,** *a.* (1882); **chloridate,** *v.;* **chloride of lime; chloride paper/shift.** O, R, W [4]

chlorite, *n. Mineral.* (1794) [G *Chlorit* (1789) < L *chloritis* a kind of green stone < Gk *chlōrîtis* < *chlōrós* greenish yellow] Any of a group of usu. greenish hydrous silicates of aluminum, magnesium, and ferrous iron. —**chloritic** (1833), **chloritize** (1963). O, R, W [3]

chloritization, *n.* (1890) *Geol.* [Transl. of G *Chloritisierung* (1887) < *chloritisieren* to replace by or transform into chlorite (< Gk *chlōrîtis* < *chlōrós* yellow green) + G *-ung,* -ing, -ization, indicating action or process] Production of or conversion into chlorite. O, W [3]

chloritoid, *n.* (1844) *Mineral.* [G (1837) < *Chlorit* chlorite (q.v.) + *-oid* -oid] A silicate of ferrous iron and aluminum with magnesium. O, W [3]

chloropal, *n.* (1826) *Mineral.* [G < Gk *chlōrós* yellow green + G *Opal* < L *opalus* < Skt *upala* stone, jewel] Nontronite, a greenish clay mineral resembling opal. O, W [3]

chlorophyllase, *n. Bot.* [G < Fr *chlorophylle* + G *-ase* -ase] An enzyme present in leaves that hydrolyzes chlorophyll. W [3]

chlorophyllide, *n. Bot.* [G *Chlorophyllid* < Fr *chlorophylle* + G *-id* -ide] One of various pigments obtained from chlorophyll by removing the phytyl radical. R, W [3]

chloropicrin, *n.* (c.1889) *Chem.* Var. **chlorpicrin** [G *Chlorpikrin* < Gk *chlōrós* yellow green + *pikrós* bitter + G *-in* -in] A colorless, sweet-smelling, oily liquid, used mainly as a soil fumigant; also called *trichloro-nitro methane* and *nitro chloroform.* O, R, W [4]

chloroplast, *n,* (1887) *Biol.* Old var. **chloroplastid(e)** (1906, 1888) [G (1883) < a short. of *Chloroplastid* < Gk *chlōrós* yellow green + *plastós* formed] A plastid containing chlorophyll. —**chloroplastic.** O, R, W [4]

choleretic, *a.* (1927) and n. (1929) *Chem.* [G *Choloreticum* (1923) < NL *choleresis* secretion of bile by the liver] *a.:* stimulating the secretion of bile by the liver; *n.:* an agent that has this effect. O, W [3]

choline, *n.* (1869) *Biochem.* [G *Cholin* (1862) < Gk *cholḗ* bile + G *-in* -ine] A strong hygroscopic base distributed widely in plant and animal products. —**choline,** *a.* (1946); **cholinic.** O, R, W [4]

chomophyte, *n.* (1909) *Bot.* [G *Chomophyt* (1905) < Gk *chôma* mound of dirt + *phytón* plant] A plant growing in rock fissures or crevices and on ledges where rock debris has accumulated. O [3]

chondri(o)-, *comb. form. Biol.* [G < Gk *chondríon* small grain, dim. of *chóndros*] Grain: granular, as in *chondriogene.* R, W [4]

chondrin, *n.* (1838) *Biol.* [G < *chondri-* (q.v.) + *-in* -in] A horny substance obtained from cartilage and often associated with gelatin. —**chondrinogen** (1872), **chondrinous.** O, W [3]

chondricont, *n.* (1911) *Biol.* [G *Chondriokont* < *chondri-* (q.v.) + Gk *kontós* pole] A fibrillar or rod-shaped chondriosome (q.v.). O, W [3]

chondriome, *n. Biol.* Var. **chondrioma** [G *Chondriom* < *chondri-* (q.v.) + *-om* -ome] A cell's chondriosomes considered as a functional unit. W [3]

chondriomere, *n. Biol.* [G *Chondriomer* < *chondri-* (q.v.) + *-mer* < Gk *méros* part] A sperm cell's chondriosomal portion. W [3]

chondriomite, *n. Biol.* [G *Chondriomit* < *chondri-* (q.v.) + Gk *mítos* thread] A chain of granular chondriosomes; a single chondriosome. R, W [3]

chondriosome, *n.* (1910) *Biol.* [G *Chondriosom* (1908) < *chondri-* (q.v.) + Gk *sōma* body] Mitochondrion: any of a class of evidently self-perpetuating lipoprotein complexes in the cytoplasm of most cells. O, W [4]

chondriosphere, *n. Biol.* [G *Chondriosphäre* < *chondri-* (q.v.) + Gk *sphaîra* sphere] An aggregated or large spherical chondriosome. W [3]

chondrite, *n.* (1883) *Geol.* [G *Chondrit* (1863) < *chondri-* (q.v.) + *-it* -ite] A stony meteorite containing chondrules. O, R, W [4]

chondritic, *a.* (1866) *Geol.* [G *chondritisch* < Gk *chondritikós* granular + G *-isch* -ic] Granular: of or having the structure of a chondrite (q.v.). O, R, W [4]

chondrodystrophy, *n.* (1893) *Path.* [G *Chondrodystrophie* (1892) < *chondri-* (q.v.) + *Dystrophie* dystrophy < NL *distrophia* < Gk *dys-* poor + *trophḗ* nourishment] Achondroplasia, a cartilage condition resulting in dwarfism. — **chondrodystrophic** (1903). O, W [3]

chondroitic acid, *n.* (1885) *Biochem.* [Transl. of G *Chondroitsäure* < *chondri-* (q.v.) + *-it* -ite + *Säure* acid] Chondroitinsulfuric acid. O, W [3]

chondroitin, *n.* (1895) *Biochem.* [G < *chondri-* (q.v.) + *-in* -in] A gummy polysaccharide acid occurring as chondroitinsulfuric acid. O, W [3]

chondromucoid, *n. Biochem.* [G *Chondromukoid* < *chondri-* (q.v.) + *mukoid* mucoid (q.v.)] An amorphous substance consisting of a protein found in cartilage matrix. W [3]

chondrosin(e), *n.* (1886) *Chem.* [G *Chondrosin* (1886) < NL *chondrosia* < Gk *chóndros* grain, cartilage + G *-in* -in(e)] A gummy, monobasic acid obtained by hydrolyzing chondroitin (q.v.). O, W [3]

chorale, *n.* (1841) *Music* Var. **choral** (1841) [G, a short. of *Choralgesang* (1566) < ML *cantus choralis* choral song] A musical hymn or sacred song (of the German Protestant Church) sung in unison by a choir or congregation; something resembling a chorale; a group who sing principally choral music. — **chorale prelude** (c.1924 *W9*). O, R, W [4]

chordotonal, *a.* (1888) *Anat.* [G (1882) < Gk *chordḗ* string + *teínein* to fasten] Concerning or being one of an insect's sensory organs believed to be responsive to vibrations. O, R, W [3]

choriocarcinoma, -s/-ta *pl.* (1901) *Med.* [G *Chorion Carcinom(a)* (1898) (now also *Karzinom*) < Gk *chórion* outer fetal membrane + *karkínōma* cancer] A malignant tumor that develops in chorionic tissue. O, R, W [4]

chorioepithelioma, *n.* (1901) *Med.* [G *Chorionephitheliom* (1898) < Gk *chórion* outer fetal membrane + L *epithelium*, Gk *epí* upon + *thḗlē* teat, nipple + G *-om* -oma < *Karzinom*] Choriocarcinoma (q.v.). — **chorioepitheliomatous** (1901). O, W [3]

Christ-child, (the), *n.* (1842) *Theol.* [Transl. of G (*das*) *Christkind* or *Christkindchen* the Christ child/small child] Christ's figure (as a child). O [4]

Christmas tree, *n.* (1789) *Theol.* [Transl. of G *Christbaum* < *Christ* Christ (< L *Christus* < Gk *Christós*) + *Baum* tree] An evergreen and now often artificial tree decorated indoors with lights, etc. at Christmas time; a feature of Christmas celebration, orig. in Germany and now held in many cities of the world. O, R, W [4]

chromaffin, *a.* (1903) *Chem.* Var. **chromaffine** (1907), **chro-**

maffinic (1913) [Prob. < G (1898) < *Chromium* chrome + *affin* < L *affīnis* akin] Stained brown with chromium salts. — **chromaffin body.** O, R, W [3]

chromatin, *n.* (1882) *Biochem.* [G (1880) < Gk *chróma* (gen. *chrṓmatos*) color + G *-in* -in] The part of a cell nucleus that can be readily stained with basic dyes; a cytoplasmic constituent with similar reactions; a complex of nucleic acid exhibiting differential staining at different periods; karyotin. — **chromatinic, chromatin diminution.** O, R, W [4]

chromatogram, *n.* (1922) *Chem.* [G *Chromatogramm* < *chromato-* + *-gramm* < Gk *chróma* (gen. *chrṓmatos*) color + *grámma* record(ed)] The result of analysis by chromatography (q.v.). O, R, W [4]

chromatography, *n.* (1937) *Chem.* [G *Chromatographie* (1906) < *chromato-* + *-graphie* < Gk *chróma* (gen. *chrṓmatos*) color + *gráphein* to write, describe] The process of using adsorption to separate solids, liquids, or gases in a solution or mixture (this is a different meaning from the 1731 sense of "description of colors"). — **chromatographic(al)** (1907, 1946); **chromatograph,** *v.* (1953) and *n.* (1958); **chromatographically** (1962). • ~ appears in terminal position in numerous compounds like **paper** (1948)/**gas** (1961)/**column chromatography.** O, R, W [4]

chromatoid, *a.* (1901) *Biol.* [G < *chromato-* + *-oid* -oid < Gk *chróma* (gen. *chrṓmatos*) color + *-oeidēs* like, similar] Chromatinlike in its affinity for stains. O, R, W [3]

chromatophore, *n.* (c.1864 *W9*) *Bot.* [G *Chromatophor* (1882) < *chro-mato-* + *-phor* < Gk *chróma* (gen. *chrṓmatos*) color + *phorós* bearing] A pigment-bearing cell; a chloroplast or chromoplast. — **chromatophoric** (1895), **chromatophorous.** O, R, W [4]

chromatoplasm, *n.* (1902) *Biol.* Var. **chromoplasm** [G *Chromatoplasma* < LL < Gk *chróma* (gen. *chrṓmatos*) color + *plásma* < *plássein* to mold] The colored parts of protoplasm. O, W [3]

chromidiogamy, *n.* (1912) *Biol.* [G *Chromediogamie* < *Chromidium* chromidium (q.v.) + Gk *gámos* marriage, union] The process whereby a chromatin undergoes syngamatic union in the form of muscle. O [3]

chromidiosome, *n.* (1912) *Biol.* [G *Chromidisom* < *Chromidium* chromidium (q.v.) + *-som* < Gk *sōma* body] The smallest chromatin particles composing the chromidial mass. O [3]

chromidium, -dia *pl.* (1906) *Biol.* [G (1902) < NL < L *chrōmium* chrome + *-idium*, a dim. suffix] A chromatin or chromatinlike granule in the cell cytoplasm. — **chromidial,** *a.* O, W [3]

chromite, *n.* (1840) *Mineral.* [G *Chromit* < *chrom-* + *-it* -ite < Gk *chróma* color] Chrome iron ore, the source of chromium and its compounds; a compound of chromic oxide and a metal oxide. — **chromite series.** O, R, W [4]

chromitite, *n.* (1910) *Mineral.* [G *Chromitit* (1908) < *Chromit* chromite (q.v.) + *-it* -ite] A rock composed chiefly of chromite. O, W [3]

chromomere, *n.* (1891 *W9*) *Biol.* [G *Chromomer* (1896) < *chromo-* + *-mer* < Gk *chróma* color + *méros* part] A visible enlargement of the chromonema (q.v.) where nucleoproteins appear to be concentrated; the central, granular part of a blood platelet. — **chromomeric** (1952). O, R, W [4]

chromonema, -ta pl. (1925) Biol. [G (1912) < Gk chrôma color + nêma thread] A chromatid's coiled, threadlike core, commonly thought to be the carrier of the genes. —**chromonemal, chromonematic, chronemic.** O, R, W [4]

chromophore, n. (1879) Biochem. [G Chromophor < chromo- + -phor < Gk chrôma color + phóros bearer] A functional group that gives rise to a molecule's color and can produce a dye. —**chromophoric** (1892), **chromophorous** (1893). O, R, W [4]

chromoplast, n. (1885) Bot. Var. **chromoplastid** (1885) [G Chromoplastid < chromo- + Plastid plastid (q.v.) < Gk chrôma color] A colored plastid usu. not containing chloroplasts; a chromatin nucleolus. —**chromoplast,** a. (1913). O, R, W [4]

chromosome, n. (1889) Biol. [G Chromosom (1888) < chromo- + -som < Gk chrôma color + sôma body] A chromatin-containing basophilic body that is considered to be the seat of the genes. —**chromosome,** a. (1912); **chromosomal** (1909); **chromosomally; chromosomic; chromosomin,** n.; **chromosomology; chromosome complement/number/set.** O, R, W [4]

chromotrope, n. (1893) and a. (1893) Chem. [G Chromotrop < chromo- + -trop < Gk chrôma color + trópos turn] (Of) one of several acids used in dyeing. —**chromotropic** (1899), **chromotropism** (1908). O, W [3]

chromotropic acid, n. (1899) Chem. [Transl. of G Chromotropsäure < Chromotrop chromotrope (q.v.) + Säure acid] A colorless crystalline acid used in dyeing. O, W [3]

chromotypography, n. (1851) Printing [Fr or G Chromotypographie < G chromo- (< Gk chrôma color) + G Typographie < ML typographia < Gk týpos impression + -graphia -graphy] The method or art of printing in chromatic colors. O, W [3]

chrysaniline, n. (1864) Chem. [G Chrysanilin < chrys- + Anilin aniline < the comb. form of Gk chrỹsós gold] A yellow crystalline base derived as a by-product in manufacturing fuchsine. O, W [3]

chrysanthemin, n. (1918) Chem. [G (1916) < NL chrysanthemum chrysanthemum + G -in -in] Asterin, cyanidin monoglucoside. O, W [3]

chrysogen, n. Chem. [G < Chryso- + -gen < the comb. form of Gk chrỹsós gold + -genēs producing] Napthacene, an orange tetracyclic hydrocarbon. O, W [3]

chrysotile, n. (1850) Mineral. [G Chrysotil < chryso- + -til < the comb. form of Gk chrỹsós gold + tílos anything plucked] A variety of serpentine, an asbestos fiber used in weaving and fireproof fabrics. O, R, W [4]

cimolite, n. (1801) Mineral. [G Zimolit < L Cimolia < Cimolus, an island in the Aegean Sea + G -it -ite] Purified fuller's earth. O, W [3]

cinchoninic acid, n. (1879) Chem. [Transl. of G Cinchoninsäure < NL Cinchona a genus of evergreen trees or shrubs growing in the valleys of the Andes (so named in honor of the Countess of Chinchon, Spain) + G -in -in + Säure acid] A white crystalline acid; 4-quinoline carboxylic acid. O, W [3]

cinnamene, n. (1873) Chem. [G Zinnamen < L cinnamum cinnamon + G -en -ene] Styrene, an aromatic hydrocarbon used in medicine and synthetic rubber. —**cinnamenyl.** O, R, W [3]

cinnoline, n. (1883) Chem. [G Cinnolin (1883) (now Chinolin) < the comb. form of china < Peruvian Sp quina China bark, actually quinaquina (< Quechua) bark of barks, i.e., the best of barks + G -ol- -ol + -in -in] A poisonous crystalline base. O, W [3]

cisleithan, a. (1870) Geogr. Var. **cis-leithan** (1870) [Ad. of G zisleithanisch < L cis this side of + Leitha, the name of a Danube tributary + G -anisch (< L -anus) -an] Situated on the western (Austrian) side of the Leitha river. O, W [3]

citrin, n. (1936) Med. [G (1936) (now also Zitrin) < L citrus citron tree + G -in -in] Vitamin P, a water-soluble flavonoid orig. obtained mainly from lemons. O, R, W [4]

civetone, n. Chem. [Prob. < G Zibeton < It zibetto < Ar zabad civet, perfume + G -on -one] A crystalline ketone that is the principal constituent of civet and that is used in perfumes. W [3]

CJD, see Creutzfeldt-Jakob disease

cladogenesis, n. (1953) Biol. [G Kladogenese (1947) < Klado- + Genese < Gk kládos branch + génesis genesis, origin, development] A process of adaptive evolution that promotes a greater variety of animals or plants. —**cladogenetic(ally)** (1957, 1957). O, R [3]

clang, n. (1867) Physics, (1895) Psych. [G Klang sound] (Physics) the sound of the fundamental tone and the harmonics; (Psych.) echoing of the words of another person; a symptom of mental disturbance. O [3]

clangful, a. (1867) Physics [Partial transl. of G klangvoll < Klang sound + -voll -ful] Sonorous—a nonce word. O [3]

clang tint, n. (1867) Music Var. **klangfarbe** (1867) [Partial transl. of G Klangfarbe < Klang sound + Farbe color] Timbre. O, W [3]

clang unity, n. (1895) Psych. [Partial transl. of G Klangeinheit < Klang sound + Einheit unity] Simplicity of the acoustic sensation of musical sound. O [3]

clarina, -s and **clarini** pl. Music [G Clarino < It clarino trumpet < L clārus clear] An instrument combining the qualities of clarinet and oboe, invented by Heckel in 1891. W [3]

clarinet(t)ist, n. (1864) Music [G Klarinettist < Klarinette (< Fr clarinette) clarinet + G -ist -ist] A performer on the clarinet. O, R, W [4]

-clasite, comb. form Mineral. [Orig. formed as G -klasit < Gk klásis break, fracture + G -(i)t -(i)te] -clase. W [3]

class-conscious, a. (1903) Sociol. [Transl. of G klassenbewußt conscious of class] Conscious of belonging to a particular social or economic class, esp. as in membership in the proletariat. —**class-consciousness.** O, R, W [4]

clastic, a. (1877) Geol. (1875) Anat. [G klastisch < klast- < Gk klastós split, fractured + G adj. suffix -isch -ic] (Geol.) of, belonging to, or being a rock consisting of broken pieces of older rocks; (Anat.) capable of being taken apart, as in an anatomical model built with separable pieces. —**clastic,** n. O, R, W [3]

-clastic, comb. form Mineral. [Orig. formed as G klastisch clastic (q.v.)] Composed of fragmented material, as in the word pyroclastic. W [3]

claviature, n. (1882–3) Music [G Klaviatur, formed < Fr clavier (< L clāvis) keyboard, in analogy to ML tastatura keyboard] The keyboard of an organ or piano; the system of fingering such a keyboard. O, W [3]

clavicylinder, *n.* (1880) *Music* [G *Klavizylinder* < Fr *clavier* keyboard + G *Zylinder* < L *cylindrus,* Gk *kýlindros* cylinder] A keyboard instrument producing its tones by friction from glass cylinders. O, R, W [3]

clavier, *n.* (1845) *Music* Old var. **klavier** [G *Klavier* < Fr *clavier* keyboard < ML *clāvis* piano, organ key] General designation during the Baroque era for the harpsichord, clavichord, and organ, later denoting mainly the clavichord; a dummy keyboard for practice. —**clavierist** (1845). O, R, W [4]

clavieristic, *a.* *Music* [Prob. < G *klavieristisch* pertaining to the clavier (q.v.)] Suitable for or relating to a keyboard stringed instrument. W [3]

cleisto-, *comb. form Bot.* Var. **cleist-, clist(o)-** [G (now also *kleisto-*) < Gk *kleistós* closed] Closed, as used in technical terms like *cleistocarp.* R, W [3]

cleistogamy, -es *pl.* (1881) *Bot.* [G *Cleistogamie* (now *Kleistogamie*) < *cleisto-* (q.v.) + -*gamie* < Gk *gameîn* to wed] The producing of small, inconspicuous flowers in addition to fully developed ones, as in the pansy. —**cleistogamous(ly)** (1874, 1885), -**gamic(ally)** (1877, 1885). O, R, W [4]

clerisy, -ies *pl.* (1818) *Ed.* [G *Clerisei* (now also *Klerisei*) < G *Kleris* (< L *clērus,* Gk *klêros*) clergy, often used contemptuously; introduced by Coleridge to express a notion no longer associated with clergy] Learned people as a class; intelligentsia. O, R, W [4]

clinkstone, *n.* (1811) *Mineral.* [Transl. of G *Klingstein* phonolite < *klingen* to ring + *Stein* stone] Phonolite, a compact volcanic rock. O, W [3]

clinoclase, *n.* (1850) *Mineral.* Var. **clinoclasite** [G *Clinoclas* (now *Klinoklas*) < *Clino-* + -*clas* < Gk *klínein* to slope + *klásis* fracture, break] Dark green, basic copper arsenate. O, W [3]

clinostat, *n.* *Bot.* [G *Klinostat* < *clino-* + -*stat* < the comb. form of Gk *klínein* to slope + NL -*stata* < Gk -*statos* one that causes to stand] A device for measuring the effect of gravity and light on the movements of a growing plant, and for changing or eliminating these movements. W [3]

clinozoisite, *n.* *Mineral.* [G *Klinozoisit* < *Klino-* + *Zoisit* zoisit (q.v.) < Gk *klínein* to slope] A monoclinic, basic silicate of calcium and aluminum. W [3]

clob(ber), *see* klaberjass

cloudburst, *n.* (1817) *Meteor.* Old var. **cloud-burst** (1817) [Transl. of G *Wolkenbruch* < *Wolken* (pl.) clouds + *Bruch* burst] A violent rainstorm; a deluge or waterspout. O, R, W [4]

Co, *see* cobalt

coagulation necrosis, *n.* (1883) *Path.* [Ad. of G *Koagulationsnekrose* (1877) < *Koagulation* + *Nekrose* < L *coāgulātio* coagulation + Gk *nékrōsis* deadening, death, decay] A necrosis where dead tissue becomes firmer and swollen, and where cells retain their general structure; also called *coagulative necrosis.* O [3]

coal blower, *n.* (1721) (archaic) [Transl. of G *Kohlenbläser* (archaic) < *Kohlen* (pl.) coals + *Bläser* blower] A contemptuous name for an alchemist; a quack. O [2]

coarticulation, *n.* (1942) *Ling.* [G *Koartikulation* (1933) < *Ko-* + *Artikulation* < L *co-* comb. form of *cum* with, together + LL *articulātio* pronunciation] Secondary articulation, the concurrent activity or positioning of another

part of the articulator (or of another speech organ) used in producing a given sound. O, R, W [3]

cobalt, *n.* (1683 *W9*) *Chem.* [G *Kobalt,* by folk etymology < *Kobold* sprite, spirit] A silver-gray, magnetic metal used in alloys and to produce blue color in porcelain etc. • ~ is short. to the symbol **Co** and to the comb. forms **cobalto-** (1842) and **cobalti-**. It appears in numerous derivatives like **-ic** (1782), **-ine** (1835), **-ous** (1863–72); **-iferous** (1863–72), **-ite** (1868), and **-ized,** as well as in many compounds like **cobalt vitriol** (1809)/**blue** (1835)/**pyrites** (1844)/**bronze** (1875)/**60** (1946). O, R, W [4]

cobaltammine, *n.* (1881) *Chem.* [Prob. < G *Kobaltammin* < *Kobalt* cobalt (q.v.) + *Ammin* ammine (q.v.)] One of numerous ammines of cobalt. O, R, W [3]

cobalt bloom, *n.* (1776) *Mineral.* Var. **cobalt-bloom** (1776) [Transl. of G *Kobaltblüthe* (now *Kobaltblüte*) < *Kobalt* cobalt + *Blüte* bloom] Erythrite, a hydrous cobalt arsenate. O, R, W [3]

cobalt glance, *n.* (1806) *Mineral.* [Ad. of G *Kobaltglanz* < *Kobalt* cobalt + *Glanz* glance] Cobaltite, a cobalt sulfarsenide. O, W [3]

cocaine, *n.* (1874) *Chem.* [G *Cocain* (now also *Kokain*) < Sp *coca* < Quechua *kúka* any of several S. American shrubs of the genus *Erythroxylon* + G -*in* -ine] A bitter crystalline alkaloid obtained from coca leaves and used as a local anesthetic but with addictive qualities; an alkaloid found in coca derived from ecgonine. —**cocaine** and **cocainized,** *a.* (1887, 1887); **cocainization** (1887); **cocainist** (1908); **cocainism; cocainize; cocaine family/plant.** O, R, W [4]

cocarboxylase, *n.* (1932) *Chem.* [G *Kokarboxylase* (1932) < L *con/cum* together with + *carbō* coal + Gk *xýlon* wood, stuff + -*ase* -ase, denoting a destroying substance] A coenzyme that is the pyrophosphate of thiamine used in the decarboxylation of pyruvic acid. O, W [3]

coccinite, *n.* (1850) *Mineral.* [G *Kokzinit* < L *coccinus* scarlet + G -*it* -ite] A native mercury iodide. O, W [3]

codamine, *n.* (1871) *Chem.* [G *Codamin* (1870) (now *Kodamin*), a blend of *Kodein* codeine (< Gk *kṓdeia* poppyhead) + G *Amin* amine < *Ammoniak* ammonia + -*in* -ine] Opium alkaloid, a crystalline alkaloid. O, W [3]

codetermination, *n.* (1949 *W9*) *Industry* Var. **codetermination** (1952), *Mitbestimmung* (q.v.) [Transl. of G *Mitbestimmung* < *mit-* with, co- + *Bestimmung* decision, determination] Orig. in the Federal Republic of Germany and then in other countries, the legal right of labor representatives to sit on management boards and help make decisions (this is different from the earlier meaning of ''a determination that determines the same matter''). O, W [4]

coelestine, *see* celestine

coelom, *n.* (1878) *Zool.* Var. **coelome** (1888), **celom** [G (now also *Zölom*) < Gk *koílōma* cavity] The body cavity of higher metazoans. —**coelomic** (1881); **coelomate,** *a.* and *n.* O, R, W [4]

coenoblast, *n.* (1883) *Zool.* [G *Coenoblastem* (now also *Zönoblastem*) < *Coeno-* + *Blastem* < Gk *koinós* common + *blastós* bud, germ] Mesendoderm, an embryonic blastomere or cell layer. —**coenoblastic** (1885). O, W [3]

coenzyme, *n.* (1908) *Biochem.* Var. **co-enzyme** (1908) [G *Koënzym* (1908) < *ko-* + *Enzym* < L *con/cum* together with + Gk *en* in + *zýmē* yeast] A nonprotein organic compound forming the active part of an enzyme system. —**coenzyme R** (1941), **coenzyme I/II.** O, R, W [4]

coffee klatsch, *see* kaffeeklatsch

cohenite, *n. Mineral.* [G *Cohenit* < the name of Emil *Cohen* (1842–1905), German mineralogist + *-it* -ite] A rare crystalline carbide of nickel, iron, and cobalt found in some meteorites. R, W [3]

Cohnheim's area, *n. Path.* [Transl. of G *Cohnheimsche Felder* < the name of Julius F. *Cohnheim* (1839–84), German pathologist + *Felder* (pl.) fields] A polygonal area found in transverse sections of striated muscle fiber. W [3]

colchicine, *n.* (c.1847 *W9*) *Chem.* [G *Colchicin* (now also *Kolchizin*) < NL *Colchicum* a genus of the family Liliaceae + G *-in* -ine] A poisonous crystalline alkaloid extracted from the meadow saffron, used to create new plant varieties and to treat acute gout. —**colchicinize, cholchicine tannate.** O, R, W [4]

cold cuts, *pl.* (1945) *Food* [Transl. of G *kalter Aufschnitt* < *kalt* cold + *aufschneiden* to cut open, slice (actually, assorted cuts of sausages and cooked meats)] Orig. U.S., an assortment of cooked meats and cheeses, sliced and served cold. O, R, W [4]

cold duck, *n.* (1969 *W9*) *Beverages* Var. **Cold Duck** (1970) [Transl. of G *kalte Ente* < *kalt* cold + *Ente* duck, ad. of *kalte Ende* cold ends, or leftover wines combined and drunk at the close of a party] An inexpensive blend of sparkling burgundy and champagne. R [4]

collagenase, *n.* (1927) *Biochem.* [G *Kollagenase* (1927) < *Kollagen* (< Gk *kólla* glue + *génesis* creation) + G *-ase* -ase, denoting a destroying substance] One of a group of proteolytic enzymes that decompose collagen and gelatin. O, W [3]

collargol, *n.* (1900) *Chem.* Old var. **collargolum** (1900), **Collargol** (1907) [G (1900) (now also *Kollargol*) < *Colloid* < Gk *kólla* glue + *árgos* silver + G *-ol* (< *Alkohol* alcohol, ult. < Ar) *-ol*] A colloidal preparation of silver used as an external antiseptic. O [3]

colleter, *n.* (1875) *Bot.* [G *Kolleter,* irreg. < Gk *kollētē* gluer] A mucilage-secreting hair with a multicellular stalk found most commonly on bud scales and higher plants (this is a different word from the French word that gave the meaning "worker in a watch-repair shop"). O, W [3]

collophane, *n.* (1892) *Mineral.* Var. **collophanite** (1892) [G *Kollophan* (1870) < Gk *kólla* glue + *phanós* clear] Any of the massive, fine-grained varieties of apatite, used in fertilizers. O, R, W [3]

collophanite, *see* collophane

Cologne brown, *n.* (1658) *Chem.* Old var. **Cologne earth** (1658) [Transl. of G *Kölner Braun/Erde* < the comb. form of *Köln* Cologne, city in Germany + *braun* brown or *Erde* earth] Vandyke brown, a pigment so named because of its use by Vandyke. O, R, W [3]

colophonite, *n.* (1808) *Mineral.* [G *Kolophonit* < *Kolophonium* colophony < Gk *kolophón* summit, conclusion + G *-it* -ite] A coarse variety of garnet with resinous luster. O, W [3]

colorature, *n.* (1828–64) *Music* [G *Coloratur* (now also *Koloratur*) (< It *coloratura*) or It] Coloratura, or musical variations. O, R, W [3]

color hearing, *n.* (1882) *Psych.* Var. **colour-hearing** (1882) [Transl. of G *farbiges Hören* (< *farbig* colored + *Hören* hearing) or Fr *audition colorée* (< *audition* hearing + *colorée* colored)] Chromesthesia, the perception of colors accompanying the hearing of words or numbers. O, W [3]

column of Türck, *n. Anat.* [Transl. of G *Türcksche Säule* < the name of Ludwig *Türck* (1810–68), Austrian physician + G *Säule* column] The direct pyramidal tract in the spinal cord. W [3]

combinative, *a.* (1888) *Ling.* [Short. of a transl. of G *kombinatorischer Lautwandel* < *kombinatorisch* combinative < *kombinieren* to combine + *Laut* sound + *Wandel* change] Of a sound change caused by a particular neighboring sound (this is different from the older, various meanings borrowed < L *combinat-*). O, W [3]

commerce, *see* commers

commers, *n.* (1855) Var. **commerz** (1855), **commerce** (1858), **kommerz, kommers** [G < Fr *commerce* < L *commercium,* orig., every type of noisy party or gathering] A social gathering at an inn or tavern, where students in German universities settle around tables for the evening, drinking beer and singing. O, W [3]

complex, -es *pl.* (1907) *Psych.* [G *Komplex* (1906) < L *complexus,* past part. of *complecti* to include, complicate, orig. introduced by Albert Neisser (1855–1916), German physician and established by Carl Gustav Jung in *Über die Psychologie der Dementia Praecox* in 1907] A system of suppressed or repressed desires or memories that dominates one's personality; broadly, an exaggerated reaction to a situation or subject (this is different from the old L borrowing that means "composed of separable parts"). —**complex,** *a.* (1913) and in compounds like **Oedipus** (1913)/ **inferiority complex.** O, R, W [4]

concertmaster, *n.* (1876) *Music* Var. **concertmeister** (1876), **concert-master** (1889) [Transl. of G *Konzertmeister* < *Konzert* concert + *Meister* master] Leader of the first violins and subleader of the orchestra. O, R, W [4]

concertstück, *n. Music* [Ad. of G *Konzertstück* < *Konzert* concert + *Stück* piece] A concertino, typically in free form. W [3]

conchite, *n.* (1900) *Mineral.* [G *Conchit* (1900) < L *concha,* Gk *conchē* mussel, shell + G *-it* -ite] Aragonite, a calcium carbonate found in mollusk shells. O [3]

concordant, *a.* (1914) *Geol.* [G *konkordant* (1896) < MFr *concordant* < L *concordāns* (gen. *concordāntis*) concordant] Of strata that conform to or are parallel in structure or bedding. O, W [3]

condensation, *n.* (1913) *Psych.* [A. A. Brill's transl. of Freud's G term *Verdichtung* < *verdichten* to thicken, condensate] The process of grouping several seemingly discrete ideas into a single symbol, esp. in dreams (this is different from the LL borrowing that means "the literal act or process of condensing"). O, R, W [4]

conditioned, (the), *n.* (1829) *Philos.* [Transl. of G *(das) Bedingte* (that which is) postulated] That which is subject to the conditions of cognition and finite existence, as opposed to the unconditioned or absolute. O [3]

condurangin, *n.* (1885) *Chem.* [G (1885) < *Kondurango* a South American vine < Quechua *kunturánku* + G *-in* -in] A poisonous glucoside found in condurango bark that is used in medicine. O, W [3]

configuration, *n.* (1925) *Psych.* [Transl. of G *Gestaltpsychologie*] Gestalt (q.v.). —**configurationism** (1925), **configurationist.** O, R, W [4]

conformal, *a.* (1893) *Math.* [G *conform* (1844) (now *konform*) < LL *cōnfōrmālis* alike in shape + E *-al*] Of, relating to, or being a map where angles and scale are preserved. —**conformally** (1893), **conformal projection** (1910). O, R, W [4]

congenital myotonia, *see* myotonia congenita

conglutin, *n.* (1879) *Chem.* [G (now *Konglutin*) < *con-* + *Glutin* < L *com-* + *glutinosis*] Casein found in almonds and lupines, used in medicine. O, W [3]

conglutinin, *n. Biochem.* [G (now *Konglutinin*—see *conglutin*) + *-in* -in] A heat-stable constituent of bovine serum; a substance or substances in blood plasma that can cause clumping. W [3]

Congo red, *n.* (1885) *Chem.* [Transl. of G *Kongorot* < *Kongo* Congo (African territory surrounding the Congo river) + *rot* red] An azo dye used in dyeing and as a chemical indicator and biological stain. O, R, W [4]

coniceine, *n. Chem.* [G *Conicein*—see *coniine*] A base obtained from the alkaloids of poison hemlock. W [3]

conichalcite, *n.* (1850) *Mineral.* [G *Conichalcit* (1849) (now also *Konichalzit*) < Gk *konía* dust + *chalkós* copper + G *-it* -ite] A hydrous basic copper calcium arsenate. O, W [3]

coniferin, *n.* (1867) *Bot.* [G (now *Koniferin*) < *Conifer* (< L) + G *-in* -in] A crystalline glucoside obtained esp. from the cambium of coniferous trees. O, R, W [3]

coniine, *n.* (1831) *Chem.* Var. **conine** (1882), **conin** [G *Koniin* < LL *conium* hemlock + G *-in* -ine] A liquid alkaloid found in poison hemlock that paralyzes the motor nerves; 2-propyl piperidine. —**coniine,** *a.* (1878). O, R, W [3]

conodont, *n.* (1859) *Archaeology* [G (now also *Konodont*) < Gk *kônos* cone + *odoýs* (gen. *odóntos*) tooth] A conical, toothlike Palaeozoic fossil earlier thought to be extinct cyclostomes' teeth, but more prob. the fossil of some unknown invertebrate. O, R, W [4]

constative, *a.* (1901) and *n.* (1906) *Ling., Philos.* [Transl. of G *konstatierend* (1900) < L *constātivus* established] *a.:* of a use of the aorist tense to indicate that the given action has taken place, rather than emphasizing its initiation or conclusion; capable of being true or false; *n.:* a statement that can be true or false. O, R [3]

contabescent, *a.* (1868) *Bot.* [G < L *contābēscentem,* present part. of *contābēscere* to waste away, introduced as a botanical term by Karl Friedrich von Gartner, German botanist, in *Beiträge zur Kenntniss der Befruchtung* in 1844, and first used in English by Darwin] Of an atrophied botanical state. O, W [3]

contentual, *a.* (1909) *Philos.* [Transl. of G *inhaltlich* < *Inhalt* content + adjectival suffix *-lich* -ual] Belonging to or concerning content. O [3]

cookbook, *n.* (1809) *Food* Brit. var. **cookery book** [Poss. transl. of G *Kochbuch* or D *kookboek* cookbook] Cookbook. O, R, W [4]

coordination number, *n.* (1908) *Chem.* [Transl. of G *Koordinationszahl* (1893) < *Koordination* + *Zahl* number < L *coōrdinātus* arranged] In a coordination complex, the number of attachments to the central atom; in a crystal, the number used in classifying various spatial arrangements of constituent groups of crystals. O, R, W [3]

copiapite, *n.* (1850) *Mineral.* [G *Copiapit* < the name of *Copiapó,* Chile + G *-it* -ite] A basic iron sulfate. O, W [3]

copper nickel, *n.* (1728) *Mineral.* [Transl. of G *Kupfernickel* < *Kupfer* copper + *Nickel* nickel, so called from its resembling copper] Arsenical nickel. O, W [3]

copper-slate, *n.* (1875) *Mineral.* [Transl. of G *Kupferschiefer* < *Kupfer* copper + *Schiefer* slate] A dark bituminous schist containing copper ore. O [3]

coproporphyrin, *n.* (1924) *Chem.* [G *Koproporphyrin* (1923) < *kopro-* < Gk *kópros* dirt, dung, feces + *porphýreos* purple-colored + G *-in* -in] A porphyrin pigment excreted by the liver in bile. O, W [3]

coquimbite, *n.* (1844) *Mineral.* [G *Coquimbit* (1841) < the name of *Coquimbo,* a province in Chile + G *-it* -ite] A hydrous ferric sulfate. O, W [3]

Coramine, *n.* (1925) *Chem.* Var. **coramin** (1935) [G *Coramin* (1924) (now also *Koramin*) a proprietary name] A trademark for nikethamide; a pyridine derivative used as a cardiac stimulant. O, W [3]

corance, *see* crants

corded ware, *n.* (1928) *Archaeology* [Transl. of G *Schnurkeramik* cord-ornamented ceramic ware] A type of ware used by the "battle-ax" neolithic people of Thuringia, Germany. —**corded-ware,** *a.* (1929). O [3]

coriandrol, *n.* (1891) *Chem.* [Orig. formed as G *Coriandrol* (1891) (now *Koriandrol*) < L *coriandrum* coriander + G *-ol* (< Öl oil) -ol] D-linalool, a liquid obtained from the oil of coriander and linalool. O, W [3]

corn brandy, *n.* (1704) *Beverages* [Transl. of G *Kornbranntwein* (or D *Korenbrandewijn*) < G *Korn* grain, corn, rye + *Branntwein* brandy] Spirits distilled from grain; whiskey. O [3]

cornel berry, -ries *pl.* (1578) *Bot.* Var. **cornel fruit** (1578) [Transl. of G *Kornelbeere* < OHG *cornulberi* berry of the cornel tree or cherry tree] The cherry-like fruit of the cornel tree or of other species of *Cornus.* O [3]

cornel tree, *n.* (1551) *Bot.* [Transl. of G *Kornellkirschbaum* < *Kornellkirsche* cornel cherry + *Baum* tree] A large shrub or low tree, the species *Cornus mas* bearing an edible cherry-like fruit. • ~ is short. to **cornel.** O [3]

cornwallite, *n.* (1850) *Mineral.* [G *Cornwallit* < *Cornwall,* the name of a county in southwest England + G *-it* -ite] A green basic copper arsenate resembling malachite. O, W [3]

corpsbruder, -s and **-bruder** *pl.* (1904) Var. **corps-student** (1904) [G (now also *Korpsbruder*) < *Corps* (< Fr) fraternity + G *Brüder* brother] A fraternity brother in a German student corps; a close comrade. O, W [3]

corpuscle of Herbst, *n. Anat.* [Transl. of G *Herbstsches Körperchen* < the comb. form of the name of Ernst F. Herbst (1803–92), German physician + *Körperchen* corpuscle] In birds, one of various tactile organs related to Pacinian corpuscles. W [3]

corpuscle of Vater, *n. Anat.* [Transl. of G *Vatersches Körperchen* < the comb. form of the name of Abraham *Vater* (1684–1751), German anatomist + *Körperchen* corpuscle] Pacinian corpuscle, a nerve-fiber capsule in the hands and feet. W [3]

corsite, *n.* (1876) *Geol.* [G *Corsit* (1866) < Fr *Corse,* the name of the island of Corsica + G *-it* -ite] An orbicular gabbro found in Corsica. O [3]

corticosterone, *n.* (1937) *Biochem.* [G *Corticosteron* (1936) (now also *Kortikosteron*) < the comb. form of L *cortex, cortico* + G *Sterol* sterol + *-on* -one] A steroid hormone produced by the adrenal cortex or made synthetically. O, R, W [4]

corybulbine, *n.* (1894) *Chem.* [G *Corybulbin* (1893) (now also *Korybulbin*), a composite of L *Corydalis tuberosa* tuberous corydalis + Gk *bolbós* onion + G *-in* -ine] A crystalline alkaloid obtained from species of *Corydalis.* O, W [3]

corycavine, *n.* (1893) *Chem.* [G *Corycavin* (1892) (now also *Korykavin*), a composite of L *Corydalis tuberosa* tuberous corydalis + *Corydalis cava* "hollow" corydalis + G *-in* -ine] A base obtained from commercial corydaline. O [3]

corydaline, *n.* (1838) *Chem.* [G *Corydalin* (now also *Korydalin*) < L *Corydalis tuberosa* tuberous corydalis + G *-in* -ine] A bitter alkaloid obtained from corydalis roots. O, W [3]

cosmos, -es *pl.* (1848) *Philos.* [G (< Gk) *Kosmos* universe] The universe viewed as an orderly, harmonious system; a transf. sense for a system of ideas, existences, etc. O, R, W [4]

cossyrite, *n.* (1882) *Mineral.* [G *Cossyrit* (1881) (now also *Kossyrit*) < *Cossyra,* the name of an island near Sicily + G *-it* -ite] A variety of aenigmatite (q.v.). O, W [3]

co-state, *n.* (1795) *Politics* [Transl. of G *Mitstaat* < *mit* co-, together + *Staat* state < L *status*] A state allied with another state. O [3]

cotarnine, *n.* (1857) *Chem.* [Prob. < G *Cotarnin* (now also *Kotarnin*), an anagram of *Narcotin* narcotine] A crystalline alkaloid obtained by the action of oxidizing agents on narcotine and used to check bleeding. —**cotarnamic/cotarnic acid** (1863–72, 1863–72). O, W [3]

cotoin, *n.* (1879) *Chem.* [G (now also *Kotoin*) < Sp *cotocoto* < Quechua *kkhotokkhoto* the bark of a Bolivian tree formerly used as an astringent + G *-in* -in] A crystalline ketone found in coto bark and formerly used in intestinal disorders. O, W [3]

cotunnite, *n.* (1827) *Mineral.* [G *Cotunnit,* named after *Cotunnius,* the latinized name of Domenico *Cotugno* (1736–1822), Italian anatomist + *-it* -ite] A soft lead chloride found in Vesuvius. O, R, W [3]

coumaran, *n. Chem.* [Prob. < G *Cumaran* (now also *Kumaran*) (< Fr *coumarine,* prob. < Pg < Tupi *cumaru* Tonka bean) + G *-in* -in] A colorless oil derived from coumarone (q.v.). R, W [3]

coumarone, *n.* (1883) *Chem.* Var. **cumarone** (1883) [Prob. < G *Cumaron* (1883) (now *Kumaron*) or < Fr *Coumarine* < Tupi *cumaru,* a native name in Guiana of the Tonka bean + G *-on* -one] Benzofuran, a heavy, oily compound found in solvent naphtha; a derivative of this. —**coumarone (-indene) resin** (1935, 1900). O, R, W [4]

counterglow, *see* gegenschein

court-marshal, *n.* (1692) *Admin.* (obs.) [Transl. of G *Hofmarschall* chief administrative officer of a princely household < *Hof* court + *Marschall* marshall The marshal

(administrator) of a prince's household. —**court-marshaless** (1833), the wife of a court-marshal. O [3]

coventrate, *v.* (1940) *Mil.* [Ad. of G *coventrieren* < *Coventry,* the name of an English town in the West Midlands + G verb suffix *-ieren* -ate] To bomb intensively; to pulverize areas of a city by concentrated bombing as was inflicted on Coventry in November 1940. —**coventrating,** *verbal n.* (1940); **coventration** (1942). O [3]

cozymase, *n.* (1924) *Biochem.* [G (1923) < a blend of *Coenzym* and *Zymase* < L *con/cum* with + Gk *en* in + *zýmē* yeast + *-ase,* a suffix identifying a destroying substance] Diphosphopyridine nucleotide, a coenzyme of numerous dehydrogenases. O, W [3]

cram, *n.* (1810) *Sociol.* [G *Kram* and Sw, Dan, and Norw *kram* stuff, rubbish, trash; G < MHG *krām* market booth < OHG *crām*] Anything unwanted; junk. W [3]

crame ware, *n.* (1667) *Commerce* [G *Kramwaare* < *Kram* cram (q.v.) + *Waare* (now *Ware*) ware] Goods sold in a crame. O [3]

cranberry, *n.* (1647 W9) *Bot.* [LG *kraanbere* or poss. < G *Kranbeere/Kränbeere,* actually *Kranichberre* < *Kran* crane + *Beere* berry] A small roundish, red acid berry of the N. American species *Vaccinium macrocarpum* and extended to the European *V. Oxycoccos;* the shrubs that bear this fruit or fruit resembling a cranberry. —**cranberry,** *v.* • ~ appears in numerous compounds like **cranberry marsh** (1748)/**sauce** (1767)/**bog** (1807)/**rake** (1849)/**bush/gourd/ tree** and **Australian** (1866)/**European** (1866)/**American/ large/small cranberry.** O, R, W [4]

crance, *see* crants

craniology, *n.* (1806) *Anthrop.* [Prob. < G *Kraniologie* < *Kranio-* + *-logie* < Gk *kraníon* skull + Gk *lógos* word, account + G *-ie* (< L *-ia*) -y] Phrenology (archaic); the anthropological study of the size, shape, and proportions of the skulls of various races. —**craniologist** (1815), **-logical** (1815), **-logically.** O, R, W [4]

cranse, *see* crants

crants, -es *pl.* (1592) (obs.) Var. **craunce** (1592), **cranse** (1596), **crance, corance** [G *Kranz* or D *krans*) < MHG, OHG *kranz* wreath, garland, whence D *krans* as in "in Killian 1599 *krants*"] Wreath, garland. O, W [3]

craton, *n.* (1944 W9) *Geol.* [G *Kraton* < Gk *krátos* strength, might + G *-on* -on] A generally immobile section of the earth's crust that forms a continent's nuclear mass or an ocean's central basin. —**cratonal** and **cratonic,** *a.* R, W [4]

craunce, *see* crants

creatinine, *n.* (1851) *Biochem.* [G *Kreatinin* < *Kreatin* < Gk *kréas* (gen. *kréatos*) flesh + G *-in* -ine] A white crystalline compound obtained by dehydrating creatine. O, R, W [4]

Credé's method, *n. Med.* [Transl. of G *Credésche Methode* (now *Credé-Prophylaxe*) < the name of Karl S. F. *Credé* (1819–92), German gynecologist + *Methode* method] The putting of a silver nitrate solution into newborn infants' eyes to prevent gonorrheal ophthalmia. W [3]

crednerite, *n.* (1850) *Mineral.* [G *Crednerit* (1847) < the name of Karl F. Heinrich *Credner* (1809–76), German geologist + *-it* -ite] A foliated native oxide of manganese and copper. O, W [3]

crematorium, -s and **-toria** *pl.* (1880) *Med.* [G (now *Krematorium*) < NL < L *cremātor* < *cremāre* to incinerate + *-ium* -ium, coined in G, according to Carr, during the debates on cremation at Gotha, Germany, in 1878] An establishment for cremation: crematory. O, R, W [4]

Crems white, *see* Krems white

Cremnitz white, *n.* (1874) *Chem.* Var. **Kremnitz white** (1874) [Transl. of G *Cremnitzerweiß (now Kremnitzerweiß)* < the name of *Kremnitz*, Czech *Kremnica,* a town now of eastern Czechoslovakia + G *weiß* white] A white lead used in inks and by artists: *Krems white* (q.v.). O, R, W [3]

creosote, *n.* (1835) *Chem.* [G *Kreosot* creosote (1832), a word orig. intended to mean ''flesh-saving'' + Gk *kréas* flesh + *sōtér* preserver] An oily, antiseptic liquid with a strong odor and a smoky, burning taste. —**creosote,** *v.* (1846) and *a.* (1851). • ~ appears in many composites like **creosoted** (1862), **creosoting** (1863), **creosoter** (1889), **creosotate, creosotic,** and **creosote bush** (1851)/**plant** (1866)/ **oil** (1889). O, R, W [4]

cresol, *n.* (1869) *Chem.* [Prob. < G (now *Kresol*), a blend of *Kreosot* creosote (q.v.) + *-ol* < *Alkohol* alcohol (ult. < Ar) -ol] One of three poisonous isomeric phenols; a mixture of the three cresol isomers derived from coal tar, used as a germicide. —**cresotic (acid)** (1863–72), **cresolene, cresorcinol, cresol red.** O, R, W [4]

cresotinic acid, *n.* (1863–72) *Chem.* [Prob. transl. of G *Kresotinsäure,* ad. < *Kreosot* creosote (q.v.) + *-in* -inic + *Säure* acid] Cresotic acid, which is derived from the corresponding cresols. O, W [3]

creutzer, *see* kreuzer

Creutzfeldt-Jakob disease, *n.* (c.1966 W9) *Med.* Var. **Jakob-Creutzfeldt disease** [Transl. of G *Creutzfeldt-Jakob-Krankheit* < the name of the German psychiatrists Hans Gerard *Creutzfeldt* (1883–1964) and Alfons M. *Jakob* (1884–1931)] A degenerative disease of the human nervous system eventuating in mental deterioration and death. • ~ is abbr. as **CJD.** R [3]

criminalistics, *n.* (c.1943 W9) *Law* [G *Kriminalistik* (1897) < *Kriminalist* criminalist (< L *crīminālis* concerning crime) + G *-ik* -ics] Scientific crime detection. O, R, W [4]

crimmel/crimmer, *see* krimmer

cristobalite, *n.* (1888) *Mineral.* Erron. var. **crystobalite** (1935) [G *Cristobalit* (1887) (now also *Kristobalit*) < the name of Cerro San *Cristóbal,* near Pachuca, Mexico + G *-it* -ite] A quartz polymorph found as crystals in volcanic rock. O, R, W [4]

critical flicker/fusion frequency, *n.* (1907) *Psych., Physiol.* Var. **(flicker) fusion frequency** (1944) [Transl. of G *Verschmelzungsfrequenz* (1903) < *Verschmelzung* fusion + *Frequenz* frequency < L *frequēns*] The threshold where intermittent light is perceived half the time as flickering and half the time as fused or continuous. O, W [3]

critical theory, *n.* (1968) *Philos.* [Transl. of G *kritische Theorie* (1937) < *kritisch* critical (< Gk *kritikós*) + G *Theorie* theory < LL *theoria* < Gk *theōría*] A dialectical, theoretical critique of society, associated with the Frankfurt School, Germany. O [3]

criticism, *n.* (1867) *Philos.* [G *Kritizismus* < *kritiz-* + *-ismus* < L *criticus* + *-ismus* < Gk *kritikós* concerning critical judgment or *kritikḗ téchnē* the art of judging, so named because it was based on a critical study of the faculty of knowledge] The critical philosophy of Immanuel Kant (1724–1804), German philosopher. O [3]

crocidolite, *n.* (1835) *Mineral.* [Ad. of G *Krokydolith* (1831) < *Krokydo-* + *-lith* < Gk *krokýs* (gen. *krokýdos*) nap of cloth + *líthos* stone] A blue variety of asbestos, suited for spinning and weaving. O, R, W [4]

crocin, *n.* (1863–72) *Chem.* [Prob. < G < L *crocus* saffron < Gk *krokós,* ult. < a Semitic source like Ar *kurkum* crocus + G *-in* -in] A yellow glycoside found in various saffron and gardenia species. O, W [3]

crocoite, *n.* (1844) *Mineral.* Var. **crocoisite** (1844) [G *Krokoit* (1838) < *Krokoisit* < Fr *crocoise* < L *crocus* (see *crocin*) + G *-it* -ite] Orig. called *crocoisite,* a native lead chromate in monoclinic crystals. O, R, W [4]

croconic acid, *n.* (1838) *Chem.* [Transl. of G *Krokonsäure,* irreg. < Gk *krokós* (see *crocin*) + G *Säure* acid] A yellow crystalline hydroxy ketone. —**croconate** (1854). O, W [3]

cronstedtite, *n.* (1823) *Mineral.* [G *Cronstedtit* (now also *Kronstedtit*) < the name of Axel F. *Cronstedt* (1722–65), Swedish mineralogist + G *-it* -ite] A black hydrous iron silicate. O, W [3]

crowberry, -ries *pl.* (1597) *Bot.* [Prob. < transl. of G *Krahenbeere* a black-blue berry of the genus *Empetrum* < the comb. form of *Krahe* crow + *Beere* berry] Any of various heaths, related plants, or their fruit, as a red crowberry. — **crowberry family.** O, R, W [4]

crown-eater, *n.* (1845) *Mil.* [Transl. of G *Kronenfresser* < *Krone* crown (gold coin) + *Fresser* gobbler] A nickname given to Swiss mercenaries who served with the French in the 16th and 17th centuries and received crowns as wages. O [3]

crownland, *n. Politics* [Transl. of G *Kronland* < *Krone* crown + *Land* land] Any of the provinces of the former Austro-Hungarian empire (this is different from the old *crown land, crown-land, crownland* land belonging to the crown). O, R, W [3]

crown prince, *n.* (1791) *Politics* Var. **crown(-)prince** (1791) [Transl. of G *Kronprinz* < *Krone* crown + *Prinz* prince] The prince who is heir apparent or designate to a throne or crown, esp. in Germany and northern Europe; someone who is esp. qualified or likely to succeed to a forthcoming vacancy. —**crown princess** (1863), **crown princeship** (1889). O, R, W [4]

crown-rash, -es *pl.* (1710) *Textiles* [Transl. of G *Kronrasch* < *Krone* crown, top quality + *Rasch* (coarse) serge] A particular quality of rash or woolen materials. O [3]

crucian carp, *n.* (1763) *Ichthy.* Var. **crusian** (1771), **crucian** [Ad. of LG *karuse/kruske* (< MLG *karuske/karusse*) or NHG *Karausche*) carplike, freshwater fish + G *-ian* -ian, ult. prob. < L *coracinus* a black fish like a perch] A European carp. O, R, W [4]

crumb structure, *n.* (1906) *Agric.* [Transl. of G *Krümelstruktur* (1882) < *Krümel* crumb + *Struktur* structure] The condition of the soil when its particles are grouped together into crumbs. O [3]

crumhorn, *see* krummhorn

cruorin, *n.* (1840) *Med.* [G < NL < L *cruor* coagulated blood + G -in -in, coined by Johannes Peter Müller (1801–58), German physiologist, in *Grundzüge der Physiologie*, 2nd ed., transl. by William Baly as *Elements of Physiology* in 1837] Hemoglobin. O [3]

crusian, *see* crucian carp

cryolite, *n.* (1801) *Mineral.* [G *Kryolith* (1799) < *kryo-* + *-lith* < Gk *krýos* ice, frost + *líthos* stone] A sodium-aluminum fluoride found in Greenland and used in making aluminum. O, R, W [4]

cryolithionite, *n. Mineral.* [G *Kryolithionit* < Gk *krýos* frost, ice, as in G *Kryolith* cryolite (q.v.) + *Lithionit* lithionite (obs. synonym of *lepidolite*)] A fluoaluminate of sodium and lithium found in the Ural Mountains. W [3]

cryoturbation, *n.* (1946) *Geol.* [G *Kryoturbation* (1936) < *Kryo-* + *-turbation* < Gk *krýos* frost, icy cold + NL *turbation* disturbance] Any physical disturbance in the soil produced by the action of frost. O [3]

cryptobiotic, *a.* (1916) *Bot.* [G *kryptobiotisch* (1884) < *krypto-* + *-biotisch* < Gk *kryptós* hidden + *biōtikós* concerning life + G *-isch* -ic] Of insects etc. that live in concealment; crytozoic. O, W [3]

cryptoclastic, *a.* (1882) *Geol.* [G *kryptoklastisch* < *krypto-* + *-klastisch* < Gk *kryptós* hidden + *klastós* split, fractured + G *-isch* -ic] Of a rock composed of microscopic fragmented particles. O, W [3]

crypt of Lieberkühn, *see* Lieberkühn's gland

cryptomere, *a.* (1909) *Biol.* [G *kryptomer* (1904) < *krypto-* + *-mer* < Gk *kryptós* hidden, secret + *méros* share, part] Denoting a latent gene or factor not detectable by inspecting the individual carrying it. —**cryptomerism.** O, W [3]

cryptovolcanic, *a.* (1921) *Geol.* [Transl. of G *kryptovulkanisch* (1905) < *krypto-* + *vulkanisch* < Gk *kryptós* hidden, secret + L *Vulcānus* Roman god of fire + G adj. ending *-isch* -ic] Of a rock structure believed to have been produced by deep, concealed volcanic activity. —**cryptovolcanism, cryptovolcano,** *n.* O, R, W [3]

cryptoxanthin, *n.* (1934) *Chem.* [G *Kryptoxanthin* (1933) < *krypto-* + *Xanthin* < Gk *kryptós* hidden, secret + *xanthós* yellow, yellow-red, reddish-brown + G *-in* -in] A red, crystalline carotenoid alcohol that is a precursor of vitamin A. O, W [4]

crystallin, *n.* (1847) *Biochem.* [G *Kristallin* < Sw < Gk *krystállinos* crystal < *krýstallos*] A globulin in the crystalline lens. O, W [3]

crystallite, *n.* (1805 *W9*) *Mineral.* [G *Kristallit* < MHG *cristal(le)* < OHG *cristalla* < Gk *krýstallos* crystal + G *-it* -ite] A small imperfect crystal formed during the initial stages of crystallization of a magma. —**crystallitic.** O, R, W [4]

crystalloblastic, *a.* (1913) *Geol.* [G *kristalloblastisch* (1903) < *kristallo-,* the comb. form of *krystall-* crystal < *-blastisch* < Gk *krýstallos* + *blastikós* budding + G *-isch* -ic] Of or pertaining to a rock's crystalline texture caused by metamorphism; of a rock's structure produced by crystals growing in a solid solution. —**crystalloblast,** *n.* O, W [3]

Cs, *see* cesium

cubanite, *n.* (1868) *Mineral.* [G *Cubanit* (1843) (now also *Kubanit*), named < *Cuba* Caribbean island < Sp *cubano* + G *-it* -ite] A copper-iron sulfide. O, W [3]

cultic, *a.* (1898) *Theol.* [G *kultisch* < *Kult* + *-isch* -ic < L *cultus* cultivation, veneration (of a divinity)] Of or pertaining to a religious cult. —**cultically** (1953). O, R, W [4]

cultish, *a.* (1926) *Sociol.* [G *kultisch* < *Kult* + *-isch* -ish < L *cultus* cultivation, reverence (of a deity)] Of, pertaining to, or suggesting a cult, esp. of an eccentric, unorthodox person. —**cultishness** (1948). O, R, W [4]

cultural sociology, *n. Sociol.* [Transl. of G *Kultursoziologie* < *Kultur* culture (< L *cultūra*) + G *Soziologie* sociology < Fr *sociologie* < L *socius* + G *-logie* -logy] The sociology of the historical processes involved in cultural phenomena. R, W [3]

culturegeschichte, *see* kulturgeschichte

culture-historical, *a. Anthrop.* [Transl. of G *kulturhistorisch* < *Kultur* culture + *historisch* < L *cultūra* + *historicus* < Gk *historikós* + G *-isch* -ic] Being or pertaining to the theory of methods of the Vienna school of ethnology. W [3]

culturology, *n.* (1939) *Anthrop.* [G *Kulturologie* (1913) < *kulturo-* + *-logie* < L *cultūra* cultivation (of the mind and body) + Gk *lógos* word, account] The science or study of culture, esp. using Leslie A. White's methodology. —**culturological(ly)** (1949), **culturologist** (1957). O, R, W [3]

cumarone, *see* coumarone

cumengite, *n. Mineral.* Var. **cumengeite** [G *Cumengit* < the name of Edouard *Cumenge* (1828–1902), French mining engineer + G *-it* -ite] An indigo-blue lead-copper chloride. W [3]

cumidine, *n.* (1850) *Chem.* [G *Cumidin* (now also *Kumidin*), a blend of *Cumin* (< L *Cuminum*) a dwarf plant of the family Umbelliferae + *-id* (< Gk *-oeidēs* similar) + G *-in* -ine] An isomeric liquid base obtained from cumene; isopropyl aniline. O, W [3]

cuminoin, *n. Chem.* [G *Kuminoin,* a combining of *Cumin* (see *cumidine*) + *-oin,* as in *Benzoin*] A white crystalline compound obtained from cumaldehyde and analogous to benzoin. W [3]

cupferron, *n.* (1910) *Chem.* [G *Kupferron* (1909) < *Kupfer* (< L *cuprum* copper + *ferrum* iron) + G *-on* -on] A crystalline salt used as a precipitant for iron, copper, and metals of the uranium group. O, R, W [3]

cuprite, *n.* (1850) *Mineral.* [G *Cuprit* (now *Kuprit*) < *cupr-* (< L *cuprum* copper) + G *-it* -ite] Red copper ore or red copper oxide. O, R, W [4]

cuproid, *n.* (1864) *Crystal.* [G (now also *Kuproid*) (so named by Wilhelm K. Haidinger (1795–1871), Austrian geologist, the discoverer of numerous minerals) < G *cupr-* + *-oid* -oid < L *cuprum* copper + Gk *-oeidēs* similar] A solid that contains 12 equal triangles and is related to a tetrahedron. O, W [3]

curcumin, *n.* (1850) *Chem.* [G *Kurkumin* < NL < Ar *kurkum* saffron + G *-in* -in] Turmeric yellow, an orange-yellow crystalline compound used to color foods. —**curcumin** S. O, W [3]

curine, *n. Chem.* [G *Curin* (now *Kurin*) < *Curare* (now *Kurare*) < Sp < Tupi *urari* lit., whomever it comes upon, that person is felled + G *-in* -ine] A crystalline alkaloid derived from tube curare. W [3]

Curort, *see* Kurort

cuscohygrine, *n. Chem.* Var. **cuskhygrine** [G *Cuskohygrin* (now also *Kuskohygrine*) < the name of Sp *Cuzco* city in Peru + Gk *hygrós* wet, damp + G -*in* -ine] An oily base cooccurring with hygrine in cusco-bark leaves. W [3]

cusconine, *n. Chem.* [Prob. < G *Cuskonin* < the name of Sp *Cuzco* city in Peru + G -*n*- + -*in* -ine] A crystalline alkaloid found in cusco bark. W [3]

cuskhygrine, *see* cuscohygrine

cyanate, *n.* (1845–6) *Chem.* [Prob. < G *Cyanat* (now also *Zyanat*) < *Cyan*- + -*at* -ate < Gk *kýanos* dark blue, enamel, lapis lazuli] A salt or ester of cyanic acid (q.v.). O, R, W [4]

cyanic acid, *n.* (1838 *W9*) *Chem.* [Transl. of G *Zyansäure* < *zyan*- (< Gk *kyáneos* dark blue) + G *Säure* acid] An unstable, poisonous acid obtained from cyanuric acid. O, R, W [4]

cyanidin, *n.* (1914) *Chem.* [G (1913) (now *Zyanidin*) < L *cyanus,* Gk *kyáneos* dark blue + G -*id* -id- + -*in* -in] An anthocyanidin that occurs widely in the form of glycosides like cyanin. O, W [3]

cyanite/kyanite, *n.* (1794) *Mineral.* [G *Zyanit* < *zyan*- (< Gk *kyáneos* dark blue) + G -*it* -ite] An aluminum silicate usu. found in blue crystals or aggregates; also called *disthene* (< the Fr word). —**cyanitic.** O, R, W [3]

cyan(o)-, *comb. form.* (1838) *Chem.* [G *cyan*- (now *zyan*-) < Gk *kyáneos* dark blue] Of a dark blue, as in *cyanotype;* containing cyanogen, as in *cyanophoric.* O, R, W [4]

cyan(o)methemoglobin, *n. Chem.* [G (now *Zyanmethämoglobin*) < *Cyan(o)*- (< Gk *kyáneos* dark blue + *metá* in between) + G *Hämoglobin* < Gk *haîma* blood + L *globus* ball, sphere, globule + G -*in* -in] A red crystalline compound obtained when hydrogen cyanide acts on cold methemoglobin or on oxyhemoglobin at body temperature. W [3]

cyanotrichite, *n.* (1854) *Mineral.* [G *Zyanotrichit* < *zyano*- + -*trichit* < Gk *kyáneos* dark blue + *thrich*- < *thríx* hair + G -*it* -ite] A blue, fibrous, basic copper aluminum sulfate. O, W [3]

cyanuramide, *n. Chem.* [G *Zyanuramid* < *zyan*- < Gk *kyáneos* dark blue + L *ūrīna,* Gk *oûron* urea + G *Amid* (< G *Ammoniak* ammonia + -*id* -ide) amide] Melamine (q.v.). W [3]

cyanuric acid, *n.* (1838) *Chem.* [Transl. of G *Zyanursäure* < *zyan*- < Gk *kyáneos* dark blue + L *ūrīna,* Gk *oûron* urine + G *Säure* acid] A weak, crystalline acid. O, R, W [3]

cyaphenine, *n. Chem.* [G *Zyaphenin* < Gk *kya*-, a short. of *kyáneos* dark blue + Fr *phénol* < Gk *phaínein* to show, glow + G -*in* -ine] A white crystalline compound formed by polymerizing benzonitrile. W [3]

cyclodialysis, *n.* (1908) *Med.* [G *Cyklodialyse* (1905) (now also *Zyklodialyse*) < NL *cyclodialysis* < Gk *kýklos* any circular body, eye + *diálysis* separating] An operation to relieve the tension in the eyeball in cases of glaucoma. O, W [3]

cyclomorphosis, -phoses *pl.* (1926) *Biol.* [G *Cyclomorphose* (1904) (now also *Zyklomorphose*) < NL *cyclomorphosis* < Gk *kýklos* cycle + *mórphōsis* a shaping] The recurrent seasonal polymorphism found esp. in marine planktonic animals. O, W [3]

Cyclon, *see* Zyklon

cyclosis, -ses *pl.* (1835) *Bot.* [G < *cyklo*- + -*se* -sis < Gk *kýklos* cycle + -*sis,* a term proposed by Carl Heinrich Schultz (1798–1871), German botanist in *Die Cyklose des Lebenssafts in den Pflanzen* in 1831] The circulation of milky juice in plant vessels, or of protoplasm within a cell. O, R, W [4]

cyclothymia, *n.* (1921) *Psych.* [G *Cyclothymie* (now *Zyklothymie*) < NL *cyclothymia* < the comb. form of Gk *kýklos* circle + *thymós* mind, temper + G -*ie* (< Gk -*ia*) -ia] A temperament characterized by rapid changes from liveliness to depression that may lead to manic-depressive insanity. —**cyclothymic** (1925), **cyclothyme,** *n.* (1925), O, R, W [4]

cyclotomy, -mies *pl.* (1879) *Math.* [Transl. of G *Kreisteilung* < *Kreis* circle + *Teilung* division] The process of dividing a circle into a given number of equal parts. —**cyclotomic** (1879). O, R, W [3]

cylindrite, *n.* (1893) *Mineral.* Old var. **kylindrite** (1893) [G *Kylindrit* (1893) < Gk *kýlindros* cylinder + G -*it* -ite] A lustrous sulfide of lead, antimony, and tin. O, W [3]

cyprine, *n.* (1823) *Mineral.* [G *Zyprin* < L *cyprum* copper + G -*in* -ine] A variety of vesuvianite colored blue by copper. O, W [3]

cysteine, *n.* (1884) *Biochem.* Var. **cystein** (1923) [G *Cysteïn* (1882) (now *Zysteïn*), based on *Cystin* with the insertion of -*e*- + -*in* -in < Gk *kýstis* bladder] A crystalline amino acid that is oxidizable to cystine and is a constituent of glutathione and many proteins. —**cysteic acid.** O, R, W [4]

cystolith, *n.* (1846) *Path.,* (1857) *Bot.* [G *Zystolith* < *zyst*- + -*lith* < Gk *cysto*-, the comb. form of *kýstē* (urinary) bladder + *líthos* stone] (*Path.*) a urinary calculus; (*Bot.*) a calcium carbonate outgrowth on the cellulose wall of certain cells of higher plants. —**cystolithic** (1846), **cystolithiasis.** O, R, W [4]

cytase, *n.* (1895) *Biochem.* [G (now also *Zytase*) < *cyt*- (now also *zyt*-) (< Gk *kýtos* hollow, receptacle, cell) + G -*ase* -ase, denoting a destroying substance] One of several enzymes occurring in the seeds of plants such as cereals that can make soluble the material of the cell walls by hydrolyzing galactan, mannan, xylan, and araban. O, W [3]

cytaster, *n.* (1892) *Biol.* [G (1882) (now *Zytaster*) < *cyt*- + *Aster* < Gk *kýtos* hollow, receptacle + L *astēr,* Gk *astér* aster] Aster: an asterlike structure not associated with the chromosomes. O, W [3]

cytidine, *n.* (1911) *Biochem.* [G *Cytidin* (1910) (now *Zytidin*), a blend of *Cytaster* + -*idine* (< Gk *kýstisos* herbal plant) + G -*id*- -id- + -*in* -ine] A crystalline nucleoside obtained by hydrolyzing ribonucleic acid and cytidylic acid. —**cytidinic, cytidylic acid.** O, R, W [4]

cyto-, *comb. form* (1859) *Biol.* Var. **cyt-, cyte-** [G (now *zyto*-) < Gk *kýtos* hollow, receptacle] Used in many technical terms to denote a cell (as in *cytochemistry*) or cytoplasm (as in *cytoplasmic*). O, R, W [4]

cytoblast, *n.* (1842) *Biol.* [G (1840) (now *Zytoblast*) < *cyto*- + -*blast* < the comb. form of Gk *kýtos* cavity, cell + *blastós* bud] The cell nucleus; Altmann's granules (q.v.); protoplast. O, R, W [3]

cytode, *n.* (1879) *Biol.* [G (1866) (now *Zytode*) < *cyt*- (now *zyt*-) + -*ode* < Gk *cyto*-, the comb. form of *kýtos* hollow, vessel, cell + -oeidēs like] An anucleate mass of protoplasm; an organism that usu. has cytodic form. O, W [3]

cytoglobin, *n. Chem.* [G (now *Zytoglobin*) < *cyto-* + *Globin* < Gk *cyto-*, the comb. form of *kýtos* hollow, vessel, cell + L *globus* ball + G *-in* -in] A nucleoprotein derivable from many glandular organs and cells. W [3]

cytolymph, *n. Biol.* [G *Cytolymphe* (now *Zytolymphe*) < *cyto-* + *Lymphe* < Gk *cyto-*, the comb. form of *kýtos* hollow, cell + L *lympha* < *limpa, lumpa* < Gk *nýmphē* nymph] Hyaloplasm (q.v.). W [3]

cytomere, *n. Biol.* [G *Cytomer* (now *Zytomer*) < *cyto-* + *-mere* < Gk *cyto-*, the comb. form of *kýtos* hollow, cell + *méros* part] A cell produced by the division of the schizont in certain coccidia; a spermatozoon's cytoplasmic component. W [3]

cytomicrosome, *n. Biol.* [G *Cytomicrosom* (now *Zytomicrosom*) < *cyto-* + *Microsom* < Gk *cyto-*, the comb. form of *kýtos* hollow, cell + *mikrós* small + *sõma* body] Mitochrondrion, a cytoplasmic microsome. W [3]

cytophilic, *a.* (c.1909 *W9*) *Biol.* Var. **cytophil** [Prob. < G *Cytophil* (now *Zytophil*) < *cyto-* + *-phil* < Gk *cyto-*, the comb. form of *kýtos* hollow, cell + *phílos* loving + E *-ic*] Having an affinity for cells. W [3]

cytoplasm, *n.* (1874) *Biol.* [G *Cytoplasma* (1848) (now also *Zytoplasma*), so named by Rudolf Albert von Koliker (1817–85), Swiss anatomist < *cyto-* + *Plasma* < Gk *cyto-*, the comb. form of *kýtos* hollow, cell + *plásma* form] (Archaic) hyaloplasm; (rare today) protoplasm; the part of a protoplast's protoplasm external to the nuclear membrane. —**cytoplasmic** (1889), **-plasmatic, -plasmically, cytoplasmic heredity/inheritance.** O, R, W [4]

cytopyge, *n.* (1888) *Biol.* [G (now *Zytopyge*) < *cyto-* + -*pyge* < Gk *cyto-*, the comb. form of *kýtos* hollow, cell + *pȳgé* rump] The place where a protozoan body discharges waste. O, W [3]

cytosine, *n.* (1894) *Biochem.* [G *Cytosin* (1894) (now also *Zytosin*) < *Cyto-* < Gk *kýtos* hollow, cell + *-ose-*, denoting a carbohydrate + G *-in* -ine] A crystalline pyrimidine base, obtainable by hydrolyzing nucleic acids and also made synthetically. —**cytosine arabinoside.** O, R, W [4]

cytosome, *n. Biol.* [G *Cytosom* (now *Zytosom*) < *cyto-* + *-som* < Gk *cyto-*, the comb. form of *kýtos* hollow, cell + *sõma* body] A cell's cytoplasmic portion. R, W [3]

cytostome, *n. Biol.* (1883) [G *Cytostom* (now *Zytostom*) < *cyto-* + *-stom* < Gk *cyto-*, the comb. form of *kýtos* hollow, cell + *stóma* mouth] The mouth of a unicellular organism. —**cytostomal, cytostomous.** O, R, W [3]

cytotoxin, *n.* (1902) *Chem.* [G (now also *Zytotoxin*) < *cyto-* + *Toxin* < Gk *cyto-*, the comb. form of *kýtos* hollow, cell + *toxikón* poison (used on arrows)] Any substance that has a toxic effect upon cells. —**cytotoxic** (1907), **cytotoxicity, cytotoxic T cell.** O, R, W [4]

cytotropism, *n.* (1909) *Biol.* [G *Cytotropismus* (now also *Zytotropismus*) < *cyto-* + *-tropismus* < Gk *cyto-*, the comb. form of *kýtos* hollow, cell + *tropé* turning + G *-ism* (< L *-ismus*) -ism] The tendency of cell masses and isolated cells to move toward or away from each other. O, R, W [3]

czarin, *n.* (1716) *Politics* (archaic) [G *Zarin* (see *czarina*) < *Zar* + fem. suffix *-in* -in] Czarina. O [3]

czarina, *n.* (1717) *Politics* Var. **tsarina** (1891), **tzarina** [G *Zarin* < *Zar* (< NL *czar* < Russ *tsar*) + L fem. suffix *-ina* -ina] The wife of a Russian czar. O, R, W [4]

D

dachs, -es/-ø *pl.* (1886) *Zool.* (colloq.) [Short. of G *Dachshund*] Dachshund (q.v.), also called *teckel*. O, W [3]

dachshund, -s/-e *pl.* (1840–50 *R*) *Zool.* Var. **dachshound** (c. 1881) [G < *Dachs* badger + *Hund* hound] A German breed of short-legged, droopy-eared dogs, adapted for chasing badgers into burrows. • ~ is transl. as **badger dog** (q.v.). O, R, W [4]

dacite, *n.* (1878) *Geol.* [G *Dazit* (1863) < *Dazien,* the German form of L *Dācia,* in antiquity the name of the territory between the Tisza, Danube, and Dniester rivers + G -*it* -ite] A variety of fine-grained, extrusive rock composed mainly of plagioclase and quartz. —**dacitic.** O, W [3]

dacryoadenalgia, *n.* (1848) *Med.* [G *Dacryoadenalgie* (1803) < Gk *dákryon* tear + *adén* gland + *álgos* pain + G -*ie* (< Gk -*ia*) -ia] Inflammation of a lachrymal gland. O [3]

dahllite, *n.* (1890) *Geol.* [G *Dahllit* (1888) < *Dahll,* the name of the Norwegian brothers and mineralogists Tellef (1825–93) and Johann (1830–77) + G -*it* -ite] Carbonate-hydroxylapatite. O, W [3]

damkjernite, *n.* *Geol.* [G *Damkjernit* < the name of *Damkjern,* Telemark, Norway + G -*it* -ite] A melanocratic dike rock with phenocrysts. W [3]

damping capacity, *n.* (1931) *Physics* [Transl. of G *Dämpfungsfähigkeit* (1923) < *dämpfen* to dampen + *Fähigkeit* ability, capacity] The ability of a material to absorb vibrational energy and dissipate it as heat. O, W [3]

Dance of Death, *see* Totentanz

danke [G short. of *(ich) danke (Ihnen/dir!)* I thank you!] Thanks. R [2]

danke schön [G short. of *(ich) danke (Ihnen/dir) schön!* thank you kindly!] Thanks very much! R [3]

Danziger, *n.* *Geogr.* [G < *Danzig,* the name of the former Free City or German city + *-er* -er] A resident or native of Danzig, esp. before the city was absorbed into Poland. W [3]

Danziger Goldwasser/danziger goldwasser, *n.* *Beverages* [G < *Danziger* the name of the city of *Danzig* (now Pol *Gdansk*), where the liqueur was first produced + G *Goldwasser* goldwater, from its sparkling, golden color] A colorless, aromatic liqueur, with flecks of gold leaf added; also called *Goldwasser, Danzig brandy,* and *goldwater.* W [3]

darapskite, *n.* *Mineral.* [G *Darapskit,* named after Ludwig *Darapsky* (1857–post 1909), Chilean scientist + G -*it* -ite] A hydrous nitrate and sulfate of sodium. W [3]

Dasein, *n.* (1846) *Philos.* Old var. **Daseyn** (1846) [G (a favorite word of Goethe) existence < *da* there + *sein* to be] In Hegelianism, existence or determinate being; in existentialism, factual reality or human existence. O, W [2]

dasylirion, *n.* (1858) *Bot.* [G (1838) < Gk *dasýs* thick + *leírion* lily] A genus (cap.) or a plant of the liliaceous family native to Mexico and the southwestern U.S., with a woody stem and small white flowers. O, W [3]

dasypeltis, *n.* (1849) *Zool.* [G (1830) < Gk *dasýs* thick + *péltē* small shield] A small, harmless, egg-eating snake of central and southern Africa. O [3]

datolite, *n.* (1808) *Mineral.* [G *Datolith* (1806) < Gk *dateîsthai* to divide + G -*lith* < Gk *líthos* stone] A basic calcium borosilicate usu. found in glassy greenish crystals. —**datolitic.** O, R, W [4]

dauerlauf, -s/-läufe *pl.* *Sports* [G < *dauernd* long-lasting (< *dauern* to last, endure) + *Lauf* run, race] A long-distance, cross-country ski race. W [3]

dauermodification, -s/-en *pl.* (1938) *Biol.* Var. **Dauermodifikation** (1938), **dauermodifikation** (1968) [G *Dauermodifikation* (1913) < *Dauer* duration < *dauern* to last + *Modifikation* < Fr *modification*] An acquired character that is temporarily transmitted through the cytoplasm and tends to disappear after a few generations. O, W [3]

dauerschlaf, *n.* *Med.* [G < *dauernd* long-lasting + *Schlaf* sleep] Psychotherapy, now rarely used, that uses drugs to induce long periods of deep sleep. R [3]

Day, (The), *n.* (1914) *Politics* [Transl. of G *(Der) Tag,* lit., (the) day] A day when an important event is expected to occur. O [3]

death instinct, *n.* (1922) *Psych.* [Transl. of Freud's G *Todestrieb* (1920) death instinct or drive)] A biological or unconscious tendency toward destruction, usu. self-destruction. O, R, W [4]

death song, *n.* (1778) *Music* Var. **death-song** (1778) [Transl. of G *Todesgesang* < the gen. of *Tod* death + *Gesang* song] A song performed immediately before death or to memorialize the dead; such a custom among the American Indians. O [3]

death wish, *n.* (1896) *Psych.* Var. **death-wish** (1896) [Transl. of G *Todeswunsch* < the gen. of *Tod* death + *Wunsch* wish] A conscious or unconscious desire for the death of oneself or another. O, R, W [4]

dechenite, *n.* (1851) *Mineral.* [G *Dechenit* < the name of Heinrich von *Dechen* (1800–89), German geologist + -*it* -ite] Natural lead metavanadate. O, W [3]

decision problem, *n.* (1939) *Math., Philos.* [Transl. of G *Entscheidungsproblem* < *Entscheidung* decision + *Problem* < L *problēma* < Gk] The deductive problem of finding a decision procedure for a class of formulas. O, W [3]

decke, -n *pl.* *Geol.* [G, lit., cover < *decken* to cover] A nappe, a large mass thrust over other rocks. W [3]

deckel, *see* deckle

decken structure, *n.* *Geol.* [Partial transl. of G *Deckenbau* (or *Deckensystem*) < *Decken* (< *Decke*) cover + *Bau* structure (or *System* system < Gk *sýstema*)] A nappe structure. W [3]

deckle, *n.* (1810) *Industry* Var. **deckel** [G *Deckel* lid, cover] Deckle edge or strap; a frame around the outside edges of a papermaking machine or of a hand mold that governs the paper width. —**deckle**, *v.;* **deckled** (1906). • ~ also appears in compounds like **deckle strap** (1810)/**edge** (1874), **deckle-edged** (1888). O, R, W [4]

defervescence, *n.* (1866) *Med.* [G *Defervescenz* (now *Deferveszenz*) < L *dēfervēscens,* present part. of *dēfervēscere* to cool off] Subsidence of a fever (this is different from the old meaning of "abatement of heat"). O, R, W [3]

deflation, *n.* (1893) *Geol.* [G (1891) sweep, first used in this sense by the German geologist Johannes Walther (1860–1937) < L *deflātus,* past part. of *deflāre* to blow off] Wind erosion of particles of rock, sand, etc. (this is different from the meaning of "act of economic or other contraction"). O, R, W [4]

defusion, *n.* (1927) *Psych.* [Transl. of Freud's G *Entmischung* (1923) a reversal of fusion, formed as an opposite to *Mischung* mixture] A reversing of the normal fusion of the instincts accompanying maturity. O, R, W [3]

dehnstufe, -n *pl. Ling.* [G < *dehnen* to stretch, lengthen + *Stufe* step, grade] In Indo-European ablaut, the lengthening of a vowel to compensate for a dropped consonant, as in E *goose,* corresponding to G *Gans;* the lengthened grade of a vowel. W [2]

dehrnite, *n. Mineral.* [G *Dehrnit* < the name of *Dehrn,* a village near Limburg, Germany, where it was discovered + *-it* -ite] Carbonate-fluorapatite. W [3]

dehydracetic acid, *n.* (1872) *Chem.* [Transl. of G *Dehydracetsäure* (1866) (now *Dehydrazetsäure*) < *dehydracet* + *Säure* acid < L *de-* de- + Gk *hýdōr* water + L *acētum* vinegar] A crystalline, cyclic compound, usu. produced by heating ethyl acetoacetate and used to treat fruit. O [3]

dehydrase, *n.* (1914) *Biochem.* [G (1913) < L *de-* de- + Gk *hýdōr* water + G *-ase* -ase, denoting a destroying substance] Dehydrogenase; dehydratase. O [3]

dehydrocholesterol, *n.* (1935) *Chem.* [G *Dehydrocholesteryl* (1935) < *dehydro-* + *Cholesteryl* < L *de-* from + Gk *hýdōr* water + *cholé* bile + *stereós* stiff, solid + G *-yl* -ol] A crystalline, steroid alchohol, the provitamin of vitamin D3. O, W [3]

delanovite, *n.* (1854) *Mineral.* Var. **delanouite** (1934) [G *Delanovit* (1854) < the name of Gaston-Ovid *Delanoue* (1836–1902), French geologist + G *-it* -ite] A rose-red, manganiferous clay. O [3]

delatynite, *n. Chem.* [G *Delatynit* < the name of *Delatyn,* a Ukranian town in the Carpathian Mountains + G *-it* -ite] A carbon-rich amber found at Delatyn. W [3]

deli, *see* delicatessen.[2]

delicatessen[1], *n.* (1893) *Food* [G *Delikatessen,* pl. of *Delikatesse* delicacy < *delikat* (< L *dēlicātus*) + G *Essen* food, meal] Ready-to-eat food products, including meats, cheeses, delicacies, relishes, etc. O, R, W [4]

delicatessen[2], *n.* (1877) *Food* [Short. of G *Delikatessengeschäft* < *Delikatessen* delicatessen[1] (q.v.) + *Geschäft* store, business] A store that sells ready-to-eat food products. —**delicatessen store** (1889)/**shop** (1893)/**dealer** (1894)/**department** (1894)/**truck** (1900)/**dinner** (1904)/**man** (1913). • ~ is short. to the colloq. **deli** (1954). O, R, W [4]

delomorphous/delomorphic, *a.* (1882) *Anat.* [G *delomorph* (1870) (< *delo-* + *-morph* < Gk *dêlos* visible + *morphē* form) + E *-ous* or *-ic*] Having fixed or definite form, as in the parietal cells of the cardiac glands. O, W [3]

delphinidin, *n.* (1914) *Chem.* [G (1914) < NL *Delphinium* larkspur + G *-id* -ide + *-in* -in] An anthocyanidin occurring widely in plants in the form of glycosides. O, W [3]

delvauxite, *n.* (1854) *Mineral.* [G *Delvauxit* (1854), ad. of Fr *delvauxine* < the name of J. S. P. J. *Delvaux* de Feuffe (1782–1863), Belgian chemist + G *-it* -ite] An ill-defined hydrous ferric phosphate. O, W [3]

demantoid, *n.* (1892) *Mineral.* [G a green variety of andradite < obs. G *Demant,* a var. of *Diamant* (< OFr) diamond + G *-oid* < Gk *-oeidēs* similar)] A green variety of andradite with a brilliant luster: a valued garnet. O, R, W [4]

denkmal, -mäler, *pl.* (1877) [G monument, memorial < *denk-,* corresponding to Gk *mnēmosýnon* a mnemonic aid + G *Mal* < MHG, OHG *meil* sign, mark] A monument, memorial. O [3]

depside, *n.* (1910) *Chem.* [G *Depsid* (1910) < Gk *dépsein* to knead + G *-id* -ide] Any of the largest organic group of lichen substances. O [3]

depsidone, *n.* (1935) *Chem.* [G *Depsidon* (1934) < Gk *dépsein* to knead + G *-id* -ide + *-on* -one, denoting the presence of a carbonyl group] Any of a group of lichen acids related to the depsides (q.v.), but that are not readily broken down by alkalis. O [3]

depth psychology, *n.* (1924 *W9*) *Psych.* [Transl. of Freud's G *Tiefenpsychologie* (1923) < the comb. form of *Tiefe* + *Psychologie* < NL *psychologia*] Psychonanalysis. —**depth psychologist** (1947), **depth-psychological** (1958). O, R, W [4]

dermatome, *n.* (1915) *Anat.* [G *Dermatom* (1898) < *derma-* + *-tom* < Gk *dérma* skin + *tómos* that which cuts] A skin area delimited by its single nerve supply (this is different from the older "surgical device and embryological" meanings). —**dermatomal**, *a.* O, R, W [4]

dermatomyositis, *n.* (1899) *Path.* [Ad. of G *Dermomyositis* (1891) < *dermato-* + *Myositis* < Gk *dérma* skin + *mŷs* (gen. *mŷos*) muscle + G (< L) *-itis* -itis, medical suffix denoting inflammation] A chronic inflammation of unknown origin affecting the skin, skeletal muscles, and subcutaneous tissue. O, R, W [3]

derrid(e), *n.* (1890) *Chem.* [G *Derrid* (1890) < *Derris* (< Gk) membrane + G *-id* -ide)] A drug extracted from derris. O [3]

desemer, *n.* [G < LG, ad. < MLG *bisemer, besemer* (of Baltic origin), describing a weight] An ancient balance: a steelyard. W [3]

determinable, (the), *n.* (1878) *Philos.* [Transl. of G *das Bestimmbare* < *das* the + *bestimmbar* capable of being determined] That which can be given a more determinate form or be more precisely specified, esp. as a general term or concept. —**determinable**, *a.* (1949). O [3]

determinant, *n.* (1893) *Biol.* [G *Determinante* (1892) < L *dētermināns,* gen. *dētermināntis,* present part. of *dētermināre* to determine, a concept introduced by August F. L. Weismann (1834–1914), German zoologist] In Weismann's theory of heredity, a hypothetical unit supposedly determining the development and character of a cell, in contrast to the gene of more recent biological theory (this is different from the old meaning of "something that identifies, determines, or aids analysis"). O, R, W [3]

determinative judgment, *n. Philos.* [Transl. of Kant's G *bestimmende Urteilskraft* < present part. of *bestimmen* to determine + *Urteilskraft* ability to judge, judgment] A judgment, developed from a general concept or universal principle, which designates the particulars. W [3]

deuteranope, *n.* (1902) *Optics* [G (1897) < Gk *deúteros* less < *deúein* to lack + *-an-* *-un-* + *óps* eye] One who is red-green color-blind. —**deuteranopia** (1901); **deuteranopic.** O, W [3]

Deutsche Blumen, *n. Art* [G < *deutsch* German + *Blume* flower] A kind of porcelain decoration of the mid-18th century. R [2]

Deutsche mark, deutsche mark, *n.* (1948) *Currency* Var. **D-mark** (1948), **DM** (1958), **Deutsch(e)mark** (1959), **deutschmark** [G < *deutsch* German + *Mark* a German monetary unit] The German mark used by the German Federal Republic in the period 1948–90; the monetary unit of the German Democratic Republic during part of that period (see *Ostmark*); the monetary unit of the reunified Germany from 1990. O, R, W [4]

Deutsches Reich, *n. Politics* [G < *deutsch* German + *Reich* realm] Official name of Germany before 1919. R [3]

Deutschmark, *see* deutsche mark

devil dog, *n.* (1915–20 R) *Mil.* [Transl. of G *Hundsteufel,* designating a U.S. Marine in World War One < *Hund* dog + *Teufel* devil] A U.S. Marine in World War One and later, used by the Marines to describe themselves. R, W [3]

devil's dung, *n.* (1578) *Bot.* [Transl. of G *Teufelsdreck* < the gen. of *Teufel* devil + *Dreck* feces, dung] Asafetida, a fetid Asian gum resin of the plant of the genus *Ferula,* formerly used as an antispasmodic. O, W [3]

devil's milk, *n.* (1578) *Bot.* [Transl. of G *Teufelsmilch* < the gen. of *Teufel* devil + *Milch* milk (or < Du *duivelsmelk*)] Any of several plants secreting acrid, milky juice; the juice itself, supposedly with curative powers. O, W [3]

dextran, *n.* (1879) *Chem.,* (1946) *Med.* [G (1874) < *dextro-* (< L *dexter, dextra* right) + G *-an* -an] Chem.: a dextrorotatory, gummy polysaccharide from starch or enzymes; Med.: partially hydrolyzed dextran, as used in solution as a plasma substitute: synthetic blood. —**clinical/ native dextran.** O, R, W [4]

diabantite, *n.* (1875) *Mineral.* [Ad. of G *Diabantachronnyn,* irreg. < *Diabase* < Gk *diábasis* transition + *chrónnyein* to stain + G *-it* -ite] Ferroan clinochlore, a basic silicate. O, W [3]

diadochite, *n.* (1850) *Mineral.* [G *Diadochit* (1837) < Gk *diádochos* successor + G *-it* -ite] A basic hydrous phosphate and sulfate of iron. O, W [3]

diakinesis, -neses *pl.* (1902) *Biol.* [G *Diakinese* (1897) < *dia-* + *Kinese* < Gk *día* through + *kínēsis* motion, movement] The final stage of meiotic prophase, characterized by the bivalents' marked contraction. —**diakinetic.** O, R, W [4]

dialogite, *n.* (1826) *Mineral.* [G *Dialogit* (c.1817) < Gk *dialogé* enumeration, estimate + G *it-* ite] Rhodochrosite, a manganese carbonate. O, R, W [3]

dianite, *n.* (1861) *Mineral.* [G *Dianit* (1860) < NL *dianium* < the name of the Roman goddess *Diana* Diana + G *-it* -ite] A variety of columbite, an iron columbate. O, W [3]

diaphorase, *n.* (1938) *Biochem.* [G (1938) < Gk *diáphoros*

varied, different + G *-ase* -ase, denoting a destroying substance] A flavoprotein enzyme that can catalyze the reduction of dyes. O, R, W [3]

diaphorite, *n.* (1868) *Mineral.* [G *Diaphorit* < Gk *diáphoros* different + G *-it* -ite] The orthorhombic form of freieslebenite (q.v.). O, W [3]

diaschisis, -ises *pl.* (1915) *Path.* [G (1906) < Gk *diáschizein* to sever] Loss of a pattern of brain activity caused by a localized injury to some other connected region of the nervous system. O, R, W [3]

diathermy, *n.* (1909 *W9*) *Med.* Var. **diathermia** [G *Diathermie* (1909) < *dia-* + *-thermie* < Gk *día* through + *thermós* hot] The passing of high-frequency electric current through tissue for medical or surgical purposes. —**medical/surgical diathermy** (1918, 1930). O, R, W [4]

diatoric, *a.* [Ad. of G *diatoros* < Gk *diátoros* pierced < *diateírein* to pierce + E *-ic*] Of an artificial tooth with a recessed base for attachment to a person's dental plate. W [3]

diazonium, *n.* and *a.* (1895, 1895) *Chem.* [G (1895) < *diaz(o)-* + *-onium* < Gk *di-* < *dís* twice + *a-* not + *zōḗ* life] (Of) the univalent cation $-N_2^+$ attached to a carbon atom in one organic radical. —**diazonium compound** (1895). O, R, W [4]

dichogamy, -mies *pl.* (1862) *Bot.* [G *Dichogamie* < *dicho-* + *-gamie* < Gk *dícho* separate, parted + *gámos* wedding + G *-ie* (<Gk *-ia*) -y] The condition where the male and female reproductive elements of hermaphroditic plants or animals produce at different times and thus ensure crossfertilization. —**dichogamous** (1859), **dichogamic.** O, R, W [3]

dicoumarin, *n.* (1886) *Chem.* Var. **Dicumarol** (1942), **dicoumarol** (1943) [G *Dicumarin* (1885) < *di-* + *Coumarin* < Gk *di-* < *dís* twice + Fr *coumarine* (< *cumaríe,* native name in Guiana of the Tonka bean) + G *-in* -in] Orig., any compound with a basic structure of two conjoined coumarin molecules; (cap.) the trademark; a white crystalline compound obtained from spoiled sweet clover hay, used as an anticoagulant; also called *bishydrocoumarin.*• ~ is commonly spelled **dicoumarol** today. O, R, W [4]

Die Brücke, *see* Brücke

diener, *n. Med.* [G servant < *dienen* to serve + nom. suffix *-er* -er, etc.] Lab helper, esp. in medical schools (this is different from the var. of E *deener* shilling). W [3]

diesel, *n.* (1894) and *a.* (1934 *W9*) *Tech.* [G < the name of Rudolf *Diesel* (1858–1913), German engineer, its inventor, a short. of *Dieselmotor/Diesellokomotive* diesel engine, diesel locomotive] (Of) Diesel's internal combustion engine; (of) an electric locomotive or other vehicle powered by diesel engines to produce its own electric power. • ~ appears in composites like **dieselize** (1946), **dieselization** (1950), **dieselized** (1958), **diesel cycle/electric/engine/-engined.** O, R, W [4]

dietrichite, *n.* (1882) *Mineral.* [G *Dietrichit* (1878) < the name of Dr. G. W. *Dietrich,* Austrian chemist of Pribam, Bohemia, who was active in the 19th century + G *-it* -ite] A hydrous sulfate of aluminum etc. of the halotrichite (q.v.) group. O, W [3]

dietzeite, *n. Mineral.* [G *Dietzeït* < the name of August *Dietze* (d. 1893?), German chemist + *-it* -ite] A yellow calcium iodochromate usu. in fibrous or columnar form. W [3]

digenite, *n.* (1850) *Mineral.* [G *Digenit* < Gk *digenḗs* of two genders, kinds + G *-it* -ite] An isometric copper sulfide with varying deficiency in copper. O, W [3]

digitalis, *n.* (1568) *Pharm., Bot.* [G (1542), coined by the German botanist Leonhard Fuchs (1501–66) as a latinization of G *Fingerhut* < *Finger* finger + *Hut* hat, guard, i.e. thimble, from the thumblike shape of the flowers containing the substance of the drug] (Cap.) a genus of Eurasian herbs with bell-shaped flowers; the dried leaf of the purple foxglove, from which a powerful heart stimulant and diuretic are obtained. —**digitalis,** *a.* (1883); **digitally** (1832); **digitalization** (1882); **digitalize** (1927). O, R, W [4]

dihydrite, *n.* (1868) *Mineral.* [G *Dihydrit* < *di-* + *hydr-* (< Gk *di-* < *dís* twofold + Gk *hýdōr* water) + G *-it* -ite] Pseudomalachite (q.v.). O, W [3]

diktat, *n.* (1933) *Politics* [G, lit., something dictated < NL *dictātum,* ult. < L *dictāre* to dictate, command] A harsh treaty or settlement imposed on a vanquished enemy, esp. said of the Treaty of Versailles in 1919; a categorical assertion. O, R, W [4]

ding an sich/Ding an sich, *pl.* **dinge an sich** (1846) *Phil.* Var. **Ding-an-sich** (1865) [G < *Ding* thing + *an sich* in itself] Thing-in-itself (q.v.). O, R, W [3]

dingus, -es *pl.* (1876) (colloq.) Old var. like **dingis** (1876) [Prob. colloq. G *Dings* or Du *dinges* someone or something whose name can't be momentarily remembered < OHG *ding* thing] A contraption or gadget whose common name is unknown or momentarily forgotten; (vulgar) penis. O, R, W [4]

dinkel, *n.* (1866) *Bot.* [G a type of wheat or spelt < OHG *dinkel* (origin unknown)] A species of wheat. O [3]

DIN system, *n.* *Industry* [G *DIN* (abbr. of *Deutsche Industrie Normen* German industry norms, i.e., standards for industrial products as set by the Deutscher Normenausschuss, a German organization that establishes and registers standards in all branches of industry) + E *system*] A system to determine the speed of photographic materials under certain conditions. W [3]

diogenite, *n.* *Geol.* [G *Diogenit* < Gk *diogenḗs* born of or descended from Zeus + G *-it* -ite] An achondritic meteorite composed mainly of orthopyroxene. W [3]

dionin(e), *n.* (1899) *Pharm.* [G *Dionin,* a former trademark] Ethylmorphine or its hydrochloride, used for its narcotic effect like that of codeine. O, W [3]

diosgenin, *n.* (1937) *Chem.* [G (1936) < NL *Dioscorea* the scientific name of the Mexican yam (ad. < the name of *Dioscoridēs,* 1st cent. Greek physician) + G *-genin* < Gk *-genēs* producing, yielding] A crystalline steroid sapogenin obtained chiefly from Mexican yams and used in synthesizing cortisone. O, R, W [3]

diosphenol, *n.* (1880) *Chem.* [Prob. < G < Gk *diósma* divine odor + G *Phenol* (< Fr *phenol* < Gk *phaino-* < *phaínein* to appear, show)] A crystalline hydroxy terpenoid ketone obtained from buchu oil, also called *buchu camphor.* O, W [3]

dip, *n.* (1894) *Lit.* [Transl. of G *Senkung* dip < *senken* to dip + *-ung*] An unstressed element in a line of alliterative verse. O [3]

dipeptidase, *n.* (1927) *Biochem.* [G (1927) < *Dipeptid* (see *dipeptide*) + *-ase* -ase, denoting a destroying substance] An enzyme that catalyzes the hydrolysis of a dipeptide but not of a polypeptide (q.v.). O, R, W [4]

dipeptide, *n.* (c.1891 *W9*) *Chem.* [Prob. < G *Dipeptid* < *di-* + *Peptid* < *di-,* comb. form of Gk *dís* twice + *peptós* cooked, digested + G *-id* -ide] A peptide that provides two molecules of amino acid by hydrolysis. O, R, W [4]

diploicin, *n.* (1904) *Biol.* [G (1904) (now *Diploizin*) < L *Diploicia canescens* a lichen + G *-in* -in] A crystalline depsidone. O [3]

diploid, *a.* (1908) *Biol.* [Prob. < G (1905) < Gk *diplóos* double + G *-id* -id] Double or twofold in a cell's arrangement or appearance; of or relating to diploidy (this is different from the Greek-derived "crystalline" meaning, esp. as a noun). —**diploidy,** *n.* (1924); **diploidize** (1930); **diploidization** (1930); **diploidic.** O, R, W [4]

diplokaryon, *n.* *Biol.* [G < Gk *diplóos* double + *káryon* nut, kernel] A nucleus having twice the diploid (q.v.) number of chromosomes. —**diplokaryotic.** W [3]

diplont, *n.* (1925) *Biol.* [G < Gk *diplóos* double + *ōn* (gen. *óntos*) being] An organism that is diploid at all stages of its life except as a gamete. —**diplontic** (1929). O, R, W [4]

diplophase, *n.* (1925) *Biol.* [G < Gk *diplóos, diploûs* twofold, double + *phásis* phase] The diploid (q.v.) phase in certain organisms' life cycle. O, R, W [3]

dirndl, *n.* (1937) *Apparel* [(Dial. Bavarian) G (< *Dirne* girl + dim. suffix, as in Bavarian *Kindl, Kindlein* < *Kind* little child), a short. of *Dirndlkleid* lit., a girl's dress] A style of women's dress with close-fitting bodice, short sleeves, low neck, and skirt copied from Alpine peasants. O, R, W [4]

dirndl skirt, *n.* (1957) *Apparel* [Partial transl. G *Dirndlrock* lit., a girl's skirt] A full skirt with a tight waistband. O, R, W [3]

dispireme, *n.* (1890) *Biochem.* Var. **dispirem** (1890) [G *Dispirem* < *di-* + *Spirem* < Gk *dís* double + *speiréma* spindle] A supposed late phase of mitotic division, now usu. considered an observational artifact. O, W [3]

dissogeny, *n.* (1896) *Zool.* Var. **dissogony** (1896) [G *Dissogonie* (1888) < Gk *dissós* double + *gónos* offspring + G *-ie* (< Gk *-ia*) -y] The occurring of sexual maturity in two distinct periods of an individual's life, as in the larval and the adult forms of certain ctenophores. O, R, W [3]

distelfink, *n.* *Zool.* [G (PaG *Dischdelfink*) goldfinch < *Distel* thistle + *Fink* finch] A traditional Pennsylvania Dutch motif designed as a stylized bird. R, W [3]

dithizone, *n.* (1929) *Chem.* [G *Dithizon* (1929), a short. of *Diphenylthiocarbazon*] A crystalline compound used as a reagent for estimating and separating lead and other metals. O [3]

diverticulosis, -loses *pl.* (1917) *Path.* [G (1914) (now also *Divertikulose*) < NL *diverticulum* a byway, deviation + *-osis,* a suffix indicating action, process, condition] An intestinal disorder where there are many diverticula. O, W [4]

DM, see deutsche mark

D-mark, *n.* (1948) *Currency* [G, a short. of *Deutsche Mark* German monetary unit] Deutsche mark (q.v.). O, R, W [4]

Doberman pinscher, *n.* (1917) *Zool.* [G *Dobermann Pinscher* pinscher developed by the German breeder K. F. Ludwig *Dobermann* (1834–94)] A large dog of a breed originating in Germany, with a smooth, short, usu. black coat. • ~ is short. to **pinscher** (1926) and **Doberman** (1928). O, R, W [4]

Dobos torte, *-n pl.* (1915) *Food* Var. **Dobos Torte** (1970), **Dobos torta** (1970), **Dobos** [G (c.1885) < the name of Jozsef C. *Dobós* (1847–1924), Hungarian pastry chef + G *Torte* torte (q.v.)] A rich sponge cake of alternate thin layers, with a mocha-chocolate filling and caramel-glaze topping. O, W [3]

docent, *n.* (1880) *Art, Ed.* [G (1755) (now *Dozent*) < L *docent-,* present part. of *docēre* to teach] A college or university teacher or lecturer, esp. in German institutions; a person who guides groups through a museum or art gallery and provides commentary. O, R, W [4]

doctorand, *n.* (1912) *Ed.* Var. **doctorandus** (1921) [G (now *Doktorand*) (< ML) *doctorandus* a candidate for a doctor's degree] A doctoral candidate. O, W [3]

dollar, *n.* (1543) *Currency* [G, ad. of earlier LG *da(l)ler* (in 1540 Alberus, Luther's student and friend, recorded the HG form *taler* along with the full form *Joachimstaler* < Sankt Joachimsthal, now *Jachymov,* a town in northwestern Bohemia, Czechoslovakia, where the first talers were made)] Orig., the English name for the German *taler* (q.v.), and now also for coins or paper currency of the northern European countries, of various Asian and Central American countries; also, now usu. paper, the standard unit of the United States; many extended senses. • ~ is a long-naturalized, productive item, as in derivatives like **Dollardom** (1852) and **dollarwise,** and in compounds like **dollar diplomacy** (1910) and **dollar store** (1872, U.S.). O, R, W [4]

dolman, *n.* (1883) *Mil.* [Fr or G *Dolman* < Turk *dolama* a short jacket] A short jacket characteristic of hussar uniforms (this is different from the older meanings of "Turkish long robe, woman's mantle"). O, R, W [3]

domeykite, *n.* (1850) *Mineral.* [G *Domeykit* (1845) < the name of Ignacio *Domeyko* (1802–89), Polish mineralogist + G *-it* -ite] Copper triarsenide. O, W [3]

dominant, *a.* (1900) *Biol.* [Transl. of Mendel's G *dominierend* (1866) (now *dominant*) dominating, ult. < OFr *dominance*] Of a hereditary character, where one allele predominates over a contrasting allele in its manifestation (this is different from various older meanings derived from Middle French or Latin). O, R, W [3]

dominigene, *n.* (1938) *Biol.* [G *Dominigen* (1935) < *dominierend* dominant (< MFr or L *domināns*) + G *Gen* < Gk *-genēs* born] A gene that modifies another gene's dominance. O, W [3]

doodle, *v.* (1816) *Music* Old var. **doudle** (1816) [Ad. of G *dudeln* < *Dudel* bagpipe < Czech or Pol *dudy*] (Dial. Brit.) to play on the bagpipe (this is different from the verb that means "to make a fool of," which may come ult. from LG *dudeldopp*). O, R, W [3]

doodlesack, *n.* (1847–78) *Music* Var. **dudelsack** [Ad. of G *Dudelsack* < *Dudel* bagpipe + *Sack* bag] (Dial. Brit.) bagpipe. O, R, W [3]

dopa, *n.* (1917) *Chem.* [G (1917), an abbr. of G *Dioxyphenylalanin* 3,4-Dihydroxyphenylalanine] A crystalline amino acid, named from the initial letters of the formative elements of *di*oxyphenyl*ala*mine, that is used to treat Parkinson's disease. O, R, W [4]

Doppelflöte/doppelflote, *n.* *Music* [G < *doppel-* double + *Flöte* flute < MFr *flaute* < OProv *flaut*] An 8-foot flute pipe-organ stop, of which each pipe has double mouths. W [3]

doppelgänger/doppelganger, *n.* (1830) Var. **doubleganger** (1830), **doppelgaenger,** **Doppelganger** [G < *doppel-* double + *Gänger* goer, as also in *Fußgänger* pedestrian and *Nachgänger* successor] A person's ghostly counterpart and companion, esp. a look-alike who haunts the person's life. O, R, W [4]

Doppler effect, *n.* (1905) *Physics* [G *Doppler-Effekt* (1843) the effect observed and explained by Christian *Doppler* (1803–53), Austrian physicist and mathematician] A change in frequency with which waves (like sound or light) from a given source reach an observer, the frequency increasing with the speed at which source and observer approach each other and decreasing with the speed at which they move away from each other. • ~ appears in compounds like **Doppler-shift,** *v.* (1971); **Doppler shift** (1955)/**radar** (1959)/**broadening** (1963)/**navigation** (1966). It is short. to **Doppler.** O, R, W [4]

dopplerite, *n.* (1863–72) *Mineral.* [G *Dopplerit* (1849), named after Christian *Doppler* (1803–53), Austrian physicist and mathematician + G *-it* -ite] An elastic acid substance found in peat beds and composed of carbon etc. O, W [3]

dorse, *n.* (1610) *Ichthy.* [G *Dorsch* or LG *dorsch* < MLG *dorsch* a young or small cod, found in the Baltic Sea] A young cod. O [3]

Dortmund, *a.* *Art* [G < the name of *Dortmund,* noted German city in Nordrhein-Westphalia on the Dortmund-Ems canal] Of an artistic kind or style prevalent in Dortmund. W [3]

double assurance, *n.* *Biol.* [Transl. of G *Doppelte Sicherung* < *doppelt* double + *Sicherung* assurance (< *sichern* to safeguard)] Dual control of differentiation caused by the synergistic interaction of a specific organizer and a particular competent embryonic tissue. W [3]

doubleganger, *see* doppelgänger

doudle, *see* doodle

douglasite, *n.* *Mineral.* [G *Douglasit* < the name of *Douglas*hall, near Stassfurt, Germany + *-it* -ite] A hydrated potassium iron chloride. W [3]

dragooner, *n.* (1639) *Mil.* (archaic) Var. in several archaic forms and as **dragoon** (< Fr *dragon*) [Prob. < G *Dragoner* < Fr *dragon*] A kind of cavalry soldier of the 17th and 18th centuries. O, W [3]

drahthaar, *n.* *Zool.* [G < *Draht* wire + *Haar* hair] A German breed of wire-haired pointers. R, W [3]

draisine, *n.* (1818) *Transportation* [Fr and G < the name of Baron Karl von *Drais* (1785–1851), its German inventor + G or Fr *-ine* -ine] A dandy horse, a cumbersome, two-wheeled velocipede. O, W [3]

dramaturg, *n.* (1988) *Theater* [Reborrowing of G *Dramaturg* dramaturge (q.v.), to name the person in charge of an old practice in German opera houses and theaters] Artistic or literary adviser to a theatrical or drama company. L2 [4]

dramaturge, *n.* (1859) *Theater* [G *Dramaturg* and Fr *dramaturge* (1787) < Gk *dramatourgós* playwright] A dramatist, esp. someone skilled in writing or revising plays; a functionary of some European theaters who selects and arranges the repertoire. O, R, W [4]

dramaturgy, *n.* (1801) *Theater* [G *Dramaturgie* (1769), used by the German critic and dramatist Gotthold E. Lessing (1729–81) in *Die Hamburgische Dramaturgie* < Gk *dramatourgía* science of the structure and laws of the drama] The technique or art of writing drama; the technical devices used in this and not found in other literary forms; dramatic or theatrical acting. —**dramaturgic(al), dramaturgically.** O, R, W [4]

Drang (nach Osten), *n.* (1906) *Politics* [G *Drang nach Osten* < *Drang* push, pressure + *nach* to(ward) + *Osten* East] The imperialistic foreign policy of Germany to expand into eastern and southeastern Europe, esp. in the 12th to 14th centuries and in the 1930s; transf. sense to economics. O, R [3]

dravite, *n. Mineral.* [G *Dravit* < the name of the *Drave/ Drava* River in Austria and Yugoslavia + G *-it* -ite] A usu. brown, magnesium-containing tourmaline. R, W [3]

dreamwork, *n.* (1913) *Psych.* [Transl. of Freud's G *Traumarbeit* < *Traum* dream + *Arbeit* work] The process by which dreams evolve so as to hide their real meaning from the dreamer's conscious mind. O, R, W [3]

Dreibund, *n.* (1914) *Politics* Var. **dreibund** [G (1882) < *drei* three + *Bund* alliance] The Triple Alliance of Germany, Austria-Hungary, and Italy formed in 1882. 0-1933, R [3]

dreikanter, -s/-ø *pl.* (1903) *Geol.* [G, lit., something with three edges < *drei* three + *Kante* edge + *-er* -er] A usu. three-faced pebble faceted by wind-blown sand: a ventifact. O, R, W [3]

Dresden, *n.* (1735) *Art* [G < the name of *Dresden,* a German city noted for its baroque art and delicate china] The Dresden style; a variety of white porcelain made there. • ~ appears in compounds like **Dresden china** (1735)/**porcelain** (1753)/**ware.** O, W [4]

drilling, *n.* (1640) *Textiles* [By folk etymology < G *Drillich* triple thread cotton weave < MHG *drilich* < L *trilīx* triple-twilled] Drill: a strong, durable cotton fabric (this is different from the "military" meaning). —**drill,** *n.* (1743), **a.** (1861). O, R, W [3]

drillmaster, *n.* (1869) *Mil.* Var. **drill-master** (1869) [G *Drillmeister* < *Drill* drill + *Meister* master] One who teaches or coaches drill, as in the military or the police. O, R, W [4]

drumfire, *n.* (1916 *W9*) *Mil.* [Transl. of G *Trommelfeuer* < *Trommel* drum + *Feuer* fire] Continuous bombardment, like the rolling of drums; fig. sense of barrage, as in political warnings. O, R, W [4]

druse, *n.* (1753) *Geol.* [G < OHG *druos* swelling] A crystalline crust lining the sides of a small rock cavity; such a cavity, O, R, W [3]

dudelsack, *see* doodlesack

duftite, *n. Mineral.* [G *Duftit* < the name of G. *Duft,* director of the Otavi Mines at Tsumeb, South-West

Africa + G *-it* -ite] A basic arsenate of lead and copper. W [3]

dumb, *a.* (1823) (colloq.) [Poss. ad. of G and PaG *dumm* or Du *dom* stupid] Dull, stupid, O, R, W [4]

dumbhead, *see* dummkopf

dummkopf, *n.* (1809) (colloq.) Var. **dumkopf** (1923), **dumbkopf** (1968) [G < *dumm* dumb + *Kopf* head] A stupid person or blockhead, used as a term of abuse. • ~ is transl. as **dumbhead** (1887). O, R, W [4]

Dungan, *see* Tungan

dunk(ard), dunker, *see Introduction* (code switching)

dur, *a. Music* [G < MHG *bedur,* ult. < L *dūrus* hard] Written in a major key, as C dur; major. R, W [3]

durchkomponiert, *a.* (1897) *Music* [G, past part. of *durchkomponieren* to set a libretto to music throughout, without leaving narrative passages; to set a strophic poem to music without regard for the strophe < *durch* through + *komponieren* < L *compōnere*] Through-composed, said of a libretto set to music without narrative passages or of a poem set to music without regard to its strophic form. O, W [3]

durchmusterung, *n.* (1892) *Astronomy* [G (1856), used by the German astronomer Friedrich Wilhelm August Argelander (1799–1875) in his *Durchmusterung des nördlichen Himmels* < *durch* through(out) + *Musterung* examination] Certain extensive catalogs of stars specifying their magnitude and approximate positions. O-1933 [2]

dusack, *n. Mil.* [G *Dussak* < Czech *tesák* sword] A kind of rough German cutlass used in the 16th century. W2 [2]

dyestuff, *n.* (1837) *Chem.* [Prob. a transl. of G *Farbstoff* < *Farbe* color, dye + *Stoff* stuff] Dye, a natural or synthetic coloring matter used to color materials. O, R, W [4]

dynamo, *n.* (1875) *Industry* [Short. of G *Dynamo(electrische) Maschine* (1867) < Gk *dynámis* power + G *elektrisch* electric + *Maschine* machine < NL *electricus* + L *māchina*] A generator, esp. a direct-current one; a person of great energy or force. O, R, W [4]

dynamoelectric, *a. Industry* Var. **dynamoelectrical** [G *dynamoelektrisch*—see *dynamo*] Concerning the change of mechanical into electrical energy or vice versa. R, W [3]

dyslexia, *n.* (1888) *Med.* [G *Dyslexie* (1883) < Gk *dys-* poor, bad + *léxis* speech] Disturbance of one's ability to read. —**dyslectic,** *a.* (1960); **dyslexic,** *n.* (1960). O, R, W [4]

dysplastic, *n.* and *a.* (1925, 1925) *Path.* [G *dysplastisch* (1921) < *dys-* + *plastisch* < Gk *dys-* bad, poor + *plastikós* < *plássein* to shape] (Of or possessing) abnormal growth or development, as in organs, cells, etc. O, R, W [4]

dysteleology, *n.* (1874) *Philos.* [Haeckel's G *Dysteleologie* (1866) < *dys-* + *Teleologie* < Gk *dys-* poor, bad + NL *teleologia* < Gk *télos* end, aim, goal + *lógos* study, word] The doctrine of purposelessness in nature, as in animals' functionless rudimentary organs; such an organ. —**dysteological** (1874), **dysteleologist** (1883). O, R, W [3]

dystrophic, *a.* (1931) *Ecology* [G *dystroph* (1925), used by the German zoologist August Thienemann (1882–1960) (< *dys-* + *-troph* < Gk *dys-* poor, bad + NL *-trophia*) + E *-ic*] Concerning a lake containing much dissolved humic matter (this is different from the older "dystrophy" meaning). O, R, W [4]

E

earth mother, *n.* (1902 *W9*) *Myth.* Var. **Earth-Mother** (1904) [Transl. of G *Erdmutter* < *Erde* earth + *Mutter* mother] A mythological spirit or being symbolizing the earth as the divine source of terrestrial life: the female principle of fertility; a sensual and maternal woman; mother earth. O, R, W [4]

earth pitch, *n. Mineral.* [Transl. of G *Erdpech* < *Erde* earth + *Pech* pitch] Maltha, a mineral tar; also called *brea.* W [3]

East Germanic, *n.* (c.1901 *W9*) *Ling.* [Prob. transl. of G *Ostgermanisch* < *ost-,* comb. form of *Osten* East + *Germanisch* Germanic] An extinct division of the Germanic branch of Indo-European languages containing Gothic and prob. some other languages. R, W [4]

ecdyson(e), *n.* (1956) *Zool.* [G (1956) < Gk *ékdysis* act of getting out, escape + *ōn* being] A steroid, present hormonally in the young forms of insects and diverse classes of arthropods, that controls molting. O [4]

ecgonine, *n.* (1864) *Chem.* [G *Ecgonin* (1862) < Gk *ékgonos* made from + G *-in* -ine] A crystalline alkaloid obtained by hydrolyzing cocaine; tropine-carboxylic acid. —**ecgonic** (1891); **ecgonate,** *n.* (1891). O, W [3]

echitamine, *n.* (1879) *Chem.* [G *Echitamin* (1878) < NL *Echites scholaris* generic plant name + G *Amin* amine] An alkaloid present in the bark of various species of *Echites.* —**echitenine** (1886), **echitine** (1906), **echitamidine** (1932). O [3]

echt, *a.* (1916) [G < LG, ult. OHG *ēhaft* proper, legal] Authentic, genuine, typical. —**echt,** *adv.* (1950). O, R, W [3]

ecology, -ies *pl.* (1873) *Ecology* Var. **oecology** (1873), **aecology** [Ad. of G *Ökologie* < Gk *oîkos* house(hold) + *lógos* word, study + G *-ie* (< Gk *-ia*) -y] A branch of science concerned with interrelationships of organisms and their environments; the pattern or totality of such relationships; human ecology. —**ecologist** (1893), **-ic(al)** (1896, 1899), **-ically** (1909), **ecological subspecies.** O, R, W [4]

ecphore/ekphore, *v.* (1917) *Psych.* [Prob. short. of G *ekphorieren* (1912) < Gk *ekphoreîn* < *ékphoros* (to be) made known] To ecphorize: to rouse or revive an engram or system of engrams from latency. —**ecphoric/ekphoric** (1921), **ecphorically** (1921), **ecphorize/ecphorise** (1923), **ecphorizable** (1923). O, W [3]

ecphoria, -s/-e *pl.* (1917) *Psych.* Var. **ekphory** (1917), **ecphory** (1921) [G *Ekphorie* (1912) < *ek-* + *-phorie* < Gk *ékphoros* made known + G *-ie* (< Gk *-ia*) -ia or -y] The rousing of an engram or engrammic system into an active state. O, W [3]

ectogenic, *a.* (1900) *Biol.* [Prob. < G *ektogen* (see *ectogenous*) + E *-ic*] Of an exogenous disease; of an ectogenous organism. O, R, W [3]

ectogenous, *a.* (1883) *Biol.* [Prob. < G *ektogen* (< NL < Gk *ektós* outside of + *-genēs* born) + E *-ous*] Capable of developing apart from its host, esp. for pathogenic bacteria. O, R, W [4]

ectotrophic, *a.* (1897 *W9*) *Bot.* Var. **ectotropic** [G *ektotrophisch* (1890) < *ecto-* + *-trophisch* < Gk *ektós* outer, outside of + *trophḗ* nutrition, nourishment + G suffix *-isch* -ic] Of the relationship between a fungus and a mycorrhiza, where the fungus or tissue covers the plant roots, and supplies digested organic nutrients to the plant, which in turn supplies minerals and water to the fungus. O, R, W [3]

edaphic, *a.* (1900) *Ecology* [G *edaphisch* (1898), used by the German botanist Andreas Franz Wilhelm Schimper (1856–1901) in *Pflanzengeographie auf physiologischer Grundlage* < Gk *édaphos* soil + G *-isch* -ic] Relating to, produced, or influenced by the soil; of the change so produced in ecological formations. —**edaphic climax** (1949), **edaphically.** O, R, W [4]

edaphon, *n.* (1927) *Ecology* [G (1913) < Gk *édaphos* soil + G *-on* -on] The community of plant and animal life in the soils. O, R, W [3]

edelweiss, *n.* (1862) *Bot.* [G *Edelweiß* < *edel* noble + *weiß* white] A small, perennial alpine plant of the genus *Leontopodium* with woolly leaves and white composite "flowers"; a New Zealand plant related to this; a plant of the *Gnaphalium* genus. —**edelweiss,** *a.* (1884). O, R, W [4]

edenite, *n.* (1842) *Mineral.* [G *Edenit* (1839) < the name of *Eden*ville, a town in the State of New York, U.S.A. + G *-it* -ite] A light-colored variety of aluminous amphibole. O, W [3]

EEG, *see* electroencephalogram

effusive, *a.* (1888) *Geol.* [G *effusiv* (1887) < L *effūsiō* outpouring] Distinguished or formed by the nonexplosive outpouring of lava (this is different from various older meanings). —**effusive,** *n.* (1895). O, R, W [4]

egeran, *n. Mineral.* [G < *Eger,* the German name of a river in the Sudeten region of Czechoslovakia (Czech *Cheb*) + G *-an* -an] A brown idocrase, a silicate. W [3]

eicosenic acid, *n.* (1923) *Chem.* Old var. **icosenic acid** (1923) [Transl. of G *Eikosensäure* (1894) < Gk *eíkosi* twenty + G *Säure* acid] An unsaturated fatty acid, of which one isomer, 9-eicosenic acid, is a minor constituent of many fish oils, and another, 11-eicosenic acid, occurs in the wax of certain plant seeds. O [3]

eider, *n.* (1743) *Zool.* [Prob. < G *Eider(ente)* < *Eider,* the name of a German river in Schleswig-Holstein, ult. < Icel (+ G *Ente* duck)] An eider duck or its eiderdown. —**eider,** *a.* (1791). O, R, W [4]

eiderdown, *n.* (1774) *Zool.* [Prob. a partial transl. of G *Eiderdaune* < *Eider* eider (q.v.) + *Daune* down] The breast feathers from an eider duck; a quilt or comforter filled with eiderdown or a similar soft matter. —**eiderdown,** *a.* (1859). O, R, W [4]

eidetic, *a.* (1924) *Psych.* [G *eidetisch,* used by the German psychologist Erich Jaensch (1883–?) < Gk *eidetikós* forming, shaping] Concerning the faculty of seeing images that revive an optical impression with almost photographic accuracy: vivid, lifelike (this is different from the Greek-derived meanings of "of an intuitionist, having the characteristics of eidos"). —eidetic, *n.* (1970); eidetically (1929); eidetics (1943). O, R, W [4]

Eifelian, *a. Geol.* (1853) Old var. **Eifel** (1879) [Fr *eifélien* or G *Eifel,* the name of a region in Germany + E *-ian*] Of or relating to a subdivision and/or the rocks of European Devonian. —**Eifelian,** *n.* (1895). O, W [4]

eigen-, *comb. form* (1930) *Math., Physics* [G *eigen* own, characteristic] Used in various technical compounds like *eigenperiod* (1940). O [3]

eigenfrequency, *n.* (1955) *Physics* [G *Eigenfrequenz* < *eigen* own, characteristic + *Frequenz* frequency < L *frequentia*] One of the frequencies at which a given oscillatory system is able to vibrate; a resonant frequency. O, W [3]

eigenfunction, *n.* (1926) *Math., Physics* [G *Eigenfunktion* < *eigen* own, characteristic + *Funktion* function < L *fūnctiōn-, fūnctiō*] The solution of a differential equation such as the Schrödinger wave equation so as to satisfy specified conditions: proper function. O, R, W [3]

eigenstate, *n.* (1955) *Physics* [Partial transl. of G *Eigenstand* < *eigen* own, characteristic + *Stand* state] A state of a quantized dynamic system that meets certain conditions. O, W [3]

eigentone, *n.* (1940) *Physics* [G *Eigenton* < *eigen* own, characteristic + *Ton* tone] A tone or one of several tones from or characteristic of a vibrating body or system; the frequency at which this occurs. O, W [3]

eigenvalue, *n.* (1927) *Physics* [Partial transl. of G *Eigenwert* < *eigen* own, proper + *Wert* value] Any of the permissible values of an eigenfunction's parameter; also called *characteristic root/value* and *proper value* (1930). O, R, W [4]

eigenvector, *n.* (1955) *Physics* [G *Eigenvektor* < *eigen* own, proper + *Vektor* vector < NL *vector* < L] Characteristic vector. • ~ is transl. as **characteristic vector.** O, R [3]

einfühlung, *n.* (1904) *Psych.* Var. **Einfühlung** (1936) [G < *sich einfühlen* to get a feeling (for), have a sympathetic understanding (of) + nom. suffix *-ung* -ing] Empathy. • ~ is transl. as **empathy** (q.v., 1904). O [3]

einkanter, *n. Geol.* [G, lit., something with one edge < *ein* one + *Kante* edge + *-er* -er] A stone having one sharp edge worn by wind-driven sand. R, W [3]

einkorn, *n.* (1884) *Bot.* [G < *ein* one + *Korn* kernel] *Triticum monococcum,* perhaps the most primitive, cultivated, 7-chromosome wheat, prob. a derivative of wild einkorn and a grass and still grown esp. in poor soils in central Europe. O, R, W [4]

eis wool, *n.* (1882) *Textiles* Var. **ice wool** (1882) [Partial transl. of G *Eiswolle* < *Eis* ice + *Wolle* wool] A fine, glossy wool yarn made of two-threaded thickness and used double for making shawls. O-1933 [3]

eka-, *comb. form* (1889) *Chem.* [G (1872) < Skt *eka* one] Denoting a predicted element that should occupy the next lower position in the same family of the periodic table, esp. for undiscovered elements like ekacesium (i.e., virginium), just below cesium. O, R, W [3]

EKG, *see* electrocardiogram

ekphore, *see* ecphore

ekphory, *see* ecphoria

el(a)eolite, *n.* (1816) *Mineral.* [G *Eläolith* < *Eläo* + *-lith* < Gk *élaion* olive oil + *líthos* stone] A variety of nephelite, a hexagonal silicate. O, W [3]

elastic (collision), *a.* (1913) and *n.* (1923 *W9*) *Physics* [G *elastisch* (1913) < Gk *elastós* flexible + E *collision*] (Of) a collision between two particles where the total kinetic energy is conserved, as is the total momentum. O, R, W [3]

elastin, *n.* (1875) *Biochem.* [G < Gk *elastós* elastic + G *-in* -in] Brittle, fibrous scleroprotein found in elastic tissue, ligaments, and artery walls. O, R, W [4]

elaterite, *n.* (1826) *Mineral.* [G *Elaterit* < Gk *elatér* driver + G *-it* -ite] Mineral rubber, a fossil resin found in the U.S. and used in varnishes and other coatings such as waterproofing. O, R, W [4]

elector, *n.* (1529) *Politics* Var. **Elector** [Short. of the transl. of G *Kurfürst* < *Kur* (now *Kür*) election, i.e., electoral + *Fürst* prince (or directly < MFr *electeur* and/or ML *elector*)] One of the German princes during the Holy Roman Empire entitled to take part in selecting the Emperor (this is different from various other "election" meanings such as a Knight Elector or an elector who votes in the U.S., Great Britain, or Ireland). O, R, W [4]

electrocardiogram, *n.* (1904) *Med.* [G *Electrocardiogramm* (1894) (now *Elektrokardiogram*) < Gk *élektron* amber (since amber was noted first to generate electricity when rubbed) + *kardía* heart + *grámma* record] A record of the electric currents that the heart produces in the body, provided by an electrocardiograph to detect abnormalities in the heart muscle. • ~ is abbr. as **EKG.** O, R, W [4]

electroencephalogram, *n.* (1934) *Med.* [G *Elektroenkephalogramm* (1929) < Gk *élektron* amber (see *electrocardiogram*) + *enképhalos* brain + *grámma* record] The tracing of the pattern of brain waves as recorded by an electroencephalograph. • ~ is abbr. as **EEG** (1936). O, R, W [4]

electron microscope, *n.* (1932) *Med.* [G *Elektronenmikroskop* (1932), used by the German physicist Ernst Brüche (1900–) < *Elektron* electron + *Mikroskop* microscope] An electron-optical instrument that uses an electron beam to radically magnify minute objects onto a screen or plate. —**electron microscopic(al)** (1933, 1945); **-copy,** *n.* (1934); **-copist** (1948). O, R, W [4]

electron optics, *n.* (1932) *Physics* [Prob. < G *Elektronenoptik* (1932) < *Elektron* electron + *Optik* optics] A branch of electronics that studies and uses electron beams analogous to those of light rays (this is different from the older "chemical" meaning). —**electron-optical** (1933). O, R, W [4]

electroviscous (effect), *n.* and *a.* (1935, 1935) *Chem.* [G *elektroviskos* (1935) < NL *electricus* produced from amber by friction < Gk *élektron* amber + LL *viscosus* sticky] (Of) the increase in viscosity in a solution or suspension as caused by an electric charge. O, W [3]

element, *n.* (1901) *Math., Philos.* [G (1882), used in this sense by the German mathematician Georg Cantor (1845–1918), ult. < L *elementum* a component unit of a series] Any of the real or conceptual entities composing a set, as in a progression of numbers or in a matrix of symbols; an entity that fulfills the criterion or criteria used to define a set (this is different from the many earlier meanings). O, R, W [4]

elemicin, *n. Chem.* [G *Elemizin* < *Elemi* the resin of a certain group of tropical trees (< NL *elemi,* prob. < Ar *al-lāmi*) + G *-iz* < L adj. suffix *-icus* + G *-in* -in] A liquid ether present in some essential oils. W [3]

eleolite, *see* elaeolite

eleonorite, *n.* (1881) *Mineral.* [G *Eleonorit* (1880) < *Eleonore,* a woman's name used as the name of a mine near Giessen, Germany + *-it* -ite] A former name for a supposed variety of beraunite (q.v.). O [3]

eliasite, *n.* (1852) *Mineral.* [G *Eliasit* < *Elias(grube)* mine, the name of a mine in Joachimsthal, now Jachymov, Czechoslovakia + G *-it* -ite] A variety of gummite (q.v.). O, W [3]

elute, *v.* (1925) *Biochem.* [Transl. of G *eluieren* < L *ēluere* (past part. *ēlūtus*) to rinse out, wash out] To use a solvent to wash away adsorbed matter from a substance, as in chromatography (this is different from the old, Latin-derived meaning of "to wash out"). O, R, W [4]

elution, *n.* (1922) *Biochem.* [G < L *ēlūtio* the rinsing or washing away] The removal of adsorbed matter by washing with a solvent (this is different from the old, Latin-derived "general chemical" meaning). O, R, W [4]

Em(b)den, *n.* (1903 W9) *Zool.* [By folk etymology, a short. of G *Emdener Gans* < *Emden,* the name of a major North Sea port in Germany + *Gans* goose] (usu. cap.) a breed of white, large domestic geese with an orange bill, or a goose of this breed. R, W [3]

embolite, *n.* (1850) *Mineral.* [G *Embolit* < Gk *embólion* insert, wedge + G *-it* -ite] A native silver chloride and bromide resembling cerargyrite. —**embolite,** *a.* O, R, W [3]

embrithite, *n.* (1854) *Mineral.* [G *Embrithit* (1837) < Gk *embrithés* heavy + G *-it* -ite] A former name for a supposed variety of boulangerite (q.v.). O [3]

Emden, *see* Embden

Emment(h)al(er)/emment(h)al(er), *n.* (1902) *Food* Var. **Emmenthal cheese** (1950) [Short. of G *Emmenthaler Käse* < *Emmenthal* (now *Emmental*) the name of a region in Switzerland + *Käse* cheese] A Swiss cheese with numerous holes. O, R, W [4]

emmer, *n.* (c.1900 W9) *Bot.* [G < OHG *amari* a form of wheat related to dinkel] *Triticum dicoccum,* a hard red wheat; any tetraploid wheat. —**emmer,** *a.* (1921). O, R, W [4]

empathy, *n.* (1904) *Psych.* [Transl. of G *Einfühlung* (q.v.) (1903) the ability to place oneself in another person's position] The capacity to imagine or vicariously experience what another person feels or thinks; the imaginative projecting of a subjective state into some object so that the object seems to be infused with it. —**empathic(ally)** (1909, 1929), **-thist** (1923), **-thize** (1924), **-thetic(ally)** (1932, 1961). O, R, W [4]

empirio-, *comb. form* (1895) *Philos.* Var. **empirico-** (1895) [G (< Gk *empería* experience), as in *Empiriokritizismus* empiriocriticism (q.v.)] Experience or experiment, as in *emperiogenic;* empirical, as in *emperico-inductive.* O, W [3]

empiriocriticism, *n.* (1897) *Philos.* Var. **empirio-criticism** (1933) [Ad. of G *Emperiokritizismus* (1894) < *empirio-* + *Kritizismus* < Gk *empeiría* experience + *kritikḗ téchnē* the art of evaluation, judgment < G *-ismus* (< L) -ism] A scientifically directed phenomenalistic type of empiricism that seeks to explain knowledge as pure experience and eliminate other elements. —**empiriocritical** (1909). O, W [3]

emplectite, *n.* (1857) *Mineral.* [G *Emplektit* < Gk *émplēktos* inwoven + G *-it* -ite] A compound of copper, bismuth, and sulfur. O, R, W [3]

emulsin, *n.* (1838) *Chem.* [G < L *ēmulsus* milked + G *-in* -in] An enzyme preparation usu. obtained from plants like almonds and mold fungi that contain glycosidases. O, R, W [3]

enanthem, *n.* (1842) *Med.* Var. **enanthema** [G *Enanthem* or NL *enanthema* < Gk *enánthēma* eruption] A mucosal eruption, as opposed to a cutaneous one. —**enanthematous.** O, W [3]

enantiomorph, *n.* (1885) *Crystal.* [G (1856) < Gk *enantíos* opposite + *morphḗ* form] Either of two enantiomorphous crystals or two crystalline forms or compounds exhibiting enantiomorphism: mirror image; also called *optical antipode.* • ~ appears in several derivatives like **-morphism** (1885), **-morphous(ly)** (1892, 1898); **-morphic** (1900); **-morphy,** *n.* (1900). O, R, W [4]

enantiotropy, *n.* (1900) *Chem.* [G *Enantiotropie* (1888) < Gk *enantíos* opposite + G *trop-* + *-ie* < Gk *tropḗ* turning + *-ia*] The existence of two different, stable forms of the same substance that at a definite transition temperature are interconvertible. —**enantiotropic** (1903). O, R, W [3]

enargite, *n.* (1852) *Mineral.* [G *Enargit* < Gk *enargḗs* clear, visible + G *-it* -ite] A copper arsenic sulfide and an important source of copper. O, R, W [3]

enchylema, *n.* (1886) *Biol.* [Prob. < G *Enchylem* (1880) < Gk *en-* in + *chylós* sap, fluid + *-ōm* swelling] Hyaloplasm (q.v.); karyolymph (q.v., though this meaning probably orig. came from Fr *enchylème*). —**enchylematous,** *a.* O, W [3]

endartery, *n.* (1880) *Path.* Var. **end-artery** (1964) [G *Endarterie* (1872) < *Ende* end + *Arterie* < Gk *artería* aorta, artery] A terminal, major artery. O, W [3]

endhand, *n. Games* [Transl. of G *Hinterhand*] The last skat player to bid in turn (this is different from the meaning of "dealer in a game with three players"). W [3]

endlichite, *n.* (1885) *Mineral.* [G *Endlich* < the name of Frederick M. *Endlich* (1851–99), American mineralogist + E *-ite*] A type of vanadinite (q.v.) with arsenic. O, W [3]

endocannibalism, *n.* (1900) *Anthrop.* [G *Endokannibalismus* (1896) < *endo-* (< the comb. form of Gk *éndon* within) + G *Kannibalismus* cannibalism < NL *canibalismus*] The practice of eating one's own family or tribe. O, W [3]

endomitosis, *n.* (1942) *Biol.* [G *Endomitose* (1939) < *endo-* < Gk *éndon* within + *mítos* thread of a warp + *-sis* fem. suffix denoting action] Chromosomal division in a nucleus without subsequent division of the nucleus. —**endomitotic** (1951), **endomitotically.** O, R, W [3]

endosulvan, *n.* (c.1965) *Chem.* [G *Endosulfan*] (An infrequent German var. spelling, like Du *Endosolvan,* of) Endosulfan, a powerful insecticide. B [3]

endothelioma, -s/-ta *pl.* (1880) *Med.* [G *Endotheliom* (1875) < *Endothelium* + *-oma,* ult. < Gk *éndon* within + *thēlế* nipple + *-ōma* tumor] A tumor of the endothelium. —**endotheliomatous** (1906). O, R, W [4]

endotrophic, *a.* (1899) *Bot.* Var. **endotropic** (1899) [G *endotropisch* (1887) < *endo-* + *-tropisch* < Gk *éndon* inside, within + *trophế* nutrition, nourishment + G adj. suffix *-isch* -ic] A fungus the hyphae of which grow inside a mycorrhiza's cells and which utilize water or organic substances from the host but release the sugars to it. O, R, W [3]

endrumpf, *n.* *Geol.* [G < *Ende* end + *Rumpf* rump, trunk] Peneplain, a large land surface worn down by erosion to nearly a plain. W [3]

energid, *n.* (1897) *Biol.* [G (1892) < Gk *energós* active + G *-id* -id] The unit of a cell's nucleus and its active cytoplasm. O, W [3]

energism, *n.* (1895) *Philos.* [G *Energismus* (1892) < *Energie* (< LL *energīa* < Gk *enérgeia* energy) + G *-ismus* (< L *-ismus*) -ism] The tenet that phenomena like mental states are explicable in terms of energy; the ethical theory that the supreme good lies in the efficient exercise of normal human activities, not in pleasure and/or happiness. — **energistic** (1931). O, R, W [3]

Englander, *n.* (1836) *Politics* [G an inhabitant or citizen of England < *England* + *-er* -er] A native or resident of England, in terms of a German comparison (this is slightly different from Sir Walter Scott's 1820 meaning of "English person" < E *England* + *-er*). O, W [3]

English disease, *n.* (1963) *Sociol.* Var. **English sickness** (1963) [Transl. of G *(die) englische Krankheit* < *englisch* English + *Krankheit* disease] Orig., a transl. of the German folk-equivalent for *rickets (Rachitis), (die) englische Krankheit,* which was first identified and fully described in the 1770s in England; a term now widely used in Europe to describe economic inefficiency and failure, also excessive absenteeism, restrictive practices, and wildcat strikes characteristic of Great Britain in the 1970s and early 1980s (this is different from the 1733 *English disease/malady* low spirits or melancholy, which was prob. transl. < Fr *la maladie anglaise*). O [4]

English sickness, *see* English disease

engram, *n.* (1908) *Psych.* Var. **engramme** [G (1904) < Gk *en* -in + *grámma* letter, record] A lasting trace or modification left in the brain's neural tissue, hypothesized to explain memory trace. —**engrammatic** (1925). O, R, W [4]

enigmatite/aenigmatite, *n. Mineral.* [Ad. of G *Ainigmatit/Änigmatit* < Gk *aínigma(t-)* puzzle, mystery + G *-it* -ite] A mineral formerly classed with the amphibole group, but actually a silicate of sodium, iron, and titanium. W [3]

enin, *see* oenin

enlighteners, *see* Illuminati

enlightenment, *n.* (1865) *Philos.* [Transl. of G *Aufklärung* (q.v.)] (Cap.) a primarily French philosophical movement of the 18th century; an attitude or spirit from this (this is different from the old meaning of "action or state of enlightening"). O, R, W [3]

enstatite, *n.* (1857) *Mineral.* [G *Enstatit* < Gk *enstátēs* adversary + G *-it* -ite] An orthorhombic magnesium silicate. —**enstatic** (1885). O, R, W [4]

entropy, *n.* (1868) *Physics, Math.* [G *Entropie* (1865), used in this sense by the German mathematical physicist Rudolf J. E. Clausius (1822–88) < Gk *en* -in, within + *tropế* turn + G *-ie* -y] A thermodynamic term for the measure of the amount of energy in a system; a measure of randomness or disorder; a term in communication theory and in wider mathematical use. —**entropic(ally)**. O, R, W [4]

entscheidungsproblem, *n.* (1922) *Math.* [G decision problem] (Transl. as) **decision problem** (q.v.). O [3]

entwicklungsroman, -e *pl. Lit.* [G < *Entwicklung* development + *Roman* novel, ult. < L *rōmānicē*] An often autobiographical novel dealing with a character's development from childhood to maturity. W [3]

environment, *n.* (1827) *Ecology* [Poss. < Carlyle's transl. of G *Umgebung* surroundings or *Umwelt* (q.v.)] The surrounding conditions under which persons, other biota, or things develop (this is different from the old meaning of "surroundings"). O, R, W [4]

enzyme, *n.* (1881) *Biochem.* [G *Enzym* (1877) < Gk *énzymos* leavened] Any of a large class of complex, naturally occurring, proteinaceous substances produced by living cells that are vital in plant and animal life. —**enzyme,** *a.* (1902); **enzymic/enzymatic** (1881, 1942); **enzym(at)ically** (1944, 1949); **enzymology; enzymologist.** O, R, W [4]

eosin(e), *n.* (1866) *Chem.* [G *Eosin* < Gk *ēós* dawn + G *-in* -in(e)] A fluorescent red dye; sodium or potassium salt of this dye, esp. used in microscopy; a dye related chemically to eosin. —**eosin,** *a.* (1885). O, R, W [4]

eosinophil(e), *n.* and *a.* (1886, 1886) *Biol.* [G *Eosinophil* (1878–79) < *Eosin* eosin (q.v.) + *-phil* < Gk *phílos* loving] (Of) a cell readily stained by eosin. —**eosinophilic/-philous** (1892, 1900), **-philia** (1900). O, R, W [4]

ependyma, *n.* (1872) *Anat.* [G *Ependym,* used in this sense by the German physician Rudolf Virchow (1821–1902) to name the lining membrane of the cerebral ventricles and of the central spinal canal < Gk *epéndyma* upper garment < *epéndyein* to put on or over] This epithelial lining membrane. —**ependymal** (1874), **ependymitis** (1889). O, R, W [3]

ephedrine, *n.* (1889) *Med.* Old var. **ephedrin** (1900) [G *Ephedrin* (1887) < NL (< Gk) *Ephedra* genus name + G *-in* -ine] A crystalline alkaloid that is extracted from mahuang or is made synthetically and is often used in relieving hay fever, asthma, etc. O, R, W [4]

epi-, *comb. form* (1911) *Chem.* [G (1911) < Gk *epí* upon, at] Sometimes prefixed to the name of a sugar or sugar derivative to indicate that a second compound which bears the prefix is an epimer of the first compound, as in *epiglucose* to mean "mannose" (this is more specialized than the older, more general meaning seen in *epicholesterol*). •A secondary use is described in the Appendix. O [3]

epichordal, *a. Biol.* [G < *epi-* + *chordal* < Gk *epí* on, upon + *chordế* intestine + G *-al* -al] Located on or above the intercranial part of the notochord. O, W [3]

epidermolysis, -molyses *pl.* (1894) *Path.* [G *Epidermolyse* (1886), formed by the German physician Heinrich Köbner (1838–?) < *epidermo-* + *-lyse* < Gk *epidermís* outermost layer of skin + *lýsis* loosening] Epidermolysis bullosa, a rare, hereditary loosening and blistering disorder of the skin. O, W [3]

epididymite, *n. Mineral.* [G *Epididymit* < *epi-* + *-didymit* as in *eudidymit* < Gk *epí* on, upon + *didŷmos* twin + G *-it* -ite] A silicate of sodium and beryllium. W [3]

epidiorite, *n.* (1887) *Mineral.* [G *Epidiorit* < *epi-* + *Diorit* < Gk *epí* on, upon + *diorízein* to distinguish + G *-it* -ite] A variety of diorite metamorphosed from pyroxemic igneous rocks. O, R, W [3]

epidosite, *n.* (1863) *Geol.* [G *Epidosit* (1845) < Gk *epídosis* a free or additional giving + G *-it* -ite] A metamorphic rock composed of green granular or fibrous epidote mixed with quartz. O, W [3]

epigenesis, *n.* (1807) *Biol.* [G *Epigenese* < *epi-* + *Genese* < Gk *epí* upon + L (Gk) *genesis* generation, used in this sense by Caspar Friedrich Wolff (1733–94), German biologist, who developed the theory to disprove the theory of preformation or evolution] The theory that an initially undifferentiated entity is first brought into existence and then gradually diversifies and differentiates (this is different from the "geological" meaning of *epigenetic*—q.v.). —**epigen(es)ist** (1875, 1816), **epigenetic** (1883). O, R, W [4]

epigenetic, *a.* (1905) *Geol.* Var. **epigenic** [G *epigenetisch* (1886) < *Epigenese* (see *epigenesis*) + adj. suffix *-isch* -ic] Of postdepositional structures or rocks formed after the depositing of the enclosing rocks. O, R, W [4]

epigenite, *n. Mineral.* [G *Epigenit* < Gk *epigenḗs* descendant + G *-it* -ite] A sulfide perhaps of copper, iron, and arsenic. W [3]

epigone, *n.* (1865) *Lit., Art* Var. **epigon** (1890) [G (1830) < L *epigonus* one of the seven sons of seven leaders defeated at Thebes according to Greek legend < Gk *epígonos* one born afterwards] An inferior, imitative follower, as in literature or art. —**epigonic, epigonous, epigonism.** O, R, W [4]

epimer, *n.* (1911) *Chem.* [G (1911) < *epi-* + *-mer* < Gk *epí* after, thereupon + *méros* part] Either of two stereoisomers of a compound with more than one differing, assymetric carbon atoms. —**epimeric** (1911). O, R, W [3]

epimerism, *n.* (1911) *Chem.* [Ad. of G *Epimerie* (1911) < *epi-* + *-mer* (see *epimer*) + *-ie* -ism] The fact or condition of containing epimers. O [3]

epiphenomenon, -a/-s *pl.* (1899) *Psych.* [Transl. of G *Begleiterscheinung* < *Begleitung* accompaniment < *begleiten* to accompany + *Erscheinung* phenomenon, appearance] A secondary phenomenon (this is different from the older "pathological, specialized psychological" meanings). O, R [3]

epistilbite, *n.* (1826) *Mineral.* [G *Epistilbit* < *epi-* (< Gk on, after) + G *Stilbit* stilbit] A zeolitic aluminosilicate of calcium. O, W [3]

epitokous/epitocous, *a.* (1896) *Biol.* [G *epitok* (1868) < Gk *epítokos* fruitful, bearing offspring + E *-ous*] Of or pertaining to the epitoke, the posterior sexual part of the body of some polychaete worms. O, W [3]

epoch-forming, *see* epoch-making

epoch-making, *a.* (1863) [Prob. transl. of G *epochemachend* (1774) < *Epoche* (< ML *epocha* < Gk *epochḗ* pause, stoppage, a significant point in time) + G *machend* < *machen* to make] Epochal: uniquely or greatly significant, orig. said mainly of scientific discoveries or treatises and now extended to any remarkable publication, event, etc. • ~ was orig. transl. as **epoch-forming** (1816) and extended to **epoch-marking** (1895). O, R, W [4]

equational division, *n.* (1920) *Biol.* [Transl. of G *Aequationsteilung* (1887) < *Aequation* (< L *aequātiō*, gen. *aequātiōnis* making alike) + G *Teilung* division] Of a chromosomal division that takes place longitudinally and results in two equal, paired segments incorporated into the daughter nuclei. O [3]

erbswurst, *n.* (1885) *Food* [G < *Erbse* pea + *Wurst* sausage] A seasoned pease flour formed into sausage shape and used in soups or served as a bean dish. O [3]

erepsin, *n.* (1902) *Med.* [G (1901), prob. < L *ēripere* < Gk *eréptesthai* devour, consume + G *Pepsin* (q.v.)] A proteolytic enzyme found esp. in the intestinal juice. O, W [4]

ergastic, *a.* (c.1896 W9) *Biol.* [G *ergastisch* (1896) < Gk *ergastikós* able to work] Of or relating to the nonliving by-products of protoplasmic action. O, W [3]

ergocornine, *n.* (1944) *Chem.* [G *Ergocornin* (1943) (now also *Ergokornin*) < *ergo-* + *Corn* (*Korn*) < Fr *ergot* cock's spur + L *cornū* horn + G *-in* -ine] A crystalline tripeptide alkaloid secured from ergotoxine. O, W [3]

ergocristine, *n. Chem.* [G *Ergokristin* < *ergo-* + *Kristall* crystal + *-in* -ine < Fr *ergot* + L *crystallum* < Gk *krýstallos*] A crystalline tripeptide alkaloid obtained from ergotoxine, formulaically slightly different from ergocornine (q.v.). W [3]

ergodic, *a.* (1926 W9) *Math.* [Ad. of G *ergoden* (1887) (now also *ergodisch*), used in this sense by the Austrian physicist Ludwig Boltzmann (1844–1906), whose statistical discoveries are also reflected in the terms *Boltzmann's constant/statistic* < *Ergod* + *-en* -ic < Gk *érgon* work + *hodós* way] Of a theorem that a trajectory in a confined space has the property by which all points of the space will be included with equal frequency in the trajectory; of a stochastic process or its property whereby every sequence or representative sample is statistically identical and thus equally representative of the whole; of the probability that any state will occur. —**ergodicity** (1949). O, W [3]

ergonomy, *n.* (1987) *Econ.* [G *Ergonomie* < *ergo-* + *-nomie* < Gk *érgon* work + L *oeconomicus* economical + G *-ie* -y] Ergonomics, the study of the ways whereby humans can operate efficiently in their environment. L1 [3]

ergotamine, *n.* (1921) *Biochem.* [G *Ergotamin* (1921) < *Ergot* (< Fr cock's spur) + G *Amin* amine] A crystalline tripeptide alkaloid found in ergot and used mainly in treating migraine. O, R, W [3]

ergotaminine, *n.* (1922) *Biochem.* [G *Ergotaminin* (1921) < *Ergotamin* ergotamine (q.v.) + *-in* -ine] A pharmacologically inactive ergot alkaloid, the mirror image of ergotamine. O [3]

erikite, *n. Mineral.* [G or Dan *Erikit* < the name of *Erik* Eric the Red, 10th-century Norwegian-Icelandic explorer of Greenland, the mineral's locality + G or Dan *-it* -ite] A silicate and phosphate of the cerium metals. W [3]

erlking, *n.* (1797) *Myth.* [Partial transl. of G *Erlkönig* alder-tree king < Herder's erron. transl. of the Dan var. *eller-*

konge instead of Dan *elverkonge* king of the elves] King of the elves; a goblin or personified natural power in Germanic and Scandinavian mythology that does mischief, esp. to children. O, R [3]

ermelin, *n.* (1555) *Zool.* (archaic) Var. **ermeline** (c. 1630) and various obs. forms [Prob. ad. of G *Hermelin* a large weasel or its fur (as influenced by E *ermine*) < MHG *hermelīn* < OHG *harmili(n)*] Ermine. O, W [3]

ersatz, *a.* (1875) and *n.* (1892) [G < *ersetzen* to replace, substitute] (of) a substitute or imitation, usu. an inferior or artificial article intended to replace a genuine item; (of) the discovery and use of such substitutes: substitution. — **hairsatz** (1943 *Algeo*). O, R, W [4]

ersatz reserve, *n.* (1875) *Mil.* [G < *Ersatz* replacement + *Reserve* reserve, actually all men subject to the draft who have not yet been called up < L *reservāre* to keep back] A reserve of the German army, as in World War Two, drawn upon to fill out understaffed units and composed of men unqualified for the regular army or landwehr (q.v.). O, W [3]

erysipeloid, *n.* (1888) *Path.* [G (1887) < *Erysipelas* + *-oid* < Gk *erythrós* red + *pélla* skin + *-oeidēs* similar] Dermatitis, esp. of the hands of persons infected by the bacillus causing swine erysipelas. O, W [3]

erythremia, *n.* (1908) *Path.* Var. **erythraemia** [G *Erythrämie* (1904) < Gk *erythrós* red + *aîma* blood] Polycythemia vera, a hemoglobic disease. —**erythr(a)emic** (1938, 1962). O, W [3]

erythroblast, *n.* (1890) *Path.* [G (1886) < *erythro-* + *-blast* < Gk *erythrós* red + *blastós* bud, germ] A polychromatic, nucleated cell recognizable as a precursor of erythrocytes; any of various cells ancestral to red blood cells. —**erythroblastic** (1908), **erythroblastemia**. O, R, W [3]

erythroblastosis, -toses *pl.* (c.1923 *W9*) *Path.* [G *Erythroblastose* (1912) < *Erythroblast* erythroblast (q.v.) < *-ose* < Gk *-sis* fem. suffix denoting action] The abnormal presence of erythroblasts in the body, specif. as a hemolytic disease of the fetus and newborn. —**erythroblastotic** (1957), **erythroblastosis fetalis/neonatorum**. O, W [4]

erzahler, *n.* *Music* [Prob. < G, lit., narrator < *erzählen* to narrate + *-er* -er] A gemshorn organ pipe. W [3]

Erzherzog, -e *pl.* *Politics* [G archduke] A prince of the Austrian imperial family; a sovereign prince. W2 [2]

Erzherzogin, -nen *pl.* *Politics* [G < *Erzherzog* archduke + fem. suffix *-in* -in] The wife of an Erzherzog (q.v.). W2 [2]

eschatocol, *n.* (1897) *Law* [G *Eschatokoll* < It *escatocollo*, Gk *eschatokóllion* end piece of a papyrus scroll] The concluding part of a protocol, containing the attestation, date, etc. O, W [3]

eschynite/aeschynite, *n.* *Mineral.* [Ad. of G *Äschynit* < *äschyn-* (< Gk *aischýnē* shame) + G *-it* -ite] A rare oxide of columbium, titanium, cerium, and some other metals. W [3]

ester, *n.* (1852) *Chem.* [G (1848) < a short. of G *Essigäther* < *Essig* vinegar + *Äther* ether, ult. < L *acētum* + *aether*] One of a class of compounds that can be hydrolyzed to yield an organic or inorganic acid and an alcohol or phenol. —**ester,** *a.* (1907). • ~ appears in composites

like **esterification** (1898), **-ify** (1966), **-ified** (1907), **-ize**, **-ifiable, ester gum** (1940). O, R, W [4]

esthetic(s), *see* aesthetic(s)

estragole, *n.* *Chem.* Var. **estragol** [G *Estragol* < *Estragon* (< Fr) a shrub (*Artemesia dracunculus*) + G *-ol* -ole] A liquid ether that has an odor like aniseed and is used in flavoring and perfumes; also called *methyl chavicol*. W [3]

etch(ing) figure, *n.* (1879) *Physics* [Transl. of G *Ätzfigur* (1869) < *ätzen* to etch + *Figur* figure < L *figūra*] (Usu. pl.) a depression on a mineral's crystal face caused by the action of a solvent, which reveals the molecular structure. O, W [3]

eternal feminine, (the), *n.* (1892) *Lit.* [Transl. of Goethe's penultimate line in *Faust* II, *das Ewig-Weibliche* < *das* the + *ewig* eternal (transl. adverbially as *eternally*) + *Weibliche* feminine] The Eternally Feminine; the feminine element in human nature. O [3]

ethnopsychology, *n.* (1886) *Psych.* [Transl. of G *Völkerpsychologie* < *Völker,* pl. of *Volk* people + *Psychologie* psychology < NL *psychologia*] The psychology of races and peoples; the study of this. —**ethnopsychological,** *a.* (1885); **-ically.** O, W [3]

ethyl, *n.* (1838) *Chem.* [G (1834), used in this sense by the German chemist Justus von Liebig (1803–73), ult. < Gk *aithér* top layer of the air + *hýlē* wood, stuff] A univalent hydrocarbon radical obtained from ethane. • ~ appears initially in many derivatives like **ethylene** (1852) and in many compounds like **ethyl alcohol** (1869). O, R, W [4]

ettringite, *n.* *Mineral.* [G *Ettringit* < *Ettringen,* the name of a German region along the Rhine + *-it* -ite] A hydrous basic sulfate of calcium and aluminum. W [3]

euchroite, *n.* (1825) *Mineral.* [G *Euchroit* < Gk *eúchroos* of nice color + G *-it* -ite] A basic, emerald-green arsenate of copper. O, W [3]

euchromatin, *n.* (1932) *Biol.* [G (1928) < *eu-* + *Chromatin* < Gk *eús* beautiful, good + *chrōmatós* colored + G *-in* -in] The genetically active portion of chromatin held to stain less intensively than does heterochromatin (q.v.). —**euchromatic** (1936). O, R, W [4]

eucolite, *n.* (1847) *Mineral.* Var. **eukolite/eukolyte** (1849, 1882) [G *Eukolit* < Gk *eúkolos* happy, easily satisfied + G *-it* -ite] A variety of eudialyte (q.v.) that is optically negative. O, W [3]

eucone, *a.* (1885) *Optics* Var. **euconic** [G (1877) < Gk *eús* good + *kônos* cone] Of certain insects' and crustaceans' eyes that have a fully developed crystalline cone in the ommatidia. O, W [3]

eucrite, *n.* (c.1899 *W9*) *Geol.* [G *Eukrit* < Gk *eúkritos* easily recognized] A meteorite constituted essentially of augite and anorthite; a very basic gabbro. —**eucritic.** R, W [3]

eucyclic, *a.* (1875) *Bot.* [G *eucyclisch* (1858) (now *euzyklisch*), used in this sense by the German botanist Alexander C. H. Braun (1805–77) < *eu-* + *cyclisch* < Gk *eús* good + L *cỹclicus,* Gk *kyklikós* ring-shaped] Of cyclic flowers with alternate isomerous whorls. O, W [3]

eudaemonism, *n.* (1827) *Philos.* Var. **eudaimonism** (1866), **eudemonism** [Prob. < G *Eudämonismus* < Gk *eudiamonía* happiness + G *-ismus* (< L) -ism] An ethical doctrine that defines moral obligation in terms of personal well-being or happiness, esp. if governed by reason. O, R, W [4]

eudaemonist, *n.* (1818) *Philos.* Var. **eudemonist** [Prob. < G *Eudämonist* < Gk *eudaímon* happy + G *-ist* -ist] An adherent of eudaemonism. —**eudemonistic(al)** (1855, 1881), **-istically.** O, R, W [4]

eudialyte, *n.* (1837) *Mineral.* [G *Eudialyt* < Gk *eudiálytos* < *eús* good + *dialytós* dissolving + G *-it* -ite] An optically positive silicate composed chiefly of zirconium, iron, calcium, and sodium. O, W [3]

euglenoid, *n.* and *a.* (1885, 1885) *Biol.* [G, used in this sense by the German biologist Christian Gottfried Ehrenberg (1795–1876) < NL *Euglena* < comb. form of Gk *eû* < *eús* good + *glḗnē* pupil of the eye + G *-oid* < Gk *-oeidēs*] (of) a member of the genus of single-celled, extremely varied aquatic flagellates; (of) such an organism. O, R, W [4]

eukolite, *see* eucolite

eulytite, *n.* (1868) *Mineral.* Var. **eulytine** (1850) [G *Eulytit* < *Eulytin* (< Gk *eúlytos* easily dissolved + G *-in*) + *-it* -ite] A bismuth silicate occurring in tetrahedral crystals. O, W [3]

euploid, *a.* (1926) *Biol.* [G (1922) < *eu-* + *-ploid* < Gk *eús* good + *diplóos* double + G *-oid* (< Gk *-oeidēs* similar)] Having each of the different chromosomes of the set in equal numbers. —**euploid,** *n.*; **euploidy,** *n.* (1933). O, W [4]

eurobin, *n. Pharm.* [G < Gk *eû* < *eús* good + Pg (< Tupi) *araroba* Goa powder + G *-in* -in] The triacetate of chrysarobin earlier used as its substitute in ointments. W [3]

euryene, *a. Physiol.* [G *euryen* < *eury-* + *-en* < Gk *eurýs* wide + *-ēnēs*, as in *prosēnēs* gentle and *apēnēs* cruel, i.e., with face turned toward someone and with averted face, respectively] Having a broad or short forehead and/or an upper facial index of 45 to 50. —**eureny,** *n.* W [3]

euryhaline, *a.* (1888) *Biol.* Var. **euryhalin** [G *Euryhalin* (1871) < Gk *eurýs* wide + *hálinos* of salt] Having the capacity to live in waters with a wide range of salinity. O, W [3]

eurytherm, *a.* (1888) *Biol.* [G < *eury-* + *-therm* < Gk *eurýs* extensive + *thermós* warm, hot] Of an organism able to live in a wide range of temperatures. —**eurythermic** (1903), **-mous** (1940), **-mal** (1964). O [3]

eurythmy, *n.* (1949 *W9*) *Dance* [G *Eurythmie* < Gk *eurythmía* rhythm] A system of harmonious body movements set to the rhythm of spoken words that Rudolph Steiner's anthroposophy (q.v.) projected for dance (this is different from the earlier Latin-derived "architectural, pathological, rhythmic" meanings, usu. spelled as *eurhythmy*). W [4]

eurytopic, *a.* (c.1945 *W9*) *Biol.* [Prob. < G *eurytop* < *eury-* + *-top* (< Gk *eurýs* extensive, wide + *tópos* place) + E *-ic*] Possessing a wide range of tolerance to variation in one or more environmental factors. —**eurotopicity.** W [4]

eustatic, *a.* (1906) *Geol.* [G *eustatisch* (1888) < *eu-* + *statisch* < Gk *eús* good + *statikós* standing still or firm + G *-isch* -ic] Pertaining to or caused by a worldwide change in sea level. —**eustatically** (1934); **eustatism** (1935); **eustasy,** *n.* (1946). O, R, W [4]

eusynchite, *n. Mineral.* [G *Eusynchit* < *eu-* < Gk *eús* good + *synchein* to mix + G *-it* -ite] Descloizite, a basic vanadate. W [3]

eutely, *n. Biol.* [Prob. < G *Eutelie* < Gk *eutéleia* thrift, economy] The condition where a body is composed of a constant number of cells, as in some lower worms and rotifers. W [3]

eutrophic, *n.* (1884) and *a.* (1931) *Biol.* [Prob. < G *eutroph* < Gk *eútrophos* providing ample nourishment + E *-ic*] (Of) an overrichness in organic or mineral nutrients that results in an excessive growth of algae and other plants, resulting in depleted oxygen and some animal extinction (this is different from the earlier "medical, well-nourished" meanings). —**eutrophication** (1947). O, R, W [4]

euxanthic acid, *n.* (1852) *Chem.* [Transl. of G *Euxanthinsäure* (1844) < Gk *eû* < *eús* good + *xanthós* yellow + G *Säure* acid] A glycoside that yields glucuronic acid and euxanthone (q.v.) by hydrolysis; purreic acid. O [3]

euxanthone, *n.* (1852) *Chem.* [G *Euxanthon* (1844) < *Euxanthin(säure)* (see *euxanthic acid*) + *-on* (< Gk fem. patronymic suffix) -one] A yellow derivative of xanthone; purrenone. O [3]

euxenite, *n.* (1844) *Mineral.* [G *Euxenit* (1840) < Gk *eúxenos* hospitable + G *-it* -ite] An oxide of calcium, titanium, tantalum, columbium, cerium, and uranium. O, R, W [3]

Ewigkeit/ewigkeit, *n.* (1857) [G < *ewig* eternal + nom. suffix *-keit* -ity] Used jocularly for *thin air,* chiefly in the phrase *into thin air.* O [3]

Ewigweibliche, (das), *n. Lit.* [Goethe's G (1832) < (*das* the) + *ewig* eternal + *weiblich* feminine] (The) eternal feminine (q.v.). R [2]

exine, *n.* (1884) *Bot.* Var. **extine** (1835/1852) [Prob. < G *Exin* < L *ex* out (of) + G *-in* -ine] The outer of the two layers forming the wall of pollen grains and other spores. O, R, W [4]

existentialism, *n.* (1919) *Philos.* [G *Existentialismus* < L *ex(s)istere* to exist, LL *existentia* state of having being (*existentālis* existential) + G (< L) *-ismus* -ism] The theory that one's individual existence precedes one's essence and that one is responsible for fashioning oneself, which, in the Christian form, leads to God; a phenomenological, introspective humanism or theory of human beings that believes that their existence cannot be exhaustively described or understood. —**existentialist,** *n.* (1945), *a.* (1946). O, R, W [4]

existenz, -es *pl. Psych.* [G < LL *existentia* state of having being] The state or fact of having being: existence. W [3]

exlex, *a.* (1909) *Law* Var. **ex-lex** (1909) [G < L *ex lex* bound by no law] Beyond the pale of the law. O, W [3]

expressionism, *n.* (1925) *Art, Lit., Music* Var. **expressionismus** (1925) [G *Expressionismus* (1911) < Fr *expression* < L *expressio* (gen. *expressionis*) expression + G (< L) *-ismus* -ism] A theory or practice in art, music, and literature, esp. in the late 19th and early 20th centuries, of depicting one's inner, subjective emotions and sensations, rather than depicting objective reality or traditional techniques. • ~ appears in earlier meanings and in compounds like **abstract expressionism** (1952). O, R, W [4]

extine, *see* exine

extrasystole, *n.* (1900) *Med.* [G (1899) < *extra-* + *Systole* contraction < L *extra* outside of, in addition] A heartbeat outside of the normal rhythm, leading to momentary arrhythmia. —**extrasystolic.** O, R, W [3]

extraversion, *n.* (1915) *Psych.* Var. **extroversion** [Jung's G < *extra-* + *Version* < L *extrā* outside of + *versus* turned < *vertere* to turn + G *-ion* -ion] Extroversion, the fact of having (and wanting to have) one's thoughts and activities exclusively directed to things outside oneself; a habitual tendency toward this. O, R, W [4]

extravert(ed), *see* extrovert(ed)

extremal, *n.* (1901) *Math.* [G *Extremale* (1900), ult. < L *extrēmus* the outermost + G *-al* (< L *-alis*) -al] A function y(x) or its graphic representation that maximizes or minimizes an integral; a surface, the integral over which is a maximum or a minimum. —**extremal,** *a.* (1950). O [3]

extremum, extrema/-s *pl.* (1904) *Math.* [G (1879) (< L *extrēmus*) extreme] A stationary value of a function that is either a maximum or a minimum, either relative or absolute. O, R, W [3]

extroversion, *see* extraversion

extrovert(ed)/extravert(ed), *a.* (1918) *Psych.* [Ad. of G *extrovertiert/extravertiert* < *extro-/extra-* + *vertiert* < L *extrā* (toward) outside + *vertere* to turn + G *-iert* -ed] Having the character of an extrovert. O, R, W [4]

eye, *see* augen

F

F, *see* Fahrenheit

Fach/fach, *n.* (1842) [G compartment, field (of interest), trade] Branch of knowledge, field of interest; fig. sense as a circumscribed branch of knowledge. O [3]

fackeltanz, -tänze *pl. Music* [G < *Fackel* torch (ult. < L *facula*) + *Tanz* dance] A pavane for a ceremonial torchlight procession earlier used to celebrate a royal marriage in some German courts; polonaise. W [3]

factice, *n.* (1896) *Chem.* Old var. **factis** (1896) [G *Factis, Faktis* a trademark] Any of various rubber-like products made by vulcanizing unsaturated vegetable oils and used mainly as compounding ingredients with rubber: synthetic rubber; (cap.) a trademark for a vulcanized oil. —**brown/white factice** (1896, 1912). O, W [3]

facticity, *n.* (1945) *Philos.* [G *Faktizität* or (Fr *facticité*) < *Faktum* fact + *-izität* (or Fr *-icité*), ult. < L *factum* + *-icitat-* -icity] Quality or condition of being a fact: factuality. O, R, W [4]

factis, *see* factice

factor group, *n.* (1897) *Math.* [Ad. of G *Factorgruppe* (1889) < *Factor* (now *Faktor*) factor (< L) + G *Gruppe* group] A group G/H, the elements of which are cosets with respect to a normal subgroup of a given group: quotient group. O, R [3]

fagine, *n.* (1838) *Chem.* [G *Fagin* (1832) < L *fāgus* beech + G *-in* -ine] A volatile, poisonous, narcotic principle present in the husks of beechnuts. O, W [3]

fagott, -e *pl. Music* [G (1616) < It *fagotto* a bundle of faggots, actually reeds, so named because of the original appearance of its attached tube] Bassoon, a fagotto (< It). O, W [3]

fagottist, *n.* (1886) *Music* [G < It *fagotto* fagott (q.v.) + G *-ist* -ist] Bassoonist, a performer on the bassoon. O, W [3]

fahlband, *n.* (1880) *Geol.* [G < *fahl* pale + *Band* band, so named for its pale color at decomposition] A stratum or band in crystalline rock containing metallic sulfides. O, R, W [3]

fahlerz, -e *pl.* (1796) *Mineral.* Var. **fahlore** (1805) [G < *fahl* ash-colored, yellow + *Erz* ore] Tetrahedrite (q.v.). O, W [3]

Fahrenheit, *n.* (1753) and *a.* (1753 W9) *Physics* [G < the name of Gabriel D. *Fahrenheit* (1686–1736), German physicist] (Pertaining to) a thermometer or scale where, under standard atmospheric pressure, water boils at 212 degrees and freezes at 32 degrees above the zero of the scale. • ~ is abbr. as **F**. O, R, W [4]

fall line, *n.* (1961) *Sports* [Transl. of G *Fallinie,* a blend of *Fall* fall + *Linie* line < L *līnea*] The natural (direct) way down a slope used for skiing (this is different from the old "geological" meaning). O, R, W [4]

faltboot, *n.* (1926) *Sports* Var. **foldboat** (1938) [Partial transl. of G *Faltboot* < *falten* to fold + *Boot* boat] A small, collapsible canoe. —**faltbooting,** *verbal n.* (1926). O, R, W [4]

famatinite, *n.* (1875) *Mineral.* [G *Famatinit* (1873) < the name of the Sierra de *Famatina,* a mountain range in northwestern Argentina + G *-it* -ite] A copper antimony sulfide. O, W [3]

family tree, *n.* (1933) *Ling.* [Transl. of G *Stammbaum* (q.v.)] A schematic diagram showing the genealogical relationships of languages of parent stock in common (this is different from the various older "nonlinguistic genealogical" meanings). O, R, W [4]

family-tree theory, *n.* (1933) *Ling.* (Transl. of G *Stammbaumtheorie* < *Stammbaum* family tree + *Theorie* theory < LL *theōria* < Gk] A theory of August Schleicher (1821–68) in historical linguistics, which produces a family-tree diagram from a parent language, and on to subbranches, as in Indo-European to Germanic to West Germanic and eventually to English (this theory is now mainly superseded by the wave theory—q.v.). O, R, W [3]

famulus, -uli *pl.* (1832) *Ed.* [G (1558) a professor's academic assistant < L *famulus* servant, assistant] A private secretary or attendant, esp. to a scholar or a magician. O, R, W [4]

fantasie, *n. Music* [G < It *fantasia* < L *phantasia* imagination] Fantasia, an instrumental composition of the 16th and 17th centuries. W9 [3]

fantasiestück, -e *pl. Music* [G < *Fantasie* (q.v., rarely) fantasy; a musical composition for instruments, free in form + *Stück* piece] Fantasia; character piece (q.v.). W [3]

fantast, *n.* (1588) Var. **phantast** [G *Fantast/Phantast* < ML *fantasta,* ult. Gk *phantastēs* boaster] A visionary or dreamer; an eccentric or fantastic person; a fantasist such as H. G. Wells. O, R [3]

farnesol, *n.* (1904) *Chem.* [G (1902) < the name of the Italian cardinal Odoardo *Farnese* (1573–1626) + G *-ol* -ol] A sesquiterpene alcohol found in various essential oils and used in perfumes. O, R, W [3]

Fasching, *n.* (1911) *Theol.* [G carnival < MHG *vaschank, vastschang,* actually, (the) serving of the fasting potion, drink] In South Germany, the carnival that begins on Epiphany (January 6) and lasts until Shrove Tuesday; transf. sense to rugby matches, etc. O, R [3]

fasnacht, *see* fastnacht

fassaite, *n.* (1814) *Mineral.* [G *Fassait* < the name of Val di *Fassa,* Venezia Tridentina, northeast Italy + G *-it* -ite] A green variety of augite. O, W [3]

fastland, *n.* (1883) *Geol.* [Ad. of G *Festland* < *fest* firm + *Land* land] Mainland, esp. upland, as distinguished from islands; the continent. O, W [3]

fastnacht, *n. Theol.* Var. **fas(s)nacht** [Short. of G *Fastnachtkuchen* < *Fastnacht* Shrove Tuesday (< *fasten* to fast + *Nacht* night) + *Kuchen* (PaG *Kuche*) cake] A cake of yeast-leavened dough traditionally eaten on Shrove Tuesday; (PaG) a festival of Christians of Germanic origin held on the day before Lent begins. R, W [3]

fatherland, *n.* (1791–1823) *Politics* [Orig. a transl. of Du *vaderland,* but as of 1864 esp. a transl. of G *Vaterland* fatherland] (Now usu.) Germany, expressed as *the Fatherland* (this is different from old meanings like "land of one's birth or forebears"). —**fatherlandish** (1832). O [3]

fatherlandless, *a.* (1898) *Politics* [Transl. of G *vaterlandlos* < *Vaterland* fatherland + *-los* without, -less] Unpatriotic. O [3]

father right, *n.* (1899) *Law* Var. **father-right** (1955) [Transl. of G *Vaterrecht* < *Vater* father + *Recht* right] The father's supremacy in a family, with descent and inheritance following the male line. O, W [3]

fatigue products/stuff/substances, *n.* (1909) *Physiol.* [Transl. of G *ermüdender Stoff/ermüdende Substanz* (1865) exhausting or tiring matter] An accumulation of toxic material once thought to result from excessive muscular activity and to cause fatigue. O [3]

fayalite, *n.* (1844) *Mineral.* [G *Fayalit* (1840) < *Fayal,* the name of an island in the Azores + G *-it* -ite] A rare iron silicate isomeric with olivine (q.v.). O, R, W [3]

Fechner's law, *n.* (1874) *Psych.* Var. **Weber-Fechner law** (q.v.) [Transl. of G *Fechner-Gesetz* (1860) < the name of Gustav Theodor *Fechner* (1801–87), German experimental psychologist and philosopher + *Gesetz* law] The principle in experimental psychology that the intensity of a sensation is proportional to the logarithm of the original stimulus. O, W [3]

feeling tone, *n.* (1892) *Psych.* [Transl. of G *Gefühlston* < *Gefühl* feeling + *Ton* tone < L *tonus* < Gk *tónos*] The specific quality of an experience or of a belief as measured by its pleasantness or unpleasantness. O, W [3]

Fehling('s) solution, *n.* (1873) *Chem.* [Transl. of G *Fehling-Lösung* < the name of Hermann von *Fehling* (1812–85), German chemist + *Lösung* solution] A blue alkaline solution of copper sulfate and Rochelle salt used in sugar analyses. O, W [3]

Fehme/fehme, -n/-s *pl.* (1829) *Politics* Var. **Vehme** (1829) [G *Fe(h)me* (see Brockhaus), *Vehme* in the Middle Ages, a district court in Westphalia, western Germany; from the 14th to the 18th century, a secret tribunal that rendered the decisions to murder political opponents and traitors in their own midst] This medieval tribunal; a unit of a secret Nazi organization devoted to identifying and executing those persons considered to be enemies of National Socialism. —**fehmic.** O (not in 2nd ed.), W [3]

Fehmgericht, *see* Vehmgericht

feldgrau, *n.* (1934) *Mil.* [G (der) *Feldgraue* (the) soldier in field-gray uniform. • ~ is transl. as **field gray** (q.v.). O [3]

feldgrau, *a.* (1929) *Mil.* Var. **field gray** (1929) [G field gray] Field gray, the regulation color of a German infantryman's uniform. O [3]

feldspar, *n.* (1757) *Mineral.* Var. **feldspath** (1757), **felspar** (1794, q.v.), and various archaic forms [G *Feldspat(h)* < *Feld* field + *Spat* (< MHG *spāt* foliated rock)] Any of a group of aluminum silicates containing potassium, sodium, calcium, or barium. —**feldspar,** *a.* (1807); **-sparic** (1811); **-sparite** (1832); **-sparry,** *a.* (1852); **-fel(d)spathic**

(1832, 1845); **fel(d)spathoid,** *n.* (1930, 1896); **feldspathization; feldspathize.** O, R, W [4]

felsenmeer, -s/-e *pl.* (1905) *Geol.* [G < *Fels(en)* rock(s) + *Meer* sea, ocean] An expanse of angular rock fragments usu. above mountain timberline; a boulder field. O, W [3]

felsobanyaite/felsobanyite, *n.* (1856) *Mineral.* [G *Felsobanyit* (1852) < *Felsobanya,* the name of a town in what was formerly Hungary, now called *Baia-Sprie,* Rumania + G *-it* -ite] An orthorhombic sulfate of aluminum. O [3]

felsophyre, *n. Geol.* [G *Felsophyr* < *felso-* (< *Felsit* < E *felsite*) + G *-phyr* < Gk *pórphyros* crimson] A porphyritic rock with a felsitic groundmass. —**felsophyric.** W [3]

felspar, *n.* (1794) *Mineral.* [Erron. ad. of G *Feldspat(h)* as a supposed borrowing from *Fels* rock, instead of from *Feld*] (Chiefly Brit.) feldspar (q.v.). O, R, W [4]

felstone, *n.* (1858) *Mineral.* [Partial transl. of G *Felsstein* < *Fels* rock + *Stein* stone] Orig., a vague term for amorphous rocks, which was generally replaced by *felsite;* now a compact, porphyritic feldspar (q.v.)—**felstone,** *a.* (1882). O [3]

fenchene, *n.* (1891) *Chem.* [G *Fenchen* (1891) < *Fenchel* fennel + *-en* -ene] Any of various isomeric, liquid terpenes, esp. obtained from fenchyl alcohol. O, W [3]

fenchone, *n.* (1891) *Chem.* [G *Fenchon* (1891) fennel + *-on* -one] An oily terpenoid ketone, used chiefly as a pine scent. O, W [3]

Fennoscandian, *a.* (1907) *Geol.* [G *fennoskandisch* (1904) < *fenno-* + *skandisch* < L *fenn(i)* Finns + *Scandia* (prob.) Sweden + G *-isch* -an] Concerning an ancient land mass in northwestern Europe comprising most of Scandinavia and Finland and the northwestern parts of the former U.S.S.R.; in extended use, Scandinavia and Finland as a political unit. —**Fennoscandia,** *a.;* **Fenno-Scandia,** *n.* (1907); **Fennoscandinavian,** *a.* (1962). O, W [4]

fenster, *n.* (1925) *Geol.* [G, lit., window < MHG *venster* < OHG *fenstar*] An opening eroded down through overthrust rock: window. O, R, W [3]

ferberite, *n.* (1868) *Mineral.* [G *Ferberit* (1863) < the name of Rudolph *Ferber,* 19th-century German mineralogist from Gera + *-it* -ite] A valuable ferrous tungstate. O, R, W [3]

fernflöte, *n. Music* [G < *fern* far, distant + *Flöte* flute (ult. < OProv *flaut*), also called *Waldflöte* forest flute] A very soft organ pipe of flute tone and 4- or 8-foot pitch. W [3]

ferrometer, *n.* (1935) *Physics* [G < *ferro-* (< the comb. form of L *ferrum* iron) + G *Meter* meter < Fr *mètre* < Gk *métron*] An instrument for determining the magnetic properties of ferromagnetic material. O [3]

fest, *n.* (1865) [G (< MHG *vest*) feast, festival < L *fēstum* feast day] A festive (or formal) gathering. • ~ is functionally shifted to a terminal comb. form, as in **talkfest** (1910), **rockfest** (1973), and **gabfest.** Mencken and Schönfelder independently collected more than 80 such derivatives. O, R, W [4]

Festschrift/festschrift, -en/-s *pl.* (1898) *Ed.* [G < *Fest* festival, celebration + *Schrift* essay, script] One or more volumes of usu. miscellaneous articles by pupils and colleagues published to honor a scholar on a special anniversary, as on a 65th birthday. O, R, W [4]

Festspiel, *n. Theater* [G < *Fest* festival + *Spiel* play] A festival play. W2 [3]

Festung Europa, *n.* (1944 *Algeo*) *Politics* [G < *Festung* fortress + *Europa* Europe, ult. < Gk *Eurṓpē*] Hitler's fortification of Europe. • ~ is transl. as **Fortress Europe** (1944). O, W (not in latest reprints of W3) [3]

fetalization, *n.* (1930) *Biol.* Var. **foetalization** (1930) [G *Fetalisation* (1926) fetalization] A retaining in higher forms' postnatal life of bodily conditions occurring when lower forms were developing: pedomorphism. —**f(o)etalized,** *a.* (1940). O, W [3]

fibrinferment, *n.* (1876) *Physiol.* [G (1872) < *fibr-* + *-in-* + *Ferment* < L *fibr-,* comb. form of L *fibra* fiber + *-in* + *fermentum*] Thrombin, a proteolytic enzyme. O [3]

fibrinogen, *n.* (1872) *Med., Biol.* [G < *fibr-* + *-in-* + *-o-* + *-gen* < the comb. form of *Fibrin* < L *fibra* fiber + Gk *-genēs* born, produced] A globulin that is produced in the liver and is converted into fibrin during blood clotting. —**fibrinogenous,** *a.* (1876); **-genopenia.** O, R, W [4]

fibrinoid, *a.* (1910) *Path.* [G (1880) < *Fibrin* (see *fibrinferment*) + *-oid* < Gk *-oeidēs,* similar, resembling] A substance that stains like fibrin and is derived from connective tissue. —**fibrinoid,** *n.* (1958). O, R, W [4]

fibroferrite, *n.* (1844) *Mineral.* [G *Fibroferrit* < *fibro-* + *Ferrit* < L *fibra* fiber + *ferrum* iron + G *-it* -ite] A basic, hydrated ferric sulfate occurring in fibrous silky tufts. O, W [3]

fidibus, -es/-ø *pl.* (1829) [G (1722) < a folk etymological ad. of Horace's *Odes,* I, 36 from "let us appease the gods with incense and lyre" (*Et ture et fidibus iuvat placere deos*) to read: "with pipe tabac (actually: smoke) and paper spills"] A paper match for lighting pipes. O, W [3]

fiedlerite, *n.* (1892) *Mineral.* [G *Fiedlerit* (1887) < the name of Karl G. *Fiedler* (1791–1853), a German commissioner of mines + *-it* -ite] A hydroxychloride of lead. O, W [3]

field devil, *n.* (1535) *Theol.* (archaic) [Transl. of G *Feldteufel* < *Feld* field + *Teufel* devil, Luther's rendition in the *Second Book of Chronicles,* XI, 15] Satyr (in Cover dale's transl. of Luther's transl. of Heb *səîrîm;* in the King James version it is pejorated to *devil*). O [3]

field gray, *n.* (1915) and *a. Mil.* Var. **field grey** (1915) [Transl. of G *feldgrau*] The regulation color of a German infantryman's uniform; this color applied to others' uniforms; the color itself. O, W [3]

field marshal/field-marshal, *n.* (1614) *Mil.* [Transl. of G *Feldmarschall* < *Feld* field + *Marschall* marshal < OFr *maréchal,* ult. of Gmc origin] The title of a military officer of the highest rank, as in the continental army or the British army, corresponding to a modern U.S. general. —**field-marshalship** (1855). O, R, W [4]

fife, *n.* (1555) *Music* [Transl. of G *Pfeife* fife] A small flute with six to eight finger holes and usually no key, used chiefly in military bands; a shrill flute stop in a pipe organ; (rare) a fifer or the sound of a fife. —**fife,** *a.* (1854) and *v.* (1598). • ~ appears in composites like **fifer** (1540), **fife and drum** (1674), **fifing** (c.1817), **fife bird** (1854). O, R, W [4]

filicic acid, *n.* (1865) *Chem.* [Transl. of G *Filixsäure* (1851) < *Filix* (< L *felix* fern) + G *Säure* acid] A phenolic anthelmintic substance obtained from filicin, esp. the common male fern. O, W [3]

filicin, *n.* (1892) *Chem.* [G (1891) < *Filix* (< L *felix* fern)

+ G *-in* -in] Filicic acid (q.v.); the mixture of active principles obtained from the male fern. O, W [3]

fillmass, *n. Chem.* [Transl. of G *Füllmasse* < *füll-* < *füllen* to fill + *Masse* mass < L *massa* < Gk *mâza*] Massecuite, used esp. in making beet sugar. W [3]

Filz, -e *pl.* (1981) *Politics* [G < MHG *vilz,* OHG *filz* powdered or ground mass, now (colloq.) tangle, niggard(liness)] Shoddiness. BDC [2]

filzocratie, -n *pl.* (1981) *Politics* [G *Filzocratie/Filzokratie* < colloq. G *Filz* Filz (q.v.) shoddiness + a short. of *Democratie/Demokratie* democracy, ult. < Gk *demokratía*] An inferior, shoddy system of political government. BDC [2]

fine structure, *n.* (1918) *Physics* [Transl. of G *Feinstruktur* (1916) < *fein* fine + *Structur* < L *strūctūra*] The presence of usu. multiplets of closely spaced lines in the spectra of certain elements that show up as single lines under low resolution; small-scale variation in structure, etc.; similar groups of energies or lines in other spectra. —**fine structure,** *a.* (1923). O, R [3]

finitary, *a.* (1952) *Math.* [Transl. of G *finit* (1934) finite (< L *fīnītus* limited), modeled on < E *unitary*] Involving only a finite number of steps in methods, proofs, etc.; having a finite number of well-defined objects and processes. O, W [3]

fireblende, *n.* (1850) *Mineral.* [Partial transl. of G *Feuerblende* (1832) < *Feuer* fire + *Blende* deceptively gleaming metal < *blenden* to blind, deceive] Pyrostilpnite, a silver antimony sulfide. O, W [3]

firm, *n.* (1744) *Commerce* [G (< It) *Firma* the binding signature in a contract < *firmare* (< L) to authenticate a contract by signing it] The title, name, or style under which a business operates; a business unit, enterprise, kind of partnership, or group of persons working together. O, R, W [4]

firn (snow), *n.* (1853) *Meteor.* [G *Firn* last year's snow < OHG *firni* old] The previous year's granulated snow that is not yet glacier ice: névé. —**firn,** *a.* (1934); **firnification** (1923); **firn line** (1958). O, R, W [4]

firstling, *n.* (1535) [Coverdale's poss. transl. of G *Erstling* firstborn < *erst-* + *-ling*] The first of its kind to appear, be produced, or come into being; extended sense to any class, kind, offspring, product, etc. —**firstling,** *a.* (1611); **firstlin(g)s,** *adv.* (1827). O, R, W [4]

fischerite, *n.* (1846) *Mineral.* [G *Fischerit* (1844) < the name of Gotthelf *Fischer* von Waldheim (1771–1853), German naturalist + *-it* -ite] A green basic aluminum phosphate. O, W [3]

Fischer-Tropsch process, *n.* (1933) *Chem.* Var. **Fischer-Tropsch synthesis** [Alteration of G *Fischer-Tropsch-Synthese* (1922–26) < the names of Franz *Fischer* (1877–1947), German chemist and Hans *Tropsch* (1889–1935), German chemist born in Czechoslovakia + *Synthese* < Gk *sýnthesis*] A process introduced by them to produce liquid and gaseous hydrocarbon fuels. O, R, W [3]

fisetin, *n.* (1865) *Chem.* [G *Fisettin* < *Fisettholz* the yellow wood of fustic + *-in* -in] A yellow, crystalline pigment obtained from the wood of fustet, sumac, etc. that was used as a dyestuff for centuries. O, W [3]

fist-law, *n.* (1831) *Law* [Transl. of G *Faustrecht* < *Faust* fist + *Recht* law] The right of the strongest. O [3]

flak, -ø pl. (1938) Mil. Var. **flack** (1975) [G < a short. of *Fliegerabwehrkanone* < *Flieger* pilot + *Abwehr* defense + *Kanone* cannon] Antiaircraft artillery or the bursting shells fired by such artillery; abusive criticism. • ~ appears in compounds like **flak-happy** (1944)/**jacket** (1956)/**curtain/ opposition**. O, R, W [4]

flamethrower, n. (1915) Mil. Var. **flammenwerfer** (1915), **flame-thrower** (1917) [Transl. of G *Flammenwerfer* < *Flamme* flame + *Werfer* thrower < *werfen* to throw] A weapon for shooting a stream of flaming gasoline, etc. at enemy troops or positions; a device to kill insects or weeds: flame gun. O, R, W [4]

flammenwerfer, see flamethrower

flaser, a. (1888) and n. Geol. [G vein in rock or wood, prob. dial. ad. of *Flader*] (Of) an irreg., usu. streaked granular lens in a micaceous interstitial rock mass, esp. found in gabbro, granite, and gneiss. O, W [3]

flavanthrone, n. (1902) Chem. Var. **flavanthrene** (1902) [G *Flavanthren* < *flav-* yellow + *-anthren* < *Anthracen* < L *flāvus* + Gk *ánthrax* coal + G *-en* -ene, the formative of the names of hydrocarbons] A yellow vat dye. O, W [3]

flavin(e), n. (1933) Biochem. [G *Flavin* (1933) < *flav-* (< L *flāvus* yellow) + G *-in* -in(e)] Riboflavin or another yellow nitrogenous pigment derived from isolloxazine (this is different from the older, Latin-derived meanings of "acriflavine, yellow dyestuff"). O, R, W [3]

flavone, n. (1897) Chem. [G *Flavon* (1895) < *flav-* (< L *flāvus* yellow) + G *-on* -one] A colorless, crystalline, tricyclic ketone; a derivative of this; a flavonoid. —**flavonoid,** a. and n. (1949). O, R, W [3]

flavonol, n. (1898) Chem. [G (1895) < *flav-* (< L *flāvus* yellow) + G *-on-* (as in *Flavon* flavone—q.v.) + *-ol* -ol] A hydroxy derivative of flavone, many of whose derivatives occur as yellow plant pigments. O, R, W [3]

flavopurpurin, n. (1879) Chem. [G < *flavo-* + *Purpurin* < L *flavo-*, comb. form of *flāvus* yellow + *purpura* crimson + G *-in* -in] A yellow crystalline compound occurring in commercial synthetic alizarin. O, R, W [4]

flextime/flexitime, n. (1972) Industry Var. **flexible (work) time, Gleitzeit** (q.v.) [Transl. of G *Gleitzeit* sliding time] A work arrangement whereby employees can generally choose their own working hours; (cap. as *Flextime*) a trademark for a timing device to record an employee's hours. O, R [4]

flimmer, n. Biol. [G flimmer, glitter] One of the delicate, lateral filaments found in some flagella: mastigoneme (this is different from the old "chatterbox" meaning). W [3]

flimmer, v. (1880) [G *flimmern* to glimmer] To glimmer or flicker, as in a candle. O, W [3]

flinkite, n. (1891) Mineral. [G *Flinkit* (1889) < the name of Gustav *Flink* (1849–1931), Swedish mineralogist + G *-it* -ite] A basic manganese arsenate in feathery forms. O, W [3]

flitter, n. (18..) Metall. [G a small metal flake, backformation < *flittern* to flitter] A small flake or bit of metal; fine metal fragments used for ornamenting. O, R, W [3]

flittermouse, -mice pl. (1547) Zool. [Transl. of G *Fledermaus* < *fleder-* < MHG *vlederen* to flutter, flitter + G *Maus* mouse] A bat; a term of playful endearment. O, R, W [3]

floss, n. (1839) Metall. [G *Floss, Flosz* pig-iron dross] Vitrified oxide or earth floating on the iron in a puddling furnace; floss hole; white cast iron for converting into steel. —**floss(-)hole** (1839). O, W [3]

fluegelhorn, see flügelhorn

flügel/flugel, n. Music [G < MHG *vlügel* wing, the shape of a grand piano] The grand piano or its predecessor. W [3]

flügelhorn, n. (1854) Music Var. **flugelhorn** (1926), **fluegelhorn** [G < *Flügel* wing + *Horn* horn] A bugle with valves differing from the cornet only in having a larger bore; a brass bugle similar to the saxhorn. —**flügelhornist.** • ~ is short. to **flugel** (1954). O, R, W [4]

flugelman, see fugleman

fluocerite, n. (1854) Mineral. Var. **fluocerine** [G *Fluocerit* (now also *Fluozerit*), ad. < Fr *fluocérine* < NL *fluor* feldspar + *cerium* cerium + G *-it* -ite] A native fluoride of cerium and related metals. O, W [3]

fluor, n. (1661) Mineral. [Ad. of Georgius Agricola's *fluores,* a transl. of the mining term *flusse,* ult. < L *fluor* feldspar] (Archaic) a mineral belonging to a group including fluorite; (chiefly Brit.) fluorite. • ~ appears in compounds like **fluorspar** (1794), **fluor acid** (1882). O, R, W [4]

fluoranthene, n. (1878) Chem. [G *Fluoranthen* (1877), an irreg. blend of *Fluoren* + *Phenanthren* < *Fluor* + *Anthracen* anthracene < Gk *ánthrax* coal] A crystalline hydrocarbon esp. found in coal-tar distillates; a derivative of this. O, W [3]

fluorapatite, n. (1882) Mineral. [G *Fluorapatit* < *Fluor* fluor + *Apatit* apatite (q.v.) + *-it* -ite] An apatite containing fluorine. O, R, W [3]

fluorophor(e), n. (1898) Chem. [G *Fluorophor* (1897) < *fluoro-* (< *Fluorit* fluorite) + *-phor* < Gk *phóros* bearing] An atomic group, which when present in a molecule, causes it to be fluorescent; a fluorescent substance. O [3]

flysch, -es pl. (1827) Geol. Var. **Flysch** (1827) [(Dial. Swiss) G something that slides or flows, prob. related to Swabian *Flins* slate, G *Flinz* slate, sandstone] A thick, extensive deposit, mainly of sandstone and common in the European Alps. O, R, W [4]

fob, n. (1653) [(Poss. akin to East Prussian) G *Fuppe* pocket, *fuppen* to pocket stealthily] A small pocket just below the front waistband in men's trousers; an ornament hanging outside a fob pocket and connected by a short chain to a watch carried in the pocket; the watch itself; a decorative device attached to a belt, zipper, or pin. —**fob,** v. (1818); **fob pocket/chain** (1837, 1885). O, R, W [4]

foehn/föhn, n. (1861) Meteor. [G *Föhn* < OHG *phonno,* ult. < L *Favōnius* warm west wind] A warm dry south wind (like the Santa Ana wind in Southern California, U.S.A.) that flows down the valleys in the Alps. —**foehn-like, foehn wind** (1910). O, R, W [4]

foetalization, see fetalization

föhn, see foehn

foldboat, n. (1938) Sports Var. **fold boat** (1969) [Transl. of G *Faltboot* faltboot (q.v.)] Faltboat. • ~ appears in derivatives like **foldboater** and **foldboating**. O, R, W [4]

folk, folk-, a. or comb. form [Transl. of G *Volk, Volks-* folk, of the people] Of, relating to, current, or existing among people. • ~ appears in numerous composites like **folkish**

(1938), **folksy** (1852), **folk medicine** (1898), **folktale** (1891). O, R, W [4]

folk art, *n.* (1921) *Art* [Prob. transl. of G *Volkskunst* < *Volk* folk + *Kunst* art] A traditional art originating among the people. —**folk art,** *a.;* **folk artist** (1934). O, R, W [3]

folk dance, *n.* (1909) *Dance* [Transl. of G *Volkstanz* < *Volk* folk + *Tanz* dance] A dance originating among and characteristic of the common people. —**folk dance,** *v.* (1927); **folk-dancer** (1937); **folk-dancing** (1967). O, R, W [4]

folk etymology, *n.* (1883) *Ling.* [Transl. of G *Volksetymologie* < *Volk* folk + *Etymologie* < Gk *etymología* investigation of the real, original sense of a word] The popular transformation of unusual words so as to give them an apparent but actually mistaken relationship to better-known words. O, R, W [4]

folklore, *n.* (1846) *Sociol.* [Transl. of G *Volkskunde* (1806) < *Volk* folk + *Kunde* knowledge] Traditional customs, beliefs, dances, etc. preserved unreflectively and orally by a people; a comparative discipline that studies such customs; a popular fantasy or unsupported belief. —**folkloric** (1883), **-ish** (1926), **-ism** (1886), **-ist(ic)** (1876, 1888). O, R, W [4]

folk psychology, *n.* (1889) *Psych.* [Transl. of G *Völkerpsychologie* < *Völker,* pl. of *Volk* folk + *Psychologie* < NL *psychologia*] Ethnopsychology; such study of primitive people. —**folk psychologist** (1918). O, W [3]

folk song, *n.* (1847) *Music* [Transl. of G *Volkslied* (1771) < *Volk* folk + *Lied* song] A song originating with or traditional among the common people; a song with such qualities. —**folksongish** (1925), **folksongy** (1934). O, R, W [4]

folk state, *n. Politics* [Transl. of G *Volksstaat* < *Volk* folk + *Staat* state, ult. < L *status*] A state with a racially homogeneous population; a state with ethnic unity. W [3]

footfolk/foot-folk, *pl.* (1859) *Mil.* [Transl. of G *Fussvolk* < *Fuss* foot + *Volk* folk] (Chiefly Brit.) foot soldiers (this is different from the Middle Ages meaning of "infantry"). O [3]

foozle, *v.* (1857) [Poss. ad. of dial. G *fuseln* to perform quick, shoddy work] To bungle; to waste one's time. —**foozle,** *n.;* **foozling** (1857); **foozler** (1896); **foozled** (1899). O, R, W [4]

forbesite, *n.* (1868) *Mineral.* [G *Forbesit* (1868) < the name of David *Forbes* (1828–76), English geologist + G *-it* -ite] A hydrous, fibrocrystalline arsenate of nickel and cobalt. O, W [3]

foreconscious, *a.* (1915) *Psych.* [Transl. of G *vorbewußt* < *vor* before + *bewußt* conscious] Preconscious: relating to that part of the mind below the threshold of immediate conscious attention, but whose perceptions and memories can be recalled without inner resistance or repression; preceding the development of self-consciousness. —**foreconscious,** *n.* (1924). O, W [3]

forehand, *n. Games* [Transl. of G *Vorderhand* < *vorder* fore + *Hand* hand] The player in skat who bids first (this is different from meanings like "tennis or racquet stroke, working foreman"). R, W [3]

forepleasure, *n.* (1910) *Psych.* [Transl. of Freud's G *Vorlust* (1905) < *vor* fore + *Lust* pleasure] Pleasure induced

by sexual stimulation that tends to lead to a more intense reaction, as in orgasm. O, R, W [3]

forerunner, *n.* (1949) *Sports* [Transl. of G *Vorläufer* (q.v.)] One or more skiers who run the course as a preliminary to a downhill skiing race (this is different from the old "harbinger, predecessor" meanings). O, W [4]

foresite, *n.* (1875) *Mineral.* [G *Foresit* < the name of G. F. *Foresi* from Porto Ferrajo, Elba + G *-it* -ite] A hydrous silicate of aluminum and calcium. O-1933 [3]

foreword, *n.* (1842) *Printing* [Transl. of G *Vorwort* < *vor* fore + *Wort* word] Introduction, as in a book, long article, speech, etc. O, R, W [4]

foreworld, *n.* (1796) *History* [Prob. transl. of G *Vorwelt* < *vor* fore + *Welt* world] The primeval or ancient world. O, W [3]

form, *n.* (1803) *Philos.* [Kant's G < L *fōrma* form] A formative mode of cognition and perception in Kantian philosophy, esp. in regard to temporal and spatial order. O, W [3]

formal concept, *n.* (1922) *Philos.* [Transl. of Wittgenstein's G *formaler Begriff* < *formal* (< L *fōrmālis* concerning the superficial form or disposition) + G *Begriff* concept] A concept in logic devoid of descriptive content that would restrict it to a particular subject matter. O [3]

formaldehyde, *n.* (1872) *Chem.* [G *Formaldehyd* < *form-* (< L *acidum formicicum* formic acid) + G *Aldehyd* aldehyde (q.v.)] A very reactive aldehyde used as a preservative, disinfectant, etc.; also called *formic aldehyde.*—**formaldehydogenic.** • ~ appears initially in **formaldehydesulfoxylate/sulfoxylic acid/tanning.** O, R, W [4]

formalism, *n.* (1934) *Math.* [G *Formalismus* (1928) < *formal* + *-ismus* < L *fōrmālis* concerning the superficial form or disposition + *-ismus* -ism] A particular mathematical theory or method of description of a physical effect or situation (this is different from older "general, theological, theatrical, literary, etc." meanings). O [3]

formant, *n.* (1901) *Ling.* [G (1894) < L *formant-* < *fōrmāns* present part. of *fōrmāre* to form] A characteristic component of a speech sound, as in resonance bands; transf. sense to a musical instrument; a morphological determinative or derivational affix. O, R, W [4]

format, *n.* (1840) *Printing* [F (< G) or G < L *fōrmātus* formed, shaped, as in *liber in quarto formatus* a volume formed in quarto] The shape and size of a publication; its general makeup or style; (by extension) the general arrangement of things, as in stamps, cameras, etc.; the arrangement of data or characters for computer or other use. —**format,** *v.* (1964); **formatting,** *verbal n.* (1964); **formatted,** *part. a.* (1965). O, R, W [4]

formation, *n.* (1898) *Ecology* [G (1838) < L *fōrmātio* formation, arrangement, shape] A community of species, as in groups of plants that have adapted themselves to similar climatic conditions (this is different from many other meanings). O [4]

form criticism, *n.* (1923) *Lit.* Var. **Formgeschichte** (1923), **form history** [Transl. of G *Formgeschichte* (1919) history of form, used in this sense by the German theologian Martin Dibelius (1883–1947) < *Form* form (< OFr < L *fōrma*) + G *Geschichte* history] A method of literary criticism chiefly applied to the Bible, by classifying scriptural units into forms like elegies, parables, sayings, etc., and then tracing the early history of these forms with the aim of discovering their original form and relating this to its historical setting. —**form critic** (1933), **form-critical** (1933). O, R, W [4]

formenkreis, -e/-es *pl. Biol.* [G < *Formen*, pl. of *Form* form (< OFr < L *fōrma*) + G *Kreis* circle] A polytypic species such as birds. W [3]

Formgeschichte, *n.* (1923) *Lit., Theol.* [G < *Form* form (< OFr < L *fōrma*) + G *Geschichte* history] Form criticism (q.v.). O [3]

formose, *n.* (1886) *Chem.* [G (1886), a blend of *Formaldehyd* + *-ose* < NL *acidum formicum* formic acid] A mixture of hexose sugars produced by condensing formaldehyde (q.v.) in the presence of diluted alkalis. O [3]

form quality, *n.* (1901) *Philos.* [Transl. of G *Gestaltqualität* (1890) < *Form* form, shape + *Qualität* quality < OFr *form* < L *fōrma* + OFr *qualite* < L *qualitat-, quālitās*] That which characterizes a mental whole as having a particular form, or being formed, or as having related parts. O [3]

Fortress Europe, *see* Festung Europa

forty-eighter, *n. Politics* [Transl. of G *Achtundvierziger* < *acht* eight + *und* and + *vierzig* forty + *-er* -er] A German who took part in the revolution of 1848, esp. one who fled to the United States. W [3]

forward lean, *n. Sports* [Transl. of G *Vorlage* forward lean < *sich vorlegen* to lean forward] The position of a skier who leans forward from the ankles. Longman [3]

foundations, *pl.* (1817) *Philos.* [Transl. of G *Grandlagen*, pl. of *Grundlage* basis, foundation] The underlying principles or logical basis of a subject, esp. as an area of study. O [3]

four-hundred-day clock, *n. Tech.* [Transl. of G *Vierhunderttageuhr* < *vier* four + *hundert* hundred + *Tage*, pl. of *Tag* day + *Uhr* clock] Anniversary clock: one that can run 400 days on a single winding. R, W [3]

four-vector, *n.* (1914) *Math.* [Transl. of G *Vierervektor* (1910) vector of four < *vierer* + *Vektor* < NL *vector*] A vector defined within four dimensions, esp. a space-time vector in the theory of relativity. —**four-vector,** *a.* (1968). O [3]

foyaite, *n.* (1878) *Mineral.* [G *Foyait* < the name of La Foia, a mountain in the Portuguese province of Algarve + G *-it* -ite] A kind of nepheline- or nephelite-syenite rock. —**foyaitic.** O, W [3]

Fractur, *see* Fraktur

fracture, *see* breaking

frage, *n. Games* [G, lit., question, bid < OHG *frāga*] The lowest bid in a card game, as in frog or skat. W [3]

fragmentist, *n.* (1874) *Lit.* [G < *Fragment* + *-ist* < L *frāgmentum* fraction + *-ist* -ist] A writer of a literary fragment or of a work surviving only fragmentarily. O, W [3]

Fraktur, *n.* (1886) *Printing* Var. **Fractur** (1886), **fraktur** (1904) [G *Fractur* (now *Fraktur*) < L *frāctūra* fracturing] A German-style black-letter text type; (U.S.) a Pennsylvania Dutch style of decorative calligraphy. O, R, W [4]

frame story/tale, *n.* (1924) *Lit.* [Transl. of G *Rahmenerzählung* < *Rahmen* frame + *Erzählung* story, tale] A story told within a frame; a story constituting a frame for another story or a series. O, W [3]

franckeite, *n.* (1893) *Mineral.* [G *Franckeit* (1893) < the name of Carl and Ernst *Francke,* German mining engineers active in Bolivian geology in the 19th cent.] A massive lead antimony tin sulfide. O, W [3]

frangulin, *n.* (1864) *Chem.* [G < NL *frangula* (< L *frangere* to break) alder buckthorn + G *-in* -in] An orange crystalline glucoside obtained esp. from the alder buckthorn. —**frangulic (acid)** (1872). O, W [3]

frank[1]**,** *n. Currency* [G *Franken* (or Flemish *frank*) franc < Fr *franc*] One of various monetary units in Belgium, Switzerland, Luxembourg, etc., orig. equivalent to the French franc (this is different from the many other meanings). • ~ is usu. spelled as E *franc.* W [3]

frank[2]**,** *n.* (1904 *W9*) *Food* Var. short. of G *Frankfurter* (*Würstchen*) frankfurter (q.v.)] Frankfurter. O, R, W [4]

Frankenthal, *a.* (1863) and *n. Pottery* [G *Frankenthaler Porzellan* porcelain made in *Frankenthal,* in the German Palatinate between 1755 and 1800 + *Porzellan* < MFr *porcelaine,* ult. < L *porcellus*] (Of) artistic faience and hard-paste porcelain made in Frankenthal then. O, W [3]

frankfurter/frankforter, *n.* (1877) *Food* Var. **frankfort/frankfurt** (1877, 1902) [G *Frankfurter* (*Würstchen*) < *Frankfurter* of or from Frankfurt, Germany + *Würstchen* sausage] A sausage of beef, pork, or chicken, in casings or skinless, orig. smoked and highly seasoned and made in Frankfurt am Main. —**turkeyfurter** (1943 *Algeo*). O, R, W [4]

frass, *n.* (1854) *Entomology* [G *Frass, Frasz* < *fressen* to devour, as borrowed by Henry T. Stainton in *The Entomologist's Companion* (1854, 2nd ed.)] Larva excrements or refuse produced by boring insects. O, R, W [3]

frau/Frau, -en/-s *pl.* (1813) [G (married) woman] A married woman; wife or housewife, sometimes disparaging; a title equivalent to *Mrs.* and cap. when preceding the German woman's name. O, R, W [4]

Frauendienst, *n.* (1879) *Sociol.* [G, orig. the title of a work by the MHG poet Ulrich von Lichtenstein (c.1200–76), written in 1255, which depicts the exaggerated chivalry toward women during the Age of the Minnesong (q.v.) < G *Frauen,* pl. of *Frau* woman + *Dienst* service] Exaggerated chivalry toward women. O [3]

fräulein/Fräulein, -s/-ø *pl.* (1689) [G < *Frau* woman + dim. suffix *-lein* little, i.e., an unmarried young woman] A young, unmarried (German) girl or woman (cap. when preceding her name); a German governess. O, R, W [4]

fraxin, *n.* (1864) *Chem.* [G < L *fraxinus* ash tree + G *-in* -in] A bitter, crystalline glucoside found esp. in the bark of the ash and the horse chestnut. O, W [3]

free, *a.* (1906) *Physics* (1965) *Chem.* [Transl. of G *frei* (1894) free, not bound] Of an electron that is not bound to an atom, molecule, and is thus able to move unrestrictedly under the influence of magnetic and electric fields (this is different from many older meanings). O [3]

free corps, *n. Mil.* [Transl. of G *Freikorps* < *frei* free + *Korps* corps < Fr *corps* corporate body] A corps of usu. German volunteer soldiers. W [3]

Free Democrat, *n. Politics* [Transl. of G *Freier Demokrat/Freidemokrat* < *frei* free + *Demokrat* democrat < Fr *democrate* a supporter of popular rule < Gk *demokratía* democracy, people's rule] A member of a conservative,

Protestant political party formed in West Germany (preceding reunification) that stresses individual freedom, esp. economically. W [4]

freibergite, *n.* (1856) *Mineral.* [G *Freibergit* (1853) < the name of *Freiberg,* a German town in Saxony + *-it* -ite] A variety of tetrahedrite containing silver. O, W [3]

freieslebenite, *n.* (1850) *Mineral.* [G *Freieslebenit* (1845) < the name of Johann K. *Freiesleben* (1774–1846), German mineralogist + *-it* -ite] A sulfide of antimony, lead, and silver. O, W [3]

fresh, *a.* (1848) [U.S. folk etymology < G *frech* saucy] Saucy, impudent (this is different from many other meanings). O, R, W [4]

friedrichsdor, *n.* (1741) *Currency* [G (1741) < the gen. of the name of *Friedrich* Frederick II (1770–1840), King of Prussia + G *-dor* < Fr *d'or* (made) of gold] A former gold coin of Prussia first struck by him; frederik (< Dan), a Danish coin. W [3]

frightfulness, *n.* (1914) *Mil.* [Transl. of G *Schrecklichkeit* (q.v.)] Action or policy to terrorize the enemy, esp. civilians, during a war (this is different from the old meaning of "quality of being frightful"). O, W [3]

Fritz, *n.* (1883) *Mil.* [G a foreigner's derogatory nickname for *Friedrich* Frederick, a common German given name] A German soldier, shell, aircraft, etc., esp. in World War One. —**Fritz,** *a.* (1932), but prob. unrelated to "on the fritz." O, R, W [3]

fröhlich, *a. Music* [G gay, joyous] Joyous, happy (used as a direction in music). W [3]

Fröhlich's/Froehlich's syndrome, *n.* (1912) *Med.* [G < the name of Alfred *Fröhlich* (1871–1953), Austrian neurologist who identified the disease called G *Fröhlich-Krankheit* + E *syndrome*] Adiposogenital dystrophy, characterized by obesity, sexual infantilism, and changes in secondary sex characteristics. O, W [3]

frontogenesis, *n.* (1931 *W9*) *Meteor.* [G *Frontogenese* (1928), used by the German meteorologist Tor Bergeron (1891–?) < *fronto-* + *-genese* < L *frōns* (gen. *frontis*) forehead, brow + *génesis* (< Gk) origin, development] The formation or development of fronts, which induce precipitation and clouds. —**frontogenetic** (1966), **frontogenetically.** O, R, W [3]

fuchsite, *n.* (1844) *Mineral.* [G *Fuchsit* (1842) < the name of Johann N. von *Fuchs* (1774–1856), German mineralogist + *-it* -ite] Chromium muscovite, a common mica. O, R, W [3]

fuehrer, *see* Führer

fugleman, *n.* (1804) *Mil.* Var. **f(l)ugelman** (1804, 1814) [G *Flügelmann* < *Flügel* wing + *Mann* man] A trained soldier formerly placed in front of a military unit at drill to serve as a model; transf. sense to a leader in general. —**fugle,** *v.* (1837); **fuglemanship** (1845); **fugling,** *verbal n.* (1858). O, R, W [4]

Führer/fuehrer, *n.* (1934) *Politics* Var. **Fuehrer** (1937) [G *Führer* leader, guide; a title taken by Hitler] Leader (q.v.); guide; *der Führer,* the Chancellor of the Third Reich, Adolf Hitler (1889–1945). —**fuhrer,** *a.* (1943). O, R, W [4]

Führer prinzip/principle, *n.* (1937) *Politics* [G *Führerprinzip,* partially transl. as *Führer principle* < *Führer*

leader + *Prinzip* principle < L *prīncipium* beginning] The principle that the Führer has the right to command, and the people have the duty to obey him. O [3]

fulgide, *n. Chem.* [G *Fulgid* < *fulg-* (< L *fulgēre* to flash, lighten) + G *-id* -ide] The anhydride of fulgenic acid; a derivative of this acid, as used in photography. W [3]

fulvene, *n. Chem.* [G *Fulven* < L *fulvus* yellow + G *-en* -ene] A yellow hydrocarbon that is a methylene derivative of cyclopentadiene; any of a series of fulvene derivatives. W [3]

funckia, *see* funkia

function, *see* Introduction

fundiform, *a.* (1854) *Anat.* [Latinized transl. of G *schleuderförmig* (1841) < *Schleuder* sling + *förmig* shaped < *Form* shape < L *fōrma*] Of a ligament of the ankle or penis that has the shape of a sling. O [3]

funkia, *n.* (1839) *Bot.* Var. **funckia** (1839) [G (< NL) *funckia* (1817) < the name of C. H. *Funck* (1771–1839), German botanist + *-ia* -ia] Hosta, a member of the genus of Asiatic liliaceous plants; a plantain lily. O, R, W [4]

furfuran, *n.* (1877) *Chem.* Var. **furfurane** (1895) [G (1877) < *Furfurol* (< L *furfur* clover) + G *-an,* as used in names of hydrocarbons] Furan, a flammable liquid compound. O, R, W [4]

furiant, *n.* (1881) *Music, Dance* [Czech and G (< Czech) < L *furiant-* < *furiāns,* pres. part. of *furare* to rage] A spirited Bohemian dance or its music. O, R, W [3]

Fürst, -en *pl. Politics* [G < MHG *vürste,* OHG *furisto* foremost, the first, i.e., prince] In Germany and Austria until 1918, a noble outranked only by a duke; a prince. W2 [2]

Fürstenbund, *n. Politics* [G (1785) < *Fürsten,* pl. of *Fürst* prince + *Bund* league] The league of German princes formed in 1785 to oppose Austria. W2 [2]

furunculosis, -oses *pl.* (1912) *Path.* [G *Furunkulose* (1894) < L *fūrunculus* furuncle, boil, (actually) little thief, (also) wild shoot + G *-ose* (< Gk *-osis*) -osis, fem. suffix of action] A highly infectious disease of salmonid fishes (this is different from the older "having furuncles" meaning). O, R, W [3]

fusel oil, *n.* (1850) *Chem.* [Ad. of G *Fuselöl* (1841) < *Fusel* cheap liquor (and the unpleasant odor it generates) + *Öl* oil < L *oleum*] An acrid, oily liquid of unpleasant odor, a by-product of fermentation, consisting chiefly of alcohols; amyl alcohol. O, R, W [4]

fusion¹, *n.* (1892) *Psych., Physiol.* [Transl. of G *Verschmelzung* (1824) fusion] A blend of separate, simultaneous sensations, ideas, etc., into a new complex so fused as to be seldom analyzable by introspection; the blending of retinal images in binocular vision (this is different from various earlier meanings). O, W [3]

fusion², *n.* (1927) *Psych.* [Transl. of Freud's G *Mischung* (1923) mixture] In Freudian theory, the union and balance of death and life instincts that exist in normal individuals. O [3]

fusion frequency, *see* critical flicker frequency

fussefall, *n.* (1547) *Politics* (archaic) [G *Fuszfall* < (*einem*) *zu Fusz* or *zu Füssen fallen* to fall at one's feet] Prostration before a sovereign. O [3]

fustin, *n.* (1864) *Chem.* [G < Fr *fustet* < ML *fustetum* sumac, fustet + G -*in* -in] A crystalline compound found in the wood of various plants like the smoke tree: dihydrofisetin. O, W [3]

futurological, *a.* [Ad. of G *futurologisch* futurological < *Futurologie* + -*isch*] Concerning futurology (q.v.). R [3]

futurology, *n.* (1946) [G *Futurologie* (1943) < *futuro-* + -*logie* < L *futūrum* future + Gk *lógos* word, study + G -*ie* (< Gk -*ia*) -y] A study that deals systematically with and attempts to forecast future possibilities based on current trends in human affairs. —**futurologist** (1967). O, R [4]

G

g, *n*. (1930) *Physics* [G, a short. of *gerade* even in number] Used to designate (a) functions like wave functions that do not change sign on inversion through the origin, and (b) atomic states, etc. represented by such functions (contrasting with the odd terms, abbr. as *u*, q.v.). O [3]

G, *see* gauss

gadolinite, *n*. (1802) *Mineral*. [G *Gadolinit* (1802) < the name of Johan *Gadolin* (1760–1852), Finnish chemist + G *-it* -ite] A vitreous silicate of iron, beryllium, yttrium, erbium, and cerium; a source of rare earths. —**gadolinite**, *a*. (1883); gadolinium (1886). O, R, W [4]

gahnite, *n*. (1808) *Mineral*. [G *Gahnit* < the name of Johan G. *Gahn* (1745–1818), Swedish chemist + G *-it* -ite] An oxide of zinc and aluminum, also called *zinc-spinel*. O, R, W [4]

galactan, *n*. (1886) *Chem*. Var. **galactosan** [G (1882), ad. of *Galactin* lactogenic hormone (< Gk *gála, gálaktos* milk + G *-in* -in), to conform with G *Dextran*] Any of various polysaccharides of plant or animal origin that yield galactose by hydrolysis. O, R, W [3]

galactonic acid, *n*. (1885) *Chem*. [Transl. of G *Galactonsäure* (1885) (now *Galaktonsäure*) < *Galactose* (< Gk *gála, gálaktos* milk) + G *-onic*, after *lactonic* containing carboxyl + *Säure* acid] A crystalline acid obtained by oxidating galactose. O, W [3]

galactosamine, *n*. (1900) *Chem*. [G *Galaktosamin* (1900) < *Galaktos* (< Gk *gála, gálaktos* milk) + G *Amin* amine < *Ammoniak* ammonia + *-in* -ine] A crystalline amino derivative of galactose. O, R, W [3]

galacturonic acid, *n*. (1917) *Chem*. [Transl. of G *Galactoronsäure* (1917) < *Galactose* + uronic (< Gk *gála, gálaktos* milk + L *ūrīna* < Gk *oûron* urine) + G *Säure* acid] The uronic acid obtained from galactose. O, W [3]

galangin, *n*. (1882) *Chem*. [G (1881) < *Galanga* < ML < Ar *khalanjān* galingale + G *-in* -in] A crystalline flavone pigment found in galingale. O, W [3]

galant, *n*. (1949) and *a*. (1953) *Music* [Fr and G < OFr *galer* to rejoice] A charming and elegant style of 18th-century music as opposed to the baroque style. O, W [3]

galanterie, -n/-s *pl*. (1911) *Music* [Fr and G < Fr *galanterie* gallantry, charm] An 18th-century name for a short, nonessential movement interpolated into the classical musical suite (this is different from the "gallantry, politeness" meanings). O, W [3]

galenite, *n*. (1868) *Mineral*. [G < *Galena* (< L) lead sulfide + G *it* -ite] Galena, a native lead sulfide. O, W [3]

Galgenhumor/galgenhumor, *n*. (1912) [G < *Galgen* gallows + *Humor* humor, ult. < L moisture] Gallows humor (q.v.). O [3]

gallacetophenone, *n*. (1881) *Chem*. [G *Gallacetophenon* (1881) (now *Gallazetophenon*) < the comb. form of L *Gallus* Gaul + *acétum* vinegar + Fr *phén(ol)* < Gk *phaínein* to shine, glow + G *-on* (< Gk *-one* female descen-

dant) -one] A yellow, crystalline compound formerly used as a mordant dye and to treat skin diseases. O, W [3]

gallisin, *n*. (1884) *Chem*. Var. **gallisine** (1890) [G (1884) < *gallisieren* to gallize < the name of Ludwig *Gall* (1791–1863), German chemist + *-in* -ine] An amorphous, unfermentable mixture obtained from commercial glucose. O [3]

galli(si)ze, *v*. (1888) *Chem*. [Transl. of G *gallisieren* < the name of Ludwig *Gall* (1791–1863), German chemist + verbal suffix *-ieren* -ize] To treat unfermented grape juice with water, acid, and sugar so as to increase the quantity of wine produced. —**gallisized**, *part. a.;* **gallisizing**, *verbal n*. (1888); gallization (1891). O [3]

gallizinite, *n*. (1837) *Mineral*. [Ad. of G *Gallitzenstein* < *Gallitzen* of Galicia + *Stein* stone] Goslarite (q.v.). O [3]

gallows humo(u)r, *n*. (1901) [Transl. of G *Galgenhumor*] Grim, ironical, or "sick" humor. O, R [4]

gamma-sitosterol, *see* sitosterol

gamont, *n*. (1912) *Biol*. [G (1904) < *Gamete* < Gk *gametḗ* a wife, *gamétēs* a husband + *on* (gen. *óntos*) being] A protozoan gametocyte. O, W [3]

gang, *n*. *Geol*. Var. **gangue** (< Fr 1809) [Fr *gangue* < (G *Gang*) and G a mineral vein or vein of ore located in a crevice] The worthless rock or vein matter in a mineral deposit; the matrix in which an ore is found (the French spelling is the common one in English today). —**gangue**, *a*. (1872). O, R, W [4]

gangart, *n*. (1811) *Mineral*. [G < *Gang* vein, lode + *Art* kind, type] Gangue (q.v.). O [3]

ganglioside, *n*. (1943) *Biochem*. [G (1942) < *Ganglion* + *-oside* < Gk *ganglión* swelling + *-ose* a suffix corresponding to *-osis*, used to form the name of fungal diseases of plants + G *-ide* -ide] Any of a group of glycolipides present chiefly in the ganglion cells of the nervous system. O, R, W [3]

gangue, *see* gang

ganophyllite, *n*. (1892) *Mineral*. [G *Ganophyllit* (1890) (or Sw) < *gano-* + *phyll-* (< Gk *gános* brightness + *phýllon* leaf) + G or Sw *-it* -ite] A hydrous silicate of manganese and aluminum. O, W [3]

Ganzfeld, *n*. (1973) and *a. Psych*. Var. **ganzfeld** [G < *ganz* entire + *Feld* field] (Of or concerned with) a method of testing for extrasensory perception where outside stimuli, esp. through sight and hearing, are neutralized so as not to interfere with internally produced imagery; (of) the blank screen used in this. B [3]

Gastarbeiter, *n*. (1970) *Industry* [G guest worker (q.v.)] Guest worker. B [3]

gasthaus, -es/-häuser *pl*. (1834) *Travel* Var. **Gasthaus** [G inn < *Gast* guest, (in some contexts) host + *Haus* house] A German inn or tavern. O, R, W [3]

gasthof, *n*. (1832) *Travel* Var. **Gasthof** (1874) [G < *Gast* guest, host + *Hof* (in this context mostly) house in the country, i.e., an unpretentious country inn] A German hotel, usu. larger than a gasthaus (q.v.). O [3]

gas-vacuole, *n.* (1902) *Bot.* [G (1895) (now *Gasvakuole*) < *Gas* gas + *Vakuole* vacuole < NL *gas*, ad. < L *chaos* + *vacuus* empty] A type of gas-containing vacuole found in some bacteria and blue-green algae. O [3]

gau, -s/-e *pl.* (1845) *Politics* [G < MHG *gou, göu* land, landscape, region, now an area settled by a Germanic tribe; a Nazi party district] A region or district in ancient German tribal organization; one of 20 party districts into which the National Socialists divided Germany and Austria (by 1942 there were 43). O, W [3]

gauge, *n.* (1920) *Physics* [Transl. of G *Maßstab* (1918) yardstick, used in this sense by the German mathematician Claus Hugo Hermann Weyl (1885–1955) < *Maß* measure + *Stab* stick, rod] Weyl's concept of measuring the vector field so as to relate length and position; a function introduced as an additional term into the equation of the potentials of a field so that the derived equations of the observable physical quantities are unchanged by that introduction (this is different from the various older meanings of "measurement, capacity, instrument, etc."). — **gauge,** *a.* (1940). O [3]

gauleiter, *n.* (1936) *Politics* Var. Gauleiter (1936) [G < *Gau* gau (q.v.) district + *Leiter* leader] A Nazi district leader; a local or petty tyrant. O, R, W [4]

gauss, -ø/-es *pl.* (1882) *Physics* Var. Gauss (1882) [G < the name of Karl Friedrich *Gauss* (1777–1855), German mathematician, astronomer, and physicist, (unofficial) unit of magnetic induction] Oersted, the cgs unit of electromagnetic induction. • ~ appears in composites like **Gaussian,** *a.* (1874); **Gaussian distribution** (1905); **gauss meter;** and in the abbr. **G.** O, R, W [4]

Ge, *see* germanium

Gebrauchsmusik, *n.* (1930) *Music* Var. gebrauchsmusik [G < gen. of *Gebrauch* use, i.e., practical use + *Musik* music < OFr *musique* < L *musica* < Gk *mousiké*] Music composed primarily for practical use and performance outside the concert field. O, R, W [2]

gedackt/gedeckt, *n.* (1855) *Music* Var. gedact (1855) [G < past part. of *decken* to cover] A labial pipe-organ stop of flute quality with its pipes closed at the top. O, W [3]

gedacktwork/gedecktwork, *n.* (1904) *Music* [Ad. of G *Gedacktwerk* < *gedackt* covered + *Werk* work] The flue stops in a gedackt (q.v.). O, W [3]

gedanite, *n.* (1887) *Mineral.* [G *Gedanit* (1878) < the ML name *Gedanum,* G *Danzig* a city now in Poland and spelled *Gdansk* + G *-it* -ite] A fossil resin resembling amber. O, W [3]

Gedankenexperiment, *n.* (1958) *Philos.* Var. **Gedanken experiment** [G < *Gedanken* thoughts + *Experiment* experiment < MFr < L *experīmentum*] An experiment carried out by proposing a hypothesis in thought and thus is made only in imagination. • ~ is transl. as **thought experiment** (q.v.). O, R, W [3]

gedeckt, *see* gedackt

gedeckt pommer, *n. Music* [G *Gedacktpommer* < *gedackt* (q.v.) + *Pommer* a wind instrument resembling a shawm] A gedackt pipe-organ mixture stop. W [3]

geest, *n.* (c.1828 *W9*) *Geol.* [G dry or sandy soil < LG] Old alluvial matter on the surface of the land; loose material formed by rock decay. O, W [4]

gegenion, *n. Physics* [G < *gegen* counter, opposite + *Ion* (< Gk) ion] Counterion, an ion with an opposite charge. R, W [3]

gegenschein/Gegenschein, *n.* (1880) *Astronomy* [G (1854) < *gegen* counter, reflective + *Schein* glow] A patch of faint elliptical nebulous light occurring in the ecliptic and opposite the sun. • ~ is transl. as **counterglow** (1888). O, R, W [4]

Gegenstandstheorie, *n. Psych.* [G < gen. of *Gegenstand* object + *Theorie* theory < LL *theoria* < Gk] A theory of objects, especially intentional ones. W [3]

Geheimrat, *n.* (1837) *Politics* Var. **Geheimer Rat** (1911) [G < *geheim* secret, confidential + *Rat* counsel, councillor] (Esp. in Germany) a privy councillor. O, W [3]

gehlenite, *n.* (1817) *Mineral.* [G *Gehlenit* (1815) < the name of Adolf Ferdinand *Gehlen* (1775–1815), German chemist + *-it* -ite] A silicate of aluminum and calcium. O, R, W [3]

geige, -n *pl. Music* [G < MHG *gīge*, Late OHG *gīga* violin] A fiddle or violin. W [2]

geigen principal, *n. Music* [G *Geigenprinzipal* < *Geige* violin + *Prinzipal* open diapason] A violin diapason. W [3]

Geiger counter, *n.* (1924) *Physics* Var. **Geiger-Müller counter** (1930), geiger [Transl. of G *Geigerzähler* < older *Geigerrohr* Geiger tube < the name of Hans *Geiger* (1882–1945), German physicist who helped develop it in 1913 + *Zähler* counter] Geiger-Müller tube; an instrument consisting of a Geiger-Müller tube and accessory electronic equipment used to record the momentary current pulsations in the tube gas; fig. sense as in political or literary measures. O, R, W [4]

Geist/geist, *n.* (1871) [G spirit, intelligence] Ghost; intelligence (see *poltergeist*). O, R [2]

Geisteswissenschaft, -en *pl.* (1909) *Philos.* [G < the gen. of *Geist* geist (q.v.) + *Wissenschaft* science, generally used in the pl. to mean all the arts and sciences; (since the middle of the 19th century, in philosophy) the humanities] The arts and/or the humanities, in contrast to the sciences. O [2]

geisteswissenschaftler, -ø *pl.* (1938) *Philos.* [G < *Geisteswissenschaft* (q.v.) + *-ler* -ler] One who studies the humanities or arts. O [2]

geistlich, *adv.* or *a. Music* [G uplifting < *Geist* spirit + adj. suffix *-lich* like] Soulful, with deep feeling (used as a direction in music). W [3]

gelände jump, *see* geländesprung

geländeläufer, *n.* (1933 *W9*) *Sports* [G < *Gelände* terrain, countryside + *Läufer* runner] A skier who is making a cross-country run: langläufer (q.v.). R, W [3]

geländesprung, *n.* (1931 *W9*) *Sports* Var. **gelände jump** [G < *Gelände* countryside, (in some contexts) slope + *Sprung* jump] A jump made from a low crouching position by using both ski poles, usu. over an obstacle. R, W [4]

Gelehrte(r), -n *pl.* (1836) *Ed.* Var. **gelehrte(r)** (1836) [G a learned person < *gelehrt* < *lehren* to instruct] A learned person; a scholar. O [2]

gelt, *n.* (1529) *Currency* [Du *geld* (< MD *ghelt*) and G *Geld* < MHG (and in many parts of Germany as late as the 17th cent.) *gelt* or *geld* payment, money] Payment, orig. in the basic sense of money such as the pay of a German army; (reborrowed later, perhaps indirectly, as slang to mean) profit or money. —**passage gelt** (1745). O, R, W [4]

gemeinde, -n *pl. Politics* [G community < MHG *gemeinde,* OHG *gimeinida* an organized community, smallest unit of government] A unit of German local government: municipality. W [2]

gemeinschaft/Gemeinschaft, -en *pl.* (1887) *Sociol.* [G, ult. < OHG *gimeinscaf* commune, association] A spontaneous social relationship between individuals based on kinship, membership in a community, or affection, in contrast with Gesellschaft (q.v.); such a community or society. O, R, W [3]

gemeinschaft-like, *a.* (1964) *Sociol.* [Ad. of G *gemeinschaftlich* < *Gemeinschaft* (q.v.) + *-lich* -like] Pertaining to a particular social relationship between individuals. O [2]

gems, -es *pl. Zool.* Var. **gemse** [G *Gemse* chamois] Chamois. R, W [3]

gemsbok, -ø/-s *pl.* (1777) *Zoology* Var. **gemsbock** (1777), **gemsbuck** (1883) [Afrikaans < G (and poss. directly also < G into E) *Gemsebock* < *Gemse* chamois + *Bock* buck] (The orig. South African name for) a large, strikingly marked oryx; one of several related oryxes. O, R, W [4]

gemshorn, *n.* (1825) *Music* [G a pipe-organ flute stop < *Gemse* chamois + *Horn* horn] A labial pipe-organ stop intermediate between a string tone and a reed tone in quality. O, W [3]

gemütlich, *a.* (1852) Var. **gemuetlich** [G pleasant, dear < *Gemüt* soul, heart + *-lich* like] Cheerful, agreeably pleasant, congenial, comfortable. O, R [3]

Gemütlichkeit/gemütlichkeit, *n.* (1892) Var. **Gemuetlichkeit** [G coziness, cheerfulness, comfort < *gemütlich* (q.v.) + nom. suffix *-keit* -ness] Kindliness, friendliness, cordiality, coziness, pleasant state or condition. O, R [3]

gene, *n.* (1911) *Biol.* [G *Gen* (1909), a short. of *Pangen* < *pan-* + *-gen* < Gk *pân* all, entire + *gen-,* ult. representing *gígnesthai* to be born, become, *génos* kind] Any of the elements of the germ plasm that specifically transmit hereditary characters. —**gene,** *a.* (1928). • ~ appears in numerous compounds like **gene bank/frequency/mutation** (1964, 1930, 1928). O, R, W [4]

genial, *a.* (1825) *Psych.* [Fr *genial* or G *genialisch* having a creative intellect < *genial* (< LL *genius* genius) + G *-isch* -ic] Characterized by genius (this is different from older meanings of "favorable, relating to the chin"). O, R, W [3]

genom(e), *n.* (1930) *Biol.* [G *Genom* (1920), a blend of *Gen* (< Gk *génos* gender, type) + G *Chromosom* chromosome] A haploid set of chromosomes and/or the total genes they contain. —**genomic.** O, R, W [4]

genotype, *n.* (1897 *W9*) *Biol.* [G *Genotypus* (now *Genotyp*) < *geno-* + *Typus* < Gk *génos* gender, type + *týpos* model, example, pattern] The genetic constitution of an individual or group; the group of individuals that share a given trait or traits; the type species of a genus. —**genotypically** (1911), **-typic(al)** (1930, 1911), **-type,** *v.* (1961); **-typicity.** O, R, W [4]

gentianose, *n.* (1888) *Chem.* [G (1882) < NL *Gentiana*

gentian + G *-ose* -ose, denoting a carbohydrate] A nonreducing trisaccharide found in fresh gentian root. O, W [3]

geocerite, *n. Mineral.* Var. **geocerain** [Ad. of G *Geocerain* (now *Geozerain*) < *geo-* (< MFr and L) + L *cēra* wax + G *-in* -in] A mineral found in brown coal and consisting of carbon, hydrogen, and oxygen. W [3]

geochemistry, *n.* (1903) *Chem.* [Transl. of G *Geochemie* (1838) < *geo-* + *Chemie* < MFr and L *ge(o)-* + ult. Ar *al-kīmiyā'*] Earth chemistry; the related geological and chemical properties of a substance. —**geochemist** (1918), **geochemical(ly)** (1957). O, R, W [4]

geoid, *n.* (1881) *Physics* [G (1872) < Gk *geoeidḗs* earthlike] An equipotential surface within or around the earth; the true figure of the earth's surface. —**geoidal,** *a.* (1881). O, R, W [4]

geomedicine, *n. Med.* [Ad. of G *Geomedizin* < *geo-* + *Medizin* < Gk *gêo-,* the comb. form of *gê* earth + L (*ars*) *medicina* (the art of) healing] A branch of medicine concerned with geographic factors in disease. —**geomedical.** R, W [3]

geophyte, *n.* (1900) *Bot.* [G *Geophyt* (1896) < *geo-* + *-phyt* < Gk *gêo-,* the combining form of *gê* earth + *phytón* growth] A perennial plant that produces its overwintering buds below the surface of the ground. —**geophytic** (1956). O, R, W [3]

geopolitical, *a.* (1902) *Politics* [Ad. of G *geopolitisch* < *Geopolitik* geopolitics (q.v.) + adj. suffix *-isch* -al] Of, pertaining to, or based on geopolitics. —**geopolitically** (1938). O, R, W [4]

geopolitician, *n.* (1941 *W9*) *Politics* Var. **geopolitiker** [Ad. of G *Geopolitiker* < *Geopolitik* geopolitics (q.v.) + *-er* -er] A specialist in geopolitics. O, R, W [4]

geopolitics, *n.* (1904) *Politics* Var. **Geopolitik** [Sw *geopolitisk* (1899) and G *Geopolitik* (1931) < *geo-* + *Politik* < Gk *gêo-,* the comb. form of *gê* earth + Fr *politique* < Gk *politikḗ* (*téchnē*) (the art of) administering] The dependence of a people's domestic and foreign politics upon the physical environment; the study of this; a Nazi expansionist doctrine somewhat based on this view (see Karl Haushofer, *Geopolitik der Panideen,* 1931); the combination of geographic and political factors characterizing a country or a geographic region. O, R, W [4]

geoscience, *n.* (1942 *W9*) *Geol.* [Transl. of G *Geowissenschaft* < *geo-* (< Gk *gêo-,* the comb. form of *gê* earth) + G *Wissenschaft* science] The science concerned with the physical environment; any of the geosciences. R, W [4]

geotropism, *n.* (1875) *Bot.* [G *Geotropismus* (1868) < *geo-* + *Tropismus* < Gk *gêo-,* the comb. form of *gê* earth + *tropḗ, trópos* change in direction, orientation + L *-ismus* < Gk *-ismos*] A tropism in which gravitational attraction is the orienting quality; a tropism in which certain plants and animals turn or move toward (rather than away from) the earth. —**geotropy** (1889). • ~ appears in compounds like **positive/negative geotropism.** O, R, W [4]

geranial, *n.* (1899) *Chem.* [G (1891), a short. of *Geraniumaldehyd* < *Geranium* (< L *geranium* a genus of herbacious plants < Gk *geránion* < *géranos* crane) + G *Aldehyd* aldchyde < NL abbr. *al. dehyd.*] The trans form of citral, a fragrant oil present in many essential oils and used in flavoring and perfumery as citral. O, R, W [3]

geraniol, *n.* (1871) *Chem.* [G (1871) < *Geranium* (see *geranial*) + G *Öl* < L *oleum* oil] A fragrant liquid alcohol that is present in many essential oils and used in soap and rose and other perfumes. O, R, W [4]

Germanist, *n.* (1831) *Ling., Lit.* [G (1828) < *German-* (< L *Germānia* European land occupied by the Germanic peoples in Roman times) + G *-ist* -ist] One learned in the German language, Germanics, and/or German literature and culture; a historian who overstresses the Germanic influence on European civilization or is influenced by German thought. —**Germanistic** (1881). O, R, W [4]

Germanistics, *n. Ling., Lit.* [G *Germanistik* < *Germanist* Germanist (q.v.) + *-ik* -ics] Germanics, the study of Germanic languages and literatures. W [3]

germanite, *n. Mineral.* [G *Germanit* < *German-* (see *Germanist*) + *-it* -ite] A copper iron germanium sulfide. W [3]

germanium, *n.* (1886) *Chem.* [G (1886) < *German-* (see *Germanist*) + *-ium* (< NL), so named by the German chemist Clemens Winkler (1838–1904), its discoverer, in honor of his country] An element placed between antimony and bismuth on the periodic table and used as a semiconductor. • ~ is symbolized as **Ge.** O, R, W [4]

germ center, *n.* (1898) *Anat.* Var. **germ(-)centre** (1898) [Transl. of G *Keimcentrum* (1884) (now *Keimzentrum*) < *Keim* germ + *Centrum* center < L *centrum* < Gk *kéntron*] A group of lightly staining cells forming the central area of a lymphoid follicle. O, W [3]

germ plasm, *n.* (1889) *Biol.* [Transl. of G *Keimplasma* (1883) < *Keim* germ + *Plasma* plasma (q.v.)] The part of the germ cells and their predecessors that, according to August Weismann's theory of heredity, bear the hereditary characters; the hereditary material in these: genes (q.v.). O, R, W [4]

gersdorffite, *n.* (1849) *Mineral.* [G *Gersdorffit* (1842) < the name of von *Gersdorff,* an Austrian family who owned the nickel mine at Schladming, Styria, Austria, c.1842 + G *-it* -ite] A sulfarsenide of nickel. O, R, W [3]

Gesamtkunstwerk, *n.* (1939) *Music* [G < *gesamt* total, encompassing + *Kunstwerk* work of art] An art work produced by an ideal synthesis of art forms such as music and drama, as theorized by Richard Wagner. O [3]

Gesellschaft/gesellschaft, -s/-en *pl.* (1887) *Sociol.* [G society < *Gesell* companion + *-schaft* -ship] A rationally developed, mechanistic relationship between individuals based on duty to society or to an organization; a society that is so characterized. O, R, W [4]

Gesellschaft-like, *a.* (1964) *Sociol.* [Ad. of G *gesellschaftlich* < *Gesellschaft* (q.v.) + *-lich* -like] Pertaining to or resembling the Gesellschaft. O [3]

gestalt/Gestalt, -s/-en *pl.* (1890) *Psych.* [G (1890) shape, form < MHG appearance, makeup, manner] An integrated structure or configuration of biological, physical, or psychological phenomena; the pattern of this. —**gestalt,** *a.* (1922). • ~ is transl. as **configuration** (q.v.). O, R, W [4]

gestaltism, *n.* (1938) *Psych.* [G *Gestaltismus* < *Gestalt* configuration + *-ismus* (< L) -ism] Gestalt psychology (q.v.). O [3]

gestaltist, *n.* (1931) *Psych.* [G < *Gestalt* configuration + *-ist* -ist] A gestalt psychologist. O, W [3]

gestalt psychologist, *n.* (1922) *Psych.* [Ad. of G *Gestaltpsychologe* < *Gestalt* configuration + *Psychologe* psychologist] One versed in, devoted to, and/or a practitioner of gestalt psychology (q.v.). O, W [3]

Gestalt psychology, *n.* (1924) *Psych.* Var. **gestalt psychology** [G *Gestaltpsychologie* < *Gestalt* configuration + *Psychologie* < NL *psychologia* < Gk *psychē* breath, soul + *lógos* word, study + G *-ie* (< Gk *-ia*) -y] A system of psychology that conceives of psychological, biological, and physiological elements as units in interrelated, configurational wholes; also called *configurationism.* O, R, W [4]

Gestaltqualität, -en *pl.* (1909) *Psych.* [G < *Gestalt* configuration + *Qualität* quality < Fr *qualité* < L *qualitat-, quālitās*] The quality of a gestalt (q.v.). O [2]

gestalt theory, *n.* (1925) *Psych.* Var. **Gestalt theory** (1925) [G *Gestalttheorie* < *Gestalt* configuration + *Theorie* theory < L < Gk *theoría*] The theory underpinning Gestalt psychology (q.v.). O [3]

Gestapo, *n.* (1934) *Politics* [G (1933), an acronym of *Geheime Staatspolizei* < *geheim* secret + *Staat* state + *Polizei* police < MFr *police, ult.* < Gk *politeía*] The feared German secret police of the Nazi regime; transf. sense to any such secret police. —**Gestapo,** *a.* (1937). O, R, W [4]

gesundheit/Gesundheit, *interj.* (1914) [G, lit., health < a short. of the wish *Gesundheit und ein langes Leben* to your health and long life, or said when someone sneezes, actually, *zur Gesundheit* may it contribute to your health, i.e., God bless you] (An expression used to wish someone) good health; bless you (said esp. to one who has just sneezed). O, R, W [4]

gewürztraminer, *n.* (?1970) *Beverages* [G < *Gewürz* spice + *Traminer* < the G name of *Tramin* Termeno, a town in the Italian Tirol + *-er* -er] A dry, Alsatian white wine with a spicy bouquet; a similar wine made elsewhere. 12 [3]

giant slalom, *n.* (1952 *W9*) *Sports* [Partial transl. of G *Riesenslalom* < *Riese* giant + *Slalom* < Norw *slalåm* actually, a slightly descending ski track or spur] A zigzag downhill race in skiing that is longer and steeper than a regular slalom. R, W [3]

gibel, *n.* (1841) *Ichthy.* [G (now *Giebel*) a fish related to a crucian carp] Crucian carp. —**gibel carp.** O, W [3]

Giemsa stain, *n.* (c.1909 *W9*) *Med.* Var. **Giemsa's stain, Giemsa** [Transl. of G *Giemsa-Färbung* < the name of Gustav *Giemsa* (1867–1948), German chemotherapist + *Färbung* staining] A stain composed of a mixture of methylene azure and eosin, used chiefly in differential staining of blood films. W [3]

giro, *n.* (1890 *W9*) *Econ.* Var. **Giro** (1907) [G < It *giro* the transfer of funds, etc.] A system that transfers credits between banks, post offices, etc., esp. as in the system operated by the British Post Office to bank and transfer money (this is different from the old Italian-derived "tour" meaning). —**giro,** *a.* (1896); **giro cheque/order** (1972, 1976); **girocracy** (1989). O [4]

gismondite/gismondine, *n.* (1823) *Mineral.* [G *Gismondin* (1817) < the name of Carlo Giuseppe *Gismondi* (1762–

1824), Italian mineralogist + G *-in* -ine] A hydrous calcium aluminum silicate. O, W [3]

gitoxin, *n. Biochem.* [G < *Digitoxin,* a blend of *Digitalis digitalis* (q.v.) + *Toxin* < Gk *toxikón* (*phármikon*) poison for arrows < *tóxon* bow + G *-in* -in] A poisonous, crystalline steroid glycoside obtainable from digitalis. W [3]

gitter, *n.* (1876) *Optics* [G < OHG *getiri* lattice, grating] A diffraction grating. —**gitter cell.** O [3]

glance, *n.* (1457–8) *Mineral.* [G *Glanz* a metal ore with a gleam, luster] Any of various mineral sulfides with a metallic luster. O, R, W [4]

glance coal, *n.* (1805) *Mining* [By folk etymology and transl. of G *Glanzkohle* < *Glanz* gleam, luster + *Kohle* coal] A hard, lustrous coal, esp. anthracite. O, W [3]

glance-ore, *n.* (1457) *Mining* (archaic) [Ad. and transl. of Du *glans ertz* or G *Glanzerz* < *Glanz* gleam + *Erz* ore] Potter's ore. O [3]

Glauber's salt, *n.* (1736) *Med.* Var. **Glauber salt** (1761) [Transl. of G *Glaubersalz,* first artificially made in 1656 < the name of Johann Rudolf *Glauber* (1604–68), German chemist + *Salz* salt] The crystalline decahydrate of sodium sulfate, used in dyeing and as a laxative: mirabilite. O, R, W [4]

glaucocerinite, *n. Mineral.* Var. **glaucokerinite** [G *Glaucokerinit* (now *Glaukokerinit*) < *glauco-* < Gk *glaukós* greenish blue + *kérinos* wax-like + G *-it* -ite] A hydrous sulfate of copper, zinc, and aluminum. W [3]

glaucodot, *n.* (1850) *Mineral.* Var. **glaucodote** (1861) [G *Glaukodot* (1849) < *glauko-* + *-dot* < Gk *glaukós* greenish blue + *dotér* giver, donor] A sulfarsenide of cobalt and iron. O, W [3]

glaucokerinite, *see* glaucocerinite

glauconite, *n.* (1836) *Mineral.* [G *Glaukonit* (1828) < Gk *glaucón* (neuter of *glaukós* greenish blue) + G *-it* -ite] A green, micaceous iron potassium silicate used for water softening: green earth. —**glauconitic** (1864), **glauconitization.** O, R, W [4]

glaucophane, *n.* (1849) *Mineral.* Var. **glaucophanite** [G *Glaukophan* (1845) < *glauko-* + *-phan* < Gk *glaukós* greenish blue + *phanés* gleaming] A silicate of aluminum, iron, and magnesium. O, R, W [3]

Gleichschaltung, -en *pl.* (1933) *Politics* Var. **gleichschaltung** (1950) [G coordination < *gleich* equal + *Schaltung* switch < *schalten* to switch] An authoritarian state's act, method, or policy of maintaining rigid, total coordination and uniformity, leading to forced standardization, as even in art. O, W [3]

Gleitzeit, *n.* (1971) *Industry* [G, a short. of *gleitende Arbeitszeit* < *Gleit-* < *gleiten* to glide, slide + *Zeit* time] Flextime (q.v.), as when company doors are open from 7 a.m. to 7 p.m., and workers can arrive when they like, provided that they are present for "core time" from 10 a.m. to 3 p.m. • ~ is transl. as **sliding time** (1972), **gliding shift/time** (1972, 1972), and **flextime.** B [3]

glessite, *n. Mineral.* [G *Glessit* < L *glessum* amber < Gmc + G *-it* -ite] A fossil, amber-like resin. W [3]

gletscher, *n.* (1762) *Geol.* Var. **Gletcher** (1932) [G (16th cent.) < *Valois glacer* ice, glacier, ult. < L *glacia* ice] A glacier. O [3]

gliding shift/time, *see* flextime, Gleitzeit

glimmer, *n.* (1683) *Mineral.* [G mica < *glimmern* to glow] Mica (this is different from the older "feeble light" meaning). O, R, W [3]

gliomatosis, -ses *pl.* (1886) *Path.* [G *Gliomatose* (1882) < *gliomat-* + *-ose* < NL *glioma,* pl. *gliomata* swelling, growth + Gk *-osis* fem. suffix of action] A diffuse overgrowth of glia cells associated with or arising from a gliomatous tumor; gliosis (q.v.). O, W [3]

gliosis, -oses *pl.* (1890) *Path.* [G *Gliose* (1882) < *gli-* + *-ose* < Gk *glía* glue + *-osis* fem. suffix of action] A proliferation of glia cells. —**gliotic.** O, W [3]

glitch, -es *pl.* (1962) *Tech.* (slang) Var. **glitsch** [Prob. backformation < G *glitschen* to slide, slip] An undesired, brief surge of electric power; a false electrical signal; malfunction or snag, as in a computer or spacecraft; a sudden change in a neutron star's period of rotation. —**glitch,** *v.* O, R [4]

globosite, *n.* (1868) *Mineral.* [G *Globosit* (1865) < *globos-* (< L *globōsus* ball-shaped, spherical) + G *-it* -ite] A fluophosphate of iron found in globular concretions that may be identical with strengite (q.v.). O [3]

globularin, *n.* (1864) *Chem.* [G < *globular* (< NL *globularia* globe daisy) + G *-in* -in] A glucoside found in the leaves of *Globularia Alypum.* 0-1933 [2]

glockenspiel, *n.* (1825) *Music* [G < *Glocke* bell + *Spiel* play] A carillon; the modern celesta; a percussion instrument consisting of a series of scaled metal bars; a pipe-organ percussion stop that tonally imitates a glockenspiel. O, R, W [4]

glucase, *n.* (1894) *Biochem.* [G (1892) (now *Glukase*) < *gluc-* (< Gk *glykýs* sweet) + G *-ase* -ase suffix denoting "enzyme"] Maltase, an enzyme. O [3]

glucke, *n.* Var. **gluck** [G interj. *gluck,* lit., clucking hen < *glucken* to cluck] A roller-canary tour imitative of a hen's clucking. W [3]

glucoheptose, *n.* (1890) *Chem.* [G (1890) < *gluco-* + *Heptose* < Gk *glykýs* sweet + *heptá* seven + G *-ose* -ose suffix denoting "carbohydrate"] Any heptose obtained from glucose. O [3]

glucosone, *n.* (1889) *Chem.* [G *Glucoson* (1889) < *gluco-* (< Gk *glykýs* sweet) + G *-ose* -ose suffix denoting "carbohydrate" + *-on* < Gk *ón* (gen. *óntos*) being] The osone derived from glucose. O, W [3]

glucovanillin, *n.* (1884) *Chem.* [G (1883) < *gluco* + *Vanillin* < Gk *glykýs* sweet + NL *vanilla* a pod of the genus *Vanilla* + G *-in* -in] A glucoside of vanillin, which provides commercial vanilla extract. O [3]

glucuronic/glycuronic acid, *n.* (1882) *Chem.* [Transl. of G *Glykuronsäure* < *glyk-* + *Uron* < Gk *glykýs* sweet + *oûron* urine + G *Säure* acid] An acid obtained by oxidating glucose. O, R [3]

gluhwein/glühwein, *n.* (1898) *Beverages* [G < *glühen* to make red hot, mull (of wine) + *Wein* wine] Mulled wine. O, W [3]

glutamic acid, *n.* (1871) *Biochem.* [Transl. of G *Glutaminsäure* (1866) < *glut-* (< L *gluten* glue) + G *Amin* amine + *Säure* acid] A crystalline amino dicarboxylic acid. O, R, W [3]

glutton, *n.* (1674) *Zool.* [Loose transl. of G *Vielfrass* < *viel* much + *Frass* immoderate appetite < *fressen* to devour, to eat like a glutton, transl. as the old E *glutton* excessive eater] A voracious European wolverine. O, R, W [4]

glycerose, *n.* (1888) *Chem.* [G (1888) (now also *Glyzerose*) < *Glycerine* (< Gk *glykerós* sweet) + G *-ose* -ose] A mixture of glyceraldehyde and dihydroxyacetone; glyceraldehyde, esp. in relation to other sugars. O, W [3]

glycine, *n.* (1851) *Biochem.* [G *Glycin* (1848) < *glyc-* (< Gk *glykýs* sweet) + G *-in* -ine] A sweet, crystalline amino acid; also called *aminoacetic acid.* O, R, W [4]

glycosamine, *n.* (1877) *Chem.* [G *Glycosamin* (1876) (now *Glykosamin*) < *Glycose* (< Gk *glykýs* sweet) + G *Amin* amine] Glucosamine; any amino sugar in which amino groups replace the alcoholic hydroxyl groups. 0 [3]

glycuronic acid, *see* glucuronic acid

glycyl, *n.* (1901) *Chem.* [G (1901) < *Glycin* glycine (q.v.) + *-yl* -yl] A univalent radical derived from glycine. O [3]

gnathostome, *n.* (1889) *Biol.* [Haeckel's G (1874) < *gnatho-* + *Stoma* < Gk *gnáthos* bent + *stóma* jaws, throat] A member of the Gnathostomata, a superclass of vertebrates with fully developed lower and upper jaws. —**gnathostome,** *a.* (1936); **gnathostom(at)ous** (1908). O [3]

gneiss, -es *pl.* (1757) *Geol.* [G *Gneis* a metaphoric rock roughly consisting of quartz, feldspar, and glimmer] A laminated or foliated metaphoric rock like granite in composition. —**gneiss,** *a.* (1845). • ~ appears in adj. derivatives like **gneissic** and **gneissy** (1757, 1757), **gneissose** (1843), **gneissoid** (1849). O, R, W [4]

Gödel's theorem, *n.* (1933) *Math.* Var. **Gödel's incompleteness theorem** [Transl. of G *Gödel-Satz* (1931) metamathematical theorem of incompleteness < the name of Kurt *Gödel* (1906–78), Austro-American physicist + G *Satz* theorem] A theorem that advanced logic and mathematics contain factual statements that are neither provable nor disprovable, thus making mathematics essentially incomplete. —**Godelian,** *a.* (1942). O [3]

God's acre, *n.* (1617) *Theol.* [Transl. of G *Gottesacker* < gen. of *Gott* god + *Acker* acre, i.e., burying ground out in the fields as opposed to the churchyard] A churchyard or cemetery, esp. one adjacent to a church. O, R, W [4]

goethite/göthite, *n.* (1823) *Mineral.* [G *Göthit* (1806), to honor the name of Johann Wolfgang von *Goethe* (1749–1832), German poet and dramatist + *-it* -ite] A hydrous iron oxide of natural rust. O, R, W [4]

Goldbach(')s conjecture, *n.* (1919) *Math.* Var. **Goldbach's theorem/hypothesis** (1919, 1960) [Transl. of G *Goldbachs Vermutung* (1742) < the name of Christian *Goldbach* (1690–1764), German mathematician + *Vermutung* conjecture] Goldbach's unproved hypothesis for the very simple problem that every even number greater than 2 can be represented as the sum of two prime numbers. O, R [3]

goldwasser/Goldwasser, *n.* (1848) *Beverages* Var. **goldwater** (1877) [Short. of G *Danziger Goldwasser* (q.v.)] Danziger Goldwasser. O, R, W [3]

Gondwanaland, *n.* (1896) *Geol.* Var. **Gondwana land** (1896) [G (1885) < the name *Gondwana,* a region of central India inhabited by the Dravidian *Gond* people + G *Land* land] A vast continental area thought to have once existed in the southern hemisphere and then separated to form South America, Antarctica, Australia, the Indian peninsula, and Africa; these land masses collectively as they exist today (this is different from the older "Indian rocks" meaning). O, R [4]

gonochorism, *n.* (1876) *Biol.* [Haeckel's G *Gonochorismus* (1866) < *gono-* + *Chorismus* < Gk *goné* origin, gender + *chōrízein* separate + G (< L) *-ismus* -ism] Dioecism; the development or evolution of sex. —**gonochoric** (1950); **gonochorismal,** *a.* O, W [3]

gonochorist, *n.* (1904) *Biol.* [Haeckel's G (1866) < *Gonochorismus* gonochorism (q.v.) + *-ist* -ist] A dioecious individual or race, esp. one in which sex is determined developmentally rather than hereditarily. —**gonochoristic** (1904). O, W [3]

gonomere, *n.* (1903) *Biol.* [G *Gonomer* (1902) < *gono-* + *-mer* < Gk *goné* origin, gender + *méros* part] A pronucleus that, after plasmogeny, retains its identity for a time and does not fuse with another nucleus in the same cell. —**gonomery,** *n.* (1920); **gonomeric** (1925). O, W [3]

gonotokont/gonotocont, *n.* (1905) *Biol.* [G *Gonotokont* (1904) < *gono-* (< Gk *goné* origin, gender) + *tokōnt-* < *tokōn,* present part. of *tokân* to be near delivery] Gonocyte; an organ or cell in which meiosis occurs. O, W [3]

gonotome, *n.* (1900) *Biol.* [G *Gonotom* (1889) < *gono-* + *-tom* < Gk *goné* origin, gender + *tomé* cutting, dividing] A block of tissue in a somite that participates in gonad formation; any somite that contains a gonad. O, W [3]

Good(-)King(-)Henry, *n.* (1578) *Bot.* [Prob. transl. of G *guter Heinrich* (lit., good Henry < the name of the English King Henry VII, 1457–1509) goosefoot (*Chenopodium*)] Goosefoot, naturalized in North America. O, R, W [4]

goosegirl, *n.* (1826) [Transl. of G *Gänsemädchen* < *Gänse* geese, pl. of *Gans* + *Mädchen* girl] A girl who tends geese; a girl gooseherd. O, W [3]

goose-step, *n.* (1806) *Mil.* [Erron. transl. of G *Gänsemarsch* lit., geese march, in G actually, *Stechschritt* or *Paradeschritt* a stiff-legged military step with limbs raised and thrust forward] A straight-legged, stiff-kneed step used by foot soldiers of some armies when passing in review; an elementary military drill. —**goose-step,** *v.* (1879 *W9*); **goose-stepper** (1923); **goose-stepping,** *n.* and *a.* (1879, 1935). O, R, W [4]

gorbasm, *n.* (1989) *Politics* [G blend (1989), as used in *Der Spiegel* < the name of the Russian political leader Mikhail *Gorbachev* (1931–) + *Orgasm* < NL *orgasmus* < Gk *orgasmós*] Extreme public enthusiasm for him, as in his German visits. L2 [4]

gorceixite, *n. Mineral.* [G *Gorceixit* < the name of Henrique *Gorceix* (1842–1919), Brazilian mineralogist + G *-it* -ite] A hydrous basic phosphate of barium and aluminum. W [3]

goslarite, *n.* (1849) *Mineral.* [G *Goslarit* (1845) < *Goslar,* the name of a German town in the Harz Mountains + *-it* -ite] A native white zinc sulfate: zinc vitriol. O, W [3]

gossypol, *n.* (1899) *Chem.* [G (1899) < *gossyp-* + *-ol* -ol < NL *Gossypium* cotton plant + L *oleum* oil] A toxic, phenolic pigment in cottonseed. O, W [3]

göthite, *see* goethite

Götterdämmerung, -en *pl.* (1909) *Myth.* [G (1876) < *Götter,* pl. of *Gott* god + *Dämmerung* twilight, as popularized by Richard Wagner's operatic title] Twilight of the gods (q.v.); fig. sense as in a complete catastrophic end of a political or social order. O, R, W [4]

Gott mit uns, *Theol.* [G < *Gott* God + *mit* with + *uns* us] God is with us; God be with us. R [3]

gougelhof, *see* gugelhupf

graben, -s/-ø *pl.* (1896) *Geol.* [G (1883) ditch, trench] A depressed segment of the earth's surface bounded by faults; a rift valley. O, R, W [4]

grade, *n.* (1872) *Ling.* [G *Grad* grade, step (< Fr *grade* < L *gradus*) or transl. of G *Stufe*] Any phase of a root or an affix that appears in an ablaut series; the characteristic vowel of this phase. O, W [3]

Graf, -en *pl.* (1630) *Politics* [G a count < MHG *grāve*, OHG *grāvo*, *grāfio* < ML *graphio* royal administrative official] A noble's title in Germany, Austria, and Sweden, equivalent to an English earl. O, R [3]

gräfin, -nen *pl. Politics* [G the wife of a count < *Graf* (q.v.) + nom. fem. suffix *-in*] Countess. AH [2]

gramenite, *n.* (1858) *Mineral.* [G *Gramenit* (1857) < L *grāmen* grass + G *-it* -ite] A grass-green variety of chloropal (q.v.). O [3]

grammatical change, *n.* (1926) *Ling.* [Transl. of G *grammatischer Wechsel*, a phonological formulation by Karl A. Verner (1846–96), Danish linguist, to explain the exceptions to Grimm's law, according to which the voiceless spirants from Indo-European changed to voiced spirants in Germanic when no preceding syllable bore the principal stress] This system of shifted consonants in the Germanic strong verb according to Verner's law; Verner's law. O, W [3]

grand, *n.* (1893) *Games* [G (c.1850), a short. of Fr *grand jeu* grand play, It *grando* grand (in grand the only trumps are the four knaves)] A round in skat in which only the four knaves (jacks) are trumps. O, W [3]

grano-, comb. form *Geol.* [G, a short. of *Granit* granite < It *granito* < L *grānum*] Denoting granite or a granitic substance (*granolith*); granitic (*granogabbro*). R, W [4]

granoblastic, *a. Geol.* [G *granoblastisch* < *grano-* (q.v.) + *blastisch* < Gk *blastós* bud + G *-isch* -ic] Of a rock that has a texture in which the fragments are irregular and angular and present a mosaic under the microscope. W [3]

granophyre, *n.* (1882) *Geol.* [G *Granophyr* (1872) < *grano-* (q.v.) + (*Por*)*phyr* porphyry < Gk *pórphyros* crimson] A porphyritic igneous rock constituted chiefly of quartz and alkalic feldspar; a similar rock with micropegmatite intergrowths. —**granophyric** (1897). O, R, W [4]

granum, grana *pl.* (1894) *Bot.* [G (1883) < L grain] Any of the discs arranged in stacks in the chloroplast (this is different from the older, Latin-derived meanings). O [3]

graphite, *n.* (1796) *Mineral.* [G *Graphit* (1789) < *Graph* (< Gk *gráphein* to write) + G *-it* -ite] The carbon mineral graphite; a dark grayish blue to dark bluish gray color. —**graphite,** *a.* (1945) and *v.* • ~ appears in many derivatives like **graphitic** (1864) and **graphitization** (1899) and in some compounds like **graphite blue** and **graphitic carbon** (1881). O, R, W [4]

grass staggers, *see* grass tetany

grass tetany/staggers, *n.* (1933) *Biochem.* [Transl. of G *Grastetanie* (1930) < *Gras* grass + *Tetanie* < Gk *tetanós* stretched out, prostrate] An often fatal cattle disease caused by a blood calcium and a magnesium deficiency. O, W [3]

grauly, *a.* (1848) [Ad. of G *gräulich* gruesome] Grisly. O [2]

graupel, *n.* (1889) *Meteor.* [G sleet, hail, prob. of Slavic origin] Granular snow pellet, also called *soft hail.* O, R, W [4]

grauwacke, *see* graywacke

Gravenstein, *n.* (1821) *Bot.* [G *Gravensteiner* < the G name of *Gravenstein,* now Dan *Graasten,* a Danish village in formerly German Schleswig-Holstein] A fine variety of large dessert apple with yellowish-red skin. O, R [3]

graywacke, *n.* (1794) *Geol.* Var. **grauwacke/greywacke** (1794, 1811) [G *Grauwacke* < *grau* gray + *Wacke* wacke, lit., gray sandstone containing feldspar and chlorite] A grayish, coarse sandstone or fine-grained conglomerate. —**graywacke,** *a.* (1832). •The G short. form *Wacke* (q.v.) was also borrowed. O, R, W [4]

greathede, *n.* (1340) *Theol.* (obs.) [Prob. partial transl. of Late MHG or Early NHG *groszheit* greatness (recorded in *Grimm* but now obs.] Greatness. O [2]

greenstone, *n.* (1805) *Geol.* [Transl. of G *Grünstein* green stone] Any of numerous green, usu. eruptive, basaltic rocks (this is different from the "nephrite" meaning). —**greenstone,** *a.* (1830). O, R, W [4]

greisen, *n.* (1878) *Geol.* [G *Greisen/Greisz* a coarse gray rock containing zinnwaldite and accessory topaz] A crystalline rock of quartz and mica. —**greisening** (1907), **greisenization** (1920). O, R, W [4]

Grenzbegriff, -e *pl.* (1787) *Philos.* [Kant's G < *Grenze* limit + *Begriff* concept] Kant's concept showing the limitation of sense experience; a limiting concept; conception of an unattained ideal. O [3]

Grenz ray, *n. Med.* [Partial transl. of G *Grenzstrahl* < *Grenze* boundary, limit + *Strahl* ray] A soft X-ray with a wavelength approaching the limit of extreme ultraviolet, used esp. to treat skin lesions; also called *infraroentgen ray.* W [3]

Grepo, *n.* (1964) *Politics* [G, a short. of *Grenzpolizei* < *Grenze* boundary, border + *Polizei* police, guard < MFr *police* < LL *politia* < Gk *politeía*] An East Berlin border guard, preceding German reunification. O [3]

greywacke, *see* graywacke

grieben, *pl. Food* [G pl. of *Griebe* crackling from goose fat] Cracklings from goose fat. W [3]

grindle, *n.* (1884–5) *Ichthy.* Var. **grindal, grindel, grinnel(l)** [G *Gründel* gudgeon or mudfish < *Grund* ground + dim. suffix *-el* -le] (U.S.) The bowfin (mudfish). O, R, W [3]

grobian, *n.* (1621) Var. **Grobian** (1621) [G < the name of the fictional patron saint of vulgar people < ML (*Sanctus*) *Grobianus* < MHG *grob* coarse, vulgar] Boor, lout; a buffoonish person. —**Grobian,** *a.* (1654); **grobianism** (1609). O, W [3]

grochauite, *n.* (1875) *Mineral.* [G *Grochauit* (1873) < *Grochau,* the name of a Silesian town, formerly in Germany and now in Poland + G *-it* -ite] A chlorite-like mineral found in small, hexagonal crystals. O [3]

grorudite, *n.* (1896) *Geol.* [G *Grorudit* (1890) < *Grorud,* the name of a town now included in northeastern Oslo, Norway + G *-it* -ite] A hypabyssal rock of alcalic feldspar, aegirine (q.v.), and much quartz. O [3]

groschen, -ø *pl.* (1617) *Currency* [G < MHG *grosch(e)*, ult. < ML *denarius grossus* thick penny] One of various German or Austrian coins over the centuries. O, R, W [4]

grossdeutsch, *a.* (1946) *Politics* [G *großdeutsch* < *groß* great + *deutsch* German] Pan-Germanic; concerning a greater Germany, including Austria. O [3]

grossflöte, -n *pl. Music* [G < *gross* large, grand + *Flöte* < It *fluoto grande* grand flute] A labial pipe-organ stop with 8-foot pitch and strong flute quality. W [2]

grossularite, *n.* (1847) *Mineral.* Var. **grossular** [G *Grossularit* < NL *Grossularia* a genus of shrubs (family saxifragaceae), from the color of some varieties resembling the gooseberry + G *-it* -ite] A variously colored garnet: (h)essonite. O, R, W [4]

grotzen, *n. Apparel* [G the dark center back strip of a pelt] This center of a fur pelt. W [3]

ground, *n.* (1400) *Theol.* [Ad. of G *Grund* ground, as used by 14th-cent. German mystics like Johannes Eckhart and Johann Tauler] The divine essence or center of the individual soul, in which mystic union lies; Godhead as the source of all that is. O [3]

ground form, *n. Ling.* [Ad. of G *Grundform* < *Grund* ground + *Form* form < OFr < L *fōrma*] A stem, root, or word considered as the base from which various forms or other words have developed (a different meaning is recorded in the Appendix). W [3]

ground-hele, *n.* (1578) *Bot.* (obs.) [Ad. of G *Grundheil* (*Veronica officinalis*) < *Grund* ground + *heil* whole, safe] This large genus of scrophulariaceous plants, O [2]

Grübelsucht, *n.* (1876) *Psych.* [G a compulsive inclination to brood < *grübeln* to brood + *Sucht* mania] A form of obsession where even the basic facts are compulsively queried. O [2]

gruenlingite, *see* grünlingite

Grundriss, -e *pl. Ed.* [G *Grundriß* basic outline < *Grund* ground + *Riß* outline] A comprehensive, systematic outline, esp. of a science. W [3]

grünerite/grunerite, *n.* (1861) *Mineral.* [G *Grünerit* (1853) < the name of Emmanuel L. *Grüner* (1809–83), Swiss-born mineralogist + G *-it* -ite] A brown variety of amphibole (hornblende). O, W [3]

grünlingite/gruenlingite, *n.* (1898) *Mineral.* [G *Grünlingit* (1897) < the name of Friedrich *Grünling* (1857–1919), German mineralogist + *-it* -ite] A sulfide and telluride of bismuth: telluric bismuth. O, W [3]

grunstein, *n.* (1796) *Mineral.* Var. **grunsten** [G < *grün* green + *Stein* stone] Greenstone (q.v.): a green porphyry of siderite and mica. —**grunstein,** *a.* (1811). O [3]

gruss, -es *pl. Geol.* [G *Grus* weathered, granular rock < MLG] A finely granulated, undecomposed rock such as granite. W [3]

guadalcazarite, *n.* (1875) *Mineral.* [G *Guadalcazarit* (1869) < the name of *Guadalcázar*, San Luis Potosi, Mexico + G *-it* -ite] A zincky sulfide of mercury. O, W [3]

guaiaretic acid, *n.* (1866) *Chem.* (Transl. of G *Guajakharzsüure* (1861) < Sp *guajaco* guaiac tree (found in Central America) + G *Harz* resin + *Säure* acid] A white compound found in guaiacum. —**guaiaretate,** *n.* (1892). O [3]

guanase, *n.* (1904) *Biochem.* [G (1904) < *Guanine* (< Sp

guano natural dung) + G *-ase*, -ase, denoting a destroying substance] An enzyme found in most animal tissues that hydrolyzes guanine to xanthine and ammonia; guanine aminohydrolase/deaminase. O, R, W [3]

guanophore, *n.* (1924) *Zool.* [G (1912), first used in this sense by the German zoologist Wilhelm Josef Schmidt (1884–?) < *Guanine* + *-phore* < Sp *guano* dung + Gk *phorós* carrying, bringing] A chromatophore containing crystals or granules of guanine, found in the skin of reptiles and fishes. O, W [3]

guanosine, *n.* (1909) *Chem.* Var. **guanosin** (1909) [G *Guanosin* (1909) < an infixed combining of *Guanine* < Sp *guano* dung + G *Ribose* ribose, an arbitrary rearrangement of some of the letters of *Arabinose*, from which the German chemist Emil Fischer (1852–1919) prepared ribose] A crystalline nucleoside that yields guanine and ribose by hydrolysis. O, W [3]

guanylic acid, *n.* (1899) *Chem.* [Transl. of G *Guanylsäure* (1898) < *guanyl-* < Sp *guan(o)* dung + G *-yl* < Gk *hýlē* wood, substance + G *Säure* acid] An amorphous nucleotide obtained from ribonucleic acid; guanosine monophosphate. O, W [3]

gudmundite, *n.* (1928) *Mineral.* [G *Gudmundit* (1928) < a short. of *Gudmundstorp*, the name of a place near Sala, Vastmanland, Sweden + G *-it* -ite] Sulfide iron, a grayish-white antimonide. O, W [3]

guest-friend, *n.* (1873) [Transl. of G *Gastfreund* host < *Gast* guest + *Freund* friend] Historically, a guest, away from the security of home environs, to whom the host provides hospitality and protection. O [3]

guest worker, *n.* (1970) *Industry* Var. **Gastarbeiter** (1970), **guestworker** (1984) [Transl. of G *Gastarbeiter* < *Gast* guest + *Arbeiter* worker] A foreign worker employed temporarily in an industrialized European country; (U.S.) a Mexican laborer legally in the U.S. B [4]

gugelhupf/gugelhof, *n.* (1886) *Food* Var. **gougelhof, kugelho(p)f** (1886, q.v.) [G *Gugelhupf/Gugelhopf* < *Gugel* monk's cowl (< MHG < ML *cuculla* a medieval type of male cap) + G *hupf-* < *hupfen* to hop, rise, descriptive of the rising part of a cake] A semisweet cake, esp. Viennese. O, W [3]

guhr, *n.* (1686) *Mining* [G *Guhr/Gur* bubbling slime rising up from rocks, akin to *gären* to ferment] A loose, earthy deposit from water found in rock cavities; (a short. of) kieselguhr (q.v.). O, W [3]

guldengroschen, -s/-ø *pl. Currency* [G < *Gulden* (< Du) guilder + G *Groschen* smallest Austrian coin, penny] An old German silver coin preceding the taler (q.v.) in the 15th century that was orig. worth one gold gulden. W [3]

guldentaler, *n. Currency* [G < *Gulden* guilder + *Taler*] Guldengroschen (q.v.). W [2]

gulose, *n.* (1891) *Chem.* [G (1891) < the transposition and omission of letters of *Glucose* < Fr < Gk *gleûkos* cider] A hexose sugar that is stereoisomeric with glucose and obtainable from xylose. O, W [3]

gümbelite, *n.* (1871) *Mineral.* [G *Gümbelit* (1870) < the name of Carl Wilhelm von *Gümbel* (1823–98), German geologist] A magnesium-bearing variety of hydromuscovite. O [3]

gummite, *n.* (1868) *Mineral.* [G *Gummit* (1868) < *Gummi* gum (< MHG < L) + G -*it* -ite] (A general term for) secondary oxides, also called *uranium-ocher*. O, R, W [4]

Gunther, *n. Myth.* [G warlord < the name of *Gunther*, a Burgundian king and Brunhild's husband in Germanic legend < Gmc **gund-*, **gunt-*, OHG *gund-* war + *herro* lord] Brunhild's husband. R [4]

Günz, *n. and a.* (1910, 1910) *Geol.* [G (1909), the name of a Danube tributary in Bavaria, Germany] (of) the first of four geologic stages distinguished by an advance of the ice during the Pleistocene glaciation of Europe. —**Gunzian,** *a.* O, R, W [4]

Günz-Mindel, *n.* (1910) *Geol.* [G < *Günz* + *Mindel* (1909), the names of two Bavarian tributaries of the Danube] The first interglacial stage between the Günz (q.v.) and the Mindel stages of ice advance. O, W [3]

guten Abend, *interj.* [G < *gut* good + *Abend* evening] Good evening. R [2]

gute Nacht, *interj.* [G < *gut* good + *Nacht* night] Good night. R [2]

guten Morgen, *interj.* [G < *gut* good + *Morgen* morning] Good morning. R [2]

guten Tag, *interj.* [G < *gut* good + *Tag* day] Good day. R [2]

Gutnish, *n.* (1892) *Ling.* Var. **Gutnic** [G *Gutnisch* Gothlandic] The dialect of Gotland, diverged from East Norse and closely related to Swedish. O, W [3]

Gutnish, *a.* (1927) *Ethnology* [G *gutnisch* Gothlandic] Of or pertaining to Gotland or its inhabitants and their customs. O [3]

guttation, *n.* (1889) *Bot.* [G (1887) < L *gutta* drop + G -*tion* -tion] A plant's exudation of moisture from an uninjured surface. O, W [4]

guvacine, *n.* (1891) *Chem.* [G *Guvacin* (1891) < Skt *guvāka* betel-nut tree + G -*in* -ine] A white, crystalline alkaloid obtained from the areca nut. O [3]

gymnasiast, *n.* (1828) *Ed.* [G < *Gymnasium* gymnasium (q.v.) + -*ast* < (NL -*asta* < Gk -*astēs*) -ast] A student in or graduate of a European gymnasium, i.e., a middle or junior and senior high school combined. O, W [3]

gymnasium, -iums/-ia *pl.* (1691) *Ed.* [G < L *gymnasium* < Gk *gymnásion* meeting place of philosophers and sophists] In Europe, esp. Germany, a secondary school designed to prepare students for the universities (this is different from the older "athletic place" meaning). • ~ is often pronounced as in German, partly to distinguish the two meanings. O, R, W [4]

H

h, *n.* (1901) *Physics* [G (1901) symbol for Planck's constant (q.v.), the elementary quantum of action] Planck's constant. O, R, W [3]

habilitate (oneself), *v.* (1881) *Ed.* [Transl. of G *sich habilitieren* (1684) < ML *habilitare* to render one able] To qualify, as in teaching at a university (this is different from older meanings like "to endow, provide the means"). O, W [4]

hacking, *n.* (1890) *Med.* [Ad. of G *Hackung* < *hacken* to chop + *-ung*] A massage with the edge of the hand. O [3]

hadromal, *n.* (1899) *Chem.* [G (1899) < *hadr-* + *-om* + *-al* (see *hadrome*)] A hydrolysis product of lignin; paraconiferyl aldehyde. O [3]

hadrome, *n.* (1898) *Bot.* Var. **hadrom** (1965) [G *Hadrom* (1884) < *hadr-* + *-ome* < Gk *hadrós* thick + *-ōma* denoting mass, tumor] The conducting tissue of the xylem, excluding fibers; the somewhat rudimentary xylem in cryptogams. O, W [3]

haematogen, *n.* (1890) *Chem.* Var. **hematogen** (1934) [G *Hämatogen* (1885) < *hämato-* + *-gen* < Gk *haîma* (gen. *haímatos*) blood + *génos* type] A yellow, iron-containing powder obtained from egg yolk and orig. projected as the precursor of hemoglobin. O [3]

h(a)ematoporphyrin, *n.* (1885) *Chem.* [G *Haematoporphyrin* (1871) < *hämato-* + *Porphyrin* < Gk *haîma* (gen. *haímatos*) blood + *pórphyros* crimson, purple] One of several isomeric porphyrins that are hydrated protoporphyrin derivatives, esp. the pigment obtained from hematin or heme. O, W [3]

h(a)emoglobin, *n.* (1869 W9) *Biochem.* [G *Hämiglobin,* ad. of *Hämoglobin* < *hämo-* (< Gk *haîma,* gen. *haímatos*) + G *Globin* (q.v.)] Methemoglobin, a basic pigment found in blood. O, R, W [4]

haemogregarine, *n.* (1908) *Biochem.* Var. **hemogregarine** [G *Haemogregarina* (1885) < *haemo-* < Gk *haîma* (gen. *haímatos*) blood + L *gregarius* gregarious + G *-in* -ine] A member of a family of coccidian parasites that infest the red blood cells of vertebrates such as giant snakes. O, W [3]

h(a)emosiderin, *n.* (c.1885 W9) *Physiol.* [G *Hämosiderin* (1888) < *hämo-* + *Siderin* < Gk *haîma* (gen. *haímatos*) blood + *sídēros* iron + G *-in* -in] A granular, ferric-oxide pigment formed by the breakdown of hemoglobin. O, R, W [3]

haff, *n.* (1859) *Geogr.* [G lagoon < (M)LG *haf* sea] A long, shallow fresh-water lagoon found at a river mouth, esp. along the German Baltic coast. O, W [3]

Hafner ware, *n.* *Pottery* [G (also *Hafnerkeramik*) < *Hafner* potter + *Ware* ware] A 16th-century German earthenware such as stove tiles and heavy vessels. W [3]

haiduk, *n.* (1615) *Mil.* (archaic) Vars. like **heyduc(k)** (1889, 1615), **heyduke** [G *Haiduck* (also *Heiduck*) < Hung *hajduk,* pl. of *hajdu* robber] A Balkan outlaw resisting Turkish rule; a Hungarian mercenary soldier of a class

eventually elevated to the nobility; a male attendant in some European countries dressed in livery resembling a Hungarian haiduk's costume. O, R, W [4]

hair salt, *n.* (1795) *Mineral.* [Transl. of G *Haarsalz* < *Haar* hair + *Salz* salt] Epsomite when in silky fibers; alunogen. O, W [3]

hairstone, *n.* *Geol.* [Transl. of G *Haarstein* < *Haar* hair + *Stein* stone] Quartz densely penetrated with hairlike crystals of rutile or another mineral: sagenite. O, W [3]

Hakenkreuz/hakenkreuz, *n.* (1918 W9) and *a.* (1931) *Politics* [G < *Haken* hook + *Kreuz* (ult. < L *cruc-, crux*) cross, symbol of the Nazi party] (Of) a swastika, esp. as the Nazi emblem. O, R, W [4]

Hakenkreuzler, -ø/-s *pl.* *Politics* [G one who wears and/or subscribes to the implications of the Nazi emblem < *Haken* hook + *Kreuzler*] A member of any German-speaking organization in Europe following World War One that uses the swastika as an emblem of extreme nationalism or anti-Semitism. W [3]

hall church, *n.* *Archit.* [Transl. of G *Hallenkirche* < *Halle* hall + *Kirche* church] A Gothic church, esp. in Germany, in which, instead of a clerestory, the aisles reach almost to the height of the nave. W [3]

halochromism, *n.* (1902) *Chem.* [Ad. of G *Halochromie* (1902) < *halo-* + *-chromie* < Gk *hálōs* a circle of light around the sun or moon + *chrōma* color + G *-ie* (< Gk *-ia*) -ism] The property of some colorless or faintly colored compounds to become brilliantly colored when acids are added. O, W [3]

halper, *v.* (1596) (obs.) [Ad. of G *holpern* (1540 in Kluge, to stumble) to vacillate (in Grimm)] To stumble or teeter; to go backward and forward. O [2]

halt, *n.* (1591–8) *Mil.* [G < imper. of *halten* to hold, stop] A military command to stop marching; a temporary stop on a march or journey; a small station where only local trains usually stop. —**haltless** (1856). O, R, W [4]

halt, *v.* (1656) *Mil.* [G < *halten* to halt] To make a halt, orig. a military term but soon a temporary stopping in a march or journey; to cause to halt or stop. O, R, W [4]

halt, *interj.* (1796) [G < imper. of *halten* to hold] Stop! O, R [4]

hamartoma, -s/-ta *pl.* (1904) *Path.* [G *Hamartom* (1904) (or NL *hamartoma* < G) < Gk *hamartánein* to go awry + *-ōma* denoting a tumor] A tumor-like mass thought to represent anomalous development of natural tissue rather than a true tumor. —**hamartomatous.** O, W [3]

hambergite, *n.* (1890) *Mineral.* [Sw or G *Hambergit* (1890) < the name of Axel *Hamberg* (1863–1933), Swedish mineralogist + Sw or G *-it* -ite] A basic beryllium borate found in prismatic crystals. O, W [3]

Hamburger, *n.* (1616) *Geogr.* [G < the name of the German city *Hamburg* + *-er* -er] A native or resident of Hamburg. —**Hamburger,** *a.* (1798). O [3]

hamburger, *n.* (1884 W9) *Food* Var. **hamburg, burger**

(q.v.) [Short. of G *Hamburg(er) Steak* < the name of the German city of *Hamburg*, where it originated] A patty of cooked ground beef; a sandwich consisting of such a patty in a split bun. —**hamburger**, *a*. O, R, W [4]

hamburg(er) steak, *n*. (1889) *Food* [G a small, flat round patty of ground beef] Ground or chopped beef; a patty of cooked ground beef served as the main course. O, R, W [4]

hamster, *n*. (1607) *Zool*. [G a small rodent with a stubby tail and pouch-like cheeks < OHG *hamustro*, ult. of Slavic origin] Any of several Old World rodents of *Cricetus* and related genera; their fur. —**golden hamster, hamstery**. O, R, W [4]

handbook, *n*. (1814) *Ed*. [Transl. of G *Handbuch* a handy but comprehensive manual covering a field of study < *Hand* hand + *Buch* book] A book that can be conveniently carried as a reference manual, esp. for tourists; a concise reference book; a bookmaker's betting book or place of business (this is different from OE *handboc* < L *manuālis*). O, R, W [4]

hannayite, *n*. (1879) *Mineral*. [G *Hannayit* (1878) < the name of James Ballantyne *Hannay* (1855-post-1926), British chemist + G *-it* -ite] A hydrous acid phosphate of magnesium and ammonium found in guano. O, W [3]

Hanswurst, *n*. *Theater* [G, lit., Jack sausage < LG *hansworst*, intended to mean a clumsy person as thick as a sausage] A farcical or burlesque stereotyped character common in German comedies of the 16th to the 18th centuries. W [3]

H antigen, *n*. *Immunology* [G, a short. of *Hauchantigen* < *Hauch* breath + *Antigen* antigen < Gk *antí* against + *-genēs* producing, causing] Flagellar antigen. W [3]

haplite, *see* aplite

haploid, *a*. (1908) *Biol*. [G (1905) < Gk *haploeidés* single] Having a single set of unpaired chromosomes; monoploid. —**haploid**, *n*. (1914); **haploidy**, *n*. (1922). O, R, W [4]

haplont, *n*. (1920) *Biol*. [G < Gk *haplóos* simple + *ón* (gen. *óntos*) being] An organism whose somatic cells are haploid at all stages of its life except as a zygote, which is diploid. —**haplontic** (1929). O, R, W [3]

hapten, *n*. (1921) *Immunology* Var. **haptene** (1921) [G (1921) < *hapt-* + *-en* < Gk *háptein* to touch, fasten] A nonantigenic substance that can become antigenic only when conjugated to a carrier protein. —**haptenic** (1932). O, R, W [4]

haptics, *n*. (1895) *Psych., Ling*. [G *Haptik* (1892) < *hapt-* (< Gk *háptein* to touch, fasten) + G *-ik* -ics] The study of touch and tactile sensations, esp. to communicate; a nonlanguage communication that conveys meaning by physical contact. —**haptical(ly)** (1899, 1964). O, R [3]

haptine, *n*. (1900) *Immunology* [G *Haptin* (1900) < *hapt-* (< Gk *háptein* to touch, fasten) + G *-in* -ine] One of diverse free receptors detached from its parent cell, circulating freely in the bloodstream and protecting against infection. O [3]

haptophore, *a*. and *n*. (1899, 1899) *Immunology* [G *Haptophor* (1898) < *hapto-* + *-phor* < Gk *háptein* to touch, fasten + *phórein* to carry] (Of) the ability to enter into combination, as in a group of atoms in a toxin's molecule that can combine with the corresponding receptors of a cell. —**haptophorous** (1902), **haptophoric** (1902). O, W [3]

haptotropism, *n*. (1900) *Bot*. [G *Haptotropismus* (1884) < *hapto-* + *-tropismus* < Gk *háptein* to attach, fasten + *trópos* change, turn + G *-ismus* (< L *-ismus*) -ism] Positive stereotropism, where plants exhibit tropic movements when touched by a foreign body. O, W [3]

hartite, *n*. (1863-82) *Mineral*. [G *Hartit* < a short. of *Oberhart*, the name of an Austrian town + *-it* -ite] A white fossil resin found in peat beds. O, W [3]

harzburgite, *n*. (1890) *Geol*. [G *Harzburgit* (1887) < the name of *Harzburg*, a German town in the Harz Mountains + *-it* -ite] A rock of the periodotite group mainly consisting of orthopyroxene and olivine (q.v.). O, W [3]

hasenpfeffer, *n*. (1892) *Food* Var. **hassenpfeffer** (1892) [G < *Hase* hare + *Pfeffer* pepper] A highly seasoned rabbit stew. O, R, W [4]

haskwort, *n*. (1578) *Bot*. [Folk etymology < G *Halskraut* < *Hals* neck + *Kraut* plant] (An old name for) two species of bellflowers. O [3]

haubitz, *see* howitz

hauchecornite, *n*. (1893) *Mineral*. [G *Hauchecornit* (1893) < the name of Wilhelm *Hauchecorne* (1828-1900), German geologist + *-it* -ite] A sulfide of nickel, bismuth, and antimony. O [3]

hauerite, *n*. (1847) *Mineral*. [G *Hauerit* (1846) < the name of the Austrian geologists Joseph Ritter von *Hauer* (1778-1863) and his son Franz Ritter von *Hauer* (1822-99) + G *-it* -ite] Native manganese sulfide. O, W [3]

hausen, *n*. (1745) *Zool*. [G < MHG *hūse(n)*, OHG *hūso*, prob. related to Norw *huse* fish head, because of its armored head] Beluga, a large white sturgeon. O, R, W [3]

hausfrau, -s/en *pl*. (1798) Var. **house-frau** (1918) [G < *Haus* house + *Frau* woman] Housewife; mistress of a household. O, R, W [4]

hausmaler, -ø *pl*. (1935) *Art* [G < *Haus* house + *Maler* painter, actually one who decorates porcelain in one's own premises] One who paints undecorated china in one's own workshop or house. O [3]

hausmalerei, *n*. (1935) *Art* [G < *Haus* house + *Malerei* painting] Painting and decorating by a hausmaler (q.v.). O [2]

hay-hut, *n*. (1903) *Agric*. [Transl. of G *Heuhütte* < *Heu* hay + *Hütte* hut] A wooden hut that covers a haystack on a mountainside. O [3]

hazel hen, *n*. (1661) *Zool*. Var. **hazel grouse** (1783), **hazelhen** [Transl. of G *Haselhuhn* < *Hasel* hazel + *Huhn* chicken] A European woodland grouse. O, R, W [4]

hazelwort, *n*. (1551) *Bot*. [Transl. of 16th-century G *Haselwurtz* < MHG *hasel*, OHG *hasal* a shrub or small tree of the genus *Corylus* + G *Wurtz* (now *Wurz* or *Wurzel*) herb, root] The herbalists' name for an asarabacca. O, W [3]

heat tonality/tone/toning, *n*. (1895) *Chem*. [Transl. of G *Wärmetönung* < *Wärme* warmth, heat + *Tönung* tuning, tonality] The sum of the heat produced by a chemical reaction and of the work done by the system. O [3]

heavy spar, *n*. (1789) *Mineral*. [Transl. of G *Schwerspat* (1774) < *schwer* heavy + *Spat* spar] Barite, a native sulfate of barium. O, R, W [4]

heckelphone, *n*. (1905) *Music* Old var. **heckelphon** (1905) [Archaic G *Heckelphon* (1904) < the name of Wilhelm *Heckel* (1856-1909), German instrument maker + *-phon*

< Gk *phōnē* sound, modeled on G *Saxophon*] A baritone oboe, pitched an octave below the normal oboe. O, W [3]

hectograph, *n.* (1880) *Printing* Var. **hektograph** (1880) [G *Hektograph* < *hekto-* + *-graph* < Fr *hect(o)-* < Gk *hekatón* hundred + *gráphein* to write] A device for making copies of a writing or drawing by transferring it to a gelatin slab treated with glycerin and then taking impressions from the gelatin; the process of doing this. —**hectograph,** *v.* (1887); **-graphic** (1887); **-graphy** (1889). O, R, W [4]

hedonal, *n.* (1900) *Chem.* [G < *hedon-* (< Gk *hēdonē* joy, pleasure) + G *-al* -al] A white crystalline compound used as a hypnotic and anesthetic until its toxic effects became known. O [3]

hedrumite*n.* (1896) *Geol.* [G *Hedrumit* (1890) < *Hedrum,* the name of a village north of Larvik, Norway + G *-it -*ite] A hypabyssal porphyritic igneous rock consisting mainly of a potash feldspar. O [3]

hedyphane, *n.* (1832) *Mineral.* [G *Hedyphan* (1830) < *hedy-* sweet + *-phan* -phane < Gk *hēdýs* pleasant + *phanós* clear] A calcium variety of mimetite (q.v.). O, W [3]

Hefner candle, *n.* (1898) *Optics* Var. **Hefner flame** (1911), **Hefnerkerze** (1914) [Transl. of G *Hefnerkerze* < the name of Friedrich von *Hefner*-Alteneck (1845–1904), German electrical engineer + *Kerze* candle (flame)] A German standard unit of luminous intensity; the light of the Hefner lamp. O, R, W [3]

Hefner lamp, *n.* (1891) *Physics* Var. **Hefner-Alteneck lamp** (1902) [G *Hefnerlampe* < *Hefner* (see *Hefner candle*) + *Lampe* lamp < OFr < L *lampas* < Gk *lámpein* to shine] A lamp of standard dimensions that burns amyl acetate. O [3]

heft, -e *pl.* (1886) *Printing* [G notebook, fascicle < *heften* to fasten together] A number of sheets of paper fastened together to help form a book; a fascicle of a serial publication. O [3]

Hegelianism, *n.* (1846) *Philos.* [G *Hegelianismus* < the name of Georg W. F. *Hegel* (1770–1831), German philosopher + *-ismus* (< L) -ism] Orig., Hegel's philosophical system of absolute idealism; a modification of Hegel's system, as in accepting his objective idealism but revising his dialectic. O, R, W [4]

heil, *interj.* (1927) *Sports* (1937) *Politics* [G hail! < MHG *heil* healthy] Hail, the traditional greeting of skiers; (later as) the Nazi salute; a greeting. —**heil,** *v.* (1938); **heiled** (1940). O, R, W [3]

heiligenschein, -s/-e *pl. Theol.* [G halo or gleaming light around the head of a divine or saintly person < *Heilige(r)* saint + *Schein* glow] A halo of light around the shadow of a person's head caused by sunlight on raindrops. • ~ has a secondary use (see Appendix). R, W [3]

Heilsgeschichte, *n.* (1938) *Theol.* [G < *Heils-,* gen. of *Heil* welfare, well-being + *Geschichte* history, i.e., the history of continuous divine action relative to humans] Sacred history, specif. the interpretation of history emphasizing God's saving acts and Christ's role in redemption. O, W [3]

heilsgeschichtlich, *a.* (1952) *Theol.* [G < *Heilsgeschichte* (q.v.) + *-lich* -like] Of Heilsgeschichte. O [2]

Heimweh, *n.* (1721) [G homesickness < *Heim* home +

Weh hurt, longing] Homesickness. • ~ is transl. as **homesickness** (1756, q.v.). O [3]

Heimwehr, *n.* (1931) *Mil.* [G < *Heim* home + *Wehr* defense] Formerly, the German or Austrian Home Defense Force. —**Heimwehr,** *a.* (1938). O [3]

Heinie, *n.* (1904) *Mil.* Var. **Heine** (1917), **H(e)iney** (1904, 1925) [G *Heini* a pet name for *Heinrich* Henry, and a colloq. aspersion of "dummy"] A German, esp. a German soldier in World War One. O, R, W [4]

heintzite, *n.* (1891) *Mineral.* [G *Heintzit* (1890) < the name of Wilhelm Heinrich *Heintz* (1817–80), German chemist + *-it* -ite] Kaliborite (q.v.). O [3]

hektograph, *see* hectograph

heldentenor, -s/-e *pl.* (1926) *Music* [G one who has the voice to sing such operatic parts < the comb. form of *Held* hero + *Tenor* (< OFr < L) tenor] A tenor voice of great brilliancy and volume, esp. suited for heroic roles in opera; (often cap.) someone with such a voice. • ~ is transl. as **heroic tenor.** O, R, W [4]

heliodor, *n.* (1913) *Mineral.* Var. **heliodore** (1952) [G < *helio-* < Gk *hélios* sun + *dōron* gift] A richly golden-colored variety of beryl found in southern Africa. O, R, W [3]

heliophyllite, *n.* (1890) *Mineral.* [Sw or G *Heliophyllit* (1888) < *helio-* + *Phyllit* < Gk *hélios* sun + *phýllon* leaf + G or Sw *-it* -ite] A yellowish oxychloride of lead and arsenic that is dimorphous with ecdemite. W [4]

hell, *v.* (1799) [G *hellen* to brighten < *hell* clear] To add luster to; to burnish gold or silver (this is different from its early meanings "to put in hell, to pour"). O [3]

hellandite, *n.* (1903) *Mineral.* [G *Hellandit* < the name of Amund *Helland* (1846–1918), Norwegian geologist + G *-it* -ite] A hydrous borosilicate of the cerium metals and calcium. O, W [3]

heller, -ø/-s *pl.* (1575) *Currency* [G < MHG *haller* < *Haller pfenninc,* i.e., a penny from Schwäbisch-*Hall,* a German town in Baden-Württemberg, where it was first struck] An old silver coin orig. issued in 13th-century Germany; a bronze coin like a penny formerly used in Austria and Germany; this unit of value; haler. O, R, W [3]

Helmholtz resonator, *n.* (1930) *Physics* [G < the name of Hermann L. F. von *Helmholtz* (1821–94), German inventor + *Resonator* < L *resonāre* to resound] A hollow acoustic vessel with two openings, one of which is pointed toward a source of sound that may be intensified in some frequencies by the resonating, enclosed air, and the other opening to be held next to one's ear. O, W [3]

Helmitol, *n.* (1903) *Pharm.* Var. **helmitol** (1933) [G (1902) a proprietary coinage] The proprietary name of a preparation of formamol; a derivative of hexamethylenetetramine that has been used as a urinary antiseptic and in treating rheumatism. O [3]

helvellic acid, *n.* (1906) *Pharm.* [Transl. of G *Helvellasäure* (1885) < NL *Helvella esculenta* a type of toadstool + *Säure* acid] A poisonous acid found in some fungi of this family. O [3]

helvetium, *n.* (1940) *Chem.* [G (1940) < NL *Helvetia* Switzerland + G (< L) *-ium* -ium] Earlier name for the radioactive element astatine. O [3]

helvite, *n.* (1818) *Mineral.* Var. **helvin(e)** (1818) [Ad. of G

Helvin (1817) < L *helvus* reddish-brown] A silicate sulfide of manganese and beryllium. O, W [3]

hematogen, *see* haematogen

hematoporphyrin, *see* haematoporphyrin

hemicellulose, *n.* (1891) *Chem.* [G (1891) (now also *Hemizellulose*) < *hemi-* + *Cellulose* < Gk *hémysis* half + L *cellula* small cell] Any of various noncellulosic polysaccharides that accompany cellulose and lignin in the cell walls of wood and green plants. —**hemicellulosic.** O, R, W [4]

hemikaryon, *n.* (1925) *Biol.* [G (1905) < *hemi-* + *Karyon* < Gk *hemi-* one of the comb. forms of *haîma* blood + *káryon* nut, kernel, nucleus] A cell nucleus possessing the haploid number of chromosomes. —**hemikaryotic** (1925). O, R, W [3]

hemimorphite, *n.* (1868) *Mineral.* [G *Hemimorphit* (1853) < *hemi-* + *Morphit* < Gk *hémysis* half + *morphé* shape + G *-it* -ite] A basic zinc silicate in transparent orthorhombic crystals; smithsonite, formerly called (U.S.) *calamine.* O, R, W [4]

hemin, *n.* (1929) *Chem.* Var. **haemin** [G *Hamin* (1929) < Gk *haima* blood + G *-in*] A red blood pigment. O [4]

hemiparasite, *n.* (1891) *Bot.* [G *Hemiparasit* (1890) < *hemi-* (< Gk *hémysis* half) + G *Parasit* < L *parasitus,* Gk *parásitos* table companion] A facultative parasite; a partially parasitic plant like mistletoe. —**hemiparasitic** (1902). O [3]

hemisaprophyte, *n.* (1895) *Bot.* [G *Hemisaprophyt* (1889) < *hemi-* + *Saprophyt* < Gk *hémysis* half + *saprós* rotten + *phytón* growth, product] A facultative saprophyte that looks like a normal plant but is alternatively parisitic or autotrophic. —**hemisaprophytic** (1895). O [3]

hemoglobin, *see* haemoglobin

hemogregarine, *see* haemogregarine

hemosiderin, *see* haemosiderin

henid, *n.* (1906) *Philos.* [G *Henide* (1905) < Gk *hén* one + *ídios* self, peculiar, coined in *Geschlecht und Charakter,* by the German philosopher Otto Weinniger (1880–1903)] A psychological dictum that it is impossible to differentiate perception and sensation in their earliest stages in lower types of organisms. —**henidical** (1909). O [3]

henism, *n.* (1881) *Phil.* [G *Henismus* < Gk *hén* (neuter of *heîs*) one + G *-ismus* (< L) -ism] Singularism, monism. O, W [3]

henotheism, *n.* (1860) *Philos.* [G *Henotheismus* < *heno-* + *Theismus* < Gk *hén* (gen. *henós*) one + *theós* god + G (< L) *-ismus* -ism] The worship of one god without denying that there may be other gods, also called *monolatry.*—**henotheist(ic)** (1884, 1880). O, R, W [4]

heortology, *n.* (1900) *Theol.* [G *Heortologie* (or Fr) < Gk *heorté* feast + *lógos* word, study] A study of religious calendars, as in the history and significance of Christian religious feasts and seasons. —**heortologist** (1900), **heortological.** O, R, W [3]

hepatin, *n.* (1886) *Biochem.* [G (1886) < *hepat-* + *-in* < Gk *hépar* (gen. *hépatos*) liver + L *-ina*] An iron-containing protein occurring in liver tissue (this is different from the older "glycogen" meaning). O [3]

hepatite, *n.* (1802–3) *Mineral.* [G *Hepatit* (1800) < *hepat-* (< Gk *hépar,* gen. *hépatos* liver) + G *-it* -ite, named for

its odor] A barite that emits a fetid odor when rubbed or heated. O, W [3]

hercynite, *n.* (1849) *Mineral.* [G *Hercynit* (1839) < L *Hercynia* (*silva*) Hercynian Forest, the Roman name for all or parts of the German sub-Alpine mountains + G *-it* -ite] A black oxide of iron and aluminum: iron spinel. O, R, W [3]

herderite, *n.* (1828) *Mineral.* [G *Herderit* (1828) < the name of Baron Siegmund August Wolfgang von *Herder* (1776–1838), German mining official + *-it* -ite] A phosphate and fluoride of beryllium and calcium. O, W [3]

heroin, *n.* (1898) *Pharm.* Var. **heroine** [G a trademark < Gk *hérōs* hero; in the Middle Ages *heroic* meant "strong, powerful" + G *-in* -in] A white, crystalline derivative of morphine with strong addictive powers, banned in most countries but still a worldwide problem. —**heroin,** *a.* (1910); **heroin baby** (1972); **heroinism.** O, R, W [4]

Herr, -en *pl.* (1653) [G master or lord, used with the last name as a courteous reference to an adult male] Mister; a German gentleman. O, R [4]

herrengrundite, *n.* (1881) *Mineral.* [G *Herrengrundit* < *Herrengrund,* now the name of a place in Hungary + G *-it* -ite] A basic hydrous sulfate of calcium and copper. O-1933 [3]

Herrenvolk/herrenvolk, -s/-völker *pl.* (1940) *Sociol.* [G < *Herr* lord, master + *Volk* people, race] Master race; the Nazi conception of the German people as born to rule inferior peoples; an appellation of other "superior" peoples. • ~ is loosely transl. as **master race** (q.v.). —**herrenvolk,** *a.* (1947). O, R, W [4]

Herrnhuter/herrnhuter, *n.* (1748) *Theol.* [G < the name of the German town *Herrnhut* (lit., Lord's care), where Count von Zinzendorf established the religious sect on his estate in 1722 + *-er; a Herrnhuter* is thus one from Herrnhut] A member of the Moravian Church. —**Herrnhut(ian)ism** (1753, 1882), **Herrnhutenism** (1879). O, W [3]

Hertz, -ø/-s *pl.* (1928) *Physics* [G a unit of frequency < the name of Heinrich R. *Hertz* (1857–94), German physicist] A unit of frequency equal to one cycle per second. —**megahertz, terahertz.** • ~ is symbolized as **Hz** and is used as an *a.* to name apparatus, concepts, etc. developed by Hertz, as in **Hertzian telegraphy** (1898)/**wave** (1900). O, R, W [4]

herzog, *n. Politics* [G a title of nobility in the rank between king and prince] Duke. W2 [3]

hessite, *n.* (1849) *Mineral.* [G *Hessit* (1843) < the name of Henri *Hess* (1802–50), Swiss chemist in Russia + G *-it* -ite] A usu. massive silver telluride. O, R, W [4]

heterecious, *see* heteroecious

heteroauxin, *n.* (1935) *Biochem.* [G (1934) < *hetero-* + *Auxin* < Gk *héteros* different + *aúxein* to grow + G *-in* -in] Indoleacetic acid, a crystalline plant hormone used to promote rooting and growth of plants. O, R, W [3]

heteroaxial, *a.* (1926) *Geol.* [G (1891) (now also *heterouchsial*) < *hetero-* + *axial* < Gk *héteros* different, strange + L *axis* axis + G *-al* -al] Having a geological structure based on two axes or sets of axes. O [3]

heterocaryotic, *see* heterokaryotic

heterochromatin, *n.* (1932) *Biol.* [G (1928) < *hetero-* + *Chromatin* < Gk *héteros* different + *chrôma* (gen. *chrômatos*) color + G *-in* -in] Variable heterochromatic chromosome material, now primarily viewed as a state rather than as a substance. —**heterochromatized**, *a.* (1941); **heterochromatization** (1941). O, R, W [4]

heterocline, *n.* (1844) *Mineral.* Old var. **heteroclin** (1844) [G *Heteroklin* (1840) < *hetero-* + *-klin* < Gk *héteros* different + *klínein* to incline] Marceline, a siliceous oxide of manganese. O [3]

heter(o)ecious, *a.* (1882) *Bot.* [Ad. of G *heteröcisch* (1866) (now *heterözisch*) < *hetero-* + *-öcisch* < Gk *héteros* different + *oîkos* house(hold) + G *-isch* -ious] Of fungi's passing through different stages in its life cycle on alternate and often unrelated hosts. —**heteroecismal**, *a.* (1884); **-cious(ness); -ciously; -cism; -cy**, *n.* O, W [4]

heterogenetic, *a.* (1918) *Path.* [G *heterogenetisch* (1913) < *hetero-* + *-genetisch* < Gk *héteros* different + *genetế* birth + G *-isch* -ic] Heterophile (q.v.); of heterogenesis. O, R, W [4]

heterogenite, *n.* (1872) *Mineral.* [G *Heterogenit* (1872) < *hetero-* + *-genit* < Gk *héteros* different + *génesis* origin + G *-it* -ite, so named because its composition differs from that of some manganese oxides] One of various hydrous oxides of cobalt, as in heterogenite-2H. O [3]

heterogony of ends, *n.* (1887) *Philos.* [Transl. of G *Heterogonie der Zwecke* (1886), coined by the German psychologist-philosopher Wilhelm Wundt (1832–1920) in his *Ethik* < *hetero-* + *-gonie* < Gk *héteros* different + *gónos* birth, origin + G *-ie* (< Gk *-ia*) -y + *der* of (the) + *Zwecke* ends] Wundt's principle that particular will directed to particular ends produces unexpected consequences leading to the development of religion and codes of moral and social behavior. O [3]

heterokaryotic/heterocaryotic, *a.* (1916) *Bot.* [G *heterocaryotisch* (1913) (now *heterokaryotisch*) < *hetero-* + *caryotisch* < Gk *héteros* different + *káryon* (gen. *káryotikos*) nut, kernel + G *-isch* -ic] Exhibiting or resulting from heterokaryosis, as in fungi, with cells of two or more genetically unlike nuclei; of, pertaining to, or containing heterokaryons. —**heterokaryosis** (1916), **heterokaryon** (1945). O, R, W [3]

heterological, *a.* (1926) *Philos.* Var. **heterologic** [Ad. of G *heterologisch* (1907) < *hetero-* + *-logisch* < Gk *héteros* different + *lógos* word] Heterologous, not having the property it denotes. —**heterologicality** (1950), **heterologically**. O, W [3]

heterolysin, *n.* (1901) *Med.* [G (1900) < *hetero-* + *-lysin* < Gk *héteros* different + *lýsis* act of loosing + G *-in* -in] A hemolysin from an animal of a different species, as when foreign blood-cells are introduced into an animal's bloodstream. O, W [3]

heteromorphosis, *n.* (1891) *Physiol.* [G *Heteromorphose* (1891) < *hetero-* + *-morphose* < Gk *héteros* different + *mórphōsis* formation] An organism's regenerative development of an abnormal or misplaced part; the producing of a malformed or misplaced organ or tissue. O, W [3]

heteronomous, *a.* (1870) *Biol.* [G *heteronom* < *heter-* + *-onom* < Gk *héteros* different + *nómos* law + E *-ous*] Subject to or involving different laws of growth, as in parts or members differentiated from the same primitive type (this is different from the older meaning of "subject to different principles"). —**heteronomously** (1909). O [4]

heteronomy, *n.* (1798) *Philos.* [G *Heteronomie* < *heter-* + *-onomie* < Gk *héteros* the other of two, different + *-onomía*, as in *autonomía* autonomy] A subjection to another being, power, or external law; the condition of lacking moral freedom; the state or quality of being heteronomous. O, R, W [3]

heterophile, *a.* (1920) and *n.* (1929) *Biochem.* Var. **heterophilic** (1929) [G *heterophil* (1917) < *hetero-* + *-phil* < Gk *héteros* different + *phílos* friendly, loving] (Of) the capacity to react immunologically with sera, etc. from organisms of another species, as used in agglutination tests for mononucleosis. —**heterophilic** (1929). O, R [3]

heteroploid, *n.* and *a.* (1926, 1926) *Bot.* [G (1916) < *hetero-* + *-ploid* < Gk *héteros* different + *-ploid* < *diplóos* double + *-oid* < *-oeidēs* similar] (Of) an organism's nucleus with a chromosome number that is neither the diploid nor the haploid number characteristic of its species. —**heteroploidy**, *n.* (1926). O, W [4]

heteropolar, *a.* (1922) *Chem.* [G (1906) < *hetero-* + *polar* < Gk *héteros* different + *pólos* < *pélein* to turn, be in motion] Of chemical bonds or crystals formed by ions of unlike poles (this is different from the earlier "electrical" meaning). O, R, W [3]

heteropolymer, *n.* (1948) *Chem.* [G < *hetero-* + *Polymer* < Gk *héteros* different + *polýs* much, many + *méros* part, share] Copolymer, a polymer formed from two or more different monomeric molecules. O, W [3]

heteropolymerization, *n.* (1931) *Chem.* [G *Heteropolymerisation* < *Heteropolymer* heteropolymer (q.v.) + *-isation* -ization] The process or action of polymerizing. O [3]

heteropycnosis, *n.* (1925) *Biol.* [G *Heteropyknose* (1907) < *hetero-* + *Pyknose* < Gk *héteros* different + *pyknós* thick + G *-se* (< Gk *-sis*) -sis, fem. suffix of action] The persistence of higher than average staining in chromosomal material; the differing condition or degree of condensation distinguishing various chromosomes (such as sex) in a nucleus. —**heteropycnotic** (1934). O, W [3]

heterotrophy[1], *n.* (1891) *Bot.* [G *Heterotrophie* (1885) < *hetero-* + *-trophie* < Gk *héteros* different + *trophế* nourishment] Some plants' abnormal mode of nutrition by utilizing a fungus surrounding the roots (rather than using root hairs). O [3]

heterotrophy[2], *n.* (1896) *Biol.* [G *Heterotrophie* (1885) (see *heterotrophy*[1])] The compound position of a shoot in relation to the horizon and the mother shoot. O [2]

heterotrophy[3], *n.* (1900) *Bot.* [G *Heterotrophie* (see *heterotrophy*[1])] A symbiotic relationship, as seen in lichens.
• ~ is not a new meaning of *heterotrophy*[1], but is a reborrowing from G *Heterotrophie*, one of the few multiple, successive borrowings from one etymon in the entire corpus. O [3]

heterotypic, *a.* (1885 W9) *Biol.* Var. **heterotypical** (1888) [G *heterotypisch* (1887) < *hetero-* + *-typisch* < Gk *héteros* different + *typikós* figurative + G *-isch* -ic] Of or being the first division of meiosis; different in kind, form, or arrangement. O, R, W [4]

heteroxanthine, *n.* (1886) *Biochem.* Var. **heteroxanthin** [G *Heteroxanthin* (1885) < *hetero-* + *Xanthin* < Gk *héteros* different + *xanthós* yellow + G *-in* -ine] A purine sometimes found in human urine; 7-methyl-xanthine. O, W [3]

heubachite, *n.* (1877) *Mineral.* [G *Heubachit* < the name of *Heubachthal* in Baden-Württemberg, Germany + *-it* -ite] Nickelian heterogenite (q.v.), a hydrous oxide that forms a crust on barite. O-1933 [2]

heumite, *n.* (1901) *Geol.* [G *Heumit(e)* (1898), named after the town of *Heum* in southern Norway (now *Brathagen-Heum*) + G *-it(e)* -ite] A hypabyssal dike-rock containing alkali feldspars and hornblende, along with smaller amounts of other rocks. O [3]

heurige, *n.* (1934) *Beverages* Var. **heuriger** (1935) [(Austrian) G *Heuriger* < *heurig* this year's new (wine)] New wine from the latest Viennese harvest; a wine garden where this is served. —**heurige(r),** *a.* (1941). O, R [3]

heuristic, *a.* (1848) *Philos.* Var. **heuristical** (1848) [G *heuristisch* (1767) < NL *heuristicus* < Gk *heurístikein* to find, discover + G *-isch* -ic] Serving to solve a problem by trial and error rather than by logic or someone else's directions; of or concerning exploratory problem-solving procedures that utilize self-educating procedures to improve performance (this is different from the older, general meaning of "serving to discover"). —**heuristically** (1935). O, R, W [4]

heuristic, *n.* (1860 *W9*) *Philos.* [G *Heuristik* < NL *heuristica* (fem. of *heuristicus*) < Gk *heurístikein* to find, discover] The art or science of heuristic procedure; heuristic argument. —**heuristics** (1963). O, R, W [4]

hexenbesen, *n.* (c.1900 *W9*) *Bot.* [G < *Hexen,* pl. of *Hexe* witch + *Besen* broom] (*Colloq.*) witches'-broom; a tufted cluster of small branches produced by an abnormal growth stimulus, such as by mistletoes or physiological disturbances. W [3]

hexerei, *n.* (1898) [(PaG) G < *hexen* to practice witchcraft + nom. suffix *-erei* -erei] Witchcraft. O, W [3]

hexite, *n.* (1899) *Chem.* [G *Hexit* < *hex* (< Gk) six + G *-it* -ite] Hexitol; hexanitrodiphenylamine, a high explosive. O [3]

hexogen, *n.* (1923) *Chem.* Var. **hexogene** [G < *hexo-* + *-gen* < Gk *héx* six + *génos* type] Cyclonite, a high explosive. O [3]

hexone, *n.* (1898) *Chem.* Var. **hexon** (1898) [G *Hexon(base)* (1898) < Gk *héx* six + *ón* being (+ G *Base* basis)] A hexone base; methyl isobutyl ketone. O, R, W [4]

heyduc, *see* haiduk

hibschite, *n.* (1907) *Mineral.* [G *Hibschit* (1905) < the name of Joseph E. *Hibsch* (1852–1940), Czech mineralogist + G *-it* -ite] A hydrogrossular, a calcium aluminum silicate-hydroxide. O, W [3]

high forest, *n.* (1879) *Bot.* [Transl. of G *Hochwald* < *hoch* high + *Wald* forest] A forest of trees wholly or mainly raised from seed; a forest of lofty trees. —**high forest,** *a.* (1953). O, W [3]

High German, *n.* (1706 *W9*) *Ling.* [Transl. of G *Hochdeutsch* < *hoch* high + *deutsch* German] The German spoken in southern and central Germany; the literary and official language of Germany, referred to as High German, as derived from West Germanic, in contrast with the languages of Low German (q.v.). —**High German consonant shift,** the second shift described by Grimm's law. R, W [4]

High Sea Fleet, *n.* (1907) *Mil.* [Transl. of G *Hochseeflotte* < *Hochsee* high sea + *Flotte* fleet] A group of ships that travel the open seas, esp. warships in times of war. O [3]

Hilbert space, *n.* (1939 *W9*) *Math.* [Transl. of G *Hilbert-Raum* < the name of David *Hilbert* (1862–1943), German mathematician + *Raum* space] A complete, infinite-dimension vector space for which a scalar product is defined. R [3]

hinterhand, *n.* *Games* [G < *hinter* behind, last + *Hand* hand] The last skat player in turn to bid. • ~ is transl. as **endhand** (q.v.). W [3]

hinterland, *n.* (1890) *Geogr.* [G < *hinter* behind + *Land* land] The land or region lying behind the coast district or remote from cities or towns; the back country; a region that provides supplies for the nation administering it; an urban zone of influence; a little-known area of knowledge: frontier; a geological moving block. O, R, W [4]

hintzeïte, *n.* (1891) *Mineral.* Var. **heintzite** (q.v.) [G *Hintze-it* (1890) < the name of Carl A. F. *Hintze* (1851–1916), German mineralogist + *-it* -ite] Orig., a contested synonym for *heintzite* (q.v.); kaliborite (q.v.). O, W [3]

hiortdahlite, *n.* (1892) *Mineral.* [Norw or G *Hiortdahlit* (1888) < the name of Thorstein Hallager *Hiortdahl* (Hjortdahl) (1839–1925), Norwegian chemist + G or Norw *-it* -ite] Orig., a synonym for *heintzite* (q.v.); now a rare fluorine-containing silicate of zirconium, sodium, and calcium. O, W [3]

hirse, *n.* (1562) *Bot.* [G < MHG *hirs(e)*, OHG *hirsi* poss. meaning "something grown or nourishing"] Millet, any of various annual cereal and forage grasses. O [3]

hirudin, *n.* (1905) *Biochem.* [G *Hirudin/Herudin* (1903) < L *hirūdo* (gen. *hirūdinis*) leech] A protein produced by leeches' buccal glands, used to prevent blood clotting; formerly a trademark. O, R, W [4]

hisingerite, *n.* (1868) *Mineral.* [G *Hisingerit* (1828) < the name of Wilhelm *Hisinger* (1766–1852), Swedish geologist + G *-it* -ite] Orig., a synonym for *gillingite;* an amorphous iron ore that is a hydrous ferric silicate. O, W [3]

histidine, *n.* (1896) *Biochem.* Var. **histidin** (1900) [G *Histidin* (1896) < *hist-* (< Gk *histíon* web, tissue) + G *-id,* as in *Oxid* oxide + *-in* -ine] A crystalline, basic amino-acid that is essential to a rat's nutrition and that is synthesized by microorganisms and plants. O, R, W [4]

histiocyte, *n.* (1924) *Physiol.* [G *Histiozyt* (1913) < *histio-* + *-zyt* < Gk *histíon* web, tissue + NL *cytus* cell < Gk *kýtos* hollow, urn, vessel] A large, phagocytic tissue cell that can become motile when stimulated. —**histiocytic** (1924), **histiocytosis** (1925), **histiocytoma.** O, W [4]

histone, *n.* (1885) *Biochem.* Old var. **histon** (1885) [G *Histon* (1884) < *hist-* + *-on* < Gk *histós* web + *-on* < *-ōnē* (fem. patronymic suffix) -one] Any of a small class of basic protein substances like globulin with marked properties, as in relation to genes. O, R [4]

historicism, *n.* (1895) *History* [G *Historismus* < *Historie* (< Gk *historikós* historical) + G (< L) *-ismus* -ism] A theory advanced esp. by German historians since the 1850s that all social and cultural phenomena are relative and historically determined and thus to be comprehended only by studying their historical context; the writing or treating of history, literature, etc. according to this theory; an intense or exaggerated concern with the past; the use of or excessive reliance on historical styles or forms, esp. in architecture. —**historicist(ic)** (1937, 1949). O, R, W [4]

historism, *n.* *History* Var. **historicism** [G *Historismus* historicism (q.v.)] A theory about sociocultural phenomena: historicism. W [3]

Hitler, *a.* (1930) *Politics* [G < the name of Adolf *Hitler* (1889–1945), chancellor of the German Third Reich and leader of the National Socialist Party] Of one who embodies Hitler's characteristics; of a dictatorial person. • ~ appears in numerous derivatives like **-ism** (1930), **-ite** (1930), **-ist** (1931), **-ize** (1933), **-ian** (1934), **-ish** (1935), **-istic** (1941), **-ized** (1943), **-esque** (1944), **-iana** (1966). O [4]

Hittorf dark space, *n.* (1916) *Physics* [Transl. of G *Hittorf-Dunkelraum,* named after Johann Wilhelm *Hittorf* (1824–1914), German scientist + *dunkel* dark + *Raum* space] Crookes dark space, the dark space between the cathode glow and the negative glow; also called *cathode dark space.* O, R [3]

hoch, *n.* (1867) and *interj.* (1870) [G an exclamation of salutation and praise < a short. of *hoch lebe* long live] (An expression of) salutation or approval. —**hoch,** *v.* (1909). O, W [3]

hochgeboren, -ø *pl.* (1905) *Sociol.* [G a person of noble birth < *hoch* high + *geboren* born] A high-born person; such persons collectively. —**hoch(wohl)geboren,** *a.* (1949, 1930). O [2]

hochheimer, *see* hock, hockamore

hochmoor, *a.* *Geogr.* [G a moor above ground-water level < *hoch* high + *Moor* fen, swamp] Of or growing on various acid peats or peaty soils. W [3]

Höchst, *a.* *Pottery* [Short. of G *Höchster Porzellan* china made since 1746 in *Höchst,* a town now a part of Frankfurt on Main + *-er* -er + *Porzellan* < ML *porcelaine,* ult. < L *porcellus*] Of, concerning, or being an 18th-century German faience or porcelain largely influenced by the styles of Meissen clayware. W [3]

hock, *n.* (1625) *Beverages* [G, a short. of the name of the German city *Hochheim*] (Chiefly Brit.) Rhine wine. — **hock,** *a.* (1851); **hock cup** (1851); **hock bottle** (1892). O, R, W [4]

hockamore, *n.* (1673) *Beverages* Var. **hochheimer** [G < the name of *Hochheim* on the Main (not on the Rhine), Germany, where the wine is made + *-er* -er] A white Rhine wine; hock (q.v.) (this is different from various "non-wine" meanings). O [3]

hoernesite, *n.* (1868) *Mineral.* Var. **hörnesite** (1968) [G *Hörnesit* (1860) < the name of Moritz *Hörnes* (1815–68), Austrian paleontologist + G *-it* -ite] Magnesium orthoarsenate. O, W [3]

hohlflöte/hohlflute, *n.* (1660) *Music* [G < *hohl* hollow + *Flöte* flute < MFr *flahute* < OProv *flaut*] A pipe-organ flute stop possessing a hollow tone. O, W [3]

hohmannite, *n.* (1888) *Mineral.* [G *Hohmannit* (1888) < the name of Thomas *Hohmann,* mining engineer in Valparaiso, Chile, who discovered the mineral + G *-it* -ite] A hydrated basic ferric sulfate. O, W [3]

holewort, *n.* (1578) *Bot.* [Transl. of G *Ho(h)lwurz* < *hohl* hollow + *Wurz* (short. of *Wurzel*) root] Hollow root (q.v.). O [3]

holiday course, *n.* (1906) *Ed.* [Transl. of G *Ferienkurs* < *Ferien* (pl.) school holidays, vacations + *Kurs* course, classes < OFr *course* < L *cursus*] A series of lectures or classes held orig. in Germany during a school holiday or vacation. O [3]

hollow root, *n.* (1578) *Bot.* Var. **holewort** (1578), **hollowwort** (1863) [Transl. of G *Ho(h)lwur(t)z,* applied to *Aristolochia*—see Grimm] The *Coryadalis tuberosa* or other species of *Corydalis.* O [3]

hollowwort, *see* hollow root

holmquistite, *n.* (1914) *Mineral.* [Sw or G *Hölmquistit* (1913) < the name of Per Johan *Hölmquist* (1866–1946), Swedish mineralogist + Sw or G *-it* -ite] A rare, basic alkali silicate of lithium, magnesium, iron, and aluminum. O, W [3]

Holocaine, *n.* (1897) *Pharm.* Var. **holocain** (1899) [G *Holocaïn* < *holo-* + *-cain* (< Gk *hólos* entire + *-cain*), modeled on G *Cocaïn* (now *Kokaïn*) cocaine] A synthetic derivative of *p*-phenetidine resembling cocaine in its effects and used as an anesthetic, esp. for the eye; (cap.) a trademark for phenacaine. O, R [4]

holocellulose, *n.* (1933) *Chem.* [G *Holozellulose* < *holo-* + *Zellulose* < Gk *hólos* entire + NL *cellula* < L *cella* cell + G *-ose* -ose, denoting a carbohydrate] The total polysaccharide fraction of wood or straw etc. composed of cellulose and hemicelluloses. O, W [3]

holomictic, *a.* (1937) *Biol.* [G *holomiktisch* (1935), used in this sense by the Austrian hydrobiologist Ingo Findenegg (1896–1974) < *holo-* + *miktisch* < Gk *hólos* entirely + *miktós* mixed + G *-isch* -ic] Of a lake's experiencing a complete circulation of water to its lowest depth during overturn. O, W [3]

holonomic, *a.* (1899) *Math.* Var. **holonomous** (1899) [G *Holonom* (1894) < *holo-* + *-nom* < Gk *hólos* whole + *nómos* law + E *-ic*] Of a constrained system where the equations that define the constraints are integrable or already free of differentials; these constraints. O [3]

holoparasite, *n.* (1891) *Biol.* [G *Holoparasit* (1890) < *holo-* + *Parasit* < Gk *hólos* entire, complete + *parásitos* table companion, sponger] An obligate parasite, which can exist only in association with its host. —**holoparasitic** (1902), **holoparasitism** (1927). O, W [3]

holoplanktonic, *a.* (1893) *Biol.* [G *holoplanktonisch* (1890) < *holo-* + *planktonisch* < Gk *hólos* whole, entire + *planktón* floating about + G *-isch* -ic] Of aquatic organisms' passing their entire life in drifting or swimming weakly in the water. —**holoplankton,** *n.* (1909). O, R, W [4]

holopneustic, *a.* (1892) *Entomology* [G *holopneustisch* (1877) < *holo-* + *pneustisch* < Gk *hólos* entire, whole + *pneustikós* for breathing < *pneîn* to breathe + G *-isch* -ic] Of insects' having all of their spiracles or tracheal stigmata open. O, R, W [3]

holosaprophyte, *n.* (1890) *Bot.* [G *Holosaprophyt* (1889) < *holo-* + *Saprophyt* < Gk *hólos* whole, entire + *saprós* rotten + *phytón* growth, product] An entirely saprophytic organism: an obligate saprophyte. —**holosaprophytic** (1895). O, W [3]

Holstein, *a.* (1865) and *n.* (1872) *Zool.* [G and Du < the name of a northwestern region of Germany] (Of) a breed of large dairy cattle; (of) a cow of this breed. • ~ is mainly < Du, where the cows were orig. raised in Friesland; the variant **Holstein-Friesian** is wholly < Du and is ambiguously short. to **Holstein.** O, R, W [4]

homatropine, *n.* (1880) *Pharm.* Var. **homatropin** (1901) [G *Homatropin* (1880) < *homo-* + *Atropin* < Gk *homós* alike, common + NL *Atropa belladonna* deadly nightshade + G *-in* -ine] A poisonous, crystalline ester of tropine and mandelic acid used as its hydrobromide to dilate the eye pupil. O, W [3]

Homburg (hat), *n.* (1894) *Apparel* [G < *Homburg,* the name of a town near Wiesbaden, Germany] A man's soft felt hat with a curled brim and creased high crown, first made and worn in Homburg, then a fashionable health resort. O, R, W [4]

hom(o)eoblastic, *a.* (1920) *Geol.* [G *homöoblastisch* (1904) < *homö-* + *blastisch* < Gk *homoîos* similar, alike + *blastós* bud + G *-isch* -ic] Of metamorphic rock composed of grains of equal size. O, W [3]

homeocrystalline, *a.* (1888) *Geol.* Var. **homoeocrystalline** (1888) [G *homöokrystallinisch* < *homö-* + *krystallinisch* < Gk *homoîos* alike, similar + *krystállinos* crystalline, translucent + G *-isch* -ine] Having the constituent minerals' crystals equally developed: granitic. O, W [3]

homeopath, *n.* (1830) *Med.* Var. **homoeopath** (1830) [G *Homöopath* (1824) < *homö-* + *-path* < Gk *homoîos* similar, alike + *páthos* suffering, illness] One who advocates or practices homeopathy. O, R, W [4]

homeopathic, *a.* (1830) *Med.* Var. **homoeopathic** (1830) [G *homöopathisch* (1824) < *Homöopath* homeopath (q.v.) + *-isch* -ic] Of or relating to homeopathy; of a diluted or analogous quality; a homeopathic medicine. —**homeopathically** (1837), **homeopathicity** (1842), **homeopathic magic.** O, R, W [4]

homeopathy, *n.* (1826) *Med.* Var. **homoeopathy** (1849) [G *Homöopathie* (c.1796) < *Homöopath* homeopath (q.v.) + *-ie* -y] A system and procedure that treats a disease by administering small doses of medicine that would in healthy persons produce symptoms like those of the disease being treated. O, R, W [4]

homeotypic, *a.* (1888) *Biol.* Var. **homeotypical** (1888), **homoeotypic** (1889) [G *homöotypisch* (1887) < *homö-* + *-typisch* < Gk *homoîos* similar, alike + *typikós* typical] Of or concerning the second division of meiosis. O, R, W [4]

homesickness, *n.* (1756) Var. **Heimweh** (1721) [Transl. of G *Heimweh* < *Heim* home + *Weh* hurt, woe] Homesickness: nostalgia. O, R, W [4]

homilite, *n.* (1881) *Mineral.* [G or Sw *Homilit* < Gk *homilía* association < *homiléein* to be in company + G or Sw *-it* -ite] A borosilicate of iron and calcium. O, W [3]

hominine, *a.* (1959) and *n.* (1961) *Anthrop.* [G (< NL) *Homininae* (1949) the projected subfamily including humans] A member of the Homoninae, which is sometimes considered as a subfamily of the family Hominidae to comprise the large-brained hominids, in contrast to the small-brained Australopithecinae hominids (this is different from the old Latin-derived "human" meaning). O [3]

homocaryotic, *see* homokaryotic

homoeo- (as in *homoeoblastic/-crystalline/-path/-pathic/-pathy/-typic*), *see* the respective *homeo-* spelling

homoeopolar, *see* homopolar

homoeothermic, *see* homoiothermic

homogamy, *n.* (1874) *Bot.* [G *Homogamie* < *homo-* + *-gamie* < Gk *homógamos* married, sharing the same wife + G *-ie* -y] The state of having flowers alike throughout, as in the maturing of the pistils and stamens at the same time; interbreeding of individuals of like or similar characteristics. —**homogamic** (1907). O, R, W [4]

homogentisic (acid), *n.* (1891) *Chem.* [Transl. of G *Homogentisinsäure* (1891) < *Homogentisin* (< Gk *homós* common, equal + *genti* < NL *Gentiana* genus name of *Gentiana lutea* + G *-sin* -sin) + *Säure* acid] A crystalline acid formed during the metabolism of phenylalanine and tyrosine. —**homogentisate** (1891). O, R, W [3]

homoiothermic, *a.* (1870) *Zool.* Var. **homoeothermal** (1870), **homoeothermic** (1889) [G *homöotherm* (1847) < *homö-* + *-therm* < Gk *homoîos* similar, alike + *thermós* warm + E *-ic*] Maintaining a relatively constant body temperature nearly independent of the environmental temperature: warm-blooded. —**homoiotherm,** *n.* (1891). O, W [4]

homokaryotic/homocaryotic, *a.* (1916) *Bot.* [G *homöcaryotisch* (1913), irreg. < *homö-* + *caryotisch* < Gk *homoîos* similar, alike + *káryon* nut kernel + G *-isch* -ic] Of a fungus' cell in the mycelium containing two or more genetically identical nuclei. —**homokaryosis** (1928), **homokaryon** (1949). O, W [3]

homophyletic, *a.* *Anthrop.* [G *homophyl* + E *-etic*] Relating to homophyly (q.v.). W [3]

homophyly, *n.* (1883) *Anthrop.* [G *Homophylie* < Gk *homophylía* the condition of being of the same race] Resemblance due to common ancestry. O, W [4]

homopolar, *a.* (1922) *Chem.* Var. **homoeopolar** [G *homöopolar* (1906) < *homö-* + *polar* < Gk *homoîos* alike, similar + NL *polaris* < L *polus* pole] Formed by or arising from the sharing of electrons between neutral atoms, without ionization; covalent. —**homopolarity.** O, R, W [4]

homopolymerization, *n.* (1931) *Chem.* Var. **homopolymerisation** (1963) [G *Polymerisation* (1930) < *homo-* + *Polymerisation* < Gk *homós* common, equal + *polýs* many + *méros* part + G *-isation* -ization] A reaction in which identical molecules are joined into a homopolymer. —**homopolymer,** *n.* (1940); **-merize** (1952); **-meric** (1971). O, W [3]

homostyly, *n.* (1887) *Bot.* [G *Homostylie* < *homo-* + *-stylie* < Gk *homós* alike + *stýlos* support] Homogony, a condition of having one kind of flowers where the gynoecium and androecium are of uniform relative length. O, R, W [3]

homotopic, *a.* (1918) *Math.* [G *homotop* (1907) < *homo-* + *-top* < Gk *homós* common, equal + *tópos* place + E *-ic*] Homeomorphic, topologically equivalent (this is different from the earlier meaning of "of the same place"). —**homotopically** (1930). O, R, W [3]

homotopy, *n.* (1918) *Math.* [G *Homotopie* (1907) < *homo-* + *-topie* < Gk *homós* common, equal + *tópos* place + G *-ie* -y] Homeomorphism, a mapping involving topological equivalence in geometric figures. O, R, W [3]

honest broker, *n.* (1878) *Politics* [Transl. of G *ehrlicher Makler* (1878), a sobriquet for Otto von Bismarck (1815–98), German chancellor] This sobriquet; a representative of a country seeking to mediate problems between opposing countries; a mediator in industrial or other disputes. O [4]

hoodlum, *n.* (1871) [Prob. < (Bavarian) G *Hodalum,* NHG *Hudellump* < G *Hudel* ragamuffin + *Lump* scoundrel]

Orig., U.S., a rowdy, thug, or mobster. • ~ appears in the derivatives **-ism** (1872), **-ish** (1883), **-ing** (1892). O, R, W [4]

hookworm, *n.* (1902) *Biol.* (1902) [Transl. of G *Hakenwurm* (1789) < *Haken* hook + *Wurm* worm] A parasitic nematode worm that attacks humans, other mammals, and a few birds, using strong, hooklike organs to attach itself to the host's intestinal lining. —**hookworm disease** (1902), **hookwormy.** O, R, W [4]

hooray, *see* hurrah

horme, *n.* (1915) *Psych.* [G a hypothetical energy as defined by Carl Gustav Jung < Gk *hormḗ* impulse] (Primarily Brit.) hypothetical, vital energy as an urge to purposive activity. —**hormism** (1948), **hormist** (1948). O, R, W [4]

hormic, *a.* (1926) *Psych.* [G *hormisch* (?1915) < Gk *hormḗ* impulse + G *-isch* -ic] Characterized by horme. —**hormic theory** (1948), **hormic psychology.** O, R, W [3]

hornblende, *n.* (1770) *Mineral.* [G < *Horn* horn (probably having reference to the color of the mineral) + *Blende* (orig.) deceptively gleaming mineral] A common variety of aluminous amphibole; amphibole. • ~ appears in composites like **-blendic** (1823), **-blendite** (1874), **-blendization,** **-blend schist** (1880). O, R, W [4]

hörnesite, *see* hoernesite

hornfels, -ø *pl.* (1854) *Geol.* [G < *Horn* horn (having reference to the rock's color and composition) + *Fels* rock] A fine-grained silicate rock. —**hornfels,** *v.* (1901); **-felsed,** *a.* (1922); **-felsing,** *verbal n.* (1930); **-felsic** (1951). O, R, W [4]

horn silver, *n.* (1770) *Mineral.* [G *Hornsilber* (or poss. Sw *hornsilver*) < G *Horn* horn (probably having reference to the mineral's color) + *Silber* silver] Cerargyrite, a native chloride of silver. O, R, W [3]

hornslate, *n.* (1791) *Mineral.* [Transl. of G *Hornschiefer*] A schistous variety of hornstone (q.v.). O [3]

hornstone, *n.* (1728) *Mineral.* [Transl. of G *Hornstein* < *Horn* horn (having reference to the mineral's color and composition) + *Stein* stone] A cryptocrystalline variety of quartz much like flint. —**hornstone,** *a.* (1796). O, R, W [4]

horst, *n.* (1893) *Geol.* [G (1883) thicket, mass, cluster < OHG *hurst* thicket, mostly on top of a rock] An elevated block of the earth's crust separated by faults from adjacent, somewhat depressed blocks. O, R, W [4]

Horst Wessel (lied/song), *n.* (1937) *Politics* [G (1927) < the name of Horst *Wessel* (1907–30), author of the words of the official anthem of the German Nazi party + *Lied* song] The German Nazi party anthem. • ~ is transl. as **Horst Wessel song** (1968). O, R [3]

houndsfoot, *n.* (1710) (archaic) [Prob. folk-etymology of G *Hundsfott* scoundrel, rascal < *Hund* hound + *-fott,* NHG *Fotz* vagina] A scoundrel or worthless rascal. —**houndsfoot,** *a.* (1814). O, W [3]

house-frau, *see* hausfrau

housemother, *n.* (1834) [Transl. of G *Hausmutter* < *Haus* house + *Mutter* mother] The mother of a household or family; a woman acting as hostess or chaperon in a dormitory, hostel, etc. —**housemotherly** (1880). O, R, W [4]

howitz, *n.* (1687) *Mil.* (obs.) Var. **haubitz** (1700) [Ad. of G *Haubitze* < Czech *houfnice* (a word introduced into Ger-

many during the Hussite wars) catapult] Howitzer (this modern word is < Du *houwitser*). O [3]

hübnerite, *see* huebnerite

huchen, *n.* (1829) *Ichthy.* Var. **hucho** (1829), **huch** [G *Huchen,* Late MHG a large, predacious fish like a salmon, found in the Danube] This large, elongated game fish. O, W [3]

huebnerite, *n.* (1867) *Mineral.* Var. **hübnerite** (1867) [G *Hübnerit* (1865) < the name of Hüttenmeister Adolf *Hübner,* 19th-cent. German mining engineer at Freiberg, Saxony + *-it* -ite] Manganese tungstate, found in columnar or foliated masses. O, R, W [3]

huegelite, *see* hugelite

huehnerkobelite, *see* hühnerkobelite

hügelite, *n.* (1914) *Mineral.* Var. **huegelite** [G *Hügelit* (1914) < the name of Baron Karl Freiherr von *Hügel,* 20th-cent. Austrian geographer + G *-it* -ite] Orig., a hydrated vanadate of lead and zinc; (later shown to be) a hydrated arsenate of lead and uranium. O [3]

hühnerkobelite, *n.* (1950) *Mineral.* Var. **huehnerkobelite** [G *Hühnerkobelit* < *Hühnerkobel,* the name of a mountain in Bavaria, Germany + *-it* -ite] Alluaudite (q.v.), a phosphate of sodium, calcium, iron, and manganese. O, W [3]

humanism, *n.* (1832) *Ed.* (1903) *Philos.* [G *Humanismus,* with reference to education, prob. coined by Niethammer in his correspondence with Hegel in 1808—(see Paul/Betz, *Deutsches Wörterbuch,* 5th edition, 1966); Georg Voigt introduced the term in its cultural–historical sense in 1859—(see Kluge/Mitzka, *Etymologisches Wörterbuch der deutschen Sprache,* 18th edition, 1960); the earliest, but now disused sense of *humanism* in English as a "belief in the mere humanity of Christ," first attested in 1812, is prob. < Fr *humanisme*] A devotion to the humanities, esp. the system of the Humanists in studying Latin and Greek classics; a way of life, doctrine, or set of attitudes centered on human needs and interests. O, R, W [4]

humboldtilite, *n.* (1826) *Mineral.* [G *Humboldtilit* (1825) < the name of Baron Alexander von *Humboldt* (1769–1859), German scientist + *-ilit* (< *Melilit* melilite) -ilite] A variety of melilite, often found in large crystals. O [3]

humboldtite, *n.* (1823) *Mineral.* [G *Humboldtit* < the name of Baron Alexander von *Humboldt* (1769–1859), German scientist + *-it* -ite] Humboldtine (a word < Fr), a ferrous oxalate. O, W [3]

humin, *n.* (1844) *Biochem.* [G < NL *humus* earth, soil + G *-in* -in] A usu. amorphous substance formed in reactions, as from humus, or a pigment from the acid hydrolysis of protein. O, W [3]

hummel, *n.* (1500–20) *Zool.* (obs.) [G and LG *hummel* bumblebee, drone] A drone; a lazy fellow. O (not in 2nd ed.) [2]

humoresque, *n.* (1880) *Music* [G *Humoreske* < *Humor* (< L) humor + *-eske* -esque, patterned after *Groteske* grotesque or *Burleske* burlesque] A musical composition typically humorous or fanciful: capriccio. O, R, W [4]

hunter, *n.* (1753) *Mil.* Var. **ja(e)ger** (1809) [Transl. of G *Jäger* (or Fr *chasseur*) hunter < *jagen* to hunt] A faithful courier: chasseur (this is different from the meanings developed < OE *huntian* to hunt). O [3]

huntmaster, *n.* (1691) *Sports* (archaic) [Transl. of G *Jä-*

germeister < *Jäger* hunter + *Meister* master] The master of the hunt; an officer who directs it. O [2]

hurrah, *interj.* (1716) Var. **hurray** (1845), **hooray** (1888), **hoorah** [Poss. < G *hurra!* the imper. of *hurren* to hasten, hurry] An exclamation or shout expressing joy, triumph, applause, or encouragement, as at public assemblies. — **hurrah,** *a.* (1835) and *v.* O, R, W [4]

hyalite, *n.* (1794) *Mineral.* [G *Hyalit* (1794) < *hyal-* (< Gk *hýalos* glass) + G *-it* -ite] Opal, a colorless, often quite clear variety. O, R, W [4]

hyalobasalt, *n. Mineral.* [G < *hyalo-* (< Gk *hýalos* transparent rock, glass) + G *Basalt*] Basalt glass. W [3]

hyalogen, *n. Biochem.* [Prob. < G < *hyalo-* + *-gen* < Gk *hýalos* transparent rock + *génos* offspring] Any of various insoluble, mucoid-related substances found in many animal structures, which yield hyalines by hydrolysis. R, W [3]

hyalo-ophitic, *a.* (1920) *Geol.* [G *hyaloophitisch* (1899) < *hyalo-* + *ophitisch* < Gk *hýalos* glass + *ophítēs* of or like a snake + G *-isch* -ic] An ophitic-like texture where the spaces of an open network of feldspar laths are occupied by glass rather than pyroxene. O [3]

hyalophane, *n.* (1855) *Mineral.* [G *Hyalophan* < *hyalo-* + *-phan* < Gk *hýalos* glass + *phanḗs* apparently] A monoclinic feldspar resembling adularia. O, R, W [3]

hyalopilitic, *a.* (1888) *Geol.* [G *hyalopilitisch* (1887) < *hyalo-* < Gk *hýalos* glass + *pîlos* felt, fungus, toadstool + G *-it* -ite + *-isch*-ic] Having innumerable needle-like microlites embedded in glass. O, W [3]

hyaloplasm, *n.* (1886) *Biol.* Var. **hyaloplasma** [Prob. < G *Hyaloplasma* < *hyalo-* + *Plasma* < Gk *hýalos* glass + LL (< Gk) *plásma* structure] A clear, apparently homogeneous ground substance of cytoplasm. —**hyaloplasmic.** O, R, W [4]

hyalosiderite, *n.* (1824) *Mineral.* [G *Hyalosiderit* < *hyalo-* < Gk *hýalos* glass + *siderítēs* of iron] A very ferruginous variety of olivine (q.v.). O, W [3]

hyalosome, *n.* (1889) *Biol.* [G *Hyalosom* (1887) < *hyalo-* + *-som* < Gk *hýalos* glass + *sōma* body] A faintly staining cell structure resembling the nucleolus. O [3]

hydantoin, *n.* (1872) *Chem.* [Prob. < a G blend of *hydro-* (< the comb. form of Gk *hýdōr* water) + G *Allantoin* allantoin (q.v.)] A crystalline, weakly acidic compound that is a di-oxo derivative of imidazole found in beet juice; a derivative of the hydantoin compound. O, R, W [3]

hydathode, *n.* (1895) *Bot.* [G (1894) < *hydat-* + *Hode* < Gk *hýdōr* (gen. *hýdatos*) water + *hodós* way, road] A pore or gland in the leaf epidermis of higher plants, associated with terminal tracheids of a vein, which discharges water from the interior; also called *water pore/stoma.* O, R, W [4]

hydatomorphic, *a. Chem.* [Ad. of G *hydatomorphose* < *hydato-* + *-morphose* < Gk *hydato-,* the comb. form of *hýdōr* (gen. *hýdatos*) water + *morphḗ* form] Of, concerning, or resulting from crystallization in aqueous solutions. —**hydatomorphism.** W [3]

hydrastinine, *n.* (1887) *Chem.* [G *Hydrastinin* (1887) < NL *Hydrastis* Hydrastis Canadensis, a North American ranunculaceous plant + an infixed G *-in* -ine + a terminal *-in* -ine] A synthetic crystalline base derived from hydrastine and used to control uterine bleeding. O, R, W [4]

hydrazine, *n.* (1887) *Chem.* [G *Hydrazin* < *hydr-* + *-azo* + *-in* -ine < the irreg. comb. form of Gk *hýdōr* water + < Fr *azote* inert, unable to support life] A fuming, corrosive, strongly reducing liquid base weaker than ammonia and used as a fuel component for rocket and jet engines and in making salts and organic derivatives. — **hydrazino-** (1907), **hydrazinium** (1927), **hydrazine hydrate.** O, R, W [4]

hydrazone, *n.* (1888) *Chem.* [G *Hydrazon* (1888) < *Hydrazin* hydrazine (q.v.) + *-on* -one] Any compound that contains the grouping >C =NNHR and that is thus a condensation product of an aldehyde or ketone with hydrazine; a substituted derivative. O, R, W [3]

hydrobenzoin, *n.* (1877) *Chem.* [G < *hydro-* + *Benzoin* < Gk *hydro-,* the comb. form of *hýdōr* water + MFr *benjoin* < Ar *luban jāwi* frankincense of Java + G *-in* -in] A crystalline compound that yields benzoin by oxidation. O, W [3]

hydroboracite, *n.* (1835) *Mineral.* [G *Hydroboracit* (1834) (now *Hydroborazit*) < *hydro-* < Gk *hydro-* the comb. form of *hýdōr* water + ML *borac, borax* borax (< Ar, ult. < Per *būrah*) + G *-it* -ite] A white hydrous calcium magnesium borate. O, W [3]

hydroborane, *n.* (1927) *Chem.* [G *Hydroboran* (1926), used in this sense by the German chemist Alfred Stock (1876–1946) < *hydro-* + *Boran* < Gk *hydro-* (the comb. form of *hýdōr* water) + NL *borax* borax + G *-an* -ane] Any hydride or boron richer in hydrogen than others containing the same number of boron atoms. O [3]

hydrochinone, *see* hydroquinone

hydrocotarnine, *n. Chem.* [Prob. < G *Hydrocotarnin* (now also *Hydrokotarnin*) < *hydro-* (< the comb. form of Gk *hýdōr* water) + G *Kotarnin,* an anagram of *Narkotin* narcotine (q.v.)] A crystalline alkaloid obtained from opium and also formed by reducing cotarnine (q.v.). O, W [3]

hydrohalite, *n.* (1861) *Mineral.* [G *Hydrohalit* (1847) < *hydro-* + *Halit* < NL *Halites* < Gk *hydro-,* the comb. form of *hýdōr* water + *háls* salt + G *-it* -ite] A hydrated chloride of sodium formed only from very cold salt water. O, W [3]

hydroid, *n.* (1887) *Bot.* [G (1883) < *hydro-* + *-oid* < Gk *hydro-,* the comb. form of *hýdōr* water + *-oeidēs* similar] An element forming part of a plant's hydrome tissue (this is different from earlier ''zoological'' meanings). O, R [4]

hydromagnesite, *n.* (1837) *Mineral.* [G *Hydromagnesit* (1827) < *hydro-* + *Magnesit* < Gk *hydro-,* the comb. form of Gk *hýdōr* water + Fr *magnésite* < Gk *magnēsía* any of several ores and amalgams < fem. of *Mágnēs* of Magnesia (*Manisa* today), ancient city in Asia Minor + G *-it* -ite] Basic magnesium carbonate. O, W [3]

hydrom(e), *n.* (1900) *Bot.* [G *Hydrom* (1883) < *hydro-* + *-om* -ome < Gk *hydro-,* the comb. form of *hýdōr* water + *mestós* full] The water-conducting part of a vascular bundle. O [3]

hydronium, *n.* (1908) *Chem.* [G (1907), a short. of *Hydroxonium* < *hydro-* (the comb. form of Gk *hýdōr* water) + NL *oxonium* < Gk *oxýs* tart, sour] A hydrated hydrogen ion, esp. oxonium. O, R, W [4]

hydropath, *n.* (1842) *Med.* [G (or Fr) < G *Hydropathie* hydropathy (q.v.)] Hydropathist, one who practices or believes in hydropathy. —**hydropathic(al)** (1843, 1844), **hydropathically.** O, R [4]

hydropathy, *n.* (1843) *Med.* [G *Hydropathie* (1825) < *hydro-* + *-pathie* < Gk *hydro-,* the comb. form of *hýdōr* water + *-patheia* enduring, suffering + G *-ie* -y] The water cure, originated in Germany to treat diseases by copious, frequent use of water, internally and externally. O, R, W [4]

hydrophilite, *n.* (1875) *Mineral.* [G *Hydrophilit* (1869) < *hydro-* < Gk *hydro-,* the comb. form of *hýdōr* water + *phílos* loving + G *-it* -ite] A rare mineral of calcium chloride: antarcticite. O, W [3]

hydroquinone, *n.* (1865–72) *Chem.* Var. **hydrochinon(e)** (1865–72) [Ad. of G *Hydrochinon* < *hydro-* + *Chinon* quinone (< *china*) < Gk *hydro-,* the comb. form of *hýdōr* water + Sp *quina* (< Quechua) china bark, actually *quinaquina* the bark of barks + G *-on* -one] A white, crystalline, strongly reducing phenol used as a developer in photography and as an antioxidant esp. for oils and fats. O, R, W [4]

hydrotalcite, *n.* (1879) *Mineral.* [G *Hydrotalkit* < *hydro-* + *Talk* + *-it* -ite < Gk *hydro-* (the comb. form of *hýdōr* water) + NL *talcum* (prob. < MFr *talc* < Ar *talq* mica)] Talc, a hydrous aluminum and magnesium hydroxide and carbonate. O, W [3]

hydrothermal, *a.* (1849) *Geol.* [G < *hydro-* + *thermal* < Gk *hydro-,* the comb. form of *hýdōr* water + *thérmē* heat + G *-al* -al] Of or relating to hot water, esp. in mineral formation or metamorphism. —**hydrothermally** (1941). O, R, W [4]

hydrotropy, *n.* (1928) *Chem.* [G *Hydrotropie* (1916) < *hydro-* + *-tropie* < Gk *hydro-,* the comb. form of *hýdōr* water + *tropē* turn, change] The solubilization of a normally only slightly soluble substance by adding an agent. O, W [3]

hydroxamic acid, *n.* (1875) *Chem.* [Transl. of G *Hydroxamsäure* (1869) < *Hydroxylamine* + *Hydroxyl* (< E) + G *Amin* amine < Gk *hydro-,* the comb. form of *hýdōr* water + *-yl* (first used in G, but ult. < the comb. form of Gk *hýlē* matter, substance) + G *Säure* acid] One of a class of weak acids that are acyl derivatives of hydroxylamine. O, W [3]

hydroxonium, *n.* (1925) *Chem.* [G (1907) < *hydro-* + *Oxonium* < Gk *hydro-,* the comb. form of *hýdōr* water + G *ox-,* a short. of *Oxygen* oxygen + *Ammonium* ammonia < Gk *ammōniakón* plant that grew in the vicinity of the temple dedicated to Jupiter Ammon in Siwa, Egypt] Hydronium (q.v.). O, W [3]

hydroxy(l)apatite, *n.* (1912) *Mineral.* [G *Hydroxylapatit* < *Hydroxyl* (< E) hydroxyl + G *Apatit* apatite (q.v.)] Apatite containing hydroxyl. O, R, W [4]

hydrozincite, *n.* (1854) *Mineral.* [G *Hydrozinkit* < *hydro-* (< the comb. form of Gk *hýdōr* water) + G *Zinkit* < *Zink* zinc + *-it* -ite] A basic zinc carbonate, also called *zinc bloom.* O, R, W [3]

hylean, *a. Geogr.* [Prob. < G *Hylaa,* region of tropical rain forest in the Amazon Basin in South America, so named by Alexander von Humboldt (1769–1859), German naturalist < Gk *Hyláia,* forested region on what is now the Dnieper River in the Ukraine < Gk *hýlē* forest + E *-an*] Covered with forest: wooded. W [3]

hymn of hate, *n.* (1914) *Lit.* [Transl. of G *Haßgesang* (1914), part of the title of an anti-British song by the German poet Ernst Lissauer (1882–1937) < *Haß* hate + *Gesang* song, hymn] This song; transf. sense to other negative writings. O [3]

hyoscyamine, *n.* (1858) *Chem.* [G *Hyoscyamin* (now *Hyoszyamin*) < NL *Hyoscyamus* the genus that produces it < Gk *hyoskýamos* fodder bean + G *-in* -ine] An extremely poisonous, crystalline alkaloid that is used as a sedative and to relieve spasms. O, R, W [4]

hypabyssal, *a.* (1895) *Geol.* [Ad. of G *hypabyssisch* (1891) < Gk *hyp-* < *hypó* under + NL *byssus* flax, linen + G *-isch* -al] Of or concerning a fine-grained igneous rock formed from magma that has solidified into other rocks; intermediate between plutonic and volcanic. O, R, W [4]

hyperchamaerrhine, *a. Anthrop.* [G *hyperchamärrhin* < *hyper-* + *Chamärrhin* < Gk *hypér* above, very + *chamaí* low + *rhís* (gen. *rhinós*) nose + G *-in* -ine] Having a very short, broad nose with a nasal index of at least 58. W [3]

hyperchromatosis, -ses *pl.* (1898) *Biol.* [G *Hyperchromatose* (1898) < *hyper-* + *Chromatose* < Gk *hypér* above, excess + *chrōma* (gen. *chrōmatos*) color + G *-ose* (< Gk *-osis* suffix of action) -osis] Hyperchromatism, the development of excess chromatin or of excessive nuclear staining in a cell or nucleus (this is different from the earlier "hyperchromia" meaning). O, W [3]

hyperergy, *n. Med.* [Prob. < G *Hyperergie* < *hyper-* (< Gk) above, very + G *Allergie* allergy (q.v.)] The state of having a degree of sensitivity toward an allergen greater than that typical of one's age group and community. —**hyperergic.** W [3]

hypereuryprosopic, *a. Anthrop.* [G *hypereuryprosopisch* < *hyper-* + *euryprosopisch* < Gk *hypér* above, excessive + *eurýs* broad + *prósōpon* face + G *-isch* -ic] Having a short, broad face with a facial index below 80. W [3]

hypereuryprosopy, *n. Anthrop.* [Prob. < G *Hypereuryprosopie* < *hyper-* + *Euryprosopie* < Gk *hypér* overly + *eurýs* broad + *prósōpon* face + G *-ie* (< Gk *-ia*) -y] The state of being hypereuryprosopic (q.v.). W [3]

hyperfine structure, *n.* (1927) *Physics* [Transl. of G *Hyperfeinstruktur* < *hyper-* + *fein* fine + *Struktur* structure < Gk *hypér* super + OFr *fine* (< L *fīnis*) + L *strūctūra*] The presence of multiplets of closely spaced lines in a spectrum that are closer together than those in a fine structure. O, R [3]

hypergol, *n.* (1947) *Aeron.* [G < *hyp(er)-* + *-erg-* + *Öl* < Gk *hypér* super + *érgon* work + L *oleum* oil] A self-igniting rocket propellant. O, R, W [3]

hypergolic, *a.* (1947) *Aeron.* [G *hypergolisch* < *hypergol* (q.v.) + *-isch* -ic] Of a hypergol. —**hypergolically.** O, R, W [4]

hyperleptoprosopic, *a. Anthrop.* [G *hyperleptoprosopisch* < *hyper-* + *leptoprosopisch* < Gk *hypér* above, excessive + *leptós* small + *prósōpon* face + G *-isch* -ic] Having a long, narrow face with a facial index of at least 93 on the living and at least 95 on the skull. W [3]

hyperleptoprosopy, *n. Anthrop.* [G *Hyperleptoprosopie* < *hyper-* + *Leptoprosopie* < Gk *hypér* overly + *leptós* small + *prósōpon* face + G *-ie* (< Gk *-ia*) -y] The state of being hyperleptoprosopic (q.v.). W [3]

hypersthenite, *n.* (1841) *Geol.* [G *Hypersthenit* < *Hyper-*

sthen hypersthen (< Fr *hypersthène* < Gk *hypér* super + *sthénos* strength) + G *-it* -ite] An aggregate of hypersthene and labradorite; hypersthenic pyroxenite. O, W [3]

hypertely, *n.* (1895) *Zool.* [G *Hypertelie* (1873) < *hyper-* + *-telie* < Gk *hypér* super + *télos* completion + G *-ie* (< Gk *-ia*) -y] The development of size, behavior patterns, imitative coloration, etc. to an extreme beyond the ground of mere utility; fig. sense, as in militarism. —**hypertelic,** *a.* (1936). O, W [4]

hypnoid(al), *a.* (1898) *Psych.* [G *hypnoid* (1893) < *hypn-* + *-oid* < Gk *hýpnos* sleep + *-oid* < *-oeidēs* similar] Of a state of consciousness where there is heightened suggestibility or dissociation, as in hysteria or in hypnosis induced by nonhypnotic means. O, R, W [4]

hypomania, *n.* (1882) *Psych.* [NL *hypomania* (< G *Hypomanie*) or directly < G (1881) < *hypo-* + *-manie* < Gk *hypó* below, under + LL *mania* madness] A mild mania. —**hypomaniac** (1910); **hypomanic,** *a.* and *n.* (1932, 1932). O, R, W [4]

hyponasty, *n.* (1875) *Bot.* [ISV or G *Hyponastie* < *hypo-* + *-nastie* < Gk *hypó* below + *nastós* close] A nastic movement where a plant organ is bent inward and upward. —**hyponastic** (1875), **hyponastically.** O, R, W [4]

hypothetical imperative, *n. Philos.* [Transl. of G *hypothetischer Imperativ* < L *hypotheticus,* Gk *hypothetikós* involving a logical hypothesis + G *Imperativ* < L *imperātīvus* commanding] The Kantian imperative of conduct that derives from expedience or practical necessity rather than from moral law. R, W [3]

hypotrichosis, *n.* (1896) *Path.* [G *Hypotrichose* (1892) < *hypo-* + *Trichose* < Gk *hypó* under + *tríchōsis* growth of hair] Congenital deficiency of hair. —**hypotrichotic** (1937). O, W [3]

hypsicranial/-cranic, *a. Anthrop.* [G *hypsikran* < *hyps-* < Gk *hýpsi* high + *kraníon* cranium + E *-ial* or *-ic*] Having a high skull with a length-height index of at least 75. —**hypsicrany,** *n.* W [3]

hypsochromic, *a.* (1892) *Chem.* [G *hypsochrom* (1892) < *hypso-* + *-chrom* < Gk *hypsós* height + *chrôma* color + E *-ic*)] Causing or characterized by a visible lightening of color when an atom or group is introduced into a compound. O, W [3]

hypsoisotherm, *n. Meteor.* [Transl. of G *Höhenisotherme* < *höhen-* high + *Isotherme* < Gk *hypso-*, the comb. form of *hýpsi* high + Fr *isotherme* < Gk *ísos* like + *thermós* hot] An isotherm drawn on a vertical section of the atmosphere and perhaps also of the ground to mark the distribution of temperature in the vertical. W [3]

hypsophyl, *n. Bot.* [NL *hypsophyllum* as transl. of G *Hochblatt* < *hoch* high + *Blatt* leaf] A floral leaf beneath the sporophylls: scale leaf or bract. —**hypsophyllar(y), hypsophyllous.** W [3]

hysterocrystalline, *n. Geol.* [G *Hysterokrystallin* < *hystero-* + *Krystallin* < Gk *hystero-*, the comb. form of *hýsteros* latter, late + L *crystallinus,* Gk *krystállinos* of ice] A condition of secondary crystallization in igneous rock. W [3]

Hz, *n.* (1958) *Physics* [Short. of G *Hertz* (q.v.), the name of the German physicist] Hertz. • ~ and similar shortenings often have a very high frequency in English, sometimes more than the full form from which they are formed. O, R, W [4]

I

ianthinite, *n.* (1927) *Mineral.* [G *Ianthinit* < L *ianthinus* < Gk *iánthinos* of violet color + G *-it* -ite] A hydrous uranium dioxide. O, W [3]

ice wine, *n.* (1982) *Beverages* Var. **ice-wine** [Trans. of G *Eiswein* < *Eis* + *Wein* wine] Very sweet wine made from overripe grapes that were frozen before harvesting. BDC [2]

ice wool, *see* eis wool

ich dien (1529) *Politics* [G < *ich* I + *dien* serve < *dienen* to serve] Motto of the Prince of Wales; the prince himself. O, R [3]

ich-laut, *n.* *Ling.* Var. **Ich laut** [G < *ich* I (actually having reference to the velar voiceless spirant spelled in German as *ch*) + *Laut* sound] This sound. W [3]

icosa- (in chem. usually spelled *eicos-*), *comb. form* (1889) *Chem.* Var. **icose-** (1895), **icosi-** [First used in G in *Eikosylen* (1879) < Gk *eíkosi* twenty] Indicating the presence in a molecule of twenty atoms of an element, usu. carbon), as in *eicosane* (1889) (this is different from the general, Greek-derived "twenty" meaning). O [3]

icosenic acid, *see* eicosenic acid

id¹, *n.* (1893) *Biol.* [G (1891), a short. by the German biologist August Weismann (1834–1914) of *Idioplasma* idioplasm (q.v.)] A hypothetical structural unit of living matter. O, W [3]

id², *n.* (1924) *Psych.* [Transl. into L of Freud's G *Es* it (1917)] The primitive, undifferentiated source of the organism's energy that reacts blindly on a pleasure–pain level and is an ultimate source of higher psychic components (see *ego*). —**id,** *a.* (1952). O, R, W [4]

idant, *n.* (1893) *Biol.* [Weismann's G (1892) (see *id¹*) < L *id* it + present part. suffix *-ant* being in a specified condition] A hypothetical structural unit arising from a series or aggregation of ids. O, W [3]

idea, *see* noumenon

ideal, *n.* (1898) *Math.* [G (1871) < the adj. use of *ideal* in *ideale Zahl* ideal number (q.v.) by the German mathematician Ernst Eduard Kummer (1810–93) < *Ideal* < Fr, ult. < Gk *idéa*] A subring of multiples of *n* in the ring of integers, with deep relevance for algebraic geometry (this is different from the various older "nonmathematical" meanings). O, R, W [3]

idealism, *n.* (1796) *Philos.* [G *Idealismus* (1786) < Fr *idéalisme* (or directly < Fr) < LL *idealis* < L *idea* (< Gk) most suitable form + G (< L) *-ismus* -ism or Fr *-isme*] A theory stating that mind or the spiritual and ideal are fundamentally important in reality; the practice of idealizing or living according to such ideals; artistic or literary theory or practice of such ideals. O, R, W [4]

ideal number, *n.* (1860) *Math.* [Transl. of G *ideale Zahl* (1846) < *ideal* (< Fr or LL) ideal + *Zahl* number] Ideal (q.v.). O [3]

ideal realism, *n. Philos.* [G *Idealrealismus* < *ideal* + *Realismus* (see *idealism*) + ML *realis* essential] Any of several

theories that combine the principles of idealism and realism, also called *real idealism.* —**ideal-real,** *n.* (1886). O, W [3]

ideal type, *n.* (1928) *Sociol.* [Ad. of G *Idealtypus* (1922) < *ideal* (see *idealism*) + *Typus* < Gk *týpos* model] A construct abstracted from the salient features or elements of social phenomena to form a unified conceptual scheme of hypothetical validity. —**ideal typical** (1936)/**typology** (1964). O, R, W [3]

Identitätsphilosophie, *n.* (1866) *Philos.* [G (1775) < *Identität* + *Philosophie* < LL *identitās* (gen. *identitātis*) identity + Gk *philosophía* love of learning] A system proposed by various German philosophers that assumes the fundamental identity of spirit and nature. O [2]

idiobiology, *n. Biol.* [G *Idiobiologie* < *idio-* (< Gk *ídios* one's own, personal, distinct) + G *Biologie* biology (q.v.)] A branch of biology concerned with the consideration of organisms as individuals. W [3]

idioblast¹, *n.* (1893) *Biol.* [G (1893) < *idio-* + *-blast* < Gk *ídios* peculiar, individual + *blastós* bud, germ] An isolated plant cell differing considerably in contents, form, or wall structure from adjoining cells. —**idioblastic.** O, R, W [4]

idioblast², *n.* (1920) *Geol.* [G (1904) (see *idioblast¹*)] A crystal within a metamorphic rock that has developed its own characteristic, later faces. —**idioblastic** (1908). O, W [3]

idiophone, *n.* (1940) *Music* [G *Idiophon* (1913) < *idio-* + *-phon* < Gk *ídios* one's own, individual + *phōnḗ* sound] A musical instrument whose sound emanates from the vibration of its elastic material such as metal or wood, as in Upper Congo drumming. —**idiophonic.** O, W [3]

idioplasm, *n.* (1889) *Biol.* [G *Idioplasma* (1884) < *idio-* (< Gk *ídios* self, individual) + G *Plasma* plasma (q.v.)] The portion of the cell protoplasm that is presumed to transmit hereditary properties, commonly equated with chromatin (q.v.). —**idioplasmatic** (1890), **idioplasmic.** O, R, W [3]

idiosome, *n.* (1893) *Biol.* [G *Idiozom* (see *idiozome*)] Idioblast¹ (q.v.); acrosome (q.v.); idiozome. O, W [3]

idioticon, *n.* (1842) *Ling.* [G (1743) < Gk *idiōtikón,* neuter sing. of *idiōtikós* idiotic] A dialect or regional dictionary. O [2]

idiozome, *n.* (1899) *Biol.* Var. **idiosome** (q.v.) [G *Idiozom* (1896) < *idio-* < Gk *ídios* self, individual + *zōma* band, belt] Acrosome (q.v.). O, W [3]

idryl, *n.* (1845) *Chem.* [G *Idyril* (1844) < *Idria* Idrija, the name of a town in Slovenia + G *-yl* -yl] A mixture of fluoranthene (q.v.) and other hydrocarbons; fluoranthene. O [3]

ignimbrite, *n.* (1932) *Geol.* [G *Ignimbrit* < L *īgnis* fire + *imber* rain + G *-it* -ite] A hard rock formed by solidification of mainly fine deposits of volcanic ash. O, R [4]

ihleite, *n.* (1876) *Mineral.* [G *Ihleit* (1876) < the name of

M. *Ihle*, a 19th-cent. Bohemian superintendent of mines at Mugrau + G *-it* -ite] Copiapite (q.v.). O, W [3]

ijolite, *n.* (1897) *Geol.* [G *Ijolith* (1891) < *Ijo*, the name of a Finnish coastal village and district + G *-lith* -lite] A plutonic igneous rock consisting essentially of augite (q.v.) and nepheline. —**ijolitic** (1938). O, W [3]

-il, *n. suffix* [G *-il* and Fr *-ile* < L adj. suffix *-ilis*] A substance related to something that is specified, as in *benzil*. W [3]

ilag, *n.* (1941) *Mil.* [G, a short. of *Internierungslager* < *Internierung* internment + *Lager* camp] A prison camp for civilians interned in Nazi Germany. O [3]

Illuminati, *pl.* (1797) *Theol.* [Ad. of G *Illuminaten* (1776), pl. < L pl. < *illuminatus* enlightened, to name a celebrated 18th-cent. Bavarian secret society holding deistic and republican principles] This society; other such freethinkers like the French Encyclopedists (this is different from the old "Spanish heretical sect" meaning). • ~ is transl. as **enlighteners** (1800). O, W [4]

illumination, *n.* (1881) *Philos.* [G (see *Illuminati*)] Enlightenment as perceived by the Illuminati (this is different from the various earlier meanings). O [2]

illustriousness, *n.* (1929) *Politics* [Transl. of G *Durchlaucht* (transl. < L *perillūstris*) < G *durch* through, i.e., thoroughly + *-laucht* (related to *leuchten* to shine) illustrious + E *-ness*] (Used with a possessive a. and often cap. as) an honorific title for German princes (this is different from the old "illustrious quality" meaning). O [3]

ilmenite, *n.* (1827) *Mineral.* [G *Ilmenit* (1827) < *Ilmen*, the name of a mountain chain in the Urals + G *-it* -ite] An oxide of iron and titanium: titanic iron ore. O, R, W [4]

ilmenorutile, *n.* (1861) *Mineral.* [G *Ilmenorutil* (1854–7) < *Ilmen*, a mountain chain in the Urals + G *Rutil* rutile (q.v.)] A black variety of rutile containing niobium. O, W [4]

ilsemannite, *n.* (1871) *Mineral.* [G *Ilsemannit* (1871) < the name of Johannes Guilielmus *Ilsemann* (1727–1822), German chemist + *-it* -ite] A massive hydrous oxide or poss. molybdenum sulfate. O, W [3]

ilvaite, *n.* (1816) *Mineral.* [G *Ilvait* (1811) < It *Ilva* Elba + G *-it* -ite] A black, crystalline silicate of iron and calcium; also called *lievrite* (q.v.). O, W [3]

imago, -es *pl.* (1916) *Psych.* [Jung's G (1916) < NL < L image] In psychoanalysis, a subconscious, idealized image of any person, including oneself (this is different from the old "adult insect" meaning). O, R, W [4]

imhofite, *n.* (1965) *Mineral.* [G *Imhofit* (1965) < the name of Josef *Imhof*, 20th-cent. Swiss collector of minerals + G *-it* -ite] A sulfide of thallium and arsenic. O [3]

imidazole, *n.* (1892) *Chem.* [G *Imidazol* (1887) < *Imid* imide, purposely altered from *Amid* amide + *-azo-* (< Fr *azote* inert, unable to support life) + G *-ol* (< *Alkohol* alcohol, ult. < Ar) -ole] A crystalline, heterocyclic base consisting of a five-membered ring: glyoxaline; any of a large class of imidazole derivatives. —**imidazoline, imidazolyl.** O, R, W [4]

imine, *n.* (1883) *Chem.* [G *Imin* (1883), a deliberate altering of *Amin* amine] Any of a class of compounds obtained from ammonia by replacing two hydrogen atoms with a bivalent hydrocarbon radical or other nonacid organic rad-

ical. —**imin(o)-** and *a.* (1903, 1903); **imino ether** (1897). O, R, W [4]

immanence philosophy, *n.* (1901) *Philos.* [Transl. of G *Immanenzphilosophie* < *Immanenz* immanence + *Philosophie* philosophy < LL *immanentem* present part. of *immanere* to dwell in, remain + L *philosophia*] The theory developed in late 19th-century Germany that reality exists only through being immanent in conscious minds. O [3]

immiserization, *n.* (1942) *Sociol.* Var. **immiseration** (1942) [Transl. of G *Verelendung* < *verelenden* to make or become wretched, miserable, impoverished + *-ung*] The act of making or situation of becoming steadily more miserable; impoverishment. —**immiserize** (1971), **immiserification.** O, W [3]

immoralism, *n.* (1907) *Philos.* [Nietzsche's G *Immoralismus* < *immoral* (< Fr or E) + G *-ismus* (< L) -ism] An ethical perspective like Nietzsche's that would replace morality with a new scale of values: a philosophical system that rejects moral law. O, R, W [3]

In, *see* indium

increment borer, *n.* (1889) *Forestry* [Transl. of G *Zuwachsbohrer* (1868) < *Zuwachs* increment + *Bohrer* drill] Accretion borer, a hollow auger used to cut a core from a tree in order to count the annual rings and estimate the accretion. —**increment boring** (1942). O, W [3]

incunabula, *pl.* (1861) *Printing* [G < L, pl. of *incūnabūlum* swaddling clothes, origin] The orig. German name for books printed before 1500; a work of art or human activity or industry of an early period (this is different from the earlier "earliest stages" meaning). —**incunabular,** *a.* (1889). O, R, W [4]

indamine, *n.* (1888) *Chem.* [G *Indamin* < L *Indicum* indigo + G *Amin* amine < NL *ammonium*] A blue dye or any of a class of organic, amino-phenyl derivatives of quinone diimine. O, R, W [4]

indazole, *n.* (1884) *Chem.* [G *Indazol* (1883) < *Indol* indole (q.v.) + an infixed *-azo-* < Fr *azote* inert, unable to support life] A crystalline, bicyclic compound; benzopyrazole ring; a derivative of indazole. O, W [3]

indigoid, *a.* (1908) *Chem.* [G (1908) < *indigo* (< Sp < L *Indicum* < Gk *Indikón* that which derives from India) + G *-oid* < Gk *-oeidēs* similar] Resembling or related to indigo, esp. in chemical structure and dyeing capacities. —**indigoid,** *n.* (1939); **indigoid (vat) dye** (1908). O, R, W [4]

indium, *n.* (1864) *Chem.* [G (1863), a rare metal of the boron group discovered by the German chemists Ferdinand Reich (1799–1882) and Theodor Richter (1824–98) from zinc ore samples at Freiburg, Germany < *indigo* (see *indigoid*) + *-ium* < NL, as in *sodium*] This metallic element, particularly used in plating airplane bearings. — **indium,** *a.* (1897). • ~ is symbolized as **In.** O, R, W [4]

individualism, *n.* (1897) *Bot.* [G *Individualismus* (1895) < Fr *individualisme* or NL *individualis* individual] A symbiotic association by two nutritionally interdependent organisms to produce a wholly different individual, as in lichens (this is different from the various "nonbotanical" meanings). O, W [3]

Indo-Germanic, *a.* (1826) *Ling.* Old var. **Indo-German** (1826) [G *indogermanisch* (1823) < *Indo-* + *Germanisch* < Gk *Indos* Indic + L *Germānus* (the) German, prob. <

Celtic] Of Indo-European, an unrecorded, prehistoric language (or its speakers) from whom the numerous Indo-European languages derived. —**Indo-Germanic**, *n.* (1877); **Indo-Germanist** (1889). O, R, W [4]

indole, *n.* (1869) *Chem.* Var. **indol** [G *Indol*, a blend of *Indigo* + *-ol* < *Alkohol*, ult. < Ar] A crystalline compound found in civet, jasmine oil, and coal tar that is used in floral perfumes; a derivative of indole. —**indoleacetic acid** (1886), **indolebutyric acid**, **indole group**. O, R, W [4]

inesite, *n.* (1889) *Mineral.* [G *Inesit* (1887) < Gk *ínes* tendon + G *-it* -ite] A hydrous silicate of manganese and calcium. O, W [3]

infusoriform, *a.* (1877) *Zool.* [Transl. of G *infusorienartig* (1849), first used in this sense by the German physiologist Rudolf Albert von Kölliker (1817–1905) < *Infusorium*, pl. *Infusorien* + *-artig* like] Designating or relating to the minute, ciliated, infective larva of the Dicyemida. —**infusoriform**, *n.;* **infusoriform larva** (1964). O, W [3]

inlaut, **-e/-s** *pl.* (1892) *Ling.* [G < *in* in, within + *Laut* sound] A medial sound or position in a syllable or word. O, R, W [3]

inner mission, *n. Theol.* [G *innere Mission* < *inner* inner + *Mission* mission < L *missiō* dispatch] A movement started in the 19th century by the Evangelical Church of Germany that partly used sisterhoods and lay brotherhoods to serve neglected, unfortunate persons through Christian lodging houses, orphanages, etc. R, W [3]

inner product, *n.* (c.1909 W9) *Math.* [G *inneres Produkt* (1844) < *inner* inner + *Produkt* product < L *prōductum* result, so named because an inner product of two vectors is zero unless one has a component within the other] Scalar product, a product of two vectors: dot product. O, R, W [3]

inner quantum number, *n.* (1923) *Physics* [Transl. of G *innere Quantenzahl* (1920) < *inner* inner + *Quantum* (< L) quantum + G *Zahl* number] A vector quantum number expressing an atom's total angular momentum excluding nuclear spin. O, W [3]

Innigkeit, *n.* (1964) *Music* [G a deep-felt sincerity] Sincerity and warmth (expressed in music). B [3]

inosinic acid, *n.* (1855) *Chem.* [Transl. of G *Inosinsäure* < *Inosin* (< Gk *ís*, gen. *inós* tissue fiber) + G *Säure* acid] An amorphous nucleotide. —**inosinate**, *n.* O, W [3]

inotropic, *a.* (1903) *Physiol.* [G *Inotrop* (1896) < *ino-* + *-trop* < comb. form of Gk *ís*, gen. *inós* fiber, muscle + *tropé* turning + E *-ic*] Influencing the contractility of muscle. —**inotropism**. O, R, W [4]

inscenation, *n.* (1897) *Theater* [Transl. of G *Inszenierung* < L *in* in + *scēna* stage + G *-ierung* -tion] *Mise en scène*, theatrical representation. O, W [3]

inselberg, **-s/-e** *pl.* (1907) *Geol.* [G (1898) < *Insel* island + *Berg* mountain] An isolated mountain, partly buried by the debris from its slopes and rising conspicuously from the surrounding plain (as in tropical Africa). O, R, W [3]

intellectualism, *n.* (1829) *Philos.* [G *Intellectualismus* (1803) (now *Intellektualismus*) < *intellectual* + *-ismus* -ism < L *intellēctuālis* intellectual + *-ismus*] The doctrine that knowledge derives from pure reason, which is considered to be the ultimate principle of reality. O, R, W [3]

intelligence quotient, *n.* (1916 W9) *Ed.* [G *Intelligenzquotient* (1912) < *Intelligenz* intelligence + *Quotient* quotient

< MFr *intelligence* < L *intelligentia* + *quotiēns*] A number determined by various intelligence tests and once heavily depended on to express a person's relative degree of intelligence. • ~ is abbr. as **IQ** (c.1960). O, R, W [4]

intendant, *n.* (1903) *Theater* [G (1775) < Fr *intendant* supervisor, administrator < L *intendēns, intendēnt-*] The administrator of a theater or opera house (this is different from the old French meanings of "public official, title, etc."). O [3]

intention movement, *n.* (1950) *Psych.* [Transl. of G *Intentionsbewegung* (1910) < *Intention* (< L *intentiō* intention < *intendēre* to intend) + G *Bewegung* movement < *bewegen* to move, motivate] An animal's movement or action that performs no function except to indicate that further movement may follow. O, R [3]

interglacial, *a.* (1867) *Geol.* [G *interglazial* (1865) < *inter-* + *glazial* < L *inter* between + *glaciēs* ice + G *-al* -al] Occurring or formed between glacial periods. —**interglacial**, *n.* (1922); **-ism** (1881); **-ist** (1893). O, R, W [4]

interimistic, *a.* (1859) [Poss. < G *interimistisch* < *Interim* (< L) + G *-istisch* -istic] Of, relating to, or done for the interim: provisional (this is different from the later "church history" meaning). O, W [3]

Interimsethik, *n.* (1910) *Theol.* Var. **interim ethic(s)** (1947) [G (1901) < *Interim* + *Ethik* < L *interim* in between + Gk *ethikós* ethical] Moral principles presented by Jesus, considered as the guide for people expecting the imminent end of the world; a code of conduct for use in a particular, temporary situation. O [2]

intermedin, *n.* (1932) *Physiol.* Var. **intermedine** (1948) [G (1932) < NL *pars intermedia* the middle part + G *-in* -in] A melanocyte-stimulating hormone. O, W [3]

interphase, *n.* (1913) *Biol.* [G (1912) < *inter-* (< L) between + G *Phase* < Fr < Gk *phásis* appearance, phenomenon] Interkinesis, the period between any two nucleic mitoses. —**interphase**, *a.* (1961); **interphasic**, *a.* O, R, W [4]

intersertal, *a.* (1893) *Geol.* [G (1870) < L *intersertus* put in + G *-al* -al] Of an igneous rock with an ophitic texture where the interstitial material is glass or a substance other than augite. O, W [3]

intersex, *n.* (1910 W9) *Biol.* [G *Intersex* (1915) < *inter-* + *Sex* < L *inter* between + *sexus* sex] A form or individual having the characteristics of both sexes: an intergrade between the sexes. —**intersexed** (1939). O, R, W [4]

intersexuality, *n.* (1916) *Biol.* Var. **intersexualism** [G *Intersexualität* (1915) < *intersexual* + *-tät* (ult. < L *inter* between + ML *sexualis* sexual + *-tas*, gen. *-tatis*) -ty)] The state or quality of being intersexual; intersexual character. O, R, W [4]

interstadial, *n.* (1914) and *a.* (1922) *Geol.* [G (1894) < Fr *interstadiaire* < L *inter* between + *stadium* < Gk *stadión* stage, state] (Of or pertaining to) a minor, temporary time of ice retreat during a glacial period. O, R, W [4]

intine, *n.* (1835) *Bot.* [Prob. < G < L *intus* within + G *-ine* -ine] The inner of two layers forming the wall of a spore like a pollen grain: endosporium. O, R, W [4]

intratelluric, *a.* (1889) *Geol.* [G *intratellurisch* (1880) < *intra-* + *tellurisch* < L *intra* on the inside, within + *tellūs* (gen. *tellūris*) earth + G *-isch* -ic] Occurring, situated, or formed deep inside the earth; of the period or stage of igneous-rock crystallization prior to eruption. O, R, W [3]

introjection[1], *n.* (1899) *Philos.* [G *Introjektion* < *intro-* + *-jektion* < L *intro* to the inside + *-iectio* < *iacere* to throw] A theory whereby objects perceived have mental counterparts as sense perceptions (this is different from the earlier meaning of "action of throwing in"). —**introjectionist** (1903), **introjectionism** (1912). O, W [3]

introjection[2], *n.* (1916) *Psych.* [G *Introjektion* (1909) (see *introjection*[1])] The process or act of introjecting body parts, ideas, or attitudes. O, R, W [4]

introversion, *n.* (1912) *Psych.* [Jung's G < NL *introversionem,* dative n. of action] The tendency, situation, or act of directing oneself inward, in mentally withdrawing from the world and external life (this is different from the old meaning of "act of turning inward, as to God"). O, R, W [4]

intuition, *see* Anschauung

inulin, *n.* (1813 *W9*) *Bot.* [Prob. < G < NL *Inula* genus of plants + G *-in* -in] A white, tasteless, indigestible polysaccharide found in various plants and used as a source of levulose. R, W [4]

inversion, *see* Walden inversion

invert soap, *n.* (1941) *Chem.* [Transl. of G *Invertseife* (1940) < *invert* (< L *invertere* to turn around or inside out) + G *Seife* soap] Cationic detergent, one of a class of synthetic detergents. O, R, W [3]

iodine number/value, *n.* (1885) *Chem.* [Transl. of G *Jodzahl* (1884) < *Jod* iodine (< Fr *iode* < Gk *iṓdēs* violet) + G *Zahl* number] The proportion of unsaturation present in an oil or fat as measured by the number of iodine or halogen grams that can be absorbed by 100 grams of the given compound. O, W [3]

iodipin, *n.* (1899) *Pharm.* [G *Jodipin* < *Jod* (< Fr *iode* < Gk *iṓdēs* violet) + L *adip-* < *adeps* fat + G *-in* -in] Iodized sesame oil. O [3]

iodism, *n.* (1832) *Path.* [Prob. transl. of G *Jodkrankheit* < *Jod* (< Fr *iode* < Gk *iṓdēs* violet) + G *Krankheit* disease + E *-ism*] An abnormal, local, systemic condition caused by excessive or prolonged use of or sensitivity to iodine. O, R, W [3]

iodobromite, *n.* (1890) *Mineral.* [G *Iodobromit* (1878) (now *Jodobromit*) < *iodo-* (< *Iod* iodine < Fr *iode* < Gk *iṓdēs* of violet color) + G *Bromit* bromine < *brom-* (< Gk *brómos* stench) + G *-it* -ite] A chloride, iodide, and bromide of silver: iodian bromargyrite. O, W [3]

iolite, *n.* (1758) *Mineral.* [G *Iolith* < *io-* + *-lith* < Gk *íon* violet + *líthos* stone] Cordierite, an orthorhombic silicate. O, R, W [3]

ionene, *n.* (1894) *Chem.* [G *Ionen* (1893) < *Ion* (< Gk) violet + G *-en* -ene] A hydrocarbon obtained by eliminating a water molecule from alpha- or beta-ionone. O [3]

ionogenic, *a.* (1912) *Chem.* [G *ionogen* (1911) < *iono-* *-gen* < Gk *íon* violet + *-genēs* producing, generating + E *-ic*] Capable of being ionized. O, R, W [3]

Ionone, *n.* (1894) *Chem.* [G *Ionon* (1893) (now *Jonon*) < *Ion* violet + *-on* < Gk *íon* + *ṓn* being] A trademark: either of two liquid ketones (alpha-ionone or beta-ionone) that are esp. used in perfumes for their strong odor of violets. O, R, W [3]

ionotropy, *n.* (1949) *Chem.* [G *Ionotropie* (1947) < *iono-* + *-tropie* < Gk *íon* violet + *-tropia* turning < *trépein* to turn] A phenomenon in which there is ordering of particles in a gel resulting from the addition of an electrolyte to a colloidal suspension. —**ionotropic.** O [3]

IQ, *see* intelligence quotient

irene, *n.* (1894) *Chem.* [G *Iren* (1893), a blend of *Ir-on* irone (q.v.) + *-en* -ene] A colorless liquid hydrocarbon obtained from naphthalene. O, W [3]

iretol, *n.* (1894) *Chem.* [G (1893), a blend of *Ir-igenin* + *-ol* < Gk *íris* (gen. *íridos*) iris + L *oleum* oil] A crystalline compound obtained from irigenin by alkaline hydrolysis. O [3]

iridin[1], *n.* (1894) *Chem.* Var. **iridine** (1966) [G (1893) < *irid-* (< Gk *íris,* gen. *íridos* iris) + G *-in* -in] A crystalline glucoside found esp. in the orrisroot (this is different from the earlier meaning of "oleoresin used as a purgative"). O, W [3]

iridin[2], *n.* (1953) *Chem.* Var. **iridine** (1969) [G (1951) (see *iridin*[1])] A protamine or mixture of protamines obtained from rainbow trout's spermatozoa. O [3]

iridosmine, *n.* (1827) *Mineral.* Var. **iridosmium** [G *Iridosmin* (1827) < *irid-* + NL *osmium* < Gk *íris* (gen. *íridos*) iris + *osmē* fragrance, smell + G *-in* -ine] A native iridium osmium alloy used for tipping pen points: osmiridium. O, R, W [4]

irigenin, *n.* (1894) *Chem.* [G (1893) < *Iridin* + *Genin* < Gk *íris* iris + *gennân* to generate, produce + G *-in* -in] A crystalline flavonoid obtained by acid hydrolysis of iridin. O [3]

irisin, *n.* (1887) *Chem.* [G (1886) < *Iris* (< Gk) iris + G *-in* -in] A polysaccharide found esp. in the rhizome of the yellow iris. O, W [3]

iritis, *n.* (1818) *Optics* [G (1801) < *Iris* (< Gk) iris + G suffix *-itis* (< Gk) qualifying disease] Inflammation of the iris of the eye. —**iritic** (1855). O, R, W [4]

Iron Cross, *n.* (1871) *Mil.* [Transl. of G *(das) Eiserne Kreuz* (1813) < *eisern* made of iron + *Kreuz* cross] A German and Austrian medal awarded for distinguished services in wars since the early 19th century. O, R [4]

Iron Curtain/iron curtain, *n.* (1945) *Politics* [Transl. of G *(ein) eiserner Vorhang* iron fireproof theatrical curtain] In the contemporary sense, a barrier of secrecy, censorship, and even military positions regarded as isolating the Soviet Union and countries in its sphere since World War Two until 1990 (*iron curtain* was used to mean "an impregnable barrier" in the theater by 1794, "any impenetrable barrier" by 1819, and "an isolating political barrier" by 1920). • ~ is a German reborrowing. O, R, W [4]

irone, *n.* (1894) *Chem.* [G *Iron* (1893) < *Iris* (< Gk) iris + *-ōn* (< Gk)] A liquid of isomeric, unsaturated ketones, used in perfumes. O, R, W [3]

iron glance, *n.* (1805–17) *Geol.* [Transl. of G *Eisenglanz* < *Eisen* iron + *Glanz* glance] Hematite, a ferric oxide. O, W [3]

iron law of wages, *n.* (1896) *Econ.* Var. **brazen law of wages** (1896) [Transl. of G *ehernes Lohngesetz* < *ehern* brazen, unerring + *Lohn* wage(s) + *Gesetz* law] The doctrine that wages tend to fall to a minimum level necessary for a worker's subsistence. O, R, W [3]

iron monticellite, *n.* (1937) *Mineral.* Var. **iron-monticellite**

(1937) [Transl. of G *Eisenmonticellit* (1914) (now also *Eisenmontizellit*) < the name of Teodoro *Monticelli* (1759–1845), Italian mineralogist + G *-it* -ite] A silicate of calcium and iron, isomorphous with monticellite. O, W [3]

isatoic acid, *n.* (1885) *Chem.* [Transl. of G *Isatosäure* (1884) < the comb. form of L *isatis,* Gk *isátis* wood, used in chemistry to form the name of *isatin* and of other bodies related to it and to indigo + G *Säure* acid] N-carboxyanthranilic acid. O [3]

isatoic anhydride, *n.* (1899) *Chem.* [Short. of G *Isatosäureanhydrid* (1889) < *Isatosäure* isatoic acid (q.v.) + *Anhydrid,* ad. < Gk *ánhydros* waterless + G *-id* -ide] A high-melting anhydride of isatoic acid obtained by oxidating isatin. O, W [3]

isepiptesis, -ses *pl.* (1875) *Ornith.* Var. **isopiptesis** (1962) [G *Isepiptese* (1855) < Gk *ísos* equal, alike + *epipt̄esis* (downward) glide, flying toward] A line connecting points that migrating birds of a given species reach on the same date. —**isepiptesial** (1875). O, W [3]

iserine, *n.* (1805) *Mineral.* Var. **iserite** (1868) [G *Iserin* (1797) < a short. of *Iserweise,* Bohemia + *-in* -in] A variety of ilmenite (q.v.). O [3]

island universe, *n.* (1867) *Astronomy* [Transl. of G *Weltinsel* (1845) < *Welt* world + *Insel* island, coined by Alexander von Humboldt (1769–1859), German natural scientist, as a poetical reference to Earth within the stellar system] An external galaxy other than the Milky Way system. O, R, W [4]

-ismus, *suffix* (1912) *Ling.* [G or L -ism] (Used like *-ism* in word formation to indicate) a typical condition or conduct, a noun formed from a proper name, or a system or principle, as in *snobismus* (and often pejoratively). O [3]

isoagglutination, *n.* (1907 *W9*) *Immunology* [G (1902) < *iso-* + *Agglutination* < Gk *ísos* equal, alike + L *agglūtinātio* adhesion] Agglutination of one individual's cells by the serum of another individual of the same species. O, R, W [4]

isobestic, *see* isosbestic

isoborneol, *n.* (1894) *Chem.* [G (1894) < *iso-* (< Gk *ísos* equal) + G *Borneol* < *Borneo,* the name of a large island in the Malay Archipelago + *-ol* (< G *Alkohol* alcohol, ult. < Ar) -ol] A volatile, crystalline terpenoid alcohol, stereoisomeric with borneol, that yields camphor by oxidation. O, W [3]

isobutyric acid, *n.* (1871) *Chem.* [Transl. of G *Isobuttersäure* (1864) < *Isobutter* (< Gk *ísos* equal + L *būtr̄yium* butter) + G *Säure* acid] A colorless liquid acid found in many plants and also obtained from isobutyl alcohol, used mainly to make esters for flavoring. O, W [3]

isochar, *n.* (1963) *Bot.* [Rendering of G *Isopsepher* (1938) < *iso-* + *Psepher* (which is rendered to E *character* and short. to *char*) < the comb. form of Gk *ísos* equal + *ps̄ephos* number + *éros* sign] A line, imaginary or plotted on a map, that links areas containing plants having similar numbers of distinguishing characteristics. O [3]

isochronous, *a.* (1895) *Archaeology* [G *isochron* (1893) < *iso-* + *-chron* < Gk *ísos* equal + *chrónos* time + E *-ous*] Originating or formed in the same period (this is different from the old "equal time" meaning). O [3]

isocitric acid, *n.* (1869) *Chem.* [Transl. of G *Isocitronsäure*

(1869) < *iso-* (< Gk *ísos* equal) + G *Citronsäure* (now *Zitronensäure*) citric acid < MFr *citron* < OProv, ad. < L *citrus* + G *Säure* acid] A crystalline acid, isomeric with citric acid, that occurs in blackberry juice. O, R, W [3]

isoclasite, *n.* (1872) *Mineral.* [G *Isoklas* (1870) < *iso-* + *-klas* < Gk *ísos* equal + *klásis* break, split + E *-ite*] A basic hydrous calcium phosphate, found in one Bohemian site. O, W [3]

isocolloid, *n.* (1915) *Chem.* [G *Isokolloid* (1911) < *iso-* + *Kolloid* < Gk *ísos* equal + *kólla* glue + *-oeid̄es* similar] A colloidal dispersion in which the disperse phase and the dispersion medium are chemically related or identical. O [3]

isoeugenol, *n.* (1883) *Chem.* [G (1882) < *iso-* (< Gk *ísos* equal) + G *Eugenol* < *Eugen,* the name of the Prince of Savoy (1663–1736), Austrian general and statesman + G *-ol* (< L *oleum* oil) -ol] An aromatic liquid phenol that occurs in ilang-ilang oil and nutmeg oil, used in perfumes and to synthesize vanillin; 4-propenyl-guaiacol. O, W [3]

isoflor, *n.* (1944) *Bot.* [Transl. of G *Isoporie* (1938) < *iso-* + *-porie* (which is rendered to E *flor*) < Gk *ísos* equal + *poreía* load] A line, imaginary or plotted on a map, that links areas containing equal numbers of plant species (see *isochar*). O [3]

isogenic, *a.* (1933) *Biol.* [G *isogen* (1913) < *iso-* + *-gen* < Gk *ísos* equal + *-gen̄es* producing, produced + E *-ic*] Having the same genotype: homozygous. O, W [4]

isogloss, -es *pl.* (1925) *Ling.* [G (1892) < *iso-* + *Gloss* < Gk *ísos* equal + L *glōssa* word requiring explanation < Gk *glōssa* tongue, language] The boundary line of a local concentration or dominance of a speech feature such as of vocabulary or pronunciation; such a line plotted on a map. —**isoglottal,** *a.* (1932); **-glottic** (1939); **-glossic** (1968); **-glossal,** *a.* O, R, W [4]

isohydric, *a.* (1887) *Chem.* [G *isohydrisch* (1887) < *iso-* + *-hydrisch* < Gk *ísos* + *hydr-,* comb. form of *hýdōr* water + G *-isch* -ic] Of or having the same ion concentration (as a hydrogen ion). O, W [3]

Isolde, *n. Myth.* Var. **Iseult, Yseult** [G < OFr *Isolt,* the name of a heroine in the Arthurian legends] In literary works in various languages, the Irish princess who was married to King Mark of Cornwall and was loved by Tristram; Tristram's wife and the King of Brittany's daughter; a female given name, esp. in German. R [4]

isoleucine, *n.* (1903) *Biochem.* [G *Isoleucin* (1903) < *iso-* + *Leucin* < Gk *ísos* equal + *leukós* shining, white + G *-in* -ine] A crystalline amino acid, isomeric with leucine, that is essential for plant and animal nutrition. O, R, W [4]

isolichenin, *n.* (1898) *Chem.* [G (1881) < *iso-* + *Lichenin* < Gk *ísos* equal + *leich̄en* to lick + G *-in* -in] The rarer of the two major lichen starches. O [3]

isolysin, *n.* (1901) *Biochem.* [G (1900) < *iso-* + *Lysin* < Gk *ísos* equal + *lýsis* solution, dissolution, loosening + G *-in* -in] Isohaemolysin, a lysis of an individual's red blood cells. O [3]

isomaltose, *n.* (1891) *Chem.* [G (1890) < *iso-* + *Maltose* < Gk *ísos* equal + NL *maltum* malt + G *-ose* (< Fr), denoting a carbohydrate] A syrupy disaccharide, isomeric with maltose, that is present in hydrol and is also obtainable by various procedures. O, W [3]

isomer, *n.* (1866) *Chem.* [Prob. < G *Isomer* (1830) (< *a.*)

< *iso-* + *-mer* < Gk *ísos* equal, alike + *méros* part] A compound, radical, or ion isomeric with one or more of its kind; a similarly isomeric nuclide: nuclear isomer. • ~ appears in numerous derivatives like **isomere** (1884), **isomerase** (1943). O, R, W [4]

isometric, *a.* (1891) *Physiol.* [G *isometrisch* (1882) < *iso-* + *metrisch* < Gk *ísos* equal + *métron* measure + G *-isch* -ic] Of, relating to, or designating muscular contraction where tension is developed, but without appreciable shortening of muscle fibers (this is different from meanings in physics, biology, mathematics, etc.). O, R, W [4]

isomorphism, *n.* (1828) *Chem., Mineral.* [Prob. < G *Isomorphismus* (1819) < *iso-* + *Morphismus* < Gk *ísos* equal + *morphé* form + G (< L) *-ismus* -ism] The quality or state of being isomorphic (this is different from the ''mathematical, psychological, linguistic'' meanings). O, W [4]

isonicotinic acid, *n.* (1883) *Chem.* [Transl. of G *Isonicotinsäure* (1883) < *iso-* + *Nicotin* (< Gk *ísos* equal + Fr *nicotine* tobacco plant < the name of Jean *Nicot,* French ambassador to Portugal, who introduced tobacco into France in 1560 + G *-in* -inic) + *Säure* acid] A crystalline acid used chiefly in synthesizing isoniazid. —**isonicotinic acid hydrazide** (1952). O, W [4]

isopiptesis, *see* isepiptesis

isopleth, *n.* (1909) *Math.* [G *Isoplethe* (1877) < Gk *isoplēthés* of equal value] An isogram on a graph (as in meteorology); a line connecting points on a map where a given variable has a specified constant value (this is different from the Greek-derived ''chemical'' meaning). —**isoplethic.** O, R, W [4]

isosbestic, *a.* (1925) *Chem.* Erron. var. **isobestic** (1954) [G *isobestisch* (1924) < *iso-* < Gk *ísos* equal + *sbestós* extinct + G *-isch* -ic] A wavelength at which light is absorbed at a constant rate by a liquid as the acidity varies. O [3]

isostere[1], *n.* (1900) *Meteor.* [G *Isoster* (1883) < *iso-* + *Ster* < Gk *ísos* equal + *stereós* firm] A line or surface connecting points of equal atmospheric density. O, R, W [3]

isostere[2], *n.* (1919) *Chem.* Var. **isoster** (1919) [G *Isoster* (1909) (see *isostere*[1])] A line on a graph indicating the pressure of a gas needed to produce a given amount of adsorption at various temperatures. O [3]

isotonic[1], *a.* (1895) *Physiol.* [G *isotonisch* (1884) < *iso-* + *tonisch* < Gk *ísos* equal + *tónos* tension + G *-isch* -ic] Of, relating to, or having the same osmotic pressure: isosmotic. —**isotonicity** (1896). O, R, W [4]

isotonic[2], *a.* (1891) *Physiol.* [G *isotonisch* (1882) (see *isotonic*[1])] Pertaining to or exhibiting equal tension in muscular contraction. —**isotonically** (1953). O, R, W [4]

isotypic, *a.* (1929) *Mineral.* [G *isotyp* (1894) < *iso-* + *Typ* < Gk *ísos* equal + L *typus,* Gk *týpos* model + E *-ic*] Of or having an identical or similar crystal structure; of or having an analogous chemical formula (this is different from the old ''biological'' meaning). O, R, W [3]

isotypy, *n.* (1938) *Mineral.* [G *Isotypie* (1894) < *iso-* + *-typie* < Gk *ísos* equal + L *typus,* Gk *týpos* model + G *-ie* -y] The character or state of being isotypic: isotypism. O, W [3]

isoxazole, *n.* (1891) *Chem.* [G *Isoxazol* (1888) < *iso-* + *Oxazol* < Gk *ísos* equal + *oxýs* sharp, sour, + *a-* not + *zōé* life + G *-ol* (< L *oleum* oil) -ol] A liquid, heterocyclic compound with a penetrating odor; a derivative of this. O, W [3]

itatartaric acid, *n.* (1872) *Chem.* [Transl. of G *Itaweinsäure* (1867), irreg. < *ita-* (< *Akonit* the common monkshood < Gk *akóniton* < *akoné* boulder) + G *Weinsäure* tartaric acid < *Wein* wine + *Säure* acid] Dihydroxytaconic acid. —**itatartrate,** *n.* (1872). O [3]

I-thou, *n.* (1937) *Theol.* [Transl. of Martin Buber's G *Ich-Du, Ich und Du* (1923) < *Ich* I + *und* and + *Du* you] The personal relationship between a human and God; transf. sense in literature and music. —**I-thou,** *a.* (1958). O [3]

i-umlaut, *n.* (1870) *Ling.* [G I-mutation] The fronting influence of an *i* or *j* on the vowel of a preceding syllable in the same word; the consequence of this fronting. —**i-umlauted,** *part. a.* (1927). O [3]

J

jacobaea, *n.* (1578) *Bot.* [NL or poss. < the popular G *Jacobs(kreuz)kraut,* named after the apostle *Jacobus/Jakobus*] The ragwort or a related South African species. — **Jacobaea lily** (1752). O [3]

jaeger, *n.* (1776) *Mil., Ichthy.* Var. **jager** (1776), **yager** (1809), **jäger** (1815) [G hunter; a marksman in the infantry] A sharpshooter or rifleman in the German or Austrian army or in a mobile light-infantry unit; a (German or Swiss) hunter; an attendant on a person of rank dressed in hunter's costume; a predatory seabird. • ~ is transl. as **hunter** (q.v.). O, R, W [4]

jalapinolic acid, *n.* (1855) *Chem.* [Transl. of G *Jalappinolsäure* (1854) < *Jalappinol* (< Sp purga de *Jalapa,* the name of a purgative plant found in Mexico + G *-ol* < *Alkohol,* ult. < Ar alcohol) + G *Säure* acid] A crystalline derivative of palmitic acid obtained by hydrolyzing jalapin. O [3]

jalpaite, *n.* (1868) *Mineral.* [G *Jalpait* (1858) < *Jalpa,* the name of a Mexican city + G *-it* -ite] A sulfide of silver and copper. O, W [3]

Janissary/janizary music, *n.* (1888) *Music* Var. **janissary music** (1888) [Ad. of G *Janitscharenmusik* < *Janitschar* < Turk *yeniceri* (in the 14th to 18th cent.) a soldier in the sultan's crack regiment + G *Musik* music < OFr *musique,* ult. < Gk *mousikê*] Music of the Janissary, the military bodyguard of Turkish sovereigns (c.1400–1826) or of military bands modeled on this; music written in imitation thereof. O, R, W [3]

jarosite, *n.* (1854) *Mineral.* [G *Jarosit* (1852) < the name of Barranco *Jaroso,* Almeria, Spain + G *-it* -ite] A basic sulfate of potassium and iron. O, R, W [4]

jass, *n.* *Games* [(Dial.) G *Jass* (now *Jaß*), prob. borrowed by Swiss mercenaries from the Dutch, a card game popular in Switzerland played with 36 cards by 2 to 4 people] A two-handed game that uses a 36-card or 32-card pack; **klaberjass** (q.v.). R, W [3]

jaulingite, *n.* *Mineral.* [G *Jaulingit* < the *Jauling,* the name of an Austrian town + G *-it* -ite] A fossil resin with high oxygen content. W [3]

joch, *n.* *Geogr.* [G mountain ridge] Col, a high pass in a mountain range usu. across a watershed; a saddlelike depression in a ridge crest. W [3]

jodel, *see* yodel

jodeler, *see* yodeler

Johannisberger, *n.* (1822) *Beverages* [G < *Johannisberg* < the name of a castle and village on the Rhine above Rüdesheim, Germany + *-er* -er] A fine wine made in Johannisberg in the Rheingau. O (not in 2nd ed.) [2]

johannite, *n.* (1835) *Mineral.* [G *Johannit* (1830) < the name of the Austrian Archduke *Johann* Baptist Joseph Fabian Sebastian (1782–1859) + G *-it* -ite] A hydrous basic uranyl copper sulfate. O, W [3]

johnstrupite, *n.* (1890) *Mineral.* [G *Johnstrupit* (1890) < the name of Frederik *Johnstrup* (1818–94), Danish geologist + G *-it* -ite] Mosandrite (q.v.). O, W [3]

joint mouse, -mice *pl.* (1886) *Med.* [Transl. of G *Gelenkmaus* (1886) < *Gelenk* joint + *Maus* mouse, so named because its movement suggests that of a mouse] (usu. pl.) a loose fragment, as of cartilage, within the cavity of a joint. O, W [3]

joint water, *n.* (1599) *Med.* [Transl. of G *Gelenkwasser* < *Gelenk* joint + *Wasser* water] Synovia, a lubricating fluid in joints. O, W [3]

jordanite, *n.* (1868) *Mineral.* [G *Jordanit* (1864) < the name of Johann Ludwig *Jordan* (1771–1853), German scientist of Saarbrücken + *-it* -ite] A monoclinic lead arsenic sulfide. O, W [3]

jordisite, *n.* (1910) *Mineral.* [G *Jordisit* (1909) < the name of Eduard Friedrich Alexander *Jordis* (1868–1917), German chemist + *-it* -ite] A black sulfide of molybdenum. O [3]

joseite, *n.* (1868) *Mineral.* [G *Joseit* (1853) < the name of Sao *José* do Paraiso, Brazil + G *-it* -ite] A native telluric bismuth. O, W [3]

Judenhetze, *n.* (1882) *Politics* [G < *Juden* (pl. of *Jude*) Jew + *Hetze* persecution] Systematic persecution of the Jews. O [2]

Judenrat, *n.* (1950) *Politics* [G < *Juden* Jews + *Rat* council] A council (of Jewish elders) representing a Jewish community in an area governed by the Nazis during World War Two. O [3]

judenrein, *a.* (1942) *Politics* [G < *Juden* Jews + *rein* pure (of)] Of a society or organization from which any Jewish members have been expelled. O [3]

Jugendstil, *n.* (1928) *Art, Archit.* Var. **jugendstil** [G (1896) < *Jugend* (the title of a Munich periodical) + *Stil* style < L *stilus*] A late 19th and early 20th century German decorative style equivalent to art nouveau. —**jugendstil,** *a.* (1950). O, R, W [3]

juglone, *n.* (1878) *Chem.* Old var. **juglon** (1887) [G *Juglon* (1877), irreg. < NL *juglans* walnut] A crystalline compound obtained from green walnut shells and having weak bactericidal and fungicidal properties. O, W [3]

Jugoslav, *see* Yugoslav

jump turn, *n.* (1924) *Sports, Dance* [Transl. of G *Umsprung* or *Drehsprung* < *um* around or *dreh-* (< *drehen* to turn) + *Sprung* jump] A turn in the air made while ski jumping; a comparable turn in dancing. O, R, W [3]

Junggrammatiker, -ø *pl.* (1922) *Ling.* Var. **junggrammatiker** (1922) [G < *jung* young + *Grammatiker* grammarian] One of a group of German historical linguists after 1870 who held that phonetic laws are universally valid and permit no exceptions. • ~ is transl. as **neogrammarian** (1885, q.v.). O, R [3]

junggrammatisch, *a.* (1958) *Ling.* [G < *Junggrammatiker* (q.v.) + *-isch* -ic] Of the Junggrammatiker. O [2]

Junker, *n.* (1554) *Politics* Var. **junker** (1865), **younker** [G a member of the (German) landed gentry < OHG *juncherro* < *junc* young + *hērro* lord, master] A usu. young German nobleman; a member of the Prussian aristocracy characterized by undemocratic views and extreme militarism; a negative transf. meaning for a member of another such group. —**Junkerism** (1866), **Junkerdom** (1870), **Junkerish** (1878). O, R, W [4]

Jura, *n.* (1829) *Geol.* [Prob. < G, named after the *Jura* mountain range between France and Switzerland < L (*mōns*) *Jura* the Jura (Mountain)] The Jurassic geological period or its rocks. —**Jura,** *a.* (1851). O, W [4]

Juso, *n.* (1971) *Politics* [G, a short. of *Jungsozialisten* < *jung* young + *Sozialist(en)* socialist(s) < L *sociālis*] Any of a group of young leftist members of the West German Social Democratic Party; a German Social Democrat. B [3]

juvenile, *a.* (1907) *Geol.* [G *juvenil* (1902) < Fr *iuvénil*, L *iuvenīlis* youthful] Originating within the earth or some other planet and brought to the surface for the first time, as in gasses or salt (this is different from the old ''young, etc.'' meanings). O [3]

K

k/K, *n. Physics, Chem.* (1901, 1901) [G, an abbr. for a formula in physics < *konstant* constant (< MFr *constant* < L) + the name of Ludwig *Boltzmann* (1844–1906), Austrian physicist] Boltzmann's constant, (q.v.) a formula in physics and chemistry for the ideal gas constant per molecule. O, R, W [4]

K, *n. Ed.* [Short. of G *Kindergarten* (q.v.)] (An abbr. for) *kindergarten,* as in *K-12* for precollege education. R [4]

ka, *n. Physics* [Short. of G *Kathode* cathode < Gk *cáthodos*] Cathode, the electrode at which electrons come into a device from the external circuit. W [3]

kafer, *n.* (1599) (obs.) *Zool.* [Prob. < G *Käfer* beetle] Chafer, a beetle. O [2]

kaffeeklatsch, -es *pl.* (1888) Var. **kaffeeklatch** (1936) *Beverages* [G < *Kaffee* coffee (ult. < Ar *qahwah*) + G *Klatsch* gossip] Gossip over coffee; a meeting, often over coffee, for informal conversation. —**kaffeeklatscher** (**1936**), **kaffeklatsching** (1956). • ~ is partially transl. as **coffee klatsch** and is short. to **klat(s)ch** (q.v.). O, R, W [4]

kainite, *n.* (1868) *Mineral.* Var. **kainit** (1877) [G *Kainit* (1865) < Gk *kainós* new + G *-it* -ite] Hydrous sulfate and chloride of magnesium and potassium, used as a fertilizer. O, R, W [2]

kairoline, *n.* (1883) *Chem.* [G *Kaïrolin* (1883) < *Kaïrin* as infixed by *-ol* -ol < Gk *kairós* favorable moment] An oily liquid with antipyretic properties. O [3]

kaiser^{*1*}, *n.* (1807) *Politics* [G emperor < OHG *keisar,* ult. < L *Caesar* < the name of Julius *Caesar* (100-44 B.C.), Roman general and statesman] The sovereign of Austria, 1804–1918 (this is different from the old meanings of "The Emperor, an emperor"), which came into E < ON *keisari,* ult. < L by c.1160). —**kaisership** (1848), **kaiserling** (1852). O, R, W [4]

kaiser^{*2*}, *n.* (1888) *Politics* [G emperor (see *kaiser*^{*1*})] The ruler of Germany, 1871–1918. • ~ is a reborrowing < G (not an altered meaning of *kaiser*^{*1*}) and occurs in composites like **-ate** (1881), **-ish** (1892), **-ism** (1914), **-istic** (1919), **-ist** (1920), **Kaiser moustache** (1938). O, R, W [4]

kaiserdom, *n.* (1914) *Politics* [Transl. of G *Kaisertum* < *Kaiser* (see *kaiser*^{*1*}) + *-tum* -dom] The office or power of a kaiser; the area ruled by a kaiser. O, R, W [4]

kaiserin, *n.* (1888 *W9*) *Politics* [G empress < *Kaiser* (see *kaiser*^{*1*}) + fem. suffix *-in* -in] The wife of a kaiser. W [3]

kaliborite, *n.* (1892) *Mineral.* [G *Kaliborit* < *kali-* (< *Alkali* alkali, ult. < Ar *al-qili* the ashes of the plant saltwort) + G *Boron* (< ML *borax* boric acid, ult. < Per *būrah*) + G *-it* -ite] A hydrous borate of magnesium and potassium. O, W [3]

kalicinite, *n.* (1922) *Mineral.* [G *Kalicinit* < Fr *calicine* (irreg. < NL *kalium* potash) + G *-it* -ite] Kalicin, an acid carbonate or bicarbonate of potassium. O, W [3]

kaliophilite, *n.* (1887) *Mineral.* [G *Kaliophilit* (1886) < *kalio-* + *-phil* (< NL *kalium* potash + Gk *phílos* loving)

+ G *-it* -ite] A potassium aluminum silicate of volcanic origin: phacellite. O, W [3]

kalkowskite, *n. Mineral.* [Ad. of G *Kalkowskyn* < the name of Ernest *Kalkowsky* (1851–1938), German mineralogist + E *-it* -ite] Basically an oxide of iron and titanium. W [3]

kallidin, *n.* (1950) *Biochem.* [G (1948), a combining of *Kallikrein* + *Peptid* + *-in* -in < Gk *kallíkreas* sweetbread + *peptós* boiled, digested] A supposedly hypotensive peptide released from a globulin by kallikrein (q.v.), which stimulates the uterus and intestine, but was later shown to be a mixture of two peptides; lysylbradykinin. —**kallidin I/II.** O [3]

kallikrein, *n.* (1930) *Biochem.* [G (1930) < Gk *kallíkreas* sweetbread + G *-in* -in] An enzyme occurring in the human pancreas and elsewhere that liberates kallidin from a blood-plasma precursor and is used therapeutically; any enzyme that liberates a kinin from a protein. O [3]

kallilite, *n.* (1892) *Mineral.* [G *Kallilith* < *kalli-* + *-lith* < Gk *kalli-,* a comb. form of *kállos* beauty + *líthos* rock, stone, being a transl. of G *Schönstein,* the name of the place where it was found] Sulfide of bismuth and nickel. O [3]

kaluszite, *n.* (1875) *Mineral.* [G *Kaluszit* (1872) < *Kalusz,* the name of a Galician town in the former USSR + G *-it* -ite] Syngenite (q.v.). O [3]

kamacite, *n.* (1890) *Mineral.* [G *Kamacit* (1861) (now *Kamazit*) < Gk *kámax* (gen. *kamakós*) vine pole, shaft + G *-it* -ite] A meteoric, nickel-iron alloy. O, R, W [4]

kamarezite, *n.* (1895) *Mineral.* [G *Kamarezit* (1893) < the name of *Kamareza,* near Laurium, Greece + G *-it* -ite] Brochantite, a hydrous copper sulfate. O, W [3]

kamerad/Kamerad, *interj.* (1914) *Mil.* [G (1639) comrade, esp. a fellow soldier < MFr *camarade*] (Used by German soldiers in World War One as) a cry of surrender, in the sense of being comrade rather than enemy. —**kamerad,** *jocular v.* (1916). O, R, W [4]

kämmererite, *n.* (1854) *Mineral.* [G *Kämmererit* (1841) (or Sw *kaemmererit* by 1842) < the name of August Alexander *Kämmerer* (1789–1858), Swedish scientist + G *-it* -ite] A reddish variety of penninite (q.v.). O, W [3]

Kammerspiel, *n. Theater* [G < *Kammer* chamber + *Spiel* play] In Germany, an intimate social drama presented in a small theater; a theater where such a drama is presented (G *Kammerspielhaus*). W2 [2]

kanone, -n *pl. Sports* [G cannon < It *cannone* ordnance piece, actually, large barrel, ult. < L *canna* barrel] An expert skier. R, W [3]

kapelle/Kapelle, -n *pl. Music* Var. **capelle** [G band, orchestra < It *cappella* (< ML) an association of musicians, actually, musicians and choir in a court chapel] The orchestra or choir of a royal or papal chapel; a musical organization, esp. an orchestra (*a cappella,* the *a.* and *adv.* form, comes directly < Ital). O, W [3]

Kapellmeister/kapellmeister, *n.* (1838) *Music* Var. **capell-meister** (1880) [G (1570) < *Kapelle* (q.v.) + *Meister* director, conductor] The musical director of a kapelle; bandmaster. O, R, W [4]

kapellmeister music, *n. Music* [G *Kapellmeistermusik* < *Kapellmeister* (q.v.) + *Musik* music < L *musica* < Gk *mousikḗ*] (Usu. disparaging) uninspired but correct music. W [3]

kaput, *a.* (1895) (slang) Var. **kaputt** (1914) [G *kaputt* (1648) (orig., trickless) done for < the phrase *caput machen* (current during the Thirty Years War) to do away with < Fr *faire capot* to lose all the tricks in a card game] Wholly defeated or destroyed; finished or worn out; hopelessly outmoded or discarded. O, R, W [4]

karabiner, *see* carabiner

Karlsbad salt, *n. Chem.* [Transl. of G *Karlsbader Salz* < the comb. form of *Karlsbad,* now *Karlovy Vary,* a town in western Czechoslovakia famous for its sulfur springs + G *Salz* salt] A mixture of mineral salts obtained from the water of certain springs; an artificial mixture of such salts. W [3]

karren, -s/-ø *pl.* (1894) *Geol.* Var. **Karren** (1924) [G *Karre* trough] The furrows, fissures, or grikes of a limestone surface. O, W [3]

karrenfeld, -s/-er *pl.* (1885) *Geol.* Var. **Karrenfeld** (1885) [G < *Karre* trough, furrow + *Feld* field] An area, usu. of limestone stripped of soil, which has been eroded to provide a landscape of small pinnacles separated by crevices. O [3]

karst, *n.* (1894) *Geol.* [G < the name of a portion of the Dinaric Alps (Serbo-Croatian *Kras,* It *Carso*] A barren limestone region of sinks, ridges, protruding rocks, and caves; a kind of topography typical of the Yugoslavian Karst. —**karst,** *a.* (1894); **-tic** (1925); **-tification** (1958); **-tology** (1968). O, R, W [4]

karstenite, *n.* (1884) *Mineral.* [G *Karstenit* (1813) < the name of Dietrich Ludwig Gustav *Karsten* (1768–1810), German mineralogist + *-it* -ite] Anhydrite (q.v.). O [3]

karyosome, *n.* (1889) *Physiol.* [G *Karyosoma* (1883) (now *Karysom*) < *karyo-* + *-som* < Gk *káryon* nut, nucleus + *sōma* body] Chromocenter, a body of chromatin in a nucleus; endsome, esp. one consisting of a nucleolar mass of heterochromatin. O, R, W [4]

karyotin, *n.* (1925) *Med.* Var. **karyotine** (1966) [G (1910), a blend of *Karyon* (< Gk *káryon* nut, nucleus) + G *Chromatin* chromatin] The usu. stainable material of a cell nucleus; the substance composing the nuclear reticulum. O, W [3]

katatonia, *see* catatonia

katoptrite/catoptrite, *n.* (1917) *Mineral.* [G *Katoptrit* (1917) (or Sw) < Gk *kátoptron* minor + G or Sw *-it* -ite] A silico-antimonate basically of bivalent manganese and aluminum. O, W [3]

katzenjammer, *n.* (1849) [G < *Katzen* (pl. of *Katze* cat) + *Jammer* distress, wail] Hangover: nausea and debility often following dissipation or drunkenness; transf. sense to distress or confusion; a discordant clamor. —**katzenjammer kids** (1897) naughty children (sufficiently mischievous to cause one to experience some of the symptoms of a hangover). O, R, W [4]

keesh, *see* kish

kegler, *n.* (1932) *Sports* Var. **keggler** (1958), **kegel(l)er** [G one who bowls < *kegeln* to bowl < *Kegel* bowling pin < OHG *kegil* stake, peg] (U.S.) a participant in a bowling game. O, R, W [4]

kegling, *n.* (1938 *W9*) *Sports* Var. **kegel(l)ing** [Ad. of *Kegeln* bowling < *kegeln* to bowl + E *-ing*] Bowling. R, W [3]

keller, *n.* (1927) [G cellar, basement] A beer cellar in Austria or Germany. —**keller,** *a.* (1968). O [3]

kephalin, *see* cephalin

keratohyalin(e), *n.* (1887) *Biochem.* [G *Keratohyalin* (1882) < *kerato-* + *Hyalin* < Gk *kéras* (gen. *kératos*) horn + *hyálinos* of glass or crystal] The substance composing the granules in the granular layer of the epidermis. O [3]

keratophyre, *n.* (1889) *Geol.* [G *Keratophyr* (1874) < *kerato-* + *-phyre* < Gk *kéras* (gen. *kératos*) horn + *phýrein* to mix] (Orig. applied to) various rocks containing highly sodic feldspars; any of several rocks resembling hornfels (q.v.); a compact porphyritic rock containing anorthoclase as its prevailing feldspar (q.v.). O, W [3]

keratoplasty, *n.* (1857) *Med.* [Ad. of G *Keratoplastik* (1824) < *kerato-* (< Gk *kéras,* gen. *kératos* horn) + G *Plastik* < Fr *plastique* < L *plastice,* Gk *plastikḗ* (*téchnē*) (the art of) shaping] Plastic surgery on the cornea, esp. grafting. —**keratoplastic** (1907). O, W [4]

kern, *n.* (1941) *Meteor.* [G < a short. of *Kernzähler* kern counter (q.v.) < *Kern* kernel + *Zähler* counter, indicator] Nucleus, a particle on which water vapor condenses in free air (this is different from various old "nonmeteorological" meanings). O, R, W [3]

kern counter, *n.* (1941) *Meteor.* [Partial transl. of G *Kernzähler* (1913) (see **kern**)] A device that counts dust and other nuclei particles. O [3]

kernel, *n.* (1909) *Math.* [Transl. of G *Kern* (1904) kernel, nucleus] (Used in integral equations) a function of at least two variables that, when multiplied by one or more functions of each of just one of the variables, constitutes the integrand of an integral relative to these other variables. O [3]

kernicterus, -es *pl.* (1912) *Path.* Var. **Kernikterus** (1912) [G *Kernikterus* (1903) < *Kern* nucleus + *ikterus* icterus < NL < Gk *íkteros* jaundice] The staining of nuclei of the brain cells and spinal cord with bile pigments, usu. affecting infants and causing permanent brain damage; the disease caused by this. —**kernicteric** (1956). O, W [3]

ket-, *see* keto-

ketazine, *n.* (1894) *Chem.* [G *Ketazin* (1891) < *keto-,* the comb. form of *Keton* ketone, identifying the compound as containing a carbonyl group + *Azot* + *-in* -ine] An azine compound formed from a ketone. O, W [3]

ketene, *n.* (1905) *Chem.* Var. **keten** (1905) [G *Keten* (1905), irreg. < *Aceton* acetone] A poisonous, gaseous carbonyl compound, used as an acetylating agent; a derivative of this. O, R, W [4]

ket(o)-, *comb. form* (1888) *Chem.* [G short. of *Keton* ketone (q.v.)] A comb. form indicating the presence of a ketone group. O, R, W [4]

ketoketen(e), *n.* (1908) *Chem.* [G *Ketoketen* (1908) < *keto-,* the comb. form of *Keton* ketone (q.v.) + *Keten* ketene (q.v.)] A ketene of the type RR'C:C:O. O [3]

ketone, *n.* (1851) *Chem.* [G *Keton* (1848), ad. < *Aceton* (now *Azeton*) < Fr *acétone* < L *acētum* vinegar, sour wine + G *-on* -one] Any of a class of organic compounds distinguished by a carbinol group attached to two carbon atoms. —**ketonic** (1876), **ketonuria** (1913), **ketonization** (1931), **ketonize** (1937), **ketone body/group** (1915). O, R, W [4]

kettle stitch, *n.* (1818) *Printing* [Ad. of G *Kettelstich* < *Kettel,* East Middle German dimin. of *Kette* chain (ult. < L *catēna*) + *Stich* stitch] In early book binding, a knot formed in the sewing thread at the ends of the book sections to fasten them together: catch stitch. O, R, W [3]

Keuper/keuper, *n.* (1844) *Geol.* [G Upper Franconian for sandstone (cf. Bavarian *Kiefer* sand, gravel), a term introduced by the German geologist Leopold von Buch (1774–1853) for the upper division of the formation referred to as the German Trias] The upper division of the Triassic period. —**Keuper,** *a.* O [3]

kibble, *n.* (1671) *Mining* (Brit.) [Folk etymology < G *Kübel* bucket] A hoisting bucket used in mining. —**kibble,** *a.* (1834); **kibble-chain** (1851). O, R, W [3]

kieselguhr, *n.* (1875) *Geol.* Var. **kieselgur** [G (1866) (now *Kieselgur*) < *Kiesel* flint, gravel + *Guhr* infusoria] Diotomaceous earth: loose or porous diatomite. O, R, W [4]

kieserite, *n.* (1862) *Mineral.* [G *Kieserit* (1861) < the name of Dietrich G. *Kieser* (1779–1862), German geologist + *-it* -ite] Hydrous magnesium sulfate. O, R, W [4]

kilch, *n.* (1881) *Ichthy.* [(Alemannic) G goiter, so named because the air bladder of this small fish inflates to look like a goiter when the fish is suddenly raised from a great depth)] (The orig. Swiss name for) a small whitefish. O [3]

killcrop, *n.* (1652) *Myth.* [Ad. of LG *kilkrop,* G *Kielkropf* changeling < G *Kiel,* prob. reflecting MG *quil* (G *Quelle*) source, well, provenience (in keeping with old beliefs that such children sprang from water or waves) + *Kropf* goiter (prob. because of their thick necks or their gluttony)] A voracious infant, popularly believed to be a fairy changeling, substituted for the human baby. O, W [3]

kinase, *n.* (1902) *Biochem.* [G *Kinas* < Gk *kínēsis* kinesis (q.v.)] Any substance that converts a zymogen into an enzyme; an enzyme that catalyzes phosphorylation processes. O, R, W [4]

kinchin, *n.* (1561) (Brit. slang) [Folk etymology < G *Kindchen,* dim. of *Kind* child] Child. —**kinchin-lay** (1838) the stealing of money from children sent on errands. O, R, W [3]

kindergarten, *n.* (1852) *Ed.* [G (1840), a term introduced by the German educator Frederich Froebel (1782–1852) for a school for preschool children < *Kinder* children + *Garten* garden] A (division of a) school below the first grade serving pupils of 4 to 6 years; the kindergarten room or building; Milner's kindergarten. —**kindergarten,** *a.* (1869), *v.;* **-ing** (1871); **-ism** (1872); **-ize.** • ~ is abbr. as **K.** O, R, W [4]

kindergartner, *n.* (1881) *Ed.* Var. **kindergartener** (1889) [A mistaken linkage of G *Kindergarten* kindergarten with *Kintergärtner* or *Kindergärtnerin,* male or female kindergarten teachers, respectively] A child attending kindergarten or of an age to do so; a teacher there. O, R, W [4]

kinder, kirche, küche (1899) [G *Kinder, Kirche, Küche* children, church, kitchen (with a fourth *K, Kleider* dress,

orig. added)] (An earlier, sexist enumeration of) the occupations, in varying order, supposedly desirable for a housewife, as further stressed by the Nazis. O [3]

kinderspiel, *n.* (1902) *Theater* [G < *Kinder* children + *Spiel* play] (Primarily Brit.) a dramatic piece performed by children. O [3]

kinesis, -ses *pl.* (1905) *Biol.* [G *kinese* (1901) < E *kinesis* < NL *kinesis* < Gk *kínēsis* motion] An organism's unoriented movement induced by a particular kind of stimulus such as light (this is different from the "cytological" meaning). O, R, W [4]

king's paprika, *n.* *Food* [Transl. of G *Königspaprika* < the comb. form of *König* king + *Paprika* < Hung. ult. < Gk *péperi*] Hungarian paprika made from whole peppers including their seeds and stalks. W [3]

kino, n. *Theater* [G short. of *Kinematograph* < Fr *cinématographe* < Gk *kínēma* motion + *gráphein* to write, describe] Primarily in Europe, a motion-picture theater; cinema. R, W [3]

kinoplasm, *n.* (1894) *Biol.* Var. **kinoplasma** [G *Kinoplasma* (1892) < *kino-* + *Plasma* < Gk *kineín* to set in motion + *plásma* structure, formation] An active protoplasmic component formerly thought to form filaments and mobile structures. —**kinoplasmic** (1900). O, W [3]

kinzigite, *n.* (1878) *Geol.* [G *Kinzigit* (1860) < the name of the *Kinzig* valley in the Black Forest, Germany + *-it* -ite] A crystalline schistose rock composed of garnet, biotite, and other minerals. —**kinzigitic** (1965). O [3]

kip, *n.* (1909) *Sports* [G *Kippe* basically, edge, tip, but here an exercise on the parallel bars as first named by Friedrich Ludwig Jahn (1778–1852), German pioneer in physical education] (U.S.) a gymnastic feat executed when hanging by the hands from the bar; a synchronized swimming movement (this is different from various "nonsports" meanings). —**kip,** *v.* (1909); **kipping,** *part. a.* (1967). O, W [3]

kipfel, *n.* *Food* [(Austrian) G, dim. of *Kipf* a type of pastry in the shape of a wheel spoke < OHG *kipfa, chipf* < L *cippus* stake, post] A crescent-shaped roll or cookie. W [3]

Kirchhoff's law, *n.* (1869) *Physics* [Transl. of G *Kirchhoff-Gesetz* (1859) (i.e., *Strahlungsgesetz* law of radiation) < the name of Gustav Robert *Kirchhoff* (1824–87), German physicist + *Gesetz* law] Either of two statements governing electric networks in which steady currents are flowing; the statement governing maximum emissivity of a body characterized by maximum possible absorption at all incident wavelengths. O, R [3]

kirsch(wasser), *n.* (1869) *Beverages* Var. **Kirsch(wasser)** [G *Kirschwasser* < *Kirsche* cherry + *Wasser* water] A dry, colorless brandy made from black cherries. O, R, W [4]

kischtimite, *n.* (1863) *Mineral.* [G *Kyschtimit* < *Kyschtym,* a city in the Ural Mountains + G *-it* -ite] A fluocarbonate of the cerium metals found in gold washings and allied to parisite (q.v.). O-1933 [2]

kish, *n.* (1812) *Metall.* Var. **keesh** [Folk etymology < G *Kies,* a short. of *Eisenkies* < *Eisen* iron + *Kies* gravel, pyrites] An impure graphite that separates on slow cooling of molten cast iron; dross on the surface of molten lead. —**kishy** (1825). O, R, W [3]

kitsch, -es *pl.* (1926) *Art, Lit., Music* Var. **Kitsch** (1926) [G a tasteless creation in any of the arts < colloq. *kitschen* to slap together] A would-be artistic product held to be of low quality; that quality of such art. —**kitsch,** *v.* (1951) and *a.* (1958). O, R, W [4]

kitschy, *a.* (1967) *Art* [G *kitschig* trashy, showy, inartistic < *Kitsch* + *-ig*] Having the characteristics of kitsch (q.v.). O, R [4]

klab, *see* klaberjass

klaberjass, *n.* (1892) *Games* Var. **klobbiyos** (1892) [G, poss. < Du *klaverjas* < *klaveren* club (in cards) + G *Jab,* prob. < Du *jassen* a card game popular in Switzerland, played with 36 cards by 2 to 4 players] A two-handed type of piquet played with 32 cards. • ~ is short. to **clabber, clob(ber), jass, klab, klob.** O, R, W [4]

klang, *n.* (1867) *Music* Var. **clang** (1867) [G sound < *klingen* to ring] Sonority, timbre. O [2]

klangfarbe, *n. Music* [G < *Klang* sound + *Farbe* color] Musical quality of a note, timbre. O [2]

klangfarbenmelodie, *n.* (1959) *Music* [G < *Klangfarbe* timbre + *Melodie* melody < LL *melodia* < Gk *meloidía*] Melody of timbres. O [3]

Klappvisier, *n. Mil.* [G < *Klappe* flap + *Visier* visor < OFr *visiere*] A visor attached by a hinged top, used on 14th-century basinets. R [3]

klaprothite, *see* klaprotholite

klaproth(ol)ite, *n.* (1872) *Mineral.* [G *Klaprothit* (1872) < the name of Martin H. *Klaproth* (1743–1817), German chemist + *-it* -ite] A sulfide of copper and bismuth. O, W [3]

klatsch/klatch, -es *pl.* (1941 *W9*) *Beverages* [G *Klatsch* gossip, a short. of *Kaffeeklatsch* (q.v.)] A gathering where there is informal conversation; a coffee party; a visit, as with an amorous result. O, R, W [4]

klavier, *see* clavier

klavierstück, *n. Music* [G < *Klavier* piano + *Stück* piece] A piano piece. O, W [3]

kleindeutsch, *a.* (1945) *Politics* [G < *klein* small + *deutsch* German, in reference to a 19th-cent. German empire led by Prussia and consisting of all the German states except Austria] Referring to or supporting the policy of a united Germany, excluding Austria. O [2]

kleindeutsche(r), *n.* (1916) *Politics* [G nominalization of *kleindeutsch* (q.v.)] A supporter of a kleindeutsch empire. O [2]

kleinite, *n.* (1907) *Mineral.* [G *Kleinit* (1905) < the name of Karl *Klein* (1842–1907), German mineralogist + *-it* -ite] A hydrous chloride and sulfate of mercury and ammonium: mercury oxychloride. O, W [3]

klementite, *n.* (1892) *Mineral.* [G *Klementit* (1891) < the name of Constantin *Klement* (1856–?), curator of the Natural History Museum in Brussels + G *-it* -ite] A variety of thuringite (q.v.) containing more magnesium than iron. O [3]

klets/klett, *see* kletterschuh

kletten prinzip, *n.* (1988) [G < *Klette* burr + *Prinzip* principle < L *principium*] A method developed by the former West German police for controlling crowds or riots. L1 [3]

kletterschuh, -e *pl.* (1920) *Sports* [G < *klettern* to climb + *Schuh* shoe] A cloth- or felt-soled boot esp. worn in

rock climbing. —**kletterschuh,** *a.* (1951). • ~ is short. to **klett** and **klets** (pl., 1963). O [3]

klinostat, *n.* (1880) *Bot.* [G < *klino-* + *-stat*] Clinostat (q.v.). O, W [3]

klippe¹, -s/-n *pl.* (1902) *Geol.* Var. **Klippe** (1902), **klip** [G crag, reef] An outlying, detached remnant of an overthrust rock mass: outlier. O, R, W [3]

klippe², *n. Currency* [G an edged coin < Sw *klippa* to trim < ON] A square or lozenge-shaped coin. R, W [3]

klipsteinite, *n.* (1868) *Mineral.* [G *Klipsteinit* (1866) < the name of August von *Klipstein* (1801–94), German mineralogist + *-it* -ite] A hydrous silicate of manganese and iron. O [3]

Klischograph, *n.* (1955) *Printing* Var. **klischograph** [G (1955), a blend of *Klischee* (printer's) block + *-graph* < Fr *cliché* cheap imitation + Gk *gráphein* to write, describe] A type of electronic engraving plate; (cap.) the trademark for this machine. O [3]

klob(biyos), *see* klaberjass

klockmannite, *n.* (1939) *Mineral.* [G *Klockmannit* (1928) < the name of Friedrich *Klockmann* (1858–1937), German mineralogist + *-it* -ite] A blue-black selenide of copper. O, W [3]

kloesse, *see* klosse

klops, -es *pl.* (1936) *Food* [(Northeast) G a small meatball] A type of meatball or meatloaf. O [3]

klösse, *pl. Food* Var. **kloesse** [G pl. of *GKloß* dumpling] 151Dumplings. R, W [3]

kloster, *n.* (1844) *Theol.* [G convent < ML *claustrum* < L *claudere* to close] A convent or monastery in Germany, Holland, etc. O [3]

knackwurst/knockwurst, *n.* (1929 *W9*) *Food* [G *Knockwurst* < *Knack* crack + *Wurst* sausage] A highly seasoned sausage that is shorter and thicker than a frankfurter. O, R, W [4]

knall-gas, *n.* (1899) *Chem.* Var. **Knallgas** (1899), **knallgas** [G < *Knall* bang + *Gas* gas < NL, ad. < L *chaos*] Any explosive mixture of gases. O [3]

knawel, *n.* (1578) *Bot.* [G *Knauel* a type of *Scleranthus*] A low, spreading, orig. European weed, *Scleranthus annuus;* one of various other plants of this genus. O, R, W [3]

knebelite, *n.* (1818) *Mineral.* [G *Knebelit* (1817) < the name of Karl Ludwig von *Knebel* (1774–1834), German poet and translator + *-it* -ite] Hydrous silicate of iron and manganese found esp. in Sweden: manganoan fayalite (q.v.). O, W [3]

Knecht Ruprecht, *n. Myth.* [G (1524) < *Knecht* manservant + the name *Ruprecht* Rupert, Robert] A sprite in German folklore who visits children before Christmas, rewarding the good but threatening the bad ones. W2 [2]

Kneipe, -n/-s *pl.* (1854) Old var. **Knipe** (1854), **Kneip** (1880)] [G, orig. *Kneipschenke* a run-down, small tavern < *kneipen* to pinch (pennies) + *Schenke* saloon] A celebratory meeting of German university students and the like, often organized as a society, at a tavern or restaurant. —**kneipe,** *v.* (1864). O [3]

Kneipp cure, *n.* (1891) *Med.* Var. **Kneipp's cure** (1891) [Transl. of G *Kneippkur* or *Kneippsche Kur* < the name of the German Catholic priest and nature healer Sebastian *Kneipp* (1821–97) + *Kur* cure < ML *cura* < L] Kneipp-ism, a treatment of disease by hydrotherapic means including walking barefoot in dewy grass. O, W [4]

knick/nick, *n.* (1932) *Geol.* [G *Knick* a sharp turn, bend < *knicken* to bend] Knickpoint (q.v.); the angle made by a pediment and the adjoining mountain slope. —**knickline.** O, W [3]

knickpoint, *n.* (1924) *Geol.* Var. **nickpoint** (1954) [G < *Knick* a sharp turn, bend + *Punkt* point] A place where there is a new erosive curve in the stream bed. • ~ is short. to **knick** (1970). O, W [3]

Knipe, *see* Kneipe

knockwurst, *see* knackwurst

knödel/knoedel, -ø/-s *pl.* (1827) *Food* [G < MHG *knödel,* dim. of *knode, knote* knot] Dumpling. • ~ has the same meaning as the Yiddish borrowing *knaidel.* O, W [3]

knopite, *n.* (1896) *Mineral.* [G *Knopit* (1894) < the name of Adolf *Knopp* (1828–93), German mineralogist + *-it* -ite] A variety of perovskite (q.v.) containing cerium. O, W [3]

knopper, -s/-n *pl.* (1879) *Bot.* [G gall nut] A kind of gall formed by a gall wasp on the leaves and immature acorns of various oaks, earlier used in dyeing and tanning. O, W [3]

knosp, *n.* (1808) *Archit.* [G *Knospe* bud] An architectural ornament shaped like a bud; a knop, knob. —**knosped** (1818). O, R, W [3]

kobold, *n.* (1635) *Myth.* [G *Kobold, Kobolt* goblin, sprite, prob. < MHG *kobe* cove + *holt* < OHG *holdo* spirit— see *cobalt*] Esp. in German folklore, a cave-inhabiting gnome or mischievous domestic spirit; a goblin. O, R, W [4]

kochubeite/kotschubeite, *n.* (1868) *Mineral.* [G *Kotschubeit* (1863) < the name of Count P. A. *Kochubei,* 19th-cent. Russian mineralogist + *-it* -ite] A rose-red, chrome-bearing clinochlore. O, W [3]

koenenite, *n.* (1902) *Mineral.* [G *Koenenit* (1902) < the name of Adolf von *Koenen* (1837–1915), German mineralogist + *-it* -ite] A basic hydroxide and chloride of sodium, magnesium, and aluminum. O, W [3]

kohlrabi, -es *pl.* (1807) *Food* [G < *Kaulirabi,* ad. < It *cavoli rape,* pl. of *cavolo rapa* cabbage beet] A cabbage with an edible stem that becomes greatly enlarged and fleshy: turnip cabbage; a plant of this type; bromatium. O, R, W [4]

Kohlrausch's law, *n.* (1888) *Chem.* [Transl. of G *Kohl-rausch-Gesetz* (1876) < the name of Friedrich Wilhelm *Kohlrausch* (1840–1910), German physicist + *Gesetz* law] A statement that the migration of an ion at infinite dilution depends on the nature of the solvent plus the potential gradient, not on the other ions that are present. O, W [3]

koilonychia, *n.* (1902) *Path.* [G (1897), used by the German doctor Julius Heller (1864–1931) < Gk *koîlos* hollow + *ónyx* (gen. *ónychos*) nail + G *-ia* (< Gk) -ia] An abnormally thin and concave condition of the fingernails, found especially in hypochromic anemias: spoon nail. O, W [3]

kolbeckite, *n.* (1928) *Mineral.* [G *Kolbeckit* (1926) < the name of Friedrich *Kolbeck* (1860–1943), German mineralogist + *-it* -ite] A blue, hydrous silicate-phosphate of beryllium, aluminum, and calcium. O, W [3]

Kolbe reaction, *n.* (1885) *Chem.* [G *Kolbe-Reaktion* < the name of Adolf Wilhelm Hermann *Kolbe* (1818–84), German chemist + *Reaktion* reaction < ML *reactionem* (nom. *reactio*)] A process for preparing salicylic acid. O [3]

kollergang, *n.* (1890) *Industry* [G < *kollern* to roll + *Gang* motion, course, route] Edge runner, a machine that crushes fibrous matter used in papermaking. O, W [3]

kominuter, *n. Tech.* [G < L *comminutus* < past part. of *comminuere* to crush + G *-er* -er] A ball mill used to grind raw materials or clinker in manufacturing Portland cement. W [3]

Kommandatura, *n.* (1937) *Mil.* Var. **Kommandantur(a)** (1937, 1949) [G *Kommandantur* < Fr *commandant* commander + G *-ur* -ura] The center of operation of a military force; a military government headquarters, esp. a Russian or NATO headquarters in a European city following World War Two. O, W [3]

kommers/kommerz, *see* commers

konditorei, -ø/-en *pl.* (1935) *Food* Var. **Konditorei** (1973) [G pastry shop < *Konditor* (< L *conditor* one who prepares tasty delicacies) + G *-ei* -ei] A confectioner's (pastry) shop. O, R, W [3]

koppelflöte, *n. Music* [G < *Koppel* tie, connection (< MHG < OFr *cople* pair) + G *Flöte* flute < MHG < OFr *flaute*] A kind of open flute-stop in a pipe organ. W [3]

koppite, *n.* (1880) *Mineral.* [G *Koppit* (1875) < the name of Hermann Franz Moritz *Kopp* (1817–92), German chemist + *-it* -ite] A pyrochlore (q.v.) containing cerium, iron, and potassium. O, W [3]

kotoite, *n. Mineral.* [G *Kotoit* < the name of Bundjiro *Koto* (1856–1935), Japanese geologist + G *-it* -ite] A borate of magnesium. W [3]

kotschubeite, *see* kochubeite

K-point, *n.* (c.1982) *Sports* [Short. and transl. of G *kritischer Punkt* < *kritisch* critical + *Punkt* point < L *criticus* + *punctum*] The point in the landing area used in ski jumping. BDC [3]

kraft (paper), *a.* and *n.* (1907, 1907) *Industry* [G *Kraft(papier)* < *Kraft* strength (+ *Papier* paper) < L *papӯrus*] A tough brown wrapping paper or board. —**sackkraft** (1963). O, R, W [4]

krantzite, *n.* (1868) *Mineral.* [G *Krantzit* < the name of August *Krantz* (1809–72), German mineralogist + *-it* -ite] A fossil resin similar to amber. O, W [3]

krapfen, -ø *pl.* (1845) *Food* [G < MHG *krapfe* pastry in the form of a hook] A bismarck, fritter. O, W [3]

kratogen, *n.* (1923) *Geol.* [G (1921) < *krato-* + *-gen* < Gk *krátōs* strength + *óros* mountain (range) + *gennân* to produce] Craton (q.v.). —**kratogenic** (1934). O, W [3]

kraurite, *n. Mineral.* [G *Kraurit* < Gk *kraurós* brittle + G *-it* -ite] Dufrenite, a hydrous iron phosphate. W [3]

krausen, *n. Beverages* [G *Krause* the foam formed during the main fermenting process of beer < *krausen, kräusen* to curl back from the edge (said of foam), curl < MHG *krusen* to curl] Fermenting wort. W [3]

krausen, *v. Beverages* [G to add herbs to brewing beer in the state of secondary fermentation (see *krausen,* n.)] To add newly fermenting wort to beer to effect natural carbonation. W [3]

kraut, *n.* (1845) *Food* [G short. of *Sauerkraut* cured cabbage] Sauerkraut (q.v.); cured cabbage or turnips. —**kraut**, *a.* (1895). O, R, W [4]

Kraut, *n.* (1918) *Mil.* Var. **kraut** (1926) [G short. of *Sauerkraut* cured cabbage] A German, esp. a soldier, usu. used disparagingly. —**Kraut,** *a.* (1929). O, R, W [4]

kreis, -e *pl. Politics* [G county, district < OHG *kreiʒ*] A unit of German local government comparable to a county. W [3]

kreittonite, *n.* (1850) *Mineral.* [G *Kreittonit* (1848) < Gk *kreittōn* stronger, better + G *-it* -ite] A black variety of gahnite (q.v.). O, W [3]

kremersite, *n.* (1854) *Mineral.* [G *Kremersit* (1853) < the name of Peter *Kremers* (1827–post-1878), German chemist + *-it* -ite] A volcanic hydrous chloride of iron, potassium, and ammonium. O, W [3]

Kremnitz white, *see* Cremnitz white

Krems white, *n.* (1854) *Chem.* Var. **Crems white** [Transl. of G *Kremserweiss* < the comb. form of *Krems,* the Austrian town where it was first made + G *weiss* white] Cremmitz white, a lead pigment used by artists and in inks. O, W [3]

krennerite, *n.* (1878) *Mineral.* [G *Krennerit* (1877) < the name of Joseph *Krenner* (1839–1920), Hungarian mineralogist + G *-it* -ite] A gold telluride. O, W [3]

kreu(t)zer, *n.* (1547) *Currency* Var. **creutzer** [G *Kreuzer* < MHG *kriuzer,* transl. of ML *denarius cruciatus,* from the cross marking the coin] A small coin used in Austria, Germany, and Hungary from the Middle Ages to the mid-19th century. O, R, W [4]

Krieg, -e/-s *pl. Mil.* Var. **krieg** [G war] War. R [2]

kriegie, *n.* (1944) *Mil.* (slang) [Short. of G *Kriegsgefangener* prisoner of war < *Krieg* + *Gefangener*] An allied prisoner of war in Germany during World War Two. O, R [3]

kriegsspiel, *n.* (1811) *Mil.* [G < *Krieg* war + *Spiel* game] A game in which blocks and flags representing contending forces and guns are moved about as though in war conditions; a form of chess. —**kriegspiel(l)er** (1916, 1891). • ~ is transl. as **war game** (1828, q.v.). O, R, W [3]

krieker, *n.* (1890) *Zool.* [Ad. of G *Kriecher* creeper (or Du *krieken* to chirp, peep)] (U.S.) a name in New Jersey and Rhode Island for the pectoral sandpiper. O, W [3]

krimmer, *n.* (1834) *Apparel* Var. **crimmer** (1834), **crimmer** (1923) [G a type of sheep long raised in the Crimean Peninsula < *Krim* Crimea + *-er* -er] A gray fur resembling astrakhan; a pile fabric resembling this. O, R, W [4]

Kriss Kringle, *n.* (1830) *Myth.* Var. **Kris Kringle** (1849) [By folk etymology < G *Christkindl(ein)* little Christ child < *Christ* + *Kindlein,* dim. of *Kind* child] Santa Claus. O, R [4]

krone, -n *pl.* (1895) *Currency* [G crown] Austria's basic monetary unit from 1892 to 1925; a coin worth one krone (this is different < Dan *krone,* representing various Scandinavian coins). O, R, W [4]

krug, *n.* (1866) *Beverages* [G mug] A beer mug or tankard. O [3]

krumhorn, *see* krummhorn

Krummholz/krummholz, -ø *pl.* (1903) *Forestry* [G (1872) < *krumm* bent, crooked + *Holz* wood] Stunted forest; elfin wood. O, R, W [4]

krummhorn, *n.* (1694) *W9) Music* Var. **krumhorn** (1864),

crumhorn [G < *krumm* bent + *Horn* horn, a reed wind instrument, popular in the 16th and 17th cent.] An obsolete reed wind instrument; cromorna, an organ reed-stop. O, R, W [4]

kuchen, -ø *pl.* (1854) *Food* [G cake] Any of several varieties of coffee cake. • ~ appears terminally and regionally in compounds like **blitz/bund/cinnamon kuchen.** O, R, W [4]

kugelblitz, *see* ball lightning

kugelho(p)f, *n.* (1886) *Food* [Ad. of G *Gugelhupf, Gugelhopf*] Gugelhupf (q.v.). O, R, W [3]

Kultur/kultur, *n.* (1914) *Sociol.* [G < L *cultūra* cultivation (of body and mind)] Culture, esp. as conceived by the Germans (used in a derogatory sense during World Wars One and Two); an advanced stage or type of social organization, with emphasis on practical efficiency rather than on humanitarian concerns; culture conceived by German expansionists as an ideal state of civilization supposedly unique to Germany. —**Kultur,** *a.* (1916). O, R, W [4]

Kulturbild, *n.* (1961) *Anthrop.* [G < *Kultur* (q.v.) + *Bild* picture] A description of a given culture. O [2]

Kulturgeschichte, *n.* (1876) *History* Var. **culturegeschichte** [G < *Kultur* (q.v.) + *Geschichte* history] A history of the cultural development of a country or area; history of civilization. O [2]

Kulturgut, *n.* (1952) [G < *Kultur* (q.v.) + *Gut* asset, possesions] A cultural asset. O [3]

Kulturhound, *n.* (1946) Var. **kulturhund** (1963) [Ad. of G *Kulturhund* < *Kultur* (q.v.) + *Hund* hound] A culture vulture, one with excessive or pretentious interest in the arts. O [3]

Kulturkampf, *n.* (1879) *History* [G < *Kultur* (q.v.) + *Kampf* battle, struggle] Conflict between the government and religious authorities, specif. the struggle (1872–87) between the Roman Catholic Church and the German government chiefly motivated by Prince Bismarck's efforts to control education and church appointments to effect political centralization. O, R, W [4]

Kulturkreis, -e *pl.* (1948) *Anthrop.* [G (1897) < *Kultur* (q.v.) + *Kreis* circle, area] A cultural group; an orig. German anthropological concept of a culture complex developed from a focal area that spreads to wide areas of the world. O, R, W [3]

Kulturstaat, *n.* (1925) *Politics* [G < *Kultur* (q.v.) + *Staat* state < L *status*] A civilized country. O [2]

Kulturträger, -ø *pl.* (1920) [G < *Kultur* (q.v.) + *Träger* carrier, bearer] A supporter or defender of civilization. O [3]

kümmel, *n.* (1864) *Beverages, Food* [G < MHG *kümel* < OHG *kumil, kumin* < L *cumēnium* < Gk *kýminon* caraway seed] A colorless, aromatic liqueur flavored with caraway seeds, cumin, etc.; Leyden cheese flavored with caraway seeds; (cap.) these seeds. O, R, W [4]

Kunstforscher, -ø *pl.* (1899) *Art* [G < *Kunst* art + *Forscher* investigator, scholar] An art historian. O [2]

Kunstforschung, *n.* (1966) *Art* [G < *Kunst* art + *Forschung* research] The study of fine art; art history. O [2]

Kunstgeschichte, *n.* (1892) *Art* [G < *Kunst* art + *Geschichte* history] Art history. O [3]

Kunsthistoriker, -ø *pl.* (1937) *Art* [G < *Kunst* art + *His-*

toriker historian < L *historia* + G *-iker*] An art historian. O [3]

Künstlerroman, *n.* (1941) *Lit.* [G < *Künstler* artist + *Roman* novel < OFr *romans*] A Bildungsroman (q.v.) about an artist. O [3]

kunstlied, -er *pl.* (1880) *Music* [G < *Kunst* art + *Lied* song] An art song, esp. a song by a German composer, in contrast to a folk song. O, R, W [3]

Kunstprosa, *n.* (1936) *Lit.* [G < *Kunst* art + *Prosa* (< L) prose] A stylized or highly literary prose. O [3]

Kupferschiefer, *n.* (1830) *Geol.* [G < *Kupfer* copper + *Schiefer* slate] A bituminous, copper-rich shale of the Permian series. O [3]

Kur, *n.* (1885) *Med.* [G < L *cura* care, treatment] A cure, mainly the taking of the waters in a German-speaking country; a spa. O [3]

Kurhaus, -es *pl.* (1855) *Med.* [G < *Kur* (q.v.) + *Haus* house] The building at a German health resort where medicinal waters are dispensed; a pump room in Germany, sometimes a similar building outside Germany. O [3]

Kurort, *n.* (1868) *Med.* Var. **Curort** (1868), **kurort** (1930) [G < *Kur* (q.v.) + *Ort* place] A health resort in Germany or other German-speaking countries. O [3]

kursaal, *n.* (1849) *Med.* [G < *Kur* (q.v.) + *Saal* hall] A set of public rooms for visitors' entertainment at a health resort in Germany or England. O [3]

kutnahorite/kutnohorite, *n.* (1907) *Mineral.* [G *Kutnahorit* (1901) < the name of *Kutna Hora*, a town in Bohemia + G *-it* -ite] A rhombohedral carbonate of calcium, manganese, magnesium, and iron. O, W [3]

kyanite, *see* cyanite

kymograph, *n.* (1867) *Med.* Var. **cymograph** [G *Kymographion* (1850) (now *Kymograph*), the name given by the German physiologist A[lfred] W[ilhelm] Volkmann (1800–77) to the instrument invented by his colleague Friedrich Wilhelm Ludwig (1816–95) < *kymo-* + *-graphion* < Gk *kŷma* wave + *gráphein* to write, describe + G *-ion*] An instrument designed to record variations in pressure or motion graphically; an apparatus for recording on a moving X-ray film an organ's motion. —**kymographic(ally)** (1885, 1942), **kymogram** (1923), **kymography** (1930). O, R, W [4]

kynurenic acid, *n.* (1872) *Biochem.* [Transl. of G *Kynurensäure* (1853) < *Kynuren* (< Gk *kyn-* < *kýōn* dog + *oûron* urine) + G *Säure* acid] A crystalline carboxyllic acid produced by tryptophan metabolism as excretion in the urine of dogs and other animals. O, W [3]

kynurenine, *n.* (1931) *Biochem.* [G *Kynurenin* (1931) < *Kynuren* (see *kynurenic acid*) + *-in* -ine] A crystalline amino acid obtained from various animals' urine, which can form kynurenic acid. O, W [3]

kyrine, *n.* (1903) *Biochem.* [G *Kyrin* (1902) < Gk *kŷros* authority, validity, (fig.) nucleus + G *-in* -ine] One of various basic substances or mixtures once projected as the nucleus of the molecular structure of the proteins from which they were hydrolyzed. O [3]

kyrosite, *n.* (1896) *Mineral.* [G *Kyrosit* (1843) < Gk *kŷros* confirmation + G *-it* -ite, so named because its specific character was thought to be confirmed] A variety of marcasite, an iron mineral containing a small amount of arsenic. O [3]

L

Lach, *see* Lech

lachsschinken, -ø/-s *pl.* (1923) *Food* Var. **lachschinken** [G < *Lachs* salmon + *Schinken* ham] Cured and smoked pork loin rolled into a sausage. O, W [3]

lacmoid, *n.* (pre-1888) *Chem.* Var. **lackmoid** [Prob. < G *Lackmoid/Lakmoid* < *Lackmus,* ad. < Du *lakmoes* a blue dye + G *-oid* -oid (< Gk *-oeidēs*) similar] A violet-blue dye that resembles litmus. O, W [3]

lactam, *n.* (1883) *Chem.* [G (1882) (now also *Laktam*), a blend of *Lacton* lactone (q.v.) + *Amid* amide] Any of a class of cyclic amides analogous to lactones and formed by eliminating a molecule of water from the amino and carboxyl groups. O, R, W [4]

lactim, *n.* (1883) *Chem.* [G (1882) (now also *Laktim*), a blend of *Lakton* lactone (q.v.) + *Imid* immide, an ad. of *Amid* amide] Any of a class of cyclic imines that are isomers of the lactams. O, W [3]

lactobionic acid, *n.* (1889) *Chem.* [Transl. of G *Lactobionsäure* (1889) < *lacto-* (< the comb. form of L *lāc,* gen. *lactis* milk) + G *Bionik* < *bio-* < Gk *bíos* life + E *-(o)nic,* as in *electronics* + G *Säure* acid] A syrupy acid produced by oxidating lactose. —**lactobionate** (1927). O, W [3]

lactoflavin, *n.* (1933) *Chem.* [G (1933) < *Lacton* lactone (q.v.) + *Flavin* < L *flāvus* yellow + G *-in* -in] Riboflavin (q.v.), a crystalline pigment. O, R, W [3]

lactol, *n.* (1925) *Chem.* [G (1925) < *Lacton* lactone (q.v.) + G *-ol* -ol < *Alkohol* alcohol, ult. < Ar *al-kuḥul*] Any cyclic compound formed by the linking of the oxygen atom in a -C(OH)-group. O [3]

lactone, *n.* (1880) *Chem.* [G *Lacton* (1880) (now also *Lakton*) < *lacto-* + *-on* -one < L *lac* (gen. *lactis*) milk + Gk *-ōnē* fem. patronymic suffix] Any of an inner-amide class of amino carboxylic acids formed by eliminating a molecule of water from the hydroxyl and carboxyl groups. —**lactonization** (1909), **lactonize** (1912), **lactonized** (1939). O, R, W [4]

lactonic (acid), *n.* and *a.* (1871, 1871) *Chem.* [Transl. of G *Lactonsäure* (1870) < *Lacton* lactone (q.v.) + *Säure* acid] (of) galactonic acid, produced from milk sugar and galactose. O, R, W [3]

laemmergeier, *see* lammergeier

lager, *n.* (c.1853 *W9*) *Beverages* [Short. of G *Lagerbier* lager beer (q.v.)] Lager beer. —**lager lout/generation** (1988, 1989 *L2*). O, R, W [4]

lager, *v.* (1946) *Beverages* [G *lagern* to store, said of unaged beer that achieves its full taste during storage] To store beer during a period of aging. —**lagering,** *verbal n.* (1965). O, R, W [3]

lager beer, *n.* (1853) *Beverages* [G *Lagerbier* < *Lager* store, storage + *Bier* beer] A light, usu. dry beer brewed by bottom fermentation from malt with hops and water, and drunk mainly in Germany and America. —**lager beer,** *a.* (1882). • ~ appears initially in compounds like **lager** beer cellar (1854)/**cask** (1855)/**brewery** (1856)/**saloon** (1856)/**shop** (1861)/**garden** (1868)/**schooner** (1869)/**wagon** (1869). O, R, W [4]

Lakenvelder/lakenvelder, *n.* *Zool.* [G short. of *Lakenfelder Haushuhn,* a domestic fowl bred in Western Hanover, Germany, as early as 1835 and that gets its name < *Laken* sheets of white linen + *Felder* fields, i.e., patches of white spread over a black field (Du *Lakenfeller*)] (Cap.) this German breed of strikingly marked black-and-white fowls; a bird of this breed. W [3]

lammergeier/lämmergeyer *n.* (1817) *Ornith.* Var. **laemmergeier, lammergeier** [G < *Lämmer* (pl. of *Lamm* lamb, a prey this vulture prefers) + *Geier* vulture] A large bird of prey, also called *bearded vulture.* O, R, W [4]

lampbrush, *n.* (1901) *Biol.* [Loose transl. and short. of G *Lampencylinderputzer* lamp glass cleaner] Lampbrush chromosome (q.v.). O [3]

lampbrush chromosome, *n.* (1911) *Biol.* [Transl. of G *Lampenbürstenchromosom* (1892) < *Lampe* + *Bürste* + *Chromosom* chromosome (q.v.)] A greatly enlarged pachytene chromosome resembling a bottle brush. O, W [4]

lamprophyllite, *n.* (1899) *Mineral.* [G *Lamprophyllit* (1894) < *lampro-* + *phyll-* + *-it* -it < Gk *lamprós* gleaming, shining + *phýllon* leaf] A rare silicate of sodium, strontium, and titanium. O, W [3]

lamprophyre, *n.* (1890) *Geol.* [G *Lamprophyr* (1874) < *lampro-* + *-phyr* < Gk *lamprós* gleaming, shining + *-phyr,* as in *porphýra* rock shell] Any of a series of dark, traplike rocks of alkaline aspect. —**lamprophyric** (1892). O, R, W [3]

lance-knight, *n.* (1530) *Mil.* [Folk-etymological transl. of erron. G *Lanzknecht* landsknecht (q.v.)] Mercenary foot-soldier, esp. one armed with a pike: landsknecht. O, W [3]

land, länder/laender/lands *pl.* (1920) *Politics* [G land, province, state (part of a country)] A semiautonomous, local unit of government in Germany or Austria. O, W [3]

landamman(n), *n.* (1796) *Politics* [(Swiss) G *Landamann* < G *Land* land + *Ammann* < MHG *ambetmann,* NHG *Amtmann* official, an officeholder] The chief magistrate's title in certain Swiss cantons. O [3]

landau, *n.* (1743) *Transportation* Old var. like **lando** (1743), **landau carriage** (1794) [G *Landauer,* short. < *Landauer Wagen* a carriage seating four, first made in *Landau,* Bavaria, Germany] A four-wheeled carriage with folding top; transf. sense as a closed automobile with a similar feature. —**landaulet(te)** (1791, 1901). O, R, W [4]

landgrave, *n.* (1516) *Politics* [G *Landgraf* < *Land* land + *Graf* count] A German count possessing certain territorial jurisdictions; a later title of certain German princes; (U.S. archaic) a county nobleman in the Carolina colony. —**landgraveship** (1669), **-gravess** (1762), **-grav(i)ate.** O, R, W [4]

landgravine, *n.* (1682) *Politics* [G *Landgräfin* < *Landgraf* landgrave (q.v.) + fem. suffix *-in*] The wife of a landgrave; a woman of that rank and power. O, R, W [3]

ländler, -ø/-s *pl.* (1876) *Dance* [G a dance that is danced "im Landt" (now "auf dem Lande") in the country rather than in the city < the name of *Landl,* in upper Austria] An Austrian couple dance of rural origin, similar to a slow waltz; music for this. O, R, W [3]

landsknecht, *n.* (1530) *Mil., Games* Var. **lance-knight** by folk etymology (1530) and various obs. forms [G < *Knecht* now a servant, soldier recruited in the *Land* (gen. *Landes*), i.e., "Imperial Domain"] A mercenary footsoldier in the German or other European armies in the 16th and 17th centuries; a faro-like card game played in Germany (and later elsewhere) at least by the 15th century. • ~ is often written in its Fr form *lansquenet* (1607), borrowed < G. O, R, W [3]

landsturm, *n.* (1814) *Mil.* Var. **Landsturm** [G the home guard, orig. the call to arms made by storm-warning bells < *Land* land + *Sturm* storm] A general levy in wartime in some European countries; the militia so called out, as opposed to the *landwehr* (q.v.); home reserves. O, R, W [3]

Landtag, *n.* (1591) *Politics* [G < *Land* land, estates + *Tag* day, diet, orig., the periodic day on which the estates of the realm in the Holy Roman Empire of the German Nation met; now the convening of the parliament in certain modern German states] Diet of the old German empire or of some modern German states. O, R [3]

landvogt, *n. Politics* [G < *Land* land + *Vogt* < OHG *fogat* < ML *vocatus,* a short. of *advocat* (NHG *Advokat* attorney)] In the Middle Ages, the governor of a German royal province or district. W [3]

landwehr, *n.* (1815) *Mil.* Old var. **Landwehr** [G < MHG *lantwer* forces called to defend the land < OHG *lantwerī*] The trained military reserve forming part of the national army in Germany, Austria, etc. —**landwehr,** *a.* (1866). O, R, W [3]

långbanite, *n.* (1887) *Mineral.* [G or Sw *Långbanit* (1887) < *Långban,* the name of a town in Värmland, Sweden + G or Sw *-it* -ite] A prismatic silicate and oxide of manganese, iron, and antimony. •As G *Långbanit* used the Sw diacritic *å,* it is difficult to determine when the orig. Swedish form was borrowed into English, or when the Swedish-borrowed German was the etymon. O, W [3]

langbeinite, *n.* (1898) *Mineral.* [G *Langbeinit* (1891) < the name of A. *Langbein,* 19th-cent. German chemist of Leopoldshall + G *-it* -ite] A double sulfate of potassium and magnesium, much used for fertilizer. O, R, W [3]

langlauf, *n.* (1927) *Sports* [G < *lang* long in distance + *Lauf* run, race] Cross-country skiing, a running or racing on skis. O, R, W [4]

langläufer, -ø/-s *pl.* (1929) *Sports* [G < *lang* long (in distance) + *Läufer* runner < *laufen* to run + *-er* -er] A cross-country skier. O, R, W [4]

langley, *n.* (1947) *Meteor.* [G (1942), used by Karl Wilhelm Franz Linke (1878–1944), German meteorologist < the name of Samuel P. *Langley* (1834–1906), American astronomer] A unit of solar energy per unit area. • ~ is symbolized as **ly.** O, R [3]

lanolin, *n.* (1885) *Chem.* Var. **lanoline** (1894) [G < L *lana*

wool + *oleum* oil + G *-in* -in] Wool grease refined for ointments and cosmetics; the cholesterol-fatty matter obtained from sheep's wool for such refinement; also called *(refined) wool fat.* —**lanolated, lanolize.** O, R, W [4]

lansfordite, *n.* (1888) *Mineral.* [G *Lansfordit* (1888) < *Lansford,* the name of a town in Pennsylvania + G *-it* -ite] Basic magnesium carbonate. O, W [3]

lanthanide, *n.* (1926) *Chem.* [G *Lanthanid* (1925), used by the Swiss-born mineralogist Victor Moritz Goldschmidt (1888–1947) < *Lanthan* lanthanum < Gk *lanthánein* to be hidden + G *-id* -ide] Any of the family of rare-earth metals with an atomic number between 57 (lanthanum) or 58 (cerium) and 71 (lutetium); the element of this series, also called *lanthanon* and symbolized as *Ln.* —**lanthanon** (1947), **lanthanoid** (1953), **lanthanide series** (1945). O, R, W [4]

lanthanide contraction, *n.* (1926) *Chem.* [Ad. of G *Lanthanidenkontraktion* (1925) < *pl.* of *Lanthanid* lanthanide (q.v.) + *Kontraktion* contraction < L *contrahere* to draw together] The decrease in size, such as in atomic and ionic radii, relative to increasing atomic number as found in the lanthanide series. O, W [3]

lanthanite, *n.* (1849) *Mineral.* [G *Lanthanit* (1845) < NL *lanthanum* < Gk *lanthánein* to be hidden + G *-it* -ite] Hydrous lanthanum carbonate. O, W [3]

lanthopine, *n.* (1888) *Chem.* [G *Lanthopin* < *lanth-* + *Opium* + *-in* -ine < Gk *lanthánein* + *ópion,* dim. of *opós* sap] A crystalline alkaloid found in opium. O, W [3]

laparoscopy, *n.* (1916) *Med.* [G *Laparoskopie* (1910), first used in this specific sense by the German physician Hans Christian Jacobaeus (1879–1937) < *laparo-* + *-skopie* < Gk *laparo-,* the comb. form of *lapára* part of the body between the ribs, hips, and flanks + G *skopeîn* to view, examine] Visual examination of the inner peritoneal cavity by inserting a laparoscope into it through the abdominal wall or vagina. —**laparoscopic** (1967), **laparoscopist** (1967). • ~ makes specific the old, general, Greek-derived meaning of "examination of the loins or abdomen." O [4]

larch, -es *pl.* (1548) and *a.* (1548) *Bot.* [G *Lärche* < MHG *lerche/larche,* ult. < L *larix* (gen. *laricis*) a coniferous tree with light-green, clustered needles] (Of) any of several coniferous trees of the genus *Larix* or the family Pinaceae that shed their needles during the fall and winter; (of) the wood of this tree. —**larchen,** *a.* (1818). • ~ appears in several compounds like **larch turpentine** (1616)/**bark** (1827)/**canker** (1891)/**pine.** O, R, W [4]

larvikite/laurvikite, *n.* (1895) *Mineral.* [G *Larvikit* (1890) < the name of *Laurvik,* now *Larvik,* a port in Norway + G *-it* -ite] An alkali-syenite rock that is widely used as a decorative stone. O, W [3]

lateritization, *n.* (1903) *Geol.* [Transl. of G *Lateritisirung* (1898) (now *Lateritisierung*) < *Laterit* + *-ization* (see *laterization*)] Laterization. O [3]

laterization, *n.* (1903) *Geol.* Var. **lateritization** (1903) [Transl. of G *Lateritisirung* (1898) (now also *Lateritisierung*), prob. back-formation of *lateritisieren* to convert into laterite < L *laterit* brick + an infixed G *-is-* + verbal suffix *-ieren*] The process of converting rock to laterite; the converting itself. —**laterized** (1911), **laterizing** (1911). O, W [4]

laterize, *v.* (1920) *Geol.* [Prob. transl. of G *lateritisieren* (see *laterization*) + *-ieren* -ize] To convert into laterite. —**lateritized**, *part. a.* (1920). O [3]

laubanite, *n.* (1888) *Mineral.* [G *Laubanit* (1887), named by the German scholar H. Traube (prob. the mineralogist Hermann Traube, b. 1856) < the Siberian place-name *Lauban,* where it was found + G *-it* -ite] Hydrous silicate of aluminum and calcium. O [3]

laudanine, *n.* (1871) *Chem.* [G *Laudanin* (1870) < *Laudanum* (< ML, prob. < L *ladanum* < Gk *lēdanon* rock-rose) + G *-in* -ine] A poisonous, crystalline alkaloid obtained from opium. O, W [3]

laudanosine, *n.* (1871) *Chem.* [G *Laudanosin* (1871), irreg. < *Laudanin* laudanine (q.v.) + *-ose-* denoting a carbo-hydrate + *-in* -ine] Another poisonous alkaloid obtained from opium; laudanine methyl ether. O, W [3]

Lauegram, *n.* (1915) *Physics* Var. **Laue photograph** (1915) [Short. of G *Laue-Diagramm* < the name of Max von *Laue* (1879–1960), German physicist + *Diagramm* diagram < Gk *díagramma*] Laue pattern, a kind of diffraction photographic record. —**Laue pattern/spot** (1940, 1940). O, W [3]

Laufen, *a.* (1927) *Geol.* [G (1909) < the name of *Laufen,* a place near Salzburg, Germany, used to name a minor retreat and advance of Alpine glaciation] This oscillating glaciation, which briefly followed the Würm (q.v.) stage. O [3]

laumontite, *n.* (1805) *Mineral.* Var. **lomonite** (1805), **laumonite** (1808) [Ad. of G *Lomontit* (1805), phonetically < the name of François Pierre Nicolas Gillet de *Laumont* (1747–1834), its French discoverer + G *-it* -ite] Hydrous silicate of calcium and aluminum. O, R, W [3]

laurionite, *n.* (1887) *Mineral.* [G *Laurionit* (1887) < *Laurion,* the name of a Greek town + G *-it* -ite] A prismatic, basic lead chloride. O, W [3]

laurite, *n.* (1866) *Mineral.* [G *Laurit* (1866), named by Friedrich Wöhler for *Laura,* the wife of Charles Arad Joy (1823–91), American chemist + G *-it* -ite] Ruthenium sulfide. O, W [3]

laurvikite *see* larvikite

lautarite, *n.* (1892) *Mineral.* [G *Lautarit* (1891) < Oficina *Lautar(o),* the name of the Chilean pampa's owner + G *-it* -ite] Prismatic calcium iodate. O, W [3]

lautenclavicymbal, *n. Music* [G *Lautenklavizymbel* < Late MHG *lūte* < MF *lut,* ult. Ar *al-ud* the (instrument of) wood + ML (< L) *clavis* (piano) key + G *Zymbel* (now *Zymbal/Zimbel*) < L *cymbalum* < Gk *kýmbalon* (ancient) cymbal] A harpsichord that has strings of gut rather than of metal. R [3]

lauter, *a. Beverages* [G clear, pure < OHG *hlūtar* pure] Clear, as in mash; clarified, as in beer. —**lauter**, *v.* W [3]

lauter tub/tun, *n. Beverages* [Partial transl. of G *Läuter-bottich* < *läutern* to purify, refine, rectify + *Bottich* vat] A brewing tank for draining off or filtering the clear liquid wort in the mash. R, W [3]

lautite, *n.* (1883) *Mineral.* [G *Lautit* (1881) < *Lauta,* the name of a town near Marienburg, Germany + *-it* -ite] An orthorhombic sulfide and arsenide of copper. O, W [3]

lautverschiebung, -en *pl. Ling.* [G < *Laut* sound + *Verschiebung* shift] Consonant shift, one change in a set of changes in one or more consonants in a given period of a language's development. W [3]

lauwine, *n.* (1818) *Geol.* Old var. **lawine** (1845) [G *Lawine* < *lau* mild < (Romansh) *lavina* < ML *labina* < L *lābi* to glide] An avalanche. O [3]

Laves phase, *n.* (1940) *Metall.* [G (1939) < the name of Fritz-Henning *Laves* (1906–78), German mineralogist + *Phase* phase < NL *phasis*] Any of a group of intermetallic compounds whose stable structure and combination mechanism are determined by the crystal lattice. O [3]

lawine, *see* lauwine

layer lattice, *n.* (1929) *Crystal.* [Transl. of G *Schichtengitter* (1925) < *Schichte* layer + *Gitter* lattice] A crystal lattice in which the atoms are arranged in special ways in layers of a few atoms thick. O [3]

lazulite, *n.* (1807) *Mineral.* [G *Lazulith* (1795), named by Martin Heinrich Klaproth (1743–1817), German chemist < the older name *Lazurstein* < ML *lazulum* (gen. *lazuli*) lapis lazuli < Ar *lāzaward*) + G *-lith* < Gk *líthos* (G *Stein*) stone] An azure-blue, hydrous phosphate of iron, magnesium, and aluminum. —**lazulite**, *a.* (1811); **lazulitic** (1853). O, R, W [4]

lazurite, *n.* (1892) *Mineral.* [G *Lasurit* (1853), so named by Franz von Kobell (1803–82), German mineralogist < ML *lazur* lapis lazuli < Ar *lāzaward* + G *-it* -ite] The chief constituent of lapis lazuli, composed of a sodium silicate containing sulfur. O, R, W [4]

Leader, *n.* (1934) *Politics* [Transl. of G *Führer* leader, It *Duce,* Sp *Caudillo*] The head of an authoritarian state (the first known recorded English use, in 1918, is transl. < *Caudillo*). O, W [3]

lead glance, *n.* (1810) *Mineral.* [Transl. of G *Bleiglanz* < *Blei* lead + *Glanz* glance (q.v.)] Galena, a lead sulfide. O, W [3]

leading motive, *see* leitmotiv

lear, *see* lehr

leb(en)-, *comb. form* [G life] •Considering the number of German borrowings with this as the initial element, it is interesting that this element gives little or no evidence of becoming productive in English to create new English words.

Lebensform, -en *pl.* (1937) *Sociol.* [Wittgenstein's G < the gen. of *Leben* life + *Form* form < L *forma*] Any type of human activity involving values (religious, artistic, political, etc.); a style of life. O [2]

lebenslust, *n.* (1890) [G < the gen. of *Leben* life + *Lust* joy] Joy of living. O [2]

lebensraum/Lebensraum, *n.* (1905) *Politics* [G < the gen. of *Leben* life, living + *Raum* space] Space in which a country can live and grow; a territory that is considered necessary for the existence of a state. • ~ is transl. as **living room** (1934), which is of course different from the old meaning of "room in a residence used for the occupants' common social activities." O, R, W [4]

lebensspur/Lebensspur, -en *pl.* (1960) *Geol.* [G (1912) < the gen. of *Leben* life + *Spur* track, trace] An organism's small track, burrow, cast, or the like left in sediment, esp. when preserved as a fossil. O [3]

Lebenswelt, *n.* (1962) *Philos.* [G < the gen. of *Leben* life + *Welt* world] World of direct, lived experience. O [3]

leberwurst, *n.* (1855) *Food* [G < *Leber* + *Wurst* sausage] Liver sausage (q.v.). O, W [3]

lebhaft, *a. Music* [G lively < MHG *lebehaft* alive] Vivace, lively (used in music as a direction). W [3]

lebkuchen, -ø *pl. Food* [G < *leb-,* prob. related to *Laib* loaf + *Kuchen* (q.v.) cake] A Christmas cookie usu. flavored with spices and honey and containing nuts and candied fruit peel. R, W [3]

Lech, *n.* (1893) *Ethnology* Var. **Lekh** (1893), **Lach** (1911) [G < ORuss *lyakh,* OPol **lech*] A member of an early Slavic people who once inhabited the area around the upper Oder and Vistula; the name of their legendary ancestor. —**Lech, a.** (1911). O [3]

Lechish, *n.* (1888) *Ling.* [G *lechisch,* the adj. form of *Lech* (q.v.)] Certain West Slavic languages, e.g., Polish, Polabian. —**Lechish, a.** (1936–37). O [3]

Lechitic, *n.* (1934) and *a.* (1935) *Ling.* [G *lechitisch,* a var. of *lechisch* and the adj. form of *Lech* (q.v.)] (of) a linguistic name for certain West Slavic languages (Polish, Kashubian, Slovincian). O [3]

ledeburite, *n.* (1912) *Metall.* [G *Ledeburit* (1909) < the name of Adolf *Ledebur* (1837–1906), German mineralogist + *-it* -ite] The eutectic found in cast iron and some high-alloy steels that is composed of austenite and cementite. O, W [3]

lederhosen, *pl.* (1936 *W9*) *Apparel* [G < MHG *lederhose* leather trousers] Knee-length leather trousers worn esp. in Bavaria and other Alpine areas. O, R, W [4]

leer, *see* lehr

lehm, *n.* (1833) *Geol.* [G loam] Loess (q.v.), as in the Rhine valley. O [3]

lehr, *n.* (1598) *Tech.* Var. **leer** (1662), **lear** (1797) [G < a short. of *Lehrofen* < *Lehre,* MHG *lēre* model, measure, tool for measuring + *Ofen* oven] A long oven in which glassware is annealed on a continuous belt. —**lehrman** (1849), **leering** (1889). O, R, W [4]

Lehrjahre, *pl.* (1865) [G < *lehren* to teach + *Jahre,* pl. of *Jahr* year] Term of apprenticeship, usu. fig. rather than a formal arrangement of a given number of years in a trade or profession. O [2]

Leibniz's law, *n.* (1941) *Math.* Var. **Leibnitz's law** [Transl. of G *Leibniz-Regel* Leibniz's rule or *Leibniz-Kriterium* Leibniz's criterium, from the name of the German philosopher Gottfried Wilhelm Leibnitz (1646–1716)] The principle of the identity of indiscernibles or individuals. O [3]

Leidenfrost phenomenon, *n.* (1967) *Physics* [Transl. of G *das Leidenfrostsche-Phänomen* (now usu. *Leidenfrost Phänomen*) < the name of Johann Gottlob *Leidenfrost* (1715–94), German physician + *Phänomen* phenomenon < LL *phaenomenon* < Gk *phaenómenon*] A phenomenon where a hot surface generates a layer of insulating vapor and so repels a liquid; a hypothetical phenomenon applied analogously to the relationship of matter and antimatter in the boundary regions where particles and antiparticles meet. B [3]

leitmotiv/leitmotif, *n.* (1876) *Music* Var. **leitmotive** (1876) [G *Leitmotiv* < *leit-* leading < *leiten* to guide + *Motiv* motif < Fr *motif*] A melodic phrase or figure, esp. in Wagnerian opera, which marks a particular character, sentiment, or situation and which recurs every time that particular element appears; fig. as in a recurring theme in literature, etc. • ~ is transl. as **leading motive** (1883). O, R, W [4]

Lekh, *see* Lech

lenition, *n.* (1912) *Ling.* [Transl. of G *Lenierung* < L *lēnis* soft + G *-ierung* -ition] In Celtic languages, the process or result of becoming lenis; a change from fortis to lenis articulation. —**lenition, a.** (1953). O, R, W [3]

Lenz's law, *n.* (1866) *Physics* [Transl. of G *Lenz-Gesetz* or *Lenz-Regel* (1834) < the name of Heinrich F. E. *Lenz* (1804–65), German-born physicist + *Gesetz* or *Regel* law] A law explaining the direction of a current produced by electromotive force due to electromagnetic induction. O, W [3]

leonhardite, *n.* (1848) *Mineral.* [G *Leonhardit* (1843) < the name of Karl Cäsar von *Leonhard* (1779–1862), German mineralogist + *-it* -ite] Partially dehydrated laumontite (q.v.). O, W [3]

leonite, *n.* (1897) *Mineral.* [G *Leonit* (1896) < the name of *Leo* Strippelmann, German director of the salt works at Westerregeln, Germany, in the 19th cent. + *-it* -ite] A hydrous sulfate of potassium and magnesium. O, W [3]

leopoldite, *n.* (1882) *Mineral.* [G *Leopoldit* < *Leopoldshall,* now a part of the German city of Stassfurt + *-it* -ite] Sylvite, a potassium chloride. O, W [3]

lepidoblastic, *a. Geol.* [G *lepidoblastisch* < ·*lepido-* + *-blastisch* < Gk *lepís* (gen. *lepídos*) scale + *blastós* bud + G *-isch* -ic] Of a texture in a metamorphic rock analogous to the scaly texture of an igneous rock. W [3]

lepidocrocite, *n.* (1823) *Mineral.* [G *Lepidokrokit* < *lepido-* < Gk *lepís* (gen. *lepídos*) scale + *krókē* thread, filament + G *-it* -ite] An iron oxide hydroxide found in some iron ores. O, R, W [3]

lepidolite, *n.* (1796) *Mineral.* [G *Lepidolith* (now *Lepidolit*) < *lepido-* + *-lith* < Gk *lepís* (gen. *lepídos*) scale + *líthos* stone] A mineral of somewhat varied composition: lithia mica. O, R, W [4]

lepidomelane, *n.* (1844) *Mineral.* [G *Lepidomelan* < *lepido-* + *-melan* < Gk *lepís* (gen. *lepídos*) scale + *mélas* (gen. *mélanos*) black] A mica: ferrian biotite (q.v.). O, W [3]

lepromin, *n.* (1932) *Med.* [G (1927) < NL *leproma* leprous tubercle < Gk *lépra* rash, formed on the analogy of words like *sarcoma* + G *-in* -in] An extract of human leprous tissue used in skin tests for leprosy. —**lepromin test** (1940). O, W [3]

leptene, *a. Anthrop.* Var. **leptenic** [G *lepten* < *lept-* (< Gk *leptós* thin, narrow) + G *-en* -ene] Of a facial index used for persons having a high and/or narrow forehead. —**lepteny,** *n.* W [3]

leptochlorite, *n. Mineral.* [Prob. < G *Leptochlorit* < *lepto-* + *Chlorit* < Gk *leptós* thin, narrow, delicate + *chlōrós* yellow green + G *-it* -ite] Any of various chlorites of indistinct crystallization. W [3]

leptome, *n.* (1898) *Bot.* Var. **leptom** (1902) [G *Leptom* (1884) < *lept-* + *-om* < Gk *leptós* thin + *sôma* body] The part of the mestome that conducts food materials; a cryptogam's somewhat rudimentary phloem. —**leptocentric** (1914). O, R [3]

leptonology, *n.* (1917) *Geol.* [G *Leptonologie* (1916) (a rendering of *Feinbaulehre der Materie*) < Gk *leptós* (neuter *leptón*) small, slight, slender + G *-logie* < L *-logia* -logy] The study of the ultimate structure of matter. O [2]

leptoprosopic, *a.* (1889) *Anthrop.* Var. **leptoprosopous** [G *leptoprosopisch* < *lepto-* < Gk *leptós* small + G adj. suffix *-isch* -ic] Of a facial index used for persons having a long and/or narrow face. O, W [3]

leptosomic/leptosome, *a.* (1931 *W9*) *Med.* Var. **leptosomatic** (1937) [G *leptosom* < *lepto-* + *-som* < Gk *leptós* narrow, thin + *sôma* body (+ E *-ic*)] Of asthenic or ectomorphic physique. O, R, W [4]

leptosome, *n.* (1931) *Med.* Var. **leptosom** [G *Leptosom* (see *leptosomic, a.*)] A person of leptosomic physique. O, R, W [4]

letovicite, *n.* (1932) *Mineral.* [G *Letovicit* (1932) (now also *Letovizit*) < the name of *Letovice*, a Czechoslovakian town in Moravia + G *-it* -ite] An acid ammonium sulfate, found in coal-mine waste-mounds. O, W [3]

Lett, *n.* (1589) *Ethnology, Ling.* [G *Lette* an inhabitant of *Lettland* (Latvia) (< OHG *letto* clay + *Land* land), ult. < Latvian *Latvi*] An individual belonging to the people called Letts; those people (Lettish) or their language; a Latvian. —**Letto-,** *comb. form* (1880). O, R, W [4]

Lettish, *a.* (1831) *Ethnology, Ling.* Var. **Lettic** [G *lettisch* < *Lette* Lett (q.v.) + adj. suffix *-isch* -ish] Of or relating to the Letts, Latvians, or their language. —**Lettish,** *n.* (1841). O, W [3]

leucaemia, *see* leukemia

leuchtenbergite, *n.* (1844) *Mineral.* [G *Leuchtenbergit* (1842) < the name of Maksimilian Leikhtenbergskii (1817–52), duke of *Leuchtenberg* + G *-it* -ite] A variety of clinochlore that often resembles talc. O, W [3]

leucite, *n.* (1799) *Mineral.* Var. **leucit** (1799) [G *Leucit* (1791) (now *Leuzit*) < *Leucit* (< Gk *leukós* white, bright) + G *-it* -ite] Silicate of aluminum and potassium found in igneous rocks, also called *amphigene.*—**leucite,** *a.* (1878); **leucitic** (1830). O, R, W [4]

leucitite, *n.* *Mineral.* [G *Leucitit* (now *Leuzitit*) < *Leucit* leucite (q.v.) + *-it* -ite] A basaltic rock mainly composed of leucite with augite and some magnetite (q.v.). R, W [3]

leucitophyre, *n.* (1879) *Geol.* [Prob. < G *Leucitophyr* < *Leucit* (see *leucite*) + *-phyr* (< Gk), as in *porphýra* rock shell] A porphyry containing leucite phenocrysts. O, W [3]

leucochalcite, *n.* (1883) *Mineral.* [G *Leucochalcit* (1881) (now *Leukochalzit*) < *leuco-* + *chalc-* + *-it* -ite < Gk *leukós* white, bright + *chalcós* ore, metal, copper] A basic arsenate of copper crystallizing as white needles. O, W [3]

leucocratic, *a.* (1909) *Geol.* [G *leukokrat* (1898) < *leuko-* + *-krat* < Gk *leukós* white, bright + *krateîn* to dominate + E *-ic*] Rich in light-colored minerals; having a light color. O, R, W [4]

leucophore, *n.* (1924) *Physiol.* [G *Leukophor* (1895) < *leuko-* + *-phor* < Gk *leukós* light, bright + *phor-* < *phérein* to bear, carry] A white chromatophore. O, W [3]

leucoplast, *n.* (1886) *Biol.* [G *Leukoplast* < *leuko-* + *-plast* < the comb. form of Gk *leukós* white, bright + *plastós* formed, shaped] A colorless plastid, specif. one capable of becoming a chromoplast. O, R, W [4]

leucosis/leukosis, -oses *pl.* (1922) *Med.* [G *Leukosis* (1908) < *leuko-* (< Gk *leukós* white, bright) + G *-sis* (< Gk fem. suffix of action) -sis] Any of the various leukemic diseases of animals (this is different from the old "pallor, albino" meaning). —**leukotic.** O, R [3]

leucosphenite, *n.* *Mineral.* [Prob. < G *Leukosphenit* < *leuko-* + *Sphenit* < the comb. form of Gk *leukós* white, bright + *sphén* wedge + G *-it* -ite] A sodium barium silicotitanate, found in white crystals. W [3]

leucoxene, *n.* *Mineral.* [G *Leukoxen* < *leuko-* + *-xen* + *-en* -ene < Gk *leukós* white, bright + *xénos* stranger] A general term for alteration products of ilmenite (q.v.). W [3]

leuk(a)emia, *n.* (1855) *Path.* Var. **leuc(a)emia** (1876) [G *Leukämie* (1848) < Gk *leuchaimía* < *leukós* white + *haîma* blood] A sometimes fatal cancerous disease of humans and other warm-blooded animals characterized by an abnormal increase in the number of leukocytes in body tissue. —**leuk(a)emic** (1876), **leukemogen(ic)** (1944, 1942). O, R, W [4]

leukosis, *see* leucosis

leuma, *n.* *Med.* [G (actually L) *Leuma (equorum)* < Gk *loimê* pestilence + L *equus* (gen. pl. *equorum*) horse] Shipping fever, a viral disease of horses: pinkeye. W [3]

levade, *n.* (1944) *Sports* [G < Fr *lever* to lift < L *levāre* to lift + G *-ade* -ade] A show-ring movement in which a horse raises its forequarters and balances. O, R, W [3]

libethenite, *n.* (1832) *Mineral.* [G *Libethenit* (1823) < *Libethen,* the name of a town in Slovakia near Banska Bystrica + G *-it* -ite] An olive-green, basic phosphate of copper. O, W [3]

libido, *n.* (1909) *Psych.* [G < L lust, desire < *libēre* to please] (Sigmund Freud's term for) psychic or emotional drive or energy, esp. when associated with the sexual instinct, and in psychoanalytic theory is derived from primitive biological drives; frequency of sexual activity; lustful striving or desire. —**libido theory** (1932). O, R, W [4]

Liebchen/liebchen, *n.* (1876) [G sweetheart < *lieben* to love + nom. dim. suffix *-chen* -kin, etc.] Someone who is very dear; (often used as a term of address) sweetheart, pet, darling. O [3]

lieber Gott, *n.* (1898) and *interj.* (1912) [G < *lieb* dear + *Gott* God] Dear God; good God. O [3]

Lieberkühn, *n.* (1867) *Optics* [G a reflector named for its German inventor Johann N. *Lieberkühn* (1711–56)] A concave reflector attached to a microscope to focus the light on an opaque object. O [3]

Lieberkühn's gland, *n.* (1844) *Med.* Var. **Lieberkühn's crypt, crypt of Lieberkühn** [Transl. of G *Lieberkühnsche Krypte* (now *Lieberkühn-Drüse* Lieberkühn's gland) < the name *Lieberkühn* (q.v.) + *Krypte* crypt < Gk *kryptós* hidden + G *-isch* -ish] A tubular gland of the intestinal mucous membrane. O, W [3]

Liebestod/liebestod, *n.* (1889) *Music* [G < the comb. form of *Liebe* love + *Tod* death] An aria or a duet proclaiming lovers' suicide, as in Wagner's death scene for Isolde; such a suicide. O [3]

Liebfraumilch, *n.* (1833) *Beverages* Var. **Liebfrauenmilch** [G *Liebfrau(en)milch* < the gen. of *Liebfrau,* as in *Liebfrauenstift,* lit., Foundation of the Virgin Mary + *Milch* milk] A white wine orig. made at Worms, Germany; loosely, a similar German white wine. O, R, W [4]

lieblich, *a.* *Music* [G pleasant, charming < *Liebe* love + adj. and adv. suffix *-lich* -ly] Sweet in tone (used in organstop names). W [3]

Liebling/liebling, -e *pl.* (1868) [G < *lieb* dear + nom. suffix *-ling* -ling] Liebchen (q.v.). O [2]

lied, -er *pl.* (1852) *Music* Var. **Lied** (1852) [G short. of *Kunstlied* < *Kunst* art + *Lied* song] Generally, a song in the German vernacular, dominantly sentimental rather than narrative; a kunstlied (q.v.), a German art song, principally of the 19th century. O, R, W [4]

Liederkranz[1], *n.* (1858) *Music* [G < *Lieder*, pl. of *Lied* song + *Kranz* wreath, collection, circle] A group of songs; a singing society of usu. males of German background. O, R [3]

Liederkranz[2], *n.* *Food* [Short. of G *Liederkranzkäse* a cheese made in the U.S. that Emil Frey named after his *Liederkranz* singing society in 1892 + *Käse* cheese] A trademark for a soft milk cheese resembling a mild Limburger. R [3]

Lieder singer, *n.* (1936) *Music* [Partial transl. of G *Liedersänger(in)* < *Lieder*, pl. of *Lied* song + *Sänger(in)* male (or female) singer] One who sings lieder (q.v.). —**liedersinging** (1937). O [3]

lievrite, *n.* (1814) *Mineral.* [G *Lievrit* (1812) < the name of Claude Hugues Lelièvre (1752–1835), French mineralogist + G *-it* -ite] Ilvaite (q.v.). O, W [3]

life-world, *n.* (1940) *Philos.* [Transl. of G *Lebenswelt* (1924, but published in 1936, q.v.), used by the Austrian-born philosopher Edmund G. A. Husserl (1859–1938) < the gen. of *Leben* life + *Welt* world] All the immediate activities, experiences, and contacts that compose an individual's world: human existence as a realm of practical activity. O [3]

lignocaine, *n.* (1954) *Med.* [G *Lignokain*, a substitution of *ligno-* for the first element in *Xylokain* < *Kokain* cocaine (q.v.) + *-in* -ine] A crystalline, aromatic amide, used in its hydrochloride form as a local anesthetic and also in tablets and creams. O, R [3]

ligroin, *n.* (1881) *Chem.* Var. **ligroine** [G tradename] Any of various petroleum naphtha fractions, chiefly used as solvents. O, R, W [4]

lillianite, *n.* (1892) *Mineral.* [G *Lillianit* (1889) < *Lillian*, the name of a mine in Leadville, Colorado + G *-it* -ite] A sulfide of bismuth and lead. O, W [3]

limbachite, *n.* (1882) *Mineral.* [Prob. < G *Limbachit* (1873), named by Friedrich August Frenzel (1842–1902), German mineralogist < the German town of *Limbach*, Saxony, now *Limbach-Oberfrohna* + *-it* -ite] A hydrous silicate of aluminum and magnesium. O [3]

limen, *n.* (1895) *Psych.* [Transl. of G *Schwelle* (1824) threshold (= L *līmen*), a short. of G *Reizschwelle* < *reizen* to stimulate + *Schwelle*] Threshold (an E transl. of *Schwelle*), the point at which a psychological or physiological effect begins to be produced. —**stimulus limen** (1895). O, R, W [4]

lime uranite, *n.* *Mineral.* [Prob. a transl. of G *Kalkuranit* < *Kalk* lime (< L *calc-*, *calx*) + G *Uranit* uranite (q.v.)] Autunite, a uranyl calcium phosphate. O, W [3]

limnic, *a.* (1911) *Geol.* [G *limnisch* (1850) < *limn-* (< Gk *límnē* lake, pond) + G adj. suffix *-isch* -ic] Of deposits like coal or peat formed in an inland body of standing fresh stagnant water like a lake or swamp. O [3]

limnite, *n.* (1868) *Geol.* [G *Limnit* < *limn-* (< Gk *límnē* lake, pond) + G *-it* -ite] Bog iron ore (this is different from the "paleontological" meaning). O, W [3]

limnoplankton, *n.* (1893) *Bot.* [Haeckel's G (1891) <

limno- + *Plankton* < Gk *límnē* lake, pond + *planktós* (neuter *planktón*) someone or something wandering about] The plankton found in fresh-water bodies like lakes. —**limnoplanktonic**. O, W [3]

limonite, *n.* (1823) *Mineral.* [G *Limonit* (1813) < Gk *leimón* meadow + G *-it* -ite] A name orig. confined to bog iron ore but now a general term for hydrous iron oxides, esp. goethite (q.v.). —**limonite**, *a.* (1874); **limonitic**. O, R, W [4]

linalool, *n.* (1891) *Chem.* Var. **linalol** [G (1891) < a blend of *Linaloe* a Mexican genus of trees + G *Öl* oil] A fragrant, liquid tertiary alcohol found esp. in Mexican linaloe oil and used in perfumes, soaps, and flavoring. —**linalyl** (1900). O, R, W [4]

linamarin, *n.* (1892) *Chem.* [G (1891) < Fr *linamarine* or directly < Fr into E, ult. < L *līnum* flax + *amārus* bitter] Phaseolunatin, a bitter, crystalline glucoside that occurs in flax and the lima bean. O, W [3]

linarite, *n.* (1844) *Mineral.* [G *Linarit* (1837) < the name *Linares*, Spain + G *-it* -ite] A basic lead copper sulfate. O, R, W [3]

lindackerite, *n.* (1857) *Mineral.* [G *Lindackerit* (1853) < the name of Joseph *Lindacker*, 19th-cent. Austrian chemist + G *-it* -ite] A green, hydrous nickel copper arsenate. O, W [3]

linden, *n.* (1577) *Bot.* [The 20th-cent. currency of the word is prob. due to its use in translations of German romance, as taken < G *Linden* (pl. of *Linde*) or as the first element in *Lindenbaum* linden tree] Linden tree (this meaning prob. orig. came from OE **linden*, but seems to have been revived in modern times from a German etymon). O, R, W [4]

linguistic island, *see* speech island

linin, *n.* (1887) *Biol.* [G (1887) < L *līnum*, Gk *línon* thread, flax + G *-in* -in] The lightly staining part of the reticulum, which is achromatic material connecting chromioles in the interphase nucleus (this is different from the earlier "chemical" meaning). O, W [3]

linn(a)eïte, *n.* (1849) *Mineral.* [G *Linneït* (1845) < the name of Carl von *Linné* (1707–78), Swedish natural scientist + G *-it* -ite] A steel-gray cobalt sulfide: cobalt pyrites. O, W [3]

linolenic acid, *n.* (1887) *Chem.* [Transl. of G *Linolensäure* (1887) < *Linolen* (< L *līnum* < Gk *línon* flax, thread + L *oleum* oil) + G *-n-* + *Säure* acid] A liquid, unsaturated, fatty acid, found as glycerides in linseed and other drying oils, which is considered essential in animal nutrition. —**linolenate** (1909). O, W [4]

Linzer torte, -n/-s *pl.* (1906) *Food* Var. **Linzertorte** (1906) [G < the comb. form of *Linz*, the name of an Austrian city + *Torte* (q.v.)] A delectable baked tart with a jam filling, decorated on top with pastry strips in a lattice pattern. O, R, W [3]

liparite[1], *n.* (1865) *Mineral.* [G *Liparit* (1847), named by the German mineralogist Ernst Friedrich Glocker (1793–1858) < Gk *liparós* shining + G *-it* -ite] Fluorite, a calcium fluoride. O [2]

liparite[2], *n.* *Geol.* [G *Liparit* < the name of the *Lipari* Islands + G *-it* -ite] Rhyolite (q.v.). W [3]

Lipizzan(er), *see* Lippizaner

lipochondrion, -ria *pl.* (1936) *Anat.* [Ad. of G *Lipochon-*

drie (1935) (< *lipo-* < Gk, the comb. form of *lípos* fat + *chondríon*, dim. of *chóndros* granule), prob. patterned after G *Mitochondrie* mitochondrion] Golgi body, a lipoid granule in the cytoplasm. —**lipochondrial** (1946). O, W [3]

lipochrome, *n.* (1887) *Biol.* [G *Lipochrom* < *lipo-* + *-chrom* < Gk *lipo-*, the comb. form of *lípos* fat + *chrô̄ma* color] Any of various pigments that are found naturally in plants and animals and that are soluble in fats or fat solvents, esp. carotenoid. —**lipochromic**. O, R, W [3]

lipoid, *n.* (1906) *Med.* [G (1901) < *lip-* + *-oid* < Gk *lípos* fat + *-oeidēs* similar] Any fat-like substance such as a lipid or lipin. —**lipoidal**, *a.* (1919); **lipoidosis** (1932). O, R, W [4]

liposome, *n.* (1910) *Biol.* [G *Liposom* (1904) < *lipo-* + *-som* < Gk *lípos* fat + *sôma* body] A fatty droplet in the cytoplasm of a cell, esp. of an egg; a minute, artificial droplet used as an experimental model for biological membranes. —**liposomal**, *a.* O, R, W [4]

Lippizaner, *n.* (1911) *Zool.* Var. **Lippizana** (1928), **Lippizan(er)** (1954), **Lippizzaner** [G < *Lippiza, Lipizza, Lippizza*, stud in Slovenia (formerly the Austrian Imperial Stud) where the strain was developed + *-er* -er] This strain or breed of spirited, mainly white, crossbred horses; a Lippizaner horse, as of the Spanish Riding School. O, R, W [4]

Liptauer (cheese), *n.* (1902) *Food* Var. **liptauer** (1955) [G *Liptauer (Käse)* < *Liptauer (Alpen)*, the G name for the Slovak portion of the Carpathian Mountains, or < G *Liptau, Lipto*, a Czechoslovakian town (+ G *Käse* cheese)] A soft cheese, orig. made in Hungary; a cheese spread of Liptauer and seasonings (as paprika); an imitation of this. O [3]

liquid crystal, *n.* (1891) *Chem.* [Transl. of G *flüssiger Krystall* (1890) < *flüssig* liquid + *Krystall* (now *Kristall*) < L *crystallum* < Gk *krýstallos* ice, rock crystal] A turbid substance that exhibits double-refraction polarization but has such low viscosity that it behaves mechanically like an ordinary liquid. —**liquid-crystal display** (1968). O, R, W [4]

liquidus, -es *pl.* (1901) *Chem.* Var. **liquidus curve** (1948) [G (< L) (1899) liquid, first used in this sense by the German chemist Hendrik Willem Bakhuis Roozeboom (1854–1907)] A curve, as on a temperature-composition diagram, above which a mixture is wholly liquid and below which it consists of solid and liquid in equilibrium: freezing-point curve. O, R, W [3]

lithiophorite, *n.* (1871) *Mineral.* [G *Lithiophorit* (1870) < *lithio-*, the comb. form of *Lithium* (< NL) lithium + G *-phor* + *-it* -ite < Gk *phorós* bearing, carrying] Hydrous oxide of aluminum, lithium, and manganese. O, W [3]

lithistid, *n.* (1885) and *a.* (1892) *Biol.* [G (1870) < NL *Lithistida* < Gk *líthos* stone + *histós* web + NL *-ida*] (Of) a siliceous sponge of the group *Lithistida*, in which the spicules form a massive reticulate skeleton. O [3]

lithography, *n.* (1813) *Art* [G *Lithographie* (c.1804–5) < *litho-* + *-graphie* < Gk *líthos* stone + *gráphein* to write] The process or art of printing or making a drawing or design on a special kind of surface: planography (this is different from the old meaning of "engraving on precious stones"). —**lithographic(al)** (1813, 1828); **-graphically** (1828); **-grapher** (1828); **-graph**, *n.* (1828), *a.* (1846). • ~

also appears in compounds like **lithographic varnish** (1903). O, R, W [4]

lithophane, *n.* (c.1890 *W9*) *Pottery* [Prob. < G *Lithophan* < *litho-* + *-phan* < Gk *líthos* stone + *phanós* bright, gleaming] Porcelain ornamented with figures that become distinct by transmitted light, as from a lampshade. —**lithophanic**. O, R, W [4]

lithophile, *a.* (1923) *Geol.* Var. **lithophil** (1923), **lithophilic** (1971) [G *Lithophil* (1923) < *litho-* + *-phil* < Gk *líthos* stone + *phílos* loving] Of elements concentrated in the silicate outer shell of the earth. O, R, W [3]

litzendraht, *n.* (1921) *Tech.* [G litz wire (q.v.)] Litz wire. O [2]

litz wire, *n.* (1927) *Tech.* Var. **Litz wire** (1927) [Partial transl. of G *Litzendraht* < *Litze* (< L *lícium* braid, cord, lace) + G *Draht* wire] A copper wire made from individually enameled strands braided together to reduce skin effect and thus high-frequency resistance. O, R, W [4]

liver sausage, *n.* (1855) *Food* [Transl. of G *Leberwurst* (see *liverwurst*] Liverwurst. O, R, W [4]

liverwurst, *n.* (1855) *Food* Var. **leberwurst** (1855), **liver sausage** (1855) [Partial transl. of G *Leberwurst* < *Leber* liver + *Wurst* sausage] Liver sausage, a seasoned sausage of cooked ground liver and lean pork trimmings stuffed into casings. O, R, W [4]

living room, *see* lebensraum

loafer, *n.* (1830) [Poss. a short. of *landloafer*, as ad. < G *Landläufer* vagabond, tramp (see *Grimm*, 6, 122) (now *Landstreicher*) < *Land* land + *Läufer* runner, or *-streicher* one who loafs] One who loafs; a lazy person. —**loafer**, *a.* (1888). • ~ also appears in several derivatives like **loafery** (1861), **loaferish** (1866). O, R, W, [4]

loan, *see* loanword

loan translation, *n.* (1933) *Ling.* [Transl. of G *Lehnübersetzung* < *(ent)lehnen* to loan, borrow + *übersetzen* to translate + *-ung*] An expression borrowed into a target language by translating its meaning into a word or words in the target language: calque. O, R, W [4]

loanword, *n.* (1874) *Ling.* Var. **loan word, loan-word** (1874) [Transl. of G *Lehnwort* < *(ent)lehnen* to loan, borrow + *Wort* word] A word of one language transferred into another language and at least partly naturalized. • ~ is short. to **loan**. O, R, W [4]

local sign, *n.* (1874) *Psych.* [Transl. of G *Lokalzeichen* < *Lokal* locality, place (< L *locus*) + *Zeichen* sign] The element in a sensation that provides the basis for one's instinctive judgment as to its locality. O [2]

loch, *n.* (1789) *Mining* [Poss. < G hole] (Brit.) in Derbyshire an open fissure in a mineral vein, esp. lead. O, W [2]

loden, *n.* (1911) *Textiles* Var. **loden cloth** (1952) [G, a short. of *Lodenmantel* < MHG *lode* coarse woolen cloth + *Mantel* mantle < L *mantellum*] A thick, orig. Tyrolean woolen cloth used for making wind- and water-resistant coats; a dark green color. • ~ appears in compounds like **loden cloak** (1916)/**green** (1969). O, R, W [4]

lodenmantle, *n.* (1914) *Apparel* [G *Lodenmantel* (see *loden*)] A thick, woolen overcoat of a style worn in southern Germany and Austria. O [3]

loellingite, *see* lollingite

loess, *n.* (c.1833 *W9*) *Geol.* Old var. **löss** (1873) [G *Löss* (now *Löß*] An unstratified covering of fine, chiefly wind-deposited loam (see different meaning in the Appendix). —**loessial** (1928), **loessal, loessland**. O, R, W [4]

loeweite/loewigite, *n.* (1862) *Mineral.* Var. **löwigite** (1862) [G *Löweit* (1846)/*Löwigit* (1861) < the name of Karl Jacob *Löwig* (1803–90), German chemist + *-it* -ite] Hydrous magnesium sodium sulfate. O, W [3]

logotherapy, *n.* (1948) *Psych.* [G *Logotherapie* (1947) < Gk *lógos* reason + G *Therapie* < NL *therapia* < Gk *therapeía* attendance, medical treatment] An existential psychotherapy that holds that one's mental health depends on awareness of meaning in one's life, e.g., from spiritual sources. O [3]

Lohengrin, *n. Lit.* [G *Lohengrin, Loherangrin* (< Fr, said to mean "the Lothringian Garin"), the son of Parsifal (q.v.)] In Germanic legend, Parsifal's son known as the Knight of the Swan and a knight of the Holy Grail; the title of an opera by Richard Wagner that premiered in 1850. R [4]

Lokal, *n.* (1903) [Short. of G *Nachtlokal* < *Nacht* night + *Lokal* club] A local bar or nightclub. O [2]

löllingite/loellingite, *n.* (1849) *Mineral.* [G *Löllingit* (1845) < *Lölling*, the name of an Austrian town + G *-it* -ite] A tin-white iron arsenide: leucopyrite. O, R, W [3]

lomonite, *see* laumontite

lonchidite, *n.* (1865) *Mineral.* [G *Lonchidit* < Gk *lonchídion*, dim. of *lónchē* spearhead + G *-it* -ite] A variety of marcasite containing arsenic. O [2]

longing, *see* Sehnsucht

longulite, *n. Mineral.* [G *Longulit* < L *longulus* lengthy + G *-it* -ite] An elongated crystallite (q.v.). W [3]

loranskite, *n. Mineral.* [G *Loranskit* < the name of Appollonie Mikhailovich *Loranski* (1847–?), Russian mining inspector + G *-it* -ite] A black columbite and titanite of the rare-earth metals. W [3]

Lorelei, *n.* (1878) *Myth.* Old var. **Loreley** (1878) [G < the name of the *Lorelei*, a siren of German legend said to inhabit the Lorelei rock on the right bank of the Rhine south of Koblenz and to entice boatmen to their destruction by her beauty and her singing] This beautiful, legendary woman; a siren; a given name for a female. O, R, W [4]

löss, *see* loess

los von Rom (1899) *Politics* [G (1897), lit., free from Rome] (The slogan of) a movement that arose in Austria and Germany in the late 19th century seeking to reduce the political influence of the Roman Catholic Church; such a slogan applied to other policies of this kind. O [3]

Low German, *n.* (1838 *W9*) *Ling.* [Transl. of G *Niederdeutsch* < *nieder* low + *Deutsch* German] The German dialects of northern Germany, esp. those used since the medieval period: Plattdeutsch (q.v.). —**Low German**, *a.* O, R, W [4]

löwigite, *see* loeweïte

loxoclase, *n.* (1846) *Mineral.* [G *Loxoklas* (1846) < *loxo-* + *-klas* < Gk *loxós* askew, oblique + *klásis* break, cleavage] A sodium-containing orthoclase (q.v.). O, W [3]

LSD (25), *n.* (1947) *Pharm.* [Abbr. of G *Lysergsäurediäthylamid* < *lyserg-* (< Gk *lýsis* dissolving, dissolution + *érgon* work, action) + G *Säure* acid + Gk *dís* twofold

+ G *Äthyl* ethyl (q.v.) + *Amid* amide (q.v.)] Lysergic acid diethylamide, a drug that causes psychotic, schizophrenic-like symptoms. O, R, W [4]

lucern, *n.* (1532) *Zool.* (obs.) [Prob. ad. of G *lüchsern* lynx] A lynx or its fur. O, W [3]

Lucullic, *a.* (1892) *Food* Var. **Lucill(i)an** (1913, 1892) [G *lukullisch* < the name of the Roman general Licinus *Lūcullus* + G *-isch*] Lucullan: profusely luxurious, esp. foods. O, W [3]

lucullite, *n.* (1819) *Mineral.* [G *Lucullit/Lucullan* (1814) < the name of the Roman general Licinus *Lūcullus*, who esp. liked this marble + G *-it* -ite or *-an*] Egyptian marble stained black by carbon. O, W [3]

Ludolph's number, *n.* (1886) *Math.* Var. **Ludolphian number** (1886) [Transl. of G *Ludolphische Zahl* (now *Ludolph-Zahl*) < the name of *Ludolph* van Ceulen (1540–1610), German mathematician who taught in the Netherlands + G *Zahl* number] The number π calculated to 35 decimal places. O [3]

ludwigite, *n.* (1875) *Mineral.* [G *Ludwigit* (1874) < the name of Ernst *Ludwig* (1842–1915), Austrian chemist + G *-it* -ite] A fibrous borate of magnesium and iron. O, W [3]

Ludwigsburg, *n.* (1863) *Pottery* [G < the name of the German town *Ludwigsburg*, where notable hard-paste porcelain was made from 1758 to 1824] This porcelain, characterized by its suitability for figure modeling. —**Ludwigsburg**, *a.* (1960). O [3]

lueneburgite, *n.* (1872) *Mineral.* Old var. **luneburgite** (1872) [G *Lüneburgit* (1870) < *Lüneburg*, a town in Hannover, Germany + *-it* -ite] A hydrous phosphate of magnesium and boron. O, W [3]

Luftwaffe, *n.* (1935) *Mil.* Var. **luftwaffe** [G < *Luft* air + *Waffe* weapon] The air force of the Third Reich. —**Luftwaffe**, *a.* (1942). O, R [3]

Luian, *see* Luwian

lujau(v)rite, *n. Geol.* [G *Luijaurit* < the name *Luijaur* Urt, Lujavr Urt, Lapland + G *-it* -ite] A melanocratic, nepheline-syenite rock. W [3]

lumichrome, *n.* (1935) *Chem.* [G *Lumichrom* (1934) < *lumi-* + *-chrom* < L *lūmen* (gen. *lūminis*) light + Gk *chrôma* color] A fluorescent crystalline compound formed by ultraviolet irradiation of riboflavin in neutral or acidic solution and that is found in ruminants' urine and milk. O, W [3]

luminescence, *n.* (1889) *Physics* [G *Lumineszenz* < L *lūmen* (gen. *lūminis*) light + *-escentia* state or process of becoming] A light emission that is not directly caused by incandescence; a light so produced. O, R, W [4]

lumisterol, *n.* (1932) *Biochem.* [G *Lumisterol/Lumisterin* (1931) < L *lūmen* (gen. *lūminis*) light + Gk *steréos* hard, firm + G *-in* or *-ol* (< *Alkohol* alcohol, ult. < Ar) -ol] A steroidal alcohol that is a stereoisomer of ergosterol and occurs as an intermediate product in producing tachysterol and vitamin D_2. O, W [3]

lumpen, *see* lumpenproletariat

lumpenproletariat, *n.* (1924) *Politics* [Karl Marx's G (1850) < *Lumpen* (pl. of *Lump*) ragamuffin + *Proletariat* proletariat, the lowest social or economic class of a community < Fr < L *prōlētārius*] The lowest and most abased members of the proletariat. —**lumpenproletarian**, *n.* (1936),

a. (1937). • ~ is short. to **lumpen**, *a.* (1944), *n.* (1949); **lumpenprole** (c.1970). O [4]

lüneburgite, *see* lueneburgite

lupeol, *n. Chem.* [Prob. ad. < G *Lupin* (< L *lupus* wolf + G *-in*) + *-ol* (< G *Alkohol* alcohol, ult. < Ar) -ol] A crystalline triterpenoid alcohol. W [3]

lupulon(e), *n.* (1919) *Chem.* [G (1916) < NL *lupulus* < L *lupus* (beer) hop + G *-on* (< Gk *-ōnē* fem. patronymic suffix) -on(e)] A bitter, crystalline ketone obtained from hops (lupulin) and that is an effective antibiotic. O, W [3]

Luvian, *see* Luwian

Luwian, *n.* (1923) and *a.* (1952) *Ethnology, Ling.* Var. **Luvian** (1924), **Luian** (1934) [Ad. of G *Luvisch* (1921) and *Luvier*, resp. < *Luvia*, in antiquity, the name given to part of Asia Minor] (of) a member of an Anatolian people contemporary with the Hittites who wrote in cuneiform; (of) their cuneiform inscriptions or language. O, R [4]

ly, *see* langley

lycomarasmin, *n.* (1945) *Chem.* [G (1945) < NL *lycopersici* < Gk *lýkos* wolf + *merasmós* < *meraísmein* to dry up, devour + G *-in* -ine] Phytotoxic dipeptide containing glycine and aspartic acid residues. O [3]

lydite, *n.* (1816) *Geol.* Var. **lydit** (1816) [G *Lydit* < *Lydien*, the name of a region in western Asia Minor + G *-it* -ite] Touchstone: Lydian stone. O, W [3]

lyochrome, *n.* (1933) *Biochem.* [G *Lyochrom* (1933) < *lyo-* + *-chrom* < Gk *lýein* to dissolve + *chrôma* color] Flavin, a yellow pigment. O [3]

lyophile, *a.* (1915) *Chem., Biol.* Var. **lyophilic** [G *lyophil* (1908) < *lyo-* + *-phil* < Gk *lýein* to dissolve + *phílein* to love] (Chem.) lyophilic; (Biol.): lyophil: of, relating to, or obtained by freeze-drying. —**lyophilize** (1938 *W9*). O, R, W [3]

lyophobic/lyophobe, *a.* (1911) *Chem.* [G *lyophob* (1908) < *lyo-* + *-phob* < Gk *lýein* to dissolve + *phobeîn* to fear (+ E *-ic*)] Not having an affinity for the dispersion medium. O, R, W [3]

lysin, *n.* (1900) *Biochem.* [G (1893) < *Lysis* (< Gk) dissolution + G *-in* -in] Any of various antibodies capable of dissolving bacteria, blood corpuscles, or the like. O, R, W [4]

lysine, *n.* (1892) *Biochem.* [Prob. < G *Lysin* (1891) < *Lysis* (< Gk) dissolution + G *-in* -in] A crystalline basic amino acid; alpha- or eta-diamino-caproic acid. O, R, W [4]

lyxose, *n.* (1896) *Chem.* [G (1896), an anagram of *xylose* < Gk *xýlon* wood + G *-ose* (denoting the presence of a carbohydrate) -ose] A crystalline aldose sugar that is the epimer of xylose and is rare in nature. O, W [3]

M

maar, -s/-e *pl.* (1826) *Geogr.* Var. **Maar** (1826) [G crater lake, prob. < ML *mara* a stagnant water] A crater (lake) of the Eifel district in Germany; a volcanic crater (lake), not in a cone and produced by explosion. O, W [3]

machtpolitik, *n.* (1916) *Politics* Var. **macht-politik** (1916) [G < *Macht* power, might + *Politik* politics < Fr *politique*] A doctrine of power politics, esp. the use of force to gain political goals. O, W [3]

macroërgate, *n.* (1901) *Entomology* Var. **macrergate** [G (1895) < *macro-* + *Ergate* < Gk *macro-*, the comb. form of *makrós* large + *ergátes* worker] An unusually large worker ant. O, W [3]

macroglobulin, *n.* (1952) *Biochem.* [G *Makroglobulin* (1948) < *makro-* + *Globulin* < Gk *macro-*, the comb. form of *makrós* large + L *globulus* globule + G *-in* -in] Any of the immunoglobulins of very high molecular weight. O [3]

macroglobulinemia/macroglobulinæmia, *n.* (1949) *Biochem.* [G *Makroglobulinämie* (1948) < *Makroglobulin* macroglobulin (q.v.) + *-ie* -ia < Gk *haîma* blood + *-ia*] An excess of makroglobulins in one's blood. —**microglobulinæmic** (1961). O [3]

macromolecule, *n.* (c.1929 *W9*) *Chem.* [G *Makromolekül* (1922) < *makro-* + *Molekül* < Gk *macro-*, the comb. form of *makrós* mass + Fr *molécule*] A very large molecule, as of proteins and nucleic acids. —**macromolecular.** O, W, R [4]

maennerchor, *see* Männerchor

magic realism, *n.* (c.1927 *W9*) *Lit.* [Transl. of G *magischer Realismus* < *magisch* magic + *Realismus* realism (q.v.)] The meticulous, realistic painting of fantastic images. — **magic realist.** R, W [3]

magnetite, *n.* (1851) *Mineral.* [G *Magnetit* (1845) < *Magnet* (< L *māgnēs,* gen. *māgnētis,* actually, stone from *Magnesia*) + G *-it* -ite] Magnetic iron oxide: lodestone. —**magnetitic, magnetite series.** O, R, W [4]

Magnetophon, *n.* (1946) *Tech.* Var. **magnetophone** (1946) [G, orig., a tradename for a German tape recorder < *magneto-* (< L, the comb. form of *māgnēs*—see *magnetite*) + G *-phon* < Gk *phōnḗ* sound] (Cap.) the trademark for this magnetic recorder; this German machine or another of German manufacture (this is different from the earlier meaning of "magnetic musical instrument"). O, W [3]

magnetoplumbite, *n.* (1926) *Mineral.* [G *Magnetoplumbit* (1925) < *magneto-* + *Plumbit* < L *magneto-*, the comb. form of *māgnēs* (see *magnetite*) + L *plumbum* lead + G *-it* -ite] A magnetic oxide of ferric iron with lead and manganese. O, W [3]

magnochromite, *n. Mineral.* [G *Magnochromit* < *magno-* (< L *magno-*, the comb. form of *māgnus* great, large) + G *Chromit* chromite (q.v.)] Magnesiochromite, an oxide of magnesium and chromium. W [3]

magnoferrite, *n. Mineral.* [G *Magnoferrit* < *magno-* +

Ferrit < L *magno-*, the comb. form of *māgnus* great, large + *ferrum* iron + G *-it* -ite] Magnesioferrite, a member of the magnetite (q.v.) series. W [3]

Magnus effect, *n.* (1921) *Physics* [G *Magnus Effekt* < the name of Heinrich G. *Magnus* (1802–70), German scientist + *Effekt* effect < L *effectus*] In propelling ships or lifting airplanes, the effect of rapid spinning on a rotating cylinder whose axis is perpendicular to a utilized current of air. O, R, W [3]

mailed fist, *n.* (1897) *Politics* [Transl. of G *gepanzerte Faust* < *gepanzert* armored < *Panzer* armor + *Faust* fist] In power politics, an armed or overbearingly threatening force; brutal or naked power, esp. coercive force. O, R, W [4]

Maitrank, *n.* (1858) *Beverages* [G < *Mai* May (< L *Māius* < *Māia* a Roman goddess) + *Trank* drink] A May drink made by putting fresh waldmeister (q.v.) into sugared, mild wine. • ~ is transl. as **May-drink** (1850). O [3]

malacon, *n.* (1854) *Mineral.* Var. **Malacone** (1954), **malakon** [G *Malakon* (1844) < Gk *malakón,* neuter form of *malakós* soft] A soft, altered form of zircon (q.v.). O, W [3]

malerisch, *a.* (1933) *Art* [G (1915) picturesque, painterly < *malen* to paint + *-isch* -ic] Of or relating to a style of painting characterized more by the merging of colors than by the more formal linear style; painterly. O [3]

malthacite, *n.* (1849) *Mineral.* Var. **malthazite** (1883) [G *Malthazit* (1837) < Gk *malthakós* soft + G *-it* -ite] A variety of fuller's earth. O [3]

maltol, *n.* (1894) *Chem.* [G (1894) < NL *maltum* malt + *-ol* (< G *Alkohol* alcohol, ult. < Ar *al-kuḥul*) -ol] A crystalline compound that occurs in pine needles, chicory, and larch bark, used for enhancing flavors and aromas; also called *larixinic acid.* O, R, W [4]

mandelic acid, *n.* (1844) *Chem.* [Partial transl. of G *Mandelsäure* < *Mandel* almond (< ML *mandala*) + G *Säure* acid] A crystalline, hydroxy acid, used for genitourinary infections; also called *amygdalic acid.* O, R, W [3]

mandelstein, *n.* (1799) *Geol.* Var. **mandelstone** [G < *Mandel* almond (< ML *mandala*) + G *Stein* stone] Amygdaloid, an igneous rock. O [3]

manganocalcite, *n.* (1852) *Mineral.* [G *Manganocalcit* (now *Manganokalzit*) < *mangan-* (see *manganosite* + *Calcit* calcite (q.v.)] A rhodochrosite (q.v.) containing calcium; a calcite containing manganese. O, W [3]

manganophyllite, *n.* (1877) *Mineral.* [G *Manganophyll* < *mangan-* (see *manganosite*) + *-phyll* < Gk *phýllon* leaf + E *-ite*] Manganoan biotite (q.v.). O, W [3]

manganosiderite, *n. Mineral.* [G *Manganosiderit* < *mangan-* (see *manganosite*) + *Siderit* siderite (q.v.)] A member of the siderite-rhodochrosite series. O, W [3]

manganosite, *n.* (1887) *Mineral.* [G *Manganosit* < *mangan-*, a short. of *Manganesium* < Fr *manganèse* < L *mag-*

nēsium < Gk *magnēsíē* (*líthos*) stone of Magnesia, in antiquity the name of cities in Asia Minor + G -*it* -ite] An emerald-green manganous oxide. O, W [3]

manganotantalite, *n. Mineral.* [G or Sw *Manganotantalit* < G *mangan-* (see *manganosite*) + *Tantalit* tantalite < NL *tantalum*] A manganiferous tantalite. W [3]

manganpectolite, *n. Mineral.* [G *Manganpectolith* < *mangan-* (see *manganosite*) + *Pectolith* pectolite (q.v.)] A manganiferous pectolite. W [3]

mangel, *see* mangel-wurzel

mangel-wurzel, *n.* (1767 *W9*) and *a.* (1779) *Bot.* Var. **man-gold-wurzel** (1800) [G < *Mangold* silver or stock beet + *Wurzel* root] (of) a coarse variety of garden beet, used for cattle food; (of) its fleshy, so-called root. • ~ is short. to **mangold** (1856), **mangel** (1883), **wurzel** (1888). O, R, W [4]

Männerchor, *n. Music* Var. **maennerchor** (Sc) [G < *Män-ner* (pl. of *Mann*) men + *Chor* chorus, choir < L *chorus* < Gk *chorós*] A men's choral group. WN20 [2]

mannose, *n.* (1888) *Chem.* [G (1888), a short. of *Mannitose* < Gk *mánna* manna + G -*ose* -ose, designating a car-bohydrate] A crystalline, aldose sugar that is known in three optically isometric forms. O, R, W [4]

manool, *n.* (1935) *Chem.* Var. **manoöl** (1935) [G (1935) < *Manoao*, the name of a New Zealand genus of coniferous trees + G -*öl* (< *Öl* oil < L *oleum*) -ol] A bicyclic di-terpenoid alcohol found in the oil of manoao wood, used in perfumes. O [3]

many-valued, *a.* (1934) *Phil.* [Transl. of G *mehrwertig* < *mehr* more (than one) + *wertig* valued < *werten* to value] Possessing three or more truth-values instead of the usual two of truth and falsehood. O, R, W [4]

maranite, *n.* (1884) *Mineral.* [G *Maranit* (1801) < the name of the Sierra de *Marāo*, Portugal + G -*it* -ite] Chi-astolite (q.v.). O [3]

marble bone (**disease**), *n.* (1922) *Path.* [Transl. of G *Mar-morknochen* < *Marmor* marble + *Knochen* bone (+ E *disease*)] An affected bone in one who has osteopetrosis; the disease itself. —**marble bones** (1922). O, W [3]

märchen/Märchen, -ø *pl.* (1871) *Lit.* [G fairy or folk tale, dim. of *Märe* tale] A fairy tale, esp. a folktale. —**märchen,** *a.* (1908). O, R, W [3]

marchpane, *see* marzipan

Marcobrunner. *n.* (1825) *Beverages* Var. **Markbrunner** (1825), **Markobrunn** (1967) [G < the name of a vineyard in the Rheingau, Germany] A Rhine white wine. O [3]

Marek's disease, *n.* (1947 *W9*) *Med.* [Transl. of G *Mareks-Krankheit* (1907) < the name of Josef *Marek* (1868– 1952), German veterinarian + *Krankheit* disease] Fowl paralysis, a cancerous disease of poultry characterized esp. by proliferated lymphoid cells; also called *range paralysis.* O, R [4]

margarodite, *n.* (1849) *Mineral.* [G *Margarodit* (1843) < LGk *margaródēs* pearl-like + G -*it* -ite] A pearly mica resembling talc. O, W [3]

margravine, *n.* (1692) *Politics* [G *Markgräfin* (or Du *markgravin*) < MHG *marcgravinne* wife of a margrave (q.v.)] A margrave's wife. O, R, W [4]

Maria-glass, *see* marienglass

maria-groschen, *see* mariengroschen

marialite, *n.* (1854) *Mineral.* [G *Marialit* (now *Marialith*) < the name of *Maria* Rose, wife of the German miner-alogist Gerhard von Rath (1830–88) + -*lit* < Gk *líthos* stone] A chlorine-containing aluminosilicate of sodium. O, R, W [3]

marienglas, *n.* (1762) *Mineral.* Var. **marienglass** (1762), **Maria-glass** (1896) [G < the comb. form of *Marie* Mary, Mother of Jesus + *Glas* glass] A name for mica and sel-enite. O [3]

mariengroschen, -ø *pl.* (1617) *Currency* Var. **maria-groschen** (1617), **maria-groschen** (1617) [G (1503) < the comb. form of *Maria* Mary, Mother of Jesus + *Groschen* groschen (q.v.)] An old German silver coin having a rep-resentation of the Madonna and Child, first minted in Gos-lar about 1505. W [3]

mark[1], *n.* (1839) *Currency* [G *Mark*, MHG *marc, marke, mark* brand] The basic monetary unit of Germany, esp. a silver coin first issued in 1875; deutsche mark (q.v.). O, R, W [4]

mark[2], *n.* (1726) *Politics* [G *Mark* < MHG *marc(h)* < OHG *marha* boundary (land)] A land area held in com-mon by a Germanic community in prehistorical or medi-eval times; (used as) part of the name of certain German principalities, esp. the Mark of Brandenburg. O, R, W [4]

Markbrunner/Markobrunn, *see* Marcobrunner

markgraf, -en *pl.* (1551) *Politics* Var. **margrave** [G < OHG *marcgrāvo* margrave (q.v.)] Margrave, a member of the German nobility comparable to a British marquess. O, R, W [3]

markworthy, *a.* (1827) [Transl. of G *merkwürdig* (now *merkenswert*) < *merken* to note + *würdig* worthy (of)] Noteworthy. O, W [3]

marmatite, *n.* (1843) *Mineral.* [G *Marmatit* < *Marmato*, the name of a town in Colombia, South America + G -*it* -ite] Ferroan sphalerite (q.v.). O, W [3]

martite, *n.* (1851) *Mineral.* [G *Martit* < L *Mārtem* (dative of *Mārs*) war < *Mārs* Roman god of war + G -*it* -ite] Hematite that is pseudomorphous after magnetite (q.v.). O, W [3]

marzipan, *n.* (1494) *Food* Var. **marchpane** (1494) [G < It *marzapane* a coin of the Middle Ages, a fancy box for confections < Ar *mawthabān* seated person, from the rep-resentation of the seated Christ on the coin] A confection of crushed almonds (or almond paste) and egg whites that is often molded into ornamental forms. —**marzipan,** *a.* (1587). • ~ appears initially in compounds like **marzipan confections** (1948)/**recipe/forms.** O, R, W [4]

mase, *n.* (1527) *Med.* (obs.) Var. **masse** (1527) [G *Maser* gnarl] A spot or freckle. O [2]

masers, *pl.* (1527) *Med.* (obs.) [G *Masern,* pl. < LG *ma-sele,* OHG *masala,* gnarly growth, boil] (A superseded name for) measles. O [2]

maskelynite, *n.* (1875) *Mineral.* [G *Maskelynit* (1872) < the name of Nevil Story-*Maskelyne* (1823–1911), English mineralogist + G -*it* -ite] A glass of plagioclase (q.v.) composition found in some meteorites. O, W [3]

masochism, *n.* (1893) *Psych.* [G *Masochismus* (1886), coined by the German psychiatrist Richard von Krafft-Ebing (1840–1902) < the name of the Austrian novelist Leopold von Sacher-*Masoch* (1836–95) + G (< L) -*ismus*

-ism] Various complex tendencies to hurt or subjugate oneself, often sexually, and now usu. viewed as a form of sexual perversion. —masochist(ic) (1895, 1904), masochistically (1936). O, R, W [4]

massa bowl, n. (1858) Pottery [Ad. and expansion of G Masse mass, in the sense of "paste" used for porcelain, bowls, etc. + E bowl] A pipe bowl made from meerschaum (q.v.) parings. O [2]

mässig, adv. (1884) and a. Music [G moderate, not exaggerated < OHG māʒig] Moderato, a direction in music. O, W [3]

mast cell, n. (c.1890 W9) Biol. [Ad. of G Mastzelle < Mast food + Zelle cell < L cella] A basophilic leukocyte; a similar, larger cell than this, which is believed to produce heparin. R, W [4]

masterpiece, n. (1579) [Transl. of D meesterstuk or G Meisterstück < Meister master + Stück piece (of work)] Chef-d'oeuvre, orig. a work by which a craftsman was awarded the guild's rank of master; something that excells in brilliance, quality, or trait; something or someone to be admired for being remarkable or singular. O, R, W [4]

master race, n. (1937 W9) Sociol. [Poss. a loose transl. of G Herrenvolk (q.v.) < Herr mister, master + Volk race, people] A race or nation considered to be preeminently great or powerful, specif. the Nazi view of themselves. O, R [4]

mastersinger, n. (1810) Music [Ad. of G Meistersinger (q.v.)] Meistersinger. O, R, W [4]

masterwort, n. (1548) Bot. [Transl. of G Meisterwurz < Meister + Wurz, a short. of Wurzel root] A herbaceous plant used esp. formerly in medicine; cow parsnip; Angelica. O, R, W [3]

mastocyte, n. Biol. [G Mastozyt, ad. < Mastzelle mast cell (q.v.)] Mast cell. W [3]

masurium, n. (1925) Chem. [G (<NL) (1925) (superseded by G Technetium) < Masuren, the G name of a region in northeast Poland + L -ium] The name first given to chemical element 43, but now replaced by technetium. O, W [3]

mat, see matted

mathematicism, n. (1933) Philos. [G Mathematizismus < Mathematik mathematics (< MFr mathematiques, ult. < Gk mathēmātikḗ) + G -ismus (< L) -ism] The view that everything can be described ult. in mathematical terms or that the universe is basically mathematical. O [3]

matriarchate, n. (1885) Sociol. [G Matriarchat, on the analogy of Patriarchat (< L pater (gen. patris) father + Gk archḗ rule) < L mater (gen. matris) mother + Gk archḗ + G -at (< L -atus suffix indicating office, function) -ate] A matriarchal domination, community, or system; matriarchy. O, R, W [4]

matted, a. (1648) Geol. Var. matte (1648), mat (1864), matt (1876) [G matt dull < Fr mat, It matto < Ar mata dead] Having a lusterless surface; matte. O, R [4]

maucherite, n. (1913) Mineral. [G Maucherit (1913) < the name of Wilhelm Maucher (1879–1930), German mineral dealer + G -it -ite] A nickel arsenide. O, W [3]

Mauerkrankheit, n. (1981) Sociol. (colloq.) [G < Mauer wall + Krankheit illness, sickness] The negative psychological effect of the Berlin Wall on West Berliners before German reunification. BDC [2]

mauger, a. [Folk etymology prob. < G mager thin, skinny] Thin, puny, emaciated. W [3]

Mauser(rifle), n. (1880) Mil. [G (1871) the M71, M84 etc. rifle < the names of the brothers Peter Paul (1838–1914) and Wilhelm Mauser (1834–82), German inventors and manufacturers of firearms] This rifle, adopted in 1871 and perfected in 1884. —Mauser, v. (1903). O, R [4]

maw(seed), n. (1730) Bot. [Transl. of G Magsamen < MHG māgesāme poppy seed] Poppy seed, esp. of the opium poppy, the exudate of which includes morphine and codeine; this seed used as birdseed. O, W [3]

Maychafer, n. (1827) Entomology [Transl. of G Maikäfer < Mai May (< L Māius < Māia Roman goddess) + G Käfer beetle] May beetle: June beetle. O [3]

May-drink, n. (1850) Beverages [Transl. of G Maitrank (q.v.) or Du meidrank] Maitrank. O [2]

mediatize/mediatise, v. (1830) Politics [Transl. of G mediatisieren < mediat < LL immediātus indirectly + G verbal suffix -ieren -ize] To reduce the rank of a prince or state to that of mediate vassal of the Holy Roman Empire; to place in a middle or intermediate position; to act as mediator. —mediatization. O, R, W [4]

meerschaum, n. (1784) Mineral. Old var. like meershaum [G a species of Alcyonacea resembling solidified foam < Meer sea, ocean + Schaum foam] Sepiolite, a hydrated magnesium silicate; this clayey material used in tobacco pipes; a pipe (mainly) of this; a kind of gravel. • ~ is trans. as sea-foam (1837). —meerschaum pipe (1812). O, R, W [4]

meiler, n. (1839) [G, prob. < ML miliarium a thousand pieces (with reference to the stacked wood)] A charcoal kiln. O [3]

mein Gott, interj. (c.1838) [G < mein my + Gott God] My God. O [3]

mein Herr (1922) [G < mein my + Herr mister, sir] (Used jocularly or ironically in addressing a German man) my (dear) Sir. O [3]

Meissen, n. (1863) Pottery [G < the name of the German town Meissen, which has made hard-paste porcelain since 1710] This famous ornamental ware, also used as table ware. —Meissen, a. (1882) • ~ appears in compounds like Meissen china/ware. O, R, W [4]

-meister, suffix (1965) [G -master, as in shlockmeister, ski-meister] (Used in nominal compounds instead of) -master. O [3]

meistergesang, -gesänge pl. Lit. [G < MHG meistergesanc] A song of the Meistersinger (q.v.); these songs as a literary genre. W [2]

meisterlied, -er pl. Lit. [G < Meister master + Lied song] Meistergesang (q.v.). W [2]

Meistersinger, -ø/-s pl. (1810) Lit. Var. mastersinger (1810) [G < Meister master + singer singer < singen to sing] A poet or musician belonging to any of various German guilds, esp. in the 15th and 16th centuries, composed chiefly of middle-class craftsmen and formed to cultivate poetry and music. O, R, W [4]

melam, n. (1835) Chem. [G (1834), coined by the German chemist Justus von Liebig (1803–73) < mel- + -am < Amin amine < NL ammonium + G -in -ine] An amorphous compound obtained from ammonium thiocyanate or as a byproduct from preparing melamine (q.v.). O, W [3]

melamine, *n.* (1835) *Chem.* Var. **Melamine** (1835) [G *Melamin* (1834) < *melam* (q.v.) + *-in* -ine] A crystalline, high-melting organic base, a cyclic trimer of cyanamide; (often cap.) a melamine resin or plastic from such a resin, used in tableware, etc. • ~ appears in compounds like **melamine formaldehyde/resin** (1941, 1941). O, R, W [4]

melanemia, *n.* (1860) *Path.* Var. **melanæmia** (1860) [G *Melanämie* (1855), coined by the German pathologist Friedrich Theodor von Frerichs (1819–85) < *melan-* < Gk *mélas* (gen. *mélanos*) + *haîma* blood] An abnormal condition in which the blood contains melanin and malaria occurs. —**melanæmic** (1878). O, W [3]

melanite, *n.* (1807) *Mineral.* [G *Melanit* (1799) < *melan-* (< Gk *mélas*, gen. *mélanos* black) + G *-it* -ite] A velvet-black garnet: titanian andradite. —**melanitic.** O, R, W [4]

melanoblast, *n.* (1902) *Biol.* [G (1896) < *melano-* + *-blast* < Gk *mélas* (gen. *mélanos*) black + *blastós* bud] A cell that produces melanin. —**melanoblastic, melanoblastoma.** O, R, W [3]

melanocerite, *n.* (1896) *Mineral.* [G *Melanocerit* (1887) (now also *Melanozerit* < *melano-* (< Gk *mélas*, gen. *mélanos* black) + G *Cerit* < *Cerium* < the asteroid *Ceres* + *-it* -ite] A complex silicate, borate, tantalate, fluoride, or other compound of cerium and other metals. O, W [3]

melanochroite, *n.* (1835) *Mineral.* [G *Melanochroit* < Gk *melanóchroos* black-colored + G *-it* -ite] Phoenicochroite (q.v.). O [3]

melanocratic, *a.* (1909) *Mineral.* [G *melanokrat* (1898) < *melano-* + *-krat* < Gk *mélas* (gen. *mélanos*) black + *krateîn* to dominate, rule + E *-ic*] Rich in predominantly dark-colored minerals. O, W [3]

melanophlogite, *n.* (1879) *Mineral.* [G *Melanophlogit* (1876) < *melano-* + *Phlogit* < Gk *mélas* (gen. *mélanos*) black + *phlóg* flame + G *-it* -ite] An impure form of silica found in sulfur. O [3]

melanophore, *n.* (1903) *Biol.* [G *Melanophor* (1895) < *melano-* + *-phor* < Gk *mélas* (gen. *mélanos*) black + *phorós* bearing] A chromatophore containing melanin: a pigment cell. —**melanophoric.** O, R, W [4]

melanoscope, *n.* (1876) *Tech.* [G *Melanoskop* (1871) < *melano-* + *-skop* < Gk *mélas* (gen. *mélanos*) black + *skopeîn* to observe] A combination of colored glasses for viewing certain optical properties of chlorophyll. O [3]

melanostibian, *n.* *Mineral.* [Ad. of G *Melanostibium* (< *melano-* + *Stibium* < Gk *mélas*, gen. *mélanos* black + L *stibium* antimony) + E *-ian*] A black oxide of iron, manganese, and antimony. W [3]

melanterite, *n.* *Mineral.* [G *Melanterit* < Fr *mélantérie* melanterite < NL *melanteria* < Gk black metallic dye or ink + G *-it* -ite] A native copperas. W [3]

meld, *n.* (1897) *Games* [G back-formation < *melden* to announce (or show a card)] The art of melding; a card or combination of cards that can be melded. O, R, W [4]

meld, *v.* (1897) *Games* [G *melden* to announce (or show a card)] To declare a card or combination of cards that has scoring or other value in the given card game; to do this as a meld. O, R, W [4]

melibiase, *n.* (1899) *Chem.* [G (1895) < Gk *méli* honey + *bi-* < L *bis* twice, twofold + G *-ase* -ase, denoting a destroying substance] An enzyme that brings about the hydrolysis of melibiose (q.v.) O [3]

melibiose, *n.* (1899) *Chem.* [G (1889), an ad. of *Melitose* < Gk *mélitos*, gen. of *méli* honey + *bi-* < L *bis* twice + G *-ose* -ose, denoting a carbohydrate] A disaccharide sugar obtained by partially hydrolyzing raffinose. O, W [3]

melis, -es *pl. Chem.* [G < Gk *méli* honey] A usu. slightly yellow, crudely refined sugar usu. prepared as a loaf. W [3]

mellite, *n.* (1801) *Mineral.* [Transl. of G *Honigstein* (1793), used in this sense by the German chemist Johann Friedrich Gmelin (1748–1804) < *Honig* honey + *Stein* stone (= L *mell-* + *-lit*)] A honey-colored, hydrous aluminum mellitate found in brown coal (this is different from the ISV-derived "pharmaceutical" meaning). O, W [3]

mellon/melon, *n.* (1835) *Chem.* Var. **mellone** [G *Mellon* (1834) < *melam* (q.v.) + *-on* -one] A compound of carbon and nitrogen obtained as a yellow powder by heating various cyanogen compounds or in preparing melamine (q.v.). O, W [3]

melodeon/melodion, *n.* (1840) *Music* [G *Melodion* (1806) < *Melodie* (< OFr < Gk *melōidía*) + quasi-Gk suffix *-ion* -ion, -eon] A keyboard instrument with graduated metal rods sounded by contact with a revolving cylinder; (U.S.) American accordion or music hall. O, R, W [4]

melon, *see* mellon

menacane, *n.* (1803) *Mineral.* [G *Menacan* < the place-name *Menachan* in Cornwall, England] Menaccanite, a variety of ilmenite (q.v.). —**menac** (1803). • ~ has a different etymon than do *menachanite/menaccanite*, which were formed directly in English by adding *-ite* to the Cornish place-name by 1795. O [3]

menarche, *n.* (1900) *Med.* [G (1895) < Gk *mḗn* month + *archḗ* beginning] The initiating of a female's menstruation: her first period. —**menarcheal** and **menarchial**, *a.* O, R, W [4]

mendipite, *n.* (1851) *Mineral.* [G *Mendipit* (1839) < the name of the *Mendip* Hills in Somerset, England, where it was found + G *-it* -ite] Oxychloride of lead. O, W [3]

Mennonite, *n.* (1565) *Theol.* [G *Mennonit* (c.1535) < the name of *Menno* Simons, Frisian religious reformer (1492–1561) + G connective *-n-* + *-it* -ite] A member of an evangelical Protestant denomination that stresses biblical authority and is opposed to infant baptism, taking of oaths, military service, and the holding of civic offices. —**Mennonite**, *a.* (1727–41), **Mennonitism.** O, R, W [4]

mensur, *n.* (1911) [G (1619) < L *mēnsūra* measure] In Germany, a fencing duel between students who use partially blunted weapons, resulting in facial scars. O [3]

menthene, *n.* (1838) *Chem.* [G *Menthen* < NL *mentha* (< L) mint + G *-en* -ene] An oily, unsaturated hydrocarbon obtained from menthol (q.v.); a tetrahydro derivative of a cymene. —**menthenol, menthenone.** O, R, W [3]

menthol, *n.* (1876) *Chem.* [G (1861) NL *mentha* (< L) mint + G *-ol* < L *oleum* oil] A secondary terpenoid alcohol occurring in peppermint oil or Japanese mint oil and also made synthetically, used in medicine and flavoring. —**mentholated** (1933), **menthol cigarette** (1952). O, R, W [4]

Mephistopheles, *n.* (c.1590) *Myth.* Old var. like **Mephostophilis** (c.1590) [G *Mephostophiles* (1587) – the current forms, *Mephistopheles* and *Mephisto*, come from Goethe's

Faust (1790, 1808, 1832)] In the German legend, the name of the evil spirit to whom Faust sold his soul; applied allusively to persons in the 17th century with reference to this chief devil as portrayed in Marlowe's *Dr. Faustus,* and in more modern times in Goethe's characterization. • ~ appears in adjectives like **-phelistic** (1837), **-phelean** (1851), **-phelian** (1853), **-phelic** (1873). O, R [4]

mercallite, *n. Mineral.* [G *Mercallit* (now *Merkallit*) < the name of Guiseppe *Mercalli* (1850–1914), Italian geologist + G *-it* -ite] Potassium acid sulfate. W [3]

mercaptan, *n.* (1834) *Chem.* [G (1834) (now *Merkaptan*) < Dan < ML *mercurium captans* a mercury-bound substance] Thiol or thioalcohol, a class of compounds analogous to the alcohols and phenols, esp. ethyl mercaptan. O, R, W [4]

mercapturic acid, *n.* (1879) *Chem.* [Short. and transl. of G *Bromphenyl-mercaptursäure* (1879) < *Mercaptan* mercaptan (q.v.) + *Urin* (< Gk *oûron* urine) + G *Säure* acid] An acid formed from cysteine and an aromatic compound usu. excreted in urine. O, W [4]

mercy seat, *n.* (1530) *Theology* Var. **Mercy-Seat, Mercy Seat** (1667) [Transl. of Luther's G *Gnadenstuhl* < the comb. form of *Gnade* mercy + *Stuhl* chair, seat, as transl. < Heb *kappōreth,* describing the gold covering placed on the Ark of the Covenant and regarded as the resting-place of God] The throne of God in Heaven, regarded as a place of divine access, atonement, or communion; (depiction of) Jesus with the Heavenly Father; transf. sense to a powerful king's throne and the favors dispensed therefrom. O, R, W [4]

meromictic, *a.* (1937) *Biol.* [G *meromiktisch* (1935) < Gk *méros* part + *miktós* mixed + G adj. suffix *-isch* -ic] Applied to a lake in which, at the fall overturn, water below a certain depth does not take part in the circulation due to its high density (as in salt concentration). O, W [3]

meroplanktonic, *a.* (1893) *Biol.* [Haeckel's G *meroplanktonisch* (1890) < Gk *méros* part + G *Plankton* plankton (q.v.) + G adj. suffix *-isch* -ic] Of the portion of the plankton that spends only part of their life-cycle drifting or swimming at or near the surface. —**meroplankton** (1909). O, W [3]

mesarch[1], *a.* (1891) *Bot.* [G (1887) < *mes-* < Gk *mésos* middle + *arché* beginning] Having metaxylem developed on both sides of the protoxylem. O, R, W [4]

mesarch[2], *a.* (1923) *Ecology* [G (see *mesarch*[1])] Of a sere's originating in a mesic habitat in ecological succession. O, R, W [3]

mescaline, *n.* (1896) *Chem.* Var. **mezcaline** (1896), **mescalin** (1900) [G *Mezcalin* (1896) (now *Mescalin/Meskalin*) < Sp *mezcal* mescal < Nahuatl *mexcalli* a liquor + G *-in* -ine] 3,4,5-trimethoxyphenyl-ethylamine, crystalline alkaloid that is the chief active principle of mescal buttons and is used to produce cataleptic symptoms in experimental psychiatry. —**mescaline,** *a.* (1913). O, R, W [4]

mesectoderm, *n. Biol.* [G *Mesektoderm* (1894) < *mes-* + *Ektoderm* < Gk *mésos* middle + *ektós* outside of + *dérma* skin] An embryonic blastomere or cell layer that is not yet differentiated into the ectoderm and mesoderm but will later give rise to both. —**mesectodermal** and **mesectodermic,** *a.* W [3]

mesenchyme, *n.* (1888) *Biol.* Var. **mesenchym** [G *Mesenchym* < *mes-* + *-enchym* < Gk *mésos* middle + *en* into + *chýma* juice] A loosely organized mesodermal connective tissue containing most of the mesoblast and giving rise to bone, cartilage, etc. • ~ appears in adjectives like **-chymal** (1886), **-chymatous** (1886), **-chyme** (1904). •*Mesenchyma* is < NL. O, R, W [4]

mesendoderm, *n. Biol.* Var. **mesentoderm** [G *Mesentoderm* (1894) < *mes-* + *Entoderm* < Gk *mésos* middle + *entós* within + *dérma* skin] An embryonic blastomere or cell layer that is not yet differentiated into endoderm and mesoderm but will later give rise to both. W [3]

mesene, *a. Physiol.* [G *mesen* < *mes-* (< Gk *mésos* middle) + G *-en,* as in *euryen* euryene (q.v.)] Having a moderate proportioned forehead with an upper facial index of certain dimensions. —**meseny,** *n.* W [3]

mesitine, *n.* (1828) *Mineral.* [G *Mesitin* (1827), a short. of *Mesitinspath* (see *mesitite*), so named because it is intermediate between magnesite and siderite (q.v.)] Mesitite, also called *mesitine spar.* O, W [3]

mesitite, *n.* (1868) *Mineral.* [G *Mesitit* (1827), a short. of *Mesitinspath* mesitine spar < Gk *mesítēs* go-between + G *-it* -ite + obs. *Spath* spar] Ferroan magnesite. O, W [3]

mesocranial, *a. Physiol.* [Prob. < G *mesokran* mesocranial < *meso-* < Gk *mésos* middle, medium + *kraníon* skull + E *-ial*] Having a skull of medium proportions and a cranial index of 75–80. —**mesocrany,** *n.* W [3]

mesolite, *n.* (1822) *Mineral.* [G *Mesolith* (1816) < *meso-* + *-lith* < Gk *mésos* middle + *líthos* stone] Hydrous aluminosilicate of calcium and sodium. O, R, W [4]

mesophase, *n.* (1929) *Biol.* [G (1929) < *meso-* + *-phase* < Gk *mésos* middle + *phásis* appearance, phase] A mesomorphic phase. O, W [3]

mesosaprobe, *n.* (1927) *Bot.* [Prob. < G *Mesosaprobie* (1908) < *meso-* < Gk *mésos* middle, medium, half + *saprós* rotted + *bíos* life + G *-ie* (< Gk *-ia*) -e] A mesosaprobic (q.v.) organism. O, W [3]

mesosaprobic, *a.* (1925) *Bot.* [Prob. < G *mesosaprobisch* (1908) < *meso-* < Gk *mésos* middle, medium, half + *saprós* rotted + *bíos* life + G adj. suffix *-isch* -ic] Being or inhabiting a moderately oxygenated environment containing considerable organic material and bacteria. O, W [3]

mesosiderite, *n.* (1868) *Geol.* [G *Mesosiderit* (1865) < *meso-* + *Siderit* < Gk *mésos* middle + *sídēros* iron + G *-it* -ite] A stony-iron meteorite in which the silicates are present as pyroxene and plagioclase. O [3]

mesothorium, *n.* (1907) *Chem.* [G (1907) < *meso-* (< Gk *mésos* middle) + G *Thorium* (< the name of *Thor,* Norse god of thunder) thorium + *-ium* < NL] Either of two radioactive products in the thorium series as intermediate between thorium and radiothorium, or a mixture of these two products, and used as a substitute for radium in luminous paints. O, W [4]

Messerschmitt, *n.* (1940) *Aeron.* [G (1939) < the name of Willy *Messerschmitt* (1898–1978), German aircraft designer] Any of various types of fighters or other German aircraft used in World War Two. —**Messerschmitt,** *a.* (1957). O, R [4]

mestome, *n.* (1885) *Bot.* Var. **mestom** [G *Mestom* < Gk *méstōma* < *mestoûn* to fill up + G *-om* -ome] The conducting tissues composed of leptome (q.v.) and hadrome (q.v.). O, W [3]

metabolic, *a.* (1845) *Biol., Chem.* [G *metabolisch* (1839), ad. < Gk *metabolikós* changeable < *metabolḗ* change + *-ikos* (= G adj. suffix *-isch* -ic)] Of, concerning, or produced by metabolism; undergoing metamorphosis; vegetative, esp. in certain cell nuclei (this is different from the old "transitional" meaning). • ~ appears in composites like **metabolical(ly)** (1880, 1913), **metabolic heat/movement/ water.** O, R, W [4]

metabolyo, *n.* (1890) *Biol.* [G *Metabolie* (1852) < Gk *metabolḗ* change + G *-ie* -y] Metamorphosis, the changing of shape as found in certain unicellular organisms; euglenoid movement. O, W [3]

metacontrast, *n.* (1950) *Psych.* [G *Metakontrast* (1910) < *meta-* + *Kontrast* < Gk *metá* afterwards + MFr *contrast*] A blurring in the aftereffect of a visual stimulus when followed shortly afterward by a second stimulus. O [3]

metakinesis¹, -eses *pl.* (1888) *Biol.* [G *Metakinese* (1882) < *meta-* + *Kinese* < Gk *metá* afterwards + *kínēsis* motion] Metaphase (q.v.). O, W [3]

metakinesis², -eses *pl. Anat.* [G *Metakinese* (1926) (see *metakinesis¹*)] Prometaphase, a stage in mitosis characterized by chromosome congression to the spindle equator. O, W [3]

metamathematics, *n.* (1926) *Math.* [G *Methamathematik* (1923) < *meta-* + *Mathematik* < Gk *metá* afterwards + L (*ars*) *mathematica* < Gk *mathematikḗ* (*téchnē*) < *máthēma* (acquired) knowledge] The philosophy of mathematics, esp. its logical syntax and formal properties and similar formal systems. —**metamathematical(ly)** (1926, 1937), **-ician** (1935). O, R, W [4]

metanephridium, *n.* (1930) *Zool.* [G (1889) < *meta-* + *Nephridium* < Gk *metá* afterwards + *nephrídios* concerning the kidney + G (< L) *-ium*] In certain invertebrates, a nephridium originating in a ciliated coelomic funnel. —**metanephridial,** *a.* (1940). O, W [3]

metaphase, *n.* (1887) *Biol.* [G (1884) < *meta-* + *-phase* < Gk *metá* afterwards + *phásis* phase, stage] The stage of mitosis that precedes the anaphase. —**metaphase plate.** O, R, W [4]

metaphyte, *n.* (1893) *Bot.* [G *Metaphyt* < *meta-* + *-phyte* < Gk *metá* afterwards + *phytón* plant] A multicellular plant. —**metaphytic,** *a.* (1900). O, W [3]

metaplasis, *n.* (1888) *Physiol.* [Haeckel's G (1866) < Gk *metaplássein* to mold into a new form] The middle or adult stage of ontogenetic development. O [3]

metastable¹, *a.* (1897) *Chem.* (1922) [G *metastabil* (1893), coined by the German chemist Wilhelm Ostwald (1853–1932) < *meta-* + *Stabil* < Gk *metá* in between + L *stabilis* stable] Distinguished by only a slight margin of stability. —**metastability** (1901), **metastably** (1938), **metastable state** (1968). O, R, W [3]

metastable², *a.* (1922) *Physics* [G *metastabil* (1919), introduced in this sense by the German-American physicist James Franck (1882–1964) and the German physician Hugo Wilhelm Knipping (1895–?) (see *metastable¹*)] Of a body or quantum-mechanical system existing at an energy level higher than that of a more stable state. O, R, W [4]

metatrophic, *a.* (1900) *Biol.* [G *metatroph* (1897) < *meta-* + *-troph* < Gk *metá* afterwards + *trophḗ* nourishment + E *-ic*] Needing complex organic sources of nitrogen and carbon for nutrition: heterotrophic. —**metatroph(y).** O, R, W [3]

metaxite, *n.* (1836) *Mineral.* [G *Metaxit* (1832) < LGk *métaxa* raw silk + G *-it* -ite, so called for its luster] A fibrous serpentine. O, W [3]

metazoa, *pl.* of **metazoon** (1874) *Zool.* [Haeckel's G (1874) < *meta-* < Gk *metá* afterwards + *zoa,* pl. of *zóōn* animal] (One of Haeckel's two great divisions of the animal kingdom, the other being protozoa) animals whose adult bodies are composed of numerous cells differentiated into tissues and organs. **metazoic** (1877); **-zoan,** *n.* (1884) and *a.* (1886); **-zoal,** *a.* O, R, W [4]

meter-angle, *n.* *Optics* [Transl. of G *Meterwinkel* (1880) < *Meter* meter (< L *metrum* < Gk *métron*) + G *Winkel* angle] A convergence unit equal to the angle between the line of sight of either eye and the median line passing between them when the eyes are focused on a point on that line one meter away. W [3]

meth(a)emoglobin, *n.* (1870) *Chem.* [G *Methaemoglobin* < *met-* (< Gk *metá* afterward) + G *Hämiglobin* haemoglobin (q.v.), discovered by the German chemist Felix Hoppe-Seyler (1825–95)] A crystalline basic pigment found in normal blood, also called *ferrihemoglobin* and *hemiglobin.* —**meth(a)emoglobulin** (1890), **meth(a)emoglobinuria** (1897). O, W [4]

Methodenstreit, *n.* (1958) [G, lit., methods struggle < *Methoden* (prob. the comb. form rather than a pl. of *Methode* method) (< L *methodus* < Gk *méthodos*) + G *Streit* controversy] Discussion or dispute of opinions about the methodology of a given field of study. O [3]

methyl red, *n.* (1910) *Chem.* [Transl. of G *Methylrot* (1909) < *Methyl,* back-formation < *Methylen* (< Fr *méthylène* < Gk *méthy* wine + *hýlē* wood, substance) + G *rot* red] A red, basic azo dye that is used similarly to methyl orange as an acid-base indicator. O, R, W [3]

Metol/metol, *n.* and *a.* (1893, 1893) *Chem.* [G (1893), coined as a proprietary name] (of) a trademark; (of) this photographic developer, sulfate of methylparamidometacresol. O, R, W [4]

metric space, *n.* (1927) *Math.* [Transl. of G *metrischer Raum* (1914) < *metrisch* metric < *Meter* meter (< L *metrum* < Gk *métron*) + G *Raum* space] A mathematical set for which a metric is defined for all pairs of elements of the set. O, R [3]

metrizable, *a.* (1927) *Math.* [Transl. of G *metrisierbar* (1924) < *Metrisation* metrization (q.v.) + adv. suffix *-bar* -able] Of a topological space that can be assigned a metric. —**metrizability** (1927). O, R [3]

metrization, *n.* (1927) *Math.* [G *Metrisation* (1924) < *metrisieren* to assign a metric < L *metrum* measure < Gk *métron*] The process of assigning a metric to an appropriate topological space. O, R [3]

mett sausage, *n.* *Food* [Partial transl. of G *Mettwurst* (q.v.)] Mettwurst. W [3]

mettwurst, *n.* (1895) *Food* Var. **mett sausage** [G < *Mett* (ground) lean pork + *Wurst* sausage] A smoked German-type sausage of lean beef and salt pork. O, W [3]

miargyrite, *n.* (1836) *Mineral.* [G *Miargyrit* (1829) < *mi-*

+ *argyr-* + *-it* -ite < Gk *meíōn* less + *árgyros* silver] A silver antimony sulfide. O, W [3]

miarolitic, *a.* (1895) *Geol.* [G *miarolitisch* (1887) < It dial. *miarolo* a kind of granite containing cavities + G *-lit* (< Gk *líthos* stone) + G adj. suffix *-isch* -ic] Characterized by irregular cavities into which well-formed crystals project; of such cavities. O, W [3]

miascite, *n.* (1854) *Geol.* Var. **miaskite** [G *Miaszit* (1814) < *Miask,* the name of a town in the Ural Mountains + G *-it* -ite] A rock occurring in the Ilmen Mountains, essentially made up of orthoclase (q.v.), nepheline (q.v.), and dark mica. O [3]

micelle, *n.* (1881) *Physics* Var. **micella** (1881), **micell** (1946) [G *Micell* (1877) (now *Mizell*) < L *micella,* dim. of *mica* crumb] A unit of structure comprising polymeric molecules or ions. —**micellar theory** (1893). O, R, W [4]

microclase, *n.* (1885) *Mineral.* [G *Mikroklas* < *mikro-* + *-klas* < Gk *mikrós* small + *klásis* cleavage, fracture] A potash-soda feldspar that occurs intercrystallized with orthoclase (q.v.). O [3]

microcline, *n.* (1849) *Mineral.* [G *Mikroklin* (1830) < *mikro-* + *-klin* < Gk *mikrós* small + *klínein* to incline] A feldspar mineral that is like orthoclase but is triclinic. —**microcline,** *a.* (1888); **microcline green.** O, R, W [4]

microlite, *n.* (1878) *Geol.* Var. **microlith** (1879) [G *Mikrolith* (1867) < *mikro-* + *-lith* < Gk *mikrós* small + *líthos* stone] A microcrystal that usu. affects polarized light (this is different from the earlier "oxide mineral" meaning). —**microlitic** (1879). O, R, W [3]

microperthite, *n.* (1885) *Geol.* [G *Mikroperthit* < *mikro-* micro- (< Gk *mikrós* small) + G *Perthit* < E *perthite* < *Perth,* the Canadian town where it was found + G *-it* -ite] A perthite (feldspar rock), the structure of which can be seen only with a microscope. —**microperthitic** (1888). O, W [3]

microphage, *n.* (1890) *Biol.* Var. **microphag** (1903) [G *Mikrophag* (or Fr *microphage*) < *mikro-* + *-phag,* a short. of *Phagozyt* < Gk *mikrós* small + *phageîn* to eat + *kytós* cavity, cell] A polymorphonuclear leukocyte. —**microphage,** *a.* (1896). O, R, W [3]

microrespirometer, *n.* (1905) *Physiol.* [G *Mikrorespirometer* (1904) < *mikro-* + *Respirometer* < Gk *mikrós* small + L *respīrāre* to breathe + Gk *métron*] A device designed to measure the respiratory activity of minute amounts of living material like individual cells. —**microrespirometric** (1905); **-metry,** *n.* (1960). O, W [3]

microsome, *n.* (1885) *Biol.* [G *Mikrosom* (1880) < *mikro-* + *-som* < Gk *mikrós* small + *sōma* body] Any of several minute structures of the cell; a particle in a particulate fraction obtained by heavy centrifugation of broken cells. • ∼ appears in adjectives like **microsomal** (1897), **microsomial, microsomic.** O, R, W [4]

Middle English, *n.* (1836) *Ling.* [Transl. of G *Mittelenglisch* (1802) < *mittel* middle + *Englisch* English < OE *Englisc* < *Engle* Angles] A period in the history of English, intermediate between the periods of Old English and New or Modern English, usually dated c.1100–1500; English as represented in manuscripts of this period; the English of this time. O, R, W [4]

middlehand, *n. Games* Var. **mittelhand** [Transl. of G *Mit-*

telhand < *mittel* + *Hand* hand] In skat, the second player to bid in turn. W [3]

milarite, *n. Mineral.* [G *Milarit* < the place-name Val *Milar,* Switzerland + G *-it* -ite] A hydrous silicate of potassium, calcium, beryllium, and aluminum. W [3]

milk line, *n.* (1893) *Biol.* [Transl. of G *Milchlinie* (1892) < *Milch* milk + *Linie* < L *linea*] The line of altered glandular tissue appearing on either side of a mammalian embryo, which gives rise in females to the mammary glands. O, W [3]

milk ridge, *n.* (1909) *Biol.* [Transl. of G *Milchleiste* (1893) < *Milch* milk + *Leiste* ridge] Milk line (q.v.). O [3]

millerite, *n.* (1854) *Mineral.* [G *Millerit* (1845) < the name of William Hallowes *Miller* (1801–80), English mineralogist + G *-it* -ite] Nickel monosulfide. O, R, W [4]

miltz, *n.* (1909) *Food* [G *Milz* spleen] The spleen as used in cooking. O [3]

milzbrand, *n. Med.* [G < *Milz* spleen + *Brand* burning, blight] The disease anthrax. W [3]

mimetite, *n.* (1852) *Mineral.* [G *Mimetit* (1845) < Fr *mimétèse* mimetite < Gk *mimētēs* imitator + G *-it* -ite] Lead chloroarsenate. O, R, W [3]

mimophyre, *n.* (1841) *Geol.* [G *Mimophyr* < *mimo-* (< Gk *mîmos* mime) + G *-phyr* < *Porphyr* porphyry (q.v.)] An uncrystallized rock resembling porphyry. O [2]

mimosine, *n.* (1937) *Pharm.* Old var. **mimosin** (1937) [G *Mimosin* (1936) < *Mimose* mimosa (< NL *mimosa*) + G *-in* -ine] A crystalline amino acid found in the lead tree and in the common sensitive plant. O, W [3]

Mindel, *n.* (1910) *Geol.* [G (1901) < *Mindel,* the name of a Bavarian river that empties into the Danube near Gundremingen, Germany] The second stage of European glaciation. —**Mindel,** *a.* (1957). O, W [3]

minenwerfer, *n.* (1915) *Mil.* [G < *Minen,* pl. of *Mine* mine + *Werfer* thrower < *werfen* to throw] A German trench mortar: minnie (q.v.). • ∼ is transl. as **mine thrower** (1915). O [3]

mineraloid, *n.* (1913) *Mineral.* [Prob. < G (1909) < *Mineral* + *-oid* < ML *minerale* + Gk *-oeidēs* similar] A substance that would have the attributes of a mineral except that it is amorphous rather than crystalline. O, R, W [3]

mine thrower, *n.* (1915) *Mil.* [Transl. of G *Minenwerfer*] Minenwerfer (q.v.). O [3]

minette, *n.* (1878) *Geol.* [G (< Fr) (1828), dim. of Fr *mine* ore, mine, first used in this sense by the French-German mineralogist Philippe Louis Voltz (1785–1840)] A dark, igneous rock composed mainly of biotite (q.v.) and orthoclase (q.v.). •The also-geological meaning of "oolitic iron ore" came to English directly from Fr *minette.* O, R, W [3]

minne-drinking, *n.* (1880) *Beverages* [Partial transl. of G *Minnetrunk* < *Minne* love + *Trunk* drink < *trinken* to drink] Orig., a practice among idolatrous Germanic tribes at grand sacrifices and banquets of downing a horn filled with mead or other fermented brew in honor of the gods or in memory of someone absent or deceased; a later practice said to survive in some German localities. O [3]

minnelied/Minnelied, -er *pl.* (1876) *Lit.* [G < *Minne* love + *Lied* song] A song by or in the style of a minnesinger (q.v.); a love song. • ~ was partially transl. as **minnesong** (q.v.). O, W [3]

Minnepoesy, *n.* (1845) *Lit.* [G < *Minne* love + E *poesy*] Minnepoetry (q.v.). O [2]

Minnepoetry, *n.* (1887) *Lit.* [G < *Minne* love + E *poetry*] The poetry of the minnesingers. O [2]

minnesang, *see* minnesong

minnesinger, *n.* (1825) *Lit., Music* Var. **Minnesinger** (1825), **minnesänger** [G (also *Minnesänger*) < *Minne* love + *Singer/Sänger* singer] One of a class of aristocratic German lyric poets and musicians of the 12th to the 14th centuries inspired by the French troubadors. —**minnesinging,** *verbal a.* (1825), *n.* O, R, W [4]

minnesong/minnesang, *n.* (1845) *Lit., Music* Var. **Minnesong** (1845) [G *Minnesang* or *Minnelied* (q.v.) < *Minne* love + *Sang* or *Lied* song] A song of the minnesingers; collectively, their songs or this musical form. O, W [3]

Minnie/minnie, *n.* (1917) *Mil.* (slang) [Folk etymology and short. of G *Minenwerfer* (q.v.) mine thrower] A German trench mortar or its projectile; either of two types of mortars, a minenwerfer or a nebelwerfer (q.v.). —**minnie,** *v.* (1930), *a.* (1930); **moaning minnie** (1941, q.v.). O [3]

Minster, *n.* (1612) *Textiles* (archaic) [G *Münster,* the name of the former capitol of Westphalia, Germany] A kind of linen cloth orig. exported from Munster. O [2]

miogeoclinal, *see* miogeosynclinal

miogeosynclinal, *a.* (1942) *Geol.* Var. **miogeoclinal** (1971) [G *miogeosynklinal* (1940) < *mio-* + *geo-* + *synklinal* < Gk *meíōn* less + *geo-,* the comb. form of *gē* earth + *sýn* together with + *klínein* to bend] Of or pertaining to a relatively stable geosyncline in which sediments accumulate without accompanying volcanism. —**miogeosyncline,** *n.* (1942). O, W [3]

mirabilite, *n.* (1854) *Mineral.* [G *Mirabilit* (1845) < NL *mirabile* wonderful + G *-it* -ite] Hydrous sodium sulfate, deposited in saline lakes, etc.: *Glauber's salt.* O, R, W [3]

mirror iron, *n. Metall.* [Transl. of G *Spiegeleisen* (q.v.)] Spiegeleisen. W [3]

misch metal, *n.* (1916 *W9*) *Chem.* Var. **mischmetal** (1924) [G *Mischmetall* < *mischen* to mix (< OHG *miskan* < L *miscēre*) + G *Metall* metal, ult. < L *metallum*] A pyrophoric alloy containing about 50% cerium plus other rare-earth metals, used in lighter flints. O, R, W [4]

Mischsprache/mischsprache, -n *pl.* (1930) *Ling.* [G (1885) hybrid language < *mischen* to mix + *Sprache* language] A language that supposedly arises from a mixture of two or more other languages. • ~ is loosely transl. as **mixed language** (1888, which is different from the same compound that means "creolized language"). O, W [2]

mispickel, *n.* and *a.* (1683, 1683) *Mineral.* [G *Mis(s)pickel,* poss. < *miss,* orig., confused, interchanged + *Buckel* back, i.e., false or deceptive lump, because the mineral was first thought to be without value] (of) arsenopyrite, an iron sulfarsenide. —**mispickly,** *a.* (1683). O, R, W [3]

mit, *prep.* (1885) *(colloq.)* [G *with,* along] With: (A) jocularly, to imitate a German's accent, as in 'come *mit* us'; (B) to omit the object of the verb and allude to German word order, which normally places prefixed verbal complements at the end of the clause, as in "I suppose Mrs. Gotkin will come *mit,*" as modeled on G *mitkommen* to come along. O [2]

Mitbestimmung, *n.* (1970) *Econ.* [G < *mit* co-, together with + *Bestimmung* determination] In Germany and some other European countries, the right of workers to take part in corporation management. • ~ is a reborrowing, this time in its phonetic form, for what has been transl. as **codetermination** (1952, q.v.) and **worker(s') participation** (1971). B [3]

mite, *v. Sociol.* [Prob. ad. of G *meiden* to avoid, shun] To impose a mite (social and economic boycott) on an Amish member for violating church law. —**mite,** *n.* [3]

mitis green, *n.* (1839) *Chem.* Var. **Mitis green** [Transl. of G *Mitisgrün* < the name of Ignatz *Mitis* (1771–1842), German manufacturer + *grün* green] (Cap.) Paris green used as a pigment; (often cap.) emerald green. O, W [3]

mitome, *n.* (1888) *Biol.* [G *Mitom* < *mit-* (< Gk *mítos* thread) + G *-om,* -ome, as in *Karzinom* carcinoma)] The supposed fibrillar reticulum of protoplasm. O, W [3]

mitosis, -oses *pl.* (1887) *Biol.* [G (1882) (now *Mitose*), coined by the German anatomist Walther Flemming (1843–1905) < *mit-* + *-(o)sis* < Gk *mítos* filament, thread + *-osis*] A complex nuclear division in which chromosomes are differentiated and halved; a cell or nucleus undergoing this division; karyokinesis, the whole process of mitosis. —**mitotic(ally)** (1888, 1890), **mitosic** (1890). O, R, W [4]

mitosome, *n.* (1891) *Biol.* [G *Mitosoma* (1889) < *mito-* + *-soma* < Gk *mítos* thread, filament + *sôma* body] A threadlike cytoplasmic inclusion, esp. one presumed to be derived from the preceding mitotic spindle. O, W [3]

Mitsein, *n.* (1955) *Philos.* [G (now also *Mitdasein/Miteinandersein*) coexistence, used by the German philosopher Martin Heidegger (1889–1976) < *mit* with + *sein* to be, being] The concept of a person's *being* in its relationship with others. O [3]

Mittagessen, *n.* (1880) *Food* Var. **Mittagsessen** (1880), **mittagessen** (1941) [G < *Mittag* noon + *Essen* meal] In Germany, a midday meal or lunch. O [3]

Mitteleuropa, *n.* (1918) *Geogr.* Var. **Mittel-Europa, Mittel Europa** (1950) [G < *mittel* middle + *Europa* (< L) Europe] Central Europe. O, R [3]

Mitteleuropa, *a.* (1931) *Geogr., Art* Var. **mitteleuropa** [G < *mittel* central + *Europa* (< L) Europe] Of or from Central Europe; of the kind or style prevalent there. O [3]

Mittel-European, *n.* (1950) *Ethnology, Politics* [G *Mitteleuropäer* < *mittel* middle, central + *Europäer* European] A Central European. O [3]

Mittel-European, *a.* (1937) *Ethnology, Politics* [G *mitteleuropäisch* < *mittel* middle + *europäisch* European < *Europa* Europe] Middle European. O [3]

mittelhand, *n. Games* [G, lit., middle hand] Middlehand (q.v.). W [3]

Mittelschmerz/mittelschmerz, -es *pl.* (1895) *Med.* [G < *mittel* middle + *Schmerz* pain] Pain that occurs between menstrual periods, usu. thought to be associated with ovulation. O, R, W [3]

mixed language, *see* Mischsprache

mixite, *n.* (1882) *Mineral.* [G *Mixit* (1879) < the name of A. *Mixa,* 19th-cent. Czech inspector of mines at Joachimsthal, Germany, where the mineral occurs + G *-it* -ite] A hydrous arsenate of copper and bismuth. O, W [3]

mixoploid, *n.* and *a.* (1931, 1931) *Biol.* [Prob. < G <

mixo- + *-ploid* < Gk *mixo-*, the combining form of *mîxis* mixture + *plóos* fold] (of) an organism that has different numbers of genomes in different cells: chimera. —**mixoploidy**, *n.* (1931). O, R, W [4]

mixoscopia/mixoscopy, *n.* (1939) *Psych.* [G *Mixoskopie* (1891) < *mixo-* + *-skopie* < Gk *mixo-*, the comb. form of *mîxis* mixture + *skopeîn* to look at + G *-ie* (< Gk *-ia*) -y] The securing of sexual pleasure or even orgasm as a result of seeing human beings or animals copulate: sexual perversion. O [3]

mixotrophic, *a.* (1900) *Biol.* [G *mixotroph* (1897) < *mixo-* + *-troph* < Gk *mixo-*, the comb. form of *mîxis* mixture + *trophikós* nursing + E *-ic*] Obtaining nourishment from a mixture of autotrophic and heterotrophic mechanisms; pertaining to such nourishment. O, W [3]

mizzonite, *n.* *Mineral.* [G *Mizzonit* < Gk *meízōn* greater + G *-it* -ite] A volcanic scapolite mineral intermediate between meionite and marialite. W [3]

mneme, *n.* (1913) *Psych.* [G (1904) < Gk memory] The persistent or recurrent aftereffects of experience on an individual or of the race; the capacity for this. — **mnemic(ally)** (1908, 1925), **mnemicness** (1941). O, R, W [3]

mnestic, *a.* *Psych.* [Prob. < G *mnestisch* < Gk *mnêstis* memory + G adj. suffix *-isch* -ic] Concerning memory or mneme (q.v.). W [3]

moaning minnie/Moaning Minnie, *n.* (1941) *Mil.* [Expansion and short. of G *Minenwerfer* (q.v.), so named from the moaning sound of the shell] This trench mortar or its shell; an air-raid siren. O [3]

mobility, *n.* (1895) *Chem., Physics* [Transl. of G *Beweglichkeit* (1876) < *bewegen* to move, be mobile + *-lichkeit*] A mathematical formula for the degree to which a charge carrier undergoes movement in a specific direction in responding to an electric field (this is different from the various French-derived ''bodily movement'' meanings). O [3]

Modernismus, *n.* (1934) *Art* [G (a liberalizing movement in Catholic theology, orig. at the beginning of the 20th cent., against the rigid constraints of the Church) < G *modern* modern + *-ismus* (< L) -ismus] Modernism, a movement in modern art that deliberately breaks away from classical and traditional methods and styles. O [3]

module, *n.* (1927) *Math.* Old var. **modul** (1937) [G *Modul* (1871) < L *modulus* measure, dim. of *modus* measure, type] Orig., a closed set that is a subset of a ring; a commutative additive group with prescribed elements and product (this is different from the numerous French- or Latin-derived meanings). —**left/right module** (1970). O, R [3]

Moeritherium, *n.* (1902) *Zool.* Var. **Mœritherium** (1902) [G (1901), used in a German essay by the British archaeologist Charles William Andrews (1866–1924) and published in *Verhandlungen des V. International Zool. Congresses* (V, 528) in 1901 < Gk *Moîros*, the name of a lake in Egypt + *theríon* wild beast] A genus of an extinct probocidean mammal; this mammal, whose remains were found in late Eocene and Oligocene beds in Upper Egypt. —**moerithere**. O, W [3]

mogul, *n.* and *a.* (1961, 1961) *Sports* [Folk etymology < (Austrian) G *Mugel* hill, bump] (of) a large bump on a ski slope. —**moguled**, *a.* (1975). O, R [4]

Mohr balance, *n.* *Pharm.* [Prob. transl. of G *Mohr-Waage* < the name of Karl F. *Mohr* (1806–79), German pharmacist + *Waage* balance] Westphal balance, a balance having the buoyancy of a float. W [3]

Mohs' scale, *n.* (1879) *Mineral.* Var. **Mohs scale** (1879), **Mohs's scale** (1897) [Ad. of G *Mohs-(Härte)skala* (1812) < the name of Friedrich *Mohs* (1773-1839), German mineralogist + *Härteskala* < *Härte* hardness + *Skala* scale] A scale of hardness in which ten reference minerals, ranging from very soft to very hard ones, are individually assigned a value of one to ten to designate their hardness; a revised, fifteen-value scale. O, W [4]

mol, *see* mole

moldavite, *n.* (1896) *Geol.* [G *Moldawit* (now also *Moldavit*) < *Moldau*, G name of the Vltava River in western Czechoslovakia + G *-it* -ite] A tektite from the Czech tektite fields; formerly, the substance composing such tektites. O [3]

mole, *n.* (1902) *Chem.* Var. **mol** (1923) [G *Mol* (1900), a short. of *Molekulargewicht* < *molekular* molecular (< ISV *molecular*) + G *Gewicht* weight] The quantity of a substance whose mass in grams is equal numerically to the molecular weight of the substance (this is different from numerous other, often earlier meanings). —**mole fraction** (1923). O, R, W [4]

moll, *a.* (1597) *Music* [G < ML *molle* < L *molle*, neuter of *mollis* soft, gentle] Composed in the minor mode, e.g., c-moll (this is different from the earlier ''soft'' meaning). O, R, W [3]

molybdite, *n.* *Mineral.* [G *Molybdit*, ad. of E *molybdine* + G *-it* -ite] Ferrimolybdite, a hydrated iron molybdate. W [3]

molybdophyllite, *n.* (1901) *Mineral.* [G *Molybdophyllit* (1901) < *molybdo-* + *-phyllit* < Gk *mólybdos* lead + *phýllon* leaf + G *-it* -ite] A hydrous silicate of lead and magnesium. O, W [3]

monadological, *a.* (1895) *Philos.* [G *monadologisch* < Gk *monás* entity + *lógos* word, reason + G adj. suffix *-isch* -cal] Concerning or based on monadology: monadic. — **monadologically** (1937). O, W [3]

monazite, *n.* (1836) *Mineral.* [G *Monazit* (1829) < Gk *monázein* to be or live alone (on account of its supposed rarity) + G *-it* -ite] A phosphate of the cerium metals and thorium often found in sand and gravel deposits. O, R, W [4]

monchiquite, *n.* (1891) *Geol.* [G *Monchiquit* (1890) < Serra de *Monchique*, the name of a mountain range in southern Portugal + G *-it* -ite] A lamprophyre (q.v.) containing small phenocrysts of augite and olivine (q.v.). O [3]

Monera, *pl.* (1869) *Zool.* [Haeckel's G, ult. < Gk *monéres* single] The kingdom or other major division of the simplest organisms; a taxon of variable rank comprising these. —**moneran**, *a.* (1877), *n.*; **moneric** (1881); **moneral**, *a.* O, R, W [3]

monergism, *n.* (1893) *Theol.* [G (< NL) and NL *Monergismus* < Gk *mónos* single, sole + *érgon* work + *-ismus* (< L) -ism] The doctrine that regeneration is exclusively the work of the Holy Spirit. •The earliest citation (1867–80) is prob. < NL; the next (1893) is < G. O, R, W [3]

monimolimnion, -limnia *pl.* (1937) *Biol.* [G (1935) < Gk *mónimos* stable + *límnē* standing water] The denser, lower, noncirculating layer of a meromictic lake. O [3]

monism, *n.* (1862) *Philos.* [G *Monismus* (1836) < *mon-* (< Gk *mónos* single, alone) + G (< L) *ismus* -ism] (A) The metaphysical doctrine that there is only one kind of substance or ultimate reality, or that reality is one indivisible organic whole; monogenesis; (B) a viewpoint, theory, or methodology that reduces phenomena to a fundamental principle; a sociological doctrine that human and nature's laws are a single, harmonious force. O, R, W [4]

monist, *n.* (1836–7) *Philos.* [G (1836) < *mon-* (< Gk *mónos* alone, single) + G (< L) *-ist* -ist] An advocate of monism (q.v.). —**monist,** *a.* (1931); **monistic(al)** 1862, 1890; **monistically** (1880). O, R, W [4]

monoblast, *n.* (1925) *Biol.* [Prob. < G (1923), used by the German professor Otto Naegeli (1871–1938) < *mono-* + *-blast* < Gk *mónos* single + *blastós* bud, shoot] A motile cell that develops into a monocyte (q.v.) of the circulating blood. O, W [3]

monocyte, *n.* (1913) *Biol.* [G *Monozyt* (1910) < *mono-* + *-zyt* < Gk *mónos* single + *kýtos* hollow, cell] A large, sluggish phagocytic leukocyte that has a single nucleus with a chromatin network. • ~ appears in the composites **monocytosis** (1914); **monocytic** (1934); **monocytoid,** *a.;* **monocytic leukemia.** O, R, W [4]

monomict, *a. Mineral.* [G *monomikt* < *mono-* < Gk *mónos* single + *miktós* mixed] Of a clastic sedimentary rock composed of a single mineral species. W [3]

monomineral(ic), *a.* (1917) *Mineral.* [G *monomineralisch* < *mono-* + *mineralisch* < Gk *mónos* single + ML *minerale* + G *-isch*] Composed entirely or almost entirely of a single mineral species. O, W [3]

mononucleotide, *n.* (1908) *Chem.* [G *Mononucleotid* (1908) < *mono-* + *Nucleotid* < Gk *mónos* single + *nucleo-*, comb. form of L *nucleus* nucleus + G *-id* (< Fr *-ide*) -ide, with *-t-* infix] A nucleotide formed from a single molecule each of phosphoric acid, a sugar, and a nitrogen base. O, W [3]

monoploid, *n.* (1928) *Biol.* [G (1927) < *mono-* + *-ploid* < Gk *monoplóos* onefold] Having or being a chromosome set composed of a single genome (q.v.). —**monoploid,** *a.* (1955); **monoploidy,** *n.* (1943). O, R, W [3]

monotone, *a.* (1905) *Math.* Var. **monotonic** (q.v.) [G *monoton* (1881) < *mono-* + *-ton* < Gk *monotónos* uniform] Of a function or quantity varying in such a way that it either never increases or never decreases; of a sequence consisting of terms that vary in this way (this is different from the earlier "acoustic and various other" meanings). O, R, W [3]

monotonic, *a.* (1901) *Math.* [G *monoton* (1881) < Fr *monotone* < LL *monotonus* < Gk *monotónos* uniform + E *-ic*] Of a function that never increases or diminishes throughout an interval; monotone (q.v.). O, R, W [3]

monotropy, *n.* (1902) *Chem.* [Prob. < G *Monotropie* (1888) < *mono-* + *-tropie* < Gk *mono-*, the comb. form of *mónos* single, alone + *tropḗ* turning + G *-ie* -y] The

existence of two different forms of the same substance, one of which is stable and the other metastable, such that the change from the unstable form to the stable one is irreversible. O, R, W [3]

monoxenous, *a.* (1940) *Biol.* [G *monoxen* (1867) < *mono-* + *-xen* < Gk *mónos* single, alone + *xénos* stranger + E *-ous*] Of a parasitic plant or animal that is restricted to a single host species during its entire lifetime. O, W [3]

monradite, *n.* (1846) *Mineral.* [G *Monradit* (1842) < the name of Dr. *Monrad* of Bergen, Norway + G *-it* -ite] A massive, granular variety of pyroxene found there. O [3]

monsoon forest, *n.* (1903) *Bot.* [Transl. of G *Monsunwälder* (1898) < *Monsun* (< E *monsoon*) + G *Wälder,* pl. of *Wald* forest] Open or partially deciduous forest found in tropical areas with seasonal heavy rainfall or prolonged drought. O, W [3]

mops, *n.* (1890) *Zool.* [G < LG, Du < LG *mopen* to make a wry face, reminiscent of this dog's surly face or < Du *moppen* to growl, grumble] A pug dog. O [3]

morbility, *n.* (1876) *Path.* [G *Morbilität* < NL *morbilitas* (gen. *morbilitatis*), ult. < L *morbus* disease] The proportion of sickness in a given area; the sick rate: morbidity. O [3]

mordent, *n.* (1806) *Music* Var. **mordant** (1906) [G < It *mordente* < *mordere* to bite] A melodic grace made by rapidly alternating a principal tone with an auxiliary one, usu. a half step below it; acciaccatura. O, R, W [4]

morgenstern, *n.* (1637) *Mil.* Old var. like **morgan sterne** (1637) [G < *Morgen* morning + *Stern* star] A medieval club with a spiked head. • ~ is trans. as **morning star** (1684). O [2]

morning-land, *n.* (1842) *Geog.* [Poss. a transl. of G *Morgenland*] The Orient: the East. O [3]

morning star, *n.* (1684) *Mil.* [Transl. of G *Morgenstern*] Morgenstern (q.v.), a shafted weapon. O, R, W [3]

moroxite, *n.* (1814) *Mineral.* [G *Moroxit* (1798) < Gk *móroxos* pipe clay + G *-it* -ite] A crystallized variety of apatite (q.v.). O, W [3]

morphine, *n.* (1828) *Chem.* Var. **morphia** (< NL, 1818) [G *Morphin* (1816), named as isolated from opium in 1806 by the German chemist Friedrich Wilhelm Sertürner (1783–1841) < L *Morpheus,* Ovid's name for the god of dreams + G *-in* -ine] A bitter, white, crystalline narcotic alkaloid base that is habit-forming, used as an analgesic and sedative and in drug addiction. —**morphine,** *v.* (1856), *a.* (c.1865). • ~ appears in composites like **-inize** (1865), **-inism** (1882), **-inist** (1894), **-inomania** (1882), **-inic** (1891), **-inization, morphine injection** (1878)/**syringe** (1897)/**meconate,** and is short. to **morph** (1912). O, R, W [4]

morph(o)-, *comb. form Biol.* [G *morph(o),* comb. form of Gk *morphḗ* form, shape] Denoting form, structure, shape, type. O, R, W [4]

morpho, *n.* (1853) *Entomology* Var. **Morpho** (1853) [G (1807) < Gk *Morphṓ,* an epithet of Aphrodite] A large tropical American butterfly of the genus *Morpho,* noted for shiny blue wings; this genus. —**morpho,** *a.* (1925). O, W [4]

morpholine, *n.* (1889) *Chem.* [G *Morpholin* (1889) < *Morphin* morphine (q.v.) with an infixed *-ol-,* so named because chemists orig. thought that its molecular structure was like that of morphine] A cyclic, secondary amine made from ammonia and ethylene oxide and used mainly as a solvent and emulsifier. O, R, W [3]

morphology[1], *n.* (1830) *Biol.* [G *Morphologie* (1817) < Gk *morphē* form + G *-logie* < Gk *lógos* word, study + G *-ie* -y] A branch of biology concerned with the form and structure of plants and animals; the structure and form of something. • ~ appears in composites like **-logical** (1830), **-logist** (1845), **-logic(ally)** (1872, 1859), **morphological index**. O, R, W [4]

morphology[2], *n.* (1869) *Ling.* [G *Morphologie* (see *morphology*[1])] A part of syntax, but differentiated from word order by stressing word formation including inflection, derivation, and compounding. —**morphologic(al) construction** (1878). O, R, W [4]

morphon, -tes *pl.* (1873) *Biol.* Var. **morphone** (1880) [Haeckel's G < Gk *morphē* form + *ón* (gen. *óntos*) being] A morphological individual, factor, or element. O [3]

morphotropy, *n.* (1900) *Mineral.* [G *Morphotropie* (1870) < *morpho-* + *-tropie* < Gk *morphē* form + *tropē* change + G *-ie* -y] Morphotropism, the modifying influence of a change in chemical constitution on crystal form; the study of this. —**morphotropic** (1899). O [3]

mosaic disease, *n.* (1894) *Med.* [Transl. of G *Mosaikkrankheit* (1886) < *mosaik* (< ML *mosaicum* colorful, of variegated composition) + G *Krankheit* disease] A virus disease that attacks plants, characterized by retarded growth and leaf discoloration, as in tobacco mosaic. O, R [4]

mosandrite, *n.* (1846) *Mineral.* [G *Mosandrit* < the name of Carl G. *Mosander* (1797–1858), Swedish chemist + G *-it* -ite] A silicate of the cerium metals, sodium, calcium, titanium, and zirconium. O, W [3]

Moselle, *n.* (1687) *Beverages* [G *Mosel,* a short. of *Moselwein* < the G name of the *Moselle* (< Fr) tributary that flows through France and joins the Rhine at Koblenz + G *Wein* wine] A light, white table wine made from grapes grown in the Moselle valley; a wine resembling this. — **Moselle wine** (1687). O, R, W [4]

mosse, *n.* (1617) (obs.) *Beverages* [G *Mass* measure] A measure of wine to be sold and drunk. O [2]

mossite, *n.* (1898) *Mineral.* [G *Mossit* (1897) < *Moss,* the name of a Norwegian city + G *-it* -ite] An oxide of iron and tantalum: part tantalite and part tapiolite. O, W [3]

motiviert, *a.* (1812) Var. **motivirt** (1890) [G, the past part. of *motivieren* to motivate < ML *motivus*] Motivated. O [3]

Motivierung, *n.* (1866) [G (1838) motivation < *motivieren* (see *motiviert*) + nom. suffix *-ung* -ing, -tion] Motivation. O [3]

mountain green, *n.* (1727) *Mineral.* (1822) *Chem.,* (1864) *Bot.* [Transl. of G *Berggrün* < *Berg* + *grün*] Malachite; green earth; malachite green, a color; a handsome West Indies plant, *Spathelia simplex.* —**mountain green,** *a.* (1796). O, W [3]

mucker, *n.* (1891) (U.S. slang) [Prob. < G grumbler, grouch, hypocrite < *mucken* < Du < MHG *mucken* to grumble] A fanatic or hypocrite; a coarse, boorish person; a tough, often vicious person. • ~ appears in composites like **muckdom** (1893), **muckish(ly)** (1904, 1906), **muckism**

(1906), **mucker-in** (1942), **mucker-upper** (1942). O, R, W [4]

muckite, *n.* *Mineral.* [G *Muckit* < the name of H. *Muck,* German mineralogist who was active in the 19th cent. + *-it* -ite] A resinous hydrocarbon that is similar to amber and is a variety of retinite. W [3]

mucoid, *n.* (1900) *Biochem.* [Prob. < G *Mukoid* < *Mucin* + *-oid* < L *mucus* mucus + Gk *-oeidēs* similar] Any of a group of complex proteins somewhat similar to mucoproteins or mucins: colloid; mucoprotein. O, R, W [4]

mull, *n.* (1928) *Ecology* [G (1879) < Dan *muld* < ON *mold* mold, dust, soil] Granular forest humus usu. consisting of a layer of mixed organic matter and mineral soil that merges gradually into the underlying mineral soil, which is characteristic of grasslands and hardwood forests. O, W [4]

multiple myeloma, *n.* (1897) *Med.* [Ad. of G *multiples Myelom* (1873) < *multipel* + *Myelom* < L *multiplex* manifold + Gk *myelós* bone + *-ōma* signifying tumor] Myelomatosis, a disease of bone marrow. O, R, W [4]

multirotation, *n.* (1890) *Chem.* [G (1890) < *multi-* + *Rotation* < L *multus* manifold + *rotāre* to turn] Mutarotation, a change in optical rotation. O [3]

mum, *n.* (1640) *Beverages* [G *Mumme* (1489) < the name of its supposed original brewer, Christian *Mumme*] A strong ale or beer made first in Brunswick, Germany. — **mum,** *a.* (1682–3). O, R, W [4]

murexide, *n.* (1838) *Chem.* Var. **murexid** (1841) [G *Murexid* < NL *murex* (< L) sea mussel + G *-id* -ide] A crystalline compound with a metallic luster, formerly used as a dye; the ammonium salt of purpuric acid. —**murexide,** *a.* (1875); **merexide reaction/test.** O, R, W [3]

muriacite, *n.* (1799) *Mineral.* [G *Muriacit* (1795) (now also *Muriazit*) < L *muria* brine + G connective *-c-* + *-it* -ite] Anhydrite (q.v.). O [3]

muromontite, *n.* (1854) *Mineral.* [G *Muromontit* (1848) < NL *Muromontium,* G *Mauersberg,* a town in western Germany + G *-it* -ite] A silicate that is perhaps identical with gadolinite (q.v.) or is a variant of clinozoisite (q.v.). O, W [3]

muscarine, *n.* (1872) *Chem.* [G *Muscarin* (1869) (now *Muskarin*) < NL *muscaria* < L *musca* fly + G *-in* -ine] A quaternary ammonium base related to choline (q.v.) that is a poisonous alkaloid found in the fungus *Amanita muscaria.*—**muscarinic(ally)** (1941, 1971). O, R, W [4]

Muschelkalk, *n.* (1833) *Geol.* [G shell limestone < *Muschel* mussel, shell + *Kalk* lime < L *calx* (dat. *calcem*)] A limestone bed of the German red sandstone formation. —**Muschelkalk,** *a.* O, W [3]

muscle spindle, *n.* (1894) *Path.* [Ad. of G *Muskelspindel* (1863) < *Muskel* (< L *musculus*) < G *Spindel* spindle] Any of numerous sensory end-organs within muscle that consist of intrafusal muscle fibers richly supplied with nerve endings and that respond to muscular stretching and contraction. O, R, W [3]

Mussulman, -mans/-men *pl.* (1950) *Politics* [G *Muselmann* Muslim < It *musulmano,* Turkish *müslüman* < Ar *muslim;* a prisoner in a Nazi concentration camp who lost the will to live and bore his/her lot fatalistically] Under the Third Reich, such a prisoner, who ult. reacted only as a brute animal (this is different from the old Turkish-derived "Muslim" meaning). O [3]

mutant, *n.* (1901) and *a.* (1903) *Biol.* [G *Mutante* (1901) (< NL *mutant*), coined by the Dutch botanist Hugo de Vries (1845–1915) in his German work *Die Mutations-theorie* (1901–3) < L *mutant-, mūtāns,* present part. of *mūtāre* to change] (Of) the product of mutation (q.v.). O, R, W [4]

mutase, *n.* (1914) *Biochem.* [G (1910) < L *mūtāre* to change + G (< L) *-ase* -ase denoting a destroying substance] An enzyme that can catalyze a dismutation or molecular rearrangements. O, W [3]

mutation, *n.* (1901) *Biol.* [G (< L) (1901) mutation] (De Vries's projected) hypothetical, abrupt, fundamental change in heredity that should produce new individuals unlike their parents, leading to new species (this is different from various older meanings). O, R, W [4]

muthmannite, *n. Mineral.* [G *Muthmannit* < the name of Friedrich Wilhelm *Muthmann* (1861–1913), German chemist + *-it* -ite] A silver gold telluride. W [3]

mutti, *n.* (1906) [G, an endearing form of *Mutter* mother] The childish or endearing form of *mother* used in German-speaking countries: Mom(my). O [3]

mycetocyte, *n.* (1924) *Entomology* [G *Mycetocyt* (1911) (now *Myzetozyt*) < Gk *mýkēs* fungus + *kýtos* cavity, cell] Any of the large cells found in various insects, usu. aggregated into paired mycetomes, which contain unicellular fungi. O, W [3]

mycetome, *n.* (1924) *Zool.* Var. **mycetom** (1924) [G *My-cetom* (1911) (now *Myzetom*) < *myce-* + *-tom* < Gk *mý-kēs* fungus + *kýtos* hollow, cell + G *-om* (Gk *-ōma*) -me, designating aggregation, swelling] Either of a pair of organs in some insects consisting of a cellular mass of mycetocytes (q.v.). —**mycetomic.** O, W [3]

mycobacterium, *n.* (1909) *Biol.* [G *Mycobakterium* (1896) (now also *Mykobakterium*) (< NL) < Gk *myco-,* irreg. comb. form of *mýkēs* fungus + G *Bakterium* < Gk *bactêrion* rod, staff] A saprophytic or parasitic bacterium that causes tuberculosis, leprosy, and other diseases in humans and other animals; the genus of this. —**mycobacte-rium paratuberculosis.** O, R, W [4]

mycorrhiza, -e/-es *pl.* (1895) *Bot.* Var. **mycorhiza** (1895) [G *Micorhiza* (1885) (now *Mikorhiza*) < NL *mycorrhiza* < Gk *myko-,* irreg. comb. form of *mýkēs* fungus + *hríza* rod] A symbiotic fungus growing in association with the roots of a seed plant, also called *fungus root;* this association. —**mycorrhiza,** *a.* (1927); **myco(r)rhizal,** *a.* (1900). O, R, W [4]

mycotic, *a. Psych.* [G *mykotisch* < *Mykose* mycosis (< NL *mycosis*), after G pairs like *hypnotisch* and *Hypnose*] Concerning or characterized by mycosis. —**mycotic pneumonia/ stomatitis.** R, W [3]

mycotrophy, *n.* (1927) *Bot.* [G *Mykotrophie* (1923) < *myko-* + *-trophie* < Gk *myko-* irreg. comb. form of *mýkēs* fungus + *trophê* nourishment + G *-ie* -y] The situation

of certain plants that have mycorrhize growing in association with their roots, as an aid in assimilating nutrients. —**mycotrophic** (1930). O, R, W [3]

myelin[1], *n.* (1867) *Biol.* (1873) *Anat.* Var. **myeline** (1867) [G < Gk *myelós* marrow + G *-in* -in(e)] (*Biol.*): a fatty substance obtainable from animal tissues like egg yolk and also from some vegetable tissues; (*Anat.*): the medullary sheath of nerve fibers about the axis cylinder, usu. containing lipids. • ~ appears in composites like **myelinic** (1876), **myelinate** (1894), **myelino-** (1897), **myelinated** (1899), **myelination** (1899), **myelinization** (1900), **myelinize** (1903), **myelin sheath** (1896). O, R, W [4]

myelin[2], *n.* (1854) *Mineral.* [G < Gk *myélinos* marrowy, so named from its appearance] A variety of kaolin. O [3]

myeloblast, *n.* (1904) *Biol.* [G (1900) < *myelo-* + *-blast* < Gk *myelós* marrow + *blastós* bud, shoot] Hemocyto-blast, a stem cell that can produce all types of blood cells; a cell derived from this immature stem-cell. • ~ appears in composites like **-ic** (1916), **-osis** (1937), **-emia, -oma, myeloblastic leukemia.** O, R, W [4]

myogen, *n.* (1896) *Biochem.* [G (1895), a short. of *Myosi-nogen* < *myo-* < Gk *myo-,* the comb. form of *mýs* (gen. *mýos*) muscle + *genés* producing] A mixture of albumins obtained from skeletal muscle plasma, as from rabbits. — **myogen A/B/I/II.** O [3]

myoglobin, *n.* (1925) *Biochem.* Var. **myohemoglobin** [G (1921) < *myo-* + *Globin* < Gk *mýs* (gen. *mýos*) muscle + L *globus* globule, sphere + G *-in* -ine] A red, iron-containing protein somewhat similar to hemoglobin. — **myoglobinuria.** O, R, W [4]

myoplasm, *n.* (1907) *Anat.* [G *Myoplasma* (1905), coined by the German pathologist Paul Schiefferdecker (1849–1931) < *myo-* + *Plasma* < Gk *mýs* (gen. *mýos*) muscle + *plásma* structure] The sarcoplasm or cytoplasm of a muscle cell. —**myoplasmic** (1970). O [3]

myotonia congenita, *n.* (1886) *Med.* Var. **congenital myo-tonia** (1886) [G < *Myotonia* (1881) (< NL < Gk *myo-,* the comb. form of *mýs,* gen. *mýos* muscle + *tónos* tone + *-ia*) + G *Congenita* (< L *con-* < *cum* with + *genitum,* past part. of *gīgnere* to beget, bring forth)] A rare, hereditary disease manifested soon after birth, which is a myotonia but without muscular wasting. O [3]

myrmekite, *n.* (1916) *Geol.* [G *Myrmekit* (1897) < Gk *myrmekía* anthill, wart + G *-it* -ite] An intergrowth of feldspar and vermicular quartz formed in the late development of an igneous rock. —**myrmekitic** (1916), **myr-mekitization** (1916). O, W [3]

myxomatosis, -atoses *pl.* (1927) *Med.* [G *Myxomatose* (1898) or transl. of *Myxomkrankheit* < *myxoma* (< NL) < Gk *mýxa* mucus + G *Krankheit* disease or *-ose* (< Gk *-osis*) -osis, fem. suffix of action] A bodily condition characterized by the presence of myxomas, specif., a highly contagious virus disease of rabbits, which has been used to control rabbits; mucoid degeneration. —**myxomatosis,** *a.* (1955); **myxomatized,** *a.* (1955). O, R, W [4]

N

Na, *see* natrium

nachlass, *n.* (1842) *Lit.* [G < *nach* after, behind + *lassen* to leave] An author's unpublished writings left after the author's death. O [3]

nachschlag, -e/-s *pl.* (1879) *Music* [G < *nach* after(wards) + *schlagen* to beat, hit] The two terminating notes that are usu. played at the end of a trill; a musical ornament containing one or more short unaccented grace notes; short, unaccented grace notes. O, W [3]

nachthorn, -hörner/-s *pl. Music* [G < *Nacht* night + *Horn* horn] A night horn, cor de nuit; an organ flute stop often in 4 foot and 2 ranks. • ~ is transl. as **night horn.** W [3]

Nachtlokal, -e *pl.* (1939) [G < *Nacht* night + *Lokal* public place] A nightclub. —**nachtlokal,** *a.* O [3]

nachtmusik, -en/-s *pl. Music* [G < *Nacht* night + *Musik* music < Fr *musique*] Serenade. W [3]

nacht und nebel (1947) [G (*bei*) *Nacht und Nebel* < *bei* during, in + *Nacht* night + *und* and + *Nebel* mist, fog] Orig. a Nazi decree in 1941; now often a situation characterized by mystery and obscurity. —**nacht und nebel,** *a.* (1963). O [3]

nagelfluh, -s/-e *pl.* (1808) *Geol.* Var. **Nagelfluh** (1808), **nagelflue** (1849) [G < *Nagel* nail, i.e., nail-like, jagged + *Fluh* conglomerate of rock, rock face] A massive conglomerate of the Miocene series in the Swiss Alps. O, W [3]

nagyagite, *n.* (1849) *Mineral.* [G *Nagyagit* (1845) < *Nagyag* (formerly Hungary, now *Săcărambu,* Romania) + G *-it* -ite] A black sulfo-telluride of lead and other metals. O, W [3]

nannoplankton, *n.* (1912) *Biol.* Var. **nanoplankton** (1974) [G (1909) (< NL) < Gk *nânos,* L *nānus* dwarf + Gk *planktós* (of organisms) floating about] The smallest forms of plankton. —**nannoplanktonic.** O, R, W [4]

napfkuchen, *n. Food* [G < *Napf* bowl, cup, pan + *Kuchen* tart, cake] A semisweet cake: gugelhupf (q.v.). W [3]

narcissism, *n.* (1820) *Psych.* Var. **narcism** (1970) [G *Narzissismus* < *Narziss* (< L *Narcissus,* Gk *Nárkissos,* a handsome youth in Greco-Roman mythology, who fell in love with his own image, died of unrequited love, and was turned into the flower narcissus) + G *-ismus* (< L *-ismus*) -ism] Inordinate fascination with oneself; egotism; erotic gratification derived from one's own attributes; a stage in one's libido development. O, R, W [4]

narcissist, *n.* (1930) *Psych.* Var. **narcist** [G *Narzissist* < *Narziss* (< L *narcissus* narcist) + G *-ist* -ist] One who indulges in narcissism (q.v.). O, R, W [4]

narcissistic, *a.* (1916) *Psych.* Var. **narcistic** [G *narzissistisch* < *Narzissist* (see *narcissist*) + *-isch* -ic] Of or relating to narcissism (q.v.)—**narcissistic personality.** O, R, W [4]

naringin, *n.* (1879) *Chem.* [G *Naringen* (1879) < Skt *nāranga* orange tree < a Dravidian language + G *-en* -in] A bitter glycoside present in grapefruit, some oranges, and other citrus fruit. —**naringenin.** O, W [3]

nasat, *n. Music* [G < Fr *nazard/nasard* having a nasal sound < L *nāsus* nose] Nazard, a mutation organ stop. W [3]

nastic, *a.* (1908) *Bot.* [G *nastisch* (1904) < Gk *nastós* flattened + G *-isch* -ic] Of the movement of a flattened organ of plants as a result of irreversible differential growth of cells or of reversible turgor pressure changes in cells of specific regions. —**nastic movement** (1908). O, R, W [4]

-nastie, *comb. form Bot.* [G (see *nasty*)] Used with initial comb. forms to create new botanical names like *epinasty.* W [3]

nasty, nasties *pl.* (1936) *Bot.* [G *Nastie* (1904) < Gk *nastós* flattened + G *-ie* (< Gk *-ia*) -y] A nastic movement. O [3]

National Socialism, *n.* (1931) *Politics* Var. **national socialism** [Ad. of G *Nationalsozialismus* < *national* (< MFr) national + G *Sozialismus* socialism < L *sociālis* + *-ismus*] Adolf Hitler's name for his Nazi doctrine of political and economic reorganization and control. O, R, W [4]

National Socialist, *a.* (1923) *Politics* Var. **national socialist** [Ad. of G *nationalsozialistisch* < *national* (< MFr) national + G *sozialistisch* socialist < L *sociālis* + *-ist*] Of a member of Hitler's National Socialist Workers' Party; of this party or doctrine. —**National Socialist,** *n.* (1931). O, R, W [4]

natrium, *n.* (1842) *Chem.* [G < NL < Fr < Sp *natrón* < Ar *natrun* <Gk *nítron* bicarbonate of soda] An old name for sodium. • ~ is short. to **Na,** now the symbol for sodium. O, R, W [4]

natr(o)-, *comb. form* (1902) *Mineral.* [G *natr(o)-* < *Natron* (see *natrium*)] Natron; sodium; used in names like *natrophilite.* O, W [4]

natrochalcite, *n.* (1908) *Mineral.* [G *Natrochalzit* < *natro-* (q.v.) + *Chalzit* < Gk *chalkós* ore, copper + G *-it* -ite] A hydrous basic sulfate of sodium and copper. O, W [3]

natrolite, *n.* (1805) *Mineral.* [G *Natrolith* (1803) < *natro-* (q.v.) + *-lith* -lite < Gk *líthos* stone] A hydrated sodium aluminum silicate: needle zeolite. O, R, W [4]

nature printing, *n.* (1855) *Art* [Transl. of G *Naturselbstdruck* < *Natur* nature (< L *nātūra*) + G *selbst* (it)self + *Druck* print] The process by which a print of an object like a leaf or lace is made on a printing surface by pressing the object into the surface. —**nature-print,** *v.* (1855), *n.;* **nature-printed** (1859). O, W [3]

Naturphilosoph, -en *pl.* (1834) *Philos.* Var. **Naturphilosopher** (1957) [G < *Natur* nature + *Philosoph* philosopher < L *nātūra* + MFr *philosophe*] One who espouses the theory of Naturphilosophie (q.v.) O [3]

Naturphilosophie, *n.* (1817) *Philos.* Var. **Natur-philosophie** (1817) [G < *Natur* nature + *Philosophie* philosophy <

L *nātūra* + *philosophia*] The theory advanced esp. by Friedrich Schelling (1775–1854) that there is an unchanging, eternal law of nature. O [3]

naumannite, *n.* (1849) *Mineral.* [G *Naumannit* (1845) < the name of Karl F. *Naumann* (1797–1873), German mineralogist + G *-it* -ite] A silver selenide found in iron-black cubes or massive. O, R, W [4]

navite, *n. Mineral.* [G *Navit* < the German name of the river *Nahe* (L *Nava*), Germany + G *-it* -ite] A coarse olivine basalt containing phenocrysts in a holocrystalline groundmass. W [3]

Nazi, *n.* (1930) *Politics* [G short. of *Nationalsozialist* National Socialist (q.v.)] A member of the former fascistic National Socialist Workers' Party, founded in 1919; a member or supporter of such a party or doctrines. • ~ appears in various derivatives like **Nazidom** (1933), **Nazify** (1933), **Nazification** (1933), **Nazifying** (1934), **Nazified** (1934), **Naziphile** (1939). O, R, W [4]

Nazi, *a.* (1930) *Politics* [G *Nazi-* concerning Nazism] Of or pertaining to a Nazi (*n.,* q.v.). —**Nazi-ish** (1939). O, R, W [4]

Nazism, *n.* (1934) *Politics* Var. **Nazi-ism** (1934), **Naziism** (1938) [G *Nazismus,* a short. of *Nationalsozialismus* National Socialism (q.v.)] The political and economic philosophy held and implemented by the National Socialist German Workers' party, led by Adolph Hitler from 1921 until his death in 1945; a Nazi-like movement or state. —**Nazist** (1938), **Nazistic** (1938). O, R, W [4]

Nd, *see* neodymium

Neanderthal, *a.* (1861 *W9*) *Anthrop.* Var. **Neandertal** (1923) [G *Neanderthaler* < the name of the *Neanderthal* valley near Düsseldorf, Germany] Of the prehistoric skull orig. found in the Neanderthal Valley near Düsseldorf, Germany, and of the extensive later finds elsewhere; of primitive or very old-fashioned persons. —**Neanderthal,** *n.* (1899); **-oid,** *n.* (1887), *a.* (1890); **-ian,** *a.* (1920), n. (1920); **-ic** (1967); **Neanderthal man/skull** (1863, 1864), etc. O, R, W [4]

Neanderthaler, *n.* (1913) *Anthrop.* Var. **Neandertaler** (1913) [G *Neandert(h)aler* < the name of the *Neandert* (q.v.) Valley + *-er* -er] A Neanderthal man. O, R, W [4]

nebelwerfer, *a.* (1943) and *n.* (1946) *Mil.* [G (1943), actually, *Granatwerfer für Nebelgranaten* a rocket mortar for propelling smoke grenades < *Nebel* mist, fog + *Werfer* mortar, thrower] (of) a six-barrelled rocket mortar used by the Germans in World War Two. O [2]

nebenkern, **-s/-e** *pl.* (1898) *Biol.* [G (1871) < *neben* next to, secondary + *Kern* nucleus] A spherical mass of mitochondria (in the proximity of the cell nucleus). O, W [3]

neck canal cell, *n.* (1887) *Bot.* [Transl. of G *Halskanalzelle* < *Hals* neck + *Kanal* canal + *Zelle* cell < L *canālis* + *cella*] A cell in the archegonium's neck of ferns and mosses. O, W [3]

necton, *see* nekton

needlestone, *n.* (1820) *Mineral.* [Transl. of G *Nadelstein* < *Nadel* needle + *Stein* stone] An earlier name for various minerals with needle-like crystals, such as natrolite (q.v.) and scolecite (q.v.): mesotype. O [3]

neëncephalon, *n.* (1917) *Anat.* Var. **neoencephalon** [G (1908) (< NL) < Gk *neós* new + *enképhalon* brain] The

philogenetically latest part of the brain, i.e., the cerebral cortex and related structures. —**neencephalic** (1917). O, R, W [4]

neeze-wort, *n.* (1548) *Bot.* (obs.) [Ad. of G *Niesewurzel* (now *Nieswurz*) (or < Du *nies-wortel*) < G *niesen* to sneeze + *Wurz(el)* root] An early name for the poisonous herb hellebore. O [3]

neftgil, *n. Mineral.* Var. **neftdegil** [G short. of *Naphthadil* < Per *naftdagil* crude oil plus a blue clay or kaolin clay] Ozokerite, a waxlike mineral. W [3]

nekton, *n.* (1893) *Biol.* Var. **necton** (1923) [G *Necton* (1890) (now *Nekton*) < Gk *nēktón* that which swims] Collectively, the forms of organic life found at various depths of the oceans or of lakes that possess the power to swim actively, in contrast to plankton. —**nektonic** (1903). O, R, W [4]

neodymium, *n.* (1885) *Chem.* [G *Neodym* (1885) (< NL) < Gk *neós* new, renewed, young + *dídymos* double + E *-ium*] A plentiful rare-earth metal whose oxide is used in coloring glass and porcelain. • ~ is symbolized as **Nd**. It has been productive in many technical names like **neodymium acetate/bromate/nitrate,** etc. O, R, W [4]

neoencephalon, *see* neencephalon

neogrammarian, *n.* (1885) *Ling.* Var. **neo-grammarian** (1885) [Transl. of G *Junggrammatiker* (q.v.)] A member of the Junggrammatiker, an important late 19th-century philological movement in Germany that had considerable impact in the development of historical linguistics. —**neogrammarian,** *a.* (1933). O, R, W [3]

neohesperidin, *n.* (1936) *Pharm.* [G (1936) a natural sweetener < *neo-* + *Hesperidin* < Gk *neós* new + *hesperid-,* stem of *Hesperídes* the nymphs of Greek mythology, used to form technical terms of botany and chemistry + G *-in* -in] A bitter glycoside of a flavone found in Seville oranges. O [3]

Neo-Kantian/neo-Kantian, *n.* (1881) *Philos.* [Ad. of G *Neukantianer* < *neu* new + *Kantianer* a Kantian] One who subscribes to the philosophy of modern thinkers in consonance with Kant's general theory of knowledge. —**Neo-Kantian,** *a.* (1886). O, R, W [3]

Neo-Kantianism, *n.* (1888) *Philos.* [Prob. ad. of G *Neukantianismus* < *neu* new + *Kantianismus* Kantianism < the name of Immanuel *Kant* (1724–1804), German philosopher + G *-ian* (< L *-ianus*) -ian, denoting characteristic + G (< L) *-ismus* -ism] A movement opposing mid-19th century idealism and materialism, as modified from Kantianism by various philosophers. O, R, W [3]

Neosalvarsan, *n.* (1912) *Pharm.* [G (1912) < *neo-* + *Salvarsan* < Gk *neós* new + L *salvāre* to heal + G *Arsenik* arsenic + L *sānus* hale, well, healthy] A trademark: neoarsphenamine; a medicinal yellow powder that was superseded by penicillin. O, W [4]

neoteny, **-nies** *pl.* (1901) *Zool.* Var. **neoteinia** [G *Neotenie* (1884) < *neo-* + *-tenie* < Gk *neós* young, new + *teínein* to stretch, expand] The gaining of sexual maturity by an animal still in its larval stage, despite the lack of genetic ability to attain mature physical form; the retention of some immature characteristics in an animal's adult stage. —**neotenic** (1901), **neotenous** (1930), **neotenously** (1963). O, R, W [4]

neotocite, *n.* (1854) *Mineral.* Old var. **neotokite** (1854) [Sw *neotokit* or G *Neotokit* (1852) (now *Neotozit*) < Gk *neótokos* newborn + Sw or G *-it* -ite] A hydrous silicate of manganese and iron. O, W [3]

nepheline-syenite, *n.* (1892) *Geol.* [G *Nephelinsyenit* (1877) < Fr *néphéline* < Gk *nephélē* mist, cloud + *Syenit* < *Syēnē*, the Greek name for Aswan, Egypt + G *-it* -ite] A rare plutonic rock resembling syenite, but containing nepheline and other qualities so as to require a different name for this mineral. O [3]

nephelinite, *n.* (1863) *Geol.* [Prob. < G *Nephelinit* < *Nephelin* < Gk *nephélē* fog, cloud + G *-in* -in + *-it* -ite] A silica-deficient volcanic rock considerably composed of nepheline. —**nephelinitic** (1909), **nephelinization** (1943), **nephelinized** (1943), **nephelinizing** (1946). O, R, W [4]

nephrite, *n.* (1794) *Mineral.* [G *Nephrit* (1780) < *nephr-* (< Gk *nephrós* kidney) + G *-it* -ite] A mineral jade, once worn as an old charm against kidney disease, hence the name of this gemstone. O, R, W [4]

nephrocyte, *n.* (1895) *Zool.* [G *Nephrocyt* (1894) (now also *Nephrozit*) < *nephro-* + *-cyte* < Gk *nephrós* kidney + *kýtos* hollow, cell] A pericardial cell, as in insects, that stores up waste products. O [3]

nephron, *n.* (1932) *Anat.* Var. **nephrone** [G (1924) < Gk *nephrós* kidney] An excretory unit, as in a vertebrate's kidney. O, R, W [4]

nephrosis, -oses *pl.* (1916) *Med.* [G *Nephrose* (1905) (< NL) < Gk *nephrós* kidney + G *-ose* (< Gk *-osis*) -osis, fem. suffix of action] A kidney disease, primarily in the renal tubules. O, R, W [4]

nephrotome, *n.* (1895) *Zool.* [G *Nephrotom* (1889) < *nephro-* + *-tom* < Gk *nephrós* kidney + *tómē* (severed) part] The part of the somite that develops into a vertebrate's excretory organs. O, W [3]

neptunium, *n.* (1877) *Chem.* [G (< NL) (1877) < G *Neptun* the planet Neptune + *-ium*] A tantalum-like mineral, once thought to be an element, that is found in some tantalite in Haddam, Connecticut (not to be confused with the radioactive element 93 of the same name). O [2]

neritic, *a.* (1891) *Biol.* [G *neritisch* (1890) < Gk *Nērēís* (gen. *Nērēídos*) daughter of the sea god Nereus; a water nymph + G suffix *-isch* -ic] Pertaining to or constituting the area of shallow water bordering seacoasts. O, R, W [4]

Nernst lamp, *n.* (1899) *Physics* [G *Nernst-Lampe* < the name of Walther Herman *Nernst* (1864–1941), German Nobel prize-winning chemist and physicist + *Lampe* lamp < L (< Gk) *lampas*] The electric incandescent lamp that he invented, esp. used in the infrared region. O, W [3]

Nernst's theorem, *n.* (1913) *Physics* [Short. of G (*das*) *Nernstsche Wärmetheorem* (1906) (now *Nernst-Wärmetheorem*) < *Nernst* (see *Nernst lamp*) + *Wärme* warmth, heat + *Theorem* < Gk *theórēma* theorem] The third law of thermodynamics. O [3]

nerol, *n.* (1903) *Chem.* [G (1902), a short. of *Neroliöl* neroli oil (q.v.)] An oily, unsaturated alcohol, present in neroli oil and many other essential oils, that is used in perfumes. O, R, W [4]

neroli oil, *n.* (1849) *Chem.* [Ad. of G *Neroliöl* < the name of Anna-Marie de la Tremoille, the wife of Prince *Nerola* of Nerole (who supposedly discovered this oil c.1670) (<

Fr *néroli* < It *neroli*) + G *Öl* oil < L *oleum* < Gk *élaion*] A fragrant, essential oil that is obtained esp. from the flowers of the sour orange and is used in perfumes and as a flavoring material; also called *orange-flower oil*. O, R, W [4]

Neue Sachlichkeit, *n.* (1929) *Art, Lit.* (1930) [G < *neue* new + *Sachlichkeit* objectivity, realism < *sachlich* objective, factual + nom. suffix *-keit* -ity, -ness]. A new realism, developed in Germany in the 1920s as a reaction against impressionism in the arts, that sought to be functional and utilitarian. O [3]

neugroschen, -ø *pl. Currency* [G < *neu* + *Groschen* (q.v.)] A Saxony groschen of a billion (1840–73). W2 [2]

neuraminic acid, *n.* (1942) *Chem.* [Transl. of G *Neuraminsäure* (1941) < *neur-* (< Gk *neûron* nerve) + G *Amin* ammine (< *Ammoniak* ammonia + *-in* -ine) + *Säure* acid] A carbohydrate amino-acid occurring as acyl derivatives. • ~ is short. to **neuraminidase** (1957), **neuraminate** (1970). O, W [3]

neurinoma, -s/-ta *pl.* (1913) *Path.* [G *Neurinom* (1910) (< NL) < Gk *neûron* nerve + *inós* muscle + G *-om* (< Gk *-ōma* denoting tumor) -oma] A neurilemmoma (tumor) or nerve cell. O, W [3]

neuroepithelium, *n.* (1885) *Optics* Var. **neuro-epithelium** (1885) [G *Neuroepithel* (1874) < NL < Gk *neûron* nerve + G *Epithel* < Gk *epí* after(ward) + *thēlē* nipple + E *-ium*] The modified epithelium in organs of special sense, as the nose or the eye; the embryonic ectoderm that gives rise to the nervous system. O, R, W [4]

neurokyme, *n.* (1908) *Psych.* [G *Neurokym* (1895) < *neuro-* < Gk *neûron* nerve + *kŷma* wave] The kinetic energy of neural discharges in the brain. O, W [3]

neuron, *n.* (1891) *Med.* Var. **neurone** (1896) [G (1891) < Gk *neûron* nerve] A nerve cell with all of its processes. —**neuronal, neuronic.** O, R, W [4]

neuropilema, *n.* (1891) *Anat.* Var. **neuropilem** (1891) [G (1890) < *neuro-* < Gk *neûron* nerve + *pílēma* felt] Neuropil (perhaps a short. of *neuropilema*), a feltwork of unmyelinated nerve fibers; the delicate ending of such a fiber. O [3]

neurotrope, *n. Anat.* [G *Neurotrop* (or Fr *neurotrope*) < G *neuro-* + *-trop* < Gk *neûron* nerve + *tropé* turning] A neurotropic agent. W [3]

neurotropism, *n.* (1905) *Anat.* Var. **neurotropy** [G *Neurotropismus* or *Neurotropie* (1900) (< NL) < Gk *neûron* nerve + *tropé* turning + G *-ismus* (< L *-ismus*) -ism or G *-ie* (< Gk *-ia*) -y] The affinity of a mass of nerve cells for another such mass. O, R, W [3]

neustic, *a. Biol.* Var. **neustonic** [Prob. < G *neustisch* < Gk *neustón* (neut. of *neustós*) swimming + G adj. suffix *-isch* -ic] Of or concerning a neuston (q.v.). R, W [3]

neuston, *n.* (1928) *Biol.* [G (1917) < Gk *neustón* (neuter of *neustós*) swimming] Minute organisms that live on the surface layer of fresh water. —**neuston,** *a.* (1957). O, R, W [4]

neutral, *a.* (1893) *Biol.* [G (1880) < L *neutrālis* neutral, introduced in this sense by Paul Ehrlich (1854–1915), German physician] Concerning biological stains or dyes derived from mixing an acid dye with a basic dye. O [3]

neutrophil, *a.* (1893) *Med.* Var. **neutrophile** (1893) [G (1880) < *neutro-* + *-phil* < the comb. form of L *neutrālis* neutral + Gk *phílein* to love] Capable of being equally stained with acid or basic dyes. —**neutrophilic** (1893), **neutrophilous** (1900), **neutrophiline**. O, R, W [4]

Neuwider/neuwider green, *n. Chem.* [Partial transl. of G *Neuwieder Grün* < the name of *Neuwied,* a German city + *grün* green + *-er* -er] A color ranging from light yellowish green to green. W [3]

Neuwied/neuwied blue, *n. Chem.* [Partial transl. of G *Neuwieder Blau* < the name of *Neuwied,* a German city + *blau* blue] The color Bremen blue. W [3]

nevyanskite, *n.* (1854) *Mineral.* Old var. **newjanskite** [G *Newjanskit* (1845) < *Newjansk,* the name of the Russian city Nevyansk + G *-it* -ite] A natural alloy principally of iridium and osmium. O, W [3]

newberyite, *n.* (1879) *Mineral.* [G *Newberyit* (1879) < the name of James Cosmo *Newbery* (1843–95), Australian mineralogist + G *-it* -ite] A crystalline acid magnesium phosphate. O, W [3]

new blue, *n.* (1897) *Chem.* [Prob. transl. of G *Neublau* < *neu* new + *blau* blue] A blue pigment or dye; French blue. O, W [3]

New English, *n. Ling.* [Transl. of G *Neuenglisch,* patterned by Henry Sweet after G *Neuhochdeutsch* < *neu* new + *Hochdeutsch* High German] The English language after about 1750 (this is different from the old meaning of "English since c.1475"). WNW [3]

New Order, *n.* (1940) *Politics* Var. **new order** (1940) [Transl. of G *die neue Ordnung* < *die* the + *neue* new + *Ordnung* regulation, order] The plan of Adolf Hitler to reorganize European countries politically according to National Socialism (q.v., this is different from the old meaning of "a new government or regime"); National Socialism. O, R [3]

Nibelung, *n.* (1861 *W9*) *Myth.* Var. **Niblung** [G < (Upper G) *nibeln* to drizzle, *Nebel* mist + *-ung* -ing] Any of a race of dwarfs who owned a magic ring and a hoard of gold that Siegfried took from them; any of Siegfried's followers; any of the Burgundian kings in the *Nibelungenlied* (q.v.). R [4]

Nibelungenlied, n. *Lit.* [G < *Nibelung* (q.v.) + *Lied* lay, song] A MHG epic poem about Siegfried by an unknown author in the early 13th century and based on Germanic legends. R [3]

nicht wahr (1924) [G < *nicht* not + *wahr* true, actually, an ellipsis of *Ist das nicht wahr?* Isn't that true *or* so?] Isn't that so, isn't it the truth? O, R [3]

nick, *see* knick

nickel, *n.* (1755) *Mineral.* [Sw or G (1754) < a short. of G *Kupfernickel* < *Kupfer* copper + *Nickel* nickel)] A silvery white, lustrous metal, hard but malleable and used in alloys and as a catalyst; a monetary term (a U.S. or Canadian coin, a trifling sum, the quantity of marijuana that five dollars will purchase). —**nickel,** *a.* (1822), *v.* (1920). • ~ appears in many derivatives like **-ine** (1786), **-ic** (1828), **-ization** (1857), **-ized** (1872), **-ing** (1875), **-ous** (1880), **-ed** (1885), and **-odeon** (1921), and also in many compounds like **nickel green/silver** *(1837, 1860) and* **nickel and dime** (1935), besides the compounds borrowed from G compounds. O, R, W [4]

nickel antigorite, *n.* (1961) *Mineral.* [G *Nickelantigorit*

(1957) < *Nickel* nickel + *Antigorit* antigorite] A nickelic variety of antigorite. O [3]

nickel bloom, *n.* (1861) *Mineral.* Var. **nickel-bloom** (1861) [Transl. of G *Nickelblüte* < *Nickel* nickel + *Blüte* blossom, bloom] Earthy annabergite. O, W [4]

nickel chlorite, *n.* (1961) *Mineral.* [G *Nickelchlorit* (1957) < *Nickel* nickel + *Chlorit* chlorite (q.v.)] A basic silicate of magnesium, nickel, and iron. O [3]

nickel glance, *n.* (1836) *Mineral.* [Ad. of G *Nickelglanz* < *Nickel* nickel + *Glanz* glance] Gersdorffite, a nickel sulfarsenide. O, W [3]

nickel iron, *n.* (1875) *Mineral.* [Prob. a partial transl. of G *Nickeleisen* < *Nickel* nickel + *Eisen* iron] Any alloy of nickel and iron, occurring naturally and meteorically. — **nickel iron,** *a.* (1946). O, W [3]

nickel spinel, *n.* (1961) *Mineral.* [G *Nickelspinell* (1957) < *Nickel* nickel + *Spinell* spinel < It *spinella,* dim. of *spina* (< L) thorn] A laboratory-produced oxide of nickel and aluminum. O [3]

nicotinic acid, *n.* (1873) *Chem.* [Transl. of G *Nicotinsäure* (1873) < *Nicotin* (< Fr) nicotine < the name of the French chemist Jean *Nicot* (1530–1600) + G *Säure* acid] A white crystalline acid that belongs to the vitamin B complex and causes pellagra when deficient in humans, also called *niacin.* O, R, W [4]

Niersteiner, *n.* (1825) *Beverages* [G a Rhine wine, hailing from < *Nierstein,* the name of a German town near Mainz + *-er* -er] A fine variety of white Rhine wine. O [3]

night horn, *see* nachthorn

nigrine, *n.* (1805) *Mineral.* [G *Nigrin* (1800) < L *niger* black + G *-in* -ine] A black ferruginous variety of rutile. O, W [3]

nihilism, *n.* (1817 *W9*) *Philos.* [G *Nihilismus* (1799) < L *nihil* nothing + G *-ismus* (< L *-ismus*) -ism] A philosophical view that totally rejects existing moral principles and values. O, R, W [4]

niobite, *n.* (1854) *Mineral.* [G *Niobit* < the name of the Greek mythological figure *Niobe,* Tantalus's daughter + G *-it* -ite] Columbite, essentially a black iron columbate. O, W [3]

niobium, *n.* (1845) *Chem.* [G (1845) (now *Niob*) < NL < Gk *Nióbē,* the name of Tantalus's daughter, who was changed into a stone while weeping for her children (Heinrich Rose, a German mineralogist who rediscovered the mineral in the Bavarian mountains of Germany, chose this name because of the mineral's occurrence in tantalum, a word very similar to *Tantalus*) + G *-ium* (< NL *-ium*) -ium] A metallic element occurring in tantalum and other minerals and used in lustrous alloy steels, also called *columbium.* —**niobium,** *a.* (1849); **niobous** (1863); **niobium pentoxide**. O, R, W [4]

nitrolamine, *n. Chem.* [G *Nitrolamin* < *nitro-* (< the comb. form of L *nitrum* nitron) + G *-lamin,* a short. of *Hydroxylamin* hydroxylamine] Any of a class of compounds derived by the action of ammonia or amines on nitrosites, etc. W [3]

nitron, *n.* (1906) *Chem.* [G (1905) < Gk *nítron* soda] A heterocyclic compound that is used in chemical analysis as a precipitant. O [3]

nitrosamine, *n.* (1878) *Chem.* [G *Nitrosamin* (1875) < *nitros-* (< Gk *nítron* soda) + G *Amin* amine < *Ammoniak* ammonia + *-in* -ine] Any of the class of compounds of the type formula >NNO. O, R, W [4]

nitrosate, *n. Chem.* [G *Nitrosat* < a short. of *Nitrosonitrat* < *Nitrose* + *Nitrat* < LL *nitrōsus* nitrous + Fr *nitrate*] Any of the class of compounds obtained from unsaturated hydrocarbons like terpenes by the action of nitrogen dioxide. W [3]

nitrosite, *n. Chem.* [G *Nitrosit* < a short. of *Nitrosonitrit* < *Nitrose* < LL *nitrōsus* nitrous + G *Nitrit* nitrite] Any of the class of compounds derived from unsaturated hydrocarbons like terpenes by the action of nitrogen trioxide or nitrous acid. W [3]

nitwit, *n.* (1922) [G < dial. *nit* not < *nicht* not + E *wit* knowledge, intelligence] A slow-witted, stupid, foolish person. —**nitwit**, *a.* (1928); **nitwitted** (1931); **nitwittery** (1936); **nitwittedness** (1952). O, R, W [4]

nix¹, -es *pl.* (1833) *Myth.* [G (*der*) *Nix* < MHG *nickes*, OHG *nihhus*, orig. bathing spirit, i.e., in Germanic folklore, a spirit living in water] A water elf. O, R, W [4]

nix², *n.* (1789) (slang) [Colloq. Du and G *Nix* < *nichts* nothing] Nobody; nothing. O, R, W [4]

nix, *adv.* (1776) (slang) [G *nix* < *nichts* nothing] No. — **nix**, *v.* to turn down (1903) and *interj.* O, R, W [4]

nixie, *n.* (1816) *Myth.* [G (*die*) *Nixe*, the fem. equivalent of *Nix* nix¹ (q.v.)] A female nix; a water nymph. O, R, W [4]

nockerl, -n *pl.* (1855) *Food* [G < *Nock* small mountain + South G dim. suffix *-erl* -erl] A rich light dumpling. — **Salzburger nockerl** (1855). O, W [3]

noematic, *a.* (1866) *Philos.* [Prob. < G *noematisch* < Gk *noēmatikós* rational < *noéma* thought + G *-isch* -ic] Of or pertaining to a noema in Husserlian philosophy. O, W [3]

nonego, *n.* (1829) *Philos.* Var. **non-ego** (1829) [Transl. of G *Nicht-Ich* < *nicht* not, non + *Ich* I, ego] The external world or object of knowledge, as opposed to the ego or the subject. —**non-egoistical** (1842). O, W [4]

nonose, *n.* (1890) *Chem.* [G (1890) < L *nōnus* ninth + G *-ose* -ose, denoting a carbohydrate] A monosaccharide with nine carbon atoms in its usu. unbranched molecules. O [3]

noodle, *n.* (1779) *Food* [Ad. of G *Nudel* noodle, poss. related to (*K*)*nödel* lump, dumpling—not attested in German before the 16th cent.] A flat narrow strip of dry dough served in soups etc.; a ribbon-shaped pasta. —**noodle soup** (1779). O, R, W [4]

noodle, *v. Food* [Prob. ad. of G *nudeln* (see *noodle*, *n.*) to fatten up] To feed poultry like geese forcibly with a long, fattening roll. W [3]

nordmarkite, *n.* (1895) *Geol.* [G *Nordmarkit* (1890) < *Nordmark*, the name of a region in Sweden + G *-it* -ite] A brown magnesium variety of staurolite. —**nordmarkitic** (1947). O, W [3]

norleucine, *n.* (1913) *Chem.* [G *Norleucin* (1913) (now *Norleuzin*) < *nor*- (< *normal* normal) prefixed to the names of organic compounds to denote the normal isomer of the compound + *Leucin* < Gk *leukós* white + G *-in* -ine] A crystalline, optically active amino-acid isomeric with leucine. O, W [3]

norvaline, *n.* (1921) *Chem.* [G (1921) < *nor*- (< *normal* normal) prefixed to the name of organic compounds to

denote the normal isomer of the compound + *Valin* < *Isovaleriansäure* isovaleric acid + *-in* -in] A crystalline, optically active amino-acid isomeric with valine. O, W [3]

nosean, *n.* (1836) *Mineral.* Old var. **nosiane** (1836) [Obs. G *Nosian* (1815) (now *Nosean*) < the name of Karl Wilhelm *Nose* + *-an* -an(e)] Noselite (q.v.). O, W [3]

noselite, *n.* (1892) *Mineral.* [G *Noselith* (1890) < the name of Karl Wilhelm *Nose* (1753?–1835), German mineralogist + Gk *líthos* stone] A sodium aluminosilicate and sulfate. O, W [3]

Nostratic, *a.* (1931) *Ling.* Var. **Nostratian** (1931) [G *nostratisch* < L *nostrās* (gen. *nostrātis*) of our country + G adj. suffix *-isch* -ic/-ian] Pertaining to a remote family of languages hypothesized to be the antecedent of Indo-European, Hamito-Semitic, Ural-Altaic, Dravidian, Kartvelian, etc. O [3]

note row, *see* tone-row

notgeld, *n.* (1970) *Currency* [G emergency money, scrip < *Not* necessity + *Geld* money] Necessary money (supplementary currency) used in Germany and some east European countries, esp. after World War One. 12 [2]

notion, *n. Philos.* [Transl. of G *Begriff* concept < *begreifen* to perceive, understand] Hegel's concept of the organized unity of a differentiated whole corresponding to a given universal: a dialectal synthesis of Being and Essence leading toward the Absolute Idea; Kant's pure concept of reason. W [3]

noumenon, -mena *pl.* (1796) *Philos.* [G (1781) < Gk *nooúmenon*, neuter present part. of *noeîn* to perceive, apprehend] Kant's concept of an object which is inaccessible to experience, but to which a phenomenon is referred for its sense; an object of purely rational comprehension. • ~ is transl. as **idea** (1871). O, R, W [4]

novákite, *n.* (1959) *Mineral.* Var. **novakite** [G *Novákit* (1959) < the name of Jiří *Novak* (1902–59), a Czech mineralogist + G *-it* -ite] A tetragonal arsenide of copper. O [3]

N.P.D./NPD, *n.* (1966) *Politics* [G < a short. of *Nationaldemokratische Partei* National Democratic Party] A neo-Nazi party. O [3]

nuclease, *n.* (1902) *Biochem.* [G *Nuklease* (1899) < *nuklea*- (< L *nucleus* nucleus) + G *-ase* -ase, denoting a destroying substance] Any plant or animal enzyme that helps hydrolyze nucleic acids, as into nucleotides. O, R, W [4]

nucleic acid, *n.* (1892) *Chem.* [Transl. of G *Nucleinsäure* (1889) (now also *Nukleinsäure*) < *nucle*- (< L *nucleus* nucleus) + G *-in* -ine + *Säure* acid, altered in English to *-ic*] Any of the two classes of complex acids in living cells—DNA and RNA. O, R, W [4]

nuclein, *n.* (1878) *Biochem.* [G < *nucle*- (< L *nucleus* nucleus) + G *-in* -in] Nucleic acid (q.v.), nucleoprotein. —**nucleinic (acid)** (1896), **nucleination**. O, W [4]

nucleolocentrosome, *n.* (1900) *Biol.* [Prob. orig. formed as G *Nucleolocentrosom* (now also *Nukleolozentrosom*) < the comb. form of *Nucleolus* nucleolus + *Centrosom* centrosome (q.v.)] Nucleocentrosome (the short. form that replaced it) or intranuclear division center. O, W [3]

nucleoid, *n.* (1938) *Biol.* [G (1937) < *nucle*- + *-oid* < L *nucleus* nucleus + Gk *-oeidēs* similar] A nucleus-like body in some bacteria that is not proved to be so. O, R, W [4]

nucleon[1], *n.* (1895) *Biochem.* [G (1895) (now also *Nukleon*) < *Nuclein* (see *nucleic acid*) + *Pepton* peptone (q.v.)] A compound like phosphorcarnic acid, which is allied to the nucleins but contains peptone instead of albumin. O [3]

nucleon[2], *n.* (1923) *Physics* [G (now also *Nukleon*) < *nucle-* (< L *nucleus* nucleus) + G *-on* -on] A proton or neutron. —**nucleonics** (1945), **nucleonic** (1946). O, R, W [4]

nucleoplasm, *n.* (1889) *Biol.* [Prob. < G *Nucleoplasma* < *nucleo-* + *Plasma* < L *nucleus* nucleus + LL *plasma* < Gk < *plássein* to mold] A nucleic protoplasm; karyolymph. —**nucleoplasmic** (1890), **nucleoplasmatic.** O, R, W [4]

nucleoprotein, *n.* (1907) *Biochem.* [G (1885) (now also *Nukleoprotein*) < *nucleo-* + *Protein* < the comb. form of L *nucleus* nucleus + Fr *protéine* protein] A conjugated protein combined from a protein and a nucleic acid such as occurs in all living cells. O, R, W [4]

nucleoside, *n.* (1911) *Biochem.* [G *Nucleosid* (1909) (now also *Nukleosid*) < L *nucleus* nucleus + G *-ose* -ose, denoting a carbohydrate + *-id* -ide] A compound formed by partially hydrolyzing a nucleotide or nucleic acid, usu. consisting mainly of deoxyribose or ribose. —**nucleosidase** (1911), **nucleoside phosphorylase.** O, R, W [4]

nucleotide, *n.* (1908) *Biochem.* [G *Nucleotid* (1908) (now also *Nukleotid*) < L *nucleus* nucleus + an infixed G *-t-* + *-id* -ide] A compound formed as an ester of a nucleoside and a phosphoric acid; a compound chemically related to this. —**nucleotidase** (1911). O, R, W [4]

null plane, *n.* (1903) *Math.* [Transl. of G *Nullebene* (1837) < *Null* (< L *nūllus*) null, zero + G *Ebene* plane] The plane containing the null lines of a given wrench that pass through a given point. O [3]

null point, *n.* (1903) *Math.* [Transl. of G *Nullpunkt* (1837) < *Null* null, zero + *Punkt* point < L *nūllus* + *punctum*] The intersecting point of the null lines of a given wrench lying in a given line. O [3]

numinous, -es *pl.* (1938) *Psych.* Var. **numinosum** (1938) [G *(das) Numinose* < L *nūmen* divine essence as a driving force + G *-ose*] A powerful, unseen presence that inspires reverence and dread, as in a psychic revelation. —**numinous,** *a.* (1951). O, W [3]

nutcracker, *n.* (1758) *Zool.* Var. **nutbreaker** (1778) [Transl. of G *Nuss brecher* < *Nuss* nut + *-brecher* cracker < *brechen* to break, crack] A dark brown, European corvine bird (*Nucifraga caryocatactes*) O, R, W [4]

nutsch (filter), *n. Chem.* [G *Nutsche* a filter used in chemical laboratories] A simple, usu. suction-operated filter adapted to batch operation. W [3]

nyctinastic, *a.* (1906) *Bot.* [G *nyktinastisch* (1904) < *nykti-* + *nastisch* < Gk *nýx* (gen. *nyktós*) night + *nastós* compressed + G adj. suffix *-isch* -ic] (Primarily Brit.) concerning the nastic raising of leaves or flowers in the morning, and their lowering or folding in the evening, as associated with diurnal changes in temperature or light-dark intensity. —**nyctinastism** (1921). O, W [4]

nyctinasty, -ties *pl.* (1936) *Bot.* [Prob. < G *Nyktinastie* (see *nyctinastic*)] (Primarily Brit.) the nastic movement associated with diurnal changes, as in the closing or opening of certain flowers. O, W [4]

O

O antigen/o antigen, *n. Immunology* [G *o(hne Hauch) Antigen* < *ohne* without + *Hauch* breath + *Antigen* antigen (q.v.)] Somatic antigen, which occurs in the wall of gram negative bacteria. W [3]

oberrealschule, -s/-n *pl. Ed.* [G < *ober* upper + *real* real, i.e., with emphasis on the sciences and modern languages + *Schule* school] A German secondary school emphasizing modern languages and the sciences (as opposed to the *Gymnasium* gymnasium—q.v.). W [2]

object libido, *n.* (1933) *Psych.* [G *Objektlibido,* also known as *Objektbesetzung* < *Objekt* object + *Libido* libido (or *Besetzung* occupation), here actually tranference of the libido to objects, whether other individuals or things < L *objectus* + G *Libido* libido (q.v.)] Erotic desire directed toward someone other than oneself (cf. *ego-libido*). O, W [3]

obscurant, *n.* (1799) *Lit.* [G *Obskurant* (1793) (or Fr *obscurant*) < L *obscūrāre* to obscure] One who tries to block enlightenment, inquiry, or reform. —**obscurant,** *a.* (1878); **-ist** (1838). O, R, W [4]

occasionalism, *n.* (1842) *Philos.* [G *Okkasionalismus* < *okkasional* < Fr *occasion* < L *occāsiō* opportunity + G (< L) *-ismus* -ism] The philosophical doctrine that asserts the inherent incapacity of mind and matter to affect each other, and explains their interaction as God's intervention. O, R, W [4]

occult bleeding, *n.* (1904) *Med.* [Transl. of G *okkulte (Magen)blutung* (1901) < *okkult* occult (< L *occultus*) + G *Magen* stomach + *Blutung* bleeding] Scanty bleeding in the gastrointestinal tract, which is hard to detect. O [3]

oceanity, *n.* (1922) *Meteor.* [G *Oceanität* (1895) < *Ocean* (< Gk *ōkeanós* ocean) + G *-ität* -ity < L *-itas* (gen. *-itatis*) nom. suffix indicating quality or condition] State or quality characteristic of a marine climate; the degree to which a climate is oceanic. O, R, W [3]

oceanography, *n.* (1859) *Ecology* [G *Oceanographie* (now *Ozeanographie*) < *oceano-* + *-graphie* < the comb. form of Gk *ōkeanós* ocean + *gráphein* to write, describe] The branch of physical geography dealing with oceans and their phenomena. —**oceanographer** (1886), **-graphic(al)** (1893, 1895), **-graphically** (1883), **biological/dynamic/physical oceanography.** O, R, W [4]

ochronosis, -noses *pl.* (1867) *Med.* [G (1866) (now *Ochronose*) < Gk *ōchrós* pale yellow + *nósos* disease + G *-osis/-ose* (< Gk *-osis*) -osis, fem. suffix of action] A rare, abnormal deposit of pigment in cartilage, etc. —**ochronotic** (1922). O, W [3]

Octoberfest, *see* Oktoberfest

octose, *n.* (1890) *Chem.* [G (1890) < *octo-* (< L *octō* eight) + G *-ose* -ose, denoting a carbohydrate] Any synthetic monosaccharide having eight carbon atoms per molecule. O, W [3]

od, *n.* (1850) *Philos.* Var. **odyl(e)** [G (1850), coined by the German philosopher Carl-Ludwig Reichenbach (1778–

1869) < ON *ōðr* feeling] A hypothetical force or natural power once thought to be held by certain individuals and to underlie magnetism and hypnotism. —**od force** (1851). O, R, W [4]

odontoblast, *n.* (1878) *Med.* [G < *odonto-* + *-blast* < the comb. form of Gk *odoús* (gen. *ódontos*) tooth + *blastós* bud, cell] A tooth cell that secretes dentin. —**odontoblastic.** O, R, W [4]

odoriphore, *n.* (1919) *Physiol.* Var. **odorophore** (1919) [G *Odoriphor* (1895) < *odor-* + infixed *-i-* + *-phor* < L *odor* (gen. *odōris*) odor + Gk *phóros* bearing, carrying] Osmophore, a chemical carrier in molecules that causes a compound to have an odor. —**odoriphoric** (1944). O, W [3]

odyl, *see* od

oecology, *see* ecology

oenin, *n. Chem.* Var. **enin** [Prob. < G *Önin* < Gk *oînos* wine] An anthocyanin pigment, found in the skin of blue grapes, which forms a crystalline fluoride. W [3]

oenocyte, *n.* (1886) *Entomology* [G *Oenocyth* (1886) (now *Önozyth*) < *oeno-* + *-cyth* < Gk *oînos* wine + *kýtos* cavity, cell] A large, probably secretory, wine-colored cell of most insects that is produced in the epidermis. —**oenocytic.** O, W [3]

offprint, *n.* (1885) *Printing* [Transl. of G *Abdruck* < *ab* off + *Druck* print] Reprint of an article, etc. —**offprint,** *v.* (1895). O, R, W [4]

off-verse, *n.* (1935) *Lit.* [Transl. of G *Abvers* < *ab* off, down + *Vers* verse < L *versus*] The second half-line of a line of Old English poetry (cf. *on-verse*). O [3]

Oflag, *n.* (1941) *Mil.* Var. **oflag** (1941) [Short. of G *Offizierslager* < *Offizier* officer + *Lager* (prisoner) camp] A German prison camp for captured enemy officers. O, R, W [4]

ohm, *n.* (1851) [G an old (wine) measure of approximately one and a half hectoliters < MGH *ame, ome,* ML *ama* a wine measure < L *(h)ama* fireman's bucket < Gk *ámē* bucket] An old German measure equivalent to 30 to 36 gallons. O [2]

Oktoberfest, *n. Beverages* Var. **Octoberfest** [G < *Oktober* October (< L *October*) + G *Fest* festival] A Munich festival in the fall, usu. featuring beer drinking; any similar festival, as in the U.S. R [4]

ol, *a.* (1907) *Chem.* [G < *-ol* (1907) < L *oleum* oil] Of a hydroxyl group or a complex containing such a group, where the oxygen atom is bonded to two metal atoms. O [3]

-ol, *suffix* (1907) *Chem.* [G (1907) < L *oleum* oil] A suffix used to create names for compounds containing hydroxyls (*glycerol* etc.). O, R, W [4]

Olbers' paradox, *n.* (1952) *Astronomy* [Ad. of G *Olbers-Paradoxen* (1826) < the name of H. Wilhelm M. *Olbers* (1758–1840), German astronomer + *Paradoxen* paradoxes < L *paradoxum* < Gk *parádoxon*] The paradox that if enough stars were distributed evenly throughout an infinite static universe, the sky ought to be as bright at night as it is during the day. O, R [3]

Oligocene, *a.* (1859) *Geol.* [Ad. of G *oligozän* (1854) < *oligo-* + *-zän* < Gk *olígos* little, few + *kainós* new] Designating or pertaining to a period of the Tertiary, between the Eocene and the Miocene. —**oligocene,** *n.* O, R, W [4]

oligoclase, *n.* (1832) *Mineral.* [G *Oligoklas* (1826) < *oligo-* + *-klas* < Gk *olígos* little + *klásis* fracture] A lime-soda, plagioclase feldspar. O, R, W [4]

oligodynamic, *a.* (1893) *Biochem.* [G *oligodynamisch* (1893) < *oligo-* + *dynamisch* < Gk *olígos* little + *dynamikós* powerful, effective] Pertaining to or produced by minute quantities of metallic ions in solution; active in or produced by small quantities. O, W [3]

oligohaline, *n.* (1951) *Chem.* [G *Oligohalin* (1922) < *oligo-* + *Halin* < Gk *olígos* little + *hálinos* of salt] Brackish water that has salinity in the range immediately above that of fresh water. O [4]

oligonite, *n. Mineral.* [G *Oligonit* < Gk *olígon* < *olígos* little + G *-it* -ite] A manganiferous variety of siderite. W [3]

oligonucleotide, *n.* (1942) *Biochem.* [G *Oligonucleotid* (1941) (now also *Oligonukleotid*) < *oligo-* + *Nucleotid* < Gk *olígos* little, few + comb. form of L *nucleus* nucleus + *-t-* + G *-id* -ide] Any polynucleotide with molecules composed of relatively few nucleotides. O, R [3]

oligopeptide, *n.* (1941) *Biochem.* [G *Oligopeptid* (1940) < *oligo-* (< Gk *olígos* little, few) + G *Peptid* peptide (q.v.)] Any peptide with molecules made up of relatively few amino-acid residues. O [3]

oligopyrene, *a. Chem.* [Prob. < G *oligopyren* < *oligo-* (< the comb. form of Gk *olígos* little) + G *Pyren* tetracyclic aromatic carbohydrate < Gk *pŷr* fire, designating chemical compounds obtained by heating + G *-en* -ene] Of a sperm cell having less than the normal amount of chromatin. W [3]

oligosaccharide, *n.* (1930) *Biochem.* [G *Oligosaccharid* (1930) < *oligo-* (< Gk *olígos* few, little) + G *Saccharid* saccharide] A carbohydrate containing few constituent monosaccharide units. O, R, W [4]

oligosaprobic, *a.* (1925) *Ecology* [G *oligosaprobisch* (1902) < *oligo-* (< Gk *olígos* little, few) + G *saprob* saprobic (q.v.) + E *-ic*] Being or inhabiting a richly oxygenated aquatic environment that contains little decayed organic matter. O, W [3]

oligotrophic, *a.* (1928) *Ecology* [G *oligotroph* (1925) < *oligo-* + *-troph* < Gk *olígos* few, little + *trophḗ* nutrition + E *-ic*] Relatively deficient in plant nutrients but usu. containing abundant oxygen, as in a lake. —**oligotrophy** (1928). O, R, W [4]

oligotropic, *a.* (1899) *Entomology* [G *oligotrop* (1884) < *oligo-* + *-trop* < Gk *olígos* few, little + *tropḗ* turning < *trépein* to turn + E *-ic*] Of bees that collect nectar from only a few kinds of flowers. O, W [3]

olivenite, *n.* (1820 *W9*) *Mineral.* [G *Olivenit* (1820) < *Oliven* (pl. of *Olive*) olive < L *olīva* + G *-it* -ite] A basic copper arsenate usu. olive green in color. O, R, W [4]

olm, *n.* (1905) *Zool.* [G < OHG *olm* olm] A European aquatic, cave-dwelling salamander. O, W [3]

ombrophilous, *a.* (1895) *Bot.* Var. **ombrophilic** [G *ombro-*

phil (1893) < *ombro-* + *-phil* < Gk *ómbros* rain + *phílos* loving + E *-ous*] Of a plant that can survive or even flourish in conditions of excessive moisture. —**ombrophily,** *n.* (1903). O, W [3]

ombrophobous, *a.* (1895) *Bot.* [G *ombrophob* (1893) < *ombro-* + *-phob* < Gk *ómbros* rain + *phóbos* fearing, shying + E *-ous*] Of a plant that is not adapted to excessive rainfall. —**ombrophoby,** *n.* (1903). O, W [3]

ommatin, *n.* (1940) *Biochem.* Var. **ommatine** (1940) [G (1939) < Gk *ómma* (gen. *ómmatos*) eye + G *-in* -in] Any ommochrome (insect eye-pigment) of low molecular weight (cf. *ommin*). O, W [3]

ommin, *n.* (1940) *Biochem.* Var. **ommine** (1940) [G (1939) < Gk *ómma* eye + G *-in* -in] An ommochrome having strong colors and high molecular weight (cf. *ommatin*). O [3]

ommochrome, *n.* (1945) *Biochem.* [G *Ommochrom* (1942) < Gk *ómma* eye + *chrôma* color] A pigment derived by condensation reactions from tryptophan found esp. in insect eyes. O, W [3]

omphacite, *n.* (1828–32) *Mineral.* [G *Omphacit* (1812) (now also *Omphazit*) < Gk *omphákitēs* green stone < *ómphax* unripe sour grape + *-ites* -ite] A grass-green pyroxene. O, W [3]

oncosine, *n.* (1854) *Mineral.* Var. **onkosin(e)** (1854, 1923) [G *Onkosin* (1834) < *onkos-* < Gk *ónkōsis* swelling + G *-in* -ine] A muscovite variety, an aluminosilicate of magnesium, potassium, and other alkali metals. O [3]

Ondatra, *n.* (1867) *Zool.* [G (1795), adopted as a generic name by the German botanist Heinrich Friedrich Link (1767–1851), ult. < Huron] *Ondatra zibethica,* a rodent genus of the North American muskrat (this is different from the meaning of "the name of the individual muskrat of this genus," borrowed into English from the French of Comte de Buffon as early as 1774). O, W [3]

ondine, *see* undine

onegite, *n. Mineral.* [G *Onegit* < the name of Lake *Onega* in the northwest of the former U.S.S.R. + G *-it* -ite] A pale amethyst gemstone containing goethite needles. W [3]

one-sided, *a.* (1813 *W9*) [Transl. of G *einseitig* < *ein* one + *-seitig* -sided < *Seite* side] Biased: concerned with only one side of a question or subject; unilateral. —**one-sidedly** (1856), **one-sidedness.** O, R, W [4]

onkosine, *see* oncosine

on-verse, *n.* (1935) *Lit.* [Transl. of G *Anvers* < *an* starting, as in *angehen* to go on + *Vers* verse < L *versus*] The first half-line of a line of Old English poetry. —**on-verse,** *a.* O [3]

oocyst, *n.* (1875) *Bot.,* (1882) *Zool.* [G (1866) (< Gk *ōón* + *kýstis* bladder, sack), as named by the German botanist Anton de Bary (1831–88) in his *Morphologie und Physiologie der Pilze, Flechten und Myxomyceten* (1866)] A receptacle for the ova of some polyzoa: zygote. O, R, W [3]

oocyte, *n.* (1895) *Biol.* [G *Ovocyte* (1892) (now *Oozyte*) < *ovo-* + *-cyte* < the comb. form of L *ōvum* egg, later < Gk *ōón* egg + *kýtos* cell, cavity] An egg mother-cell, before the egg matures. O, W [4]

oogonium, -gonia/-s *pl.* (1895) *Biol.* [G *Ovogonium* (1892), coined by the German zoologist Theodor Boveri

(1866–1915), a founder of modern cytology < NL < Gk *ōón* egg + *gónos* sprout + NL suffix *-ium*] The female reproductive germ-cell in primitive plants that produces oocytes (q.v.). —**oogonial**, *a.* O, R, W [3]

ooid, *n.* (1928) *Geol.* [G (1908) < Gk *ōoeidés* egg-shaped] Oolith, a component concretion piece of oolite. O, W [4]

oosite, *n.* (1868) *Mineral.* [G *Oosit* (1834) < the name of the *Oos* valley in Baden, Germany + *-it* -ite] A mineral related to pinite. O [3]

Operation Sea-lion, *see* Sea-lion

opthalmometer, *see Introduction*

opthalmoscope, *n.* (1857) *Optics* [G *Ophthalmoskop* (1850/1) < *opthalmo-* + *-skop* < Gk *ophthalmós* eye (ball) + *skopeîn* to view, examine] An optical instrument for viewing the interior of the eye. —**opthalmoscope,** *v.;* **-scopic(ally)** (1857, 1861); **-scopical** (1879); **-scopy,** *n.* (1864). O, R, W [4]

Oppenheimer, *n. Beverages* [G of or hailing from *Oppenheim,* the name of a town in Hesse, Germany + *-er* -er] A white wine of the Rhine wine grape from Rheinhessen. W [3]

optant, *n.* (1914) *Politics* [G (and Dan) *Optant* < L *optāns* (gen. *optāntis*) exercising an option] One who, when the territory of which one is a citizen changes its political sovereignty, opts between retaining that former citizenship or accepting the new one; generalized as one who opts. O, W [3]

optochin, *n.* (1914) *Pharm.* [Ad. of G (<NL) *Optochinum* (1913) < G *opto-* (< the comb. form of Gk *optikós* concerning the eye) + G *Chinin* quinine < Sp *quina*, ult. < Quechua] Ethylhydrocuprein(e), a quinine derivative. O [4]

optogram, *n.* (1878) *Optics* [G *Optogramm* < *opto-* + *-gramm* < Gk *optikós* concerning the eye + L *-gramma* < Gk *grámma*] An image fixed on the retina by light's photochemical reaction. —**optography.** O, W [3]

optophone, *n.* (1913) *Physics* [G *Optophon* (1912) < *opto-* + *-phon* < Gk *optikós* concerning vision + *phōnế* voice, sound] An instrument that converts light variations into sound variations corresponding to the different characters in a scanned written text, permitting blind persons to read. O, R, W [4]

order, *n.* (1933) *Physics* [Transl. of G *Ordnung* (1933) order, as introduced by Paul Ehrenfest (1880–1933), Austrian physicist] An integer characterizing a substance's change of phase equal to the order of the lowest derivatives of the free energy exhibiting a discontinuity at that change. O [3]

ordination, *n.* (1954) *Math.* [Transl. of G *Ordnung* arrangement, order] The rearranging of a set of points, from a multidimensional space, into a smaller dimension with minimal distortion; in a transf. sense, botanical ecology. O [3]

oregonite, *n.* (1960) *Mineral.* [G *Oregonit* (1959) < the name of the State of *Oregon,* where it was found + G *-it* -ite] A naturally occurring and laboratory-made arsenide of nickel and iron. O [3]

orfe, *n.* (1706) *Ichthy.* [G *Orf(e)* < L *orphus* < Gk *órphos* ide] A European cyprinoid fish popular in aquariums. —**golden/silver orfe.** O, W [4]

organelle, *n.* (1909) *Biol.* Var. **organella** (1909) [G *Orga-* *nell* < NL *organulum* (1884), dim. of L *organum* organ] Any of various specialized parts of a cell, which functions like the organs of animals with many cells. —**organellar,** *a.* (1970). O, R, W [4]

organization center/centre, *n.* (1927) *Biol.* [Transl. of G *Organisationszentrum* < *Organisation* organization + *Zentrum* center < ML *organizatio* + L *centrum*] A biological inductor; a region of a developing embryo that acts as an inductor. O, W [3]

organizator, *n.* (1924) *Biol.* [G *Organisator* (1921) < Fr *organiser* to organize, actually, provide with organs] Organizer or inductor, a substance capable, under certain circumstances, of inducing a specific type of development in embryonic or other undifferentiated tissue. O [3]

organoid, *a.* (1857) *Biol.* [Prob. < G < *organ-* + *-oid* < L *organum* < Gk *órganon* tool, instrument + L *-oidēs* < Gk *-oeidēs*] Resembling an organ in qualities or appearance, as in tumors. O, W [3]

organosol, *n.* (1892) *Chem.* [G (1892) < *organo-* + *-sol* < Gk *órganon* body organ + *-sol* < L *solūtiō* solution] Colloidal dispersion of a synthetic resin, used to make vinyl and other coatings. O, W [3]

orientable, *a.* (1935) *Math.* [Transl. of G *orientierbar* (1932) < *orientieren* to orient + *-bar* -able < Fr *s'orienter* to orient oneself, be guided by] Concerning a surface that, if each point is considered to be surrounded by a small closed curve, a clockwise or counterclockwise sense can be assigned to each curve so that they are identical for all sufficiently close points; used analogously of higher-dimension spaces. O [3]

orogen, *n.* (1923) *Geol.* Var. **orogene** (1964) [G (1921), back-formed < *Orogenie* < Gk *óros* mountain + *-genēs* producing, produced] An orogenic belt, a strip of the earth's surface that has been subjected to folding or other disformation; a region of such mountain-making disturbances. O, R, W [3]

orterde, *n.* (1930) *Geol.* [G < *Ort*, orig., point, outermost end (part) + *Erde* earth, i.e., partially hardened humus, as opposed to ortstein (q.v.)] A soil horizon with little or no cementation between the iron and the organic remains. O, W [3]

orthite, *n.* (1817) *Mineral.* [G *Orthit* (1817) < *orth-* (< Gk *orthós* straight) + G *-it* -ite] Allanite, esp. as long, slender crystals. —**orthitic** (1843). O, W [3]

orthoclase, *n.* and *a.* (1849, 1849) *Mineral.* [G *Orthoclas* (1823) (now *Orthoklas*) < *ortho-* + *-clas* < Gk *orthós* straight + *klásis* fracture] (Of) a variety of common potassium feldspar. O, R, W [4]

orthoclastic, *a.* (1878) *Mineral.* [G *orthoclastisch* (now *orthoklastisch*) < *ortho-* + *-klastisch* < Gk *orthós* straight + *klásis* fracture, *klastós* broken + G adj. suffix *-isch* -ic] Having cleavages at right angles to each other. O, R, W [3]

orthocranic, *a. Anthrop.* [G *orthokran* < *ortho-* < Gk *orthós* straight + *kraníon* skull + E *-ic*] Orthocephalic: having a relatively low head with a specified length-height index. W [3]

orthodiagraphy, *n.* (1904) *Med.* [G *Orthodiagraphie* (1900) < *ortho-* + *Diagraphie* < Gk *orthós* straight + *diagráphein* to copy, trace + G *-ie* (< Gk *-ia*) -y] A procedure for producing sketches showing an organ's exact size by projecting the shadow formed by a narrow beam of alpha X-rays onto a fluorescent screen. O [3]

orthogenesis, *n.* (1895) *Biol.* [G (1888) (now *Orthogenese*) (< NL) < Gk *orthós* straight + *génesis* genesis] The evolution or development of organic forms along definite lines in successive generations that are determined by inherent tendencies and are for the most part uninfluenced by the environment; a theory of social evolution along similar lines for all cultures. —**orthogenetic(ally)** (1899, 1911), **orthogenetics** (1937). O, R, W [4]

orthogeosyncline, *n.* (1936) *Geol.* [Ad. of G *Orthogeosynklinale* (1935) < *ortho-* + *Geosynklinale* < Gk *orthós* straight + *geo-*, comb. form of *gê* earth + *synklínein* to lean toward each other] A linear geosyncline between a continental craton and an oceanic craton. —**orthogeosynclinal** (1941). O, W [3]

orthogneiss, *n.* (1902) *Geol.* [G *Orthogneis* (1898) < *ortho-* (< Gk *orthós* straight, upright) + G *Gneis* gneiss (q.v.)] Gneiss derived from igneous rock. O, W [3]

orthohydrogen, *n.* (1929) *Chem.* Var. **ortho-hydrogen** (1929), **ortho hydrogen, Orthohydrogen** (1935) [Transl. of G *Orthowasserstoff* (1929) (analogized on the model of *Orthohelium*) < *ortho-* (< Gk *orthós* straight) + G *Wasserstoff* hydrogen] Molecular hydrogen where the two nuclei in the molecule spin in the same direction. O, R, W [4]

orthophyric, *a.* (1895) *Geol.* [G *orthophyrisch* (1887) < *ortho-* + *phyrisch* < Gk *orthós* straight + *phyr-* < *porphýreos* purple-colored (rock resulting from hardened magma) + G adj. suffix *-isch* -ic] Of the groundmass of closely packed crystals of feldspar. O, R [3]

orthoploid, *a.* (1920) *Bot.* [G (1916) < *ortho-* + *–ploid* < Gk *orthós* straight + *plóos* -fold, as in *twofold* + *-oiedēs* similar] Possessing a balanced or complete set of chromosomes. O [3]

orthopyroxene, *n.* (1903) *Mineral.* [G *Orthopyroxen* (1902) < *ortho-* + *Pyroxen* < Gk *orthós* straight + Fr *pyroxène* pyroxene] An orthorhombic pyroxene. O [3]

orthotectonic, *a.* (1956) *Geol.* [G *Orthotektonik* (1940) < *ortho-* + *Tektonik* < Gk *orthós* straight + *tektonikós* pertaining to architecture] Created by or of the nature of a geological deformation resulting in complex, crowded systems of fold belts like the Alps. O [3]

ortstein, *n.* (1906) *Geol.* [G < *Ort*, orig., point, outermost end or part + *Stein* stone, i.e., hardened humus, as opposed to *Orterde* orterde (q.v.)] Hardpan, a layer of hard soil often cemented with iron and organic matter. O, W [3]

osamine, *n. Chem.* Var. **osamin** [G *Osamin* < the L suffix *-osus* full of, designating a carbohydrate + G *Amin* ammine (q.v.)] Any of a class of compounds obtained from sugars. W2 [2]

osazone, *n.* (1888) *Chem.* [G *Osazon* (1884) < L suffix *-osus* full of, denoting a carbohydrate + Gk *-azon* < *ázōos* inert] Any of the basic crystalline compounds derived from sugars, the molecules of which contain two adjacent hydrozone groups and which are used for characterizing sugars. O, W [3]

osmiridium, *n.* (1880) *Mineral.* Var. **osmiiridium** [G (1828) < Gk *osmé* fragrance + G *Iridium* (< NL) < Gk *íris* (gen. *íridos*) rainbow + G (< L) *-ium* -ium—for G *Osm-*

iridium (1824) and *Osmium-iridium* (1821)—see OED] A naturally occurring metal alloy that was orig. described as iridosmine and is now usu. distinguished from it. O, R, W [4]

osmoceptor, *n.* (1944) *Physiol.* [G (1920) < *osmo-* + (*Re*)*ceptor* (now *Rezeptor*) receptor < Gk *osmé* smell + L *receptāre* to receive, absorb] A receptor for the sense of smell. O [3]

osmophilic, *a.* (1901) *Chem.* Var. **osmophile** [G *osmophil* (1900) < *osmo-* + *-phil* < Gk *osmé* smell + *phílos* friendly, loving + E *-ic*] Tolerating or thriving in a medium of high osmotic pressure. O [4]

osmophoric, *a.* (1901) *Chem.* [G *osmophor* (1900) < *osmo-* + *-phor* < Gk *osmé* smell + *phor-* < *phérein* to carry, conduct + E *-ic*] Of, relating to, or being an osmophore (a chemical group or a flower's scent gland). O, W [3]

osmoregulation, *n.* (1927 *W9*) *Physiol.* [G (1906) < *osmo-* + *Regulation* regulation < Gk *ósmōs* thrust, pressure + L *regulāre* to regulate] The keeping of a more or less constant osmotic pressure, esp. in an organism's body fluids. —**osmoregulator** (1935); **-late,** *v.* (1958); **-lating,** *a.* (1958); **-lating,** *verbal noun.* O, R, W [4]

osmoregulatory, *a.* (1911) *Physiol.* [Ad. of G *osmoregulatorisch* (1906) < *osmo-* + *regulatorisch* regulatory < Gk *ósmōs* thrust, pressure < L *regulāre* to regulate] Of, relating to, or effecting osmoregulation. O, W [4]

osone, *n.* (1889) *Chem.* [G *Oson* (1889) < L suffix *-osus* full of, denoting a carbohydrate + G *-on* < Gk *-ōnē*, fem. patronymic suffix] Any compound having two alpha carbonyl groups, derived by hydrolyzing an osazone (q.v.). O, W [3]

osteoblast, *n.* (1875) *Biol.* [Prob. < G < *osteo-* + *-blast* < Gk *ostéon* bone + *blastós* bud, germ] A bone-forming cell. —**osteoblastic** (1875). O, R, W [4]

osteoclast, *n.* (1872) *Biol.* [G *Osteoklast* < *osteo-* + *-klast* < Gk *ostéon* bone + *klastós* broken] One of the large multinucleated cells found in developing bone; a surgical instrument for performing osteoclasis. —**osteoclastic.** O, R, W [4]

osteodystrophia fibrosa, *n.* (1930) *Med.* [G (1924) < *Osteodistrophie* osteodystrophy (q.v.) + L *fibrōsus* fibrous] Defective ossification of bones in animals, esp. horses. O [3]

osteodystrophy, *n.* (1930) *Med.* Var. **osteodystrophia** (< NL) [G *Osteodistrophie* (1905) < *osteo-* + *Distrophie* < the comb. form of Gk *ostéon* bone + *dys-* bad + *trophé* nourishment + G *-ie* (< Gk *-ia*) -y] One of various disorders affecting the whole skeleton where there is defective bone development prob. due to faulty metabolism or a very poor diet. —**osteodystrophic, renal osteodystrophy.** O, W [3]

osteoid, *n.* (1847–9) *Med.* [Archaic G malignant tumor (1838) < *osteo-* + *-oid* < Gk *ostoeidés* bony, bone-like] Orig., an ossifying fungal tumor; now, uncalcified bone matrix. —**osteoid,** *a.* (1840 *W9*). O, W [4]

osteolite, *n.* (1875) *Mineral.* [G *Osteolith* < *osteo-* + *-lith* < Gk *ostéon* bone + *líthos* stone] Compact, impure, earthy apatite. O, W [3]

osteon, *n.* (1928) *Biol.* Var. **osteone** (1968) [G (1914) < Gk *ostéon* bone] Haversian system, a term applied to one of the tiny canals through which blood vessels and medullary matter pass in bone. O [3]

Ostmark, ø/-s pl. (1948) Currency [G < Ost East + Mark mark (q.v.)] The temporary currency of the Soviet sector of Berlin as early as 1948; the East German monetary unit of 1964–90. O, R [4]

Ostpolitik, n. (1961) Politics [G < Ost East + Politik politics < Gk politiké] West Germany's views and actions vis-à-vis its eastern neighbors, esp. Poland, prior to reunification of Germany in 1990; a similar policy of any Western nation. O, R [4]

otavite, n. (1906) Mineral. [G Otavit (1906) < Otavi, the name of a town in the north of South-West Africa, now Namibia + G -it -ite] Cadmium carbonate, naturally occurring and isostructural with calcite. O, W [3]

otosclerosis, n. (1901) Path. [G Otosklerose (< NL) (1901) < oto- + Sklerose < Gk oûs (gen. ōtós) ear + sklērós brittle, hard + G -ose (< Gk -osis, suffix of action) -osis] An ear disease where some normal tissue is replaced by spongy bone and progressively causes deafness. —**otosclerotic,** n. (1933), a. (1933). O, R, W [4]

ouch, interj. (1837) [Ad. of G autsch (echoic)] An often sudden cry of pain or dismay. O, R, W [4]

Ouija, n. (1891) Games Var. **ouija** [G < F oui yes + G ja yes] A trademark for a board with Roman alphabetical letters and other signs written on it, used for seeking spiritualistic or telepathic messages as in seances; (lower case) a spiritualistic spelling device. —**ouija board** (1895). O, R, W [4]

outer product, n. (1929) Math. [Transl. of G äusseres Produkt (1844) < äusser- outer + Produkt product < ML productum] A vector product; usu. today, a cross product, a related product of two vectors yielding a higher-ranked tensor than either of them. O, R [3]

outrun, n. (1913) Sports [Transl. of G Auslauf < aus out (of) + Lauf run < laufen to run] The level stretch at the foot of the ski slope where jumpers slide to a stop. O, W [3]

outwandered, a. (1876) Biol. [Transl. of G ausgewandert < auswandern to emigrate] Wandered away, as in cells; (e)migrated, as in peoples. O [3]

overbelief, n. (1897) Myth. Var. **Aberglaube** (1873) [Transl. of G Aberglaube < (the archaic meaning of) aber false or alternate + Glaube belief] An antiquated or superseding belief, belief in something that is unwarranted or unverifiable. O, R, W [3]

overcompensation, n. (1912 W9) Psych. [Transl. of G Überkompensation or übersteigerte Kompensation < über over or übersteigert excessive + Kompensation < L compēnsātio] Orig., Alfred Adler's term in psychological analysis for a person's excessive reaction to a feeling of inferiority, inadequacy, or guilt by making an exaggerated effort to overcome the feeling; now generalized to mean any such reaction and effort. —**overcompensatory** (1917); **overcompensate,** v. (1934); **overcompensated,** a. (1937). O, R, W [4]

overdeepened, a. (1900) Geol. [Transl. and back-formation < G Übertiefung (1899) < über over + Tiefung depression < tief deep, (ver)tiefen to deepen] Of excessively deepened, glaciated valleys of the Alpine kind. —**overdeepening,** n. (1902); **overdeepen,** v. (1905). O [3]

overfold, n. (1883) Geol. [Transl. of G Überfaltung < über over + Faltung folding < falten to fold] An overturned fold; a sigmoid fold. O, W [3]

overman, n. (1895) Philos. [Transl. of G Übermensch (1883) superman (q.v.)] Superman or beyondman (q.v.); trans. sense, as a superior being (human or comic-strip). O, R, W [4]

overnight, v. (1891) [Transl. of G übernachten < über over, as in stay over, + -nachten a back-formation < Nacht night, i.e., to spend the night (staying over)] To stay overnight. —**overnighting,** verbal n. (1948), a. (1966). O, R, W [4]

overtone, n. (1867) Physics, Music, Lit. [Ad. of G Oberton < ober upper, above, over + Ton tone < L tonus < Gk tónos] Physics: the color of reflected light; Music: any of the attendant higher tones or harmonics of a fundamental tone; a fig. sense as applied to lit. O, R, W [4]

overvoltage, n. (1907) Chem. [Transl. of G Überspannung (1899) < über over, upper, above + Spannung tension, voltage] Orig., the excess voltage required to discharge an ion at an electrode beyond the electrode's equilibrium potential; now, any excess voltage. O, R, W [4]

ovocyte, n. (1905) Biol. [G (1892) < ovo- + -cyte < L ōvum egg + Gk kýtos cavity, cell] Oocyte, a female germ cell after synapsis. O, W [4]

ovoflavin, n. (1933) Biochem. [G (1933) < ovo- + Flavin < the comb. form of L ōvum egg + flāvus yellow + G -in -in] Riboflavin, as found in egg white. O, W [3]

ovogenesis, n. (1887) Biol. [G O(v)ogenesis/O(v)ogenese (< NL) < L ōvum or Gk ōón egg + génesis genesis] Oogenesis, the production or formation of an ovum. —**ovogenetic** (1886), **ovogenous** (1890). O, W [3]

ovomucoid, n. (1894) Biochem. [G Ovomukoid (1894) < ovo- + Mukoid < L ōvum egg + mūcus mucus + G -oid (< Gk -oeídēs similar) -oid] A mucoid present in egg white. —**ovomucoid,** a. (1938). O, W [3]

ovoplasm, n. (1890) Biol. [G O(v)oplasma (< NL) < L ōvum or Gk ōón egg + plásma (the) formed, shaped] Ooplasm, an egg's cytoplasm. —**ovoplasmic** (1890). O, W [3]

ownhood, n. (1649) Philos. [Transl. of G Eigenheit < eigen own + nom. suffix -heit -hood] Egoism, depending on or desiring one's own way or will; selfhood (q.v.). O, W [3]

oxazole, n. (1888) Chem. [G Oxazol (1887) < Gk oxýs sharp, sour, tart + azōós lifeless + G -ol (< L oleum oil) -ole] A volatile, heterocyclic compound; a derivative of this. —**oxazolone** (1899), **oxazolidine** (1902). O, W [3]

oxime, n. (1891) Chem. Var. **oxim** [G Oxim (1882) < a short. of Oxygenium oxygen < Fr oxygène + Imid imide < NL ammonia ammonia] One of a group of compounds characterized by >C=NOH. —**formoxime** (1891), **acetoxime.** O, R, W [4]

oxine, n. (1927) Chem. [G Oxin < a short. of Oxychinolin (1927) < Gk oxýs sharp, tart, sour + china < Quechua quina china bark, actually quinaquina bark of barks, or the best of barks + G -ol (< L oleum oil) -ol + -in -ine] A crystalline phenolic base that is used to form various insoluble compounds, esp. used as an antibacterial agent. O, W [3]

oxonic acid, n. (1881) Chem. [Transl. of G Oxonsäure. prob. < Ox(o)-, the comb. form of Oxygenium (< Fr oxy-

gène) oxygen, indicating the presence of oxygen atoms bound to a central atom + *-on* < archaic G *Carboneum* carbon + *Säure* acid] Allantoxanic acid. O, W [3]

oxycephaly, *n.* (1895) *Anthrop.* [G *Oxycephalie* (now *Oxykephalie*), prob. < Gk *oxykephalós* sharp-headed + G *-ie* -y] A congenital deformity of the skull, also called *acrocephaly.* —**oxycephalic, oxycephalous.** O, R, W [4]

oxychromatin, *n.* (1895) *Biol.* [G (1894) < *oxy-* + *Chromatin* < Gk *oxýs* sharp, tart, sour + *chrôma* (gen. *chrómatos*) color + G *-in* -in] Oxyphilic chromatin, a supported compound of chromatin having considerable affinity for acid dyes. O, W [3]

oxygenase, *n.* (1903) *Biochem.* [G (1903) < *oxy-* + *-genase* < Gk *oxýs* sharp, tart, sour + *génesis* production, generation + G *-ase* -ase, denoting a destroying substance] Orig., a narrow meaning of oxidase; now usu. an oxidoreductase enzyme that catalyzes the introduction of molecular oxygen into an organic substance. O, R [3]

oxyproline, *n.* (1928) *Biochem.* [G *Oxyprolin* < a short. of *Hydroxyprolin* (1905) < *hydroxy-* (< *hydr-,* the comb. form of Gk *hýdor* water + *oxýs* sharp, tart, sour) + G *Prolin* < a short. of *Pyrrholidin* < Gk *pyrrós* fiery red + L *oleum* oil] Hydroxyproline, a monohydroxy derivative of the amino-acid proline. O [3]

ozokerite/ozocerite, *n.* (1837) *Mineral.* Var. **ozokerit** [G *Ozokerit* (1833) < *ozo-* + *-kerit* < Gk *ózein* to smell + *kērós* wax + G *-it* -ite] A waxlike hydrocarbon mixture with an often bad smell that is used for making candles, electrotype impressions, etc. —**ozokerit,** *a.* (1871). O, R, W [4]

ozone, *n.* (1840) *Chem.* [G *Ozon* (1840) < Gk *ózon* the fragrant < *ózein* to have a fragrance, smell] An allotropic triatomic form of oxygen with a characteristic pungent odor, esp. used in water purification, bleaching, etc.; pure, fresh air; fig. senses like aristocratic people or workers. —**ozone,** *a.* (1861); **ozonic** (1840); **ozoneless** (1887); **ozoned** (1902). • ~ appears in various compounds like **ozone layer** and **ozonic ether.** O, R, W [4]

ozonide, *n.* (1867 *W9*) *Chem.* [G *Ozonid* (1904) < *Ozon* (< Gk *ózon* the fragrant) + G *-id* -ide] Any of a group of usu. explosive compounds formed by adding ozone to the double or triple bond of certain organic compounds; the ion O_3- or its salt. O, R [4]

ozonometer, *n.* (1864) *Ecology* [G (1839) < *ozono-* + *Meter* meter < the comb. form of Gk *ózon* the fragrant + L *metrum* measure] An instrument that measures the amount of ozone in the air. —**ozonometry** (1867). O [3]

P

Pa, *see* protactinium

pachnolite, *n.* (1866) *Mineral.* [G *Pachnolit* (1863) < Gk *páchnē* hoarfrost + G -*lit* < Gk *líthos* stone] A hydrous fluoride of aluminum, sodium, and calcium. O, W [3]

paedogamy, -mies *pl.* (1910) *Biol.* Var. **pedogamy** (1910) [G *Pädogamie* (1902) < *pädo-* + -*gamie* < Gk *paîs* (gen. *paidós*) child + *gámos* marriage + G -*ie* (< Gk -*ia*) -y] In protozoa, a type of endogamy, in which two protozoans originate from the same parent cell. —**paedogamous** (1926). O, W [3]

paideia, *n. Ed.* [G < Gk *paideía* educational ideal] Training of a child's physical and mental capacities so as to effect an enlightened, culturally harmonious outlook; such an ideal development. W [3]

palace revolution, *n.* (1904) *Politics* Var. **palace coup** (1970), **palace revolt** [Ad. of G *Palastrevolution* < G *Palast* palace + *Revolution* revolution < L *palātium* + *re-volūtiō*] The overthrowing of a political leader, without civil war and usu. by other persons in the ruling circle. O, R, W [4]

palaeencephalon, *see* paleencephalon

palae-, *see* words under **paleo-**

palagonite, *n.* (1863) *Geol.* [G *Palagonit* (1846) < *Palagonia,* the name of a town on the island of Sicily + G -*it* -ite] A basaltic glass occurring as basaltic tuff in volcanic ash. —**palagonite tuff** (1863), **palagonitic** (1886). O, W [3]

palatschinken, -ø *pl.* (1929) *Food* [G *Palatschinke* < Hung *palatcsinta* < Rum *plăcintă* < L *placenta* cake] An Austrian dish of pancakes stuffed with jam. O, W [3]

paleëncephalon, *n.* (1917) *Anat.* Var. **palæencephalon** (1917), **paleoencephalon** [G *Paläencephalon* (1908) (now also *Paläenzephalon*) < Gk *palaiós* old, primitive, primeval + *enképhalos* brain] The phylogenetically older portion of the brain (cf. neencephalon). O, R, W [3]

Paleocene, *n.* and *a.* (1877, 1877 *W9*) *Geol.* Var. **Palæocene** (1877) [Prob. ad. of G *Paleozän* (now *Paläozän*) a subdivision of the Tertiary < *palao-* + -*zan*] (Of or relating to) the lowest series of the Tertiary system. O, R, W [4]

paleoëncephalon, *see* paleëncephalon

Paleogene, *n.* (1882) *Geol.* Var. **Palæogene** (1882) [G *Paläogene* < *paläo-* + -*gen* < Gk *palaiós* old, ancient + *génein* to generate, produce] The earlier division of the Tertiary strata, including the Paleocene, Eocene, and Oligocene. —**Paleogene,** *a.* O, R, W [4]

paleostriatium, -striata *pl.* (1913) *Anat.* Var. **palæostriatum** (1913) [G *Paläostriatum* (1908) (< NL) < *paläo-* + -*striatum* < Gk *palaiós* old, ancient + NL *striatus* striated + G -*ium* (< NL) -ium] The philogenetically older portion of the corpus striatum, consisting primarily of the globus pallidus. —**pal(a)eostriatal** (1921). O-S, W [3]

paligorskite, *see* palygorskite

palingenesis, -geneses *pl.* (1879) *Biol.* [G < *palin-* + *Genesis* < Gk *pálin* again + L *genesis* < Gk < the stem of *gígnesthai* to be born] Ernst Haeckel's term for the embryonic, exact reproduction of hereditary characteristics (this is different from the old Gk "theological" borrowing). O, R, W [3]

pallasite, *n.* (1868) *Geol.* [Prob. < G *Pallasit* (c.1772) < the name of Peter Simon *Pallas,* German world traveller and physician (1741–1811) + G -*it* -ite] A metallic meteorite consisting mainly of iron, also called *pallas iron.*—**pallasitic** (1956). O, W [3]

palygorskite, *n.* (1868) *Mineral.* Var. **paligorskite** (1868) [G *Paligorskit* (1862) < *Paligorsk,* the name of a town in the Ukraine + G -*it* -ite] A hydrous basic silicate of aluminum and magnesium belonging to the family of clay minerals. O, W [3]

panencephalitis, *n.* (1950) *Path.* [Prob. < G a. *panenzephalisch* and/or *Panenzephalomyolitis* (1939) < *pan-* + *enzephalisch* and/or *Enzephalomyolitis* < Gk *pân* all, entire + *enképhalos* skull + *myelós* spine + G -*itis* (< L) -itis, denoting inflammation] A rare kind of encephalitis affecting both the white matter and the gray matter, with a gradual loss of motor and mental functions. O [3]

panentheism, *n.* (1874) *Philos.* [G *Panentheismus* (1828) < *pan-* + *en-* + *Theismus* < Gk *pân* (neuter form of *pâs*) all, entire + *en* (with)in + *theós* god + L -*ismus* -ism] The religious philosophy that God includes the world as a part though not the entirety of His being. —**panentheistic** (1918), **panentheist,** *a.* (1959), *n.* (1974). O, W [3]

Pangaea/Pangea, *n.* (1924) *Geol.* [G (1920), a term prob. coined by Alfred Wegener (1880–1930), German geologist, to describe a hypothetical continent, in a theory that would provide the basis for the study of tectonic plates + Gk *pân* all + *gaîa* earth, land] A hypothetical continent that contained all the earth's mass before the Triassic period, before the continents were separated. O, R [4]

pangen, *n.* (1899) *Biol.* Var. **pangene** (1899) [G (1899) < *pan-* + -*gen* < Gk *pân* all + *génein* to produce, generate] A hypothetical, primary unit of a germ cell. O, W [3]

Pan-German, *a.* (1892) and *n.* (1899) *Politics* [Transl. of G *Alldeutschtum* < *all-* (= Gk *pân* all) + G *Deutschtum* German (culture and civilization)] *a.:* of or concerning all Germans, esp. their union into one country; *n.:* one who advocates Pan-Germanism. —**Pan-Germanic** (1900); **Pan-Germany** (1902), **Pan-Germanist,** *n.* (1909), *a.* (1939); **Pan-Germanistic** (1915). •*Pan-Germanism* (1882), which denotes the later Nazi doctrine of racial superiority and world domination, was borrowed from Fr *pangermanisme,* as transl. < G *Alldeutschtum.* O, R, W [4]

panharmonicon, *n.* (1848) *Music* [G *Panharmonikon* (1800) < *pan-* + *Harmonikon* < Gk *pân* all + *harmonikón,* neuter of *harmonikós* well-sounding] An early prototype of the orchestrion, invented in 1800 by Johann Nepomuk Maelzel (1772–1838), German inventor of the metronome. O [3]

panhaus, *see* ponhaus

panlogism, *n.* (1871) *Philos.* [G *Panlogismus* (1853) < *pan–* (< Gk) all + Gk *lógos* word, study, reason + G (< L)
-ismus -ism] The doctrine, primarily from Hegel, that absolute reality is explained only by logos or reason. — **panlogical** (1872); **panlogistic** (1893); **panlogist,** *n., a.* O, R, W [4]

pannhaas/pannhaus, *see* ponhaus

Pan-Satanism, *n.* (1894) *Philos.* [G *Pansatanismus* < *pan–* + *Satanismus* < Gk *pân* all + ML *satanās* antagonist + G (< L) *-ismus* -ism] An orig. Gnostic belief that the universe is the expression of Satan's personality. O, W [3]

pansexualism, *n.* (1917) *Psych.* [Prob. < G *Pansexualismus* < *pan–* + *Sexualismus* < Gk *pân* (neuter of *pâs*) all, entire + L *sexuālis* sexual + L *-ismus* -ism] The infusion of erotic feeling into all conduct and experience; the view that the sexual instinct motivates all desire and interest. O, W [4]

Pan-Slavism, *n.* (1846) *Politics* Old var. **Pansclavismus** (1846) [G *Panslavismus* < *pan–* (< Gk) all + G *Slavismus* traits, attitudes, etc., of the Slavic peoples < *Slav* + *-ismus* < L] Orig. the political and cultural movement stressing the various Slavic peoples' cultural ties, but later the Russian expansionism that drew support from such a movement. — **Panslavistic** (1850); **Panslavic** (1860); **Panslavist,** *a.* and *n.* (1883, 1884); **Pan-Slav,** *a.* (1903). O, R, W [4]

pantaleon, *n.* (1757) *Music* Var. **pantalon(e)** (1838, 1880) [G *Pantal(e)on* (c.1690) < the name of *Pantaleon* Hebenstreit (1667–1750), German inventor of the instrument] A large dulcimer with 100 to 250 strings, sounded by wooden mallets. O, W [4]

pantocain, *n.* (1931) *Pharm.* Var. **pantocaine** (1937) [G (now *Pantokain*) < Gk *pân* (gen. *pantós*) all, complete + Sp *coca* < Quechua *kuka* a Peruvian shrub + G *-in* -in] A hydrochloride salt of a diamino ester used as a local anesthetic. O [3]

panzer, *a.* (1940) *Mil.* [G < MHG *panzier* < OF *panciere* breastplate, suit of armor < L *pantex* (gen. *panticis*) paunch] Of or concerning a German military armored unit or vehicle. —**panzer,** *n.* (1943). O, R, W [4]

panzer division, *n.* (1940) *Mil.* [G < *Panzer* panzer + *Division* (< L) division] A German armored division used in World War Two for rapid attack. O, R, W [4]

paonidin, *see* peonidin

papill(o)edema, *n.* (1908) *Optics* [G *Papillenödem* (1895) (< NL) < G *Papille* < L *papilla* pupil of the eye + G *Ödem* < Gk *oídēma* swelling] Choked disk, a swelling of the optic disk caused by intercranial pressure on the optic nerve, esp. in brain tumors. O, W [3]

paprikahuhn, -hühner *pl.* (1905) *Food* [G < G *Paprika* (< Hung, ult. < Gk *péperi*) paprika + *Huhn* chicken] An Austrian, actually Hungarian poached chicken in a paprika-flavored cream sauce. O [3]

parabasal(body), n. (1912) *Biol.* [G *parabasal* (1911) < *para–* next to + *basal* forming a basis < Gk *pará* + L and Gk *básis* basis + G adj. suffix *-al* -al (+ E *body*)] A cytoplasmic body associated with some flagellates' kinetoplast. O, W [3]

paracrine, *a.* (1972) *Physiol.* [G *parakrin* < *para–* + *-krin* < Gk *pará* beside, next to + *krínein* to share, divide]

Concerning the action of a hormone whose effects are purely local, and of tissues that react to this hormone. O [3]

paraffin, *n.* (1838) *Chem.* Var. **paraffine** (1839) [G (1830) < L *parum* too little, scarcely + *affïnis* participating] Paraffin hydrocarbon, a saturated carbon of the methane series; paraffin wax, a crystalline substance used for making candles, sealing jars, etc.; chiefly British, kerosene. —**paraffin,** *v.* (1891) • ~ appears in numerous composites like **-ed** (1876), **-oid** (1887), **-ize** (1888), **-inic** (1891), **-y** (1902), **-er, paraffin oil/wax/scale/test** (1851, 1872, 1880, 1950). O, R, W [4]

paraganglion, -ganglia *pl.* (1907) *Anat.* [G (1900) < *para–* + *Ganglion* < Gk *pará* beside, next to + *ganglión* painless swelling under the skin] Any of numerous highly vascular groups of chromaffin tissue similar to those of the adrenal medulla and closely associated with the sympathetic nerve trunks. —**paraganglionic** (1937). O, W [3]

parageosyncline, *n.* (1936) *Geol.* [G *Parageosynklinale* (1935) < *para–* + *Geosynklinale* < Gk *pará* beside, next to + *geo-,* the comb. form of *gê* earth + *synklínein* to incline along with] A geosyncline situated within an older craton. —**parageosynclinal** (1941). O, W [3]

paragneiss, -es *pl.* (1902) *Geol.* [G *Paragneis* (1898) < *para–* (< Gk) beside, next to + G *Gneis* gneiss (q.v.)] Gneiss obtained from sedimentary rocks. O, W [3]

paragonite, *n.* (1849) *Mineral.* [G *Paragonit* (1848) < *Paragon* (< Gk, present part. of *parágein* to mislead) + G *-it* -ite] A muscovite-like mica that contains sodium instead of potassium. —**paragonitic** (1868). O, R, W [4]

parahydrogen, *n.* (1929) *Chem.* [Transl. of G *Parawasserstoff* (1929), coined on the analogy of *Parahelium* < *para–* (< Gk) beside, alongside + G *Wasserstoff* hydrogen] A molecular hydrogen where the two hydrogen nuclei spin in opposite directions and thus contribute nothing to the total angular momentum. O, W [3]

paralic, *a.* (1911) *Geol.* [G *paralisch* (1852) < Gk *páralos* close to shore + G adj. suffix *-isch* -ic] Formed or relating to interfingered continental and marine sediments. O, W [3]

parametritis, *n.* (1869) *Anat.* [G (1862) < *para–* + *Metritis* < Gk *pará* beside, next to, along + *métra* uterus + G (< L) *-itis* -itis, a suffix denoting inflammation] Inflammation of the connective tissue and fat alongside the uterus. —**parametrium** (1878), **parametrial** (1903). O, W [3]

paramitome, *n.* (1888) *Biol.* [G *Paramitom* < *para–* (< Gk) beside, next to + G *Mitom* mitome (q.v.)] The ground substance of protoplasm as distinguished from the denser mitome. O, W [3]

paraprotein, *n.* (1949) *Biochem.* [G (1940) < *para–* (< Gk) beside, next to + G *Protein* protein (q.v.)] One of various proteins found in the blood only in myelomatosis and a few other diseases. O [3]

paraproteinaemia, *n.* (1958) *Immunology* [G *Paraproteinämie* (1940) < *para–* (< Gk) beside, in addition + G *Protein* protein (q.v.) + Gk *-haemia,* a comb. form of *haîma* blood] A condition where there are paraproteins in the blood. O [3]

pararosaniline, *n.* (1879) *Chem.* [G *Pararosanilin* (1878) < *para–* (< Gk) beside + L *rosa* red + G *Anilin* < Fr *anil* < Ar *an-nil* < Skt *nīlī* indigo + G *-in* -ine] A crystalline alcohol used as a biological stain and in numerous triphenylmethane dyes. O, W [3]

parasitoid, *n.* and *a.* (1922, 1922) *Entomology* [G (< NL) *Parasitoidea* (1913) < L *parasītus* < Gk *parásitos* table companion, sponger + Gk *-oeidēs* similar] (of) a parasitic predator insect, esp. one belonging to the orders Diptera or Hymenoptra, whose larvae ult. kill their host. O, R, W [3]

parasymbiosis, -bioses *pl.* (1897) *Bot.* [G *Parasymbiose* (1897) < *para-* + *Symbiose* < Gk *pará* beside + *symbíōsis*) coexistence] The symbiosis between a fungus and an alga in a lichen thallus, in which the fungus protects the alga from high light intensity and may supply it with mineral salts, while the fungus parasitizes the living alga cells and lives on dead algae cells. —**parasymbiont,** *n.* (1921); **parasymbiotic** (1921). O [3]

parasyndesis, *n.* (1911) *Zool.* [G *Parasyndese* (1907) (< NL) < Gk *pará* beside, alongside of + *sýndesis* binding together] Parasynapsis. —**parasyndetically** (1911), **parasyndetic.** O, W [3]

paratectonic, *a.* (1956) *Geol.* [G *Paratektonik* (1940) < *para-* + *-tektonik* < Gk *pará* beside, alongside + *tektonikós* concerning structure, formation] Caused by or resembling a chiefly epeirogenic deformation that produces broad folds like those in Germany north of the Alps. O [3]

paratomy, *n.* (1930) *Zool.* [G *Paratomie* (1890) < *para-* + *-tomie* < Gk *pará* beside + *tomía* cut] Regeneration before separation, in a fission reproduction following structural organization of a new annelid individual out of blastema tissue. O, W [3]

paratonic, *a.* (1875) *Bot.* [G *paratonisch* (1868) < *para-* + *-tonisch* < Gk *pará* beside + *tónos* tension + G adj. suffix *-isch* -ic] Of plant movements resulting from external stimuli such as tropism and kinesis. —**paratonically** (1880). O, W [3]

paratrophic, *a.* (1900) *Biol.* [G *paratroph* (1897) < *para-* + *-troph* (< Gk *pará* beside + *trophikós* nourishing) + E *-ic*] Parasitically deriving needed nourishment from living organisms; parasitic. O, R, W [3]

parautochthonous, *a.* (1927) *Geol.* [Prob. < G *parautochthon* < *para-* + *autochthon* < Gk *pará* beside + *autós* self + *chthṓn* earth + E *-ous*] Intermediate in character between allochthonous and autochthonous. O [3]

pargasite, *n.* (1818) *Mineral.* [G *Pargasit* (1814) < *Pargas*, the name of a town in Finland + G *-it* -ite] A green or blue-green variety of hornblende. O, R, W [4]

parisite, *n.* (1846) *Mineral.* [G *Parisit* < the name of José *Paris*, Colombian mine owner and philanthropist (d. 1849) + G *-it* -ite] A rhombohedral fluorocarbonate. O, W [3]

parsettensite, *n.* (1924) *Mineral.* [G *Parsettensit* (1923) < *Parsettens*, the name of an Alp in the Swiss canton of Graubünden + G *-it* -ite] A basic manganese silicate. O, W [3]

Parseval, *n.* (1908) *Transportation* [G (1906) dirigible < the name of its inventor, August von *Parseval* (1861–1942), German aeronautical engineer] A kind of nonrigid dirigible orig. used in Germany. O, W [3]

Parsifal/Parzival, *n.* *Lit., Music* [G < the name of the seeker of the Holy Grail in Richard Wagner's musical

drama of that name which premiered in 1882; Wagner's choice of spelling, *Parsifal,* differs from *Parzival,* the hero's name in the epic by Wolfram von Eschenbach (c.1170–c.1220). The name derives from Chrétien de Troyes' epic *Perceval* (written before 1190) and is believed to mean "penetrator of the vale" < Fr *percer le val*] The knight in Wagner's drama or the German mythological knight of the Holy Grail. R [4]

parthenocarpy, *n.* (1911) *Bot.* [Prob. < G *Parthenokarpie* (1902) < Gk *parthénos* virgin, maiden + *karpós* fruit + G *-ie* (< Gk *-ia*) -y] The development of a fruit without fertilization of its plant. —**parthenocarpic(ally)** (1911, 1950), **parthenocarpical, parthenocarpous.** O, W [4]

partial valency, *n.* (1899) *Chem.* [G *Partialvalenz* (1899) < *partial* + *Valenz* < LL *partialis* partial + *valentia* strength, well-being] A partially unsatisfied valency to account, for example, for olefins' addition reactions and the benzene ring's stability. O [3]

particularism, *n.* (1853) *Politics* [G *Partikularismus* (c.1850) < Fr *particularisme* < NL *particularismus* < L *particulāris* of or from a part] The policy whereby a state or region goes its own political way, as opposed to a state within a federation (this is different from the earlier Fr theological and other meanings). O, R, W [4]

partschinite, *n.* (1854) *Mineral.* [G *Partschinit* (1847) < the name of Paul Maria *Partsch* (1791–1856), Viennese mineralogist + G *-it* -ite with an *-in-* infix] A silicate of aluminum, iron, and magnesium; a garnet like spessartine. O [3]

Parzival, *see* Parsifal

Paschen's law, *n.* (1903) *Physics* [Transl. of G *Paschen-Gesetz* (1889) < the name of L.C.H. Friedrich *Paschen* (1865–1947), German physicist + *Gesetz* law] The electronic formulation that at a constant temperature the breakdown voltage in a given gas is a function of the product of the gap width and pressure. O, W [3]

passgang, *n. Sports* [G *Paßgang* < *Paß* (< Fr *pas* step < L *passus*) + G *Gang* (< OHG) walk, i.e., the manner in which some quadrupeds walk by advancing both legs of one side at the same time] A method of cross-country running on skis. • ~ is partially transl. as **passwalk.** W [3]

passglas, -gläser *pl.* (1897) *Art* Var. **pass glass** (1897), **pass glas** [G < *passen* to be suitable, appropriate, hence *Pass* the right measure + *Glas* glass] A tall, decorated, cylindrical drinking glass. O [3]

passion play, *n.* (1870) *Theol., Theater* Var. **Passion Play** (1975) [Prob. < a transl. of G *Passionsspiel* < the gen. of *Passion* (< LL) passion + G *Spiel* play] A dramatic portrayal of the Passion of Christ, like that performed every ten years in Oberammergau, Germany. O, R, W [4]

passive, *n.* (1895) *Immunology* [G *passiv* (1892) < L *passīvus* enduring] Caused by or involving the introduction into the body of external antibodies. O [3]

passt-mir-nicht *Games* [G, lit., suits me not < G *passen* to suit, *mir* (dat. of *ich*) me, *nicht* not] In playing tournee, a player's right to return the first card turned up and to let the second card determine the trump suit. W [2]

passwalk, *see* passgang

Pasteur reaction, *n.* (1930) *Biochem.* [Ad. of G *Pasteursche Reaktion* (1926) < the name of the French scientist Louis *Pasteur* (1822–95) + G *Reaktion* reaction < NL reaction-] Pasteur effect, the inhibiting effect of oxygen on a fermentation process. O [3]

past-pointing, n. (1916) Med. [Transl. of G vorbeizeigen (1910) < vorbei past + zeigen to point] One's inability to point at an intended object after being spun around in a diagnostic neurological test. O [3]

-path, comb. form Med. [Back-formation < G -pathie -pathy < Gk páthos pain, illness, suffering] Denoting a practioner of a particular system of medicine, as in osteopath; denoting one who is suffering from a specified illness, as a neuropath. R, W [4]

pathbreaker, n. (1905) Var. **path breaker** (1905) [Transl. of G Bahnbrecher < Bahn path + -brecher < brechen to break] A person or something that breaks open a path; a pioneer or trailblazer. O [3]

pathbreaking, a. (1914) Var. **path-breaking** (1914) [Transl. of G bahnbrechend < Bahn path + brechend, pres. part. of brechen to break] Of trailblazing: of one or something that pioneers or opens a new path. O, W [3]

patristic, a. (c.1828 W9) Theol. [G patristisch (1822) < patr- (< L pater, gen. patris father) + G adj. suffix -istisch -istic] Of the writings of the early fathers of the Christian Church; of the basic writings of any religious group or cult. —**patristical.** O, R, W [4]

patzer, n. (1948) (slang) Games Var. **potzer** (1948) [G blunderer, bungler; blunder, blotch < patzen to blunder] A casual, inept chess player. O, R [4]

paulite, n. (1814) Mineral. [G Paulit (1812) < the name of St. Paul Island, Labrador + G -it -ite] Hypersthene, an orthorhombic pyroxene. O [3]

pearlite, see perlite

pearlstone, n. (1800) Geol. [Transl. of G Perlstein < Perle (< MFr) pearl + G Stein stone] Perlite (q.v.), "Hungarian-pearlstone" (cited in connection with the noted German traveler Alexander von Humboldt, Franconian assessor of mines in 1792–7). O, W [3]

pecking order, n. (1928) Psych. Var. **peck order** [Transl. of G Hackliste/Hackordnung (1922) < hacken to chop, peck + Liste list, arrangement or Ordnung order, sequence] A behavior pattern first observed in hens and later discovered in other social animals, in which those of higher rank within the group are able to attack those of lower rank without retaliation; transf., to a hierarchy based on status or rank. O, R [4]

pectolite, n. (1828) Mineral. Old var. **pektolite** (1828) [G Pektolith (1828) < Gk pektós rigidified + G -lith < Gk líthos stone] A whitish or grayish monoclinic mineral of sodium calcium silicate. O, R, W [3]

pedogamy, see paedogamy

pedology, n. (1912 W9) Geol. [G Pedologie (1862) (or Russ pedologiya) < G pedo- + -logie < Gk pédon ground, soil + logía knowledge, study] Soil science: the scientific study of soil. —**pedological(ly)** (1924, 1932), **pedologist** (1924), **pedologic** (1927). O, R, W [4]

pelargonidin, n. (1914) Chem. [G (1914) < Pelargonin pelargonin (q.v.) with an -id- infix] A plant pigment; an anthocyanidin derived from pelargonin. O, W [3]

pelargonin, n. (1914) Chem. [G (1914) < Gk pelargós stork + G -in -in] Chromoglucoside obtained from Pelargonium zonale. —**pelargonin chloride** (1956). O, W [3]

pellotine, n. (1895) Chem. [G Pellotin (1894) < MexSp

pellote peyote, a type of cactus, the sap of which induces hallucinations in color + G -in -ine] A crystalline, narcotic alkaloid obtained from peyote and certain other cacti. O, W [4]

penetrance, n. (1934) Biol. [G Penetranz (1926) < L penetrāre to penetrate] A gene's capacity to produce a particular effect in the organism to which it belongs. O, W [4]

penninite, n. (1868) Mineral. Var. **pennine** (1868) [G Pennin < the G name of the Penninische Alpen Pennine Alps + E -ite] A pseudo-rhombohedral mineral of the chlorite group consisting of a basic alumino-silicate. O, R, W [4]

pentaërythritol, n. (1892) Chem. [G Pentaërythrit (1892) < penta- < Gk pénte five + erythrós red + G -it -it + E -ol] A crystalline, tetrahydroxy-methyl that is widely used in the manufacture of explosives and synthetic drying oils and resins; a polyhydroxy ether alcohol. —**pentaerythritol tetranitrate** (1923). O, R, W [3]

pentathionic acid, n. (1849) Chem. [Transl. of G Pentathionsäure (1845) < penta- + thion- (< Gk pénte five + theîon sulfur) + G Säure acid, discovered by Heinrich Wilhelm Friedrich Wackenroder (1798–1854), German chemist (see Meyers)] An acid that contains five atoms of sulfur in each molecule. O, W [3]

pentosan, n. (1892) Chem. Old var. **pentosane** (1913) [G (1892) < pento- < Gk pénte five + -osan, suffix denoting a polysaccharide] Any of a widely distributed class of polysaccharides like araban or xylan. O, R, W [4]

pentose, n. (1890) Chem. [G (1890) < pento- < Gk pénte five + -ose, denoting a carbohydrate] Sugar containing five carbon atoms per molecule. —**pentoside** (1909), **pentose nucleic acid** (1934), **pentose phosphate pathway/cycle** (1960, 1963). O, R, W [4]

pentosuria, n. (1902) Med. [G (1895) < Pentose pentose (q.v.) + Gk ouría < oûron urine] The presence or excess of pentoses in the urine. —**pentosuric** (1906). O, W [3]

penuchle, see pinochle

peonidin, n. (1915) Chem. Var. **paonidin** (1915) [Ad. of G Päonin < Gk paiōnía peony + G -id- -id- + -in -in] An anthocyanidin derived by hydrolyzing peonin (q.v.). O, W [3]

peonin, n. (1915) Chem. [G Päonin (1915) < Päonie < Gk paiōnía peony + G -in -in] An anthocyanin that is the coloring matter of red peonies. —**peonin (hydro)chloride** (1956). O, W [4]

peppernut, see pfeffernuss

pepsin, n. (1844) Med. [G (1836) < Gk pépsis digestion + G -in -in(e)] An enzyme contained in gastric juice that digests most proteins into polypeptides; a digestant prepared from pepsin. —**pepsin(e),** a. (1886); **pepsinogen** (1878); **pepsinated** (1882); **pepsigogue; pepsiniferous; pepsino-; pepsitensin.** O, R, W [4]

peptide, n. (1906) Biochem. [Prob. < G Peptid (1903) < pept- (< Gk peptós cooked, digested) + G -id -ide] Any of the combinations of two or more amino acids. —**peptide,** a. (1953). • ~ appears in many composites like **peptized** (1921), **peptidic(ally)** (1949, 1964), **peptide chain/bond** (1931, 1935). O, R, W [4]

peptone, n. (1860) Biochem. [G Pepton (1849) < pept- (< Gk peptós cooked, digested) + G -on -one] Any of a class of soluble, diffusible substances produced by protein hydrolysis or digestion. —**peptone**, *a.* (1878); **-nized** (1880); **-nization** (1881); **-nizing** (1884); **-nizer** (1893); **-noid** (1893); **-nic**; **peptonelike**. O, R, W [4]

peracid, *n.* (1900) *Chem.* [Transl. of G *Persäure* (1900) < *per-* (< L) through, with + G *Säure* acid] An acid obtained from an element's highest oxidation state; peroxy acid. —**peracidity**. O, R, W [4]

Perbunan, *n.* (1938) *Chem.* Var. **perbunan** (1940) [G < *per-* (< L) through, with + G *Buna,* a clipped combining of *Butadien* and *Natrium* + *N,* chemical symbol for nitrogen] A trademark for a synthetic rubber first developed in Germany and orig. called *Buna-N.* O, R, W [3]

perchloroethylene, *n.* (1873) *Chem.* Var. **perchlorethylene** (1875) [G *Perchloräthylen* < *perchlor-* (< L *per* through, with + Gk *chlōrós* yellow-green) + G *Äthylen* ethylene < L *aethēr,* Gk *aithēr* the blue (of the atmosphere), upper air + *hýlē* stuff + G *-en* -ene] Tetrachloroethylene, a heavy, nonflammable liquid used in dry cleaning and as a solvent. O, R, W [4]

periarteritis (nodosa), *n.* (1876) *Med.* [G *Periarteritis nodosa* (1866) < NL *Periarteritis* (< Gk *perí* around, surrounding + L *artheritis* < Gk *arthritîs* inflammation of the joints) + G *nodosa* (< L) node, knot] An often fatal form of periarteritis, an acute inflammation surrounding the arteries. O, R, W [3]

periblem, *n.* (1873) *Bot.* [G (1868) < Gk *períblēma* hull, covering] The histogen that gives rise to the cortex in plants. O, R, W [3]

periclase, *n.* (1844) *Mineral.* Var. **periclasite** (1868) [G *Periklas* (1840) < It *periclasia* < Gk *períklasis* act of breaking around] A cubic mineral of native magnesia. O, R, W [3]

periclinal chim(a)era, *n.* (1916) *Biol.* [G *Periklinalchimäre* (1909) < *periklinal* (< Gk *períklines* sloping on all sides) + G *Chimäre* chimera, the monster in Greek mythology < L *Chimaera,* Gk *Chímaira,* actually, goat] A type of plant chimera (that is, mosaic) in which different tissues are diposed one with the other. O [3]

pericyte, *n.* (1925) *Biol.* [G *Pericyt* (1923) (now *Perizyt*) < *peri-* + *-cyt* < Gk *perí* round about + *kýtos* hollow, (now) cell] Any of many flattened branching cells found in the tissue around capillaries or other small blood vessels. O, W [3]

periderm, *n.* (1839) *Bot.* [G *Peridermis* (1836), a term suggested in this sense by Hugo von Mohl (1805–72), German botanist < NL *peridermis* < Gk *perí* around + *dérma* skin] The protective, secondary tissue initially developed in the epidermis or subepidermal layers of many plant stems and roots; the whole of such tissues. —**peridermal** (1884). O, R, W [4]

peridinian, *n.* (1912) *Biol.* Var. **peridinean** (1912), **peridiniean** (1935) [Ad. of G (< NL) *Peridinium* (1832) < Gk *peridinēs* whirled around + G (< L) *-ium* -ian] A dinoflagellate of the family Peridiniidae. —**peridinian**, *a.* (1935). O, W [4]

peridotite, *n.* (1878) *Geol.* [G *Peridotit* (1877) (or Fr *péridotite*) < Fr *péridotite* (of unknown origin)] Any of a group of plutonic rocks composed chiefly of olivine but containing little or no feldspar. —**peridotitic** (1886). O, R, W [4]

periglacial, *a.* (1928) *Geol.* [G *periglazial* (1909) < *peri-*

+ *glazial* < Gk *perí* around + L *glaciālis* icy, full of ice] Characteristic of or being an area beside a frozen or ice-covered area. —**periglacially** (1941). O, R, W [4]

perihaemal, *a.* (1881) *Zool.* [G *perihämal* (1877) < *peri-* + *-hämal* < Gk *perí* around + *haîma* blood + G *-al* -al] Of certain vessels and cavities in echinoderms and other invertebrates. O [3]

perine, *n.* (1895) *Bot.* [Prob. < G *Perin* (1882) < NL *perinium* < L *per* through, around, across + *-in* -in] Perinium, the sculptured outermost coat of a pollen grain. O, W [3]

peritectic, *a.* (1924) *Metall.* [G *peritektisch* (1912) < *peri-* + *-tekt* (< Gk *perí* around + *tēktikós* soluble < *tēkein* to melt) + G *-isch* -ic] Of or concerning a phase occurring between the solid phase and the liquid phase when a mixture is cooling. —**peritectic**, *n.* (1929); **peritectically** (1935); **peritectoid**, *a.* (1936). O, R, W [3]

perlite, *n.* (1833) *Geol.* Var. **pearlite** (1833) [Prob. < G *Perlit* < *Perle* (< MFr) pearl + G *-it* -ite] Volcanic glass of a concentric shelly structure, usu. in the form of enamel-like globules and used in plaster and concrete; pearlstone (q.v.). —**perlitic** (1879). O, R, W [4]

Perlon, *n.* (1941) *Chem.* Var. **perlon** (1973) [G a tradename for Nylon 6] A trademark for either of two types of nylonlike synthetic fibers. O, W [3]

permutite, *n.* (1907) *Chem.* [G *Permutit* < L *permūtāre* to exchange, interchange + G *-it* -ite] An artifical zeolite used in softening water and refining sugar; *Permutit* is a trademark for such ion-exchange materials and equipment. —**Permutit**, *a.* (1910). O [3]

pernicious anemia, *n.* (1874) *Med.* Var. **pernicious anaemia** (1874) [Ad. of G *perniciöse* (now *perniziöse*) *Anämie* (1868) < Fr *pernicieux* pernicious < L *perniciēs* peril, destruction + Gk *anaimía* anemia] A progressive, formerly usu. fatal form of anemia, resulting from a deficiency of vitamin B_{12}; infectious anemia. O, R, W [4]

perovskite, *n.* (1840) *Mineral.* Var. **perofskite** (1878) [G *Perowskit* (1839) < the name of Count Lev. Aleksevich von *Perowski* (1792–1856), Russian statesman + G *-it* -ite] A cubic mineral of calcium titanate, sometimes also containing cerium and other rare earths. —**perovskite**, *a.* (1939). O, R, W [3]

persis, -ses *pl. Chem.* Var. **persio** [G < the G name for the ancient heartland of Persia < Gk *Persís* < OPer *Pārsa*] Cudbear, a powdery paste obtained from certain lichens and used to color beverages. W [3]

personnel, -ø/-s *pl.* (1837) *Admin.* [Ad. of G *Personale* orig., servants, domestics (now *Personal* employees) (or < Fr borrowed < G) < ML *personale* servants, domestics < neuter sing. of *personalis* domestic staff < LL *persōnālis* personal, of or pertaining to a person] A body of persons employed in some service, business, orchestra, etc.; those individuals who work in an organization's business administration; the part of a business concerned with employees. —**personnel**, *a.* (1914). • ~ appears in various compounds like **personnel manager** (1926)/**department** (1943)/**carrier** (1945)/**management** (1957)/**officer** (1957)/**agency**. O, R, W [4]

perspectivism/Perspectivism, *n.* (1910) *Philos.* [G *Perspektivismus* < *Perspektive* perspective + *-ismus* < ML *perspectiva* + L *-ismus* -ism] The concept that reality is only partial because every individual views every other individual and event from a limited, special perspective; consciousness of or process of using different perspectives, as in literary criticism and artistic representation. O, R, W [4]

Perthes(') disease, *n.* (1915) *Med.* [Transl. of G *Perthes-Krankheit* (1910) < the name of Georg Clemens *Perthes* (1869–1927), German surgeon + *Krankheit* disease] A hip disease occurring in children, where necrosis of part of the femur head leads to increasing deformity of the joint. O [3]

perylene, *n.* (1910) *Chem.* [G *Perylen* (1910) < a short. of *Peridinaphthylen* < *peri-* + *di-* + *Naphthylen* < Gk *perí* around + *dís* twofold + *náptha* crude oil + G *-yl* -yl + *-en* -ene] A crystalline, aromatic hydrocarbon obtained from coal tar and providing certain organic pigments. O, W [3]

pestilence-wort, *n.* (1548) *Bot.* (obs.) Var. **pestilent-wort** [Transl. of G *Pestilenzwurz,* also shortened to *Pestwurz* < *Pestilenz* pestilence (< L *pestis*) + G *Wurz* wort] The butterbur, *Petasites vulgaris.* O [3]

petalite, *n.* (1808) *Mineral.* [G *Petalit* (1800) < Gk *pétalon* leaf + G *-it* -ite] A monoclinic silicate of aluminum and lithium, used as a source of lithia. O, R, W [3]

petri/Petri dish, *n.* (1892) *Med.* [Transl. of G *Petri-Schale* < the name of Julius *Petri* (1852–1921), German bacteriologist + *Schale* dish, bowl] A small, shallow plastic or glass dish with an overlapping cover used esp. for bacteriological cultures. O, R, W [4]

petrogenesis, -geneses *pl.* (1901) *Geol.* [G (1866) (< NL) < *petro-* + *Genesis* < Gk *pétros* stone + *génesis* creation] The origin of rocks, esp. igneous and metaphoric ones. —**petrogenetic(ally)** (1911, 1970). O, R, W [4]

petrographic province, *n.* (1886) *Geol.* Var. **petrographical province** (1886) [Prob. ad. of G *petrographische Provinz* (see *Meyers Großes Universallexikon,* 1981–6, 10, 579), and its antecedent in H. Vogelsang's ''Geognastisches Bezirk'' (geological district or province) in *Zeitschrift der deutschen geologishen Gesellschaft,* 1872/525) < NL *petrographic* + L *prōvincia*] A region of igneous rocks evidently formed during the same period of geological activity, presumably from the same magma. • ~ is short. to **province.** O, W [3]

petrolene, *n.* (1838) *Chem.* [G *Petrolen,* irreg. < *Petroleum* (< ML) + G *-en* -ene] Petroleum solvent, that part of asphalt soluble in paraffin naphtha or hexane; also called *malthene.* O, R, W [3]

petrotectonics, *n.* (1933) *Geol.* [Short. of G *petrographische tektonische Analyse* < *petro-* + *graphische* + *-tekton* + *Analyse* < Gk *pétros* rock + *gráphein* to write, describe + *tektonikós* concerning the art of building + NL *analysis*] The study of rock structure, esp. to plot the historical movements of rocks. —**petrotectonic** (1933). O [3]

petzite, *n.* (1849) *Mineral.* [G *Petzit* (1845) < the name of W. K. *Petz* (*Pecz*) (d. 1873), Hungarian geologist + G *-it* -ite] A silver gold telluride. O, W [3]

Pfalzian, *a.* (1931) *Geol.* [Ad. of G *pfälzisch(e)* (1922) < *Pfalz* the (Rhineland) Palatinate, ult. < L *palātium* palace, royal residence + G adj. suffix *-isch* -ian] Relating to or naming a minor orogenic movement in Europe that is believed to have occurred during the Permian period. O [3]

Pfannkuchen, -ø *pl. Food* Var. **Pfannekuchen** (1906) [G < *Pfanne* pan + *Kuchen* (q.v.) cake] A pancake in Germany and other German-speaking regions. O [3]

pfefferkuchen, *n.* (1870) *Food* Var. **Pfefferkuchen** (1964) [G < *Pfeffer* pepper + *Kuchen* (q.v.) cake] Gingerbread or spiced cake. O, W [3]

pfeffernuss, -nuesse *pl.* (1934) [G *Pfeffernuß* < G *Pfeffer* pepper + *Nuß* nut] A small highly spiced cake or cookie traditionally made at Christmas. • ~ is occasionally transl. as **peppernut** (1938). O, W [2]

pfennig, -s/-e *pl.* (1547) *Currency* Old var. like **phenyng** (1547) [G < OHG *pfenning* (which is related to the OE word that gave E *penny*), perhaps < L *pannus* a piece of cloth, used as an item of exchange] Various German coins, since 1971 a penny equal to 1/100 mark. • ~ is short. to **pfg.** O, R, W [4]

pfui, see phooey

pfuiteufel, *interj.* (1922) [G < *pfui* phooey (q.v.) + *Teufel* devil] An emphatic exclamation of disgust. O [3]

pH, *n.* (1909) *Chem.* [G (1909), a short. of *Potenz* power (< L *potentia*) + G *H* symbol for hydrogen] A measure of a solution's acidity or alkalinity, a negative logarithm of the effective hydrogen-ion activity or concentration (in gram equivalents per liter). O, R, W [4]

phaeochromocyte, see pheochromocyte

phaeochromocytoma, see pheochromoctyoma

phaeophorbide, see pheophorbide

ph(a)eophytin, *n.* (1907) *Biochem.* [G *Phaeophytin* (1907) (now *Phäophytin*) < *phaeo-* + *-phytin* < Gk *phaiós* dark in color + *phytón* plant + G *-in* -in] A waxy pigment, which is derived from chlorophyll, that is very similar structurally to chlorophyll; a phytyl ester of pheophorbide. O, W [3]

ph(a)eoplast, *n.* (1886) *Bot.* [G (1885) (now *Phäoplast*) < *phaeo-* + *-plast* < Gk *phaiós* dark in color + *plastós* formed] A brown chromatophore in the higher brown algae. O, W [3]

phallin, *n.* (1897) *Chem.* [G (1891) < LL *phallus* < Gk *phallós* male sex organ + G *-in* -in] A hemolytic agent obtained from the death cup toadstool and once thought to be its poisonous principle—see *phalloidin(e).* O [3]

phalloidin(e), *n.* (1938) *Chem.* [G *Phalloidin* (1938) < NL *phalloides* epithet of the death cup *Amanita Phalloides* + G *-in* -in(e)] The chief phallotoxin; a highly toxic peptide. O, W [4]

phalloin, *n.* (1959) *Chem.* [G (1957) (< LL) < Gk *phallós* male sex organ + G *-in* -in] A phallotoxin, $C_{35}H_{48}N_8O_{10}S.$ O [3]

phantast, see fantast

pharmacogenetics, *n.* (1960) *Med.* [G *Pharmakogenetik* (1959) < *pharmako-* + *Genetik* < Gk *phármakon* drug + *genetē* birth, origin + G *-ik* (< Gk *-ika*) -ic + E *-s*] The pharmacological study of how genetic factors affect drug reactions. —**pharmacogenetic** (1962), **pharmacogeneticist** (1971). O, R [3]

pharmacolite, *n.* (1805) *Mineral.* [G *Pharmakolith* (1800) < G *pharmako-* + *-lith* < Gk *phármakon* drug + *líthos* stone] A hydrous arsenate of calcium, occurring in silky fibers. O, R, W [3]

pharmacosiderite, *n.* (1835) *Mineral.* [G *Pharmakosiderit* (1813) < *pharmako-* + *Siderit* < Gk *phármakon* drug + *sídēros* iron + G *-it* -ite] A hydrous iron arsenate. O, W [3]

phasemeter, *n.* (1898) *Tech.* [G *Phasenmeter* (1894) < *Phase* phase + *Meter,* ult. < Gk *phásis* + *métron* measure] An instrument that measures the phase difference between two electromotive forces or alternating currents. O, W [3]

phellem, *n.* (1887) *Bot.* [G (1877) < Gk *phéllos* cork] Cork, a phellogen's layer of usu. suberized cells. O, R, W [4]

phenacite/phenakite, *n.* (1834) *Mineral.* [G *Phenakit* (1833) (or < Sw) < Gk *phénax* (gen. *phénakos*) deceiver, from its easily being mistaken for quartz + G *-it* -ite] Beryllium silicate, a rare crystalline mineral sometimes used as a gem. O, R, W [4]

phenanthrene, *n.* (1882) *Chem.* [G *Phenanthren* (1864), discovered by the German chemist Rudolf Fittig (1835–1910) < *phen-,* a comb. form ult. < Gk *phaínein* to appear to be + G *-anthren,* a comb. form of *Anthracen* anthracene] A tricyclic, crystalline aromatic hydrocarbon. O, R, W [4]

phenanthridine, *n. Chem.* [Prob. < G *Phenanthridin,* a blending of *Phenanthr-* (< *Phenanthren* phenanthrene, q.v.) + *Pyridin* pyridine < Gk *pŷr* denoting heat, fever, fire + G *-id-* a chemical suffix, as in *Sulfid* sulfide + *-in* -ine] A crystalline base, isomeric with acridine. W [3]

phenanthroline, *n.* (1882) *Chem.* [G *Phenanthrolin* (1882) < *phen-* + *Anthroline* < Fr *phénole* < Gk *phaínein* to shine, glow + *ánthrax* coal + G *-olin* -oline, as in *Chinolin* chinazoline (q.v.)] One of three crystalline nitrogen bases, often used as an oxidation-reduction indicator. O, W [3]

phenetole, *n.* (1850) *Pharm.* Var. **phenetol** [G *Phenetol* (1850) < Gk *phaínein* to appear, seem + G *-ol* (< *Alkohol* alcohol, ult. < Ar) -ole, with an *-et-* infix] Ethoxy benzene; ethyl phenyl ether. —**phenetole red.** O, R, W [4]

phengite, *n.* (1868) *Mineral.* [G *Phengit* < L *phengītēs* selenite, ult. < Gk *phéngos* light, luster] A variety of muscovite (prob. L and Gk are the source of the old meaning of "stone anciently used for windows"). O, W [3]

phenicochroite, *see* phoenicochroite

phenmiazine, *n. Chem.* [G *Phenmiazin* < *phen-* + *-miazin* < Gk *phaínein* to show + *méion* less + L *acidus* sharp, tart + G *-in* -ine] Quinazoline, a crystalline, aromatic compound. W [3]

phenocopy, -copies *pl.* (1937 *W9*) *Biol.* [G *Phänokopie* (1935) < *phäno-* + *Kopie* < Gk *phaínein* to seem, appear, show + ML *copia* copy (increasing the supply) < L *cōpia* supply, quantity] An abnormal, phenotypic variation induced by environmental factors, which simulates a genetically produced disorder. —**phenocopic.** O, R, W [4]

phenogenetics, *n.* (1938) *Biol.* [G *Phänogenetik* (1918) < *phäno-* + *Genetik* < Gk *phaínein* to appear, seem + *genetē̆* birth, origin + *-ika* -ic + E *-s*] Developmental genetics. —**phenogenetic(ally).** O, W [3]

phenolase, *n.* (1911) *Biol.* [G (1906), a short. of *Phenoloxydase* phenoloxydase (q.v.)] An early term for phenol oxydase (q.v.). O, W [3]

phenological, *a.* (1875) *Biol.* Var. **phenologic** (1974) [Ad.

of G *phänologisch* (1853) < *phäno-* + *logisch* < Gk *phaínomenon* appearance + *lógos* word, study + G adj. suffix *-isch* -ical] Pertaining to the relationship between climate and various periodic, biological phenomena. — **phenologically.** O, R, W [4]

phenol oxidase, *n.* (1913) *Biol.* Var. **phenoloxydase** [G (1912) < *Phenol* < Fr < Gk *phaínein* to appear, seem + G *Oxydase* < Gk *oxýs* sharp, tart + G *-ase* -ase, denoting a destroying substance] A copper-containing enzyme that promotes phenol oxidation. O, W [3]

phenomenology, *n.* (1875) *Philos.* [G *Phänomenologie* (1764), first used by Johann Heinrich Lambert (1728–77), German polymath and member of the Prussian Academy of Sciences, in his *Neues Organon* (1764) < *Phänomen* + *-o-* + *-logie* < LL *phaenomenon* < Gk *phainómenon* phenomenon + *lógos* word, study + G *-ie* -y] A Kantian division of metaphysics; Hegel's concept of the growth of knowledge; phaneroscopy; Husserl's foundations for all sciences. —**phenomenological(ly)** (1891, 1891), **phenomenologist** (1910), **phenomenological method** (1923), **phenomenologic.** O, R, W [4]

phenosafranine, *n.* (1883) *Chem.* Old var. **phenosafranin** (1883) [G *Phenosafranin* (1883) < *pheno-* + *Safranin* < Gk *phaínein* to appear + OFr, Sp *azafran* < Ar *al za'faran* saffron + G *-in* -ine] Safranine, a group of synthetic azine dyes used as a photographic desensitizer and as a biological stain. O, R, W [3]

phenotype, *n.* (1911) *Biol.* Old var. **phaenotype** (1931) [G *Phänotypus* (1909) < *phäno-* + *Typus* < Gk *phainómenon* phenomenon + *týpos* type] An organism's appearance resulting from the interaction of genotype and environment; an organism's visible characters. O, R, W [4]

phenotypic(al), *a.* (1911) *Biol.* [G *phänotypisch* < *Phänotypus* (see *phenotype*) + G adj. suffix *-isch* -ic] Of, relating to, or constituting a phenotype. —**phenotypically** (1911). O, R, W [4]

phenylalanine, *n.* (1883) *Biochem.* [G *Phenylalanin* (1883) < *phenyl-* (< Gk *phaínein* to appear + *hýlē* stuff) + G *Alanin* alanine (q.v.)] A crystalline alpha-amino acid vital to the diet of humans and lower animals. O, R, W [4]

phenylhydrazine, *n.* (1897) *Chem.* [G *Phenylhydrazin* (1875), discovered by Emil Fischer (1852–1919), German chemist < *phenyl-* (< Gk *phaínein* to appear + *hýlē* stuff) + G *Hydrazin* hydrazine (q.v.)] A toxic liquid nitrogen base made by reducing benzenediazonium chloride, used in identifying compounds and sugars. O, W [3]

phenylhydrazone, *n.* (1889) *Chem.* [G *Phenylhydrazon* (1888), discovered and named by Otto Rudolph, 19th-cent. German chemist in his *Ueber die Phenylhydrazone einiger aromatischer Aldehyde* < *phenyl* (< Gk *phaínein* to appear + *hýlē* stuff) + G *Hydrazon* hydrazone (q.v.)] A hydrazone derived from phenylhydrazine (q.v.). O, W [3]

pheochromocyte, *n.* (1929) *Med.* Var. **phaeochromocyte** (1948) [G *Phäochromocyt* (1906) (now *Phäochromozyt*) < *phäo-* + *Chromocyt* < Gk *phaiós* of dark color + *chrōma* color + *kýtos* hollow, (now) cell] A chromaffin cell, esp. in the adrenal medulla. O, W [3]

pheochromocytoma, *n.* (1929) *Med.* Var. **paeochromocytoma** (1943) [G *Phäochromozytom* (1912) (< NL) < Gk *phaiós* dark in color + *chrōma* color + *kýtos* hollow, (now) cell + G *-om* (< Gk *-ōma*) -oma, denoting swelling] A tumor in the chromaffin cells of the adrenal medulla, usu. associated with extreme hypertension. O, R, W [4]

pheophorbide, *n.* (1911) *Biochem.* Var. **phaeophorbide** (1956) [G *Phäophorbid* < *phäo-* < Gk *phaiós* dark in color + *phorbé* fodder, pasturage + G *-id* -ide] A blue-black crystalline acid derived either from chlorophyll or ph(a)eophytin (q.v.); an ester from this acid. O, W [3]

pheophytin, *see* phacophytin

pheoplast, *see* phaeoplast

Philister, *n.* (1802) [G (1693) < L *Philistaeus* or Heb *Pelišhtī*, as first quoted in Crabb Robinson's *Diary* (1802) as a transl. of a statement attributed to Goethe: "What great (i.e., wide) eyes the Philistines will make at the knight with the iron-hand"] German university students' name for townspeople or any nonstudent; Philistine: an unenlightened, uncultured person. O, R, W [3]

Philistine, *see* Philister

phloem, *n.* and *a.* (1875, 1875) *Bot.* [G (1858) < Gk *phlóos* bark, fiber + *-ēma* pass. suffix] (of) the collective name for the vascular bundle in higher plants, including sieve cells, sieve tubes, and usu. fibers etc. —**phloic, phloem ray** (1875)/ **island** (1889)/**fiber/necrosis/parenchyma.** O, R, W [4]

phlogopite, *n.* (1850) *Mineral.* [G *Phlogopit* (1841) < Gk *phlogōsós* fiery + *óps* (gen. *ōpós*) face, glance + G *-it* -ite] A magnesium mica. —**phlogopitization.** O, R, W [4]

phlorizin, *n.* (1835) *Pharm.* Var. **phloridzin** (1835), **phloridzite** (1838), **phlorhizin** (1900), **phlorrhizin** (1947) [G *Phloridzin* (1835) < Gk *phloiós, phlóos* bark + *ríza* root + G *-in* -in] A bitter glucoside extracted from the bark of various fruit trees, which is used in diabetic experiments on animals. —**phlorizinized** (1900), **phlorizinization** (1917), **phlorizinize.** O, R, W [3]

phoenicite, *n. Mineral.* [Ad. of G *Phönikit,* a short. of *Phönikochroit* phoenicochroite (q.v.)] Phoenicochroite. W [3]

phoenicochroite/phenicochroite, *n.* (1849) *Mineral.* [Ad. of G *Phönikochroit* (1839), also short. to *Phönikit* phoenicite < Gk *phoínix* purple, crimson + *chroía* color + G *-it* -ite] A basic lead chromate in deep red crystals and masses. O, W [3]

phon, *n.* (1932) *Physics* [G (1926) < Gk *phōné* sound, voice] An acoustic unit of loudness level. O, R, W [4]

phoneme, *n.* (1905) *Psych.* [G *Phonem* (1896) < Gk *phṓ nēma* sound, tone] Verbal auditory hallucination (this is different from the Fr "linguistic" borrowing *phonème*). O [3]

phonolite, *n.* (1828–32) *Geol.* [G *Phonolith* (1812) (now *Phonolit*) (or < Fr *phonolite* < G), named for the ringing sound when struck < *phono-* + *-lith* < Gk *phōné* sound + *líthos* stone] A fine-grained volcanic rock consisting primarily of alkali feldspar and nepheline, also called *clinkstone* (q.v.). —**phonolitic** (1852). O, R, W [4]

phonometry, *n.* (1936) *Ling.* [G *Phonometrie* (1936) (or Fr *phonométrie*) < G *phono-* + *-metrie* < the comb. form of Gk *phōné* sound + *-metria* < *metreîn* to measure] A method of speech analysis by statistically measuring connected speech according to intensity and frequency, as compared with informants' responses to the same data. —**phonometric.** O, R, W [3]

phooey, *interj.* (1866) (informal) Var. **pfui** (1866) [Ad. of G *pfui*, prob. echoic of the sound of spitting in disgust] An exclamation expressing disgust or repudiation. O, R, W [4]

phorbol, *n.* (1935) *Chem.* [G (1927) < *phorb-* + *Öl* < Gk *phorbé* fodder < *phérbein* to feed, nourish + L *oleum* oil] A tetracyclic compound, some of the esters of which can help promote cancer and are present in croton oil. O, R [3]

phosgenite, *n.* (1849) *Mineral.* [G *Phosgenit* (1820) < *Phosgen* (< Gk *phōs* light + *-genēs* generating, generated) + G *-it* -ite] A crystalline lead chlorocarbonate. O, R, W [4]

phosphazene, *n.* (1920) *Chem.* [G *Phosphazin* (1919) < *phosph-* + *-azin* < Gk *phōsphóros* light-bearing + *-azin* < *ázōos* inert + G *-in* -ene] Various compounds that employ a bonding system characterized by a repeating unit, used to fireproof textiles like rayon. O [3]

phosphoferrite, *n.* (1921) *Mineral.* [G *Phosphoferrit* (1920) < *phospho-* + *-ferrit* < Gk *phōsphóros* light-bearing + L *ferrum* iron + G *-it* -ite] A manganese ferrous hydrous phosphate. O, W [3]

phospholipase, *n.* (1945) *Biochem.* [G (1935) < *phospho-* + *Lipase* < Gk *phōsphóros* light-bearing + *lípos* fat + G *-ase* -ase, denoting a destroying substance] Lecithinase, an enzyme that hydrolyzes lecithins and cephalins. O, R, W [4]

phosphomonoesterase, *n.* (1932) *Biochem.* [G (1932) < *phospho-* + *Monoesterase* < Gk *phōsphóros* light-bearing + *mónos* single + G *Ester,* a short. of *Essigäther* ethylacetate + *-ase* -ase, denoting an enzyme] An enzyme that acts on monoesters to remove a terminal phosphate group from a phosphate ester. O, W [4]

phosphophyllite, *n.* (1921) *Mineral.* [G *Phosphophyllit* (1920) < *phospho-* + *Phyllit* < Gk *phōsphóros* light-bearing + *phýllon* leaf + G *-it* -ite] A brittle, hydrous phosphate. O, W [3]

phosphor, *n.* (1910) *Physics* [G (1904) < Fr *phosphore,* ult. < Gk *phōsphóros* light-bearing] Any substance that exhibits phosphorescence or fluorescence. —**phosphor,** *a.* (1971). O, R, W [4]

phosphorroesslerite, *n.* (1939) *Mineral.* [G *Phosphorrösslerit* (1939) < *Phosphor* phosphor (q.v.) + *Roesslerit* roesslerite (q.v.)] An acid hydrous phosphate of magnesium. O, W [3]

photoautotrophic, *a.* (1943 W9) *Bot.* [G *photoautotrophisch* < *Photoautotrophie* (1932) (< *photo-* + *auto-* + *-trophie* < Gk *phōt-, phōs* light + *autós* self + *trophé* nourishment) + G *-isch* -ic] Of plants and bacteria that utilize light energy and specific pigments in autotrophic processes. —**photoautotrophically.** O, R, W [4]

photocatalytic, *a.* (1913) *Chem.* [G *photokatalytisch* (1910) < *photo-* + *katalytisch* < Gk *phōt-, phōs* light + *katálysis* dissolution + G adj. suffix *-isch* -ic] Pertaining to or exhibiting catalysis of a chemical reaction by radiant energy. —**photocatalysis** (1913), **-catalyst** (1914), **-catalytically** (1923), **-catalyzer** (1926), **-catalyze,** *v.* O, R, W [3]

photocathode, *n.* (1930) *Physics* Var. **photo-cathode** (1930) [G *Photokathode* (1929) < *photo-* + *Kathode* < Gk *phōt-, phōs* light + *káthodes* the way down] A cathode that emits electrons when illuminated, so that an electric current can pass. O, R, W [4]

photocinesis, *see* photokinesis

photodynamic, *a.* (1909) *Med.* [G *photodynamisch* (1904) < *photo-* + *dynamisch* < Gk *phōt-, phōs* light + *dynamikós* powerful, effective + G *-isch* -ic] Of or causing a toxic reaction to light, esp. ultraviolet light (this is different from the earlier meaning of "relating to light energy"). —**photodynamically** (1926). O, R, W [4]

photogrammetry, *n.* (1875) *Geogr.* [G *Photogrammetrie* < *Photogramm* + *-metrie* < Gk *phōt-, phōs* light + *grámma* record + *métron* measure + *-ia*] The process of making reliable measurements by using aerial photographs to survey and make maps. —**photogrammetrical** (1891), **photogrammetric(ally)** (1906, 1906), **photogrammetrist** (1939). O, R, W [4]

photographophone, *n.* (1901) *Tech.* [G *Photographon* < G *Photograph* photograph < *photo-* + *-graph* < Gk *phōt-, phōs* light + *-graphos* delineated + *phōné* sound, voice] A device for recording and reproducing sounds through kinematographic photographs using a telephone. O [3]

photoheterotrophic, *a.* (1945) *Bot.* [G *photoheterotrophisch* < *Photoheterotrophie* (1932) < *photo-* + *Heterotrophie* (< Gk *phōt-, phōs* light + *héteros* varied + *trophé* nutrition) + G adj. suffix *-isch* -ic] Heterotrophic and securing energy from light. —**photoheterotroph(ically)** (1963, 1972). O [3]

photokinesis, -kineses *pl.* (1905) *Physiol.* Var. **photocinesis** [G *Photokinese* (1883) < *photo-* + *Kinese* < Gk *phōt-, phōs* light + *kínēsis* movement] An organism's motion or activity in response to the effect of light. —**photokinetic(ally)** (1907, 1970). O, R, W [4]

photoluminescence, *n.* (1889) *Physics* [G *Photolumineszenz* (1888) (now *Photolumineszenz*) < *photo-* (< Gk *phōt-, phōs* light) + G *Lumineszenz* < L *lūmen* (gen. *lūminis*) light + G *-escenz* < L *-escentia* essence, state or process of becoming] Luminescence produced by visible or invisible light. —**photoluminescent,** *a.* (1909). O, R, W [4]

photophilic/photophilous, *a.* (1949) *Bot.* Var. **photophil(e)** (1964, 1952) [G *photophil* (1944) < *photo-* + *-phil* < Gk *phōt-, phōs* light + *philía* love, affection + E *-ic* or *-ous*] Light-loving, thriving best in strong light. —**photophily,** *n.* (1934). O, R, W [4]

photophoresis, -reses *pl.* (1919) *Physics* [G *Photophorese* (1918) < *photo-* < Gk *phōt-, phōs* light + *phórēsis* the act of being borne, carried] The movement of small particles like dust under the influence of radiant energy like light. —**photophoretic** (1924). O, W [3]

photosynthesis, -theses *pl.* (1898) *Bot.* [Poss. < G *Photosynthese* < NL *photosynthesis* < Gk *phōt-, phōs* light + *sýnthesis* synthesis] Synthesis of chemical compounds effected with the aid of radiant energy, esp. light, which leads plants to form carbohydrates from carbon dioxide and to release oxygen from water; any photochemical synthesis of a chemical compound. —**photosynthetic(ally)** (1900, 1900); **-sized** (1910); **-size** (1921); **-sizing,** *verbal n.* (1937); **-sizer** (1958); **photosynthetic quotient** (1945)/**ratio**; **photosynthate,** *n.* O, R, W [4]

phototactic, *a.* (1882) *Bot.* [G *phototaktisch* (1878) < *photo-* + *taktisch* < Gk *phōt-, phōs* light + L *tāctus* (past part. of *tangere* to touch) + G *-isch* -ic] Of a taxis where light is the directive factor. —**phototactically** (1914). O, R, W [4]

phototaxis, -taxes *pl.* (1893) *Bot.* Var. **phototaxy** [G (1878) < *photo-* + *Taxis* < Gk *phōt-, phōs* light + *táxis* arrangement] A taxis where light is the directive factor. O, R, W [4]

phototropism, *n.* (1899) *Biol.* [G *Phototropismus* (1892) < *photo-* + *Tropismus* < Gk *phōt-, phōs* light + *tropé* the act of turning toward + G (< L) *-ismus* -ism] The innate movement toward or away from light (as a plant shoot or tube worm); a substance's reversible change in color when exposed to light. O, R, W [4]

phototropy, -ies *pl.* (1900) *Chem.* [G *Phototropie* (1899) < *photo-* + *-tropie* < Gk *phōt-, phōs* light + *-tropia* turning] A substance's reversible change in color when exposed to light. O, W [3]

phragmoplast, *n.* (1912) *Bot.* [G (1888) < Gk *phrágmos* fence, dividing wall + *plastós* formed, shaped] Cell plate; the expanded barrel-shaped structure typical of the late stages of plant mitosis. —**phragmoplastic** (1952). O, R, W [3]

phthalazine, *n.* (1893) *Chem.* [G *Phthalazin* (1886), irreg. < G *Naphtha* (< Gk) crude oil + connective G *-l-* + *-azin* < Gk *ázōos* inert + G *-in* -ine] A colorless, crystalline, heterocyclic base; a derivative of this. O, W [3]

phycobilin, *n.* (1945) *Bot.* [G (1929) < *phyco-* < Gk *phŷkos* seaweed + L *bīlis* gall + G *-in* -in] Any of a group of pigments, present in some algae cells, which are photosynthetically active. O, W [3]

phycomycete, *n.* (1887) *Bot.* [Back-formation < NL *Phycomycetes* or G (< L) *Phycomycet* (1866) (now *Phykomyzet*) < Gk *phŷkos* seaweed + *mýkēs* fungus] A fungus belonging to the class Phycomycetes. —**phycomycete,** *a.* (1932); **phycomycetous.** O, R, W [4]

phyletic, *a.* (1881) *Biol.* [G *phyletisch* (1866) < Gk *phyletikós* < *phylétes* tribesman < *phylé* tribe + G *-isch* -ic] Pertaining to the evolutionary development of a taxon or organ thereof. —**phyletically** (1893). O, R, W [4]

phylloporphyrin, *n. Chem.* [Prob. < G < *phyllo-* + *Porphyrin* < Gk *phýllon* leaf + *porphýra* purple dye] A crystalline porphyrin with a violet luster obtained by decomposing chlorophyll or ph(a)eophytin. O, W [3]

phylloquinone, *n.* (1939) *Biochem.* [Ad. of G *Phyllochinon* (1939) < *phyllo-* (< Gk *phýllon* leaf) + G *Chinon* quinone (q.v.) + G *-in* -ine] Vitamin K, which is essential in blood clotting. O, R, W [3]

phyllosilicate, *n.* (1947) *Geol.* [G *Phyllosilikat/Phillosilikat* (1938) < *phyllo-* (< Gk *phýllon* leaf) + G *Silikat* silicate < NL *silica*] A polymeric silicate characterized by SiO_4 tetrahedra linked in indefinitely extending sheets, also called *sheet-silicate*. O, R, W [3]

phylogenesis, -eses *pl.* (1875) *Biol.* [G *Phylogenese/Phylogenesis* (1866) (or < NL *phylogenesis* < G) < Gk *phýlon* tribe + *génesis* origin, creation] Phylogeny: the genesis or evolution of a race or tribe, or of an organ or feature in these. —**phylogenetic** (1877 *W9*). O, R, W [4]

phylogeny, -ies *pl.* (1870) *Bot.* [G *Philogenie* (1866) <

philo- + **-genie** < Gk *phŷlon* tribe + *-geneia* the act of being born < *-genēs* born + *-ia*] Phylogenesis (q.v.); the racial history of a given kind or organism; the history or development of some abstract thing (like a custom or word). O, R, W [4]

physalite, *n.* (1819) *Mineral.* [G *Physalith* (1817), a short. of *Pyrophysalith* pyrophysalite < Gk *pyr-* fire + *physallís* bladder, bubble + G *-lith* < Gk *líthos* stone, so named because the mineral tumesces when heated] A topaz variety. O [3]

physharmonica, *n.* (1838) *Music* Var. **physharmonika** [G *Physharmonika* (1818) < *phys-* + *Harmonika* < Gk *phŷsa* bellows + L *harmonica* (fem. of *harmonicus*) well-sounding] A small reed organ, invented in 1818, a predecessor of the harmonium; a set of reed stops built into a pipe organ. O, W [3]

physiatrics, *n.* (1858) *Med.* Var. **physiatric** (1901) [G *Physiatrik* < Gk *phýsis* nature + *iatrikós* pertaining to healing] The system or doctrine of holistic medicine; physical medicine or therapy. —**physiatrical** (1858), **physiatrist.** O, R, W [3]

physicalism, *n.* (1931) *Philos.* [G *Physikalismus* < ML *physicalis* physical + G *-ismus* (< L) -ism] The doctrine that the descriptive terms of scientific language are reducible to certain kinds of physical entities, orig. in Germany in regard to the language of physics. —**physicalist,** *a.* (1934), *n.* (1972). O, R, W [4]

physiogeny, *n.* (1879) *Biol.* [G *Physiogenie* < *physio-* + *-genie* < Gk *physio-* physio- + *-geneia* -geny] The science of the evolution of living organisms' functions; the genesis or history of this. O [3]

physiophilosoph(er), *n.* (1887) *Philos.* [Transl. of G *Naturphilosoph* (1808–11) < G *Natur* nature (see Gk *phýsis* nature and its comb. form *physio-*) + G *Philosoph* philosopher] One who espouses the physiophilosophy (q.v.) of Lorenz Oken. O [3]

physiophilosophy, *n.* (1847) *Philos.* [Transl. of G *Naturphilosophie* (1808–11) < G *Natur* nature (see Gk *phýsis* nature and its comb. form *physio-*) + G *Philosophie* < L *philosophia* < Gk] The philosophical system of nature of Lorenz Oken (1779–1851), German philosopher, intended to present the system of nature in its universal relations. O, W [3]

physode, *n.* *Bot.* [G < Gk *physōdés* full of wind] A vesicular intracellular inclusion of brown algae of uncertain function and structure. W [3]

physogastry, *n.* (1903) *Entomology* Var. **physogastrism** (1903) [G *Physogastrie* (1894) < *physo-* + *-gastrie* < Gk *phŷsa* bladder, bubble + *gastér* belly + G *-ie* (< Gk *-ia*) -y] The condition of certain insects to have their abdomens greatly distended by the growth of fat bodies, ovaries, etc. —**physogastric** (1914). O, R, W [3]

physostigmine, *n.* (1864) *Chem.* [G *Physostigmin* (1864) < *physo-* + *Stigmin* < Gk *phýsan* to breathe air into + *stígma* dot + G *-in* -ine] Eserine, a toxic alkaloid. • ~ appears in numerous chemical names like **physostigmine salicylate,** used as a myotic medicine. O, R, W [4]

phytane, *n.* (1907) *Chem.* [G *Phytan* (1907) < *phyt-* (< Gk *phytón* plant) + G *-an* -ane] A colorless liquid hydrocarbon obtained by reducing phytol. O [3]

phytase, *n.* (1908) *Biol.* [G (1907) < *phyt-* (< Gk *phytón* plant) + G *-ase* -ase, denoting an enzyme] Any of a class of enzymes found in cereals, yeast, and kidneys, which convert phytic acid into inositol and phosphoric acid. O, W [3]

Phytin, *n.* (1905) *Biol.* Var. **phytin** (1906) [G (1904) < *phyt-* (< Gk *phytón* plant) + G *-in* (< L *-inus,* denoting an element) -in] (cap.) a trademark for a calcium and magnesium salt of phytic acid, used as a medicine, nutrient, and calcium supplement; loosely, phytic acid. O, R, W [3]

phytoalexin, *n.* (1949) *Bot.* [G (1941) < *phyto-* + *Alexin* < Gk *phytón* plant + *aléxein* to hold firmly, hold on to] Orig., a substance naturally produced by plant tissues to inhibit the growth of fungal parasites when they get on the plant, but now extended to all parasites. O, R [3]

phytohormone, *n.* (1933) *Bot.* [G *Phytohormon* (1931) < *phyto-* + *Hormon* < Gk *phytón* plant + *hormé* headstart, attack, drive + G *-on* -one] A plant hormone, any substance that hormonally affects a plant. O, R, W [4]

phytol, *n.* (1907) *Biochem.* [G (1907) < *phyt-* (< Gk *phytón* plant) + G *-ol* (< *Alkohol* < Ar *al-kuḥul*) -ol] A primary alcohol obtained by hydrolyzing chlorophyll and used to synthesize chlorophyll and vitamins E and K. —**phytyl** (1911). O, R, W [3]

picamar, *n.* (1836) *Chem.* [G < *pic-* + *-amar* < the comb. form of L *pix* pitch + *amārus* bitter, coined by Carl L. Reichenbach (1780–1869), German chemist] A bitter, viscous oil obtained from wood tar. O [3]

pickelhaube, -n/-s *pl.* (1875) *Mil.* Var. **Pickel-haube** (1875), **pickel-haube** (1927) [G < *Pickel,* influenced by *Pickel* pickax + *Haube* hood, cap < early NHG *bickel-* or *beckel(haube),* MHG *beckenhube* a visorless helmet < LL *bacchinon*)] A spiked helmet worn by German soldiers in the late 19th century and into World War One; (by metonymy), a German soldier. O, W [3]

Pick's disease, *n.* (1931) *Med.* [Transl. of G *Pick-Krankheit* < the name of Arnold *Pick* (1851–1924), Austrian psychiatrist and neurologist + G *Krankheit* disease] A condition chiefly afflicting older women, characterized by deteriorating intellect, speech disturbance, and eventual dementia (this is different from the Pick's disease named for the German physician Friedel Pick). O, W [3]

picrite[1], *n.* (1814) *Mineral.* [G *Picrit* (1797) (now *Pikrit*) < *picr-* (< Gk *pikrós* bitter) + G *-it* -ite] A discarded synonym for dolomite. O [3]

picrite[2], *n.* (1868) *Mineral.* [Fr *picrite* or G *Picrit* (1866) (now *Pikrit*) < *picr-* (< Gk *pikrós* bitter) + G *-it* -ite] A granular igneous rock composed chiefly of either hornblende or augite and olivine; a kind of olivine diabase without feldspar. —**picritic** (1931). O, R, W [3]

picroilmenite, *n.* (1900) *Mineral.* [G *Pikroilmenit* (1898) < *pikro-* (< Gk *pikrós* bitter) + G *Ilmenit* ilmenite (q.v.)] Picrotitanite, a magnesium variety of ilmenite. O [3]

picrolichenin, *n.* (1862) *Biochem.* [G (1832) < *picro-* + *Lichenin* < Gk *pikrós* bitter + *leichén* lichen + G *-in* -in] Picrolichenic acid, an amaroid found in the lichen *Pertusaria amara.* O [3]

picrolite, *n.* (1816) *Mineral.* [G *Picrolith* < *picro-* + *-lith* < Gk *pikrós* bitter + *líthos* stone] A fibrous or columnar variety of serpentine. O, W [3]

picropharmacolite, *n.* (1823) *Mineral.* [G *Picropharmako-lith* (1819) < *picro-* + *Pharmakolith* < Gk *pikrós* bitter + *phármakon* drug + *líthos* stone] A hydrous arsenate of calcium resembling pharmacolite, but containing magnesium. O, W [3]

picrosmine, *n.* (1825) *Mineral.* [G *Picrosmin* (1824) < *picr-* + *Osmin* < Gk *pikrós* bitter + *osmḗ* odor, so named because of the mineral's bitter odor when moistened] A hydrous silicate of magnesium. O [3]

piedmontite, *n.* (1854) *Mineral.* [Ad. of G *Piemontit* (1853) < It *Piemonte* Piedmont, a region in Italy + G -*it* -ite] A variety of epidote, a reddish brown or black silicate. O, R, W [4]

piemontite, *n.* (1892) *Mineral.* [G *Piemontit* (1853) < the Italian name of *Piemonte* (see *piedmontite*) + G -*it* -ite] Piedmontite (though *piemontite* is closer to the Italian and German spelling and to European practice, *piedmontite* is the usual modern spelling). O [3]

piercement, *a.* (1925) *Geol.* [Transl. of G *Durchspie-ßungs(falte)* < *Durchspießung* piercement (+ *Falte* fold)] The penetration of overlying rock layers by a mobile core, often forming salt domes. O [3]

Pietism/pietism, *n.* (1697) *Theol.* [G *Pietismus* (c.1670) < L *pietās* piety + G (< L) -*ismus* -ism] A 17th-century movement originating in the German Lutheran Church and now extended to any similar Protestant movement, in reaction to excess formalism and intellectualism and stressing Bible study and personal religious experience; emphasis on devotional practices; affectation in devotion. O, R, W [4]

Pietist/pietist, *n.* (1697) *Theol.* [G (1674) < L *pietās* piety + G (< L) -*ist* -ist] One who practices Pietism or is devoutly religious; one who is excessively or affectedly religious. —**Pietist,** *a.* (1705); **pietistic(al)** (1830, 1800); **pietistically** (1884). O, R, W [4]

piezocrystallization, *n.* (1903) *Geol.* [G *Piezokristallisation* (1895) *piezo-* + *Kristallisation* < Gk *piézein* to press, compress + L *crystallus* < Gk *krýstallos* ice, rock-crystal + G (< L) nom. suffix of action or process -*isation* -ization] A crystallization of a magma, usu. distinctively or abnormally, under pressure caused by orogenic forces. O, W [3]

piezoelectricity, *n.* (1883) *Physics* [G *Piezoelectricität* (1881) (now *Piezoelektrizität*) < *piezo-* + *Electricität* < Gk *piézein* to press, compress + G *Electricität* electricity] Electric polarization caused by pressure, esp. in a crystalline substance. —**piezoelectric(al)** (1883, 1937), **piezoelectrically** (1923), **piezoelectric oscillator.** O, R, W [4]

piezomagnetism, *n.* (1901) *Physics* [G *Piezomagnetismus* (1901) < *piezo-* + *Magnetismus* < Gk *piézein* to press, compress + *líthos magnḗtēs* lit., magnet stone, actually stone from Magnesia, ancient city in Asia Minor + G (< L) -*ismus* -ism] Magnetism induced in a crystal by applying geological stress. —**piezomagnetic** (1901). O [3]

pilger, *a.* (1902) *Metall.* [G < OHG *piligrīm* < Church L *pelegrīnus* pilgrim, irreg. < L *peregrīnus* stranger, as in G *Pilger-Schrittwalzverfahren* a rolling-mill process resembling the steps of pilgrims approaching a shrine] Of a rolling mill that reduces the outside diameter of a tube without changing the tube's inside diameter. —**pilger,** *v.* (1945); **pilgering,** *verbal n.* (1902); **pilgered** (1945). O [3]

pilsenite, *n.* (1868) *Mineral.* [G *Pilsenit* < the name of Deutsch-*Pilsen* (now Plzeň, Czechoslovakia), where it was found + G -*it* -ite] An old synonym for the alloy wehrlite. O [3]

Pilsner, *n.* (1877) *Beverages* Var. **pilsner, Pilsner** (1890) [G *Pils(e)ner (Bier)* < *Pilsen,* Czech *Plzeň,* a city in Czechoslovakia where the beer was first brewed + G -*er* -er (+ *Bier* beer)] A light lager beer with a strong hop flavor. —**Pilsner glass** (1966). O, R, W [4]

pinacolin, *n.* (1866) *Chem.* Var. **pinacoline** (1913) [G *Pinakolin* (1860) < *pinak-* + *Olin* < Gk *pínax* (gen. *pínakos*) tablet + L *oleum* oil + G -*in* -in(e)] Pinacolone, a liquid ketone. —**pinacolic** (1875) O, W [3]

pinacone, *n.* (1866) *Chem.* [G *Pinakon* (1859) < *pinak-* (< Gk *pínax,* gen. *pínakos* tablet) + G -*on* -one] Pinacol, a liquid glycol. O, W [3]

pinakiolite, *n.* (1890) *Mineral.* [G *Pinakiolit* (1890) < *pinakio-* + -*lith* < Gk *pinákion* small tablet < *pínax* (gen. *pínakos*) tablet + *líthos* stone] Borate of manganese and magnesium. O, W [3]

pinene, *n.* (1885) *Chem.* [G *Pinen* (1885) < L *pīnus* pine + G -*en* -ene] An isomeric liquid terpene hydrocarbon found in turpentine oils. O, R, W [4]

pinite, *n.* (1805) *Mineral.* [G *Pinit* (1800) < the name of the *Pini* mine in Schneeberg, Saxony, Germany + -*it* -ite] A micalike, hydrous silicate of aluminum and potassium. O, R, W [4]

pinnoite, *n.* (1885) *Mineral.* [G *Pinnoit* (1884) < Hermann *Pinno* (1829?–1902), the name of a German mining official of Halle + -*it* -ite] Magnesium metaborate, usu. occurring in yellow nodular masses or tetragonal crystals. O, W [3]

pinochle, *n.* (1864) *Games* Var. **penuchle** (1864), **pinocle** (1894), **penuckle** [Poss. ad. of (Swiss) G *Binokel* < Fr *binocle* < L *bīnī* two each, double + *oculus* eye] A game of cards for two or more players; the meld of the queen of spades and jack of diamonds. —**pinochle rummy.** O, R, W [4]

pinosylvin(e), *n.* (1939) *Biol., Bot.* [G *Pinosylvin* (1939) < NL *Pinus sylvestris* + G -*in* -ine] A toxic, phenolic compound obtained from the heartwood of Scotch pine; a related antifungal compound found in pines. O, W [3]

pinscher, *see* Doberman pinscher

Pinzgau/Pinzgauer, *n.* *Zool.* [G *Pinzgau(er)* < *Pinzgau,* the name of a valley in Austria, where such horses are bred + -*er* -er] A Pinzgau horse; this Austrian breed of heavy draft horses. W [3]

piotine, *n.* *Mineral.* [G *Piotin* < Gk *piótēs* fattiness + G -*in* -ine] Saponite, a hydrous magnesium aluminosilicate. W [3]

piperazine, *n.* (1888) *Chem.* Var. **piperazidine** (1891) [G *Piperazin* (1887) < *Piperidin* < L *piper* pepper (+ -*di*- infix) + *ázōós* inert + G -*in* -ine] A crystalline, heterocyclic base that is used as an insecticide or in veterinary medicine; a derivative of this compound. O, W [4]

piperonal, *n.* (1869) *Chem.* Var. **piperonyl** [G (1869) < *Piperin* (< L *piper* pepper + G -*on*-, as in *Argon* argon) + -*al* (< G *Aldehyd* aldehyde) -al] Heliotropin, a crystalline aldehyde. —**piperonyl alcohol** (1871)/**butoxide** (1923)/**cyclonene.** O, R, W [4]

pirol, *n. Ornith.* [G < MHG *piro* (of imitative origin) golden oriole] Golden oriole. W [3]

pisanite, *n.* (1861) *Mineral.* [G *Pisanit* (1860) < the name of Félix *Pisani* (1831–1920), French chemist + G *-it* -ite] A hydrous iron sulfate containing copper. O, W [3]

pistacite, *n.* (1828–32) *Mineral.* [G *Pistazit* (1803) < L *pistacium* < Gk *pistákē* pistacia + G *-it* -ite] Epidote, a silicate of calcium, iron, and aluminum. O, W [3]

pitchblende, *n.* (1770) *Mineral.* [Partial transl. of G *Pech-blende* < *Pech* pitch + *Blende* blende (q.v.)] A massive, impure uranite. O, R, W [4]

pitchstone, *n.* (1784) *Geol.* [Transl. of G *Pechstein* (1780) < G *Pech* pitch + *Stein* stone] Volcanic glass resembling obsidian. O, R, W [4]

pithecanthropus, *n.* (1876) *Anthrop.* Var. **pithecanthrope** (1883) [G (1868) (< NL) < Gk *píthēkos* ape + *ánthrōpos* man, so named by Ernst Haeckel (1834–1919), German zoologist] The ape-man, establishing a hypothetical link between anthropoid apes and humans (this is a different meaning from Dubois's later "fossil hominid"). O, R, W [4]

pittacal, *n.* (1835) *Chem.* Var. **pitacall** (1838) [G (1835) < *pitta-* + *-cal* < Gk *pítta* pitch + *kalós* beautiful] A dark-blue, odorless, tasteless substance derived from wood tar. O [3]

pitticite, *n.* (1826) *Mineral.* [G *Pittizit* (1813) < Gk *pítta* pitch + G *-it* -ite] A massive, hydrous ferric arsenate and sulfate. O, W [3]

placode, *n.* (1909) *Biol.* [G *Plakode* (1894) < Gk *plakṓdēs* cakelike, flat] A localized thickening of a vertebrate's embryonic ectoderm that contributes to the formation of a sensory organ or ganglia. O, R, W [3]

placodine, *n.* (1856) *Mineral.* Var. **placodite** (1886) [G *Plakodin* (1841) < Gk *plakṓdēs* basically, flat + G *-in* -ine] An arsenide of nickel. O [3]

plagioclase, *n.* (1868) *Mineral.* [G *Plagioklas* (1847) < *plagio-* + *-klas* < Gk *plágios* oblique + *klásis* fracture] One of a group of triclinic feldspars. —**plagioclastic** (1869), **plagioclase feldspars.** O, R, W [4]

plagionite, *n.* (1835) *Mineral.* [G *Plagionit* (1833) < Gk *plágion* (neuter of *plágios*) oblique + G *-it* -ite] A sulfide found in lead and antimony veins. O, W [3]

plagiotropic, *a.* (1882) *Bot.* Var. **plagiotropous** (1900) [G *plagiotropisch* (c.1879) < *plagio-* + *tropisch* < Gk *plágios* oblique + *trópos* turning, direction + G adj. suffix *-isch* -ic] Relating to or exhibiting a mode of botanical growth more or less inclined away from the vertical axis. —**plagiotropically.** O, R, W [3]

plagiotropism, *n.* (1886) *Bot.* [G *Plagiotropismus* < *plagio-* + *Tropismus* < Gk *plágios* oblique + *trópos* turning, direction + G (< L) *-ismus* -ism] The state or tendency of being inclined away from the vertical axis. O, R, W [4]

plagiotropous, *see* plagiotropic

Planck's constant, *n.* (1910) *Physics* Var. **Planck constant** (1940) [Ad. of G *Planck-Konstante* < the name of Max Planck (see *Planck('s) radiation law*) + *Konstante* constant < L *cōnstānt-, cōnstāns*] The constant *h* in Planck's radiation law, which relates the energy of a quantum of electromagnetic radiation to its frequency. • ~ is symbolized as **h** (1901). O, R, W [4]

Planck('s) radiation law, *n.* (1905) *Physics* Var. **Planck's formula** (1905), **Planck('s) law** (1905, 1974), **Planck('s) radiation formula** (1911, 1974), **Planck('s) equation** (1966, 1911) [Transl. of G *Planck-Strahlungsgesetz* (c.1900) < the name of Max Karl Ernst Ludwig *Planck* (1858–1947), German physicist + *Strahlung* radiation + *Gesetz* law] A law expressing the energy density of radiation, or the emission of radiant energy. O, R, W [3]

planctonic, *see* planktonic

plank buttress, *n.* (1903) *Bot.* [Transl. of G *Plankengerüst* (1898) < *Planke* plank (< L *planca*) + G *Gerüst* scaffolding, framework] Buttress root, plank-like roots supporting the base of a tropical tree. O, W [3]

planktology, *n.* (1893) *Biol.* [G *Planktologie* (1891) < *plankto-* + *-logie* < Gk *planktón* wandering, drifting + *-logia* study] The study of plankton. —**planktologist** (1896), **planktological** (1926). O [3]

plankton, *n.* (1891) *Biol.* [G (1887) < Gk *planktón* (neut. of *planktós*) wandering, drifting] Collectively, the various suspended organisms floating or drifting at the mercy of winds, current, and tide. —**planktonology** (1896), **-tont** (1897), **-totrophic** (1946), **totrophy** (1973), **plankton indicator/recorder/net/feeder** (1925, 1926, 1952, 1956). O, R, W [4]

planktonic, *a.* (1893) *Biol.* Var. **planctonic** [G *planktonisch* (1891) < *Plankton* plankton (q.v.) + *-isch* -ic] Of, relating to, or characterizing plankton. O, R, W [4]

plappert, *see* blaffert

-plasm, *comb. form Biol.* Var. **-plasma** [G *Plasma* < Gk *plásma* structure, form] Denoting formative or formed material, as in *bioplasm* and *neoplasm.* R, W [4]

plasma, *n.* (1772) *Mineral.* [G < LL < Gk *plásma* (formed) product] A green, faintly translucent variety of quartz, anciently used for ornaments (this is different from the old medical meaning borrowed < LL *plasma*). — **plasma,** *a.* (1800); **plasma physics** (1958)/**torch** (1959). O, R, W [3]

plasmablast, *see* plasmoblast

plasma cell, *n.* (1888) *Biol.* Var. **plasma-cell** (1888) [G *Plasmazelle* (1875) < *Plasma* (< Gk formation) + G *Zelle* cell < L *cella*] A cell that is a major source of antibodies developed from a lymphocyte; also called *plasmacyte.*—**plasma-celled** (1929), **plasmacellular** (1957). O, R, W [4]

plasmacytoma, *n.* (1907) *Path.* [G *Plasmazytom* (1907) < *Plasma* + *Zytom* < Gk *plásma* formation, structure + *kýtos* hollow, (now) cell + *-om* (< Gk *-ōma*) -oma, denoting swelling, tumor] A myeloma mainly composed of plasma cells. O [3]

plasmal, *n.* (1925) *Biochem.* [G (1924) < *Plasma* (< Gk) formation + G *-al* -al] An aldehyde formed by hydrolyzing a plasmalogen (q.v.). —**plasmal reaction** (1925). O, W [3]

plasmalogen, *n.* (1925) *Biochem.* [G (1924) < the comb. form of *Plasmal* plasmal (q.v.) + infixed *-o-* + *-gen* < Gk *gennân* to create, generate] A phosphatide that precedes the development of plasmal in tissue. —**plasmalogenic** (1939). O, R, W [3]

plasmoblast, *n.* (1942) *Biol.* Var. **plasmablast** (1973) [G (1940) < *plasmo-* + *-blast* < the comb. form of Gk *plásma* formation + *blastós* bud] An immature plasma cell. —**plasmoblastic** (1970). O [3]

Plasmochin/plasmoquin(e), *n.* (1926) *Pharm.* [G *Plasmo-chin,* a proprietary name < G (< NL) *Plasmodium* < G *Plasma* (< Gk) structure + *-oeidēs* similar + G *Chin-,* as in *Chinosol* chinosol (q.v.)] A trademark for pamaquine, an antimalarial medicine. O, W [3]

plasmodesma, -ta/-s *pl.* (1905) *Botany* Var. **plasmodesmen** (1905), **plasmodesm** (1925), **plasmodesmus** [G (1901) < *plasmo-* + *Desma* < the comb. form of Gk *plásma* formation + *désma* tendon, bond] A protoplasmic connection between cells. —**plasmodesma(ta)l** (1961). O, R, W [4]

plasmogamy, *n.* (1912) *Biol.* [G *Plasmogamie* < *plasmo-* + *-gamy* < the comb. form of Gk *plásma* formation + *gámos* wedding + *-ia*] The fusion of the protoplasts of cells. O, R, W [3]

plasmogony, *n.* (1876) *Biol.* [G *Plasmogonie* < *plasmo-* + *-gonie* < the comb. form of Gk *plásma* formation + *gónos* birth + *-ia*] Plasmogamy (q.v.); abiogenesis. O, W [3]

plasmolyte, *n.* (1927) *Physiol.* [Prob. ad. of G *Plasmoly-tikum* plasmolyticum (q.v.)] Plasmolyticum. O [3]

plasmolyticum, *n.* (1943) *Physiol.* [G *Plasmolytikum* < LL < G *Plasma* (< Gk) form, structure + *lytikós* dissolving] A substance that produces plasmolysis. O [3]

plasmon, *n.* (1932) *Biol.* [G < *Plasma* plasma (q.v.) + *-on* -on] The total cytoplasmic factors considered as a system of hereditary determinants. O, W [3]

plasmoquin, *see* Plasmochin

plasmotomy, *n.* (1902) *Biol.* [Prob. < G *Plasmotomie* (1898) < *plasmo-* + *-tomie* < Gk *plásma* formation, structure + *tomé* cutting, dividing + *-ia*] A protozoan reproduction into two or more multinucleate daughter cells. —**plasmotomic** (1949). O, W [3]

plasome, *n.* (1895) *Biol.* [G *Plasom,* a short. of *Plasma-tosom* < *plasmato-* + *-som* < Gk *plásmatos* (gen. of *plásma* formation, structure) + *-ōma* -ome, denoting swelling, tumor] An old term for a biophore, a hypothetical primary constituent unit of living structures. O, W [3]

plasson, *n.* (1879) *Biol.* [G < Gk < *plássein* to form, shape] The undifferentiated protoplasm of hypothetical primitive organisms. • ~ appears humorously as plassonity (1882). O [3]

plastein, *n. Biol.* [Prob. < G < *plast-* (< Gk *plastós* molded) + G *-ein* -ein, as in *Kasein* caseine] A substance resembling protein. W [3]

plastid, *n.* (1876) *Biol.* Var. **plastide** [G *Plastid* < *plast-* (< Gk *plastós* formed, shaped) + G *-ide* -id] A small membrane-limited component of the cytoplasm of plant cells, usu. enclosing pigment, such as chlorophyll, in a chloroplast. —**plastid,** *a.* (1890); **plastidogenetic** (1899). O, R, W [4]

plastidule, *n.* (1877) *Biol.* [G *Plastidul* < *Plastid* plastid + dim. suffix *-ul* (< L) -ule] A hypothetical, minute granule of protoplasm; a plastid's structural subunit. —**plasti-dule,** *a.* (1878); **plastidulic** (1878); **plastidular.** O, W [3]

plastin, *n.* (1889) *Biol.* [Prob. < G < *plast-* (< Gk *plastós* molded) + G *-in* -in] An acidophilic constituent of protoplasm; the substance of the true nucleolus. O, W [3]

plastochron, *n.* (1929) *Bot.* Var. **plastochrone** (1938) [G (1878) < *plasto-* + *-chron* < Gk *plastós* formed + *chrónos* time] The unit of time between successive formations of leaf primordia or of pairs of such primordia in a plant's growing stem-apex. —**plastochron ratio/index** (1948, 1955), **plastochronic** (1953). O, W [3]

plastome, *n.* (1954) *Biol.* Var. **plastom** (1954) [G *Plastom,* a blending of *Plastid* plastid (q.v.) + *Genom* genome (q.v.)] The total genetic factors or information in a cell's plastids. O [3]

platelet, *n.* (1895) *Biol.* [Transl. of G *(Blut)plättchen* < *Blut* blood + *Plättchen* platelet < *Platte* plate] Blood platelet, a minute, protoplasmic disk in vertebrates' blood. —**platelet count** (1909). O, R, W [4]

platinum blue, *n.* (1908) *Chem.* Var. **platinum-blue** (1908) [Transl. of G *Platinblau* (1908) < *Platin* platinum + *blau* blue] One of a class of dark blue polymeric complexes, formed by divalent platinum with amide ligands, which may react against tumors. O [3]

Plattdeutsch, -es *pl.* (1814) *Ling.* [G (1699) (< D *Plat-duitsch*) < G *platt* flat, low (with reference to the topography of northern Germany) + *Deutsch* German] Low German (q.v.), a collective name for the various non-High German dialects. —**Plattdeutsch,** *a.* (1942). • ~ is short. to **Platt** (1814). O, R, W [4]

plattnerite, *n.* (1849) *Mineral.* [G *Plattnerit* (1845) < the name of Karl Friedrich *Plattner* (1800–58), German metallurgist + *-it* -ite] Native lead dioxide, usu. found in iron-black concretions. O, W [3]

pleasure-pain, *n.* (1894) *Psych.* [Transl. of G *Lust-Unlust* < *Lust* pleasure, joy + *Unlust* disinclination (the opposite of *Lust*), pain] Pleasantness–unpleasantness, where there is a continuum between the two as opposite poles with regard to human motivations. —**pleasure pain,** *a.* (1897). O, W [3]

pleasure principle, *n.* (1912) *Psych.* [Transl. of G *Lust-prinzip* < *Lust* pleasure + *Prinzip* principle < L *prīnci-pium*] A tendency for a person's behavior to be directed toward immediately satisfying instinctual drives and avoiding pain or discomfort. O, R, W [4]

pleiotropy, *n.* (1939) *Biol.* [G *pleiotrop* (1910) < *pleio-* + *-trop* < Gk *pleíōn* much, strong + *tropé* turning + E *-y*] A single gene's production of multiple phenotypic effects. O, R, W [4]

pleoptics, *n.* (1955) *Optics* [G *Pleoptik* (1953) < Gk *pleíōn* plenty, strong + G *Optik* < Gk *optikós* concerning vision] A method of treating amblyopia and eccentric fixation so as to make the fovea more sensitive. —**pleoptic** (1960). O, R [3]

plerome, *n.* (1875) *Bot.* Var. **plerom** [G *Plerom* (1868) < LL *pleroma* (< Gk) that which fills] The part of the apical meristem of a plant's root or stem that gives rise to the vascular tissue and pith; the stelar region in a root tip. —**plerome,** *a.* (1882). O, W [3]

Plexiglas, *n.* (1935) *Tech.* Var. **Plexiglass** (1935), **plexiglass** (1943) [G (1935), a proprietary name < *plexi-* (< L *plexus* woven) + G *Glas* glass] A trademark for a substance made from artificial resins and widely used as a plastic or acrylic resin. —**plexiglass,** *a.* (1951). O, R, W [4]

Pliensbachian, *n.* (1903) *Geol.* [G *Pliensbachien* (1858) < *Pliensbach,* the name of a town in Baden-Württenberg + *-ien* -ian] The stage of Lower Jurassic in Europe that includes the Middle Lias and part of the Lower Lias. —**Pliensbachian,** *a.* (1955). O [3]

plomb, *n.* (1904) *Med.* Var. **plombe** (1904) [G *Plombe*

(1813) filling] An inert body such as a plastic ball inserted into the chest cavity in treating pulmonary tuberculosis. O, R [3]

plumboniobite, *n. Mineral.* [G *Plumboniobit* < *plumbo-* (< L *plumbum* lead) + G *Niobit* niobite (q.v.)] A complex niobite resembling samarskite but containing lead. W [3]

plumosite, *n.* (1864) *Mineral.* [G *Plumosit* (1845) < L *plūmōsus* feathery + G *-it* -ite] Jamesonite, or feather ore. O [3]

plunder, *v.* (1632) *Mil.* [G *plündern* to plunder, take or appropriate by force] To take goods or valuables wrongly or by open force; to embezzle or commit depredations; to take plunder or pillage; to extensively use someone else's writings without acknowledgment. —**plunder,** *n.* (1643); **plundering,** *verbal n.* (1642), *a.* (1649); **plundered** (1663). • ~ appears in numerous other derivatives like **-er** (1647), **-age** (1796), **-able** (1802), **-less** (1808), **-ess** (1835), **-ous** (1845), **-ingly**. O, R, W [4]

plunderbund, *n.* (1914) *Sociol.* [An orig. colloq. U.S. compound < E to *plunder* + G *Bund* alliance, league] A league of financial, political, and commercial interests that exploit the public. O, W [3]

pluripotency, *n.* (1927) *Biol.* [G *Pluripotenz* < *pluri-* + *Potenz* < L *plūres* several + *potentia* ability] Pluripotentiality, an organism's ability to affect more than one tissue or organ. O [3]

pluton, *n.* (1933) *Geol.* [Prob. back-formation of G *plutonisch* (1928) < Gk *Ploúton* Pluto, the name of the god of the underworld + G *-isch* -ic] An intrusive body of igneous rock, esp. a deep-seated, large body. O, R, W [3]

plutonite, *n. Geol.* [G *Plutonit* < Gk *Ploúton* Pluto, the name of the god of the underworld + G *-it* -ite] A deep-seated rock. W [3]

pneumatolysis, *n.* (1896) *Geol.* [G *Pneumatolyse* (1851) < *pneumato-* + *-lyse* (< NL) < Gk *pneumato-*, the comb. form of *pneûma* air, wind, breath + *lýsis* dissolution] The chemical process of altering rock and forming minerals by metaphoric action. O, R, W [4]

pneumatolytic, *a.* (1896) *Geol.* Var. **pneumatolitic** [G *pneumatolytisch* (1851) < *pneumato-* + *-lytisch* < Gk *pneumato-*, the comb. form of *pneûma* air, wind, breath + *lytikós* able to dissolve + G *-isch* -ic] Involving or formed by hot vapors or superheated liquids under pressure. —**pneumatolytically** (1962). O, R, W [4]

pneumoconiosis/pneumokoniosis, -noses *pl.* (1881) *Med.* Var. **pneumonokoniosis** (1881), **pneumonoconiosis** (1898) [G *Pneumonokoniosis* (1866) < *pneumono-* + *Koniosis* < Gk *pneumono-*, the comb. form of *pneúmōn, pneúmonos* lung + *kónis* dust + *-osis* fem. suffix of action] A lung disease caused by the habitual inhalation of dust and other irritants. O, R, W [4]

pneumotachogram, *n.* (1926) *Physiol.* [G *Pneumotachogramm* (1925) < *pneumo-* + *Tachogramm* < Gk *pneumo-*, the comb. form of *pneûma* air, breath + *táchos* speed + *grámma* record] A record produced by a pneumotachograph (q.v.). O, W [3]

pneumotachograph, *n.* (1926) *Physiol.* [G (1925) < *pneumo-* + *Tachograph*, ult. < Gk *pneûma* breath, air, wind + *táchos* speed + *gráphein* to write, record] An instrument for measuring the rate of air flow during breathing. —**pneumotachographic** (1928), **-graphy** (1930). • ~ is short. to **pneumotach** (1975). O, W [3]

Pockels effect, *n.* (1957) *Physics* [G *Pockels-Effekt* (1894) < the name of Friedrich Carl Alwin *Pockels* (1865–1913), German physicist + *Effekt* effect < L *effectus*] A linear electrooptical effect on crystalline materials similar to the Kerr effect in liquids. O [3]

podolite, *n. Mineral.* [G *Podolit* < *Podolia*, the name of a region in the Ukraine + G *-it* -ite] A carbonate-apatite. W [3]

Poggendorff illusion, *n.* (1898) *Psych.* [Transl. of G *Poggendorff-Täuschung* (1860) < the name of Johann Christian *Poggendorf* (1796–1877), German physicist + *Täuschung* deception] An optical illusion where an actually straight line whose central portion is interrupted by two parallel lines seems to be deflected. O, W [3]

poikiloblastic, *a.* (1920) *Geol.* Old var. **poeciloblastic** (1932) [G *poikiloblastisch* (1903) < *poikilo-* + *-blastisch* < Gk *poikilós* varied + *blastós* bud + G *-isch* -ic] Of the texture or structure of a metamorphic rock containing small idioblasts; of a nucleated poikilocyte. —**poikoblast,** *n.* (1969). O, R, W [3]

poikiloderma, *n.* (1917) *Path.* [G *Poikilodermia* (1907) (< NL) < Gk *poikilós* varied + *dérma* skin] An atrophic skin condition characterized by reticular pigmentation. —**poikilodermatous** (1936). O [3]

poikilosmotic, *a.* (1905) *Physiol.* Var. **poikilo-osmotic** (1953) [G *poikilosmotisch* (1902) < *poikil-* + *osmotisch* < Gk *poikilós* varied + *ōsmotikós* pressing, shoving + G *-isch* -ic] Of an animal whose body fluids vary osmotically with fluctuations in the surrounding medium. —**poikilosmoticity** (1935), **poikilosmosis** (1939). O, W [3]

poikilotherm, *n.* (1920) *Physiol.* [G < *poikilo-* + *-therm* < Gk *poikilós* varied + *thermós* warm] A usu. cold-blooded organism, such as a frog, with variable body temperature. O, W [4]

poikilothermic, *a.* (1884) *Biol.* Var. **poikilothermal** (1885), **poikilothermous** (1933) [G *pökilotherm* (1847) (now *Poikilotherm*) < *poikilo-* + *-therm* < Gk *poikilós* varied + *thermós* warm + E *-ic*] Cold-blooded: with a body temperature that varies with the temperature of the environment. O, R, W [4]

point group, *n.* (1895) *Math., Crystall.* [Transl. of G *Punktgruppe* (1873) < *Punkt* point (< L *punctum*) + G *Gruppe* group] A mathematical set of points; a class of crystals determined by combining their symmetry elements. O, R [3]

pokal, *n.* (1868) *Beverages* [G (1572) < It *boccale* < LL *baucalis* < Gk *baúkalis* narrow-necked vessel] A large, usu. covered, German tankard of glass or silver. O, R, W [3]

poker, *n.* (1836) *Games* [Poss. ad. of G *Pocher* poker (see Paul and Betz's and Cassell's dictionaries) (or ad. of Fr *poque* a card game similar to poker)] A card game in which the players bet on holding the highest recognized combination of cards. • ~ appears in numerous compounds related to gambling, as in **poker dice** (1874)/**chip** (1879)/**face** (1919)/**-faced** (1923)/**game** (1932), and **strip poker**. O, R, W [4]

Polabish, *n.* (1877) *Ling.* Var. **Polabisch** (1955) [G *Polabisch* being Polabian < *Polab* (< Pol *po* on + *Labe* Elbe)

+ G adj. suffix *-isch* -ish] The extinct West Slavic language of the Polabians, who lived along the lower Elbe. O, W [3]

Pole, *n.* (1533) *Politics* Old var. like **Poole** [G a native or inhabitant of Poland < MHG *Polan* < Pol *Poljane, lit.*, field dwellers < *pole* field] A native or inhabitant of Poland; someone of Polish descent. —**Poless** (1828). O, R, W [4]

pole cell, *n.* (1893) *Zool.* [Ad. of G *Polzelle* (1863) < *Pol* pole + *Zelle* cell < L *cella*] A cleavage cell of various embryonic insects and some other invertebrates that ult. gives rise to the germ cells. O, W [3]

pole figure, *n.* (1943) *Metall.* [G *Polfigur* (1924) < *Pol* pole + *Figur* figure < L *pālus* stake + *figūra*] A circular, stereographic projection of a sphere showing the pole positions of one or more lattice planes of a crystalline substance or a crystal. O [3]

polianite, *n.* (1849) *Mineral.* [G *Polianit* (1844), irreg. < Gk *poliaínesthai* < *polía* grayness + G *-it* -ite, with an *-n-* infix] A variety of pyrolusite in well-formed crystals. O, R, W [3]

policlinic, *n.* (1827) *Med.* [G *Poliklinik* < *poli-* city + *Klinik* clinic < Gk *pólis* + *klinikē*] Orig., a clinic in a private house administered by advanced medical students; a dispensary or department of a hospital where outpatients are treated. O, R, W [3]

polioencephalitis, *n.* (1885) *Med.* Old var. **poliencephalitis** (1885) [Poss. < G *Polioënzephalitis* (1881) (< NL) < Gk *poliós* gray + *enképhalon* brain + G (< L) *-itis* -itis, suffix denoting inflammation] Inflammatory disease of the spinal cord and the gray matter of the brain. O, R, W [3]

polje, -s or **polja** *pl.* (1894) *Geogr.* [Serbo-Croatian *polje* or G *Polje* (< Serbo-Croatian) field] An extension depression in a karstic region, esp. in Yugoslavia. O, W [4]

pollux, -es *pl.* (1847) *Mineral.* [G < L *Pollūx*, the name of one of the Dioscuri, twin heroes or demigods of Greek mythology (the other was Castor), so named for its appearance with castorite (q.v.)]. Pollucite, an old synonym for a zeolite mineral. O, W [3]

polster, *n. Bot.* [G cushion] A cushion plant, which grows in a dense cushiony tuft to retain moisture. W [3]

poltergeist, *n.* (1848) *Myth.* [G < *Polter* noise < *poltern* (echoic) to create a dull noise + *Geist* spirit, ghost] A noisy, usu. mischievous ghost; a spirit that makes mysterious noises. —**poltergeist,** *a.* (1927); **-geistism** (1952); **-geistic** (1973). O, R, W [4]

polyaddition, *a.* (1948) *Chem.* [G (1947) < *poly-* + *Addition* < Gk *polýs* much + L *additio* addition] Of an addition reaction between two compounds that yields a polymeric product. —**polyaddition,** *n.* (1973). O [3]

polyargyrite, *n.* (1872) *Mineral.* [G *Polyargyrit* (1869) < *poly-* + *Argyrit* < Gk *polýs* much + *árgyros* silver + G *-it* -ite] A sulfide of antimony and silver. O, W [3]

polybasite, *n.* (1830) *Mineral.* [G *Polybasit* (1829) < *poly-* + *Basit* < Gk *polýs* much + *básis* basis + G *-it* -ite] Antimony silver sulfide, of iron-black color. O, R, W [4]

polyblast, *n.* (1904) *Biol.* [G (1902) < *poly-* + *-blast* < Gk *polýs* much + *blastós* bud] A wandering tissue macrophage. —**polyblastic** (1904). O, W [3]

polychromatophil(e), *a.* (1897) *Path.* Var. **polychromato-**

philic (1897) [G *Polychromatophil* (1890) < Gk *polychrōmatos* multicolored + *phílos* loving] Staining with both basic and acid dyes. —**polychromatophil(e),** *n.* O, R, W [4]

polychrome, *n.* (1801) *Chem.* [G *Polychrom* < *poly-* + *-chrom* < Gk *polýs* many + *chrôma* color] A multicolored object; variegated coloring; esculin. —**polychrome,** *a.* (1837), *v.* (1925); **-chrom(at)ic** (1849, 1839); **-chromed** (1922); **-chrom(at)ism** (1950, 1903). O, R, W [4]

polyclad, *a., n.* (1888, 1888) *Zool.* [G *Polikladie* (1884) < *poly-* + *-kladie* < NL *Polycladidea* < Gk *polýs* much + *kládos* branch + *-ia* (belonging to) the Polycladus genus of tubellarian worms; (of) a flatworm of this genus. O, R, W [3]

polycondensation, *n.* (1936) *Chem.* [G *Polykondensation* (1932) < *Poly-* + *Kondensation* < Gk *polýs* much + L *condēnsātio* condensation] A condensation reaction that produces a compound of high molecular weight; a process using such a reaction. —**polycondensate,** *n.* (1942); **-condensed,** *a.* (1967); **-condense,** *v.* (1968). O, R, W [4]

polycrase, *n.* (1845) *Mineral.* [G *Polykras* (1844) < *Poly-* + *-kras* < Gk *polýs* much + *krâsis* mixture] A black mineral of columbate and yttrium metals. O, W [3]

polycyth(a)emia, *n.* (1857) *Med.* [G *Polycythaemie* (1854) (now *Polyzythämie*) < *poly-* + *-cyt-* + *Haemie* < Gk *polýs* much + *kýtos* hollow, (now) cell + *haîma* blood + *-ia*] A blood condition where there is an abnormal increase in circulating red blood cells. —**polycyth(a)emic** (1906), **polycythemia vera.** O, W [4]

polydisperse, *a.* (1915) *Chem.* [G *polydispers* (1911) < *poly-* + *Dispers* < Gk *polýs* much + L *dispersus* disperse(d)] Characterized by dispersed particles having a range of sizes. —**polydispersity** (1927), **polydispersed** (1941). O, R, W [4]

polydymite, *n.* (1878) *Mineral.* [G *Polydymit* (1876) < *Poly-* + *Dymit* < Gk *polýs* much + *dídymos* twin] A nickel sulfide of metallic luster. O, W [3]

polyenergid, *a.* (1920) *Biol.* [G < *poly-* + *Energid* < Gk *polýs* much, many + Fr *énergie,* LL *energia,* Gk *enérgeia* working strength + G *-id* -id] Comprising several or numerous energids. O, W [3]

polygene, *a. Geol.* Var. **polygenetic** (q.v.) [Prob. < G *polygen* < *poly-* + *-gen* < Gk *polýs* many + *-genēs* generating, generated] Originating or developing in at least two ways or at least two times, such as limestone. W [3]

polygenetic, *a.* (1903) *Geol.* Var. **polygene** [G *polygen* (1897) < *poly-* + *-gen* < Gk *polýs* much + *génesis* origin, on the analogy of word pairs like *antithesis—antithetic* + E *-tic*] Of a volcano's erupting many times, resulting from more than one process (this is different from the old biological meaning). O [3]

polygenic, *a.* (1927) *Biol.* [Fr *polygenique* or G *polygen* (1913) < *poly-* + *-gen* (< Gk *polýs* much + *génos* offspring, type) + E *-ic*] Relating to or controlled by a number of genes (this is different from the old geological meaning). —**polygenic inheritance** (1941), **polygenically** (1943). O, W [3]

polygonboden, *n.* (1924) *Geol.* [G (1879) < *Polygon* (< Gk *polýgōnon* polygon) + G *Boden* ground] Patterned ground characterized by polygonal figures. O [3]

polyhalite, *n.* (1818) *Mineral.* [G *Polyhalit* (1818) < *poly-* + *Halit* < Gk *polýs* much + *háls* salt + G *-it* -ite] A hydrous sulfate of calcium, potassium, and magnesium. O, W [3]

polylithionite, *n.* (1886) *Mineral.* [G *Polylithionit* (1884) < *poly-* + *Lithionit* < Gk *polýs* much + *lítheion* stony + G *-it* -ite] A variety of lepidolite (q.v.). O [3]

polymastia, *n.* (1878) *Med.* Var. **polymasty** (1904) [G *Polymastie* < *poly-* + *Mastie* < Gk *polýs* much, many + *mastós* chest + G *-ie* < Gk *-ia*] The condition of having more than two breasts. —**polymastism** (1886); **polymastic,** *a.* (1891), *n.* (1918). O, W [3]

polymer, *n.* (1866) *Chem.* [Prob. < G (1830) < Gk *polymerés* divisible into or consisting of many parts] Any of numerous natural or synthetic compounds formed by polymerization. —**polymer,** *a.* (1929); **polymer chemist(ry)** (1948, 1950). O, R, W [4]

polymeric, *a.* (1833) *Chem.* [G *polymerisch* (1833) < *poly-mer* (< Gk *polymerés* of many parts) + G *-isch* -ic] Relating to or being any of numerous natural or synthetic compounds. —**polymerically.** O, R, W [4]

polymery, *n.* (1914) *Biol.* [G *Polymerie* (1911) < NL *polymeria* < Gk *polyméreia* the state of having many parts] The polymeric condition when some nonallelic genes can act together to produce a single effect. O, W [3]

polymict, *a.* (1931) *Geol.* [Prob. < G *polymikt* (1898) < *poly-* + *-mikt* < Gk *polýs* much + *miktós* mixed] Polymictic: of a conglomerate containing a great variety of pebbles, including granite, schist, and sediments. —**polymictic** (1935). O [3]

polymolecular, *a.* (1896) *Chem.* [G *polymolekular* (1896) < *poly-* + *molekular* < Gk *polýs* much, many + Fr *moleculaire* < L *mōlēs* mass] Having or pertaining to many molecules, esp. of different sizes; built from more than one molecule. —**polymolecularity** (1938), **polymolecule** (1951). O, W [3]

polynucleotide, *n.* (1911) *Biochem.* [G *Polynucleotid* (1906) (now *Polynukleotid*) < *poly-* (< Gk *polýs* much, many) + G *Nukleotid* nucleotide (q.v.)] A polymeric compound whose molecules are composed of many, usu. large nucleotides. O, R, W [4]

polypeptide, *n.* (1903) *Biochem.* [G *Polypeptid* (1903) < *poly-* + *Peptid* < Gk *polýs* much, many + *peptós* cooked, digested + G *-id* -ide] A polyamide yielding amino acids, but that is molecularly too small to be a protein. —**polypeptidase** (1922), **polypeptide chain** (1935), **polypeptidic.** O, R, W [4]

polyphenol oxidase, *n.* (1913) *Biochem.* Var. **polyphenoloxidase** (1913) [G (1912) < *poly-* (< Gk *polýs* many, much) + *Phenoloxydase* (q.v.)] A copper-containing enzyme that catalyzes oxidation. O, W [3]

polyphyletic, *a.* (1875) *Biol.* [G *polyphletisch* < *poly-* + *phyletisch* < Gk *polýs* much + *phyletikós* phyletic + G *-isch* -ic] Of or belonging to several tribes or families; originating as a species from more than one ancestral line: polygenetic. —**polyphyletically** (1887), **-phylesis** (1897), **-phylet(ic)ism** (1969), **-phylety, -phyletic theory.** O, R, W [4]

polyploid, *a.* (1920) *Biol.* [G (1916) < *poly-* + *-ploid* < Gk *polýs* many, much + *haploidés* simple, onefold] Of or possessing more than two homologous sets of chromosomes in each cell nucleus. —**polyploid,** *n.* (1924); **-ploidizing,** *a.* (1941); **-ploidogen(ic)** (1944); **-ploidize** (1945), **-ploidization** (1974), **-ploidic, -ploid complex/series.** O, R, W [4]

polyploidy, *n.* (1922) *Biol.* [G *Polyploidie* (1910) < *poly-* + *-ploidie* < Gk *polýs* many, much + *haploidés* simple + *-ia*] The condition of being polyploid. O, R, W [4]

polyporic acid, *n.* (1877) *Biochem.* [Transl. of G *Polyporsäure* (1877) < *Polypor* (< L *Fungus Polyporus* < Gk *polýs* many, much + *póros* pore) + G *Säure* acid] A crystalline solid that is a coloring matter found in some fungi and lichens. • ~ is short. to **polyporic,** *a.* O [3]

polysaccharide, *n.* (1892) *Biochem.* Old var. **polysaccharid** [G *Polysaccharid* (1888) < *poly-* + *Saccharid* < Gk *polýs* much, many + *sákcharon,* ult. < Skt *śarkarā* granular sugar + G *-id* -ide] A decomposable carbohydrate made up of molecules composed of monosaccharides or their derivatives bound together: polysaccharose. O, W [4]

polysaprobic, *a.* (1925) *Ecology* [G *polysaprob* (1902) < *poly-* + *saprob* < Gk *polýs* much, many + *saprós* rotten + *bíos* life + E *-ic*] Of, being, or living in an aquatic environment rich in decayed organic matter and little or no oxygen. O, W [3]

polysomatic[1], *a.* (1888) *Geol.* [G *polysomatisch* (1885) < Gk *polysómatos* multigranular + G *-isch* -ic] Composed of at least two grains or two minerals. O [3]

polysomatic[2], *a.* (1937) *Biol.* [G *polysomatisch* (1927) < Gk *polysómatos* multigranular + G *-isch* -ic] Of, relating to, or exhibiting polysomaty (q.v.). O, W [3]

polysomaty, *n.* (1937) *Biol.* [G *Polysomatie* < *poly-* + *-somatie* < Gk *polýs* many + *sóma* (gen. *sómatos*) body + *-ia*] Replication in somatic cells of the chromosome number. O, W [3]

polyterpene, *n.* (1885) *Chem.* [G *Polyterpen* (1885) < *poly-* (< Gk (*polýs* much, many) + a short. of G *Terpentin* turpentine < LL (*resina*) *ter(e)bentina* resin of the terebinth] A polymer of a terpene hydrocarbon such as rubber hydrocarbon or a thermoplastic resin. —**polyterpenoid,** *a.* (1936), *n.* (1964). O, W [3]

polytope, *n.* (1908) *Math.* [G *Polytop* (1882) < *poly-* + *-top* < Gk *polýs* much, many + *tópos* place, area] A geometrical form of more than three dimensions, corresponding to a polygon or a polyhedron in plane or solid geometry, respectively. —**polytopal,** *a.* O [3]

polytrope, *n.* (1926) *Physics* [G (1907) < Gk *polýtropos* adaptable] A polytropic[3] (q.v.) body of gas. O [3]

polytropic[1], *a.* (1838) *Entomology* [Poss. < G *polytrop* < Gk *polýtropos* adaptable + E *-ic*] Versatile; capable of altering course. O [4]

polytropic[2], *a.* (1899) *Bot.* [G *polytropisch* (1884) < Gk *polýtropos* adaptable + G *-isch* -ic] Of insects such as bees gathering nectar from many kinds of flowers. O, W [3]

polytropic[3], *a.* (1907) *Physics* [G *polytropisch* (1887) < Gk *polýtropos* adaptable + G *-isch* -ic] Relating to or specifying a body of gas or a process where volume and pressure change in such a way that the heat remains constant. —**polytropic,** *n.* (1939). O [3]

polytypism, *n.* (1944) *Geol.* [G *Polytipismus* (1915) (now also *Polytypie*) < *poly-* + *Tipismus* < Gk *polýs* much, many + L *typus* < Gk *týpos* type, kind + G *-ismus* (< L) *-ism*] A polymorphism where a substance occurs in several crystalline modifications differing only in one dimension of the unit cell. O [3]

pommer, *n.* (1878) *Music* [G < Late MHG *pumhart* instrument < MFr *bombarde* a wind instrument resembling a shawm played in the 14th cent., prob. < It *bombarda* bombard] Bombardon, a type of shawm. O, W [3]

pompernickel, *see* pumpernickel

ponhaus/ponhaws/ponhoss, *n.* (1869) *Food* Var. **pawnhaus** (1869), **panhas** (1869), **pannhaas, pan(n)haus, ponhass, ponhos** [(PaG) G *Panhas,* Westphalian *pannhass, pannharst,* the latter of which is the LG equivalent of HG *Pfanne* pan + *-harst* roasting meat (see *Der Große Duden*), i.e., a roasted mixture of buckwheat flour with sausage broth and bits of meat] Scrapple. O, W [3]

poodle, *n.* (1820 *W9*) *Zool.* Var. **Poodle** (1858) [Ad. of G *Pudel,* a short. of *Pudelhund* < *pudeln* to splash, puddle + *Hund* dog] An old breed of intelligent, active, thick-haired dogs of uncertain origin, often kept as pets or retrievers; a dog of this breed; a lackey or cat's paw; a wooly cloth or garment of this cloth. —**poodle,** *v.* (1828); **poodle-faker/faking** (1902, 1914); **poodled** (1905); **poodle cut** (1952). O, R, W [4]

poodle dog, *n.* (1820) *Zool.* [Transl. of G *Pudelhund* (see *poodle*)] Poodle, esp. a pet dog that follows its master around, or transf. derogatorily to a person. O, W [3]

popo, *n.* (1972) (U.S. slang) [G (coined in the early 1800s) in children's speech, "behind," a reduplication of G *Podex* (< L) rear, seat] Buttocks, behind. BDC [3]

porcellanite, *n.* (1796) *Mineral.* [G *Porzellanit* (1794) < *Porzellan* porcelain < MFr *porcelaine,* ult. < L *porcellus,* dim. of *porcus* pig, vulva < G *-it* -ite] A dense siliceous rock resembling unglazed porcelain on fresh fractures (this is different from porcelainite). O, W [3]

porogamy, *n.* (1902) *Bot.* [G *Porogamie* < *poro-* + *-gamie* < Gk *póros* passage, opening + *gameîn* to wed + *-ia*] In a seed plant, the pollen tube's entrance through the micropyle for fertilization. —**porogamic** (1905). O, W [3]

porphin, *n.* (1926) *Chem.* Var. **porphine** (1926) [G (1926), a short. of *Porphyrin* porphirine < Gk *pórphyros* crimson, purple + G *-in* -in] A synthetic, purple, crystalline compound consisting of four pyrrole nuclei linked through methylene carbons. O, W [4]

porphobilin, *n.* (1939) *Biochem.* [G (1939) < *porpho-* + *Bilin* < Gk *pórphyros* purple, crimson + L *bīlis* bile + G *-in* -in] One of a group of red-brown pigments produced from porphobilinogen (q. v.). O [3]

porphobilinogen, *n.* (1939) *Biochem.* [G (1939) < *Porphobilin* porphobilin (q.v.) + *-ogen,* a suffix added to names of biologically active compounds to form the names of their inactive precursors < L *genitus* born, created] A dicarboxylic acid derived from pyrrole (q.v.). —**porphobilinogenuria** (1961). O, W [3]

porphyrin, *n.* (1910) *Chem.* [G (1909) or directly into English < Gk *pórphyros* purple, crimson + G *-in* -in] Substituted porphin (q.v.), any of a large class of deep red or purple fluorescent crystalline pigments. —**porphyrinopathy** (1950). O, R, W [4]

porphyrinogen, *n.* (1913) *Biochem.* [G (1913) < *Porphyrin* porphyrin (q.v.) + *-ogen* < L *genitus* born, created] A colorless, reduced derivative of porphyrins where the four pyrrole nuclei are linked by methylene groups. O [3]

porphyrism, *n.* (1923) *Path.* [G *Porphyrismus* (1920) (now *Porphyrie*) < Gk *pórphyros* purple + G (< L) *-ismus* -ism] Porphyria, a varied metabolic disorder characterized by the excretion of abnormally large quantities of porphyrins. O [3]

porphyroblastic, *a.* (1920) *Geol.* [G *porphyroblastisch* (1903) < *porphyro-* + *blastisch* < Gk *pórphyros* purple + *blastós* bud + G *-isch* -ic] Concerning rock textures where larger, recrystallized grains occur in a finer groundmass. —**porphyroblast,** *n.* (1920) O, W [3]

portunal, *n.* (1852) *Music* Var. **portunal-flute** [G < L *Portūnālis* of Portunus, the god of harbors] An organ stop with open wooden pipes that are larger at the top than at the mouth. O [3]

posaune, -n/-s *pl.* (1724) *Music* Old var. **buzain** (1776), **busaun** [G trombone < MHG *busūne, busīne* < OFr *buisine* < L *būcina* hunting horn] A reed stop in a pipe organ imitating a trombone tone; a trombone. O, W [3]

positive logic, *n.* (1943) *Philos.* [G *positive Logik* (1934) < *positiv* + *Logik* < OFr *positif* < L *positīvus* + *logica* < Gk *logikḗ*] Circuit logic that does not operate with negations. O [3]

posit(r)on, *n.* (1933 *W9*) *Physics* [G (1935) < a blending of L *positīvus* stipulated, given, confirming + Gk *élektron*] Positron: a positively charged particle equalling the electron in mass and magnitude of charge. O, W [4]

post, *n.* (1727–41) *Tech.* [G *Posten* < It *posta* < L *posita* (*summa*) fixed sum, amount] A stack of wet sheets of handmade paper interleaved with felt; a charge of ore ready for smelting. O, R, W [3]

postament, *n.* (1738) *Arch.* [G (1645) < obs. It **postamento* < *postare* to post] A pedestal, base, or stereobate; a frame, molding, or mount for a bas-relief. O, W [3]

postreduction, *n.* (1905) *Biol.* [G (1903) (now *Postreduktion*) < *post-* + *Reduction* < L *post* after(wards) + *reductiō* reduction] A chromosomal reduction in the second meiotic cell-division. —**postreductional,** *a.* (1905); **postreductionally** (1950). O, W [3]

potamoplankton, *n.* (1902) *Biol.* [G (1898) < *potamo-* + *Plankton* < Gk *potamós* river + *plánkton* that which drifts about] The plankton in rivers and streams. O, R, W [3]

potential temperature, *n.* (1891) *Physics* [Ad. of G *potentielle Temperatur* (1888) < *potentiell* potential + *Temperatur* temperature < L *potentiālis* + *temperātūra*] The temperature that a body of gas or liquid attains if it is brought adiabatically to a pressure of 1000 millibars. O, W [3]

potentiate, *v.* (1817) *Med.* [Prob. < transl. of G *potenzieren* < *Potenz* (< L *potentia* power) + G verbal suffix *-ieren* -ate] To make powerful or effective, as in writings or medicine; to make possible; to make physiologically more active. —**potientiated,** *a.* (1834); **potentiation** (1840); **potentiating,** *a.* (1941), *n.* (1971); **potentiator** (1955). O, R, W [4]

potentize, *v.* (1857) *Med.* [Transl. of G *potentisieren* < L *potentis-* (< *potentem* powerful) + G verbal suffix *-ieren*

-ize] To make effective or potent; to improve the power of a medicine. —**potentized** (1864). O, W [3]

potzer, *see* patzer

powder-down, *a.* (1861) and *n.* (1894) *Zool.* Var. **powder-down** (1861) [Transl. of G *Puderd(a)unen (pl.)* (1840) < *Puder* powder (< Fr *poudre* < L *pulvis* powder) + G *Dune* down] (Of) some birds' down feathers, the tips of which disintegrate into powder. O, R, W [3]

power politics, *n.* (1929 *W9*) *Politics* Var. **power-politics** (1937) [Transl. of G *Machtpolitik* < *Macht* power + *Politik* politics < Gk *politikế*]] Political action based primarily on or backed by threats to use military force, rather than based on morality. —**powerpolitician, power-politician** (1940), **power-political** (1942). O, R, W [4]

Pr, *see* praseodymium

practical ability/activity, *see* praxis

practice, *see* praxis

practicum, *n.* (1904) *Ed.* [G *Praktikum* < LL *practicus* practical < Gk *praktikế (téchnē)* guide to practical action] A practical unit of work done by an advanced university student, prob. to culminate in theoretical interpretation, as in practice teaching. O, R, W [4]

Prägnanz, *n.* (1925) *Psych.* [Short. of G *Prägnanztendenz* (1923) < *Prägnanz* + *Tendenz* < L *praegnāns* full, pregnant + Fr *tendance* tendency, inclination] The tendency found in gestalt experiments for giving configurations their most concise, clearly defined interpretations. O [3]

pralltriller, *n.* (1841) *Music* [G < *prallen* to spring back + *Triller* trill < It *trillo* (prob. echoic) trill, vibration] A melodic grace produced by rapidly alternating a principal tone with an upper auxiliary tone. O, R, W [4]

Prandtl number, *n.* (1933) *Physics* [Transl. of G *Prandtlsche-Zahl* (now *Prandtl-Zahl*) < the name of Ludwig *Prandtl* (1875–1953), German physicist + *Zahl* number] The ratio of a substance's fluid viscosity to its thermal conductivity used in calculating heat transfer. O, R, W [3]

praseodymium, *n.* (1885) *Chem.* [G *Praseodym* (1885) < NL *praseodidymium* < Gk *prásios* green + *dídymos* twin] A rare-earth metallic element, resembling iron and used in the coloring of glass. • ~ is symbolized as **Pr.** O, R, W [4]

Prater, *n.* (1803) [G < It *prato* meadow] The name of a beautiful, wooded (amusement) park in Vienna. O [3]

praxis, -es and **praxes** *pl.* (1933) *Politics* [G (1838) < ML < Gk *prâxis* doing, acting] Karl Marx's adopted term for the willed action by which a philosophy or theory becomes a social actuality (this is different from the various earlier meanings). —**praxis,** *a.* (1974). • ~ is transl. as **practice** (1933), **practical ability/activity** (1968). O [3]

precision, *n.* (1885) *Math.* [G *Präcision* (1877) (now *Präzision*) < Fr *précision* clarity, precision] The reproducibility or degree of agreement of repeated measurements of a quantity. O, R, W [4]

predazzite, *n.* (1867) *Geol.* [G *Predazzit* (1843) < the name of *Predazzo,* a town in the Tyrol + G *-it* -ite] A rock composed of brucite and calcite. O [3]

predicate, *n.* (1899) *Ed.* [Ad. of G *Prädikat* < L *praedicāre* to preach] In European universities, the judgment pronounced on a student's work in an examination, i.e., *cum laude,* etc. O [3]

predicate calculus, *n.* (1950) *Math., Philos.* [Transl. of G *Prädikatenkalkül* (1928) < *Prädikat* qualifier + *Kalkül* calculus < L *praedicāre* to preach + *calculus*] Functional calculus, a branch of symbolic logic. O, R, W [4]

pregnane, *n.* (1932) *Chem.* [G *Pregnan* (1930) < L *praegnāns* pregnant, so named for its occurrence in pregnancy urine] A synthetic, saturated, steroid hydrocarbon that furnishes progestational and corticoid hormones. O, W [3]

pregnanediol, *n.* (1930) *Biochem.* Var. **pregnandiol** (1930) [G *Pregnandiol* (1930) < L *praegnāns* pregnant + Gk *dís* twofold + G *-ol* (< L *oleum* oil) -ol] A crystalline, degradation product of progesterone, esp. found in pregnancy urine. O, W [3]

pregnenolone, *n.* (1936) *Biochem.* [G *Pregnenolon* (1934) < L *praegnāns* pregnant + G *-ol* (< *Alkohol* alcohol, ult. < Ar) + *-on* -one] A synthetic hydroxy steroid ketone that yields progesterone by dehydrogenation. O, W [3]

prehnite, *n.* (1795) *Mineral.* [G *Prehnit* (1789) < the name of Colonel Hendrik Van *Prehn* (1733–85), Dutch military officer in South Africa + G *-it* -ite] A hydrous silicate of calcium and aluminum. —**prehnitiform** (1843), **prehnitic acid** (1872), **prehnitene.** O, R, W [3]

prereduction, *n.* (1905) *Biol.* [G *Praereduction* (1903) (now also *Präreduktion*) < *prae-* + *Reduction* < L *prae-* before + *reductiō* reduction] Chromosomal reduction in the first meiotic cell division. O, W [3]

presspahn, *n.* (1904) *Tech.* Var. **press-spahn** (1913) [G *Preßspahn* (now also *Preßspan*) < *pressen* to press + *Spahn* wood shaving] Pressboard used in electrical equipment. O [3]

prestabalism, *n. Philos.* [G *Prästabilismus* < *prästabilieren* < L *prae-* pre- + *stabilis* stable + G (< L) *-ismus* -ism] Leibniz's doctrine of preestablished harmony of mind and body; Kant's view of living organisms' initial reproductive tendency implanted by the first cause. W [3]

pretzel, *n.* (c.1824 *W9*) *Food* Old var. **bretzel** (1856) [G *Brezel* or the var. *Pretzel* < MHG *brēzel, prēzel,* ult. < L *bracchiātus,* Gk *brachíōn* (lower, upper) arm (respectively), because its shape suggests entwined arms] A brittle, glazed, salted cracker made of a rope of twisted dough. • ~ appears initially in a few compounds like **pretzelbender** (1936)/**-eater/bakery/sticks.** O, R, W [4]

priamel, -n *pl.* (1950) *Lit.* Var. **Priamel** (1950) [G (1482, according to Grimm), irreg. < *Praeambel* (now *Präambel*) < ML *praeambulum* that which precedes] A kind of epigrammatic verse popular in Germany in the 15th and 16th centuries; a similar form in classical Greek poetry. O [4]

primary, *a.* (1864) *Chem.* [Ad. of G *primär* (1864) primary < LL *primarius*] Characterized by substitution of one or more atoms or groups in a molecule, esp. a carbon atom that is itself bonded to another chain or ring member. O, R, W [4]

primitive, *a.* (1888) *Math.* [G *primitiv* (1888) primitive < L *prīmitīvus*] Characterizing a substitution group whose letters cannot be partitioned into disjoint proper subsets in a way preserved by all letters of the group. —**primitive recursion.** O [3]

primitive recursion, *see* recursion

priorite, *n.* (1907) *Mineral.* [G *Priorit* (1906) < the name of Granville T. *Prior* (1862–1936), English mineralogist

+ G *-it* -ite] Eschynite (q.v.), also called *blomstrandine.* O, W [3]

pristane, *n.* (1923) *Chem.* [G *Pristan* (1923) < L *pristis,* Gk *prístos* shark + G *-an* -ane] A saturated liquid hydrocarbon that occurs in liver oils of various sharks and in ambergris. O, W [3]

privatdocent, -s/-en *pl.* (1881) *Ed.* Var. **privatdozent** [G (1697) (now *Privatdozent*) < *privat* private (i.e., nontenured) + *Docent* lecturer < L *prīvātus* + *docent-, docēns*] A university teacher in German-speaking countries who is remunerated by student fees. O, R, W [4]

prochromosome, *n.* (1906) *Biol.* [G *Prochromosom* (1905) < *pro-* + *Chromosom* < L *pro-* pre- < Gk + *chrõma* (gen. *chrõmatos*) color + *sõma* body] One of the densely staining heterochromatic masses visible in a chromosome's resting nucleus. O, W [3]

prodigiosin, *n.* (1914) *Biochem.* [G (1902) < NL *prodigiosus* splendid, prodigious < L + G *-in* -in] A red crystalline pigment with antibiotic properties that is produced by a bacterium of the genus *Serratia.* O, W [3]

proembryo, *n.* (1849) *Bot.* [G (1843) < *pro-* + *Embryo* < L *pro-* pre- + *embryo* newborn (lamb)] A young embryo; in seed plants, the group of cells developed before formation of the true embryo. —**proembryo,** *a.* (1964); **proembryonic** (1875); **proembryonal.** O, W [3]

professionist, *n.* (1804) *Trades* [G tradesman < *Profession* (< MFr) profession, vocation + G *-ist* (< L *-istus*) -ist] A person pursuing a profession or trade. O, W [3]

profundal, *a.* (1928) *Ecology* [G *profund* profound, basic < L *profundus* deep + E *-al*] Applied to the area of the bed of a thermally stratified lake lying below the thermocline. —**profundal,** *n.* (1961). O, W [3]

progesterone, *n.* (1935) *Physiol.* [G *Progesteron* (1934), a blend of *Progestin* and *Luteosteron* < L *pro-* pre- + *gestātio* gestation, pregnancy + *lūteus* yellow-brown + Gk *stéreos* rigid, firm + G *-on* -one] A female steroid sex hormone secreted by corpus luteum or made synthetically, used chiefly to treat functional uterine bleeding during pregnancy. —**progesterone,** *a.* (1961); **progesteronic.** O, R, W [4]

programma, *n.* (1820) *Ed.* [G *Programm* < L < Gk *prográmma,* orig. a proclamation, manifesto] In German schools, an essay or preface preceding the annual report on the state of the school (this is different from the LL meaning of "public, usu. posted notice"). O [3]

prokinesis, *n.* (1962) *Zool.* [Ad. of G *Prokinetik* < *pro-* + *kinetik* < L *pro-* pre- < Gk + *kínēsis* movement] The capacity of some birds and lizards to raise the upper bill or jaw relative to the cranium by rotating about a hinge anterior to the eyes. O [3]

prolan, *n.* (1931) *Physiol.* [G (1929) < L *prõlēs* offspring, progeny + G *-an* -an] The name orig. given to one female sex hormone but now known to comprise either of the gonadotrophic hormones: prolan A and prolan B. O, W [3]

proline, *n.* (1904) *Biochem.* Old var. **prolin** (1904) [G *Prolin,* a short. of G *Pyrrolidin* < Gk *pyrrhós* fiery + L *oleum* oil + G *-id-* (infix) + *-in* -ine] A heterocyclic amino acid composing many proteins. O, R, W [4]

promorphology, *n.* (1878) *Biol.* [G *Promorphologie* < *pro-* + *Morphologie* < L *pro-* pre- < Gk + *morphē* form + *lógos* word, study + *-ia*] Study of the organization of the egg, esp. the localization of later developed embryonic structures. —**promorphological(ly)** (1883, 1890), **promorphologist** (1883). O, W [3]

pronormoblast, *n.* *Anat.* [Prob. < G (c.1900) < *pro-* + *normo-* + *-blast* pre-stage of a red blood corpuscle with nucleus of the approximate size and maturity of a normal blood corpuscle + L *prō* in place of + the comb. form of *nōrmālis* + Gk *blastós* bud] A cell arising from a myeloblast according to some theories of erythropoiesis, or equivalent to the erythroblast in other theories. W [3]

prontosil, *n.* (1936) *Pharm.* Var. **Prontosil** (1936) [G (1932), a proprietary name based on Sp *pronto* fast, prompt] A sulfonamide medicine: prontosil album/soluble/ rubrum, the first clinically tested sulfa drug and used in treating a wide range of bacterial infections. O, W [4]

proper, *a.* (1916) *Physics* [Transl. of G *eigen* (1908) own, proper, characteristic] Own, proper, characteristic, as applied to a vibration or oscillation. O [3]

proper function, *see* eigenfunction

proper time, *n.* (1916) *Physics* [Transl. of G *Eigenzeit* (1908) < *eigen* proper, own, characteristic + *Zeit* time] Quantities referred to the space–time system of an observer moving with the body being considered, as designated by the term *proper* (G *eigen*), as in *proper time.* O [3]

proper value, *see* eigenvalue

prophase, *n.* (1884) *Biol.* [G (1884) < *pro-* + *Phase* < L *pro-* pre- < Gk + *phásis* appearance] The first stage in mitotic development when chromosomes become visible and split into paired chromatids. —**prophase,** *a.* (1948); **prophasic** (1913). O, R, W [4]

prop root, *n.* (1905 *W9*) *Bot.* [Transl. of G *Stutzwurzel* < *stutzen* to prop, support + *Wurzel* root] A columnar root that supports or props up the plant, as in mangrove; also called *brace root.* R, W [4]

propylene imine, *n.* (1917) *Chem.* Var. **propylenimine** (1917) [Ad. of G *Propylenimin* (1917) < *Propylen* + *Imin* imine (q.v.) < L *pro-,* Gk *pró* in front of, before, in place of + *pîon* fat + *-yl* < *hýlē* substance] A synthetic, odorless, highly flammable liquid that is widely used as a binding agent with adhesives and dyes, and in the manufacture of paper and plastics. O [3]

prosauropod, *n.* (1951) *Paleon.* [G *Prosauropode* (1920) (ad. < NL *Prosauropoda*) < L *pro-* pre- < Gk + the comb. form of *saûros* lizard + *pod-* < *poûs* foot] A bipedal Triassic dinosaur ancestral to the sauropod dinosaurs. —**prosauropod,** *a.* (1965). O, W [3]

proseminary, *n.* (1774) *Ed.* [G *Proseminar* a preparatory seminar or preseminar < *pro-* + *Seminar* < L *pro-* pre- + *sēminārium*] A preparatory seminary or school (this is different from the modern educational term *proseminar*). O [3]

prosit, *interj.* (1846) *Beverages* Var. **prost** [G (1640) < L *prōsit* may it serve, third pers. sing. subj. of *prōdesse* to serve, be of use] (Used to wish) good health, esp. before drinking. O, R, W [4]

prosopagnosia, *n.* (1950) *Med.* [G *Prosopagnosie* (1948) < *prosop-* + *-agnosie* < Gk *prósōpon* face, person + *agnōsía* ignorance] One's inability to recognize a face as that of any particular person. O [3]

prosopite, *n.* (1854) *Mineral.* [G *Prosopit* (1853) < *prosop-* (< Gk *prósōpon* face, mask) + G *-it* -ite, so named for its occurrence as a pseudomorph] A hydrous fluoride of aluminum and calcium. O, W [3]

prost, *see* prosit

prostaglandin, *n.* (1936) *Pharm.* [G (1935) < *prosta-* + *glandin* < Gk *prostátēs* that which stands before or in front + L *glandula* gland + G *-in* -in] An oxygenated, cyclic fatty acid occurring in seminal fluid and male and female mammals' tissues. O, R [4]

protactinium/protoactinium, *n.* (1918) *Chem.* [G *Protactinium* (1918) (now *Protaktinium*) < *prot-* + *Actinium* < Gk *prôtos* first + *aktís* (gen. *actínos*) ray + G *-ium* (< NL) -ium, so named because its principal isotope produces actinium by radioactive decay] A rare radioactive metallic element of relatively short life. • ~ is symbolized as **Pa.** O, R, W [4]

protagon, *n.* (1869) *Biol.* [G < *prot-* + *-agon* < Gk *prôtos* first + *ágon,* neuter present part. of *ágein* to lead] A highly complex, white crystalline substance consisting of lipide mixture obtained from the brain and nerve tissue. O, W [3]

protamine, *n.* (1874) *Biochem.* [G *Protamin* (1874) < *prot-* (< Gk *prôtos* first) + G *Amin* amine] Any of a class of basic proteins that yield basic amino acids by hydrolysis and that are combined with nucleic acid in fish sperm. —**protamine,** *a.* (1935); **protamine sulfate** (1936)/**zinc insulin** (1936). O, R, W [4]

protandrous, *a.* (1870) *Bot.,* (1897) *Zool.* Var. **protandric** (1870) [Ad. of G *protandrisch* (1867) < *prot-* + *-andrisch* < Gk *prôto-,* the comb. form of *prôtos* first + L *-andrus* < Gk *-andros* < *anér* (gen. *andrós*) man + G *-isch* -ic] Having the stamens mature before the pistils or female organs do; of the appearance of male insects earlier in the season than that of their female counterparts. —**protandrism** (1890); **protandry,** *n.* (1892). O, W [4]

protanomal, *n.* (1915) *Optics* [G *Protanomale* (1907) < *prot-* + *Anomale* < Gk *prôtos* first, most important + *anómalos* uneven] A person with a form of anomalous trichromatism. O [3]

protanomaly, *n.* (1938) *Optics* [G *Protanomalie* protanomal (q.v.) + *-ie* (< Gk *-ia*) -y] Trichromatism in which an abnormal proportion of red is required to match the spectrum. O, R, W [3]

protanope, *n.* (1908) *Optics* [G *Protanop* (1897) < NL < Gk *prôtos* first, most important + *an-* un- + *óps* eye] A person with protanopia, a red-green color blindness. O, W [3]

Protargol, *n.* (1898) *Med.* [G (1897) < *Protein* protein (q.v.) + L *argentum* silver + G *-ol* (< *Alkohol* alcohol, ult. < Ar) -ol] A trademark for strong silver protein, used as a mild antiseptic and a stain. O, W [3]

proteid, *n.* (1871 *W9*) and *a.* (1872) *Biochem.* [G *Proteid* proteide (q.v.)] (Of) protein bodies or substances. O, W [3]

proteide, *n.* (1871) *Biochem.* Var. **proteid** (1872) [G *Proteid* < Gk *prōteîos* < *prôtos* first + G *-id* -ide] Any of a huge class of natural, very complex combinations of amino acids. O, W [4]

protein, *n.* (1838) *Biochem.* [G (1838) (or directly < Fr *protéine*), both < Gk *prōteîos* first place + G *-in* or Fr *ine* -in] Any one of a class of organic compounds derived by condensation of alpha-amino acids, consisting of carbon, hydrogen, oxygen, and nitrogen with a little sulfur, in complex and more or less unstable combination. O, R, W [4]

proteinase, *n.* (1929) *Biochem.* [G (1928) < *Protein* protein (q.v.) + *-ase* -ase, denoting an enzyme] An enzyme that hydrolyzes proteins, esp. to peptides: endopeptidase. O, R, W [4]

proteinosis, *n.* (1937) *Path.* [G *Proteinose* (1932), a short. of *Lipoidproteinose* < *Lipoid* + *Proteinose* (< ML *proteinosis*) < Gk *lípos* fat + *prōteîos* first place + G *-ose* (< Gk *-osis* fem. suffix of action) -osis] The abnormal collecting or disposition of protein in tissue. O [3]

protension, *n.* (1931) *Philos.* [G *Protention* (1922) < *pro-* + *Retention* (mental) retention < L *pro-* pre- + *retention-,* *retentiō*] A phenomenological extending of the consciousness of a current act or event into the future. —**protentional,** *a.* (1931). O, W [3]

Protestant, *n.* (1539) *Politics* [G or Fr *Protestant* (1529) < L *prōtēstāns,* pl. *prōtēstāntēs* protestants, dissenters] When plural, a name given to the German princes and cities who dissented from the decision reached at the Diet of Spires, reaffirming the edict of the Diet of Worms in condemning the Reformation. O, R, W [4]

prothetely, -ies *pl.* (1934) *Entomology* [G *Prothetelie* (1903) < Gk *protheîn* to run ahead + *télos* end + G *-ie* (Gk *-ia*) -y] In some insect larvae, the development of one part of the body, esp. the wings, faster than that of the other parts; a generalized sense of relatively precocious differentiation of one structure within the whole. —**prothetelic** (1940). O, W [3]

prothrombin, *n.* (1898) *Physiol.* [G (1892) < *pro-* + *Thrombin* < Gk *pro-* pre- + *thrómbos* lump, blood clot, *thrómbōsis* clotting + G *-in* -in] A protein produced in the liver normally present in blood, whose conversion into thrombin is vital in the clotting process. —**prothrombin time** (1935). O, R, W [4]

protist, -a *pl.* (1889) *Zool., Bot.* [G *Protisten* (1866) (pl. of *Protist*) < NL < Gk *prótista* (neuter pl. of *prótistos*) the very first] A member of a third kingdom of organisms, proposed by Haeckel, which differentiates unicellular and acellular organisms from multicellular plants and animals. O, R, W [4]

protista, *see* protist

protoactinium, *see* protactinium

protoblast, *n.* *Anat.* [Prob. < G < *proto-* + *-blast* < Gk *prôtos* first + *blastós* bud] The naked cell without a wall; a blastomere of the segmenting egg that gives rise to a definite part or organ. —**protoblastic,** *a.* O, W [3]

protochlorophyll, *n.* (1894) *Biochem.* [G (1893) < *proto-* + *Chlorophyll* < Gk *prôto-,* the comb. form of *prôtos* first + *chlōrós* yellow-green + *phýllon* leaf] A green, magnesium-containing pigment, which is converted to chlorophyll by light. O, W [3]

protoclastic, *a.* *Geol.* [G *protoklastisch* < *proto-* + *-klastisch* < Gk *prôtos* + **klastikós* < *klastós* broken < *kláein* to break + G *-isch* -ic] Of, concerning, or constituting the texture of certain igneous rocks. W [3]

protocol statement, *n.* (1935) *Philos.* [Transl. of G *Protokollsatz* < *Protokoll* protocol (< ML *protocollum* <

LGk *prōtokóllon*) + G *Satz* sentence, theorem, proposition] An observational statement that presents the uninterpreted results of observations and becomes a basis for scientific verification. O, R, W [4]

protoenstatite, *n.* (1939) *Mineral.* [G *Protoenstatit* < *proto-* (< Gk *prōtos* first) + G *Enstatit* enstatite (q.v.)] An unstable product of decomposed, heated talc, which is convertible to enstatite. O, W [3]

protogynous, *a.* (1870) *Bot.* Var. **protogynic** [Ad. of G *protogynisch* (1867) < *proto-* + *-gynisch* < Gk *prōtos* first + *gynḗ* wife + G *-isch* -ous, -ic] Proterogenous, where the pistil or female organ matures before the stamens or male organs do. —**protogyny** (1870). O, W [4]

protoheme, *n.* (1931) *Biochem.* Var. **protohaem** (1963) [G *Protohäm* (1931) < *proto-* + *-häm* < Gk *prōtos* first + *haîma* blood] A ferrous chelate derivative of protoporphyrin: heme. O, W [3]

protolithionite, *n.* (1892) *Mineral.* [G *Protolithionit* (1885) < *proto-* + *Lithionit* < Gk *prōtos* first + *lítheion*, neuter of *lítheios* stony, rocky + G *-it* -ite] A variety of zinnwaldite containing more lithium and less iron. O [3]

protone, *n.* (1898) *Biochem.* [G *Proton* (1898), a short. of *Protamin* (< *prot-* + *Amin* amine < Gk *prōtos* first) + G *-ton* < Gk *pépton*, neuter of *péptos* digested, cooked] Any of several peptone-like substances produced by hydrolyzing protamines. O [3]

protonephridium, *n.* (1895) *Zool.* [G (1889) (< NL) < G *proto-* + *Nephridium* < Gk *prōtos* first + *nephridíos* concerning the kidneys + G (< NL) *-ium* -ium] In vertebrates like flatworms, an excretory system composed of flame cells opening into ducts leading to exterior pores; a nephridium equipped with a solenocyte. —**protonephridial** (1963). O, W [3]

protopectin, *n.* (1908) *Biochem.* [G *Protopektin* (1907) < *proto-* + *Pektin* < Gk *prōtos* first + *pēktós* firm, hard + G *-in* -in] One of a group of water-insoluble pectic substances in plants: pectose. —**protopectinase** (1927). O, W [3]

protopetroleum, *n.* (1909) *Chem.* [G (1897) < *proto-* + *Petroleum* < Gk *prōtos* first + *pétros* stone + L *oleum* oil] An intermediate product in the forming of petroleum from organic debris. O [3]

protophloem, *n.* (1884) *Bot.* [G (1873) < *proto-* (< Gk *prōtos* first) + G *Phloem* phloem (q.v.)] The first-formed primary phloem of a vascular bundle or other primary stelar arrangement. O, W [3]

protoplasm, *n.* (1846) *Biol.* Var. **protoplasma** [G *Protoplasma* (1846) < *proto-* + *Plasma* plasma (q.v.) < Gk *prōtos* first + *plásma* structure, formation] Organized living matter; cytoplasm. —**protoplasm(at)ic** (1866), **-plasmal** (1885). O, R, W [4]

protoporcelain, *n.* *Pottery* [Prob. transl. of G *Urporzellan* < *ur-* proto- + *Porzellan* porcelain < MFr *porcelaine*] A porcelaneous ware without some of the qualities of true porcelain, as in kaolinic Chinese stoneware. 12 [3]

protothetic, *n.* (1940) *Philos.* [G *Protothetik* (1929) < *proto-* + *-thetik* < Gk *prōtos* first + *thetikós* capable of being employed] A propositional calculus on the basis of which the Polish logician Stanislaw Lesniewski (1886–1939) constructed his system of logic. —**protothetics** (1963). O [3]

prototrophic, *a.* (1900) *Bot.* [G *prototroph* (1897) < *proto-* + *-troph* < Gk *prōtos* first + *trophḗ* nourishment + E *-ic*] A plant species in which fixation of gaseous nitrogen by modular bacteria supplies most or all of the plant's nitrogen requirement. O, R, W [4]

protoxylem, *n.* (1887) *Bot.* [G (1873) < *proto-* (< Gk *prōtos* first) + G *Xylem* xylem (q.v.)] The first-formed primary system of a fibrovascular bundle or other stelar arrangement. —**protoxylem point/strand.** O, R, W [4]

protozoa, *pl.* of **protozoon** (1834) *Zool.* [Transl. into naturalized Greek elements in English < G *Urthiere* (now *Urtiere*), coined in 1818 by the German zoologist Georg August Goldfuss (1782–1848) < *ur-* (= Gk *proto-*) + *Thiere* (= Gk *zõa*) animals] Animals consisting of a single cell, the simplest or most primitive type. —**protozoic** (1838); **-zoan,** *n.* (1864), *a.* (1888); **-zoal,** *a.* (1890); **-zoology** (1904); **-zoologist** (1906); **-zoological** (1922); **-zoacidal; -zoacide; -zoea(n); -zoiasis.** O, R, W [4]

protrichocyst, *n.* (1933) *Zool.* [G *Protrichocyste* (1928) (now *Protrichozyste*) < *pro-* + *Trichocyste* < L *pro-* pre- < Gk + *thríx* (gen. *tríchos*) hair + *kýstis* blister] An undeveloped trichocyst. O [3]

prove, *v.* (1833) *Med.* [Transl. of < G *prüfen* < L *probāre* to test, probe] To test a medicine on a healthy person to determine its effects. O [3]

proviant, *n.* and *a.* (1637, 1637) *Mil.* Old var. **proveant** (1647) [G, a term brought to England by soldiers who served in the Thirty Years' War < It *provianda* < colloq. L *provenda* army provisions] (of) provender: food or provisions, esp. for an army. O, W [4]

province, *see* petrographic province

provisorium, *n.* (1957) *Politics* [G (1848) < L *providēre* to make provision + G (< L) *-ium*] A provisional or interim condition or measure. O [3]

provitamin, *n.* (1927) *Biol.* [G (1927) < *pro-* + *Vitamin* vitamin (q.v.) < L *pro-* pre- + *vīta* life + G *Amin* amine] A precursor substance that is convertible into a vitamin within an organism. —**provitamin A** (1952). O, R, W [4]

psarolite, *n.* (1859) *Geol.* Var. **psaronite** (1859) [Prob. transl. into naturalized Greek elements in English < G *Starstein* < *Star* starling + *Stein* stone = Gk *psár* + *líthos*] The silicified stems of tree ferns preserved in the Permian or Lower New Red sandstone, named for the speckled marking that they exhibit in section. O [3]

pseudoacid, *n.* (1899) *Chem.* [Transl. of G *Pseudosäure* (1899), coined by the German chemist Arthur Rudolf Hantsch (1857–1935) < *pseudo-* (< the comb. form of Gk *pseúdein* to deceive) + G *Säure* acid] A compound that is not an acid and that exists in equilibrium with or is convertible into a basic form and so can undergo some typical reactions of bases. O [3]

pseudo base, *n.* (1899) *Chem.* Var. **pseudo-base** (1899) [G (1899) < *pseudo-* + *Base* < Gk *pseudo-*, the comb. form of *pseúdein* to deceive + *básis* step, hence "the pertaining ground," basis] A compound that is not a base but that exists in equilibrium with or is capable of isomerization into a true base. —**pseudo-basic(ity)** (1921, 1927). O, W [3]

pseudobrookite, *n.* (1878) *Mineral.* [G *Pseudobrookit* < *pseudo-* (< Gk *pseudo-*, the comb. form of *pseúdein* to deceive) + G *Brookit* brookite < the name of Henry

James *Brooke* (1771–1857), English mineralogist + G *-it* -ite] An oxide of iron and titanium resembling brookite. O, W [3]

pseudocirrhosis, *n.* (1900) *Path.* [Short. of G *Pseudolebercirrhose* (1896) (now *Pseudoleberzirrhose*) < *pseudo-* + *Leber* liver + *Cirrhose* < Gk *pseudo-,* the comb. form of *pseúdein* to deceive + *kirrhós* of orange color + G *-se* (< Gk *-osis*) -sis, fem. suffix of action] Pick's disease, pericarditis. O [3]

pseudocotunnite, *n.* (1889) *Mineral.* [G *Pseudocotunnit* (1877) < It *pseudocotunnia* (see *cotunnite*) < Gk *pseudo,* the comb. form of *pseúdein* to deceive + G *-it* -ite] A potassium lead chloride found as crystals in Vesuvian fumaroles. O, W [3]

pseudogamy, *n.* (1900) *Bot.* [G *Pseudogamie* (1881) < *pseudo-* + *-gamie* < Gk *pseudo-,* the comb. form of *pseúdein* to deceive + *gameín* to wed + G *-ie* (< Gk *-ia*) -y] In an apomictic plant, development of an embryo following pollination without nuclear fission; diploid parthenogenesis. —**pseudogamous** (1932), **pseudogamic.** O, W [3]

pseudogley, *n.* (1953) *Geol.* [G (1953) < *pseudo-* + *Gley* < Gk *pseudo-,* the comb. form of *pseúdein* to deceive + Russ *glei* clay] A gley produced by waterlogging due to poor drainage of surface water, rather than by a high water table. O [3]

pseudoglobulin, *n.* (1905) *Biochem.* [G (1899) < *pseudo-* + *Globulin* < Gk *pseudo-,* the comb. form of *pseúdein* to deceive + L *globulus* globulin < L *globus* sphere] A simple protein that is soluble in pure water and saline solutions, but insoluble in half-saturated ammonium sulfate etc. O, W [3]

pseudohalogen, *n.* (1925) *Chem.* [G (1925) < *pseudo-* + *Halogen* < Gk *pseudo-,* the comb. form of *pseúdein* to deceive + *háls* (gen. *halós* salt + *-genēs* produced] Any of several radicals containing small molecules built from atoms of electronegative elements and resembling halogens in reactions. —**pseudohalide** (1925). O, W [3]

pseudomalachite, *n.* (1835) *Mineral.* [G *Pseudomalachit* < *pseudo-* + *Malachit* < Gk *pseudo-,* the comb. form of Gk *pseúdein* to deceive + Fr *malachite* < Gk *malachítēs* a stone] A hydrous basic copper phosphate resembling malachite. O, W [3]

pseudomonas, -monades *pl.* (1903 *W9*) *Biol.* [G (1897) (< NL) < Gk *pseudo-,* the comb. form of *pseúdein* to deceive + *monás* unit] A bacterium of the genus *Pseudomonas,* comprising aerobic gram-negative species that occur chiefly in soil or water, are short and rod-shaped, and produce water-soluble pigment; the genus itself. O, R, W [4]

pseudomucin, *n.* (1883) *Med.* [G (1882) < *pseudo-* + *Mucine* < Gk *pseudo-,* the comb. form of *pseúdein* to deceive + L *mūcus* mucus + G *-in* -in] The dense, semiopaque liquid in pseudomucinous cysts. —**pseudomucinous** (1901). O [3]

pseudonitrole, *n. Chem.* [G *Pseudonitrol* < *pseudo-* + *Nitrol* < Gk *pseudo-,* the comb. form of *pseúdein* to deceive + *nítron* potassium nitrate + G *-ol* (< L *oleum* oil) -ole] Any of a class of compounds formed by nitrous acid acting upon a disubstituted nitromethane. W [3]

pseudoplasm, *n.* (1847) *Med.* [Prob. < G *Pseudoplasma* < *pseudo-* + *Plasma* plasma (q.v.) < Gk *pseudo-,* the

comb. form of *pseúdein* to deceive + *plásma* formation, aggregation] Phantom tumor, which disappears spontaneously. O, W [3]

pseudopupil, *n.* (1971) *Physiol.* [G *Pseudopupille* (1891) < *pseudo-* + *Pupille* < Gk *pseudo-,* the comb. form of *pseúdein* to deceive + L *pūpilla* pupil] A black spot in the center of an insect's eye that always points in the direction of the observer. O [3]

pseudosuchian, *n.* and *a.* (1913, 1913) *Paleon.* Var. **Pseudosuchia** (1913) [Ad. of G *Pseudosuchier* < NL *Pseudosuchia* < *pseudo-* < Gk, the comb. form of *pseúdein* to deceive + *soûxos* crocodile + G *-ier* -ian] (Of) a slender Triassic reptile belonging to the suborder Pseudosuchia of Thecodontia, which is prob. near the common ancestry of birds, dinosaurs, and crocodilians. O, W [3]

pseudotillite, *n.* (1963) *Geol.* [G *Pseudotillit* (1961) < *pseudo-* (< Gk, the comb. form of *pseúdein* to deceive) + G *Tillit* tillite < *till,* origin unknown, a hard, unproductive clay subsoil + *-it* -ite] A nonglacial deposit similar to tillite (q.v.). O [3]

pseudotuberculosis, *n.* (1896) *Med.* [G *Pseudotuberkulose* (1889) < *pseudo-* (< Gk, the comb. form of *pseúdein* to deceive) + G *Tuberkulose* tuberculosis < L *tūberculum* small lump + G *-ose* (< Gk *-osis*) -osis, fem. suffix of action] One of various diseases in birds and mammals, resembling tuberculosis. O, R, W [3]

pseudowavellite, *n.* (1925) *Mineral.* [G *Pseudowavellit* (1922) < *pseudo-* (< Gk *pseudo-,* the comb. form of *pseúdein* to deceive) + G *Wavellit* wavellite < the name of William *Wavell* (d. 1829), English physician + G *-it* -ite] Crandallite, a hydrous phosphate of calcium and aluminum. O, W [3]

pseudoxanthoma (elasticum), *n.* (1900) *Path.* [G *Pseudoxanthoma* (1896) < *pseudo-* + *Xanthom* < Gk *pseudo,* the comb. form of *pseúdein* to deceive + *xanthós* yellowish + G *-oma* (< Gk *-ōma*) -oma, denoting a swelling or tumor (+ E *elasticum* [< NL] elastic)] A congenital disease of connective tissue formation leading to cardiovascular disorder and ultimately death. O [3]

psilocin, *n.* (1958) *Biochem.* [G (1958) (now *Psilozin*) < Gk *psilós* smooth, bare + G *-in* -in] An alkaloid that is the active hallucinogenic metabolite of psilocybin (q.v.). O, R [3]

psilocybin, *n.* (1958) *Chem.* [G (1958) < NL *psilocybe* < Gk *psilós* bare + *kýbē* head + G *-in* -in] An alkaloid that is the hallucinogen found in various Central American species of mushrooms, producing effects similar to those of LSD. O, R [4]

psittacism, *n.* (1896) *Philos.* [Fr *psittacisme,* as coined by Leibnitz in his *Nouveaux essais sur l'entendment humain* in 1765, or its later G form *Psittazismus* < Gk *psíttakos* parrot + G *-ismus* (< L *-ismus*) -ism] The mechanical repeating of previously received ideas or images that shows no true reasoning or feeling; automatic repetition of words or phrases, parrot-like. —**psittacistically** (1901), **psittacist** (1923). O, R, W [3]

psychanalyst, *see* psychoanalyst

psychiatric, *a.* (1847) *Psych.* Var. **psychiatrical** (1884) [G *psychiatrisch* (1808) < *psychiatr-* (< Gk *psychḗ* soul, breath + *iatrós* physician) + G *-isch* -ic] Of, relating to, or employed in psychiatry; of mental illness that can be treated medically. —**psychiatrics** (1847), **psychiatrically** (1847). O, R, W [4]

psychiatry, *n.* (1846) *Med., Psych.* [G *Psychiatrie* (1808), coined by the German physician Johann Christian Reil (1759–1813), one-time professor of medicine at the University of Berlin < *psychiatr-* or *psycho-*, ult. < Gk *psyché* soul + *iatreía* healing (see Meyer)] A branch of medicine concerned with the practice and science of treating various emotional, mental, and behavior disorders; such service in a general hospital; a text or treatise on or a theory concerned with this branch of medicine. —**psychiatrist.** O, R, W [4]

psychoanalysis, -analyses *pl.* (1898) *Psych.* [Freud's G *Psychoanalyse* (1896) (or his *psychische Analyse,* 1894) < *psycho-* + *Analyse* < Gk *psycho-*, the comb. form of *psyché* soul, breath + *análysis* dissolution, partition] A method of using dream analysis and free association to plumb psychic content and mechanisms otherwise consciously inaccessible; a method of psychotherapy; metapsychology; an area of psychotherapeutic practice; the method or practice of interpreting nonpsychiatric data clinically. —**psychoanalyze; psychoanalyse** (1911); **psychoanalysed,** *a.* ((1928). O, R, W [4]

psychoanalyst, *n.* (1911) *Psych.* Var. **psychanalyst** [Ad. of G *Psychoanalytiker* < *psycho-* + *Analytiker* analyst < Gk *psycho-*, the comb. form of *psyché* soul, breath + *análysis* + G *-er* -er] One who practices or is skilled in psychoanalysis (q.v.). O, R, W [4]

psychoanalytic, *a.* (1906) *Psych.* Var. **psychoanalytical** (1857), **psychanalytical** (1932) [G *psychoanalytisch* < *psycho-* + *analytisch* < Gk *psycho-*, the comb. form of *psyché* soul, breath + *analytikós* analytical + G *-isch* -ic] Of, relating to, or using psychoanalysis. —**psychoanalytically** (1919). O, R, W [4]

psychodiagnostics, *n.* (1932) *Psych.* [G *Psychodiagnostik* (1921) < *pseudo-* + *Diagnostik* < Gk *psycho-*, the comb. form of *psyché* soul, breath + *diágnōsis* investigative judgment, *diagnostikós* diagnostic] The science or method of investigating a subject's personality or of diagnosing a mental disorder, esp. by means of Hermann Rorschach's ink-blot test and clinical psychology. —**psychodiagnostic,** *a.* (1937). O, R, W [3]

psychogalvanic (reflex/response), *n.* (1907) *Psych.* [G *psychogalvanische* (*Reaktion*) or *psychogalvanischer* (*Reflex*) (1907) < *psycho-* (< Gk *psycho-*, the comb. form of *psyché* soul, breath) + G *galvanisch* < the name of the Italian scientist Luigi *Galvani* (1737–98) + G *-isch* -ic (+ *Reaktion* reaction < NL *reaction-,* or G *Reflex* reflex < L *reflexus*] Changes in the apparent electrical resistance of the skin in response to exciting stimuli. —**psychogalvanometer** (1935), **psychogalvanometric** (1935). O, R, W [4]

psychogram, *n.* (1918) *Psych.* [G *Psychogramm* (1911) < *psycho-* + *-gramm* < Gk *psycho-*, the comb. form of *psyché* soul + *grámma* record] A summary or diagram of one's mental life or personality, esp. when based on one's psychological history, responses to the Rorschach test, etc. (this is different from the old meaning of "spirit-writing"). O, W [3]

psychography, -ies *pl.* (1921) *Psych.* [Fr or G *Psychographie* (1911) < *psycho-* + *- graphie* < Gk *psycho-*, the

comb. form of *psyché* soul, breath + *gráphein* to write, record + G *-ie* (< Gk *-ia*) -y] The making of a psychogram (q.v.); the resulting description of one's mental characteristics and their development (this is different from the old meaning of "psychobiography"). O, W [3]

psychopathic, *a.* (1847 W9) *Psych.* [G *psychopathisch* < *psycho-* + *-pathisch* < Gk *psycho-*, the comb. form of *psyché* breath, spirit + *pathēikós* suffering + G *-isch* -ic] Of, pertaining to, or characterized by psychopathy (q.v.). —**psychopathic personality** (1932)/**hospital/ward, psychopathically** (1961). O, R, W [4]

psychopathology, -ies *pl.* (1847) *Psych.* [G *Psychopathologie* (1844) (see *psychopathy*) < *psycho-* + *Pathologie* < Gk *psycho-*, the comb. form of *psyché* breath, spirit + *páthos* suffering, illness + *lógos* word, study + G *-ie* (< Gk *-ia*) -y] The study of disordered psychological and behavioral functioning; such dysfunctioning as in mental disease or social disorganization. —**psychopathologist** (1863), **-pathologic(al)** (1891, 1892), **-pathologically** (1928). O, R, W [4]

psychopathy, -ies *pl.* (1847) *Psych.* [G *Psychopathie* (1814), coined by Ernst von Feuchtersleben (1806–49), Austrian lecturer in psychiatry < *psycho-* + *-pathie* < Gk *psyché* spirit, breath + *páthos* suffering, illness + G *-ie* (< Gk *-ia*) -y] Mental disorder; treatment of disease by hypnotism; a branch of psychometry; psychopathic personality. O, R, W [4]

psychophysics, *n.* (1878) *Psych., Med.* [G *Psychophysik* (1860), coined by the German psychologist Gustav Theodor Fechner (1801–87) and used in the title of his book *Elemente der Psychophysik* < *psycho-* + *Physik* < Gk *psycho-*, the comb. form of *psyché* soul, breath + L *physica* the study of nature] The science that deals with the problems of and general relations between mind and body, as common to psychology and physics. —**psychophysical(ly)** (1872, 1894), **-physicist** (1886), **-physic** (1887). O, R, W [4]

psychotechnics, *n.* (1926) *Psych.* Var. **psychotechnic** (1927) [Prob. < G *Psychotechnik* (1914) < *psycho-* + *Technik* < Gk *psycho-*, the comb. form of *psyché* soul, breath, wind + *téchnē* trade, dexterity] Psychotechnology. O, R, W [3]

psychotechnical, *a.* (1927) *Psych.* Var. **psychotechnic** (1932) [G *Psychotechnik* (1914) < *psycho-* + *Technik* < Gk *psycho-*, the comb. form of *psyché* sound, breath, wind + *téchnē* trade, dexterity + E *-al*)] Of the practical applications of psychology, as to industrial or military problems. O, W [3]

psychrotolerance, *n.* (1977) *Biol.* [G *Psychrotoleranz* (1933) < *psychro-* + *Toleranz* < Gk *psychrós* cold + L *tolerātiō* tolerance] The capacity to be able to grow at near-freezing temperatures. O [3]

pteridine, *n.* (1943) *Chem.* [G *Pteridin* (1941) < *pter-* (< Gk *pterón* wing, feather) + G *-idin* -idine, suffix used to form the name of many organic compounds containing nitrogen] A yellow, crystalline, bicyclic base that is a fundamental constituent in major natural products; a derivative of this, such as vitamins of the B group. O, W [3]

pteridophyte, *n.* (1880) *Bot.* [G (< NL) *Pteridophyt* (1866) < Gk *pterís* (gen. *pterídos*) fern + *phytón* plant] A plant belonging to the division Pteridophyta such as a fern or fern ally. —**pteridophyte**, *a.* (1897), **-phytic** (1898), **-phytous**. O, R, W [4]

pterin, *n.* (1934) *Chem.* Var. **pterine** (1954) [G (1925) < *pter-* (< Gk *pterón* wing, feather) + G *-in* -in, so named because this pigment is in butterfly wings] A nitrogenous compound containing the pteridine (q.v.) ring system. O, W [3]

pteryla, -e *pl.* (1867) *Ornith.* [G (1840) < NL < Gk *pterón* feather + *hýlē* stuff, substance, coined by Nietzsche in his *System der Pterylographie* (1840)—see *pterylography*] One of a number of areas on a bird's skin where feathers grow, also called *feather tract.*—**pterylosis** (1874). O, R, W [4]

pterylography, *n.* (1867) *Ornith.* [G *Pterylographie* (1840), coined by the German ornithologist Christian Ludwig Nitzsch (1782–1837) in his *Pterylographiae avium pars prior* (1833) and popularized in German by 1840 < *pterylo-* + *-graphie* < Gk *pterón* feather + *hýlē* wood, stuff + *gráphein* to write, describe + G *-ie* (< Gk *-ia* -y] The study or description of birds' pterylae (see *pteryla*). —**pterylographic** (1867), **pterylographical(ly)** (1896, 1867), **pterylological**, **pterylology**. O, W [3]

pucherite, *n.* (1872) *Mineral.* [G *Pucherit* (1871) < the name of the *Pucher* mine in Schneeberg, Saxony, Germany + *-it* -ite] A bismuth vanadate found in reddish-brown, orthorhombic crystals. O, W [3]

pumpernickel, *n.* (1663) *Food* Old var. **pompernickel** (1663) [G < *pumpern* (echoic) to flatulate + *Nickel* (a short. of *Nikolaus*) gnome (used as an oath), now referring to dark-brown bread with a slightly sweet and seasoned taste, orig. so named derisively because of its bloating effect] A sourdough, fermented bread using various proportions of rye and wheat flours. O, R, W [4]

punctograph, *n.* (1901) *Med.* [G *Punktograph* < *punkto-* + *-graph* < L *punctum* point + Gk *gráphein* to write] An instrument for determining the precise location of a foreign body embedded in bodily tissues. O [3]

pure line, *n.* (1906) *Biol.* [Transl. of G *reine Linie* (1903) < *rein* pure + *Linie* line < L *linea*] A homogeneous line of descent, as in an inbred line; a clone (this is different from the old meaning of "pure blood"). O, R, W [4]

purine, *n.* (1898) *Chem.* Old var. **purin** (1902) [G *Purin* < L *pūrus* pure < NL *uricus* uric + G *-in* -ine] A crystalline base constituted of a pyrimidine ring fused with an imidazole ring prepared from uric acid and is the parent of various uric compounds; a purine derivative, esp. a purine base. —**purine**, *a.* (1902). O, R, W [4]

purple bacterium, -ria *pl.* (1900) *Bot.* [Ad. of G *Purpurbakterium* (1888) < *Purpur* purple + *Bakterium* bacterium < NL *bacterium* < Gk *baktḗrion*] Any of a group of free-living bacteria containing bacteriochlorophyll pigment. O, R, W [3]

pursuit-flight, *n.* (1930) *Zool.* [Loose transl. of G *Reihen* (1929) row, rank, said of drakes during mating season, for the act of lining up in pursuit of a duck] A flight where at least one male bird follows or attacks a female. O [3]

putsch, -es *pl.* (1920) *Politics* [G < 15th-century Swiss G *butsch* violent crash, report, prob. echoic] A secretly planned and suddenly executed effort to overthrow a gov-

ernment; any vigorous, sudden action or campaign. —**putsching**, *verbal n.* (1968). O, R, W [4]

putz, -es *pl.* (1902) *Theol.* [(PaG) G adornment < *putzen* to adorn] Crèche: in Pennsylvania German homes, a decoration representing the Nativity scene, traditionally put under a Christmas tree. • ~ is a different word from Yiddish *putz* fool, penis. O, W [3]

Putzfrau, *n.* (1927) [G < *Putz* (< *putzen* to clean) + *Frau* woman] A charwoman or cleaning lady. O [3]

pycnia, see pyknic

pycnochlorite, *n.* (1903) *Mineral.* [G *Piknochlorit* (1903) < *pikno-* (< Gk *pycno-*, the comb. form of *pyknós* thick, dense) + G *Chlorit* chlorite (q.v.)] A chlorite with the same silicon content as clinochlore but with more iron. O [3]

pycnomorphous, *a.* (1899) *Biol.* [G *pyknomorph* (1895) < *pykno-* + *-morph* < Gk *pykno-*, the comb. form of *pyknós* thick, dense + *morphḗ* form, shape + E *-ous*] Characterized by a compact arrangement of stainable parts. • ~ is today usu. replaced by the var. *pycnomorphic*, which came into English directly from Greek. O, W [3]

pyknic, *n.* and *a.* (1925, 1925) *Anthrop.* Var. **pycnia** (1958) [G *pyknisch* (1921) (now also *pyknomorph*) < *pykn-* (< Gk *pyknós* thick, stocky) + G *-isch* -ic] (characterized by or of) a person of short stature, broad girth, and powerful muscles. O, R, W [4]

pyknoepilepsy, see pyknolepsy

pyknolepsy, *n.* (1922) *Med.* Var. **pyknoepilepsy** [G *Pyknolepsie* (1916) < *pykno-* + *-lepsie* < Gk *pyknós* thick, frequent + *lépsis* seizure] An epileptiform condition where brief attacks similar to petit mal occur many times daily. —**pyknoleptic** (1924). O, W [3]

pyocyanase, *n.* (1900) *Med.* [G (1899) (now *Pyozyanase*) < NL *pyocyaneus* < Gk *pýus* pus + *kyáneos* dark-blue + G *-ase* -ase, denoting an enzyme] An antibiotic mixture, orig. thought to be an enzyme, which is produced from the bacillus of green pus and can digest bacteria of diphtheria and cholera. O, W [3]

phyrallolite, *n.* (1822) *Mineral.* [G *Pyrallolit* (1820), coined by Nels Gustaf Nordenskold (1792–1866), Finnish mineralogist < G *pyr-* + *allo-* + *-lit* < Gk *pŷr* fire + *allós* other + *líthos* stone] An altered form of pyroxene that changes color when heated. O [3]

Pyramidon, *n.* (1898) *Pharm.* Var. **pyramidon(e)** (1903, 1898) [G (1896), a proprietary name] A trademark for aminopyrine, used as an antipyretic and analgesic. O, W [3]

pyrargyrite, *n.* (1849 *W9*) *Mineral.* [G *Pyrargyrit* (1830) < *pyr-* + *argyr-* + *-it* -ite < Gk *pŷr* fire + *árgyros* silver] Dark red silver ore, silver antimony sulfide. R, W [4]

pyrazine, *n.* (1887) *Chem.* [G *Pyrazin* (1887) < *Pyridin* pyridin, an alteration of *Pyrrol* pyrrole (q.v.) with an infixed *-az-* < Gk *ázōos* inert] A white, crystalline, heterocyclic base produced by distilling piperazine with zinc dust; also called *paradiazine*. O, W [3]

pyrazole, *n.* (1887) *Chem.* [G *Pyrazol* (1885) < *Pyrrol* pyrrole (q.v.) with an infixed *-az-* < Gk *ázōos* inert] A white, crystalline, heterocyclic weak base; a derivative of this. O, R, W [4]

pyrazoline, *n.* (1887) *Chem.* [G *Pyrazolin* (1887) < *Pyr-*

azol pyrazole (q.v.) + *-in* -ine] A dihydro derivative of pyrazole; a derivative of pyrazoline. O, R, W [3]

pyrazolone, *n.* (1887) *Chem.* [G *Pyrazolon* (1887) < *Pyrazol* pyrazole (q.v.) + *-on* -one] One of three carbonyl derivatives of pyrazoline; one of numerous pyrazolone derivatives, used as analgesics and antipyretics and in dyes. —**pyrazolone dye.** O, R, W [3]

pyrethrin, *n.* (1924) *Chem.* [G (1924) < NL *Pyrethrum* < Gk *pýrethron* a pyrethrum flower + G *-in* -in] One of two oily liquid esters of pyrethrolone with high insecticidal powers obtained esp. from pyrethrum flowers. —**pyrethrine I/II** (1924, 1924). O, R, W [4]

pyridostigmine, *n.* (1953) *Pharm.* [G *Pyridostigmin,* a blend of *Pyridin* pyridine and *Neostigmin* < Gk *néos* new + *stígma* sign, mark + G *-in* -ine] A white crystalline powder used as a medicine similar to neostigmine but with fewer side effects. —**pyridostigmine bromide** (1961). O [3]

pyrimidine, *n.* (1885) *Chem.* [Prob. < G *Pyrimidin* (1885) < *Pyridin* pyridin, with an infixed *-mi-*] A colorless, crystalline, feeble base with a penetrating odor, usu. obtained from barbituric acid; a derivative of this. —**pyrimidine,** *a.* (1924); **pyrimid(in)yl.** O, R, W [4]

pyrobelonite, *n.* (1920) *Mineral.* [G *Pyrobelonit* (1919) < *pyro-* + *Belonit* < Gk *pŷr* fire + *belónē* needle + G *-it* -ite] A hydrous basic vanadate of magnesium and lead occurring as brilliant red, needle-shaped crystals. O, W [3]

pyrochlore, *n.* (1830) *Mineral.* [G *Pyrochlor* (1826) < *pyro-* + *-chlor* < the comb. form of Gk *pŷr* fire + *chlōrós* light green, yellowish green, yellow] A brown or dark-reddish mineral isomorphous with microlite. —**pyrochlore group** (1906). O, R, W [3]

pyrochroite, *n.* (1868) *Mineral.* [G *Pyrochroit* (1864), coined by Lars Johan Igelström (1822–97), Swedish mineralogist (or directly < Sw) < G or Sw *pyro-* + *chro-* + *-it* < the comb. form of Gk *pŷr* (gen. *pyrós*) fire + *chroía* color, so named because it changes color when heated] A foliated hydroxide of manganese. O, W [3]

pyrodmalite, *n. Mineral.* [G *Pyrodmalit* (1808) < *pyr-* + *Odmalit* < Gk *pŷr* fire + *odmaléos* malodorous + G *-it* -ite] Pyrosmalite (q.v.). O [3]

pyrolusite, *n.* (1828) *Mineral.* [G *Pyrolusit* (1827) < *pyro-* + *-lusit* < Gk *pyro-,* the comb. form of *pŷr* fire + *loûsis* washing + G *-it* -ite] A native manganese dioxide, the most important ore of manganese; also called *polianite* (q.v.). O, R, W [4]

pyromagnetism, *n.* (1901) *Physics* [G *Pyromagnetismus* (1901) < *pyro-* (< Gk *pyro-,* the comb. form of *pŷr* fire) + G *Magnetismus* (< NL) magnetism] Magnetism dependent on the temperature of the material. O [3]

pyromeline, *n.* (1866–8) *Mineral.* [G *Pyromelin* (1852), coined by Franz Ritter von Kobell (1803–82), German mineralogist < *pyro-* < the comb. form of Gk *pŷr* (gen. *pyrós*) fire + *mýlinos* yellow] A hydrous sulfate of nickel. O [3]

pyromellic acid, *n.* (1851) *Chem.* [Transl. of G *Pyromellitsäure,* coined by Otto Linne Erdmann (1804–69), German chemist < *pyro-* + *Mellit* < the comb. form of Gk *pŷr* (gen. *pyrós*) + L *mel* (gen. *mellis*) honey (+ E *-ic*) + G *Säure* acid] A crystalline distillate of mellitic acid. O, W [3]

pyromorphite, *n.* (1814) *Mineral.* [G *Pyromorphit* (1813)

< *pyro-* + *Morphit* < Gk *pyro-,* the comb. form of *pŷr* fire + *morphḗ* shape, form + G *-it* -ite] A chlorophosphate of lead, also called *green lead ore.* O, R, W [4]

pyrone, *n.* (1891) *Chem.* Var. **pyron** [G *Pyron* (1885) < *pyr* (< Gk *pŷr* fire) + G *-on* -one] One of two isomeric carbonyl compounds obtained from pyrin; a derivative of one of these. —**pyrone ring** (1962). O, R, W [4]

pyronin(e), *n.* (1895) *Biol., Chem.* [G *Pyronin* < *Pyron* pyrone (q.v.) + *-in* -in(e)] Any of a class of basic synthetic xanthene dyes employed mainly as biological stains. —**pyronine B** (1960)/**Y** (1960)/**G** (1974), **pyroninophilic.** O, R, W [4]

pyrophanite, *n. Mineral.* [G *Pyrophanit* (1890) < *pyro-* + *Phanit* < Gk *pyro-,* the comb. form of *pŷr* fire + *phanós* bright + G *-it* -ite] A manganese titanate found in brilliant rhombohedral crystals. O, W [3]

pyrophyllite, *n.* (1830) *Mineral.* [G *Pyrophillit* (1829) < *pyro-* + *-phillit* < Gk *pyro-,* the comb. form of *pŷr* fire + *phýllon* leaf + G *-it* -ite] A hydrous aluminum silicate resembling talc. O, R, W [4]

pyropissite, *n.* (1866) *Mineral.* [G *Pyropissit* (1853), coined by Adolf (Johann Gustav) Kenngott (1818–97), German mineralogist < *pyro-* < the comb. form of Gk *pŷr* (gen. *pyrós*) fire + *píssa* pitch + G *-it* -ite] A mixture of hydrocarbons that resembles pitch when heated. O [3]

pyroretin, *n.* (1868) *Mineral.* [G (1854), coined by August Emanuel von Reuss (1811–73), Austrian mineralogist < *pyro-* < the comb. form of Gk *pŷr* (gen. *pyrós*) fire + *rētínē* resin] A resin occurring in brown-coal masses. O [3]

pyrosclerite, *n.* (1862) *Mineral.* [G *Pyrosclerit* (1834), coined by Franz Ritter von Kobell (1803–82), German mineralogist < *pyro-* < the comb. form of Gk *pŷr* (gen. *pyrós*) fire + *sklērós* hard + G *-it* -ite, so named because it becomes hard when heated] A green, chlorite-like mineral. O [3]

pyrosmalite, *n.* (1816) *Mineral.* Old var. **pyrodmalite** [G *Pyrosmalit* (1808) < *pyro-* + *Osmalit,* an ad. of *Pirodmalit*—see *pyrodmalite* < Gk *pŷr* (gen. *pyrós*) fire + *osmḗ* smell, *odmaléos* malodorous + G *-it* -ite] A basic iron manganese silicate. O, W [3]

pyrrhite, *n.* (1844) *Mineral.* [G *Pyrrhit* (1840) < *pyrr-* (< Gk *pyrrós* fiery red) + G *-it* -ite] Pyrochlore (q.v.) O, W [3]

pyrrhotite, *n.* (1868) *Mineral.* Var. **pyrrhotine** (1835) [G *Pyrrhotit* (1868) (now also *Pyrhotit*) < *pyrrhot-* (< Gk *pyrrótēs* fiery red) + G *-it* -ite] A widely distributed magnetic iron sulfide: magnetic pyrites. O, R, W [4]

pyrrole, *n.* (1835 *W9*) *Chem.* Old var. **pyrrol** (1849) [G *Pyrrol* < *pyrr-* + *Öl* < Gk *pyrrós* fiery red + L *oleum* oil] A weakly base, colorless, toxic, liquid, heterocyclic compound, with an odor like chloroform; a derivative of this. —**pyrrole,** *a.* (1851); **pyrrolic** (1909). O, R, W [3]

pyrrolidine, *n.* (1885) *Chem.* [G *Pyrrolidin* (1885) < *Pyrrol* pyrrole (q.v.) + *-in* -ine, with an infixed *-id-*] A flammable, fuming, secondary amine obtained from pyrrole. —**pyrrolidine nucleus** (1956)/**ring** (1963). O, R, W [3]

pyrrolidone, *n.* (1889) *Chem.* [G *Pyrrolidon* (1889) < *Pyrrol* pyrrole (q.v.) + *-on* -one, with an infixed *-id-*] A crystalline or liquid lactam used mainly in making polyvinyl pyrrolidone, also called *2(-keto) pyrrolidine.* O, W [3]

pyrroline, *n.* (1884) *Chem.* Old var. **pyrrolin** (1884) [G *Pyrrolin* (1883) < *pyrr-* + *Olin* < Gk *pyrrós* bright red + L *oleum* oil + G *-in* -ine] One of two bases intermediate between pyrrole (q.v.) and pyrrolidine (q.v.); dihydropyrrole; a fuming liquid obtained by reducing pyrrole. • ~ is different from the old synonym for *pyrrole*. O, W [3]

pyrrolizidine, *n.* (1939) *Chem.* [G *Pyrrolizidin* (1936) < *Pyrrolidin* pyrrolidine (q.v.), with an infixed *-iz-* < Gk *ázōos* inert] A colorless basic liquid with a structure of two fused pyrrolidine rings sharing a nitrogen and a carbon atom; a derivative of this. —**pyrrolizidine alkaloid** (1968). O [3]

Q

Q, *n.* (1901) *Theol.* [Abbr. of G *Quelle* source] A second, hypothetical source of the materials used in the writing of the gospels of Matthew and Luke. O, R, W [3]

Q scale, *n.* (1970) *Physics, Geol.* [Short. and expansion of G *Querwellen* (also called *Transversalwellen*) < *quer* or *transversal* transverse + *Wellen,* pl. of *Welle* wave + E *scale*] A measure of the time needed for vibrations in the earth to die down. B [3]

quader, *n. Geol.* [G a square stone, freestone, ashlar < MHG *quäder(stein)* < ML *quadrus (lapis)* < L *quadrus* having four corners] A portion of the German Upper Cretaceous system of rocks. W2 [2]

Qualitätswein, -e *pl.* (1972) *Beverages* [G < *Qualität* quality (< L *quālitās*) + *Wein* wine] Any German wine officially guaranteed as made from grapes produced in certain specified regions. B [3]

quantum, quanta *pl.* (1902) *Physics* [G (1900) < L *quantum,* neuter of *quantus* how large] The smallest quantity of radiant energy that can exist—see *Planck's constant* (this is different from the various earlier meanings of "quantity"). O, R, W [4]

quantum theory, *n.* (1911) *Physics* [Prob. ad. of G *Quantentheorie* < *Quanten* + *Theorie* < L *quantum,* neuter of *quantas* how large + *theōria* < Gk; neither W nor O identifies this as German, but the theory was developed from Max Planck's concept of radiant energy in his paper of 1900. It was extended by Einstein in 1905 and Niels Bohr in 1913 in relation to atomic structure, but its 1911 citation in English as the *quanta theory* suggests that it came from German] An extensive physical theory of matter and energy based on the concept of quanta, the *pl.* of *quantum* (q.v.). O, R, W [4]

quartz, *n.* (c.1631 *W9*) *Mineral.* [G < MHG *querch* dwarf (see *cobalt*), perhaps of Slavic origin] One of the most common minerals, composed of a silicon dioxide; a gold or sometimes silver ore, as distinguished from auriferous gravel. —**quartz,** *a.* (1789). • ~ appears in many composites like **quartzite** (1849) and **quartz lamp** (1922). O, R, W [4]

quatsch, *interj.* (1907) Var. **quatch** (1915) [G (echoic) splash, squish, (fig.) nonsense < *quatschen* to talk rubbish] Nonsense, rubbish. O [3]

Quellenforschung, *n.* (1958) *Lit.* [G < *Quellen,* pl. of *Quelle* source + *Forschung* study, investigation] Study of the sources of or influences upon a literary work. O [2]

quellung, *n. Biol.* [G swelling < *quellen* to swell + nom. suffix *-ung* -ing] Swelling of a microorganism's capsule after reaction with an antibody. W [3]

quenselite, *n.* (1926) *Mineral.* [G *Quenselit* (1925) or Sw < the name of Percy Dudgeon *Quensel* (1881–1966), Swedish mineralogist + G or Sw *-it* -ite] A basic oxide of lead and manganese occurring in black, monoclinic crystals. O, W [3]

quenstedtite, *n.* (1888) *Mineral.* [G *Quenstedtit* (1888) < the name of Friedrich A. *Quenstedt* (1809–89), German mineralogist + *-it* -ite] A hydrous sulfate of iron, very similar to copiapite (q.v.). O, W [3]

querflöte, *n.* (1876) *Music* [G < *quer* transverse + *Flöte* flute, ult. < OProv *flaut*] A transverse flute; an organ stop whose sound resembles that of a flute. O, W [3]

querl, *v.* (1830) *Sports* [G *quirlen* to turn swiftly or twirl around] To twirl, turn, or wind around. —**querl,** *n.* (1854). O [3]

quersprung, *n. Sports* [G < *quer* transverse + *Sprung* jump < *springen* to jump] A 90-degree jump or turn for avoiding an obstacle in skiing. R, W [3]

quetsch¹, *n. Tech.* [G *Quetsche* a press, wringer < *quetschen* to squeeze, press < MHG *quetschen,* poss. < L *quatere, quassāre* to shake, beat] A vat with rollers to apply chemical solutions or sizing to cloth or yarn; a roller in a quetsch. W [3]

quetsch², *n.* (1839) *Food* Var. **quetsche** (1842) [G *Quetsche,* dial. form of *Zwetsche* plum—see *quetsch¹*] A variety of plum with oval, purplish fruit; a quetsch tree. O, R, W [3]

quetsch(e), *n.* (1936) *Beverages* [G *Quetsche* < *quetschen* to squeeze < MHG] A white brandy made from quetsch plums. O, R, W [3]

quinazoline, *n.* (1887) *Chem.* [Ad. of G *Chinazolin* (1887) (now also *Qhinazolin*) < *Cinolin* chinoline (q.v.), with an infixed *-azo-* < Gk *azoos* inert] A colorless, heterocyclic, crystalline compound with an odor like that of naphthalene, used in medicine; a derivative of this compound. O, R, W [3]

quinone, *n.* (1853) *Chem.* Var. **chinone** [Ad. of G *Chinone* < *china* < Peruvian Sp *quina* china bark < Qechua *kina* + G *-on* -one] One of two isomeric crystalline compounds that are diketo derivatives of dihydro benzene: benzoquinone; one of various compounds containing quinone structures. —**quinone,** *a.* (1886). • ~ appears in numerous derivatives like **quinonoid,** *a.* (1878); **quinoid,** *a.* (1900), *n.* (1907); **quinoidal,** *a.* (1907); **quinonize; quinonization;** and in a few compounds like **quinonimine** and **quinone diimine/oxime.** O, R, W [4]

quinoxaline, *n.* (1884) *Chem.* Var. **quinoxalin** [Ad. of G *Chinoxalin* (1884) (now also *Quinoxalin*) < a combining and short. of *Chinolin* quinoline (q.v.) + *Glyoxal* < Gk *glykýs* sweet + *oxýs* tart, bitter + G *Aldehyd* aldehyde (q.v.) + *-in* -ine] A heterocyclic crystalline compound first prepared by condensing ortho phenylenediamine with glyoxal; a quinoxaline derivative. O, R, W [3]

quinquevalent, *a.* (1877) *Chem.* Var. **quinquivalent** (1877) [Transl. into Latin naturalized elements in English of G *fünfwertig* < *fünf* five + *-wertig* having the value (= L *quīnque* + *valēns, valēntis*)] Pentavalent: having a valence of five. —**quinquevalence, quinquevalency.** O, R, W [4]

quintaton, *n. Music* Var. **quintaten** [G *Quintaton,* ad. < NL *quintaten* (as influenced by G *Ton* < MHG < L *tonus*) + *quīnta* fifth] Quintadena, a pipe-organ stop producing with its own fundamental a harmonic fifth in the second octave above. W [3]

R

rackett, *n.* (1876) *Music* Var. **racket** (1891), **ranket** (q.v.) [G, described as a *Holzblasinstrument* woodwind instrument (with its etymology unknown)] A Renaissance bass instrument of the oboe family, with a tube bent upon itself in short lengths enclosed in a cylinder; also called *sausage bassoon.* O, R, W [4]

radiolite, *n.* (1855) *Mineral.* [G *Radiolith* < *radio-,* the comb. form of *Radium* radium + *-lith* -lite < NL *radium* + Gk *líthos* stone] A natrolite with radiated structure. O, W [3]

radiosonde, *n.* (1937) *Meteor.* Var. **radio-sonde** (1937), **radio sonde** (1940) [G (1931) < *Radio* radio + *Sonde* probe] A small package of meteorological instruments that is carried aloft, as by an unmanned balloon, to automatically transmit measurements of weather conditions at various heights by radio. —**radiosonde,** *a.* (1946); **radiosondage** (1939). O, R, W [4]

radon, *n.* (1918) *Chem.* [G (1918) < *Radium* radium (< L *radius* ray) + G *-on* -on] A heavy, short-lived radioactive element that is one of the inert gases and is formed by disintegrated radium; a radon isotope. —**radon seed** (1925). • ~ is symbolized as **Rn.** O, R, W [4]

raff, *a.* (c.1440) and *n.* (1667) *Bot.* [Swiss G *Räf,* G *Reff* < MHG, OHG *ref* wood, lattice frame, rack, orig. prob. meaning timber, akin to ON *raptr* rafter] (Dial. English) Lumber. —**raffman** (c.1440). O, W [3]

raffinate, *n.* (1928) *Chem.* [Ad. of Fr *raffiner* or G *Raffinat* < *raffinieren* < Fr *raffiner* to refine] A liquid residue or a less soluble residue that results from removal of impurities by solvent extraction, as in oil refining. —**raffinate,** *a.* (1941). O, R, W [3]

rain forest, *n.* (1903) *Bot.* Var. **rain-forest** (1903) [Transl. of G *Regenwald* (1898) < *Regen* rain + *Wald* forest] A dense tropical woodland in an area of high rainfall with little seasonal variation: tropical rain forest; temperate rain forest. —**rain forest,** *a.* (1956). O, R, W [4]

rainworm, *n.* (1731) *Zool.* [Prob. transl. of G *Regenwurm* < *Regen* rain + *Wurm* worm, so named because of its habit of appearing above ground during a rain] Earthworm; an adult mermithid worm. O, W [3]

ramdohrite, *n.* (1931) *Mineral.* [G *Ramdohrit* (1930) < the name of Paul Georg Karl *Ramdohr* (1890–1985), German mineralogist + *-it* -ite] A rare sulfide composed of lead, silver, and antimony. O, W [3]

rammelsbergite, *n.* (1854) *Mineral.* [G *Rammelsbergit* (1845) < the name of Karl F. *Rammelsberg* (1813–99), German mineralogist + *-it* -ite] A native nickel diarsenide. O, R, W [3]

rams, -es *pl.* *Games* [G *Rams/Rammes/Ramsch* ramsch (q.v.)] A card game similar to loo. W [3]

Ramsauer-Townsend effect, *n.* (1930) *Physics* Var. **Ramsauer effect** (1930) [G *Ramsauer-Effekt* (1921) < the name of Carl Wilhelm *Ramsauer* (1879–1955), German physicist + *Effekt* effect; as this effect was independently de-

scribed by the Irish physicist John Sealy Edward *Townsend* (1868–1957) in 1922, the name *Townsend* was added to the English term] The steep decrease to near zero, of the scattering cross-section of inert-gas atoms for electrons with energies below a critical value. O [3]

ramsch, -es *pl.* *Games* [G < Fr *ramas* heap of useless things < dial. *ramser,* alter. of *ramasser* to collect] A game in which only the jacks are trumps, and the object is to lose tricks. W [3]

randkluft, *n.* (1934) *Geol.* [G < *Rand* edge + *Kluft* crevasse] A chasm caused when glacial ice breaks away from a mountainside or stationary ice. O, W [3]

ranket, *n.* (1876) *Music* Var. **rankett** (1876), **rackett** (1876) [G *Rankett* rackett (q.v.)] A type of reed organ pipe; a rackett. O, R, W [3]

rappen, -ø *pl.* (1838) *Currency* Var. **rap(p)** (1962) [G *Rappe(n)* < MGH *rappe,* orig. a coin with the head of an eagle that was jocularly mocked as a *Rappe* raven] A small Swiss coin (centime). O, W [4]

raschel, *n.* and *a.* (1940, 1940) *Textiles* Var. **raschel knitting** (1957) [Short. of G *Raschelmaschine* raschel machine, prob. < the name of the French actress Elisa *Rachel* Félix (1821–58), who popularized the warp knitting resembling tricot, produced by such a loom, by wearing dresses made of the "tricot"] (of) a kind of knitting machine; (of) the knitting done by this machine. —**raschelled,** *a.* (1970). O, W [4]

raspite, *n.* (1898) *Mineral.* [G *Raspit* (1897) < the name of Charles *Rasp,* 19th-century Australian prospector and discoverer of the Broken Hill mines, New South Wales, where the first specimen was found + G *-it* -ite] A lead tungstate that is dimorphous with stolzite and occurs as yellow monoclinic crystals. O, W [3]

Rassenkreis, -e *pl.* *Anthrop.* [G < *Rasse* race, species + *Kreis* circle, cycle, group] A polytypic species, esp. when one type has geographically replaced another type. W [2]

rassenschander, *n.* (1937) *Politics* [Erron. ad. of G *Rassendschänder* one who commits a *Rassenschande* < *Rasse* race + *Schande* violation] The Nazi concept of violation of the purity of the Aryan "race" by marriage to someone of a different race. O [2]

raster, *n.* (1934) *Physics* [G screen < L *rāster, rāstrum* toothed hoe] A pattern or area of scanning lines that uniformly covers an area as, for example, the display on a cathode-ray tube of a television set; a fine grid placed in front of the projection screen in some stereo cinematographic systems. —**raster,** *v.* (1978); **raster display** (1934); **rastered,** *a.* (1975). O, R, W [4]

ratch, -es *pl.* (1721) *Tech.* [G *Ratsche/Rätsche* ratchet (descriptive echoic of the sound resulting from a rapid tearing of paper, cloth, etc.)] A ratchet or ratchet wheel (this is different from the archaic meaning of "firelock"). O, W [3]

Rathaus, *n.* (1611) *Politics* Var. **Rath-haus,** (1855) **Rathaus**

(1964) [G (now *Rathaus*) < *Rath* (now *Rat*) council + *Haus* house] A German town hall. O [3]

rathite, *n.* (1897) *Mineral.* [G *Rathit* (1896) < the name of Gerhard von *Rath* (1830–88), German mineralogist + *-it* -ite] A lead sulfarsenate occurring in gray, orthorhombic crystals. —**rathite II** (1953). O, W [3]

rathskeller, *n.* (1900) *Beverages* Var. **Rathskeller** (1900), **ratskeller** (1969) [G (now *Ratskeller*) < *Rath* council + *Keller* cellar, basement in a *Rathaus* (q.v.)] A restaurant in the basement of a German town hall, or one patterned after it, where beer or wine is sold. O, R, W [4]

rationalization, *n.* (1927) *Industry* [Transl. of G *Rationalisierung* (1905) < *rationalisieren* to rationalize < L *ratiō* reason, a tough-out approach] The organization of industry or a business on scientific lines. O, R, W [3]

ratskeller, *see* rathskeller

rauschpfeife, -s/-n *pl.* (1876) *Music* [G < *Rausch* < MHG *rūsch* reed + G *Pfeife* pipe] A kind of mixture stop in a pipe organ. O, W [3]

rauschquinte, *n.* *Music* [G < *Rausch* < MHG *rūsch* reed + *Quinte* fifth (in music) < ML *quinta*] Another kind of mixture stop in a pipe organ. W [3]

ravenduck, *n.* (1753) *Textiles* Var. **raven-duck, raven's duck** [Transl. of G *Rabentuch* < *Raben,* pl. of *Rabe* raven + *Tuch* cloth, canvas] A kind of canvas. O [3]

raven-stone, *n.* (1817) *Law* [Transl. of G *Rabenstein* < *Raben,* pl. of *Rabe* raven + *Stein* stone, so named because of the ravens attracted to the elevated stone on which criminals were decapitated] A place of execution; gallows or gibbet. O [3]

Rb, *see* rubidium

R-boat, *n.* (1942) *Mil.* [Ad. of G *R-Boot,* a short. of *Räumboot* minesweeper < *räumen* to clear + *Boot* boat] A German minesweeper in World War Two. O [3]

Re, *see* rhenium

reafference, *n.* (1965) *Psych.* [G *Reafferenz* (1950) < *re-* + *Afferenz* < L *re-* back, again + *affere* to bring or carry to] Sensory stimulation where the stimulus changes as a result of the subject's movements in response to the stimulus. —**reafferent,** *a.* 1965). O [3]

reagin, *n.* (1911) *Immunology* [G < *reagieren* to react < L *re-* back, again + *agere* to drive, do, act + G *-in* -in] Antibody of a specialized immunoglobulin that attaches to tissue cells in allergic individuals' blood and can passively sensitize the skin of nonallergic individuals; the complement-fixing substance in the blood of syphilitic persons that is responsible for positive Kahn or Wassermann reactions; also called *Wasserman antibody.* —**reaginic** (1931), **reaginically.** O, R, W [4]

realism, *n.* (1817 *W9*) *Philos.* [G *Realismus* philosophical realism < *real* + *-ismus* < LL *reālis* real, actual + L *-ismus* -ism] Objective preoccupation with fact or reality; a philosophical doctrine that universals exist outside the mind; epistemological realism; an artistic or literary theory of fidelity to nature or reality; preoccupation with trivial or squalid details in literature or art; a kind of conception of the administration of justice and of the science of law. O, R, W [4]

realpolitik/real politik, *n.* (1914) *Politics* [G *Realpolitik* < *real* + *Politik* < LL *reālis* essential, real, actual + Gk *politikḗ* (*téchnē*) politics] Practical politics, as based on

practical and material factors or on national interest and power, rather than on ideals. O, R, W [4]

realpolitiker, *n.* (1930) *Politics* [G < *Realpolitik* (q.v.) + *-er* -er] A person who practices, advocates, or believes in realpolitik. O, R, W [3]

realschule/Realschule, -n *pl.* (1853) *Ed.* [G < *real* (< LL *reālis* practical, essential) + G *Schule* school < OHG *scuola*] A German secondary school whose curriculum includes modern languages, science, mathematics, etc. but no classics, in contrast to a gymnasium (q.v.). O, W [3]

reason, *n.* (1809–10) *Philos.* [Transl. of G *Vernunft* (q.v.)] In German Kantianism and idealism, a person's highest mental capacity, esp. in reaching general conceptions or first principles *a priori* (this is different from the various old Latin meanings). O, R, W [3]

receptor, *n.* (1900) *Biol.* [G (1900) (now *Rezeptor*) < L *receptor* one or something that receives] A highly sensitive part of the body that, upon perceiving some environmental change, generates the resulting impulses to the central nervous system (this is different from the old meaning of "receiver"). O, R, W [4]

recessive, *n.* and *a.* (1900, 1900) *Biol.* [G *recessiv* (1865) (now *rezessiv*) < L *recēssus,* past part. of *recēdere* to recede, retreat + G adj. suffix *-iv* (< L *-ivus*) -ive] According to the Austrian botanist Gregor Mendel's law, this term describes an allele that is masked or subordinate to a contrasting, dominant allele of the gene that determines it; (of) a person whose particular recessive allele is expressed; (of) a recessive allele or factor (this is different from the old Latin meaning of "receding"). O, R, W [4]

Rechtsstaat, *n.* (1935) *Politics* Var. **Rechtstaat** (1935) [G < the gen. of *Recht* right, law + *Staat* state, ult. < L *status*] A country where the rule of law prevails. O [3]

reclamation disease, *n.* (1937) *Biochem.* [Transl. of *Urbarmachungskrankheit* (1933) < *Urbarmachung* reclamation + *Krankheit* disease] A copper-deficiency disease affecting crops, esp. cereals, grown on newly reclaimed land, where affected plants do not produce seed. O, W [3]

recurrence formula, *see* recursion formula

recursion, primitive recursion, *n.* (1934) *Math.* [G (*primitive*) *Recursion* (1934) (now *Rekursion*) (< *primitiv* < Fr *primitif* simple) < LL *recursio* running back, return] In the application of a recursive definition, the definition of a function of natural numbers by simple recursion formulas or by induction on a single argument; a recursive definition. O, R [4]

recursion formula, -s/-e *pl.* (1930) *Math.* Var. **recurrence formula** [Transl. of G *Rekursionsformel* (1871) < the gen. of *Rekursion* recursion (< LL *recursio*) + G *Formel* formula] A formula relating the value of a function for a given value of its argument or arguments to its values for other values of the argument or arguments. O, R [3]

recursive, *a.* (1934) *Math.* [Transl. of G *rekurrent* (1904) (now *rekursiv,* modeled on AmE *recursive*) < G *rekurrieren* < L *recurrere* to run back, lead back] Utilizing or being an iterated procedure where the required result at each step except the last is expressed in terms of the result or results of the next step until at the terminus there is an outright evaluation of the result. —**recursive function** (1934)/**definition** (1940). O [3]

redowa, *n.* (1845) *Dance* Old var. **redowak** (1862) [G (or

Fr) < Czech *rejdovak* < *rejdovati* to steer or whirl around, drive] Either of two popular, 19th-century Bohemian ballroom dances; a dance resembling a waltz or a polka; the music for such dances. O, R, W [4]

reduction division, *n.* (1891) *Biol.* [Transl. of G *Reduktionstheilung* (1887) < *Reduktion* reduction (ult. < L *reductiō*) + *Theilung* division (now *Teilung*)] The (first) meiotic cell division during which reduction occurs; meiosis. O, R, W [4]

reflexology, *n.* (1922; 1923 *W9*) *Psych.* [G *Reflexologie* (1912) (or Russ *refleksologiya*) < G *reflexo-* + *-logie* < L *reflexus* reflex + *-logia* account, -logy] The doctrine that organisms' behavior is composed of established patterns of simple or complex reflex responses; the scientific study of reflexes as they affect behavior; a method of foot massage for relaxing nervous tension. —**reflexological** (1927), **reflexologist** (1933). O, R, W [4]

registrature, *n.* (1762) *Ed.* [G *Registratur* archive < LL *registrare* to register] A registry. O [3]

regulation, *n.* (1902) *Biol.* [G (1898) (now *Regulierung*) < LL *regulare* to regulate] An organism's capacity to adapt its body to accommodate changes made or damage done to it, normally by interrelating the various parts so as to produce an integrated whole (this is different from the old meaning of "act of regulating" etc.). —**regulation,** *a.* (1970). O, W [4]

Reich, -e *pl.* (1921) *Politics* [G < MHG *rīch(e),* OHG *rīhhi,* ult. < Celtic] The German state during the period 1871–1945, or from 1933 to 1945 esp. in the phrase *the Third Reich.* —**Reich-buster** (1948 *Algeo*). O, R [4]

Reichsbank, *n.* (1879) *Commerce* [G < the gen. of *Reich* Reich + *Bank* bank] The central bank of the German Reich from 1875 to 1945. O, R [3]

Reichsbanner, *n.* (1924) *Mil.* [G *Reichsbanner (Schwarz-Rot-Gold)* < the gen. of *Reich* Reich + *Banner* banner, flag (+ *Schwarz* black + *Rot* red + *Gold* gold)] A German republican paramilitary organization from 1924 to 1933. O [3]

Reichsführer, *n.* (c.1933) *Politics* [G < the gen. of *Reich* Reich + *Führer* leader] The title of the chief of the Schutzstaffel (q.v.). R [2]

reichsmark, -s/-ø *pl.* (1874) *Currency* [G < the gen. of *Reich* Reich, empire + *Mark* mark (q.v.)] The German mark from 1925 to 1948, when it was replaced by the deutsche mark (q.v.). O, R, W [4]

Reichsmarschall, *n.* (1940) *Politics* [G (1940) < the gen. of *Reich* Reich, empire + *Marschall* < OFr *maréschal,* akin to OHG *marascalc* keeper of the horses] Marshal of the Greater German Reich, a title given to Hermann Göring by Hitler. O [3]

reichspfennig, -s/-e *pl. Currency* [G < the gen. of *Reich* Reich, empire + *Pfennig* (q.v.) penny] The German pfennig from 1925 to 1948; a coin of one reichspfennig. R, W [3]

Reichsrat, *n.* (1858) *Politics* Var. **Reichsrath** [G *Reichsrath* (now *Reichsrat*) < the gen. of *Reich* Reich, empire + *Rath* council] The parliament of the Austrian part of the Hapsburg Empire; the council of the German federated states until 1933. O, R [3]

reichsstadt, *n. Politics* [G < the gen. of *Reich* Reich, em-

pire + *Stadt* city] A free city of the Holy Roman Empire. W2 [2]

Reichstag, *n.* (1867) *Politics* [G < the gen. of *Reich* Reich, empire + *Tag* day] The lower house of the German parliament from 1871 to 1945; the parliament building; a transf., generalized political sense. O, R [4]

Reichstag fire, *n.* (1933) *Politics* [Transl. of *Reichstagsbrand* < the gen. of *Reichstag* Reichstag (q.v.) + *Brand* conflagration, fire] A suspicious fire that destroyed the Reichstag building on February 27, 1933. O [3]

reichst(h)aler, -ø/-s *pl. n. Currency* Var. **Reichstaler** [G < the gen. of *Reich* Reich, empire + *Taler* dollar (q.v.)] The old German taler, in circulation from 1566 to about 1750; rix-dollar. R, W [3]

reichswehr, *n.* (1920) *Mil.* [G < the gen. of *Reich* Reich, empire + *Wehr* defense] The German armed forces from 1919 to 1935. O, R [3]

Reihengräber¹, *pl. Archaeology* [G, lit., graves in rows < *Reihen,* pl. of *Reihe* row + *Gräber,* pl. of *Grab* grave] Long barrows of prehistoric graves found in southern Germany. W [3]

Reihengräber², *pl. Archaeology* [G graves in rows—see *Reihengräber¹*] (Erron. use of *Reihengräber* to refer to) the prehistoric, prob. Germanic people who are buried in the Reihengräber. W [2]

reim-kennar, *n.* (1821) *Lit.* [Prob. ad. by Sir Walter Scott of G *Reimkenner* < *Reim* rhyme + *Kenner* expert, judge] A person skilled in magic rhymes. O [3]

reineckate, *n.* (1928) *Chem.* Var. **Reineckate** (1928) [G *Reineckat* (1863) < the name of A. *Reinecke,* a 19th-cent. German chemist + *-at* -ate] Tetrathiocyanato diammino chromium compound, used in insecticides. O, W [3]

Reissner's membrane, *n.* (1872) *Physiol.* [G *Reissner-Membran* < the name of Ernst *Reissner* (1824–78), German anatomist + *Membran* < L *membrāna* membrane] A thin, cellular membrane in the inner ear. O, W [3]

reiter, *n.* (1584) *Mil.* Old var. **reyter** (1584) [G < MHG *rīter* rider] A German cavalryman, esp. of the 16th and 17th centuries. O, W [3]

Reiter's disease/syndrome, *n.* (1923) *Path.* [Transl. of G *Reiter-Krankheit* (1916) < the name of Hans *Reiter* (1881–1969), German bacteriologist + *Krankheit* disease] A disease or syndrome characterized by arthritis, urethritis, and conjunctivitis, which is usu. caused by the bacteria of the genus *Chlamydia.* O, R, W [3]

releaser, *n.* (1937) *Biol., Psych.* [Transl. of G *Auslöser* (1935) < *auslösen* to release] In the plural, sign stimuli that elicit behavior in animals of the same species (this is different from the old meaning of "one who releases"). O, R, W [4]

religionless Christianity, *n.* (1953) *Theol.* [Transl. of G *religionsloses Christentum* < *religionslos* religionless, having no religious beliefs + *Christentum* Christendom, Christianity, ult. < L *religion-, religio* + *chrīstiānus* < Gk *christianós*] Christianity viewed separately from many of the practices and doctrines of conventional religion. O [3]

rell-mouse, -mice *pl.* (1752) *Zool.* (archaic) [Ad. of G *Rell-maus* (from Grimm) (or perhaps Du *relmuis*) < G *Rell* male or *Relle* female mouse gathering hazelnuts, or (see

Adelung) < *rellen* to shell + *Maus* mouse] A dormouse. O [3]

renin, *n.* (1906) *Physiol.* [G (1897) < *ren-* + *-in* < L *rēnes* kidneys + *-in* -in] A proteolytic enzyme stored in the kidneys, which hydrolyzes hypertensinogen to hypertensin (this is different from the earlier meaning of "animal kidney's substance"). O, R, W [4]

Rentenmark, *n.* (1923) *Currency* [G < *Rente,* pl. *Renten* annuity (< Fr *rente* annuity, pension) + G *Mark* mark (q.v.)] A temporary unit of currency used in Germany in 1923, vainly to stabilize the currency, and in 1924 replaced by the reichsmark (q.v.). O, W [3]

repetitor, *n.* (1770) *Ed.* [G tutor < LL *repetitor* repeater] A private tutor, usu. in Law, at a German university or college. O [3]

repress, *v.* (1909) *Psych.* [Transl. of G *verdrängen* (1893) to crowd out, repress] In psychoanalysis, of a patient or person who is the object of study: to keep out of one's conscious mind, or suppress one's unacceptable memories or desires into the unconscious. O, R [4]

reprivatize, *v.* (1950) *Politics* [Transl. of G *reprivatisieren* < L *re-* again, back + G *privat* < L *prīvātus* private + G infin. suffix *-ieren* -ize] To make private again; to denationalize. O, R [3]

reprography, *n.* (1956 *W9*) *Tech.* [G *Reprographie,* a blend of *Reproduktion* reproduction + *Photographie* photography] The duplication and reproduction of documentary and graphic material by light rays or photographic means. O, R [4]

reserpine, *n.* (1952 *W9*) *Bot.* [G *Reserpin* (1952), a combining of *Rauwolfia* (< NL) a plant of the genus *Rauwolfia* < the name of Leonhard *Rauwolf* (c.1540–96), German botanist + ML *serpentina* serpentine] A crystalline alkaloid obtained from the roots of rauwolfias and used to treat tension and mental disorders. R, W [4]

residence city, *n.* (1961) *Politics* [Transl. of G *Residenzstadt* < *Residenz* (< ML *residentia* residence) + G *Stadt* city] Seat of a princely or royal court such as Versailles. O [3]

Residenz, *n.* (1840) *Politics* [G < ML *residentia* residence] The building where a German princely court resided before 1818; the town containing such a building. O [3]

Residenzstadt, *n.* (1961) *Politics* [G residence city (q.v.)] The seat of a princely court. O [3]

resinophore (group), *n.* (1972) *Chem.* [G *Resinophor* (1921) < *resino-* + *-phor* < L *resina* resin + Gk *phóros* bearing (+ E *group*)] A group that tends to cause polymerization and resinification when the compounds in which they are contained are heated above the boiling point. O [3]

resite, *n.* (1913) *Chem.* [G *Resit* (1909) < L *resina* resin + G *-it* -ite] C-stage (phenol-aldehyde) resin: an insoluble, infusible resin that is the final product in an alkaline condensing into a phenolic resin. O, W [3]

resitol, *n.* (1913) *Chem.* [Prob. < G (1913) (< L *resina* resin) + an infixed G *-t-* + *-ol* (< *Alkohol* alcohol, ult. < Ar)] B-stage (phenol-aldehyde) resin: a rubbery, thermoplastic resin that is the intermediate product in an alkaline condensing into a phenolic resin (see *resol* and *resite*). O, W [3]

Resochin, *n.* (1946) *Pharm.* Var. **resochin** (1946) [G a trade

name coined < L *resina* resin + *-o-* + *china* < Quechua *quina* china bark, actually *quinaquina* bark of barks, i.e., the best of barks] A proprietary name for chloroquine. O [3]

resol/resole, *n.* (1913) *Chem.* [G *Resol* (1909) < L *resina* resin + G *-ol* (< *Alkohol* alcohol, ult. < Ar) -ol(e)] A-stage (phenol-aldehyde) resin: a fusible, usu. fluid resin that is the first product in an alkaline condensing into a phenolic resin, and that is used in laminating and impregnating paper and fabrics. O, W [3]

ressentiment, *n.* (1941 *W9*) *Psych.* [G < Fr *ressentiment* hidden resentment] Resentment or frustration expressed indirectly against a hostile or indifferent person or society, esp. by belittling the values esteemed by the person or society, and accompanied by a sense of helplessness in securing redress in such a universe. • This meaning was also transferred directly from French into English as *ressentiment.* R [4]

restitution nucleus, *n.* (1927) *Biol.* [Transl. of G *Restitutionskern* (1927) < the gen. of *Restitution* (< L *restitūtiō* restitution) + G *Kern* nucleus] A cell nucleus containing twice the regular chromosome number, usu. formed by an incomplete division in mitosis. O, W [3]

Reststrahlen, pl. (1910) *Physics* [G < *Rest* rest + *Strahl* ray] Electromagnetic radiation that is reflected from a crystalline solid's surface when the frequency of the radiation approximates the frequency of vibration of the ions composing the solid. —**Reststrahl/restrahl,** *n.* (1967). O [2]

reticulin, *n.* (1899) *Med.* [G (1892) < L *rēticulum* small net + G *-in* -in] A structural protein similar to collagen and considered to be a constituent of reticular tissue. O, W [3]

reticuloendothelial, *a.* (1924) *Med.* [G (1924) (now also *retikuloendothelial*) < *reticulo-* + *endothelial* < L *rēticulum* small net, network + NL *endothelium* < Gk *éndon* within + *thēlé* nipple + G *-ial* -ial] Of, relating to, or specifying a diverse system of cells arising from mesenchyme (q.v.), comprising most of the phagocytic cells of the body and helping resistance and immunity to infection. —**reticuloendothelial system** (1924). O, R, W [4]

reticuloendotheliosis, *n.* (1926) *Med.* [G *Reticuloendotheliose* (1924) (now *Retikuloendotheliose*) < *retikulo-* + *Endotheliose* < L *rēticulum* small net, network + NL *endothelium* < Gk *éndon* within + *thēlé* nipple + G *-ose* (< Gk *-osis* fem. suffix of action) -osis] Reticulosis: abnormal leukemic or aleukemic reactions in the reticuloendothelial (q.v.) cells or their derivatives. O, W [3]

reticulosis, *n.* (1932) *Med.* [G *Retikulose* (1924), a short. of *Reticuloendotheliosis* (q.v.)] A proliferative disease of reticuloendothelial cells. O, W [3]

reticulum cell, *n.* (1912) *Med.* [G *Reticulumzell* (1889) (now *Retikulumzelle*) < *Reticulum* + *Zell* (now *Zelle*) < L *rēticulum* small net, network + *cellula* small cell] A branched, anastomosing cell of the reticuloendothelial system. O, W [3]

retinula, -e pl. (1878) *Biol.* Var. **retinule** (1924) [G (1877), dim. of *Retina* < *retin-* + *-ula* -ule < ML *retina* < *rēte* net] The neural receptor of a single facet of an insect's or crustacean's compound eye. —**retinula,** *a.* (1978); **retinulate,** *n.* (1883); **retinular** (1888). O, R, W [4]

rézbányite[1], *n.* (1868) *Mineral.* Old var. **retzbanyite** (1868)

[G *Rézbányit* (1858) < *Rézbánya,* the name of a village in Hungary, now Baita in Rumania + G *-it* -ite] An impure ore of bismuth. O [3]

rézbányite[2]**,***n.* (1884) *Mineral.* [G *Rézbányit* (1883)—see *rézbányite*[1]] A granular sulfide of copper, lead, and bismuth. O, W [3]

rhabdophane, *n.* (1878) *Mineral.* [G *Rhabdophan* < *rhabdo-* + *-phan* < the comb. form of Gk *rhábdos* rod + *phanós* clear] A hydrous phosphate of yttrium, cerium, and rare-earth elements occurring massive. O, W [3]

rhabdophanite, *n.* (1892) *Mineral.* [G *Rhabdophan* rhabdophane (q.v.) + E *-ite*] Rhabdophane. O, W [3]

rhaetizite, *n.* (1816) *Mineral.* Var. **rhetizite** (1864) [G *Rhätizit* (1815) < L *rhaeticus* of *Rhaetia,* the classical name for a section of the Alps + G *-it* -ite] A white variety of cyanite. O [3]

Rhaeto-Romanic, *n., a.* (1867) *Ling.* Var. **Rheto-Romance** (1878), **Rhaeto-Romansh, Rheto-Romansch, Rhetian** [Ad. of G *rätoromanisch* < *räto-* + *romanisch* < L *rhaeto-,* the comb. form of *rhaetus* Rhaetian + *Rōmānicus* Roman + G adj. suffix *-isch* -ic/(i)sh] (of) Friulian, Ladin, and various Romansh dialects of southeastern Switzerland, perhaps to be considered as variants of a single Romance language. O, R, W [4]

rhagite, *n.* (1874) *Mineral.* [Ad. of G *Ragit* (1874) < Gk *rag-, ráx* grape + G *-it* -ite] A hydrous arsenate of bismuth occurring in a grapelike arrangement. O [3]

rhamnose, *n.* (1888) *Biochem.* [G (1887) < L *rhamnos* breaking buckthorn, so named for its relation to the Rhamnus genus] A crystalline aldose sugar, usu. obtained by hydrolysis, but also occurring widely as combined glycosides in buckthorn berries. O, R, W [3]

Rheingold, *n.* (1935) *Transportation* Var. **Rheingold express** (1935) [G (1869), lit., gold of the Rhine, also the name of an opera by Richard Wagner, actually a short. of G *Rheingoldzug* Rheingold train (or express)] A Trans-Europe express train that connects Amsterdam and Basel, following the Rhine. O [3]

rhenium, *n.* (1925) *Chem.* [G < L *Rhēnus* Rhine + G (< L) *-ium* -ium] A very dense, refractory, rare metallic element belonging to the manganese group. • ~ is symbolized as **Re.** O, R, W [4]

rheomorphism, *n.* (1937) *Geol.* [G *Rheomorphose* (1937) < *rheo-* + *morphose* < Gk *rhéos* flow, stream + *morphé* shape, form + *-osis,* fem. suffix denoting action)] The metamorphic process by which a rock becomes conspicuously mobile and partially or wholly fused. —**rheomorphic** (1937). O, W [3]

rheotaxis, -axes *pl.* (1900) *Zool.* [G (1894) < *rheo-* + *-taxis* < Gk *rhéos* flow, stream + *táxis* arrangement, order] A taxis where there is oriented movement of an organism in response to a stream of fluid such as water. —**rheotactic(ally)** (1900, 1975). O, R, W [3]

rheotropism, *n.* (1887) *Zool.* [G *Rheotropismus* (1883) < *rheo-* + *Tropismus* < Gk *rhéos* flow, stream + *tropé* orientation, turning + G (< L) *-ismus* -ism] A tropism where there is oriented movement of an animal or plant in response to a stream of fluid such as water. —**rheotropic** (1897). O, R, W [4]

Rhetian, *see* Rhaeto-Romanic

rhetizite, *see* rhaetizite

Rheto-Romance, Rheto-Romansh, *see* Rhaeto-Romanic

rhine, *n.* (1641) *Textiles* Old var. **rine** (1641), modern var. **Riga rhine (hemp)** (1765) [Transl. of G *Reinhanf,* lit., clean hemp < *rein* + *Hanf,* by erron. association with the *Rhine* River < the name *Rhein*] A high grade of Russian hemp. O [3]

Rhine daughter/maiden, *n.* (1897) *Music* [Transl. of G *Rheintochter* < the name of the river *Rhein* Rhine + *Tochter* daughter] Any of three water maidens, guardians of the Rheingold in Wagner's *Der Ring des Nibelungen* (1853–74); transf. sense to the fair blond physique with which they are usu. depicted. O [3]

Rhinelander[1]**,** *n.* (1858) *Politics* [G *Rheinländer* < *Rheinland,* the name of the Rheinland, the part of Germany west of the Rhine + *-er* -er] A native or resident of the Rhine province of Prussia or of the Rhineland; a native speaker of a Rhenish dialect of German. O, W [3]

Rhinelander[2]**,** *n.* (1887) *Dance* [G *Rheinländer* Rhineländer[1] (q.v.)] A variety of German polka or schottische (q.v.). Also as Rheinlander South German version of a polka. O [3]

Rhine maiden, *see* Rhine daughter

Rhine wine, *n.* (1843) *Beverages* [Ad. of G *Rheinwein* < *Rhein* (the name of Germany's principal river) Rhine + *Wein* wine] A wine produced in the Rhine valley; one of a class of white wines similar to this. O, R, W [4]

rhinion, *n.* (1904) *Physiol.* [G (1888) < NL < Gk, dim. of *rhīnós* nose + L *-ion* -ion] The point where the median suture joins the nasal bones. O, W [3]

rhinophyma, -ta/-s *pl.* (1882) *Med.* [G (1881), coined by Hans Ritter von Hebra (1847–1902) < *rhino-* + *-phyma* < Gk *rhīnós* nose + *phŷma* tumor, growth] A nasal nodular swelling and congestion due to advanced acne rosacea. O, W [3]

rhizobium, -bia/-biums *pl.* (1921) *Bot.* Var. **Rhizobium** (1921) [G (1899), coined by the German botanist Albert Bernard Frank (1839–1900), ult. < Gk *rhíza* root + *bíos* life + G *-ium* (< L) -ium] A type genus of Rhizobiaceae, small soil bacteria; a bacterium of this genus. O, R, W [4]

rhizosphere, *n.* (1929) *Bot.* [G *Rhizosphäre* (1904) < *rhizo-* + *Sphäre* < Gk *rhíza* root, bud + *sphaîra* ball, sphere] The soil that is influenced chemically and bacteriologically by the plant roots in it. —**rhizosphere effect.** O, W [4]

rhodamine, *n.* (1888) *Chem.* Var. **Rhodamine** (1888) [G *Rhodamin* (1887) < *rhod-* (< Gk *rhódon* rose) + G *Amin* amine (q.v.)] Any of a class of fluorescent xanthene dyes such as rhodamine B and rhodamine 6G, used in coloring and in making organic pigments. O, R, W [4]

rhodeoretin, *n.* (1845) *Chem.* [G < *rhodeo-* + *Retin* < Gk *rhódeos* roseate < *rhódon* rose + *rētínē* resin] Convolvulin (q.v.). —**rhodeoretinole** (1845), **rhodeoretin(ol)ic** (1853, 1853). O [3]

rhodinal, *n.* (1900) *Chem.* [G (1891) < Gk *rhódinos* out of roses + G *-al* -al < *Aldehyd* aldehyde (q.v.)] Levorotatory citronellol, an unsaturated liquid alcohol. O, W [3]

rhodinol, *n.* (1892) *Chem.* [G (1891) < Gk *rhódinos* out of roses + G *-ol* -ol (< G *Alkohol* alcohol, ult. < Ar)] A liquid obtained usu. from rose oil or geranium oil, used in perfumes; rhodinal (q.v.). O, W [3]

rhodizite, *n.* (1836) *Mineral.* [G *Rhodizit* < Gk *rhódizein* to be rose red < *rhódon* rose + *-izein* -ize + G *-it* -ite, so named because it colors the blowpipe-flame red] A hydrous borate of beryllium, aluminum, lithium, sodium, and potassium. O, W [3]

rhodizonic acid, *n.* (1839) *Chem.* [Transl. of G *Rhodizonsäure* (1837) < *rhodizon-* (< Gk *rhodízein* to be rose-red) + E *-ic* + G *Säure* acid] A cyclic acid known in a colored enediol form and in a more stable tautomeric form, but usu. obtained as a colored salt. —**rhodizonate,** *n.* (1842). O, W [3]

rhodochrosite, *n.* (1836) *Mineral.* [G *Rhodochrosit* (now *Rhodochrozit*) < Gk *rhodóchrōs* rose-red + G *-it* -ite] A usu. rose-red manganese carbonate, also called *dialogite* (q.v.). O, R, W [4]

rhodonite, *n.* (1823) *Mineral.* [G *Rhodonit* < Gk *rhódon* rose + G *-it* -ite] A pale-red, triclinic manganese silicate; also called *manganese spar* and *fowlerite*. O, R, W [4]

rhodoplast, *n.* (1886) *Bot.* [G (1885) < *rhodo-* + *-plast* < Gk *rhódon* rose + *plastós* formed] A reddish chromatophore found in the red algae. O, W [3]

rhodopsin, *n.* (1886) *Biochem.* [G (1878) < *rhod-* + *-opsin* < Gk *rhódon* root + *ópsis* sight + G *-in* -in] A brilliant purplish-red, photosensitive pigment found in the retina of humans, certain fishes, and most vertebrates, which light breaks down into vetinene and opsin; also called *visual purple* (q.v.). O, R [4]

rhodusite, *n.* (1894) *Mineral.* [G *Rhodusit* (1891) < L *Rhodus,* Gk *Rhódos,* the name of an Aegean island + G *-it* -ite] A fibrous variety of riebeckite (q.v.), where magnesium replaces some of the iron. O [3]

rhombencephalon, -s/-cephala *pl.* (1897) *Anat.* [G < *rhomb-* + *Encephalon* < L *rhombus,* Gk *rhómbos* parallelogram with equal sides + Gk *enképhalos* brain] The parts of the vertebrate brain that develop from the embryonic hindbrain; the hindbrain. —**rhombencephalic** (1954). O, R, W [3]

rhyacolite, *n.* (c.1830) *Mineral.* [G *Ryakolith* < *ryako-* + *-lith* -lite < Gk *rýax* mountain stream + *líthos* stone] Sanidine (q.v.). O, W [3]

rhynchodæum, -dæa *pl.* (1894) *Zool.* [Ad. of G *rhynchodaeal* (1893), coined by the German physiological chemist Adolf Daniel Oswald (1870–1956) < *rynch-* + *-odaeal* < Gk *rhýnchos* snout + *hodaîon* < *hodaîos* along the way < *hodós* way] The cavity anterior to and partially containing the proboscis of nemertines and certain other invertebrates. —**rhynchodæal,** *a.* (1972). O [3]

rhynchokinesis, *n.* (1963) *Zool.* [Ad. of G *Rhynchokinetik* (1949) < *rhyncho-* + *Kinetik* < Gk *rhýnchos* snout + *kinētikós* moveable] The capacity of some birds and lizards to raise their upper bill or jaw relative to the cranium by extensively bending nasal and premaxillary bones. O [3]

rhynchosporium, -sporia *pl.* (1920) *Bot.* Var. **Rhynchosporium** (1971) [Transl. into English of the orig. formed G *Schnabelried* (1900) < *Schnabel* snout + *Ried* reed, using the naturalized classical elements < Gk *rhýnchos* snout + *sporá* sowing + L *-ium,* neuter of *-ius*] A fungus of this genus, which causes leaf blotch in cereals and other grasses; the disease so caused. O [3]

rhynchostome, *n.* (1894) *Zool.* [G *Rhynchostom,* coined by Oswald in 1893 (see *rhynchodæum*) < *rhyncho-* + *-stom*

-stome < Gk *rhýnchos* snout + *stóma* mouth] Proboscis-bearing gastropods' anterior opening of the rhynchodæum (q.v.). O [3]

rhyolite, *n.* (1868) *Geol.* [G *Rhyolith* (now *Rhyolit*) < *rhyo-* + *-lith* -lite < Gk *rýax* mountain stream + *líthos* stone] Orig. a variety of Hungarian trachyte; now an acid, extrusive volcanic rock containing quartz and sanidine as the lava form of granite. O, R, W [4]

rhythmite, *n.* (1946) *Geol.* [G *Rhythmit* (1936) < L *rhythmus,* Gk *rhythmós* rhythm + G *-it* -ite] A varve: each of the repeated units in a sediment formation showing a rhythmic structure. O [3]

ria, *n.* (1899) *Geogr.* [G *Rias* (1886), adopted in this sense by Ferdinand Freiherr von Richthofen (1833–1905), German geographer < the pl. of Sp *ría* estuary < *río* < L *rīvus* river] A long, narrow inlet of the sea caused by submergence of a narrow river valley (this is different from the general meaning of "creek," borrowed earlier < Sp *ría*). O, W [3]

ría coast, *n.* (1902) *Geogr.* Old var. **rias coast** (1924) [Transl. of G *Riasküste* (1886) < *Rias* (see *ria*) + *Küste* coast < L *costa*] A coast containing numerous rias. O [3]

riboflavin, *n.* (1935) *Biochem.* Var. **riboflavine** [G (1935), a blend of *Ribose* ribose (q.v.) + *Flavin* < L *flāvus* yellow + G *-in* -in] Vitamin B or vitamin G: a yellow flavin pigment found in milk, green leafy vegetables, etc.; also called *lactoflavin.* —**riboflavin phosphate.** O, R, W [4]

ribonic acid, *n. Chem.* [Transl. of G *Ribonsäure* < *Ribon-,* metathesized < *Arabinose* arabinose + E *-ic* + *Säure* acid] An acid obtained by oxidation of ribose. W [3]

ribose, *n.* (1892) *Biochem.* [G (1891), a short. of *Ribonsäure* (see *ribonic acid*) + *-ose* -ose, denoting a carbohydrate] A crystalline, aldopentose sugar occurring in many nucleosides and obtained usu. from ribonucleic acid. —**ribose,** *a.* (1920); **riboside.** O, R, W [4]

richterite, *n.* (1868) *Mineral.* [G *Richterit* (1865) < the name of Theodor *Richter* (1824–98), German metallurgical chemist + *-it* -ite] A variety of amphibole containing manganese, sodium, etc. as bases; the end member of the amphibole series containing this, but lacking manganese. O, W [3]

ricker, *n.* (1820) *Industry* [Poss. < G *Rick* pole] A spar or pole made from the stem of a young tree. O, W [3]

riebeckite, *n.* (1889) *Mineral.* [G *Riebeckit* (1888) < the name of Emil *Riebeck* (1853–85), German explorer + *-it* -ite] A black, monoclinic amphibole with much sodium and iron. O, R, W [3]

riegel, -s and (erron.) **-n** *pl.* (1910) *Geol.* [G (pl. *Riegel*) < MHG *rigel,* OHG *rigil* bar] A low transverse ridge of rock running along the floor of a glaciated valley. O, W [3]

Riemann surface, *n.* (1893) *Math.* [Prob. transl. of G *Riemann-Fläche* < the name of Georg Friedrich Bernhard *Riemann* (1826–66), German mathematician + *Fläche* surface] A geometric representation of a complex variable's function, where a multiple-valued function is presented as a single-valued function on several planes. O, R [3]

Riesling, *n.* and *a.* (1833, 1833) *Beverages* [G, a wine known in Germany as early as 1490 as *Rußling/Rüßling,* but its etymology is unknown] (of) a variety of grape or grape vine widely grown in Germany and Austria; a dry white table wine made from this grape. —**Riesling**, *a.* O, R, W [4]

riffle, *n.* (1875) *Geol.* [Prob. < G *Riff* < MLG *rif, ref* shallow, ult. < ON meaning "rib," or G *Riffel* < late MGH *rif(f)el,* OHG *rif(f)ila* saw, rake; in the plural, riblike depressions and elevations] A shoal, reef, or shallow in a stream. O, W [4]

riffle, *v.* (1754) *Geol.* [Prob. < G *riffeln* (now also *riefeln*) to create shallows < MGH *rif(f)eln, rif(f)ilon* to saw] To form grooves or riffles; to flow over a riffle. O, W [4]

riffler, *n.* (1797) *Trades* [Poss. < G *riffeln* to cut grooves into an object (or < Fr *rifloir* a kind of file)] A small, curved file-like tool used by sculptors and wood carvers. O, W [4]

Riga rhine, *see* rhine

rille/rill, *n.* (1876) *Geol.* [G *Rille* (< LG *rille,* dim. of MLG *rīde* brook, hence, small brook) long, narrow groove in the surface of something usu. made of a hard substance] One of several long, narrow trenches or valleys on the moon. O, R, W [4]

rinderpest, *n.* (1865) *Med.* [G < *Rinder* (pl.) cattle, oxen + *Pest* plague, disease < L *pestis*] An infectious, usu. fatal disease of cattle. • ~ is transl. as **cattle plague** (1866). —**rinderpest,** *a.* (1873). O, R, W [4]

ring, *n.* (1935) *Math.* [G < MHG *rinc,* OHG *(h)ring* ring] A set of elements with two particular binary operations— addition and multiplication. • ~ is different from the many earlier meanings. O, W [3]

ringelnatter, *n. Zool.* [G < *Ringel* small ring < MGH *ringel(n),* dim. of *rinc* ring + G *Natter* adder < MHG *nater,* OHG *nat(a)ra,* prob. meaning orig. that which winds or twists] A harmless ringed snake found in Europe. W [3]

ring fracture, *n.* (1919) *Geol.* [Transl. of G *Kreisbruch* < *Kreis* ring, circle + *Bruch* fracture < *brechen* to break] A conical or near-cylindrical fault associated with cauldron subsidence. O [3]

ring rot, *n.* (1920) *Agric.* [Transl. of G *Bakterien(ring)fäule* < *Bakterien,* pl. of *Bakterium* bacterium + *Ring* ring + *Fäule* rot < *faulen* to rot] A bacterial disease of potatoes, or a fungal disease of sweet potatoes; a decay in a log closely following the annual rings. O, R, W [3]

rinkite, *n.* (1886) *Mineral.* [G *Rinkit* < the name of Heinrich Johannes *Rink* (1819–93), Danish explorer + G *-it* -ite] Mosandrite (q.v.). O, W [3]

rinneite, *n.* (1909) *Mineral.* [G *Rinneit* (1908) < the name of Friedrich *Rinne* (1863–1933), German mineralogist + *-it* -ite] Potassium sodium iron chloride. O, W [3]

Rinne('s) test, *n.* (1899) *Med.* [Transl. of G *Rinne-Versuch* (1855) < the name of Heinrich Adolf *Rinne* (1819–68), German otologist + *Versuch* attempt, try, test] A diagnostic test for deafness that employs a tuning fork. O [3]

ripidolite, *n.* (1850) *Mineral.* [G *Ripidolith* (1839) (now *Ripidolit*), irreg. < *rhipid-* + *-lith* -lite < Gk *rhipido-,* the comb. form of *rhípis* (gen. *rhipídis*) fan + *líthos* stone] Clinochlore, a magnesium aluminum silicate usu. containing iron. O, R, W [3]

Riss, -es *pl.* (1910) *Geol.* [G *Riß* < the name of a Danube tributary in Austria and Germany, adopted by Albrecht Penck (in Penck and Eduard Brueckner's *Die Alpen im*

Eiszeitalter, 1901–09) to designate the third Pleistocene glaciation in the Alps] The third stage of Pleistocene glaciation in Europe. —**Riss,** *a.* (1931). O, W [4]

Riss-Würm, *n.* (1910) *Geol.* [G *Riß-Würm* (1909) < *Riß,* the name of a Danube tributary in Austria and Germany + *Würm,* the name of a lake and small stream in southern Bavaria] The third interglacial interval during the Pleistocene glaciation in Europe, preceding the Würm (q.v.). O, W [3]

ritter, -ø/-s *pl.* (1824) *Politics* [G < MHG *ritter,* MLG *riddere* (a transl. of OF *chevalier* knight), or MHG *rīter, rītaere* horseman] A knight or member of a lower order of German or Austrian nobility. O, R, W [3]

rittmaster, *n.* (1648) *Mil.* (archaic) Var. **ritmaster** (1721) [Ad. of G *Rittmeister* < *Ritt,* early MHG *rytte* troop of horsemen + *Meister* master] A cavalry captain. O, W [3]

Rn, *see* radon

Robinsonade, -s/-n *pl.* (1847) *Lit.* Var. **robinsonade** (1941), **Robinsonnade** (1967) [G (1731) < *Robinson* Crusoe, hero of Defoe's novel of that name in 1719 + G *-ade,* ult. < OProv *-ada* < LL *-ata* < fem. form of L *-atus* -ate] A fictitious narrative of usu. fantastic adventures, esp. of a person like Robinson Crusoe and his shipwreck on a desert island. O, W [3]

rocketsonde, *n.* (1949) *Meteor.* Var. **rocket sonde** (1949), **rocket-sonde** (1951) [Combining of E *rocket* + G *Sonde* probe, patterned on G *Radiosonde* radiosonde (q.v.)] A rocket-lifted package of meteorological or other scientific measuring instruments that is parachuted back to earth. O, R [3]

roemer, *see* rummer

roemerite, *n.* (1877) *Mineral.* Var. **romerite** (1903) [G *Römerit* (1858) < the name of Friedrich Adolf *Römer* (1806–69), German geologist + *-it* -ite] A hydrous sulfate of ferrous and ferric iron. O, R, W [3]

roentgenkymogram, *n.* (1913) *Med.* [G *Roentgenkymogramm* (1912) (also short. to *Kymogramm*) < the name of Wilhelm Conrad *Röntgen* (1845–1923), German physicist + *Kymogramm* < Gk *kŷma* wave + *-gramma* record] A picture obtained by recording the movements of an organ on an X-ray film. O, W [3]

roentgenkymography, *n.* (1913) *Med.* [G *Röntgenkymographie* (1912) (also short. to *Kymographie*) < the name of Wilhelm Conrad *Röntgen* (1845–1923), German physicist + *Kymographie* < Gk *kŷma* wave + *gráphein* to write, record + G *-ie* (< Gk *-ia*) -y] The process or technique of using a kymograph: kymography on a moving X-ray film. —**roentgenkymographic(ally)** (1930, 1940). O, W [3]

roesslerite, *n.* (1868) *Mineral.* Var. **rösslerite** (1903) [G *Rösslerit* (1861) < the name of Karl *Rössler,* a 19th-cent. German scientist in Hanau + *-it* -ite] Magnesium orthoarsenate. O, W [3]

roesti, -ø *pl.* (1952) *Food* Var. **rösti** (1953), **rosti** (1961) [(Swiss) G *Rösti* < *rösten* to fry] A Swiss style of homefried potatoes. O [2]

rohr bordun, *n. Music* [G < *Rohr* reed, pipe + *Bordun* bourdon < Fr *bourdon* < MFr bass horn, of imitative origin] A rohrflöte (q.v.) of 16-foot pitch. W [3]

rohrflöte, -n/-s *pl.* (1855) *Music* Var. **rohr flute** (1911) [G

< *Rohr* reed + *Flöte* flute < MFr *flahute* < OProv *flaut*] A pipe-organ stop having closed metal pipes with chimneys. O, W [3]

rohr nasat, *n. Music* [G < *Rohr* reed, pipe + *Nasat* nazard] A rohrflöte (q.v.) speaking at 2⅔-foot pitch. W [3]

rohr quinte, *n. Music* [G < *Rohr* reed, pipe + *Quinte* fifth in music < ML *quīnta* (*vōx*) fifth tone] A rohr nasat (q.v.). W [3]

rollade, -n *pl.* (1989) [G a window shutter wound on a spindle, common in Continental Europe] This kind of roller shutter. L2 [3]

roller, *n.* (1663) *Ornith.* [G (*Harzer*) *Roller* < *Harzer* < the name of *Harz,* a central German mountain range + *rollen* to roll, reverberate < MFr *rol(l)er* < L *rotulus*] Any of numerous, nonpassarine, Old World coracoid birds, usu. the *Coracias garrulus;* another bird such as a canary that sings with a long, recurrent trill. —**roller,** *a.* (1855). O, R, W [4]

rollmops, -ø/-e *pl.* (1912) *Food* Erron. var. **rollmop** (1964) [G < *rollen* to roll, i.e., rolled + *Mops* pugnosed dog, alluding to the shape of the pickled herring] A pickled, spiced fillet of herring, rolled up with pickle or onions. O, R, W [4]

Romadur, *n. Food* Var. **romadur** [G < Fr *romadour/romatour,* of unknown origin] A cheese resembling Limburger in aroma and flavor. W [3]

Romanist, *n.* (1523) (archaic) *Theol.* [Archaic G as used by Luther in 1520 < NL *Romanista* a member or adherent of the Church of Rome, or directly < NL into E] A usu. disparaging term for a Roman Catholic. —**Romanist,** *a.* (1635). O, R, W [4]

Romanze, -n *pl.* (1883) *Music* [G *Romance* < Fr < Sp folk poem < OProv *romans,* OFr *romanz* something composed in French, tale in verse] An instrumental composition of a lyrical or tender character, usu. slow, romantic, and operatic. • ~ is different from the It or Sp *romanza* meaning ''romantic or lyrical piece of music.'' O [3]

romerite, *see* roemerite

Rondsdorfer, *n. Theol.* Var. **Ronsdorfian** [G an inhabitant of *Ronsdorf,* the name of a city in northern Germany where the sect was founded + *-er* -er] A member of a small sect of 18th-century millenarians, also called *Zionite.* W [3]

roodle, *n. Games* [Ad. of G *Rudel* pack, troop, flock] A special, one hand of a round of hands in poker. W [3]

roof organization, *n.* (1948) *Econ.* [Transl. of G *Dachorganisation* < *Dach* roof + *Organisation* organization < MFr or ML *organization*] A parent organization. O [3]

root pressure, *n.* (1875) *Bot.* [Transl. of G *Wurzelkraft* (1865) < *Wurzel* root + *Kraft* force, i.e., pressure] The hydrostatic, osmotic pressure by which water rises into plant stems from the roots. O, R, W [3]

roscherite, *n.* (1916) *Mineral.* [G *Roscherit* (1914) < the name of Walter *Roscher,* 20th-cent. German collector of minerals of Ehrenfriedersdorf + *-it* -ite] A hydrous basic phosphate of beryllium, manganese, iron, and calcium. O, W [3]

rosewort, *n.* (1578) *Bot.* [Prob. transl. of G *Rosenwurz* < *Rose* rose + *Wurz,* MHG *wurz,* now almost always used in compounds, now *Wurzel* root, *Wurze* wort] Roseroot, the perennial herb *Sedum rosea,* whose roots smell like roses. O, W [3]

rosickyite, *n. Mineral.* [G *Rosickýit* < the name of Vojtech *Rosický* (1880–1942), Czech mineralogist + G *-it* -ite] A native sulphur in the gamma crystal form. W [3]

Rosicrucian, *n.* (1624) *Theol.* Many old var. like **Rosicrutian** (1653) [Irreg. and short. of G *Frater Rosae Crucis* (or directly from NL into E), a latinization of the name of the legendary Christian *Rosenkreutz,* reported to have lived 1378 to 1484 and to have founded the secret Rosicrucian Society claiming alchemistic and other powers + G *-er* -an] An adherent of this secret philosophical society in the 17th and early 18th centuries, which claimed secret and magic knowledge; a member of an organization held to be descended from the Rosicrucians and dedicated to esoteric wisdom. —**Rosicrucian,** *a.* (1662); **-crucianism** (c.1740); **-crucianize** (1833); **-crucianity** (1838); **-crucian Order** (1961). O, R, W [4]

rosolic acid, *n.* (1835) *Chem.* [Transl. of G *Rosolsäure* < *rosol-* (< L *rosa* rose + *-ol-* < G *Alkohol* alcohol, ult. < Ar) + G *Säure* acid] Aurin (q.v.); a crystalline compound made red by transmitted light, also called *coralline.* O, W [3]

rösslerite, *see* roesslerite

rosti, *see* roesti

rotameter, *n.* (c.1907 *W9*) *Chem.* Var. **Rotameter** (1911), **rotometer** [Partial transl. of G *Rotamesser* (1911) < *rota* (< L) wheel + G *Messer* meter] A proprietary name for a gauge that measures the flow of a gas or a liquid through it; an instrument for measuring curved lines. O, R, W [3]

rötheln, *n.* (1873) *Med.* [G *Röt(h)eln,* pl. < *rot(h)* red, *röten, röteln* to turn red] German measles. O [2]

Rot(h)liegende, *a.* and *n. Geol.* [G *rothliegende* (now *rotliegende*), the pl. form of *rothliegend* < *roth* (now *rot*) red + *liegend* present part. of *liegen* to lie, so named for the red sandstone beds near Eisenach, central Germany] Of, pertaining to, or being a subdivision of the European Permian. W [3]

rotometer, *see* rotameter

rotor, *n.* (1949) *Meteor.* [G (1938) < L *rotāre* to turn] A large eddy where the air circulates around a horizontal axis (this is different from the various older meanings of the Latin-derived word). O [3]

Rottweiler, *n.* (1907) *Zool.* Var. **Rottweiller** (1917) [G < *Rottweil,* the name of a city in Baden-Württemburg, southwest Germany, where the species was bred + *-er* -er] A German breed of black cattle dogs; a Rottweiler dog. —**Rottweiler,** *a.* (1962). O, R, W [4]

Rottweiler, *a.* (1989) [G *Rottweiler* (q.v.), a dog of that name with a vicious reputation] (Brit.) viciously aggressive, like the dog (this is different from the earlier adjectival meaning ''of this breed or individual dog''). L2 [4]

Rottweiler politics, *n.* (1989) *Politics* [Expansion of G *Rottweiler* (q.v.) + E *politics*] (Brit.) politics marked by vicious aggression. L2 [4]

Rotwelsch, *n.* (1841) *Ling.* Old var. **Rothwelsch** (1841) *Ling.* [G *Rothwelsch* (now *Rotwelsch*) < MHG *rot* false or *rot* beggar + *Welsch* obscure language] A form of slang or cant used by underworld people and vagrants in Germany and Austria. O [2]

Rouget cell, *n.* (1922) *Anat.* Var. **Rouget's cell** (1961) [Ad. of G *Rougetsche Zelle* (1922) < the name of Charles *Rouget* (1824–1904), French physiologist + G *Zelle* cell < OFr *celle* < L *cella*] One of the various branching cells adhering to the capillaries' endothelium: pericyte. O, W [3]

roumanite, *see* rumanite

rounce, *n.* (1855) *Games* [Irreg. poss. < G *Ramsch* < Fr *ramas* heap of useless objects < *ramasser* to gather up] A variety of ramsch (q.v.) played with a full deck of cards; a similar domino game (this is different from the older, Dutch-derived "printing" meaning). —**rounce,** *v.* (1864). O [3]

round dance, *n.* (1950) *Zool.* [Transl. of G *Rundtanz* (1923) < *rund* round (< OFr *roont* < L *rotundus*) + G *Tanz* dance] Bees' circular movement performed at the hive or nest, thought to inform other bees of a near source of food (this is different from the old meaning of "dance performed by people"). O [3]

roumanite, *see* rumanite

rubeanic acid, *n.* (1891) *Chem.* [Transl. of G *Rubeanwasserstoffsäure* < *rubean* (< L *rubeus* red) + G *Wasserstoff* hydrogen + *Säure* acid] Dithio-oxamide; an intensely colored thioamide that is a weak acid. O, W [3]

rubiacin, *n.* (1848) *Chem.* Var. **rubiacine** (1848) [G (now also *Rubiazin*) < L *rubia* the genus madder, akin to L *ruber* red + G *-in* -in with an infixed *-c-*] A yellow coloring matter obtained from madder root. O [3]

rubidium, *n.* (1861) *Chem.* [G (1861) or < NL < L *rubidus* dark red + G (< L) *-ium* -ium, so named for the two red lines in its spectrum] An alkali metallic element. —**rubidium,** *a.* (1862); **rubidic**; and in numerous compounds like **rubidium strontium** (1950). • ~ is symbolized as **Rb.** O, R, W [4]

rubinglimmer, *n.* (1836) *Mineral.* [G < *Rubin* ruby (< MHG *rubin* < ML *rubinus* < L *rubeus* red) + G *Glimmer* mica] Lepidocrocite (q.v.). O [3]

rucksack, *n.* (1866) [G < Upper G, Swiss G *ruggsack* < MHG *ruck(e)* back + G *Sack* sack] Knapsack or backpack. —**rucksacked** (1909). O, R, W [4]

rückumlaut, *n. Ling.* [G < *rück-* < *zurück* back, backward + *Umlaut* umlaut (q.v.)] The absence of umlaut of the stem vowel in the past part. and past tense of some Germanic weak verbs resulting from the loss of *i* in the following syllable before the umlaut period (as in G *brennen,*

brannte, gebrannt to burn). • ~ is transl. as **unmutation.** W [3]

Rudesheimer, *n.* (1797) *Beverages* [G < the name of *Rüdesheim,* a German city on the Rhine + *-er* -er] Any of the fine Rheingau wines produced from the vineyards near Rudesheim. O, R [3]

rumänite, *n.* (1892) *Mineral.* Var. **roumanite** (1904) [G *Rumänit* (1891) < the name of *Rumänien* Rumania + *-it* -ite] A fossil resin similar to amber, found in Rumania and used for lovely jewelry; also called *Rumanian amber.* O, R [3]

rummer, *n.* (1654) *Beverages* Old var. **romer** (1673), **roemer** (1897) [Ad. of G *Römer* < 16th-cent. *roemer* < MHG *roemsch g(e)las* Roman glass] A large, tall German wineglass with a globular top and a cylindrical bottom. O, R, W [4]

Rumpelstiltskin, *n.* (1949) *Lit.* [Ad. of G *Rumpelstilzchen* < *rumpeln* rumble + dim. of archaic *Stulz* one who limps, actually, a rumbling, noisy sprite] A vindictive dwarf in a German folktale; applied allusively to marketing. O, R [4]

rumpf, *n. Anat.* [G rump < MHG *rumph*] Core or atomic kernel: the remainder of an atom after the valency electrons are removed; the trunk of a body. R, W [3]

runcle, *n.* (1784–1815) *Food* (archaic) [(Austrian, Swiss) G *Runkel,* a short. of *Runkelrübe,* prob. related to *Runken* clump of bread or *Runzel* wrinkle, crinkle, because of its strikingly wrinkled seed + *Rübe* beet] A variety of beet, used as fodder. O [3]

rutch, *v.* [Ad. of G *rutschen* to slide < MHG (of echoic origin)] To move with a shuffling or crunching noise in hunting. W [3]

rutherfordine, *n.* (1907) *Mineral.* [G *Rutherfordin* (1906) < the name of Ernest *Rutherford* (1871–1937), English physicist + G *-in* -ine] A fibrous, orthorhombic uranyl carbonate. O, W [3]

rutile, *n.* (1803) *Mineral.* [G *Rutil* (1803) < L *rutilis* reddish] Titanium dioxide; a variously colored synthetic gem that rivals a diamond in beauty. —**rutile,** *a.* (1830). O, R, W [4]

rutin, *n.* (1857) *Chem.* Old var. **rutine** [G (1842) < L *ruta* rue + G *-in* -in] A yellow crystalline flavonol glycoside found in several plant species and used in treating hypertension and radiation injury. —**rutin,** *a.* (1868). O, R, W [3]

S

s/S, *n.* (1926), *Physics* [G (1926), an abbr. of the E borrowing *Spin,* a rendering of G *Eigendrehimpuls* characteristic impulse to turn] The quantum number of spin angular momentum of a single electron (= *s*) or of a group of electrons (= *S*). O [3]

SA/S.A., *n.* (1931) *Politics* [G, an abbr. of *Sturmabteilung* (q.v.) a uniformed, armed, political section of the Nazi Party] A Nazi political or military unit, which orig. helped bring Hitler into prominence. O, R [4]

saal, *n.* (1855) Var. **Saal** (1855) [G < MHG, OHG *sal* ult. meaning "habitation"] A large room or hall. O [3]

Saale, *a.* (1937) *Geol.* [G < the name of the *Saale* River in Germany] Of the third Pleistocene glaciation in northern Europe, equivalent to the Alpine Riss (q.v.) glaciation. O [3]

Saalian, *n.* (1931) and *a.* (1933) *Geol.* Var. *a.* **Saalic** (1969) [Ad. of G *saalisch* (1920) and *n. Saale* < the name of a tributary of the Elbe River + adj. suffix *-isch* -ian] (Specifying or relating to) a minor orogenic period in Europe that is thought to have occurred in the early Permian period. O [3]

Saar, *a.* (1905) and *n.* (1967) *Beverages* [G *Saar(wein)* < the name of the *Saar* River in Germany (+ *Wein* wine)] (Of) a white wine produced in the Saar region. O [3]

Saarlander, *n.* (1955) *Politics* [G < *Saarland,* the name of a formerly West German "Land" state, province + *-er* -er] A native or resident of Saarland. —**Saarlander,** *a.* (1980). O, R, W [3]

sabadine, *n.* (1891) *Biochem.* Var. **sabatine** (1951) [G *Sabadin* (1891) < NL *sabadilla* < Sp *cebadilla,* dim. of *cebada* oats + G *-in* -ine] A crystalline alkaloid found in sabadilla seeds, used in medicine. —**sabadine hydrochloride.** O, W [3]

sabinene, *n.* (1900) *Chem.* [G *Sabinen* (1900) < NL *sabina* < L *Juniperus sabina* savin + G *-en* -ene] A liquid, bicyclic terpene hydrocarbon found in several essential oils, esp. savin oil. O, W [3]

saccharin, *n.* (1880) *Chem.* Var. **saccharine** (1885) [G (1879) < ML *saccharum* < Gk *sákcharon,* ult. < Skt *śarkarā* sugar, gravel—this was codiscovered and so named by Ira Remsen (1846–1927), American chemist and Constantin Fahlberg (1850–1910), German chemist, in *Berichte der Deutschen Chemischen Gesellschaft* (1879, in vol. 12, p. 470)] The anhydride of saccharic acid; today a crystallide imide widely used as a sweetener or sugar substitute containing little or no food value. —**saccharin(e),** *a.* (1926–7); **saccharinic (acid)** (1881); **saccharined** (1962); **saccharinize(d)** (1971,1977). O, R, W [4]

saccharite, *n.* (1859) *Mineral.* [G *Saccharite* (1845) < Gk *sákcharon* sugar (see *saccharin*) + G *-it* -ite, so named for its resemblance to sugar] A granular, massive mineral, orig. thought to be andesite (q.v.), but now considered to be a mixture. O [3]

Sacher torte, Sachertorte, *n.* (1906) *Food* Var. **sachertorte** (1961) [G < the name of the Viennese hotelier, F. *Sacher* (1816–1907) + G *Torte* torte (q.v.)] A rich, layered chocolate torte, particularly served by the 19th- and 20th-cent. Sacher family in their hotel restaurant. O, R, W [3]

Sachlichkeit, *n.* (1930) *Art* [Short. of G *neue Sachlichkeit* (q.v.)] Objectivism or realism in the fine arts. O [3]

Sachverhalt, -e *pl.* (1922) *Philos.* [G < *Sache* thing + *Verhalt* state] A state of affairs, as in Wittgenstein's philosophy and phenomenology; an objective fact. O [2]

Sacramentarian, *n.* (1845) *Theol.* Var. **sacramenter** (1845) [Ad. of G *Sacramenter,* as used by Martin Luther (now *Sakramenter*) < *Sacrament* < MHG < LL *sacrāmentum* consecration, dedication + G *-er* -er, used pejoratively in the 16th cent. to refer to a person who considered the sacraments to be only symbolic; now used in jest to refer to someone who is annoying] A person who considers the sacraments not to be supernatural or inherently efficacious; a jesting name for someone who is annoying; a Sacramentalist. O, W [4]

saengerbund/sängerbund, *n. Music* [G *Sängerbund* < *Sänger* singer + *Bund* union, association, society] A German choral society or one composed chiefly of persons of German descent. • ~ is transl. as **singing bund** (1867 *DA*). W [3]

saengerfest/sängerfest, *n.* (1865) *Music* [G *Sängerfest* < *Sänger* singer + *Fest* fest (q.v.)] A choral festival of a saengerbund (q.v.). • ~ is transl. as **songfest** (q.v.). O, W [3]

safflorite, *n.* (1852) *Mineral.* [G *Safflorit* (1835) (now also *Saflorit* < *Safflor* safflower (ult. < Ar *asfar* yellow) + G *-it* -ite] An orthorhombic cobalt arsenide. O, W [3]

safrene, *see Introduction*

safrod, *see Introduction*

sahlite, *n.* (1807) *Mineral.* [G *Sahlit* (1800) < *Sahla,* the old name of a Swedish town + G *-it* -ite] Early name for salite (q.v.). O [3]

saibling, *n.* (1884) *Ichthy.* [Standard G use of Bavarian colloq. variant of G *Salmling,* dim. of *Salmler, Salm* < MHG *salme,* OHG *salmo,* L *salmo* salmon] A char in European mountain streams, introduced into North America; Sunapee trout. O, W [3]

salamstone, *n.* (1816) *Mineral.* [Transl. of G *Salamstein,* poss. < the Indian name *Salam* + G *Stein* stone] A blue, Sri Lankan variety of sapphire. O [3]

salband, *n.* (1811) *Geol.* [G, lit., selvage < MHG *selbende, selpende* < *selp* self (< OHG *selb*) + *Ende* end] A thin coating or crust, as in the border of an igneous dike. O, W [3]

salicet, *n.* (1852) *Music* [G (1703) (now also *Salizett*) < L *salix* (gen. *salicis*) willow + G dim. suffix (< Fr) *-et*] A pipe-organ stop similar to the salicional (q.v.), but of 2-foot or 4-foot pitch. O, W [3]

salicional, *n.* (1843) *Music* [G (now *Salizional*) < L *salix* (gen. *salicis*) willow + G suffixes *-on* + *al* -onal] A soft-toned, labial pipe-organ stop normally of 8-foot pitch. O, W [3]

salite, *n. Mineral.* [G *Salit* (1800) < *Sala,* the name of a town in Västmanland, Sweden + G *-it* -ite] A variety of diopside, a pyroxene. W [3]

salmiac, *n.* (1799) *Chem.* [G *Salmiak,* a short. of ML *sal ammoniacum*] Sal ammoniac: ammonium chloride. O, W [3]

salmine, *n.* (1896) *Biochem.* [G *Salmin* (1896) < NL *salmo* < L salmon + G *-in* -ine] A protamine secured from the sperm of the salmon and related species, used in medicine. O, W [3]

salonfähig, *a* (1905) *Sociol.* [G < *Salon* (< Fr *salon,* It *salone* festive hall) + G *fähig* capable, i.e., fit for society] Fit for polite society; socially acceptable. O [3]

salpingography, *n.* (1935) *Med.* [G *Salpingographie* (1925) < *salpingo-* + *-graphie* < Gk *sálpinx* (gen. *sálpingos*) Fallopian tubes + *gráphein* to write, recórd] The process or technique of obtaining an image of the Fallopian tubes with X-rays or ultrasound. O [3]

salta, *n.* (1901) *Games* [G < L, imper. of *saltāre* to jump] A game for two played on a checkerboard. O, R, W [3]

saltatoric, *a.* (1877) *Path.* [G *saltatorisch* < L *saltātor* < *saltāre* to jump + G adj. suffix *-isch* -ic] Relating to saltatoric spasm, a nervous disease where the patient when standing begins to leap. O [3]

saltworks, -ø *pl.* (1565) *Industry* Var. **salt-work(s)** (1565) [Transl. of G *Salzwerk* < *Salz* salt + *Werk* works] A plant where salt is made commercially. O, R, W [4]

Salvarsan, *n.* (1910) *Chem., Pharm.* Var. **salvarsan** (1910) [G (1907) a proprietary name < L *salvāre* to save, heal + G *Arsenik* arsenic + L *sānus* hale, well, sound] Arsphenamine: the proprietary name of an arsenic compound formerly used in treating syphilis. O, R [4]

samarskite, *n.* (1849) *Mineral.* [G *Samarskit* (1847) (or Fr) < the name of Col. Vasilii von *Samarski*-Bykhovets (1803–70), Russian mineralogist + G *-it* -ite] A velvet-black, rare-earth oxide. O, R, W [4]

samsonite, *n.* (1910) *Mineral.* [G *Samsonit* (1910) < the name of the *Samson* mine at Sankt Andreasberg, in the Harz Mountains, Germany + *-it* -ite] A silver manganese antimony sulfide (this is different from the usu. capitalized forms meaning ''variety of dynamite'' or ''trademark for luggage''). O, W [3]

sandburg, *n.* (1970) [G < *Sand* sand + *Burg* castle] A circular wall of wet sand that seaside bathers customarily build around themselves in Germany to mark their beach headquarters. B [3]

sand cake, *n.* (1892) *Food* [Transl. of G *Sandkuchen* or *Sandtorte* < *Sand* sand + *Kuchen* (q.v.) or *Torte* (q.v.), named for its sand-crumbling resemblance] A kind of cake that crumbles. O [3]

sandnatter, *n. Zool.* [G < *Sand* + *Natter* adder] A sand boa; a sand viper. W [3]

sängerbund, *see* saengerbund

sängerfest, *see* saengerfest

sanidine, *n.* (1815) *Mineral.* [G *Sanidin* (1808) < Gk *sanís* (gen. *sanidós*) board + G *-in* -ine] A monoclinic variety of feldspar (q.v.): glassy feldspar. —**sanidinic** (1885), **sanidinite** (1887). O, R, W [3]

sapogenin, *n.* (1862) *Chem.* [G (1854), coined < a short.

of *Saponin* (< L *sāpo,* gen. *sāpōnis* soap, of Gmc origin) + Gk *gennân* to produce + G *-in* -in] The nucleus of nonsugar residue of saponin, used in synthesizing steroidal hormones. O, W [3]

saponarin, *n.* (1902) *Chem.* Old var. **saponarine** (1923) [G (1902) < ML *sāpōnāria* soapwort + G *-in* -in] A white to yellow powdery flavonoid diglycoside orig. found in soapwort, used in medicine. —**saponaretin** (1905). O [3]

saponite, *n.* (1849) *Mineral.* [Sw or G *Saponit* (1841) < L *sāpo* (gen. *sāpōnis*) soap + G *-it* -it, as a transl. of G *Seifenstein* soapstone] A hydrous silicate of aluminum and magnesium, occurring in soft, soapy, amorphous masses, filling veins in serpentine and cavities in trap-rock. O, R, W [4]

sapotoxin, *n.* (1891) *Chem.* [G (1887), coined < ML *sāpōnāria* soapwort + G *Toxin* < Gk *toxikón* (*phármakon*) poison for arrows] A highly toxic saponin; a saponin obtained from the bark of the Chilean soapbark tree. O, W [3]

sapperment, *interj.* (1815) [G, irreg. < *Sakrament* sacrament] An oath that writers put in the mouth of their German speakers. O [2]

sapphirine, *n.* (1823) *Mineral.* Old var. **saphirine** (1866) [G *Saphirin* (1819) < *Saphir* < MHG sapphire + G *-in* -ine] A usu. granular, pale-blue magnesium aluminum iron silicate and oxide. O, R, W [4]

saprine, *n.* (1887) *Chem.* Var. **saprin** (1894) [G *Saprin* (1885) < Gk *saprós* putrid + G *-in* -ine] A ptomaine obtained from putrid flesh. O [3]

saprobe, *n.* (1932) *Biol.* Var. **saprobiont** [G *Saprobie* (1902) < Gk *saprós* putrid + *bíos* life] Any organism that obtains its food from decaying organic matter. O, R, W [3]

saprobic, *a.* (1913) *Ecology* [G *saprobisch* saprobic < *Saprobie* saprobe (q.v.) + *-isch* -ic] Characterized by an environment of decaying organic matter; pertaining to a saprobe. —**saprobical** (1961), **saprobicity** (1971), **saprobically.** O, R, W [4]

saprobiont, *see* saprobe

sapropel, *n.* (1907) *Geol.* [G (1904) < *sapro-* + *-pel* < Gk *saprós* putrid + *pēlós* clay, mud] A slimy, nitrogen-rich sediment formed of incompletely decomposed plants and animals found in anaerobic bottoms of lakes and seas; kerogen. —**sapropelite.** O, R, W [4]

sapropelic, *a.* (1901) *Chem.* [G *sapropelisch* (1901) < *Sapropel* (q.v.) + adj. suffix *-isch* -ic] Living in, characterized by, relating to, or obtained from sapropel. O, R, W [4]

sapsago, *n.* (1846) *Food* Var. **Schabzieger** (q.v., 1837) [Folk etymological var. of G *Schabzi(e)ger* < *schaben* to scrape + (Austrian, Bavarian) *Zieger* whey, whey cheese] A hard green cheese made of skim-milk curd. O, R, W [4]

sarawackite, *n.* (1882) *Mineral.* [G *Sarawakit* (1877) < the name of the Malaysian state *Sarawak,* northern Borneo + G *-it* -ite] An antimony compound found in minute crystals. O [3]

sarcine, *n.* and *a.* (1858, 1858) *Chem.* Var. **sarkine** (1887) [G *Sarkin* < *sark-* < Gk *sark-* flesh + G *-in* -ine] (of) a base existing in flesh juice. O [3]

sarcopside, *n.* (1877) *Mineral.* [G *Sarkopsid* (1868) < *sark-* + *-opsid* < Gk *sark-* flesh + *ōps* face, eye + G

-id -ide, named for its fleshlike color] A fluoride and phosphate of iron, calcium, and manganese exhibiting a flesh-red color. O, W [3]

sarcosine, *n.* (1848) *Chem.* Old var. like **sarcosin** [G *S-arkosin* (1847) < *sarcos-* (< Gk gen. *sarkós* flesh) + G *-in* -ine] A sweetish crystalline amino acid used in toothpaste; N-methyl-glycine. —**sarcosinic** (1877). O, R, W [3]

sarcosome, *n.* (1899) *Biol.* Var. **sarcosoma** [G *Sarcosom* (1890) (now *Sarkosom*) < NL *sarcosoma* < Gk *sárx* (gen. *sarkós*) flesh + *sôma* body] An anthozoan's fleshy portion as opposed to the skeleton; a large mitochondrion of a striated muscle fiber. O, R, W [4]

sarin/Sarin, *n.* (1951) *Chem.* [G, of unknown origin (*Meyers Großes Universallexiken* analyzes it as an acronym but does not identify the etyma)] A corrosive, odorless, organophosphorous nerve gas. O, W [4]

sarkine, *see* sarcine

sarmatier, *n. Zool.* [G, prob. < *Sarmatien* Sarmatia, the name of an ancient region north of the Black Sea + *Tier* animal, beast] Perwitsky, a European or Asian tiger weasel or its fur. W [3]

sassolin(e), *n.* (1807) *Mineral.* [G *Sassolin* < the name of the Lago del *Sasso* in Tuscany, Italy + G *-in* -in(e) with an infixed *-l-*] Native boric acid deposited in the hot springs of Tuscany; now usu. known as *sassolite* (1868). O, W [3]

sastrugi/zastrugi, *pl.* (sometimes as *sing.* **sastruga/zastruga**) (1840) *Geogr.* [G (< Russ *zastrúga* small ridge, groove) and directly < Russ] One of a series of many wavelike ridges of hard snow formed by the wind in the snowfields of the Antarctic and Arctic regions. O, R, W [4]

satem, *a.* (1901) *Ling.* [G *Satem(sprachen)* (1890) < Avestan *satəm* hundred + G *Sprachen* languages, so named because the initial fricative of Avestan *satəm* represents an I-E palatal stop] The linguistic name for the chiefly eastern group of Indo-European languages, distinguished by their use of sibilants, in contrast to the velar stops used in the corresponding sounds in cognate words in the western group, called *centum.* • ~ mainly appears in **satem language(s)** (1901). O, R, W [4]

sauerbraten, *n.* (1889) *Food* [G < *sauer* sour + *Braten* roast] An orig. German dish of marinated, roasted beef. • ~ is transl. as **sour beef** (1935). O, R, W [4]

sauerkraut, *n.* (1617 *W9*) *Food* Var. **sourkrout** (1617), **sourcrout** (1863) [G < *sauer* sour + *Kraut* cabbage] Finely cut cabbage that has undergone acid fermentation; a cabbage dish popular in Germany; U.S. slang for a German. • ~ appears in compounds like **sauerkraut barrel** (1888)/**eater** (1918)/**cutter** (1969)/**juice/keg** O, R, W [4]

saynite, *n.* (1858) *Mineral.* [G *Saynit* (1853) < *Sayn*, the name of its locality in Prussia + G *-it* -ite] Grünauite: a native sulfide of bismuth and nickel. O [3]

S-bahn, *n.* (1962) *Transportation* [Short. of G *Schnellbahn*, *Stadtbahn* < *schnell* fast + *Stadt* city, i.e., urban + *Bahn* rail line] In some German cities a high-speed railway line or system. O [3]

scandal of particularity, *n.* (1930) *Theol.* [Transl. of G *Ärgernis der Einmaligkeit* < *Ärgernis* annoyance, vexation + *der* (gen. of *die* of the + *Einmaligkeit* uniqueness,

singularity] The problem in perceiving the particular man, Jesus, as the universal Savior. O [3]

scapolite, *n.* (1802) *Mineral.* [G or Fr *Scapolith* (1800) (now G *Scapolit*) < L *scapus* < Gk *skâpos* rod + *líthos* stone + G or Fr *-it* -ite] One of a group of minerals intermediate between meionite and marialite resembling feldspar when massive; also called *wernerite;* a member of this group. —**scapolitized,** *part. a.* (1909); **-tization** (1932); **-tize** (1936). O, R, W [4]

scapulet(te), *n.* (1887) *Zool.* [G *Scapulette* (now *Skapulette*) < NL *scapula* shoulder (blade) + G (< Fr) *-ette* -et(te)] A fold in the manubrium's lobal base in many rhizostomous medusae. O, W [3]

scat, *see* skat

schaalstone, *see* schalstein

Schabzieger, *n.* (1837) *Food* Var. **Chapsager** (1846), **sapsago** (1846), **Schabziger** (1950) [G *Schabziger* < *schaben* to grate + *Ziger* a kind of cheese] A Swiss, hard green cooking-cheese. —**Schabzieger Käse** (1969). O, W [4]

schadenfreude/Schadenfreude, *n.* (1852) *Psych.* [G < *Schaden* damage, injury, harm + *Freude* joy, enjoyment] Malicious enjoyment obtained from the mishaps of others. O, R, W [4]

schafarzikite, *n.* (1922) *Mineral.* [G *Schafarzikit* (1921) < the name of Ferenc *Schafarzik* (1854–1927), Hungarian mineralogist + G *-it* -ite] An oxide of iron and antimony occurring in crystals. O, W [3]

schafskopf, *n. Games* Var. **schafkopf** [G blockhead < *Schafs* sheep's (gen. of *Schaf*) + *Kopf* head] Blockhead; sheepshead (q.v.). R, W [3]

schalet(e), *n.* (1943) Food Var. **schaleth** (1943) [Poss. < G *Schaleth*, a G var. of Yiddish *tsholnt*, but prob. directly from Yiddish into E (Meyer lists *Schalet* but gives no etymology)] A baked fruit pudding; a Jewish main dish of meat, potatoes, and vegetables, prepared on Friday and slowly baked overnight. O [3]

Schallanalyse, *n.* (1930) *Ling.* [G < *Schall* sound + *Analyse* analysis < NL *analysis* < Gk] A method of reconstructing the metrics of an earlier textual record by analyzing the reaction of a trained observer who responds instinctively and directly to the psychological compulsion exerted by the text on anyone who reads it aloud. O [3]

schalmei/schalmey, *n. Music* [G *Schalmei* < MHG *schal(e)mî(e)* < OFr *chalemel(le)*, LL *calamellus* tubulet] A shawm, a medieval woodwind instrument preceding the oboe family; a chalumeau, a kind of reed organ pipe. W [3]

schalstein, *n.* (1804) *Geol.* Var. **schaalstein** (1804) [G *Schaalstein* < *Schaale* skin, shell + *Stein* stone] (Archaic) wollastonite; a variety of tuffaceous rock: slaty greenstone. • ~ is partially transl. as **schaalstone** (1804). O, W [3]

schaman, *see* shaman

schapbachite, *n. Mineral.* [G *Schapbachit* < *Schapbach*, the name of a town in Baden-Württemberg, Germany + *-it* -ite] Matildite, a silver bismuth sulfide. W [3]

schappe, *n.* (1885) *Textiles* Var. **chappe** [(Swiss dial.) G raw silk waste < *schappen*, a var. of *schaben* to scrape] A fabric or yarn made of spun silk or an imitation like rayon. —**schappe,** *v.;* **schapping,** *verbal n.* (1909). O, R, W [4]

scharf, *a. Music* [G sharp, bright < MHG < OHG *scarf,* actually, cutting] A mixture stop in a pipe organ with a penetrating, bright tone. W [3]

Schatz, *n.* (1907) Var. **schatz** (1971) [G treasure < *schätzen* to value] A German term of endearment for a woman, girlfriend or female companion. •The dim. forms *Schatzi* and *Schätzi* (1956, 1970) were also borrowed. O [2]

Scheele's green, *n.* (1819) *Chem.* [Transl. of G *Scheeles-Grün* (1778) < the gen. form of the name of Karl Wilhelm *Scheele* (1742–86), German-born Swedish chemist + *grün* green] Copper acid orthoarsenate, formerly used as a pigment in wallpaper and calico printing; a strong green color. O, R, W [3]

scheelite, *n.* (1837) *Mineral.* [G *Scheelit* < the name of Karl Wilhelm *Scheele* (1742–86), German-born Swedish chemist + G *-it* -ite] A native calcium tungstate, used as a commercial source of tungsten. O, R, W [4]

Scheherazade, *n.* (1851) *Lit.* [G < Ar < Per *Shīrāzād,* the name of an Indian sultan's fictional wife who tells him such fascinating, incomplete tales nightly that he spares her life] This wife; a usu. attractive young woman who narrates long or numerous stories. —**Scheherazadian,** *a.* O, R [4]

Scheitholt, *n.* (1961) *Music* [G < *Scheit* log + dial. G < LG *holt* wood, NHG *Scheitholz* split log] An early stringed instrument of Central Europe, a precursor of the zither. O [2]

schellingism, *n.* (1865) *Philos.* [G *Schellingismus* < the name of Friedrich Wilhelm Joseph von *Schelling* (1775–1854), German philosopher + *-ismus* (< L) -ism] The system of philosophy taught by Schelling. —**Schellingian,** *a.* (1865); **Schellingist** (1895). O, R [3]

schelm, *n.* (1584?) [G (as specified in the 1584 *OED* citation) < MHG *schelm(e)* rascal, rogue—not < Du *schelm* or *skellum*] An abusive or contemptuous term for Germans meaning "rascal." O [3]

schelmish, *a.* (1634) (archaic) [G *schelmisch* < *Schelm* (q.v.) + *-isch* -ish] Rascally. O [3]

schema, -ta/-s *pl.* (1796) *Philos.* [G < L *schēma* < Gk *schêma* position, form, figure] In Kantianism a general representation produced by the imagination. • ~ is different from the various later meanings borrowed directly from Greek. O, R, W [4]

schenk beer, *n.* (c.1850 *Ks*) *Beverages* Var. **shenk beer** (q.v.) [Loose transl. of G *Schankbier* < *Schank,* MHG *schanc* a measure for dispensing liquids + *Bier* beer, now beer from the tap] A beer produced in the winter by the bottom-fermentation process. W [3]

Schering bridge, *n.* (1926) *Tech.* Var. **Schering's bridge** (1975) [Transl. of G *Schering-Brücke* < the name of Harald Ernst Malmsten *Schering* (1880–1959), German electrical engineer + *Brücke* bridge] Schering's alternating-current bridge circuit devised to measure the capacitance of conductors and to measure energy loss in insulating materials. O, W [4]

schieferspar, *n.* (1807) *Mineral.* [Ad. of G *Schieferspath* (1789) (now *Schieferspat*) < *Schiefer* slate + *Spath* spar] Slate spar. O [3]

schill, *n.* (1885) *Ichthy.* Var. **schiel** (1885) [G pike perch] A zander, a European pike perch. O [3]

schiller, *a.* (1804) and *n.* (1885) *Mineral.* [G glimmer, ir-

idescence] (of) a mineral's bronzy iridescent luster of a mineral; (of) such a coloration, as in a beetle. O, R, W [4]

schiller spar, *n.* (1796) *Mineral.* [Ad. of G *Schillerspath* (1786) (now *Schillerspat*) < *Schiller* schiller (q.v.) + *Spath* spar] An altered enstatite (q.v.). O, W [3]

schiller stone, *n.* (1804) *Mineral.* [Partial transl. of G *Schillerfels* < *Schiller* glimmer, iridescence + *Fels* rock cliff] Norite, a variety of gabbro with a silky luster. O [3]

schilling, *n.* (1753) *Currency* [G < MHG *schillinc,* OHG *scilling,* perhaps a shield-like coin] A subsidiary unit of money once used in some of the northern states of Germany; the basic monetary unit of Austria; a coin representing either of these units. O, R, W [4]

Schimpfwort, -wörter *pl.* (1949) [G, lit., swearword < *Schimpf* insult < *schimpfen* to swear + *Wort* word] An insulting, abusive epithet. O [2]

schinken, *n.* (1848) *Food* [G ham] Ham. O [3]

Schinkenwurst, *n.* (1967) *Food* [G < MHG *schinke* < OHG *schinco* thigh < *Schinken* ham + *Wurst* sausage] Ham sausage. O [3]

schizoid, *a.* (1925) *Psych.* [G (1921) < *schiz-* + *-oid* < Gk *schízein* to split + *-oiedēs* similar] Having, characterized by, or caused by a split personality; disintegrating into mutually antagonistic or contradictory parts. —**schizoid,** *n.* (1925); **schizoidal,** *a.* (1938). O, R, W [4]

schizoidia, *n.* (1940) *Psych.* [G *Schizoidie* (1922) < *schizoid* (q.v.) + *-ie* (< Gk *-ia*) -ia] A schizoid condition, esp. when assumably caused by the same genetic illness as schizophrenia. O [3]

schizont, *n.* (1900) *Zool.* [G (1900) < *schiz-* + *-ont* < Gk *schízein* to split + *ón* (gen. *óntos*) being < *eînai* to be] In some sporozoans, a multinucleate cell that divides directly into merozoites; a protozoan's cell that divides asexually into daughter cells. —**schizonticide** (1943); **schizonticidal,** *a.* (1963). O, R, W [4]

schizophrene, *a.* (1925) *Psych.* [G *Schizophren* < *schizo-* + *-phren* < Gk *schízein* to split + *phrḗn* spirit, mind] A schizophrenic: someone with a predilection toward schizophrenia (q.v.). —**schizophrene,** *n.* (1936). O, W [3]

schizophrenia, *n.* (1912) *Psych.* [G *Schizophrenie* (1910) < *schizo-* + *-phrenie* < Gk *schízein* to split + *phrḗn* spirit, mind + G *-ie* (< Gk *-ia*) -ia] A mental disorder of complex etiology that occurs in various forms, all characterized by disturbed thinking and withdrawal from social activities into a fantasy life usu. with delusions and hallucinations; split personality. —**schizophrenic,** *a.* (1912), *n.* (1926); **schizophrenically** (1963). O, R, W [4]

schlafrock, *n.* (1836) *Apparel* [G < *schlafen* to sleep + *Rock* coat, gown] A dressing gown. O [2]

schlag, *n.* (1969) *Food* [G short. of *Schlagobers* (q.v.)] Schlagobers. O, R [3]

schläger, -ø *pl.* [G < MHG *sleger,* OHG *slagari* one who hits] A straight, long, blunt-tipped sword used in duels by German university students. W [2]

schlagobers, -ø *pl.* (1938) *Food* [Austrian G < G *schlagen* to beat, whip + *Obers* that which is on top, i.e., cream < *oben* on top] Whipped cream; coffee with whipped cream. O [2]

schlagsahne, -ø *pl.* (1907) *Food* [G < *schlagen* to beat, whip + *Sahne* cream] Whipped cream. O [3]

schlamperei, *n.* (1961) [G mess, slovenliness <

Schlamp(er) slob < *schlampen,* prob. echoic, to slurp < late MHG to dress slovenly, to let clothes hang on oneself] Muddleheadedness or slovenliness, esp. to designate a supposed South German and Austrian trait. O [3]

Schlemm's canal, *n. Optics* Var. **canal of Schlemm** [Transl. of G *Schlemmscherkanal* < the gen. of the name of Friedrich Schlemm (1795–1858), German anatomist + *Kanal* < L *canālis*] A circular canal within the sclerocorneal junction of the eye. W [3]

schlich, *n.* (1677) *Geol.* Var. **slickens**[2] (q.v.) [G *Schlick* slime, mud < MHG *slich*] Slime: very fine ore produced by wet crushing; slick (q.v.). O, W [3]

schlicht, *a.* (1944) *Math.* [G simple, plain < LG < MLG *slicht* bad] Pertaining to a (simple) analytic function in complex variable theory. O [3]

Schlieffen, *n.* (1919) *Mil.* Var. **Schlieffen plan** (1919) [G (1905) < the name of Alfred, Graf von *Schlieffen* (1833–1913), German general) (Relating to) Schlieffen's pre-1905 plan to invade and defeat France, as modified and applied in 1914. O [4]

schlieren, *pl.* (1885) *Geol.* [G < dial. G, the pl. of *Schlier* < MHG *slier* mud, clay] Small masses or streaks differing in mineral composition within the main body of an igneous rock; comparable streaks or regions in a transparent medium like a fluid. —**schlieric** (1921). • ~ appears in various compounds as an *a.,* as in **schlieren photograph** (1953)/**illumination** (1966). O, R, W [4]

schlieren apparatus, *n.* (1895) *Optics* [Ad. of G *Schlieren-Apparat* (1864) < *Schlieren* (q.v.) + *Apparat* apparatus < L *apparātus*] A device for observing and recording schlieren in transparent media. O [3]

schlieren method, *n.* (1899) *Optics* [G *Schlierenmethode* < *Schlieren* (q.v.) + *Methode* method < MFr or LL *methodus*] A method of observing and recording schlieren in transparent media. O, R [4]

schloss/Schloss, -es/-er *pl.* (1617) *Sociol.* [G castle, lock < *schliessen* to lock, close] A German castle or manor house. O, R, W [3]

schmeiss, -es *pl. Games* [G *Schmeiß,* the imper. of *schmeißen* to fling, throw away] A bid in klaberjass (q.v.) that requires one's opponent to accept that trump or suit or concede the hand. W [3]

Schmeisser, *n.* (1950) *Mil.* [G < the names of Hugo and Louis *Schmeisser,* 20th-cent. German small-arms designers] One of various German types of submachine gun, in use since 1918. —**Schmeisser,** *a.* (1963). O [3]

schmelz/schmelze, -es *pl.* (1854) *Industry* [G *Schmelz* enamel] Any of various kinds of decorative glass, esp. one used to flash white glass. —**schmelz,** *a.* O, W [3]

Schmelzglas, *n.* (1935) *Industry* [G < *schmelzen* to melt, fuse, liquify + *Glas* glass] Schmelz (q.v.); a glass of several colors that have been allowed to mingle before the vessel is formed. O [3]

schmerz, -es *pl.* (1911) *Psych.* Var. **Schmerz** (1925) [G < *schmerzen* to smart, hurt] Regret, grief, sorrow, pain. O [3]

Schmidt camera, *n.* (1978) *Astronomy* [G *Schmidt-Kamera* < the name of Bernhard Voldemar *Schmidt* (1879–1935), Estonian-born German optician + *Kamera* camera < LL *camera*] A camera utilizing a Schmidt system, used extensively in photofluorography and astronomy. O, W [3]

Schmidt number, *n.* (1955) *Tech.* [Transl. of G *Schmidt-Zahl* < the name of Ernst Heinrich Wilhelm *Schmidt* (1892–1935), German physicist + *Zahl* number] A dimensionless number analogous to the Prandtl number (q.v.), used in studying convective mass transfer. O [3]

Schmidt telescope, *n.* (1939) *Astronomy* [Short. and ad. of G *Schmidt-Spiegelteleskop* < the name of Bernhard Voldemar *Schmidt* (1879–1935), Estonian-born German optician + G *Spiegel* mirror + *Teleskop* telescope < Gk *teleskopós* farseeing] A photographic reflecting telescope; Schmidt camera (q.v.). O, R, W [4]

schmierkase, *n.* (1905) *Food* Var. **schmierkäse** [G < *schmieren* to smear, spread + *Käse* cheese] Cottage cheese (actually, cream cheese). O, R, W [3]

schnapper, *n.* (1827) *Ichthy.* Var. **snapper** (1827) [G < a short. of *Fliegenschnäpper* < *Fliegen* flies + *Schnäpper* < *schnappen* to snap, snatch, catch] (Fly)snapper: any of numerous active carnivorous fishes, important as food and in sport fishing. —**schnapper,** *a.* (1859). O, R, W [4]

schnapps, -ø *pl.* (1818) *Beverages* Var. **schnaps** [G *Schnaps* < LG *snaps,* orig., a mouthful, a quick swallow, ad. < G *schnappen* to snap, snatch] Any of various distilled liquors, esp. strong Holland gin. O, R, W [4]

schnauzer, *n.* (1923) *Zool.* [(Swiss) G *Schnauz(er)* whiskers, mustache, ad. < *Schnauze* snout; (vulgar) trap, gap; mouth] A wire-haired terrier of the Schnauzer breed; this old German breed. • ~ appears terminally in **giant/miniature/standard schnauzer.** O, R, W [4]

schnecken, *pl. Food* [G snails < *Schnecke* < MHG *snecke,* OHG *snecko,* actually, creeping animal] A cinnamon bun (rolled in the shape of a snail). R, W [3]

schneider, *n.* (1886) *Games* [G, lit., tailor < *schneiden* to cut, in English, an ellipsis of German *aus dem Schneider sein* to have exceeded the limits of *Schneider,* that is, the cut-off point; to have more than 30 points in skat] Various winning or losing points in skat, sheepshead (q.v.), or gin rummy; the scoring effect of a schneider. —**schneider,** *v.* (1935), *a.* O, R, W [3]

schnell, *adv.* or *a. Music* [G fast] Quickly: in a rapid manner, used as a direction in music. W [3]

schnitz/snits, -ø *pl. Food* Var. **snitz** [G (PaG, South G) slice, cut; sliced dried fruit < *schnitzen* to whittle, ad. < *schneiden* to cut] Sliced dried fruit, esp. apples. W [3]

schnitz and knepp, *pl.* (1869 *Sc*) *Food* (U.S. colloq.) PaG var. **schnitz un knepp** [Irreg. and partial transl. of colloq. G (South German, Swiss German, Austrian, PaG) *Schnitz un Knopp(e)* < *Schnitz* schnitz (q.v.) + *un* and + *Knopp,* pl. *Knoppe* dumpling] A dish of dried apples and dumplings, sometimes boiled with smoked ham. W [3]

schnitzel, *n.* (1854) *Food* [G < Late MHG *snitzel* cut, chop, dim. of *Schnitz* schnitz (q.v.)] A seasoned, garnished veal cutlet. • ~ appears terminally in compounds like **weiner** (1862)/**paprika** (1948) **schnitzel.** O, R, W [4]

schnorkel, *n.* and *a.* (1944, 1944) *Mil.* Var. **schnorchel** (1944), **schnorkle** (1946 *Algeo*), **snorkel** (1949 *Algeo,* q.v.) [G *Schnorkel* < dial. *Schnorchel, Schnorgel* mouth, snout, ad. < *schnorchen* to snore; akin to *schnarchen* to snore] (of) a tube or paired tubes housing air hoses that can be extended above the water surface to operate submerged submarines; (of) a submarine fitted with such apparatus. O, R, W [4]

schnurkeramik, *n.* (1902) *Archaeology* Var. **Schnurkeramik** (1902) [G < *Schnur* string + *Keramik* ceramics, pottery < Fr *céramique*] Corded ware: a Neolithic pottery decorated with imprinted string or cord. O, W [3]

scholzite, *n. Mineral.* [G *Scholzit* (1949) < the name of Adolf *Scholz,* 20th-cent. German mineral-collector of Regensburg + *-it* -ite] A hydrated basic phosphate of zinc and calcium. O [3]

schönfelsite, *n. Mineral.* [G *Schönfelsit* < the name of *Altschönfels,* Saxony, Germany + *-it* -ite] A feldspar-free basalt with phenocrysts of augite and olivine (q.v.) in a dense groundmass of various minerals. W [3]

schooner-sail, *n.* (1952) *Sports* [Transl. of G *Schonersegel* foresail < *Schoner* schooner + *Segel* sail] Foresail. O [3]

schorl, *n.* (1761) *Mineral.* Var. **shorl, schorlite** (q.v.) [G black tourmaline, an old word that might have come from the name of the German locality *Schörlau* village] A black tourmaline; (archaic) any of a large number of dark-colored minerals other than tourmaline. —**schorlaceous** (1794), **schorl rock** (1811), **schorl schist** (1885). O, R, W [4]

schorlite, *n.* (1794) *Mineral.* (archaic) Var. **shorlite** (1794) [G *Schorlit* (1788) < *Schörl* black tourmaline + *-it* -ite] Schorl (q.v.); pycnite, a massive columnar topaz. O, R, W [3]

schottische, *n.* (1849) *Dance* [G *(der) Schottische* < *(der) schottische Rundtanz* < *(der* the) + *schottisch* Scottish + *Rundtanz* round dance] A Scottish dance, a round dance in duple measure resembling the polka; the music for it. —**schottische,** *v.* (1865); **Highland/Military Schottische** (1882, 1894). O, R, W [4]

Schottky-barrier, *n.* (1949) *Physics* [G *Schottky-Barriere* (or *-Sperrschicht*) (1938, 1939) < the name of Walter *Schottky* (1886–1976), German physicist + *Barriere* barrier < MFr (or *Sperrschicht* < *sperren* to block + *Schicht* layer] An electrostatic depletion layer formed at a metal's interface, causing the junction to serve as an electrical rectifier. —**Schottky-barrier,** *a.* (1964). O [3]

Schottky-effect, *n.* (1925) *Physics* [G *Schottky-Effekt* (1914) < the name of Walter *Schottky* (1886–1976) + *Effekt* effect < MFr < L *effectus*] An increase in the thermionic current in a vacuum tube when there is a lowering of the energy needed to remove electrons from the cathode. O, R, W [3]

Schrammel band, *see* Schrammel quartet

Schrammelmusik, *n.* (1967) *Music* [G < the names of Johann (1850–97) and Josef (1852–94) *Schrammel,* Austrian musicians + G *Musik* music < OFr *musique,* ult. Gk *mousiké*] Music arranged for or played by a Schrammel quartet (q.v.). O [3]

Schrammel quartet, *n.* (1924) *Music* Var. **Schrammel band** (1963) [G *Schrammelquartett* < the names of Johann (1850–97) and Josef (1852–94) *Schrammel,* Austrian musicians + G *Quartett* quartet < It *quartetto* < L *quartus*] A light-music ensemble composed of two violins, a guitar, and now an accordion, popularized in Vienna by the Schrammels. O [3]

schrank, *n. Furniture* [G < Late MHG enclosed space < MHG *schranc,* OHG *scranc* webbing] (Regional U.S.) a

two-door clothes cabinet used by the Pennsylvania Dutch. R [3]

schraufite, *n.* (1896) *Mineral.* [G *Schraufit* (1875) < the name of Albrecht *Schrauf* (1837–97), Austrian mineralogist + G *-it* -ite] A blood-red fossil resin found in schistose sandstone. O (not in 2nd ed.) [3]

Schrecklichkeit, *n.* (1915) *Mil.* [G horror < *schrecklich* terrible, horrible + nom. suffix *-keit* -ness etc.] Horror or terrorism, esp. action or policy in warfare to terrorize the enemy; fig., as in parents' relationship with their children. • ~ is transl. as **frightfulness** (1914, q.v.). O, R [3]

schreibersite, *n.* (1849) *Mineral.* [G *Schreibersit* (1849) < the name of Karl Franz Anton von *Schreibers* (1775–1852), Viennese museum director + G *-it* -ite] A meteoric phosphide of iron and nickel, also called *rhabdite.* O, R, W [3]

Schreierpfeife, -n *pl.* (1939) *Music* [G < *Schreier* screamer < *schreien* to scream + *Pfeife* pipe < OHG *pfīfa*] An old woodwind of the schryari variety; a loud, straight-capped shawm. O [3]

Schriftsprache, *n.* (1931) *Ling.* [G < *Schrift* script + *Sprache* language, actually literary or standard language] The conventional, standardized written form of a language; (occasionally) a regional variation of this. O [3]

schroeckingerite, *n.* (1875) *Mineral.* Var. **schröckingerite** (1875) [G *Schröckingerit* (1873) < the name of Baron J. von *Schröckinger,* 19th-cent. Austrian mineralogist of Joachimsthal, Bohemia + G *-it* -ite] A hydrous carbonate, sulfate, and fluoride of sodium, calcium, and uranyl. O, W [3]

Schröder stairs/staircase, *n.* (1898) *Optics* [Transl. of G *Schröder-Treppe* (1858) < the name of H. G. F. *Schröder* (1810–85), German mathematician and physicist + *Treppe* flight of stairs, staircase] An optical illusion from a staircase drawn without convergence of receding parallel lines, whereupon one appears to look down at the top and then up at the underside of the staircase as the perspective reverses. O [3]

schrother, *n. Tech.* [Poss. < G *Schröter* grinder < *schroten* < MHG *schröten* < OHG *scrōtan* to chop or grind coarsely] Shredder: an operator of a machine that flakes metal scrap. W [3]

schrötterite, *n.* (1844) *Mineral.* [G *Schrötterit* (1839) < the name of Anton *Schrötter* (1802–75), German mineralogist + *-it* -ite] A former name for greenish opaline specimens of allophane. O [2]

schrund, *n.* (1870) *Geol.* [Short. of G *Bergschrund* (q.v.)] Bergschrund: a crevasse. —**schrund line** (1904). O, W [3]

Schubertiad, -en *pl.* (1869) *Music* [G *Schubertiade* < the name of Franz *Schubert* (1797–1828), Austrian composer + G *-iade* (modeled on G *Olympiade* < Gk *Olympías,* gen. *Olympíados,* Russian *olimpiada*) -iad] A concert party or recital devoted solely to performing songs and music by Schubert. O [3]

schuchardtite, *n.* (1885) *Mineral.* [G *Schuchardtit* (1882) < the name of Theodor *Schuchardt,* 19th-cent. German dealer in minerals + *-it* -ite] A green, hydrated silicate of nickel, resembling chlorite. O [3]

schuetzenfest, *n.* (1870) *Sports* [G *Schützenfest* < *Schützen,* pl. of *Schütze* marksman + *Fest* festival] A

shooting match, as at a picnic or entertainment. —
Schuetzen rifle. O, W [3]

Schuetzen rifle, *see* schuetzenfest

schuhplatteln, *v.* (1895) *Dance* [G to dance a schuhplattler
(q.v.)] To perform a schuhplattler. O [3]

schuhplattler, *n.* (1905) *Dance* Var. **Schuh plattler** (1926)
[G < dial. G *Schuochplattlar* < *Schuh* shoe + *Plattler*
one who slaps one's palms against one's shoes < *platteln*
to slap one's palms against one's thigh, seat, soles + *-ar*
-er] A Bavarian and Austrian courtship dance, where the
man slaps his thighs and heels. O, W [3]

Schuhplattltanz, *n.* (1874) *Dance* [G < *Schuhplattler*
(q.v.) + *Tanz* dance] A Bavarian and Austrian courtship
dance. O [2]

Schu mine, *n.* (1944) *Mil.* Var. **S-mine** (1944, q.v.) [Prob.
a short. of G *Schützenmine* < *schützen* to protect + *Mine*
mine] A type of German antipersonnel mine used in
World War Two. O [3]

schungite/shungite, *n.* (1892) *Mineral.* [G *Schungit* (1886)
< *Schunga/Shunga,* a Russian village on the Finnish bor-
der + G *-it* -ite] A hard, amorphous carbon occurring in
schists. O, W [3]

Schupo, *n.* (1923) *Politics* Var. **schupo** (1923) [G, a colloq.
short. of *Schutzpolizei* < *Schutz* protection + *Polizei* police < LL *polītīa* < Gk *politeía*] In Germany, a police-
man; the police force. O [3]

schuss, *a.* (1937) and *n.* (1947) *Sports* [G *Schuß,* lit., a shot
< OHG *schuʒ*] (of) a straight, high-speed skiing run down
a slope; (of) such a skiing course. —**schussboomer** (1959
W9), **schussbooming** (1961), **schussboom.** O, R, W [4]

schuss, *v.* (1937) *Sports* [Short. of G *Schußfahren* to make
a high-speed run on skiis down a slope < *Schuss* (q.v.)
+ *fahren* to go, travel] To schuss. —**schussing,** *verbal n.*
(1961). O, R, W [4]

Schutzbund, *n.* (1927) *Politics* [G, a short. of *Republika-
nischer Schutzbund* < *Schutz* protection, defense + *Bund*
league, alliance] An Austrian Social Democratic paramilitary, army-like group, disbanded in 1933. O [3]

Schutzbündler, -ø *pl.* (1974) *Politics* [G < *Schutzbund*
Schutzbund (q.v.) + *-ler* -ler, a person connected with
something] A member of the Schutzbund. O [2]

Schutzstaffel, -n *pl.* (1930) *Mil.* Var. **schutzstaffel** (1968)
[G, orig. a bodyguard < *Schutz* protection + *Staffel* de-
tachment] An elite unit of fanatical Nazis wearing black
uniforms, in charge of internal security and later organized
into a military division. • ~ is short. to **S.S.** (1932). O, R
[3]

schwa, *n.* (1895) *Ling.* Var. **shwa** (1933) [G < Heb *shéwa'*
a reduced, unaccented vowel *-e*] The mid-central, neutral
vowel (/ə/). —**schwa,** *a.* (1934). O, R, W [4]

Schwabacher, *n.* (1910) *Printing* [G < *Schwabach,* the
name of a town in central Bavaria, Germany + *-er* -er] A
German, black-letter typeface used in the 15th and 16th
centuries. —**Schwabacher,** *a.* (1922). O [3]

schwaerm, *see* schwärm

Schwann cell, *n.* (1906) *Biol.* [G *Schwann-Zelle* (1839) <
the name of Theodor *Schwann* (1810–82), German physiologist + *Zelle* cell < OFr *celle* < L *cella*] One of the
cells that enfold the axons of peripheral nerve fibers and
that may form a myelin sheath. O, R [3]

schwärm, *n.* (1926) Var. **schwaerm** (1926) [G idol, darling,

akin to *schwärmen* to rave, adore] An enthusiasm or craze,
esp. an erotic attachment for someone of the same or different sex; a "crush." O [3]

schwärm, *v.* (1913) [G *schwärmen* to rave, adore] To feel
or show passion or enthusiasm. O [3]

schwärmer, *n.* (1884) [G a dreamer or unrealistic enthusiast, a religious zealot < *schwärmen* to rave, adore] An
enthusiast or zealot. O [2]

schwärmerei/Schwärmerei, *n.* (1845) [G rapture, fanaticism < *schwärmen* to rave, be enthusiastic] Rave, rapture;
? religious zeal or fanaticism; schwärm (q.v.). O, R, W
[3]

schwärmerin, *n.* (1927) [G, fem. form of *Schwärmer*
(q.v.)] A female schwärmer. O [2]

schwärmerisch, *a.* (1894) [G visionary, rapturous, enthusiastic < *schwärmen* to rave, adore + adj. suffix *-isch*
-ish, -ic] Extravagant, very enthusiastic, infatuated. O [2]

schwartz, *see* schwarz

schwartzbrot/schwarzbrot, *n.* *Food* [G *Schwarzbrot* bread
made largely of rye < *schwarz* black, dark + *Brot* bread]
Black bread (q.v.). W [3]

schwarz, *n.* (1880) *Games* Var. **schwartz** (1880) [G black;
winning all or none of the tricks in a card game] The
winning of all the tricks in schafskopf (q.v.) or skat; the
scoring effect of such winning. —**schwartz,** *v.* (1880), *a.*
(1886). O, W [3]

schwarzbrot, *see* schwartzbrot

schwarzlot, *n.* (1925) *Pottery* Var. **Schwarzlot** (1925) [G <
schwarz black + *Lot* solder, lead weight] A kind of decoration used on 17th-century German and Dutch glass, and
later on German and Austrian pottery and porcelain, usu.
of black enamel. O [3]

schwegel, *n.* *Music* [G < MHG *schwegel(e)* < OHG *swe-
gala* a woodwind] Old name for a flute, either transverse
or vertical; a flue organ pipe. W [3]

schwein(e)hund, *n.* (1941) [G *Schweinehund* < *Schwein*
pig + *Hund* dog, as a term of abuse] Swine, bastard, or
filthy dog. • ~ was earlier transl. as **swine dog/hound**
(1916). O [3]

Schweinerei, *n.* (1906) Var. **schweinerei** (1965) [G, lit., pig-
gishness, a filthy mess < *Schwein* pig + abstract noun
suffix *-erei*] Obnoxious behavior; a scandal; a repulsive
event or object. O [3]

Schweizerdeutsch, *see* Schwyzertütsch

schweizerkäse, *n.* *Food* [G < *Schweizer,* the attrib. of
Schweiz Switzerland + *Käse* cheese] Swiss cheese. W2
[2]

Schwenkfelder, *n.* (1882–3) *Theol.* Var. **Schwenkfeldian**
(1562), **Schwenckfelder** (1882–3) [G (now *Schwenckfelder*)
< the name of the Silesian Protestant mystic Kaspar von
Schwenkfeld (1489–1561) + *-er* -er] A follower of the sect
founded by him, esp. of their modern church in Pennsylvania. O, R, W [3]

Schwyz, -ø *pl.* *Zool.* Var. **Schwyzer** [G < the name of the
Swiss canton *Schwyz*] Brown Swiss: a hardy breed of
dairy cattle originating in Switzerland. W [3]

Schwyzertütsch, *n.* (1934) *Ling.* Var. **Schwyzerd(e)utsch**
(1934), **Schweizerdeutsch** (1963) [(Swiss) G < *Schwyzer*
pertaining to Switzerland + *Tütsch* (= *Deutsch*) German]
The Swiss name of their dialect or variant; a Swiss
German or these people collectively. O, R, W [3]

scissor cut, *n.* (1931) *Art* [Transl. of G *Scherenschnitt* < *Schere* scissors + *Schnitt* cut] A silhouette that has been cut freehand with scissors. —**scissor-cutting,** *verbal n.* (1931). O [3]

sclereid, *n.* (1896) *Bot.* Var. **scler(e)ide** (1934, 1919) [G (1885) (now *Sklereid*) < *sclere-* (< Gk *sklērós* hard) + G *-id* -id] A particular kind of sclerenchymatous cell of a higher plant. O, W [3]

scleromyxœdema, *n.* (1964) *Path.* Var. **sceleromyxedema** (1964) [G *Skleromyxödem* (1954) < *sklero-* + *-myxödem* < Gk *sklērós* hard + *mýxa* slime, mud + *oídēma* growth] Lichen myxedematosis, a skin disease causing distorted features and lichenous eruptions. O [3]

sclerophyll, *n.* (1911) *Bot.* [G *Sklerophyll* (1898) < *sklero-* + *-phyll* < Gk *sklērós* hard + *phýllon* leaf] A plant with clusters or layers of thick-walled cells resistant to evaporation and thus water loss. —**sclerophyll,** *a.* (1926). O, R, W [3]

scolecite, *n.* (1823) *Mineral.* [G *Skolezit* (1813) < *skolez-* (< Gk *skólex* worm) + G *-it* -ite] A zeolite mineral that is a hydrous silicate of aluminum and calcium (this is different from the later botanical meaning). O, R, W [4]

scolopale, *n.* (1912) *Entomology* [G < a short. of *(das) skolopale Körperchen* (1882) < Gk *skólopos,* gen. of *skólops* spike + G *-al* -al + *Körperchen* corpuscle < L *corpusculum*] The rod-like structure within the sheath of a scolopidium (q.v.); the sheath itself. O [3]

scolopidium, -pidia *pl.* (1939) *Entomology* [G *Skolopidium* (1923) < NL *scolopidium* < Gk *skólopos,* gen. of *skólops* spike + L *-idium,* modeled on *Immatidium* one of the elements corresponding to a small, simple eye that make up an arthropod's compound eye] An insect's chordotonal (q.v.) organ, an elongated sensory organ. O, W [3]

scolopophore, *n.* (1888) *Entomology* Var. **scolophore** (1925) [G *Scolopophor* (1881) (now *Skolopophor*) < *scolopo-* + *-phor* < Gk *skólopos,* gen. of *skólops* spike + *phor-* < *phérein* to carry, bear] An insect's integumentary, prob. auditory sense-organ. O, W [3]

scolopophorous, *a.* (1935) *Entomology* Var. **scolopophorous** [G *Scolopophor* scolopophore (1881, q.v.) + E *-ous*] Of an insect's sensory end-organ; having the elongated tubular form of a scolopidium (q.v.). O, W [3]

scolops, *n.* (1935) *Entomology* [G (1923) < Gk *skólops* spike] The rod-like structure inside a scolopidium's sheath: scolopale (q.v.). O [3]

scopine, *n.* (1923) *Chem.* [G *Scopin* (1892) (now also *Skopin*) < L *scopolia* henbane < the name of Giovanni Antonio *Scopoli* (1723–88), Italian naturalist + G *-in* -ine] A colorless, crystalline, heterocyclic amino acid, formed by hydrolyzing scopolamine (q.v.). O, W [3]

scopolamine, *n.* (1892) *Chem.* [G *Scopolamin* (1891) (now also *Skopolamin*) < *scopol-* (< L *scopolia* henbane) + G *Amin* amine] A syrupy, poisonous alkaloid used as a sedative and in lie detector tests: hyoscine (q.v.). O, R, W [4]

scopoleine, *n.* (1885) *Chem.* [G *Scopoleïn* (1876–80) < *scopol-* (< L *scopolia* henbane—see *scopine*) + G *-in* -ine with an infixed *-e-*] A crystalline alkaloid extracted from Japanese belladonna. O [3]

scorodite, *n.* (1823) *Mineral.* Old var. **skorodite** (1823) [G *Skorodit* (1818) < Gk *skórodon* garlic + G *-it* -ite, named

for its odor when heated] A hydrous ferric arsenate. O, W [3]

scotophil, *a.* (1952) *Biol.* Var. **scotophile** (1960), **skotophil** (1972) [G *skotophil* (1944) < *skoto-* + *-phil* < Gk *skótos* darkness + *phílos* loving] Relating to a phase of the circadian cycle of an animal or plant when light does not affect reproductive activity. —**scotophilic** (1960); **scotophily,** *n.* (1960). O [3]

S.D.S., *n.* (1968) *Politics* [G *SDS* (1946), a short. of *Sozialistischer Deutscher Studentenbund* Socialist German Student Union < *Sozialistischer* socialist + *Deutscher* German + *Studentenbund* students' league] The militant Federation of German Socialist Students in West Germany. O [3]

Se, *see* selenium

sea-foam, *n.* (1837) *Mineral.* [Transl. of G *Meerschaum*] Meerschaum (q.v.) (this is different from the medieval "froth on the sea" meaning). O, R, W [3]

Sea-lion, Operation Sea-lion, *n.* (1940) *Mil.* [Transl. of G *Seelöwe* < *See* sea + *Löwe* lion] The German code name for Hitler's plan to invade England after the fall of France in World War Two. O [3]

secession, *n.* (1890) *Art* Var. **sezession** (1890) [G *Sezession* < L *sēcessiō* separation, here used in connection with *Viennese Secession* (1897)] A radical movement in art that began in Vienna and was parallel with and approximately contemporaneous with French art nouveau; this movement's style. O, R, W [3]

Secessionist, *n.* (1972) *Art* Var. **Sezessionist** (1967) [G *Sezessionist* < **Sezession** Secession (q.v.) + G (< L) *-ist* -ist] A member of the secession movement in art. O [3]

secession style, *n.* (1973) *Art* Var. **Sezessionstil** (1978) [Ad. of G *Sezessionsstil* (1905) < *Sezession* secession (q.v.) + *Stil* style] The Vienna version of art nouveau, called *Jugendstil* (q.v.) in Germany. O [3]

secondary, *a.* (1864) *Chem.* [Ad. of G *secundär* (1864) (now *sekundär*) < Fr *secondaire* < L *secundārius* following in sequence] In Germany, orig. descriptive of alcohols and now descriptive of organic compounds other than amines, etc., where the characteristic functional group is located on a saturated carbon atom that is bonded to two other carbon atoms (this is of course different from the many earlier meanings borrowed from the orig. Latin word). O [4]

second fronting, *n.* (1939) *Ling.* [Transl. of G *Zweite Aufhellung* (1914) < *zweite* second + *Aufhellung* lit., brightening up] A sound change in varieties of Old English, where the vowels *æ* (produced by an earlier fronting) and *a* become *e* and *æ,* respectively. O [3]

secretin, *n.* (1902) *Physiol.* [G (1902) (now *Sekretin*) < *secret* (< L *sēcrētus* separated) + G *-in* -in] A hormone that is released from the upper intestine and that may stimulate pancreatic secretion. O, R, W [4]

secretor, *n.* (1941) *Physiol.* [Transl. of G *Ausscheider* (1932) < *ausscheiden* to secrete] One who produces and excretes water-soluble substances like tears and urine; one that secretes. —**secretor,** *a.* (1956). O, W [4]

sectorial, *n.* and *a.* (1927, 1927) *Bot.* Var. **sectorial chimera** (1934) [Short. of G *Sektorialchimäre* (1909) < *sektorial* (< LL *sector* sector + G adj. suffix *-ial* -ial) + *Chimäre* illusion < the beast of Greek mythology, actually Gk *chí-*

maira goat] (of) a chimera in which different types of tissues grow side by side and occupy distinct sectors of varying sizes (this is different from the old "tooth" meaning). —**sectorially** (1963). O, W [4]

Seebeck effect, *n.* (1903) *Physics* [G *Seebeck-Effekt* (1822–3) < the name of Thomas Johann *Seebeck* (1770–1831), Russian-born German physicist + G *Effekt* effect < MFr *effect* < L *effectus*] The thermoelectric effect whereby an EMF is produced in a thermocouple; the phenomenon of thermoelectricity. O, R [3]

Seger cone, *n.* (1894) *Tech.* [Transl. of G *Seger-Kegel* < the name of Hermann August *Seger* (1839–93), German engineer + *Kegel* cone] A pyrometric cone, any of a series of small numbered cones or pyramids made of different substances that collectively form a scale of fusing points and are used to indicate approximate temperatures inside kilns etc. O, R, W [3]

Sehnsucht, *n.* (1847) [G yearning, longing < *Sehnen* yearning + *Sucht* passion, craze, sickness] Yearning or wistful longing. • ~ is transl. as **longing** (1955). O [3]

seidel, *n.* (1908 *W9*) *Beverages* [G, orig. a liquid measure < MHG *sīdel* < L *situla* (wine) jug] A large beer mug; the quantity that such a mug can contain. O, R, W [4]

Seilbahn/seilbahn, *n.* (1963) *Sports* [G < *Seil* cable + *Bahn* railway, (rail)road] A cable railway; an aerial cableway—see *S-bahn.* O [3]

Sekt, *n.* (1920) *Beverages* [G < *Sek* < Fr *vin sec* sweet wine] A German sparkling wine or champagne. O, R [3]

selachyl alcohol, *n.* (1922) *Chem.* [G *Selachylalkohol* (1922) < *Selachyl* (< NL *Selachii* < Gk *sélachos* shark + G *-yl* < Gk *hýlē* substance) + G *Alkohol* alcohol, ult. < Ar *al-kuḥul*] An oily, liquid, unsaturated alcohol found in fish oils. O, W [3]

selenium, *n.* (1818) *Chem.* [Prob. < G *Selen* (1818), named in German by the Swedish chemist Baron Jons Jakob Berzelius (1779–1848) < Gk *selénē* moon + an added E *-ium* (< L) on the analogy of *tellurium* when *Selen* was borrowed] A rare, toxic element resembling tellurium, which is widely used in electronics, pigments, etc. —**selenium cell** (1880)/**eye** (1893)/**dioxide/oxychloride/rectifier/red.** • ~ is symbolized as **Se.** O, R, W [4]

self-estrangement, *n.* (1878) *Psych.* [Transl. of G *Selbstentfremdung* < *selbst* self + *Entfremdung* estrangement] Estrangement from one's natural self, esp. when resulting from the alienatory development of consciousness or from pressures within a complex industrialized culture. —**self-estranged,** *a.* (1910). O [3]

selfhood, *n.* (1649) *Philos.* Var. **ownhood** (q.v.) [Transl. of G *Meinheit* or *Selbheit* < *mein* my or *selb-* self + nom. suffix *-heit* -hood] The state of having an individual identity; such an individual; individuality; self-centeredness. O, R, W [4]

self-portrait, *n.* (1831) *Art* [Transl. of G *Selbstportrait* or *Selbstbildnis* < *selbst* self + *Portrait* or *Bildnis* portrait] A self-made portrait made by an artist; one's own picture of one's personality or character. O, R, W [4]

seligmannite, *n. Mineral.* [G *Seligmannit* < the name of Gustav *Seligmann* (1849–1920), German collector of minerals + *-it* -ite] An orthorhombic copper arsenic sulfide. W [3]

seltzer (water), *n.* (1741) *Beverages* Old var. **selters water**

(1741) [Transl. of G *Selterswasser* < the name of the spring in the town of Nieder *Selters* in the district of Wiesbaden, Germany + *Wasser* water] An effervescent mineral water; highly carbonated water, as used in soft drinks and various alcoholic drinks. O, R, W [4]

sema, **-s/-ta** *pl.* (1938) *Ling.* [G (1935) < Gk *sẽma* sign] A seme, the smallest unit of meaning. O [3]

semester, *n.* (1827) *Ed.* [G (1773) < L *sēmēstris* of six months] A college half-year; either of the two periods of instruction into which an academic year is often divided. —**semestr(i)al, semester hour.** O, R, W [4]

semidine, *n.* (1893) *Chem.* [G *Semidin* (1893) < *semi-* (< L *semi* half) + G *-din* (< *Benzidin*) -dine] One of various aromatic compounds. —**semidine reaction** (1893)/**transformation** (1938). O [3]

seminar, *n.* (1889) *Ed.* [G (1524) < L *sēminārium* seminary] In German and some British universities, a group of graduate students engaged under a professor in original research; the course of study pursued in a seminar; the class itself or the classroom; a meeting for instructional purposes. —**seminar,** *a.* (1948). O, R, W [4]

semiopal, *n.* (1794) *Mineral.* [Transl. of G *Halbopal* (1788) < *halb* half + *Opal* < L *opalus* < Gk *opállios* < Skt *úpala* stone] An impure opal. O, W [3]

semipermeable, *a.* (1883) *Chem.* [Transl. of G *halbdurchlässig* (1881) < *halb* half, semi- + *durchlässig* permeable] Partly but not wholly permeable, as in a membrane selectively permeable to some usu. small molecules, esp. water. —**semipermeability** (1900). O, R, W [4]

Semitic, *a.* (1813) *Ethnology, Ling.* [G *semitisch* < *Semit(e),* prob. NL *semita* Semite < the name of *Sem* Noah's eldest son + G adj. suffix *-isch* -ic] Of, pertaining to, typical of, or constituting the Semites or their languages; in modern times usu. a reference to the Jewish rather than the Arab peoples. —**Semitic,** *n.* (1875); **-icize** (1859); **-icized,** *a.* (1863); **-icizing,** *n.* (1885); **-icism** (1907); **Semitic languages.** O, R, W [4]

semmel, **-s/-ø** *pl.* *Food* [G < MHG *semel(e)* < OHG *semala* fine wheat flour < L *simila,* ult. prob. < Semitic] A baked, crisp bread roll. O [3]

senegin, *n.* (1830) *Chem.* [G < NL < *(Polygala) senega* Senega root < E *senega* + G *-in* -in] Senega saponin, obtained from senega root and used as an expectorant. O, W [3]

Senn, *n.* (1882) *Agric.* [G < Late MHG *senne* < OHG *senno,* perhaps actually one who milks] A shepherd in the Alps. O [3]

sennhutt, *n.* (1868) *Agric.* Var. **senn-cabin** (c.1822) [G *Sennhütte* < *Senn* (q.v.) + *Hütte* hut] A shepherd's Alpine hut. O [3]

sensibilisin, *n. Med.* [Prob. ad. of G *sensibilisieren* to sensibilize < Fr *sensibiliser* < L *sēnsibilis* sensitive + G (< L) *-ismus* -ism] Anaphylactin, an antibody thought to cause anaphylaxis. W [3]

sensillum, **-silla** *pl.* (1925) *Zool.* [G (1895), coined by the German biologist Ernest Haeckel < the dim. of L *sēnsus* sense, perception] A simple, epithelial sensory receptor, esp. in arthropods, consisting of a cell or a small group of cells with a nerve connection. O, R, W [4]

sentential calculus, *n.* (1937) *Philos.* [Transl. of G *Satzkalkül* < *Satz* sentence, proposition + *Kalkül* calculus <

L *calculus*] Propositional calculus, a basic branch of symbolic logic. O, R, W [4]

separate, *n.* (1886) *Printing* [G *Separatum* < L *sēparāre* to separate] An offprint of an article from a periodical; an article or document published separately. O, R, W [4]

sepiolite, *n.* (1854) *Geol.* [G *Sepiolith* (1847) < *sepio-* + *-lith* < Gk *sépion* cuttlebone + *líthos* stone] Meerschaum (q.v.). O, R, W [4]

septanose, *n.* (1933) *Chem.* [G (1933) < *sept-* seven + *-anose* (< L, as in *Furanose*) -ose, being a suffix denoting a carbohydrate] A structure containing a seven-member ring, as in some sugars; a sugar of this structure. —**septanose,** *a.* (1934); **septanoside** (1974). O [3]

septet/septette, *n.* (1828) *Music, Lit.* [G *Septet* < *sept-* (< L *septem* seven) + *-et(te)*] A composition for seven instruments; transf. sense of a group of seven objects or people, or of a poem or stanza of seven lines. O, R, W [4]

septicine, *n.* (1876) *Chem.* [G *Septicin* < L *sēpticus,* Gk *sēptikós* putrefied + G *-in* -ine] An alkaloid formed from putrefecation. O [3]

sericite, *n.* (1854) *Mineral.* [G *Sericit* (1852) < L *sēricus* silken + G *-it* -ite] Muscovite, a fine-grained, silky mica. —**sericite,** *a.* (1884); **sericitization** (1893); **sericitized,** *a.* (1935); **sericitize.** O, R, W [3]

serine, *n.* (1880) *Chem.* [Prob. < G *Serin* (1865) < L *sēricum* silk + G *-in* -ine] A colorless, crystalline amino acid that is found widely in animal proteins; ß-hydroxy alanine. • ~ appears in names of various enzymes like **serine proteases** (1974). O, R, W [4]

serum sickness, *n.* (1908) *Med.* Var. **serum disease** (1908) [Transl. of G *Serumkrankheit* (1903) < *Serum* (< L) serum + G *Krankheit* disease] An allergic reaction to injected foreign serum, manifested by fever, etc. O, R, W [4]

servus, *interj.* (1893) [Austrian G (< L) *Servus* (your) servant!] An informal formula of greeting or farewell employed in Austria and southern Germany. O [2]

seston, *n.* (1916) *Biol.* [G (1912) < Gk *sēstón* filtered < *sēthein* to strain, filter] Minute material moving in water, such as plankton, nekton, and plant debris. —**sestonic** (1941). O, W [3]

setzling, *n.* (1688) *Ichthy.* (archaic) [Irreg. G < *setzen* to set, plant, deposit, stock + dim. nom. suffix *-ling* -ling] Fry, the young of fish. O [3]

sextet, *n.* (1841) *Music* [G *Sextett* < a Latinization of It *sestetto* sestet < *sei* (< L *sex*) six] A composition for six voices or instruments or in six voice parts; the musicians who perform this (this is different from the literary or "group or set of six" meaning). O, R, W [3]

sextole/sextolet, *n.* (1854) *Music* [G *Sextole* [G (< L *sextus* sixth) + G *-ole,* as in *Quintole* fifth] Sextuplet: a group of six musical notes to be played in the time ordinarily given to four. O, W [3]

Sezessionstil, *see* secession style

shabrack, *n.* (c.1808) *Mil.* Var. **shabraque** (1865, a Fr word < G) [G *Schabracke* < Hung *csáprág* < Turk *çaprak* saddle cloth] A saddle cloth, often of goatskin, once used by European cavalry. O, R, W [3]

shabub/shawbubbe, *n.* (1548) *Bot.* (obs.) [Prob. ad. of G *schabab* black coriander < *schab ab,* the imper. of *ab-*

schaben (slang) to shove off] An old name for a *Lunaria* plant. O [2]

shale, *n.* (1747) *Geol.* [Poss. < G *Schal(stein)* a laminated limestone or *Schal(gebirge)* layer of stone in a stratified range of mountains (this meaning is close to the English sense) < MHG *schāl(e)* < OHG *scāla* (+ *Stein* stone or *Gebirge* mountain range)] A finely stratified or laminated fissile rock; a variety of this rock (this is different from the older, various nongeological meanings). —**shal(e)y,** *a.* • ~ appears initially in compounds like **shale naphtha** (1855)/**oil** (1857)/**tar** (1857)/**shaker** (1959)/**clay.** O, R, W [4]

shaman, *n.* (1698) *Theol.* Var. **schaman(e)** [Russ *shaman* and/or G *Schamane* < Russ *shaman* < Tungus *šaman,* ult. < Skt *śramaṇa* Buddhist monk, ascetic] A priest or priest-doctor, orig. among various northern Asian peoples, who uses magic in healing and divining; someone who is regarded to have access to the spirit world, usu. through a trance. —**shaman,** *a.* (1780); **-ism** (1780); **-ian** (1802); **-ist,** *n.* (1842), *a.* (1882); **-istic** (1854); **-ite** (1871); **-ic** (1899); **-izing,** *verbal n.* (1949); **-ess** (1977). O, R, W [4]

shandite, *n.* (1950) *Mineral.* [G *Shandit* (1949) < the name of Samuel James *Shand* (1882–1957), Scottish-American geologist + G *-it* -ite] A sulfide of nickel and lead occurring in yellow rhombohedral crystals. O, W [3]

shark, *n.* (1599) Old var. **shirk** (1639, q.v.) [By folk etymology influenced by E *shark,* prob. < G *Schurke* scoundrel, perhaps related to OHG *fiurscurgo* lit., *fiur* fire + *scurgo* one who feeds it, i.e., stoker] Scoundrel, rogue; British customs officer; one who excells in something. O, R, W [4]

sharpshooter, *n.* (1802) *Mil.* [Transl. of G *Scharfschütze* < *scharf* sharp + *Schütze* marksman] One of various kinds of marksmen, including in sports; a leafhopper; the one in charge of explosives in oil-well drilling; a kind of Bahamanian catboat; a kind of shovel. —**sharpshooting,** *verbal n.* (1806). O, R, W [4]

sharp-shot, *n.* (1725) *Mil.* [Transl. of G *Scharfschuss* (now *-schuß*) < *scharf mit Patronen schiessen* to shoot with live ammunition + *Schuss* shot] Ball cartridge; a firing with this. O, W [3]

shawbubbe, *see* shabub

sheatfish, -es *pl.* (1589) *Ichthy.* Old var. **sheath fish** (1589) [Prob. by folk etymology < G *Schaid(e)* < OHG *sceida* sheatfish, catfish] A large, long catfish inhabiting central or eastern European rivers; extended to any of various large catfishes. O, R, W [3]

sheepshead, *n.* (1886) *Games* [Transl. of G *Schaf(s)kopf* < *Schaf(s)* sheep's + *Kopf* head] An earlier, simpler form of skat, also called *schafskopf* (q.v.). O, R, W [3]

shelf ice, *n.* (1910) *Geogr.* [Transl. of G *Schelfeis* (1908) < *Schelf* (< E *shelf*) + G *Eis* ice] An extensive ice sheet that extends into the water, usu. the sea, but originates on land: barrier ice. O, R, W [4]

shenk beer, -ø/-s *pl.* (1872) *Beverages* [G *Schenkbier* < *schenken* to pour, fill + *Bier* beer] A very weak, insipid beer. O [3]

shewbread/showbread, -ø/-s *pl.* (1530) *Theol.* [Transl. of G *Schaubrot* < *schauen* to show + *Brot* bread, used by Luther prob. as a loose transl. of Heb *'lech'em pā'nīm,* Vulgate *panes propositionis*] Any of the twelve loaves of

consecrated unleavened bread used in Jewish worship. —
shewbread, *a.* (1611). O, R, W [4]

shice, *n.* (1859) *Currency* (slang) Var. **shise** (1877) [Ad. of
G *Scheiss* (now *Scheiß*) excrement] Base money; nothing;
something worthless. O [3]

shicer, *n.* (1846) *Mining* (slang) Var. **shiser** (1846) [G
Scheisser (now *Scheißer*) contemptible person, one who
defecates] A worthless person; also Australian senses: a
defaulter or welscher, a failure, an unproductive mine. O,
R, W [3]

shield, *n.* (1906) *Geogr.* [Transl. of G *Schild* (1888) shield,
introduced in this sense by Eduard Suess in his *Das Antlitz
der Erde,* 1888, II, III, ii, 42] A vast, seismically stable
mass of chiefly Precambrian basement rock in the earth's
crust, forming the nuclear mass of a continent; the dome
of a shield volcano (q.v.). • ~ often appears initially and
capitalized in compounds like **Canadian Shield** (1906). O,
R, W [4]

shield-knave, *n.* (1627) *Mil.* (archaic) [Transl. of G *Schild-
knabe* (now *Schildknappe*) < *Schild* + *Knabe* knave,
bearer, boy, youth] Shield bearer. O [3]

shield volcano, *n.* (1911) *Geol.* [Transl. of G *Schildvulkan*
(1910) < *Schild* shield + *Vulkan* volcano < It *vulcano*
< L *Vulcānus*] A volcano built from successive eruptions
of lava, with a base many times larger than its height. O,
W [4]

shiffer, *n.* (1683) *Geol.* (archaic) [G *Schiffer* (now *Schiefer*)
slate] Slate. O [3]

ship of fools, *n.* (1509) *Lit.* [Transl. of G *(Das) Narrenschiff* (1494) < *(das* the) + *Narren,* pl. of *Narr* fool +
Schiff ship, the title of a satirical novel by Sebastian Brant,
and transl. into English by Alexander Barclay in 1509] A
ship whose passengers symbolize various types of folly or
vice, as in a title reused by the novelist Katherine Anne
Porter. O [3]

shirk, *n.* (1639) (archaic) Old var. like **shirke** (1639) [Prob.
ad. < G *Schurke*—see *shark*] A sponger, cheater, swindler: shark. O, W [3]

shise, *see* **shice**

shiser, *see* **shicer**

shiver, *n.* (1729) *Geol.* Old var. **shiffer** (1683) q.v. [Poss.
ad. of G *Schiefer* < MHG *schiver(e)* < OHG *scivaro* chip
of stone or wood] A stone of slaty or schistous character.
—**shiver,** *a.* (1804). O [3]

shiver, *v.* (1728) *Geol.* [Prob. ad. of G *schiefern* to split
into thin plates] To split along the line of geological cleavage. O [3]

shiver spar, *n.* (1804) *Mineral.* [By folk etymology < G
Schieferspar < *Schiefer* shiver (q.v.) + *-spar* spar, spath]
Slate spar, a variety of calcite. O, W [3]

shock troops, *pl.* (1917) *Mil.* [Transl. of G *Stoßtruppen,*
pl. of *Stoßtrupp* < *Stoß* thrust, shock + *Truppe* troop]
Men esp. suited and selected for use in particular military
assault-operations. —**shock-trooper** (1934). O, R, W [4]

shorl, *see* **schorl**

shorlite, *see* **schorlite**

shortswing, *n. Sports* [Transl. of G *Kurzschwung* < *kurz*
short + *Schwung* swing < *schwingen* to swing] A skiing
technique used for high speed, as in slalom racing. W [3]

shot effect, *n.* (1921) *Tech.* Var. **Schroteffekt** (see Appendix) [Transl. of G *Schroteffekt* < *Schrot* small shot or

buckshot + *Effekt* effect < MFr *effet* (<L *effectus*] Random fluctuations in the number of electrons emitted per
second from a hot cathode, producing shot noise (sputtering or popping noises in an audio amplifier); generalized
to any such fluctuation. O, R, W [3]

shotter, -ø *pl.* (1911) *Geol.* [G *Schotter,* akin to G *Schutt*
rubble, debris < *schütten* to pour, shed, pile up] Layered
sand and pebbles deposited by a river. O [2]

showbread, *see* **shewbread**

shrend, *v. Tech.* [Prob. ad. of obs. G *schrinden* < OHG
scrintan to burst, crack open] To break into shivers from
internal stresses, as does untempered glass. W [3]

shruff, *a.* (1541–2) and *n.* (1618) *Mineral.* [Poss. < G
Schroff < MHG *schrof(fe)* formerly a fragment of mineral
(Jacobsson in Grimm), now a craggy cliff] (Of) old brass
or copper. • ~ is a bit different from the ME item meaning
"dross of metals." O [3]

shungite, *see* **schungite**

shwa, *see* **schwa**

sial, *n.* (1922) *Geol.* Var. **Sial** (1924) [G (1922), changed
< *Sal* (1920) to avoid confusion in meanings < a blend
of NL *Silicium* silicon + *Aluminium* aluminum] The discontinuous outer portion of the earth's crust represented
by the continental masses, which are composed mainly of
rocks rich in silica and alumina (cf. *sima*); the material
composing these masses. —**sialic** (1924). O, R, W [4]

siallite, *n.* (1933) *Geol.* [G *Siallit* (1926), back-formation
< *siallistisch* < NL *silicium* silicon + G *Aluminium* alu-
minum + *-it* -ite] Weathered rock constituted mainly of
hydrous aluminum silicates that are highly leached of alkalis. —**siallitic** (1933). O [3]

sibling species, *n.* (1940) *Anthrop.* [Transl. of G *Geschwis-
terarten* < *Geschwister* siblings + *Arten,* pl. of *Art* spe-
cies] One of two or more reproductively isolated
populations that are morphologically nearly or completely
indistinguishable. O, W [3]

Sicherheitsdienst, *n.* (1947) *Politics* [G < *Sicherheit* security + *Dienst* service] The security group of the Schutzstaffel (S.S., q.v.) of the Nazi party. —**Sicherheitsdienst,** *a.*
(1966). O [2]

siderite, *n.* (1850) *Mineral.* [G *Siderit* (1844) < *sider-* (<
Gk *sídēros* iron) + G *-it* -ite] A native ferrous carbonate
that occurs as rhombohedral crystals and is a valuable iron
ore, also called *spathic iron* and *chalybite* (this is different
from the older meanings of "loadstone, quartz," etc.). O,
R, W [3]

sideroachrestic, *a.* (1961) *Path.* [G (< NL *sideroachres-
tica) sideroachrestisch* (1957) < Gk *sidero-,* the comb.
form of *sídēros* iron + *áchrēstos* useless + G adj. suffix
-isch -ic] Specifying or relating to hypochromic anemia
where impaired synthesis of hemoglobin renders useless
any treatment with iron. O [3]

siderochrome, *n.* (1961) *Biochem.* [G *Siderochrom* (1960)
< *sidero-* + *-chrom* < Gk *sídēros* iron + *chrôma* color]
One of various compounds that help transport iron in bacteria. O [3]

sideromelane, *n. Geol.* [G *Sideromelan* < *sidero-* +
-melan < Gk *sídēros* iron + *mélan, mélas* black] Obsidian, a usu. black volcanic glass. W [3]

siderophile, *a.* (1923) *Geol.* Var. **siderophil** (1923), **sidero-
philic** (1971) [G *siderophil* (1923) < *sidero-* + *-phil* <

Gk *sidero-*, the comb. form of *sídēros* iron + *phílos* loving] Concerning elements usu. found in metallic phases rather than combined as silicates or sulfides. O, R, W [4]

siderosis[1], *n.* (1890) *Med.* [G *Siderose* (1866) < NL *siderosis* < Gk *sídēros* iron + *-osis* fem. suffix of action] Pneumonoconiosis suffered by iron workers who inhale iron particles; such deposit in a tissue. —**siderotic** (1932). O, R, W [3]

siderosis[2], *n.* (1895) *Optics* [G *Siderose/Siderosis* (1891) < NL *siderosis bulbi* < Gk *sídēros* iron + *-osis*, fem. suffix of action] A condition where the lens of the eye is stained by rust derived from an embedded iron particle. O [3]

siderotil, *n.* (1897) *Mineral.* Var. **siderotilate** [G (1891) (now also *Siderotyl*) < *sidero-* + *-til* < Gk *sídēros* iron + *tílos* anything plucked, fiber] A hydrous ferrous sulfate occurring as triclinic fibrous crusts and needles. O, W [3]

Siegfried, *n. Music, Lit.* [G < the name of the hero *Siegfried* of Wagner's Ring cycle and of the MHG epic poem, the *Nibelungenlied* (q.v.)] The hero Siegfried in the cycle and the poem; a male's given name. R [4]

Siegfried Line, *n.* (1918 *W9*) *Mil.* [Ad. of G *Siegfriedlinie* < the name of *Siegfried* (q.v.) + *Linie* line < L *linea*] The Hindenberg line, a line of fortifications in France occupied by the Germans during World War One; a similar line constructed along Germany's western frontier before World War Two. O, R [4]

Sieg Heil/heil, *n.* (1940) and *interj.* (1944) *Politics* [G, lit., hail victory] The victory salute by the Germans during the Nazi regime. —**Sieg Heil**, *v.* (1967); **sieg-heiling**, *part. a.* (1968). O, R [4]

sifflöt, *n. Music* [G *Sifflöte*, prob. influenced by *Flöte* as < Fr *sifflet* small whistle] A whistle flute; a small flute organ stop that has a whistling tone. W [3]

silane, *n.* (1916) *Chem.* [G *Silan* (1916), a blend of *Silizium* silicon + *Methan* methane] Silicon hydride, a large class of hydrides analogous to hydrocarbons of the methane series. —**silanize** (1962); **-ized**, *part. a.* (1962); **-izing**, *verbal n.* (1968); **-ization** (1968). O, R, W [3]

silicone, *n.* (1863) *Chem.* [G *Silicon* (1863) (now *Silikon*) < L *silex* (gen. *silicis*) silicic acid + G *-on* -one] An organic compound analogous to a ketone; an organic siloxane (q.v.); an organosilicon compound used commercially. —**silicone**, *a.* (1944); **silicone resin** (1944)/**rubber** (1944). O, R, W [4]

silktail, *n.* (1685) *Ornith.* Var. **silk-tail** (1685) [Transl. of G *Seidenschwanz* < G *Seide* silk + *Schwanz* tail] (Dial. Brit.) a Bohemian waxwing or chatterer. O, W [3]

siloxane, *n.* (1917) *Chem.* [G *Siloxan* (1917), a combining of *Silicon* silicone + *Oxygen* oxygen + *-an* -ane < L *silex* + Fr *oxygène*] Silane (q.v.) in which hydrogen is partly replaced by oxygen. —**siloxane**, *a.* (1941). O, R, W [4]

silumin, *n.* (1922) *Metall.* [G, a combining of *Silicon* + *Aluminum* < L *silex* silicic acid + NL *alumina* aluminum] One of a series of casting alloys of aluminum containing a small amount of silicon; also called *Alpax*. O [3]

silver glance, *n.* (1805) *Mineral.* Var. **silver-glance** (1805) [Transl. of G *Silberglanz* < *Silber* silver + *Glanz* glance (q.v.)] Argentite (q.v.). O, W [3]

silverling, *n.* (1526) *Currency* (archaic) [G *Silberling* <

OHG *silabarling* < *silabar* silver + dim. suffix *-ling* -ling] A shekel, a small silver coin. O, W [3]

sima, *n.* (1909) *Geol.* [G (1909), a combining of *Silicium* silicon + *Magnesium* magnesium] A basic igneous rocklayer, rich in silica and magnesia, that underlies the sialic continental masses and forms the crust under the oceans; the material composing this (this is different from the architectural meaning). —**simatic** (1942). O, R, W [3]

simultanagnosia, *n.* (1936) *Psych.* [G *Simultanagnosie* (1924) < *simultan* (< L) simultaneous + G *Agnosie* < Gk *agnōsía* ignorance] The lack or loss of one's ability to experience perceived elements as part of a whole, such as the details of a picture. O [3]

sinapine, *n.* (1838) *Chem.* Old var. **sinapin** (1838) [Orig. formed as G *Sinapin* < L *sinapis* mustard + G *-in* < L] An alkaloid occurring in mustard seeds. O, R, W [3]

sindaw, *n.* (1548) *Bot.* (archaic) [G *Sindau* (also *Sinnau, Sinau*) < *sin-* ever-, as in *singrün* evergreen + dial. *Dau* (now *Tau*) < MHG, OHG *tou* dew] Lady's mantle, a common European herb of the genus *Alchemilla.* O [3]

sinflood, *n.* (1550) *Theol.* Var. **sinne flood** [Transl. of G *Sündflut*, as altered by folk etymology in analogy with *Sünde* sin < OHG, MHG *sinvluot* (< *sin-* ever + *vluot* flood), late MHG *süntfluot*, early NHG *sündfluod*] Deluge. O [3]

sinfonie, -n *pl. Music* [G < It *sinfonia* symphony] A symphony. W [2]

singing bund, *see* saengerbund

Singspiel/singspiel, *n.* (1876) *Music* [G < *singen* to sing + *Spiel* play < *spielen* to play] A semidramatic musical work interspersing song and dialogue, comparable to the opera comique. O, R, W [4]

sinker, *n.* (1863) *Bot.* Old var. **senker** (1863) [G *Senker* process, shoot < *senken* to lower] A process of a mistletoe's root system, where the mistletoe sends suckers into the bark of the host plant; one of such suckers. O [3]

sinopite, *n.* (1868) *Mineral.* [G *Sinopit* (1847) < L *sinopis*, ult. < Gk *Sinōpē*, the name of a town in Turkey + G *-it* -ite] A brick-red, clayish earth used anciently as a paint. O, W [3]

sinter, *n.* (1780) *Geol.* [G < OHG *sintar* dross, slag] A deposit formed by the evaporating of lake or spring water; the product of sintering; cinder. —**sinter**, *v.* (1871); **sintery**, *a.* (1863); **sintering**, *verbal n.* (1871), *a.* (1907); **sintered**, *a.* (1877); **sinter plant** (1938). O, R, W [4]

sinter coal, *n.* (1854) *Geol.* [Ad. of G *Sinterkohle* < *Sinter* sinter (q.v.) + *Kohle* coal] Cherry coal. O [3]

sinus gland, *n.* (1938) *Zool.* [Transl. of G *Sinusdrüse* (1937) < *Sinus* (< L) curvature + G *Drüse* gland] A small, glandular structure in a crustacean's eyestalk, comparable to a vertebrate's neurohypophysis. O, W [3]

sisel, *n.* (1785) *Zool.* Old var. **zisel** (1785), **zizel** (1833, q.v.) [Ad. of G *Zeisel* (< MHG *zīsel*, prob. < Czech *sysel*) suslik] A suslik, a kind of ground squirrel. O, W [3]

siserskite/sysertskite, *n.* (1850) *Mineral.* Old var. **sisserskite** (1850) [G *Sisserskit* (1845) < *Syssertsk* near Sverdlovsk + G *-it* -ite] Iridosmine (q.v.). O, W [3]

siskin, *n.* (1562) *Ornith.* [Ad. of dial. G *Sisschen* or *Zeischen* finch, perhaps ult. of imitative origin] A small, sharp-billed finch; one of various birds resembling a siskin; also called *aberdevine*.—**siskin,** *a.* (1783); **siskin-green,** *a.* (1805–17); **pine/red siskin.** O, R, W [4]

sisserskite, *see* siserskite

sitosterol, *n.* (1898) *Biochem.* Var. **gamma-sitosterol** [Ad. of G *Sitosterin* (1897) < *sito-* + *-sterol* < Gk *sîtos* grain + *stereós* rigid + G *-in* -ol] One of several common sterols or sterol mixtures, esp. the beta form, obtained from cottonseed, soybeans, etc. and used in organic synthesis. O, R, W [4]

situation ethics, *n.* (1955) *Philos.* [Ad. of G *Situationsethik* (1950) < *Situation* (< Fr) situation + *Ethik* ethics < MFr *ethique,* ult. < Gk *ēthikḗ*] An ethical belief by which acts are judged within their situational contexts instead of by inflexible moral principles. O, R [3]

sitz bath, *n.* (1849) Var. **sitz-bath** (1899) [Ad. of G *Sitzbad* < *sitzen* to sit + *Bad* bath < OHG *sizzen* + *bad*] A tub for bathing in a sitting position; a hip bath; the bath so taken; such a bath as used therapeutically. O, R, W [4]

Sitzfleisch, *n.* (1930) [G < *sitzen* to sit + *Fleisch* flesh] The ability to endure or persevere in a given activity; transf. sense to extended distance runs. O [3]

Sitz im Leben, *n.* (1934) *Theol.* Var. **Sitz-im-Leben** (1955) [G < *Sitz* seat, place + *im* in (the) + *Leben* life] In Biblical scholarship, the circumstances out of which a tradition developed, as judged to determine the form of the tradition: form criticism (q.v.). O [3]

sitzkrieg, *n.* (1940) *Mil.* Var. **Sitzkrieg** (1940) [G < *Sitz* act of sitting + *Krieg* war] Static warfare, characterized by a relative absence of active hostilities, esp. the phony war of Sept. 1939 to May 1940; a phony war. O, R, W [4]

sitzmark, *n.* (1935) *Sports* [G *Sitzmarke* < *sitzen* to sit + *Marke* mark] A depression left in the snow by a skier's falling backward; such a fall. O, R, W [4]

Sjögren's syndrome, *n.* (1938) *Path.* [G *Sjögrens-Syndrome* (1937) < the name of Henrik Sjögren (1899–?), Swedish ophthalmologist + G *Syndrom* syndrome < NL *syndrome* < Gk] A condition characterized by chronic inflammatory swelling of the lachrymal glands and by the multiplicity of autoantibodies in the blood; also called *sicca syndrome.* O [3]

skat, *n.* (1864) *Games* Var. **scat** (1864) [G (1817), so named by Friedrich Hempel of Altenburg, Germany, then the center of playing-cards manufacturing < It *scarto* discarding] A three-handed card game of German origin. O, R, W [4]

skimeister, *n.* *Sports* [G < *Ski* ski + *Meister* master, ult. < L *magister*] A skier with the best overall record in various skiing competitions; a professional skier or ski instructor. W [2]

skorodite, *see* scorodite

skotophil, *see* scotophil

skutterudite, *n.* (1850) *Mineral.* [G *Skutterudit* (1845) < *Skutterud,* the name of a village in southern Norway + G *-it* -ite] An arsenide of cobalt and nickel. O, R, W [3]

slacken, *n.* (1670) *Metall.* Var. **slakin** [Ad. of obs. G *Schlacken* (now *Schlacke*) < LG, MLG *slagge* slag] In smelting, slag mixed with ores to promote their fusion. O, W [3]

slackstone, *n.* (1683) *Metall.* (archaic) [Transl. of G *Schluckstein* (see Grimm) < *Schlacken* slacken (q.v.) + *Stein* stone] A form of slag. O [3]

slakin, *see* slacken

slattern, *n.* (1639) [By folk etymology, prob. < G *schlottern* to hang loosely, waddle, slouch < MHG *slottern, slattern* < *sloten* to stagger, shake] One who is negligent of one's habits, appearance, or surroundings, esp. a dirty, slovenly woman; a slut or prostitute. —**slattern,** *a.* (1716), *v.* (1747); **slatternly,** *a.* (c.1680), *adv.* (1750); **slattern(li)ness** (1745, 1811). O, R, W [4]

slave morality, *n.* (1907) *Philos.* [Transl. of G *Sklavenmoral* (1886) < *Sklave* slave + *Moral* morality] A Nietzschean concept of a morality characteristic of the weak, which rests upon resentment of the powerful and exalts virtues like meekness and obedience. O [3]

slenker, *v.* (1658) (archaic) [Ad. of G *schlenkern* < Late MHG *slenkern* to dangle, swing] To dangle or swing. O [3]

slick, *n.* (1683) *Mining* [Ad. of G *Schlich* finely pulverized washings of ore or rock; dry, pulverized rock in mining] Finely pounded ore. —**slick,** *a.* (1892). O [2]

slickens[1], *n.* *Geol.* Var. **schlich, slik** [Prob. ad. of G *Schlick* mud, slit < Du < MLG *slik* < *sliken* to glide] Fine silt deposited by a stream's flood waters; slickenside. W [3]

slickens[2], *n.* (1882) *Tech.* [Ad. of G *Schlich* slick (q.v.) < MHG, OHG *slich* (see Paul-Betz), prob. also akin to G *schleichen* to slink] Finely pulverized material from a quartz mill; in hydraulic mining, the sluiced-away washings of lighter earth. O, W [3]

sliding time, *see* Gleitzeit

slight, *v.* (1640–4) *Archit.* [Prob. ad. of Du *slechten* or G *schlichten,* MHG *slihten* to raze, make smooth] To level a building; to raze a fortification (this is different from several older meanings like "make level," "disdain or ignore," "act or do work carelessly," etc.). O, W [3]

slobberhannes, -es *pl.* (1877) *Games* [Ad. of G *Schlabberhan(ne)s* sloppy eater, gossiper < standard Early NHG *schlabbern* to eat sloppily, gossip + *Han(ne)s,* a nickname < *Johann(es)* John] A four-person variation of the game of hearts, in which one avoids winning the first and last tricks and any trick containing the queen of clubs. O, W [3]

Slovene, *n.* (1883) *Politics, Ling.* Var. **Slovenian** [G (now *Slowene*) < OSlav *Slověne,* supposedly derived from the stem of *slovo* word, *slovisti* to speak] One of a southern Slavic group of people usu. classed with the Croats and Serbs and residing in Slovenia; a native or resident of Slovenia, also called *Wend;* their language. —**Slovene,** *a.* (1902). O, R, W [4]

slum, *n.* (1874) *Mining* [Poss. ad. of G *Schlamm* < MHG *slam* slime, mud] (U.S.) slime: mud from metallic ore; a passageway at the bottom of a mining pit (this is different from older meanings like "room" or "ghetto area"). O, W [3]

S-matrix, *n.* (1945) *Physics* [G *Matrix-S* (1943) < LL *matrix* a public record, register] A scattering matrix: a matrix of probability amplitudes occurring in the expression of the initial wave functions in a scattering process relative to all possible final wave functions. O [3]

smearcase/smierkase, *n.* (1829) *Food* Var. **smear-case** (1848) [Ad. of G *Schmierkäse* (q.v.)] Cottage cheese; any other soft cheese suitable for spreading. O, R, W [4] smerlin, *n.* (1627) *Ichthy.* (archaic) [Ad. of G *Schmerling,* dim. of G *Schmerl* loach] A loach or groundling. O [3]

smiercase, *see* smearcase

S-mine, *n.* (1944) *Mil.* Var. S mine (1944) [Short. of G *Schützenmine* infantryman mine < *schützen* to protect + *Mine* mine < MFr] One of several German antipersonnel mines used in World War Two. O [3]

smiring, *n.* (1655) *Ornith.* (archaic) [Ad. of G *Schmiering* (defined in Grimm as "eine Art Sand- oder Strandläufer" a type of sandpiper] A variety of sandpiper. O [3]

smouse, *v.* (1775) *Food* Var. smouze (1775) [Prob. ad. of G *schmausen* to feast] To feast; to consume, as a delicacy. O [3]

snallygaster, *n.* (1940) *Myth.* [Poss. ad. of G *schnelle Geister* < *schnell* fast, quick, slick + *Geister,* pl. of *Geist* spirit, character] A mythical monster chiefly reported from rural Maryland, U.S.A., said to prey on children and poultry. O, W [3]

snapper, *see* schnapper

snits, *see* schnitz

snollygoster, *n.* (1846) *Politics* Var. snollygaster [Poss. related to G *snallygaster* (q.v.), the earliest known record of which is later] An unprincipled, shrewd person, esp. a politician. O, R, W [3]

snorkel, *n.* (1947 *W9*) *Sports* [G *Schnorkel* schnorkel (q.v.)] A breathing tube that enables one to engage in shallow or deeper underwater activities; a schnorkel; (cap.) a U.S. proprietary name. —snorkel, *a.* (1954), *v.* (1959). O, R, W [4]

snorkle, *n.* (1340) (obs.) [Poss. ad. of G *Schnörkel* curve, flourish] A wrinkle or crease. O [3]

snow eater, *n.* (1886) *Meteor.* Var. snow-eater (1886) [Transl. of G *Schneefresser* < *Schnee* snow + *Fresser* devourer, eater] Chinook: a warm, dry wind that blows in the U.S. Rocky Mountains. O, W [3]

snow-hammer, *n.* (1802–3) *Ornith.* [Transl. of G *Schneeammer* < *Schnee* snow + *Ammer* finch] A snow finch. O [3]

snow pear, *n.* (1860) *Food* Var. snow-pear (1884) [Transl. of G *Schneebirne* < *Schnee* snow + *Birne* pear] A European pear used esp. to make pear cider. O, R, W [3]

social democracy, *n.* (1888) *Politics* [Ad. of G *Sozialdemokratie* (1848) < *sozial* social + *Demokratie* democracy < L *sociālis* + (L)L *dēmocratia* < Gk *dēmokratía*] The policies and principles of social democrats or of a party of such people. O, R, W [4]

Social Democrat, *n.* (1877) *Politics* [Ad. of G *Sozialdemokrat* (1848) < *sozial* social + *Demokrat* democrat < L *sociālis* + Fr *démocrate*] A member of a Social Democratic Party; one who advocates a peaceful, democratic transition to socialism. O, R, W [4]

social democratic, *a.* (1870) *Politics* [Ad. of G *sozialdemokratisch* (1849) < *Sozialdemokrat* social democrat (q.v.) + adj. suffix *-isch* -ic] Relating to or constituting social democracy. O, W [4]

solarization, *n.* (1925) *Bot.* [G *Solarisation* (1913) < *solar* + *-isation* < L *sol* sun + *-isation* -ization] The inhibiting of photosynthesis by means of extended exposure to high light intensities (this is different from the old "photographic" meaning). O [3]

solidus, solidi *pl.,* *a.* (1901) and *n.* (1904) *Chem.* [G (1899)

< L *solidus* solid, firm] (of) a line or surface on a temperature-composition diagram for a binary system, below which a mixture exists only as a solid and above which it consists of liquid and solid in equilibrium (this is different from the various older "monetary" meanings from the same Latin source). O, R, W [3]

solum, -s and sola *pl.* (1928) *Geol.* [Short. of G *Solumhorizont* (1922) < *Solum* soil (< L) earth + G *Horizont* (< L) horizon] The upper part of a soil profile where predominant soil-formation predominantly occurs, also called *true soil* (this is different from the old "legal" meaning). O, R, W [3]

solvolysis, -lyses *pl.* (1916) *Chem.* [G *Solvolyse* (1910) < *solvo-* + *-lyse* < L *solvere* to dissolve + Gk *lýsis* dissolution, loosening] A chemical reaction of a dissolved substance and a solvent, usu. producing one or more new compounds. —solvolytic(ally) (1916, 1974). O, R, W [4]

somatocoel, *n.* (1955) *Zool.* [G (1912) < *somato-* + *-cœl* < Gk *sōma,* gen. *sōmatos* body + *koilía* body cavity] Each of two paired cavities in an echinoderm's embryo that develop into the main body cavity in the adult echinoderm. —somatocoelic (1976). O [3]

somatogamy, *n.* (1949) *Biol.* [G *Somatogamie* (1916) < *somato-* + *-gamie* < Gk *sōma,* gen. *sōmatos* body + *gameîn* to wed + G *-ie* (< Gk *-ia*) -y] The nuclear association constituting the precondition for transition from the saprophytic to the parasitic mode of life. —somatogamous (1950). O [3]

somatogenic, *a.* (1889) *Biol.* Var. somatogenetic [G *somatogenisch,* coined by August Weismann (1825–74), German biologist < *somato-* + *genisch* < Gk *sōma* (gen. *sōmatos* body) + *gennân* to create, generate + G *-isch*] Arising in, affecting, or acting through somatic cells. —somatogenic variation. O, R, W [4]

somatopsychic, *a.* (1902) *Psych.* [G *somatopsychisch* (1892) < *somato-* + *psychisch* < Gk *sōma,* gen. *sōmatos* body + *psyché* soul + G adj. suffix *-isch* -ic] Of or relating to awareness of one's own body; stemming from or relating to the effects of bodily illness on the mind. O [3]

somewhat, *n. Philos.* [Transl. of G *etwas* something, somewhat] In Hegelian philosophy, a reality that is limited by negation (this is different from the numerous older meanings.) W [3]

sonder, *a.* (1909) and *n.* (1917) *Sports* (U.S.) [G *sonder-* special, a short. of *Sonderklasse* sonderclass (q.v.)] (of, relating to, or specifying) a class of small racing yachts or a yacht of this class. O [3]

Sonderbund, *n.* (1847) *Politics* [G < *sonder-* separate + *Bund* (q.v.) alliance, league] A league formed by the seven Roman Catholic cantons of Switzerland in 1843 and defeated during the civil war of 1847. —Sonderbund, *a.* (1922). O [3]

sonderclass, *n.* (1913) *Sports* [Ad. of G *Sonderklasse* < *sonder-* separate, special + *Klasse* class < Fr *classe* < L *classis*] A special class of small racing yachts. O, R [3]

Sonderkommando, *n.* (1951) *Politics* [G (by (1614) < *sonder-* special + *Kommando* command, detachment, ult. < LL *commandāre*] A detachment of prisoners in a Nazi concentration camp responsible for disposing of the dead; a member of such a detachment. O, R [3]

song cycle, *n.* (1899) *Music* [Transl. of G *Liederzyklus* <

Lieder, pl. of *Lied* song + *Zyklus* cycle < LL *cyclus* < Gk *kýklos*] A cycle of songs intended to constitute one musical entity, as in having the same general subject. O, R, W [4]

songfest, *n.* (1912) *Music* [Transl. of G *Sängerfest* saengerfest (q.v.)] An informal session of group singing of folk or popular songs; in Germany, a song festival organized by one or more singing societies. O, R, W [4]

song form, *n.* (1884) *Music* [Transl. of G *Liedform* (1839) < *Lied* song + *Form* form < L *fōrma*] The form of a dance, song, or similar short composition in binary or ternary measure. O, W [3]

song without words, *n.* (1871) *Music* [Transl. of G *Lied ohne Worte* < *Lied* song + *ohne* without + *Worte,* pl. of *Wort* word] An instrumental composition in the style of a song (as in Mendelssohn's *Lieder ohne Worte*). O [3]

sontag, *n.* (1862) *Apparel* [G a kind of cape < the name of Henriette *Sontag* (1806–54), German vocalist] A kind of crocheted or knitted cape that many Western women wore in the second half of the 19th century. O, R, W [3]

Sorb, *n.* (1843) *Ethnology, Ling.* Var. **Sorbian** [G *Sorbe* Sorb, a member of a West Slavic tribe < *Sorbian serb*] Wend (q.v.); Wendish; their language. O, W [4]

sorb apple, *n.* (1548) *Bot.* Var. **sorb** [Ad. of G *Sorbapfel* (< *Sorbus* < L mountain ash) + G *Apfel* apple] The service tree or its fruit. **—sorb apple,** *a.* (1578). O, R [4]

sorge, *n.* [G concern, worry < OHG *sorga*] Concern, care, near-anxiety. W [3]

soteriological, *a.* (1879) *Theol.* [Ad. of G *soteriologisch* < *Soteriologie* soteriology (< *soterio-* + *-logie*—see *soterology*) + adj. suffix *-isch* -ical] Of or relating to soteriology or salvation. **—soteriologic.** O, R, W [4]

soteriology, *n.* (1864) *Theol.* [G *Soteriologie,* Fr *sotériologie* (see *soterology*)] The doctrine of salvation (this is different from the older meaning of "promoting and preserving health"). O, R, W [4]

soterology, *n.* (1882–3) *Theol.* [G *Soterologie* < *sotero-* + *-logie* < Gk *sōtér* savior + *lógos* word study + G *-ie* (< Gk *-ia*) -y] The doctrine of Christology, as opposed to soteriology (salvation). O [2]

sots, *n.* (1799 *Sc*) *Food* [Ad. of G (PaG) *Satz* yeast (see Grimm)] Yeast. W [3]

sound-history, *n.* (1933) *Ling.* [Transl. of G *Lautgeschichte* < *Laut* sound + *Geschichte* history] History of the sounds in a given language. O [3]

sound-law/sound law, *n.* (1874) *Ling.* [Transl. of G *Lautgesetz* < *Laut* sound + *Gesetz* law] Phonetic law, a formula deduced from observed data to express the development of a sound or combination of sounds under given conditions and time within a linguistic area. O, R, W [3]

sound shifting, *n.* (1880) *Ling.* Var. **sound-shift** [Transl. of G *Lautverschiebung* < *Laut* sound + *Verschiebung* shift] Phonetic change: consonant changes as defined by Grimm's law, etc. O, W [3]

sour beef, *see* sauerbraten

sourcebook, *n.* (1899) *Ed.* Var. **source book** [Prob. a blend of the transl. of G *Quelle* source + E *book,* in analogy with G *Quellenforschung, Quellengeschichte*] A book or collection of sources or original documents; a limited collection of research sources for use in a school or college course. O, R, W [4]

sourcrout, *see* sauerkraut

spaad, *n.* (1594) *Mineral.* (archaic) [G *Spad(e),* var. of *Spat* spath (q.v.)] A variety of gypsum, talc, or spar, or a powdered preparation from one of these, mainly used to form molds to cast metal objects. O [3]

space group, *n.* (1901) *Crystal.* [Transl. of G *Raumgruppe* (1891) < *Raum* space + *Gruppe* group] Any of 230 sets of symmetry operations, derived from the point groups by including translated symmetry, screw axes, and glide planes, as used to classify crystal structures. O, R, W [3]

space-time, *n.* (1915) *Physics* Var. **space-time continuum** (1927), **spacetime** (1940) [Transl. of G *Raumzeit(-Welt)* < *Raum* space + *Zeit* time (+ *Welt* world)] In Einstein's theory of relativity, the four-dimensional manifold or continuum produced by the fusion of time and three-dimensional space so as to contain all events; the whole or a portion of physical reality that is such a four-dimensional array; the primordial reality that contains only spacial and temporal qualities. O, R, W [4]

space wave, *n.* (1913) *Physics* [Transl. of G *Raumwelle* (1911) < *Raum* space + *Welle* wave] A radio wave that passes from transmitter to receiver either by reflection from the ground or else directly through space without reflection. O [3]

Spackle, *n.* (1928) *Tech.* Var. **spackle** (1951) [Prob. ad. of G *Spachtel,* a short. of *Spachtelkitt* < L *spat(h)ula* small mixing spoon + OHG *kuti, quiti,* actually resin] A trademark for a compound usu. of gypsum plaster, which is used to fill holes or cracks in a surface before painting. **—spackle,** *v.* (1971); **spackling (compound)** (1940, 1941). O, R, W [4]

spadaite, *n.* (1843) *Mineral.* [G *Spadait* (1843) < the name of Lavinio *Spada* de Medici (1801–63), Italian writer and mineralogist + G *-it* -ite] A hydrous magnesium silicate. O, W [3]

spady, *a.* (1683) *Mineral.* (archaic) [Obs. G *spadig,* var. of *spat(h)ig* spath-like] Of the nature of or containing spath (q.v.). O (not in 2nd ed.) [2]

Spaetlese, *see* Spätlese

spaetzle/spätzle, -ø/-s *pl.* (1933) *Food* [G *Spätzle,* dial. dim. of *Spatz,* sparrow, dumpling < MHG *spaz, spatze,* nickname for MHG *spare,* OHG *sparo* sparrow] A type of German noodle made of a batter of eggs, milk, and flour, as run through a coarse colander into a boiling liquid. O, R, W [3]

spalt, *n.* (1668) *Geol.* (archaic) [G crevice < *spalten* to split, cleave < OHG *spaltan*] A white, scaly, shining stone, often used to promote the fusing of metals. O [2]

spalt, *v.* (1733) *Geol.* [Prob. < G *spalten* to split (off)] (Dial.) to split off or splinter. **—spalting,** verbal *n.* (1733). O, W [3]

Spandau, *n.* (1918) *Mil.* Var. **spandau** (1929) [G < *Spandau,* the name of a district in Berlin, where the machine gun was manufactured] This German gun used during World War One; other machine guns of German design during World War Two. **—Spandau (machine) gun** (1918, 1944). O [3]

spanner, *n.* (1639) *Mil., Trades* [G < *spannen* to stretch or tense] (*Archaic*) the instrument for spanning the spring in a wheel-lock firearm; a contrivance in early steam engines for moving themselves; (chiefly Brit.) a kind of hand wrench; a pendulum attachment for an ordinary sextant to provide an artificial horizon; an embroidery machine worker who adjusts frames and fabric. —**spanner wrench, spannerman.** O, R, W [4]

sparagmite, *n.* (1882) *Geol.* [G *Sparagmit* (1829) < Gk *spáragma* fragment, fraction + G *-it* -ite] A generic term for the feldspathic sandstones that occur in late Pre-Cambrian formations in Scandinavia. O [3]

sparesome, *a.* (1864) *Econ.* [Ad. of G *sparsam* economical] Economical. O [2]

spargelstone, *n.* (1804) *Geol.* [Transl. of G *Spargelstein* < *Spargel* asparagus + *Stein* stone] Asparagus stone. O (not in 2nd ed.) [3]

spark counter, *n.* (1935) *Physics* [Transl. of G *Funkenzähler* (1935) < *Funken,* pl. of *Funke(n)* spark + *Zähler* counter] A charged-electrode counter for detecting charged particles. O [3]

Spartacist, *a.* (1919) and *n.* (1920) *Politics* Var. **Spartakist** (1925) [G *Spartakist* (1918) < the German name of *Spartakus,* Thracian leader of the slave revolt against Rome from 73 to 71 B.C. + G (< L) *-ist* -ist] (Of) a member of the German socialist extremists during World War One, dedicated to revolution and establishment of a socialist government, as incited by the political tracts of Karl Liebknecht, who adopted the slave leader's name as a pseudonym. O, R [4]

Spartacus group/league, *n.* (1918) *Politics* [Transl. of G *Spartakusbund* < *Spartakus* Sparticist (q.v.) + *Bund* league, federation] The Spartacists. O [3]

Spartakist, *see* Spartacist

spasmoneme, *n.* (1901) *Zool.* [G *Spasmonem* (1892) < *spasmo-* + *-nem* < Gk *spasmós* pulling, convulsion + *nêma* thread] A contractile organelle in stalked protozoans, which contracts and thus withdraws the animal from possible danger. O, W [3]

spath, *n.* (1763) *Mineral.* (archaic) [G (now *Spat*) spar] Spar, a usu. cleavable mineral. —**spathic** (1788). O, R, W [3]

Spätlese, -n *pl.* (1926) *Beverages* Var. **Spaetlese** (1951) [G < *spät* late + *Lese* harvest] A white wine produced (esp. in Germany) from grapes picked later than the main harvest. O [3]

spätzle, *see* spaetzle

S.P.D., *n.* (1921) *Politics* [G *SPD,* an abbr. of *Sozialdemokratische Partei Deutschlands* Social Democratic Party of Germany, until 1890 *Sozialistische Arbeiterpartei Deutschlands* Germany's Socialist Labor Party] (West) Germany's Social Democratic Party, continuing after reunification in 1990. O [3]

species being, *n.* (1959) *Sociol.* [Transl. of G *Gattungswesen* (1797) < *Gattung* type, species + *Wesen* being] Marx's term for a person's objective consciousness of life and the mastering of the natural world through work, which distinguishes humans from other animals; humankind when considered in relation to such qualities. O [3]

speciestaler, *n. Currency* [G *Speziestaler* < *Spezies* specie (< L species) + G *Taler* taler (q.v.)] A reichstaler (q.v.), an old German taler. W [3]

speck, *n.* (1633) *Food* [Du *spek* (< MDu *spec*) and G

Speck < MHG < OHG *spek* bacon] (Chiefly dial.) fat meat, as in bacon, whale blubber, or hippopotamus fat cured as bacon. —**speck,** *a.* (1820). O, W [3]

speckstone, *n.* (1794) *Geol.* (archaic) [Transl. of G *Speckstein* < *Speck* speck, bacon + *Stein* stone] Soapstone or its Chinese variety; agalmatolite. O [3]

spectrometer, *n.* (1874) *Physics* [G *Spektrometer* < *spektro-* + *-meter* (or < Fr *spectromètre*) < the comb. form of L *spectrum* spectrum + *metrum* measure] An instrument that measures the index of refraction; such an instrument that can measure the spectra observed with it. — **spectrometry** (1891), **-metric(ally)** (1903, 1953), **-metrist** (1958), **mass spectrometer** (1932), **prism spectrometer.** O, R, W [4]

spectroscope, *n.* (1861) *Physics* [G *Spektroskop* < *spektro-* + *-skop* (or Fr *spectroscope*) < the comb. form of L *spectrum* spectrum + Gk *skopeîn* to view] An instrument that forms and visually examines optical spectra. —**spectroscope,** *v.* (1881); **-scopic(al)** (1864, 1870); **-scopist** (1866); **-scopy** (1870); **-scopically** (1871); **-scopic binary** (1896)/**parallax.** O, R, W [4]

speech/linguistic island, *n.* (1888) *Ling.* [Transl. of G *Sprachinsel* < *Sprache* language + *Insel* island] A speech community located within a different speech community. O, R, W [3]

speis, *see* speiss

Speisesaal, *n.* (1871) *Food* [G < *speisen* to dine + *Saal* hall] A dining room or hall in German-speaking countries. O [3]

speiskobalt, *n.* (1872) *Mineral.* Var. **speiss-cobalt** (*1872*), **speiss cobalt** (1877) [G *Speiskobalt* or *Smaltin* (1872) < *Speise* (here) metallic mixture + *Kobalt* cobalt (q.v.)] Smaltite, an arsenide composed of cobalt and nickel. O, W [3]

speiss, -es *pl.* (1796) *Metall.* Old var. **speis** (1796) [G *Speise,* lit., food < *speisen* to eat, dine; feed] A mixture of impure metallic arsenides produced in smelting. O, R, W [4]

speiss-cobalt, *see* speiskobalt

spelt, *see* speltz

speltoid, *a.* and *n.* (1920) *Bot.* [G *speltoid* and *Speltoid* (1917) < *spelt* spelt (q.v.) + *-oid* < Gk *-oeidēs* similar, resembling] (of) a type of wheat having some characteristics of spelt. —**speltoidy,** *n.* (1944). O, W [3]

speltz, *n.* (1562) *Bot.* Var. **spelt** (1000, borrowed < LL) [G *Spelt, Spelz* < OHG *spelza* < LL *spelta*] Spelt; one of various varieties of emmer (q.v.). • ~ evidently had little currency and no continuous history in English until the 16th century. O, R, W [3]

sphaerite, *n.* (1886) *Mineral.* [G *Sphärit* (1867) < *sphär-* (< Gk *sphaîra* ball, sphere) + G *-it* -ite] A hydrous aluminum phosphate in globular concretions. O, W [3]

sphaerocobaltite, *n.* (1877) *Mineral.* [G *Sphärokobaltit* (1847) < *sphäro-* (< Gk *sphaîra* ball, sphere) + G *Kobaltit* cobaltite] A carbonate of cobalt, also called *cobaltocalcite.* O, W [3]

sphalerite, *n.* (1868) *Mineral.* [G *Sphalerit* (1847) < Gk *sphalerós* deceptive + G *-it* -it] Zincblende, zinc sulfide; also called *blackjack, blende, false galena.* O, R, W [4]

spherulite, *n.* (1823) *Geol.* Old var. **sphærulite** (1823) [Ad. of G *Sphärolit* (1816) < the comb. form of Gk *sphaîra* ball, sphere + *líthos* stone] A small spheroidal mass found in rock, esp. one consisting of many crystals that have grown radically from a point. O, W [4]

spiegeleisen, *n.* (1868 *W9*) *Metall.* [G < *Spiegel* mirror, surface + *Eisen* iron] A variety of pig iron used in steelmaking. • ~ is short. to **spiegel** (1881), partially transl. as **spiegel(-)iron** (1883), and fully transl. as **mirror iron.** O, R, W [3]

spiegel-iron, *see* spiegeleisen

spiel, *n.* (1896) (colloq.) [G (*Vor*)*spiel* humbug < *vorspielen* to humbug] A voluble, usu. high-flown line of talk, esp. to lure persons to a movie, sale, etc.; a swindle or dishonest line of business. O, R, W [4]

spiel[1], *v.* (1870 *W9*) (colloq.) [G *spielen* to humbug] To talk in a voluble, often high-flown manner; to talk glibly or perform. O, R, W [4]

spiel[2], *v.* (1859) *Music* [G *spielen* to play (music), to gamble] To play music; to gamble. —**spieling,** verbal *n.* (1859). O, W [3]

spieler, *n.* (1859) (colloq.) Old var. **speeler** (1886) [G *Spieler* player or (*Vor*)*spieler* humbugger] Player or gambler; barker; swindler; a voluble speaker; a gambling club. O, R, W [4]

Spielraum, *n.* (1921) *Philos.* [G (1896) < *Spiel* play + *Raum* room] Orig. in probability theory, the range of possibilities considered in projecting the likelihood of a hypothesis or the probability of an outcome. O [2]

spillflöte, *n. Music* [G < *Spille* spindle + *Flöte* flute < MFr *flahute* < OProv *flaut*] A spindle-shaped, half-covered pipe-organ flue stop. W [3]

spilosite, *n.* (1882) *Geol.* [G *Spilosit* < Gk *spílos* spot + G *-it* -ite] A schistose rock formed by contact metamorphism of clay slate. O, W [4]

spin, *n.* (1525) *Biol.* (obs.) [G *Spinne, Spünne* nipple (see Grimm)] A teat. O [3]

spindle, *n.* (1894) *Anat.* [G *Spindel* (1863) < MHG *spindel, spinnel,* OHG *spin(n)ala,* ad. < *spinnen* to spin] Muscle spindle, a spindle-shaped nerve ending. O, R, W [4]

spindle tree, *n.* (1548) *Bot.* [Transl. of G *Spindelbaum,* lit., spindle tree] A small, shrubby tree used esp. for spindles and skewers. —**spindle tree,** *a.* (1857). O, W [4]

spinnbar, *a.* (1944) *Biol.* [G (see *spinnbarkeit*)] Spinnable; having the quality of spinnbarkeit. O [3]

spinnbarkeit, *n.* (1938) *Biol.* Var. **Spinnbarkeit** (1938) [G (1936) < *spinnbar* capable of spin + nom. suffix *-keit* -ity] The characteristic of a viscous liquid, esp. the cervical mucus, to be drawn into strands; spinnability. O [3]

spinor, *n.* (1931) *Physics* [G (1929) < *spinnen* to spin + nom. suffix *-or* -or] A quantity resembling a vector with complex constituents in two- or four-dimensional space, used in the mathematics of relativity theory. —**spinorial,** *a.* (1968). O, R, W [3]

spiran(e), *n.* (1911) *Chem.* [G *Spiran* < the comb. form of L *spīra,* Gk *speîra,* denoting "spiro" + G *-an* -an(e)] A spiro compound. O, W [3]

spireme, *n.* (1889) *Biol.* Var. **spirem** (1889) [G *Spirem* < Gk *speírēma* spindle, thread] A continuous thread observed in the cell nucleus during mitosis. O, R, W [4]

spir(o)-, *comb. form* (1908) *Chem.* [G (1900), introduced in this sense by Adolf Johann Friedrich Wilhelm von Baeyer (1835–1917), German chemist < L *spīrāre* to breathe]

An initial element used in names of organic compounds containing one or more systems of two molecular rings with a single atom common to both (*spiropentane*). O, R, W [3]

spitz, -es *pl.* (1842) *Zool.* Var. **spitz dog** (1842), **Spitz** (1845), **spitzhund** [G, a short. of *Spitzhund* < *spitz* pointed (with reference to the shape of the dog's muzzle and ears) + *Hund* dog] One of various dogs native to northern areas (with pointed muzzle and pricked ears). O, R, W [4]

spitzer, *n. Mil.* [G, a short. of *Spitzgeschoß* < *spitz* pointed + *Geschoß* missile, bullet] A metal-jacketed, pointed bullet. W [3]

spitzflöte/spitzflute, *n.* (1855) *Music* Var. **Spitzflöte** (1966) [G *Spitzflöte* < *spitz* pointed + *Flöte* flute < MFr *flahute* < OProv *flaut*] A labial pipe-organ stop with conical pipes of flute quality. O, W [3]

spitzhund, *see* spitz

splitter, -ø *pl.* (1546) (archaic) [G chip, splinter (or < LG)] A splinter (this is different from numerous other meanings). O, W [3]

splitter, *v.* (1860) [G (*zer*)*splittern* to splinter] To splinter or break into fragments. O, W [3]

spongin, *n.* (1868) *Biochem.* [G < L *spongia* < Gk *spóngos* sponge + G *-in* -in] A scleroprotein occurring as flexible fibers in the skeleton of many sponges. O, R, W [4]

spongioblastoma, -s/-ta *pl.* (1918) *Path.* [G *Spongioblastom* < NL *spongioblastoma* < Gk *spóngos* sponge + *blastós* bud + G *-om* (< Gk *-ōma*) -oma, denoting a swelling or tumor] A malignant tumor, usu. of the brain or central nervous system, composed of spongioblasts. O, W [3]

spongioplasm, *n.* (1886) *Biol.* [G *Spongioplasma* (1885) < *spongio-* + *Plasma* plasma (q.v.) < Gk *spóngos* sponge + *plásma* structure, formation] Cytoreticulum, a meshwork of cells and their processes. —**spongioplasmic** (1886). O, W [3]

spook, *n.* (1801) *Myth.* [Du *spook* or poss. G *Spuk* ghost] A specter, ghost; (slang) a queer, strange person or a Negro; (slang) ghost-writer; spy. —**spook,** *v.* (1871). • ~ appears in numerous derivatives like **-y** (1854); **-iness** (1890); **-ery** (1893); **-ist** (1902); **-ing,** *verbal n.* (1919); **-ed,** *a.* (1937); **-ily** (1955); **-ish.** O, R, W [4]

sporonin, *n.* (1928) *Biochem.* [G (1928), irreg. < *sporo-* (< Gk *sporá* seed, sowing) + G *-n-* + *-in* -in] An inert substance composing the resistant outer wall of spores. O [3]

sporopollenin, *n.* (1931) *Biochem.* [G (1931) < *sporo-* + *Pollenin* < Gk *sporá* seed, sowing + L *pollen* fine dust + G *-in* -in] An inert substance, mainly composed of polysaccharides, that makes up the resistant outer wall of pollen grains and spores. O [3]

Sprachgefühl/sprachgefühl, *n.* (1902) *Ling.* [G < *Sprache* language + *Gefühl* feeling] One's intuitive feeling for what is linguistically appropriate or persuasive; one's sensibilities about the established usage in a language. O, R, W [3]

Sprechgesang, *n.* (1925) *Music* Var. **sprechgesang** [G, lit., sung speech < *sprechen* to speak + *Gesang* song] A dramatic vocal style intermediate between speech and singing. O, R [3]

Sprechstimme, *n.* (1922) *Music* Var. **sprechstimme** (1968)

[G (1871) < *sprechen* to speak + *Stimme* voice] Arnold Schönberg's term for the voice of a performer singing according to the principles of Sprechgesang (q.v.); loosely, Sprechgesang. O, R [3]

springerle, *n.* *Food* [(Alemannic) G < dim. of *Springer* jumper < *springen* to jump, with reference to the dough of which the cookie is made, which, when left overnight to rise, rises abruptly] A rock-hard cookie usu. flavored with anise and traditionally eaten at Christmas by German-speaking families. • ~ appears in compounds like **springerle forms** (1938)/**cracker** (1940)/**molds** (1940 *Sc*). W [3]

springwort, *n.* (1889) *Bot.* [Transl. of G *Springwurz* < *springen* to jump + *Wurz, Wurzel* root, wort] A fabled herb having supposedly magic powers. O [3]

spritz, *v.* (1935) *Beverages* [(PaG., dial.) G *spritz(en)* to squirt] (Dial. U.S.) to sprinkle, spray, or squirt. —**spritz**, *n.* (1935); **spritzing**, *verbal n.* (1976). O, R, W [3]

spritzer, *n.* (1961) *Beverages* [G a small amount of liquid, like a ''shot'' of soda water] A drink of or a mixture of white wine with soda water. O, R, W [3]

spritzig, *a.* (1949) *Beverages* [G of a sparkling, highly carbonated wine < *spritzen* to squirt + adj. suffix -*ig* -y] Of sparkling wines. —**spritzig**, *n.* (1968). O [3]

sprosser, *n.* (1871) *Ornith.* [G, akin to *Sprosse* step on a ladder—this bird's name was prob. suggested in relation to a tree trunk with its broken-off limbs, it being the oldest form of ladder on which to perch] A thrush nightingale found in eastern Europe and Asia. O [3]

spurlos versenkt, *a.* (1918) *Mil.* [G < *spurlos* without a trace + *versenkt* sunk < *versenken* to sink] Sunk without a trace; lost from sight. • ~ appears in partial transl. as **sunk spurlos** (1922). O [2]

square-free, *a.* (1960) *Math.* [Transl. of G *quadratfrei* < *Quadrat* square + *frei* free] Of an integer that equals the product of a set of different primes or is not divisible by a perfect square. O [3]

S.S., *see* Schutzstaffel

staatenbund, *n.* *Politics* [G < *Staaten*, pl. of *Staat* state + *Bund* league] A league of states where each of the states retains some degree of sovereignty; a confederacy, as opposed to Bundesstaat (q.v.). W [3]

stab, *n.* (1929) *Med.* [G rod (1911), a short. of the use by Viktor Schilling of *stabförmig* rod-shaped, *Stabkern* rod-nucleus] White blood cells characterized by a nucleus in the form of a twisted or bent rod. O [3]

stab, *a.* (1929) *Med.* [Short. of G *stabförmig* (1911) < *Stab* rod + *förmig* having the shape or form of] Concerning a stab (see the noun form) or stabs. O [3]

stab cell, *n.* (1972) *Med.* Var. **staff cell** [Ad. of G *Stabzelle* < *Stab* rod, staff + *Zelle* cell < L *cella*] A young blood granulocyte containing a densely staining nucleus in the form of a single bent or twisted rod. O, W [3]

stachyose, *n.* (1890) *Chem.* [G (1890) < *stachy-* < NL *stachys* corn cob + G *-ose* (< Gk *-ose*) -ose, denoting a carbohydrate] A sweet, crystalline tetrasaccharide found esp. in the tubers of Chinese artichoke. O, W [3]

Stadthaus, *n.* (1839) *Politics* Var. **stadthaus** [G < *Stadt* city, town + *Haus* house] A German town hall. O [3]

stadthouse, *n.* (1646) *Politics* [Ad. of G *Stadthaus* (q.v.) or Du *stadhuis* < *stad* + *huis* house] A town hall, esp. in Holland or a former Dutch colony. O [3]

staff¹, *n.* (1700) *Mil.* [Transl. of G *Stab*, as in *Generalstab* general staff] A group of officers assisting a commanding officer such as a general in carrying out his duties. —**staff**, *a.* O, R, W [4]

staff², *n.* (1892) *Industry* [Prob. short. of G *staffieren* to trim, decorate—see *staffage*] A building material with a plaster-of-paris base used ornamentally in exterior walls. O, R, W [3]

staffage, *n.* (1872) *Art* [G, a short. of *Staffagefigur* < *staffieren* to decorate, ult. < OFr *estoffer* + G (< Fr) -*age* -age + G *Figur* figure < L *figūra*] Animal or human figures added as subordinate elements in an artist's painting of a landscape. O, W [3]

staff cell, *see* stab cell

staffelite, *n.* (1868) *Mineral.* [G *Staffelit* (1866) < *Staffel*, the name of a town in Hesse, Germany + -*it* -ite] Carbonate-fluorapatite, also called *francolite* (see *apatite*). O [3]

Stahlhelm, *n.* (1927) *Mil.* [G (1918) < *Stahl* steel + *Helm* helmet, so named for the German steel helmets worn in World War I] A German veterans' organization with monarchistic, authoritarian tendencies, formed after World War One. —**Stahlhelmer** (1927). • ~ is transl. as **Steel Helmet** (1925, q.v.). O [3]

stalag/Stalag, *n.* (1941) *Mil.* [G, a short. of *Kriegsgefangenen-Stammlager* < *Kriegsgefangenen* prisoners of war, *pl.* of *Kriegsgefangener* + *Stammlager* base or main camp for prisoners of war, as opposed to *Oflag* officers' prisoner-of-war camp and to *Dulag* transshipment camp for such prisoners] In Nazi Germany, a prisoners' camp for noncommissioned officers or enlisted men. O, R, W [4]

Stalag Luft, *n.* (1947) *Mil.* [G < *Stalag* stalag (q.v.) + *Luft* air] In Nazi Germany, a prisoners' camp for Air Force personnel. O [3]

stambook, *n.* (1662) *Printing* (archaic) [Partial transl. of G *Stammbuch*, orig., lit., a family register, now a diary or journal < *Stamm* stem + *Buch* book] Journal or memorandum book. O [3]

Stammbaum, *n.* (1939) *Ling.* [G (1863) pedigree < *Stamm* stem + *Baum* tree—in modern German linguistics, the usage is *Stemma* a diagram portraying the structure of a sentence] A family tree of languages. • ~ is transl. as **family tree** (q.v.). O [2]

Stammbaumtheorie, *n.* (1954) *Ling.* [G (1863) < *Stammbaum* (q.v.) pedigree + *Theorie* theory < LL *theōria* < Gk] Formulated by August Schleicher, a linguistic pedigree theory of languages. • ~ is transl. as **family-tree theory** (1933, q.v.). O [3]

Stammtisch, *n.* (1938) *Food* [G, lit., regularly reserved table < *Stamm* (here) fraternity + *Tisch* table] A table reserved for regular patrons of a restaurant, tavern, etc. O [3]

Standartenführer, *n.* (1943) *Mil.* [G < *Standarten* flags or pennants of a military unit, the *pl.* of *Standarte* + *Führer* leader] During the Third Reich, the commanding officer of a unit of the Schutzstaffel (q.v.) or Sturmabteilung (q.v.). O [3]

stand oil, *n.* (1908) *Chem.* [Ad. of G *Standöl* < *Stand* standing + *Öl* oil, so named for its formerly being prepared by allowing linseed oil to stand] Linseed oil or another thickened drying-oil, used in varnishes and printing inks. O, R, W [4]

standpoint, *n.* (1829) [Ad. of G *Standpunkt* standpoint < *Stand* standing + *Punkt* point < L *punctum*] Orig., a position from which objects are physically viewed and judged; a position for judging details and generalizations. O, R, W [4]

stannite, *n.* (1851) *Chem.* (1896) [G *Stannit* (now *Stannat*) < L *stāgnum* (*stannum*) a mixture of silver and lead, zinc + G *-it* -ite] A salt formed in solution by treating a stannous salt with excess alkali. • ~ is different from the sulfide of copper, iron, and tin that has the same name but evidently derives from Fr *stannine*. O, W [3]

stark, *adv.* or *a. Music* [G strong, intensive < OHG *starc*] Loudly, forte, used as a direction in music. W [3]

starosty, *n.* (1710) *Politics* Var. **starostie** (1710), **starostee** (1840) [G *Starostei* or Fr *starostie* < Polish *starostwo* the domain of a Polish nobleman] In the former Polish kingdom, the domain of a starosta, a Polish nobleman who held a castle and domain bestowed by the king. O [3]

statelich, *adv.* (1610) (archaic) [G *statlich* (now *stattlich*) stately, distinguished] In a stately manner. O [2]

state socialism, *n.* (1879) *Politics* [Ad. of G *Staatssozialismus* < *Staat* state (< L *status*) + G *Sozialismus* socialism] A socialism that would use the power of the state to equalize opportunity and income. O, R, W [4]

state socialist, *n.* (1879) and *a. Politics* [Ad. of G *Staatssozialist* < *Staat* state (< L *status*) + *Sozialist* socialist] (of) an advocate of state socialism (q.v.). —**state socialistic** (1879). O, R, W [4]

states-system, *n.* (1834) *Politics* [Ad. of G *Staatensystem* < *Staaten*, pl. of *Staat* state + *System* system < L *status* + LL *systēma* < Gk] The federating of several contiguous nation-states to preserve the actual balance of power. O [3]

statist[1], *n.* (1802) *Math.* [Back-formation of G *Statistik* statistics (1787, q.v.)] One who works with statistics: a statistician (this is different from the old "political" meaning). O, R, W [4]

statist[2], *n.* (1807) *Theater* [G < L *status*, past part. of *stare* to stand + G (< L) *-ist* -ist] A supernumerary actor, a walk-on. O [3]

statistic, *n.* (1789) *Math.* [G *Statistik* statistics (q.v.) or English back-formation < *statistics*] One datum or term in a statistical collection; a quantity projected from a statistical sample to estimate a population parameter. O, R, W [4]

statistics, *n.* (usu. *sing.* but can be a **-ø** *pl.*) (1787) *Math.* [G *Statistik* < NL *statisticus* of the state of affairs, statistical < L *status* state + G *-istik* (< L *-isticus*) -istics] A subject concerned with masses of numerical data; (when pl.) a collection of such data. —**statistical,** *a.* (1787) and in various compounds like **statistical mechanics** (1885), **statistically** (1821), **statistician** (1825), **statisticize** (1879), **statisticism.** O, R, W [4]

stave rime, *n.* (1888) *Lit.* [Poss. a transl. of G *Stabreim* (1837) < *Stab* stave, staff + *Reim* rhyme < OFr *rime*, OHG *rim*] Alliteration; an alliterating word in a line of alliterative verse. O [3]

stearrhœa, *see* steatorrhea

steatorrhea/stearrhœa, *n.* (1842) *Med.* [G (1824) < *stear-*

+ *-rhœa* < Gk *stéar*, gen. *stéatos* fat + *hroía* flux] The excessive excretion of fat in one's stools. O [3]

steckling, *n. Bot.* [G < *stecken* to stick, plant (young plants) + dim. *-ling* -ling] A beet, carrot, or other late-planted plant of a biennial root crop that is usu. stored and replanted for their seeds. W [3]

Steel Helmet, *n.* (1925) *Mil.* [Transl. of G *Stahlhelm* (1918, q.v.)] A member of the Stahlhelm; the organization itself. —**steel-helmeted,** *a.* (1926). O, R [3]

Stefan-Boltzmann law, *n.* (1898) *Physics* Var. (**Stefan's**) **law** (1898), **Stefan-Boltzmann constant** (1954) [Transl. of G *Stefan-Boltzmann-Konstante* (1879–84) < the names of the Austrian physicists Josef *Stefan* (1835–93) and Ludwig Eduard *Boltzmann* (1844–1906) + G *Konstante* constant < L *constant-*] The constant in the Stefan-Boltzmann law of physics. O, R, W [3]

steifkin/stiebkin, *n.* (1617) *Beverages* (archaic) [Prob. ad. of G *Stäufchen,* dim. of *Stauf* cup, jar] A measure (serving) of wine. O [3]

stein, *n.* (1885) *Beverages* [G, a short. of *Steinkrug* or *Steingut* < *Stein* stoneware + *Krug* mug, jug or *Gut* goods (or *Biersteinkrug* beer mug)] A large earthenware mug; any thick such mug for beer; the quantity of beer that it holds. O, R, W [4]

Steinberger, *n.* (1833) *Beverages* Var. **Steinberg** (1894) [Short. of G *Steinberger Wein* < *Steinberg,* the name of a vineyard in the Rheingau, Germany + *Wein* wine] A choice Rhenish wine. O [3]

steinbock, *n.* (1683–4) *Zool.* Var. **steinbokt** (1695), **steinboc** (1859) [G wild goat < *Stein* stone < MHG, OHG *stein* actually, the hard, firm one + *Bock* buck] A wild goat of the genus *ibex;* the Alpine ibex. • ~ is a different word from *steenbok* < Afrik *steenbok.* O [3]

Steinhäger, *n.* (1959) *Beverages* [G < *Steinhagen,* the name of a town in Westphalia, Germany] A spirit produced from juniper berries; a measure or glassful of this. O [3]

steinkern, *n. Paleon.* [G < *Stein* stone + *Kern* kernel, grain] A fossil that is a stony mass or filling inside a hollow object like a bivalve shell. R, W [3]

steinwein, *n.* (1833) *Beverages* [G, a combining of a short. of the name of the *Stein*mantel vineyards near Würzburg, Germany + *Wein* wine] A dry white wine produced near Würzburg and sold in a bocksbeutel (q.v.). O [3]

stellerite, *n.* (1909) *Mineral.* [G *Stellerit* (1909) < the name of Georg Wilhelm *Steller* (1709–46), German naturalist + *-it* -ite] A zeolite found as tubular orthorhombic crystals. O [3]

stem, *v.* (1904) *Sports* [Ad. of G *stemmen* to brace (against)] To decelerate on a traverse descent by stemming one or both skis, by forcing the ski heel into the snow. O, R, W [4]

stem-book, *n.* (1592) (archaic) [Ad. of G *Stammbuch* (< *Stamm* stem + *Buch*) or Du *stamboek*] An album. O [3]

stem-building, *n.* (1870) *Ling.* [Transl. of G *Stammbau* < *Stamm* stem + *Bau* structure, building < *bauen* to build] The forming of stems from roots. O [3]

stem father, *n.* (1879) *Anthrop.* [Transl. of G *Stammvater* < *Stamm* stem + *Vater* father] A tribal ancestor. O [3]

stemform, *n.* (1900) *Bot.* [Transl. of G *Stammform* < *Stamm* stem + *Form* form] The ancestral form. O, W [3]

stem-house, *n.* (1762) *Sociol.* [Transl. of G *Stammhaus* (now *Stammsitz*) < *Stamm* stem + *Haus* house or *Sitz* seat, residence] A family's ancestral mansion. O [3]

stemmatic, *a.* (1958) *Lit.* [G *stemmatisch* < *Stemmata,* pl. of *Stemma* stemma (see *Stammbaum*) + adj. suffix *-isch* -ic] Concerning the reconstruction of interrelationships between the various readings of manuscripts of a text; relating to a textual stemma or stemmata. —**stemmatic theory** (1968). O [3]

stemmatics, *n.* (1949) *Lit.* [G *Stemmatik* (1937) < *Stemmata,* pl. of *Stemma* stemma (see *Stammbaum*) + *-ik* -ics] The research area that seeks to reconstruct the tradition of the transmission of a text or texts (esp. in manuscript form) on the basis of the relationship between the readings of the various surviving witnesses. O [3]

stemple/stempel, *n.* (1653) *Mining* [Prob. < G *Stempel* wooden post < MLG *stempel,* MHG *stempfel,* akin to G *stampfen* to pound, crush, tamp] A wooden crossbar in a mine shaft; such a bar used as a ladder. O [3]

stenothermal, *a.* (1881) *Zool.* Var. **stenothermic** (1926) [Prob. < G *stenotherm* (1871) < *steno-* + *-therm* < Gk *stenós* limited + *thérmē* heat + E *-al*] Able to withstand only small variations in temperature. —**stenotherm,** *n.* (1888). O, W [4]

stenotopic, *a.* (1949) *Zool.* [Prob. < G *stenotop* < *steno-* + *-top* < Gk *stenós* limited + *tópos* place + E *-ic*] Having a restricted adaptability to environmental changes and thus having restricted geographical distribution. O, W [4]

stephanite, *n.* (1849) *Mineral.* [G *Stephanit* (1845) < the name of Archduke Victor *Stephan* of Austria (1817–67) + G *-it* -ite] An orthorhombic sulfide of silver and antimony. O, R, W [3]

stereochemical, *a.* (1890) *Chem.* [Ad. of G *stereochemisch* (1888) < *stereo-* + *chemisch* (see *stereochemistry*)] Concerning the stereochemical properties or configuration of something. —**stereochemically** (1890). O, R, W [4]

stereochemistry, *n.* (1890) *Chem.* [Ad. of G *Stereochemie* (1890) < *stereo-* + *Chemie* chemistry < Gk *stereós* limited + ult. Ar *al-kīmiyā'*] A branch of chemistry concerned with the spatial molecular arrangement of atoms or groups of atoms; such a spatial relationship and its effects on a substance containing it. —**stereochemist** (1937). O, R, W [4]

stereochrome, *n.* (1854) *Art* [G *Stereochrom* < *stereo-* + *-chrom* < Gk *stereós* limited + *chrôma* color] A picture made by stereochromy (q.v.). —**stereochrome,** *a.* (1896). O, R, W [3]

stereochromy, *n.* (1945) *Art* [G *Stereochromie* < *stereo-* + *-chromie* < Gk *stereós* limited + *chrôma* color + G *-ie* (< Gk *-ia*) -y] A process of mural painting that uses water glass: water-glass painting. —**stereochromatic(ally)** (1859, 1845), **-chromic** (1845), **-chromatize** (1907), **-chromically.** O, R, W [3]

stereocomparator, *n.* (1901) *Astronomy* [G *Stereokomparator* < *stereo-* + *Komparator* < Gk *stereós* limited + L *comparāre* to compare] A stereoscope used to make topographic measurements by comparing stereoscopic photographs of the same region or of a celestial area. —**stereocomparagraph.** O, W [3]

stereome/stereom, *n.* (1885) *Bot., Zool.* [G *Stereom* < Gk *steréōma* solid body] Rigid, strengthening cellular tissue

of a plant; exoskeletal material of an invertebrate. O, W [3]

stereoplanigraph, n. (1906) *Tech.* [G < *stereo-* + *Planigraph* < Gk *stereós* limited + comb. form of L *plānus* plane + Gk *gráphein* to write, record] A machine that plots a topographic map of an area semiautomatically from aerial, stereoscopic photographs. O, W [3]

-sterone, *comb. form Chem.* [G blend of *-steron* (< *Sterol* sterol) + *Keton* ketone (q.v.), prob. first used in *Androsteron* (1934, see *androsterone*)] A formative element used in naming steroids. O [3]

stich, *n.* *Games* [G sting, prick < *stechen* to pierce (fig., a card that a player takes by "nailing it," as in a jousting match or felling it, so to speak, with a card of higher rank)] A trick in pinochle and some other card games that has special scoring value because it is the last trick. • ~ is different from the "literary" item borrowed from Greek. R, W [3]

stictic acid, n. (1868) *Chem.* [Transl. of G *Stictinsäure* (1846) < *stictin-* (< Gk *stiktós* spotted) + G *-in* -ic + *Säure* acid] A depsidone found in many lichens. O [3]

stiebkin, *see* steifkin

stift, n. (1637) *Theol.* [G bishopric < MHG *stift* < *stiften* to found, organize] The domain of a German prince-bishop. O [3]

stigmasterol, *n.* (1907) *Biochem.* [Ad. of G *Stigmasterin* (1906) < *Stigma* + *Sterin* < Gk *stigmá* sign + *stereós* rigid, firm + G *-in* -ol] A crystalline steroid alcohol present in Calabar beans and soybean oil, used in synthesizing progesterone. O, R, W [4]

stilleite, n. (1957) *Mineral.* [G *Stilleit* (1956) < the name of Hans *Stille* (1876–1966), German geologist + *-it* -ite] A native zinc selenide found as cubic crystals. O [3]

still-stand, *n.* (1637) *Mil.* [Short. of G *Waffen-Stillstand* < *Waffen* weapons + *Stillstand* standstill] Armistice (this is different from the meaning of E *standstill*). O [3]

stilpnomelane, *n.* (1850) *Mineral.* [G *Stilpnomelan* (1827) < *stilpno-* + *-melan* < Gk *stilpnós* gleaming + *mélas,* gen. *mélanos* black] A hydrous silicate of iron and aluminum. O, W [3]

stilpnosiderite, *n.* (1823) *Mineral.* [G *Stilpnosiderit* (1814) < *stilpno-* + *Siderit* siderite (q.v.) < Gk *stilpnós* gleaming + *sídēros* iron + G *-it* -ite] An old term for limonite (q.v.). O, W [3]

Stimmung, *n.* (1909) Var. **stimmung** (1923) [G disposition, mood] Spirit, mood, atmosphere. O [3]

stinkstone, *n.* (1804) *Geol.* [Poss. a transl. of G *Stinkstein* < *stinken* to emit a fetid odor + *Stein* stone, or else an English compound modeled on G *Stinkstein*] A rock that gives off a fetid odor when struck, because of decomposed matter in it. O, R, W [4]

stippen, *n.* *Food* [G, pl. of *Stipp* < MLG *stip(pe)* (dark) speck, ad. of *stippig* of fruit with pits and likely to have a bitter taste] Bitter pit, a nonparasitic fruit disease. W [2]

stock[1], *n.* (1882) *Mining* [G, a short. of *Erzstock* < *Erz* ore + *Stock* mass] Ore bodies commonly referred to as chimneys; igneous rock intruding upward into older formations. O, R, W [3]

stock[2], *n.* *Sports* Var. **alpenstock** (q.v.) [G, a short. of *Alpenstock* < *Stock* stick + *Alpen* Alps] A stick, esp. one used by skiers, as in the Alps. W [3]

stockwork, *n.* (1808) *Mining* Old var. **stockwerk** (1808) [Ad. of G *Stockwerk* tier, story < *Stock* tier + *Werk* work] A system of mining ore when it lies in solid masses so as to be mined in stories or chambers; a rock mass, esp. of tin ore, that can be profitably mined. O, W [3]

stole fee, *n.* (1845) *Theol.* [Transl. of G *Stolgebühr(en)* < *Stol* (< L *stola*, Gk *stolé* surplice, rainment) + G *Gebühr*, pl. *Gebühren* fee] A fee paid by a lay member to a priest for administering a Catholic sacrament or rite. O, W [3]

stollen/Stollen, -ø/-s *pl.* (1906) *Food* Var. **Stolle** (1906) [G *Stolle(n)* fruit loaf shaped like a post, a post] A sweet yeast fruit loaf. O, R, W [4]

stollen, -ø *pl. Music, Lit.* [G < MHG *stolle* in meistergesang the repeated section that supports the epistrophe, a support or post] A repeated section in meistergesang (q.v.), comparable to the exposition in classical sonata. W [3]

stolzite, *n.* (1868) *Mineral.* [G *Stolzit* < the name of Joseph Alexis *Stolz* (1803–96), Bohemian scientist + G *-it* -ite] A native lead tungstate, isomorphous with wulfenite (q.v.). O, W [3]

stomium, stomia *pl.* (1905) *Bot.* [G (< NL) (1901) < Gk *stómion*, dim. of *stóma* mouth] The thin-walled cells of a fern's annulus, which ruptures to release the spores; an anther's opening, through which dehiscence occurs. O, W [3]

stook, *n.* (1859) *Apparel* (slang) Var. **stoock** (1895) [Poss. ad. of G *Stück* piece] A pocket handkerchief. **—stook-buzzer** (1859), **stook-hauler** (1859) one who steals pocket handkerchiefs. O [3]

Storm and Stress, *n.* (1855) *Lit.* Var. **storm and stress** (1879) [Transl. of G *Sturm und Drang* (q.v.)] A movement in German literature about 1770–82 that extravagantly represented violent passion and rebelled against French literary conventions; a transf. sense to a stormy period in a person's life. O, R, W [3]

storm-bell, *n.* (1837) [Transl. of G *Sturmglocke* < *Sturm* storm + *Glocke* bell] An alarm bell. O [3]

storm-clock, *n.* (1819) [Folk etymology and transl. of G *Sturmglocke* < *Sturm* storm + *Glocke* bell] A storm-bell (q.v.). O [3]

storm collar, *n.* (1908) *Meteor.* [Transl. of G *Sturmkragen* < *Sturm* storm + *Kragen* collar] The long low roll of cloud that accompanies a squall or thunderstorm. O-1933 [3]

storm troops, *pl.* (1917) *Mil.* [Transl. of G *Sturmtrupp* < *Sturm* storm + *Trupp* troop, military unit] Shock troops; (sometimes cap.) members of the Nazi's Sturmabteilung (q.v.). **—storm trooper** (1933); **storm-troop,** *a.* (1939), *v.* (1974); **storm-trooping,** *a.* (1960). O, R, W [4]

stoss, *a.* (1848) *Geol.* [G push, thrust < *stossen* to push, thrust] Facing an overriding, impinging glacier; designating the side of an object that faces a flow of water or ice, as opposed to the lee side. O, R, W [4]

stosston, *n. Ling.* [G *Stoßton* < *Stoß* stop, push, as in certain words in Danish + *Ton* sound] A glottal stop or catch, esp. one like the strong Danish stöd. W2 [2]

strafe, *v.* (1915) *Mil.* Var. **straff** (1917) [Short. of G *Gott strafe England* may God punish England, a popular German slogan during World War One] To rake with fire at close range, orig. with artillery and later with machine guns from low-flying planes; to censure strongly. **—strafe,** *n.* (1915); **strafer** (1916); **strafing,** *a.* (1979). O, R, W [4]

strahlite, *n.* (1823) *Mineral.* [Partial transl. of G *Strahlstein* < *Strahl* ray, sunbeam + *Stein* stone (= Gk *líthos* stone] Actinolite (q.v.). O [3]

Strandbad, *n.* (1939) *Sports* Var. **Strand-Bad** (1939) [G < *Strand* (sea) shore, beach + *Bad* bath, pool] A German bathing area by natural waters; an open-air swimming pool. O [2]

stranskiite, *n.* (1960) *Mineral.* [G (1960) < the name of Iwan N. *Stranski* (1897–1979), Bulgarian-born German chemist + G *-it* -ite] An arsenate of zinc and copper, occurring as blue triclinic crystals. O [3]

strass, *n.* (1820) *Chem.* [Fr *stras(s)* or G *Strass* a lead "paste" containing glass for the manufacture of synthetic stone, prob. < the name of Josef *Strasser,* 18th-cent. German jeweller who is said to have invented it] A brilliant flint glass with a high lead content used in making gems; an imitation gem of strass: paste. **—strass,** *a.* (1908). O, R, W [4]

stratosphere, *n.* (1908) *Geol.* [G *Stratosphäre* (1901), used in the obs. sense of stratified layers that make up the earth's surface < *strato-* + *Sphäre* < L *strātum* layer + Gk *sphaîra* ball, sphere] Stratified deposits in the structure of the earth's crust (this is different from the French "meteorological" borrowing). O [3]

stratovolcano, *n.* (1885) *Geol.* [Transl. of G *Stratovulkan* (1866) < *strato-* + *Vulkan* volcano < L *strātum* layer + *Vulcānus* Roman god of fire] A volcano composed of erupted cinders and ash plus layers of lava flow. O, W [3]

straw fiddle, *see* stroh fiddle

streamling, *n.* (1694) *Ichthy.* [Poss. a transl. of G *Strömling* a small Baltic herring referred to as *gestromt* striped, because of its dorsal striping < MHG *strām* striped + G dim. suffix *-ling* -ling] A type of small herring found in the Baltic and in some Swedish lakes. O [3]

street, *n.* (1927) *Physics* Var. **vortex street** (1927) [Transl. of G *Straße* street, a short. of *Wirbelstraße* vortex street] A pattern of vortices forming two parallel lines. O [3]

strengite, *n.* (1881) *Mineral.* [G *Strengit* < the name of Johann August *Streng* (1830–97), German mineralogist + *-it* -ite] A hydrous iron phosphate that is isomorphous with variscite (q.v.). O, W [3]

strength through joy, *n.* (1935) *Sports* [Transl. of G *Kraft durch Freude* (1933) < *Kraft* strength + *durch* through + *Freude* joy] A German movement founded by the National Socialist Party in 1933 to encourage physical and cultural recreation among working people. **—strength through joy,** *a.* (1939). O [3]

streptostylic, *a.* (1901) *Zool.* [Back-formation of G *Streptostylica* (1856), the name of a reptile group < *strepto-* + *Stylica* < Gk *streptós* woven, twisted + *stŷlos* column, post] Of a reptile's having free articulation of the quadrate bone with the squamosal. **—streptostyly,** *n.* (1925). O, W [3]

streusel, *n.* (1909) *Food* [G, lit., something strewn < *streuen* to scatter + dim. suffix *-el* -el] A crumbly topping or filling for cakes, made from fat, sugar, flour, and sometimes nuts; a confection with such a topping. **—streusel cake** (1909). O, R, W [4]

streuselkuchen, *n.* (1910) *Food* [G < *Streusel* streusel (q.v.) + *Kuchen* cake] Coffee cake with a streusel topping. O, R, W [3]

strigovite, *n.* (1875) *Mineral.* [G *Strigovit* (1869) < NL *Strigovia*, G *Striegau*, the name of a district in Silesia, now Strzegom, Poland + G -*it* -ite] A basic silicate of aluminum and iron. O (not in 2nd ed.), W [3]

stroh, *a.* (1867) *Music* [G *stroh*-, as in *Strohfiedel* straw fiddle, an archaic name for an early xylophone, because its wooden staff rested on a bed of straw] Designating an early type of xylophone with a wooden staff resting on a bed of straw, not to be confused with a stringed instrument called the *Stroh violin* or *Stroh fiddle*, also referred to in German as *Strohfiedel*, named for its inventor Charles Stroh, who manufactured it in England from 1901 to 1924. O [3]

stroh fiddle, *n.* (1902) *Music* (archaic) Var. **Strohfiedel** [Prob. ad. of G *Strohfiedel* straw fiddle—see *stroh*] A xylophone in which the wooden staffs were placed on a bed of straw; now also applied to a violin or a cello invented by Charles (son of Augustus, inventor of various stringed instruments) Stroh of London in 1901, in which the usual body is replaced by an aluminum plate connected to an amplifying horn. •Transl. as **straw fiddle**. O (under *straw*) [2]

stroll, *v.* (1603) [Prob. < dial. G *strollen* (now *strolchen*) to stroll, vagabond, or bum] To saunter or ramble; to move from place to place seeking profit or occupation. —**stroll**, *n.* (1623); **stroller** (1608); **strolling**, *a.* (1709), n. (1717). O, R, W [4]

stromatolite, *n.* (1930) *Geol.* [G *Stromatolith* < *stromato*- + -*lith* < Gk *strṓma*, gen. *strṓmatos* cover, layer + *líthos* stone] A laminated calcareous sedimentary mass made from bacteria or algae. —**stromatolitic** (1933). O [4]

stromatolith, *n.* (1916) *Geol.* [G (1908) stromatolite (q.v.)] Stromatolite. —**stromatolithic** (1916). O, R [3]

stromeyerite, *n.* (1835) *Mineral.* [G *Stromeyerit* < the name of Friedrich *Stromeyer* (1776–1835), German chemist + -*it* -ite] A lustrous silver copper sulfide. • ~ has a French synonym borrowed into English, *stromeyerine*. O, W [3]

stromuhr, *n. Med.* [G < *Strom* stream, flow + *Uhr* clock, hour] A rheometer that measures the amount and speed of blood flowing through an artery. W [3]

strong, *a.* (1841) *Ling.* [Transl. of Jakob Grimm's G *stark* strong] Of the type of conjugation of ablaut verbs with changing vocalic stems, such as E *sing—sang—sung*, because of their capacity to form the past tense and present and past participles without taking the usual dental suffix, as do the so-called regular or weak (q.v.) verbs; in German grammars, of adjectives comparably declined without the use of an -(e)n suffix. O, R, W [3]

strongpoint, *n.* (1915) *Mil.* [Transl. of G *feste Stellung* < *fest* firm, strong + *Stellung* position, trench] A specially fortified position in a defense system; transf. sense to political or religious strongpoints (this is different from the older meaning of "forte"). O, W [4]

strubbly, *a.* [Ad. of G *strubbelig* < late MHG *strubbelich* shaggy] (U.S. dial.) untidy, unkempt. W [3]

strudel, *n.* (1893) *Food* [G, lit., whirlpool < late MHG *strudel, strodel* whirl, spiral, descriptive of the spiral cross-section of rolled dough from which it is made] A

baked dessert pastry of Austrian origin made with sheets of very thin dough filled with fruit layers. O, R, W [4]

struma, -e *pl.* (1931) *Med.* [NL *struma* or G *Struma (lymphomatosa)* (1912) < L *strūma* enlargement + *lymphomatosa* lymphomatous] A swelling of an organ, esp. the thryoid, as in goiter (this is different from the old "botanical" meaning). O, R, W [3]

strunzite, *n.* (1958) *Mineral.* [G *Strunzit* (1957) < the name of Karl Hugo *Strunz* (b.1910), German mineralogist + -*it* -ite] A hydrated basic phosphate of iron and manganese. O [3]

strüverite, *n.* (1896) *Mineral.* [G *Strüverit* (1876) < the name of Giovanni *Strüver* (1842–1915), Italian mineralogist + G -*it* -ite] Chloritoid (q.v.) (this is different from the later Italian borrowing that means "titanium oxide"). O [3]

struvite, *n.* (1850) *Mineral.* [Sw *struveit* or G *Struvit* (1846) < the name of Heinrich Christian Gottfried von *Struve* (1772–1851), Russian diplomat-geologist + Sw or G -*it* -ite] A hydrous phosphate of ammonium and magnesium. O, W [3]

Stube/stube, *n.* (1946) *Beverages* [G, a short. of *Bierstube, Weinstube* a tavern dispensing beer and wine (+ *Bier* beer or *Wein* wine) < MHG *stube*, OHG *stuba* heated room] An establishment serving alcoholic beverages, esp. beer: bierstube (q.v.). O, W [3]

studerite, *n.* (1868) *Mineral.* [G *Studerit* (1864) < the name of the Swiss mineralogist Bernhard *Studer* (1794–1887) + G -*it* -ite] A variety of tetrahedrite (q.v.) containing zinc and arsenic. O (not in 2nd ed.) [2]

Stuka, *n.* (1940) *Mil.* Var. **stuka** (1942) [G, a short. of *Sturzkampfflugzeug* < *Sturz* plunge, crash + *Kampf* battle + *Flugzeug* airplane] A German dive bomber, esp. as used in World War Two. —**stuka**, *v.* (1946). O, R [4]

stull, *n.* (1778) *Mining* [Prob. ad. of G *Stollen* < MHG *stolle* < OHG *stollo* post, prop, support] A round timber used to support the sides of a mine; a platform or framework for supporting miners, waste, or ore; one of the props for this platform. —**stull**, *a.* (1874). O, R, W [4]

stulm, *n.* (1684) *Mining* [Poss. ad. of G *Stollen* post, support (see *stull*); here, a slightly rising passageway leading to a mine dug into a slope] An adit into or a level in a mine. O, W [3]

stummel, *n.* [G stamp, butt, a short. of *Stummelpfeife* < *Stummel* stump, butt + *Pfeife* pipe] The shank and bowl of a tobacco pipe. W [3]

stupp, *n. Chem.* [G, prob. akin to OHG *stoub* dust] A black, sooty deposit obtained by distilling mercury ores. W [3]

sturine, *n.* (1896) *Biochem.* Var. **sturin** [G *Sturin* (1896) < L *sturionem* sturgeon + G -*in* -ine] A protamine found in sturgeons' spermatozoa. O, W [3]

Sturmabteilung, *n.* (1923) *Politics* [G < *Sturm* storm, attack + *Abteilung* detachment] A Nazi paramilitary force, made up of storm troopers or Brownshirts (q.v.) and notorious for its violence until 1934, when it was purged and reorganized. • ~ is abbr. as **SA** (1931, q.v.). O, R [3]

Sturmbannführer, *n.* (1955) *Mil.* [G battalion leader < *Sturm* storm, attack + *Bannführer*, lit., pennant, flag, unit leader] An officer in the Schutzstaffel (q.v.). O [3]

Sturm und Drang, *n.* (1844) *Lit.* Var. **sturm und drang** [G (1776), lit., storm and stress] A passionate German literary movement in the late 18th century. • ~ is transl. as **Storm and Stress** (1855, q.v.). O, R, W [4]

stylize, *v.* (1898 *W9*) *Art* Brit. var. **stylise** (1904) [Transl. of G *stilisieren* < *Stil* style (< L *stilus* stake) + irreg. G verbal suffix *-isieren* (in imitation of Fr *-ier*) *-ize*] To adapt to a given style; conventionalize. —**stylization** (1908), **stylizer.** O, R, W [4]

stylotypite, *n. Mineral.* [Ad. of G *Stylotyp* < *stylo-* + *-typ* < the comb. form of Gk *stýlos* column, pilaster, post + LL *typus* type + E *-ite*] An orthorhombic sulfide of antimony, silver, copper, and iron. W [3]

styphnic acid, *n.* (1850) *Chem.* [Transl. of G *Styphninsäure* (1846), irreg. < Gk *styphnós* astringent + G *-in* -ic + *Säure* acid] An explosive astringent acid produced usu. by nitration of resorcinol. O, W [3]

sublimation, *n.* (1910) *Psych.* [LL transl. of Freud's G *Sublimierung* or else directly < G < L *sublimāre* to elevate, ennoble + G *-ung* -tion] The refining and discharging of instinctual energy, esp. sexual, in socially acceptable ways (this is different from the numerous earlier meanings). O, R, W [4]

subsidiarity, *n.* (1936) *Theol.* [Short. and transl. of G *Subsidiaritätsprinzip* (1931) < *Subsidiarität* + *Prinzip* < L *subsidiārius* serving in a subsidiary way + *prīncipium* origin, beginning, basis] The principle that a central, usu. church authority should have a subsidiary function, restricted from tasks that can be performed effectively at immediate or local levels; transf. to political and sociological senses. O, W [3]

substantialist, *n.* (1657) *Theol.* [G < L *substantiālis* substantial + G *-ist* (< L) -ist] One of a 16th-century Lutheran sect who believed that original sin is not accidental in human nature but belongs to its substance; a Flacian; one who believes in philosophical substantialism. O [3]

suction pressure, *n.* (1922) *Bot.* [Transl. of G *Saugkraft* (1916), lit., suction force] The force with which a cell can take in water, being the difference between the pressure of the cell walls on the cell contents, and the osmotic pressure of those contents. O [3]

Sudetic, *a.* (1907) *Geogr.* [G *sudetisch* < *Sudeten* Sudeten Mountains + adj. suffix *-isch* -ic] Sudeten: of or relating to the Sudeten region. O [3]

sudoite, *n.* (1963) *Mineral.* [G *Sudoit* (1962) < the name of Toshio *Sudo* (b.1911), Japanese mineralogist + G *-it* -ite] A dioctahedral series of phyllosilicates. O [3]

suevite, *n.* (1938) *Geol.* [G *Suevit* < L *Suevia, Suebia* Swabia, a region in Bavaria + G *-it* -ite] Orig., a tuff found in the Ries crater, near Nördlingen, Germany; now a type of welded braccia associated with impact craters, suggesting impact metamorphism. O [3]

sugarbird, *n.* (1688) *Ornith.* [Transl. of G *Zuckervogel* lit., sugarbird] (Archaic) canary bird; a bird of the genus *Certhiola,* found in the West Indies and South America. • ~ is different from the *sugarbird* transl. from Du *suikervogel,* which denotes African sunbirds and honey eaters. O [3]

sulfane, *n.* (1955) *Chem.* Brit. var. **sulphane** (1968) [G (1953) < *sulf-* (< L *sulfur*) + G *-ane* -ane] Any of the various sulfur hydrides. O [3]

sulfatase, *n.* (1924) *Biochem.* Brit. var. **sulphatase** (1980) [G (1924) < *sulfat-* (< L *sulfur*) + G *-ase* -ase] One of

various esterases found chiefly in mammals' tissues which catalyze the hydrolysis of sulfuric esters. O, W [3]

sulfate of carbyle, *see* carbyl sulfate

sulfonal, *n.* (1889) *Chem.* Brit. var. **sulphonal** (1890) [G (1886) a trademark < *Sulfon* sulfone (q.v.) + *-al* -al] Sulfonmethane, a crystalline, hypnotic sulfone, also used as a sedative. —**sulphonal,** *a.* (1892). O, W [3]

sulfone, *n.* (1872) *Chem.* Brit. var. **sulphone** (1876) [Prob. < G *Sulfon* < *sulf-* (< L *sulfur* sulfur) + G *-on* -on] Any of a group of organic compounds distinguished by the sulfonyl group doubly united by means of its sulfur usu. with carbon; diaminodiphenyl sulfone or a derivative, used in treating leprosy. • ~ has produced a large number of derivatives (**sulphonic,** 1873) and some compounds (**sulfonyl chloride,** 1920). O, R, W [4]

sulphane, *see* sulfane

sulphatase, *see* sulfatase

sulphonal, *see* sulfonal

sulphone, *see* sulfone

sulze, n. *Food* [(South G, Austrian, Swiss) G *Sülze* < MHG *sülze* < OHG *sulza* brine, gelatine] Calf's-foot jelly. W [2]

sunk spurlos, *see* spurlos versenkt

superhuman, *n.* (1896) *Philos.* [Transl. of G *Übermensch* (q.v.)] Superman (q.v.). O, W [3]

superman, *n.* (1903) *Philos.* [Transl. of G *Übermensch* (q.v.), Nietzsche's philosophical term] An ideal, superior human being, as one produced by selective breeding (as later theorized by the Nazis) or in an evolutionary fight for survival; someone of extraordinary power or accomplishments; a fictional, exaggerated hero, as in comic strips. —**supermanly,** *a.* (1905); **-manliness** (1907); **-manhood** (1910); **-manism** (1916). O, R, W [4]

superstructure, *n.* (1944) *Geol.* [Transl. of G *Oberbau* (1935) < *ober* above, super + *Bau* structure] The overlying layer of an orogenic belt that is unaffected by metamorphism and plutonic activity (this is different from various other, usu. older meanings). O [3]

suppression, *n.* (1894) *Psych.* [Short. and transl. of the German psychologist Wilhelm Wundt's G term *Verdrängung* (*Vorlesungen über die Menschen- und Tierseele*) (1863) < *verdrängen* to drive out, crowd out, suppress] A phenomenon of binocular vision where the image of one eye predominates, causing partial or complete disappearance of the image of the other eye (this is different from the various, older meanings primarily borrowed from L *suppressiō*). O [3]

suprasterol, *n.* (1931) *Biochem.* [Ad. of G *Suprasterin* (1930) < *supra-* + *Sterin* < L *supra* above, over + *stereós* narrow, limited + G *-in* -ol] Either of a pair of optically active polycyclic isomers derived from vitamin D. —**suprasterol I/II** (1931, 1931). O [3]

sursassite, *n.* (1928) *Mineral.* [G *Sursassit* (1926) < *Sursass* the Rhaeto-Romanic name of Oberhalbstein in Switzerland + G *-it* -ite] A hydrous silicate of manganese and aluminum. O, W [3]

surturbrand, *n.* (1760) *Mineral.* Old var. like **sortebrand** (1760) [G < Icel *Surtarbrandr* (or directly into E < Icel) < Icel *Surtar,* gen. of *Surtr,* the name of a fire-giant in Scandinavian mythology + *brandr* brand] A variety of lignite in the Faeroes and Iceland. O, W [3]

susannite, *n.* (1845) *Mineral.* Old var. **suzannite** (1845) [G *Suzannit* (1845) < the name of the *Susanna* mine, Leadhills, Scotland + G *-it* -ite] Leadhillite, a basic sulfate and carbonate of lead. O, W [3]

suspensoid, *n.* (1909) *Chem.* [G (1908) < *suspens-* + *-oid* < L *suspendere* to suspend + Gk *-oeidēs* similar] A colloidal system where the dispersed particles are solid; a lyophobic sol. O, R, W [4]

svanbergite, *n.* (1857) *Mineral.* [Sw or G *Svanbergit* (1954) < Sw < the name of Lars Frederik *Svanberg* (1805–78), Swedish chemist + Sw *-it* -ite] A basic sulfate and phosphate of aluminum and strontium, in the beudantite group. O, W [3]

Swab, *n.* (1663) *Ethnology* [Colloq. G *Schwab(e)* Swabian] Swabian: a native or inhabitant of the medieval duchy or modern area of Swabia, Germany. O, R [3]

swallowwort, *n.* (1548) *Bot.* [Transl. of NHG *Schwalbenwurz* < *Schwalbe* swallow + *Wurz* wort, root] Any of several plants of the family Asclepiadaceae (this is different from the "celandine" meaning, which comes < Du *swaelemwortel,* now *zwaluwenkruid*). O, R, W [3]

Swan Knight, *n.* (1911) *Myth.* [Transl. of G *Schwanenritter* < *Schwan* swan + *Ritter* knight] A personage in medieval Germanic literature, like Lohengrin, son of Parsifal (q.v.), accompanied by a swan. O [3]

swan maiden, *n.* (1868) *Myth.* [Transl. of G *Schwanenjungfrau* < *Schwan* swan + *Jungfrau* maiden] A supernatural maiden in Germanic mythology having the power to transform herself into a swan by using a magical object, as a robe of swan feathers. O, R, W [4]

swan shift, *n.* *Myth.* [Transl. of G *Schwanenhemd* or *Schwanengewand* < *Schwan* swan + *Hemd* or *Gewand* garment, shift] The robe of swan feathers by means of which a supernatural maiden—the swan maiden (q.v.) or *Schwanenjungfrau,* the Valkyrie (q.v.)—can transform herself into a swan. O, R [3]

swan song, *n.* (1831) *Myth.* Var. **swan-song** (1831) [Transl. of G *Schwanengesang* or *Schwanenlied* < *Schwan* swan + *Gesang* or *Lied* song] The legendary, extremely sweet, last song of a dying swan; a terminal appearance, declaration, or work, esp. by an author or composer. O, R, W [4]

swarmer, *n.* (1765) (archaic) [G *Schwärmer* (or Du *zwermer*) < G *schwärmen* (1664) or Du *zwermen* to swarm, rove] (usu. *pl.*) fireworks. O [3]

swatchel, *n.* (1854) (slang) [Poss. ad. of G *schwätzeln,* freq. of *schwätzen* to blab, chatter] Chatter; the name for Mr. Punch in a Punch-and-Judy show; swazzle: the instrument that produces Mr. Punch's squeaky voice. —**swatchel box** (1854)/**cove** (1864). O [3]

swedenborgite, *n. Mineral.* [G *Swedenborgit* < the name of Emanuel *Swedenborg* (1688–1772), Swedish scientist and philosopher + G *-it* -ite] An oxide of beryllium, sodium, and antimony. W [3]

sweeny, *n.* (1813) *Med.* Var. **sweeney** (1813), **swinney** [Folk etymology < (PaG, Alemmanic) G *Schwinne* (see Grimm) emaciation of a limb from exhaustion or illness] An atrophy of a horse's shoulder muscles or other muscles. O, R, W [3]

swermer, *n.* (1585–7) *Theol.* (obs.) [Early Mod G *Schwermer* (now *Schwärmer*), a favorite word of Luther's for Anabaptists < *schwermen* (now *schwärmen*) to swarm, rove, rave] A sectarian; a fanatic. —**Swermian** (1585–7). O [3]

swindle, *v.* (1782) [Prob. ad. of G *schwindeln* to swindle] To take someone's money or property by deception or fraud; to practice the art of a swindler. • ~ is described in most dictionaries as being a back-formation of the noun *swindler* (1774), which is surely the usual pattern for creating such verbs; however, *swindler* and the verb *swindle* came into English almost contemporaneously. The 50-year later appearance of the noun *swindle* suggests that it, like its verb homonym, may have come into English independently from their respective German etyma. An alternative description would be to consider both the verb and noun *swindle* as back-formations of *swindler,* or possibly the noun *swindle* as a functional shift of its verb homonymic predecessor. Regardless of the true etymology, the following English derivatives were formed from the verb *swindle:* **swindling;** *verbal n.* (1788), *a.* (1795); **swindleable** (1874); **swindlingly** (1887). O, R, W [4]

swindle, *n.* (1833) [Prob. ad. (1780) of G *Schwindel* (1780) swindle] The act or process of defrauding or swindling; fraud: an instance of swindling; an exorbitant price for something. • ~ is different from the obs. homonym borrowed by 1559 < Early Mod Du *swindel* giddiness, vertigo. —**swindle sheet** (1923). O, R, W [4]

swindler, *n.* (1774) [Prob. ad. of G *Schwindler* (1691) giddy-minded person, cheat < *schwindeln* to be giddy, swindle] A person who swindles: cheat, harper. O, R, W [4]

swine-hound, *see* schwein(e)hund

swine's feather, *n.* (1635) *Mil.* Var. **swine's-pike** (1638) [Transl. of G *Schweinsfeder* < *Schwein* swine + *Feder* feather] (formerly) a spear implanted in the ground to defend against cavalry, or a stake fixed like a bayonet on a musket rest. O, W [3]

swinestone, *n.* (1794) *Mineral.* [Transl. of G *Schweinstein* < *Schwein* swine + *Stein* stone, so named for its unpleasant odor] A bituminous limestone that usu. gives off a bad odor when hit: stinkstone (q.v.). O, W [3]

swinney, *see* sweeny

swordling, *n.* (1562) *Bot.* (obs.) [Transl. of Early NHG *swertling, swertlinch* (now *Schwertlilie*), a rendering of L *gladiolus*] A yellow iris or a blue flag. O [3]

Sylvaner, *n.* (1928) *Beverages* [G *Sylvaner/Silvaner* a kind of grapevine first developed in Germany, prob. < L *Sylvānus* Silvanus, the name of the Roman god of woods and trees + G *-er* -er] A German white wine grape; a California grape resembling the German one; a wine made from either of such grapes. —**Sylvaner,** *a.* (1963). O, R, W [4]

sylvestrene, *n.* (1877) *Chem.* [G *Sylvestren* (1877) < NL *Pinus silvestris* pine found in woods < L *sylvester, -tris* + G *-en* -ene] A liquid terpene hydrocarbon or a mixture of two particular isomeric terpenes, extracted from pine oil. O, W [3]

sylvinite, *n.* (1896) *Mineral.* [G *Sylvinit* < *Sylvin* sylvine (< Fr) + G *-it* -ite] A commercial name for a mixture of halite and sylvite, the form in which sylvite usu. occurs. O, W [3]

symbiont, *n.* (1887) *Biol.* [Prob. < G, irreg. < Gk

symbiðn, symbióein to live together] An organism living in symbiosis, usu. the smaller member as opposed to the larger host. —**symbiontic(ism)**. O, R [4]

symbiosis, -ses *pl.* (1877) *Biol., Psych.* [G *Symbiose* < Gk *symbíōsis* cohabitation < *symbiðn, symbióein* to live together, first used in this sense by the German zoologist Johann Friedrich Brandt (1802–79)] A mutually beneficial association of two or more dissimilar types of organisms, often in a very close union: mutualism; mutual cooperation between social groups or persons, esp. in ecological interdependence; such a relationship, as between an infant and its mother. —**symbiotic(al)**, **-tically**, **-tics**, **-tism**, **symbiose**. O, R, W [4]

sympathisch, *a.* (1911) Erron. var. **sympatisch** (1922) [G (1847) agreeable < *Sympathie* (< L *sympathīa*) < G *-isch* -ic] Suitable, agreeable, usu. applied to persons rather than to landscapes, etc. O [2]

sympathogonia, *pl.* (1934) *Med.* [Ad. of G *Sympathogonien* (pl., 1906) < *sympatho-* + *-gonien* < Gk *sympathḗs* sympathetic + *gónos* bud, offshoot] Any of three undifferentiated embryonic cells of the sympathetic nervous system, which may give rise to a tumor. O [3]

symphilism, *n.* (1903) *Entomology* [Ad. of G *Symphilie* (1896) < Gk *symphilía* mutual love, harmony] Symphily (q.v.): a mutually helpful symbiosis existing between ants or termites and some other insects that they feed and tend as guests, which in turn may yield a sweet substance as food for the "hosts." O, W [3]

symphily, *n.* (1899) *Biol.* [G *Symphilie* < Gk *symphilía* mutual love, harmony] Commensalism characterized by mutual benefit or attraction, as between some ants or termites and various "guest" insects. —**symphilous** (1903); **symphile,** *n.* (1910); **symphilic** (1919). O, W [3]

symphonic poem, *n.* (1864) *Music* [Transl. of G *symphonische Dichtung* < It *sinfonia* < L *symphōnia* multi-voice musical presentation < Gk *symphōnía* < *sýmphōnos* harmonious + G *-isch* -ic + *Dichtung* poetry, poem] An extended orchestral work, usu. in one movement and based on an extramusical idea like a literary theme. O, R, W [4]

symplasma, *n.* (1908) *Med.* [G (1903) < *sym-* + *Plasma* < Gk *sym-* < *sýn* together, with + *plásma* formation, structure] A degenerating maternal syncytium, formed by the breaking down of the cell walls of the placenta's outer layer. —**symplasmatic** (1923). O [3]

symplast¹, *n.* (1894) *Bot.* [G (1880) < *sym-* + *-plast* < Gk *sym-* < *sýn* with, together + *plastós* formed, shaped] Coenocyte: a multinucleate protoplasmic mass created by repeated nuclear division without cell fission; an organism with such a structure. —**symplastic (growth)** (1916). O, W [3]

symplast², *n.* (1938) *Bot.* [G (1930)—see *symplast¹*] The interconnected plant protoplasts, all bounded by a continuous plasmalemma. O [3]

symplectic, *a.* (1916) *Geol.* [Ad. of Gk *symplektikós* or G *symplektisch* (1850) < *symplekt-* (< Gk *symplektikós* of intertwining < *sym-* < *sýn* with, together + *pléssein* to beat, hit) + G adj. suffix *-isch* -ic] Being or pertaining to an intimate intergrowth of two different minerals in a rock or its texture (this is different from the old "fish" meaning borrowed directly < Gk). O, W [3]

symplesite, *n.* (1844) *Mineral.* [G *Symplesit* (1837) < *sym-* + *-plesit* < Gk *sym-* < *sýn* with, together + *plēsiázein* to bring together + G *-it* -ite] A hydrous ferrous arsenate occurring as green triclinic crystals. O, W [3]

syn-, *comb. form* (1894) *Chem.* [G, first used by the German chemist Arthur Rudolf Hantzsch (1857–1935) in 1894 to specify certain geometrical isomers of organic compounds containing C=N or N=N] (Usu. italicized) such a designation, as in *syn-compound* (1894). • ~ is of course different from the various, much older meanings derived ult. < Gk *syn-*. O, W [3]

synadelphite, *n.* (1892) *Mineral.* [G *Synadelphit* (1884) < *synadelphós* one who has a sibling < Gk *sýn* with, together + *adelphós* brother + G *-it* -ite] A basic arsenate of manganese often containing other elements. O, W [3]

synantherin, *n.* (1877) *Chem.* [G (1834) < *syn-* + *Antherin* < Gk *sýn* with, together + NL *anthera* < Gk *anthḗrá, anthērós* flower-like + G *-in* -in] A form of inulin obtained from the tubers of Composites. O-1933 [3]

synchisite, *n.* (1901) *Mineral.* Var. **synchysite** (1901) [G *Synchisit* (1901), ad. < Gk *sýnchysis* mixture, confusion + G *-it* -ite] A fluocarbonate of cerium, lanthanum, and calcium. O, W [3]

syncyanosis, -noses *pl.* (1945) *Bot.* [G *Syncyanose* (1914) (now also *Synzyanose*) < *syn-* + *Cyanose* < Gk *sýn* with, together + *kyanéos* dark-blue + G *-ose* (< Gk *-osis*) -osis, fem. suffix of action] The relationship between the host and a unicellular blue-green alga that lives within it symbiotically; the organisms themselves. O [3]

syndesis, -deses *pl.* (1909) *Biol.* [G (1904) (now *Syndese*) < NL *syndesis* < Gk *sýn* with, together + *désis* a binding, pairing] Synapsis: the process of association of homologous parental chromosomes with chiasma formation. O, R, W [3]

synechthry, *n.* (1899) *Entomology* Erron var. **synecthry** (1899) [G *Synechthrie* (1896) < *syn-* < Gk *sýn* with, together + *échthros* hostile, inimical + G *-ie* (< Gk *-ia*) -y] (Term proposed by Erich Wasmann in 1896 for) hostile commensalism, where the insects that live in the ant colonies are unwelcome guests, as opposed to symphily (q.v.). O, W [3]

synecology, *n.* (1910) *Ecology* [Ad. of G *Synökologie* (1902) (now *Synekologie* < *syn-* + *Ökologie* < Gk *sýn* with, together + *oîkos* + *lógos* word, study + G *-ie* (< Gk *-ia*) -y] A branch of ecology concerned with the relationships among living plants or animal communities and their environments. —**synecological** (1922), **-logist** (1938), **-logic(ally)**. O, R, W [4]

syngenite, *n.* (1875) *Mineral.* [G *Syngenit* (1872) < Gk *syngenḗs* related + G *-it* -ite, so named for its relationship to polyhalite (q.v.)] Calcium and potassium sulfate, also called *kaluszite*. O, W [3]

synorogenic, *a.* (1936) *Geol.* [G *synorogen* < *Synorogenese* (1924), a coining by the German geologist Hans Stille (1876–1966) < *syn-* + *Orogenese* < Gk *sýn* with, together + *óros* mountain (range) + *génesis* origin, origination + E *-ic*] Formed or occurring during an orogenic movement. O, W [3]

synsemantic, *a.* (1929) *Ling.* [G *synsemantisch* (1908) < *syn-* + *semantisch* < Gk *sýn* with, together + *semantikós* designating meaning + G adj. suffix *-isch* -ic] Concerning a word or phrase that has no meaning outside its context; meaningless in isolation. O [3]

syntaxis, -taxes pl. (1909) Geol. [Transl. of G Schaarung (now Scharung) in Eduard Suess's Das Antlitz der Erde (1901–9) < G scharen to converge into a group] An arrangement of mountain ranges or fold axes that converge toward a common point. O [3]

synthalin, n. (1927) Pharm. [G (1926), a blend of synthetisch synthetic + Insulin insulin < Gk synthetikós + NL insula] A synthetic, toxic diguanidine that has the hypoglycemic effect of insulin when taken orally; decamethylene-diguanidine dihydrochloride. —**synthalin B** (1936)/**A.** O [3]

synthol, n. (1924) Chem. [G (1923), a blend of synth- < synthetisch synthetic + -ol < Alkohol alcohol (< Ar)] A synthetic, orig. German motor fuel made from carbon monoxide and hydrogen, orig. by the Fischer-Tropsch process. —**synthol process.** O, R, W [3]

syntony, n. (1925) Psych. [G Syntonie (1922) < Gk syntonía (< sýn with, together + tónos sound + -ia) + G -ie -y] The condition of having a responsive, lively temperament that may lead to manic-depressive psychosis (this is different from the old "electrical" meaning). — **syntonic** (1925). O [3]

syntrophy, n. (1897) Biol. [G Syntrophie (1897) < syn- + -trophie < Gk sýn with, together + trophḗ nourishment + G -ie (< Gk -ia) -y] A lengthy relationship between the members of two different species or bacterial strains where usu. both members benefit nutritionally from the other's presence. —**syntrophism** (1946), **syntrophic** (1950). O [3]

synusia, -e pl. (1924) Ecology Var. of **synusium** (1924) [Ad. of G Sinusie, a term adapted by Helmut Gams in 1918 < Gk synousía community, society] A structural unit of an important ecological community usu. composing a particular stratum of that community. —**synusial,** a. O, W [3]

sysertskite, see siserskite

systrophe, n. (1886) Biol. [G (1885) < Gk sy- with, together + strophḗ turning] A phenomenon of response reaction of living protoplasm, where chlorophyll grains lump together when exposed to bright light. O [3]

szaboite, n. (1883) Mineral. [G Szaboit (1878) < the name of József Szabó (1822–94), Hungarian geologist + G -it -ite] A variety of hypersthene. O [3]

szaibelyite, n. (1866) Mineral. [G Szaibelyit (1861) (now Szajbelyit) < the name of Stephan Szaibely (1777–1855), Hungarian mine surveyor + G -it -ite] A hydrous magnesium borate. O, W [3]

Szekler/Szekel, n. and a. (1843, 1843) Ethnology, Ling. [G Szekler < Hung Székely, an ethnic Magyar name < székel to inhabit] (Of) a member of the Transylvanian branch of the Magyar people; (of) their Hungarian dialect written in their own runic alphabet. O, W [3]

szmikite, n. (1892) Mineral. [G Szmikit (1887) < the name of Ignaz Szmik, 19th-cent. Hungarian mining official at Felsöbánya, Rumania + G -it -ite] Hydrous manganese sulfide isomorphous with kieserite and szomolnokite (q.v.). O, W [3]

szomolnokite, n. Mineral. [G Szomolnokit < Szomolnok (now Smolnik), the name of a locality in Slovakia + G -it -ite] Hydrous ferrous sulfate isomorphous with kieserite (q.v.). W [3]

T

Taborite, *n.* (1646) *Theol.* [Poss. < G *Taborit* < *Tábor,* the name of a Bohemian town south of Prague + G -*it* -ite] A member of the extreme wing of the Hussites led by Jan Ziska. O, R, W [3]

tabulatur, *n.* (1574) *Music, Lit.* [G (1511), prob. < NL *tabulatura* musical notation, ult. < L *tabula* tablet, table + -*atus* -ate] The system of rules for musical and poetical compositions established by the Meistersinger; an early instrumental musical notation: tablature. W [3]

tachylyte, *n.* (c.1864 *W9*) *Mineral.* Var. **tachylite** (1888) [G *Tachylit* (1826) < Gk *tachýs* fast + *líthos* stone < G -*it* -ite] Basalt glass, a black mineral. —**tachylitic** (1888). O, R, W [4]

tachyscope, *n.* (1889) *Tech.* [Orig. formed as G *Tachyskop* < *tachy-* + -*skop* < Gk *tachýs* fast + *skopión* looking] An early animated-picture machine where the photographic transparencies are rotated and viewed through an aperture: a kind of kinetoscope. O, W [3]

tachysterol, *n.* (1933) *Biochem.* [Ad. of G *Tachysterin* (1932) < *tachy-* + -*sterin* < Gk *tachýs* fast + *stereós* firm, rigid + G -*in* -ol] An oily liquid isomer of ergosterol and lumisterol, which on further irradiation produces vitamin D_2. O, W [3]

tactoid, *n.* (1929) *Chem.* [G *Taktoid* (1929) < *takt-* + -*oid* < Gk *taktós* arranged (in order) + -*oeidēs* similar] A tiny, elongated, spindle-shaped particle found in a tactosol (q.v.). O, W [3]

tactosol, *n.* (1929) *Chem.* [G *Taktosol* (1929) < *takto-* + -*sol* < Gk *taktós* arranged (in order) + MLG *sole* brine] A sol containing tactoids. O, W [3]

taenite, *n.* (1868) *Mineral.* [G *Tänit* (1861) < *tän-* (< Gk *tainía* ribbon) + G -*it* -ite] A nickel-iron alloy found massively in most meteorites (this is different from the earlier meaning of "feldspar variety"). O, W [3]

Tafelmusik, *n.* (1876) *Music* Var. **tafel musik** (1969), **tafelmusik** (1980) [G < *Tafel* tablet, festive table, banquet + *Musik* music < OFr *musique,* ult. < Gk *mousikế*] A kind of music esp. popular in the 18th century for performing at a banquet or other such meal; a special printing of such music so that two or more persons can read their parts from the same page. O [3]

Tafelwein, -e *pl.* (1972) *Beverages* Var. **tafelwein** (1972) [G < *Tafel* tablet, large table + *Wein* wine] A poorer quality of wine: table wine. O [3]

tafoni, *pl.* (1942) *Geol.* [G, pl. (1894) < dial. Corsican *tafóni* holes, hollows] Shallow, rounded hollows in weathered rock. O [3]

tagilite, *n.* (1868) *Mineral.* [G *Tagilith* (now *Tagilit*) < (Nizhni) *Tagil,* the name of a town near Sverdlovsk + G -*lith* < Gk *líthos* stone] A hydrous basic copper phosphate occurring in bright green masses. O, W [3]

takt, *n. Music* [G short. of *Taktschlag,* lit., emphatic touch < *takt* (< L *tāctus* touched < *tangere* to touch) + G *Schlag* beat] A musical beat or pulse, measure, or tempo. W [3]

taler/thaler, -s/-ø *pl.* (1787) *Currency* [G *Thaler,* a short. of *Joachimsthaler* < St. Joachimsthal in Bohemia, now Jáchymov] One of many large silver coins minted by some German states from the 15th to the 19th centuries: a German dollar. O, R, W [3]

tall oil, *n.* (c.1926 *W9*) *Chem.* Var. **tallol** [Ad. of G *Tallöl* (< Sw *tallolja*) and directly < Sw < *tall* pine + *olja* oil] A black liquid resin that is a by-product of the manufacture of chemical pulp and that is used in making paint, driers, soaps, etc. O, R, W [4]

talmi gold, *n.* (1868) *Metall.* [G (1863), irreg. < the name of its French inventor *Tallois* + G *Gold* gold] A brass alloy made to resemble gold, used in trinkets and costume jewelry: Abyssinian gold. O, R, W [3]

talweg, *see* thalweg

tamarugite, *n.* (1890) *Mineral.* [G *Tamarugit* < a short. of *Pampa de Tamarugal,* the name of a desert plateau in northern Chile + G -*it* -ite] A hydrous sulfate of sodium and aluminum; a sodium alum. O, W [3]

tapeinocranic, *a. Anthrop.* [G *tapeinokran* < Gk *tapeinós* low + *kraníon* skull + E -*ic*] Having a low skull flattened in front. —**tapeinocrany,** *n.* W [3]

taphrogenesis, *n.* (1923) *Geol.* [G *Tafrogenese* (1922) < *tafro-* + -*genese* < Gk *táphros* ditch, trench + *génesis* origin] The forming of large-scale geological structures by particular faulting, esp. as caused by tensional forces in the crust. O [3]

tarn cap, *n.* (1856) *Myth.* Var. **tarn-cap** (1856) [Ad. of G *Tarnkappe* < *tarnen* to camouflage, mask, screen + *Kappe* cap < LL *cappa*] In Wagner's opera *Der Ring des Nibelungen,* a magic cap that renders the wearer invisible. O [3]

tarnhelm, *n.* (1877) *Myth.* Var. **tarn-helm** (1877) [G < *tarnen* to camouflage + *Helm* helmet] In Wagner's opera, the tarn cap (q.v.) that renders the wearer invisible or enables the wearer to change appearance at will. —**tarnhelmed,** *a.* (1971). O [3]

tarnowitzite, *n.* (1866) *Mineral.* [G *Tarnowitzit* (1841) < *Tarnowitz,* now *Tarnowokie Gory,* the name of a town in Silesia, Poland + G -*it* -ite] A plumboan variety of aragonite (q.v.) found there. O [3]

tarras. *see* trass

taster, *n.* (1884) *Zool.* [G feeler, antenna < *tasten* to touch, feel] In some Hydrozoa, a modified zooid located on the polypstem, somewhat resembling a polypite but without a mouth; a hydrocyst or feeler (this is different from the medieval meaning of "one or a device that tastes"). O [3]

Taube, *n.* (1913) *Mil.* [G pigeon, dove < MHG *tūbe,* OHG *tūba*] A German monoplane with recurved, pigeon-shaped wings, used in World War One. O (not in 2nd ed.) [2]

Tauchnitz, *a.* (1856) *Printing* [G (1841) < the name of

Christian Bernhard, Baron von *Tauchnitz* (1816–95), who published a collection of volumes on British and American authors for sale on the Continent] Of one or more of these volumes. —**Tauchnitz**, *n.* (1863). O [3]

Taufer, *n. Theol.* Var. **taufer** [G one who baptizes < *taufen* to baptize] Dunker (q.v.), one who baptizes. W [3]

tauriscite, *n.* (1868) *Mineral.* [G *Tauriszit* (1855) < a short. of L *Pagus Tauriscorum,* the name of a locality in the Swiss canton of Uri + G *-it* -ite] Native hydrous ferrous sulfate. O, W [3]

tautomerism, *n.* (1886) *Chem.* Var. **tautomery** (1886) [Ad. of G *Tautomerie* (1885), coined by Peter Conrad Laar (1853–1929), German chemist < Gk *tautó* the same + *méros* part + G *-ie* -y, here -ism] The ability of certain organic compounds to behave in different reactions as if they possessed at least two different structures. —**tautomeric** (1890); **-mer,** *n.* (1903); **-merize,** *v.* (1934); **-merizable** (1934); **-merization** (1934). O, R, W [4]

taxameter, *n.* (1890) *Transportation* Mod. var. **taximeter** (1898 < Fr) [G < ML *taxa* charge, tax + G *-meter* meter < Fr *mètre* < Gk *métron*] Taximeter, as on a taxicab. O, W [3]

taximeter, *see* taxameter

taxis, *pl.* **taxes** (1899) *Biol.* [G (1898) (now *Taxie*), first used in this sense by the German biochemist Friedrich Czapek (1868–1921) < Gk *táxis* arrangement] An organism's irritable reaction to an external stimulation like light (this is different from the various older meanings directly < Gk *táxis*). O, R, W [4]

taxite, *n. Geol.* [G *Taxit* < *tax-* (< Gk *táxis* arrangement, ordering) + G *-it* -ite] Any volcanic rock of schlieric or clastic appearance caused by the combined flows of different colors, textures, composition, and granularity. —**taxitic.** W [3]

taxon, *pl.* **taxa** (1929) *Bot.* [G (1926), back-formation of *Taxonomie* (< Fr) taxonomy] A taxonomic group such as a genus or species; transf. sense to other forms of life. O, R [4]

Te, *see* tellurium

technicum, *n.* (1932) *Ed.* [G *Technikum* or Russ *tekhnikum* (< G) < Gk *technikón,* neuter of *technikós* technical] A technical college, esp. in the former U.S.S.R. O, W [3]

tectogene, *n.* (1937) *Geol.* [G *Tektogen* (1926) < *tekto-* + *-gen* < Gk *téktōn* carpenter, builder + *genḗs* producing, generating] A long, narrow, down-warped belt in the earth's crust, postulated as an early phase in forming an island arc or a mountain range. —**tectogenic** (1937). O, W [3]

tectogenesis, *n.* (1937) *Geol.* [G *Tektogenese* (1926) < *tekto-* + *-genese* < Gk *téktōn* carpenter, builder + *génesis* origin, creation] The forming of the greatly distorted rock structures typical of mountain ranges. —**tectogenetic** (1975). O [3]

tectology, *n.* (1883) *Biol.* [G *Tektologie* < *tekto-* + *-logie* < Gk *téktōn* builder + *lógos* word, study + *-ia* -y] The suborder of morphology as projected by the German biologist Ernst Haeckel (1834–1919) that structurally views an organism as composed of organic individuals of different orders as distinct from the stereometric view. —**tectological.** O [3]

tectonite, *n.* (1933) *Geol.* [G *Tektonit* < *tekton-* (< Gk

carpenter, builder) + G *-it* -ite] A rock the fabric of which shows that it underwent differential movement during its formation. O, W [3]

tectosilicate, *n.* (1947) *Mineral.* [G *Tektosilikat* (1938) < *tekto-* + *Silikat* < Gk *tektonikḗ téchnē* architecture, art of building + L *silex* (gen. *silicis*) silica + G *-at* -ate] A polymeric silicate containing a three-dimensional network or structure. O, R, W [3]

tektite, *n.* (1909) *Geol.* [G *Tektit* (1900) < Gk *tektós* molten + G *-it* -ite] A small, rounded. glassy body of prob. meteoric origin found esp. in Australia, Indonesia, and the former Czechoslovakia. —**tektitic.** O, R, W [4]

teleology, *n.* (1740) *Philos.* [NL *teleologia,* Fr *téléologie,* and G *Teleologie* (1728)—the G is < *teleo-* + *-logie* < Gk *teleo-,* the comb. form of *télos* earth + *lógos* word, study + G *-ie* (< Gk *-ia*) -y] The study or doctrine of ends or final causes, esp. in regard to nature; such ends in regard to a divine providence; such study to explain any natural phenomenon; entelechy. —**teleologist.** O, R, W [4]

telestereoscope, *n.* (1864) *Physics* [G *Telestereoskop* < *tele-* + *-stereo* + *-skop* < Gk *tele-,* the comb. form of *télos* end, consummation, completeness + the comb. form of *stereós* rigid, firm, spacious + *skopeín* to view] A binocular telescope. O, R, W [3]

Teller mine, *n.* (1943) *Mil.* [Partial transl. of G < *Teller* plate + *Mine* mine] A disk-shaped antitank mine used by the Germans in World War Two. O [3]

tellurism, *n.* (1843) *Zool., Physics* [G *Tellurismus* (1822) < L *tellūrem* (dative of *tellus*) earth + G (< L) *-ismus* -ism] A magnetic power or principle, orig. proposed by the German physician Dietrich Georg Kieser (1779–1856), which supposedly pervades all nature and all organisms and produces the phenomena of animal magnetism (this is different from the later "soil" meaning borrowed < Fr *tellurisme*). O [3]

tellurium, *n.* (1800) *Chem.* [G (1798) < NL < L *tellūrem* (dative of *tellūs*) earth + *-ium,* discovered and named by the German chemist Martin Heinrich Klaproth (1743–1817) in Crell's *Chem. Annalen,* 1798, I, 100, prob. in contrast to *uranium*] A rare, semimetallic element. —**tellurium,** *a.* (1834). • ~ is symbolized as **Te** and appears in numerous composites like **telluric acid** and **tellurium dioxide** (1866). O, R, W [4]

telome, *n.* (c.1935 *W9*) *Bot.* [G *Telom* < *tel-* + *-om* < Gk *tel-,* the comb. form of *télos* end, consummation + *-ōma* swelling] Vascular plants' basic unit of structure, either as a terminal branchlet or as the most fundamental unit of the plant body. —**telomic.** W [3]

telophase, *n.* (1895) *Biol.* [G (1894) < *telo-* + *-phase* < Gk *télos* end + *phásis* phase] The final phase of mitosis, where the new nuclei are differentiated and usu. accompanied by cytoplasmic division into new daughter cells. —**telophasic** (1907). O, R, W [3]

telotaxis, *n.* (1934) *Zool.* [G (1919), coined by the German zoologist Alfred Kuhn (1885–1968) in *Die Orientierung der Tiere im Raum* < *telo-* + *-taxis* < Gk *télos* end + *táxis* arrangement] An organism's directional movement so as to keep a particular stimulus such as light acting on its sense receptor(s). O, R, W [3]

tendencious, *see* tendentious

tendency drama, *n.* (1838) *Lit.* [Ad. of G *Tendenzdrama*

< *Tendenz* tendency + *Drama* drama < ML *tendentia* + LL *drāma* (< Gk)] A play written with an unexpressed but specific purpose. O [3]

tendency wit, *n.* (1916) *Psych.* [Transl. of G *Tendenzwitz* < *Tendenz* tendency (< ML *tendentia*) + *Witz* wit] A determination to self-criticism. O [3]

tendency-writing, *n.* (1875) *Lit.* [Transl. of G *Tendenzschrift* < *Tendenz* tendenz (q.v.) + *Schrift* writing, literary work < *schreiben* to write] A literary work written with a deliberate tendency or purpose. O [3]

tendentious, *a.* (1900) *Lit.* Var. **tendencious** (1905) [Ad. of G *tendenziös* < Fr *tendencieux* < ML *tendentia* tendency] Composed, written, or characterized by a deliberate tendency or purpose. —**tendentiousness** (1920), **tendentiously** (1924). O, R, W [4]

tendenz, -en *pl.* (1896) *Lit.* [G (1791) < ML *tendentia* tendency, inclination] Tendency: orig., the trend or purpose of a discourse; now a dominating purpose or attitude influencing the content and structure of a literary work. O, W [3]

tendenzroman, -e *pl.* (1855) *Lit.* Var. **Tendenzroman** (1885) [G < *Tendenz* tendenz (q.v.) + *Roman* novel < OFr *romans, romanz*] A novel in which the characters and incidents are selected with a view to exemplifying a principle: tendency novel. • ~ is partially transl. as **tendenz novel** (1896). O [3]

tensor, *n.* (1916) *Physics* [G (1898), first used in this sense by the German physicist Woldemar Voigt (1850–1919) in *Die fundamentalen physikal. Eigenschaften der Kristalle* (p. vi) < NL *tensor* < L *tensus,* past part. of *tendere* to stretch] A generalized vector containing more than three components, each being a function of the coordinates of an arbitrary point in space of an appropriate quantity of dimensions (this is different from the earlier "anatomical, mathematical" meanings). O, R, W [4]

tephroite, *n.* (1868) *Mineral.* [G *Tephroit* (1823) < Gk *tephrós* ash gray + G *-it* -ite] A manganese orthosilicate of an ash-gray or reddish color. O, R, W [3]

teratolite, *n.* (1868) *Mineral.* [G *Teratolith* (1839) (now *Teratolit*) < *terato-* + *-lith* < Gk *téras, terat-* marvel, prodigy + *líthos* stone, so named because of its supposed sovereign qualities] An impure hydrous silicate of aluminum. O [3]

terminism, *n.* (1860) *Theol.* [G *Terminismus* (17th cent.), first used in this sense by the Leipzig theologian Adam Rechenberg (1642–1721) < NL *terminus* + G *-ismus* (< L) -ism] The terminists' controversial doctrine: God has set a certain term for the probation of individuals, after which the offer of grace is lost (this is different from the earlier "Ockhamism" meaning). —**terministic** (1860). O [3]

terminology, -logies *pl.* (1801) *Philos.* [G *Terminologie* (1786), as used by Christian Gottfried Schütz in his correspondence with Kant < *termino-* + *-logie* < ML *terminus* term + Gk *lógos* word, study + G *-ie* (< Gk *-ia*) -y] The scientific study of the etymology of terms; the terms used in a specific subject; nomenclature. —**terminological(ly)** (1906, 1861), **terminologist** (1894). O, R, W [4]

terpane, *n.* (1902) *Chem.* [G *Terpan* (1894) < *Terpentin* turpentine (< LL *ter(e)binta* resin of the terebinth) + G

-an -ane] Menthane, esp. the para isomer that provides many terpenoids (q.v.). O, W [3]

terpenoid, *n.* (1933) *Chem.* [G (1933) < *terpen-* + *-oid* < *Terpentin* turpentine (see *terpane*) + Gk *-oeidēs* similar] One of a class of compounds having an isoprenoid structure like that of terpene hydrocarbons. O, W [3]

terrace, *see* trass

tertschite, *n.* (1953) *Mineral.* [G *Tertschit* (1953) < the name of Hermann *Tertsch* (1880–1962), Austrian mineralogist + G *-it* -ite] A rare, hydrated, fine-fibered calcium borate. O [3]

testosterone, *n.* (1935) *Biochem., Pharm.* [G *Testosteron* (1935) < *testo-* (< L *testis* testis) + a blend of G *Steroid* steroid + *Hormon* hormone < Gk *hormōn*] An androgenic, steroid hormone that stimulates the development of male secondary attributes, obtained esp. from bulls' testes or synthetically and used in medicine chiefly as esters.—**testosterone propionate** (1937). O, R, W [4]

tetradymite, *n.* (1850) *Mineral.* [G *Tetradymit* (1831) < Gk *tetrádymos* fourfold + G *-it* -ite, so named for its occurrence in compound twin crystals] A sulfotelluride of bismuth. O, R, W [4]

tetrahedrite, *n.* (1868) *Mineral.* [Ad. of G *Tetraëdrit* (1845) < LGk *tetráedros* having four faces + G *-it* -ite] A fine-grained sulfide of lead, zinc, mercury, or silver; a valuable ore of silver. O, R, W [4]

tetraodontoxin, *see* tetrodotoxin

tetrapeptide, *n.* (1906) *Biochem.* [G *Tetrapeptid* < *tetra-* + *Peptid* < Gk *tetra-* < *téttares* four + *peptós* boiled, cooked + G *-id* -ide] An oligopeptide where the molecule has four amino-acid residues. O [3]

tetrodotoxin, *n.* (1911) *Biochem.* Var. **tetraodontoxin** [G (1911) < *Tetrodon* + *Toxin* < NL *Tetrodon* the scientific family name for the puffer + *toxin* toxin + G *-in*] A poisonous compound obtained from the Japanese globe or puffer fish. O, R, W [4]

tetryl, *n.* (1909) *Chem.* Var. **Tetryl** (1909) [G *Tetril* (now *Tetryl*) < Gk *tetra-* < *téttares* four + *-yl* < *hýlē* wood, substance] A yellow crystalline explosive used as a detonator; methyl-picryl-nitramide (this is different from the earlier "tetracarbon" meaning). O, R, W [4]

text linguistics, *n.* (1973) *Ling.* [G *Textlinguistik* < *Text* text + *Linguistik* linguistics < MFr *texte* < ML *textus* + L *lingu-*] The belief that the natural domain of linguistic theory consists of texts, or discourses, rather than sentences. O [3]

textura, *n.* (1922) *Printing* Var. **textur** (1922) [G *Textur(a)* < L *textūra* web, texture] A kind of typeface orig. used in the earliest printed books; the handwriting on which this is based. —**textura,** *a.* (1970). O [3]

thaler, *see* taler

thalweg, *n.* (1831) *Geol.* Var. **talweg** (1937) [G (now *Talweg*) < *Thal* valley + *Weg* way] A line following the lowest part of a valley, river, or lake; the center of a waterway's chief navigable channel, which can serve as the boundary between two states. O, R, W [3]

thanatocoenosis/thanatocoenose, *n.* (1953) *Ecology* [G *Thanatocoenose* (1926) (now *Thanatozönöse*) < *thanato-* + *-coenose* < Gk *thánatos* death + *koínōsis* participation < *koinós* common] A group of fossils occurring at the same site but sometimes not representing a former bio-coenosis. O [3]

tharandite, *n.* (1850) *Mineral.* [G *Tharandit* (1817) < *Tharand(t),* the name of a town in Saxony, Germany + *-it* -ite] A type of dolomite found in greenish-yellow crystals. O [3]

theca (folliculi), pl. **thecae** (1857) *Zool.* [G (1837) < Gk *thḗkē* storage place + (L *folliculus* small leather pouch, sack)] A layer of dense stoma enveloping a Graafian follicle. • ~ differs from the old "receptacle, botanical" meanings. O, R, W [3]

theologaster, *n.* (1621) *Theol.* [G (1518), used by Luther < ML < L *theologus* theologian + *-aster,* a suffix denoting partial resemblance] A shallow theologian, esp. one who pretends to command deep theological knowledge. —**theologastric** (1894). O, W [3]

theonomy, *n.* (1890) *Theol.* [G *Theonomie* (1838) < *theo-* + *-nomie* < Gk *theós* god + *nomía* rule] Government by God; the state of being subject to God's rule and authority. O, R, W [3]

theralite, *n.* (1898) *Geol.* [G *Theralith* (1887) (now *Theralit*) < *theral* (< Gk to hunt, pursue) + G *-lith* < Gk *líthos* stone, perhaps so named because one's success in hunting it down was thought to be assured] One of various mafic, intrusive, igneous rocks. O, R [3]

thermal bremsstrahlung, *n.* (1972) *Physics* [Expanded < G *Bremsstrahlung* bremsstrahlung (q.v.)] The electromagnetic radiation produced by the thermal motion of a plasma's charged particles. O [3]

Thermit/thermite, *n.* (1900) *Chem.* [G *Thermit* < *therm-* (< Gk *thermós* hot) + G *-it* -ite] (A trademark for) a mixture of aluminum powder and powdered iron oxide that produces intense heat, as used in welding and in incendiary bombs. • ~ appears initially in compounds like **thermite process** (1905)/**welding** (1906)/**reaction** (1915). O, R, W [4]

thermochromism, *n.* (1911) *Chem.* Var. **thermochromy** (1911) [Ad. of G *Thermochromie* (1904) < *thermo-* + *-chromie* < Gk *thermós* warm + *chrôma* color + G *-ie* (< Gk *-ia*) -ism] The phenomenon whereby some substances experience a reversible change of color when heated or cooled. O, W [3]

thermoluminescence, *n.* (1897) *Physics* [G *Thermolumineszenz* < *thermo-* (< Gk *thermós* hot, warm) + G *Luminiszenz* luminescence (q.v.)] Phosphorescence produced in a previously excited substance like quartz upon gentle heating, used in dating ancient pottery; also called *thermophosphorescence.* —**thermoluminescent** (1899). O, R, W [4]

thermolysis, *n.* (1875) *Chem., Physiol.* [G *Thermolyse* (1874) < *thermo-* + *-lyse* < Gk *thermós* hot + *lýsis* loosening] The separating or decomposing of a compound into its elements by the action of heat; the dissipation of heat from the body. —**thermolytic** (1890), **thermolyze.** O, R, W [3]

thermonatrite, *n.* (1859) *Mineral.* [G *Thermonatrit* (1845) < *thermo-* + *Natrit* < Gk *thermós* hot + Fr *natron* < Ar *naṭrūn* < Gk *nítron* nitre + G *-it* -ite] A native hydrous sodium carbonate found in various saline lakes and alkali soils. O, W [3]

Thiazine, *n.* (1900 *W9*) *Chem.* Var. **thiazole** (1887) [Ad. of G *Thiazol* (1887) < Gk *theîon* sulfur + *az-* the comb. form of *ázōos* lifeless, inert + G *-in* -ine] A trademark used for a dyestuff; one of a class of dyes that contain a ring of one nitrogen, one sulfur, and four carbon atoms in the molecule, such as thionine and methylene blue. O, R, W [4]

thiazole, *see* thiazine

thing-in-itself, *pl.* **things-in-themselves** (1798) *Philos.* [Transl. of Kant's G *ding an sich* (q.v.)] Something considered for itself, apart from the subjective modes of human thought and perception: metaphysical reality. O, R, W [3]

thin-layer chromatography, *n.* (1957) *Pharm.* [Transl. of G *Dünnschicht-Chromatographie* (1956) < *dünn* thin + *Schicht* layer + *Chromatographie* chromatography (q.v.)] Chromatography where compounds are separated on a thin layer of adsorbent material like silica gel or charcoal. — **thin-layer chromatogram/chromatographic.** O, R [3]

thiobacillus, -cilli *pl.* (1951) *Biol.* [G *Thiobazillus* (1904) < *thio-* + *Bazillus* < Gk *theîon* sulfur + L *bacillus* rod] A small, rod-shaped bacterium that derives energy from oxidized sulfur and sulfur compounds; (cap.) this genus of sulfur bacteria. O, R, W [3]

thiochrome, *n.* (1935) *Biochem.* [G *Thiocrom* (1935) < *thio-* + *-crom* < Gk *theîon* sulfur + *chrôma* color] A yellow, solid, tricyclic alcohol found in yeast and used in determining thiamine. O, W [3]

thioglycol(l)ic acid, *n.* (1877) *Chem.* [Transl. of G *Thioglycolsäure* (1877) (now *Thioglykolsäure*) < *Thioglycol* (< Gk *theîon* sulfur + *glykýs* sweet + G *-ol* < *Alkohol* alcohol, ult. < Ar) + G *Säure* acid] A foul-smelling liquid mercapto acid that is used in setting cold waves and as depilating agents. —**thioglycol(l)ate,** *a.* (1980). O, W [3]

thionyl, *n.* (1866) *Chem.* [G *Thionil* (1857) < *thion-* (< Gk *theîon* sulfur) + G *-yl* -yl] A bivalent radical or cation of sulfuric acid, used esp. in names of inorganic compounds like *thionyl chloride:* sulfinyl. O, R, W [4]

Third Reich, *n.* (1923) *Politics* [Partial transl. of G *Drittes Reich* < *dritt-* third + *Reich* (q.v.)] Germany under the rule of Hitler and the Nazi party, 1933–45; Hitler's regime. O, R [4]

thixotropy, *n.* (1927) *Chem.* [G *Tixotropie* (1927) (now *Thixotropie*) < *tixo-* + *-tropie* < Gk *thíxis* touch + *tropḗ* turning + G *-ie* (< Gk *-ia*) -y] The capacity of various gels to become fluid when agitated and to resolidify when left to stand. —**thixotropic(ally)** (1927, 1963). O, R, W [4]

tholeiite, *n.* (1866) Old var. **tholeite** (1866) *Geol.* [G *Tholeiit* (1841) (now *Tholeyit*) < *Tholei,* now *Toley,* the name of a village in northeast Saar, Germany + *-it* -ite] Formerly, a kind of basaltic rock with little or no olivine and possessing an intersertal texture; in recent use, any basaltic rock usu. containing augite and a calcium-poor pyroxene, and having a higher silica and lower alkali content than do alkali basalts. —**tholeitic** (1922). O [3]

thoron, *n.* (1918) *Chem.* [G (1918), formed by Curt Schmidt (1863–?), German chemist < *Thorium* (< the name of the Norse god *Thor* < ON *Thorr*) + G *-on* -on] A heavy, radioactive, gaseous isotope produced from decomposed thorium; also called *thorium emanation*. O, R, W [3]

Thorotrast, *n.* (1932) *Med.* Var. **thorotrast** [G (1930) < *thoro-* (< *Thorium*—see *thoron*) + a short. of *Kontrast* contrast < MFr *contrast*] (A U.S. trademark for) a colloidal solution of thorium oxide used as a radiopaque medium. O, W [3]

thoroughwax, *n.* (1548) *Bot.* Var. **thorow wax** (1548) [Transl. of G *Durchwachs(kraut)* < *durch* through + *wachsen* to wax, grow (+ *Kraut* herb), so named because the stem seems to be growing through the leaves] The herb hare's-ear; a boneset. O, W [3]

thortveitite, *n.* (1912) *Mineral.* [G *Thortveitit* < the name of Olaus *Thortveit*, a 20th-cent. Norwegian collector of minerals in Iceland + G *-it* -ite] A silicate of scandium and yttrium. O, R, W [3]

thought experiment, *n.* (1945) *Philos.* Var. **Gedanken experiment** (q.v.) [Transl. of G *Gedankenexperiment*] An imaginary experiment carried out under ideal conditions and with ideal apparatus, but in thought only. O, R, W [3]

thought-world, *n.* (1947) *Philos.* [Transl. of G *Gedankenwelt* < *Gedanken*, pl. of *Gedanke* thought + *Welt* world] The combination of beliefs, mental attitudes, assumptions, and concepts about the world characteristic of a given people, place, time, etc. O [3]

Thousand-Year Reich, *n.* (1946) *Politics* [Partial transl. of G *Tausendjähriges Reich* < *tausendjährig* lasting a thousand years + neuter suffix *-es* + *Reich* realm] The German Third Reich (1933–45), envisioned by the Nazis as established for an indefinite duration. O [3]

three-valued, *a.* (1932) *Philos.* [Transl. of G *dreiwertig* < *drei* three + *-wertig* having values, orig. transl. into German < Pol *trójwartósciowej*] Having three truth-values instead of the usual two of falsehood and truth. O, R, W [3]

threose, *n.* (1901) *Chem.* [G (1901), ad. by the German chemist Otto Ruff (1871–1939) < *Erythrose* erythrose < Gk *erythrós* red + G *-ose* -ose, denoting a carbohydrate] A syrupy, aldo-tetrose sugar that is the epimer of erythrose. O, W [3]

thrombasthenia, *n.* (1935) *Med.* [G *Thrombasthenie* (1918) < *thromb-* + *Asthenie* < Gk *thrómbos* congealed blood + *asthenés* powerless + G *-ie* (< Gk *-ia*) -ia] Pseudohemophilia, a condition where there is prolonged bleeding despite having a normal number of blood platelets. O, W [3]

thrombocyte, *n.* (1893) *Biol.* [G *Thrombocyt* (1892) (now *Thrombozyt*) < *thrombo-* + *-cyt* < Gk *thrómbos* congealed blood + *kýtos* cavity, ult. cell] Blood platelet; a cell with a similar clotting function. —**thrombocytic.** O, R, W [3]

thrombocyth(a)emia, *n.* (1966) *Med.* [G *Thrombozythämie* (1929) < *thrombo-* + *Zythämie* < Gk *thrómbos* congealed blood + *kýtos* cavity, ult. cell + *haima* blood + G *-ie* (< Gk *-ia*) -ia] Thrombocytosis, esp. when a persistent or primary condition. O [3]

thrombocytopenia, *n.* (1923) *Med.* [G *Thrombocytopenie* (1920) < *thrombo-* + *Cytopenie* < Gk *thrómbos* congealed blood + *kýtos* cavity, ult. cell + *pénēs* poor + G *-ie* (< Gk *-ia*) -ia] A condition where there is a persistent reduced number of blood platelets, as in hemorraging. —**thrombocytopenic (purpura)** (1925, 1978). O, W [3]

thrombolite, *n.* (1844–64) *Mineral.* [G *Thrombolith* (1838) (now *Thrombolit*) < *thrombo-* + *-lith* < Gk *thrómbos* curd + *líthos* stone, so named for its appearance] A copper antimony oxide. O [3]

through-composed, *a.* (c.1903 *W9*) *Music* [Transl. of G *durchkomponiert* (q.v.)] Of a song or aria where each stanza or strophe has its own musical setting. O, R, W [4]

thumbling, *n.* (1867) [Transl. of G *Däumling,* dim. of *Daumen* thumb] A tiny, thumb-sized person: manikin; dwarf or pigmy. O, W [3]

thumerstone, *n.* (1796) *Mineral.* (archaic) Var. **thumite** (1868) [Partial transl. of G *Thumerstein* (1788) < *Thumer* deriving from *Thum,* the name of a town in Saxony, Germany + *-er* -er + *Stein* stone] Axinite, a complex borosilicate. O [3]

thumite, *see* thumerstone

Thuringer/Thüringer, *n.* (1923 *W9*) *Food* Var. **Thüringer sausage** [G *Thüringer(wurst)* of or from Thuringia < L *Thuringia,* the name of an historic region in Germany (+ G *Wurst* sausage)] A mildly seasoned summer sausage. O, R, W [4]

thuringite, *n.* (1844) *Mineral.* [G *Thuringit* (1832) < L *Thuringia* (see *Thuringer*) + G *-it* -ite] A ferrian variety of chamosite, of the chlorite group. O, W [3]

thylakoid, *n.* (1962) *Bot.* [G (1961) < Gk *thylakoidés* sac-like] Each of the fluid-filled, membranous sacs within a chloroplast where photochemical reactions occur. O, R [3]

thymine, *n.* (1894) *Biochem.* Var. **thymin** (1894) [G *Thymin* < *thym-* (< Gk *thýmos* thymus) + G *-in* -ine] A crystalline, pyrimidine base orig. described by Albrecht Kossel, obtained by hydrolyzing deoxyribonucleic acid and fish spermatozoa; thymopoietin, a hormone secreted by the thymus. —**thyminic (acid)** (1898). O, R, W [4]

thymoma, *-s/-ta pl.* (1919) *Path.* [G *Thymome* (1910) < Gk *thýmos* thymus + *-ōma* as in *carcinoma,* swelling, tumor] A tumor that can develop in the tissue elements of the thymus gland. O, W [3]

Ti, *see* titanium

tiemannite, *n.* (1868) *Mineral.* [G *Tiemannit* (1855) < the name of Johann Carl Wilhelm *Tiemann* (1848–99), German scientist + *-it* -ite] A native mercuric selenide with metallic luster. O, R, W [4]

till, *n.* (1611) *Printing* [Prob. ad. < G *Tülle* socket, mouth of a pitcher < MHG *tülle* < OHG *tulli* socket for an arrowhead] A horizontal piece used in an early handpress to support the sleeve with the spindle and screws. O, R, W [3]

tillite, *n.* (1907) *Geol.* [G *Tillit* (1906) < *Till* (origin unknown) + *-it* -ite] A sedimentary rock of glacial till compacted into hard rock. O, R, W [3]

Tilsit (cheese), *n.* (c.1932 *W9*) *Food* Var. **Tilsiter** (1961) [Transl. of G *Tilsiter (Käse)* < *Tilsit,* the name of a town in East Prussia, now Sovetsk, the former U.S.S.R. (+ G *Käse* cheese)] A mild, semihard, yellow cheese orig. made in Tilsit. O, R, W [4]

time spirit, *n.* (1831) *Sociol.* [Transl. of G *Zeitgeist* (q.v.)] Zeitgeist. O, W [3]

tingle-tangle/tingel-tangel, *n.* (1911) *Theater* [G *Tingel-*

tangel, echoic of the musical sounds emanating from a Berlin night club] A disreputable or cheap music hall or nightclub, esp. in Germany; a cabaret (this is different from the old, reduplicated item that means "confused bells"). O [3]

tinguaite, *n.* (1893) *Geol.* [G *Tinguait* (1887), the name of the mountain spur Serra de *Tinguá,* west of Rio de Janeiro, Brazil + G *-it* -it] A hypabyssal rock mainly of alkali feldspar, aegirite, and nepheline. O [3]

tinzenite, *n.* (1924) *Mineral.* [G *Tinzenit* (1923) < *Tinzen,* the name of a mountain in Graubünden, Switzerland + G *-it* -ite] A basic silicate of calcium, manganese, and aluminum found at Tinzen. O, W [3]

titanaugite, *n.* (1933) *Mineral.* [G *Titanaugit* (1892) < *Titan* + *Augit* augite, ult. < Gk *Titán,* the name of a member of a family or superhuman race of giants in ancient Greek mythology + L *augītes* a precious stone < Gk < *augē* brightness] A basaltic variety of augite, rich in titanium (q.v.). O, W [3]

titanite, *n.* (1858) *Mineral.* [G *Titanit* (1795) < *Titanium*—see *titanaugite*) + G *-it* -ite] A silicate of calcium and titanium (q.v.): sphene. O, R, W [3]

titanium, *n.* (1796) *Chem.* [G (1795) < NL < Gk *Titán* (see *titanaugite*) + L *-ium,* discovered independently and named by Martin Heinrich Klaproth (1743–1817), German chemist, in *Beiträge zur chemischen Kenntnis der Mineral-Körper* (1795, 1:244), on the analogy of *uranium,* as previously named by him; titanium was earlier discovered by the English chemist William Gregor (1761–1817) in 1791 and unsuccessfully named *Menakanet*] A lustrous, high-melting, metallic element that is the ninth most abundant element in the earth's crust and is used as structural material in aircraft, chemical equipment, etc. • ~ is symbolized as Ti and appears initially in numerous compounds like **titanium (di)oxide** (1877, 1885)/**white** (1920)/**sponge** (1950)/**tetrachloride** (1955)/**carbide.** O, R, W [4]

titanomagnetite, *n.* (1900) *Mineral.* [G *Titanomagnetit* (1898) < *titano-* (< the comb. form of Gk *Titán*—see *titanaugite*) + G *Magnetit* magnetite (q.v.)] A variety of magnetite containing titanium. O, W [3]

Tithonian, *a.* (1871) *Geol.* [Ad. of G (1865) *tithonisch* < L *Tithōnus* < Gk *Tithōnós* a figure in ancient Greek mythology, the lover of the goddess Eros + G adj. suffix *-isch* -ian] Designating a stage of the European Upper Jurassic. O [3]

toadstone¹, *n.* (1558) *Geol.* [Poss. a transl. of G *Krötenstein* < comb. form of *Kröte* toad + *Stein* stone] A name formerly used for various stones or fossil objects likened to a toad in color or shape, the most valuable of which were esp. worn as a charm; a bufonite. —**toadstone,** *a.* (1855). O, R, W [4]

toadstone², *n.* (1784) *Geol.* [Poss. a folk etymological var. and transl. of G *Todstein* < *Tod* death + *Stein* stone, i.e., inert stone, one of the synonyms for rhodonite (q.v.), such as G *Totspat* dead spar] A name orig. given to igneous, usu. basaltic rock by lead miners in Derbyshire, England, where some additional mining terms appear to be of German origin. O, W [3]

Tobias night, *n.* (1960) *Sociol.* [Partial transl. of G *Tobiasnacht* < *Tobias* (from *Tobit* 8:1–3) + *Nacht* night] Any of the first three nights of marriage in which the next of kin sleeps between the newlyweds for all three nights to protect them at a time when their resistance to evil is supposedly at its lowest ebb. O [3]

Tocharish, *n.* (1910) *Ling.* Var. **Tokarish** (1926) [G *Tocharisch* Tocharian < Fr *tocharien* < Gk *Tochároi* the name of an extinct Central Asian people who spoke Tocharian + G adj. suffix *-isch* -ish] The Tocharian language; the Indo-European branch containing this language. O, W [3]

Todtentanz, *see* Totentanz

Tokarish, *see* Tocharish

tomogram, *n.* (1936) *Med.* [Prob. < G *Tomogramm* < *tomo-* + *-gramm* < Gk *tómos* slice, section + *grámma* record] A roentgenogram made by tomography (q.v.). O, R, W [4]

tomography, *n.* (1935) *Med.* [Prob. < G *Tomographie* < *tomo-* + *-graphie* < Gk *tómos* slice, section + *gráphein* to write + G *-ie* (< Gk *-ia*) -y] A procedure in medical roentgenography where details in one plane of body tissue are made sharp and clear, while details of adjoining planes are blurred. —**tomograph** (1935), **tomographic(ally)** (1935, 1939). O, R, W [4]

tonalite, *n.* (1879) *Geol.* [G *Tonalit* (1864) < Passo del *Tonale,* the name of a pass through the Italian Alps + G *-it* -ite] A grandular igneous rock containing quartz, andesine (q.v.), and some orthoclase; any quartz-diorite. —**tonalitic** (1963). O, W [3]

tone color, *n.* (1881) *Music* Var. **tone colour, tone-colour** (1881) [Transl. of G *Klangfarbe* < *Klang* sound, tone + *Farbe* color] Timbre; the tonal quality of an instrument or voice, or the effect of a combination of such qualities in performing music. —**tone-coloring,** *n.* (1895–6); **tone-coloured.** O, R, W [3]

tone painting, *n.* (1897) *Music* [Transl. of G *Tonmalerei,* Richard Wagner's term, which, he admits, "may be used in jest" (see *Oxford Dictionary of Music*)] The art of using varying timbres and sound symbolism for musical effects, as in impressionistic composition. —**tone-painter** (1903). O, R, W [3]

tone poem, *n.* (1889) *Music* [Transl. of G *Tongedicht* < *Ton* tone + *Gedicht* poem] Symphonic poem (q.v.), an orchestral composition with a literary subject or suggestive of poetic images or sentiments. O, R, W [4]

tone poet, *n.* (1874) *Music* [Transl. of G *Tondichter* < *Ton* tone + *Dichter* poet] A composer of musical tone poems or program music. —**tone poetry** (1890). O, W [4]

tone-row, tone series, *n.* (1936) *Music* Brit. var. **note row** [Transl. of G *Tonreihe* < *Ton* tone + *Reihe* row] Twelve-tone row, or notes of the chromatic scale. O, R, W [4]

tonofibril, *n.* (1901) *Anat., Entomology* Var. **tonofibrilla** [G *Tonofibrille* (1899) < *tono-* + *Fibrille* < Gk *tónos* tension, pitch, tone + L *fibra* fiber] A bundle of reinforcing intracellular or extracellular fibrils; an insect's noncontractile fibril that passes from a myofibril through the epidermis into the cuticle. O, W [3]

tonoplast, *n.* (c.1888 W9) *Bot.* [G < *tono-* + *-plast* < Gk *tónos* tension + *plastós* formed, molded] A protoplasmic membrane surrounding a plant-cell vacuole. O, R, W [3]

tonstein, *n.* (1961) *Geol.* [G < *Ton* clay + *Stein* stone] A kaolinitic rock commonly found in association with coal seams; a thin band of this rock. O [3]

toot, *n.* (1890 *Sc*) [Ad. of G (PaG *dutt*) *Düte/Tüte* paper bag < MLG *tute* horn] A small paper bag (this is different from the numerous older meanings). R, W [3]

topochemical, *a.* (1920) *Chem.* [Ad. of G *topochemisch* (1920) < *topo-* + *chemisch* chemical < Gk *tópos* place + ult. Ar *al-kīmiyā'*] Of, relating to, or being topochemistry, in a locally confined chemical reaction. —**topochemically** (1962). O, W [3]

topological space, *n.* (1926) *Math.* [Transl. of G *topologischer Raum* (1914) < *topologisch* topological (< Gk *tópos* place + *lógos* study + G *-isch* -ical) + *Raum* space + *-er* -er] A set with a collection of subsets or open sets that satisfy certain properties. O, R [4]

torbernite, *n.* (1852) *Mineral.* [G *Torbernit* (1792) < the name of *Torbern* Olof Bergman (1735–84), Swedish chemist + G *-it* -ite] A hydrous phosphate of uranium and copper, also called *copper uranite* and *chalcolite*. O, R, W [3]

Torschlusspanik, *n.* (1963) *Sociol.* [G *Torschlußpanik* < *Torschluß*, lit., closing time < *Tor* gate + *Schluß* closing up, end + *Panik* panic < Gk *panikós*] An aging person's anxiety that life's opportunities may now have been closed; an aging woman's fears about lost youthful (esp. sexual) excitement. O [2]

torte, -n/-s *pl.* (1555 *W9*) *Food* [G < It *torta* < LL *tōrta* round bread, pastry] A usu. richly frosted cake or pastry baked in a large flat form (this is different from the obs. Latin-derived "bread" meaning). O, R, W [4]

Tortonian, *a.* (1885) *Geol.* [G *Tortonien* (1857) < *Tortona*, the name of a town in northern Italy] Of, relating to, or specifying a stage of the upper or middle Miocene in Europe. —**Tortonian,** *n.* (1931). O [3]

tosyl, *n.* (1938) *Chem.* [G (1933), a short. of *Toluolsulfonyl* < a combining of *Toluol* toluol + *Sulfonyl* sulfonyl] The para isomer of the univalent radical toluenesulfonyl. —**tosylate,** *v.* (1938), *n.* (1963); **tosylating,** *a.* (1972); **tosylated** (1974); **tosylation.** O [3]

Totenkopf, *a.* (1943), *n.* (1981) *Mil.* [G, lit., death's head < comb. form of *Tote* dead person + *Kopf* head] (pertaining to) a member of a division of the SS in Nazi Germany, which wore a death's head insignia. O [2]

Totenkopf division, *n.* (1943) *Mil.* [G, lit., Death's Head Division] An SS division in Nazi Germany—see *Totenkopf.* O [2]

Totenkopfverband, -e *pl.* (1943) *Mil.* [G, lit., Death's Head Detachment] An SS detachment in Nazi Germany—see *Totenkopf.* O [2]

Totentanz, *n.* (1964) *Lit.* Var. **Toden Tans** (1789), **Todtentanz** (1937) [G (*der*) *Tote* the dead (person) + *Tanz* dance] Dance of Death; a dance or procession in which Death, represented as a skeleton, leads the living or other skeletons to the grave; dance macabre; fig., in a negative military sense. • ~ is transl. as **Dance of Death** (1789). O [3]

tourill, *n.* *Chem.* [G, prob. < Fr *tourie* flask, carboy] An absorption vessel in which a gas is passed over a liquid, as in removing moisture. W [3]

tournee, *n.* *Games* Var. **tourne** [G *Tourné/Tournee* < Fr *tourné*, past part. of *tourner* to turn] A variety of skat

where the player turns over a card from the skat as trump and can exchange two cards for the skat cards. W [3]

tower karst, *n.* (1954) *Geol.* [Partial transl. of G *Turmkarst* (1954) < *Turm* tower + *Karst* chalky formation] A type of karst characterized by isolated steep hills. O [3]

toxoid, *n.* (c.1894 *W9*) *Med.* [G < *tox-* + *-oid* < ML *toxicus* poisoned + Gk *-oeidés* similar] A toxin such as of diptheria or tetanus, which has been treated so that it can induce the formation of antibodies when injected, but without being toxic. O, R, W [4]

toxophore, *n.* (1899) *Med.* [G *Toxophor* (1898) < *toxo-* + *-phor* < Gk *toxo-*, the comb. form of *tóxon* poison (used on arrowheads) + *phóros* bearing] A particular group of atoms in a toxin's molecule that contain its toxic properties. O [3]

toxophorous, *a.* (1902) *Med.* Var. **toxophoric** (1902) [G *toxophor* (1898) < *Toxophor* toxophore (q.v.) + E *-ous*] Pertaining to toxophore, having actively poisonous properties. O, W [3]

trabant, *n.* (1617) *Biol., Astronomy* [G lifeguard, armed attendant, satellite < Czech *drabant* mercenary < Per *darwān* doorkeeper] An armed guard; a lifeguard; a short segment separated from a chromosome's main body; satellite. O, W [3]

trace fossil, *n.* (1956) *Paleon.* [Transl. of G *Spurenfossil* (1932) < *Spur* trace + *Fossil* fossil < L *fossilis* dug up] A fossil that preserves the tracks, trails, and burrows rather than the soft-bodied animal itself. O, R [3]

tracheid, *n.* (1875) *Bot.* Var. **tracheide** (1875) [Prob. < G *Tracheide* (1863) < *trache-* (< Gk *trachýs*, fem. *tracheîa* rough, coarse-looking) + G *-ide* -id] A long, tubular, water-conducting cell that is peculiar to xylem; a vascular wood-cell. —**tracheidal,** *a.* (1891). O, R, W [4]

trachybasalt, *n.* (1888) *Geol.* [G < *trachy-* + *Basalt* < Gk *trachýs* coarse, rough + L *basaltēs* basalt] A rock intermediate in composition between trachyte and basalt. O, R, W [3]

Traminer, *n.* (1851) *Beverages* [G hailing from *Tramin* < It *Termeno*, the name of a village in northern Italy + G *-er*] One of several varieties of vine and grape widely grown in Germany and elsewhere; the white wine with perfumed bouquet made from this grape. —**Traminer,** *a.* (1972). O [3]

transcendent, *a.* (1803) *Philos.* [G (< L) *trānscendentem* (1789), dative sing. of present part. of *trānscendere* to transcend, used by Kant to describe something that transcended his own list of categories] Transcending or wholly outside of experience or knowledge (this is different from the various older meanings). O, R, W [4]

transcendent, *n.* (c.1810) *Philos.* Var. **transcendant** (c.1810) [Ad. of Kant's G—see **transcendent,** a.] Something that is beyond the bounds of human thought and cognition (this is different from the old "Aristotelian" and other meanings). O, W [3]

transcendental, *a.* (1798) *Philos.* [Kant's G (< L)] Of or concerning the a priori, necessary conditions of human experience as determined by the constitution of the mind itself; in contrast with the adjective transcendent (q.v.), of a partial transcending of human knowledge, particularly that which is determined by the contingent particularity of experience (this is different from the old "Aristotelian" and other meanings); of a Kantian-like philosophy. • ~ appears initially in various compounds like **transcendental logic** (1798)/**idealism** (1872)/**aesthetic/dialectic/ego/object**. O, R, W [4]

transcendentalism, *n.* (1803) *Philos.* [Kant's G *Transcendentalismus* (see *transcendental*) + *-ismus* (< L) -ism] The Kantian doctrine or tendency emphasizing a priori conditions of experience and knowledge, or the unknowable quality of ultimate reality; an idealistic, post-Kantian doctrine. O, R, W [4]

transcendentality, *n.* (1846) *Philos.* [Ad. of G *Transcendentalität* < *transcendental* (q.v.) + *-ität* -ity] Transcendental quality or state. O, R, W [4]

transference, *n.* (1916) *Psych.* [Transl. of G *Übertragung* (1895) transference < *übertragen* to transfer, pass on to + *-ung* -ence] A patient's redirection to someone else (such as the psychoanalyst) of various emotions, esp. those unconsciously retained from childhood (this is different from the old "conveying, legal" meanings). O, R, W [4]

transfinite, *a.* (1903) *Math.* [G *transfinit* (1903) < *trans-* + *finit* < L *trāns* trans-, across, beyond + *fīnītus* end] Going beyond or exceeding any finite number or magnitude; being a power of an aggregate whose cardinal number is not finite. —**transfinite,** *n.* O, R, W [4]

transfluence, *n.* (1949) *Geol.* [G *Transfluenz* (1909) < L *trānsfluentia* < *trānsfluere* to flow through or across] A quantitative flow of glacial ice across a preglacial watershed, with its consequent major erosion. O [3]

transvestism, *n.* (1913) *Med.* [G *Transvestismus* < L *trāns* trans- + *vestīre* to clothe + G (< L) *-ismus* -ism] The action or practice of adopting or having the desire to adopt the dress and manner and often the sexual role of the opposite sex. —**transvestic** (1961). O, R, W [4]

transvestite, *n.* (1910) *Med.* [G *Transvestit* < L *trāns* trans- + *vestīre* to dress + G (< L) *-it* -ite] Someone addicted to wearing the clothes of the opposite sex. — **transvestite,** *a.* (1925). O, R, W [4]

transvestitism, *n.* (1919) *Med.* [G *Transvestitismus* < *Transvestit* transvestite (q.v.) + *-ismus* (< L) -ism] Transvestism (q.v.). —**transvestitist** (1936), **transvestitic** (1977). O, R, W [3]

trass, -es *pl.* (1796) *Geol.* Old Du var. **tras** (1793), **tarras** (1793), **terrace** [Du *trass* or G, lit., a mound of earth (< Du *tras* < *terras*) < Fr *terrasse* terrace] Yellow, metamorphosed volcanic ash, esp. found on the lower Rhine and used in hydraulic cement. O, W [4]

trautonium, *n.* (1931) *Music* [G (1930), a short. of the name of Friedrich *Trautwein* (1888–1956), German acoustical engineer & its inventor + *-ium* (< L), as modeled on G *Euphonium*, ult. < Gk] An electronic instrument that can produce notes of any pitch. O [3]

tremulant, *n.* (1862) *Music* [G < It *tremolante* tremulant] A tremolo (stop), a device on an organ that mechanically interrupts the flow of tone periodically and produces a tremulous sound. O, W [3]

treponema, -s/-ta *pl.* (1908) *Biol., Med.* Var. **treponeme** (1908) [G (1905), coined by the German microbiologist Fritz Richard Schaudinn (1871–1906) < Gk *trépein* to turn + *nêma* filament, thread] A genus or an anaerobic

spirochete of this genus, certain species of which are parasitic in and pathogenic for humans and warm-blooded animals, and some of which cause syphilis and yaws. — **treponemal,** *a.* (1913); **-nematosis** (1927); **-nemicidal,** *a.* (1933); **-nematous; -nemiasis; -nemicide.** O, R, W [4]

treppe, *n.* *Med.* [G (< MHG), lit., step, flight of stairs] The graduated sequence of increasingly vigorous contractions resulting when a corresponding sequence of identical stimuli is applied to a rested muscle. W [3]

triacid, *n.* (1896) *Chem.* [Short. of G *Triacidlösung* < *Triacid* (< Gk *tría*, neuter of *treîs* + G *Acid* acid < L *acidus* sharp, sour) + G *Lösung* solution] An acid such as phosphoric or citric acid that has three acid hydrogen atoms. —**triacid,** *a.* (1929); **triacid triglyceride** (1945)/**solution**. O, R, W [4]

trialism, *n.* (1908) *Politics* [G *Trialismus* < *tri-* + *-alismus*, as in *Dualismus* < L *tria* < *trēs* three + *-ismus* -ism] A federation or union of three countries or states (this is different from the "triadism" meaning). O, W [3]

Triassic, *n.* (1841) *Geol.* Var. **Trias** (1841) [G *Trias* < LL < Gk the number three + E *-ic*, so called because it is typically subdivided in Germany into the triad of Bunter Sandstein, Muschelkalk, and Keuper] The series of strata beneath the Jurassic and above the Permian. O, R, W [4]

Triassic, *a.* (1841) *Geol.* [G *triassisch* < *Trias* (see *Triassic,* n.) + adj. suffix *-isch* -ic] Of or belonging to the Triassic period or system of rocks, including the plants, amphibians, etc. that lived in that period. O, R, W [4]

trichalcite, *n.* *Mineral.* [G *Trichalcit* (now *Trichalzit*) < *tri-* + *Chalcit* < Gk *trich-* < *thríx* hair + *chalkós* ore, copper + G *-it* -ite] Tyrolite (q.v.). W [3]

trichite, *n.* (1868) *Geol.* [G *Trichit* (1867) < *trich-* (< Gk < *thríx* hair) + G *-it* -ite] A hairlike crystallite found singly or clustered in some vitreous rocks (this is different from the "zoological" meaning). —**trichitic** (1879). O, R, W [4]

trichoblast, *n.* (1882) *Bot.* [G < *tricho-* + *-blast* < Gk *tricho-*, the comb. form of *thríx* hair + *blastós* bud] Idioblast (q.v.). O, W [3]

trichogen, *n.* (1898) *Entomology* [G < *tricho-* + *-gen* < Gk *tricho-*, the comb. form of *thríx* hair + *genḗs* producing] A hypodermal cell of insects and other arthropods, which produces their chitinous hairs or spinules. —**trichogenic.** O, W [3]

trichome, *n.* (1875) *Bot., Entomology* [G *Trichom* < Gk *tríchōma* growth of hair] A plant's epidermal hair structure; a tuft of bright hair on myrmecophilous insects that attracts ants; one of these insect hairs. —**trichomic.** O, R, W [4]

trichoplax, *n.* (1897) *Zool.* [G (1883), coined by the German zoologist Franz Eilhard Schulze (1840–1921) < *tricho-* < Gk, the comb. form of *thríx* hair + *pláx* plate] A minute marine animal with a completely ciliated discoid body formed of three layers of cells, prob. a larval hydrozoan; (cap.), the genus of this animal. O, W [3]

tridymite, *n.* (1868) *Mineral.* [G *Tridymit* (1866) < Gk *trídymos* threefold + G *-it* -ite, named for its common occurrence in trillings] A silicon dioxide found in trachyte and other igneous rocks. O, R, W [3]

trigonite, *n.* *Mineral.* [G *Trigonit* < *trigon-* (< L *trigonum* triangle) + G -*it* -ite] An acid lead manganese arsenite. W [3]

trimerite, *n.* (1896) *Mineral.* [G *Trimerit* < Gk *trimerés* of three parts + G -*it* -ite] A silicate of beryllium, manganese, and calcium. O, W [3]

Trinkhalle, *n.* (1873) *Med.* Var. **trinkhalle** (1971) [G, lit., dining hall < *trinken* to drink + *Halle* hall, large gathering place] A place at a spa where people secure and drink the medicinal water; a pump room or refreshment stall. O [3]

trinklied, -er *pl. Music* [G < *trinken* to drink + *Lied* song] A drinking song. W [2]

tripeptide, *n.* (1903) *Chem.* [Prob. < G *Tripeptid* < *tri-* (< L) three + G *Peptid* peptide (q.v.)] A peptide that produces three molecules of amino acid by hydrolysis. O, W [3]

triphyline, *see* triphylite

triphylite, *n.* (1836) *Mineral.* Var. **triphyline** (1836) [Ad. of G *Triphylin* < *tri-* three + *Phylin* < L *tri-* + Gk *phylé* tribe, clan + G -*in* -ine/-ite] An orthorhombic phosphate of iron, lithium, and manganese isomorphous with lithiophilite. O, R, W [4]

triplite, *n.* (1850) *Mineral.* [G *Triplit* (1813) < *tripl-* (< Gk *triplóos* threefold) + G -*it* -ite, so named for its threefold cleavage] A phosphate of iron, manganese, calcium, and magnesium. O, R, W [3]

trippkeite, *n.* (1881) *Mineral.* [G *Trippkeit* (1880) < the name of Paul *Trippke* (1851–80), Polish mineralogist + G -*it* -ite] A tetragonal arsenite of copper. O, W [3]

tripton, *n.* (1931) *Biol.* [G (1917) < Gk, neuter of *triptós* that which is rubbed or pounded] The nonliving debris such as humus or organic remains suspended in a body of water. O, W [3]

tritanopia, *n.* (1915) *Optics* [G *Tritanopie* (1911), coined by the German physiologist Johannes von Kries (1853–1928) < *trit-* < the Gk comb. form of *trítos* third + *anopía* blindness, so named because only a third of the colors of the spectrum can be detected by a tritanope] A dichromatic color blindness where the spectrum is seen in tones of green and red, also called *blue-yellow blindness*. —**tritanopic** (1915), **tritanope** (1974). O, R, W [4]

tritomite, *n.* (1856) *Mineral.* [G *Tritomit* (1850) < Gk *trítomos* thrice cut + G -*it* -it, so named because the crystals leave trihedral cavities in the gangue] A complex fluosilicate of thorium, cerium, and other bases. O, W [3]

trivalence, *n.* (1888) *Chem., Biol.* Var. **trivalency** (1888) [Transl. of G *Dreiwertigkeit* into naturalized Latin elements in English < G *drei* (= L *tri-*) three + G -*wertig* (= L *valēns*, gen. *valentis* having the value of) + G nom. suffix -*keit*] The quality or state of being trivalent; a trivalent chromosome group. O, R, W [4]

trivalent, *a.* (1868) *Chem., Biol.* [Transl. of G *dreiwertig*— see *trivalence*] Having a valence of three; triple, as used to describe a group of homologous chromosomes. O, R, W [4]

Trockenbeerenauslese, -n *pl.* (1963) *Beverages* [G < *trocken* dry + *Beeren,* pl. of *Beere* berry + *Auslese* selection] A superior, sweet German white wine, made from selected overripe single grapes. O [2]

troctolite, *n.* (1883) *Geol.* Old var. **troktolite** (1883) [G

Troktolit (1875) < Gk *tróktēs* a sea fish + G -*lit* -lite < Gk *líthos* stone, named for the resemblance to a trout's speckled skin] Gabbro that is composed mainly of labradorite and olivine. O, W [3]

trögerite/troegerite, *n.* (1872) *Mineral.* [G *Trögerit* (1871) < the name of R. *Tröger,* 19th-cent. German mining offical at Schneeberg, Saxony + -*it* -ite] A radioactive, hydrous arsenate of uranium. O, W [3]

troglobiont, *n.* (1924) *Zool.* Var. **troglobion** (1924), **troglobite** (1953) [Ad. of G *Troglobie* (1854) (now also *Troglobiont*) < *troglo-* < Gk *tróglē* hole, cave, cavity + *bión* living] An animal living entirely in the dark areas of caves, esp. in lightless waters. —**troglobi(o)tic** (1971, 1982). O, R, W [3]

troglophil(e), *n.* (1924) *Zool.* [G *Troglophil* (1854) < *troglo-* + -*phil* < Gk *tróglē* hole, cave + *phílos* loving] A cave-dwelling animal that does not live entirely in the dark. (cf. *troglobiont*). O [3]

troilite, *n.* (1868) *Mineral.* [G *Troilit* < the name of Domenico *Troili* (1722–92), Italian natural scientist who discovered it in a meteorite that fell in 1766 + G -*it* -ite] A native ferrous sulfide found in meteorites. O, R, W [3]

troktolite, *see* troctolite

trollflower, *n.* (1578) *Bot.* Old var. **troll flower, troll-flower** (1578, 1879) [Partial transl. of G *Trollblume* < *Troll-,* prob. < archaic *trollen* to roll + *Blume* flower, a name suggested by the flower's round shape] Globeflower, a plant with globose flowers or clusters. O, W [3]

trollop, *n.* (1615) [Prob. ad. of dial. G *Trolle* trollop, prostitute < G *Trulle*] Wench, slattern; woman of loose morals; anything dangling or dragging untidily. —**trollop,** *v.* (1854); **trolloping,** *a.* (1733); **trollopy,** *a.* (1748); **trollopish** (1864). O, R, W [4]

trommel, *n.* (1877) *Mining* [G cylindrical drum < MHG *trumel*] A usu. cylindrical or conical screen mounted on a revolving longitudinal shaft, used to wash and size ores. O, R, W [4]

trondhjemite, *n.* (1922) *Geol.* [G *Trondhjemit* (1916) < *Trondjhem* (now *Trondheim*) the name of a Norwegian seaport + G -*it* -ite] Any leucratic tonalite (q.v.), esp. one where the plagioclase is oligoclase. O, R [3]

tropane, *n.* (1919) *Chem.* [G *Tropan* < a short. of NL *atropa belladonna* deadly nightshade + G -*an* -ane] A bicyclic tertiary amine obtained from various plants and is the parent compound of atropine, cocaine, and related alkaloids. O, W [3]

trophochromatin, *n.* (1909) *Biol.* [Ad. of G *trophochromatisch* (1902) < *tropho-* + *chromatisch* < Gk *trophé* nutrition + the comb. form of *chrôma* color + G -*in* -in] A chromatin that stains intensely with iron hematoxylin but is considered as being concerned with vegetative functions only. O, W [3]

trophogenic, *a.* (1957) *Ecology* Var. **trophogenous** [G *trophogen* (1931) < *tropho-* + -*gen* < Gk *trophé* nutrition + *gennân* to produce + E -*ic*] Of the upper level of a lake, where inorganic matter is photosynthesized to produce oxygen and organic matter (this is different from the earlier "entomology" meaning). O, W [3]

trophoplast, *n.* (1885) *Bot.* [G < *tropho-* + *-plast* < Gk *trophē* nutrition + *plastós* formed] A plant plastid. O, W [3]

tropotaxis, -taxes *pl.* (1934) *Biol.* [G (1919), coined by the German biologist Alfred Kühn (1885–1968) in *Die Orientierung der Tiere im Raum* < *tropo-* + *taxis* < Gk *trópos* direction, turning + *táxis* arrangement, ordering] A taxis in which an animal orients itself and moves in response to the difference in stimulation of two separate end-organs. —**tropotactic(ally)** (1940, 1940). O, W [4]

trub, *n. Beverages* [G precipitation, ad. < *trübe* turbid] In the brewing process, a haze formed and removed during the boiling or cooling of wort. W [3]

trull, *n.* (1519) [G *Trulle* prostitute, prob. related to *Troll* troll—see *trollop*] (Obs.) a girl or lass; a strumpet or prostitute. O, R, W [4]

truth-function, *n.* (1909) *Philos.* [Transl. of G *Wahrheitsfunktion* < *Wahrheit* truth + *Funktion* function < L *fūnctiō*] A sentential or propositional function, the truth-value (q.v.) of which depends totally on the truth-values of its arguments. —**truth-functional(ly)** (1947, 1950), **truth-functionality** (1950). O, R, W [4]

truth table, *n.* (1921) *Philos.* [Transl. of G *Wahrheitstafel* < *Wahrheit* truth + *Tafel* table] A tabular representation as to the truth or falsity of some proposition in terms of the possible truth-values (q.v.) of its elements; a transf. sense in computing. O, R, W [4]

truth-value, *n.* (1903) *Philos., Math* [Transl. of G *Wahrheitswerth* < *Wahrheit* truth + *Werth* (now *Wert*) value, worth] The truth or falsity of a proposition or statement; one of the interpreted or uninterpreted values present in a formula in a many-valued logic. —**truth-value,** *a.* (1966). O, R, W [4]

trypan blue, *n.* (1909) *Med.* [Transl. of G *Trypanblau* < *Trypan* (< NL *Trypanosoma* < Gk *trýpanon* borer + *sôma* body) + G *blau* blue, so named because it is trypanocidal] A diazo dye used as an intravitam stain and in veterinary medicine. O, W [3]

trypan red, *n.* (1905) *Med.* [Transl. of G *Trypanrot* < *Trypan* (< NL *Trypanosoma* < Gk *trýpanon* borer + *sôma* body) + G *rot* red] A drug used in cases of trypanosomiasis. O, W [3]

tryptophan, *n.* (1890) *Biol.* Var. **tryptophane** (1922) [G (1890) < a combining of *Trypsin* trypsin + *-phan,* irreg. < Gk *trýein* to devour, pulverize + *phaínesthai* to appear to be] A crystalline, aromatic amino acid essential in vertebrates' diet; beta-3-indoly-alanine. —**tryptophanase** (1932 < Japanese), **tryptophan synthetase** (1955). O, R, W [4]

tsarina, *see* czarina

tschermigite, *n.* (1868) *Mineral.* [G *Tschermigit* < *Tschermig,* the name of a town in Bohemia + G *-it* -ite] Alum: ammonium double sulfate. O, W [3]

tsumebite, *n.* (1913) *Mineral.* [G *Tsumebit* (1912) < *Tsumeb,* the name of a town in Namibia + G *-it* -ite] A hydrous, basic phosphate of lead and copper found in green monoclinic crystals. O, W [3]

tubocurarine, *n.* (1898) *Pharm.* [G *Tubocurarin* < *tubo-* + *Curarin* < L *tubus* tube + Sp *curare* < Tupi *urari,* actually, whoever gets it, falls or drops + G *-in* -ine] A toxic isoquinoline alkaloid, obtained chiefly from a South American vine, and which is the main active ingredient of curare. O, R, W [3]

Tungan, -ø/-s *pl.* (1875) *Ling., Ethnology* Var. **Dungan** [G *Tunganen/Dunganen* < Jagatai *Döngan,* prob. < *dönmek* to convert] A member of a Mongolized, usu. Muslim, Turkish people in China and Turkestan; these people or their language. O, W [3]

tunker, *see Introduction*

turanose, *n.* (1890) *Chem.* [G *Turanos* or poss. also < Russ *turanoza* (1889) < Per *Tūrān* Turkestan + G *-ose* -ose, a suffix denoting a carbohydrate, so named because it is obtained from a manna found in Turkestan] A crystalline reducing disaccharide sugar; 3-α-glucosyl-fructose. O, W [3]

turbary pig, *n.* (1908) *Zool.* [Transl. of G *Torfschwein* (1862) < *Torf* turf, peat + *Schwein* pig] A prehistoric, domesticated pig first found in turbaries in Swiss neolithic lake-dwellings. • ~ is shortened to **turbary,** a. O [3]

turbary sheep, *n.* (1908) *Zool.* [Transl. of G *Torfschaf* < *Torf* peat, turf + *Schaf* sheep] A small, domesticated, prehistoric sheep first found in turbaries in Swiss neolithic lake-dwellings. O [3]

turn, *v.* (1888) *Sports* [G *turnen* < OHG *turnēn* to turn < L *tornāre* to turn on a lathe] To practice or do gymnastic exercises. O, R, W [3]

turner, *n.* (1853) *Sports* [G one who performs gymnastic exercises < *turnen* to perform gymnastic exercises + *-er* -er] A gymnast: a member of a turnverein (q.v.). • ~ is different from various earlier meanings and appears in compounds like **turnerbund** (1880 *DA*) and **turner club/hall/movement.** O, R, W [4]

turnerfest, *see* turnfest

turnfest, *n.* (1856 *DA*) *Sports* Var. **turnerfest** (1871) [G < *turnen* to perform gymnastic exercises + *Fest* fest (q.v.)] A gymnastic meet. *DA* [3]

turnhalle, *n. Sports* Var. **turnhall** [G < *turnen* to perform gymnastic exercises + *Halle* hall] Gymnasium, a building where gymnasts practice. W [3]

turnverein, *n. and a.* (1852, 1852) *Sports* [G < *turnen* to perform gymnastic exercises + *Verein* association, club] (in the U.S.) (of) an athletic club of gymnasts and athletes, orig. for German immigrants and also expanded to foster citizenship and cultural programs. O, R, W [3]

tusch, *n. Music* [G, prob. < Fr *touche* touch < *toucher* to touch lightly, as in a blast from a band including wind instruments] A fanfare or flourish of brass wind instruments and drums. W [3]

tusche, *n.* (1885) *Printing* Var. **tushe** (1885) [G India ink, back-formation < *tuschen* to ink up < Fr *toucher* to touch lightly] A black liquid composition used in lithography to draw, paint, and etch; lithographic drawing ink. —**tusche,** *a.* (1940); **tuscher.** O, R, W [4]

Twilight of the Gods, *n.* (1768) *Myth.* [Transl. of G *Götterdämmerung* (q.v.) and ON *ragnarökkr*] The Germanic gods' ultimate destruction in a cataclysmic battle with evil, from which a new order will arise. O, R, W [4]

twilight sleep, *n.* (1912) *Med.* [Transl. of G *Dämmerschlaf* (c.1905), coined by the German gynecologist Carl Joseph Gauss (1875–1957) < *Dämmer* dusk, twilight + *Schlaf* sleep] Partial narcosis induced by injection of scopolamine and morphine to dim or efface pain, esp. in childbirth. O, R, W [4]

tyrolite, *n.* (1854) *Mineral.* [Ad. of G *Tirolit* (1845) < *Tirol,* the name of an Austrian Alpine region + G -*it* -ite] A hydrous hydroxide, arsenate, and carbonate of copper and calcium. O, W [3]

tzarina, *see* czarina

U

u¹, *n.* (1930) *Math., Physics* [G, a short. of *ungerade* uneven, odd] A function, esp. a wave function, that changes sign on inversion through the origin, atomic states, etc., represented by this function. O [3]

u², *conj.* [G abbr. of *und*] And. R, W [3]

U, *see* uranium

U-bahn, *n.* (1938) *Transportation* Var. **U-Bahn** (1938) [G subway < *U* (abbr. of *Untergrund* underground) + *Bahn* railroad] The subway in one of various major cities in Germany and Austria. O [3]

über alles (1967) *Politics* [G < *über* above + *alles* everything] Above all else; (prob. from a misunderstanding of the German national anthem, "Deutschland über alles") supreme. O [2]

Überfremdung, *n.* (1965) *Politics* [G < *überfremden* to give (excessive) foreign character to < *über* over + *fremd* foreign + *-ung* -ing] The admitting or presence of too many foreigners as workers. O [2]

überhaupt, *adv.* (1875) [G < Late MHG *überhoubet* (glancing) above the head(s) (of the animals), i.e., without counting (them)] In general; as such; considered as a whole; par excellence. O [2]

Übermensch, -en *pl.* (1902) *Philos.* Var. **Uebermensch** (1902) [G < *über* above, super + *Mensch* human (being)] An ideal superior man, as conceived by Nietzsche. • ~ is transl. as **overman** (1895), **beyondman** (1896), **superman** (1903). O, R [3]

übermenschlich, *a.* (1920) *Philos.* [G < *Übermensch* (q.v.) + *-lich* -like] Having the quality of an Ubermensch; superhuman. O [2]

übermenschlichkeit, *n.* (1931) *Philos.* [G < *übermenschlich* (q.v.) + *-keit* -hood] The quality of a superman; superhumanity. O [2]

U-boat, *n.* (1913) *Mil.* [G *U-Boot* < a short. of *Unterseeboot* undersea boat] A German or Austrian submarine. — **U-boat,** *a.* (1918). O, R, W [4]

Uebermensch, *see* Übermensch

uhlan, *n.* (1753) *Mil.* Var. **ulan** (1753) [G *U(h)lan* lancer < Pol *ulan* < Turk *oglan* lad, servant] A lancer, orig. Tatar, introduced into European armies in Poland and Prussia. —**uhlan,** *a.* (1812); **uhlaner** (1886). O, R, W [4]

ullmannite, *n.* (1868) *Mineral.* [G *Ullmannit* (1850) < the name of Johann Christoph *Ullmann* (1777–1821), German mineralogist + *-it* -ite] A nickel antimonide and sulfide, usu. with some arsenic (this is different from the earlier meaning of "phosphate of manganese and iron"). O, W [3]

umangite, *n.* (1891) *Mineral.* [G *Umangit* (1891) < Sierra de *Umango,* the name of a mountain range in Argentina + G *-it* -ite] Native copper selenide. O, W [3]

umbelliferone, *n.* (1868) *Chem.* [G *Umbelliferon* < NL *umbelliferae,* fem. pl. of *umbellifer* umbelliferous + G *-on* -one] A crystalline phenolic lactone present in many plants; 7-hydroxy-coumarin. O, R, W [3]

Umgangssprache, *n.* (1934) *Ling.* [G colloquial speech < *Umgang* intimate association + *Sprache* language] The vernacular language between standard and dialectal speech customarily used as a means of communication between the two. O [2]

Umklapp (process), *n.* (1937) *Physics* Var. **umklapp process** (1976) [Partial transl. of G *Umklapprozeß* (1919) < *umklappen* to fold up or down, flip, ectropionize + *Prozeß* process] Thermal interactions in a crystal lattice where their total momentum is not conserved, and the momentum of the initial excitations is reversed. • ~ is short. to **U/u process** (1960, 1975). O [3]

umland, *n.* *Geogr.* [G < *um-* around + *Land* land < OHG *lant*] The area adjacent to a town or village that is linked by common cultural and economic activities. W [3]

umlaut, *n.* (1844) *Ling.* [G < *um* denoting "change" + *Laut* sound] A change in a vowel induced by partial assimilation to a succeeding vowel or semivowel; a vowel produced by this; the diacritic indicating this change. — **umlaut,** *v.* (1852 *W9*), *a.* (1873); **umlauted,** *a.* (1852); **umlauting,** *verbal n.* (1943), *a.* (1977); **umlaut vowel** (1879). O, R, W [4]

Umwelt, -en *pl.* (1964) *Philos.* [G surroundings, environment < *um-* around + *Welt* world] The complex of edaphic, climatic, and biotic factors that acts upon an ecological community or organism and ult. determines its form and survival. • ~ was poss. earlier trans. as **environment** (1827, q.v.). O [2]

unberufen, *interj.* (1858) [G a superstitious exclamation meaning "touch wood" < prefix *un-* not + *berufen* called upon] Knock on or touch wood, so as not to lose one's good luck! O [2]

underman, *n.* (1910) *Sociol.* [Transl. of Nietzsche's G *Untermensch* < *unter* under + *Mensch* human being, man] A person with subhuman attributes, the opposite of *Übermensch* (q.v.) (this is different from the very old meaning of "subordinate, inferior person"). O [3]

understanding, *n.* (1809) *Philos.* [Transl. of G *Verstand* < MHG *verstant* < OHG *firstand* < *firstantan* to understand] One's capacity to formulate and use categories and concepts, or to judge and make inferences, as distinguished from reason—in Kantian and German idealism, this is the highest quality of framing general conceptions or of directly apprehending universals (this is different from the various earlier meanings of the word). O, R, W [4]

undine, *n.* (1821) *Myth.* Var. **ondine** (1821) [G (1811) < NL *undina* as found in Paracelsus' *De Nymphis* (1658), of unknown origin, rather than < L *unda* (water) wave + *-ina* (fem. of *-inus*) -ine, as some scholars have assumed; it was popularized in 1811 by the German novelist Friedrich de la Motte-Fouqué (1777–1843) in his short story "Undine"] A water nymph. • ~ was spelled as *undina* in a NL transl. of *De Nymphis* (1658). O, R, W [3]

Unding, *n.* (1932) *Psych.* [G impossibility, absurdity] A vague abstraction or concept lacking any properties. O [2]

und so weiter (1885) Var. **undsoweiter** (1930) [G < *und* and + *so* so + *weiter* (further) on] And so forth, et cetera. O, R [2]

unheimlich, *a.* (c.1877) [G sinister, uneasy, dismal < *un-* not + *heimlich* familiar] Uncanny, weird. O [2]

univalent, *a.* (1898) *Biol.* [G (1890), first used in this sense by the German biologist Oskar Hertwig (1849–1922) < NL *univalens* < *uni-* the comb. form of L *ūnus* one, single + *valens* having the value of] Of a chromosome's lacking a synaptic mate: single (this is different from the earlier "chemical valence" meaning). O, R, W [3]

universal quantifier, *n.* (1936) *Philos.* [Transl. of G *allgemeiner Quantifikator* (1930) < *allgemein* general, universal + *Quantifikator* quantifier < ML *quantificare* to amount to < L *quantus* (see *quantum*) + *facere* to make] A logical quantifier referring to all values of a given variable in a formula. O, R, W [3]

unmutation, *see* rückumlaut

unpleasure, *n.* (1919) *Psych.* [Transl. of G *Unlust* < *un-* un- + *Lust* (< OHG) joy, pleasure] The sense of anxiety or inner pain resulting from one's blocking of the ego's instinctual impulse, as the opposite of the sense resulting from pleasure (this is different from the old meaning of "unpleasantness, lack of pleasure"). O [3]

untergang, *n.* (1938) *Sociol.* [G decline < *untergehen* to go down or decline] An unstoppable decline, esp. one that leads to the destruction of civilization or culture. O [2]

Untermensch, -en *pl.* (1964) *Ethnology, Sociol.* [G < *unter* under, inferior + *Mensch* human being] (With particular reference to the Nazi regime of 1933–45) a racially inferior or subhuman person—see *underman.* O [2]

unteroffizier, *n.* (1917) *Mil.* [G noncommissioned officer < *unter* under + *Offizier* officer < MFr *officier* < ML *officiarius*] A German noncommissioned officer. O [2]

upbeat, *n.* (1869) *Music* [Transl. of G *Auftakt* auftakt (q.v.)] The last, unaccented beat in a musical measure; anacrusis; a fig. sense indicating a positive or optimistic mood or development. O, R, W [4]

U process, *see* Umklapp process

ur-, *prefix* (1864) [G accented prefix *ur-* < MHG < OHG, orig., to begin with] Denoting primitive, earliest, original (this is different from the "urine" and "tail" meanings). O, R [4]

uracil, *n.* (1890) *Biochem.* [G (1885), a combining of *Urin* urea + *Acetsäure* acidic acid + *-il* -ile] A crystalline, heterocyclic compound; 2,4-dihydroxy-pyrimidine; a derivative of this compound. O, R, W [4]

uralite, *n.* (1835) *Mineral.* [G *Uralit* (1831) < the name of the *Ural* Mountains + G *-it* -ite] An amphibole produced by altering pyroxene: hornblende. —**uralitic** (1845); **uralitization** (1888); **uralitized,** *a.* (1909); **uralitize; uralite-porphyry** (1868)/**syenite** (1888). O, R, W [4]

uraninite, *n.* (1879) *Mineral.* [G *Uraninit* < *Uranium* uranium (q.v.) + *-it* -ite] Pitchblende or another mineral altered by radioactive decay; the most important uranium ore. O, R, W [4]

uranism, *n.* (1895) *Med.* [G *Uranismus* < L *Urania,* the love goddess Aphrodite + G (< L) *-ismus* -ism] Homo-sexuality, esp. between physically normal males. —**uranist** (1895). O, W [3]

uranite, *n.* (1794) *Mineral.* [G *Uranit* (1789) < *uran-* (< Gk *Ouranós* Uranus) + G *-it* -ite] A general term for minerals of the autunite and metaautunite groups. —**uranitic** (1796), **uranite group/lime.** O, R [3]

uranium, *n.* (1797) *Chem.* [G (c.1790), as discovered and named by the German chemist Martin Heinrich Klaproth (1743–1817) < L *Uranus* the name of the planet + G *-ium* (< L)] A heavy, radioactive, metallic element that is used in atomic energy and as a source of uranium 235. • ~ is symbolized as U and appears in many composites like **uraniumaire**) (as in *millionaire*) and **uranium lead** (1914). —**uranium,** *a.* (1837). O, R, W [4]

uranocircite, *n.* (1850) *Mineral.* [G *Uranocircit* < *urano-,* the comb. form of L *Uranus* uranium + Gk *kírkos* hawk (transl. of G *Falken* in *Falkenstein,* a city in central Germany + *-it* -ite] A hydrous barium uranium phosphate. O, W [3]

uranophane, *n.* (1868) *Mineral.* [G *Uranophan* < *urano-* + *-phan* < the comb. form of L *Uranus* Uranus + *phaínein* to make visible] A hydrous silicate of uranium and calcium. O, W [3]

uranopilite, *n.* (1868) *Mineral.* [G *Uranopilit* < *urano-* < the comb. form of L *Uranus* Uranus + *pîlos* felt + G *-it* -ite] A hydrous basic sulfate of uranium. O, W [3]

uranosphaerite, *n.* (1868) *Mineral.* Var. **uranospherite** [G *Uranosphaerit* < *urano-* + *sphaer-* < the comb. form of L *Uranus* Uranus + *sphaîra* ball, sphere + G *-it* -ite] A hydrous bismuth uranate. O, W [3]

uranospinite, *n.* (1885) *Mineral.* [G *Uranospinit* < *urano-* < the comb. form of L *Uranus* Uranus + *spínos* siskin, actually, its green feathers + G *-it* -ite, named for its color] A hydrous calcium uranium arsenate in green crystals. O, W [3]

uranotantalite, *n.* (c.1868) *Mineral.* [G *Uranotantalit* < *urano-* + *Tantal* < the comb. form of L *Uranus* Uranus + Gk *Tántalos* Tantalus + G *-it* -ite] Samarskite, a black orthorhombic mineral. O, W [3]

uranothallite, *n.* (c.1868) *Mineral.* [G *Uranothallit* < *urano-* + *thall-* (< the comb. form of L *Uranus* Uranus + *thallós* shoot, stalk) + G *-it* -ite] Liebigite, a hydrous uranium calcium carbonate. O, W [3]

uranothorite, *n.* (c.1868) *Mineral.* [G *Uranothorit* < *urano-* + *Thorit* < the comb. form of L *Uranus* Uranus + G *Thor* Thor + *-it* -ite] A uraniferous variety of the rare mineral thorite. O, W [3]

uranotil(e), *n.* (c.1868) *Mineral.* [G < *urano-* < the comb. form of L *Uranus* Uranus + *tílos* fiber] Uranophane (q.v.). O, W [3]

urazine, *n. Chem.* [G *Urazin* < L *ūrīna,* Gk *oûron* urine + L *acidus* sharp + G *-in* -ine] A crystalline amino derivative of urazole (q.v.): para-urazine. W [3]

urazole, *n. Chem.* [G *Urazol* < L *ūrīna,* Gk *oûron* urine + *ázōos* inert + *-ol* -ole] A crystalline, weakly acidic compound derived from triazole; a derivative of this. W [3]

Urfirnis, -es *pl.* (1912) *Pottery* Var. **urfurnis** (1957) [G < *ur-* ur- (q.v.) + *Firnis* varnish, veneer] A form of early Greek pottery; a lustrous paint found on this. O, W [3]

urgrund, *n. Philos.* [G < *ur-* primal + *Grund* ground, foundation] An ultimate cosmic principle or primal cause. W [3]

Urheimat, *n.* (1934) *Archaeology, Ling.* [G < *ur-* primal + *Heimat* homeland, home] The primeval place of origin of a people or a language. O, R [3]

uridine, *n.* (1911) *Biochem.* [G *Uridin* (1910) < *ur-* < *Uracil* uracil (q.v.) + *-idin* < *Pyramidin* pyramidine] A crystalline nucleoside that, in the form of phosphate derivatives, plays an important role in carbohydrate metabolism; 1-D-ribosyl-uracil. **—uridyllic acid.** O, R, W [4]

urning, *n.* (1883) *Med.* Var. **Urning** (1883) [G (1864), irreg. < L *Urania* the love goddess Aphrodite + G *-ing* -ing] A male homosexual. O, W [3]

urochs, *see* aurochs

urochloralic acid, *n.* (1875) *Biochem.* [Transl. of G *Urochloralsäure* (1875) < *uro-* + *chloral* < *uro-*, the comb. form of Gk *oûron* urine + *chlōrós* yellow green + G *-al-* < *Alkohol* (< Ar) alcohol + G *Säure* acid] A crystalline glycoside formed in the urine after chloral hydrate has been administered. O, W [3]

uroglaucin, *n.* (1846) *Chem.* Var. **uroglaucine** (1863) [G < *uro-*, the comb. form of Gk *oûron* urine + *glaukós* green blue + G *-in* -in] A blue pigment found in humans' urine during certain diseases such as scarlet fever. O [3]

uroporphyrin, *n.* (1915) *Biochem.* [Ad. of G *Urinporphyrin* (1915) < *Urin* urine (< L *ūrīna* < Gk *oûron* urine) + G *Porphyrin* porphyrin (q.v.)] One of four isomeric porphyrins closely related to the coproporphyrins. O, W [3]

uroporphyrinogen, *n.* (1924) *Biochem.* [G (1924) < *uro-* (< the comb. form of Gk *oûron* urine) + G *Porphyrinogon* porphyrinogen (q.v.)] A porphyrinogen where the pyrrole rings have side chains as in a uroporphyrin (q.v.). O [3]

urostealith, *n.* (1846) *Chem.* [G *Urostealit* (1845) (now *Urostealith*) < *uro-* + *Stealit* < *uro-*, the comb. form of Gk *oûron* urine + *stéar* fat + *líthos* stone] A peculiar fatty substance occurring in some urinary calculi. **—urostealith,** *a.* (1872); **urostealite** (1854). O [3]

urotropine, *n.* (1895) *Med.* Old var. **urotropin** (1895) [G *Urotropin* (1895) < *uro-* (the comb. form of Gk *oûron* urine) + G *-tropin* < *Atropin* atropine (q.v.)] Hexamethylenetetramine, a crystalline, weak base made from ammonia. O, W [3]

uroxanthine, *n.* (1846) *Chem.* Var. **uroxanthine** (1858) [G < *uro-* (< the comb. form of Gk *oûron* urine) + G *Xanthin* xanthine] Indican, a plant glucoside. O [3]

urrhodin, *n.* (1846) *Chem.* Var. **urrhodine** (1863) [G *Urorhodin* < *ur-* + *Rhodin* < Gk *uro-*, a comb. form of Gk *oûron* urine + *rhódon* rose + G *-in* -in] A red granular matter or pigment found in the urine during certain diseases. **—urrhodinic** (1886). O [3]

Urschleim, *n.* (1921) *Biol.* [G < *ur-* (q.v.) + *Schleim* mud, slime] (Early biologists' concept of) the original form of life; protoplasm. O [2]

Ursprache, -en *pl.* (1908) *Ling.* Var. **ursprache** (1922) [G < *ur-* ur- (q.v.) + *Sprache* speech, language] A parent language; a protolanguage reconstructed from the evidence of later languages. O, R, W [3]

Urtext, *n.* (1932) *Ling.* Var. **urtext** (1959) [G < *ur-* (q.v.) + *Text* text < ML *textus*] An original text; a text's earliest version. **—urtext,** *a.* (1963). O, R [4]

user-friendly, *a.* (1977) *Tech.* [Transl. of G *benutzerfreundlich* < *Benutzer* user < *benutzen* to use, make use of + *freundlich* friendly] Having the quality for ease of use by anyone, esp. said of computers. **—user-friendliness** (1982). O, R [4]

usw [G abbr. of *und so weiter* and so forth] And so forth. R, W [3]

uvarovite, *n.* (1837) *Mineral.* Var. **uwarowite** (1855), **ouvarovite** [Ad. of G *Uvarowit* (1832) < the name of Count Sergei Semeonovich *Uvarov* (1786–1855), president of the St. Petersburg Academy + G *-it* -ite] Calcium-chromium garnet. O, R [4]

V

V-1, *see at* V-one
V-2, *see at* V-two

vagile, *n.* (c.1890 *W9*) *Biol.* [Prob. < G *vagil* < L *vagus* wandering, straying + G -*il* -ile] Of an organism's or group of organisms' capacity to move about or be dispersed in a given environment. —**vagility** (1937). O, R, W [4]

valence, *n.* (1869) *Chem.* Var. **valency** (1869) [G *Valenz* (1868) < *Quantivalenz* (1865) < *quanti-* + *Valenz* < L *quanti-*, the comb. form of *quantum* how much + *valens* (gen. *valentis*) having the value of] The degree of chemical combining power of an element or radical; a unit of this power. O, R, W [4]

valence electron, *n.* (1908) *Physics* Var. **valency electron** (1908) [G *Valenzelektron* (1908) < *Valenz* valence (q.v.) + *Elektron* electron] Any of the electrons in an atom's outer incomplete shell, which are responsible for the atom's chemical properties. O, R, W [3]

valentinite, *n.* (1860) *Mineral.* [G *Valentinit* (1845) < the controversial name of Basil *Valentine* (prob. a pseudonym for Johannes Thölde), 16th-cent. German alchemist and physician + -*it* -ite] White antimony. O, R, W [3]

Valhalla, *n.* (1768) *Myth.* Var. **Walhalla** (1851) [G *Walhalla* < ON *valholl* gathering place or residence of the slain in battle, slaughter (or directly < ON)] In Norse mythology, Odin's hall where warriors who have died in battle are received, as popularized in Richard Wagner's Ring cycle; a special place or sphere for honoring notable persons: shrine. O, R, W [4]

valine, *n.* (1907) *Biochem.* [G *Valin* (1906), a short. of *Valerinsäure* < NL *Valeriana* valerian + G -*in* -ine + *Säure* acid] A crystalline amino acid that is essential in vertebrates' diet and is a general constituent of proteins, used as a nutrient in medicine and culture media. O, R, W [3]

valinomycin, *n.* (1955) *Pharm.* [G (1955), a blending of *valino-*, the comb. form of *Valin* valine (q.v.) + *Mycin* < Gk *mýkes* fungus + G -*in* -in] A dodecapeptide produced in the fungus *Streptomyces fulvissimus* that has antibiotic powers against some bacteria. O, R [3]

Valkyrie, *n.* (1768) *Myth.* Var. **Valkyr** (1841), **Walkyrie** [Ad. of G *Walküre* and ON *valkyrja*, with the G also < ON] Any of twelve warrior maidens of the Norse god Odin who choose and take to Valhalla (q.v.) the worthy heroes on the battlefield. —**Valkyrian,** *a.* (1847). O, R, W [4]

value-added tax, *n.* (1935) *Econ.* Var. **added-value tax** [Transl. of G *Mehrwertsteuer* < *mehr* more, i.e., added + *Wert* value + *Steuer* tax] A tax added to the value of an article or its constituent material at each stage during its production or distribution. O, R [4]

value judgment, *n.* (1892) *Lit., Philos.* Brit. var. **value judgement** [Transl. of G *Werturteil* < *Wert* value + *Urteil* judgment] A judgment as to the merit or demerit of a given subject, generalization, or thing. O, R, W [4]

valuta, *pl.* **valutas/valute(n)** (1893) *Econ.* [G < It (or directly < It) < LL *valūta* < L *valēre* to be worth] The agreed-on (exchange) value of a currency in terms of some other currency; foreign exchange in a usable or available form. O, R, W [3]

vanadinite, *n.* (1855) *Mineral.* [G *Vanadinit* < *Vanadin* vanadium (ult. < ON *Vanadis* the Scandinavian goddess Freya) + G -*it* -ite] A lead vanadate and chloride of the apatite group. O, R, W [4]

vanadite, *n.* (1835) *Chem.* [G *Vanadit* < *Vanadin* (see *vanadinite*) + -*it* -ite] Hypovanadate, an oxide of vanadium. O, W [3]

vanthoffite, *n.* (1902) *Mineral.* [G *Vanthoffit* (1902) < the name of Jacobus Hendricus *van't Hoff* (1852–1911), Dutch chemist + G -*it* -ite] A sulfate of sodium and magnesium. O, W [3]

vaporimeter, *n.* (1878) *Chem.* [G < *vapori-*, the comb. form of L *vapor* steam + G *Meter* meter < L *metrum* < Gk *métron*] An instrument that measures the volume or pressure of vapor, especially the one used in alcoholometry. O, R, W [4]

Variscan, *a.* (1906) *Geol.* [Ad. of G *variscisch* < ML *Variscia*, ancient name of the Vogtland district, Saxony, Germany + G adj. suffix -*isch* -an] Of, relating to, or specifying a mountain system that once extended from southern Ireland and Britain through central France and Germany into Poland, or the orogeny that formed it during the late Paleozoic division. O [3]

variscite, *n.* (1850) *Mineral.* [G *Variscit* (1837) (now *Variszit*) < ML *Variscia*, ancient name of the Vogtland district, Saxony, Germany + G -*it* -ite] A hydrated aluminum phosphate that is sometimes substituted for or confused with turquoise; also called *utahlite*. O, R, W [3]

Varroa, *n.* (1974) *Entomology* Var. **varroa** (1979) [G (1904) < the name of Marcus Terentius *Varro* (B.C. 116–27), Roman scholar] A small mite, *Varroa jacobsoni*, which is a fatal parasite of the honeybee in East Asia and has spread widely in modern times; varroa infection of bee colonies. O [3]

Vaseline, *n.* (1874) *Pharm.* Var. **vaseline** (1874) [G *Vaselin* (1872), orig. a trademark used for petrolatum, irreg. < *Wasser* water + Gk *élaion* oil + G -*in* -ine] A trademark for petrolatum, a greasy substance used as an ointment or lubricant; its greenish-yellow color as used in manufacturing glass; glass of this color. —**vaseline,** *v.* (1891); **vaselining,** *verbal n.* (1921); **vaselined,** *a.* (1942). O, R, W [4]

vashegyite, *n.* *Mineral.* [G *Vashegyit* (1823) < *Vashegy*, the name of a village in the former Czechoslovakia + G -*it* -ite] A hydrated basic aluminum phosphate. W [3]

vaterite, *n.* (1913) *Mineral.* [G *Vaterit* (1911) < the name of Heinrich *Vater* (1859–1930), German chemist and mineralogist + -*it* -ite] A relatively unstable form of calcium carbonate. O, W [3]

Vaterland, *n.* (1852) *Politics* [G < *Vater* father + *Land* land] A German's fatherland. • ~ is transl. as (the) **Fatherland** (q.v.). O [3]

Vater's ampulla, *see* ampulla of Vater

väyrynenite, *n.* (1954) *Mineral.* [G *Väyrynenit* (1954) < the name of Heikki Allan *Väyrynen* (1888–1956), Finnish geologist + G -*it* -ite] A phosphate and fluoride of beryllium and manganese. O [3]

V-bomb, *n.* (1944) *Mil.* Var. **V-weapon** (1944) [Short. and loose transl. of G *Vergeltungswaffe* (see *V-1, V-2*) or expansion of G *V,* an abbr. of this German compound] Any German V-1, V-2, or similar weapon. O, W [4]

Vehme, *see* Fehme

Vehmgericht, -e *pl.* (1829) *Politics* Var. **Vehme-gericht** (1829), **Fehmgericht** (1879) [G, lit., secret court < *Vehme* + *Gericht* court, tribunal] A powerful secret tribunal in Westphalia, Germany, in the twelfth to the 16th century; transf. to other sources of unfair judgments. —**Vehmic** (1829), **Vehmist** (1841). O, R [4]

velocity potential, *n.* (1867) *Math.* [Transl. of G *Geschwindigkeitspotential* (1858) < *Geschwindigkeit* speed, velocity + *Potential* potential < LL *potentiālis*] A scalar function of position where the negative gradient equals the velocity when there is irrotational flow of a fluid. O, W [3]

velt-marshal, *n.* (1709) Old var. **veldt-marshal** (1774), **velt-mareschal** (1819) *Mil.* [Ad. of G *Feld-Marschall* (as influenced by obs. Du *velt* field) < G *Feld* field + *Marschall* marshal] Field marshal (cap. when a part of one's title). O, W [2]

veneer, *n.* (1702) *Furniture* Old var. like **venear** (1702) [Transl. of G *Furnier* a thin layer of higher quality on top of a base of inferior quality < *furnieren* < Fr *fournir* to furnish, supply with] A thin sheet of wood taken from a log and adapted to adhere to a smooth surface; material for veneering; something resembling or functioning like a wood veneer, as in a superficial covering; an outward show or appearance; a dental crown. —**veneer,** *a.* (1845); **veneerer.** • ~ appears terminally in various compounds like **veneer crown** (1927)/**graft/moth/pitch.** O, R, W [4]

veneer, *v.* (1728) *Furniture* [Transl. of G *furnieren* to supply with a veneer < Fr *fournir*] To overlay or plate a poorer material with a thin layer of finer wood for finish or decoration; to glue together, as in making plywood; to give an attractive surface, esp. to conceal a defect or superficiality. —**veneered,** *a.* (1766). O, R, W [4]

veneering, *n.* (1706) *Furniture* Var. **faneering** (1670), **fineeringe** (common in the 18th cent.) [Transl. of G *Furni(e)rung* or *Fourni(e)rung* (see *veneer,* n.)] Veneer; a veneered surface; the process of applying veneer. —**veneering,** *a.* (1846). O, R, W [4]

ventil, *n.* (1876) *Music* [G, prob. < Fr *ventelle* small valve, sluice < MFr *ventaille* < ML *ventile*] A valve in various wind instruments such as an organ. —**ventil,** *a.* (1876). O, W [3]

ventral canal cell, *n. Bot.* [Transl. of G *Bauchkanalzelle* < *Bauchkanal* ventral canal (< *Bauch* stomach + *Kanal* canal < L *canālis*) + *Zelle* cell < L *cella*] One of a primitive plant's cells of the axial row resulting from the

division of an archegonium's central cell, just below the neck. W [3]

Venusberg, *n.* (1855) *Myth.* [G < *Venus* (< L) the name of the Roman goddess of love + G *Berg* mountain] Venus's court in German legend and esp. in Wagner's *Tristan,* situated in caverns in the Hörselberg mountain; any environment in which sexual pleasure is the primary characteristic. —**Venusbergian,** *a.* (1896). O, R [4]

verboten, *a.* (1912) [G forbidden] Strictly forbidden; not allowed. —**verboten,** *n.* O, R, W [4]

Verein/verein, -e/-s *pl.* (1853 DA) *Sociol.* [G association; society < *vereinen* to unite] A usu. political or social union or organization. • ~ appears in **turnverein** (q.v.). R, W [2]

Verfremdung, *n.* (1945) *Lit., Sociol.* [G alienation < *verfremden* to estrange] Alienation; estrangement; distancing. O [2]

Verfremdungseffekt, *n.* (1951) *Lit.* [G < *Verfremdung* (q.v.) + *Effekt* effect < L *effectus*] Alienation effect, esp. Bertolt Brecht's dramatic technique of estrangement. O [2]

vergence, *n.* (1960) *Geol.* [G *Vergenz* (1930) < L *vergere* to verge toward, incline] The direction in which a fold is overturned or inclined (this is different from the "optical" meaning). O [3]

Vernunft, *n. Philos.* Var. **vernunft** [G (< OHG) understanding put to conscious use] Reason (q.v.), as opposed to verstand (q.v.), or understanding. • ~ is transl. as **reason** (1809). W [3]

Veronal, *n.* (1903) *Chem.* Var. **veronal** [G, poss. < L *Verona,* the name of a city in Italy + G -*al* -al] Diethylmalonyl-urea, a substance used in medicine; a U.S. trademark for barbital. —**veronal,** *a.* (1904). O, W [3]

Versöhnung, *n.* (1867) [G reconciliation] A reconciliation of opposites. O [2]

verst, *n.* (1555) [Fr *verste* and G *Werst* < Russ *verstá* line, measure of length] This unit of length. O, R, W [4]

verstand, *n. Philos.* [G the ability to perceive and evaluate] Understanding (q.v.), as distinguished from Vernunft (q.v.). W [3]

Verstandsmensch, -en *pl.* (1879) [G < *Verstand* understanding + *Mensch* human being] A realist; a matter-of-fact person. O [2]

Verstehen[1], *n.* (1934) *Sociol.* [G the process of comprehending individual as well as interrelated acts and purposes] The employing of empathy to apprehend human acts and behavior so as to interpret historical and sociological developments. O [2]

Verstehen[2], *n. Philos.* Var. **verstehen** [G the intuitive comprehension of cultural history etc.] An intuitive method or theory of interpreting human culture, esp. through the understanding of symbolic relationships. W [3]

verstehende, *a.* (1933) *Sociol.* [G, the infl. present part. of *verstehen* (see *Verstehen*[1])] Using Verstehen. O [2]

vesuvian, *n.* (1796) *Mineral.* [G *Vesuv* (1795) < *Vesuv* the name of the Italian volcano Vesuvius + -*ian* < L *Vēsūvius* + -*ianus* -ian] Idocrase, a complex silicate found orig. in ancient Vesuvian lavas. —**vesuvianite** (1888). O, W [3]

vesuvin, *n.* (1885) *Chem.* [G < *Vesuv* + -*in* -in—see vesuvian] Bismarck brown (q.v.). O, W [3]

veszelyite, *n.* (1875) *Mineral.* [G *Veszelyit* (1874) < the name of A. *Viszely,* a 19th-cent. Hungarian mining engineer + G -*it* -ite] A hydrated basic copper and zinc phosphate. O, W [3]

vicariance, *see* vicariism

vicariant, *n.* (1952) *Ecology* [G *Vikariant* (1836) < L *vicārius* substituting] One of a group of plants or animals that have evolved out of effective contact with each other from an ancestral stock in common, esp. in similar but separated habitats. O [3]

vicariant, *a.* (1952) *Ecology* [Transl. of archaic G *vikarirend* (1836) (now *vikariierend*) < L *vicārius* substituting + G -*end*] Of or being varieties, species, communities, etc. that have evolved as a vicariant (q.v.). O [3]

vicariism, *n.* (1939) *Ecology* Var. **vicarism** (1939), **vicariance** (1957) [G *Vikarismus* or *Vikarianz* < L *vicārius* substituting + G -*ianz* or -*ismus* < L] The existence of vicariant forms; the differentiation or subdivision of a population as explained by geographical barriers and climate. O [3]

Vienna circle, *n.* (1934) *Philos.* [Transl. of G *Wiener Kreis* (1922) < *Wiener* of Vienna + *Kreis* circle] A group of empirical philosophers, mathematicians, and scientists active in Vienna from the 1920s to 1938 who mainly studied methods of verifying statements, the formalizing of language, and the unification of science, while eliminating metaphysics: logical positivism. O [3]

violan(e), *n.* (1850) *Mineral.* [G *Violan* (1838) < L *viola* violet + G -*an* -an(e)] A fine blue or violet diopside. O, W [3]

violaxanthin, *n.* (1931) *Biochem.* [G (1931) < L *viola* violet + G *Xanthin* xanthin < Gk *xanthós* yellow + G -*in* -in] A crystalline carotenoid pigment obtained from daffodils, yellow pansies, and other plants. O, W [3]

virial, *n.* (1870) *Physics* [G < L *vires* (pl.) strength, power + G -*ial* -ial] Half the product of the stress caused by the repulsion or attraction between two particles in space multiplied by the distance between them, or (for more than two particles) half the sum of such products taken for the whole system. —**virial,** *a.* (1965). O, R, W [3]

virial coefficient, *n.* (1902) *Physics* [G (1901) (now *Virialkoeffizient*) < *virial* (q.v.) + *Coefficient* (< NL) coefficient] For an ideal gas or similar collection of particles, each of the (temperature-dependent) coefficients of inverse powers of V in a polynomial series as used to estimate the quantity pV/RT. O [3]

visual purple, *n.* (1877) *Med.* [Transl. of G *Sehpurpur* (1877), evidently first used by the German physiologist Wilhelm Kühne (1837–1900) < *sehen* to see + *Purpur* purple] Rhodopsin, a red, photosensitive pigment found in the retinas of certain fishes and most higher vertebrates. O, R, W [4]

vitamin, *n.* (1912) *Biol.* Var. **vitamine** (1912) [Prob. < G, a blend of L *vīta* life + G *Amin* amine, as coined by the Polish-American biochemist Casimir Funk (1884–1967), who thought that vitamins were amines] One of various organic substances held to be essential to nutrition; fig. use, as in literary vitamins. —**vitamin,** *a.* (1921). • ~ appears in a large variety of compounds, esp. in names like **vitamin C** (1919)/**A** (1920) etc., and in derivatives like **vitaminless** (1914); -**ic** (1926); -**izing,** *a.* (1930); -**ized,** *a.* (1940); -**ization** (1942); -**ize** (1944); -**ology.** O, R, W [4]

vitamin D₂, *n.* (1932) *Pharm.* [G (1931) < *Vitamin* vitamin (q.v.) + D_2] A crystalline unsaturated alcohol, usu. made by irradiating ergosterol, which is added to dairy products to supplement diets; also called *calciferol* or *ergocalciferol.* O, R, W [4]

vitamin D₃, *n.* (1936) *Pharm.* [G (1936) < *Vitamin* vitamin (q.v.) + D_3] The predominant form of Vitamin D in most fish-liver oils and esp. added to poultry feeds; also called *cholecalciferol.* O, R, W [4]

vitamin H, *n.* (1937) *Pharm.* [G (1931) < *Vitamin* vitamin (q.v.) + *H,* abbr. of *Haut* skin] Biotin, a growth vitamin of the vitamin B complex. O, R, W [4]

vitamin S-66, *n.* (1912) *Pharm.* [Prob. < G *Vitamin* vitamin (q.v.) + *S-66*] An organic substance used for nutrition. O [3]

vitrophyre, *n.* (1882) *Geol.* [G *Vitrophyr* < *vitro-* + -*phyr* < L *vitro,* the comb. form of *vitrum* glass + Gk *pórphyros* purple] Porphyritic glassy rock. —**vitrophyric** (1890). O, W [3]

vivianite, *n.* (1823) *Mineral.* [G *Vivianit* (1817) < the name of John Henry *Vivian* (1785–1855), English mineralogist + G -*it* -ite] Blue iron ore, a hydrous ferrous phosphate. —**vivianitized,** *part. a.* (1870). O, R, W [3]

vogesite, *n.* (1891) *Geol.* [G *Vogesit* (1887) < *Vogesen,* the German name for the *Vosges* mountain range in northeast France + G -*it* -ite] A lamprophyre mainly consisting of hornblende or augite phenocrysts. O [3]

voglite, *n. Mineral.* [G *Voglit* < the name of Josef Florian *Vogl,* 19th-cent. Austrian mineralogist + G -*it* -ite] A green hydrous carbonate of uranium, copper, and calcium. W [3]

vogt, *n.* (1762) *Theol.* Old var. **vooght** (< Du, 1694), **vaught** (1694) [G steward (or Du *voogd, voogt*) < MHG *voget,* OHG *fogat* < ML *vocātus* < L *advocātus* attorney] Bailiff, steward, or similar official. O [2]

Volk, (Das), *n.* (1933) *Politics* [G < *das* the + *Volk* people] The German people, esp. according to the ideology of Nazi National Socialism. • ~ has old homonyms in English borrowed from Du or Afrik *volk* Afrikaner people or an Afrikaner's colored employees, as well as similarly borrowed derivatives like *volkspele* Afrikaner folk dances. O [2]

Völkerwanderung, -en *pl.* (1855) Var. **Volkswanderung** (1855) *Politics* [G < *Völker,* pl. of *Volk* people + *Wanderung* migration, as transl. < L *migrātiō gentium*] The migration of whole nations, esp. that of the Germanic peoples, Huns, and Slavs in Europe from the 2nd century A.D. to about the 11th century, culminating in the Norsemen's settling in France and England. —**Völkerwanderung,** *a.* (1961). O, W [3]

völkisch, *a.* (1939) *Politics* [G pertaining to the people < *Volk* people + adj. suffix -*isch* -ic] Populist, nationalist, or racist, esp. in the Nazi ideology. O [2]

volkonskoite, *n.* (1844) *Mineral.* Old var. **wolchonskoite** (1844) [G *Wolchonskoit* (1831) < the name of Prince *Wolchonskoy,* a minister at the imperial court in St. Petersburg, Russia, around 1830 + G -*it* -ite] An amorphous clay mineral of the smectite group, where there is some substitution by chromium. O [3]

volksdeutsch, *a.* (1937) *Politics* [G of the German people, concerning an ethnic German living outside of Germany < *volks-,* the comb. form of *Volk* people + *deutsch*

German] Concerning an ethnic German, used with or without regard for the proper German inflections, as in "a Volksdeutsche woman, the old Volksdeutsch grannie." O [3]

Volksdeutscher, -deutsche *pl.* (1961) *Politics* [G (*ein*) *Volksdeutscher,* pl. *Volksdeutsche* (see *volksdeutsch*) + *-er* -er] An ethnic German who was living outside Germany, was repatriated by the Nazis, and then was expelled into West Germany after World War Two. O, R, W [3]

Volksgeist, *n.* (1936) *Sociol.* [G < the gen. of *Volk* people + *Geist* spirit] The spirit or genius characterizing the thought or feeling of a people or nation. O [2]

Volkskammer, *n.* (1949) *Politics* [G < the gen. of *Volk* people + *Kammer* chamber, parliament] The parliament of the German Democratic Republic, preceding reunification in 1990. O [2]

Volkslied, -er *pl.* (1858) *Lit.* Var. **volkslied** (1977) [G < *Volks-,* the gen. of *Volk* folk, people + *Lied* song] (A German) folksong. • ~ has a homonym borrowed from Dutch with approximately the same meaning. O, R, W [4]

Volksoper, *n.* (1928) *Music* [G < the gen. of *Volk* people, folk + *Oper* opera < L *opera*] The light opera house in Vienna. O [2]

Volkspolizei, *n.* (1964) *Politics* [G < the gen. of *Volk* folk, people + *Polizei* police < LL *polītīa* < L < Gk *politeía*] A police force of the German Democratic Republic. O [3]

Volkspolizist, *n.* (1974) *Politics* [G < the gen. of *Volk* folk, people + *Polizist* policemen (see *Volkspolizei*) + *-ist*] A member of the police force of the German Democratic Republic until German reunification in 1990. O [3]

Volkssturm, *n.* (1944) *Mil.* [G < the gen. of *Volk* people + *Sturm* storm, attack] A territorial army conscripted by the Nazis late in World War Two composed of men and boys unfit for regular military service. —**Volkssturm,** *a.* (1969). O, R [2]

Volkswagen, *see* VW

Volkswanderung, *see* Völkerwanderung

voltzite, *n.* (1835) *Mineral.* Old var. **voltzine** (1836) [G *Voltzit* (1833) < the name of Phillipe L. *Voltzit* (d. 1840), French mining engineer + G *-it* -ite] A native zinc oxysulfide. O, W [3]

voluntarianism, *n.* (1896) *Philos.* [G *Voluntarismus* (1883), coined by the German sociologist Ferdinand Tönnies (1855–1936) in *Zur Entwicklungsgeschichte Spinozas* but popularized by Wilhelm Wundt < L *voluntārius* + G *ismus* (< L) -ism] A theory that conceives the will (rather than the intellect) to be the dominating factor in an individual or in the constitution of the world (this is different from the earlier "voluntaryism" meaning and the later U.S. "labor union" one). O, R, W [3]

volutin, *n.* (1908) *Biochem.* Var. **volutine** (1908) [G (1903) < *volut-* (< NL *volutans* a specific epithet of the bacterium *Spirillum volutans* < L *volūtāns* < *volūtāre* to roll) + G *-in* -in] A basophilic compound, which is prob. a nucleic acid compound, occurring widely as granules in microorganisms' cytoplasm or vacuoles. O, R, W [3]

von, *prep.* [G from, now also a predicate of nobility] From, as used in names like *Paul von Hindenburg* to indicate place of origin or to denote noble rank. R [3]

V-1, *n.* (1944) *Mil.* Var. **V-one** [G, symbolizing *V-Eins,* a short. of *Vergeltungswaffe-Eins* < *Vergeltung* reprisal + *Waffe* weapon + *Eins* one] Robot bomb: a German missile used in World War II. O, R, W [4]

Vorlage/vorlage, -s/-ø *pl.* (c.1936 *W9*) *Sports* [G < (*sich*) *vorlegen* to lean forward] A skiing position in which one leans forward from the ankles but usu. not lifting the heels from the skis; skiing trousers. O, R, W [4]

vorlage, *n.* (1965) *Printing* [G model, prototype] The original book or manuscript from which one or more copies are made. O [3]

vorlaufer, *n.* (1961) *Sports* [G < *vor* before, ahead + *Läufer* runner] A skier who travels a course before a race so as to set the standard by which the competitors are to be marked. • ~ is transl. as **forerunner** (1949). O [3]

vorspiel, -e/-s *pl.* (1876) *Music* Var. **Vorspiel** (1876) [G < *vor* before, preceding + *Spiel* play] A prelude or overture. O, R, W [3]

Vorstellung, -en *pl.* (1807–8) *Phil., Psych.* [G idea, concept, mental image] An idea, image, mental picture; the ability to think in mental pictures. O, R [3]

vortex street, *see* street

Vöslauer, *n.* (1920) *Beverages* Var. **Voslauer** (1960) [G < the name of Bad *Vöslau,* a town in Austria + *-er* -er] An Austrian white or red table wine from Vöslau in the Vienna Woods. O [2]

vrbaite, *n.* (1913) *Mineral.* [G *Vrbait* (and poss. also < Czech) < the name of Karel *Vrba* (1845–1922), Bohemian mineralogist + G *-it* -ite] A sulfide of thallium, arsenic, and antimony. O, W [3]

V-2, *n.* (1944) *Mil.* Var. **V-two** [G, symbolizing *V-Zwei,* a short. of *Vergeltungswaffe-Zwei* < *Vergeltung* revenge, reprisal + *Waffe* weapon + *Zwei* two] A German rocket-propelled bomb used as a missile in World War Two, a later model than V-1 (q.v.). O, R, W [4]

VW, *n.* (1958) *Transportation* Var. **Volkswagen** (1958) [Short. of G *Volkswagen* < the gen. of *Volk* people + *Wagen* car] The brand name of a type of small German car intended for popular use. O [4]

V-weapon, *see* V-bomb

W

wacke, *n.* (1803) *Geol.* Old var. like **wacca** (1803) [G < MHG *wacke* < OHG *waggo* large stone] Graywacke (q.v.), a silty or clayey sandstone. O, R, W [4]

Waffen SS, *n.* (1943) *Mil.* [G an armed unit of the SS < *Waffen* weapons + *SS*, a short. of *Schutzstaffel* (q.v.)] In Nazi Germany during World War Two, a combat unit of the SS. O, R [3]

waggle dance, *n.* (1950) *Zool.* Var. **wagging dance** (1950) [Transl. of G *Schwänzeltanz* (1923) < *schwänzeln* to wag the tail < *Schwanz* tail + *Tanz* dance] A movement performed by honeybees at their nest or hive, believed to signal the location of food to other bees. O, R [3]

wagnerite, *n.* (1825) *Mineral.* [G *Wagnerit* (1821) < the name of Franz Michael von *Wagner* (1768–1851), German mining official + *-it* -ite] A magnesium fluorophosphate. O, W [3]

Walden inversion, *n.* (1911) *Chem.* Old short. var. **inversion** (1864–72) [Transl. of G *Waldensche Umkehrung* (1906) < the name of Paul *Walden* (1863–1957), Latvian chemist + G *Umkehrung* turning around, inversion] Orig., the reversed direction of optical rotation, but now an inversion of configuration of an optically active compound into another one, which sometimes results in changing the direction of optical rotation. O, W [3]

Waldflute, *n.* (1852) *Music* Var. **Waldflöte** (1876) *Music* [Partial transl. of G *Waldflöte* < *Wald* woods, forest + *Flöte* flute < MFr *flahute* < OProv *flaut*] A soft pipe-organ flute stop, now of 8-foot and 4-foot pitch. O, W [3]

waldglas, *n. Industry* [G < *Wald* forest + *Glas* glass, so called because it was made by glassmakers in the forests of Bohemia and the Fichtelgebirge] Common medieval and Renaissance green glassware. R [3]

waldgrave, *n. Admin.* [Ad. of G *Waldgraf* < *Wald* forest + *Graf* count] In medieval Germany, an officer who had jurisdiction over a royal forest, and in the Rhine districts a hereditary title among the higher nobility: a kind of count. O, R [3]

waldgravine, *n. Admin.* [G, fem. of *Waldgraf* waldgrave (q.v.)] A waldgrave's wife. O [3]

waldhorn, *n.* (1852) *Music* [G < *Wald* woods, forest + *Horn* (< OHG) horn] The old, valveless French horn, for which Beethoven wrote; a pipe-organ reed stop with a tone resembling that of a natural horn. O, W [3]

waldmeister, *n. Bot.* [G < *Wald* woods, forest + *Meister* master or officer, perhaps so named because of its "masterful" healing power] Sweet woodruff, a scented herb. W [3]

waldrapp, *n.* (1924) *Ornith.* [G < *Wald* forest + *Rappe* (black) raven, so named because of its scintillatingly black feathers] A hermit ibis, *Geronticus eremita*, found in parts of the African Maghreb and the Middle East. O [3]

Walhalla, *see* Valhalla

Walkyrie, *see* Valkyrie

wallpecker, *n.* (1990) [Short. and transl. of G *Mauerspecht*

wall woodpecker] Any private individual who chipped off pieces of the Berlin Wall when it was being officially demolished in 1989–90. L2 [3]

Walpurgis Night, *n.* (1822) *Myth.* Var. **Walpurgisnacht** (1822), **walpurgis night** (1823) [Partial transl. of G *Walpurgisnacht* < *Walpurgis,* the name of the Catholic saint Walburga + *Nacht* night] Witches' sabbath or the Eve of St. Walburga, when, according to German belief as late as the Renaissance, witches and spirits exercise their powers; transf. sense to something with an orgiastic or nightmarish quality. O, R, W [4]

walpurgite, *n.* (1872) *Mineral.* [Ad. of G *Walpurgin* < the name of the *Walpurgis* vein in a mine at Schneeberg, central Germany + *-it* -ite] A hydrous bismuth uranium arsenate and oxide. O, W [3]

Walther, *a.* (1920) and *n.* (1968) *Mil.* [G < the name of the German family *Walther,* a firm of firearm manufacturers] (of) a pistol and/or rifle made by the Walthers. O [3]

waltherite, *n. Mineral.* [G *Waltherit,* poss. < the name of Johannes *Walther* (1860–1937), German geologist + *-it* -ite] An ill-defined carbonate of bismuth having prismatic crystals. W [3]

waltz, *n.* (1781) *Music* [Ad. of G *Walzer* < *walzen* to roll, turn < OHG *walzan*] A round dance in ¾ time; the music for this; a composition in ¾ time usu. intended for concert performance; (slang) something accomplished with ease. —**waltz,** *a.* (1826); **waltzlength** (1958); **waltzlike; waltz jump/time/swing.** O, R, W [4]

waltz, *v.* (1712 W9) *Dance* [Ad. of G *walzen*—see *waltz,* *n.*] To dance a waltz; to move in a whimsical, lively, often aimless manner; to move in a noisy or attention-seeking manner; to proceed without difficulty; (U.S.) to transport or convey something. —**waltzer** (1811); **waltzing,** *n., a.* (1811, 1811). • ~ appears in various verb phrases like **to waltz up** (1887)/**off** (1935)/**into** (1974)/**Matilda** (1917). O, R, W [4]

waltz king, *n.* (1908) *Music* [Transl. of G *Walzerkönig,* an epithet given to the Viennese composer Johann Strauss (1825–99)] This epithet for Strauss. O [3]

wander-bird, *n.* (1924) [Transl. of G *Wandervogel* (q.v.)] Wandervogel. O [3]

wander-book, *n.* (1844) *Travel* [Transl. of G *Wanderbuch* < *wandern* to wander, travel + *Buch* book] A (journeyman's) passport; a guidebook. O-1933 (not in 2nd ed.) [3]

Wanderjahr, -es *pl.* (1893) [G (see *wanderyear*)] Formerly a year when an apprentice traveled to improve skills before beginning a career; wanderyear. O, R [3]

wanderlust, *n.* (1902) *Travel* [G < *wandern* to wander, travel + *Lust* joy, desire] A longing to wander or travel. —**wanderluster** (1927); **-lusting,** *part. a.* (1936); **-lustful.** O, R, W [4]

Wandervogel, -ø/-vögel *pl.* (1928) [G, lit., bird of passage < *wandern* to wander, hike + *Vogel* bird, as in hiking through nature as free as birds] A member of the German youth organization established by Hermann Hoffmann c.1895 to promote outdoor activity and folk culture, in reaction against the materialistic values of middle-class city life, and so named by Karl Fischer (1881-1941), a leader of the organization; a hiker or rambler. —**wander-vogeling**, *n.* (1924). O [2]

wanderyear, *n.* (1880) *Travel* Var. **wander-year** (1880), **Wanderjahr** (1893) [Transl. of G *Wanderjahr* < *wandern* to travel, wander + *Jahr* year] A year of travel or wandering, esp. before one begins one's profession or trade. O, R, W [3]

Wankel engine, *n.* (1961) *Tech.* [Transl. of G *Wankelmotor* (1953) < the name of Felix Wankel (1902–88), German mechanical engineer + *Motor* (< L) engine] A kind of rotary, internal-combustion engine. • ~ is short. to **wankel** (1967) and also appears as an *a.* (1967). O, R [4]

Warasdin, *n.* (1802) *Mil.* [G *Warasdiner* (a kind of soldier) from *Warasdin,* the name of a town in Croatia (Magyar *Varasd*) + G *-er* -er] A former Slavonian soldier dressed like a Turk, with a sugar-loaf bonnet instead of a hat and armed with a fuze and a pistol. O [2]

war game, *a.* (1828) and *n.* (1891) *Mil.* [Transl. of G *Kriegspiel*] (Of) a simulated campaign or battle to test concepts rather than equipment or troops, usu. conducted in conferences; (of) an umpired training maneuver involving military units in simulated combat. —**war-game**, *v.* (1970); **war-gaming** (1954); **war-gamer** (1967). O, R, W [4]

warlord, *n.* (1856) *Mil.* [Transl. of G *Kriegsherr,* often used as a title of the German emperor, similar to *Commander-in-Chief* as the U.S. President's title] A supreme military leader. —**warlordship** (1913). • ~ differs somewhat from the homonymic translation of Chin *junfa,* which apparently provided the derivative *warlordism* (1962), and from the Chin phonetic transfer *tuchun* Chinese military governor or warlord during the period 1916–25. O, R, W [4]

wasserman, *n.* (1590) *Myth.* (obs.) [G *Wassermann,* lit., water-man] As opposed to a mermaid, a sea monster partly in the form of a man that destroys ships. • ~ is short. to **wasser** (1600). O [3]

Wassermann reaction, *n.* (1909) *Med.* Var. **Wasserman test** (1909) [G *Wassermann-Reaktion* (1906) < the name of the German bacteriologist August Paul *Wassermann* (1866–1925) + *Reaktion* < NL *reaction*-] A test in which syphilitic antibodies are detected by a complement-fixing reaction; a test that uses this reaction to detect syphilis. • ~ is short. to **Wasserman** (1909). O, R, W [4]

water cure, *n.* (1842) *Med.* [Transl. of G *Wasserkur* < *Wasser* water + *Kur* cure < ML *cūra* < L] Hydropathy or hydrotherapy, the empirical or scientific use of water in treating disease; a torture where the victim is forced to drink large quantities of water in a short time. —**water-curing**, *n.* (1849); **water-curer** (1900). O, R, W [4]

waterdust, *n.* (1873) *Tech.* Var. **water-dust** (1873) [Prob. a loose transl. of G *Wasserdunst* < *Wasser* water + *Dunst* steam, vapor] Clouds or fog composed of extremely fine particles of water. O, W [3]

watershed, *n.* (1803) *Geogr.* [Prob. a transl. of G *Wasserscheide* (commonly used as a scientific term by 1800) <

Wasser water + *Scheide* separation, boundary] Water parting; a region bounded peripherally by such a parting and ult. draining into a watercourse or basin; something added to a structure primarily to shed water; fig. sense, as in a crucial or dividing line or factor. —**watershed**, *a.* (1962). O, R, W [4]

water violet, *n.* (1597) *Bot.* [Prob. a transl. of G *Wasserveilchen*] Water gillyflower, a featherfoil. O, W [3]

water-weasel, *n.* (1611) *Zool.* [Transl. of G *Wasserwiesel* < *Wasser* water + *Wiesel* weasel] An otter. O [3]

wattevilleite, *n. Mineral.* [G *Wattevillit* < the name of Baron Oscar de *Watteville* (1824–1901), Parisian scholar + G *-it* -ite] A hydrous sulfate of sodium and calcium. W [3]

wave theory, *n.* (1933) *Ling.* Var. **Wellentheorie** (1933) [Transl. of G *Wellentheorie* < *Welle* wave + *Theorie* theory < LL *theōria* < Gk] A theory in historical linguistics to explain features in common among adjacent areas, where linguistic changes spread like waves from a focal area, in contrast to the family-tree theory (q.v.). O, R, W [3]

way wiser, *n.* (1651) *Tech.* [Transl. of G *Wegweiser* < *Weg* way + *Weiser* pointer < *weisen* to point, direct] An instrument to measure and indicate the distance traveled, usu. by road but also on the sea; guidepost; fig. sense, as in measuring conjecture. O [3]

Wb, *see* weber

weak, *a.* (1833) *Ling.* [Transl. of G *schwach,* used by Jakob Grimm to describe the type of verb conjugation that adds a dental suffix to form the preterit and perfect forms, such as *leben-lebte-gelebt;* in German grammar, adjectives declined by adding an *-(e)n* inflection; such inflection in English and other Germanic languages. O, R, W [4]

weakling, *n.* (1526) *Theol., Sociol.* [Tyndale's transl. of Luther's G *Weichling* < *weich* soft + nom. suffix *-ling* -ling, ult. a transl. of Gk *malakós*] (Obs.) an effeminate or unmanly person, as grouped with fornicators and other sinners; extension to any human or animal that is weak in body or mind or character or spiritual faith/achievements. —**weakling**, *a.* (1557). O, R, W [4]

weapon salve, *n.* (1631) *Med.* [Poss. a transl. of G *Waffensalbe*] A salve once superstitiously believed to heal a wound if applied to the weapon that made the wound; fig. sense to healing the Church's wounds. O, W [3]

wear-and-tear pigment, *n.* (1928) *Biochem.* [Transl. of G *Abnutzungspigment* < *Abnutzung* wear and tear < *abnutzen* to use up, wear out + *Pigment* pigment < L *pīgmentum* coloring matter, dye] A pigment that accumulates in aging cells. O [3]

weber, *n.* (1876) *Physics* [G < the name of Wilhelm *Weber* (1804–91), German physicist] (A now-discarded term for) a coulomb or an ampere; a unit of magnetic flux. • ~ is symbolized as **Wb**. O, R, W [3]

Weber-Fechner/Weber's law, *n.* (1890) *Psych.* [Transl. of G *Weber-Gesetz* < the name of the German physiologist Ernst Heinrich *Weber* (1795–1878) and of the German psychologist Gustav Theodor *Fechner* (1801–87) + *Gesetz* law] Their neurophysiological generalization (and concept) that approximates the intensity of a sensation to the intensity of a stimulus. O, W [3]

Weber number, *n.* (1937) *Physics* Var. **Weber's number**

(1937) [Transl. of G *Webersche Zahl* (1932) < attrib. form of the name of Moritz *Weber* (1871–1951), German naval engineer + *Zahl* number] A dimensionless quantity used in studying surface tension, waves. and bubbles; the square root of this quantity. O [3]

Weber's law, *see* Weber-Fechner law

wedeln, *n.* (1957) *Sports* [G < *wedeln* to wag the tail, sway < *Wedel* tail] A skiing technique, developed in Austria, using swiveling movements of the hips to make high-speed turns. —**wedel**(n), *a.* (1963, 1973). O, R [4]

wedel(n), *v.* (1961) *Sports* [G *wedeln* to wag, sway] To sway one's hips in downhill skiing to make short parallel turns; transf. sense to skateboarding. —**wedel(l)ing,** *n.* (1977, 1979). O [3]

weenie, *see* wiener

Wehmut, *n.* (1907) [G sadness, melancholy] Sadness, melancholy, nostalgia, wistfulness. O [3]

wehrlite, *n.* (1861) *Mineral.* [G *Wehrlit* (1838) < the name of Adolf *Wehrle* (1795–1835), Austrian mining official + G *-it* -ite] A peridotite mainly containing olivine and monoclinic pyroxene (this is different from the French-borrowed term meaning ''alloy of bismuth and tellurium''). O [3]

Wehrmacht, *n.* (1935) *Mil.* [G < *Wehr* defense + *Macht* might, force] The German name of the German armed forces from 1921 until the end of World War Two. —**Wehrmacht,** *a.* (1945). O, R, W [3]

Weichsel, *n.* (1934) *Geol.* [G, the name of the Polish river Vistula] The fourth, final stage of glaciation in northern Europe, equivalent to the Alpine Würm (q.v.). —**Weichselian,** *n.* (1968), *a.* (1969). O [3]

Weil's disease, *n.* (1889) *Path.* [Transl. of G *Weilkrankheit* (1886) < the name of Adolf *Weil* (1848–1916), German physician + *Krankheit* disease] Spirochetal jaundice, a sometimes fatal leptospirosis characterized by fever, chills, muscle pains, and hepatitis, caused by infection from rat urine. O, R, W [3]

Weimaraner, *n.* (1943) *Zool.* [G < *Weimar,* the name of the German city where the species was first bred + *-aner*] A German breed of large, short-haired sporting dogs; a dog of this breed. O, R, W [4]

weiner, *see* wiener

weinschenkite, *n.* *Mineral.* [G *Weinschenkit* < the name of Ernst H. O. K. *Weinschenk* (1865–1921), German mineralogist + *-it* -ite] Churchite, a hydrous phosphate of rare earths. W [3]

Weinstube, *n.* (1899) *Beverages* [G < *Wein* wine + *Stube* room] A small German saloon. O [3]

Wein, Weib, und Gesang (1885) [G (1869), popularized as the title of a Strauss waltz < *Wein* wine + *Weib* women + *und* and + *Gesang* song] Wine, women, and song, proverbially considered by men as essential to carefree entertainment and pleasure. O [2]

weisbachite, *n.* *Mineral.* [G *Weisbachit* < the name of Albin Julius *Weisbach* (1833–1901), German mineralogist + *-it* -ite] A variety of anglesite containing barium. W [3]

weisenheimer, *see* wisenheimer

weiss beer, *n.* *Beverages* [Partial transl. of G *Weißbier* < *weiß* white + *Bier* beer] A light-colored, effervescent beer. R, W [3]

weissite, *n.* (1836) *Mineral.* [G *Weissit* < the name of Christian Samuel *Weiss* (1780–1856), German crystallographer or Louis Weiss, owner of the Good Hope Mine, in Gunnison County, Colorado, USA + G *-it* -ite] A bluish black copper telluride. O, W [3]

weissnichtwo, *n.* (1833) [G *(ich) weiß nicht wo* (I) know not where, i.e., somewhere far off] An indefinite or imaginary city or place, named in Thomas Carlyle's satirical work *Sartor Resartus.* W [3]

Weisswurst, *n.* (1963) *Food* [G < *weiß* white + *Wurst* sausage] A whitish variety of bratwurst, made chiefly of veal. O [3]

welcome money, *n.* (1977) [Transl. of G *Begrüßungsgeld* < *Begrüßung* greeting, welcome + *Geld* money, cash—see *gelt*] Payment to the East Germans and Poles by the West German welfare program, esp. before German reunification in 1990; a similar payment by charities. BDC [3]

Wellentheorie, *see* wave theory

well-ordered, *a.* (1902) *Math.* [Transl. of G *wohlgeordnet* (1883) < *wohl* well + *geordnet* ordered, arranged < *ordnen* to order, arrange] Of an ordered set in which each of its nonempty subsets has a first or least element (this is different from the old meaning of ''having a good order''). —**well-ordered set** (1902); **well-ordering,** *a.* (1941), *n.* (1963); **well-order,** *v.* (1944). O [4]

wels, -es *pl.* (1880) *Ichyth.* [G < MHG *wels,* related to NHG *Wal* whale] Sheatfish, a European river catfish. O, W [3]

Welsbach, *a.* (1887) *Industry* [G < the name of the German engineer Carl Auer Freiherr von *Welsbach* (1858–1929), who invented the gas mantle] Of a burner producing gaslight by combustion through use of a mantle; of the U.S. trademark for this burner. —**Welsbach burner** (1887)/**lamp** (1901)/**mantle** (1912). O [4]

Welsh bean, *n.* (1585) *Food* (obs.) [Transl. of G *Welsche Bohne* < *welsch* Welsh + *Bohne* bean] The French or kidney bean. O [3]

Weltanschauung, -s/-en *pl.* (1868) *Phil.* Var. **weltanschauung** (1972) [G < *Welt* world + *Anschauung* opinion, view] World view, a philosophical view of the universe; a philosophy or view of life; cosmological conception of society and its institutions, as held by its members. • ~ is transl. as **world view** (1858). O, R, W [4]

Weltansicht, *n.* (1892) *Philos.* [G *Welt* world + *Ansicht* view] Weltanschauung (q.v.). • ~ is transl. as **world view** (1858). O [2]

Weltbild, *n.* (1934) *Sociol.* [G < *Welt* world + *Bild* picture] A view of life. O [2]

Weltliteratur, *n.* (1827) *Lit.* Var. **Weltlitteratur** (1913) [G < *Welt* world + *Literatur* literature < L *litterātūra*] A literature of all countries and peoples; a universal literature. • ~ is transl. as **world literature** (1831, q.v.). O [2]

Weltpolitik, *n.* (1903) *Politics* Var. **weltpolitik** [G < *Welt* world + *Politik* politics < Fr *politique*] International politics; an individual country's policy toward the world at large; a political view of world affairs. O, W [3]

Weltschmerz, -es *pl.* (1875) *Philos.* Var. **weltschmerz** (1923) [G < *Welt* world + *Schmerz* pain] An apathetic or pessimistic feeling about life or the state of the world, in contrast with what that state could ideally be; a sentimental sadness or vaguely yearning attitude. O, R, W [4]

Wend, *n.* (1786) *Ethnology* [G *Wende* < OHG *Winida* an old name for a Serb] A member of a Slavic people living in eastern Germany up to the Baltic Sea during early medieval times and now surviving along the middle and upper Spree River; also called *Sorb* (q.v.); Wendish (q.v.). —**Southern Wends** (1822). O, R, W [4]

Wendish, *n.* (1617 *W9*) *Ethnology, Ling.* Old var. like **Windish** (1887) [G *Wendisch* < *Wende* Wend (q.v.) + *-isch* -ish] The Wends or their West Slavic language. O, R, W [4]

Wendish, *a.* (1614 *W9*) *Ethnology, Ling.* [G *wendisch* < *Wende* Wend + adj. suffix *-isch* -ish] Pertaining to the Wends or their language; Sorbian. O, R, W [4]

wenzel, *n.* *Games* [G, lit., servant, knave < the popular Bohemian given name *Wenzel,* a short. of the Czech name *Wenzeslaus* Wenceslas, a patron saint] A jack or knave, a playing card in skat ranking usu. just below the queen. W [3]

werewolf, -wolves *pl.* (1945) *Politics* [G *Werwolf* or *Wehr-wolf* werewolf < MHG *werwolf* < OHG *wer* man or MHG *wer(e),* G *Wehr* defense + *Wolf* wolf, so named for their sinister killings] A member of a right-wing paramilitary German resistance movement, intent on sabotaging the Allied occupation of Germany at the end of World War Two (this is different from the old meaning of "lycanthrope"). O [3]

wertfrei, *a.* (1909) *Philos.* [G < *Wert* worth, value + *frei* free] Free of value judgment, as in conclusions in the sciences; morally neutral. O [3]

Wertfreiheit, *n.* (1944) *Sociol.* [G < *wertfrei* wertfrei (q.v.) + *-heit* -hood] The quality of being wertfrei. O [2]

Wesen, *n.* (1854–5) *Sociol.* [G being, essence, nature < *sein* to be] A person's nature, as revealed in characteristic behavior; the distinctive nature or essence of something. O [2]

westfalite, *n.* (1896) *Mil.* [G *Westfalit* < *Westfalisch* Westphalian, as used in the name of the original manufacturing company] One of three varieties of high explosives, with ammonium nitrate as the main ingredient. O [3]

Westmark/westmark, *n.* (1948) *Currency* Var. **west-mark** (1948) [G < *West* < *Westen* West + *Mark* mark (q.v.)] The currency unit of West Germany, as differentiated from the Ostmark (q.v.) of East Germany, preceding reunification in 1990. O [3]

Westpolitik, *n.* (1970) *Politics* [G < *West* < *Westen* West + *Politik* politics < Fr *politique*] A Communist country's policy of having trade and diplomatic relations with a non-Communist country. R [3]

widow-maker, *n.* (1975) (slang) *Mil.* [Transl. of G *Witwe-macher* < *Witwe* widow + *Macher* maker < *machen* to make, a German nickname for the American Lockheed F-104 Starfighter, 178 of which fatally crashed in Germany] One of these military aircraft; extended by the U.S. military to a grenade launcher (this is different from the Shakespearean meaning of "a killer or potential killer," as caused by a falling limb). O [3]

Wiedemann-Franz law, *n.* (1924) *Physics* [Transl. of G *Wiedemann-Franz-Gesetz* (1853) < the names of Gustav H. *Wiedemann* (1826–99) and Rudolph *Franz* (1827–1902), German physicists + *Gesetz* law] The law stating that at a given temperature the ratio of the thermal to the electrical conductivity has nearly the same value for most metals. O, W [3]

Wie geht's [G, lit., how goes it, similar to Fr *comment allez vous* how are you] How are you. R [3]

Wien bridge, *n.* (1922) *Physics* [Transl. of G *Wien-Brücke* < the name of Max *Wien* (1866–1938), German physicist + *Brücke* bridge] A bridge circuit devised by Wien for measuring or comparing capacitances. —**Wien bridge oscillator** (1967). O, W [3]

wiener, *n.* (1867) *Food* Erron. var. **weiner** (1889), **wienie** (1867 *W9*), **weenie** [G, a short. of *Wienerwurst* < *Wiener* from Vienna + *Wurst* sausage] (Frankfurter) sausage; wienerwurst (q.v.). —**wiener roast** (1920)/**party/roll/sandwich.** O, R, W [4]

Wiener Kreis, *n.* (1932) *Philos.* [G title *Der Wiener Kreis* < *der* the + *Wiener* Viennese + *Kreis* circle] Vienna circle (q.v.), a philosopher's circle where logical positivism first took the definite form of a school. O [3]

Wiener schnitzel, *n.* (1862 *W9*) *Food* [G < *Wiener* Viennese + *Schnitzel* schnitzel, veal cutlet (q.v.)] A breaded veal cutlet, garnished with lemon, capers, etc. in the Viennese style. O, R, W [4]

wienerwurst, *n.* (1889 *W9*) *Food* [G—see *wiener*] Vienna sausage; frankfurter. O, R, W [3]

wienie, *see* wiener

wiesenboden, *n.* *Geol.* [G < *Wiesen* (pl. of *Wiese* meadow) + *Boden* ground, soil] Any of an intrazonal group of meadow soils rich in organic matter. W [3]

Wildflysch, *n.* (1929) *Geol.* Var. **wildflysch** (1981) [G (1872) < *wild* wild, irregularly distributed + *Flysch,* perhaps related to Swabian *Flins* slate, NHG *Flinz* slab of slate, sandstone] Flysch containing large, irregularly distributed blocks and occupying jumbled beds. O [3]

Wildgrave, *n.* (1762) *Admin.* [Transl. of G *Wildgraf* wild game < MHG *wiltgrāve* < *wilt* game + *grāve* count (title)] Formerly, the chief magistrate of an uncultivated or forest region in Germany; such a hereditary ruler in the Rhineland. O [3]

Wildgravess, *n.* (1762) *Admin.* [Transl. of G *Wildgräfin* < *Wild* wild game + *Gräfin* countess] The wife of a Wildgrave (q.v.). O [2]

Wilhelmstrasse, *n.* (1914) *Politics* [G < *Wilhelm* William + *Straße* street] The name of a Berlin street, where the German foreign office was located until 1945; the German foreign office and its policies during that period. O, R [4]

willemite, *n.* (1850) *Mineral.* [G (or Du) *Willemit* (1829) < G *Willem,* the name of Wilhelm I (1772–1843), king of the Netherlands + G *-it* -ite] A native silicate of zinc. O, R, W [3]

will to art (1929) *Art* [Transl. of G *Wille zur Kunst* < *Wille* will + *zur* to (the) + *Kunst* art] A supposed human need and instinct for the beautiful. O [3]

will to power (1896) *Politics* [Transl. of G *Wille zur Macht* < *Wille* will + *zur* to (the) + *Macht* power] According to Nietzsche and later in Alfred Adler's individual psychology, a supposed driving force behind human behavior that should result in self-mastery, but if frustrated can become the drive to dominate others; the desire to have authority over others. O, R, W [4]

wind cap, *n.* (1940) *Music* [Transl. of G *Windkapsel* < *Wind* wind + *Kapsel* capsule < L *capsula*] An instrument with a reed cap. —**wind-cap,** *a.* (1940). O [3]

wind rose, *n.* (1846) *Meteor.* [G, lit., rose of winds < *Wind* wind + *Rose* rose < L *rosa*] A diagram indicating, for one place, the strength and frequency of winds from different directions; a diagram indicating the occurrence of other phenomena (this is of course different from the old botanical meaning). O, R, W [4]

wineberg, *n.* (1870) *Bot.* [Partial transl. of G < *Wein* wine + *Berg* mountain] Vineyard. O [3]

wine-bibber, *n.* (1535) *Beverages* [Coverdale's transl. of Luther's G *Weinsäufer* < *Wein* wine + *Säufer* bibber < *saufen* to drink heavily] (Literary and archaic) one who overindulges in wine; (archaic) the African genet, which likes palm wine. —**wine-bibbing,** *n.* (1549), *a.* (1593); **wine-bibbery** (1832). O, R [4]

wine-card, *n.* (1851) *Beverages* [Transl. of G *Weinkarte* < *Wein* wine + *Karte* card < MFr *carte,* ult. < Gk *chártēs*] Wine list, a list of the wines obtainable in a given restaurant. O [3]

winegarden, *n.* (1535) *Beverages* [Transl. of G *Weingarten* < *Wein* wine + *Garten* garden] Vineyard. O, R [3]

wine gardener, *n.* (1535) *Beverages* [Transl. of G *Weingärtner* < *Wein* wine + *Gärtner* gardener] One who tends a vineyard. O [3]

wine harvest, *n.* (1535) *Beverages* [Transl. of G *Weinernte* < *Wein* wine + *Ernte* harvest] The ingathering of grapes. O [3]

wine-hill, *n.* (1906) *Beverages* [Transl. of G *Weinhügel* < *Wein* wine + *Hügel* hill] Vineyard. O [3]

wine kernel, *n.* (1535) *Beverages* [Transl. of G *Weinkern* < *Wein* wine + *Kern* kernel] Grapestone, grape-seed sediment in wine. O [3]

wine-stock, *n.* (1535) *Beverages* [Transl. of G *Weinstock* < *Wein* wine + *Stock* (lit., stick) vine] Grapevine. O [3]

wine stone, *n.* (1526) *Beverages* [Transl. of G *Weinstein* < *Wein* wine + *Stein* stone] Argol, a crystalline crust deposited in wine casks during aging. O, W [3]

wine vinegar, *n.* (1617) *Beverages* [Transl. of G *Weinessig* < *Wein* wine + *Essig* vinegar] Vinegar made from wine, as opposed to malt vinegar. O [3]

wine-yellow, *n.* (1876) *Chem.* [Transl. of G *weingelb* < *Wein* wine + *gelb* yellow, so named for the color of the wine] A pale to grayish yellow. O, W [4]

wirble, *n.* (1848) [G *Wirbel* whirl, swirl, turmoil] Whirl. O [3]

wirble, *v.* (1848) Var. **wirbel** (1932) [G *wirbeln* to whirl about] To turn round and round, whirl. O [3]

wirrwarr, *n.* (1865) [G chaos, confusion, hubbub, echoic < echoic, archaic *wirren* to jumble, confuse] A welter, confusion. O [2]

Wirt, *n.* (1858) *Travel* Old var. **Wirth** (1858) [G host, innkeeper] The landlord of a German inn. O [2]

Wirtschaft¹, *n.* (1850) *Econ.* Old var. **Wirthschaft** (1850) [G household] Domestic economy, housekeeping. O [2]

Wirtschaft², *n.* (1903) *Travel* [G, a short. of *Gastwirtschaft* unpretentious inn] Wirtshaus (q.v.). O [2]

Wirtschaftswunder, *n.* (1959) *Econ.* Var. **wirtschaftswunder** (1980) [G < *Wirtschaft* economy + *Wunder* wonder, miracle] West Germany's economic miracle in making a vast, lasting recovery in its economic state and standard of living following World War Two; transf. sense to other countries. O [2]

Wirtshaus, -häuser *pl.* (1829) *Travel* Old var. **wirthshaus** (1829) [G country inn] A hostelry or inn in German-speaking countries. O [3]

wisenheimer, *n.* (1904) Var. **wiseheimer** (1904), **weisenheimer** (1957) [Combining of E *wise* + G *-enheimer,* analogized on G names like *Guggenheimer* and *Oppenheimer,* meaning "someone who hails from the mythical German town of Wisenheim"] Wiseacre, a know-it-all. —**wisenheimer,** *a.* (1937). O, R, W [4]

wisent, *n.* (1866) *Zool.* [G < MHG *wisent* < OHG *wisant* a bison-like wild ox] A European bison: aurochs (q.v.). O, R, W [4]

wish-fulfi(l)lment, *n.* (1901) *Psych.* [Transl. of Freud's G *Wunscherfüllung* (1900)] The gratifying of a desire, usu. symbolic, as in daydreams, neurotic symptoms, dreams, etc. —**wish-fulfilling,** *a.* (1922). O, W [4]

wismuth, *n.* (1587) *Chem.* (archaic) Old var. like **wisemute** (1587) [G bismuth (q.v.)] Bismuth. O [3]

Wissenschaft, *n.* (1834) *Ed.* [G science, field of study] Knowledge and its pursuit; learning, scholarship; science. O [2]

Wissenschaftslehre, *n.* (1846) *Philos.* [G (1794), the name of the theory of rigid scientific methodology devised by the German philosopher Johann Gottlieb Fichte (1762–1814) < *Wissenschaft* (q.v.) + *Lehre* theory, doctrine] Theory or philosophy of knowledge. O [2]

witherite, *n.* (1794) *Mineral.* [G *Witherit* (1784), irreg. < the name of William *Withering* (1741–99), English physician + G *-it* -ite] A native barium carbonate. O, R, W [4]

wittichenite, *n.* (1868) *Mineral.* [G *Wittichenit* (1853) < *Wittichen,* the name of a town in Baden-Württemberg, Germany + *-it* -ite] A native sulfide of bismuth and copper. O, W [3]

wittingite, *n.* (1868) *Mineral.* [G *Wittingit* (1849) < *Wittingi,* the name of a town in Finland, where found + G *-it* -ite] A variety of neotocite, a hydrous silicate of manganese and iron. O [3]

witwall, *n.* (1544) *Ornith.* Old var. like **witwol** (1544) [Obs. G *witwal, wittewal* (now *Widewal, Wiedewal*) golden oriole < MHG *wit(t)ewal* < *wite* wood + *-wal* (of unknown origin)] (Obs.) the green oriole; (dial. Brit.) the European great spotted woodpecker. O, W [3]

woehlerite/wöhlerite, *n. Mineral.* [G *Wöhlerit* < the name of Friedrich *Wöhler* (1800–82), German chemist + *-it* -ite] A silicate of zirconium, niobium, calcium, sodium, and other minerals. W [3]

Wohnbereich, -e *pl.* (1981) *Sociol.* [G habitat, residential district < *Wohn* (< *wohnen* to reside) + *Bereich* area] (Protected) residential area. BDC [2]

wolchonskoite, *see* volkonskoite

wolfachite, *n. Mineral.* [G *Wolfachit* < *Wolfach,* the name of a town in Baden-Württemberg, Germany + *-it* -ite] A mineral of nickel, arsenic, antimony, and sulfur. W [3]

wolf dog, *n.* (1652) *Zool.* [Transl. of G *Wolfshund* < *Wolf* wolf + *Hund* dog] Any of several varieties of large dogs formerly kept to hunt wolves such as the Irish wolfhound; a cross between a domestic dog and a wolf; wolfhound (q.v.) O, R, W [4]

wolfhound, *n.* (1786 *W9*) *Zool.* [Transl. of G *Wolfshund* < *Wolf* wolf + *Hund* hound] Any of several varieties of large dogs kept for hunting wolves; wolf dog. O, R, W [4]

wolf pack, *n.* (1941) *Mil.* [Expansion and transl. of G *Rudel* pack, as in a wolf pack] A tactical unit of two or more submarines or fighter planes that make a coordinated attack; a roaming gang of roughneck teenagers (this is different from the old meaning of "a group of wolves hunting together"). O, R, W [4]

wolf-pack tactics/system, *n.* *Mil.* [Expansion and transl. of G *Rudeltaktik/system* < *Rudel* (wolf) pack + *Taktik* tactics (< NL *tactica* < Gk *taktikḗ*) or *System* < LL *systēma* < Gk] The tactics or system used by a wolf pack of German submarines against Allied ships during World War Two. W [3]

wolfram, *n.* (1757) *Chem.* [G *Wolfram, Wolfrom, Volfram,* of unknown origin, but influenced by *Wolf* wolf, from the wolfing, devouring effect the ore has on zinc when it is mixed with the metal in the smelting furnace, or from the fact that it is said to look like wolf feces] Tungsten; wolframite (q.v.). —**wolframine** (1854), **-ate** (1860), **-ic acid** (1860), **-inium, wolfram(o)-, wolfram ocher** (1868)/**lamp** (1907)/**steel.** O, R, W [4]

wolframite, *n.* (1864) *Mineral.* [G *Woframit* < *Wolfram* + *-it* -ite] An iron manganese tungstate: wolfram (q.v.). O, R, W [4]

wonder child, *n.* (1896) Var. **wonder-child** (1896) [Trans. of G *Wunderkind* < *Wunder* marvel + *Kind* child] Child prodigy; wunderkind (q.v.). O, R, W [3]

wonder-sight, *n.* (1845) *Meteor.* [Transl. of G *Wundergesicht* < *Wunder* wonder + *Gesicht* sight(ing)] A strange and marvelous sight. O [3]

wonderworld, *n.* (1851) Var. **wonder-world** (1851) [Transl. of G *Wunderwelt* < *Wunder* wonder + *Welt* world] Wonderland, a fairy-tale world or a real place exciting great admiration or wonder. O, W [3]

woodchat, *n.* (1705) *Ornith.* [Prob. an erron. transl. of G *Waldkatze/Waldkater* < *Wald* wood + *Katze* cat, *Kater* tomcat, rather than from *Rotkopfswürger* woodchat] One of various Asiatic birds of the family Turdidae; woodchat shrike. O, R, W [4]

wood opal, *n.* (1816) *Mineral.* [Transl. of G *Holzopal* < *Holz* wood + *Opal* opal < L *opalus* < Skt *úpala*] Wood petrified with opal. O, W [3]

wood tin, *n.* (1787) *Mineral.* Var. **wood-tin** (1787) [Transl. of G *Holzzinn* < *Holz* wood + *Zinn* tin] Cassiterite, a tin dioxide. O, W [3]

word class, *n.* (1914) *Ling.* [Leonard Bloomfield's transl. of G *Wortklasse* < *Wort* word + *Klasse* class < Fr *classe* < L *classis*] One of various linguistic form classes composed of words, esp. in regard to the parts of speech of a language: form class. O, R, W [4]

word-lore, *n.* (1861) *Ling.* [Transl. of G *Wortlehre* < *Wort* word + *Lehre* lesson, doctrine, teaching] The study of words, their forms, and their history: morphology; the doctrine of word formation. —**word-lorist** (1929). O, R, W [3]

workers' participation, *see* Mitbestimmung

work lead, *n.* (1471–2) *Metall.* [Transl. of G *Werkblei* < *Werk* work + *Blei* lead] Lead bullion, which contains impurities like gold and silver. O, W [3]

worldall, *n.* (1847) *Philos.* [Transl. of G *Weltall* < *Welt* world + *all* all] The universe; the world considered as a unit. O [3]

world-famous, *a.* (1837) [Carlyle's transl. of G *weltberühmt* < *Welt* world + *berühmt* famous] Known the world over. O, R [3]

world history, *n.* (1837) *History* [Carlyle's transl. of G *Weltgeschichte* < *Welt* world + *Geschichte* history] History interweaving the events of the entire world; a school or university course in this. —**world-historic(al)** (1876, 1854). O [4]

worldline, *n.* (1916) *Physics* Var. **world-line** (1916) [Transl. of G *Weltlinie* (1913) < *Welt* world + *Linie* line] The succession of points in time-space that are occupied by a particle. O, R [3]

world literature, *n.* (1831) *Lit.* [Carlyle's transl. of Goethe's G *Weltliteratur* (q.v.)] A corpus drawn from the various national literatures that is considered as literature throughout the world; the sum of such literature; a school or college course in this. O [4]

world-old, *a.* (1840) [Transl. of G *weltalt* < *Welt* world + *alt* old] As old as the world. O [3]

world point, *n.* (1923) *Physics* Var. **world-point** (1923) [Transl. of G *Weltpunkt* (1913) < *Welt* world + *Punkt* point < L *punctum*] A point in space-time; a given point in space at a given time. O, R [3]

world politics/policy, *n.* (1896) *Politics* [Transl. of G *Weltpolitik* < *Welt* world + *Politik* politics < Gk *politikḗ*] Politics or policy based on considerations affecting the world as a whole. —**world-politician/political** (1905, 1958). O, R [3]

world power, *n.* (1866) *Theol., Politics* [Transl. of G *Weltmacht* < *Welt* world + *Macht* might, power] Orig., the theological sense of worldly power; now a nation or state powerful enough to affect "world politics" (q.v.). O, R, W [4]

world soul, *n.* (1848) *Philos.* [Transl. of G *Weltseele* < *Welt* world + *Seele* soul] The animating principle or spirit that relates to the physical world as the human soul relates to the human body. O, R, W [4]

world spirit, *n.* (1846) *Philos.* [Transl. of G *Weltgeist* < *Welt* world + *Geist* spirit] World soul; the spirit of the world in its everyday aspects and activities. O, R, W [3]

world view, *n.* (1858) *Philos.* [Transl. of G *Weltanschauung* or *Weltansicht* (q.v.)] Weltanschauung (q.v.). —**world-viewer** (1862). O, R, W [4]

Wörter und Sachen, *a.* (1937) and *n.* (1957) *Ling.* [G, lit., words and things] (Of) an aspect of comparative dialect study involving the forms of words referring to concrete objects and processes. O [3]

wound hormone, *n.* (1921) *Bot.* [Transl. of G *Wundhormon* (1921), coined by the Austrian botanist Gottlieb Haberlandt (1854–1945) < *Wunde* wound + *Hormon* (< Gk) hormone] A substance produced in a plant in response to a wound to stimulate healing. O, W [3]

wulfenite, *n.* (1849) *Mineral.* [G *Wulfenit* (1845) < the name of Franz Xavier von *Wulfen* (1728–1805), Austrian mineralogist + G -*it* -ite] A native lead molybdate, also called *yellow lead ore*. O, R, W [4]

wunderbar, *a.* [G wonderful] Marvelous. WNW [3]

Wunderkind/wunderkind, -er/-s *pl.* (1891) *Music* [G < *Wunder* marvel + *Kind* child] A child prodigy, esp. in music; one who succeeds early in a competitive or highly difficult profession or field; a Whiz Kid. •~ is transl. as **wonder child** (1896)/**boy** (1922). O, R, W [4]

Würm, *n.* (1910) *Geol.* [G (1909) < the former name of a German lake (now *Starmberger See*) in Bavaria] The fourth and final Pleistocene glaciation in Europe. —**Wurmian,** *a.* (1927), *n.* (1967). O, R, W [4]

wurst, *n.* (1855) *Food* [G sausage] Sausage, esp. the German type; a German sausage. —**wurst business/market** (*Sc*). O, R, W [4]

wurzel, *see* mangel-wurzel

wüstite, *n.* (1928) *Mineral., Chem.* Var. **wustite** [G *Wüstit* (1927) < the name of Ewald *Wüst* (1875–1934), German geologist + -*it* -ite] An artificial mineral that is almost unknown in nature, consisting of ferrous oxide. O, W [3]

X, Y, Z

X, *see* X chromosome

xanthin, *n.* (1838) *Chem.* Var. **xanthine** (1839) [G *Xanthin* or Fr *xanthine* < Gk *xanthós* yellow + G *-in* (or Fr *-ine*) *-ine*] A yellow, carotenoid coloring matter found in madder; the insoluble part of this (this is different from the "uric compound" meaning). —**xanthin,** *a.* (1868). O, R, W [3]

xanthoconite, *n.* (1868) *Mineral.* [G *Xanthokon* (1840) < *xanth-* (< Gk *xanthós* yellow) + *kónis* sand + E *-ite*] A silver arsenic sulfide of a dull red or brown color. O, W [3]

xanthogen, *n.* (1823) *Chem.* [Short. of G *Xanthogensäure* (1822) < *Xanthogen* < *xantho-* + *-gen* (< Gk *xanthós* yellow + *-genēs* produced, producing) + G *Säure* acid] Either of two univalent radicals, both of which are derived from xanthic acid. —**xanthogenate, xanthogenic acid.** O, W [3]

xanthophore, *n.* (1903) *Zool.* [G *Xanthophor* (1895) < *xantho-* + *-phor* < Gk *xanthós* yellow + *phorós* bearing, bringing] A chromatophore found in fishes and crustaceans that contains a yellow, usu. carotinoid pigment. O, W [3]

xanthophy(l)l, *n.* (1931) *Chem.* [G (1931) < *xantho-* + *-phyll* < Gk *xanthós* yellow + *phýllon* leaf] One of several yellow carotenoid pigments found in plants, such as carotenols or ketones (this is different from the French-derived homonym with a similar meaning). —**xanthophyllic** (1941), **xanthophyllous.** O, R, W [4]

xanthophyllite, *n.* (1844) *Mineral.* [G *Xanthophyllit* (1840) < *xantho-* + *-phyllit* < Gk *xanthós* yellow + *phýllon* leaf + G *-it* -ite, so named for its color] Seybertite or clintonite, a yellowish, brittle mica. O, W [3]

xanthopterin, *n.* (1926) *Chem.* [G (1925) < *xantho-* + *pter-* + *-in* < Gk *xanthós* yellow + *pterón* wing] An amphoteric pigment present in mammal urine and the wings of yellow butterflies that can be converted into leucopterin. O, W [3]

xanthosiderite, *n.* (1868) *Mineral.* [G *Xanthosiderit* < *xantho-* + *Siderit* siderite < Gk *xanthós* yellow + *sídēros* iron + G *-it* -ite] Goethite, a native hydrous oxide of iron in yellow to brown crystals. O, R, W [3]

xanthoxenite, *n.* (1920) *Mineral.* [G *Xanthoxen* (1920) (< *xantho-* + *-xen* < Gk *xanthós* yellow + *xénos* guest, stranger) + E *-ite*] A basic hydrous phosphate of calcium and ferric iron, occurring as yellow triclinic crystals. O, W [3]

X chromosome, *n.* (1902) *Biol.* [G *X-Chromosom* (1891) < the symbol *X* + *Chromosom* chromosome] A sex chromosome carrying genes for femaleness in humans and most mammals. • ~ is short. to **X** (1902). O, R, W [4]

xenoblast, *n.* (1920) *Mineral.* [G (1903) < *xeno-* + *-blast* < Gk *xénos* strange + *blastós* bud] A metamorphic rock that has its outlines bounded by neighboring crystals. —**xenoblastic** (1931). O, W [3]

xerogel, *n.* *Chem.* [G < *xero-* + *-gel* < Gk *xerós* dry + *-gel* < Fr *gelatine* (orig., a kind of thick broth) < It *gelatina* < *gelato,* past part. of *gelare* to freeze, congeal] A solid formed by drying a gel with unhindered shrinking. W [2]

xonotlite, *n.* (1868) *Mineral.* [Ad. of erron. G *Xonaltit* (1866) (now *Xonotlit*) < the name of Tetala de *Xonotla,* a village in Pueblo, Mexico + G *-it* -ite] A massive hydrous silicate of calcium. O, W [3]

X organ, *n.* (1938) *Biol.* Var. **x organ** (1959) [G *Organ X* or *X Organ* (1931), so named because it was earlier indicated by *X* in a published diagram < L *organum* < Gk *órganon*] A group of neuroendoctrine cells in some crustaceans' eye-stalks, which secrete a hormone that inhibits the Y organ's production of molting hormone. O [3]

X ray, *n.* (1896) *Physics* Var. **X-ray** (1896), **x-ray** (1948) [Transl. of Röntgen's G *X-Strahlen* < *X* (reflecting the fact that he could not explain the essential nature of the rays) + *Strahlen,* pl. of *Strahl* ray] An electromagnetic radiation possessing the nature of visible light that can act on photographic plates and films and on fluorescent screens; a photograph produced by this. • ~ appears in many compounds like **X-ray microscope** (1948). —**X-ray,** *a.* (1896), *v.* (1899). O, R, W [4]

xylem, *n.* (1873 W9) *Bot.* [G < *xyl-* (< Gk *xýlon* wood) + G *-em* -em, as in *Phloem*] A complex tissue in higher plants' vascular systems, typically constituting their woody portion. —**xylem fiber/parenchyma/ray.** O, R, W [4]

xylite, *n.* (1843) *Chem., Mineral.* [G *Xylit* < *xyl-* (< Gk *xýlon* wood) + G *-it* -ite] A volatile liquid produced from methanol; a mineral that is an impure silicate of iron found in fibrous masses. —**xylitic** (1843). O [3]

xylitol, *n.* (1891) *Chem.* [G *Xylit* (1891) (< *xyl-* < Gk *xýlon* wood + G *-it* -ite) + E *-ol*] A sweet, crystalline, pentahydroxy alcohol produced by reducing xylose and also found in some plant tissues. O, R, W [3]

xylochlore, *n.* (1862) *Mineral.* [G *Xylochlor* (1853) < *xylo-* + *-chlor* < Gk *xýlos* wood + *chlōrós* green] An altered form of apophyllite, found in olive-green crystals in volcanic rock in Iceland. —**xylochloric** (1862). O [3]

xyloretin, *n.* (1852) *Chem.* [G (1840) < *xylo-* + *Retin* < Gk *xýlos* wood + L *rēte* net + G *-in* -in] A white crystalline resin found in fossil pinewood. O [3]

xyloretinite, *n.* (1868) *Chem.* [G *Xyloretin* xyloretin (q.v.) + E *-ite*] Xyloretin. O [3]

xylotile, *n.* (1864) *Mineral.* [G *Xylotil* < *xylo-* < Gk *xýlos* wood + *tílos* down, fine hair] A hydrous iron magnesium silicate obtained by altering asbestos or chrysolite; also called *mountain wood.* O, W [3]

yager, *n.* (1804) *Mil.* [Ad. of G *Jäger*—see *jaeger*] Jaeger; a rifle with a large bore and short barrel once used in the U.S. O, R, W [3]

ylid(e), *n.* (1951) *Chem.* [G *Ylid* (1944) < *-yl* + *-id,* the former pointing to the form of the atomic bond, and the latter to that of the ion bond in the compound (see *Meyer*)] A neutral compound having a negatively charged carbon atom bonded directly to a positively charged atom of an element like sulfur, phosphorus, or nitrogen. —**ylidic** (1970). O [3]

yodel, *v.* (1838) *Music* Var. **jodel** (1876), old var. like **you-dle** (1838) [Ad. of G *jodeln* < echoic *jo*] To sing or warble by interchanging the ordinary and falsetto voice, as the Swiss and Tyrolean mountaineers do; to shout or call in such a way; to yodel a tune. —**yodel,** *n.* (1849). O, R, W [4]

yodeler, *n.* (1880) *Music* Var. **jodeler** [Ad. of *Jod(e)ler* < *jodeln* to yodel (q.v.) + *-er* -er] One who yodels. O, R, W [4]

young grammarian, *n.* (1922) *Ling.* [Transl. of G *Junggrammatiker* (q.v.)] Junggrammitiker, a neogrammarian. —**young-grammarian,** *a.* (1947). O [3]

younker, *see* Junker

youth hostel, *n.* (1929) *Travel* [Transl. of G *Jugendherberge* < *Jugend* youth + *Herberge* hostel] A hostel offering cheap, plain overnight accommodations for young travelers and holiday-goers. —**youth-hostel,** *a.* (1929), *v.* (1972); **youth hostel(l)er** (1933), **youth hostelling,** *n.* (1947). O, W [4]

Yseult, *see* Isolde

yttrofluorite, *n. Mineral.* [G *Yttrofluorit* < *yttro-* + *Fluorit* < NL *yttrium* + *fluorite*] A fluorite containing yttrium earths. W [3]

Yugoslav, *n.* (1853) *Ethnology* Var. **Jugoslav** (1867) [Ad. of G *Jugoslawe* (or Fr *Yougoslave* < G) < Serb *jugo-* < *jug* south + G *Slawe* Slav < ML *Sclavus*] A member of various groups of Serbs, Croats, and/or Slovenes; a native or resident of the former Yugoslavia. —**Yugoslav,** *a.* (1853); **Yugoslavian,** *a.* (1923), *n.* (1949); **Yugoslavic; Yugoslavia.** O, R, W [4]

zander, -ø/-s *pl.* (1854) *Ichthy.* [G < MLG *sandat* (perhaps of Slavic origin) pike perch] A central European pike perch. O, R, W [4]

zastruga, *see* sastruga

zauberflote, *n. Music* [G < *Zauber* magic + *Flöte* flute (< MFr *flahute* < OProv *flaut*) in G *Die Zauberflöte* (*The Magic Flute*), an opera first performed in 1791 with music by Wolfgang Amadeus Mozart (1756–91), Austrian composer] A stopped flute pipe-organ stop of harmonic length. W [3]

Z band, *see* Z line

Z disk/disc, *n.* (1972) *Biol.* [Transl. of G *Z-Scheibe,* a short. of *Zwischenscheibe* intermediate disk] A thin disk of fibrous protein passing through striated muscle fiber that indicates the boundaries of contiguous contractile units. • ~ is competing with the continuing **Z line/band** (1916, 1950, q.v.). B [3]

zeaxanthin, *n.* (1929) *Biochem.* [G (1929) < *Zea,* the scientific name for maize or Indian corn + *Zanthin* xanthin (q.v.)] A yellow carotenoid alcohol that is the chief pigment of yellow Indian corn. O, W [3]

zebrina, *n.* (1946) *Bot.* [G (1849) < *Zebra* (< It) zebra, with reference to its striped leaves + G *-ina* -ina] A creeping recumbent herb of the genus of this name found in Mexico and New Mexico, U.S.; (cap.) this genus. O, W [3]

Zechstein, *a.* (1823) *Geol.* [G, lit., mine stone < *Zeche* + *Stein*] Of or pertaining to a subdivision of the European Permian. O, W [3]

zehner, *n. Currency* [G dime, a short. of *Zehnpfennigstück* < *zehn* ten + *Pfennig* pfennig (q.v.) + *Stück* piece, coin] A former bullion coin in Austria and Germany, the equivalent of ten kreutzers (q.v.). W2 [2]

zeilanite, *n.* (1851) *Mineral.* [G *Zeilanit* < *Zeilan,* the German name for the island of Ceylon (now Sri Lanka) + *-it* -it] Ceylonite, a dark variety of spinel containing iron. O [3]

zeitgeber, -ø/-s *pl.* (1964) *Physiol.* [G (1954), lit., timer < *Zeit* time + *Geber* giver < *geben* to give or indicate] A recurrent event like temperature, lightness, or darkness that acts as a cue in regulating an organism's biological clock. O [3]

Zeitgeist, *n.* (1848) *Sociol.* Var. **zeitgeist** (1884) [G < *Zeit* time + *Geist* spirit] Spirit of the times. • ~ is transl. as **time spirit** (1831). O, R, W [4]

zeophyllite, *n. Mineral.* [G *Zeophyllit* < an infixing of *phyll-* into *Zeolit* zeolite < Gk *zeîn* to boil, seethe + *líthos* stone, from its boiling and swelling under a blowpipe + *phýllon* leaf, so named from its occurrence in small plates] A basic silicate and fluoride of calcium, often containing iron. W [2]

Zeppelin, *n.* (1900) *Aeron.* [G < the name of its builder, Count Ferdinand von *Zeppelin* (1838–1917)] A rigid airship or dirigible; broadly, an airship. • ~ is short. to **Zep,** *n., a.* (1915, 1915), *v.* (1919). —**zeppelin,** *v.* (1916); **-ite** (1916); **-ist(ic)** (1937, 1930). O, R, W [4]

zeunerite, *n.* (1873) *Mineral.* [G *Zeunerit* < the name of Gustav *Zeuner* (1828–1907), German physicist + *-it* -ite] A supposedly hydrous copper uranium arsenate analogous to torbenite (q.v.) etc., but that in natural specimens is usu. metazeunerite. O, W [3]

zieger, *n. Food* Var. **ziger** [G greencheese < MHG, OHG *ziger*] Whey cheese. W [3]

Zigeuner, -s/-ø *pl.* (1841) *Sociol.* [G gypsy < Late MHG *zigîner*] A male gypsy. O [3]

Zigeunerbaron, *n.* (1963) *Sociol.* [G < *Zigeuner* (q.v.) + *Baron* baron] A gypsy baron, in allusion to Johann Strauss' operetta *Der Zigeunerbaron* (1885). O [2]

Zigeunerin, -nen *pl.* (1845) *Sociol.* [G < *Zigeuner* (q.v.) + *-in* -in] A female gypsy. O [2]

zimbalon, *n.* (1910) *Music* Var. **zimbalom** (1910), **zimbaloon** [G < Hung *cimbalom* < It *cembalo* dulcimer, cymbal] Cymbalom. O, R, W [3]

zimbel, *n.* (1910) *Music* [G < MHG < L *cymbalum,* Gk *kýmbalon* cymbal] Cymbal. O, W [3]

zimentwater, *n. Mining* [Partial transl. of G *Zementwasser* < *Zement* (< MFr *ciment* < L *caementum*) cement + G *Wasser* water] A water found in copper mines, i.e., water impregnated with copper. W2 [2]

zinc, *n.* (1641 W9) *Chem.* [G *Zink,* poss. < *Zinke* (< OHG *zinko*), i.e., *Zacke* tine, spike, the manner in which the metal distillate forms on the walls of the smelting oven] A bluish-white crystalline metallic element; a bluish gray color; galvanized iron; a zinc-covered bar of a cafe or pub; the cafe itself. • ~ is symbolized as **Zn,** acts as an *a.* (1796) and *v.* (1841), and appears in many composites (zinic, 1860), esp. in compounds (**zinc chloride**, 1851). O, R, W [4]

zinc blende, *n.* (1842) *Mineral.* [G < *Zink* zinc (q.v.) + *Blende* blende (q.v.)] Sphalerite (q.v.). O, R, W [4]

zinc bloom, *n.* (1842) *Mineral.* [Partial transl. of G *Zinkblüthe* (1808) < *Zink* zinc (q.v.) + *Blüthe* (now *Blüte*) bloom, blossom] Hydrozincite, a basic zinc carbonate. O, W [3]

zincite, *n.* (1854) *Mineral.* Old var. like **zinkite** [G *Zinkit* < *Zink* zinc (q.v.) + *-it* -ite] A hexagonal zinc oxide; a zinc ore found in New Jersey, U.S.; also called *red zinc ore.* O, R, W [4]

zinckenite, *see* zinkenite

zingel, *n.* (1803) *Ichthy.* [G a small, yellow-brown perch found in the Danube and its tributaries, prob. a dial. var. of *Zindel*, a dim. of MHG *zind* spike, girth < L *cingulum, cingula* girdle] A small, brownish-green edible perch having a round, elongated body and a pronounced snout. O, W [3]

zinke, *n.* (1776) *Music* Var. **zink** (1889), old var. like **zincke** (1776) [G *Zink* zinc (q.v.)] Cornet; a loud reed-stop in an organ. O, W [3]

zinkenite, *n.* (1835) *Mineral.* Var. **zinckenite** [G *Zinkenit* (1826) < the name of Johann Karl Ludwig *Zinken* (1798–1862), German mineralogist + *-it* -ite] A steel-gray sulfide of lead antimony. O, R, W [3]

zinkite, *see* zincite

zinnober, *a.* (1895) *Chem.* Old var **zinnobar** (1895) [G < MHG *zinober* < OFr *cenobre* < L *cinnabaris* < Gk *kinnábari* a triagonal, mostly red, gleaming mineral] Chrome green. O [3]

zinnwaldite, *n.* (1861) *Mineral.* [G *Zinnwaldit* (1845) < *Zinnwald*, the name of a town in eastern Germany + *-it* -ite] A kind of mica containing lithium and iron. O, R, W [3]

zippeite, *n.* (1854) *Mineral.* [G *Zippeït* (1845) < the name of Franz Xaver Maximilian *Zippe* (1791–1863), Austrian mineralogist + G *-it* -ite] A hydrous sulfate of uranium. O, W [3]

Zips, *n. Sociol.* [G *Zipser* someone from *Zips*, the name of a formerly Hungarian region settled in the 12th and 13th cent. by peasants and craftsmen from German Silesia and Bavaria + *-er* -er] An inhabitant of Spis, an area in northeastern Slovakia. W2 [2]

zircon, *n.* (1794) *Mineral.* [G (now usu. *Zirkon*) < Fr *jargon* < It *giargone*, ult. < Per *zargun* golden (in color)] A native tetragonal silicate of zirconium usu. occurring in square prisms. —**zircon**, *a.* (1804); **-ia** (1797); **-ic** (1804); **-ite** (1814); **-ate** (1851); **-ian**, *a.* (1853); **-itic** (1895); **-iferous**; **-oid**; **-yl**; **zircon-**. O, R, W [4]

zirconium, *n.* (1808) *Mineral.* [G (1789) < *Zircon* zircon (q.v.) + *-ium* (< L) -ium, identified in zircon oxide and named by the German chemist Martin Heinrich Klaproth (1742–1817), whose name is associated in the OED with *zirconia* but not with *zirconium*] A strong, ductile, metallic element used in vacuum tubes, steel making, and nuclear reactors. • ~ is symbolized as **Zr** and appears initially in the names of numerous chemical compounds like **zirconium oxide** (1868)/**dioxide/hydride/silicate**. —**zirconium**, *a.* (1868). O, R, W [4]

zirklerite, *n. Mineral.* [G *Zirklerit* < the name of the 20th-cent. German mining official *Zirkler,* director of the Aschersleben Potash Works + *-it* -ite] A basic hydrous chloride of magnesium, calcium, iron, and aluminum. W [3]

zischägge, *n. Mil.* [G, lit., slip peak] A type of helmet, a burgonet, used by the 16th and 17th-cent. Germans and East Europeans. R [3]

zisel, *see* sisel, zizel

zither, *n.* (1850) *Music* Var. **zittern** (1868) [G < OHG *zitera, cithara* < L *cithara* < Gk *kithára* zither] A folk instrument, used at first chiefly in Bavaria and Austria, consisting of a flat wooden sound-board over which 4 to 5 melody strings and as many as 37 accompaniment strings are stretched. —**zither**, *a.* (1850), *v.* (1906); **zitherist** (1887). O, R, W [4]

zizel, *n.* (1785) *Ornith.* [Ad. of G *Ziesel*, a short. of *Zieselmaus* ground squirrel < MHG *zisel*, prob. < Czech *sysel*] Suslik, a ground squirrel. 0 [3]

Z line, *n.* (1916) *Biol.* Var. **Z band** (1950) [Transl. of G *Schicht z* (1873) < *Schicht* row + *z*, a short. of *Zwischenscheibe*—see Z disk] A transverse stripe within striated muscle fibers. O [3]

Zn, *see* zinc

zoisite, *n.* (1805) *Mineral.* [G *Zoisit* < the name of the Austrian scholar and financier of mineral-collecting expeditions, Baron Sigismund von *Zois* Eidelstein (1747–1819) + G *-it* -ite] A native silicate of aluminum and calcium, also called *thulite.* —**zoisitization**. O, R, W [4]

Zollverein, *n.* (1843) *Econ.* Var. **zollverein** (1893) [G < *Zoll* toll customs + *Verein* union] A customs union, as in the German one formed in 1843. —**zollvereinist**. O, R, W [3]

zonolimnetic, *a. Ecology* [G *zonolimnetisch* < *zono-* + *limnetisch* < *Limnet* (< Gk *zṓnē* + *límnē* pool) + G adj. suffix *-isch* -ic] Of or relating to a specific zone in depth, particularly for freshwater planktonic animals. W [3]

zoochlorella, -e *pl.* (1889) *Ecology* Var. **Zoochlorella** (1889) [G (1881), coined by the German anatomist Karl Andreas Heinrich Brandt (1854–1931) < *zoo-* + *Chlorella* < Gk *zoôn* living organism, animal + *chlōrós* green + dim. L suffix *-ella* -ella] One of the numerous minute green algae that usu. live symbiotically in the cytoplasm of some protozoans and other invertebrates. O, W [3]

zooxanthella, -e *pl.* (1889) *Ecology* [G *Zooxanthelle* (1881), coined by Brandt (see *zoochlorella*) < *zoo-* + *Xanthelle* < Gk *zoôn* living organism, animal + *xanthós* yellow + dim. L suffix *-ella* -ella] One of the numerous yellow-brown, symbiotic dinoflagellates that live in the cytoplasm of some radiolarians, coral polyps, and other marine invertebrates. O, W [3]

zope, *n.* (1880) *Ichthy.* [G, prob. < Slav (cf. Russ *sapá*)] *Abramis ballerus*, a type of carp found in rivers and lakes that empty into the North Sea and the Baltic] A common bream. O [3]

Zr, *see* zirconium

zugtrompete, *n.* (1938) *Music* [G < *Zug* tug, pull + *Trompete* trumpet < MFr *trompette*] A slide trumpet. O [2]

Zugunruhe, *n.* (1950) *Ornith.* [G < *Zug* flight, flock, migration + *Unruhe* restlessness, disquiet] Migratory restlessness, esp. birds' migratory drive. O [3]

zugzwang, *n.* (1904) *Games* Var. **Zugzwang** [G < *Zug* move (in chess) + *Zwang* compulsion] A position in chess when a player is required to move a piece, but cannot do so without disadvantage; the requirement to do this or some other unpleasant action. • ~ often appears in the phrase ''in Zugzwang'' (1935). O, R, W [3]

zum Beispiel [G < *zum* for + *Beispiel* example] For example. W2 [2]

zwanziger, *n.* (1828) *Currency* [G, a short. of *Zwanzig-kreuzer(stück)* < *zwanzig* twenty + *Kreuzer* kreutzer (q.v.) (+ *Stück* piece)] A former Austrian or German silver coin worth twenty kreutzers. O, W [3]

zwetschenwasser, *n.* *Beverages* [G, lit., plum water < *Zwetsche* (< L *damascēnus* plum from Damascus, ult. < Ar) + G *Wasser* water] A colorless plum brandy. W [3]

Zwickau prophet, *n.* *Theol.* [G *Zwickauer Prophet* (1522), so named by Luther < *Zwickauer* hailing from Zwickau, eastern Germany + *Prophet* < L *prophēta* < Gk *prophḗtēs*] A member of a 16th-century Anabaptist sect based in Zwickau, whose leaders like Nikolaus Storch and Thomas Drechsel claimed to have prophetic powers. W [3]

zwieback, -ø/-s *pl.* (1894) *Food* [G, lit., twice-baked < *zwie* twice + *backen* to bake] A biscuit or usu. sweet rusk that is first baked and then toasted until crisp. O, R, W [4]

zwieselite, *n.* (1861) *Mineral.* [G *Zwieselit* (1841) < *Zwiesel,* the name of a town in Bavaria, Germany + *-it* -ite] A monoclinic variety of triplite. O [3]

zwinger, *n.* *Mil.* [G < Late MHG *twingere, zwinger* keep, i.e., outer courtyard, enclosure] A fortress protecting a city. W [3]

zwischenspiel, *n.* *Music* [G < *zwischen* between + *Spiel* play] A musical interlude, esp. the instrumental ones between the stanzas of a song, or the *tutti* sections in a concerto: intermezzo. W [3]

zwischenzug, *n.* (1941) *Games* [G < *zwischen* intermediary, between + *Zug* move (in chess)] An interim or temporizing move in chess. O [3]

zwitterion, *n.* (1906) *Chem.* [G (1897) < *Zwitter* hybrid + *Ion* (< Gk) ion] A dipolar ion, in which the ion or molecule has separate positively and negatively charged atoms or groups. —**zwitterionic** (1946). O, R, W [4]

zygadite, *n.* (1861) *Mineral.* [G *Zygadit* < Gk *zygádēn* in pairs + G *-it* -ite] A variety of albite occurring in tabular twin crystals. O [3]

zygomycetes, *pl.* (1874) *Bot.* [G *Zygomyceten* conjugations (1872) < L < Gk *zygón* + *mýkēs* fungus + L *cytus* cell] A class of saprophytic and parasitic fungi in which sexual reproduction is by fusing usu. similar gametangia to produce a zygospore, and asexual reproduction is by means of nonmobile spores. —**zygomycetous** (1928). O [3]

zygosome, *n.* (1905) *Biol.* [G *Zygosom* (1904) < *zygo-* + *-som* < Gk *zygón* yoke, conjugation + *sôma* body] A bivalent chromosome. O [3]

zygospore, *n.* (1864) *Bot.* [G *Zygospor* < *zygo-* (< Gk *zygón* yoke, conjugation) + G *Spor* < OHG *spori* soft, putrid, suffering from dry rot < Gk *sporá*] A plant spore formed by conjugation of two similar sexual cells, as in certain fungi and algae. —**zygosporic** (1906). O, R, W [4]

Zyklon, *n.* (1926) *Tech.* Var. **zyklon** (1939), **Cyclon** (1944) [G a trademark, perhaps < Gk *kyklós* cycle] Hydrogen cyanide as derived from a carrier in the form of small tablets, used as a fumigant and formerly as a poison gas in Nazi death camps, usu. Zyklon B. O [3]

zymogen, *n.* (1877) *Biochem.* [G (1875) < *zymo-* + *-gen* < Gk *zýmē* sour dough + *-genēs* producing] An inactive protein precursor of an enzyme, also called *proenzyme.* —**xymogen,** *a.* (1896); **-ic** (1884); **-ous.** O, R, W [4]

PART IV
APPENDIX

SECONDARY SOURCES USED IN THE APPENDIX OF SUPPLEMENTARY LOANWORDS

These sources generally do not include dates of first use in English for borrowings from foreign languages.

Ad   Adkins, Lasky, Roy A. Adkins, and David Charles, eds. *A Thesaurus of British Archaeology.* London: New Abbott, 1982

Al   Allen, Edward Moninton. *Harper's Dictionary of the Graphic Arts.* New York: Harper & Row, 1983

Ap   Apel, Willi, ed. *The Harvard Dictionary of Music.* Cambridge, MA: Harvard University Press, 1969

Bo   Boger, Louise Ade, ed. *The Dictionary of World Pottery and Porcelain.* New York: Charles Scribner's Sons, 1971

Cam   *Cambridge University Press Files.* March 1986

Can   Cannon, Garland. "German Loanwords in English." *American Speech* 65 (1990): 260–65

Car   Carr, Charles T. *The German Influence on the English Vocabulary.* Society for Pure English 41. Oxford: Clarendon Press, 1934

Cu   Cummings, Parke, ed. *The Basic Dictionary of Sports.* New York: A. S. Barnes, 1949

Do   Douglas, J. D., Walter E. Elwell, and Peter Toon, eds. *The Concise Dictionary of the Christ Tradition.* Grand Rapids, MI: Zondervan, 1989

Ei   Eichhoff, Jürgen. "Deutsches Lehngut und seine Funktion in der amerikanischen Pressesprache." *Jahrbuch für Amerikastudien* 17 (1972): 156–212

Fl   Fleming, John, Hugh Honour, and Allen Lane, eds. *The Penguin Dictionary of Decorative Arts.* London: Penguin Books, 1977

Fr   Freiberger, W. F., ed. *The International Dictionary of Applied Mathematics.* Princeton, NJ: D. Van Nostrand, 1960

Go   Gould, Julius, and William L. Kolb, eds. *A Dictionary of Social Science.* New York: Free Press, 1964

Gr   Gray, H. J., and Alan Isaacs, eds. *A New Dictionary of Physics.* London: Longman Groups, 1975

Hai   Haislund, Niels. "German Loanwords in English." *Kopenhagener germanische Studien* 1 (1969): 126–38

Har   Hartog, Jan de. *The Lambs War.* New York: Harper & Row, 1980, pp. 10–11

Ho   Hope, Thomas E. *Lexical Borrowing in the Romance Languages.* New York: New York University Press, 1971, pp. 610–19

Il   Illingworth, Valerie, ed. *The Macmillan Dictionary of Astronomy.* 2nd ed. London: Macmillan, 1985

Jac   Jackson, Benjamin Daydon, ed. *A Glossary of Botanical Terms.* 4th ed. Dehra Dun, India: Bishen Singh Mahendra Pal Singh, 1986

Jar   Jarka, Horst. "The Language of Skiers." *American Speech* 38 (1963): 202–8

Ka   Kann, Hans-Joachim, "The Burger Family." *Jahrbuch für Amerikastudien* 17 (1972): 212–15

Ka1   —"Deutsches Lehngut in TIME (1973 und 1974)." *Lebende Sprachen* 20 (1975): 134 f

Ka2   —"DDR-Deutsch in TIME Magazine (1963–1973)." *Zeitschrift für Dialektologie und Linguistik* 42 (1975): 63 f

Ka3   —"Entlehnungen aus dem Deutschen in TIME." *Muttersprache* 84 (1974): 430 f

Ka4   —"Neue Germanismen in TIME 1980." *Der Sprachdienst* 25 (1981): 94 f

Ka5   —"Neue Germanismen in TIME 1984." *Der Sprachdienst* 29 (1985): 38 f

Ka6   —"Neue Germanismen in TIME 1985." *Der Sprachdienst* 30 (1986): 39 f

Ka7   —"Neue Germanismen in TIME 1987." *Der Sprachdienst* 32 (1988): 77 f

Ka8   —"Neue Germanismen in TIME 1989." *Der Sprachdienst* 34 (1990): 99 f

Ke   Kennedy, Michael. *The Oxford Dictionary of Music.* New York: Oxford University Press, 1985

Ku   Kurath, Hans. "German Relics in Pennsylvania English." *Monatshefte* 37 (1945): 96–102

La   Landau, Sidney I., ed. *International Dictionary of Medicine and Biology.* 3 vols. New York: John Wiley and Sons, 1986

Lap   Lapedes, Daniel N., ed. *McGraw-Hill Dictionary of Scientific and Technical Terms.* New York: McGraw-Hill, 1974

Le   Leach, Maria, and Jerome Fried, eds. *Funk and Wagnalls Standard Dictionary of Folklore, Mythology, and Legends.* New York: Funk & Wagnalls, 1972

Li   Liedtke, Herbert. "The Evolution of the Ski-Lingo in America." *Monatshefte* 35 (1943): 116–124

Lu   Lucie-Smith, Edward, ed. *The Thames and Hudson Dictionary of Art Terms.* London: Thames and Hudson, 1984

Men   Mencken, H. L. *The American Language.* 4th ed. New York: Alfred A. Knopf, 1947

Men1   —*The American Language, Supplement I.* New York: Alfred A. Knopf, 1945

Men2   —*The American Language, Supplement II.* New York: Alfred A. Knopf, 1948

Mer   Meringer, R. "Wörter und Sachen." *Indogermanische Forschung* 16 (1924): 101

Ne   *The New Dictionary of American Slang.* Ed. Robert L. Chapman. New York: Harper & Row, 1986 (based on Harold Wentworth and Stuart B. Flexner, eds., *Dictionary of American Slang.* New York, Crowell, 1975)

Pa   Parker, Sybil P. *McGraw-Hill Dictionary of Physics.* New York: McGraw-Hill, 1985

Pe   Pei, Mario. *Glossary of Linguistic Terminology.* New York: Columbia University Press, 1966

Po   Poggendorff, J. C., *et al. J. C. Poggendorffs biographisch-literarisches Handwörterbuch für Mathematik, Astronomie, Physik mit Geophysik, Chemie, Kristallographie und verwandte Wissenschaftsgebiete,* hrsg. von der Sächsischen Akademie der Wissenschaften zu Leipzig. Leipzig: J. A. Barth, 1863–

Pr   Preger, Wilhelm. *Geschichte der deutschen Mystik.* 3 vols. Leipzig: Dorffling & Franke, 1874–93. Reprinted 1960

Ra   Ramsay, L. G. G., ed. *The Complete Encyclopedia of Antics.* New York: Hawthorn Books, 1962

Re   *Reader's Digest.* December 1990, pp. 31, 154

Ro   Rohrer, Christian. *Die Tempelgesellschaft.* Stuttgart: Hoffman, 1920

Ru   Runes, Dagobert D. *Runes Dictionary of Philosophy.* New York: Philosophical Library, 1983

Sa   Safire, William, ed. *Safire's Political Dictionary.* 3rd ed. New York: Random House, 1978

Sc   Schönfelder, Karl-Heinz. *Deutsches Lehngut im amerikanischen Englisch.* Halle (Saale): VEB Max Niemeyer, 1957

Se   Seymour-Smith, Charlotte, ed. *Dictionary of Anthropology.* Boston: G. K. Hall, 1986

Spo   Spong, John S. *Rescuing the Bible from Fundamentalism.* San Francisco, New York: HarperCollins, 1991, pp. 22 f

Spr   *Der Sprach-Brockhaus,* mit einem Vorwort von F. A. Brockhaus. 7th ed. Wiesbaden; F. A. Brockhaus, 1966

Su   Suess, Eduard. *Das Antlitz der Erde.* Prag, Wien: F. Tempsky, 1901. Vol. 3: 1

Th   Thompson, Oscar, ed. *International Cyclopedia of Music and Musicians.* 9th ed. New York: Dodd, Mead, 1964

Thr   Thrush, Paul W., ed. *A Dictionary of Mining and Related Terms.* Washington, D.C.: U.S. Department of the Interior, 1968

Ti   *Time* (Special German Unification Edition), pp. 10 ff

To   Walton, E. K., B. A. O. Randall, M. H. Battey, and O. Tomkeieff, eds. *The S. I. Tomkeieff Dictionary of Petrology.* New York: John Wiley and Sons, 1983

Ve   Veatch, J. O., and C. R. Humphreys. *Water and Water Use Terminology.* Kakaunu, WI: Thomas Printing and Publishing, 1966

Wi   Witherhouse, Ruth D., ed. *The Macmillan Book of Archaeology.* London: Macmillan, 1983

SUPPLEMENTARY LOANWORDS

abbau, *n. Biol.* (rare) [G <*ab* down + *Bau* structure, i.e., demolition, reduction, decomposition] Catabolism or its products. La

abdämpfen, *v. Music* [G < *ab* down + *dämpfen* dampen, i.e., to tone down (actually, an imper. form of the verb)] (A notation to) mute, esp. in connection with timpani. Ap, Ke

Abglitt, *n. Ling.* [G < *abgleiten* to slide off] A partial synonym for off-glide or Absatz (q.v.). Pe

ablösen, *v. Music* [G < *ab* off, away + *lösen* to dissolve, loosen, remove (actually, an imper. form of the verb)] (A notation to) separate the notes, i.e., play staccato. Ke

abnehmend, *a. Music* [G < present part. of *abnehmen* to decrease] (A notation to play) diminuendo. Ap, Ke

abraumsalze, *pl. Mining* Var. (in transl.) **Abraum salts** (see main Dictionary) [G < *Abraum* top layer of soil, etc. over minerals + *Salze,* pl. of *Salz* salt] At one time, salts regarded as waste during the excavation of ore, but now known to contain valuable potash salts. To

ABS, *n. Transportation* [G abbr. of *Antiblockiersystem* < *anti-* (< Gk) against + G *blockieren* to block + *System* system < L *systēma* < Gk] Antilock braking system. Cam

Absatz, *n. Ling.* [G pause, stop, break < *absetzen* to pause, interrupt] According to Henry Sweet, the final phase in the articulation of a phoneme, during which the vocal organs return to their neutral position or assume one in anticipation of forming another sound. Pe

absetzen, *v. Music* [G < *ab* off, away from, apart + *setzen* to set (actually, an imper. form of the verb)] (A notation) to separate either notes or phrases. Ap

abstossen, *v. Music.* [G *abstoßen* < *ab* away from, apart + *stoßen* to push, actually an imper. form of the verb] (A notation) to play staccato; in organ playing, to cease using a stop. Ap, Ke

abteilung, *n. Mining* [G < *abteilen* to divide, partition off + nom. suffix *-ung* -ing] A part of a district of a mine assigned to the care of a fireman or deputy; a stratigraphical formation or series. Thr

abtropfung, *n. Med.* [G < *abtropfen* to drip or trickle down + nom. suffix *-ung* ing] The process of maturation of pigmented nevi cells during which those next to the basal layer move to the dermal layer of the epidermis. La

abwechseln, *v. Music* [G < *ab* off + *wechseln* to change, i.e., to alternate (actually, an imper. form)] (A notation to) change (used with reference to orchestral instruments alternating with one another in the hands of the same player). Ke, Th

Achtelpause, *n. Music* [G < *Achtel* eighth + *Pause* pause < Gk *paûsis*] A quaver (eighth) rest. Ap, Ke

Achtfuss, *n. Music* [G < *acht* eight + *Fuß* foot] An eight-foot (stop). Ap

actuality[1], *n. Philos.* [Transl. of G *Wirklichkeit* reality < *wirklich* real + nom. suffix *-keit* -ity] In Edmund Husserl, actual individual existence in space and time, as contrasted with mere possibility. Ru

actuality[2], *n. Philos., Psych.* [Ad. of G *Aktualität* < *aktual* actual < LL *āctuālis* + G *-ität* -ty] The character of conscious processes as lived in by the ego, in contrast with "actuality" of conscious processes more or less far from the ego. Ru

adergneiss, *n. Geol.* [G < *Ader* vein, artery + *Gneis* gneiss] Arterite, i.e., gneiss or schist veined by a network of granitic veinlets. To

Adlerglas, *n. Art* [G < *Adler* eagle + *Glas* glass] A tall, cylindrical German type of drinking glass, with or without a cover, decorated in enamel with a double eagle of the Holy Roman Empire displaying on its wings the 56 armorial bearings of the confederate families ruling the empire; also called *Adlerhumpen* or *Reichsadlerhumpen.* Fl

Adlerhumpen, *see* Adlerglas

aesthetic judgment, *n. Philos.* [Transl. of G *ästhetische Urteilskraft* < *ästhetisch* aesthetic + *Urteilskraft* < the gen. of *Urteil* judgment + *Kraft* power, strength] The power of judgment exercised upon data supplied by the feelings or sense of beauty. Ru

affection, *see* doctrine of affection

Affekt, *see* mit Affekt

affektepilepsie, *n. Med.* [G < *Affekt* fervor, strong emotion, passion + *Epilepsie* epilepsy < L *affectus* + Gk *epilēpsia*] An obs. term for hysterical convulsion. La

affektvoll, *a. Music* [G < *Affekt* fervor (< L *affectus*) + G *voll* full (of)] (A direction to play) with fervor. Ke

Affenkapelle, *n. Art* [G < *Affen,* pl. of *Affe* ape, monkey + *Kapelle* orchestra, band] A German type of singerie in porcelain, consisting of about 26 figures, made in Meissen between 1750 and 1760. Fl

Affenspalte, *n. Med.* [G < the comb. form of *Affe* ape, monkey + *Spalte* fissure, cleft] Sulcus lunatus. La

359

AG, *n. Commerce* [G abbr. of *Aktiengesellschaft* < *Aktie,* pl. *Aktien* stock + *Gesellschaft* company] (The German equivalent of) Inc. (i.e., incorporated). Ti

agenda, *n. Theol.* (regional) [G *Agende* < L *agenda* things to be done < *agere* to do, act] Agendum, i.e., the order of worship (in Protestant Christianity). Men

Akkord, *n. Music* [G < Fr *accord* < *accorder* to tune (harmonize instruments)] A chord. Ke

akkordieren, *v. Music* [G < Fr *accorder* to tune (harmonize) instruments] To tune. Ke

aldo-, *comb. form Chem.* [G comb. form < *Aldehyd* aldehyde (see main Dictionary)] Relating to an aldose. La

algebraization, *n. Philos.* [Transl. of G *Algebraisierung* < *algebraisieren* to convert into algebraic symbols < *Algebra* algebra (ult. <Ar *al-jabr*) + G verbal suffix -*isieren* < Fr -*iser* -ize, -ise + G nom. suffix -*ung* -ing, -tion, etc.] In Husserl, substitution of algebraic symbols (intermediate terms) in which the material context of an objective sense is experienced. Ru

allgemeingültig, *a. Philos.* [G < *allgemein* general(ly) + *gültig* valid] Said of a proposition or judgment that is universally valid or necessary. Ru

alpenstich, *n. Med.* [G < *Alpen,* comb. form denoting Alpine + *Stich* stab, sting, stroke] An epidemic form of Alpine pneumonia. La

alraun, *n. Myth.* [G mandrake] (The German name for) the mandrake or a similar root, as the bryony, used in magic. Le

Altgeige, *n. Music* [G < *Alt* (< L *vox alta*) + *Geige* violin] Viola. Ke

am Frosch, *Music* 'obG < *am* at the + *Frosch* nut, frog (of the fiddle bow)] (Direction to use the portion of the violin bow nearest the right hand) at the nut. Ap, Ke

am Griffbrett, *Music* [G < *am* at the + *Griffbrett* fingerboard < *Griff* grip, handle < *greifen* to take hold + *Brett* board] (Direction in violin playing to bow) near or at the fingerboard. Ap

am Steg, *Music* [G < *am* at the, on the + *Steg* bridge (of a violin, etc.)] (Direction in violin playing, to bow) at the bridge. Ap, Ke

andächtig, *a. Music* [G < *Andacht* devotion + adj. suffix -*ig* -y, etc.] (Direction to play) with devotion. Ap

and how!, *interj.* [Transl. of G *und wie* and how] And how! (an exclamation used to confirm someone else's assessment). Men

Angang, *n. Myth.* [G < *angehen* to approach] An ominous encounter, usu. limited to the first person or animal met in going on or returning from a journey. Le

Anhang, *n. Music* [G < *anhängen* to attach, supplement] A supplement, i.e., a coda in the musical sense; in musicological terminology, a section appended to a critical edition of a work containing variant readings, material of doubtful attribution, etc. Ke

anker, *n.* [G < ML *anc(h)eria* small vat] A unit of capacity equal to 10 U.S. gallons; a unit to measure liquids, esp. honey, oil, vinegar, spirits, and wine. Pa

Anlage, *n. Bot.* [G predisposition, hereditary factor(s)] Ru-

diment, inception, primordium, fundament. (See *anlage* in main Dictionary.) Jac

anmutig, *a. Music* [G < *Anmut* charm, grace + adj. suffix -*ig* -y] (A notation to play) with charm and grace. Ke

Ansatz, *n. Music* [G < *ansetzen* (point, place at which, or manner in which) to begin, initiate] In singing, the proper adjustment of the vocal apparatus; in playing wind instruments, the proper adjustment of the lips; in violin playing, attack. Ap

Ansbacher, *n. Beverages* (rare) [G short. of *Ansbacherbier* < *Ansbacher* of or from Ansbach, the name of a city in Bavaria, Germany + *Bier* beer] A beer orig. brewed in Ansbach. Sc

Anschlag, *n. Music* [G < *anschlagen* (manner in which) to strike, touch] Sometimes called *double appogiatura,* but actually consisting of the notes immediately below and above the principal notes; in piano playing, touch. Ap, Ke

Ansichtslosigkeit, *n. Philos.* [G, lit., the state of being devoid of a point of view < *ansichtslos* having no opinion, without a point of view (coined specif. in imitation of *aussichtslos* without any hope, hopeless) + nom. suffix -*igkeit* -ity] Objectivity or an unmediated approach to bare fact. Ru

apochromat, *n. Med.* [G back-formation < *apochromatisch* < Gk *apó* down, away + *chrôma* (gen. *chrômatos*) color + G adj. suffix -*isch* -ic] An apochromatic objective without secondary spectrum. La

appearances, *pl. Philos.* [Transl. of G *Erscheinungen* (pl.) manifestations < *erscheinen* to appear, become evident + nom. suffix -*ung* -ing, -ance] In Kant, applied to things as they are for human experience, as opposed to things as they are for themselves. Ru

appresentation, *n. Philos.* [G *Appräsentation* < L *ap-* < *ad* toward + Fr *présentation* portrayal] In Edmund Husserl, the function of a presentation proper as motivating the experiential positing of something else as present along with the strictly presented object. Ru

Arbeitstier, -e *pl.* (1987) *Sociol.* [G workhorse < the gen. of *Arbeit* work + *Tier* animal] Workhorse. Ka8

architectonic(s), *n.* (1838) *Philos.* [Ad. of G *Architektonik* < L *architectonicus* < Gk *architektonikós* of a master builder] In Kant, the formal scheme, structural design, or method of elucidation of a system. Ru

Atempause, *n. Music* [G < *atmen* to breathe + *Pause* pause < L *pausa*] A very short rest used in instrumental performances for the sake of articulation in phrasing. Ap

at-handedness, *n. Philos.* [Transl. of G *Zuhandenheit* < *zuhanden* close at hand + nom. suffix -*heit* -(ed)ness] In Martin Heidegger, a deficient form of the more basic relationships, as opposed to those described by on-handedness. Ru

Atmungsferment, *n. Med.* [G < the gen. of *Atmung* breathing, respiration + *Ferment* enzyme < L *fermentum* yeast] Warburg's respiratory enzyme. La

Atomzahl, *n. Geol.* [G (1871) < *Atom* atom (< Gk *átomos*) + G *Zahl* number] The sum of the atoms and metals contained in a unit weight of rock. To

auf der G, *Music* [G, lit., on or at the G string] (A notation to initiate the sound) at the G string. Ke

aufgeregt, *a. Music* [G < past part. of *aufregen* to excite] (A notation to play in an) excited (mode). Ap

Aufhebung, *n. Ling.* [G suspension, neutralization] Neutralization or the temporary suspension in some position or environment of an otherwise functioning phonemic difference or distinction. Pe

aufwuchs¹, *n. Biol.* [G growth < *auf* on, upon + *Wuchs* growth] Organism(s) attached to an underwater substrate without penetrating its surface. Ve

aufwuchs², *n. Med.* [G < *auf* on, upon + *Wuchs* growth, shape] Periphyton. La

Augen-gabbro, *n. Geol.* [G < *Augen,* pl. of *Auge* eye + *Gabbro* gabbro] A dynamically metamorphized gabbro intermediate in structure between flaser-gabbro and gabbro-schist, with well-developed, lozenge-shaped masses of the original rock preserved among the recrystallized laminae. To

Augen-granulite, *n. Geol.* [G *Augengranulit* < *Augen,* pl. of *Auge* eye + *Granulit* granulite] A granulite containing lozenge-shaped aggregates of quartz, feldspar, or garnet, surrounded by fine-grained aggregates of the same mineral and mica. To

Augenmigmatite, *n. Geol.* [G *Augenmigmatit* < *Augen,* pl. of *Auge* eye + *Migmatit* migmatite] A foliated migmatite with pinkish orthoclase augen (see main Dictionary). To

Augen-mylonite, *n. Geol.* [G *Augenmylonit* < *Augen,* pl. of *Auge* eye + *Mylonit* mylonite] A mylonite with augen structure. To

Augensalz, *n. Geol.* [G < *Augen,* pl. of *Auge* eye + *Salz* salt] (A local German term for) nodules of coarse halite embedded in certain horizons of Alpine salt deposits. To

Augen-schist, *n. Geol.* [Prob. partial translation of G *Augenschiefer* < *Augen,* pl. of *Auge* eye + *Schiefer* slate, schist] A schist with small augen or eyes of feldspar or other minerals. To

augen structure, *n. Geol.* [G *Augenstruktur* < *Auge,* pl. *Augen* eyes + *Struktur* (< L *structūra*) structure] A structure in some gneisses and granites in which certain mineral constituents were squeezed into elliptical or lens-shaped forms and, esp. if surrounded by parallel flakes of mica, resemble eyes. To

ausbrenner, *n. Beverages* (regional trade jargon) [G < *ausbrennen,* lit., to burn out or off] A jet device for burning old pitch off the inner surfaces of kegs before applying a new seal. Men2

Austausch coefficient, *n. Physics* [G *Austauschkoeffizient* < *Austausch* exchange, interchange + *Koeffizient* coefficient < NL *coefficient-, coefficiens*] A measure of turbulent mixing, i.e., the product of mass and transverse distance travelled in a unit of time by a fluid in turbulent motion as it passes through a unit area that is conceived as lying parallel to the general direction of flow. Lap, To

austempering, *verbal n. Metall.* [G *aus* out, de- + E *tempering*] The quenching of a ferrous alloy from a temperature above the transformation range. Lap

Auszug, *n. Music* [G < *ausziehen* to extract, make an ab-stract] An arrangement, usu. for piano, of an opera, oratorio, etc. Ap, Ke

autoklastisch, *a.* (1894) *Geol.* Var. **autoclastic** [G < Gk *autós* directly + *klastikós* < *klastós* broken] A term applied to rocks that have been brecciated in place by mechanical processes. To

axiological, *a. Philos.* [Ad. of G *axiologisch* < the comb. form of Gk *áxios* worth + *logikós* pertaining to reason + G *-isch* -ical] In Husserl, of or pertaining to value or theory of value (the latter term understood as including disvalue and value-indifference). Ru

Backsteingothik, *n. Art* [G < *Backstein* brick + *Gothik* (now *Gotik*) Gothic] The simplified, brick-built, 19th-cent. Gothic architecture typical of North Germany. Lu

Baden culture, *n. Archaeology* [Ad. of G *Badener Kultur* < *Badener* of or hailing from *Baden,* the western part of the state of Baden-Württemberg + *Kultur* culture < L *cultūra*] A third millennium B.C. Copper Age culture group of vast extent in eastern Europe. Wi

Bahnung, *n. Med.* [G < *bahnen* to make or pave the way + nom. suffix *-ung* -ing] The increased ease of transmission of a nerve impulse in fibers of the central nervous system by repeated stimulation. La

Bankkrieg, *n.* (1990) *Commerce* [G, lit., bank (or economic) war, coined on the analogy of *Blitzkrieg* and *Sitzkrieg* (see main Dictionary)] Economic warfare. Re

base wax, *n. Sports* [Transl. of G *Grundwachs* < *Grund* base, bottom + *Wachs* wax] A wax applied to the dry running surface of the ski as a protection against moisture and wearing. Jar

basic hornfels, *n. Geol.* [Compounding of E *basic* + G *Hornfels* hornfels (see main Dictionary)] A hornfels derived from a basic igneous rock. Ti

Bassettflöte, *n. Music* Var. **Bassflöte** [G < It *bassetto,* dim. of *basso* bass + *Flöte* flute] A 17th and 18th century name for a recorder of low pitch. Ke

Bassflöte, see Bassettflöte

bass trombone, *n. Music* [Transl. of G *Baßposaune* < *Baß* bass + *Posaune* trombone] A wind instrument with a range to F or E below the tenor trombone B-flat. Ke

bass trumpet, *n. Music* [Ad. of G *Baßtrompete* < *Baß* bass + *Trompete* trumpet < MF *trompette*] A wind instrument made of brass; a valve trombone pitched in C. Ke

bast, *n. Bot.* [G < inner bark, fiber < MHG, OHG *bast* fiber] The inner fibrous bark of the lime tree; phloëm (see main Dictionary); fibrous tissue providing mechanical support. Jac

bebend, *a. Music* [G < present part. of *beben* to reverberate] (A direction to play) with a tremolo. Ke

bedächtig, *a. Music* [G < *Bedacht* deliberation + adj. suffix *-ig* -y, i.e., deliberate] (A notation to play) unhurriedly, with deliberation. Ke

beer-schiessen, *n. Beverages* (regional trade jargon) [G *Bierschießen* < *Bier* beer + *Schießen* shooting, (here, fig.) dispensing (time)] A beer break. Men2

beer-shooter, *n. Beverages* (regional trade jargon) [Transl. of G *Bierschießer* < *Bier* beer + *Schießer* dispenser] A person who dispenses beer to workers whenever they take a beer break. Men2

begeistert, *a. Music* [G < past part. of *begeistern* to enthuse, inspire] (A notation to play) with enthusiasm, inspired(ly). Ke

Begleitung, *n. Music* [G < *begleiten* to accompany + nom. suffix *-ung* -ing, -ment)] Accompaniment. Ap, Ke

Begriffsgefühl, *n. Philos.* [G < the gen. of *Begriff* concept + *Gefühl* feeling] The faculty of eliciting feelings, images, or recollections associated with concepts or capable of being substituted for them. Ru

behaglich, *n. Music* [G < *Behagen* comfort, ease + adj. suffix *-lich* -ly] (A notation to play) with ease. Ap

behend(e), *a. Music* [G < MHG *behende,* orig. adv. *bi-hende* at hand, handy] (A notation to play) nimbly, quickly. Ap

beherzt, *adv. Music* [G < past part. of *beherzen* to be of courage] (A notation to play) boldly. Ke

beklemmt/beklommen, *a. Music* [G < past part. of *beklemmen* to oppress, cause anguish] (A notation to play as if feeling) oppressed or being heavy of heart. Ke

belsnickle, *n.* (1823 *DA*) *Theol.* (regional) Var. **bells-nickel, bell-snickle, beltznickle, bensnickel** [Folk-etymological ad. of G *Pelznickel* (orig. *Pelzmichel* < *Pelz* pelt, fur + *Michel* fellow, person) a person disguised in furs] A boogieman accompanying St. Nicholas on his rounds. Sc

belustigend, *a. Music* [G < present part. of *belustigen* to amuse, cheer up] (A notation to play) with gaiety. Ke

bergmahl/bergmeal, *see* bergmehl (in main Dictionary)

berg till, *n. Geol.* [Prob. partial transfer of G *Berg* < *Eisberg* (ice)berg (see main Dictionary) + E *till*] Detrital matter dropped in lacustrine clay by melting icebergs. To

Bernstein, *n. Geol.* [G amber < LG < MLG *bern(e)stein* < *bernen* to burn + *stein* stone] Amber. To

beruhigend, *a. Music* [G < present part. of *beruhigen* to calm, quieten] (A notation to create a mood that is) calming, quieting. Ap, Ke

beruhigt, *a. Music* [G < past part. of *beruhigen* to calm, soothe] (A direction calling for a sound that is) calm, relaxed. Ap, Ke

beschleunigt, *a. Music* [G < past part. of *beschleunigen* to accelerate] (A notation to play) at a faster tempo. Ap

Besetzung, *n. Music* [G < *besetzen* to cast or fill parts or to designate instruments + nom. suffix *-ung* -ing] Casting, instrumentation, and/or designation of voices employed in a composition. Ap

bestand, *n. Bot.* [G < *bestehen* to exist; resist] Durable form. Jac

bestimmt, *a. Music* [G < past part. of *bestimmen* to decide] (A notation to play) with resolve, decisive(ly). Ap, Ke

Bewußtsein überhaupt, *Philos.* [G < *Bewußtsein* consciousness + *überhaupt* in general, on the whole as such] Consciousness conceived as a real entity over and above individual consciousness. Ru

beziehungswahn, *n. Med.* [G < the gen. of *Beziehung* reference + *Wahn* erron. opinion, delusion, madness] Psychiatric delusion of reference. La

bicycle Bahn, -en *pl.* (1989) *Transportation* [Compounding of E *bicycle* + G *Bahn,* or partial transl. of *Fahrrad* bicycle + *Bahn* track, path, lane] A bicycle lane. Ka8

blatterstein, *n.* (1823) *Geol.* [G < *Blatt,* pl. *Blätter* leaf + *Stein* stone, i.e., slate-like or tuffaceous stone] (A local German name for) variolite. To

Blitz-krampf, *n. Med.* [G < *Blitz* lightning + *Krampf* cramp, spasm] Convulsion or infantile massive spasm. La

Blitz-Nick-und-Salaam-krampf, *Med.* [G < *Blitz* lightning (speed) + *Nick-* < *nicken* to nod + *und* and + *Salam* (< Ar) salaam + G *Krampf* cramp, spasm] Salaam convulsion. La

blown fifth, *n.* (1928) *Music* [Transl. of G *Blasquinte* < *blasen* to blow + *Quinte* (< MFr) fifth] A fifth of 678 cents, as established by E. M. Hornbostel in his paper on musical norms. Ap

BMW, *n. Transportation* [G abbr. of *Bayerische Motoren Werke* Bavarian Motor Works] (By extension) the name of a luxury car manufactured by the BMW in Munich. Ti

bodenplatte, *n. Med.* [G < *Boden* bottom, floor + *Platte* plate] Bottom or floor plate. La

bogen structure, *n. Geol.* Var. **bogenstruktur** [G < *Bogen* arch + *Struktur* structure < L *strūctūra*] The structure of glassy tuffs, composed largely of curved shards of glass. To

bogen texture, *n.* (1893) *Geol.* [Partial transl. of G *Bogenstruktur* < *Bogen* bow + *Struktur* (< L *strūctūra*) structure, texture] A term for the texture of vitric tuffs composed largely of shards and bows of glass formed by the explosive disruption of vesicles in lavas. To

Bonner Durchmusterung, *n.* (1859–62) *Astronomy* [G < *Bonner* hailing from *Bonn,* Germany + *Durchmusterung* a star catalog] A general star catalog prepared by the Prussian astronomer Friedrich Argelander (1799–1875), published in Bonn (1859–62). Il

Böttichertanz, *n. Dance* [G < *Bötticher* cooper + *Tanz* dance] A carnival dance performed in Munich, Germany, every seven years, in which two lines of men polka through quadrille variations and longways formations; also called *Schäfflertanz.* Le

Brandwirtschaft, *n. Archaeology* [G < *Brand* burn + *Wirtschaft* economy] Burn beating, i.e., the burning of vegetation and the use of ashes in the neolithic period to enhance the fertility of the soil. Ad

breit, *a. Music* [G < It *largo*] (A notation calling for a pace that is) slow and expressive. Ap, Ke

brennschluss, *n. Aeron.* [G < *brennen* to burn + *Schluß* conclusion, cessation] The cessation of burning in a rocket, resulting from complete consumption of the propellant, from deliberate shutoff, or from other causes. Lap, To

Brummeisen, *n. Music* [G < *brummen* to hum + *Eisen* iron, actually an elastic metal tongue] Jew's harp. Ap

Brummstimmen, *pl. Music* [G < *brummen* to hum + *Stimme,* pl. *Stimmen* voice] Humming without words, i.e., bouche fermée or bocca chiusa. Ap

Brustwerk, *n. Music* [G < *Brust* breast + *Werk* works] A special group of smaller organ pipes in the middle, anterior to or beneath the organ, between the large pedal pipes. Ap, Ke

bub, *n.* (1837) *Sociol.* [Poss. < G *Bub* or *Bube* boy] Boy, lad, brother. Men1

Bügelhorn, *n.* *Music* [G < *Bügel* bow + *Horn* horn] A generic term for bugle. Ap

Bühnenmusik, *n.* *Music* [G < the comb. form of *Bühne* stage + *Musik* (< L *mūsica*) music] Incidental music for plays; in operas, music played on the stage itself. Ap

bullkater, *n.* *Myth.* [G < *Bulle* bull + *Kater* tomcat] A supposed Silesian field spirit. Le

can be [Transl. of G *kann sein,* a short. of *es kann sein,* lit., it can be, it is possible] (It's) possible. Men

cant hook, *n.* *Tech.* [Prob. transl. of G *Kanterhaken* < *Kanter* < Late MHG *kanter* < It *cantiere,* ult. < L *cantherius* wooden beam + G *Haken* hook] A pole for lumbering, like a peavey without a spike at the tip. Men1

cheaters, *pl.* *Sports* (colloq.) [Transl. of G *Mogler,* pl. cheaters] Metal skis. Jar

chip carving, *see* Kerbschnitt

choral prelude, *n.* *Music* Var. **chorale prelude, choral vorspiel** [Partial transl. of G *Choralvorspiel* < *Choral* choral + *Vorspiel* prelude] An organ composition based on a Protestant chorale and designed to be played before the chorale is sung by the congregation. Ke

coffee cake, *n.* (1885 *DA*) *Food* [Prob. transl. of G *Kaffeekuchen* < *Kaffee* (< Ar *qaḥwa*) coffee + G *Kuchen* cake] An enriched, often fruited bread, at times topped with streusel, and glazed with melted sugar. Sc

coffee-klatsch campaign, *n.* *Politics* [Ad. and compounding of G *Kaffeeklatsch* kaffeeklatsch (see main Dictionary) + E *campaign*] A type of political campaign in cities and towns in the course of which a candidate meets small groups of voters at a "coffee hour." Sa

compathy, *n.* *Philos.* [Transl. of G *Miteinanderfühlen* < *mit* with + *einander* one another + *Fühlen* feeling] The sense of human beings' feeling with each other the same psychical (not physical) pain. Ru

confused, *a.* *Philos.* [Transl. of G *verworren* confused, past part. of *verwirren* to confuse] In Husserl, not given distinctly or articulately, with respect to implicit components. Ru

conscious, *a.* *Philos.* [Transl. of G *bewußt* aware, conscious] In Husserl, (in a broader sense) noematically intentional; conscious of something; (in a narrower sense) "actual," belonging to the cogito. Ru

consequence, *n.* *Philos.* [Ad. of G *Konsequenz* result < L *cōnsequentia* consequence] In Husserl, the relation of formal-analytic inclusion that obtains between noematic senses. Ru

consequence logic, *n.* *Philos.* [Ad. of G *Konsequenzlogik* < *Konsequenz* consequence (q.v.) + *Logik* logic, ult. < Gk *logikḗ*] Pure apophantic analytics; a level of pure formal logic in which the only thematic concepts of validity are consequence, inconsequence, and compatibility. Ru

constituted, *a.* *Philos.* [Transl. of G *konstituiert* < past part. of *konstituieren* < Fr *constituer* < L *cōnstituere* to

set up, determine] In Husserl, resultant from consecutive analyses. Ru

constitution, *n.* *Philos.* [G *Konstitution* < L *cōnstitutio* < *cōnstituere* to set up, determine] In Husserl, in a broader sense, intentionally in its character as producing; on the one hand, intentionally identical and different *objects of conclusion* with more or less determinate objective sense, and, on the other hand, more or less abiding *ego-habitudes:* said to be more constitutive; in a narrower sense, the structure of intentionality in its character as rational, i.e., as productive of valid objects and correct, justified habits. Ru

cook cheese, *n.* *Food* (1941) (regional) Var. **kochkäse** (1948) [Transl. of G *Kochkäse* < *kochen* to cook + *Käse* cheese] A cooked smearcase (see main Dictionary), with or without caraway seeds. Sc

Córdoba Durchmusterung, *n.* *Astronomy* [G < *Cordoba,* the name of Córdoba, Argentina, the observatory where the Bonner Durchmusterung was continued and completed in 1930 + *Durchmusterung* a star catalog] This continuation and completion. Il

Culmbacher, *n.* (1932) *Beverages* (rare) [G short. of *Culmbacherbier* (now *Kulmbacherbier*) < *Kulmbacher* of or from *Kulmbach,* the name of a city in Bavaria, Germany + *Bier* beer] A beer orig. brewed in Kulmbach. Sc

cut a face (colloq.) [Prob. a transl. of G *ein Gesicht schneiden,* lit., to cut a face, but meaning fig. to make faces] To make faces, grimace. Men1

Dämpfung, *n.* *Music* [G < *dämpfen* to dampen, mute + nom. suffix *-ung* -ing] Muting, or pianoforte soft pedalling. Ke

darmbrand, *n.* *Med.* [G < *Darm* intestine + *Brand* burning, fire, conflagration] A severe, often fatal jejunitis, now known as *pigbel.* La

dauben pollen, *n.* *Bot.* [G < *Daube* stave + *Pollen* (< NL) pollen] Stave pollen, a modification of schalen or spalten pollen (q.v.), with broadened fissures, having stave-like insertions (found in the flora of tropical Africa). Jac

Deckelpokal, *n.* *Pottery* [G < *Deckel* cover + *Pokal* goblet, cup] (A German term for a) covered cup of metal or glass. Bo

deckplatte, *n.* *Med.* [G < *Decke* cover (< *decken* to cover) + *Platte* plate] Roof plate or membrana tectoria. La

derb, *a.* *Music* [G < MHG *derp* hard, firm] (A notation calling for music that is) robust (in sound). Ke

deuter cells, *n.* *Bot.* Var. **Pointer cells** [G *Deuter* interpreter < *deuten* to interpret + E *cells*] A row of large parenchymatous cells, empty or containing starch, which occur in the middle nerve of mosses. Jac

Dewey blitz, *n.* *Politics* [E *Dewey* + G *Blitz* blitz (see main Dictionary)] The second-ballot drive by the advocates of Thomas Dewey (1901–71), a candidate for the presidency of the U.S., that enabled him to wrest the nomination from Senator Robert Taft in the 1948 Republican convention. Sa

dimmer foehn, *n.* *Meteor.* [Compounding of E *dimmer* +

G *Foehn, Föhn* foehn (see main Dictionary)] A rare form of foehn where, during a very strong wind from the south, a pressure difference of 12 millibars or more exists between the south and north side of the Alps. Lap

dirndled, *a.* (1969) *Apparel* [G *Dirndl* dirndl (see main Dictionary) + E suffix *-ed*] Of a person clad in a dirndl. Ka3

distinctness, *n. Philos.* [Transl. of G *Deutlichkeit* < *deutlich* clear, distinct + nom. suffix *-keit* -ness] In Husserl, explicit articulateness with respect to syntactic components. Ru

DIW, *n. Econ.* [G abbr. of *Deutsches Institut für Wirtschaftsforschung* < *deutsch* German + *Institut* institute + *für* for + *Wirtschaftsforschung* economic research] The name of the Economic Forecasting Institute in Berlin. Ti

DM day, *n. Currency* [G *DM* (a short. of *Deutschmark* German mark;–see main Dictionary) + E *day*] October 3, 1990, the day on which East Germans were able to exchange their Ostmarks for West Germany's Deutschmarks on a one-for-one basis and creating large economic problems for the newly reunited Germany. Ti

doctrine of affection, *n. Music* [Transl. of G *Affektionslehre* (1702) < the gen. of *Affektion* (< L *affection-, affectio*) affection + *Lehre*, formulated by the German musicologist and organist Andreas Werckmeister (1645–1706) et al.] An aesthetic theory of the late baroque period describing how to express affections in music like sorrow and hate. Ap

Donau glaciation, *n. Geol.* [Compounding of *Donau*, the G name for the Danube + E *glaciation*] A Pleistocene glacial time unit in the European Alps. Lap

dope slope, *n. Sports* (colloq.) [Transl. of G *Idiotenhang* or *Idiotenhügel* < *Idiot* idiot, (slang) dope + *Hang* slope or *Hügel* hill, rise] (Humorous reference to a) gentle ski slope used by beginners. Jar

Dorngeholz, *n. Bot.* Var. **Dorngestrauch**, (in transl.) thornbrush, thorn scrub [G < *Dorne* thorn + *Gehölz* copse < *Holz* wood] A vegetation class dominated by tall succulents and profusely branching, smooth-barked hardwoods that vary in density from mesquite bush in the Caribbean to open spurge thicket in Central Africa. Lap

Dorngestrauch, *n. Bot.* [G < *Dorne* thorn + *Gesträuch* shrub(s) < *Strauch* shrub] Dorngeholz (q.v.). Lap

dosen pollen, *n. Bot.* [G < *Dose* box + *Pollen* (< NL) pollen] Dosen pollen, elliptic pollen with three longitudinal stripes and a pore in each (found in the flora of tropical Africa). Jac

drachen, *n.* (1927) *Mil.* [G drake, kite, cited as a war word in William Edward Collinson's *Contemporary English*, 1927] Kite. Car

Drehsprungstemme, *n. Sports* [G < *drehen* to turn + *Sprung* jump + *Stemme* lift, hoist] A stunt on the high bar consisting of a back giant swing with half a twist to a giant forward swing. Ra

du lieber Gott (1980) [G < *du* you + *lieber* (inflected form of *lieb*) dear + *Gott* God] Dear God. Ka8

düsenwind, *n. Meteor.* [G < the comb. form of *Düse* jet + *Wind* wind] The mountain-gap wind of the Dardanelles. Lap

düster, *a. Music* [G < LG < MLG *düster* rather dark, somber] Somber (used as a direction in music). Th

egological, *a. Philos.* [Ad. of G *egologisch* < L *ego* I + *logicus* < Gk *logikós* consistent] Of or pertaining to the ego or to egology. Ru

egological reduction, *n. Philos.* [Ad. of G *egologische Reduktion* < *egologisch* egological (q.v.) + *Reduktion* < L *reductiō* leading back (to a smaller number)] In Husserl, phenomenological reduction involving *epoché* with respect to one's own explicit and implicit positing of concrete egos or an ego other than one's own. Ru

eifrig, *a. Music* [G < *Eifer* ardor + adj. suffix *-ig* -y] With ardor (used as a direction in music). Th

eigen equation, *n. Physics, Math.* [Partial transl. of G *Eigen(wert)gleichung* < *eigen* characteristic (+ *Wert* value) + *Gleichung* equation] A characteristic equation. Lap

eigenfunction expansion, *n. Math.* [G *Eigenfunktion* eigenfunction (see main Dictionary) + E *expansion*] By using spectral theory for linear operators defined in spaces comprised of functions, in certain cases the operator equals an integral or series involving its eigenvectors. Lap, Le

eigenvalue problem, *n. Physics, Math.* [Partial transl. of G *Eigenwertproblem* < *Eigenwert* eigen value (see main Dictionary) + *Problem* problem < L (< Gk) *problēma*] Sturm-Lionville problem. Lap

eilend, *a. Music* [G < present part. of *eilen* to hasten] In haste (used as a direction in music). Ap

Einklang, *n. Music* [G < *einklingen* = *zusammenklingen* to sound together or in harmony] Simultaneous performance of the same note or melody by various instruments or by the whole orchestra, either at exactly the same pitch or in a different octave. Ap

eins, zwei, drei, *Math.* [G one, two, three] The first three numbers used in counting. Men

Einsatz, *n. Music* [G < *einsetzen* to set in, start; institute] Attack; entrance of an orchestral part. Ap

Einschluss thermometer, *n. Chem.* [G *Einschluß* inclusion (< *einschließen* to enclose, include) + E *thermometer*] An all-glass, liquid-filled thermometer, with a temperature range of $-201°$ to $360°$ C. Lap

Einsfühlung, *n. Philos.* [G combining of *sich eins fühlen mit* to be at one or of a mind with + nom. suffix *-ung* -ing, etc.] The emotional and dynamic understanding of nature as the operational field of living forces. Ru

Einstellung, *n. Med.* [G < (*sich*) *einstellen* (*auf*) to take a position (with regard to), to have an attitude (toward) + nom. suffix *-ung* -ing] A pronounced tendency to respond in a certain way to a particular stimulus; a predisposition toward a relatively fixed or rigid pattern; a mental set. La

Einzelkunst, *n. Art* [G < *einzel-* single, solitary + *Kunst* art] A primitive or paleolithic art: the art of depicting unrelated persons, animals, and objects. Lu

eisen platinum, *n. Metall.* [Partial transl. of G *Eisenplatin* < *Eisen* iron + *Platin* platinum] Ferroplatinum, a dark gray to almost black, native platinum alloy containing sufficient iron to be attracted to a magnet. Thr

eisenwolframite, *n. Mineral.* [G *Eisenwolframit* < *Eisen* iron + *Wolframit* wolframite (see main Dictionary)] An iron tungstate mineral, $FeWO_4$. Thr

eiserner Hut, *n. Geol.* [G < *eisern* iron-like, made of iron + *Hut* hat] Iron hat or gossan. Thr

eiweissmilch, *n. Med.* [G < *Eiweiß* eggwhite + *Milch* milk] Albumen milk, i.e., milk made from the white of eggs. La

elementary idea, *n. Sociol.* [Transl. of G *Elementargedanke,* coined by Adolf Bastian (1826–1905), director of the Berlin Museum of Ethnology < *elementar* (< L *elementārius*) elementary, elemental + G *Gedanke* idea] One of similar, rudimentary responses shared by all human beings, which are modified only by environmental conditions and historical factors. Go

Ellenbogengesellschaft, *n. Sociol.* [G < *Ellenbogen* elbow + *Gesellschaft* society] Elbow society, i.e., the West German push-and-shove society as opposed to the docile East German social mode of behavior. Ti

empfindsamer Stil, *n. Music* [G < *empfindsam* sensitive, sentimental + *Stil* style] The North German style of the second half of the 18th century, represented by W. F. Bach, et al. Ap

empfindungsvoll, *a. Music* [G < the gen. of *Empfindung* feeling + *voll* full] With feeling (used as a direction in music). Ke, Th

empty, *a. Philos.* [Transl. of G *leer* blank, empty] In Husserl, without intuitional fullness; materially indeterminate. Ru

Entartete Kunst, *n. Art* [G < *entartet* degenerate + *Kunst* art] The name of an exhibition, held in Munich in 1937, of all types of avant-garde art disapproved of by the Nazi party. Lu

entschieden, *a. Music* [G < past part. of *entscheiden* to resolve] With resolve (used as a direction in music). Ap, Th

epi-, *comb. form Geol.* [G (1907) < Gk *epí* upon, at] A prefix suggested by C. W. von Gümbel in 1888 as a qualifier to the names of rocks that have suffered a change in mineral composition, and by Ulrich Grubenmann in 1907 as a qualifier to rocks belonging to the upper zone of metamorphism. To

ergriffen, *a. Music* [G < past part. of *ergreifen* to touch, move, seize] (Deeply) moved (used as a direction in music). Ap

Erlebnis, *n. Philos.* [G < *erleben* to experience + nom. suffix *-nis* -ness, etc.] The mind's identification with its own emotions and feelings. Ru

erlöschend, *a. Music* [G < present part. of *erlöschen* to die down, become extinguished] Fading or dying away (used as a direction in music). Ap, Th

ermattend, *a. Music* [G < present part. of *ermatten* to tire, weary, weaken] Letting down, weakening (used as a direction in music). Ap, Th

erniedrigen, *a. Music* [G to lower, debase < *er-* verbal prefix meaning 'to come to pass' + *niedrig* low + in-

finitive suffix *-en*] (Musical notation to) lower the pitch. Th

ernst(haft), *a. Music* [G < *Ernst* earnestness (+ *-haft* like)] With dignified resolve (used as a direction in music). Ap

erntefieber, *n. Med.* [G < *Ernte* harvest + *Fieber* (< L *febris*) fever] Harvest fever. La

erschüttert, *a. Music* [G < past part. of *erschüttern* to agitate] Agitated (used as a direction in music). Th

ersterbend, *a. Music* [G < present part. of *ersterben* to die away < *sterben* to die] Dying or fading away (used as a direction in music). Ap, Th

erweitert, *a. Music* [G < past part. of *erweitern* to enlarge, widen < *weit* wide] Paced, slow and steady (used as a direction in music). Ke

erz cement, *n. Mining* [Ad. of G *Erzzement* < *Erz* ore + *Zement* cement < L *caementum*] A ferruginous hydraulic cement formerly made in Germany. Thr

erzürnt, *a. Music* [G < past part. of *erzürnen* to anger, irritate, agitate] Agitated (used as a direction in music). Th

Eulenkrug, *n. Pottery* [G < the comb. form of *Eule* owl + *Krug* jug] A German type of jug in the form of an owl, made of thin, glazed earthenware, found c.1540. Bo

evidence, *n. Philos.* [Ad. of G *Evidenz* < L *ēvidentia* manifestness] In Husserl, (in a narrow sense) consciousness of an intended object as itself given; (in a broad sense) "evidence" may be either mediate or immediate. Ru

evident, *a. Philos.* [G < L *ēvidēns* (gen. *ēvidentis*) certainty, meaning certain, obvious] In Husserl, said of both evidence and the object of evidence. Ru

exemplification, *n. Philos.* [Transl. of G *Exemplifizierung* < *exemplifizieren* to exemplify < L *exemplum* example + *facere* to make, serve as] In Husserl, the relation of an entity to any eidos or any universal type under which it falls as an instance. Ru

facetier pollen, *n. Bot.* [G *Facettierpollen* < *Facette* polished surface < *facettieren* to facet + *Pollen* (< NL) pollen] Pollen with faceted surfaces (found in the flora of tropical Africa). Jac

fact, *n. Philos.* [Transl. of G *Sachverhalt* circumstance, state of affairs or of *Tatsache/Faktum* fact < L *factum* done, past part. of *facere* to do] In Husserl, an object having categorical-syntactic structure, i.e.: (A) that which simply is, as contrasted with that which is necessarily; (B) that which is actual, as contrasted with that which is merely possible; (C) that which is, regardless of its value; (D) that which is nonfictive. Ru

Fahrvergnügen, *n.* (1990) *Transportation* [G < *fahren* to travel, drive + *Vergnügen* pleasure] Pleasure in driving a car. Ti

faith, *n. Philos.* [Transl. of G *Glaube* belief < *glauben* to believe] The acceptance of ideas that are theoretically indemonstrable, yet necessarily entailed by the indubitable reality of freedom. Ru

fallmaster, *n. Admin.* (regional) [Ad. of G *Fallmeister* knackerman] The town official who removes animal carcasses. Men1

APPENDIX

Fallstreifen, -ø pl. Meteor. [G < fallen to fall + Streifen strip, streak] Wisps or streaks of water or ice particles falling out of a cloud but evaporating before reaching the earth's surface as precipitation. Lap

falten pollen, n. Bot. [G < Falte fold + Pollen (< NL) pollen] Fold pollen with smooth surfaces and three-deep longitudinal grooves in each (found in the flora of tropical Africa). Jac

Fasenacht, n. Theol. Var. **Fastnacht** (see main Dictionary) [G < fasten to fast + Nacht night] In Germany, the festival immediately preceding Lent, Shrove Tuesday, called Fasching in Bavaria and Austria. Le

Fastnachtsbär, n. Myth. [G < the gen. of Fastnacht Shrovetide + Bär bear] A male wrapped in straw and wound with ropes who is led from house to house to dance with all females of the household and receive food, drink, and money in return. Le

Federmesser, n. Archaeology [G penknife < Feder feather, quill (pen) + Messer knife] Erron. transl. as penknife point (points of this type are typical constituents of assemblages of flint tools in northern Europe dating to the last few millennia of the last ice age). Wi

feeling, n. Philos. [Transl. of G Gefühl feeling] In Husserl, (A) noetic processes of valuing, i.e., liking, disliking, preferring; (B) nonintentional, "hyletic" processes or states, immanent in the stream of consciousness. In Kant, a conscious, subjective impression that does not involve cognition or representation of an object. Ru

feierlich, a. Music [G < Feier festivity + adj. suffix -lich like] Solemn, festive (used as a direction in music). Ke

fleckfieber, n. Med. [G < Fleck spot, blemish + Fieber fever < L febris] Louse-borne epidemic typhus or petechial fever. La

fleckschiefer, n. Geol. [G (1858) < Fleck spot, speck + Schiefer slate] A variety of spotted slate or schist characterized by minute specks or spots of determinable or determinate material. To

flehend, a. Music [G < present part. of flehen to entreat] Entreating (used as a direction in music). Ke

fliessender, a. Music [Ad. of fließend flowing, smooth] Smoother, more flowing (used as a direction in music). Ke

flip-over process, n. Physics Var. **Umklapp process** (see main Dictionary) [Transl. of G Umklapprozeß < umklappen to fold up (or down), flip, ectropinonize + Prozeß process < L processus] Interactions in a crystal lattice in which their total momentum is not considered and the momentum of the initial excitations is reversed. Pa

Flötenuhr, n. Music [G < Flöte, pl. Flöten flute, pipe + Uhr clock] A set of small pipes and bellows operated by a clockwork. Ap

flott, a. Music [G "snappy"–ult. related to fließen flow] Lively (used as a direction in music). Ap

flüssig, a. Music [G < Fluß flow + adj. suffix -ig -y, -ing] Flowing, fluid (used as a direction in music). Ap

foehn cloud, n. Meteor. [Partial transl. of G Föhnwolke < Föhn foehn (see main Dictionary) + Wolke cloud] (Usu. in the plural) lenticular clouds formed in the lee of mountains during foehn conditions. Lap

foehn sickness, n. Meteor. [Partial transl. of G Föhnkrankheit < Föhn foehn (see main Dictionary) + Krankheit sickness] A phenomenon in humans in Alpine regions, marked by adverse psychological and physiological effects during prolonged periods of foehn wind. Lap

forefield, n. (1919) Mil. [Transl. of G Vorfeld forefield, as quoted by William Edward Collinson in "German 'War-Words'" in Modern Language Review 14 (1919): 87] Forefield. Car

forellengranulit, n. Geol. [G (1862) < Forelle trout + Granulit granulite < LL grānulum + G -it -ite] Spotted granulite, a compact granulite with spots due to crystals of hornblende. To

formalization, n. Philos. [Transl. of G Formalisierung < formalisieren to formalize, portray formally + nom. suffix -ung -ing]. In Husserl, (A) (objective:) ideational "abstraction" from the determination of an object as belonging in the same material region; (B) (noematic:) substitution, in a noematic-objective sense, i.e., the sense signified by a sentence, of the moment "what you please" for every determinate core of sense, while retaining all the moments of categorical form. Ru

formkohle, n. Mining [G < Form form (< L fōrma) + G Kohle coal] A variety of incoherent brown coal, apparently without any cementing material whatsoever. Thr

fortfahren, v. Music [G < fort forward + fahren to travel, i.e., to continue] (Musical direction to) go forward, continue. Ke

founded, a. Philos. [Transl. of G fundiert based on, having a base] In Husserl, (A) the character of one noetic-noematic stratum as presupposing the presence of another, founding stratum; (B) the character of an act-correlate as something founded. Ru

Frau Hütt, n. Myth. [G < Frau Dame + Hütte hut < MHG hütte, OHG hutta he/she/that which covers, envelops] In the Tyrol, a rock resembling a mythological woman turned to stone for wasting food. Le

Frau Welt, n. Myth. [G < Frau Dame + Welt World] A superhuman paramour considered by medieval German clerics to be the devil. Le

frei, a. Music [G < MHG vrī < OHG frī free, ult., protected] Free, unrestrained (used as a direction in music). Ap

Fremdwort n. Ling. [G, lit., foreign word, foreignism] An established but unacculturated borrowing from another language. Can

fricadelles, pl. (1892) Food (regional) Var. **fricadilloes, fricatelles, fricadellen** [Prob. < G Fricadellen (1692) (now Frikadellen) < Fr fricadelles (pl.) fried meat balls] Fried meat balls made of stale bread, chopped meat, and onions, and served with hot catsup. Sc

frisch, a. Music [G < MHG vrisch < OHG frisc fresh, healthy, frisky] Brisk (used as a direction in music). Th

Frosch, see am Frosch

fruchtgneiss, n. (1896) Geol. [G Fruchtgneis < Frucht fruit + Gneis gneiss] A contact metamorphized, coarsely layered rock. To

fruchtschiefer, n. (1858) Geol. [G < Frucht fruit + Schie-

366

fer slate, schist] A variety of spotted slate or schist characterized by concretionary spots resembling berries or peas. To

Führerbunker, *n.* (1984) *Politics* [G < *Führer* (see main Dictionary) leader + *Bunker* bunker (see main Dictionary)] Hitler's bunker. Ka5

fulfillment, *n. Philos.* [Transl. of G *Erfüllung* realization, fulfillment < *erfüllen* to realize, fulfill + nom. suffix *-ung* -ing] In Husserl, synthesis of identification, based on conscious processes. Ru

Füllstimmen, *pl. Music* [G < *füllen* to fill + *Stimme,* pl. *Stimmen* voice, i.e., accessory or supplementary voices] A middle strand in the texture of a choral or instrumental composition that may be considered to be purely accessory; an added oral part; the mixture stop of an organ. Ap, Ke

ganz gut, Var. **sehr gut** [G < *ganz* quite, entirely (or *sehr* very) + *gut* good, well] (Phrase used in response to the question: *"Wie geht's?"* How are you?) Quite *or* pretty *or* very well. Men, Sc

garbenschiefer, *n.* (1858) *Geol.* [G < the comb. form of *Garbe* sheaf + *Schiefer* slate, schist] A variety of spotted slate or schist characterized by concretionary spots suggesting sheaves. To

Gastwort, *n. Ling.* [G, lit., guest word] A tenuous, unadapted borrowing from another language. Can

gebunden, *a. Music* [G < past part. of *binden* to bind, tie] Tied or slurred, legato (used as a direction in music). Ap, Th

gedämpft, *a. Music* [G < past part. of *dämpfen* to dampen, mute] Of brass instruments, muted; of drums, muffled; of a pianoforte, soft-pedalled (used as a direction in music). Ke

gedehnt, *a. Music* [G < past part. of *dehnen* to stretch (out)] Stretched out, slow (used as a direction in music). Ap

gefühlsvoll, *a. Music* [G < the gen. of *Gefühl* feeling + *voll* full] With feeling (used as a direction in music). Ap

gegenhalten, *n. Med.* [Short. of G *entgegenhalten* < *entgegen* against + *halten* to hold, i.e., to hold toward or against, that is, to offer resistance to] Paratonia or uneven resistance to passive movement of the limbs. La

gehalten, *a. Music* [G < past part. of *halten* to hold, sustain] Sustained (used as a direction in music). Ap

gehend, *a. Music* [G < present part. of *gehen* to go, proceed] Andante (used as a direction in music). Ap, Th

gekneipt, *a. Music* [G < past part. of *kneipen* to pinch, pluck] Plucked, pizzicato (used as a direction in music). Th

gelande, *v. Sports* [Short. of G *Geländesprung* < *gelände jump* (see main Dictionary) < *Gelände* countryside, (skiing) slope + *Sprung* jump] To execute a gelande jump. Jar

gelandy, -ies *pl.* (1972) *Sports* Var. **gelände jump** [Short. of G *Geländesprung* < *Gelände* countryside, (in some contexts) slope + *Sprung* jump] A jump made from a low crouching position with the aid of both ski poles. Ka3

gelassen, *a. Music* [G < past part. of MHG *gelazen* to be serene] Calm, serene (used as a direction in music). Ap, Th

gemächlich, *a. Music* [G < MHG *gemechlich,* OHG *gimahīh* at a comfortable pace] Leisurely (used as a direction in music). Ap, Th

gesangvoll, *a. Music* [G < *Gesang* song + *voll* full] Tuneful, songlike, cantabile (used as a direction in music). Ap, Th

geschleift, *a. Music* [G < past part. of *schleifen* to drag] Legato (used as a direction in music). Th

gesteigert, *a. Music* [G < past part. of *steigern* to increase] Crescendo or sforzando (used as a direction in music). Ap, Th

gestellstein, *n.* (1778) *Geol.* [G < *Gestell* frame, rack + *Stein* stone] (An old German name for) greisen (see main Dictionary). To

getragen, *a. Music* [G < past part. of *tragen* to carry, sustain] Sustained (used as a direction in music). Th

gezogen, *a. Music* [G < past part. of *ziehen* to stretch (out)] Portamento (used as a direction in music). Ap, Th

glatter pollen, *n. Bot.* [G < *glatt* smooth + *Pollen* (< NL) pollen] Smooth pollen devoid of prominent markings (found in the flora of tropical Africa). Jac

gleitend, *a. Music* [G < present part. of *gleiten* to glide] Glissando (used as a direction in music). Th

gleitgestein, *n. Geol.* [G < *gleiten* to slide + *Gestein* rocks] Rutsch breccia. To

glutwolke, *n.* (1914) *Meteor.* [G < *Glut* glow, heat + *Wolke* cloud] (A German term for) *nuée ardente.* To

gon, *n. Physics* [G < Gk *gonía* angle, corner] A unit of angle (in Germany) equal to 1/100 of a right angle. Gr

Gott im Himmel (1980) [G < *Gott* God + *im* in + *Himmel* heaven] Good heavens. Ka8

graben lake, *n. Geol.* [G *Graben* rift, ditch + E *lake*] A lake that is the result of a graben faulting, also called *rift lake.* Ve

Green, *n.* (1980) *Politics* [Transl. of G *(die) Grünen* < *(die* the) + the inflected nom. form of *grün* green] A member of a faction or a group of members (the Greens) in the German Bundestag, whose principal concern is that of the environment. Ka8

Grenzsignal, *n. Ling.* [G < *Grenze* border, boundary + *Signal* (< ML *signale*) signal, sign] Trubetzkoy's term for juncture. Pe

Grenz tube, *n. Physics* [G *Grenze* edge, border, limit, margin + E *tube*] A tube with a low absorption window so that X-rays produced at voltages below about 10^4 volts can be transmitted. Gr

Griffbrett, *see* am Griffbrett

Grossdeutschland, *n. Politics* [G < *groß* great, (here) Greater + *Deutschland* Germany] Greater Germany, i.e., a Germany that includes Austria in its sphere. Ti

ground form, *n. Bot.* [Ad. of G *Grundform* (see main Dictionary for *ground form*)] The original, sometimes hypothetical form from which other forms have been derived by morphological variation. Jac

Grubenhäuser, *pl. Archaeology* [G < *Grube,* pl. *Gruben*

pit + *Haus,* pl. *Häuser* house, dwelling] Pit huts over rectangular excavations, a type of early medieval dwelling in northern Europe, sunk into the ground to a depth of between 0.2 and 1.0 meters; also called *grubhuts.* Ad, Wi

grubhuts, *see* Grubenhäuser

gummi bears, *pl.* (1986) *Food* [Partial transl. of G *Gummibären* < *Gummi* rubber + *Bären,* pl. of *Bär* bear] Name given to a chewable type of candy in the shape of tiny bears. Ka6

gürtel pollen, *n. Bot.* [G, lit., girdle pollen] Girdle pollen having a zone of varied markings (found in the flora of tropical Africa). Jac

haarscheibe, *n. Med.* [G < *Haar* hair + *Scheibe* disk] A hair disk. La

Hallenkirche, *n. Art* [G < *Halle* hall + *Kirche* church] A church whose nave and aisles are (almost) of equal height, also transl. as *hall church* (see main Dictionary). Lu

hand cheese, *n.* (1941) *Food* (regional) Var. **handkäse** (1890) [Transl. of G *Handkäse* < *Hand* hand + *Käse* cheese] A white, ball-shaped hard cheese strewed with caraway seeds. Sc

hartsalz, *n. Geol.* [G < *hart* hard + *Salz* salt] (A German term for) a rock composed of halite, sylvite, and kieserite. To

hartschiefer, *n. Geol.* [G < *hart* hard + *Schiefer* slate, schist] A strongly layered and partly schistose rock resulting from dynamic metamorphism and associated with other rocks of mylonitic habit in which alternating layers have been produced from ultramylonite by recrystallization and metamorphic differentiation. To

hastig, *a. Music* [G < *Hast* haste, hurry + adj. suff. *-ig* -y] With haste, hurried, impetuous (used as a direction in music). Ap, Th

Haufenbecher, *n. Pottery* [G < *Haufen* heap + *Becher* beaker] A late 16th and early 17th century type of German set of beakers, one fitting into the other, usu. of silver; also called *Setzbecher.* Bo, Cu

hauptsalz, *n. Geol.* [G < *Haupt* head, main- + *Salz* salt] (A German term for) a rock composed of halite, carnallite, and kieserite. To

Hecht vault, *n. Sports* [Partial transl. of G *Hechtsprung* long fly] A vault over the long axis of a (long) horse with a straight body and straight legs. Ra

heftig, *a. Music* [G violent, impetuous < MHG *heftec* insistent; *heifte* impetuous] Violent (used as a direction in music). Ap

heiligenschein, *n. Physics* [G < *Heilige(r)* saint + *Schein* glow] A diffuse white ring surrounding the shadow cast by the observer's head upon a dew-covered lawn when the solar elevation is low and, therefore, the distance from observer to shadow is great (see main Dictionary for *heiligenschein*). Pa

Heinzelmännchen, *pl. Myth.* [G < *Heinzel,* dim. of *Heinz* + *Männchen,* dim. pl. of *Mann* man] In German folk belief, friendly dwarfs or elves who perform chores for people they like when everyone is asleep. Le

heiter, *a. Music* [G merry < MHG *heiter,* OHG *heitar* shining] Merry (used as a direction in music). Th

Heldenflöte, -n *pl.* (1973) *Music* [G < the comb. form of *Held* hero, here "heroic" in the sense of "Wagnerian" + *Flöte* flute] An (organ) flute (stop) in the range of the voice of a *heldentenor* (see main Dictionary). Ka1

hell, *a. Music* [G clear, bright < MHG *hel* gleaming] Clear, bright (used as a direction in music). Th

herzstoss, *n. Med.* [G *Herzstoß* stroke, heart attack < *Herz* heart + *Stoß* push, thrust, blow, jolt] An apex beat or cardiac systole. La

high-kraeusen, *n. Beverages* (regional trade jargon) [Combining of E *high* + ad. of G *Krause* krausen (see main Dictionary)] A thick collar of foam on fermenting beer. Men2

hinterlander, *n.* (1973) [G *Hinterland* hinterland (see main Dictionary) + E nom. suffix *-er*] Someone from the back country. (The German name for a backwoodsman or "hick" is *Hinterwälder.*) Ka1

Historie, *n. Theol.* [G history, story] The study of the Gospels as mere historical records. Do

Hitler Youth, *n. Politics* [Transl. of G *Hitlerjugend* < the name of Adolf *Hitler* (see main Dictionary) + *Jugend* youth] A Nazi youth organization. Ka7

HO, *n. Commerce* [G abbr. of *Handelsorganisation* < the gen. of *Handel* trade + *Organisation* (< ML) organization] A monopolistic department store chain in the former GDR (q.v.). —**HO (retailing) outlets.** Ti

hoch!, *interj.* [G, lit., high] An exclamation, usu. in praise of a person; Hurrah! Men

Hochschnitt, *n. Pottery* [G < *hoch* high + *Schnitt* cut] A 17th and 18th century German revival of a technique of engraving glass in cameo rather than in intaglio, leaving the decoration in relief. Bo, Lu

hof¹, *n. Med.* [G < MHG, OHG *hof* (origin unknown), lit., courtyard, specif., ring or circle; corona] The hollow in the cytoplasm of a cell that lodges the nucleus; a lucent area in the cell protoplasm. La

hof², *n. Bot.* [G court, halo] The areola of a bordered pit; Rosen's expression for a clear, granule-free space surrounding the nucleus or nucleolus. Jac

hofbrau, *n. Beverages* Var. **hofbräu, huffbrow** [G, lit., court brew] The name of a beer brewed in the State Hofbräuhaus in Munich, Germany, founded in 1539 by Duke Wilhelm V of Bavaria. Men

hohlraum, *n. Physics* Var. (in transl.) **black body** [G < *hohl* hollow + *Raum* space] An ideal body that would absorb all incident radiation and reflect none. Lap

hold on! (colloq.) [Poss. ad. of G *halt an!* stop! < *anhalten* to stop] Wait (a minute)! Stop (there)! Men2

hornbast, *n. Bot.* [G < *Horn* horn + *Bast* inner bark, fiber] A tissue of obliterated groups of sieve-tubes, esp. thickened and horny texture. Jac

hortungskörper, *n. Med.* [G < the gen. of *Hortung* hoarding < *Hort* treasure < MHG, OHG *hort* heap, actually that which is covered or hidden + *Körper* body] Senile amyloid or other matter found in body organs of aged individuals. La

huffbrow, *see* hofbrau

hurtig, *a. Music* [G nimble, swift, ult. < OFr *hurter* to propel] Quick, nimble (used as a direction in music). Ap

Ich, *n. Philos.* [G ego, I < *ich* I] The final, ultimate, conscious subject; the functional, dynamic unity of consciousness. Ru

intentional analysis, *n. Philos.* [Ad. of G *intentionale Analyse* < *intentional* purposeful, with intention + *Analyse* analysis < Gk *análysis*] In Husserl, explication and clarification of the essential structure of actual and potential (horizontal) synthesis by virtue of which objects are intentionally constituted. Ru

it listens well (colloq. and regional) [Prob. < G *es hört sich gut an* it sounds good, corrupted to *es* it + *hört* listens + *gut* good, well] It sounds good. Men1

Jungfrauenbecher, *n. Art* [G < the comb. form of *Jungfrau* maiden, virgin + *Becher* beaker] A wager-cup in the form of a girl with a wide-spreading skirt holding a bowl above her head, used at wedding feasts, first seen in Germany about 1575. Cu

Kaiser's Geburtstag, *n. Beverages* (regional trade jargon) [G < the gen. form of *Kaiser* emperor + *Geburtstag* birthday] Payday. Men2

kammrad pollen, *n. Bot,* [G, lit., cogwheel pollen] Cogwheel pollen having regular projections in the equatorial region (found in the flora of tropical Africa). Jac

Kapo, *n. Mil.* [G short. of Fr *caporal* captain, leader, corporal (not to be confused with E *capo* < It *capo* chief, head)] (In concentration camp jargon) a prisoner in charge of other prisoners. Har

karherberge, *n. Bot.* Var. **Karflur** [G < *Kar* hollow dug out by glaciers + *Herberge* hostel (or *Flur* meadow)] Collectively, plants occurring in hollows high in the mountains. Jac

Kerbschnitt, *n. Archaeology* [G < *kerben* to notch + *Schnitt* cut] A technique used in decorating wood or pottery, also called *chip carving.* Wi

kernschwund, *n. Med.* [G < *Kern* nucleus + *Schwund* disappearance, decline, decay] A congenital deficiency of cellular nuclei in the central nervous system. La

K feldspar, *n. Mineral.* Var. (in transl.) **potassium feldspar** [Abbr. and ad. of G *Kaliumfeldspath* < *Kalium* potassium + *Feldspath* feldspar] Any alkali feldspar (orthoclase, microline, sonidine, adularia) containing the molecule $KA^1Si_3O_3$. Lap

kilopond, *n. Physics* [G < *Kilo* kilo, short. for *Kilogramm* kilogram + *Pond* < Fr *kilogramme* + L *pondus* weight] The weight of falling mass of one kilogram at normal acceleration; a unit of force: kilogram-force, also short. to *kp.* La

kilopond-meter, *n. Physics* [G *Kilopondmeter/Meterkilopond* < *Kilopond* kilopond (q.v.) + *Meter* meter, ult. < Gk *métron*] A unit of torque: kilogram-force meter, also short. to *kpm* or *mpk.* La

kindergraph, *n.* (1925) (obs.) [Blend of G *Kinder,* pl. of

Kind child + E *photograph*] A photograph of a child. Men1

klagend, *a. Music* [G < present part. of *klagen* to lament] Lamenting (used as a direction in music). Ap

klar, *a. Music* [G clear < MHG *klār* < L *clarus* resounding; bright] Clear, distinct (used as a direction in music). Ap

klebschiefer, *n.* (1923) *Geol.* [G < *kleben* to stick, adhere + *Schiefer* slate, schist] A type of polishing slate that contains concretions of menilite. To

klei soil, *n. Geol.* [Partial transl. of G *Kleiboden* < *Klei* < MLG, OS *klei* loam + *Boden* soil] (A local German name for) marsh soil. To

kneifend, *a. Music* [G < present part. of *kneifen* to pinch, pluck] Plucking, pizzicato (used as a direction in music). Ap, Ke

knötchen pollen, *n. Bot.* [Short. of G *Knötchendosenpollen* < *Knötchen* nodule + *Dose* box + *Pollen* (< NL) pollen] Nodule pollen having a tuberculate surface (found in the flora of tropical Africa). Jac

knotenglimmerschiefer, *n.* (1860) *Geol.* [G < *Knoten* node + *Glimmer* mica + *Schiefer* slate, schist] A nodular mica-schist. To

knotenschiefer, *n.* (1838) *Geol.* [G < *Knoten* node + *Schiefer* slate, schist] A variety of spotted slate or schist characterized by conspicuous subspherical or polyhedral clots, often composed of definitely individualized minerals. To

kochkäse, *see* cook cheese

Kornmutter, *n. Myth.* [G < *Korn* grain, rye + *Mutter* mother] In German mythology, the spirit of growing grain. Le

Kornwolf, *n. Myth.* [G < *Korn* grain, rye + *Wolf* wolf] In German mythology, a field spirit that dwells in the last sheaf; hence, the reaper who reaps the last sheaf is also called *Kornwolf* and is expected to act the part. Le

kp, *see* kilopond

kpm, *see* kilopond-meter

kräftig, *a. Music* [G < *Kraft* strength, vigor + adj. suffix *-ig* -y] Strong, vigorous (used as a direction in music). Ap

kraft pulp, *n. Industry* [Partial transl. and short of G *Kraftpapierbrei* < *Kraftpapier* kraft paper (see main Dictionary) + *Brei* pulp] Sulfate pulp. Al

kraft pulping, *n. Chem.* Var. **Kraft process** (see *kraft paper* in main Dictionary) [G *Kraft* + E *pulping*] A wood-pulping process in which sodium sulfate is used in the caustic soda pulp-digestion liquor. Lap

Krautstrunk, *n. Pottery* [G < the comb. form of *Kraut* cabbage + *Trunk* draught] (The German name for) a glass tumbler, dating from the 15th century, made of green glass and covered with prunts resembling the stem of a cabbage. Bo

Kreuz König, *n. Dance* [G < *Kreuz* cross + *König* king] A German folk dance for two couples interlacing hands and arms. Le

Kristallnacht, -nächte *pl.* (1980) *Politics* Var. **Krystallnacht** [G < *Kristall* crystal + *Nacht* night] The night of the pogrom against the Jews of Germany on November 9,

1938, particularly in Berlin, where innumerable display windows of Jewish business establishments were smashed. Har, Ka8, Ti

kuehlschift, *n. Beverages* (regional trade jargon) [Irreg. < G *Kühlschiff* < *kühlen* to cool + *Schiff* vessel] Cooling tank. Men2

kuhreihn, *n. Dance* [G < *Kühe,* pl. of *Kuh* cow + *Reihen* song, dance] A cowherdsman's dance in the Swiss Alps. Le

Kunstkammer, *n. Art* [G < *Kunst* art + *Kammer* chamber (private) museum] A princely or private 16th or 17th century assemblage of art objects and curiosities, also called *Wunderkammer* (q.v.). Lu

Kunstwollen, *n. Art* [G < *Kunst* art + *Wollen* will, intention, desire] Artistic intention. Lu

lager, *n.* (1987) *Politics* [G camp < a short. of *Konzentrationslager* concentration camp, a term first used in 1901 in English in connection with the type of camp instituted by Lord Kitchener during the South African War (1899–1902), where noncombatants of an area were placed] A (Nazi) concentration camp. (see *lager* in main Dictionary). Ka7

langer Samstag, *n. Commerce* [G < *lang* long + *Samstag* Saturday] Long Saturday, i.e., the first Saturday of each month when German stores are allowed to stay open all day. Ti

langsam, *a. Music* [G slow < MHG *lancsam,* OHG *langsam* time-consuming] Slow (used as a direction in music). Ap, Ke

laukastein, *n.* (1853) *Geol.* [G < *Lauka,* the name of a locality near Bansko, Slovakia + G *Stein* stone] An aragonite concretion with a radial structure. To

Lauterbach, *n. Dance* [G < the town of that name in Hessia, Germany] A type of waltz named for the town and river of Lauterbach. Le

lebending, *a. Music* [G lively, alive < MHG *lebendec,* OHG *lebendīg* alive] Lively (used as a direction in music). Ap

lederhosened, *a.* (1972) *Apparel* [G *Lederhosen* lederhosen (see main Dictionary) + E suffix -*ed*] Of a person clad in lederhosen. Ka3

Lehnwort, *n. Ling.* (Regional) [G *loanword*–see main Dictionary] Loanword (cf. *Gastwort* and *Fremdwort*). Can

leidenschaftlich, *a. Music* [G < *Leidenschaft* passion + adj. suffix -*lich* -ly] Passionate(ly) (used as a direction in music). Ap

leise, *a. Music* [G soft(ly) < MHG *līse,* OHG (adv.) *līso* gently, barely audible] Soft or softly (used as a direction in music). Ap

let it be!, *interj.* [Transl. of G *lass* (or *laß*) *es sein,* lit., let it be < *lassen* to let + *es* it + *sein* to be] Let the matter rest. Men

linsen pollen, *n. Bot.* [G < *Linse* lens + *Pollen* (< NL) pollen] Lens pollen doubly convex in form (found in the flora of tropical Africa). Jac

living room, *n.* (1825) *Sociol.* [Poss. an American transl. of G *Wohnzimmer* < *wohnen* to dwell, reside, live + *Zim-*

mer room] The principal room in a residence used for social activities (see *lebensraum* in main Dictionary). Men

loess, *n. Bot.* [G *Löss/Löß* loam, prob. < Alemannic *lösch* loose] Drifting dust detained and consolidated by vegetation. Jac

Love-death, *n.* (1984) *Music* [Transl. of G *Liebestod* < the comb. form of *Liebe* love + *Tod* death] An aria or a duet proclaiming the suicide of lovers (see *Liebestod* in main Dictionary). Ka6

lückenschädel, *n. Med.* [G < the comb. form of *Lücke* gap, breach + *Schädel* skull] Craniofenestria. La

luftig, *a. Music* [G airy < *Luft* air + adj. suffix -*ig* -y] Airy (used as a direction in music). Ke

lumpenization, *n.* (1975) *Sociol.* [Ad. of G *Lumpen,* pl. of *Lump* ragamuffin, down-and-out person + E nom. suffix -*ization*] The creation of a lumpenproletariat (see main Dictionary). Ka2

lustig, *a. Music* [G merry < *Lust* joy, mirth + adj. suffix -*ig* -y] Merry, cheerful (used as a direction in music). Ap

lute harpsichord, *n. Music* Var. **lautenclavicymbal** (see main Dictionary) [Transl. of G *Lautenklavizymbal* < the comb. form of *Laute* lute + *Klavizymbal* harpsichord] A harpsichord with gut instead of metal strings, so called because of its lute-like sound. Ap, Ke

mächtig, *a. Music* [G < *Macht* power, might + adj. suffix -*ig* -y] Powerful (used as a direction in music). Ke

mahlstick, *n. Art* Var. **Rest stick** [Partial transl. of G *Mahlstock* (now *Malstock*) < *malen* to paint + *Stock* stick] A long stick, held by a painter in one hand to support and steady the other hand holding the brush. Lap, Le, Lu

majestätisch, *a. Music* [G with majesty, dignity < *Majestät* majesty (< L *māiestāt-, māiestās*) + G adj. suffix -*isch* -ic] Majestic (used as a direction in music). Th

mandelstein, *n. Geol.* [G < *Mandel* almond + *Stein* stone] (An old German term for) an amygdaloidal rock, usu. basalt. To

mangankiesel, *n. Geol.* [G < *Mangan* manganese (< ML *magnesia*) + G *Kiesel* flint, silica] A quartz-schist that contains large quantities of manganese carbonate. To

markiert, *a. Music* [G < past part. of *markieren* to mark, stress < Fr *marquer* < It *marcare, marca* sign, mark] Clearly accented, stressed (used as a direction in music). Ap, Ke

markig, *a. Music* [G < *Mark* essence, vigor + adj. suffix -*ig* -y] Vigorous (used as a direction in music). Ap, Ke

marschgemäß, *a. Music* [G at a marching pace < *Marsch* march + *gemäß* in keeping with] In marching style (used as a direction in music). Th

Massenfilter, *n. Chem.* Var. **Quadruple spectrometer** [G < the comb. form of *Masse* mass + *Filter* filter] A type of mass spectroscopy in which ions pass along a line of symmetry between four parallel cylindrical rods; an alternating potential superimposed on a steady potential between pairs of rods that filter out all ions except those of a predetermined mass. Lap

mässig, *a. Music* [G measured < *Maß* measure + adj. suffix -*ig* -y] Moderate (used as a direction in music). Th

Mauer, *n. Archaeology* [G < the name of a village near Heidelberg, Germany] A pre-Neanderthal lower jaw found in a sand pit at Mauer near Heidelberg in 1907. Wi

mehlnährschaden, *n. Med.* [G < *Mehl* meal, flour + *nähren* to nourish, feed + *Schaden* damage, injury] A children's disorder similar to kwashiorkor. La

metzel soup, *n. Food* (regional) [Ad. of G *Metzelsuppe* < *metzeln* to slaughter < ML *macellare* to kill, ult. < Heb *makhela* to strike down + G *Suppe* soup] Sausage broth. Sc

Metzgersprung, *n. Dance* [G < *Metzger* butcher + *Sprung* leap] A running dance of the butchers' guild, popular in Munich and Nuremberg. Le

Michelsberg (culture), *n. Archaeology* [Ad. of *Michelsberger Kultur* < *Michelsberger* of or hailing from Michelsberg in the Rhineland + *Kultur* culture < L *cultūra*] A neolithic culture of the late 4th and early 3rd millennia B.C., found mostly in the Rhineland and stretching from Belgium in the north to Switzerland in the south. Wi

migrant melisma, -ta *pl. Music* [Transl. of G *Wandermelisma* (*-en* pl.) < *wandern* to wander, migrate + Gk *mélisma* song, tune] A term introduced by Peter J. Wagner in the 1930s for a phrase in a Gregorian chant that recurs in a number of melodies of the same type. Ap

Milchglas, *n. Art* [G, lit., milk glass] White glass, translucent like milk, first made in the 15th century in Venice with oxide of tin. Fl

Mindelheim, *n. Archaeology* [G < the name of a town west of Munich] An early Hallstatt culture cemetery of the 7th century B.C. whose graves contain distinctive melon-shaped urns and wide open bowls, heavily decorated with incised geometric designs. Wi

mission-festival, *n. Theol.* (regional) [Transl. of G *Missionsfest* < the gen. of *Mission* mission + *Fest* festival, feast] A festival of the German Evangelical Church. Men

mit Affekt *Music* [G < *mit* with + *Affekt* (< L *affectus*) fervor] (A direction to play) with fervor. Ke

mit Andacht, *see* andächtig

mit Aufschwung *Music* [G < *mit* with + *Aufschwung* rise; impetus] With rising passion (used as a direction in music). Ke

mit Eile, *see* eilend

mit Empfindung *Music* [G < *mit* with + *Empfindung* feeling] With feeling (used as a direction in music). Ap

mitleidig, *a. Music* [G compassionate < *Mitleid* compassion + adj. suffix -*ig* -y, (here) -ly] Compassionate (used as a direction in music). Th

mittel, *a. Printing* [G *mittel-* middle, medium] (The German name for) 14-point type. Al

mit Wärme *Music* [G < *mit* with + *Wärme* warmth] With warmth (used as a direction in music). Ap

moneybund, *n. Commerce* (obs.) [Orig. colloq. U.S. compound of E *money* + G *Bund* alliance, league, as in *plunderbund* (see main Dictionary)] Money oligarchy. Men

mox nix, *interj.* (1954) (colloq.) Var. **max nix** [Folk etymological ad. of G (*es*) *macht nichts* (*aus*) < (*es* it) + *ausmachen* to matter + *nichts* nothing] (It) doesn't matter, makes no difference. Ka7, Ne

mpk, *see* kilopond-meter

murkstein, *n. Geol.* [G < *Murk* (now *Murkel*) fragment, crumb + *Stein* stone] An old name for granulite. To

Mutterrecht, *n. Anthrop.* [G < *Mutter* mother + *Recht* right] Mother right, a term employed by Johann Jakob Bachofen (1815–87), Swiss historian and anthropologist, describing woman's place in the earliest form of human society. Se

nachdrücklich, *a. Music* [G emphatic < *Nachdruck* emphasis + adj. suffix -*lich* -ly] Emphatic, expressive (used as a direction in music). Ap

nachlassend, *a. Music* [G < present part. of *nachlassen* to let up] Relaxing, slackening (used as a direction in music). Ap

Nachschlag, *n. Music* [G < *nach* after, accessory + *Schlag* beat, impact, (here:) striking of a piano key] The two terminating notes that are usually played at the end of a trill; any ornamental note or notes added after another note. Ap, Ke

nagelkalk, *n. Geol.* [G < *Nagel* nail, tine + *Kalk* lime] (A German name for) limestone having a cone-in-cone structure, also called *tutenmergel* or *tutenkalk* (q.v.). To

nährlösung, *n. Bot.* [G < *nähren* to nourish + *Lösung* solution] A nutrient solution for laboratory cultures, by mycologists usu. restricted to a solution of horse dung. Jac

natural notes, *pl. Music* Var. **Natural tones** [Transl. of G *Naturtöne* < *Natur* (< L *nātūra*) nature + G *Ton*, pl. *Töne* tone, note] Of brass instruments: notes neither flattened nor raised. Ke, Th

natürlich, *a. Music* [G natural < *Natur* nature (< L *nātūra*) + G adj. suffix -*lich* -ly, -like] Natural, *naturale*. Ke

nebenkörper, *n. Med.* [G < *neben* accessory, additional + *Körper* body < L *corpus*] A protistan hyperparasite, once viewed as an accessory body in a marine ameba's cytoplasm. La

nem, *n. Med.* [Abbr. of G *Nahrungseinheit Milch* < *Nahrungseinheit* nutritional unit + *Milch* milk] A nutritional unit (of milk). La

Neue Wilden, *pl. Art* [G *die neuen Wilden*, lit., the new wild ones] A name given esp. to the German and Austrian neoexpressionists during the 1970s, including Georg Baselitz, Rainer Fetting, and Julian Schnabel. Lu

Nicht-Ich *Philos.* [G < *nicht* not + *ich* I, used nominally to mean *ego*] Anything that is not the subjective self. Ru

Nickkrampf, *n. Med.* [G < *nicken* to nod + *Krampf* cramp, spasm] Nodding spasm. La

niederblätter, *pl. Bot.* [G < *nieder* nether + *Blätter*, pl. of *Blatt* leaf, rendered in Gk as *káta* nether + *phýlla*, pl. of *phýllon* leaf] The early leaf-form of a plant or shoot, as cotyledons, bud-scales, rhizome-scales, etc. Jac

Niederschlag, *n. Music* [G < *nieder* down + *Schlag* beat] Down-beat. Ap, Ke

nix come arous (1844 *DA*) (colloq.) Var. **nix come erous, nixcumerous** (1943) [Folk-etymological ad. of G *nichts kommt dabei heraus* < *nichts* nothing + *kommt* comes or will come + *dabei* by it + *heraus* out] Nothing will come as a result of it; it will lead to or yield nothing. Sc

Nuppenbecher, *n. Art* [G (now *Noppenbecher*) < *Nuppe* (*Noppe*) nub, knot + *Becher* beaker] A 15th-century drinking glass ornamented with drops of glass applied to the outer surface and drawn out to a point. Fl

oberhefe, *n. Bot.* [G < *ober* upper, i.e., floating + *Hefe* yeast] The floating yeast in bread-making. Jac

oberwind, *n. Meteor.* [G < *ober* upper + *Wind* wind] A night wind from the mountains or upper ends of lakes; a wind of the Salzkammergut in Austria. Lap

on-handedness, *n. Philos.* [Transl. of G *Vorhandenheit* availability < *vorhanden* available, existing + nom. suffix -*heit* -ness, etc.] The existence of things in a mode of thereness, lying passively in a neutral space. Ru

outer bremsstrahlung, *n. Physics* [E *outer* + G *Bremsstrahlung* bremsstrahlung (see main Dictionary)] Bremsstrahlung involving the acceleration of a charged particle coming from outside the atom whose nucleus produces the acceleration, and in which the energy loss by radiation is much greater than that by ionization, usu. seen in electrons with energies greater than about 50 MeV (million electron volts). Lap

Panzer-Forderer snaking conveyor, *Mining* [G *Panzerförderer* < *Panzer* armor + *Förderer* conveyor + E *snaking* + redundant *conveyor*] An armored conveyor that is moved forward behind the coal plough by means of a traveling wedge pulled along by the plough or by means of jacks or compression-air-operated rams attached at intervals to the conveyor structure. Lap

papierkrieg, -e *pl.* (1973) *Admin.* [G < *Papier* paper (ult. < Gk *pápyros*) + G *Krieg* war] Paper war; red tape. Ka1

Pappenheimer, *n. Mil.* [G < the name of Gottfried Heinrich, Count *Pappenheim* (1594–1632), Austrian general] A heavy rapier with a swept hilt incorporating two large perforated shells used during the first half of the seventeenth century. Cu

pathetisch, *a. Music* [G < LL *pathēticus* < Gk *pathētikós* suffering, enduring, passionate] With great emotion (used as a direction in music). Ap, Ke

pendelluft, *n. Med.* [G < *Pendel* pendulum + *Luft* air, vent] Nonsynchronous lung ventilation. La

perlsucht, *n. Med.* [G < *Perle* (< MFr *perle*) pearl, bead + G *Sucht* malady, disease] Pearl disease; tuberculosis. La

pig's maw, *n. Food* Var. **schwartenmagen** [Folk-etymological rendering of G *Schwartenmagen* hog's head cheese; or as Grimm explains it, *Schweinemagen mit Speck, Schwarte und Blut gefüllt* –a pig's maw stuffed with bacon, cracklings, and blood)] Collared pork head. Sc

politzerization, *n.* (1879) *Med.* [G *Politzern* or *Politzerization* (1879) < the name of Adam *Politzer* (1835–1920), Austrian otologist, inventor of a soft rubber bulb, called the *Politzer bag,* used to inflate the middle ear by increasing air pressure in the nasopharynx] Inflation of the middle ear by means of a Politzer bag. La

polkissen, *n. Med.* [G < *Pol* pole + *Kissen* cushion, pad] Juxtaglomerular cells. La

postulate, *n. Philos.* [G *Postulat* < L *postulātum,* neuter of *postulātus,* past part. of *postulāre* to demand, ask for, premise] In Kant, (A) an indemonstrable practical or moral hypothesis, such as the reality of God, freedom, or immortality; (B) any of the principles of the general category of modality, i.e., "postulates of empirical thought." Ru

potentiality, *n. Philos.* [Ad. of G *Potentialität* the state or condition of being possible < *potential* (< L *potentia*) potential + G nom. suffix -*ität* -ity] In Husserl, the character common to conscious processes of positing or setting an object, whether in the form of beliefs, values, or volitions. Ru

prächtig, *a. Music* Var. **Prachtvoll** [G pompous, resplendent < *Pracht* splendor, pomp + adj. suffix -*ig* -y] With much dignity, pomp (used as a direction in music). Ke

practical, *a. Philos.* [Transl. of G *praktisch* < LL *practicus* < Gk *praktikós* aimed at action, active] In Husserl, of or pertaining to such conscious processes as reach fulfillment in behavior. Ru

predicaments, *pl. Philos.* [Transl. of G *Prädikamente* (pl.) < LL *praedicamentum* prior direction] In Kant, name of the innate a priori forms of the understanding. Ru

pretzel-bender, *n.* (slang) [G *Brezel* pretzel (see main Dictionary) + E *bender,* lit., one who shapes the pretzels] (A jocular reference to) a whimsical person. Sc

principal coordination, *n. Philos.* [G *Prinzipalkoordination* < *prinzipal* main, principal + *Koordination* < L *prīncipālis* first, foremost + LL *coordination*- coordination] In Kant, the correlative functioning of object and subject. Ru

PS, *n.* (1986) *Transportation* [G abbr. of *Pferdestärke* horsepower < *Pferd* horse + *Stärke* power] Horsepower. Cam

pure, *a. Philos.* [Transl. of G *rein* clean, pure] In Kant, strictly that which is unmixed with anything sensuous or empirical. Ru

quartzwacke, *n. Geol.* [G < *Quartz* quartz + *Wacke* graywacke] Orig., a sandstone with less than 10% of unstable mineral constituents; now, a sandstone with 10% or more of matrix, but less than 10% rock and detrital feldspar. To

quellkuppe, *n. Geol.* [G < *quellen* to well up + *Kuppe* dome] A lava plug or dome. To

quellung reaction, *n. Biol.* [G *Quellung* swelling (< *quellen* to swell + nom. suffix -*ung* -ing) + E *reaction*] Swelling of the capsule of a bacterial cell, caused by contact with serum-containing antibodies capable of reacting with polysaccharide material in the capsule. Lap

quetschflächen, *pl. Geol.* [G < *quetschen* to squeeze + *Fläche,* pl. *Flächen* surface] Curved surfaces that are bound in lavas, the result of compressed plastic masses; also called *quetsch lava.* To

rahmen pollen, *n. Bot.* [G < *Rahmen* frame + *Pollen* (< NL) pollen] Frame pollen with six small and three broad streaks between the poles (found in the flora of tropical Africa). Jac

rasch, *a. Music* [G < MHG *rasch,* OHG *rasc* swift, rapid] Quick, rapid (used as a direction in music). Ap

Rassenschande, *n. Sociol.* [G < the comb. form of *Rasse* race + *Schande* shame] A crime against Nazi racial laws. Har

rational will, *n. Sociol.* [Transl. of G *Kürwille* < *küren* to choose + *Wille* will] The will that provides the social-psychological underpinning for *gesellschaft* (see main Dictionary). Go

rauh, *a. Music* [G coarse < MHG *rûch* hairy, OHG *rûh* orig., plucked] Coarse (used as a direction in music). Th

raus!, *interj.* (colloq.) Var. **rous, rous mit 'im** [G *'raus* (erron. or colloq.) < *heraus* (*mit dir, ihm,* etc.) or *hinaus* (*mit dir, ihm.* etc. out (with you, him, etc.)] Out! Ka, Men

reibungsbreccia, *n. Geol.* [G *Reibungsbreccie* < the gen. of *Reibung* friction + *Breccie* < Fr *brèche,* ult. Gmc fracture, break] Fold breccia, i.e., a breccia resulting from the folding of rock consisting of sharp fragments embedded in a fine-grained matrix like sand or clay. To

Reichsadlerhumpen, *see* Adlerglas

Reihengräberfeld, *n. Archaeology* [G < *Reihen,* pl. of *Reihe* row + *Gräber,* pl. of *Grab* grave + *Feld* field] A classic type of graveyard of the 5th to 7th centuries, normally found on the south-facing slope of a river in France, the Low Countries, and Western Germany, with graves lined in rows. Wi

richtig, *a. Music* [G < MHG *rihtec,* OHG *rihtîg* correct, right, precise] Precise (used as a direction in music). Th

Riesenfelge, *n. Sports* [G giant swing] Giant circle, a complete swing around the high bar, either forward or backward, with one's body and arms extended. Ra

Riesenpokal, *n. Art* [G < the comb. form of *Riese* giant + *Pokal* cup] The name usu. given to the huge cups, standing up to 40 inches in height and usually gilt, intended for ostentation rather than use, made in Germany in the 16th century. Cu

rillenstein, *n. Geol.* [G < the comb. form of *Rille* rill + *Stein* stone] A corroded pebble having a surface covered with an angular pattern of rills. To

ringbinden, *pl. Biol.* [G < *Ring* ring + *Binde,* pl. *Binden* ties] Striated muscle cells in a circumferential, helical pattern. La

ringschwiel(e), *n. Med.* [G < *Ring* ring + *Schwiele* callosity] A circular secondary cataract. La

rippen pollen, *n. Bot.* [G < *Rippe* rib + *Pollen* (< NL) pollen] Rib pollen with longitudinal ribs having punctuated markings on them (found in the flora of tropical Africa). Jac

Rohrblatt, *n. Music* [G < *Rohr* reed + *Blatt* membrane] A reed of the clarinet, oboe, etc. Ap

Rohrwerk, *n. Music* [G < *Rohr* reed + *Werk* works] Reed department of the organ. Ap, Ke

Rollschweller, *n. Music* [G < *Rolle* roller + *Schweller* sweller, a pedal-operated volume control in organs] General crescendo pedal of an organ that gradually brings out all the stops. Ap, Ke

roterde, *n. Geol.* [G < *rot* red + *Erde* soil] Red clay that resulted from weathered, basic igneous rock. To

Rückbildung, *n. Ling.* [G back-formation] Back- or regressive formation. Pe

rückflusskaldera, *n. Geol.* [G < *Rückfluß* reflux, backflow, reverse flow + *Kaldera* (< LL *caldaria*) caldera] Withdrawal caldera. To

ruh-cellar, *n. Beverages* (regional trade jargon) [Partial transl. of G *Ruh(e)keller* (or *Gärkeller*) < *ruhen* to repose, rest (or *gären* to ferment) + *Keller* cellar, vat] A cellar (or vat) where maturing beer is stored. Men2

ruhig, *a. Music* [G < *Ruhe* calm, repose, quiet + adj. suffix *-ig* -y] Peaceful (used as a direction in music). Ke

run into flak, *verb phrase Politics* [Compounding of E *run into* + G *Flak* flak (see main Dictionary] To meet some unexpected opposition or criticism. Sa

runder pollen, *n. Bot.* [G < *rund* round + *Pollen* (< NL) pollen] Round pollen, pollen spherical in form (found in the flora of tropical Africa). Jac

Rut(h)e, *n. Music* [G *Rute* rod, switch, birch, brush] A type of brush used to beat the bass drum to obtain the special effect called for by Richard Strauss. Ap, Th

rutsch breccia, *n. Geol.* [G *Rutschbreccie* < *rutschen* to slide, glide + *Breccie* < Fr *brèche,* ult. Gmc fracture, break] A tectonic form of breccia composed of lens-shaped rock fragments cleaved along their glide surfaces. To

salic, *n.* (1903) *Mineral.* [G *Salik* < NL *silica* < L *silex,* gen. *silicis* hard stone + NL *alumina* < L *alûmen,* gen. *alûminis* alum, coined by Eduard Sueß, or Suess (1834–1914), Austrian geologist, in *Antlitz der Erde,* 3 vols., 1895–1909] One of the two principal groups of minerals. Car

Samtteigdrucke, *pl. Art* [G < *Samt* velvet + *Teig* dough + *Druck,* pl. *Drucke* print] Prints known in French as *empreintes veloutées* and in English as *flock prints.* Cu

sanft, *a. Music* [G gentle, easy, soft, placid < MHG *senfte,* OHG *semfti* (adv. MHG *sanfte,* OHG *samfto*) orig., well-fitted or suited] Soft, gentle (used as a direction in music). Ap, Th

Saujude, -n *pl. Sociol.* [G < *Sau* sow, hog, pig, swine + *Jude* Jew] Jewish pig. Ti

Schäfflertanz, *n. Dance* [G < *Schäffler* cooper + *Tanz* dance] A carnival dance performed in Munich, Germany, every seven years, in which two lines of men polka through quadrille variations and longways formations.

schalen pollen, *n. Bot.* [G < *Schale* shell + *Pollen* (< NL) pollen] Shell pollen with three slits that do not reach the poles and are without pores, and with the pollen tubes emerging from the slits (found in the flora of tropical Africa). Jac

schalkhaft, *a. Music* [G < *Schalk* rogue + adj. suffix *-haft* -like] Playful (used as a direction in music). Ap, Th

schalstein porphyry, *n. Geol.* [Prob. < G *Schalstein* schalstein (see main Dictionary) a variety of tufaceous rock + E *porphyry*] A porphyritic tuff composed of diabase. To

scharf betont, *a. Music* [G < *scharf* sharp, emphatic + *betont* accented] With emphatic accent (used as a direction in music). Ke

scharnitzer, *n. Meteor.* [G < *Scharnitz,* the name of a town in the Austrian Tyrol + G nom. suffix *-er*] A cold, northerly wind of long duration in the Tyrol, Austria. Lap

schaurig, *a. Music* [G chilling, ult. < MLG *schüdden* to (cause to) shake + adj. suffix *-ig* -y] Chilling (used as a direction in music). Th

schelmisch, *a. Music* [G < *Schelm* rogue + adj. suffix *-isch* -ish] Roguish (used as a direction in music). Th

schistose hornfels, *n. Geol.* [Prob. compounding of E *schistose* + G *Hornfels* hornfels (see main Dictionary)] A hornfels with a relict stratified structure. To

schlafkrankheit, *n. Med.* [G < *Schlaf* sleep < *schlafen* to sleep + *Krankheit* sickness] American, Gambian, or Brazilian trypanosomiasis or sleeping sickness. La

schlafsucht, *n. Med.* [G < *Schlaf* sleep + *Sucht* disease, sickness] Hypersomnia; Kleine-Levin syndrome. La

schlammfieber, *n. Med.* [G < *Schlamm* mud, slime + *Fieber* (< L *febris*) fever] A form of leptospiral jaundice. La

schlaucher, *n. Beverages* (regional trade jargon) [G < *Schlauch* hose + *-er* -er] A workman employing a hose to rinse out empty vats. Men2

schleppend, *a. Music* [G < present part. of *schleppen* to drag] Dragging, heavy (used as a direction in music). Ap, Ke

schlieren, *pl. Physics* [G *Schlieren,* pl. of *Schliere* streak, flaw, impurity] In atmospheric optics, parcels of air having densities sufficiently different from their surroundings so that they may be discerned by means of refraction anomalies in transmitted light. (See *schlieren* in main Dictionary.) Lap

schlieren arch, *n. Geol.* [Prob. < G *Schlieren* schlieren + E *arch*] A plutonic mass with platy schlieren having an arch in the border zones that is absent in the interior. To

schlieren dome, *n. Geol.* [Prob. < G *Schlieren* schlieren + E *dome*] A plutonic mass with platy schlieren that fairly covers the entire surface in the shape of a dome. To

schlieren lava, *n. Geol.* [Prob. < G *Schlieren* schlieren + E *lava*] A lava displaying heterogenous, drawn-out streaks. To

schlieren method, *n. Optics* [G *Schlierenmethode* < *Schliere,* pl. *Schlieren* flaw, impurity + *Methode* method, ult. < Gk *méthodos*] An optical technique that detects density in a fluid flow. Lap

schlusskoagulum, *n. Med.* [G < *Schluß* closing, shutting, ending + *Koagulum* coagulation < L *coāgulāre* to coagulate] Closing coagulum. La

schmachtend, *a. Music* [G < present part. of *schmachten* to yearn] Yearning, longing (used as a direction in music). Ke

schmelzend, *a. Music* [G < present part. of *schmelzen* to melt] Melting away (used as a direction in music). Ke

schmetternd, *a. Music* [G < present part. of *schmettern* to blare] In horn playing: blaring (used as a direction in music). Ke

Schnabelkrug, *n. Art* [G < *Schnabel* beak + *Krug* jug] A type of Rhenish stoneware jug, having a beak-like spout, made in the early 17th century. Fl

schnell or **schneller,** *a. Music* [G fast or faster < MHG,

OHG *snel* orig., energetic] Fast or faster (used as a direction in music). Ap, Ke

Schnelle, *n. Art* [G jug < *schnellen* to fling, toss (suggestive of the motion required to empty the vessel] A tall, slender, tapering tankard, usu. of stoneware, made in Cologne and Westerwald in the 16th century. Fl

Schnitzelbank, *n. Music* [G < *schnitzen* to whittle, turn + *Bank* (work) bench] A cumulative German drinking song introduced in the U.S. by German settlers of Pennsylvania, Milwaukee, and elsewhere. Le

schollendome, *n. Geol.* [Partial transl. of G *Schollenkuppe* < *Schollen,* pl. of *Scholle* clod, sod; flake, layer, stratum + *Kuppe* dome] (A German name for) tumulus. To

schoppen, *n.* (1931) *Beverages* (regional) [G half a pint, a glass of that size < dial. Fr *choppene* (< OFr *chopine* < MLG) or < G *Schoppen,* ult. < MLG *shōpen* scoop] A large glass or tankard; the quantity of beer that it holds (as a stein–see main Dictionary). Sc

Schroteffect, *n. Physics* [G, lit., (buck)shot effect] A random fluctuation in the number of thermions per second emitted from the filament of a valve, such as a vacuum tube, that gives rise to sputtering or popping noises in the amplifier. • ~ is transl. as **shot effect** (see main Dictionary). Gr

schuppen structure, *n. Geol.* Var. **Imbrecite structure, shingle structure** [Partial transl. of G **Schuppenbau** < *Schuppe,* pl. *Schuppen* scale, flake, shingle + *Bau* structure < *bauen* to build] A sedimentary structure characterized by shingling, i.e., the arrangement of pebbles by currents so that they slope in the same direction and overlap like shingles on a roof. Lap

schwartenmagen, *see* pig's maw

schweizer cheese, *n. Food* Var. **schweizerkäse** (see main Dictionary) [Partial transl. of G *Schweizerkäse* < the attrib. form of *Schweiz* Switzerland + *Käse* cheese] Swiss cheese. • ~ is transl. as **Swiss cheese.** Sc

schwelle, *n. Med.* [G threshold < MHG *swella,* OHG *swelli* bearing beam] Threshold. La

schwermütig, *a. Music* [G < *schwer* heavy + *-mütig* of heart, spirit] Heavy-hearted, melancholy, mournful (used as a direction in music). Th

Schwungstemme, *n. Sports* [G uprise] Uprise, a direct rise to a support from the end of a front or back swing on the parallel bar, or the backswing on the high bar. Ra

schwungvoll, *a. Music* [G < *Schwung* verve, animation + *voll* full] Animated, spirited (used as a direction in music). Ap

scultetus, *n. Med.* [G < the name of Jan *Scultetus* (the latinized form of *Scholz*), a German surgeon] An S-bandage. La

seelenvoll, *a. Music* [G < *Seele* soul + *voll* full] Soulful (used as a direction in music). Ap

sensibility, *n. Philos.* [Transl. of G *Sinnlichkeit* < *sinnlich* sensual, sentient + nom. suffix *-keit* -ity, etc.] In Kant, the faculty by means of which the mind receives sensuous intuition. Ru

sensitiver Beziehungswahn, *n. Med.* [G < *sensitiv* sensitive (< ML *sensitivus*) + G *Beziehungswahn* (q.v.) delusional penchant for references] A state of having hypersensitive ideas of reference, often induced by a sense of conflict between the patient's feelings and his or her own moral or ethical standards. La

Setzbecher, *pl. Art* [G < *setzen* to set, stack + *Becher* beaker] A number of beakers fitted into and stacked upon one another, also called *Haufenbecher* (q.v.). Bo, Cu

Siebenschritt, *n. Dance* [G < *sieben* seven + *Schritt* step] A couple dance that originated in the Tyrol and is performed by moving in a counterclockwise circle. Le

Siebensprung, *n. Dance* [G < *sieben* seven + *Sprung* leap] A men's dance corresponding to the Basque *zaspi jausiak*. Le

singend, *a. Music* [G < present part. of *singen* to sing] Cantabile (used as a direction in music). Ke, Th

sittlichkeit, *n.* (1927) *Philos.* [G < *sittlich* moral, proper + nom. suffix *-keit* (here) -it, as quoted in William Edward Collinson's *Contemporary English,* 1927] Morality. Car, Ru

ski bunny, *n. Sports* [Transl. of G *Schihaserl* < *Schi* ski + *Haserl* bunny, dim. of *Hase* rabbit] In skiing, a beginner, usu. a female. Jar

smearbund, *n. Politics* (obs.) [Orig. colloq. U.S. compounding of E *smear* + G *Bund* alliance, league, formed on the analogy of *plunderbund* (see main Dictionary)] A band of defamers, e.g., of the Jews. Men

snollygaster, *n. Sociol.* [Folk etymology < G *schnelle Geister schnell* fast, swift, crafty + *Geister,* pl. of *Geist* spirit, character] According to U.S. President Harry Truman, a male born out of wedlock (see *snollygoster* in main Dictionary). Sa

so long, *interj.* (1860) [Poss. transl. of G (*adieu*) *so lange* < Fr *à dieu* to God (I commend you), good-bye + G *so lange* that long, i.e., until we meet again] Good-bye. Men

Sondergotik, *n. Art* [G (1913) < *sonder-* separate, special + *Gotik* Gothic] Mid-14th to 16th century German Gothic architecture, marked by elaborate vaulting and filigree tracery. Lu

spalten pollen, *n. Bot.* [G < *Spalte* fissure + *Pollen* (< NL) pollen] Fissure pollen with three longitudinal fissures, sometimes with pores in them (found in the flora of tropical Africa). Jac

spangen pollen, *n. Bot.* [G < *Spange* clasp + *Pollen* (< NL) pollen] Clasp pollen with three main ribs, with three pores in the equatorial region and one between each of two of the smaller ribs (found in the flora of tropical Africa). Jac

Sphäriker, *n. Philos.* [In G a proponent of *Sphärik* spherics < *Sphäre* sphere, domain + *-ik* < L *sphaera* + *-icus* -ic(s)] A term used by Friedrich Froebel (1782–1852), Swiss educator, to designate those, including himself and Pestalozzi, who believe in or realize in practice the totality or wholeness of a human being, in whom all polarities, such as mind and emotion, and spirit and soul are united. Ru

Spinnbarkeit relaxation, *n. Physics* [G *Spinnbarkeit* (< *spinnbar* capable of spin + nom. suffix *-keit* -ity) + E *relaxation*] A rheological effect illustrated by the pulling away of liquid threads when an object that has been immersed in a viscoelastic fluid is pulled out. Pa

spöttisch, *a. Music* [G < *Spott* mockery, scorn, derision + adj. suffix *-isch* -ish] Mocking (used as a direction in music). Ke, Th

Sprachvergnügen, *n. Ling.* [G < *Sprache* language (< *sprechen* to speak) + *Vergnügen* joy, pleasure] Joy in speaking. Ti

sprudel, *n.* (1906) *Beverages* [G, lit., (hot) spring, well; mineral water] The name of a mineral water from Carlsbad, now Czech Karlovy Vary. Car

sprudelstein, *n. Geol.* [G < *Sprudel* hot spring, mineral + *Stein* stone] A calcareous oölith resulting from the agitation of waters at hot springs. To

spur, *n. Physics* [G trace, track, trail < MHG *spur, spor,* OHG *spor* actually, footprint] As a result of secondary ionization, usu. the side track of a cluster of ionized molecules branching off from the path of a charged particle where ionization and excitation occurred. Fr

squanderlust, *n.* (1933) [Parody of G *Wanderlust* (see main Dictionary) a longing to travel] An inclination to squander. Men

square notation, *n. Music* [Transl. of G *Quadratnotation* < *Quadrat* square + *Notation* (< L) notation] A term introduced by Friedrich Ludwig in *Repertorium organorum* (1910) to designate the notation of the School of Notre Dame. Ap

stachel pollen, *n. Bot.* [G < *Stachel* spine + *Pollen* (< NL) pollen] Pollen having a spiny surface with pores ranging from three to many (found in the flora of tropical Africa). Jac

standhaft, *a. Music* [G < *Stand* stand + *-haft* -fast, as in *steadfast*] Resolute (used as a direction in music). Th

stark or **stärker,** *a. Music* [G strong, loud or stronger, louder < MHG *starc,* OHG *star(a)ch* orig. prob. stiff, rigid] Strong or stronger, loud or louder (used as a direction in music). Ke

Stasi, *n. Politics* [G abbr. of *Staatssicherheitsdienst* < *Staat* state + the gen. of *Sicherheit* security + *Dienst* service] The (former) East German security service; extended sense as a member of this service. Ti

staukuppe, *n. Geol.* [G < *Stau* slack water (< *stauen* to dam up, congeal) + *Kuppe* dome] Tholoid. To

Steg, *see* am Steg

Steigeisen, *n. Sports* [G crampon] Crampon, a steel framework with spikes attached that is affixed to boots to give them traction on icy terrain: climbing iron. Ra

steinmark, *n. Geol.* [G < *Stein* stone + *Mark* pulp] A porcelain clay, which Agricola described in *De re metallica* in 1546 (printed in 1556). To

stem turn, *n. Sports* [Partial transl. of G *Stemmbogen* < *stemmen* to brace (against) + *Bogen* arch < *biegen* to bend, turn] A change in direction by placing one's weight on one ski and propelling oneself with the other in a semicircle. Jar

sterbend, *a. Music* [G < present part. of *sterben* to die (away)] Dying (away) (used as a direction in music). Ap, Th

stich welding, *n. Metall.* [G *Stich* spot + E *welding*] A series of spot resistance welds. Lap

stillstand, *n. Geol.* [G < *stillstehen* to stand still] The stationary state of a land area, a continent, or an island with respect to the interior of the earth or to sea level. Lap

stink coal, *n. Geol.* [Transl. of G *Stinkkohle* < *stinken* to stink + *Kohle* coal] Brown coal that has an oily odor on burning. To

STM, *n. Physics* [G abbr. of *Stromtunnelmikroskop* (1981) < *Strom* current + *Tunnel* (< MFr) tunnel + G *Mikroskop* microscope < NL *microscopium*] A microscope that permits the study of a surface by applying voltage to a probe tip that enables electrons to tunnel through the gap between the tip and the surface as it goes over it, enabling a computer to draw a map of the shape and contour of atoms. Re

stockend, *a. Music* [G < present part. of *stocken* to hesitate, falter] Gradually slackening in time (used as a direction in music). Ke

stosszahlansatz, *n. Math.* [G < *Stoß* (here) collision + *Zahl* number + *Ansatz* (here) (point of) onset] An assumption made by Ludwig Boltzmann in support of his H-theorem, according to which there is no correlation between velocities and positions of different particles so that the number of collisions undergone by a particle is independent of its position or velocity and depends only on the cross section for collisions. (See *Boltzmann constant* in main Dictionary.) Fr

straff, *a. Music* [G taut, tight, stretched < Late MHG *straf* taught] Firm (used as a direction in music). Ap

straw fiddle, *n. Music* Var. **Strohfiedel** [Transl. of G *Strohfiedel* < *Stroh* straw + *Fiedel* fiddle (see *stroh* in main Dictionary)] A xylophone in which the wooden staffs were placed on a bed of straw; now also applied to a violin or a cello invented by Charles Stroh of London in 1901, in which the usual body is replaced by an aluminum plate connected to an amplifying horn. Ap, Th

Sturm, der, *n. Art* [G < (*der* the) + *Sturm* storm] An art magazine and gallery, founded in 1910 and 1912, respectively, to foster the (then) new generation of expressionists. Lu

stürmisch, *a. Music* [G < *Sturm* storm + adj. suffix -*isch* -ish, -y] Stormy (used as a direction in music). Ke

Stutzkehre, *n. Sports* [G < *stützen* to support + *kehren* to turn] A turn from a stunt on the parallel bars, in a front swing, to a support facing in the opposite direction. Ra

Swiss cheese, *see* schweizerkäse

Tafel slope, *n. Physics* [G *Tafel* table, plate, mesa + E *slope*] The (two-dimensional) slope of a curve of overpotential or electrolytic polarization in volts versus the logarithm of current density. Pa

Templist, *n.* (1881) *Theol.* [G (1861) < *Tempel* temple + -*ist* -ist < L *templum* + -*ist*] A member of the Temple Society (*Tempelgesellschaft,* orig. called *Gemeinde der Jerusalemfreunde* Society of the Friends of Jerusalem), founded by the German pietist Christoff Hoffman (1815–

85) in 1861 in Wittemberg as a Unitarian society, free of any ties to scripture or dogma. Car, Ro

Tempo wie vorher *Music* [G < *Tempo* tempo (ult. < L *tempus*) + G *wie* as + *vorher* before] Tempo primo (used as a direction in music). Ke, Th

thalweg[1], *a. Physics* [G (now *Talweg*) < *Tal* valley + *Weg* way, road] Of water seeping through the ground below the surface in the same direction as a surface stream-course (see *thalweg* in the main Dictionary). Lap

thalweg[2], *a. Geol.* [G (see *thalweg* in Dictionary)] Of a line crossing all contour lines on a land surface perpendicularly. Lap

Theatertreffen, *n. Theater* [G < *Theater* theater (ult. < Gk *théatron*) + G *Treffen* festival, meet] A theater festival. Ti

theke, *n. Bot.* [G < L *thēca* sac, capsule < Gk *thḗkē* storage place, chest] (Sometimes used for) the theca (ascus) of lichens. Jac

thick milk, *n. Food* (regional) [Transl. of G *dicke Milch* < *dick* thick + *Milch* milk] Sour milk. Ku

thunder machine, *n. Music* [Transl. of G *Donnermaschine* < *Donner* thunder + *Maschine* machine < L *māchina*] A device introduced by Richard Strauss to simulate thunder (not to be confused with the *bronteon* - G *Bronteion*). Ap

Tongeschlecht. *n. Music* [G < *Ton* tone (ult. < Gk *tónos*) + G *Geschlecht* sex, gender] The indication whether a chord or key is major or minor. Ap

tonstein, *n. Geol.* [G < *Ton* clay + *Stein* stone] (A German term) initially designating altered, feldspar-rich rockssuch as trachite or felsite; now used to refer to fine-grained, compact, nonlaminated rocks found as thin banks in beds of coal that consist in large part of kaolinite. To

totsäufer, *n. Beverages* (regional trade jargon) [G, lit., one who causes others to drink themselves to death < *sich totsaufen* to drink oneself to death] A customer's man. Men2

Trabi, *n.* (1991) *Transportation* [Short. of G *Trabant* the name of an automobile with a two-stroke engine built in the former East Germany] This automobile. Ka4

transcendental illusion, *n. Philos.* [Transl. of G *transzendentaler Schein* < *transzendental* transcendental (< ML *trānscendentālis*) + G *Schein* appearance, illusion] An illusion resulting from the tendency of the mind to accept the *a priori* forms of reason. Ru

Trendforschung, *n. Sociol.* [G < *Trend* trend + *Forschung* research] Trend research (to discover what is in and what is out). Ti

tropho-, *prefix Bot.* [Comb. form of Gk *tropho-*, as in *tróphimos* nursling, renders G *Amme* nurse, as in *Ammenbiene* nursing drone] A prefix in plant names denoting ''nursing, nourishing.'' Jac

tutenkalk, *n. Geol.* [G < *Tute* cone + *Kalk* lime] (A German name for) limestone having a cone-in-cone structure, also called *nagelkalk* (q.v.). Lap, To

tutenmergel, *n. Geol.* [G < *Tute* cone + *Mergel* marl] (A

German term for) limestone having a cone-in-cone structure, also called *nagelkalk* (q.v.). To

TV blitz, *n. Politics* [E *TV* + G *Blitz* blitz (see main Dictionary)] A concentrated advertising of a candidate's merits during the last week of a political campaign, as in Ross Perot's blitz in the 1992 U.S. presidential campaign. Sa

Umgangssprache, *n. Ling.* [G < the comb. form of *Umgang* association, (daily) intercourse, interaction + *Sprache* language] The vernacular. Pe

umgekehrte Schreibung, *n. Ling.* [G < *umgekehrt* inverse, reverse + *Schreibung* spelling] A misspelling due to the writer's uncertainty by reason of a change in pronunciation. Pe

Umkehr effect, *n. Physics* [G *Umkehr* reversal + E *effect*] Due to the presence of the ozone layer, an anomaly of the relative zenith intensities of scattered sunlight at certain wavelengths in the ultraviolet as the sun approaches the horizon. Pa

VEB, *n. Commerce* [G abbr. of *volkseigener Betrieb* < *volkseigen* state-owned + *Betrieb* company, plant] In the former East Germany, a state-owned company or plant. Ti

verhallend, *a. Music* [G < present part. of *verhallen* to fade away] Fading away (used as a direction in music). Ap

verlierend, *a. Music* [G < present part. of *verlieren* to lose, decrease] Diminishing, attenuating (used as a direction in music). Ke

verlöschend, *a. Music* [G < present part. of *verlöschen* to die down, become extinguished] Dying down (used as a direction in music). Ke

verschwinded, *a. Music* [G < present part. of *verschwinden* to vanish, disappear] Disappearing (used as a direction in music). Ap, Ke

verstärken, *v. Music* [G to increase] Reinforce (the sound, used as a direction in music). Ap

Vesperbild, *n. Art* [G < *Vesper* (< L) vespers + G *Bild* picture, painting] Pietà. Lu

vicar, *n. Theol.* (regional) [G *Vikar* < Late MHG *vicār(i)* < L *vicārius* substitute or stand-in for a cleric; a graduate student with a background in theology; (in Switzerland) a substitute teacher] A theological student. Men

Volksarmee, *n. Mil.* [G < the gen. of *Volk* people + *Armee* army, ult. < ML *armāta*] The armed forces of (former) East Germany. Ti

volksfest, *n.* (1893 *DA*) (regional) [G < the gen. of *Volk* people, folk + *Fest* festival, feast] Folk festival. Sc

Vopo, *n. Politics* [G short. of *Volkspolizei* < the gen. of *Volk* people + *Polizei* police, ult. < Gk *politeía*] (Former East Germany's) People's Police. Ti

waben pollen, *n. Bot.* [G < *Wabe* honeycomb + *Pollen* (< NL) pollen] Honeycomb pollen having an areolate surface (found in the flora of tropical Africa). Jac

wacke mandelstein, *n. Geol.* [G < *Wacke* wacke (see main

Dictionary) + *Mandelstein* mandelstein (q.v.)] Weathered amygdaloidal basalt. To

wackestone, *n. Geol.* [G *Wacke* wacke (see main Dictionary) + E *stone*] A mud-supported carbonate rock with a grain content of more than 10%. To

waldplattenstein, *n. Geol.* [G < *Wald* forest, woods + *Platten,* pl. of *Platte* plate, slab + *Stein* stone] Lozero. To

wanderlustful, *a.* [G *Wanderlust* (see main Dictionary) a longing to travel + E *-ful*] Having a strong desire to travel. Men

(mit) Wärme, *Music* [G < *mit* with + *Wärme* warmth] With warmth (used as a direction in music). Ap

wasserhelle (cells), pl. *Med.* [G < *Wasser* water + *Helle* brightness, clarity or *hell* bright, clear (+ E *cells*)] Water-clear cells present in adenoma of the parathyroid gland La

wehmütig, *a. Music* [G < *weh-* sad + *-mütig* of mind, heart] Sad, melancholy (used as a direction in music). Ap

weich, *a. Music* [G soft, tender] Tender, light, and sometimes minor (used as a direction in music). Th

weisstein, *n. Geol.* [G < *weiß* white + *Stein* stone] (An old German name for) leucocritic granite, granulite, felsite, or aplite. To

Wesensschau, *n. Philos.* [G < the gen. of *Wesen* essence, being + *Schau* sight, view, review] In Husserl, the immediate grasp of essences. Ru

Wesenswissen, *n. Philos.* [G < the gen. of *Wesen* essence, being + *Wissen* knowledge] The knowledge of essences conditioned by the elimination of acts that posit reality and by the inclusion of pure devotion to the qualities of objects as such. Ru

westwork, *n. Art* [Ad. of G *Westwerk* westside works] The western portion of the nave of a Carolingian, Ottonian, or Romanesque church, generally presenting an impressive multistoried facade with towers on the exterior. Lu

windkessel, *n. Med.* [Short. of G *Druckwindkessel* < *Druck* pressure + *Wind* wind + *Kessel* chamber] A blast pressure tank, i.e., a device similar to a compressed air chamber in a steam engine or pump. La

witzelsucht, *n. Med.* [G < *witzeln* to affect wit, make jokes + *Sucht* disease, sickness] A penchant toward excessive and abnormal joviality, characteristically caused by lesions of the frontal lobe. La

wuchtig, *a. Music* [G < *Wucht* weight, force + adj. suffix *-ig* -y] Weighty, heavy (used as a direction in music). Ap

Wunderkammer, -n pl. (1986) *Art* [G < *Wunder* wonder, marvel + *Kammer* chamber, cabinet (see Grimm)] Curio cabinet, the forerunner of the modern museum of art and science. Ka7

würdig, *a. Music* [G < *Würde* dignity + adj. suffix *-ig* -y] Stately, with dignity (used as a direction in music). Ap

zart, *a. Music* [G < MHG, OHG *zart* tender] Tender, soft (used as a direction in music). Ap

zitterbewegung, *n. Physics* [G < *zittern* to tremble, vibrate + *Bewegung* motion] An oscillating motion of an electron in some interpretations of the Dirac electron theory. Fr

zitternd, *a. Music* [G present part. of *zittern* to tremble]

Trembling, tremolando (used as a direction in music). Th

zögernd, *a. Music* [G < present part. of *zögern* to hesitate] Delaying, i.e., rallentando (used as a direction in music). Ke

zuckerguss, *n. Med.* [G < *Zucker* sugar (ult. < Skt *śarkarā*) + G *Guß* icing] A thickening of the serosal surface of certain organs, such as the spleen and liver. La

Zunftbecher, *n. Art* [G < *Zunft* guild + *Becher* beaker] A late 17th-century enameled glass beaker displaying a heraldic device or other guild symbol. Fl

zurückgehend, *a. Music* [G < present part. of *zurückgehen* to return] Returning (to the original tempo, used as a direction in music). Th

zurückhaltend, *a. Music* [G < present part. of *zurückhalten* to hold back] Holding back, i.e., rallentando (used as a direction in music). Ap, Ke

zustandsumme, *n. Math.* [G < *Zustand* state + *Summe* sum < L *summa*] In a partition function, the sum or product of the overall energy states of the system. Fr

zweikanter, *n. Geol.* [G < *zwei* two + *Kante* edge] A pebble with two sides formed by wind action. To

Zwiebelmuster, *n. Art* [G < *Zwiebel* onion + *Muster* pattern] A type of porcelain made in Meissen since 1739, featuring designs of formalized leaves, flowers, and peaches mistaken for onions. Fl

zwischengebirge, *n. Geol.* [G < *zwischen* intermediate, in between + *Gebirge* mountain range] A mountainous region between two mountain chains in an orogen that has remained relatively undisturbed. To

Zwischenglas, *n. Art* [G < *zwischen* between + *Glas* glass] An 18th-century German glass vessel engraved and decorated with gold on the outside and encased in a sheath of glass. Fl

Zwischengoldglas, *n. Art* [G < *zwischen* between + *Gold* gold + *Glas* glass] Decorations of gold leaf sandwiched between a two-layered type of glass. Lu

zwischenscheibe, *see* Z line (in main Dictionary).

zwitter-rock, *n. Geol.* [Partial transl. of G *Zwitterstein* < *Zwitter* hybrid + *Stein* stone] A variety of greisen containing casiterite and other ore minerals. To

SUPPLEMENTARY LOANWORDS ARRANGED BY SEMANTIC FIELDS

Administration: fallmaster, papierkrieg (2 items)

Aeronautics: bremsstrahlung

Anthropology: mutterrecht

Apparel: dirndled

Archaeology: Baden culture, Brandwirtschaft, Federmesser, Grubenhäuser, Kerbschnitt, Mauer, Michelsberg (culture), Mindelheim, Reihengräberfeld (9)

Art: Adlerglas, Adlerhumpen, Affenkapelle, Backsteingothik, Einzelkunst, Entartete Kunst, Hallenkirche, Jungfrauenbecher, Kunstkammer, Kunstwollen, mahlstick, Milchglas, Neue Wilden, Nuppenbecher, Reststick, Riesenpokal, Samtteigdrucke, Schnelle, Setzbecher, Sondergotik, Sturm, Vesperbild, westwork, Wunderkammer, Zunftbecher, Zwiebelmuster, Zwischenglas, Zwischengoldglas (28)

Astronomy: Bonner Durchmusterung, Córdoba Durchmusterung (2)

Biology: abbau, aufwuchs, quellung reaction, ringboden (4)

Beverages: Ansbacher, ausbrenner, beer-schiessen, Culmbacher, high-kraeusen, hofbrau, Kaiser's Geburtstag, kuehlschift, ruh-cellar, schlaucher, schoppen, sprudel, totsäufer (13)

Botany: anlage^2, bast, bestand, dauben pollen, deuter cells, Dorngeholz, Dorngestrauch, dosen pollen, facetier pollen, falten pollen, glatter pollen, groundform^2, gürtel pollen, hof^2, hornbast, kammrad pollen, karflur, karherberge, knötchen pollen, linsen pollen, loess^2, nährlösung, niederblätter, oberhefe, rahmen pollen, ring pollen, rippen pollen, runder pollen, schalen pollen, spalten pollen, spangen pollen, stachel pollen, theke, tropho-, waben pollen (35)

Chemistry: aldo-, Einschluss thermometer, Kraft pulping, Massenfilter (4)

Commerce: AG, Bankkrieg, HO, langer Samstag, moneybund, VEB (6)

Currency: DM day

Dance: Böttichertanz, Kreuz König, kuhreihn, Lauterbach, Metzgersprung, Rheinländer, Schäfflertanz, Siebenschritt, Siebensprung (9)

Economics: DIW

Food: coffee cake, cook cheese, fricadelles, gummi bears, hand cheese, metzel soup, pig's maw, schweizer cheese, thick milk (9)

Geology: adergneiss, Atomzahl, Augen-gabbro, Augen-granulite, Augenmigmatite, Augen-mylonite, Augensalz, Augen-schist, Augen structure, autoklastisch, basic hornfels, berg till, Bernstein, blatterstein, bogen structure, bogen texture, Donau glaciation, eiserner Hut, epi-, fleckschiefer, forellengranulit, fruchtgneiss, fruchtschiefer, garbenschiefer, gestellstein, gleitstein, hartsalz, hartschiefer, hauptsalz, klebschiefer, klei soil, knotenglimmerschiefer, knotenschiefer, laukastein, mandelstein, mangankiesel, murkstein, nagelkalk, quartzwacke, quellkuppe, quetschflächen, reibungsbreccia, rillenstein, roterde, rückflusskaldera, rutsch breccia, schalstein porphyry, schistose hornfels, schlieren arch, schlieren dome, schlieren lava, schollendome, 'schuppen structure, sprudelstein, staukuppe, steinmark, stillstand, stink coal, thalweg[2], tonstein, tutenkalk, tutenmergel, wacke mandelstein, wackestone, weisstein, zweikanter, zwischengebirge, zwitter-rock (68)

Industry: kraft pulp

Linguistics: Abglitt, Absatz, Aufhebung, Fremdwort, Gastwort, Grenzsignal, Rückbildung, Sprachvergnügen, Umgangssprache, umgekehrte Schreibung (10)

Mathematics: eigen equation, eigenfunction expansion, eigenvalue problem, eins . . . zwei . . . drei, stosszahlansatz, zustandsumme (6)

Medicine: abtropfung, affektepilepsie, Affenspalte, alpenstich, apochromat, Atmungsferment, aufwuchs, Bahnung, beziehungswahn, Blitz-krampf, Blitz-Nick-und-Salaam-krampf, bodenplatte, darmbrand, deckplatte, Einstellung, eiweismilch, erntefieber, fleckfieber, gegenhalten, haarscheibe, herzstoss, hof[1], hortungskörper, kernschwund, Lückenschädel, mehlnährschaden, nebenkörper, nem, Nickkrampf, pendelluft, perlsucht, politzerization, polkissen, ringschwiel(e), schlafkrankheit, schlafsucht, schlammfieber, schlusskoagulum, schwelle, scultetus, sensitiver Beziehungswahn, wasserhelle, windkessel, witzelsucht, zuckerguss (45)

Metallurgy: austempering, eisen platinum, stich welding (3)

Meteorology: dimmer foehn, düsenwind, Fallstreifen, foehn cloud, foehn sickness, glutwolke, graben lake, oberwind, Scharnitzer (9)

Military: drachen, forefield, Kapo, Pappenheimer, Volksarmee (5)

Mineralogy: eisenwolframite, K feldspar, salic (3)

Mining: abraumsalze, abteilung, erz cement, formkohle, Panzer-forderer snaking conveyor (5)

Music: abdämpfen, ablösen, abnehmend, absetzen, abstossen, abwecheslnd, Achtelpause, Achtfuss, affektvoll, Akkord, akkordieren, Altgeige, am Frosch, am Griffbrett, am Steg, andächtig, Anhang, anmutig, Ansatz, Anschlag, Atempause, auf der G, aufgeregt, Auszug, Basettflöte, bass trombone, bass trumpet, bebend, bedächtig, begeistert, Begleitung, behaglich, behend(e), beherzt, beklemmt, belustigend, beruhigend, beruhigt, beschleunigt, Besetzung, bestimmt, blown fifth, breit, Brummeisen, Brustwerk, Bügelhorn, Bühnenmusik, choral prelude, Dämpfung, derb, düster, eifrig, eilend, Einklang, Einsatz, empfindsamer Stil, empfindungsvoll, entschieden, ergriffen, erlöschend, ermattend, erniedrigen, ernst(haft), erschüttert, ersterbend, erweitert, erzürnt, feierlich, flehend, fliessender, Flötenuhr, flott, flüssig, fortfahren, frei, frisch, Füllstimmen, gebunden, gedämpft, gedehnt, gefühlsvoll, gehalten, gehend, gekneipt, gelassen, gemächlich, gesangvoll, geschleift, gesteigert, getragen, gezogen, gleitend, hastig, heftig, heiter, Heldenflöte, hell, hurtig, klagend, klar, kneifend, kräftig, langsam, lebendig, leidenschaftlich, leise, Love-death, luftig, lustig, lute harpsichord, mächtig, majestätisch, markiert, markig, marschgemäß, mässig, migrant melisma, mit Affekt, mit Aufschwung, mit Empfindung, mitleidig, mit Wärme, nachdrücklich, nachlassend, Nachschlag, natural notes, natürlich, Niederschlag, pathetisch, prächtig, rasch, rauh, richtig, Rohrblatt, Rohrwerk, Rollschweller, ruhig, Rut(h)e, sanft, schalkhaft, scharf betont, schaurig, schelmisch, schleppend, schmachtend, schmelzend, schmetternd, schnell, Schnitzelbank, schwermütig, schwungvoll, seelenvoll, singend, spöttisch, square notation, standhaft, stark, sterbend, stockend, straff, straw fiddle, stürmisch, Tempo wie vorher, thunder machine, Tongeschlecht, verhallend, verlierend, verlöschend, verschwindend, verstärken, Wärme (mit), wehmütig, weich, wuchtig, würdig, zart, zitternd, zögernd, zurückgehend, zurückhaltend (178)

Mythology: alraun, Angang, bullkater, Fastnachtsbär, Frau Hütt, Frau Welt, Heinzelmännchen, Kornmutter, Kornwolf (9)

Optics: schlieren method

Philosophy: actuality[1], actuality[2], aesthetic judgment, algebratization, allgemeingültig, Ansichtslosigkeit, appearances, appresentation, architectonic(s), athandedness, axiological, Begriffsgefühl, Bewußtsein überhaupt, compathy, confused, conscious, consequence, consequence logic, constituted, constitution, distinctness, egological, egological reduction, Einfühlung, empty, Erlebnis, evidence, evident, exemplification, fact, faith, feeling, formalization, founded, fullfilment, Ich, intentional analysis, Nicht-Ich, on-handedness, postulate, potentiality, practical, predicaments, principal coordination, pure, sensibility, sittichkeit, Sphäriker, transcendental illusion, Wesensschau, Wesenswissen (51)

Physics: Austausch coefficient, eigen equation, eigenvalue problem, flip-over process, gon, Grenz tube, heiligenschein[2], hohlraum, kilopond, kilopond-meter, outer bremsstrahlung, schlieren, schroteffect, spinnbarkeit relaxation, spur, STM, Tafel slope, thalweg[1], Umkehr effect, zitterbewegung (20)

Politics: Führerbunker, Green, Grossdeutschland, Hilter Youth, lager, run into flak, smearbund, Stasi, TV blitz (9)

Pottery: Deckelpokal, Eulenkrug, Haufenbecher, Hochschnitt, Krautstrunk (5)

Printing: mittel

Sociology: Arbeitstier, bub, elementary idea, Ellenbogengesellschaft, living room, lumpenization, Rassenschande, rational will, Saujude, snollygaster, Trendforschung (11)

Sports: base wax, cheaters, dope slope, Drehsprungstemme, gelande, gelandy, Hecht vault, Riesenfelge, Schwungstemme, ski bunny, Steigeisen, stem turn, Stutzkehre (13)

Technology: cant hook

Theater: Theatertreffen

Theology: agenda, belsnickle, Fasenacht, Historie, mission festival, Templist, vicar (7)

Transportation: ABS, bicycle Bahn, BMW, Fahrvergnügen, PS, Trabi (6)

Miscellany: and how, anker, can be, cut a face, du lieber Gott, ganz gut, Gott im Himmel, hinterlander, hoch!, hold on!, it listens well, kindergraph, let it be!, mox nix, nix come araus, pretzel-bender, raus!, so long!, squanderlust, volksfest, wanderlustful (21)